APA Handbook of
Research Methods in Psychology

APA Handbooks in Psychology® Series

APA Addiction Syndrome Handbook—two volumes
    Howard J. Shaffer, Editor-in-Chief
APA Educational Psychology Handbook—three volumes
    Karen R. Harris, Steve Graham, and Tim Urdan, Editors-in-Chief
APA Handbook of Adolescent and Young Adult Development—one volume
    Lisa J. Crockett, Gustavo Carlo, and John E. Schulenberg, Editors
APA Handbook of Behavior Analysis—two volumes
    Gregory J. Madden, Editor-in-Chief
APA Handbook of Career Intervention—two volumes
    Paul J. Hartung, Mark L. Savickas, and W. Bruce Walsh, Editors-in-Chief
APA Handbook of Clinical Geropsychology—two volumes
    Peter A. Lichtenberg and Benjamin T. Mast, Editors-in-Chief
APA Handbook of Clinical Psychology—five volumes
    John C. Norcross, Gary R. VandenBos, and Donald K. Freedheim, Editors-in-Chief
APA Handbook of Community Psychology—two volumes
    Meg A. Bond, Irma Serrano-García, and Christopher B. Keys, Editors-in-Chief
APA Handbook of Comparative Psychology—two volumes
    Josep Call, Editor-in-Chief
APA Handbook of Consumer Psychology—one volume
    Lynn R. Kahle, Editor-in-Chief
APA Handbook of Contemporary Family Psychology—three volumes
    Barbara H. Fiese, Editor-in-Chief
APA Handbook of Counseling Psychology—two volumes
    Nadya A. Fouad, Editor-in-Chief
APA Handbook of Dementia—one volume
    Glenn E. Smith, Editor-in-Chief
APA Handbook of Ethics in Psychology—two volumes
    Samuel J. Knapp, Editor-in-Chief
APA Handbook of Forensic Neuropsychology—one volume
    Shane S. Bush, Editor-in-Chief
APA Handbook of Forensic Psychology—two volumes
    Brian L. Cutler and Patricia A. Zapf, Editors-in-Chief
APA Handbook of Giftedness and Talent—one volume
    Steven I. Pfeiffer, Editor-in-Chief
APA Handbook of Human Systems Integration—one volume
    Deborah A. Boehm-Davis, Francis T. Durso, and John D. Lee, Editors-in-Chief
APA Handbook of Industrial and Organizational Psychology—three volumes
    Sheldon Zedeck, Editor-in-Chief
APA Handbook of Intellectual and Developmental Disabilities—two volumes
    Laraine Masters Glidden, Editor-in-Chief
APA Handbook of Men and Masculinities—one volume
    Y. Joel Wong and Stephen R. Wester, Editors-in-Chief
APA Handbook of Multicultural Psychology—two volumes
    Frederick T. L. Leong, Editor-in-Chief

APA Handbook of Neuropsychology—two volumes
    Gregory G. Brown, Tricia Z. King, Kathleen Y. Haaland, and Bruce Crosson, Editors
APA Handbook of Nonverbal Communication—one volume
    David Matsumoto, Hyisung Hwang, and Mark Frank, Editors-in-Chief
APA Handbook of Personality and Social Psychology—four volumes
    Mario Mikulincer and Phillip R. Shaver, Editors-in-Chief
APA Handbook of Psychology and Juvenile Justice—one volume
    Kirk Heilbrun, Editor-in-Chief
APA Handbook of Psychology, Religion, and Spirituality—two volumes
    Kenneth I. Pargament, Editor-in-Chief
APA Handbook of the Psychology of Women—two volumes
    Cheryl B. Travis and Jacquelyn W. White, Editors-in-Chief
APA Handbook of Psychopathology—two volumes
    James N. Butcher, Editor-in-Chief
APA Handbook of Psychopharmacology—one volume
    Suzette M. Evans, Editor-in-Chief
APA Handbook of Research Methods in Psychology, Second Edition—three volumes
    Harris Cooper, Editor-in-Chief
APA Handbook of Sexuality and Psychology—two volumes
    Deborah L. Tolman and Lisa M. Diamond, Editors-in-Chief
APA Handbook of Sport and Exercise Psychology—two volumes
    Mark H. Anshel, Editor-in-Chief
APA Handbook of Testing and Assessment in Psychology—three volumes
    Kurt F. Geisinger, Editor-in-Chief
APA Handbook of Trauma Psychology—two volumes
    Steven N. Gold, Editor-in-Chief

APA Handbooks in Psychology

APA Handbook of Research Methods in Psychology

SECOND EDITION

VOLUME 1
Foundations, Planning, Measures, and Psychometrics

Harris Cooper, *Editor-in-Chief*

Marc N. Coutanche, Linda M. McMullen, A. T. Panter, David Rindskopf, and Kenneth J. Sher, *Associate Editors*

AMERICAN PSYCHOLOGICAL ASSOCIATION

Copyright © 2023 by the American Psychological Association. All rights reserved. Except as permitted under the United States Copyright Act of 1976, no part of this publication may be reproduced or distributed in any form or by any means, including, but not limited to, the process of scanning and digitization, or stored in a database or retrieval system, without the prior written permission of the publisher.

Chapter 14 was coauthored by an employee of the United States government as part of official duty and is considered to be in the public domain.

The opinions and statements published are the responsibility of the authors and editors, and such opinions and statements do not necessarily represent the policies of the American Psychological Association.

Published by
American Psychological Association
750 First Street, NE
Washington, DC 20002
https://www.apa.org

Order Department
https://www.apa.org/pubs/books
order@apa.org

Typeset in Berkeley by Circle Graphics, Inc., Reisterstown, MD

Printer: Sheridan Books, Chelsea, MI
Cover Designer: Mark Karis

Library of Congress Cataloging-in-Publication Data

Names: Cooper, Harris M., editor. | American Psychological Association, issuer.
Title: APA handbook of research methods in psychology / editor-in-Chief
  Harris Cooper; associate editors Marc N. Coutanche, Linda M. McMullen,
  A.T. Panter, David Rindskopf, and Kenneth J. Sher
Description: Second Edition. | Washington, DC : American Psychological
  Association, [2023-] | Series: APA handbooks in psychology | Revised
  edition of APA handbook of research methods in psychology, c2012. |
  Includes bibliographical references and index. | Contents: v. 1. Foundations,
  planning, measures, and psychometrics -- v. 2. Research designs: quantitative,
  qualitative, neuropsychological, and biological -- v. 3. Data analysis and research publication
Identifiers: LCCN 2022020492 (print) | LCCN 2022020493 (ebook) |
  ISBN 9781433837135 (v. 1 ; hardcover) | ISBN 9781433841330 (v. 2 ; hardcover) |
  ISBN 9781433841354 (v. 3 ; hardcover) | ISBN 9781433841323 (v. 1 ; ebook) |
  ISBN 9781433841347 (v. 2 ; ebook) | ISBN 9781433841361 (v. 3 ; ebook)
Subjects: LCSH: Psychology--Research--Methodology--Handbooks, manuals, etc. |
  Psychology--Research--Handbooks, manuals, etc.
Classification: LCC BF76.5 .A73 2023 (print) | LCC BF76.5 (ebook) |
  DDC 150.72/1--dc23/eng/20220802
LC record available at https://lccn.loc.gov/2022020492
LC ebook record available at https://lccn.loc.gov/2022020493

https://doi.org/10.1037/0000318-000

Printed in the United States of America

10 9 8 7 6 5 4 3 2 1

Contents

Volume 1: Foundations, Planning, Measures, and Psychometrics

Editorial Board xi
About the Editor-in-Chief xiii
About the Associate Editors xv
Contributors xix
A Note From the Publisher xxiii
Introduction: Objectives of Psychological Research and Their Relations
to Research Methods xxv

**Part I. Philosophical, Ethical, and Societal Underpinnings
of Psychological Research** 1

Section 1. Philosophical Issues for Research in Psychology 3

Chapter 1. Perspectives on the Epistemological Bases for Qualitative Research 5
    Carla Willig
Chapter 2. Frameworks for Causal Inference in Psychological Science 23
    Peter M. Steiner, William R. Shadish, and Kristynn J. Sullivan

**Section 2. Ethical and Professional Considerations in Conducting
Psychological Research** 57

Chapter 3. Ethics in Psychological Research: Guidelines and Regulations 59
    Adam L. Fried and Kate L. Jansen
Chapter 4. Ethics and Regulation of Research With Nonhuman Animals 83
    Sangeeta Panicker, Chana K. Akins, and Beth Ann Rice

Section 3. Cultural and Societal Issues in Conducting Psychological Research 95

Chapter 5. Cross-Cultural Research Methods 97
    David Matsumoto and Fons J. R. van de Vijver
Chapter 6. Research With Populations That Experience Marginalization 115
    George P. Knight, Rebecca M. B. White, Stefanie Martinez-Fuentes,
    Mark W. Roosa, and Adriana J. Umaña-Taylor

Part II. Planning Research 133

Chapter 7. Developing Testable and Important Research Questions 135
        Frederick T. L. Leong, Neal Schmitt, and Brent J. Lyons
Chapter 8. Searching With a Purpose: How to Use Literature Searching
        to Support Your Research 151
        Diana Ramirez and Margaret J. Foster
Chapter 9. Psychological Measurement: Scaling and Analysis 169
        Heather Hayes and Susan E. Embretson
Chapter 10. Sample-Size Planning 189
        Ken Kelley, Samantha F. Anderson, and Scott E. Maxwell
Chapter 11. Workflow and Reproducibility 211
        Oliver Kirchkamp
Chapter 12. Obtaining and Evaluating Research Funding 227
        Jonathan S. Comer and Amanda L. Sanchez

Part III. Measurement Methods 247

Section 1. Behavior Observation 249

Chapter 13. Behavioral Observation 251
        Roger Bakeman and Vicenç Quera

Section 2. Self-Report 275

Chapter 14. Question Order Effects 277
        Lisa Lee, Parvati Krishnamurty, and Struther Van Horn
Chapter 15. Interviews and Interviewing Techniques 297
        Anna Madill
Chapter 16. Using Intensive Longitudinal Methods in Psychological Research ... 327
        *Masumi Iida, Patrick E. Shrout, Jean-Philippe Laurenceau,
        and Niall Bolger*
Chapter 17. Automated Analyses of Natural Language in Psychological Research . 361
        Laura K. Allen, Arthur C. Graesser, and Danielle S. McNamara

Section 3. Psychological Tests 381

Chapter 18. Objective Tests as Instruments of Psychological Theory and Research . 383
        David Watson
Chapter 19. Norm- and Criterion-Referenced Testing 407
        Kurt F. Geisinger
Chapter 20. The Current Status of "Projective" "Tests" 433
        Robert E. McGrath, Alec Twibell, and Elizabeth J. Carroll
Chapter 21. Brief Instruments and Short Forms 451
        *Emily A. Atkinson, Carolyn M. Pearson Carter, Jessica L. Combs Rohr,
        and Gregory T. Smith*

Section 4. Chronometric and Psychophysical Measures 467

Chapter 22. Eye Movements, Pupillometry, and Cognitive Processes 469
    Simon P. Liversedge, Sara V. Milledge, and Hazel I. Blythe
Chapter 23. Response Times 493
    Roger Ratcliff
Chapter 24. Psychophysics: Concepts, Methods, and Frontiers 511
    Allie C. Hexley, Takuma Morimoto, and Manuel Spitschan

Section 5. Measures in Psychophysiology 529

Chapter 25. The Perimetric Physiological Measurement of Psychological
    Constructs 531
    Louis G. Tassinary, Ursula Hess, Luis M. Carcoba, and Joseph M. Orr
Chapter 26. Salivary Hormone Assays 565
    Linda Becker, Nicolas Rohleder, and Oliver C. Schultheiss

Section 6. Measures in Neuroscience 579

Chapter 27. Electro- and Magnetoencephalographic Methods in Psychology 581
    Eddie Harmon-Jones, David M. Amodio, Philip A. Gable,
    and Suzanne Dikker
Chapter 28. Event-Related Potentials 605
    Steven J. Luck
Chapter 29. Functional Neuroimaging 631
    Megan T. deBettencourt, Wilma A. Bainbridge, and Monica D. Rosenberg
Chapter 30. Noninvasive Stimulation of the Cerebral Cortex 655
    Dennis J. L. G. Schutter
Chapter 31. Combined Neuroimaging Methods 673
    Marius Moisa and Christian C. Ruff
Chapter 32. Neuroimaging Analysis Methods 697
    Yanyu Xiong and Sharlene D. Newman

Part IV. Psychometrics 721

Chapter 33. Reliability 723
    Sean P. Lane, Elizabeth N. Aslinger, and Patrick E. Shrout
Chapter 34. Generalizability Theory 745
    Xiaohong Gao and Deborah J. Harris
Chapter 35. Construct Validity 769
    Kevin J. Grimm and Keith F. Widaman
Chapter 36. Item-Level Factor Analysis 793
    Nisha C. Gottfredson, Brian D. Stucky, and A. T. Panter
Chapter 37. Item Response Theory 809
    Steven P. Reise and Tyler M. Moore
Chapter 38. Measuring Test Performance With Signal Detection Theory
    Techniques 837
    Teresa A. Treat and Richard J. Viken

Index 859

Editorial Board

EDITOR-IN-CHIEF

Harris Cooper, PhD, Hugo L. Blomquist Professor, Emeritus, Department of Psychology and Neuroscience, Duke University, Durham, NC, United States

ASSOCIATE EDITORS

Marc N. Coutanche, PhD, Associate Professor of Psychology, and Research Scientist in the Learning Research and Development Center, University of Pittsburgh, Pittsburgh, PA, United States

Linda M. McMullen, PhD, Professor Emerita, Department of Psychology, University of Saskatchewan, Saskatoon, SK, Canada

A. T. Panter, PhD, Senior Associate Dean for Undergraduate Education, College of Arts and Sciences, and Professor, L. L. Thurstone Psychometric Laboratory, The University of North Carolina at Chapel Hill, Chapel Hill, NC, United States

David Rindskopf, PhD, Distinguished Professor of Educational Psychology and Psychology, City University of New York Graduate Center, New York, NY, United States

Kenneth J. Sher, PhD, Chancellor's Professor, Curators' Distinguished Professor of Psychological Sciences, Emeritus, Department of Psychological Sciences, University of Missouri, Columbia, MO, United States

About the Editor-in-Chief

Harris Cooper, PhD, is the Hugo L. Blomquist Professor, Emeritus, in the Department of Psychology and Neuroscience at Duke University. His research interests follow two paths. The first concerns research synthesis and research methodology. His book *Research Synthesis and Meta-Analysis: A Step-by-Step Approach* (2017) is in its fifth edition. He is the coeditor of the *Handbook of Research Synthesis and Meta-Analysis* (3rd ed.; 2019). In 2007, Dr. Cooper was the recipient of the Frederick Mosteller Award for contributions to research synthesis methodology given by the International Campbell Collaboration. In 2008, he received the Ingram Olkin Award for distinguished lifetime contribution to research synthesis from the Society for Research Synthesis Methodology. Dr. Cooper also studies the application of social and developmental psychology to education policy. In particular, he studies the relationship between time and learning.

Dr. Cooper chaired the first American Psychological Association (APA) committee that developed guidelines for information about research that should be included in manuscripts submitted to APA journals. In 2011, he published a book on the topic, *Reporting Research in Psychology: How to Meet Journal Article Reporting Standards*. In 2020, Dr. Cooper published a revised second edition of the book as *Reporting Quantitative Research in Psychology: How to Meet APA Style Journal Article Reporting Standards*.

Dr. Cooper currently serves as the editor of *American Psychologist*, the flagship journal of APA. He served as editor for the *Psychological Bulletin* from 2003 through mid-2009. *Psychological Bulletin* is in the top five social science journals in total citations and impact factor. He was the chair of the APA Council of Editors in 2006 and was a member of the committee that revised the *Publication Manual of the American Psychological Association* (2010). In 2012, Dr. Cooper became the inaugural coeditor of the *Archives of Scientific Psychology*, APA's first open methods, collaborative data sharing, open access journal. He remained as editor until 2015.

From 2009 to 2015, Dr. Cooper served as the chief editorial advisor for APA's journal publishing program. In this role, he served as a resource to the editors of APA's 70+ journals as well as the mediator of disputes between editors and authors and between authors and authors. Dr. Cooper's book *Ethical Choices in Research: Managing Data, Writing Reports, and Publishing Results in the Social Sciences* (2016) draws from the experience. The book goes beyond the proper treatment of human research subjects to examine frequently neglected ethical issues that arise after data have been collected.

Dr. Cooper served as the chair of the Department of Psychology and Neuroscience at Duke University from 2009 to 2014. He also served as chair of the Department of Psychological Sciences at the University of Missouri and director of Duke University's Program in Education. From 2017 to 2018 he served as the dean of social sciences at Duke.

About the Associate Editors

Marc N. Coutanche, PhD, is an associate professor of psychology and research scientist in the Learning Research and Development Center at the University of Pittsburgh. Dr. Coutanche directs a program of cognitive neuroscience research that uses brain imaging and behavioral studies to understand human learning, memory, and perception, particularly how the human brain transforms perceptual experience into knowledge. Addressing this question involves understanding the neural basis for successful memory encoding, the role of sleep in memory consolidation, how word learning is influenced by context, and more. In parallel, he develops and tests new computational techniques to identify and understand the neural information present within neuroimaging data. His work has been funded by the National Institutes of Health, National Science Foundation, American Psychological Foundation, and other organizations. He has published in a variety of journals that include *Trends in Cognitive Sciences*, *Cerebral Cortex*, *The Journal of Experimental Psychology: General*, *Memory & Cognition*, and *Perspectives on Psychological Science*. Dr. Coutanche received his undergraduate training in experimental psychology at Oxford University, earned a master's degree and PhD from the University of Pennsylvania, and conducted postdoctoral training at Yale University. He received a Howard Hughes Medical Institute International Student Research Fellowship and a Ruth L. Kirschstein Postdoctoral National Research Service Award, and was named a 2019 Rising Star by the Association for Psychological Science.

Linda M. McMullen, PhD, is professor emerita of psychology at the University of Saskatchewan (Canada). Over her career, she has contributed to the development of qualitative inquiry in psychology through teaching, curriculum development, and pedagogical scholarship; original research; and service to the qualitative research community.

Dr. McMullen introduced qualitative inquiry into the graduate and undergraduate curricula in her home department, taught courses at both levels for many years, and has published articles, coedited special issues, and written a book (*Essentials of Discursive Psychology*) that is part of the American Psychological Association's (APA's) series on qualitative methodologies. She is also coauthor (with Frederick J. Wertz, Kathy Charmaz, Ruthellen Josselson, Rosemarie Anderson, and Emalinda McSpadden) of *Five Ways of Doing Qualitative Analysis: Phenomenological Psychology, Grounded Theory, Discourse Analysis, Narrative Research, and Intuitive Inquiry*, which shows how the same set of data is analyzed using each of five leading qualitative methodologies. For the past couple of decades, her research has focused on discursive analyses of service providers' and service users' accounts of depression and the use of antidepressants. She is coeditor (with Janet M. Stoppard) of *Situating Sadness: Women and Depression in Social Context*.

Dr. McMullen has been engaged with building the Society for Qualitative Inquiry in Psychology (SQIP; a section of Division 5 [Quantitative and Qualitative Methods] of APA) into a vibrant scholarly society since its earliest days. She was a member of the Executive Committee from 2013 to 2021, served as its president in 2015–2016, and was elected SQIP Section Representative to the Division in 2018 for a 3-year term. In this latter capacity, she headed the multiyear process of developing an organizational structure for SQIP, codifying it in a set of bylaws, and harmonizing the SQIP bylaws with those of Division 5.

While working as a university professor, Dr. McMullen took on many leadership roles, including director of clinical training for the graduate program in clinical psychology at the University of Saskatchewan (1988–1994, 1995–1997), head of the Department of Psychology (1997–2002, 2003–2006), university leader for the Social Sciences and Humanities Research Council of Canada (2011–2013), and acting vice-dean for social sciences (2012–2014). She served as the elected faculty member on the university's Board of Governors from 2004 to 2010.

Dr. McMullen's contributions have been recognized by Division 5 of the APA (2021 Distinguished Contributions to Qualitative Inquiry Award), the Canadian Psychological Association (2003, Fellow; 2012 Distinguished Member, Section for Women and Psychology), and the Saskatchewan Psychological Association (1994 Award for Outstanding and Longstanding Service to the Profession).

A. T. Panter, PhD, is the senior associate dean for undergraduate education and a professor of psychology in the L. L. Thurstone Psychometric Laboratory at the University of North Carolina (UNC) at Chapel Hill. She received her BA from Wellesley College in 1985 and her PhD from New York University in 1989. She is past president of the American Psychological Association's (APA's) Division on Quantitative and Qualitative Psychology. As a quantitative psychologist, she develops instruments, research designs, and data-analytic strategies for applied research questions in higher education, personality, and health. Dr. Panter serves as a program evaluator for UNC's Chancellor's Science Scholars Program, a multisite adaptation of the successful Meyerhoff Program. She was also principal investigator for The Finish Line Project, a $3 million First in the World grant from the U.S. Department of Education that systematically investigated new supports and academic initiatives, especially for first-generation college students. Her books include the *APA Dictionary of Statistics and Research Methods* (2013), *The APA Handbook of Research Methods in Psychology* (1st ed.; 2012), the *Handbook of Ethics in Quantitative Methodology* (2011), *The SAGE Handbook of Methods in Social Psychology* (2004), and volumes on program evaluation for HIV/AIDS multisite projects.

At the undergraduate level, she teaches statistics, research methods, and a first-year seminar on communicating research results to others ("Talking About Numbers"). At the doctoral level, she teaches courses in research design, classical and modern approaches to instrument/survey design, and test theory and multivariate methods. Dr. Panter has received numerous awards for her teaching and mentoring, including the

Tanner Award, the J. Carlyle Sitterson Award, a Bowman and Gordon Gray Distinguished Professorship, and APA's Jacob Cohen Award for Distinguished Teaching and Mentoring. She is an APA Fellow, a member of the Graduate Record Examination Advisory Board, a former member of a Social Security Administration advisory panel related to disability determination, and a member of APA's Committee on Psychological Testing and Assessment. She regularly provides services for federal agencies, national advisory panels, and editorial boards.

Dr. Panter has been a member of the university faculty since 1989. As senior associate dean, she oversees all of the College's programs for undergraduate education: academic advising, undergraduate research, student success and academic counseling (including Learning Center, the Writing Center, Peer Mentoring, Carolina Firsts, Summer Bridge), undergraduate curricula (including the general education curriculum), instructional innovation, research and evaluation, Robertson Scholars Leadership Program, and Honors Carolina (including distinguished scholarships). Among her active work on campus, she helped design and implement the IDEAS in Action general education undergraduate curriculum, developed student learning outcomes for the university system, implemented a new holistic Thrive academic advising approach, address legal mandates related to the use of race/ethnicity in undergraduate admissions decisions, developed visualizations for key university data, and increased the number and type of high impact academic experiences for all undergraduate students.

David Rindskopf, PhD, is a Distinguished Professor at the City University of New York Graduate Center, specializing in research methodology and statistics. His main interests are in Bayesian statistics, causal inference, categorical data analysis, meta-analysis, and latent variable models. He is a Fellow of the American Statistical Association and the American Educational Research Association and is past president of the Society of Multivariate Experimental Psychology and the New York Chapter of the American Statistical Association.

Kenneth J. Sher, PhD, is Chancellor's Professor and Curators' Distinguished Professor of Psychological Sciences, Emeritus, at the University of Missouri. He received his undergraduate degree from Antioch College (1975), his PhD in clinical psychology from Indiana University (1980), and his clinical internship training at Brown University (1981). His primary areas of research focus on etiological processes in the development of alcohol dependence, factors that affect the course of drinking and alcohol use disorders throughout adulthood, longitudinal research methodology, psychiatric comorbidity, and nosology. At the University of Missouri, he has directed the predoctoral and post-doctoral training program in alcohol studies, and his research has been continually funded by the National Institute on Alcohol Abuse and Alcoholism for more than 35 years. Dr. Sher is a Fellow of the American Association for the Advancement of Science, Association for Psychological Science, and American Psychological Association (APA), and his research contributions have been recognized by professional societies, including the Research Society on Alcoholism (where he was awarded the Young Investigator Award, the Distinguished Researcher Award, and the G. Alan Marlatt Mentoring Award) and APA (Distinguished Scientific Contribution Award and the Distinguished Career Contributions to Education and Training from the Division on Addictions and a presidential citation), as well as by the University of Missouri (where he received the Chancellor's Award for Research and Creativity, the President's Award for Research and Creativity, and the SEC Faculty Achievement Award/Professor of the Year), the National Institutes of Health (a MERIT Award, a Senior Scientist and Mentoring Award, and a Mark Keller Lectureship), and Indiana University (Richard C. Atkinson Lifetime Achievement Award). Throughout his career he has been heavily involved in service to professional societies (e.g., he served as president of the Research Society on Alcoholism and served on the APA's Council of Representatives, Board of Scientific Affairs, and Policy and Planning Board, chairing the latter two of these bodies). Dr. Sher also has a long history of service to scholarly publications, serving as an associate/field editor for both disciplinary journals (*Clinical Psychological Science, Journal of Abnormal Psychology,* and *Psychological Bulletin*) and specialty journals (*Journal of Studies on Alcohol and Drugs* and *Alcoholism: Clinical and Experimental Research*). He recently served as acting editor for *Clinical Psychological Science*. His current work is focused on attempting to define the "core" of addiction and developing methods to improve the diagnosis of alcohol use disorders and other psychological disorders.

Contributors

Chana K. Akins, PhD, Department of Psychology, University of Kentucky, Lexington, KY, United States

Laura K. Allen, PhD, Educational Psychology Department, University of Minnesota, Minneapolis, MN, United States

David M. Amodio, PhD, Department of Psychology, University of Amsterdam, Amsterdam, The Netherlands

Samantha F. Anderson, PhD, Department of Psychology, Arizona State University, Tempe, AZ, United States

Elizabeth N. Aslinger, PhD, Powers Laboratory, Yale University School of Medicine, New Haven, CT, United States

Emily A. Atkinson, MS, Department of Psychology, University of Kentucky, Lexington, KY, United States

Wilma A. Bainbridge, PhD, Department of Psychology, The University of Chicago, Chicago, IL, United States

Roger Bakeman, PhD, Department of Psychology, Georgia State University, Atlanta, GA, United States

Linda Becker, PhD, Department of Psychology, Friedrich-Alexander-Universität Erlangen-Nürnberg, Erlangen, Bayern, Germany

Hazel I. Blythe, PhD, Department of Psychology, Northumbria University, Newcastle-Upon-Tyne, England

Niall Bolger, PhD, Department of Psychology, Columbia University, New York, NY, United States

Luis M. Carcoba, MD, PhD, Department of Psychology, The University of Texas at El Paso, El Paso, TX, United States

Elizabeth J. Carroll, PhD, Center for Health and Counseling Services, Ramapo College of New Jersey, Mahwah, NJ, United States

Carolyn M. Pearson Carter, PhD, Carter Psychology LLC, Indianapolis, IN, United States

Jonathan S. Comer, PhD, Center for Children and Families, Department of Psychology, Florida International University, Miami, FL, United States

Megan T. deBettencourt, PhD, Institute for Mind and Biology and Department of Psychology, The University of Chicago, Chicago, IL, United States

Suzanne Dikker, PhD, Department of Psychology, New York University, New York, NY, United States

Susan E. Embretson, PhD, School of Psychology, Georgia Institute of Technology, Atlanta, GA, United States

Margaret J. Foster, MSLIS, MPH, University Libraries, Texas A&M University, College Station, TX, United States

Adam L. Fried, PhD, Clinical Psychology Program, Midwestern University, Glendale, AZ, United States

Philip A. Gable, PhD, Department of Psychological and Brain Sciences, University of Delaware, Newark, DE, United States

Xiaohong Gao, PhD, Independent Consultant, Coralville, IA, United States

Kurt F. Geisinger, PhD, Buros Center for Testing, Department of Educational Psychology, The University of Nebraska–Lincoln, Lincoln, NE, United States

Nisha C. Gottfredson, PhD, Department of Health Behavior, Gillings School of Global Public Health, The University of North Carolina at Chapel Hill, Chapel Hill, NC, United States

Arthur C. Graesser, PhD, Department of Psychology and Institute for Intelligent Systems, University of Memphis, Memphis, TN, United States

Kevin J. Grimm, PhD, Department of Psychology, Arizona State University, Tempe, AZ, United States

Eddie Harmon-Jones, PhD, School of Psychology, The University of New South Wales, Sydney, New South Wales, Australia

Deborah J. Harris, PhD, College of Education, University of Iowa, Iowa City, IA, United States

Heather Hayes, PhD, Learning Analytics and Quality, Western Governors University, Millcreek, UT, United States

Ursula Hess, PhD, Department of Psychology, Humboldt University, Berlin, Germany

Allie C. Hexley, DPhil, Department of Experimental Psychology, University of Oxford, Oxford, Oxfordshire, England

Masumi Iida, PhD, T. Denny Sanford School of Social and Family Dynamics, Arizona State University, Tempe, AZ, United States

Kate L. Jansen, PhD, Clinical Psychology Program, Midwestern University, Glendale, AZ, United States

Ken Kelley, PhD, Information Technology, Analytics, and Operations Department, Mendoza College of Business, University of Notre Dame, Notre Dame, IN, United States

Oliver Kirchkamp, PhD, Faculty of Business and Economics, Friedrich Schiller University of Jena, Jena, Germany

George P. Knight, PhD, Department of Psychology, Arizona State University, Tempe, AZ, United States

Parvati Krishnamurty, PhD, Bureau of Labor Statistics, Bethesda, MD, United States

Sean P. Lane, PhD, Department of Psychological Sciences, Purdue University, West Lafayette, IN, United States

Jean-Philippe Laurenceau, PhD, Department of Psychological and Brain Sciences, University of Delaware, Newark, DE, United States

Lisa Lee, PhD, NORC at the University of Chicago, Chicago, IL, United States

Frederick T. L. Leong, PhD, Department of Psychology, Michigan State University, East Lansing, MI, United States

Simon P. Liversedge, PhD, School of Psychology, University of Central Lancashire, Preston, Lancashire, England

Steven J. Luck, PhD, Center for Mind and Brain, University of California, Davis, Davis, CA, United States

Brent J. Lyons, PhD, Schulich School of Business, York University, Toronto, ON, Canada

Anna Madill, PhD, School of Psychology, University of Leeds, Leeds, England

Stefanie Martinez-Fuentes, MS, T. Denny Sanford School of Social and Family Dynamics, Arizona State University, Tempe, AZ, United States

David Matsumoto, PhD, Department of Psychology, San Francisco State University, San Francisco, CA, United States

Scott E. Maxwell, PhD, Department of Psychology, University of Notre Dame, Notre Dame, IN, United States

Robert E. McGrath, PhD, School of Psychology and Counseling, Fairleigh Dickinson University, Teaneck, NJ, United States

Danielle S. McNamara, PhD, Department of Psychology, Arizona State University, Tempe, AZ, United States

Sara V. Milledge, PhD, School of Psychology, University of Central Lancashire, Preston, Lancashire, England

Marius Moisa, PhD, Department of Economics, University of Zurich, Zurich, Switzerland

Tyler M. Moore, PhD, Department of Psychiatry, University of Pennsylvania, Philadelphia, PA, United States

Takuma Morimoto, PhD, Department of General Psychology, Justus-Liebig-Universität Gießen, Gießen, Germany; Department of Experimental Psychology, University of Oxford, Oxford, Oxfordshire, England

Sharlene D. Newman, PhD, Alabama Life Research Institute, University of Alabama, Tuscaloosa, AL, United States

Joseph M. Orr, PhD, Department of Psychological and Brain Sciences, Texas A&M University, College Station, TX, United States

Sangeeta Panicker, PhD, Public Responsibility in Medicine and Research, Boston, MA, United States

A. T. Panter, PhD, College of Arts and Sciences and L. L. Thurstone Psychometric Laboratory, The University of North Carolina at Chapel Hill, Chapel Hill, NC, United States

Vicenç Quera, PhD, Quantitative Psychology Section, Faculty of Psychology, University of Barcelona, Barcelona, Spain

Diana Ramirez, MLIS, Sterling C. Evans Library, Texas A&M University, College Station, TX, United States

Roger Ratcliff, PhD, Department of Psychology, The Ohio State University, Columbus, OH, United States

Steven P. Reise, PhD, Department of Psychology, University of California, Los Angeles, Los Angeles, CA, United States

Beth Ann Rice, PhD, Department of Psychology, Slippery Rock University, Slippery Rock, PA, United States

Nicolas Rohleder, PhD, Department of Psychology, Friedrich-Alexander-Universität Erlangen-Nürnberg, Erlangen, Bayern, Germany

Jessica L. Combs Rohr, PhD, Houston Methodist Hospital, Houston, TX, United States

Mark W. Roosa, PhD, T. Denny Sanford School of Social and Family Dynamics, Arizona State University, Tempe, AZ, United States

Monica D. Rosenberg, PhD, Department of Psychology, The University of Chicago, Chicago, IL, United States

Christian C. Ruff, PhD, Department of Economics, University of Zurich, Zurich, Switzerland

Amanda L. Sanchez, PhD, Penn Center for Mental Health, Perelman School of Medicine, University of Pennsylvania, Philadelphia, PA, United States

Neal Schmitt, PhD, Department of Psychology, Michigan State University, East Lansing, MI, United States

Oliver C. Schultheiss, PhD, Department of Psychology, Friedrich-Alexander-Universität Erlangen-Nürnberg, Erlangen, Bayern, Germany

Dennis J. L. G. Schutter, PhD, Department of Experimental Psychology, Helmholtz Institute, Utrecht University, Utrecht, The Netherlands

William R. Shadish, PhD, Deceased

Patrick E. Shrout, PhD, Department of Psychology, New York University, New York, NY, United States

Gregory T. Smith, PhD, Department of Psychology, University of Kentucky, Lexington, KY, United States

Manuel Spitschan, PhD, Max Planck Institute for Biological Cybernetics, Tübingen, Germany; Department of Sport and Health Sciences, Technical University of Munich, Munich, Germany

Peter M. Steiner, PhD, Department of Human Development and Quantitative Methodology, University of Maryland, College Park, MD, United States

Brian D. Stucky, PhD, Mercer, Los Angeles, CA, United States

Kristynn J. Sullivan, PhD, Merced County Public Health Department, Merced, CA, United States

Louis G. Tassinary, JD, PhD, School of Performance, Visualization and Fine Arts, Texas A&M University, College Station, TX, United States

Teresa A. Treat, PhD, Department of Psychological and Brain Sciences, University of Iowa, Iowa City, IA, United States

Alec Twibell, PhD, School of Psychology and Counseling, Fairleigh Dickinson University, Teaneck, NJ, United States

Adriana J. Umaña-Taylor, PhD, Harvard Graduate School of Education, Cambridge, MA, United States

Fons J. R. van de Vijver, PhD, Deceased

Struther Van Horn, PhD, National Center for Health Statistics, Hyattsville, MD, United States

Richard J. Viken, PhD, Department of Psychological and Brain Sciences, Indiana University, Bloomington, IN, United States

David Watson, PhD, Department of Psychology, University of Notre Dame, Notre Dame, IN, United States

Rebecca M. B. White, PhD, MPH, T. Denny Sanford School of Social and Family Dynamics, Arizona State University, Tempe, AZ, United States

Keith F. Widaman, PhD, Graduate School of Education, University of California, Riverside, Riverside, CA, United States

Carla Willig, PhD, Department of Psychology, City University of London, London, England

Yanyu Xiong, MS, Department of Psychological and Brain Sciences, Indiana University, Bloomington, IN, United States

A Note From the Publisher

The *APA Handbook of Research Methods in Psychology, Second Edition*, is the 36th publication and the first subsequent edition to be released in the American Psychological Association's *APA Handbooks in Psychology*® series, instituted in 2010. The series comprises both single volumes and multivolume sets focused on core subfields or on highly focused content areas and emerging subfields. A complete listing of the series titles to date can be found on pages ii–iii.

Each publication in the series is primarily formulated to address the reference interests and needs of researchers, clinicians, and practitioners in psychology. Each also addresses the needs of graduate students for well-organized and highly detailed supplementary texts, whether to "fill in" their own specialty areas or to acquire solid familiarity with other specialties and emerging trends across the breadth of psychology. Many of the sets additionally bear strong interest for professionals in pertinent complementary fields (i.e., depending on content area), be they corporate executives and human resources personnel; psychiatrists; doctors, nurses, and other health personnel; teachers and school administrators; counselors; legal professionals; and so forth.

Under the direction of small and select editorial boards consisting of top scholars in the field, with chapters authored by both senior and rising researchers and practitioners, each reference commits to a steady focus on best science and best practice. Coverage converges on what is currently known in the particular topical area (including basic historical reviews) and the identification of the most pertinent sources of information in both the core and evolving literature. Volumes and chapters alike pinpoint practical issues; probe unresolved and controversial topics; and highlight future theoretical, research, and practice trends. The editors provide guidance to the "dialogue" among chapters through internal cross-referencing that demonstrates a robust integration of topics. Readers are thus offered a clear understanding of the complex interrelationships within each field.

With content edited and authored by some of the most respected members of the largest association of psychologists in the world, the *APA Handbooks in Psychology* series is an indispensable and authoritative reference resource for researchers, instructors, practitioners, and field leaders alike.

Introduction: Objectives of Psychological Research and Their Relations to Research Methods

This is the second edition of the *APA Handbook of Research Methods in Psychology*. It is the first handbook in the APA series to undergo revision. This seems only appropriate given the handbook's broad overview of research methods used throughout scientific psychology. Not surprisingly, research methods have evolved over the past 10 years since the first edition, and there was much new material to cover. Of 103 chapters in the revised handbook, 27 cover new topics or revisit topics but have been rewritten, 75 have undergone revision, many extensively, some with smaller changes and updated references. One chapter has been reprinted.

METHODS OF KNOWING

The American philosopher Charles Peirce (1839–1914) claimed that we use five different ways to decide what we believe is true about our world (Feibleman, 1969). First, we believe some things are true because authorities we trust tell us so. Sometimes, we know these authorities personally, such as our parents and teachers. Sometimes, they are very distant from us, such as the writers of ancient religious texts. Other times, authorities are less far removed but still not personally known, for example, the authors in a handbook on research methods.

Second, we know things are true because we have heard them repeated many times. Peirce called this the *method of tenacity*, or the *a priori method*. Here, something is believed because it has always been believed (longevity) or because we have heard it repeated many times. We could include in this method the commonsense adages with which we are all familiar, such as "birds of a feather flock together" or "a stitch in time saves nine."

Third, we observe or experience things ourselves and our senses tell us they are true. The sun warms things up, for example.

Fourth, we know that some things are true because they can be logically derived; they are the product of rational analysis. Without getting into the formalities of logical

---

My sincere thanks go to the five associate editors of this handbook, Marc N. Coutanche, Linda M. McMullen, A. T. Panter, David Rindskopf, and Kenneth J. Sher. The latter three also served as editors on the first edition. They deserve equal billing with me as editors. They also provided feedback on this introduction, although any mistakes remain my doing. A special note of thanks goes to Kristen Knight, APA project editor, for her diligence and organizational efforts.

deduction, if a premise known to be true tells us that "all males have an Adam's apple," and we observe a men's intercollegiate fencing match, then logic dictates we believe that these fencers have Adam's apples under their masks.

The problem with each of these first four methods of knowing is that they are fallible. Two trusted authorities can disagree, suggesting that one (at least) must be wrong. Tenacious beliefs can lead us astray because conditions change over time, or what seems like common sense is not so sensible after all (remember, in addition to birds of a feather flocking together "opposites attract," and although a stitch in time may be frugal, "haste makes waste"). Our senses can deceive us, for example, through the application of different frames of reference, as demonstrated by optical illusions. Are the soccer balls in Figure 1 the same size?

Finally, a logical deduction is based on the validity of the premises, which may be wrong. Or, the logic itself may be faulty even though the premises are true, as when we affirm the consequent ("All male fencers have an Adam's apple," and "Spencer has an Adam's apple"; therefore, "Spencer is a fencer").

Peirce's final method of knowing was the scientific method. We can think of the scientific method as a combination of observation and rational analysis, or observation using a set of logical rules that should lead to veridical conclusions about the world. Peirce expected the scientific method to lead to knowledge that was exactly the same for every person, uninfluenced by idiosyncratic frames of reference. He held out the hope for truly objective knowledge.

FIGURE 1. Optical illusion involving two balls of the same size. Adapted from "The Representation of Perceived Angular Size in Human Primary Visual Cortex," by S. O. Murray, H. Boyaci, and D. Kersten, 2006, *Nature Neuroscience*, 9, pp. 429–434 (https://doi.org/10.1038/nn1641). Copyright 2006 by Springer Nature. Adapted with permission.

THE FLAWED BUT SELF-CRITICAL NATURE OF SCIENTIFIC INVESTIGATION

Peirce's grand vision for science, especially when applied to the social and behavioral sciences, is viewed by many in the 21st century as naive, at best. Vigorous debate prevails about whether knowledge is ever attainable without being infused with the theory of the observer (Godfrey-Smith, 2021; Kuhn, 1996). And studies that turn the methods of science on itself (the sociology of science) suggest that even when the search for objective knowledge is a desirable (and an obtainable) goal, the scientific process, in practice, is still replete with appeals to authority, idiosyncratic observation, and failures of rationality (Merton, 1957, 1979).

Perhaps it is best, then, to thank Peirce for having pointed out potential flaws in the ways that we acquire knowledge. And, although his belief in the existence of objective truth is open to debate, he argued that the application of rationally derived rules to observation was a self-correcting system. Over time, he asserted, by putting the claims of our authorities, observations, tenacious beliefs, and logical deductions to repeated empirical testing (with further observation and rational analysis), our erroneous beliefs would be replaced by *truer* ones.

The view of rational analysis as self-correcting captures only a secondary characteristic of the scientific method, in the case of social science, the scientific study of thought, feeling, and behavior. At the heart of the scientific ethos is the notion of critical analysis. That is, a scientific posture requires that we be skeptical of *any* truth claim, no matter from where it comes, even from science itself. Scientists test ideas in multiple ways from multiple perspectives with the *failure to disprove* after rigorous testing as the goal of their efforts.

Let's use Figure 1 to construct an example. In an ideal world, a scientist says,

> My observation suggests that the upper ball is larger than the lower ball. Now, let's try to prove that my observation is wrong.[1] As a public demonstration, I will use my thumb and forefinger to measure the diameter of the lower ball; then, holding my hand steady, I will move my measurement to the upper ball.

The measurement would suggest that the balls were roughly equal in diameter. Another scientist might then point out that my thumb and forefinger could not be held perfectly steady and suggest a ruler be used. The ruler would still suggest that the balls were equal in diameter. The process might continue with progressively more precise and careful measurement. Eventually, the observing scientists would come to agree that the hypothesis that the balls were the same size could not be rejected, or that evidence they were different sizes had failed repeated tests.

Next, the scientists would turn their attention to discovering why their eyes had deceived them. Then, as plausible evidence accumulated about *why* the reliance on simple observation was flawed (perhaps gathered by conducting experiments that manipulate the angle of the converging walls or the shadows in Figure 1), confidence in the conclusion about the state of nature, or the laws of visual perception, will grow.

---

[1] To be more precise, in the tradition of null hypothesis testing the scientist might say, "I propose an alternative to the hypothesis that the two balls have equal diameter. I propose that the upper ball is larger. Now, let's try to reject the equal diameter hypothesis."

A self-critical posture requires that truth claims never be believed with absolute certainty, only with greater or lesser certainty. This is what is most unique and, I think, exciting about the scientific posture. It is also one tenet that binds the chapters in this handbook. All of the chapter authors would agree that psychological scientists must take a critical stance toward what they call "knowledge."

SCIENCE AND DEMOCRACY

There is much to admire in this self-critical stance to knowledge acquisition. Importantly, in the 10 years since the first edition of this handbook, the need for critical thinking has mushroomed into a serious societal concern. Polarized thinking that is immune to evidence has driven deep divides in the body politic (Rutjens et al., 2018). While the self-critical methods outlined herein are essential to the solution of so many social problems, science itself is under attack and needs defense.

Timothy Ferris (2010) claimed that science is inherently antiauthoritarian because of its skeptical stance. In fact, he claimed that science and liberal democracy, that is, a social system that values human rights and freedom of action, go hand in hand. One cannot flourish without the other. Ferris wrote,

> The very process of doing first-rate science—of making important discoveries rather than merely refining old ideas—depends on unfamiliar and unpopular ideas being freely promulgated, discussed, and in some instances accepted. The fact that millions of people today are open to new ideas and skeptical about political and intellectual authority is largely due to the rise of science. (p. 4)

So, I would add another attribute shared by the authors of chapters in this handbook: open-mindedness. At the same time scientists accept no truth claim uncritically they also turn no idea away prima facie, on its first appearance.

Maintaining this posture of "open-minded skepticism" is no easy task. Finding the proper balance between foregoing prejudgment and embracing doubt, while holding in abeyance our only-too-human desire for certainty (and for *our* certainties to be deemed the correct ones), is the scientist's principal challenge. And psychological scientists have a particularly difficult task. They must hold to open-minded skepticism while studying their own species in contexts in which they themselves act. Unlike the physicist who can remain relatively detached from the behavior of atoms, psychological scientists can have a personal stake in what they discover about human nature, the good and the bad. So, is open-minded skepticism impossible? Perhaps. Flawed in its execution? More often than we might desire. Worth the effort? Certainly.

In the pages of this handbook, you will find descriptions of many techniques that psychologists and others have developed to help them pursue a shared understanding of why humans think, feel, and behave the way they do. These are the tools that we use to conduct our rational, self-critical, and open-minded analyses.

THE HANDBOOK'S ORGANIZATION

Organizing the chapters of this handbook was a huge challenge. Psychology's methods defy simple categorization because of their cross-disciplinary (and subdisciplinary) heritages. Many methods presented are similar to one another on some dimensions but far apart on others. So, deciding which dimensions to prioritize has nontrivial implications for where a method appears. In addition, prioritizing some dimensions over others can border on arbitrary and be based on oversimplified characterizations of any methodology's capacities for guiding discovery. Many methods can be used for more than one purpose. We have tried to put these "Swiss Army knives" of methodology in the toolbox compartment of their most frequent use. In addition, traditions of use within subdisciplines dictated that some methods appear close together, even if grouping them defied the logic of our dimensional analysis. And, some methods are so unique that they were hard to place anywhere. These methods are no less important because of their singularity; indeed, if they are the only way to answer a question, their uniqueness can make them especially valuable.

So, as you scan the table of contents and contemplate our choices for clustering and ordering the presentation of methods, I am certain that you will be perplexed by some of our choices. Other schemes could fit equally well, or better. Below, I try to capture the high-order dimensions that informed our placement of chapters, beginning with those that relate to the earliest decisions that a researcher makes when choosing methods.

FINDING THE METHOD THAT FITS THE QUESTION

There is an old joke in which a person is searching the ground beneath the halo of a streetlight.

> A stranger emerges from the dark and asks, "What are you looking for?"
> "My car keys," replies the searcher.
> The stranger sees nothing under the light and inquires, "Where did you lose them?"
> "Over there," says the searcher, pointing down the street.
> The stranger asks, "So why are you looking here?"
> "Because this is where the light is," the searcher explains.

Clearly, this searcher's method does not fit the objective. Similarly, psychological researchers must choose methods that fit the research question that they want to answer, not the method that is available or that they know best. No matter how luminous a method is, if the questions it can answer do not correspond to the knowledge sought, the researcher will remain in the dark.

You could think of this handbook as a collection of streetlights. Each method contained herein is meant to help you shed light on thought, feeling, and behavior over a different expanse and from a different angle. As I alluded to, another frequent metaphor compares research methods with a toolbox. Here, methodology provides the hammers, screwdrivers, wrenches, and rulers that psychological researchers use when they ply their trade.

You will read repeatedly in the chapters that follow that your first task as a psychological researcher is to pick the method best suited to answer the question that motivates you. You will be told not to search where the light is or bang a nail with a screwdriver. Instead, you will learn to choose the method that best answers your question. The contributors hope that this handbook will expand the topics that you can illuminate and increase the size of your toolbox. We hope to provide you with new ways to answer old questions as well as to raise new questions, perhaps ones you did not realize could be asked.

At the broadest level, when choosing a method you make decisions about (a) what measurement and data collection techniques best capture the thoughts, feelings, and behaviors that interest you; (b) what research design best fits the question that you want to answer; and (c) what strategies for data analysis best match the characteristics of your measurements and design.

The simplest choice for organizing the presentation of material is the temporal sequence in which you will make these decisions. This is roughly what we have done. So, the earliest chapters in Volume 1, Part I, address the broadest questions related to research designs. These involve both (a) which research designs are most appropriate for which question and (b) how to think about the ethicality the research that address your question, and (c) how to conduct research with participants drawn from more diverse populations.

Next, the chapters in Volume 1, Part II, help you with the research planning process, including how to develop a testable hypothesis, find the pertinent literature, secure the resources you need, and choose measures and what people to study. Part III of the first volume describes the plethora of measurement techniques that psychologists most often use to collect data and how to determine whether the measurement techniques that you might choose are the best ones for your purpose. For this revised edition of the handbook, significant changes were made to the discussions of chronometric and psychophysical measures (Section 4) and the measures used in psychophysiology and neuroscience (Sections 5 and 6).

Part IV contains chapters-looking at different ways to assess the trustworthiness of measures. These help you determine whether your measures can (or did) allow you find the answers you sought.

In Volume 2, Parts I through VII, the chapters return to issues of research design. They present for your consideration a panoply of options, further divided along more nuanced distinctions in their objectives (discussed in the following section, Interpretive Inquiry, Description, and Causal Explanation).

Chapters on techniques for data analysis follow in Volume 3, Part I, again with special attention to the fit between design, measurement, and analysis. Finally, issues and choices you must consider when you write up your research to share with the community of psychologists are discussed in the handbook's concluding chapters, in Volume 3, Part II.

INTERPRETIVE INQUIRY, DESCRIPTION, AND CAUSAL EXPLANATION

To choose the research design that best fits your research question, you need to consider some questions about your research aims. Are you seeking to (a) undertake an interpretive inquiry, (b) provide a description of an event, or (c) develop a causal explanation for the event or relation that interests you? Are you hoping to discover how individuals change over time or what makes groups of individuals different from one another, on average? The handbook begins with three examinations (including this Introduction and Chapters 1 and 2) that help you understand the differences between these types of questions. Then, in Volume 2, the chapters map specific research designs onto specific research questions.

Interpretive Research

To choose between interpretive or descriptive research, you must also answer the following question: Do you want to uncover the impetus to thoughts and actions that exist for the actors themselves or do you have your own theory or perspective to guide your data collection? Carla Willig (Chapter 1 in this volume) helps you decide whether your question naturally fits in the former category, suggesting an interpretive inquiry design. She suggests that qualitative research designs are most appropriate when the interpretation of an event by participants is your goal or when your question falls into one of these categories:

- What does something feel like?
- How is something experienced?
- How do people talk about something and with what consequences?
- How do people make sense of an experience?
- How do they construct its meaning? What does this allow them to do or not to do? To feel or not to feel?
- How does a particular event unfold? How do participants experience the event? What may be its consequences? For them and for others?

Willig makes the point that these approaches to psychological research are most appropriate when the researchers do not want to impose their own (or someone else's) theory or perspective on the thoughts, feelings, or actions of the people that they are studying. Rather, the researchers want to uncover the impetus to behavior that exists for the actors themselves. Cultural anthropologists refer to this as using an *emic* approach to describing behaviors and (conscious or unconscious) beliefs.

Qualitative designs (detailed in Volume 2, Part I) use a range of data, including spoken or written narratives from interviews and informal conversations; archival data contained in public records and private diaries; and visual data from photographs, film, and video. Although these data are often obtained from relatively few participants, large-scale, primarily quantitative, studies have increasingly employed a range of qualitative methods to explore a diverse range of questions. In recent years, the desirability of using multiple methods in research has become increasingly evident and is being adopted more often. Volume 2, Part II contains new chapters that address the use of multiple methods for collecting both qualitative and quantitative evidence in the same study.[2]

It is also possible to take an *etic* approach to research, or to provide a description of an event. Here, the researchers' theories and beliefs are applied to the situations that they study. These forms of descriptive research often focus on a few specific characteristics of events or individuals chosen a priori by the researcher. Participants are then sometimes broadly sampled and they respond to questions developed by the researchers to investigate particular aspects of the person or situation. Similar to qualitative research, the researchers make no attempt to manipulate the participants' circumstance. Similar to quantitative research, the data collected will be in numerical form and examined through statistical procedures.

Causal Explanatory Research

If your answer to the first question was (c), that you were seeking a causal explanation for an event or relation, then you will be looking for a different type of research design. When an investigator is in search of a causal connection, research cannot be undertaken

---

[2] For an interesting take on the similarities and differences between quantitative and qualitative approaches, see Shweder (1996): "The true difference between the approaches is not over whether to count and measure but rather over what to count and measure, and over what one actually discovers by doing so" (p. 179).

without some theoretical underpinning. Sometimes the theory is explicit, sometimes implicit, but it is always there. Theory tells us what variables to focus on as potential causes and effects, or how to divide the world into meaningful chunks.

Even with a theory to guide you, however, coming to a firm conclusion that one event has caused another may be more problematic than it seems at first.[3] In fact, "How do we know a cause when we see one?" is a question that has vexed philosophers of science for centuries. To understand why, we need to digress into a bit of science history.

The Scottish philosopher David Hume (see *A Treatise on Human Nature*, 1739–1740/1978) set out the dilemma for us (and, some would say, led social scientists astray; see Maxwell, 2004). Hume argued that for something to be considered a cause, (a) the cause and the effect had to happen together, (b) the cause had to occur before the effect, and (c) there had to be a *necessary connection* between the two events. Agreeing on whether Hume's first two conditions prevail in a particular search for a causal relationship is relatively straightforward. A researcher needs to show that Events A and B co-occur more often than would be expected by chance (although chance, being the iffy thing it is, implies that we can never make this determination with absolute certainty). The temporal sequence of events is typically observable with a high degree of reliability (although sometimes events occur nearly simultaneously, and sometimes effects, in psychology at least, are caused by the anticipation of other events).

Hume's (1739–1740/1978) third condition presents the greatest challenge to researchers in search of causes. Hume argued that we can never know with perfect certainty that the event we are calling the cause was the necessary connection that produced the effect.

A thought experiment will clarify his claim. Suppose I placed my coffee cup on the edge of my desk. My elbow slid into a book that then knocked the cup to the floor. What caused the coffee cup to fall? If we were to ask a group of people who observed the event to independently identify the cause of the spill, we would be confronted with multiple nominations. Most observers would say "the book" or "your elbow," but the more playful in the group might nominate "a gust of air" or even perhaps "a poltergeist." Are they wrong? Can you prove it *conclusively*?

Hume (1739–1740/1978) asserted that events happen in an unending flow and that even designating where one event ends and the next begins is subjective, that is, requires a prior theory or perspective that is supplied by the observer.[4] Therefore, he claimed, whenever we identify a *cause*, it remains possible to argue for other causes in two ways. First, we can identify another event that takes place *between* the asserted cause and effect. So, if I claim my elbow caused the coffee cup to fall, you can counterclaim that it was the book that provided the necessary connection. Yet another observer (especially a physicist) could claim *gravity* was the cause. After all, without gravity, the coffee cup would have remained suspended in air. Events preceding my errant elbow might also be viable alternate nominations—it was my writing deadline that caused me to be sitting at my desk.

Second, Hume (1739–1740/1978) argued that causal systems are open to outside influences. That is, an outside event can enter the claimed causal sequence. The "gust of air" or "poltergeist" explanation for my coffee spill would be outside

---

[3]See Cooper (2007) for my first presentation of this material on Hume (1739–1740/1978).
[4]Note how this harkens back to the criticisms of Peirce.

"an elbow-book-gravity-spill" causal system. Could an invisible mischievous spirit have knocked the cup just a nanosecond before the book hit it?

If we accept Hume's (1739–1740/1978) argument that we never know causes with complete certainty, then how are we to proceed to answer the question "What events cause other events to happen?" Steiner et al. (Chapter 2 in this volume) present the three influential frameworks that most psychologists use—drawn from social science, statistics, and computer science—to decide how evidence can be mapped onto causal claims so as to make the claim more or less plausible. Each strategy has implications for how data will be collected and analyzed. Oversimplifying, these strategies suggest that if causal explanation is what you seek, you next must answer the question "Are you interested in (a) testing the implications of a causal model or (b) manipulating a possible cause to see whether it has the presumed effect?" Depending on where your interest lies, you would choose either a design that involves causal modeling or a manipulation of experimental conditions.

Causal modeling. Research designs that propose and test causal models and do not involve experimental manipulations could be categorized as *quantitative descriptive research*. Researchers who use modeling approaches play out the *implications* of different causal assumptions and, therefore, produce results that bear on the plausibility of causal relations (Neimark & Estes, 1967). This is especially true of researchers who build and test structural equation models. Steiner et al. (Chapter 2 in this volume) point out that causal models are often intended to provide an exhaustive description of a network of linkages, which when coupled with certain assumptions (this is where Hume's, 1739–1740/1978, ghost haunts us) imply causal relationships.

Typically (and again oversimplifying), the modeling approach begins when researchers propose a sequence of interconnections that they believe captures the underlying causes of thought, feeling, or behavior. Then, they use one of numerous approaches to see how well the model and the data fit. They examine the co-occurrence of events in a multivariate, temporally sequenced framework. So, for example, I might propose that the sales of research methods handbooks are caused by (a) the editor's level of compulsiveness, which affects (b) the level of expertise of those chosen to be associate editors. Next, the expertise of the associate editors affects (c) who is chosen to be chapter authors. Then, the expertise of the chapter authors influences (d) the audience's perception of the value of the book and, finally, (e) their decision to buy the handbook.

Rodgers (2010) viewed the ascendance of mathematical and statistical modeling in psychology as nothing less than a (quiet but much needed) epistemological revolution. For one thing, most causal models focus on multivariate and temporally sequenced descriptions of behavior. These are typically more complex, and more complete, than the descriptions that you might find tested in many other approaches to studying causal relationships. Also, users of the modeling approach are less interested in testing a model against a null hypothesis ("Is this model better than no model at all?") but rather against an alternative model ("Is this model better than another proposed model?"). So, my model of handbook sales might be compared with one in which the publisher's advertising budget was also included.

Experimental and quasi-experimental designs. When researchers control aspects of the experimental situation by the purposive manipulation of an event, typically they do so to identify a cause-and-effect relation between one or a few presumed causes and one or a few effects rather than to investigate a complex and comprehensive model.

Designs are called *experimental* when they involve purposive manipulation of different conditions within the study. In this case, a study is conducted to isolate and draw a direct link between one event (the cause) and another (the effect). In studies that employ random assignment of participants to conditions, both the introduction of the event and who is exposed to it are controlled by the researchers (or other external agents), who then leave the assignment of conditions to chance. This approach is the best we have to ensure that on average the groups will not differ before the purposive manipulation. Therefore, we can be most confident (but not completely confident) that any differences between the conditions that we have created were caused by the manipulation, rather than preexisting differences between the participants in one condition from those in another.[5]

Designs with purposive manipulations can also be *quasi-experimental*. Here, the researchers (or some other external agents) control the introduction of the experimental manipulation but do not control precisely who may be exposed to it. In these designs, the researchers must find ways other than random assignment to equate participants in the various conditions so as to render less plausible the notion that preexisting differences between participants can explain any differences that they find on the outcome measures (the effects).

Individual-Change and Group-Difference Research

Before your quest for a research design can move from the general to the specific, you must also answer the question "Are you interested in understanding (a) how an individual (or more generally, a single unit) behaves or changes over time or (b) what makes one group different from another group, on average?" Let me give an illustration that demonstrates why this distinction is so important.

We know that sometimes learning, understanding, or cognitive change comes to a person as a sudden "aha" experience (Kounios & Beeman, 2009). The person gets it pretty much all at once, and a noticeable change in thinking becomes immediately evident and remains thereafter. Different people may have aha experiences after different numbers of exposures to an event or stimulus. For example, the top panel of Figure 2 displays the scores of six hypothetical people on a questionnaire regarding their perception of the need for energy conservation. The imaginary participants were exposed to 10 proconservation messages in the same sequence.[6] Each message highlighted a different reason for conserving energy—health threats from pollution, climate change, reduced costs, energy independence, and so on. On the basis of the data in this figure, the best description of how a person's perspective on the need for conservation changed would be to say that each person experienced a cognitive change on viewing a particular message, after which their perspective became noticeably more proconservation and remained so. But the message that precipitated the change was different for different people, and one person never changed at all.

---

[5]But we can never be completely certain that the characteristic of the manipulation that we claim is causal was the productive element because our experimental and comparison conditions can be viewed as differing on many characteristics. Hume's ghost again.

[6]You would not want to do this in a real experiment because it confounds the particular stimuli with the order. In this imaginary scenario, you must assume that order has no influence, so that differences between people are due to the message.

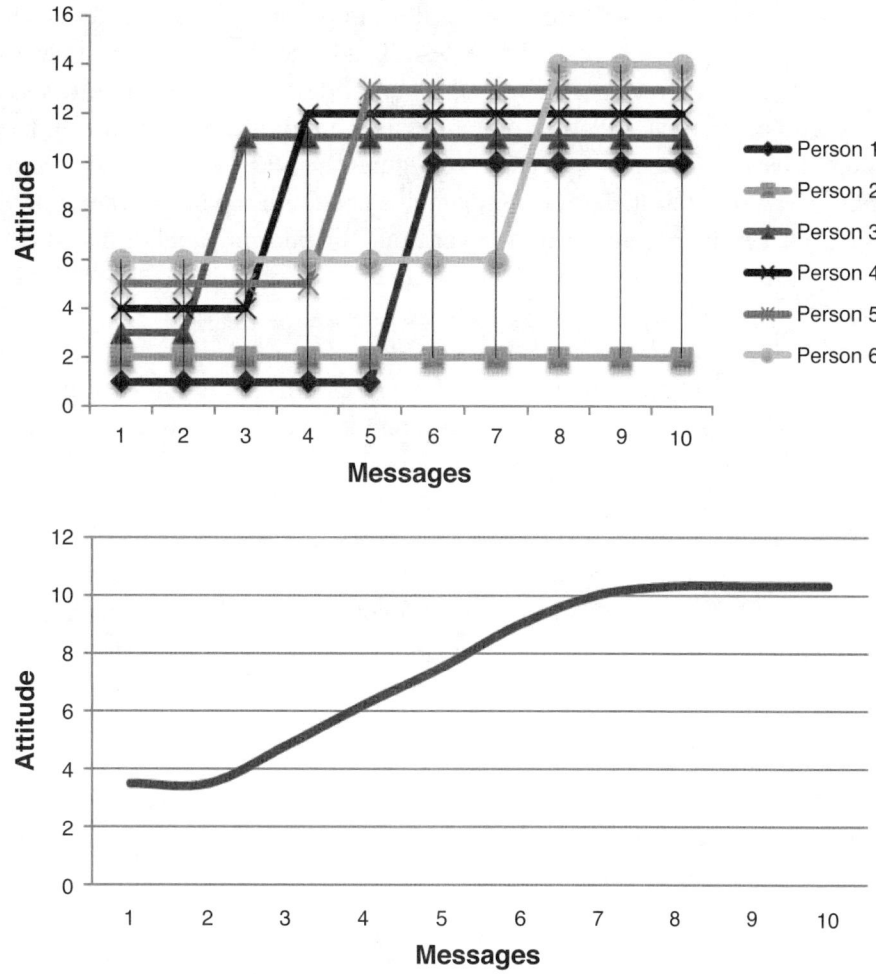

FIGURE 2. Hypothetical graphs of six individuals' change in attitude (top panel) and group-averaged attitudes of those six people (bottom panel) toward energy conservation after viewing 10 proconservation messages with different themes.

The bottom panel of Figure 2 provides a graph of how the same data look if averaged across the six people. A much different picture emerges. Looking at this graph, if you were to *assume* the group average effect accurately reflected what was happening to each individual person, you would say that after the second exposure, each person gradually changed their perspective on conservation after viewing each message. After eight exposures, no additional change took place. Clearly, this would be an incorrect characterization of the process occurring at the level of the individual person. That said, the group-averaged data could be used to describe how change occurred for the group as a whole, as a single unit. Thus, the correct interpretation of the group-averaged data would be to say that when a group was exposed to proconservation messages, the group average attitude changed gradually after the second exposure, but there was no additional change after eight exposures. This would be an accurate description of how the group behaved over exposures, but it would not adequately describe any single member within the group.

Whether you are interested in the individual or group-averaged effect depends on the context in which your question is being asked. Sometimes the group average does represent the behavior of a single unit. So the bottom panel of Figure 2 is a description of, say, how one city's perspective might be described if the 10 messages were weekly programs aired on a local television channel. Then, the city becomes the unit, not the individuals who populate it. If your problem focuses on understanding how individual units change over time, then the top panel of Figure 2 provides you with six replications of the phenomena of interest. The bottom panel is irrelevant to your question. If your focus is on how a group average changes over time, the bottom panel provides you with one instance of this and the top panel is irrelevant.

Summary of Design Considerations

Figure 3 lays out the relations between the four questions about a research question. The figure needs to be read from both the top and the bottom to arrive at the designs in the middle. This is because two questions, those about interpretive, descriptive, or explanatory research (at the top) and single-unit versus differences-between-groups-of-units research (at the bottom), are independent of one another. Which of the two other questions you answer depends on how you answer the question about interpretation, description, or explanation. A theory-discovery or theory-specified approach is available to you once you have decided that your question is interpretive or descriptive. If your question is explanatory, it is theory driven by definition, but you must decide whether the question involves modeling the causal implications of the theory or estimating its causal effect via an experimental manipulation.

The handbook uses the answers to these questions to organize the chapters on research design found in Volume 2. Interpretive research designs that emphasize a qualitative

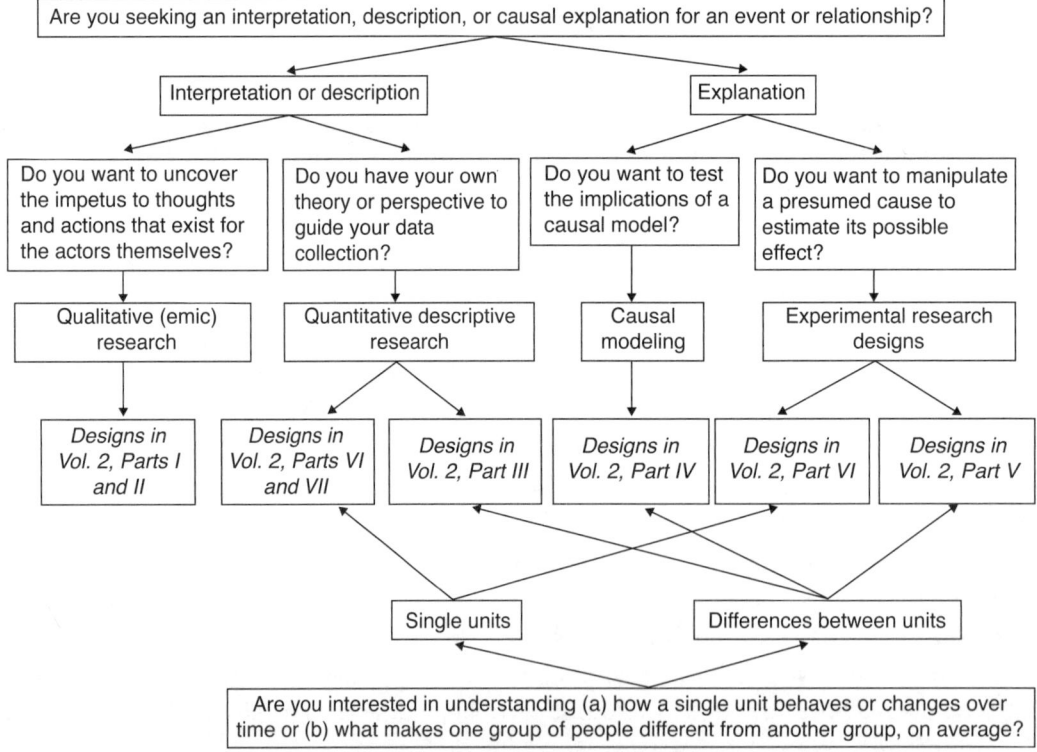

FIGURE 3. Relations between research questions, research designs, and the organization of parts in the *APA Handbook of Research Methods in Psychology*.

approach are detailed in Part I. Most of these designs also focus on questions that involve describing the current state or change in an individual unit of interest or a small sample of individuals. Part II looks at issues at the transition point between qualitative and quantitative research, as well as issues that arise in research with particular populations and settings that go beyond their simple participation in research.

Volume 2, Parts III through VII, introduce designs that emphasize an etic (or theory-specified), more quantitative approach to research. Volume 2, Part III, presents issues in sampling for quantitative studies. Although the techniques described herein will be of interest to all researchers, they would be of special interest to those who are conducting descriptive research. So, for example, if you are collecting data on the impact of growing up in a single-parent home, this section will assist you in planning your strategy for sampling respondents, help you consider issues you will encounter in collecting data from participants over time, and help you determine how you might use the internet. Volume 2, Part IV, focuses on designs that build and test the implications of causal models. You will find here approaches that differ in the type of data that they employ (sometimes even simulated data) and in the assumptions that are made as part of the data analysis (e.g., Bayesian modeling). Volume 2, Part V, focuses on research with experimental manipulations, in which participants are deliberately treated differently. Section 1 of Part V distinguishes these designs depending on how participants were assigned to their experimental conditions. Section 2 of Part V describes many of the unique problems that psychologists face when they conduct experimental research in applied settings.

In Volume 2, Part VI, designs are introduced that focus on theory-testing questions, rely heavily on quantification, and are used to study change in individual units. These designs all require multiple measurements of the same dependent variable(s) over a period of time. They can be used to study change that is either (a) naturally occurring, for example, as when a researcher wants to describe how a person's cognitive abilities change as they age, or (b) purposively manipulated, as when a researcher examines an older adult's cognitive ability before and after an intervention that is meant to improve memory.

The designs in Volume 2, Part VII, are labeled "Neuropsychology" and "Genetic Methods in Psychology." Here you will find designs for theory-driven research that derive largely from the more biological end of psychology's family tree.

MEASUREMENT METHODS AND PSYCHOMETRICS

After you have a good grasp of your research question and the general design of your study, you need to choose the means of measuring the variables of interest to you. You must answer the question "What measures best capture the variables of interest?" Volume 1, Parts III and IV, of the handbook help you consider your choices and pick the measure that best answers your question.

Units of Analysis

As a science matures, it adopts, adapts, and invents new techniques for looking at the world. Certainly, the ruler that we used to examine the optical illusion in Figure 1 was not invented for that purpose alone. Rather, we realized its relevance to our problem and commandeered it for our cause. And, as you look at the contents of Volume 1,

Parts III and IV, it will be obvious to you that this handbook describes an enormous array of rulers. Some of these rulers were invented by psychologists, but many were invented for other purposes to study phenomena of interest in other disciplines.

It is possible to think of the sciences as falling along a continuum that distinguishes them according to the size of the things that they study or their unit of analysis or investigation. So chemists, generally speaking, study things that are physically smaller than the things studied by biologists, whose units of study often are smaller than those studied by psychologists, whose units often are smaller than those studied by sociologists. Of course, the overlap in topics of interest is great, so at the margins the distinction between disciplines breaks down; it becomes difficult, if not impossible, to identify where one scientific discipline ends and the next begins. A psychologist who studies group identity is more likely to share an intellectual heritage with many sociologists than with a psychologist who studies the role of neurotransmitters in depression, whose work may be more akin to that of a neurobiologist.

Along with a blurring at the margins of disciplines comes the transfer of measurements and methods between disciplines. Not surprisingly, then, in this handbook, you will find measurement techniques (as well as research designs and statistical techniques) with histories that locate their roots in numerous fields of study, including economics, political science, sociology, anthropology, neurobiology, and genetics. This is a good thing for our discipline. Psychologists have come to recognize that a complete picture of any phenomenon requires that it be examined through multiple methods, applying multiple rulers. To fully understand schizophrenia, for example, psychological scientists might need to survey its prevalence in a population, examine family dynamics, observe, interview, and test individuals with the disorder, conduct brain scans, and map genes.

Because of psychology's interdisciplinary range, the array of methods covered in this handbook is daunting. But the variety of methods that psychologists use is indicative of our discipline's strength and vitality. The authors of the handbook chapters are motivated by a search for answers, no parochialism here. They share the belief that their own method of choice cannot develop a complete picture of the world or, really, any discrete phenomenon in it. Rather, each method supplies a small piece of the puzzle. It is only when the puzzle pieces are fit together that a complete picture emerges.

Volume 1, Part III, of the handbook offers many different techniques of measurement. The sections are roughly organized according to the size of their unit of analysis. It begins with the largest units and proceeds to the smallest. So, Section 1 presents techniques that measure peoples' overt individual behavior, which are typically available for others to view. Sections 2 and 3 largely describe measures for which people provide verbal or written data about what they are thinking, what they are feeling, or how they behave. Sections 4, 5, and 6 reduce the unit of analysis even further, to psychophysical and psychophysiological measures and then to measures that are biological in nature.

The chapters in Volume 1, Part IV, help you answer a second question about your measures: "How well does your chosen measure represent the variable that interests you?" This question again requires you to consider fit, but now between a concept, or latent variable, and the means that are used to measure it. Put simply, the variables involved in psychological research need to be defined in two ways, conceptually and operationally. *Conceptual* definitions describe qualities of the variable that are independent of time and space and can be used to distinguish events that are and are not instances of the concept. For example, a conceptual definition of *aggression* might be "behavior intended to cause pain or harm." Conceptual definitions can differ in breadth, that is, in the number of events that they capture. So, if the terms *pain* and *harm* are interpreted broadly, then *aggression* could include verbal as well as physical acts.

To relate concepts to concrete events, a variable must also be operationally defined. An *operational* definition is a description of the observable characteristics that allows us to determine whether a behavior or event represents an occurrence of the conceptual variable. So, an operational definition of *aggression* might include "shouting, or vocalizations above a specified decibel level" if verbal aggression is included but not so if only physical harm is included. The chapters in Volume 1, Part IV, present the criteria and many of the techniques that psychological researchers use to assess whether a measure is a good fit for a construct.

The Value of Multiple Operations

As you think about measures for a study, it is important to keep in mind that it is generally a good idea to include more than one operationalization of the constructs that interest you. Webb et al. (1999) set out the classic arguments for the value of having multiple operations to define the same underlying construct. They defined *multiple operationism* as the use of many measures that share a conceptual definition "but have different patterns of irrelevant components" (p. 35). Having multiple operations of a construct has positive consequences because

> once a proposition has been confirmed by two or more independent measurement processes, the uncertainty of its interpretation is greatly reduced. . . . If a proposition can survive the onslaught of a series of imperfect measures, with all their irrelevant error, confidence should be placed in it. (Webb et al., 1999, p. 35)

Of course, Webb and colleagues (1999) were quick to point out that our confidence in a finding is first and foremost accomplished by "minimizing error in each instrument and by a reasonable belief in the different and divergent effects of the sources of error" (p. 35) across the measures that we include.

An example shows how this works. Suppose in a study you measure the level of aggression between two people in three different ways: by unobtrusively observing participants' physical contact, by self-reported desire to harm one another, and by taking a physiological measure of arousal (one from Volume 1, Part III, Section 1; one from Section 2; and one from Section 5). You can be confident that these measures do not share irrelevant sources of error. Observed behaviors might be open to misclassification (a slap on the back might be coded as an act of aggression but really be one of friendship), but self-reports and physiological arousal less so. Self-reports are more open to responding in a socially desirable manner than unobtrusive observations or physiological measures. People become aroused by both love and hate but rarely self-report hate when love is the answer.

Now suppose your study was meant to test the hypothesis that the likelihood of aggression is related to state anxiety. If all three of your measures revealed similar predicted relations to measures of state anxiety or responded similarly to manipulations meant to increase state anxiety (say, the sounding of an alarm),[7] this would allow you to

---

[7] Of course, multiple measures of state anxiety are as desirable a feature of your study as multiple measures of aggression.

rule out the irrelevant influences (misinterpretation by observers, social desirability, etc.) on your three aggression measures as the cause of the relation. If results are inconsistent across operations, having the three measures allows you to speculate on what the important differences between operations might be and refine your theory about how the two constructs are related.

There is another benefit to including multiple operations in research. Predictions are often made from theories on the basis of presumed causal processes that include multiple steps, or causal linkages. These are the focus of causal modeling studies (Volume 2, Part IV), and they also pertain to other research designs. So, we might speculate that hearing an alarm increases state anxiety by increasing uncertainty and physiological arousal. In turn, uncertainty and arousal increase the likelihood of aggression. By including a measure of arousal in your study, along with observed and self-reported aggression measures, your study also tests this mediating mechanism.

Of necessity, the chapters in Volume 1, Part III, present their array of measurement methods largely as discrete choices. And, in Volume 1, Part IV, the methods for appraising a measure's fit with the construct of interest largely address the adequacy of each measure separately. But as you design a study, you should not think that you must choose one measure or another. Instead, when you consider which measure best captures your construct of interest, remember that no measure is perfect. And, to the extent reasonable, the more measures—that do not share the same imperfections and that test more than one linkage if a causal chain is hypothesized—the better.

QUANTITATIVE DATA ANALYSIS

Once you have chosen your design and measures, the next question you must answer is, "What data analysis procedure corresponds to your research design and the characteristics of your measures?" Volume 3, Part I, presents a compendium of your options for analysis. Section 1 presents different techniques that you can use to get to know your data as a whole. Special attention is paid to discovering distributional or other characteristics of data (e.g., outliers, missing values) that might dictate your approach to analysis or that might need to be addressed before your more substantive analysis should proceed. Section 2 presents some approaches to describing your data and techniques that you might use to communicate your findings to others.

Volume 3, Part I, Sections 3 to 5, presents both basic and advanced techniques for analyzing and interpreting social and behavioral science data. The chapters are organized first according to the number of dependent or outcome measures in the analysis. In Section 3 you will find methods that are used when you want to relate a single dependent or outcome variable (e.g., self-reported aggression) to one or more independent or predictor variables (e.g., state anxiety, age, sex).

In Volume 3, Part I, Section 4, statistical techniques are presented that apply to studies involving, in their most basic case, a single outcome or criterion measure that has been measured more than once, over time. So, if the chapter on "Collecting Longitudinal Data: Present Issues and Future Challenges" (Volume 2, Part III, Chapter 18) is of interest to you, you will likely find an analytic strategy here that meets your needs.

The methods in Volume 3, Part I, Section 5, pertain to data analyses in which you have many measures and make no distinction between which variables are independent or dependent, predictor or criterion. Most frequently, these techniques are used to uncover the abstract, or latent, variables that underlie a set of observed, or manifest, variables. For example, we might use an exploratory factor analysis to determine the number of factors underlying a multi-item measure of aggression or a confirmatory factor analysis (on the same instrument) to test the theory that the tendency toward physical and verbal aggression are independent (i.e., knowing how likely people are to hit you tells you nothing about how likely they are to call you a nasty name). Within Volume 3, Part I, Sections 3 to 5, you will also find a distinction in analytic choices depending on whether they pertain to (a) variables that are measured continuously or (b) variables that place people (or other units) into classes. Some of these techniques take into account the categorical nature of variables in your analyses, whereas others help you to discover what these categorical distinctions among respondents might be.

So, to find the chapters of greatest interest to you in these sections, first you will need to answer three questions: (a) Does your research problem distinguish independent or predictor variables from dependent or outcome variables? (b) Are your variables measured over time? (c) Are your variables continuous or categorical, either in how they are conceptualized or how they are measured? Of course, in many instances your answers to these questions will be complex. Within the same study, for example, you might want to reduce the number of dependent variables by constructing a composite (e.g., factor analyze the observation, self-report, and physiological measures of aggression) and then use the composite in a regression analysis (one dependent variable) with other, multiple indicators. Or, you will have some continuous and some class variables. As you read the chapters, you will find that one great advance in statistical science has been the recent development of sophisticated techniques that permit the integrated analysis of data that vary in their characteristics and the number of variables involved.

Volume 3, Part 1, Section 6, presents methods for studies that take into account (and capitalize on) the interdependence of responses from multiple participants who are in interaction with one another. The units of analysis can be anywhere from a dyad (e.g., a husband and wife) to a large group (e.g., a sports team, workers in an office). Because the responses of individuals in these networks are dependent on the responses of others, the data analysis strategy must take this into account. Equally important, sometimes the research question focuses on the nature of the interdependence.

Finally, in Volume 3, Part I, Section 7, you will find two chapters that present some of the special issues that arise, and some special statistical techniques that are used, when researchers reanalyze or integrate data that was collected by others. In one instance, secondary data analysis, you work with raw data that might have been collected for another purpose (e.g., arrest rates and climate data in cities are used to test the relation between crime and temperature). In the other instance, meta-analysis, the statistical results of previous research becomes the raw data in a quantitative research synthesis.

Effect Sizes, or Relation Strength, and Their Interpretation

The chapters in Volume 3, Part I, look remarkably different from those that would have appeared *in* such a work a generation ago, far more so than the other parts of the handbook. Before the past three decades, testing the null hypothesis was the gold standard for drawing inferences about whether data revealed significant relations. More recently, the exclusive use of null hypothesis significance testing has become controversial, with some arguing that the practice should be abandoned entirely (Cohen, 1994). An American Psychological Association (APA) task force recommended that researchers need to ask of their data not only, "Are these variables related, yes or no?" but also "How strong of a relationship is there?" (Wilkinson & Task Force on Statistical Inference, 1999).

Prominent among the methods used to describe data is the estimation and interpretation of *effect sizes*, or "the degree to which the phenomenon is present in the population" (Cohen, 1988, p. 9). With the coming of age of effect size estimation came the importance of understanding the difference between statistical significance and *clinical* or *practical* significance. The latter requires extrastatistical interpretation of the data. To assess practical significance, researchers (and others) must wrestle with the question of how strong a relation needs to be before it can be deemed meaningful or important (see Cooper, 2008).

The answer to this question always depends on the context in which the research takes place. Cohen (1988) suggested some general definitions for small, medium, and large effect sizes in the social sciences. In defining these adjectives, he compared different average effect sizes that he had encountered across disciplines in the behavioral sciences. However, Cohen did not intend his labels to serve as guides for the *substantive* interpretation of relations by social scientists. Rather, he intended his rules to assist with power analyses in planning future studies, a very different objective. Using Cohen's definitions to interpret the substantive importance of an effect size misapplies his work.

In fact, there is no fixed scale for the substantive interpretation of the size of a relation, and there is no substitute for knowing the research context of the specific question. Here is a simple example. Assume that we have the results of a study that evaluated an intervention that was conducted with 200 participants, 100 each in the intervention and control condition, and a dichotomous measure of success or failure. Using Cohen's definitions, an increase in success rate from 45% in the control condition to 55% in the intervention condition would be considered a small effect (equivalent to $r = .10$ explaining 1% of the variance). However, what if this effect were found on a measure of "suicides among previous attempters" and the intervention was access to online psychological services? Personally, I would not be inclined to label this effect "small," practically speaking. However, if the study measured whether previous suicide attempters did or did not endorse the statement "life is worth living" after a year of daily psychotherapy "small effect" certainly would come to my mind.

In this example, I tried to demonstrate that the interpretation of effect sizes rests heavily on (a) the intrinsic value placed on the outcome variable (how valuable is even a small difference?) and (b) the cost of the intervention. Also, when interpreting the magnitude of effects, it is informative to use contrasting elements that are closely related to the topic at hand. For example, what other interventions have been used to prevent suicide among previous attempters? If the hotline and several other interventions have been tried and found to have no effect, suddenly the daily therapy effect starts to look larger, worth pursuing further.

Effect sizes also need to be interpreted in relation to the methodology used in the primary research. So, studies with more intensive treatments (e.g., more frequent therapy sessions), more sensitive research designs (within-subject rather than between-subject), and measures with less random error can be expected to reveal larger effect sizes, all else being equal.

Although null hypothesis testing is not ignored, the contents of this handbook clearly demonstrate the shifting of emphasis from "yes or no?" to "how much?" questions. In all of the chapters on data analysis, you will find a primary emphasis on estimating and interpreting the magnitude of relations.

Promoting Transparency in Research Methods

Over the past decade, psychological scientists have increasing come to embrace the tenets of open science, a movement meant to "increase openness, integrity and reproducibility of research" (Center for Open Science, 2020). Among the changes in practice espoused by the open science movement are (a) the registration of study methods and analysis strategies before a study has begun collecting data, (b) the sharing of data once it has collected, (c) complete and transparent reporting of research methods and data, and (d) direct access for the public and policy makers to research articles and results, regardless of their economic circumstance. Open science practices are meant to facilitate the replication of study methods and results and to allow for more complete evaluations of the strength and weaknesses of research. With greater transparency and accessibility will come greater trust in and increased use of the findings of psychological science.

The question you must answer about reporting your research is: "What do readers need to know about your study so they can (a) evaluate its trustworthiness; (b) replicate it, if they wish; and (c) use it along with other studies to synthesize research on your topic?" Note that this question uses the word *need* rather than the word *want*. This is because the standards for reporting research have become considerably more detailed in the past decade. This is especially true since the publication of the seventh edition of the APA's *Publication Manual* (APA, 2020). The *Publication Manual* includes tables and figures containing the journal article reporting standards (or the JARS; Appelbaum et al., 2018) that summarize the information editors, reviewers, and readers expect to see in your work.

Why are reporting standards needed? Two developments in psychology—indeed, in all the behavioral, social, and medical sciences—have led to an increased emphasis on complete research reporting. First, social science evidence is being increasingly used in public policy decision making. This use places new importance on understanding how research was conducted and what it found (APA Presidential Task Force on Evidence-Based Practice, 2006). Policy makers and practitioners who wish to make decisions that are informed by scientific evidence want to know how reliable the information they are considering is and in what context the data were collected. This dictates that research reports be comprehensive in their descriptions of methods and results.

Second, psychological scientists studying basic processes have found that as evidence about specific hypotheses and theories accumulates, greater reliance is being placed on syntheses of research, especially meta-analyses (see Valentine et al., Volume 3, Chapter 24, this handbook). Psychologists who use meta-analysis summarize findings, but they also use variations in research methods to find clues to the variables that might mediate differences in findings. These clues emerge by grouping studies on the basis of distinctions in their methods and then comparing their results. For example, a meta-analyst might group studies of the relation between state anxiety and aggression depending on what type of aggression measure was used: observation, self-report, or physiological. What are the implications if only one type of measure reveals a relation? This synthesis-based evidence is then used to guide the next generation of problems and hypotheses to be studied in new data collections. Meta-analysis requires detailed descriptions of what you have done. Without complete reporting of methods and results, the utility of your study is diminished.

In Cooper (2018), I introduced each item listed in the JARS as well as an explanation of why it was deemed important for inclusion. The bottom line is that without complete reporting, the value of your study for the users of your findings will be diminished.

The final part of the handbook addresses issues related to open science. It includes three chapters that address data management and the integrity of the research reporting process. The chapters in Volume 3, Part II, look at how to plan for managing your data, including documentation and storage so that it is easily understood by others (Chapter 25), what practices in data analysis that should be avoided so that your results are more easily replicable (Chapter 26), and a broader overview of ethical issues that arise in research not associated with the treatment of research participants (Chapter 27). All these chapters are new to the second edition of the handbook.

CONCLUSION

"Introductions" to edited works are required to address what the chapters that follow have in common as well as how the differences between chapters are to be understood. Writing such a chapter for a handbook as broad in scope as this one has required that I touch on similarities at lofty levels of abstraction, such as the methods by which people know things and the relation of science to democracy.

But I have been able as well to uncover some very down-to-earth examples of similarities in the chapters. For example, as I have noted several times, a principle shared by all of the authors is that the research methods you choose should be appropriate to answer the question that you pose. This dictum seems almost too obvious to state. Let us not fool ourselves, however. The opposing desire to use the tool you know even if it's not a perfect fit is often hard to resist. Hopefully, this handbook will expand your toolbox so that this latter approach loses its appeal.

Describing the differences between chapters and how they can be understood has presented an equally formidable challenge. It was easy to begin with the sequence of method choices—assessing the ethics and feasibility of different approaches, then choosing measures, a research design, statistical techniques, and ending with research reports—although we know that in practice these choices are never as linear as they appear in books.

Bringing an equally linear order to the array of research designs, measurements, and analytic techniques available to psychological scientists was the most difficult task. Different approaches to psychological research begin with different epistemic assumptions and then travel through subdisciplines with different traditions. Like the species that we study, the methods used by psychological scientists defy simple categorization. But this is a good thing (even if it causes trouble for editors). After all, if science is humankind's greatest achievement (and I think it is), then isn't turning the lens of science on ourselves the ultimate expression of our uniqueness?

Harris Cooper
Editor-in-Chief

References

American Psychological Association. (2020). *Publication manual of the American Psychological Association* (7th ed.).

APA Presidential Task Force on Evidence-Based Practice. (2006). Evidence-based practice in psychology. *American Psychologist, 61*(4), 271–285. https://doi.org/10.1037/0003-066X.61.4.271

Appelbaum, M., Cooper, H., Kline, R. B., Mayo-Wilson, E., Nezu, A. M., & Rao, S. M. (2018). Journal article reporting standards for quantitative research in psychology: The APA Publications and

Communications Board task force report. *American Psychologist, 73*(1), 3–25. https://doi.org/10.1037/amp0000191

Center for Open Science. (2020). *COS: Center for Open Science.* https://www.cos.io/

Cohen, J. (1988). *Statistical power analysis for the behavioral sciences.* Erlbaum.

Cohen, J. (1994). The earth is round ($p < .05$). *American Psychologist, 49*(12), 997–1003. https://doi.org/10.1037/0003-066X.49.12.997

Cooper, H. (2007). *Evaluating and interpreting research syntheses in adult learning and literacy.* National Center for the Study of Adult Learning and Literacy. https://doi.org/10.1037/e549792010-001

Cooper, H. (2008). The search for meaningful ways to express the effects of interventions. *Child Development Perspectives, 2*(3), 181–186. https://doi.org/10.1111/j.1750-8606.2008.00063.x

Cooper, H. (2018). *Reporting quantitative research in psychology: How to meet journal article reporting standards.* American Psychological Association. https://doi.org/10.1037/0000103-000

Feibleman, J. K. (1969). *An introduction to the philosophy of Charles S. Peirce.* MIT Press.

Ferris, T. (2010). *The science of liberty.* HarperCollins.

Godfrey-Smith, P. (2021). *Theory and reality: An introduction to the philosophy of science* (2nd ed.). University of Chicago Press. https://doi.org/10.7208/chicago/9780226771137.001.0001

Hume, D. (1978). *A treatise on human nature.* Oxford University Press. (Original work published 1739–1740)

Kounios, J., & Beeman, M. (2009). The *Aha!* moment: The cognitive neuroscience of insight. *Current Directions in Psychological Science, 18*(4), 210–216. https://doi.org/10.1111/j.1467-8721.2009.01638.x

Kuhn, T. S. (1996). *The structure of scientific revolutions* (3rd ed.). University of Chicago Press. https://doi.org/10.7208/chicago/9780226458106.001.0001

Maxwell, J. A. (2004). Causal explanation, qualitative research, and scientific inquiry in education. *Educational Researcher, 33*(2), 3–11. https://doi.org/10.3102/0013189X033002003

Merton, R. K. (1957). Priorities of scientific discovery. In N. Storer (Ed.), *The sociology of science: Theoretical and empirical investigations* (pp. 635–659). University of Chicago Press.

Merton, R. K. (1979). *The sociology of science: Theoretical and empirical investigations.* University of Chicago Press.

Murray, S., Boyaci, H., & Kersten, D. (2006). The representation of perceived angular size in human primary visual cortex. *Nature Neuroscience, 9*, 429–434. https://doi.org/10.1038/nn1641

Neimark, E. D., & Estes, W. K. (1967). *Stimulus sampling theory.* Holden-Day.

Rodgers, J. L. (2010). The epistemology of mathematical and statistical modeling: A quiet methodological revolution. *American Psychologist, 65*(1), 1–12. https://doi.org/10.1037/a0018326

Rutjens, B. T., Heine, S. J., Sutton, R. M., & van Harreveld, F. (2018). Attitudes toward science. *Advances in Experimental Social Psychology, 57*, 125–165. https://doi.org/10.1016/bs.aesp.2017.08.001

Shweder, R. A. (1996). Quanta and qualia: What is the "object" of ethnographic research? In R. Jessor, A. Colby, & R. A. Shweder (Eds.), *Ethnography and human development: Context and meaning is social inquiry* (pp. 175–182). University of Chicago Press.

Webb, E. J., Campbell, D. T., Schwartz, R. D., Sechrest, L., & Grove, J. B. (1999). *Unobtrusive measures.* SAGE.

Wilkinson, L., & the Task Force on Statistical Inference. (1999). Statistical methods in psychology journals: Guidelines and explanations. *American Psychologist, 54*(8), 594–604. https://doi.org/10.1037/0003-066X.54.8.594

Part I

PHILOSOPHICAL, ETHICAL, AND SOCIETAL UNDERPINNINGS OF PSYCHOLOGICAL RESEARCH

Section 1

PHILOSOPHICAL ISSUES FOR RESEARCH IN PSYCHOLOGY

CHAPTER 1

PERSPECTIVES ON THE EPISTEMOLOGICAL BASES FOR QUALITATIVE RESEARCH

Carla Willig

This chapter reviews and clarifies the various ways in which qualitative researchers approach the creation of knowledge. Qualitative research can take many forms. Within the general rubric of qualitative research, we find a wide range of activities that are driven by different goals, deploy different research strategies, and generate different kinds of insights. This means that although all qualitative research shares some important attributes (and these are identified in the next section), it also is characterized by fundamental differences in epistemological orientation. In other words, qualitative researchers can take a range of different positions in relation to questions about the nature and status of any knowledge claims that may be made on the basis of their research. This chapter maps out the range of epistemological positions available to qualitative researchers and discusses the implications for the way in which qualitative research is conducted and evaluated.

The chapter is structured as follows: In the first section, we remind readers of the nature and purpose of qualitative research in general. We identify the most important characteristics of qualitative research, those which are shared by all forms of qualitative research (see the section What Is Qualitative Research?). In the second section, Differences Among Qualitative Approaches, we discuss the different strands within the qualitative research endeavor. Here, we focus on the different types of knowledge that can be generated on the basis of different approaches to qualitative enquiry. In the third section, Epistemological Frameworks, we introduce the various epistemological frameworks that underpin these different approaches. In the final section, Evaluation, we discuss their implications for the evaluation of qualitative research.

WHAT IS QUALITATIVE RESEARCH?

Qualitative research is primarily concerned with meaning. Qualitative researchers are interested in subjectivity and experience. They want to understand better what their research participants' experiences are like, what they mean to them, how they talk about them, and how they make sense of them. Qualitative researchers try to capture the quality and texture of their research participants' experiences and aim to understand the implications and consequences of those experiences for the participants and for other people. Qualitative research addresses the following types of questions:

- What does something feel like? For example, a qualitative researcher might want to find out what it is like to be the only man in an all-female workplace.

- How is something experienced? For example, we may want to conduct qualitative research into the experience of being made redundant.
- How do people talk about something and with what consequences? For example, we may analyze naturally occurring conversations about housework and explore subject positions available to men and women within this.
- How do people make sense of an experience? For example, we may want to find out how people who live with chronic pain explain and interpret their experience and how this shapes the way that they manage their pain.
- How do they construct the meaning of an experience? What does this allow them to do or not to do? To feel or not to feel? For example, a qualitative study could explore the ways in which people who have been injured in a road traffic accident talk about this experience and how this allows them to position themselves in relation to the accident.
- How does a particular (social or psychological) event unfold? How do participants experience the event? What may be its consequences? For them or for others? For example, we may want to find out how the end of an intimate relationship comes about, how those involved experience such an ending, what *breaking up* means to them, and how it may shape their views of future relationships.

Qualitative research does not, and cannot, answer questions about relationships between variables or about cause-and-effect relationships. Qualitative research is concerned with the description and interpretation of research participants' experiences. It tends to prioritize depth of understanding over breadth of coverage, and, as such, the knowledge it generates tends to be localized and context specific. Qualitative researchers do not aim to generalize their findings to general populations, and they do not aim to develop predictive models of human behavior. Instead, qualitative researchers tend to work in a *bottom-up* fashion, exploring in depth relatively small amounts of data (e.g., a small number of semistructured interviews, an individual case, or a set of documents relating to a specific event), working through the data line by line. As a result, any insights generated on the basis of qualitative analysis tend to be context specific and are not generalizable to general populations. Qualitative research, however, can extend its reach by informing theory development (Eakin & Gladstone, 2020) or by conducting metasyntheses (e.g., Finfgeld-Connett, 2018; see also Volume 2, Chapter 2, this handbook), and it is important to acknowledge that there are conceptualizations of generalization that do not rely on statistics and that these can be relevant to qualitative research (e.g., *Qualitative Psychology*: special section on generalizability, 2021; Roald et al., 2021).

Common features of qualitative research include the following:

- **Presents findings in accessible language.** Because qualitative research aims to capture and convey the meanings research participants attribute to their experiences and actions, research findings tend to take the form of verbal accounts. Such qualitative accounts may vary in the extent to which they are descriptive or interpretative, in the extent to which they utilize expert discourse (e.g., psychological terminology), and in the extent to which they deploy poetic language or a prose style. Qualitative research findings, however, tend *not* to be represented by numbers or equations, they do *not* involve statistical calculations, and they do *not* draw conclusions about probabilities of occurrences or covariations of phenomena within a population.
- **Views meaning in context.** Qualitative researchers are concerned with how individual research participants make sense of specific experiences within particular contexts. This means that any meanings identified are specific to the context within which they are constructed and deployed by the participants. For example, to understand what it means to somebody to get married, we need to know something about the individual's life history and their social and cultural context as well as their situation at the time of the interview. Qualitative research, therefore, tends not to draw conclusions about what something

might mean in general. Indeed, from a qualitative perspective, it is questionable whether such generalized meanings do, in fact, exist.
- **Incorporates researcher reflexivity.** Because qualitative researchers are concerned with meaning and interpretation, they need to pay particular attention to the ways in which their own beliefs, assumptions, and experiences may shape (both limit and facilitate) their reading of qualitative data. For example, whether the researcher has personal experience of the phenomenon under investigation is important, and the nature of that experience (or indeed its absence) needs to be thought about as it inevitably will frame the researcher's approach to the topic. Researcher reflexivity ought to be an integral part of any qualitative study because meaning is always *given* to data and never simply identified or discovered within it.
- **Studies the real world.** Qualitative research is concerned with participants' life experiences, which means that ideally qualitative data ought to be collected in situ, that is, where and when the experiences of interest actually take place. Such naturally occurring data include tape recordings of conversations in real-life contexts, such as homes, workplaces, or over the telephone, as well as video recordings of social interactions such as those at football matches, pubs, or clubs. Because collecting naturally occurring data is not always ethically or practically possible, however, a lot of qualitative data takes the form of transcripts of semistructured interviews with people who have agreed to talk about their experiences. Either way, whether in situ or in the form of description and reflection after the event, qualitative data always are concerned with real life, that is, with events and experiences that take place irrespective of whether the researcher studies them. Experimentation has no place in qualitative research (unless the aim is to study the experience of taking part in an experiment).
- **Is primarily inductive.** Unlike hypothetico-deductive research, qualitative research does not set out to test hypotheses derived from existing theories. On the contrary, most qualitative research deliberately brackets the researcher's theoretical knowledge to allow novel insights and understandings to emerge from the data.

As such, most qualitative research aspires to an inductive model of knowledge generation. Exceptions to this do exist, however, and these are discussed in the section titled Differences Among Qualitative Approaches. Also, most if not all qualitative researchers recognize that pure induction is an impossibility given the role of the researcher in the research process and that without some kind of theoretical lens data collection and analysis cannot take place. The challenge to the qualitative researcher is to enable the data set to speak for itself (as far as possible) and to surprise the researcher rather than to simply confirm or refute their expectations.

DIFFERENCES AMONG QUALITATIVE APPROACHES

Drisko (1997) developed Glaser's (1992) analogy of qualitative research as a "family of approaches" by suggesting that "in this family there are some close relations, some distant relations, some extended kin, some odd cousins, and a few nasty divorces" (p.186). Differences among qualitative approaches to research can go deep, and some varieties of qualitative research methodology are incompatible with one another. The various formal philosophical and epistemological positions available to qualitative researchers are mapped out in the section Epistemological Frameworks. In this section, we prepare the ground by identifying the major points of tension around which the family of qualitative research organizes itself. These points of tension include (a) the role of theory, (b) description versus interpretation, (c) realism versus relativism, and (d) politics.

The Role of Theory

As indicated in the section What Is Qualitative Research? although most qualitative research adopts an inductive model of knowledge generation, some qualitative approaches also include a deductive element. For example, grounded theory methodology involves a process of testing emerging theoretical formulations against incoming data, thus moving between developing and testing theory as the research progresses toward saturation. For example, a researcher may want to understand what caused a fight between rival fans at a football match. The researcher begins the research with no assumptions about what happened and by interviewing bystanders, witnesses, and participants in the fight. Preliminary analysis of the data generates a hypothesis about what triggered the event and the researcher returns to the field and conducts further interviews with particular individuals to test the hypothesis and to develop it into a coherent account of how the fight came about. In this case, the theory that is being tested is the emergent theory that has been conceived on the basis of an inductive process and does not involve the application of preexisting theoretical perspectives.

Alternatively, approaches such as psychoanalytic case studies draw on existing theoretical frameworks (e.g., Freudian or Kleinian theories) to account for the manifest content of the data. For example, the researcher may attribute theory-driven meanings to an interviewee's behaviors during the interview and conclude that the interviewee's long pauses, hesitations, and incomplete sentences signify resistance to acknowledging underlying feelings, such as anger or anxiety. In these cases, theory is imported from outside of the study into the research. Another example of deliberate and purposeful importing of theory into qualitative research is provided by critical approaches, such as Marxist or feminist analyses, whereby a preestablished perspective is applied to interpret the data (see Drisko, 1997). Imported theoretical perspectives supply a lens through which the data can be read, thus generating insights into particular dimensions of experience that have been identified as being of interest to the researcher or as being important for social or political reasons long before the data have been collected.

Description Versus Interpretation

Qualitative approaches also vary in the extent to which they aspire to move beyond the data and to interpret what is being presented. That is to say, they vary in the extent to which they take data "at face value." Some qualitative approaches, such as descriptive phenomenology, stay close to research participants' accounts of their experience as the aim of such research is to capture, clarify, and represent the quality and texture of those experiences. Here, analyzing data means paying close attention to what is being said by the participant, grasping and distilling its meaning, and systematically representing it to others (see Volume 2, Chapter 5, this handbook).

Other approaches, such as interpretative phenomenology, aspire to go further and to give meaning to participants' experiences beyond that which the participants may be able or willing to attribute to it. In other words, even without the application of a particular theory to the data (see the section What Is Qualitative Research?), it is possible to extract meanings that are not immediately obvious to even the person who has produced the account (i.e., the research participant). For example, existential themes such as fear of death or fear of meaninglessness may be expressed only indirectly and by way of analogy in the research participant's account, yet an interpretative analysis may conclude that they underpin and, indeed, give a deeper meaning to the account.

These two positions (descriptive vs. interpretative) are sometimes referred to as "hermeneutics of meaning recollection" (descriptive) and "hermeneutics of suspicion" (interpretative) (see Langdridge, 2007, Chapter 4, on Ricoeur and hermeneutics; see also Giorgi, 1992, for a discussion of the differences between interpretative science and descriptive science, and Willig, 2012, for more on the ethics of interpretation in qualitative analysis).

Realism Versus Relativism

Qualitative researchers need to think carefully about the kinds of knowledge claims they wish to make on the basis of their research. They need to ask themselves to what extent their research aims to shed light on reality (i.e., on how things are in the world) and to what extent it critically interrogates the way in which such (social) realities are constituted. Discussions about realism and relativism in qualitative research are complicated by the fact that both the status of the data (as realist or relativist) *and* the status of the analysis of the data (as realist or relativist) need to be established. It is important to recognize that these are two distinct but equally important considerations that easily can get confused or conflated.

To start with the status of the data, qualitative researchers can take a realist position that takes data (e.g., research participants' accounts) at face value and treats them akin to witness statements, that is to say, as a description of events that actually took place in the real world. From such a position, the researcher would take great care to ensure that the data collected are accurate and truthful by ensuring that the conditions under which accounts are produced are favorable (e.g., that participants feel safe and nondefensive, and that nothing will prevent them from opening up and telling the truth). Alternatively, the researcher can adopt a relativist position in relation to the status of the data, which means that research participants' accounts are of interest *not* because they inform the researcher about what is actually going on in the world (e.g., what really happened to the participant) but rather because they tell the researcher something about how the participants are constructing meaning in their lives. In such a case, the researcher is not concerned with the truth value of what participants are telling them; instead, the aim of the research is to generate rich and detailed accounts that will enable the researcher to gain a better understanding of the participant's meaning-making activities.

Moving on to the status of the analysis, again, two broad positions are available to the researcher: a realist position that aspires to the production of accurate and valid knowledge about what is going on, either in the social world, in terms of (a) events that are taking place in this world (this is in line with the realist position on the status of the data) *or* (b) actions that research participants are taking when they construct meaning (this is in line with the relativist position on the status of the data). In both cases, the researcher's (metaphorical) task is to hold up a mirror to reflect accurately what is going on either in the world out there or inside the mind of the research participant. This means that it is possible to adopt a realist position (i.e., holding up the mirror) in relation to relativist data (i.e., the research participant's constructions). Such a position claims that the researcher can accurately and truthfully represent the participant's subjective world (i.e., their constructions of meaning). Alternatively, the research can adopt a relativist position in relation to the analysis. This would mean abandoning any truth claims regarding the analytic insights produced, arguing instead that what is being offered is the researcher's reading of the data, which tells us just as much (or more) about the researcher (and their meaning-making activities) as it does about the participants or indeed about the social world. It could be argued that a very fine line exists between this type of research and the sorts of activities that an artist may engage in, such as writing a poem about the beauty they see in the eyes of their beloved or creating an expressionist painting of their garden (see Willig, 2019, for more on this).

Politics

Qualitative research can have an explicitly political dimension in that some qualitative researchers are motivated by a desire to give voice to otherwise underrepresented or oppressed social groups.

Indeed, feminist scholars were instrumental in introducing and promoting qualitative research methods in psychology. Because qualitative research tends to be bottom-up (allowing the voices of research participants to be heard) and because it tends to be inductive (avoiding the imposition of existing concepts and categories), qualitative research can be used as part of an empowerment agenda. Qualitative research also can be practiced in an egalitarian, participatory, and collaborative way (such as in action research or some types of ethnography in which the research participants set the agenda and shape the direction of the research), thus allowing the researcher to challenge established power relations between (expert) researchers and (naïve) research participants.

More interpretative versions of qualitative research (see the section Differences Among Qualitative Approaches) adopt a more conventional "knowing" stance, embracing the role of an expert who, as a result of familiarity with the relevant psychological literature, may be able to understand the participants better than they can understand themselves. For example, Hollway and Jefferson's (2000) approach to qualitative analysis was based on the premise that people "may not know why they experience or feel things in the way that they do [and] are motivated, largely unconsciously, to disguise the meaning of at least some of their feelings and actions" (p. 26). Thus, qualitative researchers have a range of options regarding the political orientation of their research activities. Although qualitative research often is associated with a liberal, egalitarian social agenda, not all qualitative research adopts this perspective.

EPISTEMOLOGICAL FRAMEWORKS

The previous section demonstrated that qualitative researchers can adopt a wide range of positions regarding the meaning and status of the kind of knowledge their research generates (or, indeed, regarding the extent to which the production of knowledge is possible or desirable in the first place). Epistemological positions are characterized by a set of assumptions about knowledge and knowing that provide answers to the question "What and how can we know?" Paradoxically, although we tend to think about research as being about finding answers to questions through some form of systematic process of empirical enquiry, the starting point of any research project is,
in fact, a set of assumptions about the world we are studying (i.e., ontological assumptions) and about what it means to know something and how we can obtain knowledge of something (i.e., epistemological assumptions). These assumptions are not themselves based on anything other than philosophical reflection. This is inevitable, and it is important that researchers are aware of, clear about, and prepared to acknowledge and *own* their ontological-epistemological position. This is not always easy because the most fundamental assumptions we make about the world are often unacknowledged and implicit; that is, we take them for granted. This section maps out the range of epistemological positions available to qualitative researchers and discusses their relationships with one another. It also suggests ways in which researchers can identify and clarify their own assumptions.

Perhaps the easiest way for a researcher to access the assumptions they make is to ask themselves a series of questions (see also Willig, 2021, Chapter 1), such as the following:

- What kind of knowledge do I aim to create?
- What are the assumptions that I make about the (material, social, and psychological) world(s) that I study?
- How do I conceptualize the role of the researcher in the research process? What is the relationship between myself and the knowledge I aim to generate?

The remainder of this section looks at the range of possible answers to these three questions and provides examples of research designs informed by the epistemological positions indicated by such answers. Positions and their concomitant designs will be grouped into three broad approaches that are characterized by the type of knowledge they aim to create: (a) realist knowledge, (b) phenomenological knowledge, and (c) social constructionist knowledge (see Figure 1.1 for a summary).[1]

---

[1] Authors use a range of different terms and labels to describe various ontological-epistemological positions. The best way to explain one's position within the context of a item of research is probably by identifying the assumptions that underpin one's chosen research question and approach and to then locate the position associated with those assumptions within a particular published classification system. There are quite a number of these (e.g., Crotty, 1998; Guba & Lincoln, 2005; Hansen, 2004; Madill et al., 2000; Moon & Blackman, 2017; Ormston et al., 2013; Ponterotto, 2005), so it is important to be clear and explicit about whose system one is using.

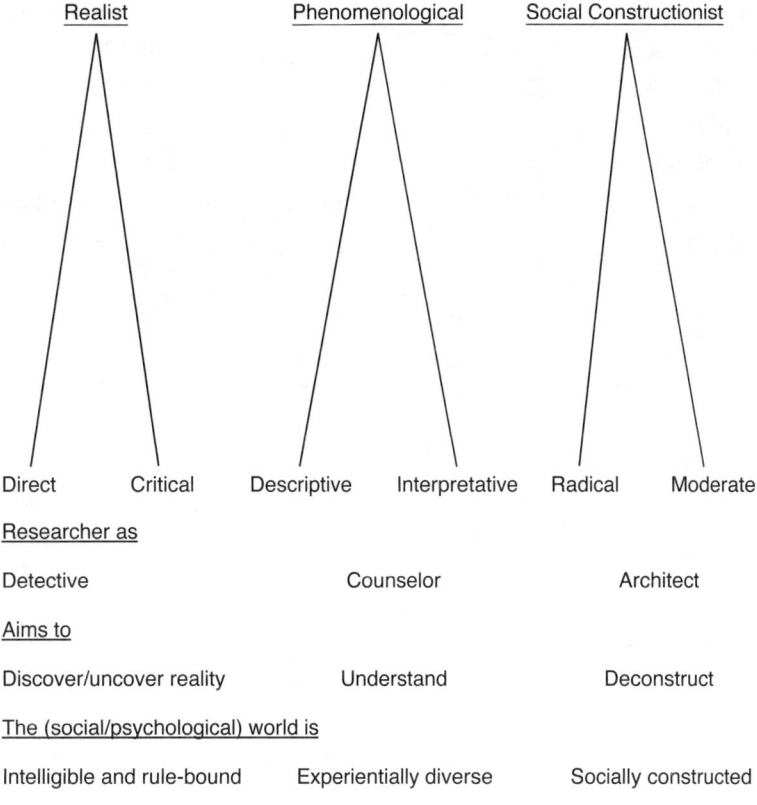

FIGURE 1.1. Three types of knowledge.

Realist Knowledge

Qualitative researchers can use qualitative methods of data collection and analysis to obtain a rich, accurate, detailed, and comprehensive picture of (some aspects of) the social world or of human psychology. The type of knowledge sought in this case aspires to capture and reflect as truthfully as possible something that is happening in the real world and that exists independently of the researcher's, and indeed the research participants', views or knowledge about it. The sorts of things a researcher who aspires to generate this type of (*realist*) knowledge might study include social processes (e.g., what happens when a new member joins an established reading group or what happens when an organization implements a new equal opportunities policy) and psychological mechanisms or processes (e.g., how a person who suffers from panic attacks plans a journey on public transportation, how people who lost a parent at an early age approach intimate relationships).

The assumption underpinning this type of research is that certain processes or patterns of a social or psychological nature characterize or shape the behavior or the thinking of research participants, and these can be identified and conveyed by the researcher. This means that the researcher assumes that the (material, social, psychological) world they investigate potentially can be understood, provided that the researcher is skilled enough to uncover the patterns, regularities, structures, or underlying rules of social engagement that characterize it and that generate the social or psychological phenomena we witness (and that constitute one's data). The researcher can succeed or fail in this process, which means that they aspire to generate valid and reliable knowledge about a social or psychological phenomenon that exists independently of the researcher's awareness of it. As such, this type of research is characterized by a discovery orientation (see Madill et al., 2000). The role of the researcher in this situation is akin to that of a detective who uses their skills, knowledge, and experience to uncover hitherto hidden facts and who, through their labor, makes what appeared puzzling or mysterious intelligible. The kinds of methods used by qualitative researchers who aim to produce this type of (realist) knowledge include (realist versions of) ethnography and grounded theory methodology as well as such varieties of interpretative analysis as psychoanalytic approaches (but these methods also can be used from within a less realist epistemological framework, which is discussed in the section Varieties of Realist Knowledge).

Phenomenological Knowledge

Alternatively, qualitative research can aim to produce knowledge about the subjective experience of research participants (rather than about the social or psychological patterns or processes that underpin, structure, or shape such subjective experiences, as realist knowledge does). In this case, the researcher aspires to capture something that exists in the world (namely, the participants' feelings, thoughts, and perceptions—that is, their experiences); however, no claim is being made regarding its relationship with other facets of the world or indeed regarding the accuracy of the participants' accounts of their experiences (e.g., whether a phenomenological account of an embodied experience such as anger or anxiety matches up with objective physiological measures such as blood pressure or galvanic skin response). Such research aims to understand experience (rather than to discover what is "really" going on). In other words, it does not matter whether what a research participant describes is an accurate reflection of what happened to them or a fantasy; instead, the type of knowledge the researcher is trying to obtain is *phenomenological* knowledge—that is, knowledge of the quality and texture of the participant's experience. For example, a researcher might want to find out what it is like to be living with a diagnosis of psychosis or how a participant experiences the process of going through a divorce. Finding that a participant experiences herself as "rejected by the whole world," for example, constitutes phenomenological knowledge irrespective of whether the participant really is being rejected by everyone she encounters.

The task of the researcher in this type of research is to get as close as possible to the research participant's experience—to step into that person's shoes, and to look at the world through their eyes, that is to say, to enter their world. Here, the role of the researcher is similar to that of the *person-centered counselor* who listens to the client's account of their experience empathically, without judging and without questioning the external validity of what the client is saying. This means that the researcher assumes that there is more than one *world* to be studied. This is because researchers who seek this type of knowledge are interested in the experiential world of the participant (rather than the material, social, or psychological structures that may give rise to particular experiences—for example, the biochemical changes associated with psychosis or the social processes that can give rise to stereotyping); what appear to be the "same" (material, social, psychological) conditions (e.g., a divorce, a diagnosis, an accident) can be experienced in many different ways, and this means that there are potentially as many (experiential) worlds as there are individuals. A researcher who attempts to generate this type of knowledge asks, "What is the world like *for this participant*?" (rather than "What is the world like and what is it about the world that makes a particular experience possible?"). The kinds of methods used by qualitative researchers who aim to produce this type of (phenomenological) knowledge, unsurprisingly, tend to be phenomenological methods (such as interpretative phenomenological analysis or descriptive phenomenology, but be aware that phenomenological methods engage with the process of interpretation in a variety of ways that are discussed in the section Varieties of Phenomenological Knowledge later in this chapter).

Social Constructionist Knowledge

Finally, a qualitative researcher can adopt a much more skeptical position in relation to knowledge and argue that what is of interest is not so much what is really going on (realist approach to knowledge) or how something is actually experienced by participants (phenomenological approach) but rather how people talk about the world and, therefore, how they construct versions of reality through the use of language. Here, the type of knowledge aspired to is not knowledge about the world or knowledge about how things are (experienced) but rather knowledge about the process by which such knowledge is constructed in the first place. This means that questions about the nature of social and psychological events and experiences are suspended and instead the researcher is concerned with the social construction of knowledge. Because language plays such an important part in the construction of knowledge, qualitative researchers who adopt a *social constructionist* orientation to knowledge generation tend to study discourses and the ways in which they are deployed within particular contexts. For example, a researcher might analyze the language used in policy documents about antisocial behavior to understand how the phenomenon of concern—"antisocial behavior"—is constructed within these documents and how the discourses used in the documents position those who are constructed as the targets of proposed interventions.

Such an approach to research is based on the assumption that all human experience is mediated by language, which means that all social and psychological phenomena are constructed in one way or another. It also means that all knowledge about the world and experience of the world is very much socially mediated and that individual experiences are always the product of internalized social constructions. In other words, when participants are telling the researcher about their experiences, they are not seen to be giving voice to an inner reality (as in phenomenological research) or to be providing information about social or psychological processes (as in realist research); instead, the researcher is interested in how socially available ways of talking about the phenomenon of interest (i.e., discourses) are deployed by the participant and how these may shape the participant's experience. Here, the role of the researcher is to draw attention to the constructed nature of social reality and to trace the specific ways in which particular phenomena are constructed through discourse and to reflect on the consequences of this for those who are affected (that is to say, who are "positioned") by these social constructions. As such, the role of the researcher is akin to that of an architect who looks at the phenomenon of interest with a view to how it has been constructed and from what resources and materials. The most commonly used method to produce this type of (social constructionist) knowledge is discourse analysis (of which there are several versions, including discursive psychology, Foucauldian discourse analysis, and critical discourse analysis); however, other methods, such as narrative analysis and memory work, also can be used. See Burr (2015) for a very clear introduction to social constructionism.

Within these three basic approaches to conceptualizing the types of knowledge sought by qualitative researchers, each theme has variations (usually in the form of more or less radical versions). In the following section, we identify a variety of positions within each approach to knowledge generation.

Varieties of Realist Knowledge

Realist aspirations to knowledge generation range from what is sometimes referred to as naïve to more critical varieties. Naïve *realist* approaches are characterized by the assumption that a relatively uncomplicated and direct relationship exists between what presents itself (the data, the evidence) and what is going on (the reality we want to understand). In other words, we assume that the data more or less directly represent (mirror, reflect) reality. For example, if we wanted to find out how people make decisions about whether to have an HIV antibody test and we interviewed individuals who recently made such a decision, a naïve realist approach would dictate that we take participants' accounts at face value and that we accept that their accounts constitute accurate descriptions of how they made their decision. The task of the researcher, therefore, would be (a) to ensure that participants feel safe and comfortable enough to provide the researcher with accurate and detailed accounts and (b) to analyze the accounts in such a way as to produce a clear and systematic model of the decision-making process (or the variety of pathways for decision making if that is what the accounts indicate).

To call such research "naïve realist" is to belittle it. The label *naïve* does imply a criticism, and it is unlikely that a researcher would ever willingly describe their own research as naïve realist—even if they subscribed to the assumptions about knowledge generation that are associated with this label. Also, some very valuable research aims to "give voice" to otherwise-marginalized individuals and communities and is underpinned by the assumption that what participants are telling the researcher about their experiences (e.g., of suffering, of exploitation, of oppression) reflects a social reality that needs to be exposed, acknowledged, and understood. Again, to call such research "naïve" is to disparage and devalue research that clearly does have its uses and significance. Perhaps a less value-laden term such as *direct realism* would be preferable.

Critical realist approaches to knowledge generation differ from the more direct (or naïve) version in that they are formed on the basis of the assumption that although the data can tell us about what is going on in the real (i.e., material, social, psychological) world, it does not do so in a self-evident, unmediated fashion. In other words, a critical realist approach does not assume that the data directly reflect reality (like a mirror image); rather, the data need to be interpreted to provide access to the underlying structures that generate the manifestations that constitute the data. For example, if we carry out a participant observation of the social rituals and practices that characterize life within a particular community, the data we collect (in the form of recordings of observations, conversations, interviews, documents, and photographs that capture life in the community, perhaps) would provide us with information about what members of the community do, how they relate to one another, and how they structure and manage their social life. The data, however, would not tell us, directly and explicitly, what it might be (e.g., historically or politically) that drives, shapes, and maintains these structures and practices. To understand this, we need to move beyond the data and draw on knowledge, theories, and evidence from outside the particular study and use these to account for what we have observed. For instance, a community's history, its relations with neighboring communities or particular geographic conditions may help the researcher explain why people do what they do.

Crucially, from a critical realist standpoint, it is not necessary (in fact, we would not usually expect) that research participants be aware of the underlying mechanisms or conditions that inform their overt behaviors and experiences. Research informed by psychoanalytic theory is a good example of critical realist research in that it is assumed that the underlying (in this case, psychological) structures that generate the manifest, observable phenomena (e.g., behaviors, symptoms, dreams, slips of the tongue) are not necessarily accessible to those who experience them (i.e., the research participants, the patients). This assumption, however, does not mean that such structures are not "real." Critical realist research can vary in the extent to which it proclaims the existence of underlying structures and mechanisms with anything approaching certainty. Some researchers have presented their analyses with caution and the proviso that the interpretations offered are just that—interpretations that represent possibilities rather than certainties (e.g., Frosh & Saville-Young, 2008). Others have taken a much more knowing stance and present their analyses as insights into how things (actually, really) are (e.g., how people function psychologically or how communities are formed; see Hollway & Jefferson, 2000).

Varieties of Phenomenological Knowledge

The researcher attempts to use phenomenological knowledge to increase their understanding of research participants' experience.

As such, phenomenological knowledge is *insider knowledge*—that is, knowledge that is used to shed light on phenomena through an understanding of how these phenomena present themselves in or through experience; that is to say, how they appear to somebody within a particular context. Differences exist, however, in the extent to which phenomenological knowledge bases itself on the researcher's interpretation of research participants' experience. This means that phenomenological approaches to knowledge generation range from descriptive to interpretative varieties. *Descriptive phenomenology* is very much concerned with capturing experience "precisely as it presents itself, neither adding nor subtracting from it" (Giorgi, 1992, p. 121). Descriptive phenomenology does not aim to account for or explain the experience or to attribute meanings to it that are imported from outside of the account of the actual experience. In other words, it does not go beyond the data. For example, a descriptive phenomenologist might be interested in the phenomenon of being surprised. To understand this phenomenon better, the researcher might conduct a series of semistructured interviews with individuals who recently have experienced a surprise (such as winning a prize, being invited on an unexpected holiday, or receiving a letter from a long-lost friend). The analysis of the interviews would aim to generate an understanding of what characterizes the experience of being surprised; in other words, the researcher would want to know what it is that people experience when they are surprised—for instance, the person may experience a sense of a loss of control, of ambivalence, or of uncertainty about how to respond, and perhaps also feelings of joy and excitement. We do not know what characterizes the experience until we have conducted a phenomenological analysis of the data and, as a descriptive phenomenologist, we should not allow our own experiences, expectations, and assumptions regarding the experience of surprise to inform our analysis of the data. The end product of a descriptive phenomenological study would be an account of the structure of the phenomenon of being surprised that is formed entirely on the basis of participants' accounts of their experiences.

By contrast, *interpretative phenomenology* does not take accounts of experience "at face value" in the same way; instead, interpretative phenomenologists do move beyond the data in that they step outside of the account and reflect on its status as an account and its wider (social, cultural, psychological) meanings. As Larkin et al. (2006) put it in their discussion of interpretative phenomenological analysis, such interpretative analysis "positions the initial 'description' in relation to a wider social, cultural, and perhaps even theoretical, context. This second-order account aims to provide a critical and conceptual commentary upon the participants' personal 'sense-making' activities" (p. 104). For example, an interpretative phenomenologist might want to explore the experience of women who have tried and failed to conceive with the help of in vitro fertilization. The researcher would start the research process in much the same way as a descriptive phenomenologist and conduct semistructured interviews with women who recently have had this experience. The next step (still in line with descriptive phenomenology) would be to engage with the interview transcripts with the aim of entering the participant's world, understanding what it has been like for the participants to go through the experience, and producing a description of the experience that captures its quality and texture and that portrays its structure and essence.

The interpretative phenomenologist acknowledges that understanding the participant's experience presupposes a process of making sense of the participant's account in the first place; in other words, the researcher needs to give meaning to the account to understand it. Through a hermeneutic circle of giving and recovering meaning, therefore, the researcher is intimately implicated in making sense of the participant's account of a failure to conceive a child. In a further interpretative move, the researcher may contextualize the participants' experience by reflecting on the social and economic structures within which women experience reproduction or on the social and cultural expectations and norms that prevail at the time of data collection. The aim of such reflection would be to make (further) sense of participants' experiences and to understand better how such experiences are shaped by the context within which they occur.

Descriptive and interpretative versions of phenomenological research, therefore, differ in their approach to reflexivity. Although descriptive phenomenologists believe that it is possible to produce descriptions that capture and comprehend the phenomenon as it presents itself, interpretative phenomenologists argue that it is not, in fact, possible to produce a pure description of experience in any case and that description always involves a certain amount of interpretation. At the most basic level, it is argued, one's choice of words shapes the meaning of what they are trying to convey and this means that, inevitably, the researcher adds meaning to the data.

Varieties of Social Constructionist Knowledge

By way of contrast with realist approaches, the social constructionist perspective is often described as *relativist*. It is relativist in the sense that it questions the "out-there-ness" of the world and that it rejects the idea that objects, events, and even experiences precede and inform our descriptions of them. Indeed, it rejects the notion of description altogether and replaces it with that of construction. Social constructionism is relativist in the sense that it conceptualizes language as a form of social action that constructs versions of reality; here, it is discourse that constructs reality rather than reality that determines how we describe or talk about it. More or less radical strands of social constructionism exist, however, and not all social constructionist researchers would describe themselves as relativists. This means that social constructionist approaches to knowledge production can range from *radical* to more *moderate* versions. Research that is concerned with the ways in which speakers within a particular social context strategically deploy discursive resources to achieve a particular interactional objective may be conducted from a radical relativist position. Such a position demands that the researcher abandons any ambition to gain access to the participants' inner experience or indeed to understand how they make sense of their experience. Instead, the researcher assumes that participants will construct different versions of reality (i.e., of their experiences, their histories, their memories, their thoughts and feelings) depending on the social context within which they find themselves and the stake that they have in this context.

In other words, from a radical social constructionist perspective, there is nothing of interest outside of the text. Reality is what participants are constructing within a particular interaction through discourse. This reality does not survive the context within which it has been constructed, as a different reality will be constructed to suit the next context. This means that the radical version of social constructionism foregrounds the variability and flexibility of accounts. It aims to understand how and why discursive objects and positions are constructed in particular ways within particular contexts, and it explores the consequences of such constructions for those who are using them and those who are positioned by them (i.e., the speakers in a conversation). For example, a researcher might be interested in how people who have decided to commence psychotherapy introduce themselves to their new psychotherapist and how they explain why they are there. To obtain suitable data, the researcher would need to obtain recordings of first sessions of a number of therapist–client dyads. These recordings would be transcribed and then analyzed. The aim of the analysis would be to identify the ways in which the participants in the sessions deploy discursive resources and with what consequences. For instance, the researcher might observe that some clients begin by pointing out that they had waited until they had reached the "end of their tether" before making the appointment. The researcher might observe that by doing this, clients position themselves within a moral discourse and construct themselves as deserving of help because they have tried very hard to sort out their own problems before asking for help. Clients may also disclaim an (undesirable) identity, perhaps that of a "needy" person, by emphasizing that they have never sought help before and that their present visit to the therapist was an exceptional event. In this way, clients might position themselves as responsible adults whose help-seeking is not a sign of weakness or of psychopathology.

The important thing to remember is that a radical social constructionist researcher would not be interested in the validity of these accounts—indeed, they would not believe in the relevance or even the possibility of establishing these accounts' validity. In other words, it is irrelevant whether clients really are seeking help for the first time or whether they really are (or feel) weak, strong, or needy. The point of social constructionist research is to examine localized, context-specific discursive productions (e.g., of the self as "adult," as "strong," "normal," or "deserving") and their action orientation and consequences within the specific context. In other words, the radical social constructionist researcher would be interested only in the particular reality constructed for the purposes of a specific conversation.

By contrast, more moderate (i.e., less relativist) approaches to social constructionist research would want to go beyond the study of localized deployments of discursive resources and make connections between the discourses that are used within a particular local context and the wider sociocultural context. For example, the researcher might be interested in exploring contemporary therapy culture more generally, looking at self-help texts, television shows that reference psychotherapy, and "problem pages" in newspapers and magazines, in which experts answer letters from troubled readers. Having identified dominant discourses surrounding psychotherapy in the 21st century, the researcher might then explore the ways in which such discourses position people (e.g., as damaged by their past, as in need of expert help, as responsible for working through their issues) and with what consequences (e.g., as a society, we may expect individuals to invest in their mental health and well-being). By grounding discourses in social, cultural, economic, and material structures, more moderate social constructionist researchers are making reference to something outside of the text. They invoke a reality that preexists and indeed shapes the ways in which individuals construct meaning within particular contexts. This means that the moderate social constructionist position has an affinity with the *critical realist* position (see the section Varieties of Realist Knowledge). Although radical social constructionists emphasize people's ability to play with discursive resources and to use them creatively to construct the social realities that suit their needs at a particular moment in time, moderate social constructionists are more concerned with the ways in which available discourses can constrain and limit what can be said or done within particular contexts.

Figure 1.1 provides a summary of what characterizes the three different types of knowledge that qualitative researchers can aim to produce. In this chapter, I have kept the use of specialist (philosophy of science) terminology to a minimum and instead have focused on a description of the assumptions (about the nature of knowledge, about the world, about the role of the researcher) that underpin and characterize the three approaches and that define their differences. I have argued that what matters is that we ask the right questions about a study (i.e., What kind of knowledge is being produced? What are the assumptions that have been made about the world that is being studied? What is the role of the researcher in the research process?) and that these answers will help us to identify (and make explicit) its epistemological foundations. I would argue that how we then label a particular epistemological position is of secondary importance as long as we are clear about its parameters. Those who are familiar with the qualitative research methodology literature will be aware that, as Ponterotto (2005) pointed out, there are numerous classification schemas in the literature that aim to classify approaches to qualitative research in meaningful and helpful ways and that use terminology lifted from the philosophy of science. For example, we find references to "modernisms, postmodernism, social constructionism, and constructivism" (Hansen, 2004); "positivism, postpositivism, constructivism-interpretivism, and critical-ideological" approaches (Ponterotto, 2005); and "positivism, postpositivism, critical theory, constructivism, and participatory" approaches (Guba & Lincoln, 2005).

Such classification schemas often are developed within the context of formulating a critique of quantitative research in cases in which qualitative (often referred to as "new paradigm") approaches are contrasted with quantitative (often characterized as *positivist* and *postpositivist*) approaches. Such critiques are important in their own right, but it is not necessarily helpful to present classifications of qualitative epistemologies within such a context. A preoccupation with contrasting quantitative with qualitative perspectives can lead to a homogenizing of qualitative research and a lack of attention to the differences between qualitative approaches. As a result, we often find representations of both quantitative and qualitative perspectives that lack sophistication and differentiation and that (despite the use of erudite terminology) actually simplify and sometimes even caricature both perspectives. Often, a simple dichotomy between a positivist (old paradigm) quantitative perspective and a constructivist (new paradigm) qualitative perspective is constructed (and this usually positions the former as flawed and in need of replacement by the latter; see also Shadish, 1995, for a discussion of common errors and misrepresentations in epistemological debates in the social sciences). The problem with such dichotomous classifications is that they do not acknowledge the full range of qualitative epistemologies that, as indicated, can reach from naïve (or better, direct) realism to radical social constructionism. In other words, not all qualitative research is constructivist, not all of it is relativist, and not all of it is interpretivist. Furthermore, as discussed in the section Differences Among Qualitative Approaches, references to these terms do not mean anything until we have clarified whether we are applying them to describe the status of the data (e.g., as descriptions of reality, as witness statements, as individual constructions, as social constructions) or to the status of our analysis (e.g., as accurate knowledge of reality, as an interpretation, as a construction, as an artistic production).

EVALUATION

How can we assess the quality and value of a particular piece of qualitative research? Given that qualitative research is concerned with meaning, and given that it usually takes the form of descriptions or interpretations of research participants' context-specific experiences and practices, it follows that the criteria traditionally used to evaluate quantitative research (i.e., reliability, representativeness, generalizability, objectivity, and validity) are not applicable to qualitative research. Does this mean that qualitative research cannot, or should not, be evaluated? Does it mean that in qualitative research "anything goes"? Opinion is divided on this subject, with some qualitative researchers (e.g., Forshaw, 2007) rejecting the whole notion of "method" in qualitative research (and with it any aspirations to "rigor"), proposing that the aim of qualitative research ought to be to produce ideas that resonate with readers and that generate debate rather than to produce insights that claim to have some validity or even truth value. Postqualitative research perspectives also reject the notion that qualitative research generates "knowledge" (see Brinkmann, 2017, for an overview and a critique). From this point of view, it is not meaningful to assess the value of qualitative research in terms other than its creativity and originality.

Others (myself included; see Willig, 2007, 2019, 2021) disagree with this argument, proposing instead that qualitative research involves a process of systematic, cyclical, and critical reflection whose quality can be assessed. Like everything else in qualitative research, however, evaluation is not a simple or a straightforward matter. This is because the criteria we use for evaluating a qualitative study must be informed by the study's epistemological position. In other words, to be able to evaluate a study's contribution to knowledge in a meaningful way, we need to know what it was the researchers wanted to find out and what kind of knowledge they aimed to generate. Several authors have compiled lists of generic criteria for evaluating qualitative research (e.g., Elliott et al., 1999; Henwood & Pidgeon, 1992; Yardley, 2000), and although some overlap exists between these, as I have argued elsewhere, "it is clear that authors approach the question of evaluation from the particular standpoint afforded by their own preferred methodological approach" (Willig, 2021, p. 314).

I concur with Madill et al. (2000) and Reicher (2000), who have argued that no such thing as a unified qualitative research paradigm exists and, therefore, that the criteria we use to evaluate qualitative studies need to be tailored to fit the particular methodology they are meant to appraise. For example, Madill et al. proposed that *objectivity* (i.e., the absence of bias on the part of the researcher) and *reliability* (i.e., the extent to which findings have been triangulated) are criteria that can be applied meaningfully to evaluate realist research, whereas from a radical constructionist point of view, any criteria that are concerned with the accuracy or authenticity of accounts would be meaningless. Instead, to evaluate such studies, we would need to assess their *internal coherence* (i.e., the extent to which the analytic narrative "hangs together" without internal contradictions), to establish *deviant case analysis* (i.e., the extent to which the limits of the applicability of the analytic insights have been identified), and *reader evaluation* (i.e., the extent to which the study is perceived by its readers to increase their insights and understanding). Finally, an evaluation of what Madill et al. described as *contextual constructionist* research (and that is compatible with the phenomenological perspective identified in this chapter) requires scrutiny of the study's use of reflexivity and the extent to which it explores (and ideally theorizes) the relationship between accounts (i.e., both the participants' accounts, that is to say the data as well as the researcher's analytic account) and the context(s) within which these have been produced. Finlay and Gough (2003) proposed that different "versions of reflexivity" reflect different epistemological orientations so that

> for some, reflexivity is celebrated as part of our essential human capacity, while for others it is a self-critical lens. Some researchers utilize reflexivity to introspect, as a source of personal insight, while others employ it to interrogate the rhetoric underlying shared social discourses. Some treat it as a methodological tool to ensure "truth," while others exploit it as weapon to undermine truth claims. (p. ix)

This means that reflexivity can be used in different ways and for different purposes. For example, for a *direct realist* researcher, reflexivity can be a way of acknowledging and bracketing off personal expectations and assumptions so that they do not make their way into the analysis and distort (or even silence) the participant's voice that is trying to make itself heard. By contrast, an interpretative phenomenological researcher may draw on their own emotional response to what the participant is saying to uncover meanings within it that are not immediately obvious to the participant. Finally, a radical social constructionist researcher can use reflexivity to trace the ways in which their own contributions to the conversation with the participant have positioned the participant and how this may have shaped the interview.

Again, these differences have implications for the evaluation of a qualitative study in that the use of reflexivity within the design of the study needs to be assessed in its own terms. In other words, we need to ask whether reflexivity has been used in a way that is compatible with the epistemological orientation of the study and whether the use of reflexivity within the study's design has met its own objectives. From our discussion of evaluation so far, it should have become clear that to make meaningful evaluation possible, a study's author needs to clearly identify the study's epistemological position. Therefore, the most important criterion for evaluating qualitative research ought to be epistemological reflexivity (i.e., the extent to which a study clearly and unambiguously identifies its epistemological stance) as this is a precondition for any further evaluation. Indeed, Madill et al. (2000) concluded that "qualitative researchers have a responsibility to make their epistemological position clear, conduct their research in a manner consistent with that position, and present their findings in a way that allows them to be evaluated appropriately" (p. 17). To help reviewers evaluate qualitative research effectively, qualitative psychologists have recently drawn up guidance that acknowledges these complexities (e.g., Levitt et al., 2018; Shaw et al., 2019).

CONCLUSION

The aim of this chapter is to review and clarify the various ways in which qualitative researchers approach the production of knowledge. Qualitative researchers aim to produce three types of knowledge, and these were given the labels *realist*, *phenomenological*, and *social constructionist*. Each of these types of knowledge was shown to be formed on the basis of different answers to questions about the nature and status of knowledge claims, the assumptions the researcher makes about the social and psychological worlds they are studying, and the role of the researcher in the research process. Different methods of data collection and analysis are required to generate the different types of knowledge, and the evaluative criteria we use to assess the value and quality of a qualitative study may differ depending on the type of knowledge the study aspires to produce. To develop these epistemological arguments and to clearly distinguish among the three positions, we have foregrounded their differences. In this concluding section, I return to the bigger picture and reflect on the ways in which the three approaches complement one another. Each research project is motivated and driven by a research question that specifies on which aspect or dimension of social or psychological reality the study aims to shed light. No study ever seeks to simply study (the meaning of) life as such or to understand the world in general. Even realist research only seeks to establish the truth about something in particular rather than simply the truth. In addition, every study will have to work within a set of practical constraints (e.g., available time and finances) that set limits to what it can aspire to find out.

All this means that even the most carefully designed study can never achieve more than to shed light on one small part of a much bigger whole. It could be argued, therefore, that the three types of knowledge identified in this chapter, rather than constituting alternative visions of what valid or useful knowledge should look like, are simply providing three different angles from which to view human experience. They shed light on three different aspects of human experience. From this point of view, qualitative research is about attempting to discover new aspects of a totality that never can be accessed directly or captured in its entirety. Pluralistic qualitative research designs have increased in popularity precisely because they explicitly acknowledge and build upon such an understanding (e.g., Frost & Bailey-Rodriguez, 2021).

To illustrate this way of thinking and to illustrate what a pluralistic amplification of meaning may involve, let us imagine a researcher who wants to understand what happens when someone is diagnosed with a terminal illness. First, the researcher might want to listen to first-person accounts of this experience. To this end, she conducts semistructured interviews with a number of participants who have gone through it. At this point, the researcher adopts a realist approach, taking the accounts at face value. She produces a thematic analysis that aims to capture and systematically represent how the participants experienced the process of being given their diagnosis. She identifies a number of interesting patterns in relation to the ways in which participants were treated by medical staff and perhaps also in the ways in which the participants' loved ones responded to the situation. The research could end here, having produced some useful and important insights.

Let us assume that the researcher has the time and motivation to continue with the research. Let us also assume that the researcher had noticed that, despite their many shared experiences with medical staff and loved ones, the participants gave quite different meanings to their illness. She also noticed that this seemed to inform the participants' sense of themselves as a terminally ill patient and how they felt about their illness. To better understand these differences, the researcher arranges further interviews with the participants, this time using a phenomenological approach to explore their subjective experience in greater depth. This phase of the research generates a further set of themes, this time capturing the existential dimensions of the experience of being diagnosed with a terminal illness and the range of existential meanings that can be given to such an experience. Again, the research could end at this point.

Let us assume, however, that the researcher is still willing and able to continue with her project. She reflects on the fact that all the participants included references to the question of responsibility (for the illness) and that many of them grappled with issues around blame (for the illness) in their accounts. She decides that she wants to find out more about this and adopts a social constructionist approach, focusing on the use of discourses of individual responsibility within the context of terminal illness. She returns to the data (both sets of interviews) and analyzes them again, this time using a discourse analytic approach. To contextualize her participants' use of discourse in their constructions of meaning around their terminal diagnosis, the researcher analyzes newspaper articles and television documentaries about terminal illness and compares the discursive constructions used in those documents with those deployed by the participants.

Much more could be done to shed further light on the experience of being diagnosed with a terminal illness, but let us take pity on our hypothetical researcher and stop here. It remains for us to conclude that, rather than being mutually exclusive, realist, phenomenological, and social constructionist forms of knowing can be thought of as providing access to different aspects of our social and psychological world(s) and that our choice of which one(s) to mobilize within the context of a particular research project is a question of knowing what we want to know on this particular occasion.

References

Brinkmann, S. (2017). Humanism after posthumanism: Or qualitative psychology after the "posts." *Qualitative Research in Psychology, 14*(2), 109–130. https://doi.org/10.1080/14780887.2017.1282568

Burr, V. (2015). *An introduction to social constructionism* (3rd ed.). Routledge.

Crotty, M. (1998). *The foundations of social research. Meaning and perspective in the research process.* Sage.

Drisko, J. W. (1997). Strengthening qualitative studies and reports: Standards to promote academic integrity. *Journal of Social Work Education, 33*(1), 185–197. https://doi.org/10.1080/10437797.1997.10778862

Eakin, J. M., & Gladstone, B. (2020). "Value-adding" analysis: Doing more with qualitative data. *International Journal of Qualitative Methods, 19*, 1–13. https://doi.org/10.1177/1609406920949333

Elliott, R., Fischer, C. T., & Rennie, D. L. (1999). Evolving guidelines for publication of qualitative research studies in psychology and related fields. *British Journal of Clinical Psychology, 38*(3), 215–229. https://doi.org/10.1348/014466599162782

Finfgeld-Connett, D. (2018). *A guide to qualitative meta-synthesis.* Routledge. https://doi.org/10.4324/9781351212793

Finlay, L., & Gough, B. (Eds.). (2003). *Reflexivity: A practical guide for researchers in health and social sciences.* Blackwell. https://doi.org/10.1002/9780470776094

Forshaw, M. J. (2007). Free qualitative research from the shackles of method. *The Psychologist, 20*(8), 478–479.

Frosh, S., & Saville-Young, L. (2008). Psychoanalytic approaches to qualitative psychology. In C. Willig & W. Stainton Rogers (Eds.), *The Sage handbook of qualitative research in psychology* (pp. 109–126). Sage.

Frost, N., & Bailey-Rodriguez, D. (2021). Doing qualitatively driven mixed methods and pluralistic qualitative research. In S. Bager-Charleson &

A. McBeath (Eds.), *Enjoying research in counselling and psychotherapy* (pp. 137–160). Palgrave Macmillan/Springer Nature.

Giorgi, A. (1992). Description versus interpretation: Competing alternative strategies for qualitative research. *Journal of Phenomenological Psychology*, 23(2), 119–135. https://doi.org/10.1163/156916292X00090

Glaser, B. (1992). *Basics of grounded theory analysis*. Sociology Press.

Guba, E. G., & Lincoln, Y. S. (2005). Paradigmatic controversies, contradictions, and emerging influences. In N. K. Denzin & Y. S. Lincoln (Eds.), *The Sage handbook of qualitative research* (3rd ed., pp. 191–215). Sage.

Hansen, J. T. (2004). Thoughts on knowing: Epistemic implications of counselling practice. *Journal of Counseling and Development*, 82(2), 131–138. https://doi.org/10.1002/j.1556-6678.2004.tb00294.x

Henwood, K. L., & Pidgeon, N. F. (1992). Qualitative research and psychological theorizing. *British Journal of Psychology*, 83(1), 97–111. https://doi.org/10.1111/j.2044-8295.1992.tb02426.x

Hollway, W., & Jefferson, T. (2000). *Doing qualitative research differently: Free association, narrative and the interview method*. Sage. https://doi.org/10.4135/9781849209007

Langdridge, D. (2007). *Phenomenological psychology: Theory, research and method*. Pearson Prentice Hall.

Larkin, M., Watts, S., & Clifton, E. (2006). Giving voice and making sense in interpretative phenomenological analysis. *Qualitative Research in Psychology*, 3(2), 102–120. https://doi.org/10.1191/1478088706qp062oa

Levitt, H. M., Creswell, J. W., Josselson, R., Bamberg, M., Frost, D. M., & Suárez-Orozco, C. (2018). Journal article reporting standards for qualitative research in psychology: The APA Publications and Communications Board task force report. *American Psychologist*, 73(1), 26–46. https://doi.org/10.1037/amp0000151

Madill, A., Jordan, A., & Shirley, C. (2000). Objectivity and reliability in qualitative analysis: Realist, contextualist and radical constructionist epistemologies. *British Journal of Psychology*, 91(1), 1–20. https://doi.org/10.1348/000712600161646

Moon, K., & Blackman, D. (2017, May 2). A guide to ontology, epistemology, and philosophical perspectives for interdisciplinary researchers. *Integration and Implementation Insights*. https://i2insights.org/2017/05/02/philosophy-for-interdisciplinarity/

Ormston, R., Spencer, L., Barnard, M., & Snape, D. (2013). The foundations of qualitative research. In J. Ritchie, J. Lewis, C. McNaughten Nicholls, & R. Ormston (Eds.), *Qualitative research practice: A guide for social science students and researchers* (pp. 1–25). Sage.

Ponterotto, J. G. (2005). Qualitative research in counselling psychology: A primer on research paradigms and philosophy of science. *Journal of Counseling Psychology*, 52(2), 126–136. https://doi.org/10.1037/0022-0167.52.2.126

Reicher, S. (2000). Against methodolatry: Some comments on Elliott, Fischer, and Rennie. *British Journal of Clinical Psychology*, 39(1), 1–6. https://doi.org/10.1348/014466500163031

Roald, T., Køppe, S., Bechmann Jensen, T., Moeskjær Hansen, J., & Levin, K. (2021). Why do we always generalize in qualitative research? *Qualitative Psychology*, 8(1), 69–81. https://doi.org/10.1037/qup0000138

Shadish, W. R. (1995). Philosophy of science and the quantitative-qualitative debates: Thirteen common errors. *Evaluation and Program Planning*, 18(1), 63–75. https://doi.org/10.1016/0149-7189(94)00050-8

Shaw, R. L., Bishop, F. L., Horwood, J., Chilcot, J., & Arden, M. A. (2019). Enhancing the quality and transparency of qualitative research methods in health psychology. *British Journal of Health Psychology*, 24(4), 739–745. https://doi.org/10.1111/bjhp.12393

Willig, C. (2007). Qualitative research: The need for system [Letter to the editor]. *The Psychologist*, 20(10), 597.

Willig, C. (2012). *Qualitative interpretation and analysis in psychology*. Open University Press.

Willig, C. (2019). What can qualitative psychology contribute to psychological knowledge? *Psychological Methods*, 24(6), 796–804. https://doi.org/10.1037/met0000218

Willig, C. (2021). *Introducing qualitative research in psychology* (4th ed.). McGraw Hill Open University Press.

Yardley, L. (2000). Dilemmas in qualitative health research. *Psychology & Health*, 15(2), 215–228. https://doi.org/10.1080/08870440008400302

CHAPTER 2

FRAMEWORKS FOR CAUSAL INFERENCE IN PSYCHOLOGICAL SCIENCE

Peter M. Steiner, William R. Shadish, and Kristynn J. Sullivan

Causal inference is central to psychological science. It plays a key role in psychological theory, a role that is made salient by the emphasis on experimentation in the training of graduate students and in the execution of much basic and applied psychological research. For decades, many psychologists have relied on the work of Donald Campbell and his colleagues to help guide their thinking about causal inference (e.g., Campbell, 1957; Campbell & Stanley, 1963; Cook & Campbell, 1979; Shadish et al., 2002). It is a tribute to the power and usefulness of Campbell's work that its impact has lasted more than 60 years. Yet the decades also have seen new theories of causation arise in disciplines as diverse as economics, statistics, and computer science. Psychologists often are unaware of these developments, and when they are aware, often struggle to understand them and their relationship to the language and ideas that dominate in psychology. This chapter reviews some of the more recent developments of frameworks for causal inference, using Campbell's familiar work on validity types and threats as a touchstone from which to examine two alternative frameworks: the potential outcomes framework (e.g., Imbens & Rubin, 2015; Rubin, 1974, 1978) and structural causal models and their respective graphical representation (e.g., Pearl, 2009b; Spirtes et al., 1993; Wright, 1921). For convenience's sake, we refer in this chapter to the different frameworks for causal inference as (a) the *validity typology/threats* (VT) framework, which is mainly associated with the work by Campbell, Cook, and Shadish (Shadish et al., 2002); (b) the *potential outcomes* (PO) framework, introduced by Neyman in 1923 (Splawa-Neyman et al., 1990) and Rubin (1974) and further explicated by Holland (1986); and (c) the *structural causal models* (SCM) with their implied *causal graphs* as put forward by Wright (1921), Spirtes et al. (1993), or Pearl (2009b).

In outlining and comparing the three frameworks, we focus predominantly on conceptual rather than applied statistical aspects, that is, how do the frameworks define causal effects and how do they formalize the causal assumptions

---

We are grateful for helpful discussions and comments by Thomas Cook, Yi Feng, Bryan Keller, Yongnam Kim, Ana Kolar, and Patrick Sheehan.

When I was asked to revise this chapter and join Will Shadish and Kristynn Sullivan as coauthor for the second edition of the handbook, I felt honored but was also intrigued. Honored because Will Shadish was one of my most important mentors introducing me to the world of causal inference. Intrigued because my own thinking on causal inference frameworks—as addressed in this chapter—has evolved. I suspect that my ideas may have changed in ways with which Will might not have always agreed, but he would have enjoyed discussing and debating them—as would I. In revising this chapter, I have edited the content to reflect my own perspectives on causal inference as a way to continue the conversation with Will and include a dedicated memorandum to Will. For Will Shadish's and Kristynn Sullivan's perspectives on causal inference, the interested reader may consult the first edition of the handbook. I also want to thank Kristynn Sullivan for having me take the lead on this revision.

https://doi.org/10.1037/0000318-002
APA Handbook of Research Methods in Psychology, Second Edition: Vol. 1. Foundations, Planning, Measures, and Psychometrics, H. Cooper (Editor-in-Chief)
Copyright © 2023 by the American Psychological Association. All rights reserved.

required for causal inference. The discussion of causal assumptions is crucial because without them it is impossible to infer causal relations. Data alone do not warrant any causal inference. Pearl and Mackenzie (2018) put it bluntly: "Data are profoundly dumb about causal relationships" (p. 14); Cartwright (1994, Chapter 2) proclaimed "no causes in, no causes out," meaning that causal conclusions cannot be deduced purely from probabilities or data alone, they always rest on causal background information. The needed background information comes from subject matter theory about the presumed data-generating process (DGP) and the implemented research design. The credibility of causal conclusions increases with the strength of subject matter theory and researcher control over the data-generating mechanism (e.g., via randomization or experimental control of treatment conditions and settings). Research designs that rely on the fewest and weakest assumptions should be preferred because "the credibility of inferences decreases with the strength of the assumptions maintained" (the law of decreasing credibility; Manski, 2013).

Given the importance of causal background information for drawing causal conclusions from observed data, we will, therefore, compare the causal frameworks with regard to four main questions. First, what are their philosophical foundations regarding causation? Second, how do they define what a cause and an effect is? Third, how do they formalize and explain the causal assumptions, and, in particular, how do they link subject matter theory to causal assumptions? This is a crucial question because understanding and defending causal assumptions matters most in actual research practice. Fourth, how do they identify causal effects from observed data, and, related to this, which research designs do they advocate to facilitate causal identification?

Before we focus on these questions, we briefly introduce each of the three causal frameworks and outline their key components. The introduction to SCM will be longer than for VT and PO because of its higher degree of formalization that requires graph terminology, graphical concepts, and the translation of subject matter theory into a structural model and a causal graph. Moreover, most readers are presumably less familiar with SCM than with VT and PO such that a more detailed exposition of SCM seems justified. For a better understanding, we use an example to demonstrate the application of graphical concepts. In discussing the assumptions and identification of causal effects, we will not make any parametric functional form or distributional assumptions, that is, we focus on the causal assumptions that are sufficient for nonparametric identification but do not address statistical assumption necessary for the estimation of identified causal effects from finite data. Since this chapter does not focus on specific designs and statistical methods for causal inference, interested readers may consult, for instance, Angrist and Pischke (2009), Cunningham (2021), Hernán and Robins (2020), Imbens and Rubin (2015), Morgan and Winship (2015), Reichardt (2019), Rosenbaum (2002, 2009), Rubin (2006), or Shadish et al. (2002). Comparisons of the three frameworks have been published before. West and Thoemmes (2010) and Shadish (2010) provided a comparison of VT and PO, while Imbens (2020) compared PO and SCM. For more details about the history of the three causal frameworks, see the corresponding chapter of the first edition of this handbook (Shadish & Sullivan, 2012).

KEY COMPONENTS OF THE THREE CAUSAL FRAMEWORKS

It is impossible to comprehensively describe all three frameworks in detail and to do justice to their manifold contributions to the theoretical and applied literature on causation, philosophy, statistics, and research designs for causal inference. Instead, we take a somewhat narrow perspective and focus on the three frameworks' key components that formalize and define causation and state the assumptions required to identify causal effects from observed data.

Throughout the entire section, we use an example to illustrate and discuss the key concepts and issues. Assume that researchers want to evaluate whether an online cognitive behavior therapy (CBT) for depressed high school students helps in reducing their depression. To assess CBT's effectiveness, they compare the online CBT treatment ($T = 1$) to a standard in-person treatment directly administered in clinics ($T = 0$). The outcome measure of interest is the Beck Depression Inventory (Y), which is also measured at baseline as depression pretest score (P) together with a set of sociodemographic variables (S) including sex and age. In addition, data on medication use, including substance use, are collected with a questionnaire at the pretest and posttest (M_0 and M_1, respectively). Low-resolution brain electromagnetic tomography (LORETA) and functional magnetic resonance imaging (fMRI) are used to measure the cognitive-affective mechanism of each student at the pretest and posttest (C_0 and C_1, respectively). The cognitive-affective mechanism is assumed to directly affect depression. Thus, besides the treatment indicator (T) and the depression posttest (Y), researchers plan on having six measured (sets of) variables: four baseline variables (P, S, M_0, C_0) and two postintervention variables (M_1, C_1).

Validity Typology and Validity Threats Framework

The core of VT is its *validity typology* and the associated *threats to validity* that originate back to Campbell (1957) and was then subsequently extended by Campbell and Stanley (1966), Cook and Campbell (1979), and Shadish et al. (2002). VT uses the validity typology and its associated validity threats to take a pragmatic, practice-oriented approach to the design of new studies and critique of already completed studies that probe cause-effect relationships. At its start, VT outlined a key dichotomy that scientists make two general kinds of inferences from experiments (Campbell, 1957, p. 297): (a) "did, in fact, the experimental stimulus make some significant difference in this specific instance" and (b) "to what populations, settings, and variables can this effect be generalized?" Campbell labelled the former inference *internal validity* and the latter *external validity*, although he often interchanged the term *external validity* with *representativeness* or *generalizability*. Later, the dichotomy was expanded into four validity types (Cook & Campbell, 1979; Shadish et al., 2002):

- **Internal validity.** The validity of inferences about whether the observed association between treatment status T and outcome Y reflects a causal impact of T on Y. Thus, internal validity is about the assumptions required for *causal inference*.
- **Statistical conclusion validity.** The validity of inferences about the association (covariation) between the presumed treatment T and outcome Y. Thus, this validity type is about the assumptions required for making *statistical inference* from the realized randomization or sampling outcomes to the underlying target populations of possible treatment assignments and participants.
- **Construct validity.** The validity with which inferences are made from the operations and settings in a study to the theoretical constructs those operations and settings are intended to represent. It is about the correct labelling of variables and accurate *language use*.
- **External validity.** The validity of inferences about whether the observed cause-effect relationship holds over variations in participants, settings, treatments, outcomes, and times. External validity directly relates to the assumptions required for *generalizing* effects.

Since any causal inference goes beyond the simple description of observed associations or mean differences obtained from a single study with a sample of participants in a given setting and at a specific point in time, valid inference requires that all four validity criteria must be met. The validity types give VT a broad sweep both conceptually and practically, pertinent to quite different designs, such as randomized controlled trials (RCTs), observational studies, or single case studies. The boundaries between the validity types are artificial but consistent with common categories of discourse among scholars.

Threats to validity address the errors researchers may make about the four kinds of inferences involving statistics, causation, language use, and generalizability. The validity threats are the second core part of VT. Regarding internal validity, researchers evaluating the effect of CBT on depression might use observational data from a nonrandomized experiment to infer CBT's effectiveness. In making causal claims they may be wrong in many ways: Without the availability of a control group, the observed difference in the depression pre- and posttest scores may be caused by some events other than the CBT intervention, for instance by pandemic-induced lockdowns during the intervention (*threat of history*) or by regression to the mean if participants are selected based on their depression pretest scores (*threat of regression to the mean*). In a study with a nonequivalent control group, the observed group difference in depression may have been caused by differential selection of study participants into treatment conditions (*threat of selection*) or by differential study attrition (*threat of attrition*). In addition to the four threats highlighted here, the list of internal validity threats also includes *maturation, instrumentation, testing, ambiguous temporal precedence*, and their interactions (Shadish et al., 2002). The presentation of all threats for all four validity types is beyond the scope of the present chapter, but they are listed and discussed in Shadish et al. (2002; see also Reichardt, 2019).

Of the four validity types, VT always has prioritized internal validity, saying that "internal validity is the prior and indispensable condition" (Campbell, 1957, p. 310) and that "*internal validity* is the *sine qua non*" (Campbell & Stanley, 1963, p. 175, emphasis in the original). Thus, VT focuses on the design of high-quality randomized and quasi-experiments that aim for high internal validity, claiming that it makes no sense to experiment without caring if the result is a good estimate of whether the treatment worked for the participants in the given setting and time.

The classification and propagation of the strongest *research designs for causal inference*—randomized experiments, regression discontinuity designs, interrupted time series designs, and nonequivalent control group designs—can be considered as the third key feature of VT. Research designs are classified by the degree they reduce "the number of plausible rival hypotheses available to account for the data. The fewer such plausible rival hypotheses remaining, the greater the degree of 'confirmation'" (Campbell & Stanley, 1963, p. 206). This is typically achieved by active experimental control over (a) the treatment conditions, (b) assignment of study participants to treatment conditions, (c) the setting of the experiment, and (d) the measurement of covariates and the outcome (including their timing). The validity types and corresponding threats that are so central to VT are intended to guide applied researchers in systematically identifying and actively preventing potential issues that may invalidate causal inference.

To achieve high internal and statistical conclusion validity for the CBT study, researchers should consider a randomized block or randomized matched pairs design. Researchers could, for instance, first form matched pairs of study participants with the same or a very similar depression pretest score, maybe even within blocks of female and male participants, and then randomly assign participants within matched pairs. Blocking and pair-matching creates comparable treatment groups and increases the study's power and, thus, its statistical conclusion validity (avoidance of a Type II error). Randomization within matched pairs increases internal validity because it rules out confounding bias due to differential selection of participants into conditions and provides a solid basis for frequentist inference (hypothesis testing). In addition, researchers would carefully choose the setting and control the implementation of both the online CBT and standard in-person control condition, and select meaningful proximal and distal outcome measures according to subject matter theory.

Since even strong research designs are rarely perfectly implementable, particularly in field settings, VT encourages researchers to use additional *design elements* to address plausible validity threats (Shadish et al., 2002, p. 157).

Among them are techniques that keep participants and treatment administrators unaware of treatment conditions, repeated pre- and posttest measurements of the outcome of interest, nonequivalent outcome measures (i.e., measures that are presumable unaffected by the treatment), multiple measures of baseline covariates, multiple comparison groups, or switching replications where in a second phase of the study the control group receives the treatment and the treatment group serves as the control. Consider the CBT example: If researchers are worried about differential attrition from their RCT, they should first think about incentives to mitigate attrition. In addition, they should take baseline measures (P, S, M_0, C_0) and then empirically probe whether attrition led to group differences in their observed measures. If so, statistical adjustment should be considered, but there is no guarantee that attrition bias can be successfully addressed. Moreover, study participants knowing that they got assigned to the control condition could get demoralized and, thus, become more depressed, which affects not only their cognitive-affective mechanism (C_1) and medication use (M_1) at the posttest but also the depression posttest (Y). Ideally, participants should be unaware of the type of treatment they receive and the alternatives. If keeping participants unaware is not possible, evaluating the average changes $E(C_1 - C_0)$ and $E(M_1 - M_0)$ for the control group may help assessing the presence of resentful demoralization (a threat to construct validity).

The focus of VT, then, is on the reduction of contextually important, plausible threats to validity as well as the addition of well-thought-out design features. If possible, it is better to rule out a threat to validity with design features than to rely on statistical adjustments and subject matter judgment to assess whether a threat is plausible after the fact. The emphasis on design over analysis was summed up well by Light et al. (1990): "You can't fix by analysis what you bungled by design" (p. viii). Simply put, design rules (Shadish & Cook, 1999).

With the emphasis on prevention of validity threats through design, VT has always been on the lookout for new designs and design improvements. This includes inventing the regression discontinuity design (Thistlethwaite & Campbell, 1960), or prioritizing comparative interrupted time series designs with a control series, nonequivalent comparison group designs with high-quality measures to remove confounding bias, and complex pattern-matching designs. The latter refer to designs that make complex predictions in which a diverse pattern of results must occur, using a study that may include multiple non-randomized designs each with different presumed biases, "The more numerous and independent the ways in which the experimental effect is demonstrated, the less numerous and less plausible any singular rival invalidating hypothesis becomes" (Campbell & Stanley, 1963, p. 206; Reynolds & West, 1987). More recent design improvements and extensions include comparative regression discontinuity designs (Tang et al., 2017; Wing & Cook, 2013) or multivariate regression discontinuity designs (Papay et al., 2011; Wong et al., 2013). Useful design principles and elements directly related to VT have been proposed by Reichardt (2000, 2019) and Rosenbaum (2009, 2017).

VT has also strongly informed and contributed to the literature on within-study comparisons (WSCs, also called design replication studies) and causal replication studies. WSCs empirically evaluate whether and under which conditions quasi-experimental designs are able to reproduce the effect estimates of randomized experiments (Cook et al., 2008; Wong & Steiner, 2018a; Wong et al., 2018). Failures to reproduce the effect estimates suggest that the quasi-experimental designs suffered from internal validity threats (i.e., violations of causal assumptions). The goal of these studies and subsequent meta-analyses is to provide applied researchers guidance for improving their quasi-experimental designs to successfully address most common threats to internal validity. Causal replication is another field in which research designs and design elements that have long been advocated by VT become more important again (Shadish et al., 2002; Wong et al., 2021). The causal assumptions underlying direct replication efforts and validity threats have been discussed by Wong and Steiner (2018b) and Steiner et al. (2019).

Potential Outcomes Framework

The PO framework is mostly associated with Donald B. Rubin, who popularized the potential outcomes notation for causal inference with observational studies (Rubin, 1974, 1978, 2004). As pointed out by Rubin, Neyman introduced the notion of "potential yields" in 1923 in the context of randomized experiments in agriculture (translated and reprinted in Splawa-Neyman et al., 1990). Thus, the PO framework is often referred to as the Neyman-Rubin or Rubin causal model. A brief history of the potential outcomes approach can be found in Imbens and Rubin (2015) and Imbens (2020). For a broader, more philosophical discussion, see Holland (1986). The PO framework has two core components: the potential outcomes notation and the assignment mechanism. The first component, the *potential outcomes*, formalizes the notation for the outcomes a study participant would obtain if assigned to different treatment conditions. For simplicity, we discuss the case with two treatments only, that is, one treatment condition and one control condition that serves as contrast for assessing the treatment's impact. With a binary treatment variable T, using $T = 1$ for the treatment condition and $T = 0$ for the control condition, and an outcome variable Y, we obtain two fixed (nonstochastic) potential outcomes: The potential treatment outcome $Y(T = 1) = Y(1)$, which is observed if a participant were exposed to the treatment condition and the potential control outcome $Y(T = 0) = Y(0)$, which is observed if exposed to the control condition.

The main advantage of using potential outcomes is that they allow for a precise definition of individual and average causal effects (often referred to as the causal estimand). For a single participant i and a given setting under investigation, the individual causal effect (ICE) is defined as the difference between the potential control and treatment outcome, $ICE_i = Y_i(1) - Y_i(0)$ (we use subscripts i only when needed for improved clarity). The average causal effect (ACE, often also referred to as the average treatment effect, ATE) is then the average across all individual effects, $ACE = E[Y_i(1) - Y_i(0)]$, where the expectation can be taken across all participants either of the sample or the target population of interest. Thus, the ACE is the difference in average outcomes if all units were assigned to the treatment instead of the control condition. Since the same participant cannot be exposed simultaneously to the treatment and control condition, one of the two potential outcomes is observed only, either $Y_i(1)$ or $Y_i(0)$. As a consequence, neither ICE nor ACE can directly be estimated from observed data. Rubin (1978) and Holland (1986) referred to this a the "fundamental problem" of causal inference. The observed outcome, Y_i, can be written as a function of the potential outcomes and the treatment status, $Y_i = Y_i(1)T_i + Y_i(0)(1 - T_i)$, while the unrealized potential outcome remains counterfactual. Though many authors use the terms *potential* and *counterfactual outcomes* interchangeably (e.g., Morgan & Winship, 2015; VanderWeele, 2015), Rubin (2005) stated that "these values are not counterfactual until after treatments are assigned, and calling all potential outcomes 'counterfactuals' certainly confuses quantities that can never be observed" (p. 325). Thus, potential outcomes are formulated from a prefactual perspective where one will be realized and becomes a fact, while the other remains counterfactual. Since the definition of counterfactuals requires a realized factual outcome together with a concept of most similar (counterfactual) worlds or a structural model with invariance assumptions across counterfactual worlds (Lewis, 1973, 2004; Paul & Hall, 2013; Pearl, 2009b), we do not consider potential and counterfactual outcomes as interchangeable.

ICE and ACE are causally identified and estimable from observed data only if strong causal assumptions are met. Since the estimation of ICE requires much stronger assumptions than the estimation of ACE, PO mostly focuses on average causal effects. PO formulates two main sets of assumptions: the *stable-unit-treatment-value assumption* (SUTVA) with regard to the potential outcomes and assumptions about the *assignment mechanism*, the second core part of PO.

SUTVA has two parts: the *no interference* and the *no hidden variations in treatments* assumption (Imbens & Rubin, 2015). The *no interference assumption* requires that each participant's pair of potential outcomes is unaffected by the other participants' treatment exposure. This assumption is commonly violated if peer effects are present. In the CBT example, this assumption could be violated if high school students with depression symptoms are randomly assigned to treatments within schools and learn about each other's treatment status. Then, students in the control condition may get demoralized and more depressed or they may try to do as well without CBT (i.e., resentful demoralization and compensatory rivalry, Shadish et al., 2002). Spillover effects are another example that might occur when students exposed to CBT tell their peers in the control condition about their training and experience. These SUTVA violations imply that each participant no longer has only two potential outcomes but a large set of potential treatment and control outcomes depending on its own and the other participants' treatment exposure (Hong & Raudenbush, 2006; Imbens & Rubin, 2015).

The second part of SUTVA requires that there is *no hidden variation of treatments*. That is, all participants receive the same version of the treatment and control condition. For instance, if multiple versions of an online CBT intervention are (unintentionally) administered, then no causal claims with regard to a single specific CBT intervention can be made. One can only assess the average effect of all treatment versions together (provided they can be considered as randomly assigned to students or schools). The effect of the treatment conditions on potential outcomes could also depend on the mode of assignment or administration and, thus, introduce hidden variation. For instance, the potential outcomes of the depression posttest may depend on whether CBT was randomly assigned, assigned based on need according to the depression pretest, or whether CBT can be voluntarily chosen by the eligible student population (with or without incentives).

These modes of assignment may trigger resentful demoralization or compensatory equalization efforts to a different degree. If SUTVA holds, then causal effects are easier to identify, interpret, and estimable with less complex statistical methods. Thus, research designs that make SUTVA more likely should be used. For instance, to avoid spill-over effects, resentful demoralization, or compensatory equalization and rivalry, researchers should consider a cluster-randomized trial that randomly assigns the CBT intervention at the school level rather than the student level.

The second core component of PO is the *assignment mechanism* by which units do or do not receive treatment. Together with SUTVA, it is the reliable knowledge of the assignment mechanism that allows researchers to identify average causal effects. One of the most frequently used assignment mechanism is random assignment as in completely randomized experiments, randomized block or matched pairs designs, or cluster-randomized trials. The key to identifying the ACE is knowledge of each participant's *assignment probability*. The probabilities can vary across participants, but they must be known and strictly between zero and one ($0 < P(T_i) < 1$) such that the assignment mechanism is *probabilistic* (also referred to as *positivity assumption*; Imbens & Rubin, 2015; Rubin, 2004). For instance, with constant assignment probabilities in a completely randomized experiment, the ACE is identified and estimable as difference in the mean outcome of the treatment and control group.

Without random assignment the situation is more complex. Instead of randomization, assignment may be based on observed variables with either a known or unknown assignment mechanism. An example for a known assignment mechanism is the regression discontinuity design in which treatment assignment is made solely with respect to a cutoff score on an observed assignment variable. Due to the deterministic assignment, however, the ACE is identified only for the subpopulation scoring right at or in the very close vicinity of the cutoff (Hahn et al., 2001). Lee and Lemieux (2010) showed that the regression discontinuity design is equivalent to a randomized experiment at the cutoff.

An example where assignment is based on known and observed variables but the mechanism itself is unknown are observational studies (also referred to as nonexperiments). For instance, researchers or administrators might assign the CBT and control intervention to high school students based on their depression pretest score and observed sociodemographic characteristics but in a vague, informal way without eligibility criteria in place (thus, it is not a regression discontinuity design). Since the variables involved in the assignment process are known, the assignment probabilities can be estimated from the observed data. The assignment probabilities are referred to as *propensity scores* and often used to estimate the ACE via matching, stratification, or weighting adjustments (Rosenbaum & Rubin, 1983). In both examples, knowing and reliably measuring the assignment-relevant variables guarantees that the assignment mechanism is *unconfounded*. If assignment is in addition *individualistic* (i.e., the assignment probabilities of each participant do not depend on the other participants' assignment probabilities) and *probabilistic* (i.e., each participant has a nonzero probability of receiving each treatment condition), then the assignment mechanism is called *regular* (Imbens & Rubin, 2015; Rubin, 2004). All these restrictions on the assignment mechanism are formalized in potential outcomes notation (see Imbens & Rubin, 2015).

The often referenced *strong ignorability* assumption refers to the combination of an unconfounded and probabilistic assignment and is regularly used in connection with propensity scores techniques to estimate the causal effect (Imbens & Rubin, 2015; Rosenbaum & Rubin, 1983). More formally, the strong ignorability assumptions states the requirement that potential outcomes must be independent of treatment assignment given a set of observed covariates X, $\{Y(0), Y(1)\} \perp T|X$ (unconfounded), and the assignment probabilities must be positive, $0 < P(T|X) < 1$ (probabilistic).

If, for our CBT example, SUTVA holds and strong ignorability is met conditional on the set observed baseline covariates $X = \{P, S, C_0, M_0\}$, then ACE is identified and given by

$$ACE = E[Y(1) - Y(0)]$$
$$= E\left\{\begin{array}{l} E(Y|T=1, P=p, S=s, C_0=c, M_0=m) \\ -E(Y|T=0, P=p, S=s, C_0=c, M_0=m) \end{array}\right\}$$

That is, the ACE can be expressed in terms of observable conditional expectations, where the difference in inner expectations evaluates the treatment effect for each possible $P \times S \times C_0 \times M_0$ value combination and the outer expectation takes the weighted average with respect to the joint distribution of the four conditioning variables $\{P, S, C_0, M_0\}$ (Imbens & Rubin, 2015). Since unconfoundedness is empirically not testable, subject matter theory is required to carefully choose the variables and to assess whether the observed baseline measures successfully remove the entire confounding bias. In the absence of reliable subject matter theory, researchers frequently try to adjust for all measured baseline variables (e.g., match on all measured baseline variables or the corresponding propensity score). Variables measured after the onset of the treatment (C_1, M_1) should not be used because they could potentially block mediated effects.

For *irregular assignment mechanisms* with unobserved confounding, that is, the assignment probabilities are unknown and cannot be estimated from the observed variables because unfoundedness is not met, researchers need to rely on different identification strategies. Examples are instrumental variable estimators that exploit a known source of exogenous variation (Angrist et al., 1996; Angrist & Pischke, 2009), difference-in-differences or gain score estimators that aim at offsetting rather than blocking confounding bias (Angrist & Pischke, 2009; Y. Kim & Steiner, 2021b), or principal stratification (Frangakis & Rubin, 2002). Most of these identification strategies have been successfully used by economists and statisticians long before PO found its way into economics and statistics, but the potential outcomes notation allowed for an exact (nonparametric) definition of the estimators' causal meaning and their underlying causal identification assumptions. For instance, the local average treatment effect of the nonparametric regression discontinuity estimator (Lee & Lemieux, 2010), the complier average treatment effect of the instrumental variable estimators (Angrist et al., 1996), or the average treatment effect for the treated of the difference-in-differences estimator (Lechner, 2011) are estimands that received their unambiguous causal definition from PO.

Though the focus of this chapter is on causal theories rather than statistical methods, one cannot ignore the importance of the statistical contributions directly related to PO. Besides the standard matching and propensity score techniques for causal inference (Rubin, 2006), these include propensity score methods for clustered data structures (Hong & Raudenbush, 2006; J.-S. Kim & Steiner, 2015; Thoemmes & West, 2011; Zubizarreta & Keele, 2017) or time-varying treatment regimens (Robins, 2000; Vandecandelaere et al., 2016), doubly-robust estimators that combine propensity score and regression adjustments (Bang & Robins, 2005; Lunceford & Davidian, 2004), principal stratification analysis (Frangakis & Rubin, 2002), causal mediation analysis (Imai et al., 2010; VanderWeele, 2015), comparative and multivariate regression discontinuity designs (Reardon & Robinson, 2012; Tang et al., 2017; Wong et al., 2013), randomized encouragement designs (Frangakis et al., 2002), causal generalization (Stuart et al., 2011; Tipton, 2012), or causal replication (Wong & Steiner, 2018b).

In addition, PO has also helped to advance variance estimation and hypothesis testing for RCTs and observational studies (Imbens & Rubin, 2015; Pashley & Miratrix, 2020, 2022; Schochet, 2016). Steyer and colleagues proposed a stochastic theory of causal effects that explicitly considers the potential outcomes as random variables, where each individual potential outcome has its own distribution, and directly allows for fallible variables in its notation, formal definitions and identification results (Mayer et al., 2014; Steyer et al., 2000).

Structural Causal Models and Causal Graphs

The origins of SCMs and causal graphs date back to Wright (1921), Burks (1926), Tinbergen (1930), and Haavelmo (1943) and somewhat later to Blalock (1964) and Duncan (1975). With the publication of two influential textbooks by Spirtes et al. (1993) and Pearl (2009b, first edition in 2002) the popularity of causal graphs and SCMs for causal inference strongly increased. Though causal graphical models could be discussed without an underlying SCM, the more stringent SCM assumptions not only allow for counterfactual analyses but also foster a better understanding of causal graphs (Peters et al., 2017). The key components of SCM are a *nonparametric structural model* with its associated *causal graph*, the concept of an *intervention* formalized by the *do*(.) operator and *do*-calculus, and a set of *graphical rules* to define and identify causal effects.

Causal inference with SCMs starts with subject matter theory about the real-world data-generating process (DGP) that must be translated into a set of nonparametric structural assignments and its associated causal graph. In practice, researchers start by drawing the causal graph and postulate an underlying SCM without explicitly formulating it. As an example consider an observational study to evaluate CBT's effect on depression. The causal graph of the presumed DGP is shown in Figure 2.1 where each arrow indicates the direction of a causal effect. The causal graph reflects researchers' belief about how the data were generated. From interviews or focus group discussions with clinicians, the researchers may have learned that study participants were assigned to CBT ($T = 1$) or a standard treatment ($T = 0$) solely based on their depression pretest score (P) but without formal eligibility criteria in place. It is known, however, that participants with higher depression scores were more likely assigned to CBT than participants with lower scores. Since prior research also

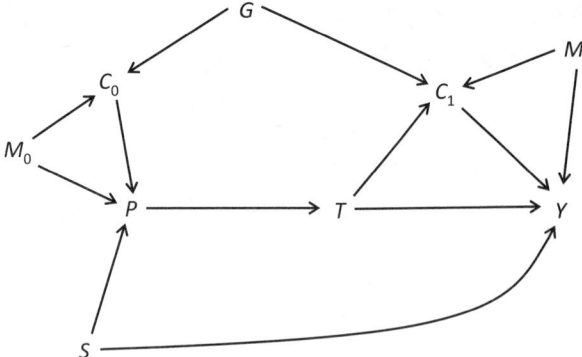

FIGURE 2.1. Causal graph (directed acyclic graph) for the evaluation of a cognitive behavior therapy (T) on depression (Y). The other variables are a depression pretest (P), a set of socioeconomic variables (S), genetic variants (G), the cognitive-affective mechanism (C_0, C_1), and medication/substance use (M_0, M_1) at the pretest and posttest, respectively.

suggests that the cognitive-affective mechanism directly affects the depression pretest (P) and posttest (Y), researchers took LORETA and fMRI measures of participants' cognitive-affective mechanism at the baseline (C_0) and after the end of the intervention (C_1). Empirical evidence of prior research also showed that a set of genetic variants (G) affects study participants' cognitive-affective mechanism (C_0, C_1). Moreover, researchers assumed that sociodemographic background variables (S = {sex, age, and potentially several other variables}) affect the response to depression measurements, and that medication use (M_0, M_1) affects the cognitive-affective mechanism and depression measurements at the pretest and posttest, respectively. Since our interest is in the total effect of CBT on depression, drawing the posttreatment variables C_1 and M_1 would not be needed. Given that researchers collected data on these variables, however, it makes sense to draw them, though we are not discussing causal mediation analysis in this chapter.

Most important in the graph are the missing arrows because they encode independence relations. For instance, researchers assumed that neither sociodemographic factors (S) nor the measures obtained from the imaging of the cognitive-affective mechanism (C_0) affected the clinicians' therapeutic decision (T). The causal graph shows many more pairwise independence relations, some of them unrealistic (e.g., between S and (C_0, C_1), G and (P, Y), or M_0 and M_1), but these simplifications allow for a clearer, less complex discussion of SCM's "toolbox." Moreover, the simplified graph likely fails to show all potential *common causes* between each pair of variables. For instance, medication use (M_0, M_1) and the cognitive-affective mechanism (C_0, C_1) might be jointly influenced by the quality of friendships and family relationships. In order to obtain a *causal* graph, all common causes between each pair of variables must be drawn (if unobserved common causes are presumed but difficult to label one may use biheaded, dashed arrows to indicate the dependence of variables). Again, for demonstration purposes we keep the graph simple but assume that the graph is causal (i.e., no common causes were omitted). At the end of this section, the graph of a more realistic scenario is briefly discussed.

Another important aspect is that the variables are drawn independent of whether they are observed or unobserved. For instance, assume that not all or none of the genetic variants (G) affecting the cognitive-affective mechanism (C_0, C_1) were measured. The same may hold for the cognitive-affective mechanism. This highlights that causal graphs represent subject matter theory about the presumed DGP rather than the observed data alone.

Before we formally state the structural model that underlies the causal graph in Figure 2.1, we briefly introduce basic graph terminology (Table 2.1 lists most important terms and concepts). *Variables* in the graph are connected by *directed edges* (arrows), which indicate causal relations in the direction of the arrow. SCM also makes use of kinship terminology. Consider for instance the treatment variable T in the causal graph. Then, T has only a single *parent* (P) but two *children* (C_1 and Y). We can also determine all *ancestors* of T (P, M_0, C_0, G, S) or all *descendants* that are in this case identical to the two children C_1 and Y.

If a graph contains only directed edges (i.e., simple arrows but no biheaded edges) and no cycles (no causal paths revert back to an already visited variable) the graph is called a *directed acyclic graph* (DAG). Though Figure 2.1

TABLE 2.1
Graph Terminology and Examples

	Variables (nodes)
Common cause	A variable that simultaneously affects two other variables in the graph. G is a common cause of C_0 and C_1: $C_0 \leftarrow G \rightarrow C_1$.
Collider (collider variable)	A collider variable on a path has two incoming arrows (but no outgoing arrows), i.e., two arrows collide in the variable. C_0 is a collider on the path $T \leftarrow P \leftarrow M_0 \rightarrow C_0 \leftarrow G \rightarrow C_1 \rightarrow Y$.
Confounder (confounding variable)	A confounder is the root variable on a confounding path. A root variable of a path has two outgoing arrows (but no incoming arrows). G is a confounder on the path $T \leftarrow P \leftarrow C_0 \leftarrow G \rightarrow C_1 \rightarrow Y$.
Direct cause	X is a direct cause of Y if an arrow leaves X and directly points into Y. T is a direct cause of Y because $T \rightarrow Y$.
Indirect cause	X is an indirect cause of Y if X and Y are connected by a causal path (chain) from X to Y with at least one intermediary variable on the path. T is an indirect cause of Y because $T \rightarrow C_1 \rightarrow Y$.
	Kinship relations
Ancestors	The ancestors of a variable X are all direct or indirect causes of X. T has five ancestors: P, M_0, C_0, G, and S. P has four ancestors: M_0, C_0, G, and S.
Children	The children of a variable X are all variables that are directly caused by the X. T has two children: C_1 and Y. P has one child: T.
Descendants	The descendants of a variable X are all variables that are directly or indirectly caused by X. T has two descendants: C_1 and Y. P has three descendants: T, C_1, and Y.
Parents	The parents of a variable X, $pa(X)$, are all direct causes of X. T has only a single parent: P. P has three parents: M_0, C_0, and S.
	Paths
Causal path	A path where all arrows point into the causal direction. $T \rightarrow C_1 \rightarrow Y$
Collider path	A noncausal path with a collider variable. $T \leftarrow P \leftarrow M_0 \rightarrow C_0 \leftarrow G \rightarrow C_1 \rightarrow Y$
Confounding path	A noncausal path without a collider variable. $T \leftarrow P \leftarrow C_0 \leftarrow G \rightarrow C_1 \rightarrow Y$
Chain	A chain is a causal path with (at least) one intermediary variable. $T \rightarrow C_1 \rightarrow Y$ or $P \rightarrow T \rightarrow Y$
Fork	A fork is a noncausal path with a common cause as single intermediary variable. $C_1 \leftarrow T \rightarrow Y$ or $P \leftarrow M_0 \rightarrow C_0$
Noncausal path	A path where at least one arrow points into a different direction (against the causal flow). $T \rightarrow C_1 \leftarrow M_1 \rightarrow Y$ or $T \leftarrow P \leftarrow C_0 \leftarrow G \rightarrow C_1 \rightarrow Y$
Open and blocked (closed) paths	An open path transmits causal or noncausal (spurious) association. A blocked or closed path does not transmit any association. The confounding path $T \leftarrow P \leftarrow C_0 \leftarrow G \rightarrow C_1 \rightarrow Y$ is open and transmits spurious association via confounder G. Conditioning on G, P, C_0, or C_1 would block the confounding path. The collider path $T \leftarrow P \leftarrow M_0 \rightarrow C_0 \leftarrow G \rightarrow C_1 \rightarrow Y$ is "naturally" blocked by C_0 and does not transmit any association. Conditioning on C_0 (or a descendant of) would open the collider path and transmit spurious collider association—unless it is blocked by any other noncollider middle variable on the path (P, M_0, G, or C_1).
Path	A path between two variables is an unbroken and nonintersecting sequence of arrows that may go along or against the direction of the arrows. $T \rightarrow C_1 \leftarrow G \rightarrow C_0 \leftarrow M_0 \rightarrow P \rightarrow S \rightarrow Y$ or $C_1 \leftarrow M_1 \rightarrow Y \leftarrow S$.

(continues)

TABLE 2.1

Graph Terminology and Examples (Continued)

	Associations
Causal association	Association between two variables transmitted along open direct and indirect causal paths.
Collider association	Spurious association between two variables transmitted along one or more open (unblocked) collider paths.
Confounding association	Spurious association between two variables transmitted along one or more open confounding paths.
Noncausal association	Spurious association between two variables transmitted along one or more open noncausal paths (i.e., open confounding or collider paths).
	Graph-related concepts
Blocking	Blocking aims at preventing a single or multiple paths from transmitting association. If a path is blocked by a set of variables **X** (including the empty set), no association is transmitted.
Conditioning/adjusting	Conditioning on or adjusting for a set of variables **X** (to block a single or multiple paths) is achieved, for instance, by controlling for **X** in a regression analysis, matching on **X**, or stratifying or blocking by **X**. Conditioning also occurs when subgroups are considered or when only cases without any missing data are analyzed.
d-separation	Given a set of variables **X**, if **X** blocks all causal and noncausal paths between the two variables. If **X** is the empty set, then two variables are d-separated if they are neither connected by a causal path nor any open noncausal (confounding) paths. If two variables are d-separated they are marginally or conditionally independent (in the probabilistic sense, provided the causal Markov and faithfulness assumptions are met).
Intervention/$do(.)$ operator	A hypothetical (thought) manipulation of the treatment variable of interest. The hypothetical exposure of the entire population to the CBT is denoted by $do(T = 1)$ and replaces the structural treatment assignment in the SCM with the fixed assignment $T := 1$.

Note. Most examples refer to the treatment and outcome variable, T and Y, of the causal graph in Figure 2.1, but the explanations apply to any pair of variables in a causal graph.

shows a causal DAG, we use the more general term *causal graph*, which allows for biheaded dashed edges to represent hidden variables that induce unobserved confounding (such graphs are also called acyclic directed mixed graphs; Shpitser, 2019).

A *path* is a sequence of nonintersecting adjacent edges. If all arrows of a path that connects an ordered pair of variables point into the causal direction, it is a *causal path* and transmits causal association. For instance, $T \rightarrow C_1 \rightarrow Y$ is a causal path connecting the causally ordered variables T and Y (i.e., the treatment must temporally precede the outcome). A *noncausal path* has at least one arrow pointing against the causal order (e.g., $T \leftarrow P \leftarrow C_0 \leftarrow G \rightarrow C_1 \rightarrow Y$) and may or may not transmit noncausal (spurious) association. Whether a noncausal path transmits spurious association depends on the presence or absence of collider variables on the path. A *collider* (on a path) is a variable in which two arrows collide. For instance, C_0 is a collider on the noncausal path $T \leftarrow P \leftarrow M_0 \rightarrow C_0 \leftarrow G \rightarrow C_1 \rightarrow Y$. Collider paths do not transmit any association because a collider "naturally blocks" any flow of association (unless it is conditioned on via matching or as a control variable in a regression; see the paragraph on blocking below).

Noncausal paths that do not contain a collider transmit confounding association. For instance, $T \leftarrow P \leftarrow S \rightarrow Y$ transmits confounding association between T and Y, with the root node S being the *confounder* because S simultaneously affects T (indirectly via P) and Y. Note that we define confounders graphically as common causes (Peters et al., 2017) rather than variables of a minimally sufficient adjustment set that remove the entire confounding bias (Hernán & Robins, 2020). For the graph in Figure 2.1, Exhibit 2.1 lists all causal and noncausal paths that connect T and Y. As the table shows, the direct and indirect causal associations transmitted from T to Y are confounded by the noncausal associations transmitted along two noncausal paths. All other paths between

EXHIBIT 2.1

Causal and Noncausal Confounding and Collider Paths Connecting Treatment T and Outcome Y in the Causal Graph in Figure 2.1

Causal paths (causal association)

$T \to Y$
$T \to C_1 \to Y$

Confounding paths (confounding association)

$T \leftarrow P \leftarrow S \to Y$
$T \leftarrow P \leftarrow C_0 \leftarrow G \to C_1 \to Y$

Collider paths (no association)

$T \leftarrow P \leftarrow C_0 \leftarrow G \to C_1 \leftarrow M_1 \to Y$
$T \leftarrow P \leftarrow M_0 \to C_0 \leftarrow G \to C_1 \to Y$
$T \leftarrow P \leftarrow M_0 \to C_0 \leftarrow G \to C_1 \leftarrow M_1 \to Y$
$T \to C_1 \leftarrow M_1 \to Y$
$T \to C_1 \leftarrow G \to C_0 \to P \leftarrow S \to Y$
$T \to C_1 \leftarrow G \to C_0 \leftarrow M_0 \to P \leftarrow S \to Y$

T and Y are collider paths that are naturally blocked and, thus, do not transmit any association. As we discuss later, the goal in causal inference is to neutralize noncausal associations transmitted along noncausal paths while leaving the causal associations transmitted along causal paths unaffected.

Two graphical concepts, blocking and *d*-separation, play an important role in the analysis of graphs (Pearl, 2009b; Pearl et al., 2016). A single path connecting two variables, U and V, is *blocked* by a set of variables **Z** (when conditioned on) if

- the path contains a chain of variables $U \to C \to V$ or a fork $U \leftarrow C \to V$ and variable C is in set **Z**, or
- the path contains a collider $U \to C \leftarrow V$ and the collider C is not in **Z**, and no descendant of C is in set **Z** either.

A blocked path does not transmit any association while an open (unblocked) path transmits association. In statistical analyses, blocking is typically achieved by conditioning on control variables via matching, subclassification, or regression adjustments. Consider the path $T \to C_1 \leftarrow M_1 \to Y$, which is naturally blocked by collider C_1. Thus, as long as C_1 is not in the conditioning set **Z**, the second condition is met and the path remains blocked. If we were to condition on the collider C_1, the parents of the collider, $pa(C_1) = \{T, M_1\}$, would become spuriously associated, which unblocks the collider path and induces collider bias between T and Y.

Here is a brief explanation for the spurious collider association (see Elwert & Winship, 2014, for a thorough treatment): Though T and M_1 are independent according to the graph in Figure 2.1, that is, they are not connected via any association-transmitting causal or confounding paths, CBT exposure (T) becomes predictive of medication use (M_1) after one learns about (i.e., conditions on) the state of the cognitive-affective mechanism (C_1). Assume that the cognitive-affective mechanism of a participant who did not receive CBT indicates no depression pattern. Then, the absence of an effective CBT treatment allows us to predict that medication use likely caused the absence of a cognitive-affective depression pattern (i.e., we obtain a negative spurious association between T and M_1). Note that conditioning on a descendant of a collider rather than the collider itself would also introduce spurious association between the collider's parents.

An unblocked collider path can still be blocked, however, if the path also contains a chain or a fork (first condition). Since our example path, $T \to C_1 \leftarrow M_1 \to Y$, contains the fork $C_1 \leftarrow M_1 \to Y$, the open collider path after conditioning on C_1 can still be blocked by M_1. Thus, three different sets **Z** are able to block the path $T \to C_1 \leftarrow M_1 \to Y$: $\{\}$, $\{M_1\}$, and $\{C_1, M_1\}$. The empty set $\{\}$ is sufficient because the collider C_1 naturally blocks the path. $\{M_1\}$ blocks the path in addition to the natural blocking by collider C_1, and $\{C_1, M_1\}$ blocks the path because M_1 intercepts the spurious association induced by conditioning on collider C_1.

d-separation considers not only a single path between U and V but *all* paths between the two variables. If a variable set **Z** blocks every single path between variables U and V, then U and V are *d*-separated conditional on **Z**. *d*-separation implies that U and V are conditionally independent.

From the graph in Figure 2.1 it is apparent that T and Y cannot be d-separated because the direct causal path $T \to Y$ cannot be blocked (it would require a mediator on the path to be blocked). However, it is easy to verify that P and Y can be d-separated by multiple sets, with the smallest set being $Z = \{G, S, T\}$. d-separation can be used to derive all marginal and conditional independencies implied by the causal graph and to subject them to empirical (non)parametric independence tests (at least those that involve observed variables only). The graph in Figure 2.1 has 23 missing arrows that results in 10 marginal and 655 conditional independences (determined using the *dagitty* package in R, Textor et al., 2016; for the corresponding online application, see http://www.dagitty.net/).

Now we can formally define the SCM as a collection of *structural assignments*, that is, each variable X_{ij} (for subject i and variable $j = 1, \ldots, J$) in a causal graph has a data-generating (structural) equation, $X_{ij} := f_i^{X_j}(pa(X_{ij}), U_i^{X_j})$, where $f_i^{X_j}$ is a nonparametric function of the parents of X_{ij}, $pa(X_{ij})$, and the independent stochastic noise variables $U_i^{X_j}$ that represent all idiosyncratic causes of X_{ij}. The SCM for the causal graph in Figure 2.1 is then given by the following structural assignments:

$$G_i := f_i^G(U_i^G)$$
$$M_{0i} := f_i^{M_0}(U_i^{M_0})$$
$$P_i := f_i^P(S_i, M_{0i}, C_{0i}, U_i^P)$$
$$M_{1i} := f_i^{M_1}(U_i^{M_1})$$
$$Y_i := f_i^Y(T_i, S_i, M_{1i}, C_{1i}, U_i^Y)$$
$$S_i := f_i^S(U_i^S)$$
$$C_{0i} := f_i^{C_0}(G_i, M_{0i}, U_i^{C_0})$$
$$T_i := f_i^T(P_i, U_i^T)$$
$$C_{1i} := f_i^{C_1}(G_i, M_{1i}, T_i, U_i^{C_1})$$

The functions f_i contain a subscript i to explicitly highlight that each participant may have its own nonparametric or parametric functional form, including interactions, higher order terms, or any transformations. That is, no linearity or constant effects nor additive noise terms are assumed. However, each participant is restricted to the same set of parental variables, though not every parental variable may have an influence on each participant's left-hand side variable. The SCM also indicates that each variable in the graph has an independent noise term $U_i^{X_j}$ which are not explicitly drawn in the graph. Note that the structural model also assumes that each participant's structural assignments depend only on the values of its own parental variables and noise terms but are completely unaffected by other participants' decisions, behaviors or outcomes (i.e., no interference). Given the SCM, the joint distribution of all the observed and unobserved variables, $P(G, S, M_0, C_0, P, T, M_1, C_1, Y)$, follows deterministically from the joint distribution of the corresponding noise terms, $P(\mathbf{U})$, where $\mathbf{U}$ is the vector of all $U_i^{X_j}$.

For an SCM and its corresponding causal graph, the $do(.)$ operator is used to define the causal effect by a *hypothetical (thought) intervention*, $do(T = t)$, that sets the treatment for all participants to a specific choice $T = t$. Then, the causal effect of the intervention $do(T = t)$ is given by the *intervention distribution* of the outcome, for instance, the distribution of the depression score Y if one were to expose the entire population (or sample) to the CBT intervention, $P(Y|do(T = 1))$. Often researchers are interested only in the expectation of the intervention distribution, $E(Y|do(T = 1))$, or the treatment-control contrast that evaluates the ACE, $E(Y|do(T = 1)) - E(Y|do(T = 0))$. Graphically, the intervention can be conceived of removing all arrows going into T because treatment status is no longer determined by the value of its parents but solely by the hypothetical intervention $do(T = t)$, and the structural assignment $T_i := f_i^T(P_i, U_i^T)$ is replaced by $T_i := t$. Then, T and Y are only connected by two open paths, the direct and indirect causal paths $T \to Y$ and $T \to C_1 \to Y$, respectively, implying that our hypothetical intervention aims at evaluating the total causal effect.

Since the $do(.)$ operator refers to a hypothetical intervention on the entire population, probabilities and expectations containing the $do(.)$ operator are not observable but must be inferred from the data together with the causal assumptions implied by the structural model and its graph. In addition to the marginal and conditional independences encoded in the causal graph, three further assumptions are needed (Pearl, 2009b; Peters et al., 2017). First, the *Markov and faithfulness assumptions* guarantee that the graphical dependence and independence relations (obtained via *d*-separation) are identical to probabilistic dependence and independence, respectively (note that the Markov assumption is already implied by the structural model). Second, a *consistency assumption* requiring that the hypothetically conceived intervention $do(T = t)$ is consistent with the observed treatment status, that is, we can only infer effects for treatments that have actually been implemented in practice. And third, an *invariance assumption* claiming that all structural assignments of the SCM, except for the intervention assignment, remain invariant if one were to actually intervene in the real-world DGP and not only hypothetically. The invariance assumption is also referred to as *autonomy assumption* and often implied by the meaning of the adjective *structural* (Pearl, 2009a, 2009b). The invariance assumption implies that a real-world intervention (say all eligible students with depression symptoms get exposed to CBT) neither affects the functional relations $f_i^{X_j}$ nor the distribution of noise terms $U_i^{X_j}$ of all structural assignments $X_{ij} := f_i^{X_j}(pa(X_{ij}), U_i^{X_j})$, except for the assignment of the intervention variable. For instance, the data-generating mechanism for the outcome, $Y_i := f_i^Y(T_i, S_i, M_{1i}, C_{1i}, U_i^Y)$, remains unaffected by a real-world intervention $do(T = t)$, only the values for T and C_1 change because of the intervention: $T_i = t$ and $C_{1i} := f_i^{C_1}(G_i, M_{1i}, T_i = t, U_i^{C_1})$. The intervention affects the distribution of descendant variables only "mechanically" through the implied changes in the values of their parental variables $pa(X_{ij})$. Thus, the intervention is conceived as a "local surgery" without side effects (Pearl, 2009b). If, under these assumptions, the intervention distributions $P(Y|do(T = t))$ can be recovered from observable (*do*-free) marginal and conditional probabilities and expectations, the causal effect is said to be *identified*.

The goal of a causal identification analysis then is to block the confounding associations transmitted along noncausal paths while leaving the causal paths open because they transmit the causal associations of interest. SCM provides a set of graphical identification criteria and a *do*-calculus that allow researchers to check whether the ACE or the corresponding intervention distributions are identified via conditioning from the observed data and the presumed causal graph. Conditioning methods include regression or matching adjustments because they (implicitly) evaluate conditional distributions and expectations. Here we discuss only a single criterion, the adjustment criterion, but other criteria like the front-door criterion (Pearl, 2009b) exist. Alternatively, one may use the *do*-calculus, which is complete, that is, it will provide an adjustment formula whenever the causal effect is nonparametrically identifiable (Huang & Valtorta, 2006; Shpitser & Pearl, 2006). The *do*-calculus is implemented in program packages like *causaleffect* in R (Tikka & Karvanen, 2017), which allows researchers to automatically check for identifiability and to obtain nonparametric adjustment formulas.

The *adjustment criterion* states that the ACE is identified if it is possible to purge all noncausal associations from the observed association between T and Y such that only the causal associations remain (the more popular *backdoor criterion* is slightly more restrictive and not complete). In graphical terminology, ACE is nonparametrically identified if we find an adjustment (i.e., conditioning) set of observed variables, **X**, such that

1. **X** blocks all noncausal paths from T to Y, and
2. no variable in **X** is on a causal path from T to Y or descends from a variable on a causal path from T to Y.

One apparent choice for the adjustment set are the treatment variable's parents. In our CBT example the depression pretest score is the single parent, $\mathbf{X} = pa(T) = \{P\}$. From Exhibit 2.1 it becomes clear that P blocks the two confounding paths without unblocking any of the six naturally blocked collider paths because P is either not a collider on those paths (first four paths) or the paths are naturally blocked by other collider variables (last two paths). Since P neither blocks the causal paths nor is a descendant of C_1 (which is on the causal path from T to Y), both conditions of the adjustment criterion are met. Then, for the valid adjustment set $\mathbf{X} = \{P\}$, the *do*-calculus provides a nonparametric adjustment formula for the ACE

$$E(Y|do(T=1)) - E(Y|do(T=0))$$
$$= \sum_p \{E(Y|T=1, P=p) - E(Y|T=0, P=p)\}$$
$$\times P(P=p).$$

Assuming discrete pretest values, the adjustment formula computes for each pretest score p the difference in the treatment and control group's mean outcome and then takes the weighted average across these mean differences. Given a large enough sample size, the conditional expectations and the marginal probability can be estimated directly from the data. For continuous variables, the sum is replaced by the integral and estimation regularly requires parametric functional form assumptions.

Now assume that the pretest score (P) is not available to the analyst such that P is no longer a candidate for the adjustment set. Then, provided all other variables are reliably measured, the adjustment criterion is met by 10 adjustment sets (determined with the *dagitty* R package): $\{S, G\}$, $\{S, G, M_0\}$, $\{S, G, C_0\}$, $\{S, C_0, M_0\}$, $\{S, G, C_0, M_0\}$, $\{S, G, M_1\}$, $\{S, G, M_0, M_1\}$, $\{S, G, C_0, M_1\}$, $\{S, C_0, M_0, M_1\}$, and $\{S, G, C_0, M_0, M_1\}$. The first and last five sets only differ with respect to the additional posttreatment variable M_1 (i.e., omitting or including M_1 does not make a difference for the identification result). Note that the adjustment criterion requires neither the inclusion of all baseline variables in the adjustment set nor the exclusion of posttreatment variables. Further, assume that no measures of the genetic variants (G) were taken (in addition to the missing pretest P), then the researchers are left with only two choices to block all confounding paths: $\{S, C_0, M_0\}$ or $\{S, C_0, M_0, M_1\}$. Note that $\{S, C_0\}$ is not a valid adjustment set since C_0 is a collider on four noncausal paths (see Exhibit 2.1). For three of them, conditioning on C_0 is not an issue because S or collider C_1 (naturally) blocks the paths, but one path would remain open:

$T \leftarrow P \leftarrow M_0 \rightarrow C_0 \leftarrow G \rightarrow C_1 \rightarrow Y$. Since G and P are not available, conditioning on M_0 in addition to $\{S, C_0\}$ is the only option left. Though adjusting for C_1 would also block this specific collider path, it is not an option since it would block the indirect causal path $T \rightarrow C_1 \rightarrow Y$ and unblock the two collider paths $T \rightarrow C_1 \leftarrow M_1 \rightarrow Y$ and $T \leftarrow P \leftarrow M_0 \rightarrow C_0 \leftarrow G \rightarrow C_1 \leftarrow M_1 \rightarrow Y$ (the latter jointly with C_0). Thus, for the adjustment set $\mathbf{X} = \{S, C_0, M_0\}$, the adjustment formula for the ACE is given by

$$E(Y|do(T=1)) - E(Y|do(T=0))$$
$$= \sum_s \sum_c \sum_m \begin{cases} E(Y|T=1, S=s, C_0=c, M_0=m) \\ -E(Y|T=0, S=s, C_0=c, M_0=m) \end{cases}$$
$$\times P(S=s, C_0=c, M_0=m).$$

Even with huge sample sizes, estimating the conditional expectations and probabilities almost always requires some (semi)parametric assumptions. For instance, regression or matching adjustments can be used to estimate the ACE.

To briefly demonstrate the graphical analysis with a more realistic scenario, consider the causal graph in Figure 2.2, where treatment selection now depends on the imaging results of the cognitive-affective mechanism (M_0) and socio-

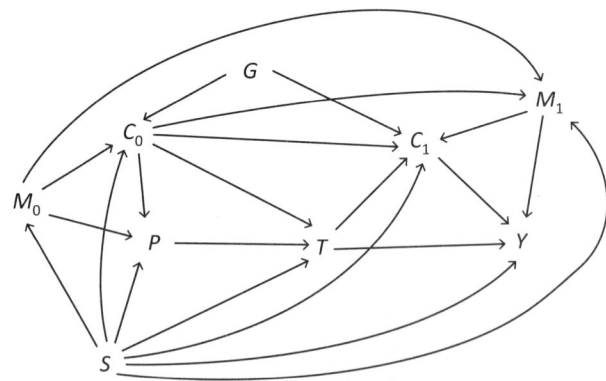

FIGURE 2.2. Causal graph (directed acyclic graph) for the evaluation of a cognitive behavior therapy (T) on depression (Y). The other variables are a depression pretest (P), a set of socioeconomic variables (S), genetic variants (G), the cognitive-affective mechanism (C_0, C_1), and medication/substance use (M_0, M_1) at the pretest and posttest, respectively.

economic variables (S) in addition to the depression pretest (P). The graph also encodes fewer independence relations between other variable pairs. For instance, socioeconomic characteristics now affect the cognitive-affective mechanism (C_0, C_1) and medication use (M_0, M_1). The graph encodes now only two marginal but still 104 conditional independencies that could be subjected to empirical independence tests (if all variables would be observed). As before, we have two causal paths that connect the CBT intervention (T) and the depression posttest (Y). But we have many more noncausal paths connecting T and Y: 68 open confounding paths and 246 naturally blocked collider paths. Using the adjustment criterion, we obtain 13 admissible adjustment sets, provided all variables in the graph are reliably measured. If the genetic variants (G) are unobserved six adjustment sets remain, with $\{C_0, P, S\}$ and $\{C_0, M_0, S\}$ being the two minimal sets with the fewest variables. Thus, in addition to the cognitive-affective mechanism (C_0) and the selection-relevant socioeconomic factors (S), researchers may condition on the depression pretest (P) or a reliable measures of medication use (M_0) to identify the causal CBT effect.

If the set of observed variables fails to meet the adjustment criterion because not all required variables have been (reliably) measured a causal effect might still be identifiable. For instance, the front-door criterion might apply or, more generally, one uses the *do*-calculus to check for nonparametric identifiability. Even if the *do*-calculus fails, alternative (non)-parametric identification strategies for (conditional) ACEs can be employed. Useful graphical representations and identification criteria were published for the most frequently used methods, including instrumental variable estimators (Brito, 2010; Brito & Pearl, 2002), difference-in-differences or gain score estimators (Y. Kim & Steiner, 2021a, 2021b), and regression discontinuity designs (Steiner et al., 2017). Another strategy is to rely on linearity and distributional assumptions that pave the way for structural equation modeling (SEM; e.g., Bollen, 1989; Hancock & Mueller, 2013). Causal identification criteria for linear SEM have been discussed by Brito and Pearl (2002, 2006) and Chen and Pearl (2015).

Causal graphs and respective identification criteria are also available for causal mediation analysis (Pearl, 2001, 2014; Shpitser, 2013), causal inference under interference (Ogburn & VanderWeele, 2014), the recoverability of causal effects in the presence of missing data due to nonresponse or attrition (Mohan & Pearl, 2019; Thoemmes & Mohan, 2015), or the generalizability of causal effects, called transportability (Bareinboim & Pearl, 2012, 2013; Pearl & Bareinboim, 2018). As for the identification analysis of ACE, the respective graphical criteria provide direct guidance for researchers in determining whether and with which variables the causal assumptions for causal mediation, recoverability, or transportability are met.

SCMs and their graphical representation also play a crucial role in causal search (Pearl, 2009b; Spirtes et al., 1993) and counterfactual analysis (Pearl, 2009b; Pearl et al., 2016). Causal search exploits *v*-structures, that is, collider structures where a collider's parents are not connected by a direct causal relation. Counterfactual analysis investigates individual and conditional causal effects that cannot be investigated by the population-level $do(.)$ operator. Counterfactuals formalize statements like the following: Student u's depression score would have been $Y_{T=1}(u) = y$ had she received CBT ($T = 1$) instead of the standard intervention ($T = 0$), which resulted in an observed depression score of $Y = Y_{T=0}(u) = 37$. While the identification and estimation of individual counterfactuals typically requires fully specified (parametric) SCMs, population-level counterfactuals are often nonparametrically identifiable (e.g., average mediation effects). SCMs and graphical discussions have also been very instructive in explaining paradoxes named after Simpson, Lord, and Berkson (Pearl et al., 2016; Pearl & Mackenzie, 2018), omitted variables bias (Steiner & Kim, 2016), collider bias issues (Ding & Miratrix, 2015; Elwert & Winship, 2014), or the causal structure of suppressor variables (Y. Kim, 2019). Accessible introductions to SCM can be found in Cunningham (2021), Elwert (2013), Morgan and Winship (2015), Pearl and Mackenzie (2018), or Rohrer (2018). More technically oriented introductions are Pearl (1998, 2009a, 2010) and Pearl et al. (2016).

COMPARISON OF THE THREE CAUSAL FRAMEWORKS

We have described the basic features of VT, PO, and SCM, and we now compare and contrast the three approaches. Specifically, we address several of the three framework's core characteristics, including philosophies of causation on which they rely, the definitions of cause and effect, the formulation of causal assumptions and identification, the importance of causal generalization and replication, the extent to which they integrate and formalize qualitative subject matter theory, and the preference of experimental research designs.

Philosophies of Causation

Though VT's, PO's, and SCM's main focus is on causal inference with observed data, they have their own philosophical foundations. Here we provide a very brief but pointed discussion of their main philosophical foundations, that is, the philosophical account of causation used to define the meaning of *T causes Y*. More detailed expositions of each framework's philosophical and epistemological orientation can be found in Cook and Campbell (1979), Shadish et al. (2002), Holland (1986), Halpern and Pearl (2005a, 2005b), Pearl (2009b), and Spirtes et al. (1993).

Cook and Campbell (1979) described VT's philosophical foundations as "derived from Mill's inductivist canons, a modified version of Popper's falsificationism, and a functionalist analysis of why cause is important in human affairs" (p. 1). VT explicitly acknowledges the impact of the work of the philosopher John Stuart Mill on causation. In particular, the idea that identifying a causal relationship requires showing that (a) the cause came before the effect, (b) the cause covaries with the effect, and (c) there are no plausible alternative explanations for the effect other than the cause. The threats to validity that VT outlines directly reflect these requirements. For instance, the threats to internal validity include Mill's first temporal requirement (ambiguous temporal precedence) and the remaining threats (history, maturation, selection, attrition, testing, instrumentation, regression to the mean) are examples of alternative explanations that must be eliminated to establish causation. VT also acknowledges the influence of Mill's methods of eliminative induction to discover and demonstrate causal relationships (Mackie, 1980; White, 2000). VT's preference for strong (quasi)experimental designs and certain design features are direct offshoots of this influence. In following Mill, VT thinks about experimental methods as strategies to eliminate noncausal or unintended causal variations. In defining a cause, VT relies on Mackie's definition of a cause as an "insufficient but necessary part of an unnecessary but sufficient condition" that brings about the effect (INUS condition; Mackie, 1980). That is, a cause of interest might show an effect only if the cause is implemented in a setting or context where support factors are present but suppression factors are absent. From philosopher Karl Popper (1959), VT places the idea of falsifying hypotheses in a crucial role (Cook, 1985).

Given VT's reliance on Mill and Mackie in defining cause-effect relationships, one can characterize the causal foundations of VT as a (probabilistic) *regularity account* of causation, that is, a succession of cause-effect relations that is instantiated with regularity in some context according to some presumed fundamental laws (Mackie, 1980; Paul & Hall, 2013). For the CBT example, this implies that the CBT intervention affects the cognitive-behavioral mechanism and subsequently reduces depression in not only a single instance but regularly in many subjects exposed to CBT. Since regularity accounts rely on the covariation of observed facts about what happens with some regularity to define cause-effect relations, without resorting to causal terminology or concepts like an intervention or an active manipulation of the cause, VT takes a *reductionist* perspective on causation (Paul & Hall, 2013; Woodward, 2016). Note that reductionism does not preclude active manipulations of treatment conditions in practice (e.g., in an RCT). To the contrary, experimental control over treatments and the entire context of a (quasi)experiment allows VT to establish the treatment-control contrast as an INUS condition, rule out most plausible validity threats, and, thus, increase the chances to observe an effect with some regularity that warrants a causal interpretation.

PO is less intimately tied to the formal philosophical literature. This is so because potential outcomes are defined as primitive causal entities without explicit reference to a specific context or a more formal causal structure like in SCM. However, the prefactual definition of potential outcomes with respect to a treatment and control condition (Rubin, 2007, 2008) suggests that (a) the cause must precede the effect and (b) that cause-effect relations are conceptually defined by a hypothetical manipulation of the treatment-control contrast ("NO CAUSATION WITHOUT MANIPULATION"; Holland, 1986; emphasis in the original). Thus, PO can be characterized as a *manipulationist* or *interventionist account* of causation (Cartwright, 2007; Woodward, 2003, 2016). PO is *nonreductionist* because the definition of potential outcomes and of the causal effect is based on the causal notion of a manipulation (Imbens & Rubin, 2015).

Interestingly, in defining potential outcomes, PO does not explicitly address whether the treatment and control condition under investigation must be (hypothetically) implemented in identical or even similar settings. It explicitly demands only that the potential treatment and control outcomes must refer to the same person and moment in time (Holland, 1986; Imbens & Rubin, 2015; Rubin, 1974). However, potential outcomes and subsequently the definition of a causal effect obtain a more meaningful causal interpretation via SUTVA, which introduces invariance assumptions across treatment conditions by requiring no interference and no hidden variations in treatment conditions (Rubin, 1978, 2007, 2019). But whether the implementation of the treatment and control condition in different settings should be considered as hidden variation in treatments or as a defining part of the treatment-control contrast remains unclear.

PO's lack of a thorough philosophical foundation is not surprising since it was conceptualized from statistical theory for randomized experiments to provide a clearly defined causal estimand for the difference in average outcomes of the randomized treatment and control groups (Rubin, 1974; Splawa-Neyman et al., 1990). However, the minimal causal structure of potential outcomes has its clear advantage because it allows other causal accounts to use PO as an interface to statistical analysis. Scholars of both VT and SCM make extensive use of methods developed or justified under PO when it comes to estimating causal effects from observed data.

In contrast to PO, SCM provides a fully developed and mathematized theory of causation that relies on a structural model and the concept of a hypothetical intervention to define causation (Halpern & Pearl, 2005a, 2005b; Pearl, 2009b; Spirtes et al., 1993). The structural model formalizes the context in which causal effects and counterfactuals obtain a precise context-specific meaning (Menzies, 2004; Woodward, 2003). Moreover, the stochastic nature of the structural assignments in SCM links causation to probability theory and statistics. The $do(.)$ operator formalizes the hypothetical intervention that is necessary to define the causal effect in substantive and probabilistic terms. Thus, SCM is a fully mathematized *interventionist* and *structural account* of causation (Cartwright, 2007; Woodward, 2003, 2016). SCM offers a *nonreductionist* perspective on causation because cause-effect relations are defined without any reference to observable facts (i.e., covariation between variables) but within a structural model using the causal notion of an intervention.

A structural model represents a fully articulated causal model that allows SCM to not only precisely define causal effects but also to directly derive potential and counterfactual outcomes for all possible interventions. Thus, potential outcomes are defined in SCM conditional on the structural model and are, therefore, conceptually more restrictive than in PO where they are model-independent, primitive causal entities. Using the structural assignment for the depression outcome of the CBT example, the "structural" potential outcomes are defined as $Y_i(t) := f_i^Y(T_i = t, S_i, M_{1i}, C_{1i}, U_i^Y)$, for $t \in \{0,1\}$ (Halpern, 1998; Pearl, 2009b, also refers to them as potential responses). Similarly, counterfactual outcomes are rigorously defined in SCM with respect to the structural model but they differ from Lewis's counterfactual outcomes that directly emanate from a reductionist counterfactual rather than nonreductionist structural account of causation (Lewis, 1973; Paul & Hall, 2013). That is, SCM-based potential and counterfactual outcomes rely on strong but potentially unrealistic invariance assumptions that require that the true DGP (i.e., its functional assignments and noise terms, except for the treatment) remains unaffected by any conceivable intervention. Factual and counterfactual worlds must be identical except for the well-defined and implemented treatment conditions. In practice this might be difficult to achieve. Consider the CBT example, where the online CBT intervention may be of different duration and take place at different times and locations (at home) than the alternative clinical in-person intervention. The difference in timing and setting likely results in different treatment-unrelated experiences and social interactions while commuting to the clinic, or differences in the use of idle time that, in addition, could also change the functional form f_i^Y of the outcome-generating structural assignment. If these differences between the treatment and control world affect the depression outcome, then the potential and counterfactual outcomes as defined in SCM do not reflect realistic potential or counterfactual situations (but under Lewis's "most similar world" conceptualization they would).

This example highlights one of the main differences between SCM and the other two causal inference frameworks (PO and VT). The complete reliance on a structural model suggests that causal claims are strictly model-dependent, that is, they should be confined to the specific model under investigation. Pearl and Mackenzie (2018) acknowledged the model-dependence of SCM by talking about "'provisional causality,' that is, causality contingent upon the set of assumptions that our causal diagram advertises" (p. 150). The economist Heckman (2006), who emphasized the importance of structural models and corresponding counterfactuals for research and science, strongly defended the provisional nature of causal claims: "A model is in the mind. As a consequence, causality is in the mind" (p. 2). For a similar position, see also Blalock (1964), "we shall conceptualize causality in terms of simplified models" (p. 15). However, the validity of a postulated model can be empirically probed, at least partially, by testing the implied independence assumptions and orientations of arrows (by using d-separation and exploiting v-structures).

In contrast, PO and VT are less model-dependent because their causal foundations do not involve structural models. To avoid strong reliance on model-dependent assumptions for observational studies, PO and VT prefer to use research designs where all or most plausible validity threats have been ruled out by design (Imbens, 2020; Shadish et al., 2002). For instance, instead of using observational data together with an SCM or causal graph of the presumed DGP to identify and estimate the causal effect of CBT on depression, PO and VT would rather suggest to implement a high-quality RCT with design elements that prevent potential validity threats including interference, hidden treatment variations, resentful demoralization, noncompliance, or attrition. One may argue that PO and in particular VT prefer to identify and estimate causal effects conditional on the research design rather than a presumed SCM. Since Nature does not behave consistently, particularly not according to an SCM or a causal graph, PO's and VT's preferred approach to causal inference can be characterized as "skillful interrogation of Nature" because Nature "responds to the form of the question as it is set out in the field and not necessarily to the question in the experimenter's mind" (from Joan Fisher Box's biography of R. A. Fisher; Box, 1978, p. 140). VT, however, also acknowledges that a single experiment provides rarely sufficient and conclusive evidence because it is not a clear window that reveals nature directly to us. To the contrary, experiments yield hypothetical and fallible knowledge that is often dependent on context and imbued with many unstated theoretical assumptions. Consequently, experimental results are partly relative to those assumptions and contexts and might well change with new assumptions or contexts. (Shadish et al., 2002, p. 29)

Given the context-dependence and the impossibility that all plausible validity threats can be ruled out with certainty, even for well-implemented RCTs, VT is in general sceptical about precise quantifications of an effect's magnitude and causal generalizations.

Theory of Cause

One of the most important aspects in causal inference is the definition of what a cause and an effect is. In general, careful definitions and theories about the cause play a minor role in PO and SCM, while VT puts more emphasis on it (West & Thoemmes, 2010). Central to all three frameworks, however, is that the cause must be manipulable. Though VT's philosophical foundation does not rely on the notion of an intervention or manipulation to define causation, VT puts strong emphasis on researcher control of treatment conditions, that is, their implementation and assignment to study participants. For this purpose, treatments must be manipulable. PO's definition of potential outcomes explicitly relies on practical manipulability of causes. If a causal agent of interest cannot be manipulated it does not qualify as a cause. Thus, PO hesitates to consider participant attributes like gender or race as potential causes because manipulating these attributes would fundamentally change the participant, that is, the participant would no longer be the same (Imbens & Rubin, 2015). In contrast, in SCM all variables can be causes as long as one can imagine a hypothetical intervention on the specific attribute (Pearl, 2009b). Whether such an intervention can be realized in practice is of less importance in SCM.

Once a cause of interest has been determined, all three frameworks require that the conceptualized cause is or has been implemented as intended. For instance, if CBT is the treatment of interest, then CBT must have been implemented as conceptually intended. PO formalized this requirement as "no hidden variations in treatment" assumption (which is part of SUTVA). SCM requires the same, that is, the intended treatment has been implemented with a probability of one (consistency assumption). Importantly, this also must hold for the control condition if the ATE of a well-defined treatment-control contrast is of interest. Thus, if unintended variations in the treatment or control condition occur, the causal effect of interest is not identified. In terms of VT, this means that the causal construct of interest is not consistent with the implemented or observed cause variable. Thus, VT would diagnose a threat to construct validity and require that the cause must be redefined and correctly labelled with respect to the treatment-control contrast actually implemented. The same can be done in PO and SCM, but their formal conceptualizations begin with clearly defined treatment and control conditions (Imbens & Rubin, 2015).

One difference between the three frameworks is that VT has paid more attention to a theory of cause than the aspects just discussed. The only knowledge we have about the cause in an experiment often may be the actions the researcher intentionally took to manipulate the treatment. This is quite partial knowledge. VT aspires to more, which is reflected specifically in the development of construct validity for the cause (Cook & Campbell, 1979). For example, experimental treatments are not single units of interventions but rather multidimensional packages consisting of many components. VT adopted Mackie's (1980) conception of cause as a constellation of features, the INUS condition, of which researchers often focus on only one, despite the fact that all of the features must be in place to produce an effect (Cook & Campbell, 1986; Shadish et al., 2002). Overall, VT has a more functionally developed theory of cause than either PO or SCM. This probably speaks to the different goals the frameworks have. VT aspires to a generalized causal theory, one that covers most aspects of the many kinds of inferences a researcher might make from various types of cause-probing studies. PO and SCM have a narrower purpose: to define an effect clearly and precisely for a given but not necessarily well-explicated context.

Definition of Causal Effects

In following Mill and Makie's reductionist regularity account, VT has treated effects as differences or covariations between two observed facts about what happened rather than hypothetical or potential outcomes under thought interventions. For example, VT conceptualizes the CBT effect as a comparison of what happened to the CBT group and what happened to the control group, or in the absence of a control group, as a comparison of what happened before the CBT intervention versus what happened after the intervention. The "causal" label is attached to the effect if the researcher is confident that the (quasi)experimental research design rules out all plausible alternative explanations (i.e., threats to internal and construct validity). This is not a precise mathematical definition, but quantifying the magnitude of the causal effect has originally been of less importance in VT than establishing the existence of a causal effect via causally valid research designs. Thus, VT never had an explicit and precise definition of a causal effect until it started to adopt PO to more rigorously formalize the statistical analyses of quasi-experiments (Reichardt, 2019; Shadish et al., 2002).

One of PO and SCM's strengths is their explicit conceptual definition of a causal effect. PO uses potential outcomes notation to define individual and then average causal effects: $ACE = E[Y_i(1) - Y_i(0)]$. SCM uses the $do(.)$ operator to define intervention distributions as the basic effect of a cause (i.e., intervention), $P(Y \mid do(T = t))$, which then is used to define different causal estimands like $ACE = E(Y|do(T = 1)) - E(Y|do(T = 0))$. The main difference between PO's and SCM's definition is that PO does not need a structural model to define the effect of a treatment-control contrast. In contrast, SCM starts with a structural model and a set of assumptions (faithfulness, consistency, and invariance) and then defines causal effects by applying the $do(.)$ operator to the causal graph and the SCM with its implied joint probability distribution. In comparison to PO, SCM's definition of a causal effect is completely model-dependent and, thus, has a correspondingly contextualized meaning. The graphical determination of an intervention's effect from the manipulated graph has the advantage that it reveals all the causal paths that directly or indirectly (via mediators) transmit causal associations. Such a graphical analysis helps researchers in deciding whether all causal paths are of interest (i.e., the total effect) or whether some of them should be blocked if possible, for instance, any causal paths due to unintended compensatory equalization or rivalry in the control group. Moreover, SCM provides a framework for assessing counterfactuals and for defining causal effects that require counterfactual reasoning like the natural direct and indirect effects in causal mediation analysis (Pearl, 2009b).

Causal Identification

Causal identification addresses the conditions under which a causal effect can be parametrically or nonparametrically inferred from an observed data set. The focus here is on *causal assumptions* required for causal inference rather than statistical assumptions that are needed for a consistent estimation of effects and sound statistical inference. That is, causal identification is not concerned about uncertainty due to random assignment or sampling (estimation of causal effects is briefly addressed in the next section).

As discussed before, in VT an effect is causally identified with respect to a given research design if all plausible threats to internal and construct validity can be credibly ruled out. Though this is a precise statement, VT does not provide mathematically or statistically formalized identification criteria or assumptions as PO and SCM do. For each assignment mechanism, PO formalizes the identification assumptions in terms of potential outcomes notation. PO's main focus is on randomized experiments and regular assignment mechanisms for observational studies. That is, if SUTVA holds and if assignment is probabilistic and unconfounded, then the ACE is identified. As a special case we mentioned above the strong ignorability assumption. If ACE is identified, then PO provides a nonparametric identification result that can be used to derive nonparametric or parametric estimators for the causal effect.

Other than for VT, main proponents of PO do not endorse all estimators and assumptions of irregular assignment mechanisms (with unobserved confounding). For instance, PO hesitates to exploit variations in treatment and control conditions over time as typical for gain score or difference-in-differences estimators or (comparative) interrupted times series estimators (Imbens & Rubin, 2015). This is so because PO considers the same participants at two time points as different units and, thus, not comparable. Nonetheless, assumptions for these estimators like the common trend assumption have also been formalized within the PO framework. See also Holland (1986), who discussed causal transience and temporal stability assumptions for repeated measurement settings in terms of potential outcomes.

In SCM, identification assumptions are typically formulated as graphical criteria like the adjustment criterion or front-door criterion. More generally, the *do*-calculus provides a machinery that automatically checks for nonparametric identification. The outcome of a graphical identification analysis is a (*do*-free) nonparametric adjustment formula that could be used to directly estimate the causal effect if the data set were sufficiently large. A distinct feature of the identification analysis in SCM is that it guides researchers in selecting and conditioning on a clearly defined set of covariates. It is also explicit about the variables that researchers should not use for their adjustments.

Thus, the main differences between the three frameworks are the degree of formalization of the identification criteria and the context. VT identifies a causal effect with respect to an actually implemented research design and the absence of validity threats, PO does so with respect to the known or presumed assignment mechanism (formalized in probabilistic terms using potential outcomes), and SCM provides an identification result conditional on a fully formalized structural model.

Estimation of Causal Effects and Statistical Inference

Since our focus is on the three framework's approach to causation and the causal assumptions required to identify causal effects rather than statistical estimation and inference, we briefly highlight only a few estimation and inference aspects. Moreover, when it comes to estimating and testing causal effects, proponents of the three frameworks use the same type of estimators, though they might differ in their preferred identification strategies.

With regard to estimation and inference, an enormous wealth of methods has originated particularly from the PO framework. Again, this is not surprising because the minimal causal structure of potential outcomes is well suited for demonstrating the statistical methods' relevance for causal inference. The most frequently used estimation and inference methods include propensity score matching or stratification, inverse-probability of treatment weighting, principal stratification, marginal structural mean models, doubly-robust estimators that combine propensity score estimators with an additional regression adjustment, weighting estimators for mediation analysis, instrumental variable estimators, difference-in-differences or gain score estimators, or nonparametric regression discontinuity estimators (Angrist & Pischke, 2009; Hernán & Robins, 2020; Imbens & Rubin, 2015; Morgan & Winship, 2015; Reichardt, 2019; Rosenbaum, 2002, 2009; Rubin, 2006; VanderWeele, 2015). For RCTs, nonparametric inference procedures and variance estimators have been suggested (Imbens & Rubin, 2015; Pashley & Miratrix, 2020, 2022; Schochet, 2016).

Causal Generalization and Replication

Traditionally, generalizability of causal findings has always played an important role in VT in form of construct and external validity, though at the beginning of VT (e.g., Campbell, 1957; Campbell & Stanley, 1966) the emphasis was by far more strongly focused on internal validity, maybe with the exemption of the multitrait-multimethod matrix for studying construct validity (Campbell & Fiske, 1959). Cook and Campbell (1979) extended the theory of construct validity of both the treatment and the outcome, and identified possible alternatives to random sampling that could be used to generalize findings from experiments. Cook (1990, 1991) developed both theory and methodology for studying the mechanisms of generalization, laying the foundation for what became three chapters on the topic in Shadish et al. (2002; Cook, 2004). For example, meta-analytic techniques now play a key role in analyzing how effects vary over different persons, locations, treatments, and outcomes across multiple studies.

PO has made contributions to causal generalization by promoting response surface modeling, meta-analysis, and analysis of effect heterogeneity and effect mediation (e.g., Frangakis & Rubin, 2002; Rubin, 1990, 1992), but rarely overtly tied these methods to the generalization of causes. More recently, however, causal generalization became an active research area in which the generalization of causal effects has been formalized under PO and statistical methods have been suggested (e.g., Stuart et al., 2011, Tipton, 2012). The same development occurred in SCM where causal generalization is referred to as transportability of causal effects. Bareinboim and Pearl (2012, 2013) and Pearl and Bareinboim (2018) introduced selection graphs, graphical criteria, and nonparametric identification results for transportability. In comparison to VT, PO and SCM provide formalized assumptions, identification results, and statistical methods, but they mostly focus on generalizability across populations and settings only. VT is also interested in generalizing cause-effect relations across variations in treatments and outcome constructs and measures (see also West & Thoemmes, 2010).

VT has also contributed to the literature on causal replication. First, VT used within-study comparisons (WSCs), also called design-replication studies, to replicate the results of a randomized experiment with quasi- or nonexperimental study designs (Cook et al., 2008, 2009; Pohl et al., 2009; Shadish et al., 2008, 2011; Steiner et al., 2010, 2011). The purpose of WSCs and their meta-analysis is to demonstrate whether and under which conditions quasi- or nonexperimental methods are able to reproduce causal effects of high-quality RCTs in actual research practice. Those studies revealed that certain variable sets, particularly pretest measures of the outcome and variables that directly index the selection process, are often effective in removing most of the selection bias. Thus, these results provide practical guidance for researchers without strong subject matter theory about the DGP. Wong and Steiner (2018a) and Steiner and Wong (2018) formalized the assumptions required for a causal interpretation of WSC results (using potential outcomes notation) and discussed measures for assessing replication success. They then extended the concepts to direct and conceptual replication efforts, introduced a causal replication framework, and demonstrated how to use switching replication or stepped wedge designs to address validity threats to causal replication (Steiner et al., 2019; Wong et al., 2021; Wong & Steiner, 2018b). Carefully implemented causal replication designs warrant causal explanations of replication failures and, thus, allows researchers to systematically explore the generalizability boundaries of causal effects across populations, settings, treatments, and outcomes.

Integration and Formalization of Subject Matter Theory

All three frameworks strongly rely on subject matter theory because threats to validity and causal assumptions can only be assessed with knowledge about the presumed DGP regarding treatment assignment and the outcome. All three frameworks are explicit about the importance of subject matter theory for causal inference. The challenge for practice is that the most crucial causal assumptions are empirically not testable (e.g., the unconfoundedness assumption, adjustment criterion, absence of differential selection). To avoid reliance on overly strong assumptions, researchers often use (quasi)experimental designs and design elements to rule out or indirectly probe validity threats. Subject matter knowledge, however, also guides the design of strong studies that allow for credible causal claims. Where the frameworks differ, however, is in the degree of formalization of subject matter knowledge and how it is linked to the causal assumptions.

VT uses nontechnical natural language to define and discuss the identification of causal effects. The validity typology and threats directly reflect aspects of actual research practice, that is, issues that emerged from implementations of research designs to evaluate the effectiveness of treatments or programs. The practice-oriented approach of VT is apparent from its major methodological publications (e.g., Cook & Campbell, 1979; Reichardt, 2019; Shadish et al., 2002). Applied examples are used to carefully explain variations of each validity threat and how design elements can be used to eliminate, mitigate, or probe the threats. Thus, for researchers with sufficient subject matter knowledge and familiarity with VT, the list of validity threats provides direct and systematic guidance in designing, implementing, and analyzing experimental and observational studies. VT's practice orientation is one of its major strength. Without a formally precise definition of causation, researchers can nonetheless implement high-quality studies that warrant causal interpretations. Traditionally, this has been the main approach in research areas relying mostly on RCTs. VT also provides general guidance with regard to the credibility of specific quasi-experimental research designs or the importance of measuring variables like the pretest of the outcome to create comparable (unconfounded) groups in nonequivalent control group designs. VT does not provide, however, rigorously formalized assumptions or criteria for the identification of a causal effect. VT does not consider this as a drawback, because it is in general sceptical about successfully ruling out *all* threats to validity in practice. Due to its practice orientation, VT can be characterized as a practitioner's guide to causal inference.

PO uses potential outcomes notation and probability theory to define causal effects and to formalize identification assumptions. The main purpose of PO is to demonstrate formally under which conditions (i.e., assignment mechanisms) an effect estimator warrants a causal interpretation. Whether the causal assumptions provide direct guidance from a subject matter point of view is of less concern. Consider an observational study, where a causal interpretation of effect estimates is warranted only if SUTVA and strong ignorability (i.e., unconfounded and probabilistic assignment) hold. Though these formal assumptions cover essentially all threats to internal and construct validity, they do not offer direct guidance for applied researchers. For instance, the unconfoundedness assumption that demands that the potential outcomes are independent of treatment assignment given a set of observed covariates, $\{Y_i(0), Y_i(1)\} \perp T_i \mid \mathbf{X}_i$, is uninformative about which covariates to measure in designing a study or to select when analyzing the data. PO highlights, of course, the importance of subject matter theory for selecting covariates but does not provide detailed guidance for researchers about how to meet the assumptions. If applied guidance is provided, it is often rather general. For instance, PO advocates to balance treatment groups on all observed baseline variables to establish a *credible* inference (Rubin, 2007, 2009). However, a credible inference may not necessarily meet the unconfoundedness assumption as the set of observed covariates might induce collider bias or strongly amplify any remaining confounding bias (Ding & Miratrix, 2015; Steiner & Kim, 2016). Though researchers well-versed with formal notation and statistical theory are able to give the assumptions context-specific meaning, many applied researchers have difficulties in deriving meaningful guidance from the abstract assumptions. Since PO's main focus is on the causal import of statistical methods (e.g., matching or instrumental variable estimators), it can be characterized as a statistician's guide to causal inference. The minimal causal structure of potential outcomes mostly helps statisticians and methodologists in linking new methods and estimators to causal inference.

SCM uses probabilistic and graphical terminology to define causal effects and identification criteria for a given structural model. This requires, however, a fully formalized causal model about the presumed DGP as causal input. The adjustment criterion, for instance, can only be applied once subject matter theory has been translated into a causal graph. Drawing realistic causal graphs is demanding, but it is the key causal input that enables researchers to apply graphical tools to derive testable independence relations, check whether a causal effect is identified and which variables to condition on, and to obtain a nonparametric adjustment formula. R packages like *dagitty* or *causaleffect* automatize this process (Textor et al., 2016; Tikka & Karvanen, 2017). Though the results of a graphical causal analysis depend on a "correctly" drawn graph, SCM does not (yet) provide sufficient applied guidance on translating subject matter theory into causal graphs. The examples used to discuss and introduce causal graphs rarely address how to add unreliably measured constructs, validity threats like history effects, or composite variables like socioeconomic status or the body-mass index to the graph. One reason for the lack of guidance might be that causal effects are almost never nonparametrically identified once graphs accurately reflect all validity threats. How researchers with fallible measures and negative identification results should proceed or how they should avoid such issues to begin with is not addressed by SCM. Given the current absence of guidance for actual research practice, SCM can be characterized as a theoretician's guide to causal inference.

To summarize, among the three frameworks, SCM has the highest degree of formalization. It provides a graphical and symbolic language to formalize qualitative subject matter theory about the presumed DGP and to link the study-specific DGP to causal identification. Thus, SCM requires researchers to explicate the presumed DGP by creating a causal graph ideally before data are collected. This is likely to be a long-term iterative process as the scientific theory bolstering the graph is developed, tested, and refined. It is, however, a process that cannot be avoided regardless if one chooses to encode assumptions in a graph or in any other alternative notational system or language like the potential outcomes notation or the validity typology with its associated threats.

Research Designs for Causal Inference

Since VT is in general sceptical about causal claims, it has a strong emphasis on experimental control over treatment assignments, treatment conditions, measurements, and settings. Experimental control allows researchers to actively rule out validity threats by design, such that causal inference relies on the fewest and weakest causal assumptions possible. Control over the assignment mechanism via random assignment or assignment based on a covariate (as in a regression discontinuity design) has two main advantages: the assignment mechanism is known and is often quite simple (which facilitates unbiased estimation). Due to the prioritization of internal over external validity, VT favors RCTs and the strongest quasi-experimental designs over (nonexperimental) observational studies. Among the quasi-experimental designs, standard and comparative regression discontinuity designs have a higher credibility than nonequivalent control group designs and comparative interrupted time series designs. In addition, VT always advocates the use of additional design elements either to protect against plausible validity threats or to detect and statistically control for them.

PO prefers research designs with regular, that is, probabilistic and unconfounded, assignment mechanisms, particularly those where the mechanism is known like in RCTs. If the assignment mechanism is regular but unknown, then PO relies on statistical matching or propensity score adjustments. For irregular assignment mechanisms, either with unobserved confounding or deterministic assignments, PO advocates instrumental variable estimators and regression discontinuity designs (Imbens, 2020). PO is less sympathetic to (comparative) interrupted time series and difference-in-differences designs because they identify the causal effect by comparing control and treatment outcomes across time rather than across independent groups at the same time (this is so because subjects at different time points are not considered as being comparable). Thus, with the exemption of instrumental variables, which are not favored by VT, and interrupted time series designs, PO and VT tend to recommend the same randomized or quasi-experimental designs for causal inference (Imbens, 2020).

SCM has no preference for specific research designs, in particular it does not assign a privileged status to RCTs or quasi-experimental designs because it is not concerned about challenges in drawing credible graphs from incomplete or uncertain knowledge about the presumed DGP. A causal graph of a randomized experiment is just as good as a causal graph of an observational study. SCM trusts in researchers' reliable knowledge of the DGP but advocates that the data are collected only after the causal model has been posited (Pearl & Mackenzie, 2018, p. 16). Research designs with control over treatment assignment, conditions and settings, however, typically result in better knowledge of the DGP and, thus, reliable causal graphs with more independence relations that facilitate a positive causal identification result (Steiner et al., 2017). For observational studies, SCM has a comparative advantage over VT and PO because it requires researchers to explicitly formalize subject matter theory about the presumed DGP and its assumptions in a causal graph, which then is used to automatically check for identifiability of causal effects, select bias-removing adjustment sets of variables, and derive testable independence relations via d-separation and subject them to empirical tests.

CONCLUSION

The description and comparison of the three causal frameworks revealed that they profoundly differ in their main conceptual and philosophical foundations. First, they differ in their degree of formalization of (a) subject matter theory about the presumed DGP and (b) the assumption required to identify a causal effect. SCM requires that qualitative subject matter theory about the DGP be translated into a nonparametric structural model and its associated causal graph. As a consequence, causal identification criteria and the *do*-calculus are contingent on the postulated DGP of the study under investigation. VT requires the researcher to systematically link subject matter theory to the catalogued validity threats and design studies that address at least the most plausible threats. This is done without any mathematical or probabilistic formalization (maybe with the exemption of statistical conclusion validity). PO is fully formalized but is less explicitly linked to subject matter theory about the presumed DGP.

Second, the three frameworks differ in how they define and quantify causal effects and in their linkage to statistical estimation and testing. SCM provides a precise model-dependent definition of a causal effect in terms of intervention distributions. PO also has a precise definition of individual and average causal effects but is less explicit about the context (because it does not require a structural model). PO's strength, however, is its direct linkage to statistical methods. VT's definition of a causal effect is the least formally quantified one since a causal effect is given by the association remaining after all validity threats have been ruled out.

Third, the frameworks differ in their prioritization of research designs. VT and PO prefer to use subject matter knowledge to design causal studies that rely on the fewest and weakest assumptions possible while SCM exploits formalized subject matter knowledge to identify causal effects for any given study. Whether the graph represents an RCT or an observational study does not make a difference.

Despite these conceptual differences, the three causal frameworks barely differ in their preferred choice of statistical methods. Whenever possible, they choose nonparametric over parametric methods, thereby avoiding overly strong functional form and distributional assumptions. Both VT and SCM strongly rely on statistical methods that were developed under or linked to causal inference via PO.

VT's and SCM's subject matter theory-oriented perspective on causal inference has clear advantages over PO in teaching causal inference to applied researchers. Due to their direct link to subject matter theory, either via generally understandable validity threats or graphical representations of the presumed DGP, students are able to understand better main causal assumptions and their direct implications for actual research practice on an intuitive level. This then helps them in implementing stronger research designs, choosing appropriate identification and estimation strategies, and in critically assessing whether causal claims are (un)warranted. It is not surprising, therefore, that textbooks advocating VT have been very popular in the social sciences (Cook & Campbell, 1979; Reichardt, 2019; Shadish et al., 2002) and that causal graphs, along with potential outcomes notation, are now finding their way into textbooks on causal inference with quasi-experiments and observational studies, particularly so in the applied sciences of economics, epidemiology, and sociology (Cunningham, 2021; Hernán & Robins 2020; Morgan & Winship, 2015). However, good examples and guidance in drawing reliable causal graphs from subject matter theory that also reflect validity threats other than selection, attrition, and nonresponse are still missing.

Given the different orientation, strengths, and weaknesses of the three causal frameworks, we argue that they should be jointly used in research practice because together they provide a richer, more powerful and reliable toolbox in planning and analyzing causal studies. VT's validity typology and threats provide excellent guidance for identifying plausible threats and help in drawing a more realistic causal graph for the planned research design. Once the presumed DGP of the planned study has been translated into a graph, SCM provides the tools to precisely define the causal effect for the given graph and to check for its identifiability. The identification result informs the researchers which variables must be reliably measured and used for statistical adjustments. Moreover, empirically testable independence assumptions can be automatically derived from the graph. PO then provides a perfect link from SCM's identification results to statistical estimation and testing.

Given VT's and PO's emphasis on strong research designs, many researchers have already successfully used VT and PO together: In planning an experimental study they consider most plausible validity threats; in analyzing the data they rely on PO's causal effect definition and its analytic tools. Translating subject matter theory about the DGP and potential validity threats into a causal graph and using SCM's graphical tools would further improve actual research practice because graphs make the most important causal assumptions explicit and, thus, invites constructive criticism by members of the research community who believe that the assumptions are not met and the causal conclusions unwarranted. Moreover, SCMs and causal graphs prevent researchers from inconsistencies between their beliefs and actions, that is, from design and analysis decisions that unintentionally contradict their beliefs about the DGP (e.g., by conditioning on a known collider; Hernán & Robins, 2020).

The crucial point here is that causal graphs must be drawn according to the best knowledge about the DGP, including most plausible validity threats, for the given treatments, outcomes, participants, and setting of the study. Qualitative methods for causal explanation might be particularly helpful here for eliciting treatment selection mechanisms and outcome generating processes prior to designing or analyzing observational studies (Maxwell, 2004). It would be a major mistake to draw graphs from observed data only, ignoring potential confounding issues and other validity threats, and then believe that the obtained graph has any causal bearing with respect to actual DGP. However, when serious efforts are made in drawing realistic graphical representations of the DGPs, the graphs' transparency about the crucial identifying assumptions helps in shifting the focus away from discussions about the appropriate choice and implementation of statistical methods to theory-driven discussions about the credibility of causal assumptions (i.e., about the absence of validity threats). After all, the credibility of causal assumptions warrants causal claims.

References

Angrist, J. D., Imbens, G. W., & Rubin, D. B. (1996). Identification of causal effects using instrumental variables. *Journal of the American Statistical Association*, *91*(434), 444–455. https://doi.org/10.1080/01621459.1996.10476902

Angrist, J. D., & Pischke, J.-S. (2009). *Mostly harmless econometrics. An empiricist's companion*. Princeton University Press. https://doi.org/10.1515/9781400829828

Bang, H., & Robins, J. M. (2005). Doubly robust estimation in missing data and causal inference models. *Biometrics*, *61*(4), 962–973. https://doi.org/10.1111/j.1541-0420.2005.00377.x

Bareinboim, E., & Pearl, J. (2012). Transportability of causal effects: Completeness results. *Proceedings of the Twenty-Sixth National Conference on Artificial Intelligence* (pp. 698–704). AAAI Press.

Bareinboim, E., & Pearl, J. (2013). A general algorithm for deciding transportability of experimental results. *Journal of Causal Inference*, *1*(1), 107–134. https://doi.org/10.1515/jci-2012-0004

Blalock, H. M. (1964). *Causal inferences in non-experimental research*. University of North Carolina Press.

Bollen, K. A. (1989). *Structural equations with latent variables*. John Wiley & Sons. https://doi.org/10.1002/9781118619179

Box, J. F. (1978). *R. A. Fisher: The life of a scientist*. John Wiley and Sons.

Brito, C. (2010). Instrumental Sets. In R. Dechter, H. Geffner, & J. Halpern (Eds.), *Heuristics, probability and causality: A tribute to Judea Pearl* (pp. 295–309). College Publications.

Brito, C., & Pearl, J. (2002). A graphical criterion for the identification of causal effects in linear models. *Proceedings of the AAAI Conference*, Edmonton, Canada.

Brito, C., & Pearl, J. (2006). Graphical condition for identification in recursive SEM. *Proceedings of the Twenty-Third Conference on Uncertainty in Artificial Intelligence* (pp. 47–54). AUAI Press.

Burks, B. S. (1926). On the inadequacy of the partial and multiple correlation technique. *Journal of Experimental Psychology*, *17*, 532–540.

Campbell, D. T. (1957). Factors relevant to the validity of experiments in social settings. *Psychological Bulletin*, *54*(4), 297–312. https://doi.org/10.1037/h0040950

Campbell, D. T., & Fiske, D. W. (1959). Convergent and discriminant validation by the multitrait-multimethod matrix. *Psychological Bulletin*, *56*(2), 81–105. https://doi.org/10.1037/h0046016

Campbell, D. T., & Stanley, J. C. (1963). Experimental and quasi-experimental designs for research on teaching. In N. L. Gage (Ed.), *Handbook of research on teaching* (pp. 171–246). Rand McNally.

Campbell, D. T., & Stanley, J. C. (1966). *Experimental and quasi-experimental designs for research*. Rand McNally.

Cartwright, N. (1994). *Nature's capacities and their measurement*. Oxford University Press. https://doi.org/10.1093/0198235070.001.0001

Cartwright, N. (2007). *Hunting causes and using them: Approaches in philosophy and economics*. Cambridge University Press. https://doi.org/10.1017/CBO9780511618758

Chen, B., & Pearl, J. (2015). *Graphical tools for linear structural equation modeling* (Tech. Rep. R-432). Department of Computer Science, University of California, Los Angeles. https://doi.org/10.21236/ADA609131

Cook, T. D. (1985). Postpositivist critical multiplism. In L. Shotland & M. M. Mark (Eds.), *Social science and social policy* (pp. 21–62). Sage.

Cook, T. D. (1990). The generalization of causal connections: Multiple theories in search of clear practice. In L. Sechrest, E. Perrin, & J. Bunker (Eds.), *Research methodology: Strengthening causal interpretations of nonexperimental data* (pp. 9–31) (DHHS Publication No. PHS 90–3454). Department of Health and Human Services.

Cook, T. D. (1991). Clarifying the warrant for generalized causal inferences in quasi-experimentation. In M. W. McLaughlin & D. C. Phillips (Eds.), *Evaluation and education: At quarter-century* (pp. 115–144). National Society for the Study of Education. https://doi.org/10.1177/016146819109200606

Cook, T. D. (2004). Causal generalization: How Campbell and Cronbach influenced my theoretical thinking on this topic, including in Shadish, Cook, and Campbell. In M. Alkin (Ed.), *Evaluation roots: Tracing theorists' views and influences* (pp. 89–112). Sage. https://doi.org/10.4135/9781412984157.n5

Cook, T. D., & Campbell, D. T. (1979). *Quasi-experimentation: Design and analysis issues for field settings*. Rand McNally.

Cook, T. D., & Campbell, D. T. (1986). The causal assumptions of quasi-experimental practice. *Synthese*, *68*(1), 141–180.

Cook, T. D., Shadish, W. R., & Wong, V. C. (2008). Three conditions under which experiments and observational studies produce comparable causal estimates: New findings from within-study comparisons. *Journal of Policy Analysis and*

Management, 27(4), 724–750. https://doi.org/10.1002/pam.20375

Cook, T. D., Steiner, P. M., & Pohl, S. (2009). How bias reduction is affected by covariate choice, unreliability, and mode of data analysis: Results from two types of within-study comparisons. *Multivariate Behavioral Research*, 44(6), 828–847. https://doi.org/10.1080/00273170903333673

Cunningham, S. (2021). *Causal inference: The mixtape*. Yale University Press.

Ding, P., & Miratrix, L. W. (2015). To adjust or not to adjust? Sensitivity analysis of M-bias and butterfly-bias. *Journal of Causal Inference*, 3(1), 41–57. https://doi.org/10.1515/jci-2013-0021

Duncan, O. D. (1975). *Introduction to structural equation models*. Academic.

Elwert, F. (2013). Graphical causal models. In S. Morgan (Ed.), *Handbook of causal analysis for social research* (pp. 245–273). Springer. https://doi.org/10.1007/978-94-007-6094-3_13

Elwert, F., & Winship, C. (2014). Endogenous selection bias: The problem of conditioning on a collider variable. *Annual Review of Sociology*, 40(1), 31–53. https://doi.org/10.1146/annurev-soc-071913-043455

Frangakis, C. E., & Rubin, D. B. (2002). Principal stratification in causal inference. *Biometrics*, 58(1), 21–29. https://doi.org/10.1111/j.0006-341X.2002.00021.x

Frangakis, C. E., Rubin, D. B., & Zhou, X.-H. (2002). Clustered encouragement designs with individual noncompliance: Bayesian inference with randomization, and application to advance directive forms. *Biostatistics*, 3(2), 147–164. https://doi.org/10.1093/biostatistics/3.2.147

Haavelmo, T. (1943). The statistical implications of a system of simultaneous equations. *Econometrica*, 11(1), 1–12. https://doi.org/10.2307/1905714

Hahn, J., Todd, P., & Van der Klaauw, W. (2001). Identification and estimation of treatment effects with a regression-discontinuity design. *Econometrica*, 69(1), 201–209. https://doi.org/10.1111/1468-0262.00183

Halpern, J., & Pearl, J. (2005a). Causes and explanations: A structural-model approach—Part I: Causes. *The British Journal for the Philosophy of Science*, 56(4), 843–887. https://doi.org/10.1093/bjps/axi147

Halpern, J., & Pearl, J. (2005b). Causes and explanations: A structural-model approach—Part II: Explanations. *The British Journal for the Philosophy of Science*, 56(4), 889–911. https://doi.org/10.1093/bjps/axi148

Halpern, J. Y. (1998). Axiomatizing causal reasoning. In G. F. Cooper & S. Moral (Eds.), *Uncertainty in artificial intelligence* (pp. 202–210). Morgan Kaufmann.

Hancock, G. R., & Mueller, R. O. (Eds.). (2013). *Quantitative methods in education and the behavioral sciences: Issues, research, and teaching. Structural equation modeling: A second course* (2nd ed.). IAP Information Age Publishing.

Heckman, J. J. (2005). The scientific model of causality. *Sociological Methodology*, 35(1), 1–97. https://doi.org/10.1111/j.0081-1750.2006.00164.x

Hernán, M. A., & Robins, J. M. (2020). *Causal inference: What if*. Chapman & Hall/CRC.

Holland, P. W. (1986). Statistics and causal inference. *Journal of the American Statistical Association*, 81(396), 945–960. https://doi.org/10.1080/01621459.1986.10478354

Hong, G., & Raudenbush, S. (2006). Evaluating kindergarten retention policy: A case study of causal inference for multilevel observational data. *Journal of the American Statistical Association*, 101(475), 901–910. https://doi.org/10.1198/016214506000000447

Huang, Y., & Valtorta, M. (2006). Pearl's calculus of intervention is complete. In *Proceedings of the 22nd Annual Conference on Uncertainty in Artificial Intelligence* (pp. 217–224).

Imai, K., Keele, L., & Tingley, D. (2010). A general approach to causal mediation analysis. *Psychological Methods*, 15(4), 309–334. https://doi.org/10.1037/a0020761

Imbens, G., & Rubin, D. (2015). *Causal inference for statistics, social, and biomedical sciences: An introduction*. Cambridge University Press. https://doi.org/10.1017/CBO9781139025751

Imbens, G. W. (2020). Potential outcome and directed acyclic graph approaches to causality: Relevance for empirical practice in economics. *Journal of Economic Literature*, 58(4), 1129–1179. https://doi.org/10.1257/jel.20191597

Kim, J.-S., & Steiner, P. M. (2015). Multilevel propensity score methods for estimating causal effects: A latent class modeling strategy. In L. van der Ark, D. Bolt, W. C. Wang, J. Douglas, & S. M. Chow (Eds.), *Quantitative psychology research*. Springer Proceedings in Mathematics & Statistics, Vol. 140 (pp. 293–306). Springer, Cham. https://doi.org/10.1007/978-3-319-19977-1_21

Kim, Y. (2019). The causal structure of suppressor variables. *Journal of Educational and Behavioral Statistics*, 44(4), 367–389. https://doi.org/10.3102/1076998619825679

Kim, Y., & Steiner, P. M. (2021a). Causal graphical views of fixed effects and random effects models. *British Journal of Mathematical and Statistical Psychology*, 74(2), 165–183. https://doi.org/10.1111/bmsp.12217

Kim, Y., & Steiner, P. M. (2021b). Gain scores revisited: A graphical models perspective. *Sociological Methods & Research*, 50(3), 1353–1375. https://doi.org/10.1177/0049124119826155

Lechner, M. (2011). The estimation of causal effects by difference-in-difference methods. *Foundations and Trends in Econometrics*, 4(3), 165–224. https://doi.org/10.1561/0800000014

Lee, D. S., & Lemieux, T. (2010). Regression discontinuity designs in economics. *Journal of Economic Literature*, 48(2), 281–355. https://doi.org/10.1257/jel.48.2.281

Lewis, D. (1973). *Counterfactuals*. Blackwell.

Lewis, D. (2004). Causation as influence. In J. Collins, E. Hall, & L. Paul (Eds.), *Causation and counterfactuals* (pp. 75–106). MIT Press.

Light, R. J., Singer, J. D., & Willett, J. B. (1990). *By design: Planning research in higher education*. Harvard University Press. https://doi.org/10.4159/9780674040267

Lunceford, J. K., & Davidian, M. (2004). Stratification and weighting via the propensity score in estimation of causal treatment effects: A comparative study. *Statistics in Medicine*, 23(19), 2937–2960. https://doi.org/10.1002/sim.1903

Mackie, J. L. (1980). *The cement of the universe: A study of causation*. Oxford University Press. https://doi.org/10.1093/0198246420.001.0001

Manski, C. F. (2013). *Public policy in an uncertain world: Analysis and decisions*. Harvard University Press. https://doi.org/10.4159/harvard.9780674067547

Maxwell, J. A. (2004). Using qualitative methods for causal explanation. *Field Methods*, 16(3), 243–264. https://doi.org/10.1177/1525822X04266831

Mayer, A., Thoemmes, F., Rose, N., Steyer, R., & West, S. G. (2014). Theory and analysis of total, direct, and indirect causal effects. *Multivariate Behavioral Research*, 49(5), 425–442. https://doi.org/10.1080/00273171.2014.931797

Menzies, P. (2004). Difference-making in context. In J. Collins, N. Hall, & L. Paul (Eds.), *Causation and counterfactuals* (pp.139–180). MIT Press.

Mohan, K., & Pearl, J. (2019). *Graphical models for processing missing data* (Tech. Rep. R-473). https://ftp.cs.ucla.edu/pub/stat_ser/r473-L.pdf

Morgan, S. L., & Winship, C. (2015). *Counterfactuals and causal inference: Methods and principles for social research* (2nd ed.). Cambridge University Press.

Ogburn, E. L., & VanderWeele, T. J. (2014). Causal diagrams for interference. *Statistical Science*, 29(4), 559–578. https://doi.org/10.1214/14-STS501

Papay, J. P., Murnane, R. J., & Willett, J. B. (2011). Extending the regression-discontinuity approach to multiple assignment variables. *Journal of Econometrics*, 161(2), 203–207. https://doi.org/10.1016/j.jeconom.2010.12.008

Pashley, N. E., & Miratrix, L. W. (2020). Insights on variance estimation for blocked and matched pairs designs. *Journal of Educational and Behavioral Statistics*, 46(3), 271–296. https://doi.org/10.3102/1076998620946272

Pashley, N. E., & Miratrix, L. W. (2022). Block What You Can, Except When You Shouldn't. *Journal of Educational and Behavioral Statistics*, 47(1), 69–100. https://doi.org/10.3102/10769986211027240

Paul, L. A., & Hall, N. (2013). *Causation. A user's guide*. Oxford University Press. https://doi.org/10.1093/acprof:oso/9780199673445.001.0001

Pearl, J. (1998). Graphs, causality, and structural equation models. *Sociological Methods & Research*, 27(2), 226–284. https://doi.org/10.1177/0049124198027002004

Pearl, J. (2001). Direct and indirect effects. In *Proceedings of the Seventeenth Conference on Uncertainty in Artificial Intelligence* (pp. 411–420). Morgan Kaufmann.

Pearl, J. (2009a). Causal inference in statistics: An overview. *Statistics Surveys*, 3, 96–146. https://doi.org/10.1214/09-SS057

Pearl, J. (2009b). *Causality: Models, reasoning, and inference* (2nd ed.). Cambridge University Press. https://doi.org/10.1017/CBO9780511803161

Pearl, J. (2010). The foundations of causal inference. *Sociological Methodology*, 40(1), 75–149. https://doi.org/10.1111/j.1467-9531.2010.01228.x

Pearl, J. (2014). Interpretation and identification of causal mediation. *Psychological Methods*, 19(4), 459–481. https://doi.org/10.1037/a0036434

Pearl, J., & Bareinboim, E. (2018). *Transportability across studies: A formal approach* (Tech. Rep. R-372). Cognitive Systems Laboratory, Department of Computer Science, UCLA.

Pearl, J., Glymour, M., & Jewell, N. (2016). *Causal inference in statistics: A primer*. Wiley.

Pearl, J., & Mackenzie, D. (2018). *The book of why. The new science of cause and effect*. Basic Books.

Peters, J., Janzing, D., & Schölkopf, B. (2017). *Elements of causal inference. Foundations and learning algorithms*. The MIT Press.

Pohl, S., Steiner, P. M., Eisermann, J., Soellner, R., & Cook, T. D. (2009). Unbiased causal inference from an observational study: Results of a within-study comparison. *Educational Evaluation and Policy Analysis, 31*(4), 463–479. https://doi.org/10.3102/0162373709343964

Popper, K. R. (1959). *The logic of scientific discovery*. Basic Books.

Reardon, S. F., & Robinson, J. P. (2012). Regression discontinuity designs with multiple rating-score variables. *Journal of Research on Educational Effectiveness, 5*(1), 83–104. https://doi.org/10.1080/19345747.2011.609583

Reichardt, C. S. (2000). A typology of strategies for ruling out threats to validity. In L. Bickman (Ed.), *Research design: Donald Campbell's legacy* (Vol. 2, pp. 89–115). Sage.

Reichardt, C. S. (2019). *Quasi-experimentation. A guide to design and analysis*. Guilford Press.

Reynolds, K. D., & West, S. G. (1987). A multiplist strategy for strengthening nonequivalent control group designs. *Evaluation Review, 11*(6), 691–714. https://doi.org/10.1177/0193841X8701100601

Robins, J. M. (2000). Marginal structural models versus structural nested models as tools for causal inference. In M. E. Halloran & D. Berry (Eds.), *Statistical models in epidemiology, the environment, and clinical trials* (Vol. 116, pp. 95–133). Springer. https://doi.org/10.1007/978-1-4612-1284-3_2

Rohrer, J. M. (2018). Thinking clearly about correlations and causation: Graphical causal models for observational data. *Advances in Methods and Practices in Psychological Science, 1*(1), 27–42. https://doi.org/10.1177/2515245917745629

Rosenbaum, P. R. (2002). *Observational studies* (2nd ed.). Springer-Verlag. https://doi.org/10.1007/978-1-4757-3692-2

Rosenbaum, P. R. (2009). *Design of observational studies*. Springer.

Rosenbaum, P. R. (2017). *Observation and experiment: An introduction to causal inference*. Harvard University Press. https://doi.org/10.4159/9780674982697

Rosenbaum, P. R., & Rubin, D. B. (1983). The central role of the propensity score in observational studies for causal effects. *Biometrika, 70*(1), 41–55. https://doi.org/10.1093/biomet/70.1.41

Rubin, D. B. (1974). Estimating causal effects of treatments in randomized and nonrandomized studies. *Journal of Educational Psychology, 66*(5), 688–701. https://doi.org/10.1037/h0037350

Rubin, D. B. (1978). Bayesian inference for causal effects: The role of randomization. *Annals of Statistics, 6*(1), 34–58. https://doi.org/10.1214/aos/1176344064

Rubin, D. B. (1990). A new perspective. In K. W. Wachter & M. L. Straf (Eds.), *The future of meta-analysis* (pp. 155–165). Sage.

Rubin, D. B. (1992). Meta-analysis: Literature synthesis or effect-size surface estimation? *Journal of Educational Statistics, 17*(4), 363–374. https://doi.org/10.3102/10769986017004363

Rubin, D. B. (2004). Teaching statistical inference for causal effects in experiments and observational studies. *Journal of Educational and Behavioral Statistics, 29*(3), 343–367. https://doi.org/10.3102/10769986029003343

Rubin, D. B. (2005). Causal inference using potential outcomes. *Journal of the American Statistical Association, 100*(469), 322–331. https://doi.org/10.1198/016214504000001880

Rubin, D. B. (2006). *Matched sampling for causal effects*. Cambridge University Press. https://doi.org/10.1017/CBO9780511810725

Rubin, D. B. (2007). The design versus the analysis of observational studies for causal effects: Parallels with the design of randomized trials. *Statistics in Medicine, 26*(1), 20–36. https://doi.org/10.1002/sim.2739

Rubin, D. B. (2008). For objective causal inference, design trumps analysis. *The Annals of Applied Statistics, 2*(3), 808–840. https://doi.org/10.1214/08-AOAS187

Rubin, D. B. (2009). Should observational studies be designed to allow lack of balance in covariate distributions across treatment groups? *Statistics in Medicine, 28*(9), 1420–1423. https://doi.org/10.1002/sim.3565

Rubin, D. B. (2019). Essential concepts of causal inference: A remarkable history and an intriguing future. *Biostatistics & Epidemiology, 3*(1), 140–155. https://doi.org/10.1080/24709360.2019.1670513

Schochet, P. Z. (2016). *Statistical theory for the RCT-YES software: Design-based causal inference for RCTs, Second Edition*. Technical Report (NCEE 2015-4011). U.S. Department of Education, Institute of Education Sciences, National Center for Education Evaluation and Regional Assistance, Analytic Technical Assistance and Development.

Shadish, W. R. (2010). Campbell and Rubin: A primer and comparison of their approaches to causal inference in field settings. *Psychological Methods, 15*(1), 3–17. https://doi.org/10.1037/a0015916

Shadish, W. R., Clark, M. H., & Steiner, P. M. (2008). Can nonrandomized experiments yield accurate answers? A randomized experiment comparing random to nonrandom assignment. *Journal of* the *American Statistical Association*, *103*(484), 1334–1344. https://doi.org/10.1198/016214508000000733

Shadish, W. R., & Cook, T. D. (1999). Design rules: More steps towards a complete theory of quasi-experimentation. *Statistical Science*, *14*(3), 294–300.

Shadish, W. R., Cook, T. D., & Campbell, D. T. (2002). *Experimental and quasi-experimental design for generalized causal inference*. Houghton Mifflin.

Shadish, W. R., Galindo, R., Wong, V. C., Steiner, P. M., & Cook, T. D. (2011). A randomized experiment comparing random and cutoff-based assignment. *Psychological Methods*, *16*(2), 179–191. https://doi.org/10.1037/a0023345

Shadish, W. R., & Sullivan, K. J. (2012). Theories of causation in psychological science. In H. Cooper, P. M. Camic, D. L. Long, A. T. Panter, D. Rindskopf, & K. J. Sher (Eds.), *APA handbook of research methods in psychology: Foundations, planning, measures, and psychometrics* (Vol. 1, pp. 23–52). American Psychological Association. https://doi.org/10.1037/13619-003

Shpitser, I. (2013). Counterfactual graphical models for longitudinal mediation analysis with unobserved confounding. *Cognitive Science*, *37*(6), 1011–1035. https://doi.org/10.1111/cogs.12058

Shpitser, I. (2019). Identification in graphical causal models. In M. Maathuis, M. Drton, S. Lauritzen, & M. Wainwright (Eds.), *Handbook of graphical models* (pp. 381–403). Chapman & Hall/CRC.

Shpitser, I., & Pearl, J. (2006). Identification of joint interventional distributions in recursive semi-Markovian causal models. In *Proceedings of the 21st National Conference on Artificial Intelligence*, (Vol. 2, pp. 1219–1226). AAAI Press.

Spirtes, P., Glymour, C., & Scheines, R. (1993). *Causation, prediction, and search*. Springer. https://doi.org/10.1007/978-1-4612-2748-9

Splawa-Neyman, J., Dabrowska, D., & Speed, T. (1990). On the application of probability theory to agricultural experiments. Essay on principles. Section 9. *Statistical Science*, *5*(4), 465–472. https://doi.org/10.1214/ss/1177012031

Steiner, P. M., Cook, T. D., & Shadish, W. R. (2011). On the importance of reliable covariate measurement in selection bias adjustments using propensity scores. *Journal of Educational and Behavioral Statistics*, *36*(2), 213–236. https://doi.org/10.3102/1076998610375835

Steiner, P. M., Cook, T. D., Shadish, W. R., & Clark, M. H. (2010). The importance of covariate selection in controlling for selection bias in observational studies. *Psychological Methods*, *15*(3), 250–267. https://doi.org/10.1037/a0018719

Steiner, P. M., & Kim, Y. (2016). The mechanics of omitted variable bias: Bias amplification and cancellation of offsetting biases. *Journal of Causal Inference*, *4*(2), 20160009. https://doi.org/10.1515/jci-2016-0009

Steiner, P. M., Kim, Y., Hall, C. E., & Su, D. (2017). Graphical models for quasi-experimental designs. *Sociological Methods & Research*, *46*(2), 155–188. https://doi.org/10.1177/0049124115582272

Steiner, P. M., & Wong, V. C. (2018). Assessing correspondence between experimental and nonexperimental estimates in within-study comparisons. *Evaluation Review*, *42*(2), 214–247. https://doi.org/10.1177/0193841X18773807

Steiner, P. M., Wong, V. C., & Anglin, K. (2019). A causal replication framework for designing and assessing replication efforts. *Zeitschrift für Psychologie mit Zeitschrift für Angewandte Psychologie*, *227*(4), 280–292. https://doi.org/10.1027/2151-2604/a000385

Steyer, R., Gabler, S., von Davier, A. A., Nachtigall, C., & Buhl, T. (2000). Causal regression models I: Individual and average causal effects. *Methods of Psychological Research Online*, *5*(2), 39–71.

Stuart, E. A., Cole, S. R., Bradshaw, C. P., & Leaf, P. J. (2011). The use of propensity scores to assess the generalizability of results from randomized trials. *Journal of the Royal Statistical Society. Series A (Statistics in Society)*, *174*(2), 369–386. https://doi.org/10.1111/j.1467-985X.2010.00673.x

Tang, Y., Cook, T. D., Kisbu-Sakarya, Y., Hock, H., & Chiang, H. (2017). The comparative regression discontinuity (CRD) design: An overview and demonstration of its performance relative to basic RD and the randomized experiment. *Advances in Econometrics*, *38*, 237–279. https://doi.org/10.1108/S0731-905320170000038011

Textor, J., van der Zander, B., Gilthorpe, M. S., Liskiewicz, M., & Ellison, G. T. H. (2016). Robust causal inference using directed acyclic graphs: The R package "dagitty." *International Journal of Epidemiology*, *45*(6), 1887–1894. https://doi.org/10.1093/ije/dyw341

Thistlethwaite, D. L., & Campbell, D. T. (1960). Regression-discontinuity analysis: Alternative to the ex post facto experiment. *Journal of Educational Psychology*, *51*(6), 309–317. https://doi.org/10.1037/h0044319

Thoemmes, F., & Mohan, K. (2015). Graphical representation of missing data problems. *Structural Equation Modeling*, *22*(4), 631–642. https://doi.org/10.1080/10705511.2014.937378

Thoemmes, F. J., & West, S. G. (2011). The use of propensity scores for nonrandomized designs with clustered data. *Multivariate Behavioral Research*, *46*(3), 514–543. https://doi.org/10.1080/00273171.2011.569395

Tikka, S., & Karvanen, J. (2017). Identifying causal effects with the R package *causaleffect*. *Journal of Statistical Software*, 76(12), 1–30. https://doi.org/10.18637/jss.v076.i12

Tinbergen, J. (1930). Determination and interpretation of supply curves: An example. *Zeitschrift für Nationalökonomie*, 1(5), 669–679. https://doi.org/10.1007/BF01318500

Tipton, E. (2013). Improving generalizations from experiments using propensity score subclassification. *Journal of Educational and Behavioral Statistics*, 38(3), 239–266. https://doi.org/10.3102/1076998612441947

Vandecandelaere, M., Vansteelandt, S., De Fraine, B., & Van Damme, J. (2016). Time-varying treatments in observational studies: Marginal structural models of the effects of early grade retention on math achievement. *Multivariate Behavioral Research*, 51(6), 843–864. https://doi.org/10.1080/00273171.2016.1155146

VanderWeele, T. J. (2015). *Explanation in causal inference: Methods for mediation and interaction.* Oxford University Press.

West, S. G., & Thoemmes, F. (2010). Campbell's and Rubin's perspectives on causal inference. *Psychological Methods*, 15(1), 18–37. https://doi.org/10.1037/a0015917

White, P. A. (2000). Causal attribution and Mill's methods of experimental inquiry: Past, present and prospect. *British Journal of Social Psychology*, 39(3), 429–447. https://doi.org/10.1348/014466600164589

Wing, C., & Cook, T. D. (2013). Strengthening the regression discontinuity design using additional design elements: A within-study comparison. *Journal of Policy Analysis and Management*, 32(4), 853–877. https://doi.org/10.1002/pam.21721

Wong, V. C., Anglin, K., & Steiner, P. M. (2021). Design-based approaches to causal replication studies. *Prevention Science*. Advance online publication. https://doi.org/10.1007/s11121-021-01234-7

Wong, V. C., & Steiner, P. M. (2018a). Designs of empirical evaluations of non-experimental methods in field settings. *Evaluation Review*, 42(2), 176–213. https://doi.org/10.1177/0193841X18778918

Wong, V. C., & Steiner, P. M. (2018b). Replication designs for causal inference. In *EdPolicyWorks working paper series,* No. 62; EdPolicyWorks Working Paper Series.

Wong, V. C., Steiner, P. M., & Anglin, K. L. (2018). What can be learned from empirical evaluations of nonexperimental methods? *Evaluation Review*, 42(2), 147–175. https://doi.org/10.1177/0193841X18776870

Wong, V. C., Steiner, P. M., & Cook, T. D. (2013). Analyzing regression-discontinuity designs with multiple assignment variables: A comparative study of four estimation methods. *Journal of Educational and Behavioral Statistics*, 38(2), 107–141. https://doi.org/10.3102/1076998611432172

Woodward, J. (2003). *Making things happen: A theory of causal explanation.* Oxford University Press.

Woodward, J. (2016). Causation and manipulability. In E. N. Zalta (Ed.), *The Stanford encyclopedia of philosophy* (Winter 2016 Edition). Stanford University. https://plato.stanford.edu/archives/win2016/entries/causation-mani/

Wright, S. (1921). Correlation and causation. *Journal of Agricultural Research*, 20(7), 557–585.

Zubizarreta, J. R., & Keele, L. (2017). Optimal multilevel matching in clustered observational studies: A case study of the effectiveness of private schools under a large-scale voucher system. *Journal of the American Statistical Association*, 112(518), 547–560. https://doi.org/10.1080/01621459.2016.1240683

SECTION 2

ETHICAL AND PROFESSIONAL CONSIDERATIONS IN CONDUCTING PSYCHOLOGICAL RESEARCH

CHAPTER 3

ETHICS IN PSYCHOLOGICAL RESEARCH: GUIDELINES AND REGULATIONS

Adam L. Fried and Kate L. Jansen

Ethical decision making in psychological research requires knowledge of the rules and regulations governing its practices as well as the ability to identify and resolve complex ethical conflicts. As outlined in the American Psychological Association's *Ethical Principles of Psychologists and Code of Conduct* (2017), psychologists have a professional responsibility to act in ways that maximize benefits of research and minimize harms, to promote trust in the research process and in the results of science, to engage in honest and truthful scientific practices, to distribute the benefits and burdens of science evenly between all persons, and to design and implement research procedures that recognize and respect individual differences.

Researchers use several sources of information when faced with ethical questions, including their knowledge of research and methodology and the advice of colleagues, team members, and institutional representatives. To conduct psychological research competently, researchers also must possess a reasonable understanding of the purpose and application of state and federal regulations, laws, and other rules governing research; institutional research rules; and professional guidelines and enforceable standards governing research. Researchers also must have the ability to integrate these resources and apply them to their particular situation to address complex ethical dilemmas. Although an understanding of these resources is integral to ethical decision making in the responsible conduct of research, there are times when the researcher's ethics question cannot be easily answered or when these resources are insufficient to resolve certain complex questions adequately. Rather than offering a final answer, these resources may be better viewed as tools for the thoughtful researcher to use in resolving ethical questions.

Research involves a pursuit of knowledge that often contributes to the betterment of society by informing practices, policies, and services. Broadly defined, *research* is "the systematic investigation, including research development, testing, and evaluation, designed to develop or contribute to generalizable knowledge" (Protection of Human Subjects, 2017). Researchers who work with human participants must balance the goals of maintaining standards of good science while also protecting the welfare and promoting the autonomy of participants. Although these goals may be seen as competing and potentially at odds, they need not and should not be.

The atrocities of the Nazi war crimes as well as other high-profile research studies that have resulted in substantial harm to particularly vulnerable participants (such as the Tuskegee syphilis study [Brandt, 1978] and the Willowbrook hepatitis study [D. J. Rothman & Rothman, 1984])

https://doi.org/10.1037/0000318-003
APA Handbook of Research Methods in Psychology, Second Edition: Vol. 1. Foundations, Planning, Measures, and Psychometrics, H. Cooper (Editor-in-Chief)
Copyright © 2023 by the American Psychological Association. All rights reserved.

have contributed to an erosion of public trust in the biomedical and behavioral sciences. More recently, important questions about the integrity of the research enterprise and the validity of science have surfaced that may threaten the health and safety of the public. Institutions, regulatory bodies, and professional associations have responded to these developments by creating and enforcing rules that prevent or resolve ethical conflicts in the scientific community. These historic and recent examples underscore the critical importance of competent ethical decision making and planning.

This chapter provides an introduction to ethical issues and resources in psychological research with human participants, including an overview of federal regulations, institutional oversight, and professional guidelines, and discusses major concepts in research ethics related to the planning and execution of behavioral research (more information about issues related to research dissemination can be found in Volume 3, Chapter 27, this handbook). In this chapter we also discuss approaches to science-in-ethics decision making when addressing novel ethical questions and challenges in which standard regulations and professional guidelines may offer incomplete solutions.

FEDERAL REGULATIONS: HISTORY AND SCOPE

The history of regulations governing research often is traced back to the Nuremberg Code (1949), which was enacted after the public learned of the atrocities associated with the work of Nazi scientists during World War II. The Nuremberg Code introduced several important principles governing research with human subjects, including informed consent procedures and the right of participants to withdraw participation.

Following the Nuremberg Code, the Declaration of Helsinki of the World Medical Association (1964/2008) elaborated on points contained in the Nuremberg Code and included topics such as nontherapeutic biomedical research with human participants. Finally, the Belmont Report (National Commission for the Protection of Human Subjects of Biomedical and Behavioral Research, 1979) provided the basis for federal biomedical and behavioral research regulations. In addition to a brief discussion of the Belmont Report, two other important federal regulations and laws are discussed as they relate to research in the next sections: the Code of Federal Regulations and the Health Insurance Portability and Accountability Act of 1996.

The Belmont Report

The National Commission for the Protection of Human Subjects of Biomedical and Behavioral Research was created through the National Research Act of 1974. The commission's charge was to identify and summarize the basic ethical principles to guide investigators conducting biomedical and behavioral research, with the resulting document known as the Belmont Report (National Commission for the Protection of Human Subjects of Biomedical and Behavioral Research, 1979).

Divided into three main sections, the Belmont Report laid the foundation for regulations and professional guidelines governing biomedical and behavioral research. Notably, the report (a) distinguished between the goals and methods of research and professional practice; (b) highlighted the foundational ethical principles guiding human subjects research, including respect for persons, beneficence, and justice (these principles are discussed as they apply to psychological research in the section describing the American Psychological Association [APA] "Ethical Principles of Psychologists and Code of Conduct" [the APA Ethics Code; APA, 2017]); and (c) identified and described three basic requirements of research: informed consent procedures, risk–benefit analysis, and participant selection and recruitment, which focused on issues of justice in terms of bearing the burdens of research and enjoying the benefits of science. From the Belmont Report, the federal regulations for research were born.

Code of Federal Regulations

The U.S. Department of Health and Human Service (DHHS) has codified regulations governing research with human subjects in the United States in its *Code of Federal Regulations* (CFR) Title 45, Part 46: Protection of Human Subjects (Protection of Human Subjects, 2017), known as the "Common Rule." This portion of the code is divided into several parts, with sections describing general rules and principles and institutional review board registration procedures, and sections governing biomedical and behavioral research with specific vulnerable populations (such as children, prisoners, pregnant women, human fetuses, and neonates). The Office of Human Research Protections (an office within the DHHS) monitors institutions (who, in turn, monitor the investigators) to ensure compliance with federal regulations. For example, in most studies, adverse reactions to study methods must be reported to their institution's review board, which, in turn, may be required to report to the Office of Human Research Protections for monitoring and possible investigation. More information about CFR rules and designations are discussed in the section Institutional Oversight.

Health Insurance Portability and Accountability Act of 1996

In response to the increasingly common practice of electronic transfer of health-related data among health care professionals, and in an effort to increase patient access to health-related records, the U.S. Congress enacted the Health Insurance Portability and Accountability Act of 1996 (HIPAA). This law has significant effects on records privacy and disclosure, the electronic transmission of data, and data security for both practice and research.

HIPAA governs protected health information (PHI), or individually identifiable health data, among covered entities (which includes health plans and health care providers, employers, and health care clearinghouses). Data that are completely deidentified; do not relate to the past, present, or future health of an individual; and are not created or received by a covered entity are not considered PHI.

HIPAA affects certain types of psychological and biomedical research. Researchers who are covered entities and collect or store PHI have specific obligations under the HIPAA, including providing participants with a description of their privacy rights and how their data are used and implementing procedures to ensure that data are secure and that only authorized representatives have access to these records. For example, investigators should be aware that for HIPAA-covered research, participants may be able to access certain types of health records under this law. Investigators may be able to temporarily deny access to these records while the research is ongoing, but only if the participant has agreed to this during the consent process. Furthermore, participants may be able to access these records once the research is complete. In most cases, for PHI data to be created, used, or disclosed for research purposes, a signed authorization (for the limited use of the research project) must be executed by the individual or personal representative.

In 2009 the Health Information Technology for Economic and Clinical Health Act was enacted (the American Recovery and Reinvestment Act of 2009, Public Law 111-5, 123 Stat 115, 2009). Largely designed to promote the use of health information technology, such as electronic medical records, this act also has notable implications for psychological researchers utilizing PHI. Under this act, any breach of HIPAA-protected information, including data used for research, must be reported and is subject to penalties.

Investigators should be aware that HIPAA rules have implications for children, adolescents, and those who have legal authority to act on behalf of minors (Fisher, 2004). In most cases, the legal guardian (known as the *personal representative* for the person who lacks legal authority to make health care and research participation decisions) is considered the authorized decision maker for the party.

INSTITUTIONAL OVERSIGHT

In addition to federal regulations, many institutions may enact and enforce institutional rules governing research, often coordinated by the institutional review board (IRB). The overall aim of an IRB is to protect the rights and welfare of research participants. To accomplish this aim, the IRB reviews, evaluates, approves, and oversees research protocols submitted by investigators within their particular institution to ensure compliance with the institutional and federal rules related to the practice of research.

Submitting Protocols to the Institutional Review Board

Applications to the IRB (which are submitted by investigators) typically include background and overview of the study (including research aims), recruitment procedures, description of participants (including inclusion and exclusion criteria), methods of data collection, confidentiality procedures, potential risks and benefits to the participant, detailed procedures for monitoring and reporting any adverse reactions, and the informed consent form. The IRB chair or committee, which often is composed of a variety of professionals from the institution, and a community representative who is not officially affiliated with the institution, review the application. If warranted, the chair or committee asks the investigator(s) to attend a meeting of the IRB committee to answer questions raised by members of the committee or to clarify areas of concern. Based on the information related to the proposed study, the IRB determines the appropriate level of review. The level of review determines the process the study application follows for approval as well as subsequent oversight of the research. The IRB may then approve the protocol, request that the investigator make revisions, or deny the application and provide the investigator with the reasons for the denial (Bankert & Amdur, 2005).

Formal approval from a research review committee or board (such as an IRB) is required in most cases, and investigators are responsible for determining whether such approval is required from their institution (Standard 8.01, Institutional Approval; APA, 2017). Certain types of research may qualify as exempt from IRB review (i.e., certain types of research on normal education practices). It is recommended, however, that researchers avoid making this determination alone, and in fact many institutions require their IRBs to make this decision (Prentice & Oki, 2005). Under the National Research Act of 1974, investigators whose research is funded by federal monies must seek approval from their institution's IRB before initiating any research. In addition, institutions may require all studies considered to be research (including those not funded by federal monies) to be submitted for IRB review. Further, demonstration of IRB approval (or determination of exemption) is a common requirement for publication in many academic journals.

Once a protocol is approved, the IRB has no further role in the research itself. However, the IRB is charged with overseeing the research process, and investigators who do not comply with their IRB's rules or procedures risk their research being suspended or terminated by the institution. IRBs also require periodic reviews of the research protocols. For example, informed consent forms often are approved only for a limited period of time (e.g., 1 year), after which the investigator(s) must apply for renewal of the project from the IRB.

Institutional Review Board Determinations and the Revised Common Rule

In 2017, the Federal Policy for the Protection of Human Subjects, or Common Rule, underwent substantive updates and changes. Expected compliance with the changes began in 2019. Though many of the core components of the Common Rule remained the same, several of the updates impact social science researchers. Specifically, several definitions included in the policy were updated. "Benign behavioral intervention" was expanded to exclude interventions that the subjects might find offensive or embarrassing. Further, the definition of clinical trials was expanded to include prospectively assigned subjects to evaluate the effectiveness of an intervention on behavioral health related outcomes.

Perhaps the most significant change to the Revised Common Rule is the introduction of broad consent. Broad consent is intended to serve as another option to informed consent or waiver of consent. The use of broad consent allows researchers to get permission for the use of PHI or identifiable data (including biospecimens) for later studies, including later studies not specified at the time of data collection. It should be noted, however, that if a subject declines broad consent, the data cannot be used and is not eligible for later use or future waived consent. Researchers should familiarize themselves with the contents of the Common Rule, and specifically the changes made under the Revised Common Rule when designing research and submitting to IRBs.

As previously mentioned, IRBs will use information in the study application to estimate level of risk and subsequent degree of oversight. *Minimal risk* is a classification of research that is described in federal regulations as involving procedures that are commensurate with activities encountered in daily life or routine physical or psychological examinations (45 C.F.R. § 46.102i). Research protocols classified as minimal risk may provide a justification for IRBs to approve certain types of research with no prospect for direct benefit with certain vulnerable populations, allow researchers to submit protocols under expedited review procedures, or waive informed consent procedures.

PROFESSIONAL GUIDELINES FOR PSYCHOLOGICAL RESEARCH: THE APA ETHICS CODE

The APA Ethics Code (APA, 2017) provides guidance and specific rules for psychologists and students who are engaged in related professional tasks, including research. In its effort to merit public trust, establish the integrity of the profession, and regulate the professional behaviors of those in the field, the Ethics Code represents a collective agreement among psychologists on the profession's moral principles as well as the enforceable standards related to the work of psychologists.

The Ethics Code (APA, 2017) includes five principles that are applicable to the professional work of psychologists. These principles do not represent specific rules or enforceable policies related to professional conduct but rather are aspirational in nature and frame the values that psychologists, in their everyday work, strive to fulfill. The enforceable standards (which articulate the rules that psychologists are to follow) are derived from five basic principles, which are described in the following sections as they apply to research activities.

Principle A: Beneficence and Nonmaleficence

This principle recognizes that psychologists aspire to maximize good results and minimize harms in the context of their work. Psychologists promote the welfare of others by attempting to prevent potential harms that may result from participation in a professional activity. If harms cannot be prevented or already have occurred, psychologists have a duty to minimize negative consequences and to remedy harms when possible. The principle of Beneficence and Nonmaleficence applies not only to those with whom the professional works directly (such as research participants) but also to broader groups, such as organizations, institutions, and society at large.

Principle B: Fidelity and Responsibility

Psychologists engage in behaviors that merit the trust of those with whom they work as well as the public in general, and they recognize that behaviors contrary to these principles threaten the integrity of the profession. This principle of Fidelity and Responsibility reflects the integral role of trust in the successful discharge of psychological activities. For example, individuals who consent to participate in research on potentially illegal activities, such as drug use, trust psychologists to hold to their promises of confidentiality. Researchers who behave in an unethical manner violate their responsibilities and obligations to participants, society, and science in general, and they harm the integrity of the profession.

Principle C: Integrity

To promote and maintain the integrity of the profession, psychologists must be honest in the scientific practice of psychology. This requires openness and truthfulness with the individuals with whom they work (e.g., research participants, IRBs, funding agencies) as well as accuracy in the planning, implementation, and dissemination of scientific results. For example, the Ethics Code (APA, 2017) includes strict rules mandating psychologists to report research findings in an honest and truthful fashion, and not to fabricate results, plagiarize or otherwise misrepresent the work of others as their own.

Principle D: Justice

Psychologists must take steps to provide all individuals with fair and equitable treatment and appropriate access to the benefits of science. As such, investigators ensure that the burdens and risks of research are not borne exclusively by any one group or individual but rather are distributed equally. Similarly, the benefits of scientific developments and breakthroughs should not be limited to certain groups. For example, many randomized treatment research protocols include provisions to provide the investigative treatment to the nonexperimental (control) group if shown to be effective or successful.

Principle E: Respect for People's Rights and Dignity

This principle reflects psychologists' commitment for respect of the rights of all individuals to privacy and self-governance and requires that psychologists recognize and respect individual differences in such ways that minimize vulnerabilities and maximize strengths. For example, colearning techniques and researcher consultation (discussed in the section Evidence-Based and Participant-Informed Approaches to Research Ethics) with prospective participant groups and communities help investigators develop scientific aims and research procedures that are sensitive to the research population and specific study context (Fisher, 2002; Fisher & Masty, 2006; Fisher & Wallace, 2000; Fried & Fisher, 2017).

AMERICAN PSYCHOLOGICAL ASSOCIATION STANDARDS

In addition to the five aspirational principles, the Ethics Code (APA, 2017) includes 10 sets of enforceable standards, each describing an area of professional conduct. The next sections highlight some major areas and standards that are particularly relevant for research with human subjects. The following is not meant to be an exhaustive summary, and the reader is advised to consult the ethics code in its entirety.

Informed Consent

Informed consent is a core concept in the responsible conduct of biomedical and behavioral research. As reflected in federal regulations and professional guidelines, valid informed consent procedures demonstrate science's respect for the self-determination of research participants to make informed, rational, and voluntary decisions about participation, while also protecting vulnerable populations from participation decisions that may be harmful or lead to exploitation. Respect for participant autonomy and regard for human welfare are critical components to the scientific enterprise.

Aforementioned historical incidents, such as the Tuskegee syphilis study (Brandt, 1978) and the Willowbrook hepatitis study (D. J. Rothman & Rothman, 1984), led to an erosion of public trust in science in general, and, specifically, trust in investigators' methods. Over the past several decades, a paradigm shift has occurred in the participant–investigator relationship, from a paternalistic approach in which scientists and professionals often influenced participation decisions to one that emphasizes and respects the autonomous decision-making abilities of participants (Fried & Fisher, 2008). To that end, informed consent procedures are seen as a way to ensure that participants make informed, voluntary, and rational decisions with respect to participating in a particular study. Consistent with this goal, informed consent procedures were updated under the Revised Common Rule (Protection of Human Subjects, 2017). Under the new policy, researchers must begin with a "concise and focused presentation of key information" that will help the subject determine if they would like to participate (45 C.F.R. § 46.116). Key information may include that the subject is agreeing to participate in research, the participation is voluntary, the purpose of the research and the procedure the subject is going to complete, the potential risks and benefits to participation, and alternatives to participation that might be available. These components should be applied as appropriate to the specific study.

Informed consent for behavioral and biomedical research must meet three main requirements. First, consent must be *informed*, which requires that important and relevant aspects of the research project must be communicated to the participant in a manner that can be readily understood by participants, including relevant research procedures, time and duration of participation, methods of confidentiality, types of scientific methods employed, methods of group assignment (e.g., experimental and control groups), and the purpose of the research. The second requirement is that consent must be *voluntary*; participation in a study must not be unduly coerced and participants should be advised of their right to terminate participation. The third requirement for valid informed consent is that it be *rational*. Participants should be able to appreciate and apply the research-related information being presented (including the risks and benefits of participation) to their personal situation, weigh the risks and benefits, and communicate a decision about participation (Appelbaum & Grisso, 1995).

Informed nature of consent. To make a truly informed decision about research participation, relevant information about the study must be communicated to participants. Participants, therefore, are entitled to be informed of all relevant aspects of a particular study that would reasonably be expected to influence their decision to participate, including a statement describing the purpose and procedures of the study (including expected duration of participation), foreseeable risks and benefits, confidentiality procedures and the limits of these, any compensation or other types of incentives for participation, that the study involves research (rather than a prescribed treatment), the voluntary nature of participation (and any consequences for withdrawal of participation), and the investigator's contact information (APA, 2017; Fisher, 2017). To avoid possible coercion and participant misinterpretations, federal regulations (45 C.F.R. § 46.116) require that the language of the informed consent process be understandable to the participants, including attention to primary language and education levels of the participant. For example, when creating consent and assent procedures for a research project for adults with intellectual disabilities, the investigators should consider consulting with disability professionals to select language and format that are commensurate with the participants' education and ability levels. Finally, participants must be afforded an opportunity to ask relevant questions about the research and have them answered by research staff. Opportunities to have information repeated and to ask questions have been emphasized as particularly important in certain types of biomedical research or studies conducted in treatment settings, as the length and complexity of consent documents as well as the technical nature of the study methods may require additional explanation and consideration (Perry & Wöhlke, 2019; Wilson et al., 2008).

The following sections briefly outline some common components of the informed consent process. The nature and emphasis of each consent element, including the types of information provided and the aspects and considerations in the voluntary nature of participation, will differ on the basis of the type of study and the specific research populations. Readers are encouraged to consult additional sources for clarification about informed consent procedures specific to their own projects.

Risks and benefits. The CFR requires researchers minimize research risks to participants (45 C.F.R. § 46.111(a)(1)) and ensure an adequate balance of research risks and benefits (45 C.F.R. § 46.1119(a)(2)). The informed consent process is an opportunity for researchers to communicate the benefits and risks of participation in an open and honest manner and provides the participant with sufficient information to autonomously weigh the risks and benefits in a meaningful way to assist their participation decision. Possible benefits of research projects may vary depending on the type of study and the participant, and may include benefits (such as experimental treatments or psychological and psychosocial assessments) that may not be readily available outside of the research setting. For example, some studies, such as those that include an intervention component, may represent the possibility of considerable benefit to participants that have disorders or conditions for which few empirically supported treatments are available.

Researchers must be careful to address potential misperceptions about the nature of the research and potential outcomes related to the intervention. For example, therapeutic misconceptions (i.e., the belief that group assignment or experimental treatment decisions are based on the individual treatment needs of a particular participant; Appelbaum et al., 1987) may be common in certain types of intervention research. In addition, participants may either over- or underestimate the research benefits and risks, known as *therapeutic misestimation* (Fisher et al., 2008; Horng & Grady, 2003; Jansen, 2014). These misperceptions can be addressed by describing in detail the experimental nature of the intervention, clarifying the known benefits and risks of the intervention, and clarifying that it is unknown whether the intervention will be of benefit to the particular condition. Research has demonstrated that tailoring consent information related to therapeutic misconception may facilitate understanding and reduce erroneous beliefs about the research (Lally et al., 2014).

Other studies, such as survey or observational research, may represent little direct benefit to the participant (aside from a possible altruistic benefit the participant may derive from contributing to the scientific study of a particular phenomenon or condition). It may be difficult for investigators to determine an accurate risk–benefit calculus with certain types of psychological research for which there is no prospect of direct benefit. However, there is increasing research on participant perspectives of risks and benefits associated with specific types of research that may assist investigators in better estimating participant experiences. For example, research on participants who participated in trauma-related research suggests that while there may be some immediate distress, it was often not extreme and participants found the experience to be overall a positive one (Jaffe et al., 2015).

Research risks also vary considerably, depending on the nature of the study and its methods. Almost all research represents some potential risk, such as iatrogenic effects of treatments, possible breaches of confidentiality, or potential negative reactions (e.g., emotional distress) to research procedures or subject matter. For example, investigators conducting research that surveys the incidence and nature of trauma should consider including a statement that participation in this project may elicit negative memories or emotions related to past traumatic events. Researchers can address these types of risks by including a "prefer not to answer" option for sensitive questions and by addressing possible immediate or future negative reactions resulting from participation (discussed further in the section Research Debriefing). The nature of these risks should be clearly articulated to participants along with methods the researcher is using to minimize these risks.

Confidentiality. Risks to privacy in research often are related to confidential personally identifiable information being accessed or viewed by unauthorized individuals. High-profile data breaches pose risks to the public and to public trust in research (National Academies of Sciences, Engineering and Medicine, 2017). Methods to protect confidentiality associated with the specific research project must be described clearly to prospective participants before any data collection (Standard 4.02, Discussing the Limits of Confidentiality; APA, 2017). For example, a psychologist conducting survey research over the internet should inform prospective participants about the relevant limits of confidentiality using this medium of data collection, such as threats of third-party viewing of data (APA, 2017; Fisher & Fried, 2003) as well as the methods used to maintain data security (e.g., password-protected computers, firewalls, data encryption). Methods of maintaining data security for noninternet research also should be communicated, such as the use of a participant coding system, secure storage of data, and deidentifying data sets. There are also ways that researchers can design data collection methods to minimize potential loss of confidentiality (including the chances that someone could identify individuals through collected research), including minimizing, when possible, the amounts and types of personally identifiable information collected and restricting access to personally identifiable information (National Academies of Sciences, Engineering and Medicine, 2017). For example, researchers should consider whether they need to include participants' date of birth and may instead simply ask a participant's age.

Researchers should consult state and federal laws regarding mandated reporting and duty-to-warn requirements, such as in the cases of child or elder abuse or specific threats of harm to a third party, and communicate such requirements to prospective participants. For example, research psychologists conducting psychotherapy trials may be held to the same duty-to-warn requirements as practicing psychologists in nonresearch settings when provided information by clients that meets the state or local reporting law criteria (Appelbaum & Rosenbaum, 1989; Chenneville, 2000; Fisher, 2017).

Randomized group assignment. Intervention research that involves the use of experimental treatments to determine either the efficacy of a particular treatment or the comparative benefit of an experimental intervention against another treatment requires that the researcher inform prospective participants about specific details related to group assignment (Standard 8.02b, Informed Consent to Research; APA, 2017). For example, the use of a control group in a randomized trial requires the researchers to inform participants about (a) the possibility that they will not be assigned to the treatment group and may be placed in the control group, (b) the nature of random assignment, (c) the nature of the intervention and control groups (e.g., no-treatment, placebo, wait-list), and (d) the benefits and risks of assignment to each group (Standard 8.02b, Informed Consent to Research; APA, 2017). As noted above in the Risks and Benefits section, participants may express confusion about randomization, especially in treatment-based research, and may erroneously believe that the condition to which they have been assigned is based upon their personal health needs or that the condition is recommended based upon their health conditions (Stines & Feeny, 2008). Finally, investigators should ensure clinical equipoise between the two conditions, meaning that there is no established clinical or empirical superiority between the comparative and the intervention treatment (Freedman, 1987; K. J. Rothman & Michels, 1994; Weijer & Miller, 2004).

Participant compensation and possible costs. Investigators should clarify the nature and type of payments or other compensation offered (if any) to individuals in exchange for participation in a study. The informed consent process should indicate clearly any conditions or prerequisites for receiving the compensation (e.g., all study materials must be completed in their entirety for the participant to be eligible for compensation). In addition, any costs (including out-of-pocket expenses) that may be incurred by the participant (or their insurance), such as fees associated with tests, assessments, and treatments as well as the research-related expenses that will be covered by the researchers or sponsors, also should be clearly outlined (Hunt, 2005). Compensation is discussed further in the section Inducements for Research Participation.

The voluntary nature of informed consent. Voluntary consent has been viewed as an essential component of the protection of participant welfare and rights (Freedman, 1975) and is a second requirement for valid informed consent. That is, participants should not be unduly influenced to participate in research, such as through unfair or coercive compensation or conditions that make their receipt of normal health care services contingent on their participants. Inducements that far exceed or otherwise are not commensurate with the research requirements and making adjunct treatments or other services that ordinarily would be provided to the individual contingent on research participation are examples of situations that may threaten the voluntary nature of consent. Research with particularly vulnerable populations, such as prisoners, the chronically mentally ill, the poor, or the intellectually disabled, require that investigators be particularly sensitive to unanticipated or unintentional sources of coercion and consider instituting additional procedures to ensure that participation is completely voluntary. Clinical researchers should also take steps to ensure the voluntary nature of consent; research suggests that individuals in health care settings may experience pressure to participate by providers and/or research staff (Grady et al., 2014).

During the informed consent process, the nature and purpose of the assessments and interventions should be clarified, with attention given to potential differences between research and treatment. The consent process should include information about potential consequences related to the decision to decline or withdraw participation, especially when participants are recruited in certain service-provision settings, such as counseling and treatment centers or social services agencies. This type of design may present a potentially coercive situation in which a participant may not adequately distinguish between voluntarily participating in research and receiving professional services. Such confusion may lead to the erroneous belief that the provision of psychological services is contingent on the individual's participation in research (Fisher & Goodman, 2009; Fried & Fisher, 2017), especially if the person conducting the research is also providing or involved in the provision of services. In such cases, the investigator has an added responsibility to ensure that the two roles (and differences between the two) as well as the extent to which participation in the research project will be distinguishable from the other services participants already or are entitled to receive, are clearly communicated and that participants understand that refusal to participate or withdrawal of participation will not result in a reduction or disruption of services or other negative consequence (Fisher, 2017; Fisher et al., 2002; Garland et al., 2008).

For example, a researcher conducting an anonymous study of substance abuse symptoms secondary to depression in an outpatient psychotherapy clinic specializing in mood disorders should make clear the nature of the assessments (paper-and-pencil self-report), the purpose (to assess symptoms of substance abuse to understand better the relationship between substance abuse and depression), the nature of confidentiality (anonymous data collection), the use of such information (only for research purposes and will not be communicated to the client's primary therapist nor associated with the client's treatment records), and that declining to participate in the research will in no way affect the services the participant is currently or may be eligible to receive at the treatment center.

Inducements for research participation and the voluntary nature of consent. Psychologists often offer incentives and compensation (such as gift certificates, cash, tangible goods, and class credit) in recognition of the participants' value (or to offset the cost) of the time and effort spent as a participant in a study. Researchers who offer inducements not only must make sometimes difficult determinations about what type and level of compensation is fair so as to not undervalue participation but also avoid coercing participation, especially among vulnerable populations.

Payments to research participants has long been a controversial topic, and questions have been raised about the degree to which payments unduly influences the decision to participate in a study (Macklin, 1981). Concerns exist that participants may lie or conceal information to meet inclusion criteria for a particular study if the inducements are excessive (Fisher et al., 2013), potentially leading to harm to participants or others, or providing inaccurate or misleading knowledge that may partially invalidate the results of a particular study. Researchers also grapple with questions as to whether some participants should be compensated differently from other participants, due to the nature of their participation, specific burdens of participation and/or time and effort spent participating (Persad et al., 2019).

For some research designs, professional services (such as assessment and/or treatment) are provided as compensation for participant time and effort. In these cases, researchers must make clear the exact nature of the services being offered (including limitations) and the terms of the exchange (i.e., if the participant must complete all aspects of data collection or is entitled to receive services if they complete only part; Standard 8.06, Offering Inducements for Research Participation; APA, 2017). Furthermore, participants also must be provided with information about the right to decline or withdraw participation, and be provided with referrals and alternative affordable services, if available and appropriate.

Payment in-kind. Arguments for and against participant compensation in forms other than cash (known as *payment in-kind*), such as goods or certificates in exchange for goods, continue to be debated. On the one hand, cash money may represent a significant decisional influence on those with limited financial means, perhaps unintentionally coercing participation in research in which they otherwise would not have participated without such incentive (Grady, 2001). On the other hand, researchers who actively avoid compensating with cash because of concerns about what participants may do with the money (e.g., procure illegal drugs, gamble) may be hindering participant autonomy by a priori deciding that cash is not appropriate for the participant. In addition, alternatives to cash may not be seen as being of equal value in terms of compensation (Schonfeld et al., 2003). Finally, the use of incentives in lieu of cash may unintentionally communicate certain judgments toward participants or have other negative effects. For example, research has suggested that participants may find that research that purposely provides alternative incentives in lieu of cash to be paternalistic and offensive (Oransky et al., 2009).

Required university-based research and the voluntary nature of consent. Some education institutions (e.g., colleges and universities) require participation in research studies as part of the curriculum, as a component of a specific class (e.g., an introductory psychology course), or to obtain extra credit. Such experiences may provide students with a first-hand learning experience about the nature of research and participation, and research suggests that students generally find participating in studies to be educationally valuable (Roberts & Allen, 2013). Institutions that require research participation must be sensitive to the possibility that students may not wish to participate in the research being offered by the institution at the time, or in research in general. Therefore, to avoid possible coercion and exploitation, the APA Ethics Code (Standard 8.04b, Client/Patient, Student, and Subordinate Research Participants; APA, 2017) requires that students be given a nonresearch choice that is equitable in terms of time and effort to participation in a research study. These may include attending a related education lecture or completing a writing assignment.

The rational nature of informed consent.
The final requirement of informed consent is that the decision to participate in research must be rational. That is, the participant must have the capability to understand the relevant information about the research study and evaluate the pros and cons of participating (as it relates to his or her particular situation) to arrive at a well-reasoned participation decision. These considerations become particularly relevant when working with individuals who have certain clinical disorders (such as schizophrenia), children and adolescents, and individuals with intellectual disability, as their capacity to comprehend the information necessary to arrive at a rational participation

decision may be particularly vulnerable. As such, informed consent procedures with these at-risk groups may pose special challenges to the rational understanding of relevant research procedures and rights.

To ensure rational consent, investigators must determine participant consent capacity. This determination can be complex, as researchers attempt to balance the goals of protecting participant welfare by preventing ill-informed decisions that may be harmful or exploitative with the aim of preserving autonomy. Psycholegal standards used in the determination of consent capacity have been proposed by Appelbaum and Grisso (1995) and include that the individual (a) understands the purpose, procedures, and basic informed consent information relevant to the study; (b) appreciates the risks and benefits of participation in the specific research as it will affect him or her personally; (c) is capable of weighing the risks and benefits of participation in the study to make the best decision for that participant; and (d) is capable of communicating a decision about participation.

Informed consent with vulnerable populations. The informed consent and assent process with vulnerable and at-risk populations often presents novel and unique ethical dilemmas. Individuals who have poor or questionable consent capacity should be provided with resources and protections against ill-informed decisions that may result in harmful consequences (Delano, 2005). The presence of a disability, however, may not be indicative of consent capacity. For example, research suggests that adults with mild intellectual disabilities perform as well as adults without intellectual disability on several aspects of consent comprehension (Fisher et al., 2006). Investigators may consider assessing consent capacity (e.g., through the MacCAT-CR; Appelbaum & Grisso, 2001) and instituting alternative research procedures to address possible capacity vulnerabilities, such as altering the informed consent process to increase comprehension (e.g., reading the information to participants, using language that is easier to understand, repeating consent information throughout the study, assessing their comprehension throughout the process), developing advanced research directives, or appointing surrogate decision makers (DuBois, 2007). Research suggests that interventions to improve informed consent comprehension, especially ones that are interactive between investigator and participant, may be more effective than traditional informed consent processes (Glaser et al., 2020).

Informed consent for clinical research with individuals with psychiatric conditions. Many recent and historic research studies that have been seen as abusive and harmful have included vulnerable populations who lack adequate decision-making skills. Individuals with decisional impairments (including conditions that actually or reasonably would be expected to compromise cognitive functioning related to decision making) present researchers with unique questions about the appropriateness of standard informed consent procedures. Children and adolescents with psychiatric disorders represent especially vulnerable populations, in which developmental levels or psychiatric symptoms (or a combination thereof) may impair their ability to adequately understand or voluntarily consent or assent to participation (Hoagwood, 2003).

The presence of a psychiatric disorder or intellectual disability does not in and of itself necessarily render a participant unable to provide valid informed consent. For example, research with psychiatric populations suggests that the presence of a psychiatric disorder (Carpenter et al., 2000; Turrell et al., 2011) or hospitalization history (Kovnick et al., 2003) may be individually poor indicators of consent capacity, because significant variation exists within these characteristics (Fried & Fisher, 2008). Variation may exist between conditions; for example, research suggests that individuals with more severe symptoms associated with bipolar disorder (Klein et al., 2019) and unipolar depression (Hindmarch et al., 2013) may have more difficulty with appreciating consent information.

Informed consent for research with children and adolescents. Children have the right to expect that they will be treated fairly and their interests will be protected by researchers (Fisher, 2017). Investigators should be aware that research with children and adolescents often is guided by specific laws, regulations, and guidelines that may differ from those governing research with adults. Aside from the fact that most children and adolescents may not be able to consent independently and legally to participation in a research study, many do not have the cognitive skills to weigh independently the risks and benefits of participation, making their ability to provide rational and voluntary consent questionable (Bruzzese & Fisher, 2003; Fisher & Masty, 2006). To protect children and adolescents from potentially making harmful decisions with regard to research participation, when informed consent is mandatory, regulations and professional codes of conduct, in most cases, require consent from a legally authorized party. Certain exceptions exist, such as when the research project has been approved by an IRB to dispense with informed consent or when seeking consent from a guardian may pose a risk or otherwise not be in the best interests of the child. In such cases, researchers should consider alternative consent methods, such as the appointment of a consent advocate or representative to ensure that participants' rights and welfare are protected (Fisher, 2004).

In addition to formal consent from parents, the APA Ethics Code (Standard 3.10b, Informed Consent; APA, 2017) requires that researchers provide child and adolescent participants with relevant information about the prospective study when appropriate so that they may make a decision (assent or dissent) about participation. Research suggests that adolescents may expect to be active participants in consent discussions and deliberate with parents about decisions (Grady et al., 2014). In most cases, a child's decision against participating in research should be respected. Exceptions may include certain types of clinical research for which the study may represent an opportunity for treatment for an otherwise relatively untreatable condition or disorder; in these cases, assent should not be sought if the child's or adolescent's dissent will not be honored (Fried & Fisher, 2017; Masty & Fisher, 2008; W. C. Rossi et al., 2003). Consent information should still be conveyed to the child or adolescent and opportunities to ask questions and discuss the research should be afforded.

Investigators working with children should note that even with explanations about research procedures and participant rights, children may not fully understand or believe that their participation is voluntary and they are free to withdraw at any time. One must remember that although children and adolescents may lack the cognitive ability to provide truly informed consent, methods and techniques can be used to improve consent capacity (Abramovitch et al., 1995; Bruzzese & Fisher, 2003; Tymchuk, 1992). Researchers who are considering conducting research with children and adolescents should familiarize themselves with the appropriate informed consent literature to design consent procedures that are respectful of both areas of comprehension strength and weakness (Fisher et al., 2006; Fisher & Fried, 2010; Fisher & Ragsdale, 2006; Fried & Fisher, 2008).

School-based research may be governed by a number of federal regulations, laws (e.g., Family Educational Rights and Privacy Act of 1974; Protection of Pupil Rights Amendment of 2004), and professional guidelines. Some child and adolescent researchers use *passive consent* methods in schools and other settings, in which legal guardians are given information about an upcoming study and must alert the school or researchers if they object to their child participating in the research. This practice is controversial, and it has been argued that it violates the spirit and intent of informed consent (Fisher, 2004; Hicks, 2005). Passive consent procedures are generally not considered consistent with federal regulations or the APA Ethics Code (APA, 2017) except in specific circumstances, such as when the IRB has granted a waiver of guardian consent (in which case researchers may still inform a guardian of the research before his or her child participates) or when research meets Standard 8.05, Dispensing With Informed Consent for Research (Fisher, 2017).

Waiver of informed consent. Certain types of research may qualify for a waiver of informed consent under federal regulations (Protection of Human Subjects, 2017) and the APA Ethics Code (APA, 2017). In general, an IRB may consider waiving informed consent requirement procedures in a few circumstances, including (a) the research represents minimal risk (as described, a type of research category used in federal research regulations that is synonymous with everyday occurrences, such as normal tasks associated with school or work, physician check-ups, or employment assessments) and, therefore, is not expected to cause significant physical or emotional distress or harm; (b) waiver of the informed consent will not negatively affect the rights and welfare of participants; (c) the waiver is necessary to complete the research feasibly; and (d) information about the study will be provided to participants whenever feasible and appropriate.

Any waiver of informed consent must be granted by an IRB or other research review group, which will complete a risk–benefit analysis with respect to the proposed research and waiver and then determine whether the study meets the appropriate criteria (Elliot, 2006). Researchers should note that even if an IRB grants a waiver of informed consent, the board still may require the researcher to implement debriefing procedures. Standard 8.05, Dispensing With Informed Consent for Research (APA, 2017), specifies the types of research in this category, which includes certain studies conducted in schools; research designs in which personal and otherwise-identifiable information is not associated with research data (and cannot be linked), such as anonymous or naturalistic designs; certain types of archival research; and certain analyses of job or organizational effectiveness (in which the employment status of the individual would not be at risk and confidentiality is protected).

Deception Research

Investigators engage in deception when they either deliberately misinform or purposely do not provide a participant with information that might reasonably be expected to affect their decision to participate in a research study (Fisher, 2005; Fisher & Fyrberg, 1994; Sieber, 1982). Deception research has been and continues to be a controversial method of scientific inquiry because of the delicate balance of risks and benefits inherent in the design. On the one hand, deception research has the potential to generate valuable and beneficial knowledge that otherwise would be unattainable with research that uses nondeceptive techniques. On the other hand, it has been argued that deception research violates the autonomy and self-determination of individuals and may harm the integrity of the relationship between participant and investigator (Sieber, 1982).

It has been argued that deception research deprives the individual of the ability to make a truly informed decision about participation because the individual has not been given a priori the correct or comprehensive information about the purpose or nature of the study (Fisher, 2017; Sieber, 1982). Because of the unique and potentially significant risks associated with deception research (compared with nondeceptive techniques), the APA Ethics Code (APA, 2017) requires that research that employs deceptive techniques must demonstrate that (a) the use of such methods are "justified by the study's significant prospective scientific, educational, or applied value" and (b) nondeceptive techniques and methods are not scientifically practical or appropriate. With respect to this final condition, Fisher (2017) noted that researchers who elect to use deceptive techniques over nondeceptive alternatives because of time, effort, or cost considerations may be in violation of this standard. In addition to the scientific requirements, the APA Ethics Code prohibits deceptive techniques when the research would cause physical pain or significant emotional discomfort or distress. Deciding whether to use deceptive techniques is often a complicated question. Investigators often benefit from consultation with colleagues or other resources, such as the Windsor Deception Checklist (Pascual-Leone et al., 2010) a 10-item checklist to assist investigators (and review boards) with determinations as to whether deceptive techniques are ethically appropriate and justified.

One frequent question in deception research is whether and when participants should be told about deceptive techniques (commonly referred to as *dehoaxing*). The APA Ethics Code (APA, 2017) requires that participants be informed of any deceptive techniques "as early as is feasible," which provides the researcher with some leeway in terms of timing. Although it is certainly preferable to inform participants about the use of deceptive techniques at the end of their research participation, the scientific validity of certain studies may be compromised if other prospective participants are informed about the nature and purpose of the techniques (i.e., through word of mouth from past participants). For this reason, the Ethics Code permits psychologists to wait until the end of data collection to inform participants of the use of deceptive techniques.

It is important to distinguish between debriefing (which is required in most research protocols and provides individuals with information about the study after participation, whether or not deceptive techniques have been used) and dehoaxing (which applies to deceptive techniques). Reactions to dehoaxing techniques can range from participants experiencing embarrassment, discomfort, and anger to participants verbalizing an understanding of the scientific need for the research to employ deceptive techniques (Fisher & Fyrberg, 1994). Psychologists must take steps to desensitize participants or alleviate potentially negative reactions following dehoaxing. Sieber (1983) recommended that dehoaxing techniques should address potential participant mistrust and lost confidence in scientific research as well as provide the individual with a feeling of satisfaction about their participation by conveying the social or scientific benefits of the research project.

Researchers should be aware and prepare for the possibility that participants may not reveal negative reactions to the researcher at the time of dehoaxing or debriefing (Fisher & Fyrberg, 1994) and, therefore, techniques should address potentially delayed or long-lasting negative reactions. Finally, the APA Ethics Code (APA, 2017) requires that once participants learn of the deceptive techniques used in the study, they be given the option to withdraw their data from analysis.

Research Debriefing

Standard 8.08, Debriefing (APA, 2017), requires that researchers debrief participants after most studies by providing them with relevant information about the study and giving them an opportunity to ask questions (either immediately after the study or at a later date, by providing contact information). Debriefing also offers an opportunity for the researcher to address any harm that may have occurred as a result of participation in the study. This may be especially important in certain types of clinical research, research with children and vulnerable populations, and research that taps emotionally provocative subject matter, such as trauma. Debriefing may also be viewed as a type of "knowledge transfer" that provides education and/or skills related to the research topic to participants (McShane et al., 2015). Debriefing also provides an opportunity to provide participants with resources relevant to the study topic.

Unlike dehoaxing, debriefing techniques apply to all types of research and provide an opportunity to correct any misconceptions or erroneous beliefs about the study or their participation (APA, 2017). In certain studies, debriefing may significantly compromise the scientific validity of a study or harm participants (e.g., eliciting negative feelings, such as embarrassment, anxiety or stress, or anger). This is particularly common with children, who may lack the ability to understand the purpose of research or the nature of the procedures (Fisher, 2017; Sieber, 1983). Similar to the determination of when it is appropriate to dispense with informed consent, the decision to exclude or otherwise alter standard debriefing procedures should be done in consultation with an institution's IRB or research review group.

Investigators must remember that their responsibility to participants does not end with the completion of data collection. Rather, researchers must be committed to preventing or minimizing harm that may result from participation in the study (Keith-Spiegel & Koocher, 1985) and consider that participants may not necessarily disclose harms during the debriefing session (Fisher & Fyrberg, 1994).

Confidentiality

Protecting confidentiality not only reflects the fidelity and responsibility that exist toward the people with whom researchers work but also exemplifies respect for people's rights to autonomy and privacy. Promises of confidentiality help to ensure that participants feel secure in providing honest and accurate answers to research questions and participate fully in study-related tasks. Without such confidentiality methods, participants may fear or experience significant types of harm, including embarrassment, and emotional, legal, financial, or social harm, depending on the nature of the data and breach.

Methods to ensure confidentiality are required in both federal regulations (Protection of Human Subjects, 2017) and professional guidelines governing research. For example, 45 C.F.R. § 46.111 requires that institutional approval for research cannot be granted without adequate methods to protect confidential data (when appropriate), such as methods to maintain security, coding, storage, and disposal. In addition, the APA Ethics Code (APA, 2017) includes several standards with respect to confidentiality and disclosures (see Standard 4.01, Maintaining Confidentiality; Standard 4.04, Minimizing Intrusions on Privacy; and Standard 4.05, Disclosures). The applicability of such regulations and standards depends on the type of research being conducted. For example, researchers collecting data via the internet may employ specific and unique methods for maintaining confidentiality (e.g., firewall protection, data encryption) that may differ significantly from those used in other research data collection mechanisms, such as those used in audio or video observational data or paper-and-pencil surveys. Researchers should consult relevant literature, professional guidelines, and their IRB about appropriate methods of maintaining data security and confidentiality and ensure their competence in using specific technologies in data collection (see Standard 2.01, Boundaries of Competence).

As indicated in the section Informed Consent, researchers may be mandated to disclose certain information learned during the research process. Knowing when it is necessary to disclose confidential information may not always be clear, especially when research concerns potentially illegal and dangerous behaviors, such as alcohol and drug use, possibility of suicide, and violence.[1] Investigators may be able to anticipate the types of disclosures and reports that they may have to make as it relates to their areas of research and should consult federal, state, and local laws and the institutional regulations governing disclosures and reporting as well as identify local community agencies and health care facilities that could be used as referral sources (Fisher & Goodman, 2009). For example, researchers who propose to study levels of anger and frustration among full-time caretakers of elderly family members should consult local, state, and federal laws (as well as with colleagues and their IRB) to determine any elder abuse and neglect reporting requirements and procedures. Researchers should include such information in the informed consent process as well as information about low-cost counseling resources, respite services, and relevant support groups.

Researchers who are collecting data on potentially sensitive information should consider applying for a *certificate of confidentiality* (Public Health Service Act, Section, 301(d), 42 U.S.C. Section 241(d)) before the commencement of data collection. Research that meets specific criteria and is partially or fully funded by the National Institutes of Health may be issued such a certificate without application. See https://grants.nih.gov/policy/humansubjects/coc/what-is.htm for additional information, including significant amendments related to the 21st Century Cures Act. The certificate, offered by National Institutes of Health and other HHS agencies, protects the

---

[1] See Fisher and Goodman (2009) for an excellent discussion of confidentiality and disclosure procedures in nonintervention research with dangerous and illegal behaviors.

investigator (and those associated with data collection) from being compelled (either by law enforcement, subpoena, or otherwise) to produce identifiable and sensitive research data that may expose a research participant to potential harm (e.g., legal or financial). Researchers should be aware that the certificate of confidentiality does not absolve them of mandatory reporting requirements, such as in the case of child or elder abuse, and there may be other exceptions in which a researcher may disclose information. Furthermore, as a matter of policy, DHHS staff may request access to research data that otherwise is protected by the certificate of confidentiality. The intent, scope, and limitations of the certificate of confidentiality should be communicated clearly to prospective participants during the informed consent process.

Conflicts of Interest

Attention to conflicts of interest in biomedical and behavioral research has increased in recent years. Conflicts of interest are potentially harmful when a researcher's or reviewer's professional judgment or decision making is influenced by some other interest (e.g., professional advancement, financial gain, commercial interests). Investigators who conduct studies without disclosing potentially significant conflicts of interests risk the integrity of the profession by tingeing research results with a degree of uncertainty and doubt about the degree to which (if at all) the conflict or potential conflict (such as ties with a private or corporate sponsor or institution) may have influenced the planning, collection, interpretation, or dissemination of the research data. Such conflicts also have the potential to further threaten the public's trust in science (Goldner, 2000). Examples of potential conflicts of interest in biomedical and behavioral research may include certain industry-sponsored research and financial or employment relationships between the investigator or research institution and a company, institution, or group that may have some interest in the outcome of a particular study.

As a result of increased attention to these issues, regulatory and professional bodies have begun to address conflicts of interest more directly. The APA's Task Force on External Funding has published recommendations regarding conflicts of interest in research, publication, and other areas of professional activity (Pachter et al., 2007). APA Ethics Code's standard about conflicts of interest (Standard 3.06, Conflict of Interest, APA, 2017) focuses on conflicts that may impair the professional work of a psychologist or have the potential to harm or exploit those with whom they work. Finally, other stakeholders (e.g., federal grant funding agencies) often also have conflict of interest rules that may impact the conduct and publication of psychological research.

Evidence-Based and Participant-Informed Approaches to Research Ethics

Traditionally, researchers and review boards have used their own moral compass to make ethical determinations about research-related questions, such as determining an acceptable risk–benefit calculation and appropriate recruitment and informed consent processes. Research methods and protections were often "one size fits all" and not specific to the research population studied or the methods used. Within the past 20 years, interest has grown in approaches that attempt to better fit ethical procedures to the research situation. This requires a better understanding of participant's experiences with, perspectives on, and expectations about various aspects of research. Researchers use several methods to do this, including reviewing empirical research findings on research ethics questions and soliciting information from stakeholders, such as community members, to provide input on appropriate ethical research methods.

Empirical research on research ethics provides investigators with critical information about participant experiences in research, perceptions of risks and benefits, and the appropriateness and effectiveness of informed consent methods. For example, empirical research has provided the field with critical information about consent capacity among individuals with various types of psychological conditions, such as schizophrenia

(Palmer et al., 2005), bipolar disorder (Klein et al., 2019), and substance use disorders (Jeste & Saks, 2006). Research has also been used to inform interventions that may be effective in improving consent capacity among individuals with consent-related vulnerabilities (Glaser et al., 2020). Finally, research can help us to better understand the experiences of participants who complete surveys that ask questions about suicide and trauma, providing researchers and review boards with a more accurate risk–benefit analysis (Jaffe et al., 2015).

Contemporary approaches to ethical decision-making frame research aims and procedures as a product of the association between the investigator and participant in the research context. Goodness-of-fit approaches frequently have been used to shape informed consent procedures with populations with questionable consent capacity (Fisher, 2003; Fisher & Goodman, 2009). Rather than exclusively focusing on consent vulnerabilities associated with the specific population, a goodness-of-fit approach views consent capacity interactively in terms of the participant and research context and seeks to explore methods of modifying the research process and environment to increase capacity (Fisher, 2003; Fisher & Fried, 2010; Fisher & Goodman, 2009; Fisher & Masty, 2006; Masty & Fisher, 2008). For example, research with individuals with intellectual disabilities requires careful consideration with regard to the appropriateness of standard informed consent procedures within the specific scientific context, as standard informed consent methods may lead to harm or exploitation because of weaknesses in consent comprehension (Fisher et al., 2006). A goodness-of-fit approach would include consideration of alternative methods to ensure that consent is informed, voluntary, and rational, such as reviewing consent capacity research conducted with similar populations, assessing the consent capacity of participants, modifying the consent language, using multimedia methods to present consent information, employing educational tools to enhance consent capacity, and including other individuals in the consent process to provide guidance to participants (e.g., family members, consent advocates, consent surrogates; Fisher, 2003; Fried & Fisher, 2008).

Another approach used by researchers working with human participants is colearning and community consultation, which recognizes that certain types of research designs and procedures may represent differing levels of risk, depending on the population (Fisher & Fried, 2010). According to this perspective, individuals may hold certain views toward research (including reactions, attitudes, and perspectives about scientific motives and methods, and researchers) that may have serious implications for the methods used by researchers and the type and level of protections instituted. To adequately shape research methods to the specific research–participant environment, investigators must learn more about the population from their participants and communities (Fisher, 2002; Fisher & Fried, 2010; Fisher & Masty, 2006; Fisher & Wallace, 2000). Colearning approaches encourage moral discourse between participant and investigator to construct optimal scientific methods and adequately resolve ethical questions (Fisher, 1999; Fisher & Fried, 2010; Fisher & Goodman, 2009; Fisher & Masty, 2006; Fisher & Ragsdale, 2006). Consultation with participant communities represents a valuable opportunity for researchers to gain support for the proposed study and enhance trust among participants (Fisher et al., 2002; Hoagwood, 2003; Melton et al., 1988). Such methods may be especially important for traditionally disenfranchised communities who may distrust not only the motives of investigators but also the methods of the scientific enterprise in general (Fisher & Wallace, 2000).

Research with vulnerable or impaired populations requires careful and thoughtful consideration on the part of investigators. Even well-intentioned scientists can unknowingly cause harm through their work, such as through the use of culturally insensitive research tools or dissemination methods that stigmatize groups of people or communities. Although participant perspectives can never replace or override the investigator's responsibility to conduct ethically sound and scientifically valid research, community consultation can provide investigators with important knowledge to contribute to selection and implementation of optimal research procedures (Fisher & Fried, 2010).

CONCLUSION

The responsible conduct of research with human participants often requires investigators to engage in sometimes-challenging ethical decision making in response to complex dilemmas, irrespective of the type of research and participants or the level of experience of the researcher. Psychologists often engage federal regulations, state and local laws, IRBs, and the APA Ethics Code (APA, 2017) to inform their professional behaviors. Although these resources provide guidance with respect to planning, executing, and disseminating research, at times they may appear to be in conflict with each other or may be silent on certain issues, without a clear resolution. Such situations require psychologists to engage in a decision-making process that both respects the welfare, rights, and autonomy of participants while also preserving the scientific integrity of the research and fulfilling the investigator's obligations and professional responsibilities. Effective science-in-ethics decision making, while informed by these resources as well as the moral compass of the investigators, advice of colleagues, and guidance of IRBs, often requires consideration of how the research environment interacts with participant views, strengths, and vulnerabilities. Evidence-based and participant-informed research ethics may provide a helpful framework for scientists to shape research methods and practices to the specific research situation.

References

Abramovitch, R., Freedman, J. L., Henry, K., & Van Brunschot, M. (1995). Children's capacity to agree to psychological research: Knowledge of risks and benefits and voluntariness. *Ethics & Behavior, 5*(1), 25–48. https://doi.org/10.1207/s15327019eb0501_3

American Psychological Association. (2017). *Ethical principles of psychologists and code of conduct* (2002, Amended June 1, 2010, and January 1, 2017). https://www.apa.org/ethics/code/index.aspx

Appelbaum, P. S., & Grisso, T. (1995). The MacArthur Treatment Competence Study. I: Mental illness and competence to consent to treatment. *Law and Human Behavior, 19*(2), 105–126. https://doi.org/10.1007/BF01499321

Appelbaum, P. S., & Grisso, T. (2001). *The MacArthur competence assessment tool for clinical research (MacCAT-CR)*. Professional Resource Press.

Appelbaum, P. S., & Rosenbaum, A. (1989). *Tarasoff* and the researcher: Does the duty to protect apply in the research setting? *American Psychologist, 44*(6), 885–894. https://doi.org/10.1037/0003-066X.44.6.885

Appelbaum, P. S., Roth, L. H., Lidz, C. W., Benson, P., & Winslade, W. (1987). False hopes and best data: Consent to research and the therapeutic misconception. *The Hastings Center Report, 17*(2), 20–24. https://doi.org/10.2307/3562038

Bankert, E. A., & Amdur, R. J. (Eds.). (2005). *Institutional review board: Management and function* (2nd ed.). Jones & Bartlett.

Brandt, A. M. (1978). Racism and research: The case of the Tuskegee syphilis study. *Hastings Center Report, 8*(6), 21–29.

Bruzzese, J. M., & Fisher, C. B. (2003). Assessing and enhancing the research consent capacity of children and youth. *Applied Developmental Science, 7*(1), 13–26. https://doi.org/10.1207/S1532480XADS0701_2

Carpenter, W. T., Jr., Gold, J. M., Lahti, A. C., Queern, C. A., Conley, R. R., Bartko, J. J., Kovnick, J., & Appelbaum, P. S. (2000). Decisional capacity for informed consent in schizophrenia research. *Archives of General Psychiatry, 57*(6), 533–538. https://doi.org/10.1001/archpsyc.57.6.533

Chenneville, T. (2000). HIV, confidentiality, and duty to protect: A decision-making model. *Professional Psychology: Research and Practice, 31*(6), 661–670. https://doi.org/10.1037/0735-7028.31.6.661

Delano, S. J. (2005). Research involving adults with decisional impairment. In E. A. Bankert & R. J. Amdur (Eds.), *Institutional review board: Management and function* (2nd ed., pp. 373–377). Jones & Bartlett.

DuBois, J. (2007). *Ethics in mental health research: Principles, guidance, and cases*. Oxford University Press.

Elliot, M. M. (2006). Research without consent or documentation thereof. In E. A. Bankert & R. J. Amdur (Eds.), *Institutional review board: Management and function* (2nd ed., pp. 216–221). Jones & Bartlett.

Family Educational Rights and Privacy Act (FERPA), 34 C.F.R. Part 99, 20 U.S.C.S. §1232g (1974)

https://www.cdc.gov/phlp/publications/topic/ferpa.html

Fisher, C. B. (1999). Relational ethics and research with vulnerable populations. In National Bioethics Advisory Commission (Ed.), *Reports on research involving persons with mental disorders that may affect decision making capacity* (Vol. 2, pp. 29–49). National Bioethics Advisory Commission.

Fisher, C. B. (2002). Participant consultation: Ethical insights into parental permission and confidentiality procedures for policy relevant research with youth. In R. M. Lerner, F. Jacobs, & D. Wertlieb (Eds.), *Handbook of applied developmental science* (Vol. 4, pp. 371–396). SAGE.

Fisher, C. B. (2003). Goodness-of-fit ethic for informed consent to research involving adults with mental retardation and developmental disabilities. *Mental Retardation and Developmental Disabilities Research Reviews*, 9(1), 27–31. https://doi.org/10.1002/mrdd.10052

Fisher, C. B. (2004). Informed consent and clinical research involving children and adolescents: Implications of the revised APA ethics code and HIPAA. *Journal of Clinical Child and Adolescent Psychology*, 33(4), 832–839. https://doi.org/10.1207/s15374424jccp3304_18

Fisher, C. B. (2005). Deception research involving children: Ethical practices and paradoxes. *Ethics & Behavior*, 15(3), 271–287. https://doi.org/10.1207/s15327019eb1503_7

Fisher, C. B. (2017). *Decoding the ethics code* (4th ed.). SAGE.

Fisher, C. B., Cea, C. D., Davidson, P. W., & Fried, A. L. (2006). Capacity of persons with mental retardation to consent to participate in randomized clinical trials. *The American Journal of Psychiatry*, 163(10), 1813–1820. https://doi.org/10.1176/ajp.2006.163.10.1813

Fisher, C. B., & Fried, A. L. (2003). Internet-mediated psychological services and the American Psychological Association ethics code. *Psychotherapy: Theory, Research, Practice, Training*, 40(1-2), 103–111. https://doi.org/10.1037/0033-3204.40.1-2.103

Fisher, C. B., & Fried, A. L. (2010). Ethical issues and challenges in applied research in child and adolescent development. In V. Malhomes & C. Lomanoco (Eds.), *Applied research in adolescent development* (pp. 131–152). Taylor & Francis.

Fisher, C. B., & Fyrberg, D. (1994). Participant partners: College students weigh the costs and benefits of deceptive research. *American Psychologist*, 49(5), 417–427. https://doi.org/10.1037/0003-066X.49.5.417

Fisher, C. B., & Goodman, S. J. (2009). Goodness-of-fit ethics for nonintervention research involving dangerous and illegal behaviors. In D. Buchanan, C. B. Fisher, & L. Gable (Eds.), *Research with high-risk populations: Balancing science, ethics, and law* (pp. 25–46). American Psychological Association. https://doi.org/10.1037/11878-001

Fisher, C. B., Hoagwood, K., Boyce, C., Duster, T., Frank, D. A., Grisso, T., Levine, R. J., Macklin, R., Spencer, M. B., Takanishi, R., Trimble, J. E., & Zayas, L. H. (2002). Research ethics for mental health science involving ethnic minority children and youths. *American Psychologist*, 57(12), 1024–1040. https://doi.org/10.1037/0003-066X.57.12.1024

Fisher, C. B., & Masty, J. K. (2006). Community perspectives on the ethics of adolescent risk research. In B. Leadbeater, T. Reicken, C. Benoit, M. Jansson, & A. Marshall (Eds.), *Research ethics in community-based and participatory action research with youth* (pp. 22–41). University of Toronto Press.

Fisher, C. B., Oransky, M., Mahadevan, M., Singer, M., Mirhej, G., & Hodge, D. (2008). Marginalized populations and drug addiction research: Realism, mistrust, and misconception. *IRB: Ethics & Human Research*, 30(3), 1–9.

Fisher, C. B., & Ragsdale, K. (2006). A goodness-of-fit ethics for multicultural research. In J. Trimble & C. B. Fisher (Eds.), *The handbook of ethical research with ethnocultural populations and communities* (pp. 3–26). SAGE. https://doi.org/10.4135/9781412986168.n1

Fisher, C. B., True, G., Alexander, L., & Fried, A. L. (2013). Moral stress, moral practice, and ethical climate in community-based drug-use research: Views from the front line. *AJOB Primary Research*, 4(3), 27–38. https://doi.org/10.1080/21507716.2013.806969

Fisher, C. B., & Wallace, S. A. (2000). Through the community looking glass: Reevaluating the ethical and policy implications of research on adolescent risk and sociopathology. *Ethics & Behavior*, 10(2), 99–118. https://doi.org/10.1207/S15327019EB1002_01

Freedman, B. (1975). A moral theory of informed consent. *The Hastings Center Report*, 5(4), 32–39. https://doi.org/10.2307/3561421

Freedman, B. (1987). Equipoise and the ethics of clinical research. *The New England Journal of Medicine*, 317(3), 141–145. https://doi.org/10.1056/NEJM198707163170304

Fried, A. L., & Fisher, C. B. (2008). The ethics of informed consent for research in clinical and abnormal psychology. In D. McKay (Ed.),

Handbook of research methods in abnormal and clinical psychology (pp. 5–22). SAGE.

Fried, A. L., & Fisher, C. B. (2017). Ethical issues in child and adolescent psychotherapy research. In J. R. Weisz & A. E. Kazdin (Eds.), *Evidence-based psychotherapies for children and adolescents* (3rd ed., pp. 449–465). Guilford Press.

Garland, A. F., McCabe, K. M., & Yeh, M. (2008). Ethical challenges in practice-based mental health services research: Examples of research with children and families. *Clinical Psychology: Science and Practice, 15*(2), 118–124. https://doi.org/10.1111/j.1468-2850.2008.00119.x

Glaser, J., Nouri, S., Fernandez, A., Sudore, R. L., Schillinger, D., Klein-Fedyshin, M., & Schenker, Y. (2020). Interventions to improve patient comprehension in informed consent for medical and surgical procedures: An updated systematic review. *Medical Decision Making, 40*(2), 119–143. https://doi.org/10.1177/0272989X19896348

Goldner, J. A. (2000). Dealing with conflicts of interest in biomedical research: IRB oversight as the next best solution to the abolitionist approach. *The Journal of Law, Medicine & Ethics, 28*(4), 379–404.

Grady, C. (2001). Money for research participation: Does in jeopardize informed consent? *The American Journal of Bioethics, 1*(2), 40–44. https://doi.org/10.1162/152651601300169031

Grady, C., Wiener, L., Abdoler, E., Trauernicht, E., Zadeh, S., Diekema, D. S., Wilfond, B. S., & Wendler, D. (2014). Assent in research: The voices of adolescents. *Journal of Adolescent Health, 54*(5), 515–520. https://doi.org/10.1016/j.jadohealth.2014.02.005

Hicks, L. (2005). Research in public schools. In E. A. Bankert & R. J. Amdur (Eds.), *Institutional review board: Management and function* (2nd ed., pp. 341–345). Jones & Bartlett.

Hindmarch, T., Hotopf, M., & Owen, G. S. (2013). Depression and decision-making capacity for treatment or research: A systematic review. *BMC Medical Ethics, 14*, 54. https://doi.org/10.1186/1472-6939-14-54

Hoagwood, K. (2003). Ethical issues in child and adolescent psychosocial treatment research. In A. E. Kazdin & J. R. Weisz (Eds.), *Evidence-based psychotherapies for children and adolescents* (pp. 60–75). Guilford Press.

Horng, S., & Grady, C. (2003). Misunderstanding in clinical research: Distinguishing therapeutic misconception, therapeutic misestimation, and therapeutic optimism. *IRB: Ethics & Human Research, 25*(1), 11–16. https://doi.org/10.2307/3564408

Hunt, K. M. (2005). Explaining the cost of research participation. In E. A. Bankert & R. J. Amdur (Eds.), *Institutional review board: Management and function* (2nd ed., pp. 236–240). Jones & Bartlett.

Jaffe, A. E., DiLillo, D., Hoffman, L., Haikalis, M., & Dykstra, R. E. (2015). Does it hurt to ask? A meta-analysis of participant reactions to trauma research. *Clinical Psychology Review, 40*, 40–56. https://doi.org/10.1016/j.cpr.2015.05.004

Jansen, L. A. (2014). Mindsets, informed consent, and research. *Hastings Center Report, 44*(1), 25–32. https://doi.org/10.1002/hast.237

Jeste, D. V., & Saks, E. (2006). Decisional capacity in mental illness and substance use disorders: Empirical database and policy implications. *Behavioral Sciences and the Law, 24*(4), 607–628. https://doi.org/10.1002/bsl.707

Keith-Spiegel, P., & Koocher, G. P. (1985). *Ethics in psychology: Professional standards and cases.* Crown.

Klein, C. C., Jolson, M. B., Lazarus, M., Masterson, B., Blom, T. J., Adler, C. M., DelBello, M. P., & Strakowski, S. M. (2019). Capacity to provide informed consent among adults with bipolar disorder. *Journal of Affective Disorders, 242*, 1–4. https://doi.org/10.1016/j.jad.2018.08.049

Kovnick, J. A., Appelbaum, P. S., Hoge, S. K., & Leadbetter, R. A. (2003). Competence to consent to research among long-stay inpatients with chronic schizophrenia. *Psychiatric Services, 54*(9), 1247–1252. https://doi.org/10.1176/appi.ps.54.9.1247

Lally, M., Goldsworthy, R., Sarr, M., Kahn, J., Brown, L., Peralta, L., & Zimet, G. (2014). Evaluation of an intervention among adolescents to reduce preventive misconception in HIV vaccine clinical trials. *Journal of Adolescent Health, 55*(2), 254–259. https://doi.org/10.1016/j.jadohealth.2014.01.006

Macklin, R. (1981). "Due" and "undue" inducements: On paying money to research subjects. *IRB: Ethics & Human Research, 3*(5), 1–6. https://doi.org/10.2307/3564136

Masty, J., & Fisher, C. (2008). Ethics of treatment and intervention research with children and adolescents with behavioral and mental disorders. *Ethics & Behavior, 18*(2-3), 139–160. https://doi.org/10.1080/10508420802063897

McShane, K. E., Davey, C. J., Rouse, J., Usher, A. M., & Sullivan, S. (2015). Beyond ethical obligation to research dissemination: Conceptualizing debriefing as a form of knowledge transfer. *Canadian Psychology, 56*(1), 80–87. https://doi.org/10.1037/a0035473

Melton, G. B., Levine, R. J., Koocher, G. P., Rosenthal, R., & Thompson, W. C. (1988). Community consultation in socially sensitive research. Lessons from clinical trials of treatments for AIDS. *American Psychologist, 43*(7), 573–581. https://doi.org/10.1037/0003-066X.43.7.573

National Academies of Sciences, Engineering and Medicine. (2017). *Federal statistics, multiple data sources and privacy protections: Next steps.* The National Academies Press.

National Commission for the Protection of Human Subjects of Biomedical and Behavioral Research. (1979). The Belmont Report: Ethical principles and guidelines for the protection of human subjects in research. In B. Steinbock, J. D. Arras, & A. J. London (Eds.), *Ethical issues in modern medicine* (6th ed., pp. 738–745). McGraw-Hill.

Nuremberg Code. (1949). *Trials of war criminals before the Nuremberg military tribunals under Control Council Law No. 10* (Vol. 2). U.S. Government Printing Office. https://collections.nlm.nih.gov/catalog/nlm:nlmuid-01130400RX2-mvpart

Oransky, M., Fisher, C. B., Mahadevan, M., & Singer, M. (2009). Barriers and opportunities for recruitment for nonintervention studies on HIV risk: Perspectives of street drug users. *Substance Use & Misuse, 44*(11), 1642–1659. https://doi.org/10.1080/10826080802543671

Pachter, W. S., Fox, R. E., Zimbardo, P., & Antonuccio, D. O. (2007). Corporate funding and conflicts of interest: A primer for psychologists. *American Psychologist, 62*(9), 1005–1015. https://doi.org/10.1037/0003-066X.62.9.1005

Palmer, B. W., Dunn, L. B., Appelbaum, P. S., Mudaliar, S., Thal, L., Henry, R., Golshan, S., & Jeste, D. V. (2005). Assessment of capacity to consent to research among older persons with schizophrenia, Alzheimer disease, or diabetes mellitus: Comparison of a 3-item questionnaire with a comprehensive standardized capacity instrument. *Archives of General Psychiatry, 62*(7), 726–733. https://doi.org/10.1001/archpsyc.62.7.726

Pascual-Leone, A., Singh, T., & Scoboria, A. (2010). Using deception ethically: Practical research guidelines for researcher and reviewers. *Canadian Psychology, 51*(4), 241–248. https://doi.org/10.1037/a0021119

Perry, J., & Wöhlke, S. (2019). Dealing with misconception in biomedical research. *Journal of Empirical Research on Human Research Ethics, 14*(5), 428–432. https://doi.org/10.1177/1556264619831589

Persad, G., Fernandez Lynch, H., & Largent, E. (2019). Differential payment to research participants in the same study: An ethical analysis. *Journal of Medical Ethics, 45*(5), 318–322. https://doi.org/10.1136/medethics-2018-105140

Prentice, E. D., & Oki, G. (2005). Exempt from Institutional Review Board review. In E. A. Bankert & R. J. Amdur (Eds.), *Institutional review board: Management and function* (2nd ed., pp. 93–96). Jones & Bartlett.

Protection of Human Subjects, 45 C.F.R. § 46 (2017). https://www.ecfr.gov/current/title-45/subtitle-A/subchapter-A/part-46

Protection of Pupil Rights Amendment, 34 C.F.R. part 98. 20 U.S.C. §1232–34 (2004). https://studentprivacy.ed.gov/topic/protection-pupil-rights-amendment-ppra

Roberts, L. D., & Allen, P. J. (2013). A brief measure of student perceptions of the educational value of research participation. *Australian Journal of Psychology, 65*(1), 22–29. https://doi.org/10.1111/ajpy.12007

Rossi, W. C., Reynolds, W., & Nelson, R. M. (2003). Child assent and parental permission in pediatric research. *Theoretical Medicine and Bioethics, 24*(2), 131–148. https://doi.org/10.1023/a:1024690712019

Rothman, D. J., & Rothman, S. M. (1984). *The Willowbrook wars.* Harper & Row.

Rothman, K. J., & Michels, K. B. (1994). The continuing unethical use of placebo controls. *The New England Journal of Medicine, 331*(6), 394–398. https://doi.org/10.1056/NEJM199408113310611

Schonfeld, T. L., Brown, J. S., Weniger, M., & Gordon, B. (2003). Research involving the homeless: Arguments against payment-in-kind (PinK). *IRB: Ethics & Human Research, 25*(5), 17–20. https://doi.org/10.2307/3564602

Sieber, J. E. (1982). Deception in social research I: Kinds of deception and the wrongs they may involve. *IRB: Ethics & Human Research, 4*(9), 1–5. https://doi.org/10.2307/3564511

Sieber, J. E. (1983). Deception in social research III: The nature and limits of debriefing. *IRB: Ethics & Human Research, 5*(3), 1–4. https://doi.org/10.2307/3564548

Stines, L. R., & Feeny, N. C. (2008). Unique ethical concerns in clinical trials comparing psychosocial and psychopharmalogical interventions. *Ethics & Behavior, 18*(2-3), 234–246. https://doi.org/10.1080/10508420802064333

Turrell, S. L., Peterson-Badali, M., & Katzman, D. K. (2011). Consent to treatment in adolescents with anorexia nervosa. *International Journal of Eating Disorders, 44*(8), 703–707. https://doi.org/10.1002/eat.20870

Tymchuk, A. J. (1992). Assent process. In B. Stanley & J. E. Sieber (Eds.), *Social research on children and adolescents* (pp. 128–139). SAGE.

Weijer, C., & Miller, P. B. (2004). When are research risks reasonable in relation to anticipated benefits? *Nature Medicine, 10*(6), 570–573. https://doi.org/10.1038/nm0604-570

Wilson, S., Draper, H., & Ives, J. (2008). Ethical issues regarding recruitment to research studies within the primary care consultation. *Family Practice, 25*(6), 456–461. https://doi.org/10.1093/fampra/cmn076

World Medical Association. (2013). World Medical Association Declaration of Helsinki: Ethical principles for medical research involving human subjects. *JAMA, 310*(20), 2191–2194. https://www.wma.net/wp-content/uploads/2016/11/DoH-Oct2008.pdf

CHAPTER 4

ETHICS AND REGULATION OF RESEARCH WITH NONHUMAN ANIMALS

Sangeeta Panicker, Chana K. Akins, and Beth Ann Rice

Psychological research with nonhuman animals has played and continues to play a significant role in advancing our understanding of processes of learning, memory, perception, motivation, and emotion (Carroll & Overmier, 2001). Relatively recent contributions include the development of treatment for various clinical disorders, such as behavioral therapies to alleviate chronic pain (e.g., Burma et al., 2017), therapeutic drugs (e.g., Nogueira et al., 2017), and biofeedback-based therapies (e.g., Nagai et al., 2018). Furthermore, nonhuman animal models have provided invaluable information about mechanisms underlying psychological disorders, including depressive (Planchez et al., 2019) and anxiety disorders (Lezak et al., 2017). The knowledge gained from these studies has been critical to the development of more effective treatments for anxiety disorders (Lezak et al., 2017) and other conditions (Sartori & Singewald, 2019).

This chapter provides a broad overview of research with nonhuman animals in the United States, starting with the distinction between research ethics and research regulation and the difference between animal "rights" and animal welfare, followed by a summary of the system for regulatory oversight and compliance, and concluding with responsibilities of individuals involved in the conduct of such research.

RESEARCH ETHICS VERSUS RESEARCH REGULATIONS: WHAT'S THE DIFFERENCE?

The terms *research ethics* and *research regulation* often are used synonymously. On the one hand, loose usage of these two terms can be problematic—it can lead to loss of focus and thoughtless adherence to the letter of the law rather than the spirit of the law (regulation). On the other hand, it emphasizes the important relationship between the ethical principles that undergird the conduct of research and regulations that have evolved in response to a perceived need for oversight of the research enterprise.

The ethics of research with nonhuman animals may, on first consideration, appear more complicated than the ethics of research with human participants. For instance, when viewed within the framework of individual rights and freedoms, as enshrined in the practice of obtaining consent and assent from prospective participants, the ethics of conducting research with species incapable of providing consent may be regarded as problematic.[1] There are, therefore, ongoing

---

[1] *Consent* is a legal term that applies only to individuals who have reached the age of maturity. Recognizing and respecting children as individuals, however, requires researchers to obtain not only permission from the child's parent(s) but also assent from the child. In the case of adults who are incapable of giving valid consent for a number of reasons a legally appointed representative acts in the individual's best interest (and when possible the assent of the compromised individual prevails).

https://doi.org/10.1037/0000318-004
APA Handbook of Research Methods in Psychology, Second Edition: Vol. 1. Foundations, Planning, Measures, and Psychometrics, H. Cooper (Editor-in-Chief)
Copyright © 2023 by the American Psychological Association. All rights reserved.

efforts to establish a framework for nonhuman animal research ethics, similar to the widely accepted ethical framework for research with human participants described in the Belmont Report (National Commission, 1979), as evidenced by the framework recently proposed by DeGrazia and Beauchamp (2019). It can be argued, however, that imposing such a human-centered framework on other species is inherently inappropriate as it imposes a human construct on other species. Furthermore, discussions of the ethics of research with nonhuman animals are most often, if not always, rooted in one of the many western philosophical traditions.

The current global research environment, however, warrants an ethical framework that is not rooted in a specific philosophical tradition but rather one that is secular and democratic. In 2004, Dess and Foltin proposed one such framework for research ethics broadly (i.e., to include research with both humans and other animals). The framework, which they called an *ethics cascade,* consists of a series of questions to help teachers promote civil dialogue with students about the ethics of nonhuman animal research. The questions begin by addressing broad issues, such as identifying the arbiter of morality, and gradually become more focused on specific issues, such as the ethics of selecting one method over another comparable one. While Dess and Foltin proposed the model as a pedagogical tool, it also serves as a framework for ethical decision-making at the societal level. Another framework proposed by Bennett and Panicker (2016, see Figure 1, p. 1294) for research with chimpanzees is also applicable to all animal research, in general.

Both models provide a systematic framework within which nation states make considered decisions regarding if, how, and what types of scientific research will be conducted and supported within its borders. While there may be differences in ideological and cultural beliefs of individuals and subgroups within a society, societal level decisions regarding support for such research are determined by the choices and positions adopted by the vast majority of its citizens and will likely evolve over time. For example, until relatively recently, stem cell research was considered taboo and banned in the United States. With growing recognition of its vast potential to address critical health issues, however, the general public became more accepting of stem cell research, albeit with strict oversight in a highly regulated and restricted manner. Similarly, in countries around the world where citizens value science, scientific research, and recognize the critical role of research with nonhuman animals in generating knowledge and sustaining the health and well-being of humans, other animals, and the environment, governments have developed institutional structures and processes for the oversight and conduct of such research. At the same time, mechanisms for accountability and oversight of such research have also been instituted at various levels, including the enactment of laws and issuance of regulations at the federal level, establishment of policies by research sponsors and funding agencies, and adoption of guidelines and codes of conduct by scientific societies. These oversight mechanisms not only require balancing the well-being of the research animals with the potential benefits of the research but also compel serious consideration of the ethics of action (i.e., conducting research) and inaction (i.e., not conducting research) in terms of the impact on society and the planet.

As evidenced by the long history of biomedical and behavioral research with nonhuman animals,[2] the institutions and infrastructure established to support the conduct of such research, and the continuously evolving regulatory oversight mechanisms for such research, globally societies have clearly decided that conducting research

---

[2] Readers should note the use of the term *animal* throughout this chapter. As Hodos and Campbell (1990) pointed out, evolution is not linear with humans as the most perfectly evolved. Rather, evolution is branching, with *Homo sapiens* being only one of the more recently evolved limbs. Referring to laboratory animals as *infrahuman* or tacitly removing humans from the category of animals (as in the phrase *humans and animals*) has struck many behavioral scientists as inappropriate (Dess & Chapman, 1998; Poling, 1984). Therefore, to recognize this logic we use the term *nonhuman animals*.

with such animals has value and is ethically defensible and responsible (GNS Delegates, 2020; National Research Council, 2011; Vasbinder & Locke, 2016). That being the case, what are our ethical obligations to our nonhuman animal research subjects? Conducting research with nonhuman animals is a privilege that society grants scientists—how should this privilege be respected and preserved?

ANIMAL RIGHTS VERSUS ANIMAL WELFARE: WHAT'S THE DIFFERENCE?

Most people believe that nonhuman animals should be afforded protections. Significant differences exist, however, in the goals and tactics of individuals and organizations who subscribe to animal rights ideology versus those who believe in animal welfare. It is important that the public understand these differences. Individuals and groups that identify as animal rights advocates (also referred to as animal protectionists) fall on a broad spectrum, with some ascribing to the belief that any and all human endeavors that involve other animals is tantamount to exploitation of those animals, while others oppose one or more specific human activities that involve other animals, including, but not limited to, raising and slaughtering livestock for human or animal consumption, hunting, zoos, guide dogs for the disabled, search and rescue dogs, and pet ownership (Wrenn, 2012, provided a broad overview of the different animal protectionist perspectives on "animal use" by humans). Many animal rights advocates also condemn any and all research with nonhuman animals regardless of the potential benefits of the research. In contrast, animal welfare advocates endorse the responsible use of animals to satisfy certain human needs and also believe that humans have an obligation to treat animals humanely. Animal welfare advocates, including scientists who conduct research with nonhuman animals, believe that humans are responsible for providing the animals in their care with basic needs, including food, water, shelter, and health, and ensuring that they do not experience unnecessary suffering and minimizing suffering to the greatest extent possible when pain and distress are unavoidable.

CONCERN FOR LABORATORY ANIMAL WELFARE

Often, opponents of research with nonhuman animals posit that scientists are lax about animal care or even that they wantonly neglect the research animals in their care for the benefit of their research careers (Arluke, 1988; Reinhardt, 2003). Contrary to this position, however, researchers are morally and ethically responsible not only for the care of research animals but also for ensuring the scientific validity of research findings that requires adequate care of the animals (Poole, 1997). Inadequately cared for and maltreated animals are likely to experience behavioral and physiological changes that may increase the variability of experimental results and introduce confounds. In the event that the research study requires that animals experience pain or discomfort, scientists are obligated to justify it and to minimize its extent.

Alternatives to Animal Research

Opponents of nonhuman animal research also claim that, despite the availability of alternatives to the use of such animals in basic biomedical and behavioral research, scientists are loath to use these alternatives either because they are resistant to change (Gruber & Hartung, 2004) or because of their blatant disregard for these animals' well-being (Rusche, 2003). The following are two important points that need to be clarified:

1. Proponents of alternatives often conflate animal research and animal *testing,* which involves testing the safety and toxicity of drugs, biologics, cosmetics, industrial and household chemicals, etc., for many of which nonanimal alternatives have been developed and are widely used (Knight & Breheny, 2002).
2. Nonanimal alternatives have been developed for specific *procedures* employed in animal research, for example, in vitro production of monoclonal antibodies has replaced the use of the ascites mouse.

While these alternatives have eliminated the need for using nonhuman animals in specific tests and procedures, nonhuman animals continue to play a critical role in basic and applied biomedical and behavioral research. It is also important to note that consideration of alternatives to the use of nonhuman animal models in research is not merely an academic exercise but both an ethical imperative and a regulatory requirement. The ethical imperative requires researchers not only to consider the best possible animal model for a particular study but also to ensure that there is no viable nonanimal alternative. Current regulations require a literature search for alternatives such as tissue culture and computer simulations that must be conducted before receiving approval to use animals for research purposes. Often, fundamental research questions cannot be addressed with these alternatives because the answers can be found only by studying intact organisms. Plants are not a viable alternative because they do not have a nervous system. Tissue cultures might be used to study cellular processes, but how these processes operate in live organisms cannot be studied without an intact organism. Computer simulations are becoming more and more sophisticated; however, they require knowledge obtained from live, behaving organisms and cannot be used to generate new information about behavior. Although these alternatives continue to become more advanced, they are nowhere near adequate substitutes nonhuman animals in psychological studies aimed at understanding behavior and the brain mechanisms underlying both healthy and maladaptive behaviors and disorders.

Research Animals in Perspective

The number of animals used in research is relatively small compared with the number of animals used for other purposes. The Food and Agriculture Organization of the United States (2020) reported that the number of animals used for food averaged around 10 billion animals in 2018, whereas in that same year, an estimated 14 million were used for research (Taylor & Alvarez, 2019). Additionally, recent reports indicate that, in the United States, people eat more ducks per year and consume over 1,800 times the number of pigs than the number used in research; people eat over 340 chickens for every animal used in research covered by the Animal Welfare Act (P.L.98-544; 1966) (USDA-APHIS, 2020; USDA-ERS, n.d.).

Regardless, however, of the specific contexts and ways in which humans engage with and use other animals, ensuring the well-being of the animals involved is paramount. Regulatory standards for the care and treatment of nonhuman animals in research are more stringent and burdensome than those that apply to any other human endeavor involving other animals, such as food production, entertainment, and pet ownership (Bennett & Panicker, 2016, see Table 1, p. 1287). Yet, regulations for conducting animal research have steadily increased over the years (National Academies of Sciences, Engineering, and Medicine, 2016; National Science Board, 2014). Although the increase in regulations is welcomed by some, particularly those who are opposed to the use of animals to benefit humans in any form (Grimm, 2020), others believe that the increase in regulations does little, if anything, to truly improve laboratory animal well-being but rather unnecessarily impedes the progress of science—science that would not only benefit humans, but nonhuman animals as well (Haywood & Greene, 2008; National Academies of Sciences, Engineering, and Medicine, 2016; National Science Board, 2014). Often those leading the charge for increasing regulatory restrictions on research with nonhuman animals are those that believe any and all research with nonhuman animals is unethical and should be abolished (Grimm, 2016a, 2016b, 2019). The continual push for additional regulatory requirements for the conduct of animal research, therefore, is questionable (Bennett & Ringach, 2016; Mitchell et al., 2021).

Questions have also been raised about whether animal research regulations are established on the basis of actual knowledge about the needs of nonhuman animals or on the basis of what humans consider is best for the animals (Bayne, 2005; Benefiel et al., 2005). In fact, the use of anthropomorphic criteria to establish regulatory requirements and guidelines for the well-being of a laboratory animal has in some cases negatively impacted the quality of life of the laboratory animals. For example, enrichment added to mice cages increased aggression, reduced resistance to infection, and resulted in a hostile housing environment (Barnard et al., 1996). Animal care regulations, therefore, must be based on specific knowledge about different species and their needs, rather than on unsubstantiated assumptions about what is most comfortable for other animals (Bennett et al., 2018; Dutton et al., 2018).

OVERSIGHT OF RESEARCH WITH NONHUMAN ANIMALS IN THE UNITED STATES

Research with nonhuman animals has multiple levels of oversight, many of which are overlapping. The original Laboratory Animal Welfare Act (AWA), also known as the Pet Protection Act, was passed by Congress in 1966 and was intended to prevent the theft of pet dogs and cats and their subsequent sale for research purposes. The current AWA includes the original law and several amendments passed by Congress over the years, with the most recent enacted in 2013. The Animal and Plant Health Inspection Service (APHIS) at the United States Department of Agriculture (USDA) is mandated by the AWA to oversee animal welfare for animals that are covered under the Act. Research animals that are covered under the AWA regulations include warm-blooded animals with the exceptions of rats (of the genus *Rattus*), mice (of the genus *Mus*), and birds bred for the purpose of research. Birds, however, are protected under U.S. Public Health Service (PHS) Policy (2015).

The PHS policy differs from the AWA in that it covers all vertebrates and applies to all institutions that receive PHS funding. The National Institutes of Health (NIH) Office of Laboratory Animal Welfare (OLAW) oversees the care and use of vertebrate animals at these institutions and requires them to file an Animal Welfare Assurance with OLAW, stating how they will comply with the PHS policy. The assurance is reviewed and approved by OLAW and holds the institution directly accountable. It represents a commitment that the institution will comply with the PHS policy, with the *Guide for the Care and Use of Laboratory Animals* (the *Guide*; National Research Council, 2011), and with the animal welfare regulation. A sample Animal Welfare Assurance can be found on the OLAW website (https://olaw.nih.gov/resources/documents/assur.htm).

Both USDA regulations and PHS policy require that each facility where research with animals is conducted establish an Institutional Animal Care and Use Committee (IACUC) to provide oversight. At a minimum, the IACUC must include a veterinarian, a practicing scientist experienced in animal research, a person whose primary concerns are in nonscientific areas, and a person who is unaffiliated with the institution except as a member of the IACUC. The IACUC is charged with determining whether activities involving animals that occur at the institution are in accordance with the regulations.

In accordance with OLAW, the IACUC is federally mandated to perform the following responsibilities:

- Review the institution's program for humane care and use of animals at least every 6 months.
- Inspect all of the institution's animal facilities at least once every 6 months.
- Prepare reports of the IACUC evaluations and submit the reports to the institutional official. The reports must distinguish significant deficiencies from minor deficiencies. If program or facility deficiencies are noted, the reports must contain a reasonable and specific plan and schedule for correcting each deficiency.
- Review concerns involving the care and use of animals at the institution.
- Make written recommendations to the institutional official regarding any aspect of the institution's animal program, facilities, or personnel training.
- Review and approve, require modifications in (to secure approval), or withhold approval of activities related to the care and use of animals.

- Review and approve, require modifications in (to secure approval), or withhold approval of proposed significant changes regarding the use of animals in ongoing activities.
- Be authorized to suspend an activity involving animals.

Investigators must understand that the IACUC has the authority to suspend an activity (protocol) that it previously approved. Suspension of an activity is a matter of ensuring institutional compliance, and it typically is done only when a researcher is conducting an activity with animals that has not received prior approval. It is the investigator's responsibility to seek approval (usually by submitting a new protocol or an amendment) for any new animal-use activity before conducting it.

In addition to federal oversight, nonhuman animal research may also be subject to state laws and regulations. Furthermore, many local governments such as states and municipalities have laws, regulations, and ordinances that impact animal research that is conducted within their jurisdictions.

OBTAINING IACUC APPROVAL

Before any study involving animals may begin, all animal use activities must be documented in a protocol and be reviewed and approved by the IACUC. A sample proposal application for animal research can be found on the OLAW website (https://olaw.nih.gov/resources/documents/animal-study-prop.htm). Following submission of a protocol, the IACUC typically assigns a designated reviewer and a veterinarian from the committee to conduct the review. The regulations, however, allow an opportunity for every IACUC member to request discussion of a protocol at a convened committee meeting.

The IACUC protocol application requires sufficient information about the project to evaluate whether the proposed activities comply with the regulations. The first part of the protocol application involves writing a nontechnical synopsis that should describe the project in layperson's language and address the use of animals in the project. Investigators are asked to list all internal and external funding sources related to the proposed studies. Federal policies require the IACUC to confirm that vertebrate animal studies that are described in grants coincide with descriptions in IACUC protocols.

Another key feature of the protocol review is adequate justification for the use of animals and for the number of animals being requested. Based on the conviction that animal research is critical to furthering knowledge, contributing to scientific advances that benefit society, Russell and Burch (1959) originally proposed the three Rs—replacement, reduction, and refinement—as principles to guide the discovery of humane techniques for animal research. *Replacement* refers to whether animal use can be replaced by computer modeling, cell cultures, or with a phylogenetically lower species. As discussed, these alternatives typically are not likely to replace nonhuman animals in psychological research. Nevertheless, adequate justification for not using these alternatives is required in the protocol. *Reduction* refers to reducing the number of animals necessary to satisfy the experimental objectives. Investigators are required to justify the number of animals requested and provide evidence for why this number is necessary for the scientifically valid interpretation of the results. A statistical power analysis is an acceptable way to justify the number of animals needed for an experiment. If a power analysis is not possible, a citation of previous research is acceptable. *Refinement* refers to utilizing methods to minimize pain and distress. Typically, this involves justifying the use of invasive techniques or the nonalleviation of potentially painful procedures with analgesics or other pain-relieving drugs. Investigators are expected to conduct a literature search to ensure that they are not duplicating the proposed research, that alternatives are not suitable for replacing animals in their experiments, and that they are using the least painful procedures without detracting from the scientific merit of the experiments.

The protocol application requires investigators to describe any expected adverse consequences that the animals may experience as a result of the procedures, such as loss of appetite, postoperative discomfort, or pain at an injection site. The investigator is asked to describe how animals will be monitored. This allows the veterinary staff to be preemptive of any adverse consequences and address them promptly when they arise.

PAIN AND DISTRESS

As defined by animal welfare regulations, the USDA uses specific Humane Animal Use Categories to classify the extent to which the animals may experience pain or distress in a particular research protocol. There is no Category A. Category B generally is restricted to animals used solely for breeding or holding purposes. These are animals that are not being experimentally manipulated. One example of this might be observing an animal in the wild without manipulating it or its environment. Category C applies to animals involved in research, testing, or education protocols in which they are not subjected to more than slight or momentary pain or distress. Animals receiving routine procedures such as blood collection would fall in this category. Animals used in teaching, research, surgery, or tests involving pain or distress for which appropriate anesthetic, analgesic, or tranquilizing drugs are used are assigned to Category D. An essential component of any Category D protocol is the inclusion of an appropriate treatment (anesthesia, analgesia, euthanasia, etc.) to prevent, reduce, or eliminate the pain and distress. Animals that are typically assigned to Category E are used in teaching, experiments, research, surgery, or tests involving pain or distress in which the use of anesthetic, analgesic, or tranquilizing drugs would adversely affect the interpretation of the results. An explanation of the procedures that produce pain or distress in these animals and the reasons such drugs will not be used must be provided to and approved by the IACUC. Typically, Category E protocols are those in which administration of analgesics or anesthetics would interfere with the study and invalidate the results. Category E animal use protocols receive increased IACUC, USDA, and PHS scrutiny.

USDA regulations define a *painful procedure* as "any procedure that would reasonably be expected to cause more than slight or momentary pain or distress in a human being to which that procedure was applied." The IACUC is required to determine whether the investigator has considered alternatives to potentially painful or distressful procedures. When the potential for pain or distress exists, researchers are expected to monitor animals carefully and to relieve the pain or distress whenever possible. This may be accomplished by administration of anesthetics or analgesics. By regulation, a specific scientific justification must be provided whenever anesthetics or analgesics are withheld, which might be necessary when the drugs would interfere with the interpretation of experimental data.

Relatively few animals that are used in research are assigned to Pain Category E. In the Annual Report of Animal Usage for fiscal year 2018 (USDA, 2020), APHIS reported that of about 800,000 animals used in research that are covered under AWA, only about 7% were assigned to Pain Category E. According to their estimates, the majority of animals used in research are assigned to categories with either no pain or momentary pain.

COMPLIANCE AND OTHER CONSIDERATIONS

Federal laws require that IACUCs perform annual reviews of animal studies. These reviews request the number of animals used in the past year and any unanticipated problems that were encountered while conducting the research. If an investigator fails to submit an annual report, the IACUC may inactivate the protocol until one is submitted. An investigator cannot conduct animal research on that particular protocol until it is reactivated.

In addition to annual protocol reviews to ensure that investigators comply with the care and use of animals, institutions have established procedures for individuals to report concerns about animal care and use or other noncompliance issues. Typically, the names and phone numbers of contact persons are posted in the area where animal research is conducted. If the person reporting the incidence wishes to remain anonymous, this typically is granted. If the incidence that is reported involves an animal welfare issue or a human safety concern, the institution may take immediate action, including suspension of the research activity and notification to the appropriate officials. If an activity is suspended, the incident and the actions taken by the committee are reported to APHIS and any agency funding that activity. In the event that immediate action is not required, the IACUC typically forms a subcommittee made up of IACUC members who then determine the course of action and whether further investigation is necessary. If the subcommittee decides that further investigation is needed, they will gather information and complete a report that includes supporting documentation, such as records, a summary of the concerns as they relate to the regulations, and a course of action. The IACUC reviews this report and then may request additional information, determine that no evidence or basis for the concern exists, or determine that the concern is valid. If allegations of animal mistreatment or protocol noncompliance are verified, the IACUC can apply sanctions. Examples of potential sanctions include monitoring the individual or testing that involves animals, mandating specific training to avoid future incidents, or temporarily or permanently revoking the investigator's privilege to conduct research with animals.

The importance of instituting a detailed plan for dealing with unanticipated events that can severely compromise research animal care and well-being was underscored by the COVID-19 pandemic when lockdowns and stay-at-home orders shuttered research facilities and rendered routine care of laboratory animals impossible or extremely difficult. While the pandemic may be seen as an anomaly and rare occurrence, other events such as natural disasters or laboratory break-ins can have a severe impact on nonhuman animal research programs. The National Research Council (2011) *Guide for the Care and Use of Laboratory Animals*, therefore, recommends that institutions develop detailed contingency crisis management plans that include descriptions of actions that will be taken to prevent animal pain and distress, including criteria for euthanizing research animals and how animals necessary for critical research activities will be cared for and maintained. In some cases, in addition to the *Guide*, researchers may want to use a comprehensive planning approach that is congruent with the National Preparedness System (FEMA, 2015) to develop plans for prevention, protection, and mitigation as well as response and recovery for animal research programs.

THE ROLE OF OTHER ORGANIZATIONS

In addition to ensuring compliance with local, state, and federal laws, many institutions also seek voluntary accreditation from the Association for Assessment and Accreditation of Laboratory Animal Care (AAALAC) International. AAALAC International is a private, nonprofit organization that assesses institutional animal care and use programs and certifies that the program not only meets the minimum standards for animal care required by law, but that it also meets additional standards and criteria set by AAALAC International. Once accredited, institutions are inspected every three years to determine whether they retain their accreditation.

The Institute for Laboratory Animal Research (ILAR) housed within the National Academies of Science, Engineering, and Medicine is charged with providing independent, objective advice to the federal government, the scientific community, and the public about the humane care and treatment of animals in research. Using the principles of the three Rs (refinement, reduction, and replacement) as a foundation, it evaluates and disseminates information on issues related to the ethical use of animals in scientific research. ILAR has produced numerous publications, including the *Guide for the Care and Use of Laboratory Animals* (2011), *Occupational Health and Safety in the Care and Use of Research Animals* (1997), *Recognition and*

Alleviation of Pain in Laboratory Animals (2009), and the *ILAR Journal*.

Professional organizations also play a role in ensuring laboratory animal welfare. For example, the American Psychological Association (APA) has a long-standing Committee on Animal Research and Ethics (CARE). CARE publishes various resources for researchers and students, including *Guidelines for Ethical Conduct in the Care and Use of Animals* (APA, 2012) that recommends procedures for psychologists who conduct nonhuman animal research. Anyone who publishes in APA journals is required to conduct their research with animals in accordance with these guidelines.

Although not directly involved in the oversight of research with nonhuman animals, organizations such as Public Responsibility in Medicine and Research (PRIM&R) and Scientific Center for Animal Welfare (SCAW) play an important role in ensuring compliance with all relevant laws and regulations at the local institutional level. Both organizations provide opportunities for the continuing education and training of IACUC staff and members on compliance with federal regulations and policies. Federal entities such as OLAW and the Animal Welfare Information Center at the USDA also engage in educational activities to keep the research community abreast of evolving regulations and policies.

OUR RESPONSIBILITY AS RESEARCHERS

As stewards of the nonhuman animal research enterprise, researchers have a dual obligation to ensure the humane care and treatment of laboratory animals and to gain and maintain public trust in the enterprise. To achieve this goal, researchers need to ensure that the public has an appreciation for the value of research with nonhuman animals. Counteracting misinformation about research that is perpetrated by entities that are against all nonhuman animal research, purely on ideological grounds, is critical. To that end, students from elementary school to graduate school need to be provided with a strong fact-based education about the conduct of nonhuman animal research, whether basic or applied, as well as the invaluable contributions that such research has made and continues to make to improving the lives of people and other animals.

Maintaining public support also requires responsible use of resources. New and often redundant regulations (e.g., annual inspections and varying recordkeeping requirements by multiple oversight bodies) can make the conduct of such research more burdensome and can squander scarce resources on oversight mechanisms that have little, if any, impact on the well-being of the research animals (National Academies of Sciences, Engineering, and Medicine, 2016; National Science Board, 2014; Thulin et al., 2014). New regulations should be accompanied by increased protection of the welfare of the research animal. The research community should work with regulatory agencies toward ensuring science-based regulations and policies that more effectively protect the welfare of these animals while also ensuring the responsible use of resources (especially public funding) for scientifically and ethically sound research that could improve lives.

References

American Psychological Association. (2012). *Guidelines for ethical conduct in the care and use of animals*. https://www.apa.org/science/leadership/care/guidelines

Animal Welfare Act, Pub. L. 89-544, U.S.C. Title 7, §§ 2131–2156 (1966).

Arluke, A. B. (1988). Sacrificial symbolism in animal experimentation: Object or pet? *Anthrozoos*, 2(2), 98–117. https://doi.org/10.2752/089279389787058091

Barnard, C. J., Behnke, J. M., & Sewell, J. (1996). Environmental enrichment, immunocompetence, and resistance to *Babesia microti* in male mice. *Physiology & Behavior*, 60(5), 1223–1231. https://doi.org/10.1016/S0031-9384(96)00174-6

Bayne, K. (2005). Potential for unintended consequences of environmental enrichment for laboratory animals and research results. *ILAR Journal*, 46(2), 129–139. https://doi.org/10.1093/ilar.46.2.129

Benefiel, A. C., Dong, W. K., & Greenough, W. T. (2005). Mandatory "enriched" housing of laboratory animals: The need for evidence-based evaluation. *ILAR Journal*, 46(2), 95–105. https://doi.org/10.1093/ilar.46.2.95

Bennett, A. J., Bailoo, J. D., Dutton, M., Michel, G. F., & Pierre, P. J. (2018, June 7). *Psychological science applied to improve captive animal care: A model for development of a systematic, evidence-based assessment of environmental enrichment for nonhuman primates.* https://doi.org/10.31234/osf.io/79xky

Bennett, A. J., & Panicker, S. (2016). Broader impacts: International implications and integrative ethical consideration of policy decisions about US chimpanzee research. *American Journal of Primatology, 78*(12), 1282–1303. https://doi.org/10.1002/ajp.22582

Bennett, A. J. & Ringach, D. L. (2016). Animal research in neuroscience: A duty to engage. *Neuron, 92*(3), 653–657. https://doi.org/10.1016/j.neuron.2016.10.034

Burma, N. E., Leduc-Pessah, H., Fan, C. Y., & Trang, T. (2017). Animal models of chronic pain: Advances and challenges for clinical translation. *Journal of Neuroscience Research, 95*(6), 1242–1256. https://doi.org/10.1002/jnr.23768

Carroll, M. E., & Overmier, J. B. (Eds.). (2001). *Animal research and human health: Advancing human welfare through behavioral science.* American Psychological Association. https://doi.org/10.1037/10441-000

DeGrazia, D., & Beauchamp, T. L. (2019). Beyond the 3 Rs to a more comprehensive framework of principles for animal research ethics. *ILAR Journal, 60*(3), 308–317. https://doi.org/10.1093/ilar/ilz011

Delegates, G. N. S. (2020). *Neuroethics as a science engagement strategy for excellence in global neuroscience.* https://www.globalneuroethicssummit.com/gns-2019

Dess, N. K., & Chapman, C. D. (1998). "Humans and animals"? On saying what we mean. *Psychological Science, 9*(2), 156–157. https://doi.org/10.1111/1467-9280.00030

Dess, N. K., & Foltin, R. W. (2004). The ethics cascade. In C. K. Akins, S. Panicker, & C. L. Cunningham (Eds.), *Laboratory animals in research and teaching: Ethics, care, and methods* (pp. 31–39). American Psychological Association.

Dutton, M. B., Pierre, P. J., Bailoo, J. D., Warkins, E., Michel, G. F., & Bennett, A. J. (2018). A model quantitative assessment tool for nonhuman primate environmental enrichment plans. *bioRxiv.* Advance online publication. https://doi.org/10.1101/341206

FEMA. (2015). *National preparedness goal* (2nd ed.). https://www.fema.gov/sites/default/files/2020-06/national_preparedness_goal_2nd_edition.pdf

Food and Agriculture Organization of the United States. (2020). *FAOSTAT.* http://www.fao.org/faostat/en/#home

Grimm, D. (2016a). Conservatives, liberals team up against animal research. *Science.* https://doi.org/10.1126/science.aal0405

Grimm, D. (2016b). NIH to review its policies on all nonhuman primate research. *Science.* https://doi.org/10.1126/science.aaf4090

Grimm, D. (2019). 2020 U.S. spending bill restricts some animal research, pushes for lab animal retirement. *Science.* https://doi.org/10.1126/science.aba6454

Grimm, D. (2020). NIH hosts nonhuman primate workshop amidst increased scrutiny of monkey research. *Science.* https://doi.org/10.1126/science.abb3952

Gruber, F. P., & Hartung, T. (2004). Alternatives to animal experimentation in basic research. *ALTEX, 21*(4.1 Suppl.), 3–31.

Haywood, J. R., & Greene, M. (2008). Avoiding an overzealous approach: A perspective on regulatory burden. *ILAR Journal, 49*(4), 426–434. https://doi.org/10.1093/ilar.49.4.426

Hodos, W., & Campbell, C. G. G. (1990). Evolutionary scales and comparative studies of animal cognition. In R. P. Kenser & D. S. Olton (Eds.), *The neurobiology of comparative cognition* (pp. 1–20). Erlbaum.

Institute for Laboratory Animal Research. (1997). *Occupational health and safety in the care and use of research animals.* National Academies Press.

Institute for Laboratory Animal Research. (2009). *Recognition and alleviation of pain in laboratory animals.* National Academies Press.

Knight, D. J., & Breheny, D. (2002). Alternatives to animal testing in the safety evaluation of products. *Alternatives to Laboratory Animals, 30*(1), 7–22. https://doi.org/10.1177/026119290203000103

Lezak, K. R., Missig, G., & Carlezon, W. A., Jr. (2017). Behavioral methods to study anxiety in rodents. *Dialogues in Clinical Neuroscience, 19*(2), 181–191. https://doi.org/10.31887/DCNS.2017.19.2/wcarlezon

Mitchell, A. S., Hartig, R., Basso, M. A., Jarrett, W., Kastner, S., & Poirier, C. (2021). International primate neuroscience research regulation, public engagement and transparency opportunities. *NeuroImage, 229,* 117700. https://doi.org/10.1016/j.neuroimage.2020.117700

Nagai, Y., Aram, J., Koepp, M., Lemieux, L., Mula, M., Critchley, H., Sisodiya, S., & Cercignani, M. (2018). Epileptic seizures are reduced by autonomic biofeedback therapy through enhancement of fronto-limbic connectivity: A controlled trial and neuroimaging study. *EBioMedicine, 27,* 112–122. https://doi.org/10.1016/j.ebiom.2017.12.012

National Academies of Sciences, Engineering, and Medicine. (2016). *Optimizing the nation's investment in academic research: A new regulatory framework for the 21st century.* https://doi.org/10.17226/21824

National Commission for the Protection of Human Subjects and Behavioral Research. (1979). *The Belmont report: Ethical principles and guidelines for the protection of human subjects of research.* https://www.hhs.gov/ohrp/regulations-and-policy/belmont-report/read-the-belmont-report/index.html

National Research Council. (2011). *Guide for the care and use of laboratory animals* (8th ed.). National Academies Press.

National Science Board. (2014). *Reducing investigators' administrative workload for federally funded research.* https://www.nsf.gov/pubs/2014/nsb1418/nsb1418.pdf

Nogueira, A., Pires, M. J., & Oliveira, P. A. (2017). Pathophysiological mechanisms of renal fibrosis: A review of animal models and therapeutic strategies. *in vivo, 31*(1), 1–22. https://doi.org/10.21873/invivo.11019

Planchez, B., Surget, A., & Belzung, C. (2019). Animal models of major depression: Drawbacks and challenges. *Journal of Neural Transmission* (Vienna, Austria), *126*(11), 1383–1408. https://doi.org/10.1007/s00702-019-02084-y

Poling, A. (1984). Comparing humans to other species: We're animals and they're not infrahumans. *The Behavior Analyst, 7,* 211–212. https://doi.org/10.1007/BF03391905

Poole, T. (1997). Happy animals make good science. *Laboratory Animals, 31*(2), 116–124. https://doi.org/10.1258/002367797780600198

Reinhardt, V. (2003). Compassion for animals in the laboratory: Impairment or refinement of research methodology? *Journal of Applied Animal Welfare Science, 6*(2), 123–130. https://doi.org/10.1207/S15327604JAWS0602_04

Rusche, B. (2003). The 3Rs and animal welfare—Conflict or the way forward? *ALTEX 20*(3.1 Suppl.), 63–76.

Russell, W. M. S., & Burch, R. L. (1959). *The principles of humane experimental technique.* Methuen.

Sartori, S. B., & Singewald, N. (2019). Novel pharmacological targets in drug development for the treatment of anxiety and anxiety-related disorders. *Pharmacology & Therapeutics, 204,* 107402. https://doi.org/10.1016/j.pharmthera.2019.107402

Taylor, K., & Alvarez, L. R. (2019). An estimate of the number of animals used for scientific purposes worldwide in 2015. *Alternatives to Laboratory Animals, 47*(5–6), 196–213. https://doi.org/10.1177/0261192919899853

Thulin, J. D., Bradfield, J. F., Bergdall, V. K., Conour, L. A., Grady, A. W., Hickman, D. L., Norton, J. N., & Wallace, J. M. (2014). The cost of self-imposed regulatory burden in animal research. *The FASEB Journal, 28*(8), 3297–3300. https://doi.org/10.1096/fj.14-254094

U.S. Department of Agriculture, Animal and Plant Health Inspection Service. (2020). *Annual report animal usage by fiscal year: Fiscal year 2018.* https://www.aphis.usda.gov/animal_welfare/annual-reports/Annual-Report-Summaries-State-Pain-FY18.pdf

U.S. Department of Agriculture, Economic Research Service. (n.d.). *Livestock and meat domestic data.* https://www.ers.usda.gov/data-products/livestock-meat-domestic-data/

U.S. Public Health Service. (2015). *Public health service policy on humane care and use of laboratory animals.* https://olaw.nih.gov/sites/default/files/PHSPolicyLabAnimals.pdf

Vasbinder, M. A., & Locke, P. (2016). Introduction: Global laws, regulations, and standards for animals in research. *ILAR Journal, 57*(3), 261–265. https://doi.org/10.1093/ilar/ilw039

Wrenn, C. (2012). Abolitionist animal rights: Critical comparisons and challenges within the animal rights movement. *Interface, 4*(2), 438–458.

SECTION 3

CULTURAL AND SOCIETAL ISSUES IN CONDUCTING PSYCHOLOGICAL RESEARCH

CHAPTER 5

CROSS-CULTURAL RESEARCH METHODS

David Matsumoto and Fons J. R. van de Vijver

The study of culture has blossomed into one of the most important areas of research in psychology. Articles involving cultural variables appear more today than ever before in mainstream journals in developmental, clinical, personality, and social psychology as well as in many specialty journals. Theorists are increasingly incorporating culture as an important variable in models of psychological processes.

Psychological scientists can take many methodological approaches to the study of the association between culture and psychological processes, and an in-depth review of all methodologies is beyond the scope of this chapter. Instead, we focus on cross-cultural comparative research, in which two or more cultural groups are compared on some psychological variables of interest. This method is the backbone supporting the growth of cultural science in psychology, regardless of theoretical approach or perspective. Although differences existed between methodologies associated with "cross-cultural psychology" and "cultural psychology," today both clearly use cross-cultural comparisons as the method of choice when conducting research.

Cross-cultural comparisons offer many potential advantages. They test the boundaries of knowledge and stretch the methodological parameters under which such knowledge is created and vetted in psychology. They highlight important similarities and differences across cultures. They bring researchers in disparate and divergent cultures together for a common cause. Their findings promote international and intercultural exchange, understanding, and cooperation. They contribute to a broader and deeper understanding of human behavior and the mind, and they inform theories that accommodate both individual and cultural sources of variation (Berry et al., 2002).

There are risks and liabilities as well, the foremost of which is the production of cultural knowledge that is incorrect because of flawed methodology. Cross-cultural research brings with it a host of methodological issues that go beyond monocultural studies, some of which we discuss below. To be sure, good cultural science is first and foremost good science, and many concepts that ensure the methodological rigor of any quality scientific enterprise are applicable to cross-cultural research as well. Being knowledgeable about issues unique to cross-cultural studies, however, is important because the risk of producing cultural knowledge that is incorrect or not replicable is too great if these methodological pitfalls are not understood and addressed.

Unfortunately, since the publication of the first edition of this work, Fons J. R. van de Vijver passed away. His authorship is retained here to reflect his original and ongoing contributions.

https://doi.org/10.1037/0000318-005

APA Handbook of Research Methods in Psychology, Second Edition: Vol. 1. Foundations, Planning, Measures, and Psychometrics, H. Cooper (Editor-in-Chief)

Copyright © 2023 by the American Psychological Association. All rights reserved.

Cross-cultural research also brings with it ethical issues and challenges, many of which are quite similar to those faced when conducting monocultural research (Pack-Brown & Braun Williams, 2003) using convenience samples of U.S. college students. Thus, we refer interested readers to the *Ethical Principles of Psychologists and Code of Conduct* (the Ethics Code; American Psychological Association [APA], 2017), which outlines five ethical principles for the conduct of psychologists: Beneficence and Nonmaleficence, Fidelity and Responsibility, Integrity, Justice, and Respect for People's Rights and Dignity.

This chapter is divided into two parts, first introducing readers to methodological issues that need to be addressed when conducting cross-cultural research, and then to ethical issues unique to cross-cultural research. With regard to method, many resources are available to readers that discuss the issues raised in greater depth (e.g., Matsumoto & van de Vijver, 2011); here, we consider the material only briefly. With regard to ethics, few resources are available, and we consider our work a living document, a start and definitely not an end of a dialogue.

METHODOLOGICAL ISSUES

Cross-cultural research methodology is unique in several ways, one of which is captured in the following two key terms.

Bias and Equivalence

Bias refers to differences in concept or methodology that do not have the same meaning across cultures (Matsumoto & Juang, 2023). One area of bias is measurement: A cross-cultural study shows bias if differences in measurement outcomes (categorizations or scores) do not correspond to cross-cultural differences in the construct purportedly measured by the instrument. If scores are biased, individual differences within a culture (within-culture differences) do not have the same meaning as cultural differences (between-culture differences). For example, scores on a coping questionnaire that show bias may be a valid measure of coping if compared within a single cultural group, whereas cross-cultural differences identified on the basis of this questionnaire may be influenced by other factors, such as translation issues, item inappropriateness, or differential response styles. Differences resulting from bias are not random, but rather systematic. Replication of a study with a biased instrument in similar samples will show the same biased results.

Equivalence refers to similarity in conceptual meaning and empirical methods across cultures. For example, conceptual questions may exist concerning whether diagnostic categories have the same meaning across cultures, if obsessive–compulsive disorder is similar across the cultures studied, or if people from different cultures with the same diagnosis present the same symptoms. Empirical questions also exist, for instance do scores on personality scales have the same meaning within and between cultures? With regard to measurement, bias threatens the equivalence of assessment outcomes across cultures; when bias is minimized in instruments, measurement outcomes are equivalent and comparable across cultures.

Bias and equivalence are flip sides of a coin. The absence of bias signals equivalence, and the presence of cross-cultural bias is associated with nonequivalence. Research on cross-cultural bias and equivalence highlights different issues and a joint consideration of them provides a more comprehensive view of how valid cross-cultural comparisons can be made.

Bias. Bias signals the presence of nuisance factors (Poortinga, 1989). If scores are biased, their meaning can be culture or group dependent and differences in assessment outcomes need to be accounted for, at least partially, by complimentary psychological constructs or measurement artifacts. Bias is not inherent to all instruments but arises in application of instruments in two or more cultural groups; thus, instruments may be biased when scores from specific cultural groups are compared.

We discuss three major types of bias: construct, method, and item bias (see Table 5.1 for an overview). *Construct bias* refers to differences in

TABLE 5.1
Overview of Types of Bias and Ways to Deal With It

Type and source of bias	How to deal with it?
Construct bias	
■ Only partial overlap in the definitions of the construct across cultures ■ Differential appropriateness of the behaviors associated with the construct (e.g., skills do not belong to the repertoire of one of the cultural groups) ■ Poor sampling of all relevant behaviors indicative of a construct (e.g., short instruments) ■ Incomplete coverage of the relevant aspects/facets of the construct (e.g., not all relevant domains are sampled)	■ Decentering (i.e., simultaneously developing the same instrument in several cultures) ■ Convergence approach (i.e., independent within-culture development of instruments and subsequent cross-cultural administration of all instruments) ■ Consult informants with expertise in local culture and language[a] ■ Use samples of bilingual participants[a] ■ Conduct local pilot studies (e.g., content analyses of free response questions)[a] ■ Nonstandard instrument administration (e.g., "thinking aloud")[a]
Method bias	
■ Incomparability of samples (e.g., differences in education and motivation)[b] ■ Differences in administration conditions, physical (e.g., noise) or social (e.g., group size)[b] ■ Ambiguous instructions for respondents or guidelines for research administrators[b] ■ Differential expertise of administrators[c] ■ Tester, interviewer, and observer effects (e.g., halo effects)[c] ■ Communication problems between respondent and interviewer (in the widest sense)[c] ■ Differential familiarity with stimulus materials[c] ■ Differential familiarity with response procedures[d] ■ Differential response styles (e.g., social desirability, extremity tendency, acquiescence)[d]	■ Cross-cultural comparison of nomological networks (e.g., convergent-discriminant validity studies, monotrait–multimethod studies) ■ Connotation of key phrases (e.g., similarity of meaning of key terms such as "somewhat agree") ■ Extensive training of interviewers and administrators ■ Detailed manual/protocol for administration, scoring, and interpretation ■ Detailed instructions (e.g., with adequate examples and/or exercises) ■ Include background and contextual variables (e.g., education background) ■ Gather collateral information (e.g., test-taking behavior or test attitudes) ■ Assessment of response styles ■ Conduct test–retest, training, or intervention studies
Item bias	
■ Poor translation or ambiguous items ■ Nuisance factors (e.g., items may invoke additional traits or abilities) ■ Cultural specifics (e.g., differences in connotative meaning and/or appropriateness of item content)	■ Judgmental methods (e.g., linguistic and psychological analysis) ■ Psychometric methods (e.g., differential item functioning analysis)

Note. From *Cross-Cultural Research Methods in Psychology* (pp. 23–24), by D. Matsumoto and F. J. R. van de Vijver (Eds.), 2011, Cambridge University Press. Copyright 2011 by Cambridge University Press. Reprinted with permission.
[a]Also used for dealing with method bias. [b]Sample bias. [c]Administration bias. [d]Instrument bias.

meaning of psychological concepts across cultures, and can be caused by incomplete overlap of construct-relevant behaviors, leading to construct inequivalence. An empirical example can be found in Ho's (1996) work on filial piety, defined as a psychological characteristic associated with being "a good son or daughter." The Chinese conception, which includes the expectation that children should assume the role of caretaker of elderly parents, is broader than the corresponding Western notion. An inventory of behavior related to filial piety based on the Chinese conceptualization covers aspects unrelated to a Western notion, whereas a Western-based inventory will leave important Chinese aspects uncovered. Construct bias can be caused by differential appropriateness of the behaviors associated with the construct in the different cultures.

Method bias is a label for all sources of bias resulting from cross-cultural differences in data collection methods (often described in methods section of empirical papers). Three subtypes of method bias are distinguished here, depending on whether the bias comes from the sample, administration, or instrument. Sample bias is more likely to jeopardize cross-cultural comparisons when the cultures examined differ in many respects; a large cultural distance often increases the number of alternative explanations that need to be considered. For example, a sample from the West African tribe of Burkina Faso is likely to be quite different from a sample of U.S. undergraduates (Tracy & Robins, 2008), and cultural differences are easier to obtain because of these sample differences.

Administration bias refers to differences in procedures used to administer an instrument. For example, when interviews are held in respondents' homes, physical conditions (e.g., ambient noise, presence of others) are difficult to control. Respondents may be more prepared to answer sensitive questions in a self-completion mode than in a face-to-face interview.

Instrument bias refers to systematic cultural differences in the meaning of items in instruments that confound cross-cultural comparisons; it is a common source of bias in tests. Piswanger (1975) administered a figural inductive reasoning test to high school students in Austria, Nigeria, and Togo (educated in Arabic). The most striking findings were cross-cultural differences in item difficulties related to identifying and applying rules in a horizontal direction (i.e., left to right). This was interpreted as a bias because of the different directions in writing Latin-based languages as opposed to Arabic.

Closely related to instrument bias is *item bias*, which refers to anomalies at the item level and also is called differential item functioning (Camilli & Shepard, 1994; Holland & Wainer, 1993). According to a definition widely used in education and psychology, an item is biased if respondents with the same standing on the underlying construct (e.g., they are equally intelligent) do not have the same score on the item because of different cultural meanings. Item bias can arise in various ways, such as poor item translation, ambiguities in the original item, low familiarity with or appropriateness of the item content in certain cultures, and the influence of culture-specific nuisance factors or connotations associated with item wording. For instance, Gomez et al. (2008) examined behaviors associated with oppositional defiance disorder. Australian, Malaysian Malay, and Malaysian Chinese parents had to rate their children on behaviors such as "is touchy," "argues," and "blames others." The item about being touchy was more prevalent among Malaysian parents in comparison to the other items. The authors interpreted this difference as a consequence of the lower tolerance of deviant behavior by Malaysian parents compared with Australian parents.

Equivalence. We describe four nested types of (in)equivalence that are hierarchical. Construct inequivalence refers to constructs lacking in shared meaning across cultures, which precludes comparison. Claims of construct inequivalence can be grouped into three broad subcategories, which differ in degree (partial or total). The first and strongest claim of inequivalence is found in studies that opt for a strong emic, relativistic viewpoint, which argues that psychological constructs are inextricably tied to their natural context and cannot be studied outside this context. Any cross-cultural comparison is then erroneous as psychological constructs are cross-culturally inequivalent. Some writers have argued, for example, that certain aspects of morality—definitions of morality and its domains, concepts of justice, and so on—are inextricably bound with culture, and thus cannot be understood outside a specific cultural context and thus cannot be compared across cultures (Miller, 2001; Shweder, 1999).

A second type of concept inequivalence is exemplified by psychological constructs associated with specific cultural groups, including culture-bound syndromes such as *taijin kyofusho*, a Japanese concept referring to an intense fear that one's body is discomforting or insulting for others by its appearance, smell, or movements (Kleinknecht et al., 1997; Russell, 1989; Tanaka-Matsumi, 1979). These culture-specific concepts are often marked by words that exist in one language but not in others, such as the German *schadenfreude* or the Korean concepts *dapdaphada* and *uulhada* (Schmidt-Atzert & Park, 1999). Studying these concepts across cultures would be very difficult.

The third type of concept inequivalence is empirically based and found in cross-cultural studies in which data do not show any evidence for comparability of constructs across cultures; inequivalence is the consequence of a lack of comparability of scores cross-culturally. For example, Van Haaften and van de Vijver (1996) administered Paulhus's Locus of Control Scale measuring intrapersonal, interpersonal, and sociopolitical aspects among various groups of illiterate Sahel dwellers. The three aspects could not be identified by factor analysis in any group.

The flip side of empirically based concept inequivalence is known as *structural equivalence*, which refers to whether or not an instrument administered in different cultural groups measures the same construct(s) in all groups. In operational terms, this condition requires identification of underlying dimensions (factors) in all groups, and examination of whether the instrument produced the same factor structure in all groups. When the same factor structure of an instrument is found across groups, structural equivalence is said to exist (and concept inequivalence does not). Examinations of the number and content of factors of the five-factor model of personality, for example, are attempts at demonstrating structural equivalence (McCrae et al., 2000). Parenthetically, demonstrations of structural equivalence do not necessarily imply that the same items load on the factors or that the items mean the same things across cultures; those issues are addressed by metric or measurement unit equivalence (described two paragraphs below in this same section).

Functional equivalence is a specific type of structural equivalence that refers to identity of nomological networks (i.e., associations with other constructs). A questionnaire that measures, say, openness to new cultures shows functional equivalence if it measures the same psychological constructs in each culture, as manifested in a similar pattern of convergent and divergent validity (i.e., nonzero correlations with presumably related measures and zero correlations with presumably unrelated measures).

Tests of structural equivalence are applied more often than tests of functional equivalence. The reason is not statistical or technical. With advances in statistical modeling (notably path analysis as part of structural equation modeling), tests of cross-cultural similarity of nomological networks are straightforward. However, nomological networks are often based on combinations of psychological scales and background variables, such as socioeconomic status, education, and sex. In the absence of guiding theoretical frameworks, the use of psychological scales to validate other psychological scales can easily lead to an endless regress in which each scale used for validation has to be validated (see Byrne & Matsumoto, 2021, for extended discussion).

Metric or *measurement unit equivalence* refers to whether measurement scales of instruments have the same units of measurement but a different origin (e.g., Celsius and Kelvin scales in temperature measurement). This type of equivalence assumes interval- or ratio-level scores (with the same measurement units in each culture). Measurement unit equivalence applies when a source of bias shifts the scores of different cultural groups differentially, but it does not affect the relative scores of individuals within each cultural group. For example, social desirability and stimulus familiarity influence questionnaire scores more in some cultures than in others, but they may influence individuals within groups in similar ways. When the relative contribution of both bias sources cannot be estimated, the interpretation of group comparisons of mean scores remains ambiguous.

Finally, *scalar* or *full score equivalence* assumes both an identical interval or ratio scale and an identical scale origin across cultural groups. Only in the case of scalar (or full score) equivalence can direct cross-cultural comparisons be made and conclusions drawn that average scores obtained in two or more cultures are different or equal. Beuckelaer et al. (2007) examined the equivalence of a global organizational survey measuring six work climate factors as administered across 25 countries. Using structural equation modeling, the authors found scalar equivalence only for comparisons of English-speaking countries and metric equivalence for the other countries.

Studies with cultural groups that have large cultural distances from each other are likely to be more threatened by biases and inequivalence. Studies that do not include contextual factors and that target level-oriented cultural differences also are more threatened by biases and inequivalence.

A Taxonomy of Cross-Cultural Studies

Cross-cultural studies can be characterized by the research questions addressed and designs used to address them (see also van de Vijver, 2009). One distinction is between exploratory and hypothesis testing studies. Exploratory studies attempt to increase our understanding of cross-cultural differences by documenting similarities and differences. Most often these involve quasi-experimental designs in which two or more groups are compared on some target variable(s) of interest.

Researchers tend to stay "close to the data" in exploratory studies. Hypothesis-testing studies make larger inferential jumps by testing theories of cross-cultural similarities and differences. Unfortunately, the validity of these inferential jumps is often threatened by cross-cultural biases and inequivalence.

The methodological strengths and weaknesses of exploratory and hypothesis testing studies mirror each other. The main strength of exploratory studies is their broad scope for identifying cross-cultural similarities and differences, which is particularly important in under-researched domains or in understudied populations. The main weakness of such studies is their limited capability to address the causes of the observed differences. The focused search for similarities and differences in hypothesis-testing studies leads to more substantial contribution to theory development and explicit attempts to deal with rival explanations, but such searches are less likely to discover interesting differences outside of the realm of the theory tested. These studies are likely to involve experiments manipulating key variables considered to be the active cultural ingredients that produce differences in the first place, or unpackaging studies, which involve such variables as covariates or mediators in quasi-experimental designs.

Hypothesis testing studies often include contextual factors in their design. Contextual factors may involve characteristics of the participants (such as socioeconomic status, education, and age) or their cultures (such as economic development and religious institutions). From a methodological perspective, contextual factors involve any variable that can explain, partly or fully, observed cross-cultural differences (Poortinga et al., 1987). Including such factors in a study will enhance its validity and help rule out the influence of biases and inequivalence because an evaluation of their influence can help to (dis)confirm their role in accounting for the cultural differences observed. For example, administering a measure of response styles can evaluate to what extent cross-cultural differences on extroversion are influenced by these styles.

Cross-cultural studies can also be distinguished by what is compared across cultures. Structure-oriented studies involve comparisons of constructs (is depression conceptualized in the same way across cultures?), their structures (can depression be assessed by the same constituent elements in different cultures?), or their associations with other constructs (do depression and anxiety have the same relationship in all countries?). Structure-oriented studies focus on associations among variables and attempt to identify similarities and differences in these associations across cultures. Level-oriented studies involve comparisons of mean scores (do individuals from different cultures show the same level of depression?).

From a methodological perspective, structure-oriented studies are simpler than level-oriented studies, which usually are more open to alternative interpretations. For example, suppose that a neuroticism questionnaire has been administered in two countries and that the two countries differ in extremity scoring (i.e., the use of extreme values on the scales). If all items are phrased in the same direction (which is often the case in personality measurement), cross-cultural differences in extremity scoring will be confounded with potentially valid differences in neuroticism. Consequently, cross-cultural differences in means are difficult to interpret. As long as extremity scoring affects only the item means and leaves item correlations and covariances unchanged, the factor structure, which often is examined in structure-oriented studies, will not be affected.

Cross-cultural research can also be distinguished by their level of analysis. Individual-level studies are the typical type of study in which individual participants' data are the units of analysis. Ecological- or cultural-level studies use countries or cultural groups as units of analysis; data may be obtained from individuals, but their means are used as data points in analyses. Country data can also be obtained from other aggregated sources (e.g., population statistics, average temperature or rainfall).

Hofstede's (1980, 2001, 2011) classic work is an example of an ecological level study. Raw data came from more than 117,000 employees of a multinational business organization spanning over 20 languages and seven occupational levels (Hofstede, 2001). Respondents completed a 160-item questionnaire, of which 63 were related to work values. Hofstede conducted analyses on country means of the 63 items and generated the well-known cultural value dimensions of Individualism versus Collectivism, Power Distance, Uncertainty Avoidance, Masculinity versus Femininity, Long- versus Short-term Orientation, and Indulgence versus Restraint.

Findings from ecological-level studies do not necessarily translate to individual-level phenomena, and vice versa, and interpreting findings from one level to another is known as the ecological fallacy (Campbell, 1958). The classic work in this field is Robinson's (1950) study, which demonstrated that even though a small, positive correlation (0.118) existed between foreign birth and illiteracy when individual-level data were analyzed, strong negative correlations were obtained when data were aggregated across individuals by region (−0.619) or state (−0.526). Similar types of differences in findings have been obtained in many other areas such as individualistic versus collectivistic self-construals (Harb & Smith, 2008; Hardin, 2006; Hardin et al., 2004).

Finally, individual- and cultural-level data can be combined in multilevel studies, which use data from both levels and incorporate the use of multilevel modeling statistics that examine the association of data at one level to data at another. A multilevel study was used to demonstrate that country-levels of self-directedness and civility moderated the associations of financial satisfaction and trust of in-group members to subjective well-being (Lun & Bond, 2016). Another examined 51 years of data on individualistic values and practices across 78 countries and demonstrated that individualism is on the rise around the world and cultural differences are linked primarily to changes in socioeconomic status (Santos et al., 2017).

A Priori Procedures to Deal With Bias

Researchers can deal with the various issues of bias and inequivalence before they start their research (a priori procedures) and after data have been collected (a posteriori procedures). These are not either–or alternatives; optimally, researchers can and should apply both procedures. Here, we discuss various issues that can be addressed in both.

Identifying the appropriate research question. By far the most important part of any study, cross-cultural or not, is knowing what research questions to ask in the first place. Because cultural differences are relatively easy to obtain, especially with greater cultural distances between groups compared, researchers should remember that the purpose of conducting research is to contribute to a body of knowledge (the literature), and any consideration of research designs starts with a comprehensive and functional knowledge of that literature so that research questions and studies address gaps in that knowledge and contribute back to the literature. When researchers focus on designing studies without considering adequately what research question should be addressed, they run the risk of obtaining findings that are not novel or insightful. Sophisticated statistical techniques and elegant research designs cannot salvage a lack of contribution.

Designing cross-cultural studies. Identifying gaps in literature leads to research questions to be addressed in a study, which in turn leads to questions about research methodology. Questions related to the taxonomy above apply here: Is the study exploratory or hypothesis testing? Should it include contextual variables? Is it structure- or level-oriented? No one study can do everything, and in our opinion, doing something of limited scope very well is better than conducting a study that addresses a lot not so well.

The field has gone much beyond the need to merely document differences between two or more cultures on any psychological variable. Because of cultural distances and the ease of data collection nowadays, documenting differences on anything is fairly easy. Instead, a major challenge that cross-cultural researchers face today concerns how to isolate cultural sources of such differences, and to identify cultural (vs. noncultural) ingredients that produced those differences. The empirical documentation of the contribution of those cultural ingredients to differences are what cross-cultural research designs need to pay close attention to (see Matsumoto & Yoo, 2006, for a more complete discussion of theoretical and empirical issues). For example, is the source of the differences to be explained cultural or not? Examining this question forces researchers to have a definition of what culture is and to find ways of objectively measuring it.

Once cultural ingredients that produce differences are hypothesized, a level-of-analysis issue arises. Cultural variables exist on group and individual levels. Studies can be entirely on the individual or cultural level or can involve a mixture of the two in varying degrees with multiple levels. Different variables at different levels of analysis bring with them different theoretical and methodological implications and require different interpretations back to the research literature. When individual-level cultural variables are incorporated in a study, researchers need to distinguish between them and noncultural variables on the individual level such as personality. Variables are not cultural just because researchers declare them so; rationales based on theory and data are needed.

Another question that researchers must face concerns their theoretical model of how things work. A commonly held view is that culture produces differences in a top-down manner, a theoretical bias held by many (i.e., that culture "influences" or "affects" X). For example, many cultural differences in the literature are interpreted using the Individualism versus Collectivism (IC) framework (Hofstede, 2001; Triandis, 1995), such that cultural differences on XXX (insert psychological variable of interest) between cultures A and B were influenced by IC differences between the cultures. Presumably, the individualistic nature of culture A "caused" a certain score whereas the collectivistic nature of culture B "caused" a different score, again presumably through cultural learning that resulted in the differences observed. But how do we know that to be true, and how does one demonstrate that empirically? Individual-level psychological processes and behavior may affect culture in a bottom-up fashion, in which behavior or psychological traits emerge organically as adaptations to the environment and not through macro-level cultural learning, and concepts such as IC may be conceptual abstractions produced to explain a more organic process. Or, both top-down and bottom-up processes occur simultaneously. Regardless of one's theoretical perspective, researchers should adopt research designs that are commensurate with their beliefs and models.

Unpackaging studies. Cross-cultural research is largely based on quasi-experimental designs, and as such, when differences are found, drawing conclusions about the source of those differences is impossible. When cross-cultural scientists draw such conclusions in quasi-experimental designs, this mistaken inference is known as the cultural attribution fallacy (Matsumoto & Yoo, 2006). One way to address this limitation in quasi-experimental designs is to include context variables that operationalize meaningful dimensions of culture and then empirically test the degree to which those variables account for cultural differences. Quasi-experimental designs that include context variables are known as unpackaging studies.

Bond and van de Vijver (2011) discussed the nature of these studies and how unpackaging variables can be included in cross-cultural research. Statistical techniques exist (e.g., mediation analyses) that allow researchers to justify empirically the degree to which unpackaging variables account for cultural differences. For instance, Singelis et al. (1999) demonstrated that cultural differences in an ability to be embarrassed could be explained by independent versus interdependent self-construals.

Dealing with language and translations. Of the methodological issues that face cultural scientists, none is more unique to cross-cultural research than the fact that cross-cultural studies often require the collection of data in two or more linguistic groups. A major issue that faces cross-cultural researchers concerns how to deal with language, especially in terms of the instruments and procedures of a study. As such, issues concerning equivalence between the languages used in the study become of paramount importance. Even if words are translated into different languages, the resulting translations may not be equivalent to the originals. Hambleton and Zenisky (2011) described 25 criteria with which to evaluate the adequacy of translations done for cross-cultural research, spanning such topics as general translation questions, item format and appearance, grammar and phrasing, passages and other item-relevant stimulus materials, and cultural relevance or specificity. The evaluation sheet offered to readers is an especially useful tool for researchers.

Sampling. When doing cross-cultural work, accessing participants from a local introductory psychology participant pool is often impossible (and may be undesirable). Thus, another way in which issues concerning equivalence and bias affect cross-cultural work is sampling. Samples across cultures easily differ on many demographic characteristics, and these demographics often confound any observed differences; thus, conclusions about observed differences on psychological variables may need to be interpreted in terms of relevant background characteristics, such as differences in education instead of cultural differences. Boehnke et al. (2011) discussed issues concerning sampling on both individual and cultural levels and provided guidelines for researchers that allow for empirically justified conclusions to be drawn, while at the same time being sensitive to particular needs and issues associated with samples from different cultures.

Designing questions and scales. Another way in which people of different cultures may differ is in the use of response scales. Although early cross-cultural research viewed different cultural biases in the use of scales as nuisance variables that needed to be controlled, theoretical and empirical perspectives today view such biases as potentially important aspects of culture and personality (Smith, 2004). Johnson et al. (2011) discussed these issues, paying close attention to concerns about socially desirable responding, acquiescence, and extreme responding, and provided useful guidelines and suggestions for cultural scientists.

A Posteriori Procedures to Deal With Bias

Researchers comparing cultures can take steps after data are collected to address measurement equivalence. Multiple data analytic methods are available to investigate and establish structural equivalence in structure- and level-oriented studies (Byrne & Matsumoto, 2021; Fischer & Fontaine, 2011; Sireci, 2011). For structural-oriented studies, techniques include multidimensional scaling, principal component analysis, exploratory factor analysis, and confirmatory factor analysis; for level-oriented studies, techniques include delta plots, standardization, Mantel-Haenszel, item response theory, likelihood ratio tests, and logistic regression.

As mentioned earlier, multilevel studies involve data at multiple levels that are nested (e.g., data from individuals with specific personalities collected in specific situations, within specific cultures located in specific ecologies). Multilevel data allow for the possibility of analyzing associations among data at different levels (provided they were assessed), allowing researchers to document empirically associations between ecological, cultural, individual, and situational variables and individual-level means or associations among variables. In recent years, techniques for analyzing multilevel data have blossomed and can be used if data are available from large numbers of cultures. In particular, multilevel random coefficient models may be appropriate for handling the types of nested data in cross-cultural research, providing numerous statistical advantages over statistical techniques based on ordinary least squares analyses. We encourage researchers to take advantage of such techniques (Nezlek, 2011; and see Matsumoto et al., 2007a, for an example).

Obtaining statistically significant results in cross-cultural research is fairly easy because of the relative ease with which researchers can often obtain large sample sizes. Statistical significance, however, does not necessarily reflect practical importance in the real world, and applying group differences globally to individuals can facilitate unnecessary stereotypes. Researchers can supplement their interpretations of findings with appropriate measures of effect size. Matsumoto and colleagues (Matsumoto et al., 2001, 2011) have identified several effect size measures that may be especially useful in cross-cultural research, especially when accompanied by confidence intervals. These effect sizes include the standardized difference between two sample means, probability of superiority, eta squared, and partial omega squared. Interpretations of the meaning of cross-cultural differences always should be made on the basis of the appropriate effect size estimates.

ETHICAL ISSUES IN CROSS-CULTURAL RESEARCH

Cross-cultural research is associated with a host of ethical issues that researchers should be aware of. In this section, we discuss issues concerning design, participation, sensitive topics, interpretation of findings, and impact of research on communities.

Ethical Issues Regarding Design

As with all research, issues related to design are fundamental and must be considered before contact is initiated with human participants and data collected.

Awareness of stereotypes. One of the biggest ethical dilemmas facing cross-cultural researchers is the potential for their findings to be used to vindicate stereotypes (overgeneralized attitudes or beliefs) about cultural groups. In our view, vindication is quite different from testing the accuracy of stereotypes. The latter involves researchers' conscious knowledge of stereotypes and their efforts to test the validity and boundaries of these stereotypes; presumably, such conscious knowledge also would inform researchers of the need to be aware of their potential influence on the research process. Vindication refers to researchers' ignorance of such stereotypes, and thus their potential lack of awareness of how these stereotypes may affect their decisions about research unconsciously. Researchers' early understanding of this issue and utilization of research designs that can minimize the possibility of stereotypes to affect decisions is paramount.

Cultural informants. The involvement of cultural informants, at least on the level of advisors and at best on the level of collaborators, is a must in cross-cultural research. Cultural informants and collaborators should be engaged from the beginning of any study, providing needed advice and guidance about whether to conduct the study, appropriateness of the theory and hypotheses to be tested, and the adequacy and appropriateness of the research design.

The involvement of cultural informants can help to avoid many of the ethical issues discussed in this section as well as cultural bias in interpreting results, described later. We strongly encourage researchers to seek out such informants or collaborators at the earliest stages of their studies and to work collaboratively with them throughout the research process. Most scientific organizations such as the APA have guidelines or criteria for authorship, and we encourage researchers to ensure that informants contribute their share of intellectual material to the research to gain authorship.

Ethical Issues Regarding Participation

Not all participants around the world are recruited and participate in research in the same way as those in the United States. In this section, we discuss issues related to recruitment, consent, and confidentiality.

Recruitment. In the United States, participants in most psychology studies are recruited from undergraduate psychology participant pools, mostly from introductory psychology classes, who view descriptions of studies and enroll voluntarily and of their free will. In many cases, this process is administered by software that can be accessed by any computer connected to the internet. Participants have minimal intervention by anyone else asking for their participation. Participation in research is a process well known to students in many U.S. universities.

But many other countries do not have an undergraduate participant pool, and different procedures are used to recruit participants. Oftentimes, course instructors request their students to participate, which may make students may feel compelled to participate in a study that they otherwise would not choose voluntarily because of the researcher's perceived status or possible consequences for noncompliance to the requesting instructor. This may border on coercion or undue influence and is an ethical dilemma (in addition to concerns about data quality). Researchers should avoid any recruitment procedures that involve actual or perceived coercion to participants.

Informed consent. In the United States, conducting research involving human participants without first receiving approval from an institutional review board (IRB) is impossible. IRB guidelines require researchers to obtain consent from participants before collecting most types of data. Most countries have procedures and prescriptions that are less elaborate than those in the United States. In some places, not only is obtaining an IRB approval unnecessary but so is obtaining consent from human participants. This raises ethical dilemmas for researchers: Do we obtain consent from participants in cultures in which obtaining consent is not necessary or even frowned upon? Will all participants understand the concept of consent in the same way? What does consent mean in different cultures and who is authorized to give and obtain consent? If we do obtain consent from our participants, how do we obtain it? Many participants in many cultures likely will view consent documents with skepticism or fear. Will they understand such a process and feel comfortable about giving consent?

Regardless of whether obtaining consent is necessary, we believe that researchers should strive to ensure that (a) informed consent is obtained and understood by participants, (b) invasion of privacy is minimized, and (c) consent is obtained only in a manner that minimizes coercion or undue influence. How can this process be done in a culturally competent manner?

In our experience, many of the same consent procedures can be utilized around the world, if delivered in a skillful and culturally competent manner by research teams. This manner involves a truthful and honest description of study procedures and associated risks and benefits, combined with genuine interest in participants and their welfare. If written consent is required, forms need to be translated in a competent and culturally appropriate manner. Involving cultural informants as collaborators or experimenters can help ensure that researchers are making the most diligent of efforts in this difficult ethical area of research. Moreover, cultural informants can evaluate what kind of information should be emphasized; for example, consent forms can contain abstruse legalese that may be useful to define the rights and duties of the parties but that is not meaningful to participants unfamiliar with such legalese. Informed consent issues are more likely to arise if a Western institution sponsors a study and the IRB of the country that provides the funds and/or the country in which the study is conducted do not have similar requirements regarding approvals.

Confidentiality. In the United States, we have many rules, regulations, and guidelines concerning the need to maintain confidentiality of data sources. Such rules do not exist in many other countries, and collaborators or cultural informants may not be aware of such needs or procedures. Even though a country may not have such rules or regulations, data should be kept confidential, and access given only to the research team. Participants in other countries may worry about who has access to their data, especially if they have made statements about issues that are politically, socially, or morally sensitive in their cultures. Some researchers may consider smuggling data out of a country because of this worry, but doing so would raise its own ethical concerns. Clearly, participants in research should be free of such anxiety concerning the use of their data when they provide it and afterward, and researchers should take extra precautions to ensure that this is indeed the case.

Sensitive Topics

When conducting cross-cultural research, being aware of sensitive topics and issues is important and raise interesting ethical problems for researchers (Trimble & Fischer, 2005). We mention three of these topics to raise awareness: sex and sexuality, human rights issues, and deception.

Sex and sexuality. The United States and much of Western and Northern Europe are cultures in which sex and sexuality issues can be discussed relatively openly in everyday discourse; thus, conducting research on sex and sexuality is relatively easier in these cultures. In many other cultures of the world, however, these topics are taboo, especially among youth or women. Researchers must exercise caution when conducting research on these topics in cultures in which they are taboo. Cross-cultural differences in scores on items or scales measuring sex-related topics may not be difficult to find, but are difficult to interpret. The same is true of drug use.

In some cultures, LGBTQ issues are severe taboos, punished in some societies by social isolation, physical mistreatment, and in some cases even death. Researchers studying LGBTQ issues in such cultures may be subject to the same kinds of repercussions, which strongly prohibit the generation of much useful research information in those cultures. Additionally, obtaining individuals to volunteer to participate in such studies is difficult for fear of their safety. In such cultures, added anxiety may exist that the research project itself is part of an organized activity, either by activist groups or government, to identify LGBTQ individuals. Such concerns exist not only for people who live in those cultures but also for individuals who emigrate to other countries; they may still fear for their lives. Thus, for the same reasons, conducting such a study on LGBTQ immigrants in the United States or other countries may be difficult. We have conducted such studies (Mireshghi & Matsumoto, 2008) and they raise interesting and important questions concerning recruitment and consent.

Even if issues concerning sex and sexuality are not a direct focus of the study, they may be indirectly related because of questions concerning these issues on standard personality questionnaires. For example, two items on the Intercultural Adjustment Potential Scale, a scale designed to assess the potential to adjust to a multicultural environment (Matsumoto et al., 2007b), are "sex education is a good thing" and "when a man is with a woman, he is usually thinking of sex." Despite the fact that these and many other items are designed to indirectly tap personality constructs and are imbedded within literally tens or hundreds of other items, they may be taboo in certain cultures. We have conducted studies in which cultural informants have reviewed the items and recommended or required deletion of these questions as well as items that ask about attitudes concerning drugs.

Human rights issues. Cultures differ considerably on many practices and issues that U.S. citizens often find difficult to understand and even offensive. These include abortion attitudes and practices, circumcision or female genital mutilation, and the punishment of women accused of premarital sex or extramarital affairs. (Conversely, many cultures find U.S. attitudes and practices offensive as well.) These are important social issues that are worthy of study; yet, as with issues concerning sex and sexuality, they may be taboo and difficult if not impossible to study in other cultures, and even within the United States.

Another consideration is the track record of countries in which researchers wish to work with regard to human rights issues. Many countries have been accused of human rights violations, and how these violations have been and are dealt with, in some cases, may form part of an important context within which research may occur. Researchers should know about these issues and gauge the degree to which they may affect the research and whether doing the research in the first place is wise.

Deception. Deception is used in many studies in the United States, and when used, it must gain IRB approval so that its use does not introduce undue risks to participants. Participants must be fully debriefed about deception at the end of a study and must give their informed consent to use the data. In countries without IRBs, however, conducting research that involves deception is easier, and care should be taken by engaging cultural informants as collaborators who can gauge the necessity of the deception, by enacting procedures that ensure the full debriefing of the participants, and by obtaining consent to preserve individual participant integrity.

Studying sensitive topics in a culturally insensitive manner is likely to yield invalid results, thus posing a methodological dilemma. It also has the potential to treat participants and cultures in a disrespectful manner, and this, too, is an ethical problem. We do not argue for a ban on research on sensitive topics, but we do suggest that such research be undertaken with care, precision, and sensitivity for the topics studied in regard to the cultures in question.

Ethical Issues Regarding Interpretations
Cultural biases. Researchers should be aware that they may interpret findings through their own cultural filters, and these biases can affect their interpretations to varying degrees. For example, if a mean response for Americans on a rating scale is 6.0 and the mean for Hong Kong Chinese is 4.0, one interpretation is that the Americans scored higher on the scale, while the Hong Kong Chinese suppressed their responses and avoided using the extremes of the scale. But how do we know the Chinese are suppressing their responses? What if Americans exaggerated their responses? What if the Chinese mean response of 4.0 is actually more "correct," and the American response is inaccurate? What if we surveyed the rest of the world and found that the overall mean was 3.0, suggesting that both the Chinese and the Americans inflated their ratings? In other words, the interpretation that the Chinese are suppressing their responses is made on the basis of an implicit assumption that U.S. data are correct and that we can use our cultural frame to interpret the results.

Whenever researchers make a value judgment of a finding, it may be bound by cultural bias. Interpretations of good or bad, right or wrong, suppressing or exaggerating, important or not are all value interpretations that may be made in a cross-cultural study. These interpretations may reflect the value orientations of the researchers as much as the cultures included in the study. As researchers, we may make those interpretations without giving them second thought—and without malicious intent—only because we are so accustomed to seeing the world in a certain way. As consumers of research, we may agree with such interpretations when they agree with the ways we have learned to understand and view the world, and we often will do so unconsciously.

Potential dangers. Documenting differences across cultures may pose ethical dilemmas because those documented differences can be used to perpetuate stereotypes. For example, demonstrating differences between Americans and South Koreans, or European Americans and African Americans, is fairly easy, and making statements that overgeneralize those findings to all members of those groups is potentially damaging because doing so essentially pigeonholes individuals into social categories and applies those findings to everyone in those groups. That is, cross-cultural research (or more precisely, the incorrect interpretation of cross-cultural data) can be used to ignore large degrees of individual differences in human behavior, and cross-cultural researchers need to be aware of this potential when designing their studies.

Findings from cross-cultural comparisons also can be used to oppress members of certain groups. A good example is the apartheid regime in South Africa. Tests designed in the Western Hemisphere were administered to different cultural groups without any consideration for the massive education, cultural, and linguistic differences in the population (Meiring et al., 2005). After the abolishment of apartheid in 1994, many Blacks in South Africa treated psychological testing with suspicion because it had become associated with the justification of their unfair treatment in society. The interpretation of African American differences in intelligence also has spurred a great debate on such issues in the United States in the past 40 years (Jacoby et al., 1995; Jensen, 1969).

Researchers thus need to be aware that findings could be used in these ways and have the obligation to take active steps to avoid misuse of their findings. This obligation starts with asking the right research questions, ensuring the tempered and nuanced interpretation of findings, and incorporating information not only about between- but also about within-group differences in their data (e.g., by using appropriate effect size statistics and interpreting data in relation to these statistics; see the discussion above). This obligation also extends to correcting misinterpretations of one's findings by others who cite one's research.

Overgeneralization of findings is especially easy in quasi-experimental designs that do not include contextual variables that can unpack the nature and source of cultural differences (i.e., exploratory studies). As mentioned above, these designs facilitate researchers in committing cultural attribution fallacies. Documenting meaningful differences among cultures is important, but so too is researchers' awareness of limitations of such designs in contributing to knowledge about sources of such differences. For these reasons, cross-cultural researchers should consider designs that go beyond the mere documentation of differences and attempt to isolate cultural ingredients that account for the differences, either through experimentation or unpackaging studies.

Impact of Research on the Community

A focus on the ecology of individual participants in research and designing research and interventions at the community level suggest a long-term commitment to the locale as part of the research process. So-called one-shot or safari approaches to community-based research should be discouraged, including the low probability that such approaches would leave positive effects after the project ends or the grant money runs out. Researchers doing work in other countries and cultures should be attuned to how research can make positive impacts on the lives in the community because many other countries do not have the reciprocal cycle of access benefit that exists in the United States.

Research also must avoid actions, procedures, and interactive styles that violate local customs and understandings of the community. Our goals are for understanding and learning to occur—not cultural faux pas because of our lack of education of another culture. Incidences of this nature can be tempered by positive learning interactions with cultural experts and individual study of customs and norms. At every phase of research, including the consent process, sensitivity and attention should be given to the cultural ethos and eidos of the community.

CONCLUSION

In this chapter, we have discussed basic issues concerning cross-cultural research methodology and ethical issues associated with cross-cultural research. Undoubtedly, we have raised more questions than provided answers. In many cases, the answers for many of the issues reside in local cultural communities and not in one-size-fits-all approaches to the professional and ethical conduct of research in different cultures. Our purpose has been first and foremost to raise awareness of the complex issues that face cross-cultural researchers. Thus, this discussion should serve as the start, not the end, of a dialogue concerning cross-cultural research methodology.

References

American Psychological Association. (2017). *Ethical principles of psychologists and code of conduct* (2002, Amended June 1, 2010, with the 2016 Amendment to Standard 3.04). https://www.apa.org/ethics/code/ethics-code-2017.pdf

Berry, J. W., Poortinga, Y. H., Segall, M. H., & Dasen, P. R. (2002). *Cross-cultural psychology: Research and applications* (2nd ed.). Cambridge University Press.

Beuckelaer, A., Lievens, F., & Swinnen, G. (2007). Measurement equivalence in the conduct of a global organizational survey across countries in six cultural regions. *Journal of Occupational and Organizational Psychology, 80*(4), 575–600. https://doi.org/10.1348/096317907X173421

Boehnke, K., Lietz, P., Schreier, M., & Wilhelm, A. (2011). Sampling: The selection of cases for culturally comparative psychological research. In D. Matsumoto & F. J. R. van de Vijver (Eds.), *Cross-cultural research methods in psychology* (pp. 101–129). Cambridge University Press.

Bond, M. H., & van de Vijver, F. J. R. (2011). Making scientific sense of cultural differences in psychological outcomes: Unpackaging the magnum mysteriosum. In D. Matsumoto & F. J. R. van de Vijver (Eds.), *Cross-cultural research methods in psychology* (pp. 75–100). Cambridge University Press.

Byrne, B. M., & Matsumoto, D. (2021). The evolution of multigroup comparison testing across culture: Past, present, and future perspectives. In B. G. Adams & M. Bender (Eds.), *Methods make it or break it: The role of assessment in culture and psychology* (pp. 296–318). Cambridge University Press. https://doi.org/10.1017/9781108675475.015

Camilli, G., & Shepard, L. A. (1994). *Methods for identifying biased test items*. SAGE.

Campbell, D. T. (1958). Common fate, similarity, and other indices of the status of aggregates of person as social entities. *Behavioral Science, 3*(1), 14–25. https://doi.org/10.1002/bs.3830030103

Campbell, D. T. (1961). The mutual methodological relevance of anthropology and psychology. In F. L. Hsu (Ed.), *Psychological anthropology* (pp. 333–352). Dorsey.

Fischer, R., & Fontaine, J. R. J. (2011). Methods for investigating structural equivalence. In D. Matsumoto & F. J. R. van de Vijver (Eds.), *Cross-cultural research methods in psychology* (pp. 179–215). Cambridge University Press.

Gomez, R., Burns, G. L., & Walsh, J. A. (2008). Parent ratings of the oppositional defiant disorder symptoms: Item response theory analyses of cross-national and cross-racial invariance. *Journal of Psychopathology and Behavioral Assessment, 30*(1), 10–19. https://doi.org/10.1007/s10862-007-9071-z

Hambleton, R. K., & Zenisky, A. L. (2011). Translating and adapting tests for cross-cultural assessments. In D. Matsumoto & F. J. R. van de Vijver (Eds.), *Cross-cultural research methods in psychology* (pp. 46–74). Cambridge University Press.

Harb, C., & Smith, P. B. (2008). Self-construals across cultures: Beyond Independence-Interdependence. *Journal of Cross-Cultural Psychology, 39*(2), 178–197. https://doi.org/10.1177/0022022107313861

Hardin, E. E. (2006). Convergent evidence for the multidimensionality of self construal. *Journal of Cross-Cultural Psychology, 37*(5), 516–521. https://doi.org/10.1177/0022022106290475

Hardin, E. E., Leong, F. T. L., & Bhagwat, A. A. (2004). Factor structure of the Self-Construal Scale revisited: Implications for the multidimensionality of self-construal. *Journal of Cross-Cultural Psychology, 35*(3), 327–345. https://doi.org/10.1177/0022022104264125

Heine, S. J., Lehman, D. R., Ide, E., Leung, C., Kitayama, S., Takata, T., & Matsumoto, H. (2001). Divergent consequences of success and failure in Japan and North America: An investigation of self-improving motivations and malleable selves. *Journal of Personality and Social Psychology, 81*(4), 599–615. https://doi.org/10.1037/0022-3514.81.4.599

Ho, D. Y. F. (1996). Filial piety and its psychological consequences. In M. H. Bond (Ed.), *The handbook of Chinese psychology* (pp. 155–165). Oxford University Press.

Hofstede, G. H. (1980). *Culture's consequences: International differences in work-related values*. SAGE Publications.

Hofstede, G. H. (2001). *Culture's consequences: Comparing values, behaviors, institutions and organizations across nations* (2nd ed.). Sage Publications.

Hofstede, G. H. (2011). Dimensionalizing cultures: The Hofstede model in context. *Online Readings in Psychology and Culture, 2*(1). https://doi.org/10.9707/2307-0919.1014

Holland, P. W., & Wainer, H. (Eds.). (1993). *Differential item functioning*. Erlbaum.

Jacoby, R., Glauberman, N., & Herrnstein, R. J. (1995). *The bell curve debate: History, documents, opinions*. Times Books.

Jensen, A. R. (1969). How much can we boost IQ and scholastic achievement? *Harvard Educational Review, 39*(1), 1–123. https://doi.org/10.17763/haer.39.1.l3u15956627424k7

Johnson, T., Shavitt, S., & Holbrook, A. (2011). Survey response styles across cultures. In D. Matsumoto & F. J. R. van de Vijver (Eds.), *Cross-cultural research methods in psychology* (pp. 130–176). Cambridge University Press.

Kitayama, S., Mesquita, B., & Karasawa, M. (2006). Cultural affordances and emotional experience: Socially engaging and disengaging emotions in Japan and the United States. *Journal of Personality and Social Psychology, 91*(5), 890–903. https://doi.org/10.1037/0022-3514.91.5.890

Kleinknecht, R. A., Dinnel, D. L., Kleinknecht, E. E., Hiruma, N., & Harada, N. (1997). Cultural factors in social anxiety: A comparison of social phobia symptoms and Taijin kyofusho. *Journal of Anxiety Disorders, 11*(2), 157–177. https://doi.org/10.1016/S0887-6185(97)00004-2

Lun, V. M.-C., & Bond, M. H. (2016). Achieving subjective well-being around the world: The moderating influence of gender, age and national goals for socializing children. *Journal of Happiness Studies, 17*(2), 587–608. https://doi.org/10.1007/s10902-015-9614-z

Markus, H. R., Uchida, Y., Omoregie, H., Townsend, S. S. M., & Kitayama, S. (2006). Going for the gold. Models of agency in Japanese and American contexts. *Psychological Science, 17*(2), 103–112. https://doi.org/10.1111/j.1467-9280.2006.01672.x

Matsumoto, D., Grissom, R., & Dinnel, D. (2001). Do between-culture differences really mean that people are different? A look at some measures of cultural effect size. *Journal of Cross-Cultural Psychology, 32*(4), 478–490. https://doi.org/10.1177/0022022101032004007

Matsumoto, D., & Juang, L. P. (2023). *Culture and psychology* (7th ed.). Cengage Learning.

Matsumoto, D., Kim, J. J., Grissom, R. J., & Dinnel, D. L. (2011). Effect sizes in cross-cultural research. In D. Matsumoto & F. J. R. van de Vijver (Eds.), *Cross-cultural research methods in psychology* (pp. 244–272). Cambridge University Press.

Matsumoto, D., Nezlek, J. B., & Koopmann, B. (2007a). Evidence for universality in phenomenological emotion response system coherence. *Emotion, 7*(1), 57–67. https://doi.org/10.1037/1528-3542.7.1.57

Matsumoto, D., & van de Vijver, F. J. R. (2011). *Cross-cultural research methods in psychology*. Cambridge University Press.

Matsumoto, D., & Yoo, S. H. (2006). Toward a new generation of cross-cultural research. *Perspectives on Psychological Science, 1*(3), 234–250. https://doi.org/10.1111/j.1745-6916.2006.00014.x

Matsumoto, D., Yoo, S. H., & LeRoux, J. A. (2007b). Emotion and intercultural communication. In H. Kotthoff & H. Spencer-Oatley (Eds.), *Handbook of applied linguistics: Vol. 7. Intercultural communication* (pp. 77–98). Mouton de Gruyter.

McCrae, R. R., Costa, P. T., Jr., Ostendorf, F., Angleitner, A., Hrebíčková, M., Avia, M. D., Sanz, J., Sánchez-Bernardos, M. L., Kusdil, M. E., Woodfield, R., Saunders, P. R., & Smith, P. B. (2000). Nature over nurture: Temperament, personality, and life span development. *Journal of Personality and Social Psychology, 78*(1), 173–186. https://doi.org/10.1037/0022-3514.78.1.173

Meiring, D., van de Vijver, F. J. R., Rothmann, S., & Barrick, M. R. (2005). Construct, item, and method bias of cognitive and personality tests in South Africa. *SA Journal of Industrial Psychology, 31*(1), 1–8. https://doi.org/10.4102/sajip.v31i1.182

Miller, J. G. (2001). Culture and moral development. In D. Matsumoto (Ed.), *Handbook of culture and psychology* (pp. 151–170). Oxford University Press.

Mireshghi, S. I., & Matsumoto, D. (2008). Perceived cultural attitudes toward homosexuality and their effects on Iranian and American sexual minorities. *Cultural Diversity and Ethnic Minority Psychology, 14*(4), 372–376. https://doi.org/10.1037/a0012920

Nezlek, J. (2011). Multilevel modeling. In D. Matsumoto & F. J. R. van de Vijver (Eds.), *Cross-cultural research methods in psychology* (pp. 299–347). Cambridge University Press.

Pack-Brown, S. P., & Braun Williams, C. (2003). *Ethics in a multicultural context*. Sage. https://doi.org/10.4135/9781452231709

Piswanger, K. (1975). Interkulturelle Vergleiche mit dem Matrizentest von Formann [Cross-cultural comparisons with Formann's Matrices Test]. Unpublished doctoral dissertation, University of Vienna, Vienna, Austria.

Poortinga, Y. H. (1989). Equivalence of cross-cultural data: An overview of basic issues. *International Journal of Psychology, 24*(6), 737–756. https://doi.org/10.1080/00207598908247842

Poortinga, Y. H., van de Vijver, F. J. R., Joe, R. C., & van de Koppel, J. M. H. (1987). Peeling the onion called culture: A synopsis. In C. Kagitcibasi (Ed.), *Growth and progress in cross-cultural psychology* (pp. 22–34). Swets North America.

Robinson, W. S. (1950). Ecological correlations and the behavior of individuals. *American Sociological Review, 15*(3), 351–357. https://doi.org/10.2307/2087176

Russell, J. G. (1989). Anxiety disorders in Japan: A review of the Japanese literature on *shinkeishitsu* and *taijinkyofusho*. *Culture, Medicine and Psychiatry, 13*(4), 391–403. https://doi.org/10.1007/BF00052047

Santos, H. C., Varnum, M. E. W., & Grossmann, I. (2017). Global increases in individualism. *Psychological Science, 28*(9), 1228–1239. https://doi.org/10.1177/0956797617700622

Schmidt-Atzert, L., & Park, H.-S. (1999). The Korean concepts of *Dapdaphada* and *Uulhada*: A cross-cultural study of the meaning of emotions. *Journal of Cross-Cultural Psychology, 30*(5), 646–654. https://doi.org/10.1177/0022022199030005006

Shweder, R. A. (1999). Why cultural psychology? *Ethos, 27*(1), 62–73. https://doi.org/10.1525/eth.1999.27.1.62

Singelis, T., Bond, M., Sharkey, W. F., & Lai, C. S. Y. (1999). Unpackaging culture's influence on self-esteem and embarassability. *Journal of Cross-Cultural Psychology, 30*(3), 315–341. https://doi.org/10.1177/0022022199030003003

Sireci, S. G. (2011). Evaluating test and survey items for bias across languages and cultures. In D. Matsumoto & F. J. R. van de Vijver (Eds.), *Cross-cultural research methods in psychology* (pp. 216–243). Cambridge University Press.

Smith, P. B. (2004). Acquiescent response bias as an aspect of cultural communication style. *Journal of Cross-Cultural Psychology, 35*(1), 50–61. https://doi.org/10.1177/0022022103260380

Tanaka-Matsumi, J. (1979). Taijin Kyofusho: Diagnostic and cultural issues in Japanese psychiatry. *Culture, Medicine and Psychiatry, 3*(3), 231–245. https://doi.org/10.1007/BF00114612

Tracy, J. L., & Robins, R. W. (2008). The nonverbal expression of pride: Evidence for cross-cultural recognition. *Journal of Personality and Social Psychology, 94*(3), 516–530. https://doi.org/10.1037/0022-3514.94.3.516

Triandis, H. C. (1995). *New directions in social psychology: Individualism and collectivism*. Westview Press.

Trimble, J., & Fischer, C. (2005). *The handbook of ethical research with ethnocultural populations and communities*. SAGE.

van de Vijver, F. J. R. (2009). Types of cross-cultural studies in cross-cultural psychology. *Online Readings in Psychology and Culture, 2*(2). https://doi.org/10.9707/2307-0919.1017

Van Haaften, E. H., & van de Vijver, F. J. R. (1996). Psychological consequences of environmental degradation. *Journal of Health Psychology, 1*(4), 411–429. https://doi.org/10.1177/135910539600100401

CHAPTER 6

RESEARCH WITH POPULATIONS THAT EXPERIENCE MARGINALIZATION

George P. Knight, Rebecca M. B. White, Stefanie Martinez-Fuentes, Mark W. Roosa, and Adriana J. Umaña-Taylor

Psychological research with individuals from marginalized groups, specifically those who have been "systematically excluded from mainstream, social, economic, cultural, or political life because of power inequalities in a given society" (Causadias & Umaña-Taylor, 2018), has increased since the first edition of the *Handbook of Research Methods in Psychology* (Cooper et al., 2012). This updated chapter on research with populations that experience marginalization expands our prior focus on a limited number of social positions to consider a wider range of intersecting social positions (Crenshaw, 1989; García Coll et al., 1996), including ethnicity, race, class, religion, gender, and sexuality.

The diverse social positions exist within corresponding systems of inequality, along multiple axes of inequality including racism, nativism, classism, sexism, and heterosexism. The systems work to marginalize people of color and immigrants; those who speak languages other than English, are poor, non-Christian; and those who identify as lesbian, gay, bisexual, transgender, and/or queer (LGBTQ). Simultaneously, the systems privilege Whites, native-born, English speakers, the rich, Christians, cisgender men, and heterosexual people. Incorporating an intersectional lens (Collins, 1989; Crenshaw, 1989), we recognize that individuals exist simultaneously across multiple axes of inequality and, therefore, experience marginalization and/or privilege in multiple, overlapping, and intersecting ways.

Consistent with others (Santos & Toomey, 2018; Seaton et al., 2018), we argue that knowledge about individuals' social positions and corresponding axes of inequality must inform research designs. Research processes, including sampling, recruitment, retention, and measurement, may exclude and further marginalize individuals based on multiple and intersecting aspects of their social identities (Knight et al., 2018). Thus, research methods that have been successful based on one social identity or axis of inequality (e.g., ethnicity) may not be as effective across other, intersecting social identities and axes of inequality (e.g., ethnicity, sexuality, and class). As an example, a strategy focused on establishing partnerships with and recruiting participants from Catholic places of worship in an effort to foster trust and increase the representation of Latinx families may inadvertently decrease the chances of recruiting LGBTQ Latinx participants who may experience heightened marginalization in those settings.

Research designs that attend to intersecting social identities and axes of inequality are essential so that (a) theories can be made more universal or new ones developed, (b) practitioners can provide appropriate and effective mental health and other services to heterogeneous populations, and (c) policy makers can have the information necessary to meet the needs of a diverse society.

Though the body of work with marginalized groups continues to increase, progress in the quality of research with marginalized populations, especially those that experience overlapping systems of inequality, has been somewhat limited. The limits reflect an overreliance on methods and procedures developed by and for individuals who experience multiple and intersecting axes of privilege (e.g., cisgender, middle-income, White men and women) and, to a lesser extent, developed by and for individuals who experience marginalization along one or more axes (e.g., Latinas), but experience privileges along others (e.g., cisgender, heterosexual, middle-income, native-born). In both cases, the methods that work well for groups in one of the axes may not extend to a more heterogeneous target population (e.g., all Latinxs).

Too often researchers equate "systematic" research methods with invariant procedures (i.e., ones that are identical regardless of participants' intersecting social identities and axes of inequality). In practice, the use of invariant procedures has resulted in several sources of bias in research. For instance, although there are some nationally representative data sets that provided surveys in different languages (e.g., National Epidemiologic Survey on Alcohol and Related Conditions [Grant et al., 2015]) there are other widely used studies described as having nationally representative samples despite instrumentation being offered in English only (e.g., National Assessment of Educational Progress [Murangi et al., 2019]).

Because a significant portion of some groups are relatively recent immigrants and may not have the same facility with the English language as native speakers (Gambino et al., 2014), nationally representative studies that rely on one language of administration simply cannot achieve national representation. The representativeness of these samples may be further compromised by the use of sampling, recruitment, and retention procedures that have been defined as rigorous in the context of "colorblind" research or defined as rigorous in the context of research that attended to a limited number of intersecting social identities (e.g., research with U.S. Mexican youth who are diverse on socioeconomic status [SES]). In both cases, the methods may be less appropriate and/or less effective for capturing within-group variability on other, intersecting social positions, like gender, sexuality, and religion (e.g., Capaldi & Patterson, 1987; Gallagher-Thompson et al., 2006).

Another common source of bias from the use of invariant procedures emerges from the assumption that measures of psychological constructs developed in one group (often a group that experiences multiple axes of privilege) are equally reliable and valid for other groups (often groups that experience multiple axes of marginalization). Our chapter (Roosa et al., 2012) in the first edition of this handbook acknowledged that measures developed for middle-income, English-speaking, White youth might not be equally reliable and valid, for example, among socioeconomically diverse immigrant and non-immigrant Black youth. By incorporating an intersectional lens, we are now inviting scholars to consider that a measure developed for individuals whose social positions intersect around one region of the axes of inequality (e.g., Black, cisgender boys) may not be equally reliable and valid for groups whose social positions intersect around other regions of the axes (e.g., Black cisgender girls, Black transgender boys, and Black transgender girls). That is, items used to measure common psychological constructs (e.g., discrimination: Bauerband et al., 2019; neighborhood quality: Kim et al., 2009; self-esteem: Michaels et al., 2007) may convey different psychological meanings or have different scaling properties when used with groups differently located on the intersecting axes of inequality. Therefore, the use of invariant procedures can threaten both internal (i.e., when measures are not equally reliable or valid across groups) and external (i.e., when some subsamples are not equally representative of the populations being studied) validity.

With the increasing frequency of studies that include or focus on marginalized populations, it is time to begin addressing methodological issues that have failed to account for intersecting axes of inequality. Doing so requires culturally and contextually informed theorizing (White et al., 2016a, 2016b) to help address the specific methodological demands required to conduct research with diverse populations situated across the axes of inequality as well as to identify culturally and contextually unique influences on, or outcomes of, psychological processes.

In this chapter, we provide an introduction to three critical methodological issues that affect the research on marginalized populations: (a) improving the representativeness of samples, (b) effectively translating measures and research protocols into other languages when targeted populations exhibit language diversity, and (c) determining the equivalence of measures across diverse and intersecting social positions. Where appropriate we highlight the utility of culturally and contextually informed theorizing.

IMPROVING THE REPRESENTATIVENESS OF SAMPLES

There are several reasons to believe that marginalized populations may be more difficult to engage in the research process (Knight et al., 2009b). Although not psychological research, a particularly important example comes from the recent news and empirical reports of the relative difficulty in enrolling a representative percentage of ethnic and/or racial minority participants into coronavirus vaccine, phase three clinical trials (Chastain et al., 2020). Similarly, in psychological research, some members of marginalized populations may feel particularly vulnerable (e.g., undocumented immigrants, undocumented sexual and gender minority immigrants) and may hesitate to trust researchers because of a lack of familiarity with the research process and/or fear that their intersecting marginalized social positions place them at greater risk (Hernández et al., 2013).

In contrast, some with more privileged social class positions and those with intersecting privileged social positions may have been exposed directly and indirectly to psychological research during their educations (Ryan & Bauman, 2016), may be more likely to understand what research is, how it has benefited people like them in the past, or how participation might contribute to the common good. They, therefore, may have reduced fears and suspicions and be more likely to participate (e.g., Yancey et al., 2006). However, many individuals who are relatively privileged in terms of class (i.e., education level), may continue to be reluctant to participate in research if they are aware of studies that mistreated or misrepresented members of their racial, ethnic, immigrant, gender, or sexuality groups in previous research (e.g., Manson et al., 2004). These examples highlight how systems of inequality can intersect and affect the relative willingness of a target population to participate in research (e.g., Katz et al., 2006; Norton & Manson, 1996).

Efficient recruitment of marginalized populations is complicated because a significant portion of many minority groups are immigrants with limited English language ability (Gambino et al., 2014). Language issues may make it difficult or impossible for recent immigrants to understand recruitment processes conducted exclusively in English or to complete questionnaires or interviews in English. Additionally, low-income populations, among which ethnic/racial minorities are overrepresented, have greater residential mobility than the general population making them more difficult to locate for recruitment. Finally, low-income individuals or families are less likely to have access to a telephone or the internet at times (e.g., Knight et al., 2009b).

Despite such challenges, there are strategies that can make recruitment more efficient and generate more representative samples of marginalized populations depending upon the history of the group (e.g., previous egregious mistreatment by researchers) and local conditions (e.g., how well the group is integrated into the larger community). For many groups, recruitment and retention may be more productive if the process is designed to be consistent with their social identities, values, and lifestyles (e.g., Dumka et al., 2002; Sue et al., 1991). At a very concrete level, recruitment within groups that include immigrants means that recruiters need to be fluently bilingual and all recruitment and study materials need to be available in targeted individuals' preferred languages. A more representative sample may be obtained by being responsive to the needs of the targeted population (Rivas-Drake et al., 2016), such as providing child care if data collection may take a significant amount of time, travel reimbursement when participants are asked to transport themselves to a study location, or information about local community services (e.g., tutoring).

Equally important, recruiters also need to be culturally competent; that is, they must be familiar with the values, interaction patterns, and communication styles of potential participants and capable of applying these skills in the recruitment process. This includes, for example, understanding when to communicate at a very personal level (e.g., making comments about a targeted individual's children), how to communicate in a respectful manner with each generation and social identity in a household, and being able to decipher informal signals regarding power relationships in a household (Knight et al., 2009b). For many groups, personal interaction is culturally valued, a means of expressing respect for one another, and a means of determining the degree of trust in each other (Skaff et al., 2002). Indeed, several research teams have reported that recruitment (and retention) was most effective when communication was consistent, personal, and face-to-face (Dumka et al., 1997; García et al., 2017; Maxwell et al., 2005; Rivas-Drake et al., 2016). For individuals who have not been exposed to research, face-to-face contact provides an opportunity to make decisions about whether the recruiter or researcher is someone to trust and someone who is respectful to their own intersecting social identities. These same individuals may feel more confident about making a decision to participate if researchers extend the recruitment process to include an educational piece that explains what research is, why many consider it to be a public good, and exactly what participation would entail.

There are several incentives researchers should consider when planning recruitment and retention procedures for members of marginalized populations. For applied studies, researchers should consider appealing to the value of collectivism that generally is stronger among marginalized populations than among the middle-class majority (Knight et al., 2009b). Being asked to take part in an activity that can potentially benefit one's community, or people who share one's intersecting social identities, can be motivating. In addition, financial incentives also can be effective tools as long as they are offered in an accessible form (e.g., cash, debit cards, or gift cards instead of checks) and timely manner (e.g., at the time of the interview or other research procedure; Roosa et al., 2008). Indeed, Latinx families facing economic hardship were most satisfied about participating in research when the study was framed as benefitting their community (Haack et al., 2014). Endorsement by prominent, respected community members (e.g., church leaders) and financial incentives were also associated with participants' satisfaction, albeit less than the message about community benefits.

Recruitment may be particularly challenging with groups that are fearful of potentially negative consequences from participating in research, as may be the case with undocumented immigrants. Given that this population is at risk of fines, incarceration, and deportation if their status is revealed, researchers should take several measures to secure participants' status. For example, Hernández et al. (2013) reported that *minimal* measures should include storing names, addresses, and phone numbers in three separate documents, with information appearing in a different order within each document. Hernández and colleagues also recommended requesting a waiver for signed consent from institutional review boards, in order to prevent potential linking between participants' personal information and documentation status. Extra measures include Certificates of Confidentiality, which provide further security to undocumented participants that their private information will not be revealed by researchers in any legal or social setting. Failure to take measures to protect the confidentiality of such vulnerable populations leads to further distrust and causes participants severe harm that may be compounded by participants' other social identities, like race, ethnicity, religion, gender, sexuality, and ability.

Other groups that may be more challenging to recruit are populations that have been abused or misrepresented in previous research (e.g., Native Americans, Blacks, LGBTQ individuals), that long have been the target of discrimination from the larger society, or that have had difficult relations with their surrounding communities or with the research institution. In such cases, researchers should consider developing collaborations or partnerships with the group or with respected agencies or individuals who serve, work with, or are part of the targeted population (e.g., Beals et al., 2005; Dumka et al., 2002). Bringing respected members of the targeted research population into the research process can reduce suspicions about researchers held by members of the targeted group, increase researchers' credibility, and break down other barriers to participation in research. These partnerships can take many forms, including having members of the targeted groups or their representatives as advisors to the research, as recruiters for the project or as other research staff. It is also possible to establish more extensive partnerships with members of the targeted groups via community-based participatory research (CBPR).

In CBPR, the targeted population is an equal partner in the research enterprise from the identity of the research problem to the development and implementation of methods to interpretation of results (Beals et al., 2005; Manson et al., 2004; Rivas-Drake et al., 2016). CBPR is costly in terms of researchers' time particularly at the beginning of the research when trust is being developed, methods of communication are being established, and rules governing the partnership are being negotiated. CBPR, however, may provide a level of access to and cooperation from groups that feel socially isolated and distrustful of people outside their groups.

When research focuses on sensitive issues such as discriminatory experiences in the community, recruitment as well as the quality of data obtained may benefit from matching potential participants and research staff on race/ethnicity and, as appropriate, other aspects of social identities (Gallagher-Thompson et al., 2006; Picot et al., 2002). Another important personal characteristic of research staff may be that they are familiar with, comfortable with, and respectful toward the values and lifestyles of potential participants and can demonstrate that in their interactions (i.e., they are culturally competent; Knight et al., 2009b). For example, though many research projects make strong efforts to match participants on social positions related to race or ethnicity (e.g., Murry et al., 2008; Roosa et al., 2008), an intersectional lens suggests that considering intersecting social identities relevant to a given target population may be important. That is, recruitment and retention strategies that have been successful with heterosexual immigrant Mexican adolescents, may not be as successful with sexual and gender minority Mexican immigrants, despite the fact that they share some aspects of their social identities. Similarly, recruitment and retention strategies that have been successful with relatively diverse panethnic African Americans may not be as successful with less diverse Nigerian immigrants.

A final consideration for recruiting more representative samples of marginalized populations is the often-overlooked task of carefully defining the target population. The nature of the research question, along with an understanding of diverse and intersecting social identities, should guide the researcher to define a target population appropriately. For some research questions, it may be important to limit certain aspects of diversity so that others can be examined more closely. In this case, the research question and definition of the target population may be specific to a particular region of the axes of inequality. In other cases, it may be desirable to capture a great deal of diversity across numerous intersecting regions of the axes. In this case, researchers should ensure that their research questions and methods are appropriate for a target population that exists across a more encompassing range of the axes. In both cases, researchers must consider whether the psychological processes of interest (e.g., peer interactions) are likely to be similar and relevant across the axes of inequality represented within a target population (White et al., 2016a). They must also consider whether the extant methods (e.g., sampling, measures) are likely to be appropriate and effective across the axes (White et al., 2016a, 2016b). For example, psychologists are calling for additional research on the intensification of anti-Asian stigma and discrimination in the wake of the COVID-19 pandemic (e.g., Misra et al., 2020). One set of research questions in response to this call may lead to a design that defines the target population as U.S. Chinese immigrants who speak their native language and identify as a sexual or gender minority. A different set of research questions may lead to a design that defines the target population as Asian immigrant and nonimmigrant Americans who are diverse on language spoken. In sum, decisions to define a target population and applicable research methods need to be specified and defended, and the limitations of each need to be recognized.

Though it is commonly understood that the definition of the study population and the effectiveness of the sampling and recruitment strategies have important implications for external validity, or generalizability, that these research aspects also have important implications for internal validity is less well understood. For example, some researchers define ethnic group membership based on individuals' self-identification with a group (e.g., the participant identifies as Navajo), legal identification with a group (e.g., the participant is a Navajo tribal member; Norton & Manson, 1996), or rely on surnames or administrative data (e.g., school rosters). It is likely that each approach generalizes to slightly different underlying populations, thus having an impact on external validity.

Recruitment strategies, however, combined with the definition of the population, also affect internal validity. For example, if a researcher is interested in whether the association between racial discrimination and mental health varies among Navajo living on the reservation versus a more urban area, the degree to which the recruitment strategies are differentially effective at engaging representative samples of Navajo from these two settings undermines the internal validity of the research because the sampling and recruitment strategies are an important aspect of the operationalization of the setting variable.

An example of how to put much of this advice on recruitment into practice comes from a study of cultural and contextual influences on the development of Mexican American children conducted in the midst of an anti-Latinx, anti-immigrant political firestorm (Roosa et al., 2008). To represent the diversity of contextual influences on development, the research team began by sampling "school communities" (i.e., attendance boundaries of elementary schools) in a large metropolitan area. This resulted in 47 economically and culturally different communities represented by public, parochial, and charter schools. To assist with the recruitment process, the research team recruited prominent representatives of the Mexican American community as members of a Community Advisory Board. This Board provided advice on several aspects of the study and allowed their names to be used on recruitment materials.

Partnerships were formed with each school to implement the recruitment process. According to the Community Advisory Board, schools were generally respected and trusted institutions in the Mexican American community, which provided support for recruitment. Recruitment involved sending materials home in English and Spanish with each fifth-grade child in the selected schools. These materials explained that the study would focus on Mexican heritage families and described what participation would involve. In addition, these materials explained that results of the study would be used to guide the development of programs to help Mexican heritage children at home, school, or in the community in the future. In addition, parents were told that each person who met eligibility criteria and agreed to be interviewed would receive $45 cash. Recruitment materials directed parents who were interested in the study or wanted more information about it to provide contact information so that members of the research team could talk to them about the study and answer their questions. All Mexican heritage parents who returned recruitment materials were contacted by bilingual members of the research team, usually by telephone, and the study was explained in more detail. All interviewers were culturally competent, most had extensive experience with the Mexican American community, and about 75% were bilingual. Parents who were interested in being considered for the study were given a screening interview to determine if they met eligibility criteria. Because of the researchers' interest in the influence of Mexican culture on children's adaptation, families were eligible only if both of the target child's biological parents were of Mexican origin and there were no obvious adult socialization influences from other cultures in the home (e.g., a step-parent from another ethnic group). Over 70% of families that met all eligibility criteria completed in-home interviews.

Descriptive analyses showed that the resulting sample was very similar to the local Mexican American population according to the U.S. Census, and diverse in terms of language, nativity, education, income, and residential community (e.g., living in neighborhoods that were predominately White to predominately Latinx). Adult study participants were more likely than the Mexican American population in general to have been born in Mexico, likely a result of the strict screening criteria. The study procedures, therefore, were successful at enrolling U.S. Mexican families that existed across several axes of inequality, including racism, nativism, and classism. Less attention, however, was given to other axes of inequality, especially sexism and heterosexism. In sum, integrating the strategies described above with a knowledge of local conditions would contribute to much better representation of marginalized populations in broad-based research projects, more diverse samples in studies using ethnic homogenous designs, and more readily interpretable and generalizable results.

EFFECTIVE TRANSLATION OF MEASURES

Some marginalized populations include a substantial proportion of recent immigrants and are diverse in their comfort and fluency in English.

Measures and research protocols, hence, must often be translated into other languages to make broader participation in the research endeavor more feasible for all members of these populations. Unfortunately, poor quality translations can interfere with scientific inferences by increasing the error variance in scores, which can influence observed findings (Bernal et al., 2014).

Conceptual and semantic equivalence are critical to making scientifically credible inferences in studies that are conducted in more than one language. Conceptual and semantic equivalence are necessary to make valid comparisons across ethnic groups, to compare subsets of individuals (e.g., more vs. less acculturated), or to examine relations among constructs within a linguistically diverse ethnic group. Conceptual equivalence occurs when the original language version and a translated version of a measure assesses the same specific psychological construct. Sometimes two different language versions of the same measure may assess a somewhat different construct, which may happen when the targeted concept is meaningful in one language but not the second, or more meaningful in one language than the other (Epstein et al., 2015). Semantic equivalence, however, pertains to the mapping of meanings across languages (Epstein et al., 2015) and is achieved when the item-level ideas expressed in one language are accurately conveyed in a second language. Unlike conceptual equivalence, which is more focused on the scale scores of the measure as a whole, semantic equivalence is determined at the item level. Lack of semantic equivalence occurs if specific items are poorly translated (Angel, 2013), which is likely with literal translations rather than a semantically equivalent or meaningful translation.

Approaches to Translation

There are a number of strategies for translating measures (see Knight et al., 2009b, for a detailed review). The strategy that researchers use when translating research instruments and protocols depend largely on the purpose of their research. For example, if the goal of the research is to make cross-ethnic comparisons, conceptual equivalence must be established first to ensure that the measure being translated to a different language for a different cultural group is assessing a construct that is meaningful to that population (Hambleton, 2004). This may be less of a problem when researchers are studying a construct within one population (e.g., middle-class Mexican-origin families in the United States), but issues of semantic equivalence may be more important because items must reflect a similar meaning across different language versions. Before attempting any translation, researchers must, therefore, consider the types of equivalence that are most relevant to their research and the translation strategies that will be most appropriate given their goals.

Furthermore, it is critical to understand the specific intersecting social identities of a well-defined target population when selecting a translation team and participants for pilot testing of instruments. For quantitative research, the process of selecting translators and participants who mirror the characteristics of the target population can be costly; however, doing so may significantly increase the generalizability of the measure to the intended population. For qualitative research, this strategy will help to ensure that the questions being asked of research participants are meaningful in both target languages and that the translated data represent an accurate depiction of participants' beliefs and experiences (see Knight et al., 2009b, for a review). Finally, the evaluation of the conceptual and semantic equivalence requires a set of cross-language measurement invariance analyses (a special case of the analyses described below) guided by culturally informed theorizing.

One of the most commonly used strategies is the *back-translation approach*, in which a measure is translated from the source language into a target language by one bilingual person, the new version is translated back into the source language by a second bilingual person, and then the two English versions are compared. The person translating back to the source language should not be familiar with the original version of the measure (Bernal et al., 2014). A variation of this strategy is the double translation/double back-translation approach, where two translators produce independent translations of a measure, having a third person create a revised translated version by comparing the two translated versions and resolving any issues between them, and finally having two new translators do independent back-translations of the revised translated version (Bernal et al., 2014). An important limitation of the back-translation approach is that a comparison of the original and the back-translation could suggest equivalence (i.e., items read exactly identical), but this could be the result of translators using a shared set of adaptation rules (e.g., "frame switching") or the translations erroneously retaining aspects of the original measure such as the same grammatical structure, which made it easy to back-translate word for word into the same item (Hambleton, 2004).

Another strategy, *forward translation*, involves translating the source language version into the target language and having a team of bilingual individuals scrutinize the source and target language versions (Bernal et al., 2014). This allows judgments to be made directly about the equivalence of the source and target language versions, not by examining a back-translated version. The main weakness, however, is that a high level of inference is being made by translators (Epstein et al., 2015), all of whom are bilingual and may be making insightful guesses based on their knowledge of both languages in ways that less bicultural participants may not.

The use of bilingual translators is not ideal because they likely have more formal education, may be differentially fluent in the target language, and have had more experience with the constructs and terminology used in behavioral research, relative to target participants who prefer assessments in the target language. Bilingual translators also may be less aware of linguistic nuances of the target language and of local usage of cultural constructs that pervade the daily lives of participants. These differences reflecting various social identities (e.g., education, language use) may lead to a lack of equivalence of the translated measure and the original language version because the translators are different from the target participants.

Furthermore, research focused on the "frame switching" among bicultural and/or bilingual persons (Hong et al., 2000; Ramirez-Esparza et al., 2006) suggests that some bilinguals may internalize information from two cultures in a manner that might interfere with a functional capacity to perform conceptually or semantically equivalent translations. For instance, cultural priming manipulations have been shown to influence expressions of values, causal attribution styles, and social identity orientations among bicultural participants in research. The bicultural person, therefore, responds in a manner consistent with the ethnic culture when exposed to external cues of that culture and in a mainstream manner when exposed to mainstream cues. If the language being spoken or written serves as a strong cultural prime, it can activate (or make cognitively accessible) the system of knowledge that is associated with that specific culture and interfere with the translation process in a way that is unbeknownst to the bilingual translator. Therefore, when bilingual persons review the original and its translation, they may "make sense" with the particular cultural meaning system that is active for them at the time. Research participants, for whom translated measures are often being created, are less likely to have this dual cultural frame of reference and almost certainly not to the same degree.

A final translation approach is to employ a review team or to evaluate the translation at various steps of the process. The team can (a) translate the source language version into the target language, (b) evaluate the translated items to determine whether they are meaningful for the target population in the target language, and (c) recommend changes to the original items and/or translated items in an effort to obtain semantic equivalence (Knight et al., 2009b). This assists with establishing semantic equivalence because each translator may come up with a different translation and the team can work together to determine the most appropriate meaningful translation. The disadvantages of this approach are primarily the time and costs that it entails.

Within these various strategies, some researchers follow the practice of decentering, which involves making changes to both the source and target language versions of a measure until they are equivalent to one another. Researchers who engage in this process view the source and target language versions of measures as equally open to modification (Prieto, 1992).

An advantage of decentering is that equivalence may be easier to achieve once researchers are willing to accept changes in the original version. However, decentering can be disadvantageous if the original instrument has a history of use in the original language with accepted norms or cutoffs that can be used for comparative purposes. Because decentering could alter the psychological construct being assessed in the original version of the measure if there are extensive changes to this version, caution should be used in adopting this approach.

Selecting Translators

Aside from determining *how* to translate measures, researchers must pay close attention to *who* will serve as translators. In selecting translators, considering social positions such as national origin and geographic region is important because there is considerable variability in dialects and common vocabulary within languages and across regions. Considering other social identities, including sexual and gender minority status, may also be important. In addition to differences in accent and intonation, some words have different meanings for different groups who share a language and other words may not exist for one group, whereas they may be commonly used by another. Indeed, Delgado (2016) described how the back-translation process becomes more time-consuming as a result of having a graduate student of Honduran descent and a translation consultant of Mexican origin work together on translating measures for a Mexican-origin sample. Even though, therefore, she recommended hiring a consultant to assist with the translation process, she also noted the importance of ensuring that all members of the translation team share the same background as the targeted population.

In addition to national origin group, the socioeconomic status (SES) of the translation team should also be considered. If translators and back-translators share the same SES background, and it is different from target participants' SES, the back-translated version may be equivalent to the original, but the target language version may not be meaningful for those who will complete the measure (Ziegler & Bensch, 2013). Scholars also recommend selecting translators while considering familiarity with both languages and both cultures, knowledge of the construct being assessed, and knowledge of test construction (Al-Amer et al., 2015). Translators with these characteristics, however, may not share certain social identities with some participants.

Piloting Translated Measures to Assess Equivalence

Scholars agree that pilot testing of translated measures is necessary to provide a rigorous assessment of the conceptual and semantic equivalence of language versions (Epstein et al., 2015). An important factor to consider is the language ability of participants involved in pilot testing. If measures are piloted with relatively bilingual participants, findings may not be generalizable to a population that includes a significant number of persons who strongly prefer a non-English language because bilingual participants have additional cognitive skills (Al-Amer et al., 2015). If measures are piloted on participants who are more limited in language abilities and/or preferences, then pilot subjects likely mirror much of the target population, and there is no concern regarding generalizability to the population of interest.

In sum, issues of translation will arise in quantitative and qualitative designs. Without careful attention, problems with translation can lead to inaccurate scientific inferences. Although the process of translation can be arduous when carefully implemented, it is necessary for accurate scientific inferences and to advance understandings of psychological processes. Thus, in an effort to ensure scientific advances, the additional resources needed for research on populations that are linguistically diverse must be considered as funding agencies set their priorities.

MEASUREMENT EQUIVALENCE

Measures developed in samples who experience multiple and intersecting axes of privilege are commonly used in research with samples that experience marginalization along one or more axes of inequality (e.g., Knight et al., 2009b). Researchers, therefore, must consider the validity and reliability of these measures to ensure they function similarly across diverse groups and those with marginalized social identities. If the measurement plan does not ensure that measures of the target variables produce scores with equivalent meanings across social identity groups, the observed relations may misrepresent causal relations (Knight et al., 2009a). For example, when examining parental socialization of youths' collectivistic values longitudinally across multiple cultural groups, the observed group comparisons and longitudinal relations most likely would misrepresent the causal sequences in these groups if the measure of collectivism values does not assess collectivism equivalently across groups. In such cases, this measurement problem represents a serious threat to the internal validity of the research. Therefore, as more research samples marginalized groups, particularly those who experience marginalization across multiple axes, greater attention to *measurement equivalence* is needed to obtain valid findings.

Fortunately, there are clearly articulated empirical procedures designed to evaluate measurement equivalence of measures administered to participants from different social identity groups (see Knight et al., 2009b, and Widaman & Reise, 1997, for detailed descriptions) as well as across translated versions of measures. For studies that engage in comparisons across groups (e.g., race, ethnicity, class, gender), as well as groups with intersecting social identities (e.g., between Black men and Black women), the absence of measurement equivalence can bias the observed group differences in the relations among constructs (as well as the mean differences between groups). In addition, using a measure that was developed in research with White European American schoolchildren in a study of a culturally different population (e.g., Navajo schoolchildren) can produce misleading results if measurement equivalence was not determined prior to the study even if there will be no comparisons with other groups. In this case, the targeted variable (e.g., self-esteem, parent–child conflict) might have a different meaning or require different indicators/items in the targeted sample (e.g., Navajo schoolchildren) than in the White European American schoolchildren sample used to develop the measure.

Empirically evaluating measurement equivalence across groups requires analyses focused on the functioning of the items (or observations) on that measure, as well as the functioning of the total score created from those items/observations. Generally, the creation of a good measure of a psychological construct starts with a theory that specifies the nature of, and indicators of, the construct. Knowledge about the population of interest is instrumental in identifying the indicators of the psychological construct as they exist in the population being studied. This knowledge becomes the basis for the culturally informed theorizing needed to generate the items for that measure, as well as how the construct relates to other constructs in the population being studied. Hence, culturally informed theory describes the expected construct validity relations among psychological constructs, and the indicators of the target constructs, in the population being studied. A good measure produces a total score on the construct of interest for each individual in the population being studied that is related to other constructs as the culturally informed theory specifies, and such a measure has then *construct validity* in that population.

Unfortunately, scientifically sound judgments regarding the equivalence of a measure across groups can be very complex despite well-established analytical methods (e.g., Knight et al., 2009b). Complete *factorial invariance* and *construct validity invariance* may be difficult to establish for a number of methodological reasons (e.g., insufficient sample sizes, attenuated item responses). However, perhaps the greater challenge researchers may face is the likelihood that there are some psychological constructs for which identical factor structures and construct validity relations across intersecting social identities may not be reasonably expected because of true differences in the nature of the target construct across groups (e.g., Kim et al., 2009; Michaels et al., 2007). If there are sound culturally informed reasons to expect selected items or scale scores to function differently across groups then differences in factorial and/or construct invariance (i.e., partial invariance) may be consistent with measurement equivalence.

For example, although an item assessing the frequency of suicidal thought may be appropriate on a depression scale administered to multiple groups, less variability in responses to this item in one group because of a culturally associated religious prohibition against suicide may lead to very few individuals in that group reporting suicidal ideation and an attenuation of the association of that item with other items in that group. This item may be a good indicator of depression in all groups, but it may even indicate more serious depression when endorsed by an individual facing such a prevailing religious sanction. Awareness of this religious prohibition may lead to a culturally informed theory about the depression construct that expects somewhat different factor loading, intercept, and/or unique variance for such an item, and partial factorial invariance may be indicative of measurement equivalence.

Similarly, there may be cases in which culturally informed theory suggests some subtly different construct validity relations across groups. For example, harsh parenting and restrictive control may be an adaptive parenting strategy for economically disadvantaged youth of color who live in communities with high rates of violence (White et al., 2016b). Harsh or restrictive parenting may represent an overcontrolling quality of parental behavior for White youth in middle-class neighborhoods or have mixed implication for middle-income youth of color navigating "White" contexts. If so, these forms of parental control may relate differently to mental health outcomes across axes of inequality, and partial construct validity invariance may be indicative of measurement equivalence.

Factorial Invariance

The factorial invariance of a measure across groups can be evaluated through the examination of a sequence of multigroup confirmatory factor analyses to fit a series of hierarchically nested factor structures progressing from least to most restrictive models of invariance or item response theory approaches (Widaman & Reise, 1997). The confirmatory factor analysis determines the factor loadings, intercepts, and unique (i.e., random) errors for each item on the measure. *Configural invariance* suggests that the items are measuring the same psychological construct in each group if the same set of items/observations form a factor within each group. *Metric equivalence* exists if the practical fit indices (e.g., comparative fit index [CFI], root mean square error of approximation [RMSEA], and standardized root mean residual [SRMR]) indicate that the model constraining the factor loadings to be equal across groups fits as well as the unconstrained model. *Strong invariance* exists if, in addition to constraining the factor loadings, constraining the item intercepts to be equal across groups fits as well as a model that allows the item intercepts to vary across groups. *Strict invariance* exists if, in addition to constraining the factor loadings and intercepts, constraining the unique error variances for each item to be equal across groups fits as well as a model that allows the unique errors to vary across groups. Strict invariance means that a particular score on each individual item (e.g., 3 on a Likert-type scale of 1–5) has the same meaning for each group. At all levels of factorial invariance, partial invariance may be observed if some, but not all, of the item features (e.g., factor loadings, intercepts, unique variances) are equivalent across groups (Byrne et al., 1989).

Construct Validity Invariance

If the factorial invariance findings conform appropriately with the culturally informed theorizing, one can proceed to examine the invariance of the construct validity relations of the factor scores across groups by examining the cross-group similarities of the slopes and intercepts of the relations between the scores from the target measure and scores on measures of theoretically related constructs (see Knight et al., 2009b). Here again, the expected associations (and nonassociations) among the psychological constructs must be based on appropriate culturally informed theorizing. Invariance in *slopes* can be tested by comparing the practical fit indices for a multigroup structural equation model in which the slopes are allowed to vary across groups to a model that constrains slopes to be identical across groups. If the fit indices of the constrained slope model are satisfactory and not substantially different from the unconstrained slope models, similar comparisons are made between models that allow the *intercepts* of the relations among constructs to vary with a model that constrains the intercepts to be identical across groups. If comparisons of these hierarchically arranged structural equation models suggest that the slopes and intercepts are equal across groups, construct validity invariance exists. Partial construct validity invariance may occur if the measure of the target construct is similarly related to some construct validity variables but not others.

Empirical Examples of Measurement Equivalence

The examination of measurement equivalence is necessary because psychological constructs may have subtly different meanings for individuals with diverse intersecting social identities or play different roles in their development or adjustment. In addition, recent findings have illuminated the importance of establishing measurement equivalence across setting (i.e., study sites), both within one ethnic–racial group (i.e., Latinx; Meca et al., 2017), and among multiple ethnic–racial groups (Sladek et al., 2020). This is not surprising, because the setting or context can be another aspect of intersectionality, given that some settings are more or less privileged (Santos & Toomey, 2018) and/or more or less inclusive. Hence, analyses of measurement equivalence across cultural groups and/or languages is increasingly appearing in the empirical literature. For example, Castillo and colleagues (2020) recently demonstrated configural, metric, strong, and strict invariance of the Marianismo Beliefs Scale across language versions (English vs. Spanish), sex groups (males and females), and several Latinx subgroups (Dominican, Central American, Cuban, Mexican American, Puerto Rican, and South American). Wang and colleagues (2017) demonstrated configural, metric, strong, and strict invariance across rural, urban, and rural-to-urban Chinese adolescents for the Satisfaction With Life Scale (Diener et al., 1985). There have also been studies that have led to concerns regarding the equivalence of measures. For example, although White et al. (2011) demonstrated cross-language measurement equivalence (i.e., factorial and construct validity invariance) for the Spanish language version of the exploration and resolution subscales of the Ethnic Identity Scale (EIS: Umaña-Taylor et al., 2004), they did not find similarly clear evidence of equivalence of the affirmation subscale. White et al. (2011) concluded that reverse worded items of the affirmation scale may have been problematic for these early adolescent Mexican Americans regardless of language version, but that this difficulty may have been greater in the Spanish version. A given score on the English and Spanish versions of this subscale, therefore, may not indicate the same degree of affirmation across these language groups; and that any observed mean language or age differences, or relations, to affirmation are likely uninterpretable. Finally, more work needs to be done across other social identities (e.g., gender, sexuality) and across intersecting social identities.

CONCLUSION

Psychological research that includes or focuses on populations that experience marginalization will continue to increase in response to changes in the demography of the world in the coming years. This new research should solidify the generalizability of some of our theories, contribute to changes in others, and improve the quality of services available to diverse populations. In this chapter, we provided an introduction to three essential steps in the research process that need to be applied more commonly in studies with marginalized populations to improve the quality of research with these groups. Obtaining more representative samples of marginalized populations across multiple intersecting social identities, making sure our measures are available to potential research participants in their preferred languages, and making sure that the measures are appropriate for and equivalent across populations will greatly improve the quality of research on these populations.

The three essential research processes covered in the chapter are not, however, the only improvements that need to be made. Other topics that deserve the attention of researchers conducting studies with marginalized populations include (a) effective retention processes for longitudinal and intervention studies, (b) methods for creating or adapting interventions to be culturally attractive and competent for marginalized populations, and (c) ways to meet the ethical requirements of research with marginalized populations (see Knight et al., 2009b, for a review).

Finally, although the research processes described and recommended in this chapter represent the state of the art at this time, there clearly has been little systematic research on how to improve the validity of research with marginalized populations, particularly based on the idea that social identities are intersecting and corresponding systems of oppression are overlapping. Instead, most progress in methods for these populations has been incremental and based on trial and error. The quality of research with marginalized populations could improve dramatically with more systematic approaches to determine exactly what methods work best with populations that are diverse and experience intersecting systems of inequality based on a broad array of possible social identities.

References

Al-Amer, R., Ramjan, L., Glew, P., Darwish, M., & Salamonson, Y. (2015). Translation of interviews from a source language to a target language: Examining issues in cross-cultural health care research. *Journal of Clinical Nursing*, 24(9-10), 1151–1162. https://doi.org/10.1111/jocn.12681

Angel, R. J. (2013). After Babel: Language and the fundamental challenges of comparative aging research. *Journal of Cross-Cultural Gerontology*, 28(3), 223–238. https://doi.org/10.1007/s10823-013-9197-2

Bauerband, L. A., Teti, M., & Velicer, W. F. (2019). Measuring minority stress: Invariance of a discrimination and vigilance scale across transgender and cisgender LGBQ individuals. *Psychology and Sexuality*, 10(1), 17–30. https://doi.org/10.1080/19419899.2018.1520143

Beals, J., Novins, D. K., Whitesell, N. R., Spicer, P., Mitchell, C. M., & Manson, S. M. (2005). Prevalence of mental disorders and utilization of mental health services in two American Indian reservation populations: Mental health disparities in context. *American Journal of Psychiatry*, 162(9), 1723–1733. https://doi.org/10.1176/appi.ajp.162.9.1723

Bernal, G., Cumba-Avilés, E., & Rodriguez-Quintana, N. (2014). Methodological challenges in research with ethnic, racial, and ethnocultural groups. In E. Leong, L. Comas-Diaz, V. McLoyd, G. Nagayama Hall, & J. Trimble (Eds.), *APA handbook of multicultural psychology* (pp. 105–123). American Psychological Association. https://doi.org/10.1037/14189-006

Byrne, B. M., Shavelson, R. J., & Muthén, B. (1989). Testing for the equivalence of factor covariance and mean structures: The issue of partial measurement invariance. *Psychological Bulletin*, 105(3), 456–466. https://doi.org/10.1037/0033-2909.105.3.456

Capaldi, D., & Patterson, G. R. (1987). An approach to the problem to recruitment and retention rates for longitudinal research. *Behavioral Assessment*, 9(2), 169–177.

Castillo, L. G., González, P., Merz, E. L., Nuñez, A., Castañeda, S. F., Buelna, C., Ojeda, L., Giachello, A. L., Womack, V. Y., Garcia, K. A., Penedo, F. J., Talavera, G. A., & Gallo, L. C. (2021). Factorial invariance of the Marianismo Beliefs Scale among Latinos in the Hispanic Community Health Study/Study of Latinos Sociocultural Ancillary Study. *Journal of Clinical Psychology*, 77(1), 312–328. https://doi.org/10.1002/jclp.23031

Causadias, J. M., & Umaña-Taylor, A. J. (2018). Reframing marginalization and youth development: Introduction to the special issue. *American Psychologist*, 73(6), 707–712. https://doi.org/10.1037/amp0000336

Chastain, D. B., Osae, S. P., Henao-Martínez, A. F., Franco-Paredes, C., Chastain, J. S., & Young, H. N. (2020). Racial disproportionality in Covid clinical trials. *The New England Journal of Medicine*, 383(9), e59. https://doi.org/10.1056/NEJMp2021971

Collins, P. H. (1989). The social construction of Black feminist thought. *Signs: Journal of Women in Culture and Society*, 14(4), 745–773. https://doi.org/10.1086/494543

Cooper, H., Camic, P. M., Long, D. L., Panter, A. T., Rindskopf, D., & Sher, K. J. (Eds.). (2012). *APA handbook of research methods in psychology, Vol. 2. Research designs: Quantitative, qualitative, neuropsychological, and biological.* American Psychological Association. https://doi.org/10.1037/13620-000

Crenshaw, K. (1989). Demarginalizing the intersection of race and sex: A Black feminist critique of antidiscrimination doctrine, feminist theory and antiracist politics. *University of Chicago Legal Forum*, 1989(1), 139–167.

Delgado, M. Y. (2016). *Academic identity and Latino adolescents' academic achievement: Theoretical and empirical foundations, methodological challenges, and lessons learned.* Greater Texas Foundation.

Diener, E., Emmons, R. A., Larsen, R. J., & Griffin, S. (1985). The Satisfaction With Life Scale. *Journal of Personality Assessment*, 49(1), 71–75. https://doi.org/10.1207/s15327752jpa4901_13

Dumka, L., Garza, C., Roosa, M. W., & Stoerzinger, H. (1997). Recruiting and retaining high risk populations into preventive interventions. *The Journal of Primary Prevention*, 18(1), 25–39. https://doi.org/10.1023/A:1024626105091

Dumka, L. E., Lopez, V. A., & Carter, S. J. (2002). Parenting interventions adapted for Latino families: Progress and prospects. In J. M. Contreras, K. A. Kerns, & A. M. Neal-Barnett (Eds.), *Latino children and families in the United States: Current research and future directions* (pp. 203–231). Praeger.

Epstein, J., Santo, R. M., & Guillemin, F. (2015). A review of guidelines for cross-cultural adaptation of questionnaires could not bring out a consensus. *Journal of Clinical Epidemiology*, 68(4), 435–441. https://doi.org/10.1016/j.jclinepi.2014.11.021

Fulton, P., Tierney, J., Mirpourian, N., Ericsson, J. M., Wright, J. T., Jr., & Powel, L. L. (2002). Engaging Black older adults and caregivers in urban communities in health research. *Journal of Gerontological Nursing*, 28(2), 19–27. https://doi.org/10.3928/0098-9134-20020201-07

Gallagher-Thompson, D., Rabinowitz, Y., Tang, P. C., Tse, C., Kwo, E., Hsu, S., Wang, P. C., Leung, L., Tong, H. Q., & Thompson, L. W. (2006). Recruiting

Chinese Americans for dementia caregiver intervention research: Suggestions for success. *The American Journal of Geriatric Psychiatry*, *14*(8), 676–683. https://doi.org/10.1097/01.JGP.0000221234.65585.f9

Gambino, C. P., Acosta, Y. D., & Grieco, E. M. (2014). *English-speaking ability of the foreign-born population in the United States: 2012* (American Community Survey Reports, ACS-26). U.S. Census Bureau.

García, A. A., Zuñiga, J. A., & Lagon, C. (2017). A personal touch: The most important strategy for recruiting Latino research participants. *Journal of Transcultural Nursing*, *28*(4), 342–347. https://doi.org/10.1177/1043659616644958

García Coll, C., Lamberty, G., Jenkins, R., McAdoo, H. P., Crnic, K., Wasik, B. H., & Vázquez García, H. (1996). An integrative model for the study of developmental competencies in minority children. *Child Development*, *67*(5), 1891–1914. https://doi.org/10.2307/1131600

Grant, B. F., Chu, A., Sigman, R., Amsbary, M., Kali, J., Sugawara, Y., Jiao, R., Ren, W., & Goldstein, R. (2015). National Institute on Alcohol Abuse and Alcoholism National Epidemiologic Survey on Alcohol and Related Conditions-III (NESARC-III) Source and Accuracy Statement. https://www.niaaa.nih.gov/sites/default/files/NESARC_Final_Report_FINAL_1_8_15.pdf

Haack, L. M., Gerdes, A. C., & Lawton, K. E. (2014). Conducting research with Latino families: Examination of strategies to improve recruitment, retention, and satisfaction with an at-risk and underserved population. *Journal of Child and Family Studies*, *23*(2), 410–421. https://doi.org/10.1007/s10826-012-9689-7

Hambleton, R. K. (2004). Issues, designs, and technical guidelines for adapting tests into multiple languages and cultures. In R. K. Hambleton, P. Merenda, & C. Spielberger (Eds.), *Adapting educational and psychological tests for cross-cultural assessment* (pp. 3–38). Lawrence Erlbaum. https://doi.org/10.4324/9781410611758-6

Hernández, M. G., Nguyen, J., Casanova, S., Suárez-Orozco, C., & Saetermoe, C. L. (2013). Doing no harm and getting it right: Guidelines for ethical research with immigrant communities. In M. G. Hernández, J. Nguyen, C. L. Saetermoe, & C. Suárez-Orozco (Eds.), *Frameworks and Ethics for Research with Immigrants. New Directions for Child and Adolescent Development*, *141*, 43–60. Jossey-Bass. https://doi.org/10.1002/cad.20042

Hong, Y. Y., Morris, M. W., Chiu, C. Y., & Benet-Martínez, V. (2000). Multicultural minds. A dynamic constructivist approach to culture and cognition. *American Psychologist*, *55*(7), 709–720. https://doi.org/10.1037/0003-066X.55.7.709

Katz, R. V., Kegeles, S. S., Kressin, N. R., Green, B. L., Wang, M. Q., James, S. A., Russell, S. L., & Claudio, C. (2006). The Tuskegee Legacy Project: Willingness of minorities to participate in biomedical research. *Journal of Health Care for the Poor and Underserved*, *17*(4), 698–715. https://doi.org/10.1353/hpu.2006.0126

Kim, S. Y., Nair, R., Knight, G. P., Roosa, M. W., & Updegraff, K. A. (2009). Measurement equivalence of neighborhood quality measures for European American and Mexican American families. *Journal of Community Psychology*, *37*(1), 1–20. https://doi.org/10.1002/jcop.20257

Knight, G. P., Roosa, M. W., Calderón-Tena, C. O., & Gonzales, N. A. (2009a). Methodological issues in research on Latino populations. In F. Villaruel, G. Carlo, M. Azmitia, J. Grau, N. Cabrera, & J. Chahin (Eds.), *Handbook of U.S. Latino psychology* (pp. 49–67). Sage.

Knight, G. P., Roosa, M. W., & Umaña-Taylor, A. (2009b). *Studying ethnic minority and economically disadvantaged populations: Methodological challenges and best practices*. American Psychological Association. https://doi.org/10.1037/11887-000

Knight, G. P., Safa, M. D., & White, R. M. B. (2018). Advancing the assessment of cultural orientation: A developmental and contextual framework of multiple psychological dimensions and social identities. *Development and Psychopathology*, *30*(5), 1867–1888. https://doi.org/10.1017/S095457941800113X

Manson, S. M., Garroutte, E., Goins, R. T., & Henderson, P. N. (2004). Access, relevance, and control in the research process: Lessons from Indian country. *Journal of Aging and Health*, *16*(5 Suppl.), 58S–77S. https://doi.org/10.1177/0898264304268149

Maxwell, A. E., Bastani, R., Vida, P., & Warda, U. S. (2005). Strategies to recruit and retain older Filipino-American immigrants for a cancer screening study. *Journal of Community Health*, *30*(3), 167–179. https://doi.org/10.1007/s10900-004-1956-0

Meca, A., Sabet, R. F., Farrelly, C. M., Benitez, C. G., Schwartz, S. J., Gonzales-Backen, M., Lorenzo-Blanco, E. I., Unger, J. B., Zamboanga, B. L., Baezconde-Garbanati, L., Picariello, S., Des Rosiers, S. E., Soto, D. W., Pattarroyo, M., Villamar, J. A., & Lizzi, K. M. (2017). Personal and cultural identity development in recently immigrated Hispanic adolescents: Links with psychosocial functioning. *Cultural Diversity & Ethnic Minority Psychology*, *23*(3), 348–361. https://doi.org/10.1037/cdp0000129

Michaels, M. L., Barr, A., Roosa, M. W., & Knight, G. P. (2007). Self-esteem: Assessing measurement equivalence in a multi-ethnic sample of youth. *The Journal of Early Adolescence, 27*(3), 269–295. https://doi.org/10.1177/0272431607302009

Misra, S., Le, P. D., Goldmann, E., & Yang, L. H. (2020). Psychological impact of anti-Asian stigma due to the COVID-19 pandemic: A call for research, practice, and policy responses. *Psychological Trauma: Theory, Research, Practice, and Policy, 12*(5), 461–464. https://doi.org/10.1037/tra0000821

Murangi, K., Perkins, R. C., & Tang, J. H. (2019). *Findings and Recommendations from the National Assessment of Educational Progress (NAEP) 2017 Pilot Study of the Middle School Transcript Study (MSTS). Methodological Report. NCES 2019-031.* National Center for Education Statistics.

Murry, V. M., Harrell, A. W., Brody, G. H., Chen, Y. F., Simons, R. L., Black, A. R., Cutrona, C. E., & Gibbons, F. X. (2008). Long-term effects of stressors on relationship well-being and parenting among rural African American women. *Family Relations, 57*(2), 117–127. https://doi.org/10.1111/j.1741-3729.2008.00488.x

Norton, I. M., & Manson, S. M. (1996). Research in American Indian and Alaska Native communities: Navigating the cultural universe of values and process. *Journal of Consulting and Clinical Psychology, 64*(5), 856–860. https://doi.org/10.1037/0022-006X.64.5.856

Picot, S. J. F., Tierney, J., Mirpourian, N., Ericsson, J. M., Wright, J. T., & Powel, L. L. (2002). Engaging Black older adults and caregivers in urban communities in health research. *Journal of Gerontological Nursing, 28*(2), 19–27. https://doi.org/10.3928/0098-9134-20020201-07

Prieto, A. J. (1992). A method for translation of instruments to other languages. *Adult Education Quarterly, 43*(1), 1–14. https://doi.org/10.1177/0741713692043001001

Ramirez-Esparza, N., Gosling, S. D., Benet-Martinez, V., Potter, J. P., & Pennebaker, J. W. (2006). Do bilinguals have two personalities? A special case of cultural frame switching. *Journal of Research in Personality, 40*(2), 99–120. https://doi.org/10.1016/j.jrp.2004.09.001

Rivas-Drake, D., Camacho, T. C., & Guillaume, C. (2016). Just good developmental science: Trust, identity, and responsibility in ethnic minority recruitment and retention. In S. S. Horn, M. D. Ruck, & L. S. Liben (Eds.), *Advances in child development and behavior* (Vol. 50, pp. 161–188), Elsevier. https://doi.org/10.1016/bs.acdb.2015.11.002

Roosa, M. W., Knight, G. P., & Umaña-Taylor, A. J. (2012). *Research with underresearched populations.* In H. Cooper, P. M. Camic, D. L. Long, A. T. Panter, D. Rindskopf, & K. J. Sher (Eds.), *APA handbook of research methods in psychology* (Vol. 1, pp. 101–115). American Psychological Association. https://doi.org/10.1037/13619-007

Roosa, M. W., Liu, F. F., Torres, M., Gonzales, N. A., Knight, G. P., & Saenz, D. (2008). Sampling and recruitment in studies of cultural influences on adjustment: A case study with Mexican Americans. *Journal of Family Psychology, 22*(2), 293–302. https://doi.org/10.1037/0893-3200.22.2.293

Ryan, C. L., & Bauman, K. (2016). *Educational attainment in the United States: 2015.* U.S. Census Bureau. https://www.census.gov/library/publications/2016/demo/p20-578.html

Santos, C. E., & Toomey, R. B. (2018). Integrating an intersectionality lens in theory and research in developmental science. *New Directions for Child and Adolescent Development, 2018*(161), 7–15. https://doi.org/10.1002/cad.20245

Seaton, E. K., Gee, G. C., Neblett, E., & Spanierman, L. (2018). New directions for racial discrimination research as inspired by the integrative model. *American Psychologist, 73*(6), 768–780. https://doi.org/10.1037/amp0000315

Skaff, M. K., Chesla, C., Mycue, V., & Fisher, L. (2002). Lessons in cultural competence: Adapting research methodology for Latino participants. *Journal of Community Psychology, 30*(3), 305–323. https://doi.org/10.1002/jcop.10007

Sladek, M. R., Umaña-Taylor, A. J., McDermott, E. R., Rivas-Drake, D., & Martinez-Fuentes, S. (2020). Testing invariance of ethnic-racial discrimination and identity measures for adolescents across ethnic-racial groups and contexts. *Psychological Assessment, 32*(6), 509–526. https://doi.org/10.1037/pas0000805

Sue, S., Fujino, D. C., Hu, L. T., Takeuchi, D. T., & Zane, N. W. S. (1991). Community mental health services for ethnic minority groups: A test of the cultural responsiveness hypothesis. *Journal of Consulting and Clinical Psychology, 59*(4), 533–540. https://doi.org/10.1037/0022-006X.59.4.533

Umaña-Taylor, A. J., Yazedjian, A., & Bámaca-Gómez, M. (2004). Developing the ethnic identity scale using Eriksonian and social identity perspectives. *Identity: An International Journal of Theory and Research, 4*(1), 9–38. https://doi.org/10.1207/S1532706XID0401_2

Wang, D., Hu, M., & Xu, Q. (2017). Testing the factorial invariance of the Satisfaction With Life Scale across Chinese adolescents. *Social Behavior and Personality*, *45*(3), 505–516. https://doi.org/10.2224/sbp.6222

White, R. M. B., Burleson, E., & Knight, G. P. (2016a). Future prospects for studying ethnic and racial minority youths and families in diverse rural and nonrural contexts. In L. J. Crockett & G. Carlo (Eds.), *Rural ethnic minority youth and families in the United States: Advancing responsible adolescent development* (pp. 267–286). Springer. https://doi.org/10.1007/978-3-319-20976-0_15

White, R. M. B., Liu, Y., Gonzales, N. A., Knight, G. P., & Tein, J. Y. (2016b). Neighborhood qualification of the association between parenting and problem behavior trajectories among Mexican-origin father-adolescent dyads. *Journal of Research on Adolescence*, *26*(4), 927–946. https://doi.org/10.1111/jora.12245

White, R. M. B., Umaña-Taylor, A. J., Knight, G. P., & Zeiders, K. H. (2011). Language measurement equivalence of the Ethnic Identity Scale with Mexican American early adolescents. *The Journal of Early Adolescence*, *31*(6), 817–852. https://doi.org/10.1177/0272431610376246

Widaman, K. F., & Reise, S. P. (1997). Exploring the measurement invariance of psychological instruments: Applicants in the substance use domain. In K. J. Bryant, M. Windle, & S. G. West (Eds.), *The science of prevention: Methodological advances from alcohol and substance abuse research* (pp. 281–324). American Psychological Association. https://doi.org/10.1037/10222-009

Yancey, A. K., Ortega, A. N., & Kumanyika, S. K. (2006). Effective recruitment and retention of minority research participants. *Annual Review of Public Health*, *27*(1), 1–28. https://doi.org/10.1146/annurev.publhealth.27.021405.102113

Ziegler, M., & Bensch, D. (2013). Lost in translation: Thoughts regarding the translation of existing psychological measures into other languages. *European Journal of Psychological Assessment*, *29*(2), 81–83. https://doi.org/10.1027/1015-5759/a000167

Part II
PLANNING RESEARCH

CHAPTER 7

DEVELOPING TESTABLE AND IMPORTANT RESEARCH QUESTIONS

Frederick T. L. Leong, Neal Schmitt, and Brent J. Lyons

The purpose of this chapter is to provide guidance on developing testable and important research questions. We begin with a section that explores the process of developing a research question. This section discusses the issue of how research ideas are generated, how judgments about ideas that are worth studying are made, and how new ideas or areas of research are developed. We propose a multifaceted approach to addressing these issues, and we also make recommendations to facilitate this process. In the second section of the chapter, we explore how to generate research questions that are important, linking these suggestions to specific recommendations, such as the need to understand the research literature and having a good sense of the real-world implications. We also discuss the likely sources of "less" important research ideas and provide examples related to validity generalization and meta-analyses. In the third and final section, we review suggestions from several top researchers in order to address the issue of how to formulate testable research questions with special reference to experimental research that seeks to discover new effects, extending those effects, and identifying moderators and mediators of such effects. We also focus on the centrality of identifying, evaluating, and selecting psychometrically sound psychological tests for research within the differential psychology tradition.

DEVELOPING A RESEARCH QUESTION

Developing a research question is a multifaceted process, and inspiration for research ideas can come from a variety of sources, including, but not limited to, personal interests, personal and societal problems, other people (e.g., colleagues, professors), and printed materials, including journal articles, textbooks, and news articles. Different researchers vary widely in research topics they find interesting. Leong and Muccio (2006) compared preference in research questions to preferences in music and food.

Many psychologists study human behavior that has become meaningful to them through their own personal experiences. Personal experience is a key source of ideas as individuals attempt to make sense of their own lives (Daft, 1983). Researchers are encouraged to introspect and, at first, be their own subject (Campbell et al., 1982). Specifically referring to researchers who study the workplace, Daft stated that organizations are so rich in people, stimuli, and experiences that anyone who looks around or reflects on their own experiences will find enough puzzlements to last for a productive career. For example, an organizational psychologist who is hard of hearing may study how people with hearing loss make disclosure decisions and request accommodations when applying for work and

https://doi.org/10.1037/0000318-007
APA Handbook of Research Methods in Psychology, Second Edition: Vol. 1. Foundations, Planning, Measures, and Psychometrics, H. Cooper (Editor-in-Chief)
Copyright © 2023 by the American Psychological Association. All rights reserved.

how such decisions affect employment opportunities (Lyons et al., 2017, 2018).

One important feature of a research question is that it makes a significant and innovative contribution to the psychological literature (Petty, 2006). Developing a research question that makes a significant contribution can be a large task involving extensive reviews of literature and communication with other researchers (examples of such strategies are discussed in this chapter), but innovation is also largely initiated by a creative and, oftentimes, unexpected idea (Daft, 1983).

In a chapter outlining cognitive strategies researchers can use to find a research question, Leong and Muccio (2006) suggested a variety of idea generation resources and techniques that can be used to develop creative ideas. For example, by brainstorming, researchers can generate a list of research ideas and then select those ideas that are feasible, supported by research in the area, and are motivating. Additionally, researchers can create mental maps in order to enhance individual creativity and inspire innovative research questions (for an overview of concept mapping, see Novak, 2004). Concept maps help individuals arrange and characterize their knowledge in unique ways, highlighting novel links between knowledge concepts that can be used to provide a solution to a problem (Ausubel, 1963, as cited in Novak, 2004). Leong and Muccio also recommended the "Martian perspective" as an idea generation strategy: by looking at the world as an outsider, as "a Martian who just landed on earth" (p. 25), researchers can develop ideas that have not been thought of by others.

In addition to cognitive strategies, the real world offers many resources to aid in creative idea development. Media outlets (e.g., social media, television, internet blogs, discussion boards) are often filled with news stories and creative ideas, revealing problems that may require research to aid in their resolution. For example, during the recent COVID-19 pandemic the swift rise and sharing of information about the virus on social media (e.g., Twitter) may have parents wondering about the effects of social media exposure on their children's anxiety and ability to cope with stress (e.g., Drouin et al., 2020). As another example, recently Black Lives Matter and stories of racial violence against the Black community have received increased media attention and psychologists may ask questions about how Black employees' persistent exposure to traumatic news events affects their capacities for resilience and relationship-building at work (e.g., Leigh & Melwani, 2019).

Beyond individualized cognitive techniques and real-world reflection, idea generation also requires collaboration. Innovation comes from exposing oneself to a variety of other people and ideas; researchers cannot simply sit alone in their offices and ponder research without considering feedback from others (Campbell et al., 1982). Multiple researchers have diverse sets of experiences and perspectives on addressing issues; thus, collaboration increases the likelihood that new ideas will be discovered (see Leong et al., 2015).

Researchers are encouraged to use interpersonal strategies in order to accrue the benefits of collaboration, even seeking collaboration beyond the academy. Researchers who work in applied settings (e.g., school psychologists employed by school boards to test for children's learning disabilities) are also valuable sources of research ideas specific to issues with which they may struggle and that the academic community has not yet addressed.

Attending conventions and conferences provides researchers with ample opportunity to talk to other researchers about their ideas and gain feedback helpful for the idea development process. In order to capitalize on the vast diversity of expertise present at conferences, Leong and Muccio (2006) recommended that conference attendees listen to presentations and talk to people who have the same interests as they do and talk to people from different subfields to learn how they approach similar issues in different ways. Generally speaking, increasing interdisciplinary contact allows researchers to learn different perspectives and increase the potential for innovative research ideas.

Printed sources are invaluable for generating research ideas. The most important and relevant printed sources are primary scientific journal articles (Johnson & Christensen, 2008). Without conducting a thorough literature review of academic journals in a domain of research, researchers will not know if their question is innovative or worthwhile. Reading every published journal article about a research topic is unrealistic and probably an unnecessary task. Browsing through recent editions of journals in an area of research will provide a sense of the current issues with which researchers of that domain are concerned or struggling. Additionally, each subfield within psychology has specific journals that are highly regarded and publish a field's most exciting and well-done research. Perusing through the table of contents and abstracts of recent editions of highly regarded journals will provide a sense of the types of questions the subfield finds interesting and innovative. Beyond specific subfields, however, there are leading journals in psychology that publish high-impact studies that have relevance to a variety of psychology subfields, such as *Psychological Review* and *Psychological Bulletin*.

Beyond primary sources, research ideas can also come from secondary sources of information, such as textbooks. Authors of textbooks on psychological research methods have highlighted their value in developing research questions for students (e.g., Gravetter & Forzano, 2009; Heffernan, 2005; Mertens, 2010). Information in secondary source materials is a summarized version of the information found in primary source materials. With a goal of disseminating primary source information, secondary sources are helpful for researchers who know little about a topic area and can provide a good general overview of a domain of interest. Textbooks, however, serve as a general review of a topic area and often cite studies that are several years old, neither providing enough information for an in-depth understanding of a specific research topic nor addressing more current concerns of the research community. Textbooks, thus, can serve as a source of inspiration or a stepping-stone to guide the search for a research idea to more particular and current journal articles. In addition to textbooks, conference proceedings are published conference submissions and can also provide a current overview of specific topics with which a community of researchers are concerned. Though unpublished, theses and dissertations are scientific studies that are widely available and often have extensive literature reviews, providing a good sense of the breadth and depth of topics that are being explored by young researchers.

Considering the unlimited potential of personal observation, creative strategies and interpersonal collaboration, and the vast resources available to help develop a research question, the question still is: What type of research question is worth developing?

What Questions Are Worth Asking?

The research training that most psychologists receive does not explicitly teach students how to identify the "right" research question to ask. For the most part, training to be a researcher reflects a more traditional approach to scientific analysis (Daft, 1983). In undergraduate psychology classes or graduate-level research methods seminars, students learn about scientific rigor, experimental control, planning for and removing uncertainties that could upset the research design, etc. This traditional approach assumes that researchers know a substantial amount about the phenomenon under investigation. Petty (2006) guessed that over 90% of what is written in textbooks and scientific journals about conducting research concerns the way a study should be designed and the appropriate ways to analyze the data. Relatively little has been written about deciding what to investigate. We could also apply Leong and Muccio's (2006) food and music analogy to the diversity in perceptions amongst researchers of the qualities of worthy research questions, but there appears to be some agreement that research questions should be innovative (Daft, 1983; Petty, 2006), and contribute to a conversation among researchers regarding the particular phenomenon of interest (Daft, 1985; Huff, 2009) Ahead we mention the desirability of replications that not only confirm the original research findings but also expand it to assess the role of various contextual factors that may influence replicability and interpretation of the results.

According to Daft (1983), significant discoveries in science required researchers to go beyond the safe certainty of precision in design: If we understand the phenomenon well enough to entirely predict and control what happens, why study it at all? Daft agrees with Thomas (1974; cited in Daft, 1983) in that "good basic research needs a high degree of uncertainty at the outset, otherwise the investigator has not chosen an important problem" (p. 540). Though research design is indeed important to ensure the validity of inferences that can be drawn from a particular study, the myth that successful research comes out as predicted, more than anything else Daft believed, restricts the discovery of new knowledge in research. An innovative research question may be one that generates ambiguity about the outcomes in the study. Researchers should ask questions based on ambiguity, rather than certainty, having in mind the probability of an outcome(s). Indeed, Alvesson and Sandberg (2011) noted that research questions are innovative when they problematize existing theories (i.e., identify and challenge assumptions) which in many ways requires navigating the ambiguity of uncharted territories. Innovation is often uncontrollable. Asking a question based on ambiguity is not the same as having no predictions at all. Research that is based solely on the question "What will happen to X if I manipulate Y" is rarely of theoretical or empirical importance. Rather, the best questions are based on the possibility of achieving answers that can problematize or discriminate between theories, allowing readers of the research to think about the particular phenomenon in novel ways.

In addition to innovation, research questions also need to be relevant to the concerns of the academic community. The development of knowledge and new ideas that are of interest to the academic community cannot occur in isolation (Campbell et al., 1982): Ideas also need to make sense to others in order for them to have meaning. Huff (2009) described research as a conversation between scholars interested in exploring related phenomena. The goal of research is to develop explanations of research findings and Huff defined this process as theory development: "Theories are generalized explanations that draw from and facilitate comparison and analysis of empirical observations" (p. 44).

The nature of the theoretical contribution appears to be a key factor in the success of many research studies. Daft (1985) conducted an analysis of top reasons why submitted journal articles were rejected from highly regarded journals in the field of organization sciences: over 50% of articles were rejected because they lacked a theory that provided a foundation for asking the research question and for interpreting the results. According to Daft (1985), theory is the "story" behind the variables; it is the explanation as to why the variables are related. Without theory, a research study makes no contribution to the story of an academic community's conversation (Daft, 1985; Huff, 2009). To aid in theory construction, Daft (1985) recommended that authors think of each variable in a research study as a character in a story. First, researchers should fully describe each character and then describe how and why those characters interact with one another. Research is storytelling (Daft, 1983). The *why*, not the data, is the contribution to knowledge.

Research questions should be uncertain in their outcomes and contribute to the theoretical concerns of the academic community. Determining the innovation and theoretical contribution of a research question may require researchers to use some of the strategies outlined for developing a research question. After generating an idea and before conducting the research study, Petty (2006) recommended that researchers check their research idea by reviewing the literature and asking for feedback from other scholars apart of the conversation to which they hope to contribute. In the next section, we explore in more detail how we believe important research questions are generated.

GENERATING IMPORTANT RESEARCH QUESTIONS

Beyond the broad overview provided above, we believe three elements are critical in ensuring that we consider important research ideas.

Knowledge of the Research and Theoretical Literature

There appears to be a notion that scientific breakthroughs occur as a function of someone having a sudden insight or eureka experience. Eureka—meaning "I found it!"—was supposedly exclaimed by Archimedes when he discovered a method to determine the purity of gold. While the spontaneity of his discovery is what has been transmitted to our generation over the hundreds of years since, it is unlikely that this discovery occurred without extensive effort and thought as to how one might accomplish Archimedes' goal. A more likely sequence of events involves a process of long work and thought such as that provided in the cases of several 20th century discoveries documented in the popular book *Outliers* (Gladwell, 2008). While Gladwell (2008) acknowledged the role of opportunity and the good fortune of being at the right place at the right time, he asserted that something like 10,000 hours of intense practice or effort is required for someone to become truly expert at an endeavor and have the insight to make real breakthrough discoveries. He cited the cases of Bill Gates, the Beatles, and other groups and individuals who had some level of native ability but whose true insight or accomplishments were recognized only after extended practice. Researchers are most likely to have real insight into seemingly intractable issues when they have studied a phenomenon and the related context for a long period of time.

Concern About Practical Problems or Implications of Basic Theoretical Research

Also required is a sense of the real-world implications of a research idea. Great ideas are usually generated as a function of concern about some "applied" problem, a puzzling laboratory research finding, or inconsistencies in theoretical explanations of some finding. We think all these sources involve questions about how "the world really works." There are many examples in psychology. The first test of intelligence (Binet & Simon, 1904) was developed to provide Parisian schoolchildren appropriate educational opportunities. To help the U.S. government with the classification of thousands of army recruits, Yerkes (1921) helped the army develop a group test of ability. More recently, Schmidt and Hunter (1977) developed one version of meta-analysis to show that measured ability and job performance relationships generalized across situations removing the need, in some cases, to conduct validation studies of specific tests prior to using a test. Curiosity as to how brutality in jails could be so frequent led Zimbardo (1972) to demonstrate the conditions in which most "normal" adults would engage in similar behavior. An attempt to understand the role of physical contact in child development led to studies of attachment in monkeys (H. F. Harlow et al., 1971) and similar work in humans and the development of attachment theory and many thousands of additional studies. These are a few examples, but there are many more instances in our field in which psychologists or others have been curious about some everyday problem, sought to understand some major social issue, or were curious about the generalizability of basic laboratory research that had minimal or nonobvious applied implications when first conducted. This curiosity or need led to research questions and in some instances to major programs of research as well as new theories of human behavior.

Integrating Concern About Practical Problems, Research Literature, and Theory

Our view is that important ideas arise from theoretical insight but only when it is based on a thorough knowledge of the existing literature and a curiosity about some seemingly inexplicable research finding or an important applied problem. Practical problems provide the motivation or impetus to grapple with a problem; the research literature provides the basic knowledge and often the relevant questions; theory provides the basis for an integration of the knowledge about a problem in a way that allows generalizable new knowledge or insight to emerge.

Likely Sources of Ideas for the Novice Investigator

For a person who is relatively new to an area of study, there are a number of other sources of research ideas. Many college instructors often develop ideas as a result of class discussions or student questions. In one instance, a question in class related to cross-validated multiple correlations led to a Monte Carlo simulation, the results of which were subsequently published in *Psychological Bulletin* (Schmitt et al., 1977). In the context of a discussion about interviewer decision making in the employment interview, a student asked about how applicants made decisions in an interview. This led to a study of the decision making of interviewees at a student placement center (Schmitt & Coyle, 1976). Any participant in a graduate seminar or a research reading group can cite similar instances in which student discussions of a research study led to ideas for additional research.

Another useful practice on the part of those engaged in some project is to set aside time for "research discussions." Sometimes the planned research or project becomes so time-consuming or the project and data collection is relatively well laid out so that those executing the project do not have time to consider what they are doing and what questions they might be able to answer if they examined the data somewhat differently or they collected some additional data. It is in these situations that a person new to the research team should assert themselves in a constructive way to allow for consideration of novel research. In these meetings, we have found it useful to provide members with specific assignments (e.g., come up with at least one new idea for data collection or analysis) with the obligation that they indicate why those data might be interesting. There is no reason why new researchers cannot employ similar methods to expand or build upon the primary objectives of the project. Minutes of these meetings are taken and posted on a common website and these ideas or projects are followed up in subsequent meetings. Many of the social science/psychology projects are so large and costly that investigators should use them to examine multiple questions simultaneously. Without some specific time devoted to the generation of additional ideas, these projects are unlikely to be articulated or executed. A real success for the new researcher is when their ideas are implemented and produce publishable research products.

Another source of ideas on which to build research is to read carefully the discussion sections of journal articles in an area of interest to you. Very often the author(s) will include a "future research" section or outline what they believe to be the theoretical or practical implications of their work. These discussions can be a rich source of ideas for new studies that build on the author's work. Again, you need to understand the study being described and know the research area if you are to evaluate the authors' ideas and come up with a new study that really adds to a research area as opposed to a study that simply tweaks some aspect of the original study.

A useful way to keep track of ideas (we often lose them) is to keep a list of ideas that present themselves as you read the literature or make a puzzling observation about some phenomenon. Very often it is impossible to follow up on these questions when they first present themselves, but at some point in the future you may have more time or the opportunity to collect previously unobtainable data. Periodic review of this list may help generate a productive line of inquiry at some future time or you may decide at that point that the idea is not worth pursuing.

A great deal of research in psychology is correlational and it almost always involves multiply-determined complex phenomena. This means it is certainly likely that research findings often can and should be moderated or mediated by additional variables. To have insight into these possibilities, there is no substitute again for knowledge of the research and theory in the area. Without that knowledge, suggested moderators or mediators will often reflect naiveté and may actually already have been investigated. However, when moderators or mediators suggest a different theoretical explanation of an area of research, they can have a great impact on a field. Decomposition of the impact of multiple mediators on a dependent variable that reflect different theoretical orientations are also likely to be of broad interest and importance. What we are suggesting here is similar to Wicker's (1985) suggestion that researchers consider the context of their research; map out how it fits into a larger domain (e.g., the act of leaving an organization fits in a general process of withdrawal) or how the behavioral domain in which one is interested compares with another behavioral domain (e.g., risks taken in one's sexual behavior compared to risks driving a car or at a gambling casino).

Some Psychological Examples

Psychological investigators in all areas of investigation will likely have other examples of theoretical breakthroughs, but we think the work on validity generalization (Schmidt & Hunter, 1977, 1998) and structural equation modeling (Jöreskog, 1970) provides two illustrations of our three major points about the generation of important research ideas. Schmidt and Hunter (1977, 1998) knew the personnel selection literature very well. They observed that tests of cognitive ability were often correlated with measures of job performance but that the correlations varied greatly and were occasionally not significant statistically and near zero. At the time in the history of personnel selection during which Schmidt and Hunter were considering these issues, conventional practice involved the revalidation of tests of cognitive ability in each organization and each job for which their use as selection criteria might be proposed. However, Schmidt and Hunter also knew the literature on the stability of individual differences indicated that little change seemed to occur in the relative level of individuals on ability measures across the lifespan. This suggested that the variability in validity coefficients observed in past research might have an alternative explanation. What they knew about these various literatures and what is well established regarding sampling theory in the field of statistics stimulated their development of meta-analysis and validity generalization as well as their demonstration that some individual difference constructs were important across a wide array of organizational situations. A great deal of the variability that was observed in validity coefficients in studies of personnel selection could be explained by sampling error; when one accounts for sampling error, the credibility interval around large values of the estimated population validity was quite small indicating that one could expect sizable relations between estimates of ability and job performance in most, if not all, job situations.

This example is likely not the result of any of the idea generation methods we mentioned in the last section, but rather the result of long-term effort that produced a level of understanding that few other researchers could bring to bear on the issues in which they were interested. In the development of meta-analysis, some might argue that this is an example of problems in the methods of research that led to an innovation. We feel, however, that these were insights into research that came out of a deep understanding of how research was conducted that led to thousands of subsequent studies by the authors and others. The same process seems to be involved: recognition of a problem, long-term investigation, and deep understanding of the phenomena being studied and the resultant novel insight that has subsequently generated many studies of "refinements" to the methods and the application of the methods to a wide array of research domains.

The ideas in this section arose from several decades of experience in psychological research. While we have numerous texts and articles on how to evaluate research hypotheses and ideas and it is certainly a central part of graduate training of psychologists, there are very few treatments of how to generate important and fruitful research ideas. Some ideas about the generation and creation of hypotheses do exist in relatively old papers. For example, Lundberg (1976) listed four prerequisites for hypothesis creation. First, there must be a "knowledge of acquaintance" of a subject, which means that one has a firsthand knowledge of a subject that can serve to better inform more abstract or analytical observations. Second, one must really know the subject area; truly creative thought rarely comes "out of the blue"; it is preceded by the acquisition of a thorough knowledge of the subject area. Third, we must operate from some basic model; perhaps in organizational science such a model would be an open systems paradigm. Finally, Lundberg cited the necessity of thinking about what might be wrong with one's presumed explanation of behavior. This might be a mental exercise that is the basis for generating alternate explanations or mediators or moderators of a hypothesized relationship.

With the exception of Lundberg's (1976) third requirement, these ideas are similar to the three points made earlier; that is, the importance of background knowledge and literature, grounding in the "real world," and thinking about the relationship of some phenomenon to other constructs and perhaps some unexplored ideas. We might also remember a statement from an American Psychological Association seminar (American Psychological Association, Education and Training Board, 1959) that "worthwhile ideas do not come full blown . . ."; they are the result of "a confused mixture of observation, thinking, asking why, cherishing little unformed notions, etc." (p.172).

Role of New Methods of Inquiry

Technological improvements in our methods of measurement contribute to the range and sophistication of the research questions that we can evaluate. Jöreskog's (1970) structural equation modeling (SEM) would have been virtually impossible before the advent of computers that allow for the computational algorithms that allow estimation of SEM parameters. Today, neuroscientists are investigating many hypotheses about the relation between brain activity and behavior. Many of these hypotheses could not be evaluated without the use of electrophysiological and neuroimaging techniques. Likewise, the links among genetics, illness, and behavior are greatly facilitated by the technology that allows scientists to map the human genome. Computer simulations and computer modeling allows scientists to explore the implications of their theories and research findings for large systems that probably can never be investigated using empirical research methods. These relationships can be the source of investigations that provide more refined support for theories and hypothesized causal relationships. In all these instances and more, technology allows for the confirmation/disconfirmation of theories and prior research results and opens up new research avenues. "Big data" (L. L. Harlow & Oswald, 2016) allows the identification of relationships that were never before possible. The analysis of big data would be impossibly time-consuming without today's high speed computers. To be maximally effective in generating and investigating new research ideas, we must be conversant with a wide range of research methods or have access to a research team that provides such expertise.

In summary, we believe there are three elements to the generation of novel research ideas. First, there is no substitute for basic knowledge about a field (or multiple fields) of inquiry. Second, important ideas are usually generated as a function of some practical need or some curiosity about an unexplained laboratory or real-world observation. The research process itself is a constant source of new ideas. Third, the knowledge of extant theories concerning a phenomenon and the degree to which they can or cannot handle various empirical data will facilitate the identification of theoretical deficiencies and stimulate new insight, both practical and theoretical. Finally, we also described several ways for early career investigators to identify tractable research questions. Finally, we acknowledged the importance of technology that allows us to collect new types of data. In the next section, we describe how to determine whether an important idea can be translated into a testable research question.

We would be remiss if we did not also mention the desirability of replications. It is important to replicate all research findings, but we think it is also desirable to replicate with extensions. Most journal authors include sections in the discussion sections of their papers that suggest alternative explanations of their data or possible alternative interpretations or the influence of unmeasured variables. These discussions are useful sources of ideas for new research that both replicates the original findings but also includes consideration of these alternative explanations or nuances. In this way, we, as a research community build on and expand our body of knowledge.

FORMULATING TESTABLE RESEARCH QUESTIONS

The goals of psychological science are to describe, explain, predict, and control human behavior. These goals are hierarchical and build upon each other. We can only predict human behavior when we have identified an accurate theoretical model (and the underlying mechanisms) that explains the target behavior. In order to explain such behavior, we must first fully and accurately describe it. In formulating testable and important research questions, we need to recognize the significance and inter-connectedness of each of these four steps. Given below are some recommendations on how to proceed.

Wicker (1985) quoted Galton's observation that "the roadways of our minds are worn into very deep ruts" (p. 1094) to illustrate the point that we tend to think in repeated and routinized channels that go counter to new ideas and perspectives. Wicker distilled his recommendations into four sets of strategies as follows:

> (a) Researchers should play with ideas through a process of selecting and applying metaphors, representing ideas graphically, changing the scale, and attending to process. (b) Researchers should consider contexts. They can place specific problems in a larger domain, make comparisons outside the problem domain, examine processes in the settings in which they naturally occur, consider the practical implications of research, and probe library resources. (c) It is important for researchers to probe and tinker with assumptions through such techniques as exposing hidden assumptions, making the opposite assumption, and simultaneously trusting and doubting the same assumption. (d) Finally, it is vital that researchers clarify and systematize their conceptual frameworks. They should scrutinize the meanings of key concepts, specify relationships among concepts, and write a concept paper. (p. 1094)

The advice provided by Wicker (1985) bears careful study since it provides guidance in using this multiple and convergent approach to the operationalization of our research questions. For example, related to his suggestion to "consider contexts," he recommended placing specific problems in a larger domain. To achieve this richer and context-sensitive operationalization of our research questions, Wicker recommended that

> Once the domain has been defined, the next step is to identify the major factors or influences that bear on the topic. Each of the major factors can then be analyzed into its components or attributes, and a systematic classification scheme can be developed. By examining all logical combinations of attributes, investigators can plan research to cover appropriate— perhaps neglected—aspects of the problem. (p. 1096)

Wicker's suggestions to consider context, including attending to process, making comparisons outside the problem domain, examining the process in naturally occurring settings, and considering the practical implications of the research are all valuable strategies in a multiple and convergent approach to operationalizing.

Consistent with the idea of multiple and convergent operationalization, Wicker's (1985) suggestions also illustrate the value of using different approaches to identifying important and testable research questions. The multiple strategies suggested by Wicker remind us of the need to move beyond the "quantitative-qualitative" schism. For example, Anastasi (1958) indicated many years ago that continuing debates between nature and nurture contributions to intelligence were counterproductive and most reasonable psychologists recognize that both nature and nurture are important. Instead, Anastasi proposed that the more important question was how nature and nurture interacted to influence behavior. In identifying important research questions that are worth pursuing, we need to recognize the value and contributions of both quantitative and qualitative approaches. Qualitative research offers depth that is often missing in quantitative research and, therefore, the former can serve as a resource for the identification of research questions to be addressed by the latter method (Creswell & Plano Clark, 2017).

As such, we recommend the use of mixed methods in our research, consistent with our view of multiple and convergent operationalism. Such an integrated approach avoids the artificial dichotomies within our field, helping us to achieve both rigor and relevance challenges and to bridge the research-practice gap (i.e., research that has limited implications for the practice of psychology and practice that is not based on research evidence). The value of the mixed-methods approach is also supported by the recent crisis of replication and reproducibility (Shrout & Rodgers, 2018). This crisis illustrated the significant and complex role of contexts in behavior that is often not captured in the experiments. Whereas true experiments buy us internal validity and causal attribution, they lack external or ecological validity.

By replicating, perhaps including a suspected extraneous factor in the new experimental design, we can test various contextual factors that might have influenced the results of the first study. This is occasionally referred to as a constructive replication. Another potential possibility is to attempt to collect correlational data in an actual real-world situation. While a field study of this sort may not provide the causal attributions we may like, consistency (or inconsistency) with laboratory findings would add to our confidence in the robustness of our results as well as their relevance.

Wicker's (1985) final set of strategies includes clarifying and systematizing our conceptual frameworks, pointing to the value of approaching operationalization as model building. By scrutinizing our key concepts, specifying the relations among them and writing a concept paper to explain our model, we will increase our chance of selecting testable (and test-worthy) research questions that will then be refined into important and significant questions.

Similarly, Petty (2006) outlined strategies for formulating research questions that are particularly relevant to our current issue of operationalization and testability. Beginning with the observation that "deciding what to study is the single most important step in the research process and the one (unfortunately) on which there is the least formal guidance" (p. 466), Petty noted the importance of pursuing one's interests in order to ensure persistence and success. Another important observation from Petty is that the type of research questions that we tackle may also vary with the stage of our career. For example, an early-career investigator may not want to pursue a longitudinal study that involves years of data collection before analyses can begin. Based on his personal experience and program of research, Petty offered four specific strategies: (a) discover a new effect, (b) extend an established effect, (c) demonstrate the mediation of an established effect, and (d) demonstrate moderation of an established effect.

Petty's (2006) first strategy for conducting significant and important research involves "discovering a new effect." Discovery is the holy grail for researchers; it is exciting and has important career benefits (the effect may even be named for the researcher—e.g., the Stroop effect); however, it is likely to be achieved by senior and advanced researchers because discovery requires an in-depth knowledge of existing theories and research to discover new and important effects. Petty provided personal examples of discoveries; in addition, a series of biographies in *The Undaunted Psychologist: Adventures in Research* (Brannigan & Merrens, 1993) provides interesting personal accounts of how leading psychology researchers have come to discover new effects.

Petty's (2006) second strategy—"extending an effect"—is appropriate for beginning researchers. Like the first strategy, it requires the creativity and openness described by Wicker (1985). Having become familiar with an area of research, investigators should transport constructs or established effects into new areas. Many significant contributions in the field have been achieved by extending an effect to new domains and new problems. As Petty noted, however, it is critical that these extensions apply to "important judgments, behaviors, stimuli, and population groups rather than to unimportant ones" (p. 468). In order to ensure that "extensions" are to important questions, one may need to employ some of the approaches outlined above such as research discussions and studying the Discussion sections of journal articles carefully. Other approaches to ensuring importance of one's extension include attending conferences, departmental colloquia, and studying critical reviews of the literature, such as those published in *American Psychologist, Psychological Review, Psychological Bulletin,* and *Psychological Science.*

In addition to discovering a new effect and extending an effect, Petty (2006) proposed two strategies that are related to theory development. He recommended demonstrating the mediation of an established effect, arguing that the strategy is central to theory building in psychology. By studying why variables have the impact that they do and by studying the ways in which variables relate and influence each other, one can make significant contributions to the field. Indeed, a common criticism received from journal reviewers of research manuscripts is that the investigators selected an important research topic but failed to address the underlying mechanisms that may account for their effect. For example, in a study of depression, a researcher may find that African American patients, relative to European American ones, exhibit different rates of recovery in treatment as a function of a pre-post design assessment. The discovery of race-related differential recovery rates is important, but what mechanism within the treatment accounts for this mental health disparity is more important.

Petty (2006) suggested that one needs to "specify the underlying mechanism responsible for your effect and then conduct research in which you try to measure this process and see if it is responsible" (p. 469). Your review of the literature as well as your observations from discussions of clinical case conferences may suggest that cultural mistrust is an important mechanism that could be responsible for lower levels of therapeutic alliance among African American than European American patients, which, in turn produced differential recovery rates. Using Petty's strategy, you might design a study that includes a pre-post assessment of cultural mistrust and therapeutic alliance. Using structural equations modeling, you might find that the degree of therapeutic alliance mediates the relation between cultural mistrust and recovery rates. This explanation is likely a much more significant contribution to the field than the empirical observation of mental health disparity.

Petty's (2006) final strategy for identifying important questions to pursue in one's program of research involves demonstrating how an established effect is moderated by another variable (or variables). Essentially, the moderation strategy involves developing a model in which the established effect is proposed to hold "for certain kinds of people or in certain kinds of situations, but not in others" (Petty, 2006, p. 471). Staying with our previous example, once we have demonstrated that cultural mistrust and therapeutic alliance appears to be the mechanism that leads to poorer outcomes for African American than European American patients, we might suspect that not all African Americans will exhibit the same cultural mistrust in treatment. Indeed, our familiarity with the literature suggests that cultural or racial identity may moderate this effect. By developing and adding a measure of acculturation for African Americans (Obasi & Leong, 2009), we may go on to discover that African Americans with low levels of acculturation exhibit the highest level of cultural mistrust and the lowest level of therapeutic alliance. Moreover, these patients may be the ones who show the poorest recovery rates.

Wicker (1985) suggested that it is important to play with ideas, to examine the research area within context, and to question our research assumptions. Much in the same way, Petty (2006) offered specific recommendations to discover new effects, extend an effect, and check for mediation and moderation of an effect. Whereas Petty's advice for arriving at testable and important research questions is valuable, it is primarily presented from the perspective of experimental research, but similar ideas can be used to develop and test models in other substantive areas of psychology. For those who conduct research in other subdisciplines of psychology (e.g., individual differences, longitudinal), an important prerequisite for operationalizing your research question is to select or construct psychometrically sound tests and measures. Just as experimental research is evaluated in terms of the quality of the experimental method and manipulations, research in these other areas is evaluated in terms of the quality of the operationalization of the construct. In this regard, the selection of well-validated and psychometrically sound tests and measures is crucial.

In conducting research within the differential psychology tradition, it is essential to identify, evaluate, and select the best psychological tests and measures to operationalize one's research questions. Indeed, the development of psychometrically sound psychological and educational tests is one of psychology's major contributions to science. One useful strategy is to select psychological tests that have been commercially published. Obviously, there are advantages and disadvantages of using this strategy in operationalizing your research questions. The advantages are that most tests are psychometrically well-validated, often provide national norms for comparisons, and allow for defensible cross-study comparisons. Companies that publish these tests usually select only those that have a strong research foundation. The profits from these tests allow the companies to generate additional research in support of their tests, especially to norm and restandardize them. Selecting commercially published tests, therefore, can provide confidence in the reliability and validity of the measures used in our research studies.

There are many psychometrically sound and well-validated tests that do not end up in commercial companies, and often one has to select from noncommercially published tests. Indeed, there are some disadvantages in using commercially published tests. It costs money to acquire copies of these tests and pay for their scoring, increasing the cost of doing research. (Many companies provide discounts when their tests are used for research [rather than applied] purposes.) In addition, some commercial tests, such as the Strong Interest Inventory, have proprietary scoring algorithms that are not released to the investigators. For these protected tests, it may be somewhat difficult to examine directly the psychometric properties of the instrument and to examine items via factor analyses. The costs associated with commercial tests may discourage or prevent some investigators from using them, especially investigators with low research budgets (e.g., graduate students, investigators in developing countries). There are, however, an increasing number of noncommercial versions of commercially available tests with good psychometric properties. For example, the International Personality Item Pool (Goldberg, 1999) is a viable and no-cost alternative to the NEO Personality Inventory Revised measure of the Big Five personality model developed by Costa and McCrae (1992). More recently, Rounds and his colleagues (Armstrong et al., 2008) developed public-domain marker scales for the RIASEC (realistic, investigative, artistic, social, enterprising, conventional), a measure of the Holland model of career interests, as an alternative to the Strong Interest Inventory, Self-Directed Search, and Vocational Preference Inventory, all of which are commercially published.

Using only existing or commercially published tests also involves an assumption or element of trust that the original constructor of the test has operationalized the construct appropriately and that the items in the measure are representative of the domain of interest. Very often, researchers use an existing set of items with very little or no consideration of the context in which they are used, the wording of the items, and their appropriateness (or potential obsolescence) across different groups or changing circumstances faced by a group. A careful and critical reading of the items in an instrument may actually suggest researchable questions that will reevaluate or refocus thinking in an area of research. Suggestions and evaluations of existing instrumentation may represent a research question worthy of pursuit.

CONCLUSION

In an article providing advice to new researchers, Mayer (2008) quoted from Nobel Prize winner Santiago Ramon y Cajal's (1999) book on *Advice for a Young Investigator*: "Master technique and produce original data; all the rest will follow" (p. ix). In this chapter, we have summarized some useful techniques in developing important and testable research questions. In addition to Cajal's advice regarding the need to master technique and produce original data, we discussed an important antecedent, namely motivation. Researchers who investigate the necessary and sufficient conditions for the development of expertise have found that a basic requirement is approximately 10 years of intense deliberate practice (Ericsson & Charness, 1994; Ericsson et al., 1993). Curiosity, drive, dedication, perseverance, and other related motives are, therefore, essential in the development of expertise as a researcher. We have provided some suggestions and recommendations regarding techniques for developing important and testable research questions, but you will need the motivation to master those techniques. For this reason, we end by emphasizing again the importance of selecting research problems and questions about which you are passionate and for which you care deeply in order to provide the necessary motivation to become an expert.

Whereas we often believe that we are in complete control of our research programs, Bandura (1982) reminded us of the role of "chance factors" in human behavior. We should not underestimate the role of serendipity in research, but we should also recognize that it is how we respond to these chance occurrences that is critical. It is a truism that "chance favors the prepared mind," but it is relevant here. Cacioppo and Petty's (1982) construct of the Need for Cognition, therefore, is relevant to being prepared to recognize and benefit from these chance occurrences. They used Cohen's work to define the Need for Cognition as "a need to understand and make reasonable the experiential world" (Cohen, 1955, cited in Cacioppo & Petty, 1982, p. 117). Whether in our deliberate research planning or in our reactions to unexpected chance occurrences, the task of thinking deeply is essential to formulating or reformulating research questions that will significantly enhance our understanding of human behavior. Indeed, that is one of the major purposes of sabbaticals in universities, the opportunity to be released from the day-to-day academic duties in order to reflect, contemplate, and think deeply about our research programs. Junior faculty are often advised to schedule and protect dedicated research writing times. We propose that it is equally important to schedule and protect dedicated "thinking" times to counter Wicker's (1985) observation that "the roadways of our minds are worn into very deep ruts" (p. 1094).

Earlier in the chapter, we recommended that you review some of the personal stories of leading psychological scientists and their research careers in *The Undaunted Psychologist: Adventures in Research* (Brannigan & Merrens, 1993). Many of these stories provide interesting accounts of the variety of motives that have led these scientists to pursue their program of research and become experts in their field. Indeed, Brannigan and Merrens (1993) were motivated to edit the book based on their "frustrations with current textbooks that, albeit unintentionally, lead students to believe that research is a dry, humorless activity devoid of adventure and fun" (p. xi). In reading these stories, you will find that many of these scientists were captivated, excited, and stimulated by the research questions that they pursued. You will also find that many of them encountered problems, barriers, and set-backs, but they kept going and persisted in their scientific adventures. Research is highly complex, full of challenges, and oftentimes daunting. The underlying theme in the stories from these undaunted psychologists is that each had their own strong, personal motivation for pursuing a research question and persisting in the "mastering of techniques and producing original data" (Cajal, 1999, p. ix). We encourage you to select research questions and problems that will similarly motivate you to become undaunted psychological scientists.

References

Alvesson, M., & Sandberg, J. (2011). Generating research questions through problematization. *Academy of Management Review, 36*(2), 247–271. https://doi.org/10.5465/amr.2009.0188

American Psychological Association, Education and Training Board. (1959). Education for research in psychology. *American Psychologist, 14*(4), 167–179. https://doi.org/10.1037/h0042292

Anastasi, A. (1958). Heredity, environment, and the question how? *Psychological Review, 65*(4), 197–208. https://doi.org/10.1037/h0044895

Armstrong, P. A., Allison, W., & Rounds, J. (2008). Development and initial validation of brief public domain RIASEC marker scales. *Journal of Vocational Behavior, 73*(2), 287–299. https://doi.org/10.1016/j.jvb.2008.06.003

Bandura, A. (1982). The psychology of chance encounters and life paths. *American Psychologist, 37*(7), 747–755. https://doi.org/10.1037/0003-066X.37.7.747

Bickhard, M. H. (2001). The tragedy of operationalism. *Theory & Psychology, 11*(1), 35–44. https://doi.org/10.1177/0959354301111002

Binet, A., & Simon, T. H. (1904). Methodes nouvelles pour de diagnostic du niveau intellectuel des anormaux. *L'Année Psychologique, 11*(1), 191–244. https://doi.org/10.3406/psy.1904.3675

Brannigan, G. B., & Merrens, M. R. (1993). *The undaunted psychologist: Adventures in research*. McGraw-Hill.

Cacioppo, J. T., & Petty, R. E. (1982). The need for cognition. *Journal of Personality and Social Psychology, 42*(1), 116–131. https://doi.org/10.1037/0022-3514.42.1.116

Campbell, J. P., Daft, R. L., & Hulin, C. L. (1982). *What to study: Generating and developing research questions*. Sage.

Cone, J. D., & Foster, S. L. (1993). *Dissertations and theses from start to finish: Psychology and related fields*. American Psychological Association.

Costa, P. T., Jr., & McCrae, R. R. (1992). *Revised NEO Personality Inventory (NEO PI-R™) and NEO Five-Factor Inventory (NEO-FFI): Professional manual*. Psychological Assessment Resources.

Creswell, J. W., & Plano Clark, V. L. (2017). *Designing and conducting mixed methods research* (3rd ed.). Sage Publications.

Cronbach, L. J. (1957). The two disciplines of scientific psychology. *American Psychologist, 12*(11), 671–684. https://doi.org/10.1037/h0043943

Cronbach, L. J., & Meehl, P. E. (1955). Construct validity in psychological tests. *Psychological Bulletin, 52*(4), 281–302. https://doi.org/10.1037/h0040957

Daft, R. L. (1983). Learning the craft of organizational research. *Academy of Management Review, 8*(4), 539–546. https://doi.org/10.2307/258255

Daft, R. L. (1985). Why I recommend that your manuscript be rejected, and what You can do about it. In P. Frost & L. L. Cummings (Eds.), *Publishing in the organizational sciences* (pp. 164–182). Richard D. Irwin.

Drouin, M., McDaniel, B. T., Pater, J., & Toscos, T. (2020). How parents and their children used social media and technology at the beginning of the Covid19 pandemic and associations with anxiety. *Cyberpsychology, Behavior, and Social Networking, 23*(11), 727–736. https://doi.org/10.1089/cyber.2020.0284

Ericsson, K. A., & Charness, N. (1994). Expert performance: Its structure and acquisition. *American Psychologist, 49*(8), 725–747. https://doi.org/10.1037/0003-066X.49.8.725

Ericsson, K. A., Krampe, R. Th., & Tesch-Romer, C. (1993). The role of deliberate practice in the acquisition of expert performance. *Psychological Review, 100*(3), 363–406. https://doi.org/10.1037/0033-295X.100.3.363

Feest, U. (2005). Operationism in psychology: What the debate is about, what the debate should be about. *Journal of the History of the Behavioral Sciences, 41*(2), 131–149. https://doi.org/10.1002/jhbs.20079

Gladwell, M. (2008). *Outliers: The story of success*. Little, Brown.

Goldberg, L. R. (1999). A broad-bandwidth public-domain personality inventory measuring the lower-level facets of several five-factor models. In I. Mervielde, I. Deary, F. De Fruyt, & F. Ostendorf (Eds.), *Personality psychology in Europe* (Vol. 7, pp. 7–28). Tilburg University Press.

Grace, R. G. (2001). The pragmatics of operationism: A reply. *Theory & Psychology, 11*(1), 67–74. https://doi.org/10.1177/0959354301111006

Gravetter, F. J., & Forzano, L. B. (2009). *Research methods for the behavioral sciences* (3rd ed.). Wadsworth Cengage Learning.

Harlow, H. F., Harlow, M. K., & Suomi, S. J. (1971). From thought to therapy: Lessons from a primate laboratory. *American Scientist, 59*(5), 538–549.

Harlow, L. L., & Oswald, F. L. (2016). Big data in psychology: Introduction to the special issue. *Psychological Methods, 21*(4), 447–457. https://doi.org/10.1037/met0000120

Heffernan, T. M. (2005). *A student's to studying psychology* (3rd edition). Psychology Press. https://doi.org/10.4324/9780203015827

Huff, A. S. (2009). *Designing research for publication.* Sage Publications.

Johnson, B., & Christensen, L. (2008). *Educational research: Quantitative, qualitative, and mixed approaches* (3rd edition). Sage.

Jöreskog, K. G. (1970). A general method for analysis of covariance structures. *Biometrika, 57*(2), 239–251. https://doi.org/10.1093/biomet/57.2.239

Kerr, N. L., MacCoun, R., & Kramer, G. P. (1996). Bias in judgment: Comparing individuals and groups. *Psychological Review, 103*(4), 687–719. https://doi.org/10.1037/0033-295X.103.4.687

Leigh, A., & Melwani, S. (2019). #BlackEmployeesMatter: Mega-threats, identity fusion, and enacting positive deviance in organizations. *Academy of Management Review, 44*(3), 564–591. https://doi.org/10.5465/amr.2017.0127

Leong, F. T. L., Chandra, M., & Chandra, S. (2015). Applying the portfolio model of adaptability: A career guide to managing academic environments and departmental politics. In D. S. Dunn (Ed.) *The Oxford handbook of undergraduate psychology education* (pp. 769–781). Oxford University Press.

Leong, F. T. L., & Muccio, D. J. (2006). Finding a research topic. In F. T. L. Leong & J. T. Austin (Eds.), *A guide for graduate students and research assistants* (2nd ed., pp. 23–40). Sage.

Lundberg, C. C. (1976). Hypothesis creation in organizational behavior research. *Academy of Management Review, 1*(2), 5–12. https://doi.org/10.5465/amr.1976.4408646

Lyons, B. J., Martinez, L., Ruggs, E., Hebl, M., Ryan, A. M., Bachman, K., & Roebuck, A. (2018). To say or not to say: Different strategies of acknowledging a visible disability. *Journal of Management, 44*(5), 1980–2007. https://doi.org/10.1177/0149206316638160

Lyons, B. J., Volpone, S. D., Wessel, J. L., & Alonso, N. M. (2017). Disclosing a disability: Do strategy type and onset controllability make a difference? *Journal of Applied Psychology, 102*(9), 1375–1383. https://doi.org/10.1037/apl0000230

Mayer, R. E. (2008). Old advice for new researchers. *Educational Psychology Review, 20*(1), 19–28. https://doi.org/10.1007/s10648-007-9061-4

Mertens, D. M. (2010). *Research and evaluation in education and psychology: Integrating diversity with quantitative, qualitative, and mixed methods.* Sage.

Novak, J. D. (2004). *The theory underlying concept maps and how to construct them.* https://cmap.ihmc.us/docs/theory-of-concept-maps

Obasi, E. M., & Leong, F. T. L. (2009). Psychological distress, acculturation, and mental health seeking attitudes with people of African descent in the United States: A preliminary investigation. *Journal of Counseling Psychology, 56*(2), 227–238. https://doi.org/10.1037/a0014865

Petty, R. E. (2006) The research script: One researcher's view. In F. T. L. Leong & J. T. Austin (Eds.), *Psychology research handbook: A guide for graduate students and research assistants* (2nd ed., pp. 465–480). Sage.

Ramon y Cajal, S. (1999). *Advice for a young investigator.* MIT Press. Translation by Neely Swanson and Larry W. Swanson of *Reglas y consejos sobre investigación científica: Los tónicos de la voluntad* (1897). https://doi.org/10.7551/mitpress/1133.001.0001

Schmidt, F. L., & Hunter, J. E. (1977). Development of a general solution to the problem of validity generalization. *Journal of Applied Psychology, 62*(5), 529–540. https://doi.org/10.1037/0021-9010.62.5.529

Schmidt, F. L., & Hunter, J. E. (1998). The validity and utility of selection methods in personnel psychology: Practical and theoretical implications of 85 years of research findings. *Psychological Bulletin, 124*(2), 262–274. https://doi.org/10.1037/0033-2909.124.2.262

Schmitt, N., & Coyle, B. W. (1976). Applicant decisions in the employment interview. *Journal of Applied Psychology, 61*(2), 184–192. https://doi.org/10.1037/0021-9010.61.2.184

Schmitt, N., Coyle, B. W., & Rauschenberger, J. (1977). A Monte Carlo evaluation of three estimates of cross-validated multiple correlation. *Psychological Bulletin, 84*(4), 751–758. https://doi.org/10.1037/0033-2909.84.4.751

Shrout, P. E., & Rodgers, J. L. (2018). Psychology, science, and knowledge construction: Broadening perspectives from the replication crisis. *Annual Review of Psychology, 69*(1), 487–510. https://doi.org/10.1146/annurev-psych-122216-011845

Thomas, L. (1974). *The lives of a cell: Notes of a biology watcher*. Viking Press.

Wells, G. L. (2008). Theory, logic, and data: Paths to a more coherent eyewitness science. *Applied Cognitive Psychology, 22*(6), 853–859. https://doi.org/10.1002/acp.1488

Wicker, A. W. (1985). Getting out of our conceptual ruts. *American Psychologist, 40*(10), 1094–1103. https://doi.org/10.1037/0003-066X.40.10.1094

Yerkes, R. M. (Ed.). (1921). Psychological examining in the United States Army. *Memoirs of the National Academy Science,* Vol. 15. Government Printing Office.

Zimbardo, P. G. (1972). Pathology of imprisonment. *Transaction/Society,* 4–8.

CHAPTER 8

SEARCHING WITH A PURPOSE: HOW TO USE LITERATURE SEARCHING TO SUPPORT YOUR RESEARCH

Diana Ramirez and Margaret J. Foster

It is difficult for scholars to stay abreast of the burgeoning literature that is published each year throughout the world in their respective disciplines. Similarly, students who are beginning their immersion into the professional literature in their chosen field of study may encounter difficulty in grasping the breadth and depth of the literature on a given topic. Academics rely on databases, or indexing and abstracting resources, to search and make sense of the published literature. While databases provide a necessary portal into the literature, technology can provide a false sense of mastery, especially when anyone can easily execute a search using a familiar database or Google Scholar to identify publications on a topic. How does a researcher know when their search has retrieved sufficient results? How does a student know when their search is broad enough to retrieve citations to the most relevant studies? Planning, a well-designed search strategy, and consulting with a librarian or information professional can help answer these questions.

Literature searching is a means to achieve an end. Searching can serve a variety of purposes moving along a continuum of increasing complexity from a very basic level of known-item searching to the most complex and comprehensive searching in the service of systematic reviews and other research syntheses. This continuum can also represent varying degrees of bias typically introduced during the search process and resulting paper. Bias can occur as a result of the types of resources selected for conducting the search, the search strategy design, and the way in which references are selected from a set of search results.

Some researchers, especially those new to the process, may give little conscious consideration to matching the purpose of their search to the search strategy. Researchers sometimes fail to understand the benefits of investing time in planning a systematic search process, where appropriate, which often results in haphazard and redundant searching, duplication of effort required to screen results, and lost time. Understanding what you want to achieve with a search informs all of the steps in the search process, such as selecting the most appropriate information sources to search, deciding on search parameters, designing and modifying a search strategy appropriate to each resource, being mindful of reducing bias, and improving transparency and reproducibility. Table 8.1 outlines the steps in the search process that are discussed throughout this chapter.

https://doi.org/10.1037/0000318-008
APA Handbook of Research Methods in Psychology, Second Edition: Vol. 1. Foundations, Planning, Measures, and Psychometrics, H. Cooper (Editor-in-Chief)
Copyright © 2023 by the American Psychological Association. All rights reserved.

TABLE 8.1

Steps in the Search Process

Step	Tasks
1	Determine type of search and purpose. If a review, select review type and frame the question.
2	Consider consulting a librarian and select software tools.
3	Determine eligibility criteria and search concepts.
4	Select databases to search.
5	Search for related reviews.
6	Develop a search for the most relevant database.
7	Translate the search to other databases.
8	Select gray literature.
9	Use other search techniques.
10	Complete, document, and report the search.

STEP 1. DETERMINE THE TYPE OF SEARCH AND PURPOSE

When starting a search, one must determine the type of search, the goal of the search, and the expected output of the search. Several published articles have presented typologies of search types that could be combined into the following four types: lookup, exploratory, selective, or comprehensive (Booth, 2006; Gusenbauer & Haddaway, 2021). *Lookup* searches are quick, targeted searches to find a known item, retrieve specific facts, or identify a small number of articles. Examples of goals include searching for a mental measurement, a statistical fact or trying to find studies with particular methods in support of a protocol for a new study.

The next type is *exploratory* searching, with the main goal of discovery. The focus of the search will change along the way as new ideas and concepts are found, leading to the next topic to search. The goal could be to find a research question, a gap in the literature, or just gain a better understanding. The flexibility of an exploratory search can also be its difficulty, as without an endpoint it is difficult to know when to stop. Setting an appropriate range of publication dates, such as 2010 to 2021, to circumscribe the search and determining a date to stop updating the search will improve efficiency. or stopping point to circumscribe a search can help. Finally, the goal could be to learn more about the literature in order to do a better, more comprehensive search after more is known.

Selective searching is the process of seeking studies meeting specific criteria within a narrow sampling strategy. The limits could be by years, journals, publication types, publication status, and disciplines. The scope of the search will directly affect the potential level of generalizability and validity with the review. The narrower the sampling strategy, the more limited the potential conclusions. Selective searching is helpful when there is a short time to produce a review or the review is a brief section within a report.

A *comprehensive* search would seek all studies on the topic, looking across disciplines, languages, and years. Resources searched would include, but not be limited to, unpublished studies as appropriate such as clinical registries, government reports, or dissertations. The search needs to be planned and documented to ensure its comprehensiveness. The goal could be to test a hypothesis, to build a theory, or answer a research question by seeking all published studies on a phenomenon (Gough et al., 2019).

Lastly, one should plan the output of the search. It could be that one only needs to write a paragraph to support an argument or a portion of a paper to summarize briefly current research. If a longer review based on the search needs to be written, selecting the appropriate review method and planning accordingly is necessary for an efficient and well-done review. Several articles have developed typologies of reviews to catalog the dozens of named review types (Cooper, 1988; Gough et al., 2019; Grant & Booth, 2009; Sutton et al., 2019). These review types can be placed on a spectrum from traditional reviews to reviews with frameworks to reviews that are research studies.

The most common type of reviews are traditional reviews and are usually referred to as *narrative* reviews. This is a general term used to describe a summary of the literature. It could be brief, a few paragraphs as an introduction for a study report to provide context or a full-length paper providing an in-depth summary of a topic.

Criticisms of narrative reviews include lack of transparency in the methods, wide variations in objectivity and bias, and sampling the literature for convenience instead of a systematic survey (Rosenthal, 1991; Rosenthal & Dimatteo, 2001). There are few conducting or reporting standards for narrative reviews, although some guidance has been published, including a tool for assessing the quality of narrative reviews (Atkinson et al., 2015; Baethge et al., 2019; Baumeister & Leary, 1997; Pautasso, 2013). Despite the lack of standards, reviewers would be well served by planning, conducting, and reporting searching, selecting, and analyzing methods to improve the quality and transparency of the review.

There are reviews that follow frameworks calling for authors to provide details of methods when writing up these reviews. Examples of these *structured* reviews include mapping reviews, scoping reviews, and integrative reviews. Evidence maps or mapping reviews seek to categorize the literature to find gaps in the literature to inform future research such as further reviews or primary research on a broad topic (Grant & Booth, 2009). Scoping reviews are similar in that they seek to categorize the literature, with the difference being that scoping reviews are trying to define the conceptual and logistical boundaries of the topic, while mapping reviews have set boundaries (Sutton et al., 2019). In recent years scoping reviews have grown in popularity, leading the Joanna Briggs Institute to issue guidance for how they are conducted and Preferred Reporting Items for Systematic Reviews and Meta-Analyses (PRISMA) for developing a standard for reporting (Peters et al., 2021; Tricco et al., 2018). To frame a scoping review question, one needs to define the population, concept, and context. Table 8.2 details an example of a scoping review question. Integrative reviews seek to translate research into practice by bringing together theoretical, quantitative, and qualitative research on a given topic (Hopia et al., 2016).

Systematic reviews are different from the previously mentioned reviews as they are a research method. These reviews require explicit eligibility criteria, search methods, selection, and extraction processes to analyze studies focusing on one research question (Booth et al., 2016). Systematic review methods can be used to answer a wide range of research questions, such as effectiveness of interventions, prevalence, and diagnostic testing reliability (Munn et al., 2018b). Systematic reviews can also focus on questions best answered by qualitative research, such as the lived experience of a particular population within

TABLE 8.2

Examples of Research Questions and Question Formats

Type of review	Research question	Question format
Narrative review	What does the increased number of children with anxiety mean for schools?	No standard format
Scoping	In primary education, what has been written about social anxiety in the classroom?	Population: Elementary school Concept: Social anxiety Context: Classroom
Systematic review on intervention effectiveness	How effective are fidget toys in reducing anxiety symptoms in middle school age children with separation anxiety?	Population: Middle school students with anxiety Intervention: Fidget toys Comparison: (Optional) Outcome: Anxiety symptoms lessened
Systematic review on prevalence	What is the prevalence of separation anxiety in kindergarten to third grade?	Condition: Separation anxiety Context: School setting Population: Kindergarten–third grade
Systematic review on risk/benefit	What is the association between level of physical activity and anxiety symptoms in high school students?	Population: High school Exposure: Physical activity Outcome: Anxiety symptoms

a certain context. Table 8.2 lists some examples of research questions along with question formats.

Selecting the review type is not always an easy task. Guidance in deciding on the best review method, such as the algorithm created by Andrea Tricco, has been developed to assist researchers in matching the purpose to the review (Munn et al., 2018a; Tricco, 2019). Each purpose has strategies for determining the literature needed, selecting resources, and determining how to design the search. Even though not all purposes have a requirement for documenting and reporting the search, it is helpful to track searches. Searchers can be aided by consulting an information specialist as well as employing various software tools.

STEP 2. CONSIDER CONSULTING A LIBRARIAN AND SELECT SOFTWARE TOOLS

There are many reasons to consult with a librarian or an information professional. Most academic libraries designate a subject librarian as liaison to work with students, faculty, and researchers in one or more departments at their institutions. A subject librarian has a working knowledge of information resources that are specific to a discipline and can recommend the most appropriate resources to use. These can include reference materials, databases, and gray literature. Librarians also understand how to utilize database search platforms and related search features to design advanced searches with varying degrees of precision. A librarian can help researchers design a search strategy to match the purpose, whether the goal is to explore the literature prior to narrowing down a topic or to address a specific research question. There are advantages to consulting with a librarian prior to beginning a literature search. Consultations can lead to a more streamlined planning and search process, can improve searching skills, and can result in a more systematic and comprehensive search process. Sometimes major research synthesis projects, such as systematic reviews and meta-analyses, incorporate a librarian as a research team member and author. The librarian's roles in these projects can vary but often include working with the research team

to design a search strategy for the most relevant database and then translating it for other databases; running the searches, collecting, managing, and removing duplicate references using a citation management program; preparing references for screening by the researchers using review software; documenting the search strategy; and writing the search methods section of the article.

There are several types of tools to consider for organizing and analyzing the search results such as software for citation management, sorting articles, and overall review processes. With the number of options continuing to grow, a database of review software has been created, the Systematic Review Toolbox, providing links and reviews to both free and commercial software (Marshall & Brereton, 2015). It covers tools for more than just systematic reviews, including other types of reviews and other processes helpful in literature searching.

No matter the purpose, scope, or breadth of the search, a citation management tool is highly recommended, such as EndNote, RefWorks, Zotero, Mendley, and others (Clarivate, 2021; Corporation for Digital Scholarship, 2021; Elsevier, 2021; ProQuest, 2021). All of these bibliographic managers are designed to perform similar basic functions, namely, collecting and organizing citations, attaching PDFs to citations collected, and creating reference lists in a variety of citation styles. Where they vary is by cost, desktop options, online options, interfaces with other software, options for teamwork, and more. Many academic institutions purchase access to at least one of these tools and offer training and support. Articles have been published on how to use citation managers to support systematic searching, including deduplication, managing references, and reference searching (Bramer, 2018; Bramer et al., 2016; Peters, 2017).

Study selection software goes beyond what most citation managers can do. Selection software can manage the sorting of citations through highlighting relevant terms, quick labeling, and deduplication. In addition, these software offer the capacity for independent screening and evaluation by selectors and facilitate the resolution of disagreements. Processes such as these help to minimize selection bias in the review process. There are many free tools, such as Rayyan or SysRev (Bozada et al., 2021; Ouzzani et al., 2016). Options vary on importing and exporting capabilities, assignment of citations to users, and number of potential labels. Several articles have evaluated these tools and provide comparisons (Cleo et al., 2019; Harrison et al., 2020; Van der Mierden et al., 2019).

Software designed to assist with all of the steps of a review has been available for over a decade now and continues to evolve. Review software include options for setting eligibility criteria, managing study selection, as well as data extraction and quality assessment, and allow several users to work on one review as a team. These include commercial software, such as Covidence, DistillerSR, or EPPI-Reviewer and free online tools, such as Cadima or Colandr (Harrison et al., 2020; Van der Mierden et al., 2019). While these tools would be unnecessary for a brief review, they provide efficient management for more in-depth scoping or systematic reviews that could involve working with hundreds or thousands of citations.

There are many other types of software that may be helpful. Data extraction, or the process of collecting data from each article included in a review, can be facilitated with tools as simple as Google Form or with the more sophisticated Systematic Review Data Repository from the Agency for Healthcare Research and Quality (AHRQ; Elamin et al., 2009; Saldanha et al., 2019). Before trying out these tools, learning more about the overall review processes and standards is beneficial. Table 8.3 lists recommended books and standards.

TABLE 8.3

Books and Standards for Conducting and Reporting Reviews

Type of resource	Citations
Books	Bonato, S. (2018). *Searching the grey literature*. Rowman & Littlefield.
	Booth, A., Sutton, A., & Papaioannou, D. (2016). *Systematic approaches to a successful literature review*. Sage Publications.
	Craven, J., & Levay, P. (2018). *Systematic searching*. Facet Publishing.
	Oliver, S., Thomas, J., & Gough, D. (2017). *An introduction to systematic reviews*. Sage Publications.
Conducting standards	Higgins, J. P. T., Lasserson, T., Chandler, J., Tovey, D., Thomas, J., Flemyng, E., & Churchill, R. (2021). *Methodological expectations of Cochrane intervention reviews*. https://community.cochrane.org/mecir-manual
	The Methods Group of the Campbell Collaboration. (2017). *Methodological expectations of Campbell Collaboration intervention reviews: Conduct standards*. https://www.campbellcollaboration.org/meccir.html
	Peters, M. D. J., Marnie, C., Tricco, A. C., Pollock, D., Munn, Z., Alexander, L., McInerney, P., Godfrey, C. M., & Khalil, H. (2021). Updated methodological guidance for the conduct of scoping reviews. *JBI Evidence Implementation*, *19*(1), 3–10. https://doi.org/10.1097/XEB.0000000000000277
Reporting standards	Shamseer, L., Moher, D., Clarke, M., Ghersi, D., Liberati, A., Petticrew, M., Shekelle, P., Stewart, L. A., & PRISMA-P Group. (2015). Preferred reporting items for systematic review and meta-analysis protocols (PRISMA-P) 2015: Elaboration and explanation. *BMJ* (Clinical Research Ed.), 350, g7647. https://doi.org/10.1136/bmj.g7647
	Liberati, A., Altman, D. G., Tetzlaff, J., Mulrow, C., Gotzsche, P. C., Ioannidis, J. P., Clarke, M., Devereaux, P. J., Kleijnen, J., & Moher, D. (2009). The PRISMA statement for reporting systematic reviews and meta-analyses of studies that evaluate health care interventions: Explanation and elaboration. *PLOS Medicine*, *6*(7), e1000100. https://doi.org/10.1371/journal.pmed.1000100
	Tricco, A. C., Lillie, E., Zarin, W., O'Brien, K. K., Colquhoun, H., Levac, D., Moher, D., Peters, M. D. J., Horsley, T., Weeks, L., Hempel, S., Akl, E. A., Chang, C., McGowan, J., Stewart, L., Hartling, L., Aldcroft, A., Wilson, M. G., Garritty, C., . . . Straus, S. E. (2018). PRISMA extension for scoping reviews (PRISMA-ScR): Checklist and explanation. *Annals of Internal Medicine*, *169*(7), 467–473. https://doi.org/10.7326/M18-0850
	Rethlefsen, M. L., Kirtley, S., Waffenschmidt, S., Ayala, A. P., Moher, D., Page, M. J., Koffel, J. B., & PRISMA-S Group. (2021). PRISMA-S: An extension to the PRISMA statement for reporting literature searches in systematic reviews. *Systematic Reviews*, *10*(1), 1–19. https://doi.org/10.1186/s13643-020-01542-z

STEP 3. DETERMINE THE SEARCH PARAMETERS

Defining the parameters of the search starts with the eligibility criteria or the characteristics of the literature to be included. The criteria could be vague, such as all literature on a given topic for the past 5 years, or very narrow, limited to a particular type of study with a certain population and outcome. Depending on the desired output, the eligibility criteria may need to be established before the start or change frequently if the goal of the review is discovery. For example, scoping reviews and systematic reviews standards require eligibility criteria to be set during protocol development and kept through the review process.

The characteristics to consider in the eligibility criteria can be seen in the question frameworks detailed with examples in Table 8.4. Often a search is focused on a population that could be defined by any number of characteristics such as age, gender, geographical region, a diagnosis, or grade level in school. Depending on the type of question, one may be seeking studies on an intervention, policy, risk factor, economic issues, or other criteria. The types of studies that will be included should also be determined. Types of studies could be broad, such as empirical or quantitative, or more specific, such as randomized controlled trials. Criteria could also include particular outcomes, measures, or time of follow-up with study participants. Lastly, searchers should take into account possible limits for the search, such as year of publication, language, or disciplines.

When listing the eligibility criteria, considering how the choices made will affect the potential bias of the search is important. A type of bias to be wary of is publication bias, which occurs "when results of published studies are systematically different from those of unpublished studies" (Song et al., 2013, p. 71). Publication bias can lead to overestimating the association between two variables or effects of an intervention. To avoid publication bias, the Cochrane Collaboration and the Campbell Collaboration have set standards for searching that mandate that searches are not limited to English or to the peer review literature (Higgins et al., 2021; The Methods Group of the Campbell Collaboration, 2017). Searching for unpublished literature and non-English studies are described in later sections.

The next step is to translate the eligibility criteria into search concepts. In general, search concepts include population characteristic and

TABLE 8.4

Progression From Research Question to Search Concepts

	Case study 1	Case study 2
Topic	Broad topic	Narrow topic
Output	Scoping review	Systematic review
Question	What are the school policies related to anxiety issues in elementary school children?	What effect do fidget toys have on the academic performance of college students with social anxiety?
Question format	Population: Elementary school Concept: Anxiety issues Context: School policy	Population: College students with social anxiety Intervention: Fidget toys Outcome: Academic performance
Eligibility criteria	Any study, report, or review that includes school policies involving children in k–5th grade Language: English only Years: 2010–current Other: United States only	Randomized control trials or quasi-experimental trials with college students using fidget toys to evaluate any type of academic performance Years: 2000–current Language: No limits
Search concepts	Concept 1: Elementary school Concept 2: School policy Concept 3: Anxiety	Concept 1: College students Concept 2: Fidget toys Concept 3: Social anxiety

association or intervention terms with at least one other concept. Some population terms can be difficult to search. An example is the term "adult," which is not always clearly defined in the article abstract. Working with a librarian can help avoid pitfalls when choosing concepts for the search. Also, not all of the eligibility criteria should be added to the search. Criteria to leave out of the search include outcomes and geographical settings or limits. Outcomes for the most part should not be included as a search concept as many times outcomes are often left out of abstracts. Geographical settings should not be included as such terms are not usually mentioned in the abstract or the terms are too varied to include all. If criteria are not included in the search, they will be applied during the selection process by reviewing the full text to ensure studies are not missed. Table 8.4 details the progression from a research question to search concepts for two case studies.

STEP 4. SELECT DATABASES TO SEARCH

In some instances, selecting an appropriate database to conduct a search of the literature begins with matching the topic to the content coverage of a database. Additional considerations, as mentioned earlier, may include the type, purpose, and parameters of the search. Most bibliographic databases index and abstract a collection of publications, such as a predetermined list of journals, conferences, books, and dissertations. Some databases may include a thesaurus of controlled vocabulary used as subject tags, sometimes referred to as descriptors or subject headings, for each publication indexed. Thesaurus terms can differ greatly from one database to another as they are designed to match each database's subject discipline. The majority of databases are subscription-based and are normally accessible by students and researchers who are affiliated with a specific college, university, or other academic institution. Database offerings vary widely by institution, but many subscribe to some of the most common multidisciplinary and subject databases in support of their research and degree programs. A few databases, such as Education Resources Information Center (ERIC) and PubMed, are sponsored by U.S. federal government agencies and are freely available through the internet and are also offered for subscription on various vendor platforms.

Subject databases index the published literature of a subject area or discipline such as APA PsycInfo (psychology), ERIC (education), Sociological Abstracts (sociology), and PubMed (medicine). Each subject database may be offered on a variety of platforms, or search interfaces. For example, the American Psychological Association's (APA's) PsycInfo is available on APA PsycNet, the native platform developed by APA, as well as search platforms developed by the Elton Bryson Stephens Company (EBSCO), Ovid, and ProQuest vendors. There can be overlap in coverage between subject databases. For instance, some educational psychology journals indexed by APA PsycInfo are also indexed by ERIC. The same can be true of multidisciplinary databases. Scopus and the Web of Science index the literature in the sciences, social sciences, and humanities and have some overlap in journal coverage.

One should understand the distinctions between a database, a search platform, and a search engine. This is particularly important with respect to transparency and reproducibility when reporting search methods in a systematic review. Indicating that a search was performed in EBSCO or ProQuest does not provide specific enough information to critique or replicate the search as there are numerous databases offered on each of these search platforms. Search engines such as Google and Bing are designed to search the internet and are not traditionally classified as databases. Google Scholar is a search engine that crawls a subset of the internet having webpages with domains indicating scholarly content, such as educational sites (.edu), government sites (.gov), and organizational sites (.org). Google Scholar is often used to locate gray literature and open access publications that may not be indexed in bibliographic databases. It is also used to locate publications that may be posted to preprint repositories, such as PsyArXiv.com, academic institutional repositories, or academic social networking sites such as ResearchGate.

Other resources, such as ScienceDirect (Elsevier), Emerald Insight (Emerald), SAGE Online (SAGE), Wiley Online Library (Wiley), and Project MUSE (Johns Hopkins University Press), are often referred to as databases but are actually interfaces or platforms designed to search across content produced by a single publisher. Also, Journal Storage (JSTOR) is often described as a database but is actually an archive of digitized journal collections and books in the humanities, social sciences, and some general sciences. Content varies depending on the journal collections purchased by each academic library or institution.

Understanding and making use of a database's fields and search features provides the flexibility for a researcher to design a search strategy with the specificity needed to match a topic. Each record in a database is composed of fields, and the most common are title, author, source, date, abstract, and descriptor or subject heading but may include additional fields such as language, publication type, methodology, education level, and digital object identifier (DOI). Together, these fields describe or represent a single publication, such as a journal article or book chapter. Most databases have the following basic features in common: searching of single terms and phrases, Boolean and proximity operators to connect search terms together, wildcard and truncation symbols to search for variations in search term spellings and endings, and a search history or recent searches feature to combine two or more searches together. Using a combination of fields and database search features allows a researcher to design a search strategy with specificity beyond what is possible in a Google Scholar search.

Some of the most common databases are described in the next several sections and grouped by discipline. Table 8.5 provides database comparisons detailing the discipline, database name and vendor platform options, beginning date of content coverage, and types of publications indexed in addition to scholarly journals.

Social and Behavioral Sciences Databases

The primary database for the psychology literature is APA PsycInfo, produced by APA. It indexes nearly 2,500 peer-reviewed journals in psychology and related disciplines, as well as books, chapters, conference papers, and dissertations and includes the Thesaurus of Psychological Index Terms. APA PsycInfo also indexes the contents of two companion products. APA PsycArticles provides full text access to nearly 120 APA-published and affiliated journals. APA PsycBooks provides full text access to thousands of current APA books and chapters as well as classic and out-of-print books. Each of these databases are offered on APA PsycNet, EBSCO, Ovid, and ProQuest vendor platforms. Two additional databases are EBSCO's Psychology and Behavioral Sciences Collection and PTSDpubs, which is federally funded and freely available from the National Center for PTSD at the National Center for Veterans Affairs (https://ptsd.va.gov).

The primary database for literature in the field of education is ERIC. It is federally funded and made freely available by the Institute of Education Sciences at the U.S. Department of Education (https://eric.ed.gov). ERIC indexes journals, dissertations, and other gray literature and includes the ERIC Thesaurus. ERIC is also offered on third-party vendor platforms such as EBSCO, OCLC, and ProQuest. Additional databases to consider for topics in education and educational psychology include EBSCO's British Education Index, Child Development & Adolescent Studies, Educational Administration Abstracts, and Education Source.

If the purpose of your literature review requires a broad search of the literature, then it may be necessary to consider databases with coverage of journals in related social sciences disciplines and subject areas. Social sciences databases most commonly provided by academic institutions are ProQuest's Sociological Abstracts, which includes The Thesaurus of Sociological Indexing Terms, and EBSCO's SocINDEX and Sociology

TABLE 8.5

Bibliographic Databases

Discipline	Database (vendor platforms)	Start year	Books/chapters	Conferences	Dissertations/theses
Behavioral sciences and psychology	APA PsycArticles (APA PsycNet, EBSCO, Ovid, ProQuest)	1894			
	APA PsycBooks (APA PsycNet, EBSCO, Ovid, ProQuest)	1600s	x		
	APA PsycInfo (APA PsycNet, EBSCO, Ovid, ProQuest)	1600s	x		x
	Psychology and Behavioral Sciences Collection (EBSCO)	1990s			
	PTSDpubs (ProQuest)[a]	1871	x		x
Business	ABI/INFORM (ProQuest)	1970s			x
	Business Source Ultimate (EBSCO)	1960s	x	x	x
	Human Resources Abstracts (EBSCO)	1928			
Communication	Communication and Mass Media Complete (EBSCO)	1900			
	Communication Source (EBSCO)	1900		x	
	Linguistics and Language Behavior Abstracts (ProQuest)	1973	x	x	x
Education	British Education Index (EBSCO)	1929			x
	Child Development & Adolescent Studies (EBSCO)	1926	x		x
	Educational Administration Abstracts (EBSCO)	1965			
	Education Source (EBSCO)	1880			
	ERIC (EBSCO, OCLC, ProQuest)[a]	1966	x	x	x
Medical/health	CINAHL (EBSCO)	1937	x	x	x
	Embase (Elsevier, Ovid)	1947		x	
	Medline (PubMed, EBSCO, Ovid, OCLC, ProQuest)[a]	1809			
Multidisciplinary	Academic Search Ultimate (EBSCO)	1990s	x	x	
	Scopus (Elsevier)	1970	x	x	
	Web of Science (Clarivate Analytics)	1900	x	x	
Other languages	China Academic Journals Full-text Database	1994			
	Fuente Academica (EBSCO)	1922			
	Latin American and Caribbean System on Health Sciences Information[a]	1982	x	x	x
	MedicLatina (EBSCO)	1990s			
Population specific	Abstracts in Social Gerontology (EBSCO)	1966			
	Gender Studies Database (EBSCO)	1930	x	x	x
	LGBTQ+ Source (EBSCO)	1967	x		
	Race Relations Abstracts (EBSCO)	1903	x		
Social sciences	SocINDEX (EBSCO)	1895		x	
	Sociological Abstracts (ProQuest)	1952		x	x
	Sociology Source Ultimate (EBSCO)	1900s	x	x	

Note. APA = American Psychological Association.
[a]A free version is available.

Source Ultimate. For searches involving industrial and organizational psychology topics, consider using business databases such as ProQuest's ABI/INFORM, or EBSCO's Business Source Complete and Human Resources Abstracts. Topics on communication or psycholinguistics might benefit from searching EBSCO's Communication Source or Communication and Mass Media Complete, or ProQuest's Linguistics and Language Behavior Abstracts (LLBA). There are a number of population-specific databases covering age, race, and gender areas, such as EBSCO's Abstracts in Social Gerontology, Gender Studies Database, LGBTQ+ Source, and Race Relations Abstracts.

Multidisciplinary Databases

Sometimes the goal is to search more broadly than the journals indexed within one subject-specific database or multiple subject databases. In this case, researchers should consider searching a multidisciplinary database. EBSCO's Academic Search Ultimate (also Academic Search Premier or Academic Search Complete) indexes over 5,000 journals across the sciences, social sciences, and humanities. Similarly, Elsevier's Scopus indexes nearly 25,000 journals across multiple disciplines. Another database in this category is Web of Science, which indexes over 21,000 journals across its citation databases comprising its core collection.

Health Sciences and Medicine Databases

There are several medical databases to consider, with Medline, a database provided by the National Library of Medicine, being the largest. The free interface for Medline, PubMed, provides access to more than just Medline as it includes PubMed Central as well as free online electronic books from the National Library of Medicine (https://pubmed.ncbi.nlm.nih.gov). While PubMed is very user friendly, it does lack two search options—truncation and proximity searching. For this reason, some prefer to search Medline through other vendor platforms that offer these options such as EBSCO or Ovid. The thesaurus for Medline is called Medical Subject Headings, or MeSH for short, and the addition of thesaurus terms to an individual record can take varying lengths of time to be added so that newer items have no MeSH. Other medical databases include Cumulative Index to Nursing and Allied Health Literature (CINAHL), Embase (providing more coverage on international and pharmacology journal titles than Medline), SportDiscus, and Cochrane Library.

Databases Covering Other Languages

While many databases include English abstracts of journal articles and other citations written in non-English languages, there are more databases to search for non-English journal articles. For example, Fuente Academica is a database of full-text Spanish- and Portuguese-language scholarly journals. Medical related non-English databases include Latin American & Caribbean Health Sciences Literature (LILACS) and MedicLatina. Depending on your topic or population, you may need to consider searching one of these databases. A search on acupuncture as a treatment for depression might include a search of the Chinese literature, while a search on Zika and childhood development could include a search in Spanish language medical journals through MedicLatina.

STEP 5. SEARCH FOR RELATED REVIEWS

Before moving on, locating related reviews can be helpful. This provides a more efficient way of seeing the broader picture of the literature while sorting through less. It will also inform the uniqueness of a review question. These reviews can be analyzed for their scopes and methods to inform the scope of the review and gather useful search terms and databases. Searching for related reviews will include searching subject databases, such as APA PsycInfo, ERIC, or Medline. There are also databases that only contain reviews, such as Cochrane Reviews or Campbell Collaboration or Joanna Briggs Institute. Lastly, there are protocol registries for systematic reviews, such as Prospero, providing descriptions of reviews that are in progress (Schiavo, 2019). After reviewing the related reviews, changing the search parameters or updating the planned search may be necessary. Table 8.6 provides descriptions of these databases.

TABLE 8.6

Review and Protocol Databases

Discipline	Resource
Medical	Cochrane Library https://www.cochranelibrary.com/ Covers reviews, protocols, randomized control trials
	Joanna Briggs Institute https://jbi.global/ebp#database Covers reviews, protocols
	Prospero https://www.crd.york.ac.uk/prospero/ Covers systematic review protocols with human or animal health outcomes
Social sciences	Campbell Collaboration https://www.campbellcollaboration.org/better-evidence.html Covers reviews, evidence maps, protocols

STEP 6. DEVELOP A SEARCH FOR THE MOST RELEVANT DATABASE

Developing the search involves bringing together the search concepts, limits, and thesaurus terms from the most relevant database based on the main topic of interest. For each concept, consider various synonyms based on the related reviews, related articles, terms used by practitioners, terms used internationally, and, if the concept terms have changed over time, terms used historically depending on the years to be covered. For the first database, look for each concept in the thesaurus terms. To bring the search together, for each concept the keyword terms are OR'ed with the thesaurus terms (when available). The final search string uses ANDs to combine the concept terms (concept 1 terms AND concept 2 terms AND concept 3 terms). Table 8.7 demonstrates two case studies searched in APA PsycInfo (EBSCO) and ERIC (EBSCO), both of which have well-established thesaurus terms. For case study 1, the concept of school policy was expanded to include education policy as well after looking at the ERIC thesaurus. For case study 2, there were no thesaurus terms for fidget toys, so the search for that concept was limited to terms in the title or abstract.

After creating the search, it is important to consider having the search evaluated by an expert searcher, such as a librarian or information specialist. The Peer Review of Electronic Search Strategies (PRESS) checklist was developed to evaluate a search (McGowan et al., 2016). It consists of six elements: (a) translation of the research question into search concepts; (b) Boolean and proximity operators; (c) subject headings; (d) text word searching; (e) spelling, syntax, and line numbers; and (f) limits and filters. Table 8.8 provides descriptions and examples of search related terms from the PRESS checklist with which some readers may be unfamiliar. In addition, one should determine if studies cited in related reviews should be included and test the newly developed search with these identified articles (if they are indexed by the selected database). Using the feedback from the evaluation of the search and testing against known included articles, searchers should update the search as needed.

TABLE 8.7

Two Case Study Searches Using the Most Relevant Databases

	Case study 1	Case study 2
Database	ERIC (EBSCO)	APA PsycInfo (EBSCO)
Concept 1	Elementary school: (DE "Elementary Schools" OR DE "Elementary Education" OR DE "Primary Education") OR AB ((primary or elementary) n2 (school or education)) OR TI ((primary or elementary) n2 (school or education))	College student: (DE "College Students" OR DE "Community College Students" OR DE "Junior College Students" OR DE "Graduate Students") OR TI ((college n2 student*) or undergraduate*) OR AB ((college n2 student*) or undergraduate*)
Concept 2	Policy: ((DE "School Policy") OR (DE "Educational Policy")) OR TI ((school or education*) n3 (policies or policy)) OR AB ((school or education*) n3 (policies or policy))	Fidget toys: (TI (((fidget or sensory) n2 toy*) or spinner*) OR AB (((fidget or sensory) n2 toy*) or spinner*))
Concept 3	Anxiety: DE " Anxiety" or TI anxiety or AB anxiety	Social anxiety: DE "Social Anxiety" or TI social anxiety or AB social anxiety

Note. ERIC = Education Resources Information Center; APA = American Psychological Association; DE = descriptor field; AB = abstract field; TI = title field; n# = proximity syntax, # indicates the number of words allowed between. *Works as truncation (stem searching) in several interfaces.

TABLE 8.8

Table of Search Related Terms

Term	Description	Example	Details
Boolean	Three methods for combining terms: AND, OR, NOT AND—the intersection of two search terms; the citations retrieved must have both OR—the results can be either of the search terms NOT—the results will exclude citations containing the search term following the NOT	Depression AND anxiety Depression OR anxiety Depression NOT anxiety	
Proximity	Option in some database interfaces[a] that retrieves results with search terms that are near each other, usually in the title, abstract, or subject fields. The syntax is specific to a particular database interface.[a]	Childhood NEAR/1 development Child W2 development	ProQuest search for childhood near one word of development in any order. EBSCO search for child within one-to-two words of development in the order shown.
Syntax	Properly using codes and punctuation to format a search according to the database interface.[a]	Depression[ti] Depression.ti.	PubMed syntax requires a two-letter field type code to be listed in square brackets after the search term. Ovid syntax places a two-letter field type code between two periods after the search term.
Line numbers	Many database interfaces[a] capture each executed search and label it with a line number. Line numbers are then used to combine searches.	1. Depression 2. Anxiety 3. 1 or 2 S1 depression S2 anxiety S3 S1 AND S2	Example from Ovid interface. Line 3 combines Line 1 and Line 2. Example from EBSCO interface. Line numbers have an S in front.
Limits	Limits usually refers to circumscribing search results by language, date, or publication type.	English only 2010–2020 Peer reviewed journals	
Filters	Filters vary widely between databases and refers to options for selecting and displaying citations from a set of search results that have a particular characteristic.	PubMed examples: human, systematic reviews, free full text	PubMed provides filters for human studies, systematic reviews, and articles that are freely available as full text.

[a]Database interface: Search platform provided by database vendors such as EBSCO, Ovid, or ProQuest.

STEP 7. TRANSLATE THE SEARCH TO OTHER DATABASES

Once the first database search has been finalized, the search will need to be translated for the remaining databases. When moving from one database to another, the keyword searches can stay the same as possible, although there may be differences in syntax between interfaces. The thesaurus terms of each additional database will need to be found that match each concept. Table 8.9 provides an example for case study 2 of translating a search between three different databases from three different interfaces.

STEP 8. SELECT GRAY LITERATURE RESOURCES

After searching the databases, the next step is to consider gray literature and other search techniques. *Gray literature* is an overall term used to describe unpublished works, such as conference papers and posters, clinical registries,

TABLE 8.9

Translating the Search Between Databases for Case Study 2

Database	APA PsycInfo (EBSCO)	Medline (Ovid)	ProQuest Dissertations and Theses Global
Concept 1: College student	(DE "College Students" OR DE "Community College Students" OR DE "Junior College Students" OR DE "Graduate Students") OR TI ((college n2 student*) or undergraduate*) OR AB ((college n2 student*) or undergraduate*)	Exp Students/or ((college adj2 student* or) undergraduate*).ti,ab.	noft(((college n/2 student*) or undergraduate*))
Concept 2: Fidget toys	(TI (((fidget or sensory) n2 toy*) or spinner*) OR AB (((fidget or sensory) n2 toy*) or spinner*))	(((fidget or sensory) n2 toy*) or spinner*).ti,ab.	(((fidget or sensory) n/2 toy*) or spinner*)
Concept 3: Social anxiety	DE "Social Anxiety" or TI social anxiety or AB social anxiety	exp Anxiety/or (social adj1 anxiety).ti,ab.	(social n/1 anxiety)

Note. DE = descriptor field; TI = title field; AB = abstract field; APA = American Psychological Association; noft = anywhere except full text field; exp = explode in Medline, retrieves all MeSH (medical subject heading) terms that are more narrow than the MeSH term; n#, adj#, n/# = proximity syntax depending on the vendor platform, # indicates the number of words allowed between.

dissertations and theses, technical or government reports, and other white papers. Searching for all of these different types of reports is unnecessary; however, it is appropriate to determine which ones are likely to yield studies on a given topic. Some resources may be focused on one type of report, others on one topic, and others are very general. When an issue or topic is very recent, it is even more useful to look at unpublished reports as these are more quickly released while peer-reviewed published articles take much longer due to the process. Both Campbell Collaboration and Cochrane Collaboration standards for systematic reviews require seeking out unpublished studies such as conference papers and dissertations (Higgins et al., 2021; The Methods Group of the Campbell Collaboration, 2017). Table 8.10 provides a list and links to the resources discussed below.

General Gray Literature Sources or Search Engines

There are general sources of gray literature, with the most popular being Google and Google Scholar. One may hesitate to search either of these as the retrieval numbers for most searches is overwhelming. Techniques restricting the number of returns to more relevant citations are

- restrict to files types by adding "file:.pdf,.doc" or "file:.pdf"
- restrict to particular types of websites by adding search:.gov,.edu,.org
- plus sign (+) requires a term, while a minus sign (−) removes a term

WorldCat is the most organized of the overall gray literature search engines, such as limiting by year or report type. Carrot2 provides a different way to search either Google (limited to pdfs) or PubMed, with options to show results in visual format. Millionshort allows users to remove the top 100, 1,000, or even 1 million results to see what might have been missed.

Conference papers. Conferences vary on length of individual presentation reports, with some being only an abstract or presentation slides, and others short-to-longer papers. Locating a brief report, such as an abstract, would only provide brief details of the research. It would provide, however, a trail to seek out the author's (or authors') works, especially to find a fuller report published later. Some databases cover journals and conference papers, while others cover only conference papers.

TABLE 8.10
Gray Literature Resources

Type	Resource title
Overall gray	OpenGrey (https://doi.org/10.17026/dans-xtf-47w5)
	Million Short (https://millionshort.com/)
	World Bank Open Knowledge Repository (https://openknowledge.worldbank.org/)
	WorldCat (https://www.worldcat.org/)
Conferences	Northern Light Life Sciences Conference Abstracts[a] (https://northernlight.com/life-sciences-conference-abstracts/)
	ProceedingsFirst[a] (https://help.oclc.org/Discovery_and_Reference/FirstSearch/FirstSearch_databases/ProceedingsFirst?sl=en)
Dissertations	Open Access Theses and Dissertations (https://oatd.org/)
	ProQuest Dissertations & Theses Global[a] (https://about.proquest.com/en/products-services/pqdtglobal/)
	ProQuest Dissertations and Theses Open (https://pqdtopen.proquest.com/search.html)
Education Policy	Consortium for Policy Research in Education (https://www.cpre.org/)
	National Conference of State Legislatures-Education focus (https://www.ncsl.org/research/Education.aspx)
	National Education Policy Center (https://nepc.colorado.edu/publications/all)
Measures and instruments	Mental Measurements Yearbook[a] (https://buros.org/mental-measurements-yearbook)
	Health & Psychosocial Instruments (HaPI)[a] (https://www.ebsco.com/products/research-databases/health-and-psychosocial-instruments-hapi)
Medical	Carrot2 (https://search.carrot2.org/#/search/web)
	CDC Wide-ranging ONline Data for Epidemiologic Research (WONDER) (https://wonder.cdc.gov/)
	FDA Adverse Event Reporting System (https://www.fda.gov/drugs/drug-approvals-and-databases/fda-adverse-event-reporting-system-faers)
	Mednar (https://mednar.com/mednar/desktop/en/search.html)
Trial Registries	Clinical Trials (https://www.clinicaltrials.gov/)
	Clinical Trials-limited to mental health (https://clinicaltrials.gov/search/open/term=%22mental+health%22)
	World Health Organization International Clinical Trials Registry Platform (https://www.who.int/clinical-trials-registry-platform)

Note. CDC = Centers for Disease Control and Prevention; FDA = U.S. Food and Drug Administration.
[a]Commercial, subscription-based resource.

Dissertations and theses. Dissertations and theses provide summation reports of graduate work, with great variety in length and depth. Some databases, such as APA PsycInfo or ERIC, include selected dissertations within the scope of the database. For a broader more international search, consider ProQuest Dissertations and Theses Global. While dissertations will be longer than most reports, there may be a particular section that matches the eligibility criteria of your review and the literature review may provide additional references and insights.

Other types of reports. Depending on the topic of the search, there are other sources to consider. For example, clinical registries provide protocols of recent trials, with some being regional and others international. Cochrane Collaboration calls for specifically searching two registries, ClinicalTrials.gov and World Health Organization International Clinical Trials Registry Platform, and any other relevant registries (Higgins et al., 2021). Another potential source is Mental Measurements Yearbook, which indexes instruments, surveys, and other tools that have been published and reviewed (Buros Center for Testing, 2021). Lastly, if you are interested in adverse effects of a pharmaceutical, consider searching the FDA adverse effects database (U.S. Food & Drug Administration, 2021).

STEP 9. USE OTHER SEARCH TECHNIQUES

Besides searching a wide variety of resources, there are also different techniques to employ that can lead to more relevant studies—contacting authors, citation searching, and browsing.

All three of these are mentioned by the Cochrane Collaboration and the Campbell Collaboration in their conducting standards for comprehensive searches (Higgins et al., 2021; The Methods Group of the Campbell Collaboration, 2017). Even if the searcher is not attempting a comprehensive search, these techniques are useful to locate other relevant articles. These search techniques are also very much informed by having already found several included articles, so it would be efficient to complete sorting citations from the databases and gray literature databases before moving to these additional techniques.

Searching for and Contacting Authors or Research Groups

After sorting literature found during the database searches, authors, organizations, and research groups will be identified who write on a particular topic. Those who frequently write on the topic or have written some of the seminal works can be targeted for author searches. This technique may identify relevant related works that lacked one of the search concepts or terms in the title or abstract. In addition, if organizations are known to collect, support, or present research on a topic, reaching out through a listserv (an electronic mailing list) or other means with a call for related research could yield reports not yet seen. Lastly, directly contacting authors through emails could also be productive. While this search strategy may not be needed in quick reviews or reviews that have large evidence bases, newer or rarer research topics may benefit greatly.

Browsing

Handsearching was once a common search technique employed by literature seekers. After selecting one or more journal titles and years, the volumes were pulled off the shelf in an academic library and each issue was searched by hand. Today, browsing tables of contents online has replaced the need to pull the physical item off the shelf and with ever increasing journal titles switching to digital online formats will continue to decrease.

The Cochrane Collaboration and Campbell Collaboration no longer advocate for this type of searching. This search technique may seem unnecessary given the number of databases and other resources available for searching journals. The main need for content browsing is for those relevant journal titles (or conference proceedings) that are not well indexed. As this is title specific, an information specialist with expertise in that discipline may need to be consulted to get a list of potential journal titles.

Reference Searching

Of all the search techniques beyond databases, reference searching can be the most rewarding and important technique to employ. It is also known as *snowballing*, *ancestry search*, *chain searching*, *pearl growing*, or *citation mining*. There are two directions to consider when reference searching. Backwards search involves seeking those sources that were cited by the relevant literature, usually provided in the reference list at the end of a report. Forwards search involves seeking those that have cited the included literature, which need to be located by using a different resource. There are three main resources that can be used to locate citing references: Web of Science, Scopus, and Google Scholar. Each of these resources indexes different types of publications and will retrieve different results when looking for cited and citing references from the same article. While it is not necessary to use all three resources, if one does not index a particular report, it may be necessary to try one of the others.

STEP 10. COMPLETE, DOCUMENT, AND REPORT THE SEARCH

Completing the search involves deciding when the search is done according to the search plan or goal of the search. For searches designed for scoping and systematic reviews, a protocol should be developed before starting the review, listing all of the resources to be searched and additional search techniques to be employed. The search should continue to be updated until the manuscript is submitted for publication, if desired.

For exploratory searches, a limit should be set on when to stop, either by number of resources or a date.

Throughout the search there are key elements that need to be documented in order to track the search, evaluate, and rerun the search as needed. For each database search, there are seven items to record: database, interface, date the search was run, copy and paste actual search, any limiters or filters selected, years covered by the search, and the number of citations retrieved. For nondatabase searches, record the resources used, the process, copy and paste search terms, date, and number of citations retrieved. The PRISMA-Search standard provides guidelines on documenting the breadth of a review search, from database searching to other search techniques. It has four categories: information sources and methods, search strategies, peer review, and managing records. The goal of the standard is for the entire search process and results to be fully described, ensuring that it can be fully evaluated for transparency, reproducibility, and appropriateness given the search parameters (Rethlefsen et al., 2021).

CONCLUSION

We introduced the concept of searching the literature with a purpose in mind and the importance of understanding your goals prior to beginning a search. Then we outlined and described the accompanying steps in designing a search strategy to match the purpose and to support your research. The purposes or goals of a search fall into four major types: searching for known items, exploration of a topic, selective searching to support an idea or viewpoint, and comprehensive searching used with various research syntheses. Consulting with a librarian or information professional can often provide the guidance researchers need to plan effectively an efficient search process, taking into consideration a variety of helpful tools to manage the search and the ways a librarian can be incorporated into a research synthesis project as a team member and author. Librarians can also review your search strategy for possible improvements or help to improve your searching skills. We discussed some of the intricacies involved in developing a search strategy from determining the eligibility criteria and search concepts, to selecting relevant databases, to searching for gray literature and using other search techniques. We also touched on a number of standards on conducting and reporting of search strategies for use with systematic reviews and related research syntheses and listed a number of books for further reading. We hope that this chapter will lead researchers to recognize the importance and benefits of spending time in planning and designing searches of the literature.

References

Atkinson, K. M., Koenka, A. C., Sanchez, C. E., Moshontz, H., & Cooper, H. (2015). Reporting standards for literature searches and report inclusion criteria: Making research syntheses more transparent and easy to replicate. *Research Synthesis Methods*, 6(1), 87–95. https://doi.org/10.1002/jrsm.1127

Baethge, C., Goldbeck-Wood, S., & Mertens, S. (2019). SANRA—A scale for the quality assessment of narrative review articles. *Research Integrity and Peer Review*, 4(1), 1–7. https://doi.org/10.1186/s41073-019-0064-8

Baumeister, R. F., & Leary, M. R. (1997). Writing narrative literature reviews. *Review of General Psychology*, 1(3), 311–320. https://doi.org/10.1037/1089-2680.1.3.311

Booth, A. (2006). "Brimful of STARLITE": Toward standards for reporting literature searches. *Journal of the Medical Library Association*, 94(4), 421–429, e205.

Booth, A., Sutton, A., & Papaioannou, D. (2016). *Systematic approaches to a successful literature review*. Sage Publications.

Bozada, T., Jr., Borden, J., Workman, J., Del Cid, M., Malinowski, J., & Luechtefeld, T. (2021). Sysrev: A FAIR platform for data curation and systematic evidence review. *Frontiers in Artificial Intelligence*, 4, Article 685298. https://doi.org/10.3389/frai.2021.685298

Bramer, W. M. (2018). Reference checking for systematic reviews using Endnote. *Journal of the Medical Library Association*, 106(4), 542–546. https://doi.org/10.5195/jmla.2018.489

Bramer, W. M., Giustini, D., de Jonge, G. B., Holland, L., & Bekhuis, T. (2016). De-duplication of database search results for systematic reviews in EndNote.

Journal of the Medical Library Association, 104(3), 240–243. https://doi.org/10.3163/1536-5050.104.3.014

Buros Center for Testing. (2021). *Mental measurements yearbook*. https://buros.org/mental-measurements-yearbook

Clarivate. (2021). *EndNote* [Computer software]. https://endnote.com/

Cleo, G., Scott, A. M., Islam, F., Julien, B., & Beller, E. (2019). Usability and acceptability of four systematic review automation software packages: A mixed method design. *Systematic Reviews, 8*(1), 145–146. https://doi.org/10.1186/s13643-019-1069-6

Cooper, H. M. (1988). Organizing knowledge syntheses: A taxonomy of literature reviews. *Knowledge in Society, 1*(1), 104–126. https://doi.org/10.1007/BF03177550

Corporation for Digital Scholarship. (2021). *Zotero* [Computer software]. https://www.zotero.org/

Elamin, M. B., Flynn, D. N., Bassler, D., Briel, M., Alonso-Coello, P., Karanicolas, P. J., Guyatt, G. H., Malaga, G., Furukawa, T. A., Kunz, R., Schünemann, H., Murad, M. H., Barbui, C., Cipriani, A., & Montori, V. M. (2009). Choice of data extraction tools for systematic reviews depends on resources and review complexity. *Journal of Clinical Epidemiology, 62*(5), 506–510. https://doi.org/10.1016/j.jclinepi.2008.10.016

Elsevier. (2021). *Mendeley* [Computer software]. https://www.mendeley.com/

Gough, D., Thomas, J., & Oliver, S. (2019). *Clarifying differences between reviews within evidence ecosystems*. Springer Science and Business Media LLC. https://doi.org/10.1186/s13643-019-1089-2

Grant, M. J., & Booth, A. (2009). A typology of reviews: An analysis of 14 review types and associated methodologies. *Health Information and Libraries Journal, 26*(2), 91–108. https://doi.org/10.1111/j.1471-1842.2009.00848.x

Gusenbauer, M., & Haddaway, N. R. (2021). What every researcher should know about searching—Clarified concepts, search advice, and an agenda to improve finding in academia. *Research Synthesis Methods, 12*(2), 136–147. https://doi.org/10.1002/jrsm.1457

Harrison, H., Griffin, S. J., Kuhn, I., & Usher-Smith, J. A. (2020). Software tools to support title and abstract screening for systematic reviews in healthcare: An evaluation. *BMC Medical Research Methodology, 20*(1), 1–12. https://doi.org/10.1186/s12874-020-0897-3

Higgins, J. P. T., Lasserson, T., Chandler, J., Tovey, D., Thomas, J., Flemyng, E., & Churchill, R. (2021). *Methodological expectations of Cochrane intervention reviews*. Cochrane Community. https://community.cochrane.org/mecir-manual

Hopia, H., Latvala, E., & Liimatainen, L. (2016). Reviewing the methodology of an integrative review. *Scandinavian Journal of Caring Sciences, 30*(4), 662–669. https://doi.org/10.1111/scs.12327

Marshall, C., & Brereton, P. (2015, April 27). Systematic review toolbox: A catalogue of tools to support systematic reviews. In *EASE '15: Proceedings of the 19th International Conference on Evaluation and Assessment in Software Engineering*, Article 23. https://doi.org/10.1145/2745802.2745824

McGowan, J., Sampson, M., Salzwedel, D. M., Cogo, E., Foerster, V., & Lefebvre, C. (2016). PRESS Peer review of electronic search strategies: 2015 Guideline statement. *Journal of Clinical Epidemiology, 75*, 40–46. https://doi.org/10.1016/j.jclinepi.2016.01.021

The Methods Group of the Campbell Collaboration. (2017). *Methodological expectations of Campbell Collaboration intervention reviews: Conduct standards*. Campbell Collaboration. https://doi.org/10.4073/cpg.2016.3

Munn, Z., Peters, M. D. J., Stern, C., Tufanaru, C., McArthur, A., & Aromataris, E. (2018a). Systematic review or scoping review? Guidance for authors when choosing between a systematic or scoping review approach. *BMC Medical Research Methodology, 18*(1), 143. https://doi.org/10.1186/s12874-018-0611-x

Munn, Z., Stern, C., Aromataris, E., Lockwood, C., & Jordan, Z. (2018b). What kind of systematic review should I conduct? A proposed typology and guidance for systematic reviewers in the medical and health sciences. *BMC Medical Research Methodology, 18*(1), 5. https://doi.org/10.1186/s12874-017-0468-4

Ouzzani, M., Hammady, H., Fedorowicz, Z., & Elmagarmid, A. (2016). Rayyan—A web and mobile app for systematic reviews. *Systematic Reviews, 5*(1), 210–214. https://doi.org/10.1186/s13643-016-0384-4

Pautasso, M. (2013). Ten simple rules for writing a literature review. *PLOS Computational Biology, 9*(7), e1003149. https://doi.org/10.1371/journal.pcbi.1003149

Peters, M. D. (2017). Managing and coding references for systematic reviews and scoping reviews in EndNote. *Medical Reference Services Quarterly, 36*(1), 19–31. https://doi.org/10.1080/02763869.2017.1259891

Peters, M. D. J., Marnie, C., Tricco, A. C., Pollock, D., Munn, Z., Alexander, L., McInerney, P., Godfrey, C. M., & Khalil, H. (2021). Updated methodological guidance for the conduct of scoping reviews. *JBI Evidence Implementation, 19*(1), 3–10. https://doi.org/10.1097/XEB.0000000000000277

ProQuest. (2021). *RefWorks* [Computer software]. https://refworks.proquest.com/

Rethlefsen, M. L., Kirtley, S., Waffenschmidt, S., Ayala, A. P., Moher, D., Page, M. J., Koffel, J. B., & PRISMA-S Group. (2021). PRISMA-S: An extension to the PRISMA statement for reporting literature searches in systematic reviews. *Systematic Reviews, 10*(1), 1–19. https://doi.org/10.1186/s13643-020-01542-z

Rosenthal, R. (Ed.). (1991). *Meta-analytic procedures for social research*. Sage Publications. https://doi.org/10.4135/9781412984997

Rosenthal, R., & DiMatteo, M. R. (2001). Meta-analysis: Recent developments in quantitative methods for literature reviews. *Annual Review of Psychology, 52*(1), 59–82. https://doi.org/10.1146/annurev.psych.52.1.59

Saldanha, I. J., Smith, B. T., Ntzani, E., Jap, J., Balk, E. M., & Lau, J. (2019). The Systematic Review Data Repository (SRDR): Descriptive characteristics of publicly available data and opportunities for research. *Systematic Reviews, 8*(1), 334. https://doi.org/10.1186/s13643-019-1250-y

Schiavo, J. H. (2019). PROSPERO: An international register of systematic review protocols. *Medical Reference Services Quarterly, 38*(2), 171–180. https://doi.org/10.1080/02763869.2019.1588072

Song, F., Hooper, L., & Loke, Y. (2013). Publication bias: What is it? How do we measure it? How do we avoid it? *Open Access Journal of Clinical Trials, 5*(1), 71–81. https://doi.org/10.2147/OAJCT.S34419

Sutton, A., Clowes, M., Preston, L., & Booth, A. (2019). Meeting the review family: Exploring review types and associated information retrieval requirements. *Health Information and Libraries Journal, 36*(3), 202–222. https://doi.org/10.1111/hir.12276

Tricco, A. (2019). *What review is right for you?* https://whatreviewisrightforyou.knowledgetranslation.net/

Tricco, A. C., Lillie, E., Zarin, W., O'Brien, K. K., Colquhoun, H., Levac, D., Moher, D., Peters, M. D. J., Horsley, T., Weeks, L., Hempel, S., Akl, E. A., Chang, C., McGowan, J., Stewart, L., Hartling, L., Aldcroft, A., Wilson, M. G., Garritty, C., . . . Straus, S. E. (2018). PRISMA Extension for Scoping Reviews (PRISMA-ScR): Checklist and explanation. *Annals of Internal Medicine, 169*(7), 467–473. https://doi.org/10.7326/M18-0850

U.S. Food & Drug Administration. (2021). *FDA Adverse Event Reporting System (FAERS)*. https://www.fda.gov/drugs/drug-approvals-and-databases/fda-adverse-event-reporting-system-faers

Van der Mierden, S., Tsaioun, K., Bleich, A., & Leenaars, C. H. C. (2019). Software tools for literature screening in systematic reviews in biomedical research. *ALTEX, 36*(3), 508–517. https://doi.org/10.14573/altex.1902131

CHAPTER 9

PSYCHOLOGICAL MEASUREMENT: SCALING AND ANALYSIS

Heather Hayes and Susan E. Embretson

In science, theories are developed and evaluated via hypothesis testing for a range of phenomena from the behavior of subatomic particles to human personality. To study the phenomenon of interest, it must be operationally defined and quantified or measured. For example, a researcher wants to study aggression. How does one define aggression? Perhaps we define aggression as physical harm inflicted on another human being. Now, we need to systematically assign values to our operationally defined phenomenon so that we know how little versus how much of it there can be and the ideal way to manipulate mathematically and analyze it. This system of rules for assigning numbers to a phenomenon of interest is the essence of measurement (Campbell, 1920; Russell, 1903; Stevens, 1946). We are more interested in measuring properties of an object rather than the object itself (e.g., aggression rather than the aggressor; Torgerson, 1958), and these properties become variables once quantified. Now, aggression is established as a variable, and we can study it and collect data on it for the purpose of making inferences about it and contributing to our collective understanding of "aggression."

This process of measurement is critical to the social and behavioral sciences, as no substantive theory regarding how certain psychological variables interact or affect one another can be tested without first understanding the mathematical properties of values used to represent these variables (Michell, 1990).

As stated in Michell (1997):

> Measurement always presupposes theory: the claim that an attribute is quantitative is, itself, always a theory and that claim is generally embedded within a much wider quantitative theory involving the hypothesis that specific quantitative relationships between attributes obtain. Because the hypothesis that any attribute (be it physical or psychological) is quantitative is a contingent, empirical hypothesis that may, in principle, be false, the scientist proposing such a hypothesis is always logically committed to the task of testing this claim whether this commitment is recognized or not. (p. 359)

Moreover, the object of measurement is crucial. Measurements can refer to properties of a respondent, a stimulus (e.g., experimental treatment, cognitive task, test item) to which the respondent responds or reacts, or the intersection of these two objects as manifested in a response-focused measure. Thus, as will be elaborated upon later in the section Focus of Measurement and Testing: What Is Being Scaled?, scales vary not only in terms of the relationships among values but also how they can be applied to a variety of variable types—respondent, item, or the item response, itself.

Another unique issue emerges in psychological science and testing—namely, the latent nature of many psychological variables, such as cognitive ability, personality, attitudes, and motivation. Back to our example using aggression as a variable, suppose we wanted to study individual differences in aggression or a latent trait of "aggressiveness" or one's tendency toward aggressive acts. Given the added complexity of measuring a variable that cannot be directly observed, operational definitions are complex, often multidimensional, and not conducive to a direct or single observation. A proxy for the latent variable is a set of item scores that, hypothetically, statistically correlate with one another sufficiently to warrant a common, underlying factor that accounts for, or explains, all the variance among item scores (e.g., "aggressiveness") and, hypothetically, predicts outcomes related to aggression. Establishing a reliable and valid system of measurement, therefore, is crucial to adequately studying latent psychological phenomena so much so that there are theories surrounding these types of variables and how they are scaled or measured (e.g., classical test theory and latent trait theory). As is shown later in the section Impact of Scale Level on Statistical Inferences in Latent Trait Measurement, *latent* psychological variables and the method of measuring and comparing these variables are particularly limited by the scales of measurement that are used—more so than for observed data (McDonald, 1999). Specifically, the extent to which a measurement scale reflects real numbers (arguably defined as continuous or quantitative in nature) determines the extent to which these values can be mathematically manipulated for the purposes of studying the relationships among variables (Stevens, 1946; Townsend & Ashby, 1984). In other words, the type of analysis used to investigate the relationships among variables needs to be aligned with the scale of measurement underlying these variables. Inappropriate analysis of data, given its scaling properties, can result in misleading conclusions, particularly for latent variables (McDonald, 1999; Townsend & Ashby, 1984).

MEASUREMENT SCALES: REAL NUMBERS AND LEVELS OF MEASUREMENT

In psychology, the most well-known and frequently cited taxonomy of measurement scales is that of Stevens (1946). Alternative taxonomies have emerged (e.g., Coombs, 1950; Torgerson, 1958). Furthermore, as is demonstrated later in the section Theory and Measurement Paradigms, its validity in terms of implications for statistical analysis has been disputed by several researchers (e.g., Gaito, 1980; Lord, 1953; and see Michell, 1986, 1990). Nevertheless, his taxonomy and ideas served as a basis for the development of further, more modern measurement theory (Townsend & Ashby, 1984).

Stevens's (1946) taxonomy consists of four scale levels that differ from one another in the number of axioms that hold for the numerical values of variables and, consequently, the extent to which these differentially scaled values constitute real numbers and can be mathematically manipulated (McDonald, 1999; Torgerson, 1958). These scale levels can be found in Table 9.1. Although there are 10 axioms, they can be narrowed down to four categories based on the mathematical relations among values within the scaled variable: (a) nominal, (b) order, (c) additivity, and (d) null or origin (Hölder, 1901; McDonald, 1999).

Nominal

The nominal scale of measurement is the most basic of the four levels. Scales at this level fulfill Axioms 1, 2, and 3. Based on these axioms, the properties of two objects measured on a nominal scale can only be compared in terms of whether or

TABLE 9.1

Scale Levels

	Axiomatic property	Scale level	Permissible transformations	Permissible statistics
1	Either $a = b$ or $a \neq b$	Nominal	Isomorphic	Mode; Coefficient; chi-square
2	If $a = b$ then $b = a$			
3	If $a = b$ and $b = c$ then $a = c$			
4	If $a > b$ then a not $\leq b$	Ordinal	Monotonic	Median; Spearman correlations; interquartile range
5	If $a > b$ and $b > c$ then $a > c$			
6	$a + b = b + a$	Interval	Linear	Mean; standard deviation; Pearson correlations
7	If $a = c$ and $b = d$ then $a + b = c + d$			
8	$(a + b) + c = a(b + c)$			
9	$a + 0 = a$	Ratio	Ratio	Mean; standard deviation; Pearson correlations
10	If $a = c$ and $b > 0$ then $a + b > c$			

not they fall into the same or different categories (equality and inequality, respectively). In terms of variable representation, values take the form of exhaustive and mutually exclusive categories. Examples of observed nominal variables include gender, ethnicity, and treatment type as well as other properties for which a respondent belongs to only one of the available categories at the time of measurement. Some latent variables are also categorical. For example, in an assessment of personality disorders, respondents may differ in response strategy, such as faking good, faking bad, or honest responding, and can be identified based on latent class analysis of observed data (i.e., responses to items in an assessment of personality disorder).

Given the equivalency rule and the limited information provided by this type of scale, comparisons among respondents on a variable such as response strategy or personality type are relatively simple. Specifically, the most we can observe of data in which values are scaled as a nominal variable is two or more homogeneous groups or classes of individuals. That is, within nominal categories there is no variance of numerical values. For example, all respondents in a given variable category (e.g., females, treatment group, response strategy) are interpreted as being equivalent to one another in terms of the variable value, but all the individuals in one category are different (in value) from respondents in another category (e.g., individuals who are faking nice on a personality disorder assessment are more similar to one another in response strategy than to individuals who are faking bad). Nominal variables are also described as "qualitative" in the sense that the variables reflect qualities rather than quantities of a variable.

The limited information inherent in nominal variable values results in greater flexibility when transforming values. In fact, numbers need not be involved until coding is performed for the purpose of analysis (e.g., Cohen et al., 1983).

Ordinal

Number values that meet the requirements of Axioms 4 and 5 (in addition to the preceding identity axioms) can be classified as an ordinal level of measurement (see Table 9.1). These relationships among values are more complex than those that achieve the identity requirement because values can now be ordered along a continuum representing quantity of the variable of interest. Specifically, a dominance relation is established among any three distinct values a, b, and c, where c dominates (or is higher in value) than b, which in turn, dominates a. Values of variables measuring physical objects dominate one another in some observable manner. For example, the length of Rod A exceeds that of Rod B when the two rods are placed side by side. The Moh's Hardness Scale (Mineralogists in 1822) has a range from 1 (the softest mineral is talc) to 10 (the hardest mineral is diamond). Hardness was determined based on the extent to which each increasingly hard mineral scratched its predecessor (Torgerson, 1958). Examples of ordinal-scaled variables in psychology include attitudes and personality when item responses invoke a Likert scale (e.g., an item response that ranges from 1 for *strongly disagree* to 5 for *strongly agree*).

As a result of the latter characteristics of values at an ordinal level of measurement, transformation of variable values is more restricted than that of nominal variable values. Specifically, the transformation must preserve the ordering of values across respondents or objects. This is called a monotonic (order preserving) transformation. Examples include squaring or logging the original values.

Interval

Interval scales conform to Axioms 6, 7, and 8 as well as all preceding axioms (see Table 9.1). With these relational properties, one may now ascertain the intervals between any given set of variable values. More specifically, the *distance* (i.e., differences) between values can be ordered such that the distance between any two numerical values is greater than, equal to, or less than the difference between any other two values. Thus, numbers that achieve additivity can be mathematically manipulated by combining, concatenating, or adding them to one another. There is, however, no fixed origin or natural zero on the continuum for an interval scale. Rather, an origin is chosen arbitrarily. For example, temperature measured by Fahrenheit and Celsius have arbitrary 0s—the 0 or origin is different for Fahrenheit than for other methods of measuring temperature. Psychological variables such as intelligence and personality are often used in norm-referenced testing, and, thus, achieve interval level of measurement because an arbitrary 0 is defined to be the average score for the entire set of respondent scores.

Given the additional information gleaned about the relations among values on an interval scale of measurement—namely, order of values and distance between each set of values—transformations of original values are more limited in flexibility than for ordinal and nominal variable values. Specifically, only linear transformations preserve the interval-level information in the data and, therefore, are permissible. For example, if variable x is to be transformed to variable y, the following equation (with constants a and b) would be appropriate: $y = ax + b$. If $a = 1$ and $b = 2$, and your data contain the following set of x-values: 5, 4, 2, and 3, then linearly transformed y-values would be 7, 6, 4, and 5, respectively. Many common test scores are scaled using linear transformations so that measurements have more attractive values for means and standard deviations. Examples include SAT and GRE scores, which are scaled to have a mean of 500 and standard deviation of 100, and IQ scores, scaled to have a mean of 100, and typically a standard deviation of 15.

Ratio

Ratio-scale level variable values contain the richest quantitative information. Numbers with an underlying ratio scale demonstrate all 10 axioms and lie along a real, continuous number line. The distinguishing feature of ratio-scaled variables is the inclusion of a natural and absolute 0 as part of the scale of values, thus providing a true, fixed origin about which all other values vary. Any movement (or variation) of a given value or number from this origin occurs via units of 1. The greater the distance from the origin, the greater the variable value due to a greater accumulation of unit distances from the origin. Numerical values can now be multiplied and divided, as well as added and subtracted (as in the case with interval-level data). Examples of ratio-scaled physical properties include weight, height, and age. Psychological variables can achieve ratio scaling in certain instances as will be elaborated upon later in the chapter.

As is explained in the section Permissible Statistics: Matching Analysis With Variable Type, ratio-level data are conducive to the greatest variety in mathematical and statistical modeling due to the extensive information available. This issue will be elaborated upon when considering appropriate statistical techniques for values given differences in scale level. For now, the advantage of greater information is accompanied by a greater restriction in transformation methods compared with the previous scale levels. Namely, the original value (x) can only be multiplied by a constant (c) to create a transformed (y) value: $y = cx$. If $c = 2$, and a set of x-values are 6, 9, 2, 3, then the transformed y-values would be 12, 18, 4, 6.

SCALE LEVEL AND PSYCHOLOGICAL DATA

The four scale levels differ in the amount of information available about a variable—where real numbers containing a fixed, natural origin, and demonstrate both ordinal and additivity contain the most information. As a result, the types of inferential statistical procedures that can be performed on data vary. Parametric procedures are considered more appropriate for interval and ratio-level data, whereas nominal and ordinal data are best approached with nonparametric procedures, as will be elaborated further later in the section Permissible Statistics: Matching Analysis With Variable Type. An important issue that emerges in psychological research is whether data for commonly studied variables meet the requirements of at least the interval scale level given the statistical procedures that are popularly used to analyze this type of data (e.g., statistical tests in which the dependent variable values are assumed to be quantitative or continuous such as analyses of variance [ANOVAs], linear regression). For example, behavior counts, in terms of reported incidents in some defined context, or number of items passed or endorsed on a test are quite commonplace as psychological data. If the intention is to make inferences about a specifically defined context or a specific instrument of measurement (e.g., verbal aggression toward your coworker, Paul, yesterday morning), raw counts could be regarded as ratio-scaled because there is a natural 0 for respondents who never exhibit the behavior or fail to endorse any items in a questionnaire measure of verbal aggression.

Rarely, however, are such specific contexts of interest in psychology. That is, typically the task context or test is assumed to represent a broader domain of behavior and the purpose is to generalize from the specific task or set of test items to the broader domain from which they have been sampled (e.g., verbal aggression toward any coworker at any time of the day). That is, responses are presumed to depend on a latent variable that represents a tendency to respond in a certain way to the broader domain of interest. Thus, although behavior counts may sometimes be regarded as ratio scale, most psychological data are interpreted as depending on latent variables, whose values may not be linearly related to a specific behavioral count. Most observed psychological data, therefore, meant to represent latent variables likely only achieve ordinal scale properties.

FOCUS OF MEASUREMENT AND TESTING: WHAT IS BEING SCALED?

Up to this point, the object of interest—that which manifests or implicitly possesses some psychological variable being measured—has primarily been respondents. This fact forms the foundation for, and serves as the primary goal of, the entire testing industry. This approach to scaling is referred to as *subject centered* (Torgerson, 1958), where "subject" is synonymous with "respondent."

A second focus of scaling includes the very stimuli that are used to score a respondent's latent trait level—test items or survey statements (i.e., the stimuli of the study). More broadly defined, this *stimulus-centered* focus encompasses other forms of physical, observable stimuli that are used in perceptual and cognitive psychological research (Torgerson, 1958). Statements in an attitude survey can be compared on a variable independent of the respondent's self-perceived attitude. In this latter method, the focus of measurement shifts from respondents to stimuli, where the stimuli are the focus of measurement, and variation in values and differences among respondents are assumed to be error variance. For example, in a visual search task, the object arrays differ from one another in difficulty based on the similarity of the target object to the surrounding, distractor objects (i.e., the difficulty lies in discriminating the target object from surrounding distractors). These studies are typically designed to compare performance (i.e., speed of locating target object in the array) between groups that differ in the difficulty of the set of arrays given to them. Subsequently, ANOVA is typically used to test the effect of array difficulty on performance, where within-group variance (i.e., among the individuals within the group) is anticipated to be near zero.

Finally, a third focus of scaling is known as *response centered* (Torgerson, 1958). It is the most complex method, entailing the scaling of both respondents and items on the same property, or variable, such as the latent trait (e.g., cognitive ability, extraversion, or attitude toward gun use). More specifically, both respondents and items (or tasks) are placed on the same latent trait continuum and the distance or difference between a respondent and an item on that continuum predicts the likelihood that a respondent correctly answers an item (or the extent of endorsement, in the case of Likert-type responses). A more in-depth description of these scaling foci follows, emphasizing the difference among them in how scale levels are tested and achieved.

Subject-Centered Focus

The subject-centered method of scaling is well-known and has been used widely in the testing industry. For example, in norm-referenced testing, a goal is to compare respondents on the latent trait of interest, based on their scores relative to a population mean (Crocker & Algina, 1986; McDonald, 1999). In some cases, information is used to compare individuals to one another or predict success in an educational or organizational context. Historically, subject-centered measurement and scaling has been based in classical test theory (CTT), where the emphasis is on a total score (Gulliksen, 1950; Lord & Novick, 1968):

$$X_p = T_p + e_p. \tag{9.1}$$

X is observed test score of respondent p; T is respondent p's true score (i.e., a respondent's average score based on that particular respondent's distribution of scores if he or she took the test an infinite number of times); and e is random error that dilutes the expression of respondent p's true score. In this model, it is assumed that error is distributed normally with a mean of zero and that the correlation between error and true scores is zero. CTT statistics, such as the proportion of respondents who pass or endorse an item (p-values), item-total correlations ($r_{titemtotal}$), and test reliability (Cronbach's α.) are sample-specific. Even generalizability theory, which is based in CTT, relies on multiple samples for establishing reliability (in its various forms; Brennan, 2001; Crocker & Algina, 1986).

Although item statistics such as p-values and biserial correlations are useful in selecting items for a test form, item properties are not included in the basic model in Equation 9.1. In other words, CTT methods disregard variability among items along the latent continuum for the variable of interest, and, thus, score patterns (i.e., across items). One consequence of this disregard is that two respondents may have equal total test scores even if, between these two respondents, different items were answered correctly (i.e., different response patterns between respondents). The primary interest is differences among respondents in total test score, not item scores. Differences among item-level properties are treated as error and homogeneity among test items is preferred (Gulliksen, 1950). For example, if the purpose of the test is to maximize distinctions between respondents in the sample, items can be selected to maximize individual differences (i.e., maximizing the variance of total scores). In this case, items should be selected to have p-values within the range from .4 to .6, and item-total score correlations should be high. The impact of item properties on test variance is an important derivation in CTT (see Crocker & Algina, 1986).

More importantly, however, there is no specific model or simple method for testing assumptions regarding the scaling properties of latent trait test scores in CTT. As previously mentioned, many observed test scores meant to reflect a latent variable typically achieve only an ordinal level of measurement. Nevertheless, observed test scores are often transformed, linearly, to achieve more attractive numerical values or to better approximate a normal distribution, an assumption of many popular statistical procedures (e.g., general linear models). CTT, therefore, assumes that optimal scale properties are obtained when normal distributions of total scores are produced, which can be obtained through item selection. Further, the psychometric quality of the test for measuring the intended latent trait must be established by research that includes studies of the test's reliability and validity (Crocker & Algina, 1986; Sijtsma & Junker, 2006).

Stimulus-Centered Focus

In contrast to the subject-centered approach, stimulus-centered methods aim to locate stimuli on a unidimensional continuum representing the variable of interest. A common concern in stimulus-centered scaling is multidimensionality (i.e., differences among stimuli on multiple properties, simultaneously). This topic will not be discussed at length, but refer to Torgerson (1958) for more extensive information, particularly with respect to the statistical method most commonly used to assess multidimensionality of stimuli, multidimensional scaling.

The stimulus-centered approach was uncovered in the latter half of the 19th century by psychophysicists studying perception. Their goal was to quantify the relationship between a stimulus property (e.g., lights, tones, weights) and human perception (e.g., visual, auditory, tactile). Although these observable properties can be scaled via more precise methods (length via rulers, sound via wavelengths, weight with a scale), psychophysicists such as Weber and Fechner were interested in the psychological aspects of these properties—namely, our perception and distinction level of stimuli as a function of their value on a psychological property of interest (brightness, loudness or pitch, heaviness). For example, a series of sounds are presented in pairs and the respondent is asked, "Which is louder?"

To determine the smallest difference between two values that can be reliably detected by human senses, an index or unit of measurement was initially sought by psychophysicists such as Weber and Fechner. The result of these efforts is referred to as just noticeable differences (JNDs). For perspective, the relative strength of two stimuli is considered equal if either stimulus is chosen 50% of the time. JND was defined as a 75% accuracy rate—halfway between chance and perfect accuracy. Weber further specified that incremental increases in strength of stimuli properties are accompanied by a proportionate increase in the magnitude of a respondent's discrepancy in the sensory perception of the two stimuli values (McDonald, 1999). Thus, JNDs were considered psychological, equal units in the scaling of stimulus properties, implying that values are based on an interval scale. Fechner (1860) then postulated a log relationship between stimuli property values and sensory perception. In the latter case, values are not equally spaced along the psychological continuum, but interval properties can still be determined.

Stimulus-centered measurement was extended to latent trait and individual differences variables—specifically, attitudes—by L. L. Thurstone. For example, the seriousness of a crime such as arson relative to other crimes such as smuggling or murder could be established by having a group of respondents make pairwise comparisons for all crimes in the set, or by having respondents sort each crime into ordered categories that differed in seriousness level (Thurstone, 1927). As a result, these crimes can be ordered along a continuum of "crime seriousness." These techniques are applicable to the measurement of a variety of attitudes (e.g., abortion, gun use). In attitude measurement, stimuli are statements (or items) that differ from one another along a latent, theoretical "attitude toward gun use" continuum that ranges from negative (against use of guns) to positive (pro-gun use). Moreover, each statement is accompanied by a response format with which a respondent can indicate his or her level of agreement (with the statement). The response format for each item is either dichotomous or ordered category (i.e., Likert). Either way, the scale for the set of items is hypothesized to be interval.

Thurstone (1927) developed procedures for testing whether or not values assigned to a set of statements conform to interval scaling based on his laws of comparative judgment (for dichotomously scored items) and categorical judgment (for ordered category items responses). For the purposes of the current chapter, a brief overview of the analytic steps involved in these procedures follows. A more extensive summary of the method can be found in Torgerson (1958) and Bock and Jones (1968).

Although attitude statements or stimuli can theoretically be located on a continuum of the variable of interest, the process of confirming (and, in a sense, observing) the item locations depend upon a sample of judges who are asked to rate each item on whether or not (or the degree to which) the item reflects the variable (rather than a self-evaluation or comparison). There is likely to be variance (across judges) in the rating of an item along the continuum or the sorting of an item into one of a series of ordered categories. As a result, the "true" location of an item (i) on the continuum (Figure 9.1) is its observed mean (μ_i). The variance around this mean (σ_i^2) is viewed as error in judgment. The distance between μ_1 and μ_2, or any pair of items, also varies across judges, resulting in a normal distribution of discriminal differences and an accompanying standard deviation of differences, e.g., σ_{12}. This information, however, must be derived from empirical data in the form of judgment ratings or rankings via a set of equations associated with the law of comparative judgment (or the law of categorical judgment, which is an extension of the latter).

The law of comparative judgment can be represented in the following model:

$$S_1 - S_2 = z_{12} * \sqrt{\sigma_1^2 + \sigma_2^2 - 2r\sigma_1\sigma_2}, \qquad (9.2)$$

where S_1 and S_2 reflect the psychological (scale) values of Statements 1 and 2; z_{12} is the normal deviate corresponding to the proportion of judgments in which Statement 1 is rated higher, or stronger, than Statement 2 on the attitudinal continuum (when 1 is greater than 2, this value is positive; when 1 is less than 2, this value is negative; when 1 and 2 are equal, this value is 0); σ_1 is the discriminal dispersion of statement 1, and σ_2 is the discriminal dispersion of statement 2; and r is the correlation (or dependency) between the discriminal dispersions of Statements 1 and 2 within the same group of judges.

In its present form, the equation is insoluble due to insufficient information with which to estimate parameters. Torgerson (1958), therefore, offers a series of simplifying conditions. For example, the r is typically set to 0, as different

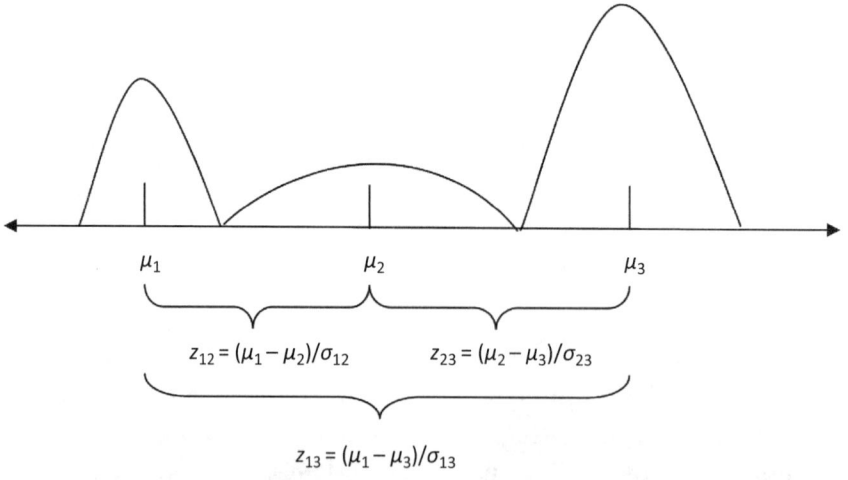

FIGURE 9.1. Discriminal distributions.

paired comparisons (discriminal processes) are assumed to be independent (e.g., comparisons for different item pairs are not dependent upon one another due to an underlying consistent bias in the judging process such as leniency, severity, or ambivalence). In latent trait measurement, this phenomenon is also referred to as *local independence* (Lord & Novick, 1968).

The remainder of the process for deriving discriminal differences involves a series of computations in which z-scores are obtained. Pairwise judgments of stimulus dominance are created by the proportion of judges (p) who rate a given item above every other item or above a given category threshold. Z-scores are then obtained for each nondiagonal element in the probability matrix based on its location in a cumulative normal distribution. When two items representing attitude toward gun use are judged as being located on the same point, the probability of endorsing one over the other is 50% ($p_{12} = .50$), and, thus, $z_{12} = .00$. For example, in the Gun Attitude Scale (Tenhundfeld et al., 2017), the item "I am confident that I could successfully defend myself using a handgun" may be perceived as equivalent to (and is equally likely to be endorsed as) the item "I would personally feel more powerful by keeping a handgun." But, if "I am confident that I could successfully defend myself using a handgun" is compared to a less supportive, negative view of gun use (e.g., "I am afraid of guns"), p_{12} will equal a lower number such as .25, in which case $z_{12} = -.68$. Or if "I am confident that I could successfully defend myself using a handgun" is compared to a stronger, positive view of gun use (e.g., "I would not hesitate to shoot an attacker on the street"), p_{12} may equal .75, in which case $z_{12} = .68$. Thus, the greater the perceived distance between two items (attitude toward gun use), the further the item moves from the center of the continuum representing "attitude toward gun use."

As depicted in Figure 9.1, and consistent with the model portrayed in Equation 9.1, the discriminal differences between each pair of statements are additive, given the interval scale theoretically underlying the statement values. Thus, $z_{13} = z_{12} + z_{23}$.

In our example, because there are three items, there will be three equations used to determine the location (mean) of statements (e.g., for Items 1 and 2: $z_{12} = (\mu_1 - \mu_2)/\sigma_{(1-2)}$). To solve this set of equations, for which the available parameter information is insufficient, the origin and units of measurement must be fixed. This may be done by setting μ_1 to 0 and, in certain simplifying conditions (Torgerson, 1958), setting the discriminal variances among items to be equal (i.e., equal distances between each pair of items), or approximately equal (given a linear change from one variance to another, using a constant value that is assumed to be small). The 0 point on the scale is arbitrary, meaning that the psychological properties of the attitude statements cannot be described by a ratio scale.

Given that these observed z-scores contain error in judgment (i.e., variance in discriminal differences across judges), additivity may not be sufficiently attained. The "true" differences between statements on a (latent) variable must be approximated by estimating values (z-scores), which can then be compared (via least squares) to determine the degree to which an interval scale underlies the data. Specifically, a matrix of theoretically "true" z-scores is produced by reducing error in the original z value matrix or averaging the column values (based on the number, n, of judgments—i.e., judges). These latter values can then be compared to the initial z-scores to determine the degree of approximation and appropriateness of treating the observed values as interval in scale.

Response-Centered Focus

The response-centered approach differs from the previous two in that both the item and respondents are placed on the same psychological continuum and scaled with respect to each other. The entire scaling procedure now becomes more complex, both theoretically and statistically. For example, two respondents—one who is high on extraversion, the other low—will exhibit a different response pattern for the same set of items that are manipulated such that they vary along the continuum of extraversion. Thus, it is now the response patterns across a set of items that is key in the process of scaling respondents. Conversely, if we have a set of respondents for whom extraversion levels vary then items can be scaled based how the respondents differ in their response patterns across items.

Like stimulus-centered methods, but different from the CTT approach to subject-centered methods, the response-centered approach contains a variety of specific models and equations that can be used to test the scaling properties of respondents and items. These models can be categorized as either deterministic or probabilistic based on how error in prediction is treated. Deterministic models do not include an error term to account for variance in response patterns not explained by either the respondent or item properties. Thus, the goal with these error-free models, which are not expected to be observed or necessarily occur in nature, is to determine the extent to which values based on this perfect scale approximated real, observed data. Probabilistic models, on the other hand, do incorporate error, allowing for comparison in fit among multiple statistical models (based on a decrease in error across incrementally more parameterized models).

Deterministic models. Two well-known deterministic models are those of Guttman (1950) and Coombs (1950). These two techniques differ primarily in how the discriminal process is theorized to occur. Similar to that of Thurstone's (1927) laws of judgment, the Guttman model is cumulative; namely, the respondent is more likely to endorse an item as the distance between respondent and item increases such that the latter surpasses the former. For example, when measuring "attitude toward gun use" (Tenhundfeld et al., 2017), a respondent may be confronted with the following statement: "I support the right to own a firearm." If the Guttman model more closely approximates the data, then respondents will disagree with the statement because it is too strong (i.e., the respondent believes guns should not be allowed under any circumstances).

In contrast, an unfolding model (e.g., Combs, 1950) assumes a proximity-based process whereby a respondent is more likely to endorse an item that is located close to their position on the latent trait continuum and, thus, will disagree with an item from either below or above. For example, the above attitude statement, is too strong in comparison with beliefs of one respondent (they disagree from below). They may be more likely to endorse the statement "A gun in the home is more likely to shoot a household member than an intruder." However, another respondent may disagree with the initial statement because they believe guns should be allowed and used in more cases. So, they disagree from above. This respondent is more likely to agree with the statement "I support the right to carry a firearm outside of the home." Or "Hunting with guns is a sport I am likely to enjoy." These, and more basic, aspects of the models are discussed in turn.

More recent models (Mokken, 1971; van Schuur, 2003) are accompanied by a series of steps in which the ordering of respondents and items can be examined visually. For example, a trace line (Figure 9.2) or item characteristic curve (ICC; see Figure 9.5) is constructed to describe the joint impact of respondent and item on response likelihood for an item. Visually, an ICC is a plot where the horizontal axis is the latent variable or trait continuum, and the vertical axis is the probability of a response (correct in the case of abilities, agreement in the case of opinions). It is the former on which the direct comparison between respondent and item value is made. Specifically, an ICC demonstrates that the discrepancy in value between respondent and item predicts the likelihood that a respondent will get a test item

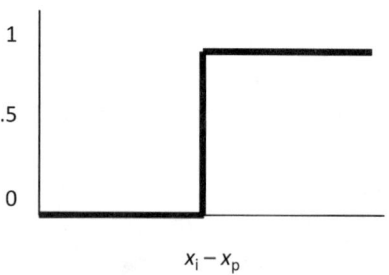

FIGURE 9.2.   Trace line for Guttman scale model.

correct. Next, the degree to which observed data approximates the model can be tested. Based on this theoretical model, the likelihood of endorsing an item is either 0 or 1. In other words, given the distance between respondent and item on the psychological continuum, the threshold for endorsing an item versus not—that is, the slope of the prediction line—is abrupt. If a respondent's location exceeds that of the item, the likelihood of item endorsement is 100% (the respondent will endorse the item), but it is 0% if the respondent is located below the item. In other words, the location of the respondent, relative to item, perfectly predicts the response.

The Guttman (1950) model only assumes ordinal-level measurement for respondents and items. This assumption can be tested visually using a scalogram and/or mathematically by calculating the coefficient of reproducibility. For the former, the steps differ, somewhat, for dichotomous versus multiple category response. First, dichotomous items or category thresholds within a single item, do not define the space/continuum but are used to divide the continuum into segments (Figure 9.3). A, B, C, and D represent midpoints, or means, for four dichotomously scored items/stimuli or multiple, ordered categories within a single item. For example, when measuring weight, item (or category response) A might represent 5–10 kg, B is 10–20 kg, C is 20–40 kg, and D is 40+ kg. If the values represent the amount of verbally aggressive behavior, defined as the number of times a respondent yells at another person, A might be less than 2 times per day, B is between 2 and 3 times a day, C is between 3 and 4 times a day, and D is 4 or more times per day. All double-digit letters (e.g., AB, BC, and so on) are midpoints between two item or stimulus points on the continuum (e.g., AB is the midpoint between items A and B). As will be explained, these latter midpoint values are useful for determining the discriminal differences in pairs of items or stimuli and determine a set of response patterns, given a respondent's location within the numbered regions.

Once the items or stimuli are constructed to vary from low to high on a variable, a respondent is presented with each stimulus and asked to rate the degree of match between the stimulus (item) and him or herself. The response-centered approach represents a different basis for item ordering than the stimulus-centered approach; namely, the ordering of items represents the ease with which the items are endorsed or passed. In the stimulus-centered approach, the responses represent judgments about the stimuli on a variable of interest and, hence, may be regarded as a relatively more objective evaluation of the stimulus properties, though this point is debatable (McDonald, 1999; Torgerson, 1958).

Given n items with a dichotomous response format, there are 2^n possible response patterns. If a 5-point Likert scale were involved, there would be 5^n possible response patterns. However, if items and respondents are scalable with respect to each other, only $n+1$ of these patterns will occur. As can be seen in Figure 9.3, these permissible patterns are associated with the number of category thresholds, and the distribution of respondents who fall into these $n + 1$ groups or classes. Remaining patterns are inconsistent with the theory surrounding the latent trait and are regarded as "errors" though, overall, some inconsistencies in patterns are expected. Mathematically, the scalability of items

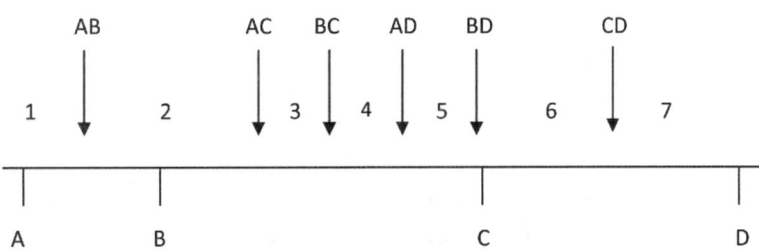

FIGURE 9.3. Category thresholds and person-type regions.

and respondents can be tested via the coefficient of reproducibility

$$C = 1 - \frac{\# \text{ total errors}}{\text{total } \# \text{ of items} * \text{total number of respondents}}, \quad (9.3)$$

which translates into the number of patterns allowable versus the number of "perfect scale" patterns. In general, a coefficient value of .90 is considered acceptable for an ordinal scale (Torgerson, 1958). Unfortunately, there are no statistical procedures for comparing fit between models representing levels of measurement (e.g., a change in chi-square or log-likelihood for ordinal vs. interval).

Coombs's (1950) unfolding model is also deterministic and involves rank ordering preferences for stimuli or items in terms of the proximity of the stimulus/item to the respondent's perceived self-standing on the same psychological continuum. However, according to this model, respondents can disagree with an item from either above or below, depending on their location relative to the item. As can be seen in Figure 9.3, item locations can be broken down into regions with midpoints between category thresholds. If there are seven regions, there are seven groups of individuals with distinct group-specific response patterns. In other words, ordering of items now depends on the location of the respondent (Figure 9.4), where the joint scale folds at the location of the respondent to determine ordering of items.

For example, in Figure 9.4, Respondent x_p is in Region 2, which exhibits the BACD pattern. However, the absolute difference between item points is not known but is relative (e.g., AB vs. CD). Thus, this scale is considered to lie somewhere between ordinal and interval (Coombs, 1950).

Probabilistic models. Probabilistic response-centered models typically fall into the category of item response theory (IRT) models (i.e., latent trait theory; Embretson & Reise, 2000; McDonald, 1999). Like the Guttman (1950) model, emphasis is placed on the correspondence between response patterns and the location of respondents and items along a psychological continuum, and this relationship can be visually represented as an ICC. More to the point, however, observed variables (e.g., item performance, endorsement, accurate response) can be used to infer and locate items and respondents on a unidimensional latent trait continuum (hence, its synonymy with "latent trait theory"). IRT models are accompanied by a series of assumptions such as "local independence" (much like when the correlations among paired-item comparisons are set to 0 in Thurstone's, 1927, models). The IRT model diverges from that of Guttman in that error is accounted for in the model by changing the mathematical expression to be the probability of endorsing the item. In other words, because error is inherent in the model, the relationship between respondent-item distance and responses can take

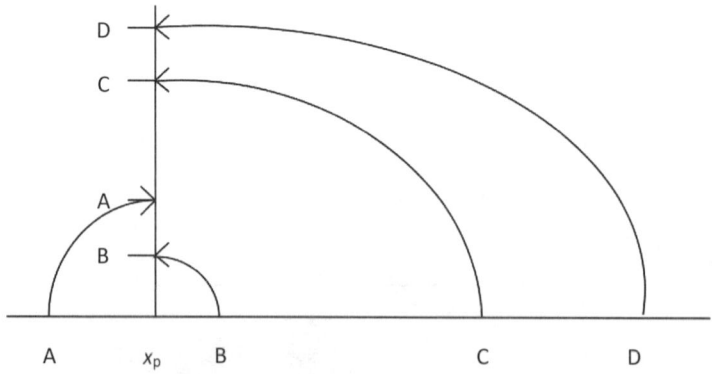

FIGURE 9.4. Folding of items around persons.

various forms that do not mirror a step function (e.g., approximations of linear, normal ogive, logistic; Lord & Novick, 1968). In Figure 9.5, three ICCs are shown—one for each of three items. The general form of the relationship between trait level and item response is the same for all items (logistic), but the parameters of the relationship such as slope and item location, or difficulty, varies across items. Moreover, IRT models and associated *hypothesized* ICCs may represent a cumulative or an ideal-point, unfolding relationship between respondent-item distance and responses (Roberts & Laughlin, 1996).

Perhaps the simplest, probabilistic response-centered model is the Rasch (1960) model

$$P(X_{is} = 1|\theta_s, \beta_i) = \frac{\exp(\theta_s, \beta_i)}{1 + \exp(\theta_s, \beta_i)}. \quad (9.4)$$

The left-hand side of the equation for the Rasch model refers to the probability of respondent *s* endorsing (or accurately responding to) item *i*; the right-hand side shows how this probability depends on the difference between the respondent's trait location (θ_s, often called *ability* even though that is not appropriate in all contexts) and the location of item *i* on the same latent trait continuum (β_i, called *item difficulty* for cognitive assessments, or *item location* for personality and attitudinal assessments). In fact, the precise distance, or interval, between respondent and item along the latent trait continuum can be estimated and is used to predict a respondent's response to the item. In other words, unlike previously discussed response-centered models in which the level of measurement is most likely ordinal, the Rasch model assumes at least interval-level variables. This unique property of Rasch models can be derived from Luce and Tukey's (1964) theory of conjoint measurement, where an outcome variable (the item response) is an additive function of two other variables (in this case, the item and respondent values). As a result, the data that are well-described by the Rasch model contain a wealth of information on both the items and respondents, and the widest

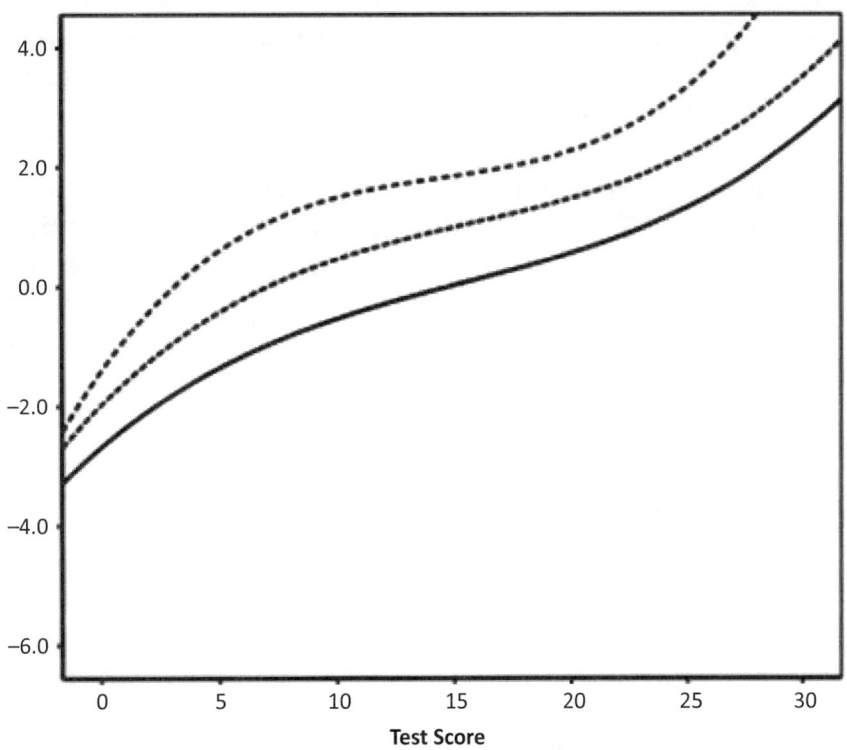

FIGURE 9.5. Item characteristics curve.

variety of statistical analyses can be applied to these data when testing a hypothesis.

Another interesting and unique feature of Rasch models is the invariant meaning of respondent and item calibrations, a property referred to as *specific objectivity*. That is, it can be shown that for any pair of trait level scores, say θ_1 and θ_2, the difference in log odds for solving *any* item β_i is given by the difference in the trait levels as follows:

$$\ln[P(X_{i1}=1)/(1-P(X_{i1}=1))]$$
$$-\ln[P(X_{i2}=1)/(1-P(X_{i2}=1))]=\theta_1-\theta_2. \quad (9.5)$$

This relationship is often shown as justifying interval-level scale properties of trait levels. Conversely, for any pair of items, the difference in log odds that *any* person will respond positively is the difference in their difficulty values. These same relationships can be shown in ratio form by taking the antilogs, which can be interpreted as a specific meaning of ratio scale properties. That is, suppose that ξ_1 and ξ_2 are the antilogs of θ_1 and θ_2, respectively. In this case, the ratio of Person 1 to Person 2 for the odds of passing *any* item is given as the simple ratio of their trait scores as follows:

$$[P(X_{i1}=1)/(1-P(X_{i1}=1))]/$$
$$[P(X_{i2}=1)/(1-P(X_{i2}=1))]=\xi_1/\xi_2. \quad (9.6)$$

Since the ratio of the trait scores for two persons, ξ_1/ξ_2, applies to any item, the scores have a ratio scale interpretation. Suppose that the antilog of item difficulties in the Rasch model are used to scale items, such that $\eta_i = \exp\beta_i$. The ratio of two rescaled item difficulties, η_1 and η_2, indicates the relative odds that the item will be passed or endorsed by any person, as follows:

$$[P(X_{2s}=1)/(1-P(X_{2s}=1))]=\eta_1/\eta_2. \quad (9.7)$$

Specific objectivity is a property that is unique to the Rasch IRT model. When educational or psychological tests are scaled with other latent trait models, however, such as the two-parameter (2PL) or three-parameter (3PL) logistic models, items can still be compared to other items without relying on population-specific, contextual information (i.e., as in norm-referenced measurement). The relationships will no longer apply directly to any item but will be modified by the additional parameters in the IRT model.

The response-centered approach has some interesting relationships to the stimulus-centered approach. Specifically, both the stimulus and response-centered approaches use a model or set of equations to test the validity of the scale level, or scalability, of items with respect to respondents and vice-versa. Thus, in the response-centered approach, respondent information is improved upon relative to CTT-based approaches by considering respondent locations with respect to item-level, rather than test-level, information. Also, Thurstone's (1927) laws of comparative and categorical judgments and Lord's (1952) probabilistic response-focused models both emphasize discriminal processes with a cumulative, dominance component (Bock & Jones, 1968). The former establishes differences between items on a property. For example, Item 1 is judged as stronger on a variable than Item 2, which is stronger than Item 3. Item 1, therefore, dominates both Items 2 and 3. The latter series of comparisons emphasizes the dominance of a respondent over an item (see Sijtsma & Junker, 2006). Thus, when latent traits are of interest, Thurstone's approach is consistent with, and could have easily evolved into the modern test theory approach—namely, IRT. Much later, however, the theoretical approaches of Lord (1953) and Rasch (1960) had an impact on the common scaling of respondents and items in psychometrics.

PERMISSIBLE STATISTICS: MATCHING ANALYSIS WITH VARIABLE TYPE

A highly debated topic in psychological measurement is which statistical analysis procedures are permissible given the scale level of the data. After Stevens (1946) developed his hierarchical taxonomy of scale levels, he (in 1951) prescribed the statistical tests appropriate for each given level (see Table 9.1). Essentially, limitations for how values of a particular scale can be transformed are extended to the type of inferential statistics that can be performed. For example, parametric statistics (e.g., *t*-tests, Pearson correlations, regression) rely on information such as means and standard deviations and, thus, are appropriate for interval and ratio-scaled data. Nominal and ordinal data, on the other hand, do not demonstrate a continuous, equal-interval range and, thus, should be examined using nonparametric statistics such as chi-square and Spearman's rank correlation, respectively.

While most scientists would agree with the restrictions on nominal-scaled data (but see Lord, 1953), there is debate regarding the treatment of data as a function of its scale level. This debate centers on two issues: (a) the basic theory underlying these restrictions—namely, the measurement paradigm, and, related to this, (b) the empirical implications for statistical inferences when an interval-scale latent variable is measured with ordinal-scaled observed scores.

THEORY AND MEASUREMENT PARADIGMS

According to Michell (1990), there are three measurement paradigms—operational, classical, and representational. In operational and classical paradigms, the relevance of Stevens' (1951) prohibitions on statistical treatment of ordinal data is contested. In these paradigms, science is viewed as the study of our numerical operations and not the study of a reality that is thought to lie beyond them. In other words, scores are measurements simply because they are reasonably consistent numerical assignments that result from a precisely specified operation. Moreover, even though nominal data are not quantitative but, rather, represent identity (e.g., football jersey numbers), researchers have argued that parametric statistical procedures can still be used for this type of data because there is no relation between measurement scales and statistical procedure (e.g., Norman, 2010; Zumbo & Zimmerman, 1993). For example, football number data do not know what mathematical operations are allowable; rather, they are numbers and, therefore, appear computable (Lord, 1953). As Townsend and Ashby (1984) commented, "Just exactly what this curious statement has to do with statistics or measurement eludes us" (p. 396). Rather, the problem with the scenario involving freshmen with lower football jersey numbers than seniors and the subsequent outrage by the comparably less value of the freshmen lies in the flawed interpretation drawn from the statistical comparison rather than in the statistical procedure, itself.

The representational paradigm is where the issue of scale level correspondence with statistical procedures is most applicable. This paradigm is most practiced in psychological measurement. In representational theory, numbers represent an empirical relational system, and, thus, these number values constitute an existing, objective structure. In this measurement paradigm, scientists argue that measurement is "the assessment of quantity" (Rozeboom, 1966, p. 224). So, nominal scale level is not included as a legitimate scale of measurement. Rather, the data must be quantitative and scaled as interval or ratio to perform parametric statistical procedures on them (Campbell, 1920).

According to a more lenient view, it is once again argued that the meaningfulness of the inferences that are made from a measure is the most important criterion in determining the adequacy of the scaling (Michell, 1990; Townsend & Ashby, 1984). That is, a measurement can produce meaningless statements such as a red football jersey being of higher value than a white football jersey. Or a statement's truth can be an artifact of the measurement scale chosen as is the case when measurement instruments vary in the extent to which ideal scale properties are achieved (e.g., interval-level data). According to Suppes and Zinnes (1963), "a numerical statement is meaningful if and only if its truth (or falsity) is constant under admissible scale transformations of any of its numerical assignments; that is, any of its numerical functions expressing the results of measurement" (p. 66). As stated by Michell (1986), however, "The question never was one of permissible statistics or of meaningfulness. It was always only one of legitimate inference" (p. 402). Thus, in this view, representational theory does not entail prescriptions about the matching of statistical procedures with scale levels (as Stevens, 1951, thought), nor does it imply anything about the meaningfulness of measurement statements. Upon closer examination of the literature, measurement paradigms and their implications for scaling and analysis are complex and conflicting, given debate over the link between scale type and statistical treatment of data. The differences among, as well as within, the various viewpoints may be responsible for most psychological researchers ignoring the implications of measurement scale for statistical inference.

IMPACT OF SCALE LEVEL ON STATISTICAL INFERENCES IN LATENT TRAIT MEASUREMENT

Based on the previous discussion, one can infer that scale levels do not necessarily correspond to statistical procedure (e.g., parametric versus nonparametric). Indeed, one can argue that meeting the assumptions of the statistical procedure chosen is most crucial because the scaling of data can take on so many forms due to the overlap among taxonomies (Harris, 2001; Howell, 1992; Warner, 2008). For example, rank and count data can be treated as interval-level data, but count can also be treated as ratio-level data. Thus, assumptions of statistical tests such as normal distribution of variable values and homogeneity of variance (e.g., *t*-test, ANOVA, general linear models) are still crucial even if the data are shown to be interval or ratio (McDonald, 1999). Nevertheless, there are situations in which the distinction between ordinal and interval is important—particularly, when measuring latent traits for which operational definitions are insufficient and the nature of the scale values must be inferred from observed data. If observed scores are intended to reflect latent scores, which are shown to be at least interval-scaled, then the relationship between latent and observed values (i.e., the transformation of one to the other) is, ideally, linear.

Several studies have demonstrated the impact of nonlinear relationships between observed and latent scores on the outcome of statistical tests and inferences about observed score means (Davison & Sharma, 1988; Maxwell & Delaney, 1985, 2004; Townsend & Ashby, 1984). Maxwell and Delaney (1985) demonstrated that when the relationship between observed and latent trait scores is logistic, the results of a *t*-test based on observed scores can be inferred for latent variables as well if and only if observed score variances are equal between groups or the test difficulty level matches the respondents' mean trait level. Similarly, Davison and Sharma (1988) showed that results of *t*-tests involving observed test scores can be generalized to the latent scores when statistical assumptions such as normality in score distributions and homogeneity of variance among scores are met. Thus, when there is a nonlinear relationship between observed and latent variables, meeting certain statistical assumptions can be sufficient for drawing inferences about the latter based on the former.

Moreover, the relationship between observed and latent scores must be monotonic. In other words, the exact form of the relationship between observed and latent scores need not be known to conduct analyses. These conditions are inadequate, however, for certain statistical procedures, such as a factorial ANOVA with interaction terms (Davison & Sharma, 1990). Specifically, factorial ANOVAs may yield significant differences in observed score means for groups of respondents who have the same true, latent trait score. Thus, meeting statistical assumptions is insufficient, and the probability density functions of dependent variables must be thoroughly examined, post hoc, to determine the appropriateness of extending results for observed scores to latent scores (Davison & Sharma, 1990). Namely, the probability density functions for multiple groups or conditions being compared must be the same, or at least overlap, if the means are different. Similar results have been found for analyses such as multiple regression (Davison & Sharma, 1990).

More recent studies have compared statistical outcomes and inferences made for CTT (subject-centered) versus IRT (response-centered) scaling of variables. In CTT, the scaling of the data (observed test scores) is debatable. The distributions of scores can be controlled by selecting items according to their difficulty levels and intercorrelations. Historically this process has entailed selecting items that yield normal distributions of scores based on the assumption that optimal scale properties are achieved when data are normally distributed. The justification for this approach can be traced to Galton (1883), who found that performance on a broad array of tasks was normally distributed. Thus, for norm-referenced tests, means and standard deviations of tests scores are computed as if the scores had an interval scale level. Then, total scores can be linearly transformed to standard scores that have meaning with respect to percentile ranks and relative frequencies on the normal distribution. According to Michell (2009), this procedure of "inferring the existence of quantity from that of mere order is aptly designated the *psychometricians' fallacy*" and it is "central to the paradigm of modern psychometrics" (p. 46). That is, achieving normally distributed scores does not, in itself, justify interval scale properties.

In contrast, estimating latent traits scores with an IRT model (particularly the Rasch model) leads to scores with interval scale and some ratio scale properties. As shown above, however, the relationship between observed test scores and latent trait scores is nonlinear. The test characteristics curves in Figure 9.5 show that while the mapping of observed test scores to latent trait estimates is nearly linear at the center of the distribution, the relationship becomes nonlinear at the extremes. That is, changes in the observed test score have greater meaning for the latent trait at the extremes.

The impact of using IRT latent trait scores versus CTT observed test scores on inferences has been compared in several studies (Embretson, 1996, 1994, 2007; Kang & Waller, 2005). In these studies, simulations are used so that the true values and relationships are known. Embretson (1996) found that interaction effects from an ANOVAs were unreliable. Using the observed score scale resulted in (a) failure to find significant interactions that existed in the latent trait scale and (b) significant interactions when none existed in the latent trait scale. Similarly, Kang and Waller (2005) found that for moderated regression analysis, Type 1 error rates were significantly higher than expected when the observed score scale was used. The IRT latent trait estimates, in contrast, yielded the expected error rate.

Other studies show that results from the observed score scale are particularly misleading when the degree of nonlinearity is increased by test inappropriateness for one or more groups that are studied. When the test is either too easy or too hard the degree of nonlinearity between latent trait scores and observed test scores increases. Embretson (1994, 2007) found that test difficulty has an impact on change and learning trend for groups of individuals who differ initially on the latent trait. That is, when using the observed test score, the greatest change across time or conditions occurs for the group for which the measure was most appropriate (i.e., trait level approximates item location or difficulty). If the groups have different initial levels on the trait, a measure may be selected to show the most change for one of these groups, even if the change on the latent trait scale is the same. These empirical studies strongly indicate that the measurement scale level has an impact on inferences depending upon the nature of the statistical procedure used to make said inferences.

SUMMARY AND CONCLUSION

Measurement and scaling are the foundations of psychological research, specifying the quantitative nature of variables under study. There is substantial variety in theory and application underlying measurement and scaling, especially in the field of psychology, due to the latent and complex nature of variables of interest. Therefore, when conducting scientific research and analysis, it is crucial to (a) establish the scale of measurement for variables of study while determining the object of focus (subject-, stimulus-, or response-centered), and (b) align the statistical method of analysis with the variable's level of measurement. This process is particularly crucial for scientists who follow the representation paradigm of measurement. Most psychologists adopt this paradigm rather than the classical and operational paradigms because the latter does not allow inferences to a domain beyond a set of observed numerical values and the scale they form, whereas the representational paradigm does. Moreover, the representational paradigm is conducive to empirically based general theories and hypothesis testing in psychology where the variables that are of interest are not directly observable and must be inferred from responses to limited sets of tasks.

When latent variables, such as cognitive ability or personality, are of primary interest, CTT or latent trait theory can be effective at testing whether the observed data approximate the latent variable, which is crucial since the observed data are used to generalize to the latent variable of interest. In CTT applications, there is a subject-centered focus in the scaling of the data, the level of measurement is confounded with statistical assumptions such as normality of data distribution and equivalence of error variances, and the relationship between observed test scores and latent trait levels changes depending on the region of the latent trait continuum in which the item is located, relative to the respondent. Thus, it is unclear (a) what level of measurement describes this type of data, (b) what the relationship is between observed scores and latent trait level, and (c) which statistical procedures are most appropriate for analysis. In IRT applications where data are inherently response-centered, interval properties can be supported because both the respondents and items are scaled along the same continuum where intervals between values are known. As demonstrated in this chapter, known interval properties of the response-centered approach is clearest with the Rasch IRT models. As a result, there is greater flexibility in the type of analysis that can be performed on this type of data.

In general, scientists who adhere to the representational paradigm of measurement should be wary of the statistical procedures used and the extent to which they are appropriate for a set of data, given the data's scale of measurement. Specifically, nonparametric statistical procedures (Chi-square, Spearman's rank correlation) should be used for hypothesis testing when data are at the nominal and ordinal levels of measurement (i.e., categorical) because the order and intervals among values in a scale are indeterminable. Parametric techniques (e.g., t-tests, ANOVA, regression) should be reserved for interval or ratio (continuous or quantitative) data because the intervals and ratios among variable values are known. If the scale level of the variable is not appropriately matched with the statistical procedure, important information in the variable values is either ignored or misrepresented. Subsequently, the results of the tests and the inferences made from the results are questionable. Correctly identifying and respecting the scaling or level of measurement for variables of study via alignment between level of measurement and statistical method is key to making reliable and accurate inferences about the behavior of variables being researched and, ultimately, making meaningful contributions to science.

References

Bock, R. D., & Jones, L. V. (1968). *The measurement and prediction of judgment and choice*. Holden-Day.

Brennan, R. L. (2001). *Generalizability theory*. Springer-Verlag. https://doi.org/10.1007/978-1-4757-3456-0

Campbell, N. R. (1920). *Physics, the elements*. Cambridge University Press.

Cohen, J., Cohen, P., West, S. G., & Aiken, L. S. (1983). *Applied multiple regression/correlation analysis for the behavioral sciences* (2nd ed.). Lawrence Erlbaum.

Combs, C. H. (1950). Psychological scaling without a unit of measurement. *Psychological Review, 57*(3), 145–158. https://doi.org/10.1037/h0060984

Crocker, L., & Algina, J. (1986). *Introduction to classical and modern test theory*. Wadsworth.

Davison, M. L., & Sharma, A. R. (1988). Parametric statistics and levels of measurement. *Psychological Bulletin, 104*(1), 137–144. https://doi.org/10.1037/0033-2909.104.1.137

Davison, M. L., & Sharma, A. R. (1990). Parametric statistics and levels of measurement: Factorial designs and multiple regression. *Psychological Bulletin, 107*(3), 394–400. https://doi.org/10.1037/0033-2909.107.3.394

Embretson, S. E. (1994). Comparing changes between groups: Some perplexities arising from psychometrics. In D. Laveault, B. D. Zumbo, M. E. Gessaroli, & M. W. Boss (Eds.), *Modern theories of measurement: Problems and issues* (pp. 213–248). Edumetric Research Group, University of Ottawa.

Embretson, S. E. (1996). Item response theory models and inferential bias in multiple group comparisons. *Applied Psychological Measurement, 20*, 201–212. https://doi.org/10.1177/014662169602000302

Embretson, S. E. (2007). Impact of measurement scale in modeling development processes and ecological factors. In T. D. Little, J. Bovaird, & N. A. Card (Eds.), *Modeling contextual effects in longitudinal studies* (pp. 63–87). Erlbaum.

Embretson, S. E., & Reise, S. P. (2000). *Item response theory for psychologists*. Lawrence Erlbaum.

Fechner, G. T. (1860). *Elements of psychophysics*. Harvard University Press.

Gaito, J. (1980). Measurement scales and statistics: Resurgence of an old misconception. *Psychological Bulletin, 87*(3), 564–567. https://doi.org/10.1037/0033-2909.87.3.564

Galton, F. (1883). *Inquiry into human faculty and its development*. Macmillan. https://doi.org/10.1037/14178-000

Gulliksen, H. (1950). *Theory of mental tests*. Wiley. https://doi.org/10.1037/13240-000

Guttman, L. A. (1950). The basis for scalogram analysis. In S. A. Stouffer, L. Guttman, E. A. Suchman, P. F. Lazarsfeld, S. A. Star, & J. A. Clausen (Eds.), *Measurement and prediction*. Princeton University Press.

Harris, R. J. (2001). *A Primer of multivariate statistics* (3rd ed.). Erlbaum. https://doi.org/10.4324/9781410600455

Hölder, O. (1901). Die axiome der quantität und die lehre vom mass [The axiom of quantity and the theory of measurement]. *Mathematisch-Physiche Klasse, 53*, 4–12.

Howell, D. D. (1992). *Statistical methods for psychology* (3rd ed.). PWS-Kent.

Kang, S.-M., & Waller, N. G. (2005). Moderated multiple regression, spurious interaction effects, and IRT. *Applied Psychological Measurement, 29*(2), 87–105. https://doi.org/10.1177/0146621604272737

Lord, F. M. (1952). *A theory of test scores*. Psychometric Monograph: Number 7.

Lord, F. M. (1953). On the statistical treatment of football numbers. *American Psychologist, 8*(12), 750–751. https://doi.org/10.1037/h0063675

Lord, F. M., & Novick, M. R. (1968). *Statistical theories of mental test scores*. Addison-Wesley.

Luce, R. D., & Tukey, J. W. (1964). Simultaneous conjoint measurement: A new type of fundamental measurement. *Journal of Mathematical Psychology, 1*(1), 1–27. https://doi.org/10.1016/0022-2496(64)90015-X

Maxwell, S. E., & Delaney, H. D. (1985). Measurement and statistics: An examination of construct validity. *Psychological Bulletin, 97*(1), 85–93. https://doi.org/10.1037/0033-2909.97.1.85

Maxwell, S. E., & Delaney, H. D. (2004). *Designing experiments and analyzing data: A model comparison perspective* (2nd ed.). Erlbaum.

McDonald, R. P. (1999). *Test theory: A unified treatment*. Lawrence Erlbaum.

Michell, J. (1986). Measurement scales and statistics: A clash of paradigms. *Psychological Bulletin, 100*(3), 398–407. https://doi.org/10.1037/0033-2909.100.3.398

Michell, J. (1990). *An introduction to the logic of psychological measurement*. Erlbaum.

Michell, J. (1997). Quantitative science and the definition of measurement in psychology. *British Journal of Psychology, 88*(3), 355–383. https://doi.org/10.1111/j.2044-8295.1997.tb02641.x

Michell, J. (2009). The psychometricians' fallacy: Too clever by half? *British Journal of Mathematical & Statistical Psychology, 62*(1), 41–55. https://doi.org/10.1348/000711007X243582

Mokken, R. J. (1971). *A theory and procedure of scale analysis with applications in political research*. De Gruyter. https://doi.org/10.1515/9783110813203

Norman, G. (2010). Likert scales, levels of measurement and the "laws" of statistics. *Advances in Health Sciences Education: Theory and Practice, 15*(5), 625–632. https://doi.org/10.1007/s10459-010-9222-y

Rasch, G. (1960). *Studies in mathematical psychology: I. Probabilistic models for some intelligence and attainment tests*. Nielsen & Lydiche.

Roberts, J. S., & Laughlin, J. E. (1996). A unidimensional item response model for unfolding responses form a graded disagree-agree response scale. *Applied Psychological Measurement, 20*(3), 231–255. https://doi.org/10.1177/014662169602000305

Rozeboom, W. W. (1966). Scaling theory and the nature of measurement. *Synthese, 16*(2), 170–233. https://doi.org/10.1007/BF00485356

Russell, B. (1903). *Principles of mathematics*. Cambridge University Press.

Sijtsma, K., & Junker, B. W. (2006). Item response theory: Past performance, present developments, and future expectations. *Behaviormetrika, 33*(1), 75–102. https://doi.org/10.2333/bhmk.33.75

Stevens, S. S. (1946). On the theory of scales of measurement. *Science, 103*(2684), 677–680. https://doi.org/10.1126/science.103.2684.677

Stevens, S. S. (1951). Mathematics, measurement, and psychophysics. In S. S. Stevens (Ed.), *Handbook of experimental psychology* (pp. 1–49). Wiley.

Suppes, P., & Zinnes, J. L. (1963). Basic measurement theory. In R. D. Luce, R. R. Bush, & E. Galanter (Eds.), *Handbook of mathematical psychology* (Vol. 1, pp. 3–76). Wiley.

Tenhundfeld, N. L., Parnes, J. E., Conner, B. T., & Witt, J. K. (2017). Development of a psychometrically valid gun attitude scale. *Current Psychology, 39*(5), 279–286. https://doi.org/10.1007/s12144-017-9761-y.

Thurstone, L. L. (1927). A law of comparative judgment. *Psychological Review, 34*(4), 273–286. https://doi.org/10.1037/h0070288

Torgerson, W. S. (1958). *Theory and methods of scaling*. John Wiley.

Townsend, J. T., & Ashby, F. G. (1984). Measurement scales and statistics: The misconception misconceived. *Psychological Bulletin, 96*(2), 394–401. https://doi.org/10.1037/0033-2909.96.2.394

van Schuur, W. H. (2003). Mokken scale analysis: Between the Guttman scale and parametric item response theory. *Political Analysis, 11*(2), 139–163. https://doi.org/10.1093/pan/mpg002

Warner, R. M. (2008). *Applied statistics: From bivariate through multivariate techniques*. Sage.

Weber, E. H. (1948). The sense of touch and common feeling, 1846. In W. Dennis (Ed.). *Readings in the history of psychology* (pp. 194–196). Appleton-Century-Crofts. https://doi.org/10.1037/11304-023

Zumbo, B. D., & Zimmerman, D. W. (1993). Is the selection of statistical methods governed by level of measurement? *Canadian Psychology, 34*(4), 390–400. https://doi.org/10.1037/h0078865

CHAPTER 10

SAMPLE-SIZE PLANNING

Ken Kelley, Samantha F. Anderson, and Scott E. Maxwell

The sample size necessary to address a research question depends on the goals of the researcher. One goal is to infer *whether* a particular effect exists and/or its direction, whereas another is to estimate the *magnitude (size)* of the effect. Sometimes both goals might be of interest.

Before we elaborate on these goals, we provide four introductory notes. First, although we focus on sample-size *planning* before data collection, sample size is important when using existing data to determine whether the questions of interest can be appropriately addressed with the available sample size. Second, we focus on a "fixed-n" approach that yields a constant suggested sample size, which differs from sequential methods, which have their own merits and limitations (e.g., Chattopadhyay & Kelley, 2016; Kelley et al., 2018; Lakens, 2014). Third, we restrict our attention to the frequentist framework, though some Bayesian methods of sample-size planning have been developed (Kruschke, 2015; Vandekerckhove et al., 2018). Finally, before delving into the process of sample-size planning, we discuss several basic elements, such as hypothesis testing, effect size, and confidence interval (CI). Attention to these fundamentals is often missed in other treatments of sample-size planning and several misuses of sample-size planning can be traced to a misunderstanding of one or more of these topics.

We begin this chapter with analogies reflecting two different goals researchers may have for their studies: one focusing on the existence of an effect—and its direction if appropriate—and the other focusing on the magnitude of the effect. We argue that the particular research question is what drives how it should be addressed statistically and, thereby, how the study should be designed. First, consider a sporting competition. In general, the most important outcome is which team wins the game, not the score itself. Of course, if the score is known, then the winner can be deduced, but of primary interest is knowing who won. Second, consider a retirement portfolio. In general, the outcome of interest is the amount the portfolio's value changed over time, not simply whether or not the portfolio changed (increased or decreased) in value. Of course, if the amount of change is known, it is also known whether the portfolio increased or decreased, but of primary interest is how much the portfolio changed.

The sports analogy reflects situations in which the dichotomous decision of whether an effect is present answers the question of interest because the existence/direction of the effect is focal. Examples of dichotomous research questions are: (a) Does the proposed model explain variance in the outcome variable? (b) Is there a relationship between a predictor and the criterion variable after other predictors have been controlled? and (c) Do the treatment and control groups have different means? For the latter two questions the direction of the effect is known if the effect is deemed statistically significant.[1]

In some situations, the question concerns estimating the magnitude of an effect, as in the portfolio example. The three research questions can be reframed in the magnitude estimation context as: (a) How much of the variance in the outcome variable is explained by the proposed model? (b) How strong is the relationship between a predictor and the criterion variable after other predictors have been controlled? or (c) How large is the mean difference between the treatment group and the control group? Each of these questions attempts to quantify the magnitude of an effect with an effect size and CI. By *effect size*, we mean "a quantitative reflection of the magnitude of some phenomenon that is used for the purpose of addressing a question of interest" (Kelley & Preacher, 2012, p. 137), with a CI used to bracket the corresponding population value with a specified degree of confidence that quantifies the uncertainty of how the estimate estimates the population value.

The different types of questions that researchers pose have different implications for appropriate methodological techniques, and, correspondingly, proper sample-size planning should explicitly depend on the type of research question. In this chapter we discuss both goals and the implications that choosing one approach over the other have for sample-size planning. We discuss sample-size planning from a power analytic perspective, when the existence of an effect or the direction of an effect is of primary interest, as well as from the accuracy in parameter estimation (AIPE; e.g., Kelley & Maxwell, 2003) perspective, when the magnitude of an effect is of primary importance (e.g., precision).[2] Because the power analytic and AIPE approaches are fundamentally different, the sample sizes necessary from the two perspectives may differ substantially, for the same model in the same population. We do not claim here that one approach is better than the other. Rather, we contend that the appropriate approach, and, thus, the appropriate sample size, is wedded to the research question(s) and the goal(s) of the study.[3]

One must realize that the same research project can pursue questions that necessitate planning using both power analytic and AIPE approaches. For example, a researcher could have a goal of obtaining an accurate parameter estimate for a particular regression coefficient (AIPE) and an additional goal of evidencing a statistically significant proportion of variance explained by the model (statistical power). Even when multiple goals exist, the researcher still has to choose a single sample size for the study. We recommend that the largest needed sample sizes be used so that the multiple goals will each individually have at least an appropriate sample size, though Jiroutek et al. (2003) discussed methods in which multiple goals can be satisfied simultaneously with a specified probability.

We now turn to discussing effect sizes and their role in research; then, we discuss the interpretation of results when existence and direction are focal and when magnitude-estimation is focal. We then describe sample-size planning for both of these goals. We subsequently consider appropriate ways to specify the parameter(s) necessary to begin a formal process of sample-size planning.

EFFECT SIZES AND THEIR ROLE IN RESEARCH

Effect sizes come in many forms with many purposes. As Kelley and Preacher (2012) discussed, the effect size of interest might refer to measures such as variability, association, difference, odds, rate, duration, discrepancy, proportionality, superiority, and degree of fit

---

[1]We formally introduce null hypothesis significance testing later.
[2]In some cases, AIPE can be used for goals in which direction is important.
[3]Of course, in research there are many other things to consider when designing a study besides sample size, such as the available resources. Nevertheless, due to the direct impact that sample size has on statistical power and accuracy of parameter estimation, its consideration is a necessary, but not sufficient, component of good study design (see, e.g., Parts VI and VII of this handbook, for selected other methodological considerations that should be considered).

or misfit among other measures that reflect quantities of interest. Effect-size estimation is the process of estimating the magnitude of an effect size in the population (even if the population value is zero).

Two Ways of Quantifying Effect Sizes: Omnibus and Targeted

An effect size of interest can be one that is *omnibus* or *targeted*. Consider multiple regression. A basic application of multiple regression considers both (a) the overall effectiveness of the model (i.e., an omnibus effect) via the squared multiple correlation coefficient as well as (b) specific relationships linking each predictor to the outcome variable (i.e., a targeted effect) while controlling for the other predictor(s) in the model, via the estimated regression coefficients. A second example is the root mean square error of approximation (RMSEA; omnibus) and path coefficients (targeted) in structural equation modeling. One-way analysis of variance (ANOVA) provides a third example, where eta-squared is an omnibus effect size that quantifies the proportion of the total variance accounted for by group status, but contrasts are targeted effects that quantify the difference between some specified linear combination of means. Both types of effect sizes can be considered in the same study.[4]

Effect sizes can also be *unstandardized* or *standardized*. An unstandardized effect size is one in which a linear transformation of the scaling of the variable(s) changes the value of the effect size. For a standardized effect size, linear transformations of the scaling of the variable(s) do not affect the value of the calculated effect size. For example, suppose there are five predictors in a multiple regression model. The squared multiple correlation coefficient remains exactly the same regardless of whether the variables in the model are based on the original units or standardized variables (i.e., z-scores). The value of the regression coefficients themselves, however, will generally differ depending on whether variables are standardized or unstandardized.

Given these two dimensions, oftentimes there will be multiple effect sizes that are of interest in a single study. Nevertheless, what is important is clearly articulating and explicitly linking the type of effect size(s) to the primary research question(s). Appropriate sample size depends heavily on the particular type of population effect size to be estimated as well as the goal(s) of the study.

Interpretation of Results

As discussed previously, there are two overarching goals for making inferences about population quantities based on sample data. The first goal focuses on the existence/direction of an effect and typically relies on null hypothesis significance testing (NHST), where an attempt is made to reject a specified null value. The second goal focuses on magnitude estimation, where an attempt is made to learn the size of the effect in the population based on an estimated effect size and its corresponding CI. We briefly review these two approaches to inference before moving on to sample-size planning.

Existence/direction: Null hypothesis significance testing. The rationale of NHST is to specify a null hypothesis, often that the value of the population effect size of interest is zero, and then test to see if the data obtained (and more extreme data) are plausible given that the null hypothesis is true. If the results obtained are sufficiently unlikely under the null hypothesis, then the null hypothesis is rejected. "Sufficiently unlikely" is operationalized as the p value from the test of the null hypothesis being less than the specified Type I error rate (e.g., .05).[5] The value of the null hypothesis depends on the situation, and the test

---

[4]To complicate matters somewhat, effect sizes can be partially omnibus and partially targeted. For example, Cramér's V can be applied to a subtable larger than a 2-by-2 table from a larger contingency table. In such a situation, the effect size represents a semitargeted (or semiomnibus) effect size. We do not consider such semitargeted effect sizes here as they are not used often and are rarely of primary interest for the outcome of a study.

[5]Recall that the technical meaning of a p value calculated in the context of a null hypothesis significance test is the probability, given that the null hypothesis is true, of obtaining results as or more extreme than those obtained.

may concern an omnibus or targeted effect size that is either unstandardized or standardized. Regardless of the specific circumstance, the logic of NHST is exactly the same.

The NHST framework has been criticized (e.g., Bakan, 1966; Cohen, 1994; Meehl, 1967; Rozeboom, 1960; see also Harlow et al., 1997; Morrison & Henkel, 1970; and Nickerson, 2000, for reviews; and McShane et al., 2019, for a recent critique). Our intent is neither to criticize nor defend this framework here. Nevertheless, by requiring statistical significance to infer *that there is an effect* and, in certain cases, by inferring *that the direction of an effect* requires a null hypothesis be specified and tested, the current state of science is such that NHST is (still) widely used and addresses a specific type of question. NHST serves as a useful guide for evaluating research results so that sampling error is not overinterpreted in an effort to reject the hypothesis that there is no effect in the population and/or to infer direction in the population.[6]

Importantly, in many cases the basic research question also involves directionality. For example, the question might be: (a) Is the population correlation coefficient positive or negative? or (b) Does the treatment group have a larger population mean than the control group? Inference for directionality usually is only meaningful for clearly defined targeted research questions. For example, consider a one-way ANOVA with more than two groups. Knowledge that there is a statistically significant *F*-test for the null hypothesis that all group means are equal does not in any way signify the direction of group differences. For a targeted test however, such as the difference between two group means, rejection of the null hypothesis clearly indicates the direction of the difference.

Magnitude estimation: Effect sizes and CIs. The rationale of CI formation comes from the realization that a point estimate almost certainly differs from its corresponding population value.

Assuming appropriate assumptions are met, the following defines a $100(1-\alpha)$% CI for some unknown parameter, where α indicates the Type I error rate: "If one repeatedly calculates such intervals from many independent random samples, $100(1-\alpha)$% of the intervals would, in the long run, correctly bracket the true value of [the parameter of interest]" (Hahn & Meeker, 1991, p. 31).

CIs often have a direct link with NHST. Often, but not always, the values contained within the $100(1-\alpha)$% CI limits are those that cannot be rejected with the corresponding NHST at a Type I error rate of α. They are often regarded as being "plausible" values of the parameter, and values outside of this region are "implausible."[7] That said, CIs do not literally provide the test of the null hypothesis, and NHST provides information not available in a CI, such as a *p* value, which provides a quantitative measure of evidence against the null hypothesis.

In addition to the link with NHST, CIs are often described with respect to their width. When a CI is wide for the particular context, there is much uncertainty about the size of the population value. As Krantz (1999) stated, "a wide CI reveals ignorance [about the population effect size] and thus helps dampen optimism about replicability" (p. 1374). All other things being equal, a narrower CI is preferred to a wider CI when interest concerns the magnitude of the population effect size. As the CI width decreases, such as when sample size increases and/or when sampling variability decreases, more values are excluded from the CI.[8] A wide CI could still be at least

---

[6] CIs can be used to evaluate null hypothesis significance testing, too, in the sense that a reject or fail-to-reject conclusion is drawn based on whether or not a specified null hypothesis is contained within the CI. However, we believe the real strength of using CIs is when estimating the magnitude of an effect size. We discuss CIs momentarily but wanted to point out that CIs can generally be used as a substitute for null hypothesis significance testing.

[7] In many cases, this one-to-one relationship between NHST framework using a Type I error rate of α and inference based on the corresponding $(1-\alpha)100$% CI holds, termed duality, but in situations in which a pivotable quantity does not exist, duality may not hold. Thus, in such situations there can be some nuanced differences between testing a null hypothesis—which is conditional on the null hypothesis being true—and using a CI—which makes no assumption about the null hypothesis. Nuances aside, for many effect sizes, such as means, mean differences, regression coefficients, among many others, duality holds.

[8] Of course, if the goal is existence/direction and NHST is used, a wide CI can still be useful if it excludes the null value.

somewhat meaningful if it excludes parameter values that would support an alternative theory and/or demonstrate practical significance.

Regardless of which approach aligns most with the research question, both the existence/direction (NHST) and magnitude estimation (effect size and CI) approaches require considerations of sample size planning. AIPE focuses solely on ensuring that an interval will be sufficiently narrow (width) for a given level of confidence with secondary attention to where the center of the interval is likely to be. This is perfectly appropriate when the goal is to obtain an accurate magnitude estimate of the parameter. On the other hand, power analysis requires specifying a hypothesized parameter value and assessing if it is contained in the confidence interval bounds while only implicitly considering width. Sample-size planning from the power analytic perspective ensures that the CI will not contain the value specified in the null hypothesis with the specified probability. Holding everything else constant, for nonnull effects, narrower intervals and larger effects provide more statistical power.

METHODS OF SAMPLE-SIZE PLANNING

The preceding discussion of hypothesis tests, effect sizes, and CIs was necessary in order to have a context for choosing and executing an appropriate sample-size planning procedure. Simply put, when interest concerns the existence and/or the direction of an effect, an a priori power analysis should be performed to plan an appropriate sample size, which yields the sample size (from a fixed-n perspective). If interest is in estimating the magnitude of an effect size, however, the AIPE approach should be used to plan an appropriate a priori sample size, which is typically a fixed-n method; but recent work allows for it to be done from a sequential estimation approach.

Determining Existence and/or Direction: Statistical Power and Power Analysis

Statistical power is the probability of correctly rejecting the null hypothesis. Statistical power is based on four quantities: (a) the size of the effect, (b) the model error variance, (c) the Type I error rate (i.e., α), and (d) the sample size. Oftentimes, the size of the effect and the model error variance are combined into a standardized effect size.[9] In many cases $\alpha = .05$, which is essentially the standard value used in psychology and related disciplines, unless there are justified reasons for some other value to be used (though, see Anderson, 2020; Benjamin et al., 2018).[10] After the Type I error rate is specified and a particular value is chosen for the hypothesized value of the standardized effect size in the population (or effect size and the error variance), statistical power depends only on sample size. This implies that sample size can be planned to obtain a desired level of statistical power based on the specified conditions.

When testing a null hypothesis, the sampling distribution of the effect size of interest is transformed to a test statistic, which is a random variable that, provided the null hypothesis is true, follows a particular statistical distribution (e.g., a central t, χ^2, F). When the null hypothesis is false, however, the test statistic follows a different distribution, namely the noncentral version of the statistical distribution (e.g., a noncentral t, χ^2, F). The noncentral version of a statistical distribution has a different mean, skewness, and variance, among other properties, compared with its central distribution analog and is defined in part by a value known as the *noncentrality parameter*, which reflects how far the noncentral distribution is shifted away from the null distribution. Whereas $\alpha 100\%$ of the sampling distribution under the null hypothesis is beyond the critical value(s), the noncentral distribution has a larger proportion of its distribution beyond the critical value(s)

---

[9]In cases where directionality is sensible, such as for a t-test of the difference between means, in addition to specifying only the Type I error rate, the type of alternative hypothesis (e.g., directional or nondirectional) must also be specified. In other situations, for tests that are inherently one-tailed, such as for an analysis of variance, such a distinction is unnecessary.

[10]One place where a Type I error rate other than .05 might be used is in the multiple comparison context, where, for example, a Bonferroni correction is used (e.g., .05/4 = .0125 if there were four contrasts to be performed).

from the central distribution. If the effect size actually came from a distribution where the null hypothesis is false, there will then be a higher probability of rejecting the null hypothesis than the specified value of α.

Having a sufficiently large area is advantageous, which translates into a high probability of the noncentral distribution beyond a critical value under the null distribution. The area of the noncentral distribution beyond a critical value of the central distribution can be quantified and is termed *statistical power*. Holding everything else constant, increases in sample size will lead to a larger area (i.e., higher probability) of the noncentral distribution being beyond the critical value from the central distribution. This happens for two reasons, specifically because (a) a larger sample size decreases variability of the null and alternative distributions, and (b) larger sample sizes lead to a larger noncentrallity parameter, both of which magnify the difference between the null and alternative distributions.

Figure 10.1 shows the null (central) and alternative (noncentral) distributions in the situation where there are four groups in a fixed effects analysis of variance design, where the null hypothesis is that the four groups have equal population means. In this situation the supposed population means are [−.5, 0, 0, .5] for a common, within-group standard deviation of 1. The effect size, f, is then .35 (see Cohen, 1988, section 8.2, for information on f). In order to have power of .80, a sample size of 23 per group (92 total) is necessary. Figure 10.1 displays this

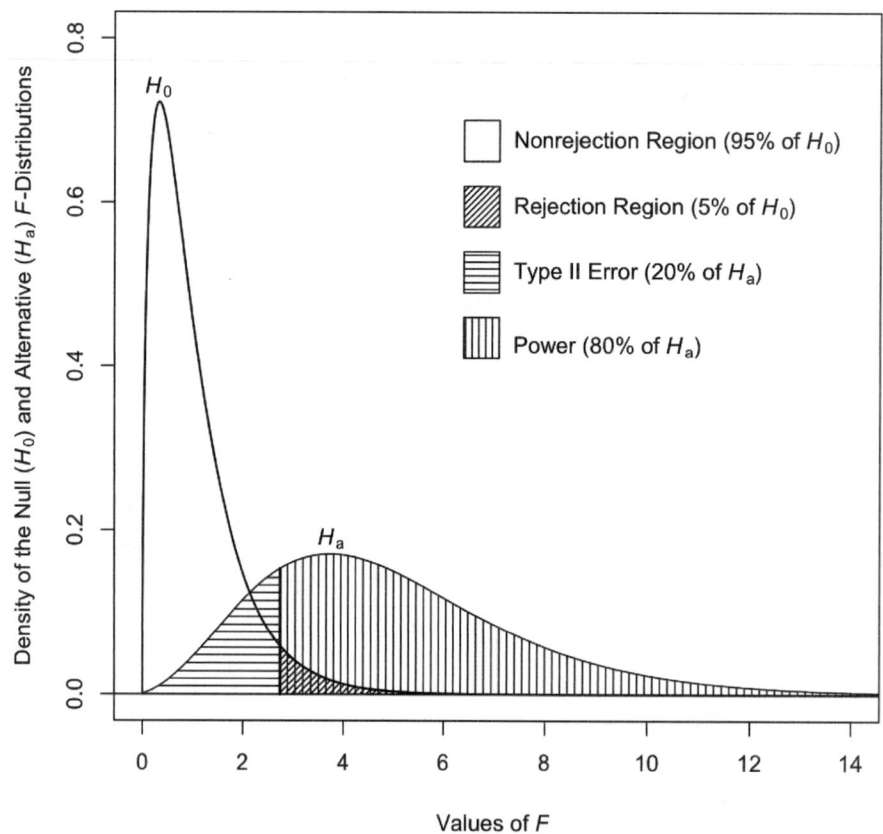

FIGURE 10.1. Illustration of the relevant areas of the null (H_0) and alternative (H_a) distributions for statistical power of .80 in a four-group fixed effects analysis of variance when the population group means are specified as −0.50, 0.0, 0.0, 0.5 for the first through fourth groups, respectively, and where the within-group standard deviation for each of the groups is 1.0, which requires 23 participants per group (92 total).

situation, where the alternative distribution has a noncentrality parameter of 11.5. As seen in the figure, the mean of the noncentral F distribution (i.e., H_a) is much greater than it is for the central F distribution (i.e., H_0). The larger the noncentrality parameter, the larger the mean of the alternative distribution, implying that, holding everything else constant, increases in the noncentral parameter increase statistical power. The effect of this is that as the noncentrality parameter becomes larger and larger (e.g., from increasing sample size), the bulk of the alternative distribution is shifted farther and farther to the right while at the same time the null distribution is unchanged, which implies that there is a smaller area of the alternative distribution that is less than the critical value from the null distribution (i.e., the probability of a Type II error is decreased, where a Type II error is the failure to reject a null hypothesis when the null hypothesis is false).

It is often recommended that statistical power should be .80, that is, there should be an 80% chance that a false null hypothesis will be rejected. Although we do not think anything is wrong with a power of .80, we want to make it clear that when α is set to the de facto standard value of .05 and power is set at .80, the probability of a Type II error $(1 - .80 = .20)$ is 4 times larger than the probability of a Type I error. Whether this is appropriate or not is based on a trade-off between false positives (Type I errors) and false negatives (Type II errors). The most appropriate way to proceed in such a situation is to consider the consequences of a Type I versus a Type II error. If an effect exists and it is not found (i.e., a Type II error has been committed), what are the implications? In some research settings there may be few if any consequences. However, if finding the effect would have been used to advance a major initiative that would greatly benefit society or a specific population, a Type II error could have major implications. In such situations the Type II error can be regarded as more important than a Type I error and consistent with that would be setting the probability of a Type II error to be more like, or even less than, the probability of a Type I error.

Estimating the Magnitude of an Effect: Accuracy in Parameter Estimation

In general, we believe that when an effect size is of interest, the corresponding CI for that effect should be of interest as well. The estimated effect size in a sample almost certainly differs from its corresponding population value. The population value of an effect is what is usually of ultimate interest in research, not an estimate from some particular sample that necessarily contains sampling error. Thus, in addition to reporting the estimated effect size (i.e., the best single point estimate of the population parameter), researchers should also report the CI limits for the population value.

One reason CIs are so important is because there can be a belief in the "law of small numbers," which states that people often employ the flawed intuition that there is a lack of variability of estimates from samples (Tversky & Kahneman, 1971). Tversky and Kahneman (1971) suggested CIs be reported because they provide "a useful index of sampling variability, and it is precisely this variability that we tend to underestimate" (p. 110). Kelley (2005) noted that reporting any point estimate "in the absence of a CI arguably does a disservice to those otherwise interested in the phenomenon under study" (p. 52). Similarly, Bonett (2008) argued that "the current practice of reporting only a point estimate of an effect size is actually a step backwards from the goal of improving the quality of psychological research" (p. 99; see also Thompson, 2002). The American Psychological Association (APA; 2010) *Publication Manual* clearly states the importance of effect sizes and CIs: "It is almost always necessary to include some measure of effect size in the Results section" and "whenever possible, provide a CI for each effect size reported to indicate the precision of estimation of the effect size" (p. 34). There has been a push in psychology and related disciplines to include effect sizes and their CIs as an alternative to or in addition to null hypothesis significance testing (e.g., Cumming, 2014; Grissom & Kim, 2005; Harlow et al., 1997; Hunter & Schmidt, 2004; Schmidt, 1996; Thompson, 2002; Wilkinson & the APA Task Force, 1999).

A wide CI reflects the uncertainty with which a parameter has been estimated. Historically, CIs were seldom reported in psychology and related disciplines. With editorial efforts, as well as directives from publication manuals, we notice that CIs are reported much more frequently than they used to be only, say, a decade ago. We believe that more work is necessary in interpreting the CI, though, rather than only reporting the upper and lower limit without actually using them. Cohen (1994) suggested that the reason more researchers did not report CIs was that their widths were often "embarrassingly large" (p. 1002), which we still believe has credibility even now. That said, wide CIs can often be avoided with proper sample-size planning from an AIPE approach, which differs from traditional methods of sample-size planning whose goal is to obtain adequate statistical power. It may seem that since there is a one-to-one relationship with regards to rejecting the null hypothesis and the null value being outside of the CI, there might be a one-to-one relationship between sample-size planning for statistical power and sample-size planning for AIPE. However, this is not the case. In particular, the goals of AIPE are satisfied even if the null value is contained within the CI as long as the interval width is narrow. The goals of power analysis can be satisfied even with a wide CI as long as the hypothesized value is not contained within the interval. Although for any CI it is known whether or not the null hypothesis can be rejected, for sample-size planning purposes the goals are fundamentally different and approached in an entirely different way. When magnitude is of interest, the computed CI should be narrow, as that signifies less uncertainty about the value of the population parameter. So, the question confronting a researcher interested in magnitude-estimation is how to choose a sample size that will provide a sufficiently narrow CI.

The approach to sample-size planning when the goal is to obtain narrow CIs has been termed, as noted, *accuracy in parameter estimation*. The goal of the AIPE approach is to plan sample size so that the CI for the parameter of interest will be sufficiently narrow, where "sufficiently narrow" is necessarily context specific. The AIPE approach to sample-size planning has taken on an important role in the research design literature, as it is known that people (a) tend to overestimate how precise an estimate is, (b) prefer not to have wide CIs, and (c) are now expected to report effect sizes and their corresponding CIs. This push in psychology (e.g., Journal Article Reporting Standards, or JARS; APA, 2010) and education (American Educational Research Association, 2006) to report effect sizes and CIs is consistent with medical research, where the Consolidated Standard of Reporting Trials (CONSORT; Moher et al., 2010) and the Transparent Reporting of Evaluations with Nonrandomized Designs (TREND; Des Jarlais et al., 2004) both state that effect sizes and CIs should be reported for primary and secondary outcomes (see Item 17 in both checklists). The new JARS also recommends a description of "sample size, power, and precision," which is consistent with our discussion here (Appelbaum et al., 2018, Table 1, p. 7). Appelbaum et al. (2018) also "emphasize the designation of hypotheses as of primary, secondary, and exploratory interest . . . these designations are meant to help convey to readers how experiment-wise results, of both null hypothesis significance tests and effect-size estimations, might be influenced by chance" (p. 9). Because of how effective CIs are as a way to convey uncertainty so that authors acknowledge how results "might be influenced by chance," it is best to avoid "embarrassingly wide" CIs (Cohen, 1994, p. 1002), which is why AIPE can be so useful. We believe that the AIPE approach to sample size planning will play an integral role in research in the coming years.

CI width is in part a function of sample size. To understand why sample-size planning for a narrow CI is termed *accuracy in parameter estimation*, consider the definition of accuracy. In statistics, accuracy is defined as the square root of the mean square error (RMSE) for estimating some parameter of interest, which is formally a function of the variance of the estimated parameter, which is inversely proportional to the precision of the estimator, and the bias of the estimator. For a fixed value of variance of the estimator, an increase in bias yields a less accurate estimate (i.e., larger RMSE), with the converse also being true. Because we seek to obtain an accurate estimate, we must consider precision and bias simultaneously. In general, the AIPE approach uses estimates that are unbiased, or at least consistent (i.e., that converge to their population value as sample size increases). It would be entirely possible to have a very precise estimate that was biased. For example, regardless of the data, a researcher could estimate a parameter based on a theory-implied value. Doing so would certainly not be statistically optimal in general, because the theory-implied value is unlikely to be correct, but the estimate would be highly precise (e.g., its variance could be zero). Because AIPE simultaneously considers precision and bias in the CI, the approach is most appropriately referred to as accuracy in parameter estimation.

Just as the Type I error rate is usually fixed at .05, as previously discussed for statistical power, the confidence level is essentially a fixed design factor, almost always set to .95. With the level of confidence fixed and with estimates for the model error variance and in some situations the size of the effect considered fixed, sample size is a factor that can be planned so that the expected CI width is sufficiently narrow. However, because the CI width is a random variable, even if the expected CI width is sufficiently narrow, any particular realization will almost certainly be either narrower or wider than desired. An optional specification allows a researcher to have some specified degree of assurance (e.g., 99%) that the obtained CI will be sufficiently narrow. That is, a modification to the standard procedure, where only the expected width is sufficiently narrow, answers questions such as "what size sample is necessary so that there is 99% assurance that the 95% CI is sufficiently narrow" (e.g., Kelley, 2008). What is "sufficiently narrow" necessarily depends on the particular context. But what is important is that the CI will bracket the population value with the specified level of confidence, which implies that the estimated effect size that the CI was based on, or its unbiased or more unbiased version, will be contained within a smaller range of plausible parameter values.[11] Because of the narrow range of plausible parameter values and the estimate of choice being within that narrow range, the estimate is one that is more accurate than one with a CI wider than that observed, all other things being equal.

Parameter Specification When Planning Sample Size

One or more nondesign factors must be specified in all of the sample-size planning procedures commonly used. The value(s) that must be specified to plan the sample size depends on the statistic(s) of interest and the type of sample-size planning procedure. For example, planning sample size for statistical power for an unstandardized mean difference between two groups requires that a mean difference and the standard deviation be separately specified. Alternatively, a standardized mean difference can be specified. Choosing relevant effect size values to use for the approaches is difficult because many times the values are unknown—in fact, learning more about the effect size may be a fundamental reason for conducting the study in the first place. But the values used can have a sizable impact on the resulting sample-size calculation. For this reason, the difficulty in estimating an effect size to use for purposes of sample-size planning has been labeled the "problematic parameter" (Lipsey, 1990).

The existing literature should ideally be the guiding sources of information for choosing

---

[11]To better understand how sample size influences the width of a CI, consider the case of normally distributed data when the population standard deviation, σ, is known and a 95% two-sided CI is of interest. Such a CI can be expressed as $\bar{x} \pm 1.96 \frac{\sigma}{\sqrt{n}}$, where $\bar{x}$ is the sample mean and n is the sample size. The estimated mean, $\bar{x}$, is necessarily contained within the CI limits. As the sample size increases, the margin of error $\left(\text{i.e., } 1.96 \frac{\sigma}{\sqrt{n}}\right)$ decreases. For example, suppose $\sigma = 15$. For a sample size of $n = 10$, the margin of error is 9.30, whereas the margin of error is 2.94 when $n = 100$. Because the range of plausible parameter values is 5.88 for the later case, it is preferred, holding everything else constant, to the former case with a CI width of 18.60. A similar relationship holds for CIs for other quantities.

parameter values when planning sample size. In some situations, even a single previous study may provide a reasonable basis for choosing a plausible effect size for a new planned study. In other situations, an ample literature may exist or perhaps meta-analyses exist estimating the effect size of interest. However, there are often biases (e.g., selective reporting, publication bias) present in estimates of these parameter values, including estimates derived from meta-analyses. Thus, when such information is available, it should be carefully and appropriately used, as we later show. Unfortunately, when such information is not available, approaches that seem to make the process easier (all too often based on rules of thumb) have generally been shown to be inappropriate (e.g., Green, 1991; MacCallum et al., 1999; Maxwell, 2004) largely because they tend to ignore one or more of the following: (a) the question of interest, (b) the effect size, (c) characteristics of the model to be used, (d) characteristics of the population of interest, (e) the research design, (f) the measurement procedure(s), (g) the failure to distinguish between targeted and omnibus effects, and (h) the desired level of statistical power and/or the width of the desired CI. In the remainder of this section, we discuss the specification of parameters for power analysis and accuracy in parameter estimation.

For power analysis, there are two common approaches for choosing parameter values. The first approach uses the best estimates available for the necessary population parameter(s), which is usually based on a review of the literature (e.g., via meta-analytic methods) or data from a pilot or previously published study. The second approach uses the minimally important effect size (MIES), based on linking the size of an effect to its meaningfulness for a theory and/or application. In using the MIES, there will be sufficient power if the magnitude of the effect size is as large as specified and even more power if the effect size is larger in the population.[12]

Both the literature review and MIES approaches are potentially useful when planning sample size, but the appropriate choice will depend on the information available and the research goals. If the goal is to plan sample size for what is believed true in the population, then the literature review approach should generally be used, with some important caveats described below. However, if the goal is to plan sample size based on the minimum value of the effect size that is of scientific and/or practical importance/interest, then the MIES approach should generally be used.

As an example of using the MIES, suppose that only a standardized mean difference of 0.20 in magnitude or larger would be of interest in a particular setting. Choosing this value for the MIES essentially implies that any value of the population standardized mean difference less than 0.20 in magnitude is of little-to-no value in the particular research context. If this is the case, then the parameter value used for the sample-size planning procedure need not be literally the true but unknown population effect size. Rather, it can be the minimum parameter value that is of theoretical or practical interest. If the population value of the effect size is larger than the chosen MIES, then statistical power will be greater than the nominal level specified. Senn (2002) addressed this idea by saying,

> the difference you are seeking is not the same as the difference you expect to find, and again you do not have to know what the treatment will do to find a figure. This is common to all science. An astronomer does not know the magnitude of new stars until he [or she] has found them, but the magnitude of star he [or she] is looking for determines how much he [or she] has to spend on a telescope. (p. 1304)

Although using the MIES to plan sample size can be useful in some situations, O'Brien and

---

[12] We use standardized effect size here so that both the unstandardized effect size and the model error variance are simultaneously considered.

Castelloe (2007) illustrated that such a method can potentially be misguided, specifically in the power analytic approach. The issue, however, is also relevant to some applications of the AIPE approach. O'Brien and Castelloe described a study where the minimally important effect size may be so small that more than 100,000 participants would be required to obtain adequate statistical power. With such a large number of patients required to detect the MIES value, the study might not be conducted because resources may not be available for over 100,000 patients (see the Discussion for a note about collaborative and multisite projects). O'Brien and Castelloe argued that their hypothetical scenario "exemplifies why confirmatory trials are usually designed to detect plausible outcome differences that are considerably larger than 'clinically relevant'" (p. 248). Thus, although the MIES approach can be useful in certain situations, it is not necessarily universally preferred as a way to plan sample size from the power analytic perspective.

Another complication of the MIES approach is that it may be difficult to determine what specific value of the effect size is truly minimally important. For example, Rosenthal (1990) discussed multiple examples where r-squared values with leading digits of .00 would universally be regarded as important. From a different perspective, Prentice and Miller (1992) illustrated how small effects can sometimes be more important than large effects. Similarly, Abelson (1985) stated that "one should not necessarily be scornful of miniscule values for percentage variance explanation" (p. 133). As Schultz and Grimes (2005) pointed out, because it is often difficult to determine the "correct" value for a minimally important effect size, researchers may be tempted to engage in a "sample size samba." When their initial value leads to a realization that too many participants are required, they may be tempted to retrofit their choice of effect size to correspond to a sample size that enables them to justify conducting the study. Unfortunately, the resultant study may be woefully underpowered to detect the effect size that was initially deemed to be important.

In contrast, the literature review approach uses effect sizes from previous (published or pilot) studies to arrive at an estimate for the likely magnitude of the effect in the planned study. Problems arise for the power analytic approach, however, when using these sample estimates at face value in sample-size planning. Specifically, the suggested sample size is often lower than needed, which results in lower than desired statistical power. This is due to publication bias and sampling uncertainty present in sample effect-size estimates. Publication bias results from statistical significance (perceived as) being used as a criterion for accepting studies for publication. The result is that effect sizes reported in published studies are systematically higher than their true (but unknown) population values. Sampling uncertainty is represented by the CIs we have described so much: Sample effect sizes are only imperfect estimates of their population values.

When using this approach, then, care should be taken to adjust prior study effect-size estimates for publication bias and uncertainty when applicable, which can be accomplished with the bias uncertainty corrected sample size (BUCSS) approach (technical details can be found in Anderson, 2021; Anderson et al., 2017; Anderson & Maxwell, 2017). Researchers specify an assumed degree of publication bias to which the prior study effect size was subjected via the alpha value required for the study results to be used in future sample-size planning. In published studies, this degree might be represented best by $\alpha = .05$, given that the study might otherwise not have been published and available to use for power analysis. But even pilot studies can be subjected to some degree of publication bias. For example, $\alpha = .50$ could be specified if a researcher determined the pilot results were only worthy of leading to a full study if $p < .5$. When using the BUCSS approach, researchers can also adjust the sample effect size for uncertainty by using the lower limit of a CI for the effect size with width that they specify. Choosing a larger CI percentage adjusts for greater amounts of uncertainty, because CIs grow wider as the percentage increases, meaning that the lower limit will be lower and, thus, a more conservative effect size value to use in sample size planning. When only uncertainty is a concern, a similar adjustment can be made using the safeguard power approach (Perugini et al., 2014).

For power analysis, holding everything else constant, the larger the magnitude of the effect size, the more statistical power a study has to detect the effect. This is not necessarily the case, however, with the AIPE approach. For example, Kelley and Rausch (2006) showed that, holding everything else constant, CIs for a sufficiently narrow expected width will require a larger sample size for larger population standardized mean differences than for smaller differences. That is, for a given expected CI width (e.g., say, 0.25 units), the sample size required for a population standardized mean difference of 0.05 requires a smaller sample size (347 per group) than does a population standardized mean difference of 1.00 (390 per group).[13]

The relationship between necessary sample size for a particular expected CI width and the size of the population standardized mean difference is monotonic in the AIPE approach—the larger the population standardized mean difference the larger the necessary sample size, holding everything else constant.[14] However, for narrow CIs for the population squared multiple correlation coefficient, the relationship between the size of the population multiple correlation coefficient and the necessary sample size for a specified width is nonmonotonic—necessary sample size for an expected CI width is maximized around a population squared multiple correlation value of around .333 (Kelley, 2008). In other situations, the size of the effect is unrelated to the CI width. Kelley et al. (2003) showed that for an unstandardized mean difference, desired CI width is independent of the population difference between means. Correspondingly, sample size from the AIPE approach does not consider the size of the unstandardized mean difference, and, thus, it is not necessary to specify the mean difference when planning sample size from the accuracy in parameter estimation approach, unlike the power analytic approach where it is necessary. The point is that the relationship between the size of the effect and the necessary sample size from the AIPE approach, holding everything else constant, depends on the particular effect-size measure.

To summarize, for power analysis, the larger the magnitude of an effect size, the smaller the necessary sample size for a particular level of statistical power, holding all other factors constant. For AIPE, however, such a universal statement cannot be made. This is the case because the way in which the value of an effect size is used in the CI procedure depends on the particular effect-size measure. There are two broad categories of effect sizes as they relate to their corresponding CIs, namely, those whose CIs depend on the value of the effect size and those whose CIs are independent of the value of the effect size. The literature on CIs serves as a guide for the way in which CIs are formed for the population value of an effect size (e.g., Grissom & Kim, 2005; Smithson, 2003). In the next section we implement some of the ideas discussed in the context of multiple regression. In particular, we provide an example in which sample size is planned for a targeted (regression coefficient) and an omnibus (the squared multiple correlation coefficient) effect size from both the power analytic and AIPE perspectives. For the former, we illustrate both the MIES approach (using the MBESS [Kelley, 2007a, 2007b, 2022] R package) and the literature review approach (using the BUCSS [Anderson & Kelley, 2020] R package). For the latter, we illustrate traditional AIPE (using MBESS; see Kelley et al., 2018, for an example of sequential AIPE).

---

[13] This is the case because, for fixed sample sizes, the larger the population standardized mean difference, the larger the noncentrality parameter, which implies a larger variance for the sampling distribution of observed standardized mean differences when the population standardized mean difference itself is larger (see Hedges & Olkin, 1985, for more details). Thus, the larger the population standardized mean difference, the larger the sample size will need to be for the same CI width.

[14] Interestingly, in the power analytic approach, the relationship between necessary sample size and the size of the population standardized mean difference is also monotonic but in the other direction—the larger the population standardized mean difference the smaller the necessary sample size for a particular level of statistical power (e.g., .90), holding everything else constant.

TABLE 10.1

Summary Statistics Taken (Means and Correlations) or Derived (Variances and Covariances) From Grant and Wrzesniewski (2010)

Variable	Mean	1.	2.	3.	4.	5.	6.	7.	8.
1. Performance	3153.70	*11923209.000*	0.00	0.14	0.03	0.13	0.27	0.31	0.34
2. Core Self-Evaluation (CSE)	5.00	0.000	*0.608*	0.23	0.00	0.15	−0.10	−0.10	0.02
3. Duty	5.11	430.360	0.160	*0.792*	0.48	0.40	−0.05	−0.01	0.10
4. Guilt	3.97	152.318	0.000	0.628	*2.160*	0.33	−0.01	0.09	0.24
5. Gratitude	4.29	507.382	0.132	0.402	0.548	*1.277*	0.10	0.25	0.29
6. CSE x Duty	0.23	923.236	−0.077	−0.044	−0.015	0.112	*0.980*	0.38	0.38
7. CSE x Guilt	0.00	1017.182	−0.074	−0.008	0.126	0.268	0.357	*0.903*	0.26
8. CSE x Gratitude	0.15	1139.11	0.151	0.086	0.342	0.318	0.461	0.240	*0.941*

Note. Variances are in the principle diagonal and are italicized, covariances are in the lower diagonal, and correlation coefficients are in the upper diagonal. Sample size is 86. Adapted from "I Won't Let You Down . . . or Will I? Core Self-Evaluations, Other-Orientation, Anticipated Guilt and Gratitude, and Job Performance," by A. M. Grant and A. Wrzesniewski, 2010, *Journal of Applied Psychology, 95*(1), p. 115 (https://doi.org/10.1037/a0017974). Copyright 2010 by the American Psychological Association.

Sample-Size Planning for Multiple Regression: An Organizational Behavior Example

Core self-evaluations are fundamental, subconscious conclusions that individuals reach about themselves, their relationships to others, and the world around them (e.g., Judge et al., 1997). Grant and Wrzesniewski (2010) noted that "little research has considered how core self-evaluations may interact with other kinds of individual differences to moderate the relationship between core self-evaluations and job performance" (p. 117). They then tested a model where a measure of Performance (financial productivity over a 3-week period) was modeled as a linear function of core self-evaluations, duty, anticipated guilt, anticipated gratitude, as well as the three two-way interactions of core self-evaluations with the remaining three predictors. The duty predictor, which quantifies the "tendency toward dependability and feelings of responsibility for others" (p. 111), was a driving force of the research, especially with respect to how it is moderated by core self-evaluation.

To test the model, data were collected from 86 call-center employees. Descriptive statistics are contained in Table 10.1, with the results from a standardized regression model (i.e., a regression model applied to standardized scores) given in Table 10.2.[15] Results show that two regression coefficients are statistically significant, namely, the interaction of core self-evaluation with duty and the interaction of core self-evaluation with gratitude. Although duty was found to have an interaction with core self-evaluation on performance, the conditional effect of duty when core self-evaluation equals zero (i.e., at the mean) has a 95% CI for the population value that ranges from −0.038 to 0.456. Notice that zero is contained in the CI for the conditional duty regression coefficient, which is in line with the NHST results (the *p* value for duty is .097). Additionally, the interaction of anticipated gratitude and core self-evaluation was statistically significant. The squared

---

[15]Grant and Wrzesniewski (2010) fit the unstandardized model given in Table 10.2. CIs for regression coefficients and the squared multiple correlation coefficient were not given in Grant and Wrzesniewski but are provided here. The standardized solution is used here because the standardized regression coefficients quantify the expected change in the dependent variable in standard deviation units for a one-standard-deviation change in the particular regressor. For example, a standardized regression coefficient of .20 means that a 1 unit (corresponding to 1 standard deviation) change in the regressor will have a .20 unit (corresponding to .20 standard deviation) change on the dependent variable. Standardized regression coefficients have a straightforward interpretation and interest is in relative performance, not literally modeling the total 3-week productivity of employees.

TABLE 10.2

Standardized Regression Model of Interest of Summary Statistics Taken (Means and Correlations) or Derived (Variances and Covariances)

Regressor	Coefficient	95% CI limits
1. Core Self-Evaluation (CSE)	−0.016	[−.224, .192]
2. Duty	0.210	[−.038, .456]
3. Guilt	−0.142	[−.380, .098]
4. Gratitude	−0.052	[−.285, .182]
5. CSE x Duty	0.057	[−.185, .299]
6. CSE x Guilt	0.242*	[.016, .467]
7. CSE x Gratitude	0.278*	[.032, .521]
R^2	.203*	[.01, .31]
Adjusted R^2	.132	

Note. Values in brackets represent the lower and upper 95% CI limits. All CIs are based on noncentral methods because the effect sizes are standardized and are calculated with the MBESS R package. The *t*-statistic associated with "duty" (used in the literature review example in Grant & Wrzesniewski, 2010) was reported to be 1.66 in the original study. Data from Grant and Wrzesniewski (2010).
*$p < .05$.

multiple correlation coefficient for the entire model was .201 ($p = .01$) with 95% CI limits for the population value of [.01, .31]; the adjusted squared multiple correlation coefficient was .132.

Although the overall model was statistically significant and there were two statistically significant interactions, none of the four conditional effects (Duty, Anticipated Gratitude, Core Self-Evaluation, and Gratitude) reached statistical significance. Because of the importance of understanding how much duty is associated with performance, as well as understanding how much performance can be explained by such a model, suppose that a follow-up study based on Grant and Wrzesniewski (2010) needs to be planned. How might sample size be planned in such a context? We will demonstrate sample-size planning and provide necessary code but, due to space restrictions, are unable to provide a detailed explanation of the functions used. However, Kelley (2007a) reviewed methods of estimating effect sizes and forming CIs for the corresponding population value, Kelley and Maxwell (2008) and Anderson (2021) provided a more thorough treatment of sample-size planning in a regression context.

THE POWER ANALYTIC APPROACH TO SAMPLE-SIZE PLANNING

When interest concerns the existence of an effect, the power analytic approach to sample-size planning should be used. The following two subsections illustrate power analysis for a regression coefficient using the literature review approach (using the BUCSS R package) and for the squared multiple correlation coefficient using the MIES approach (with the MBESS R package).

Statistical Power for a Targeted Effect (β_k)

Although the regression coefficient for the conditional effect of duty was not statistically significant in the Grant and Wrzesniewski (2010) study, theory suggests that it is a nonzero positive value. It is possible that the Grant and Wrzesniewski study did not have sufficient power to detect this specific effect. Evidence that the conditional duty regression coefficient in the population is a positive value would come from a statistically significant positive regression coefficient, signifying that when the other predictors are at their mean (i.e., zero), duty has a linear impact on performance. Using a Type I error rate of .05 and a two-sided null hypothesis significance test, we seek to answer the question "What size sample is necessary in order to have statistical power of .80 to reject the null hypothesis that the conditional duty regression coefficient equals zero?"

When using the literature review approach, the sample information from previous published or pilot studies can be used to inform researchers as to the effect-size input needed for the sample-size planning. However, as mentioned previously, this approach should use software that makes appropriate adjustments for publication bias and uncertainty. The BUCSS R package and corresponding web applications (Anderson & Kelley, 2020) have functionality for both ANOVA and regression.

The relevant function here is `ss.power.reg1()`, which conducts sample size planning for a single regression coefficient in a multiple regression model. The following code can be entered:

```
ss.power.reg1(t.observed = 1.66,
N = 86, p = 7, alpha.prior = .5,
alpha.planned = .05,
assurance = .6, power = .8)
```

In this code, `t.observed` is the *t*-statistic associated with the regression coefficient in question (here, the duty coefficient), `N` is the total sample size of the previous study, `p` is the number of predictors in the model, `alpha.planned` is the planned study Type I error rate, and power is the desired level of statistical power. The value `alpha.planned` represents the degree of publication bias assumed for the sample effect-size information, or the *p* value necessary for the previous study effect in question to be used to plan a new study. If the coefficient in question is deemed to be a driving force of the study getting published, .05 is often used here. However, in this case, Duty was nonsignificant and, thus, the level of publication bias on this particular parameter is lower. A value of .5, therefore, was entered here to assume that the effect would need to at least be trending toward the direction of significance to be worth a follow-up study. Finally, assurance represents the amount of uncertainty adjustment, given that sample information is always subject to sampling error. Entering .5 here does not add an uncertainty adjustment, while values from .51 to .99 imply an increasing adjustment for uncertainty. An assurance of .6 was used here.

The suggested sample size is 631, much larger than the previous study used because the most likely size of the duty coefficient is small and the initial goals for and power analysis of the previous study are unknown. We chose to demonstrate this particular example using the literature review approach because for targeted effects in regression, coming up with theoretically minimum values for the necessary parameters a priori without prior information can make the MIES approach difficult, given that many such values are often needed (Anderson, 2021; Maxwell, 2000).

We instead demonstrate the MIES approach for the omnibus effect in the example that follows.

Statistical Power for the Omnibus Effect

In some applications of multiple regression, no single predictor is of primary importance. Correspondingly, it is sometimes of interest only to have a model that, overall, accounts for a statistically significant portion of the variance of the outcome variable. Of particular, if interest is in obtaining a statically significant test of the squared multiple correlation coefficient. Unlike sample-size planning for a targeted regression coefficient, in order to plan sample size for statistical power of the squared multiple correlation coefficient, the only population value that must be known or estimated is the squared multiple correlation. This makes the MIES approach simpler to employ (although, of course, the literature review approach can still be used if deemed more appropriate and if prior information is available). Suppose that the researchers deem that a squared multiple correlation of .15 represents a minimally important effect size.

The `ss.power.R2()` MBESS function can be used to plan sample size for a specified value of power for the test of the squared multiple correlation coefficient. The function is used this way:

```
ss.power.R2(Population.R2=.15,
alpha.level=.05, desired.power =
0.95, p=7)
```

where `Population.R2` is a theoretical population value of the squared multiple correlation coefficient (the MIES in this case), `alpha.level` is the planned study nominal Type I error rate, `desired.power` is the intended level of statistical power, and p is the number of predictors in the regression model. Implementation of the above function returns a necessary sample size of 131. Thus, in order to have statistical power of .95 for which some of the variability in the dependent variable (here performance) is being accounted in the population by the set of predictors, where the minimally important squared multiple correlation coefficient is .15 with seven predictors and a Type I error rate of .05, a sample size of 131 is necessary.

THE AIPE APPROACH TO SAMPLE-SIZE PLANNING

When interest concerns the magnitude of an effect size, the AIPE approach to sample-size planning should be used.

AIPE for a Targeted Effect

The 95% CI from the Grant and Wrzesniewski (2010) study for the standardized conditional duty regression coefficient is [−.038, .456]. This CI is so wide that it illustrates the lack of knowledge about the population value of the standardized conditional duty regression coefficient. Correspondingly, it is really not clear how much of an impact, if any, the conditional effect of duty has on performance when the other predictors are zero. Although theory suggests that the conditional duty should have a positive impact on performance, the magnitude of that impact is important. Suppose there is a desire to have a 95% CI for the conditional duty regression coefficient that is .20 units wide. The population parameters that must be known or estimated for an application of AIPE to a standardized regression coefficient are the squared multiple correlation, the squared multiple correlation from a model not including the predictor of interest, and the standardized regression coefficient.[16] In the present example, we use the sample values from Grant and Wrzesniewski without adjusting for publication bias and uncertainty, unlike in the previous example demonstrating sample size planning for power. Although the former may be a more realistic approach, BUCSS has not been fully developed for situations in which the interval width depends on the population effect size, which may be poorly estimated due to publication bias inherent in the literature. This is an active area of research, which we suspect will grow in importance in the future.

The function ss.aipe.src() from the MBESS R package can be used as

```
ss.aipe.src(Rho2.Y_X=.20,
Rho2.k_X.without.k=.34,
p = 7, beta.k=.21, width=.20,
conf.level =.95, assurance=NULL)
```

where width is the desired CI width, Rho2.Y_X is the squared multiple correlation, Rho2.k_X.without.k is the squared multiple correlation coefficient predicting the *k*th predictor variable from the remaining p-1 predictor variables. Implementation of the above function returns a necessary sample size of 482. Notice that assurance=NULL is specified above, which implies that an assurance parameter is not incorporated into this sample-size planning procedure. Thus, approximately half of the time the CI will be wider than the desired value of .20. By specifying some assurance value (a value greater than .50 but less than 1), however, the modified sample size can be obtained. For example, if the desired assurance is .99, the above code can be modified as

```
ss.aipe.src(Rho2.Y_X=.20,
Rho2.k_X.without.k=.34,
K = 7, beta.k=.21,width=.20,
conf.level =.95, assurance=.99)
```

where assurance is the desired level of assurance and conf.level is the confidence level of interest. Implementation of the above function returns a necessary sample size of 528, which then assures that 99% of CIs formed using this procedure will be no wider than the desired value of .20.

AIPE for the Omnibus Effect

The 95% CI from the Grant and Wrzesniewski (2010) study for the population squared multiple

---

[16] The value of the regression coefficient is necessary in this case because we are working with a standardized solution. In the case of an unstandardized solution, however, the CI for the (unstandardized) regression coefficient is independent of the CI. Correspondingly, it is unnecessary to know or estimate an unstandardized regression coefficient in the context of AIPE. See Kelley and Maxwell (2008) and Kelley (2007a) for more details. The power analytic approach for both unstandardized and standardized regression coefficients requires the known or estimated population value of the regression coefficient.

correlation coefficient was [.01, .31]. Such a wide range for the plausible values of the population squared multiple correlation coefficient is undesirable, as the proportion of variance that is accounted for the model may be close to 0 or around 30%, correspondingly, with very different interpretations of how well the seven predictors are able to account for the variance of performance in the population.

Suppose one desires a width of .15 for the CI for the population squared multiple correlation coefficient. The only population parameter that must be presumed or estimated for an application of AIPE to the squared multiple correlation coefficient is the squared multiple correlation itself, like in the context of statistical power. The function ss.aipe.R2() from the MBESS R package can be used as

```
ss.aipe.R2(Population.R2=.20,
width=.15, conf.level=0.95, p=7,
assurance=NULL)
```

where the parameters are the same as noted previously. Implementation of the above yields a necessary sample size of 361. The above code does not incorporate an assurance parameter. Modifying the code to incorporate an assurance parameter of .99 leads to

```
ss.aipe.R2(Population.R2=.20,
width=.15, conf.level=0.95, p=7,
assurance=.99)
```

which returns a necessary sample size of 403.

Remember that the appropriate sample size depends on the research question. For illustrative purposes, we planned sample size for several different goals in the same hypothetical future study, which would ordinarily not be the case. If, however, multiple goals are of interest, then we recommend using the largest of the planned sample sizes.

DISCUSSION

Sample-size planning has been discussed in numerous book-length treatments (e.g., Aberson, 2019; Bausell & Li, 2002; Chow et al., 2018; Cohen, 1988; Dattalo, 2008; Davey & Savla, 2010; Kraemer & Blasey, 2016; Lipsey, 1990; Machin et al., 2018; Murphy et al., 2014). Despite the push for the use of effect sizes and CIs, the listed books do not contain as much emphasis on the AIPE approach as they do on power analysis. Because a single chapter cannot compete with book-length treatments for depth (e.g., the how-to's) or breadth (e.g., the number of designs), we hope our chapter provides a big-picture view of the overarching principles that should be considered when designing a study and planning an appropriate sample size. We also want to emphasize that sample-size planning is an active area of methodological research. As new statistical methods are developed, investigations of sample-size planning are typically needed to assure that the potential benefits of the new methods are met. Space limitations preclude full consideration of such advances, but we cite Schultzberg and Muthén (2018) illustrating the importance of sample-size planning for dynamic structural equation modeling.

Gardner and Altman (1988) encouraged medical studies to move away from null hypothesis significance testing and to focus on CIs. They also cautioned, however, that "CIs convey only the effects of sampling variation on the precision of the estimated statistics and cannot control for non-sampling errors such as biases in design, conduct, or analysis" (p. 747). Correspondingly, if biases creep into a research design, not only can the population value be estimated in a biased fashion, the wrong quantity can be estimated very precisely. That is to say, a narrow CI could be obtained that brackets the wrong population quantity. The importance of considering the various types of validity when planning a study is an issue that needs to be taken very seriously (e.g., Shadish et al., 2002).

We have thus far avoided an important potential consequence of careful sample-size planning: situations in which it becomes obvious that a single researcher is unable to invest the necessary time or resources in implementing a study that requires a larger sample size than is realistically achievable or can be achieved from a single site (e.g., if there are not enough of the particular type of participants available). In these situations, collaborative research and multisite studies can be quite beneficial. Collaboration in psychology has been gaining momentum, as evidenced by large-scale projects such as Many Labs (Klein et al., 2018) and the Psychological Science Accelerator (Moshontz et al., 2018). Relatedly, methodologists have noted a potential benefit of multiple smaller studies in terms of reducing excess heterogeneity among effects in the psychological literature (Kenny & Judd, 2019).

Without careful consideration of the issues we have discussed, one of the most common questions asked when planning research, namely, "What sample size do I need?" cannot adequately be addressed. Having a solid grasp of the foundational issues and appropriately linking the question of interest to the most appropriate type of sample-size planning will facilitate the process of sample-size planning. Once these issues are addressed, a software program can generally be used to plan the appropriate sample size. A critical evaluation of the process of sample-size planning will lead to better designed studies that we believe will facilitate a more cumulative and productive research literature.

References

Abelson, R. P. (1985). A variance explanation paradox: When a little is a lot. *Psychological Bulletin*, 97(1), 129–133. https://doi.org/10.1037/0033-2909.97.1.129

Aberson, C. L. (2019). *Applied power analysis for the behavioral sciences* (2nd ed.). Taylor & Francis. https://doi.org/10.4324/9781315171500

American Educational Research Association. (2006). *Standards for reporting on empirical social science research in AERA publications*.

American Psychological Association. (2010). *Publication manual of the American Psychological Association* (6th ed.).

Anderson, S. F. (2020). Misinterpreting *p*: The discrepancy between *p* values and the probability the null hypothesis is true, the influence of multiple testing, and implications for the replication crisis. *Psychological Methods*, 25(5), 596–609. https://doi.org/10.1037/met0000248

Anderson, S. F. (2021). Using prior information to plan appropriately powered regression studies: A tutorial using BUCSS. *Psychological Methods*, 26(5), 513–526. https://doi.org/10.1037/met0000366

Anderson, S. F., & Kelley, K. (2020). Bias-uncertainty corrected sample size (Version 1.2 or more recent) [R Package].

Anderson, S. F., Kelley, K., & Maxwell, S. E. (2017). Sample-size planning for more accurate statistical power: A method adjusting sample effect sizes for publication bias and uncertainty. *Psychological Science*, 28(11), 1547–1562. https://doi.org/10.1177/0956797617723724

Anderson, S. F., & Maxwell, S. E. (2017). Addressing the "replication crisis": Using original studies to design replication studies with appropriate statistical power. *Multivariate Behavioral Research*, 52(3), 305–324. https://doi.org/10.1080/00273171.2017.1289361

Appelbaum, M., Cooper, H., Kline, R. B., Mayo-Wilson, E., Nezu, A. M., & Rao, S. M. (2018). Journal article reporting standards for quantitative research in psychology: The APA Publications and Communications Board task force report. *American Psychologist*, 73(1), 3–25. https://doi.org/10.1037/amp0000389

Bakan, D. (1966). The test of significance in psychological research. *Psychological Bulletin*, 66(6), 423–437. https://doi.org/10.1037/h0020412

Bausell, R. B., & Li, Y.-F. (2002). *Power analysis in experimental research: A practical guide for the biological, medical, and social sciences*. Cambridge. https://doi.org/10.1017/CBO9780511541933

Benjamin, D. J., Berger, J. O., Johannesson, M., Nosek, B. A., Wagenmakers, E. J., Berk, R., Bollen, K. A., Brembs, B., Brown, L., Camerer, C., Cesarini, D., Chambers, C. D., Clyde, M., Cook, T. D., De Boeck, P., Dienes, Z., Dreber, A., Easwaran, K., Efferson, C., . . . Johnson, V. E. (2018). Redefine statistical significance. *Nature Human Behaviour*, 2(1), 6–10. https://doi.org/10.1038/s41562-017-0189-z

Bonett, D. G. (2008). CIs for standardized linear contrasts of means. *Psychological Methods*, 13(2), 99–109. https://doi.org/10.1037/1082-989X.13.2.99

Casella, G., & Berger, R. L. (2002). *Statistical inference* (2nd ed.). Cengage Learning.

Chattopadhyay, B., & Kelley, K. (2016). Estimation of the coefficient of variation with minimum risk: A sequential method for minimizing sampling error and study cost. *Multivariate Behavioral Research*, 51(5), 627–648. https://doi.org/10.1080/00273171.2016.1203279

Chow, S.-C., Shao, J., Wang, H., & Lokhnygina, Y. (2018). *Sample size calculations in clinical research* (3rd ed.). Taylor & Francis.

Cohen, J. (1988). *Statistical power analysis for the behavioral sciences* (2nd ed.). Erlbaum.

Cohen, J. (1994). The world is round (*p* <. 05). *American Psychologist, 49*(12), 997–1003. https://doi.org/10.1037/0003-066X.49.12.997

Cumming, G. (2014). The new statistics: Why and how. *Psychological Science, 25*(1), 7–29. https://doi.org/10.1177/0956797613504966

Dattalo, P. (2008). *Determining sample size: Balancing power, precision, and practicality*. Oxford University Press. https://doi.org/10.1093/acprof:oso/9780195315493.001.0001

Davey, A., & Savla, J. (2010). *Statistical power analysis with missing data: A structural equation modeling approach*. Routledge.

Des Jarlais, D. C., Lyles, C., Crepaz, N., & the TREND Group. (2004). Improving the reporting quality of nonrandomized evaluations of behavioral and public health interventions: The TREND statement. *American Journal of Public Health, 94*(3), 361–366. https://doi.org/10.2105/AJPH.94.3.361

Gardner, M. J., & Altman, D. G. (1988). Calculating CIs for regressions and correlation. *British Medical Journal, 296*(6631), 1238–1242.

Grant, A. M., & Wrzesniewski, A. (2010). I won't let you down . . . or will I? Core self-evaluations, other-orientation, anticipated guilt and gratitude, and job performance. *Journal of Applied Psychology, 95*(1), 108–121. https://doi.org/10.1037/a0017974

Green, S. B. (1991). How many subjects does it take to do a regression analysis? *Multivariate Behavioral Research, 26*(3), 499–510. https://doi.org/10.1207/s15327906mbr2603_7

Grissom, R. J., & Kim, J. J. (2005). *Effect sizes for research: A broad practical approach*. Erlbaum.

Hahn, G. J., & Meeker, W. Q. (1991). *Statistical intervals: A guide for practitioners*. John Wiley & Sons.

Harlow, L. L., Mulaik, S. A., & Steiger, J. H. (1997). *What if there were no significance tests?* Erlbaum.

Harris, R. (2001). *A Primer of multivariate statistics* (3rd ed.). Erlbaum. https://doi.org/10.4324/9781410600455

Hedges, L., & Olkin, I. (1985). *Statistical methods for meta-analysis*. Academic Press.

Hunter, J. E., & Schmidt, F. L. (2004). *Methods of meta-analysis: Correcting error and bias in research findings* (2nd ed.). Sage. https://doi.org/10.4135/9781412985031

Jiroutek, M. R., Muller, K. E., Kupper, L. L., & Stewart, P. W. (2003). A new method for choosing sample size for CI-based inferences. *Biometrics, 59*(3), 580–590. https://doi.org/10.1111/1541-0420.00068

Jones, L. V., & Tukey, J. W. (2000). A sensible formulation of the significance test. *Psychological Methods, 5*(4), 411–414. https://doi.org/10.1037/1082-989X.5.4.411

Judge, T. A., Locke, E. A., & Durham, C. C. (1997). The dispositional causes of job satisfaction: A core evaluations approach. *Research in Organizational Behavior, 19*, 151–188. https://doi.org/10.1037/0021-9010.83.1.17

Kelley, K. (2005). The effects of nonnormal distributions on confidence intervals around the standardized mean difference: Bootstrap and parametric confidence intervals. *Educational and Psychological Measurement, 65*, 51–69. https://doi.org/10.1177/0013164404264850

Kelley, K. (2007a). CIs for standardized effect sizes: Theory, application, and implementation. *Journal of Statistical Software, 20*(8), 1–24. https://doi.org/10.18637/jss.v020.i08

Kelley, K. (2007b). Methods for the behavioral, educational, and social sciences: An R package. *Behavior Research Methods, 39*(4), 979–984. https://doi.org/10.3758/BF03192993

Kelley, K. (2008). Sample size planning for the squared multiple correlation coefficient: Accuracy in parameter estimation via narrow CIs. *Multivariate Behavioral Research, 43*(4), 524–555. https://doi.org/10.1080/00273170802490632

Kelley, K. (2022). *MBESS: The MBESS R Package* (Version 4 or more recent). https://CRAN.R-project.org/package=MBESS

Kelley, K., Darku, F. B., & Chattopadhyay, B. (2018). Accuracy in parameter estimation for a general class of effect sizes: A sequential approach. *Psychological Methods, 23*(2), 226–243. https://doi.org/10.1037/met0000127

Kelley, K., & Maxwell, S. E. (2003). Sample size for multiple regression: Obtaining regression coefficients that are accurate, not simply significant. *Psychological Methods, 8*(3), 305–321. https://doi.org/10.1037/1082-989X.8.3.305

Kelley, K., & Maxwell, S. E. (2008). Power and accuracy for omnibus and targeted effects: Issues of sample size planning with applications to multiple regression. In P. Alasuuta, L. Bickman, & J. Brannen (Eds.), *The Sage handbook of social research methods* (pp. 166–192). Sage. https://doi.org/10.4135/9781446212165.n11

Kelley, K., Maxwell, S. E., & Rausch, J. R. (2003). Obtaining power or obtaining precision. Delineating methods of sample-size planning. *Evaluation & the Health Professions, 26*(3), 258–287. https://doi.org/10.1177/0163278703255242

Kelley, K., & Preacher, K. J. (2012). On effect size. *Psychological Methods*, 17(2), 137–152. https://doi.org/10.1037/a0028086

Kelley, K., & Rausch, J. R. (2006). Sample size planning for the standardized mean difference: Accuracy in parameter estimation via narrow CIs. *Psychological Methods*, 11(4), 363–385. https://doi.org/10.1037/1082-989X.11.4.363

Kenny, D. A., & Judd, C. M. (2019). The unappreciated heterogeneity of effect sizes: Implications for power, precision, planning of research, and replication. *Psychological Methods*, 24(5), 578–589. https://doi.org/10.1037/met0000209

Klein, R. A., Vianello, M., Hasselman, F., Adams, B. G., Adams, R. B., Jr., Alper, S., Aveyard, M., Axt, J. R., Babalola, M. T., Bahník, Š., Batra, R., Berkics, M., Bernstein, M. J., Berry, D. R., Bialobrzeska, O., Binan, E. D., Bocian, K., Brandt, M. J., Busching, R., . . . Nosek, B. A. (2018). Many Labs 2: Investigating variation in replicability across samples and settings. *Advances in Methods and Practices in Psychological Science*, 1(4), 443–490. https://doi.org/10.1177/2515245918810225

Kraemer, H. C., & Blasey, C. (2016). *How many subjects? Statistical power analysis in research* (2nd ed.). Sage. https://doi.org/10.4135/9781483398761

Krantz, D. H. (1999). The null hypothesis testing controversy in psychology. *Journal of the American Statistical Association*, 44(448), 1372–1381. https://doi.org/10.1080/01621459.1999.10473888

Kruschke, J. K. (2013). Bayesian estimation supersedes the t test. *Journal of Experimental Psychology: General*, 142(2), 573–603. https://doi.org/10.1037/a0029146

Kruschke, J. K. (2015). *Doing Bayesian data analysis: A tutorial with R, JAGS, and Stan* (2nd ed.). Academic Press.

Lai, K., & Kelley, K. (2011). Accuracy in parameter estimation for targeted effects in structural equation modeling: Sample size planning for narrow CIs. *Psychological Methods*, 16(2), 127–148. https://doi.org/10.1037/a0021764

Lakens, D. (2014). Performing high-powered studies efficiently with sequential analyses. *European Journal of Social Psychology*, 44(7), 701–710. https://doi.org/10.1002/ejsp.2023

Lipsey, M. W. (1990). *Design sensitivity: Statistical power for experimental research*. Sage.

MacCallum, R. C., Widaman, K. F., Zhang, S., & Hong, S. (1999). Sample size in factor analysis. *Psychological Methods*, 4(1), 84–99. https://doi.org/10.1037/1082-989X.4.1.84

Machin, D., Campbell, M. J., Tan, S. B., & Tan, S. H. (2018). *Sample sizes for clinical, laboratory, and epidemiology studies* (4th ed.). Wiley-Blackwell. https://doi.org/10.1002/9781118874905

Maxwell, S. E. (2000). Sample size and multiple regression analysis. *Psychological Methods*, 5(4), 434–458. https://doi.org/10.1037/1082-989X.5.4.434

Maxwell, S. E. (2004). The persistence of underpowered studies in psychological research: Causes, consequences, and remedies. *Psychological Methods*, 9(2), 147–163. https://doi.org/10.1037/1082-989X.9.2.147

McShane, B. B., Gal, D., Gelman, G., Robert, C., & Tackett, J. (2019). Abandon statistical significance, *The American Statistician*, 73(Suppl.), 235–245, https://doi.org/10.1080/00031305.2018.1527253

Meehl, P. E. (1967). Theory-testing in psychology and physics: A methodological paradox. *Philosophy of Science*, 34(2), 103–115. https://doi.org/10.1086/288135

Moher, D., Hopewell, S., Schulz, K. F., Montori, V., Gøtzsche, P. C., Devereaux, P. J., Elbourne, D., Egger, M., & Altman, D. G. (2010). CONSORT 2010 explanation and elaboration: Updated guidelines for reporting parallel group randomised trials. *British Medical Journal*, 340, c869. https://doi.org/10.1136/bmj.c869

Morrison, D. E., & Henkel, R. E. (Eds.). (1970). *The significance test controversy: A reader*. Aldine.

Moshontz, H., Campbell, L., Ebersole, C. R., IJzerman, H., Urry, H. L., Forscher, P. S., Grahe, J. E., McCarthy, R. J., Musser, E. D., Antfolk, J., Castille, C. M., Evans, T. R., Fiedler, S., Flake, J. K., Forero, D. A., Janssen, S. M. J., Keene, J. R., Protzko, J., Aczel, B., . . . Chartier, C. R. (2018). The psychological science accelerator: Advancing psychology through a distributed collaborative network. *Advances in Methods and Practices in Psychological Science*, 1(4), 501–515. https://doi.org/10.1177/2515245918797607

Murphy, K. R., Myors, B., & Wolach, A. (2014). *Statistical power analysis: A simple and general model for traditional and modern hypothesis tests* (4th ed.). Taylor & Francis. https://doi.org/10.4324/9781315773155

Nickerson, R. S. (2000). Null hypothesis significance testing: A review of an old and continuing controversy. *Psychological Methods*, 5(2), 241–301. https://doi.org/10.1037/1082-989X.5.2.241

O'Brien, R. G., & Castelloe, J. (2007). Sample-size analysis for traditional hypothesis testing: Concepts and issues. In A. Dmitrienko, C. Chuang-Stein, & R. D'Agostino (Eds.), *Pharmaceutical statistics using SAS: A practical guide* (pp. 237–272). SAS Institute.

Perugini, M., Gallucci, M., & Costantini, G. (2014). Safeguard power as a protection against imprecise power estimates. *Perspectives on Psychological Science*, *9*(3), 319–332. https://doi.org/10.1177/1745691614528519

Preacher, K. J., & Kelley, K. (2011). Effect size measures for mediation models: Quantitative strategies for communicating indirect effects. *Psychological Methods*, *16*(2), 93–115. https://doi.org/10.1037/a0022658

Prentice, D. A., & Miller, D. T. (1992). When small effects are impressive. *Psychological Bulletin*, *112*(1), 160–164. https://doi.org/10.1037/0033-2909.112.1.160

Rosenthal, R. (1990). How are we doing in soft psychology? *American Psychologist*, *45*(6), 775–777. https://doi.org/10.1037/0003-066X.45.6.775

Rozeboom, W. W. (1960). The fallacy of the null-hypothesis significance test. *Psychological Bulletin*, *57*(5), 416–428. https://doi.org/10.1037/h0042040

Schmidt, F. L. (1996). Statistical significance testing and cumulative knowledge in psychology: Implications for training of researchers. *Psychological Methods*, *1*(2), 115–129. https://doi.org/10.1037/1082-989X.1.2.115

Schultzberg, M., & Muthén, B. (2018). Number of subjects and time points needed for multilevel time series analysis: A simulation study of dynamic structural equation modeling. *Structural Equation Modeling*, *25*(4), 495–515. https://doi.org/10.1080/10705511.2017.1392862

Schulz, K. F., & Grimes, D. A. (2005). Sample size calculations in randomised trials: Mandatory and mystical. *The Lancet*, *365*(9467), 1348–1353. https://doi.org/10.1016/S0140-6736(05)61034-3

Senn, S. J. (2002). Power is indeed irrelevant in interpreting completed studies. *British Medical Journal*, *325*(7375), 1304. https://doi.org/10.1136/bmj.325.7375.1304

Shadish, W. R., Cook, T. D., & Campbell, D. T. (2002). *Experimental and quasi-experimental designs for generalized causal inference*. Houghton-Mifflin.

Smithson, M. (2003). *CIs*. Sage. https://doi.org/10.4135/9781412983761

Thompson, B. (2002). What future quantitative social science research could look like: Confidence intervals for effect sizes. *Educational Researcher*, *31*(3), 25–32. https://doi.org/10.3102/0013189X031003025

Tversky, A., & Kahneman, D. (1971). Belief in the law of small numbers. *Psychological Bulletin*, *76*(2), 105–110. https://doi.org/10.1037/h0031322

Vandekerckhove, J., Rouder, J. N., & Kruschke, J. K. (2018). Editorial: Bayesian methods for advancing psychological science. *Psychonomic Bulletin & Review*, *25*(1), 1–4. https://doi.org/10.3758/s13423-018-1443-8

Wilkinson, L., & the Task Force on Statistical Inference. (1999). Statistical methods in psychology journals: Guidelines and explanations. *American Psychologist*, *54*(8), 594–604. https://doi.org/10.1037/0003-066X.54.8.594

CHAPTER 11

WORKFLOW AND REPRODUCIBILITY

Oliver Kirchkamp

Why should researchers worry about workflow? Isn't it obvious how statistical analysis should be carried out? Statistical analysis should be straightforward. Details of the analysis follow from the data and from the question. Unfortunately, it is not so easy. In this chapter, I present some views on statistical workflow. I hope that an efficient statistical workflow can help us, as researchers, in three ways: in documenting clearly what analysis we carry out, in making our analysis more consistent, and in facilitating the communication of our analysis.

Is Statistical Workflow Obvious?

There are many good (and different) ways (and statistical methods) to answer a given research question. Data and research questions alone are often not enough to determine the details (and the outcome) of the statistical analysis. Simmons et al. (2011) warned that "flexibility in data collection, analysis, and reporting" has substantial impact on results. Steegen et al. (2016) demonstrated that with only a sufficiently large number of possible and plausible analyses for a single data set, one obtains a distribution of very different results. To illustrate that this multiplicity of different results is more than a theoretical problem, Silberzahn et al. (2018) gave the same data (data about 146,028 dyads of soccer players and referees) and the same research question to 29 teams of researchers. The research question was simple: Are soccer referees more likely to give red cards to players with dark skin than to players with light skin? With the same data, different teams of researchers made different, all justifiable but subjective, decisions regarding the type of the model, the treatment of dependent observations, the control variables, etc. Hence, different teams came to different conclusions. Answers of the different teams ranged from 11% *fewer* to 193% *more* yellow and red cards for players with dark skin. Silberzahn et al.'s example shows that what may look to each team of researchers like innocent details of the statistical analysis has a substantial influence on results. Proper and complete documentation of the details of the statistical analysis is necessary to reproduce results.

Consistency

A second problem of statistical analysis is that, even if we had a clear plan how to proceed, the analysis is done by humans. We all make mistakes. Veldkamp et al. (2014) used a sample of 430 articles from six top psychology journals. They found that "63% of the articles contained at least one *p*-value that was inconsistent with the reported test statistic" (p. 1). Nuijten et al. (2016) considered a sample of 16,695 articles with null-hypotheses significance tests (NHST) published

https://doi.org/10.1037/0000318-011
APA Handbook of Research Methods in Psychology, Second Edition: Vol. 1. Foundations, Planning, Measures, and Psychometrics, H. Cooper (Editor-in-Chief)
Copyright © 2023 by the American Psychological Association. All rights reserved.

in eight major psychology journals. They found that "across all journals and years 49.6% of the articles with NHST results contained at least one inconsistency" (p. 1209). Sometimes these inconsistencies have spectacular consequences. Reinhart and Rogoff (2010) used a spreadsheet to study how economic growth is influenced by debt. Herndon et al. (2014) tried to reproduce Reinhart and Rogoff (2010) and found that "coding errors, selective exclusion of available data, and unconventional weighting of summary statistics lead to serious errors that inaccurately represent the relationship between public debt and GDP growth" (p. 257). Hermans and Murphy-Hill (2015) analyzed a corpus of 9,120 Excel spreadsheet files containing formulae. They found that 24% of the analyzed spreadsheets contained at least one Excel error. Powell et al. (2008) and Kulesz and Wagner (2018) provided a more detailed discussion of spreadsheet errors. In short: researchers are only humans. Humans are not made to carry out all steps of a statistical analysis in a perfectly consistent way. Still, a good workflow might help. Below, I will sketch some ideas that might help improve consistency.

Reproducibility

A third issue we want to address here is reproducibility. Authors want other researchers to be able to reproduce and understand their analysis. What does "reproduce" actually mean? Plesser (2018) and Barba (2018) discussed how the terms "reproducibility" and "replicability" could be used. Here we follow the convention used by Claerbout and Karrenbach (1992): We call a result *reproducible* if, with the same data and the same routines, we obtain the same result. Cacioppo et al. (2015) called reproducibility "a minimum necessary condition for a finding to be believable and informative" (p. 6).

Why should reproducibility be a problem at all? If we start from the same data, and if we perform the same analysis, what could go wrong? Buckheit and Donoho (1995) warned that without proper documentation many things can go wrong: Computational methods are easily lost, researchers can't reproduce their own work, they can't communicate their work, and they can't reproduce the work of others.

Yale Law School Roundtable on Data and Code Sharing (2010) demanded that researchers make "computational research details readily available" (p. 8). Stodden (2011) recommended releasing research data and code, so that data and code can be inspected by others. Currently, we are far from a situation in which other researchers can reliably understand the work of their peers. Chang and Li (2021) attempted to reproduce the analysis of publications from 13 economics journals. They used the data and code provided by the authors of the original papers. Only 33% of the papers could be reproduced without contacting the original authors. After contacting the authors, this percentage rose to 49%. Wicherts et al. (2006) attempted to obtain data reported in 141 articles published by the American Psychological Association. For 73% of the articles the data could not be obtained.

An efficient workflow should help us to document and to communicate our statistical methods with less effort, and, thus, improve reproducibility.

Replicability

So far, we have pointed out three issues. The details of our analysis might not be sufficiently clear, our analysis might not be entirely consistent, and it might be hard to communicate our methods to other researchers. Each of these three issues makes it difficult to reproduce our research. This lack of reproducibility contributes to a lack of replicability. Here we use the term "replicability" to denote the ability to obtain similar results, based on *new* data. Replicability seems to be an issue in the profession. The Open Science Collaboration (2015) attempted to replicate 100 studies taken from three psychology journals. The authors found that only 47% of effect sizes from the original study were in the 95% confidence interval of the replication effect size. Camerer et al. (2016) attempted to replicate 18 studies from two economics journals. They found that only for 66.7% of their replications was the effect size from the original study in the 95% confidence interval of the replication effect size. Similar findings were obtained by Camerer et al. (2018).

There are several reasons why results might not be replicable. John et al. (2012) suspected that researchers might engage in questionable research practices, ranging from selective reporting to falsifying data. Munafò et al. (2017) warned that scientists are easily misled to see structure in randomness. Only one of the several problems identified by Munafò et al. seems to be related to the analysis of data and testing. Nevertheless, we suspect an inefficient workflow and a lack of documentation can be major obstacles to reproducing results. An inefficient workflow might be one of the reasons behind difficulties in replicability.

A Subjective View

In this chapter, I want to present some ideas what can be done to improve workflow. A better workflow should save time, facilitate communication with coauthors and readers and improve the quality of our work.

Statistical analysis involves several tasks, from reading data, cleaning data, and describing data to developing, estimating, and testing statistical models and reporting results. Some publications on workflow (e.g., Gelman et al., 2020) concentrate on the second part, that is, they concentrate on fitting a series of models, on developing and selecting better models, and on efficient reporting of results. Other authors (e.g., Gandrud, 2020; Wickham & Grolemund, 2017) focus on data preparation and on writing readable code (see also Kernighan & Plauger, 1978). When we talk about workflow in the following, we want to include both aspects: data preparation and the development of models.

In the next section, I will talk about reproducibility, that is, about steps we can take to document our work and to link the statistical analysis to the paper. Such readable documentation will help us understanding own work when come back to it after a break, after a paper was submitted to a journal, for example. Obviously, good documentation will also help other researchers who want to reproduce our research. I will discuss literate programming as a tool to provide documentation, briefly discuss version control, and address a few practicalities in the subsequent section.

DOCUMENTING WORK

I assume that the individual steps of statistical analysis are documented as code, that is, as a sequence of commands. Many statistical packages offer not only a command line interface (CLI) but also a graphical user interface (GUI). A GUI allows one to describe steps of the analysis visually using menus and dialogues. This visual approach can be useful to creatively explore different options of the analysis. To finally document our analysis, however, we need a textual description—a code. Most GUIs can generate this textual description of our analysis, that is, a sequence of commands, as a log file.

Literate Programming

In this section, we ask how we can connect code, that is, our instructions to a computer to read and process data, with our paper. We could treat these two tasks, writing code and writing a paper, as independent tasks. However, connecting both tasks can save time and can improve consistency.

Knuth (1992) described the idea of "literate programming." Instead of instructing a computer what to do, we first explain in a natural language what we want the computer to do. The same document contains not only the instructions to the computer but also information addressed to a human. One process, *weaving*, translates this document into readable documentation. Another process, *tangling*, creates from the same document the code for the computer.

This approach can be applied to empirical work. Temple Lang (2001) proposed integrating a statistical language with text in natural language to generate a report. Leisch (2002) presented with `Sweave` a package for `R`, which integrates the statistical analysis with the text of the paper. Xie (2015) and Xie et al. (2018) developed `knitr`, an extended package for this purpose.

It is possible to write the text that combines statistical commands and the natural language part of a report in just any text editor. One could use a program like R on the command line to translate this text into the final document. However, it is much more convenient to use an integrated development environment (IDE) for this task. An IDE is a front-end that usually provides a specialized editor, syntax highlighting, autocompletion, and facilities to develop code and build the desired output. Rossini et al. (2001) presented with ESS an integration into Emacs. Gandrud (2020) described how RStudio uses knitr to process R markdown documents.

R is not the only statistical language available. Haghish (2016) proposed the markdoc package, which supports literate programming in Stata. Rodríguez (2017) proposed markstat. Lenth and Højsgaard (2007) presented SASweave, a tool for SAS.

Research appears in many different formats, such as a paper, a handout, a book, but also as slides in a presentation, blogs, or dashboards. Xie et al. (2018) provided a comprehensive overview on how literate programming can be harnessed to generate different types of output.

With a nonliterate style of work, our methods (i.e., the commands for data preparation and the statistical analysis) and text would be organized in different documents. The distribution of text and methods over different documents becomes a problem when both, methods and text, develop over time. Which version of the text refers to which version of the methods? How can we figure out which version of the statistical methods was used to create the results in a given version of the text?

With literate programming we can organize the text of the paper and our methods in a single document. During our research, this document will change. Literate programming helps us to remain consistent. Regardless of whether new data arrives, whether we decide to organize and clean the data in a different way, or whether we change details in our analysis, in all these cases a single compilation of the document is sufficient to reflect these changes and to obtain a new and consistent version.

Some researchers might be used to writing their text with the help of a markup language like LaTeX or markdown, that is, to describe explicitly structure and formatting of the text. Others might be used to editing software that follows a "what you see is what you get" approach. In the following we will assume that the underlying file is represented in a markup language. It does not matter whether this file is edited with the help of a front-end that presents a more visual appearance (e.g., the "visual editor" in RStudio) or with a front-end that presents the structure and the bare markup.

Combining Text and Statistics

Different weave dialects follow slightly different conventions, but they all seem to have the following in common: The "standard" mode of a text is just the text in a natural language. A special command switches the compiler to a mode where the following lines are interpreted as commands in a statistical language (e.g., R). Another command switches the compiler back to the text in a natural language. For example, in Rmd (R markdown) the formatting and the structure of the text are expressed in the markdown language. Embedded in the markdown text are chunks of statistical commands. These chunks are separated from the text, in Rmd, for example, with three grave accents. Everything between an initial line like the following:

```
```{r}
```

and a closing line like this one:

```
```
```

is a "chunk." The chunk will be interpreted as commands for R. Similarly, in Rnw (R-noweb), text is written in LaTeX. In Rnw, everything between an initial line like the following:

```
<<>>=
```

and a closing line like the following one:

```
@
```

is a chunk and interpreted as commands for R. During compilation, graphs, tables and other results are generated from these chunks. Results are inserted back into the text or kept in memory to be used in later chunks. The combined document would then be translated to a pretty format, for example, pdf, odt, docx, and html.

If, in a chunk, we only want the results of a command, but not the code in the paper, we add an option to the opening line:

```
```{r, echo=FALSE}
thisCodeWillBeExecutedButNotShown()
```
```

Similar options fine-tune which parts of output are shown, how figures are rendered, etc.

Reading and cleaning of data. Now we can include all statistical operations in transparent way in our document. Let us start with reading our raw data. To be more robust, we would not assume data were read from a fixed list of files. To be more flexible, we only assume that filenames follow a pattern. In this example, the directory data contains all csv files for our project. The next chunk reads all the csv files and combines them into one single data frame. If more raw data arrive (and if the data follow the same pattern), we simply compile the document again to update our results.

In this example, we also use comments. In R, the character # denotes comments. These comments help us to remember what our code is supposed to do when we return to work after a break. These comments are also vital to help coauthors or critical reviewers to understand the code.

```
```{r}
library(dplyr)
list.files("data", "*.csv",
    full.names=TRUE) %>% ## get list
                        ## of files
  lapply(read.csv) %>%       ## read
                   ## different files
  bind_rows ->         ## combine
                   ## different files
    rawData             ## store in
              ## a variable rawData
```
```

Most data sets need cleaning. In the raw data, variables may have cryptic names, values might be coded in a way that is not suitable for analysis, etc. Since *all* steps of the statistical analysis are documented, cleaning is documented as well. Our document might include a small program, which does the cleaning, checks the coding of the data, and/or renames and recodes if necessary, etc.

Inline Results

Of course, conveniently combining text and statistics requires some discipline when writing the paper. We would not write in our introduction:

```
Our analysis includes 12 sessions
with 120 participants...
```

Today these numbers might be correct. Later, with more data or with different criteria for which participants to include, these numbers must be updated. Papers develop, the models we use for our analysis change, our criteria regarding which observations to include change, and, thus, results in our paper change, too. Minor changes in our analysis should not require a tedious update of many small results in our paper. Literate programming can help us here.

Instead of entering fixed numbers, we simply give instructions about how to calculate these numbers from the data. Early in the document we include a chunk where we calculate the statistics we need. Assuming that the variables sessionID and partID provide unique ids for sessions and participants, we could write the following:

```
```{r}
numSession <-
          length(unique(sessionID))
numPart    <-length(unique(partID))
```
```

Once we have calculated the variable numSession and numPart in the above chunk, we can use the calculated results in the text. So, in our text we would write the following:

```
Our analysis includes
`r numSession` sessions with
`r numPart` participants.
```

The `r numSession` and the `r numPart` are "inline expressions," i.e., the values of numSession and numPart will be calculated when we compile, and then inserted into the text.

We could perform all these steps manually: We could edit the document in the editor of our choice and then compile the document from within R by manually invoking the knit function. A front-end, like RStudio (or Emacs with ESS), can be a convenient help to perform these steps automatically. If, in the front-end, we create a new R markdown document from the File menu, the front-end should allow us to choose a template for the document. The front-end also allows us to choose an output format (html, pdf, docx, ...). In the editor, when we hit the Knit button, the front-end calculates the statistics, renders the figures, and creates the document in the desired format.

No matter whether we use a front-end or whether we compile manually, compiling the document creates the output with the current results inserted where we had written `r numSession` or `r numPart`. In the same way, we would include *p* values, estimated effect sizes, etc., in the text.

Generating Tables

Here is a slightly more involved example. We calculate three variants of a simple OLS regression. We store the results in variables model1, model2, and model3

```
model1<-lm(mpg~hp,       data=mtcars)
model2<-lm(mpg~hp+wt,    data=mtcars)
model3<-lm(mpg~hp+wt+cyl,
                         data=mtcars)
```

Now we want to display our estimation results as a table. Here we use the huxtable package from R to present estimation results as a table. Should our data change or should the specification of the model change, this table (and all other tables that are affected by the change) would reflect these changes automatically. The following two commands,

```
library(huxtable)
huxreg(model1, model2, model3)
```

produce this output:

	(1)	(2)	(3)
(Intercept)	30.099***	37.227***	38.752***
	(1.634)	(1.599)	(1.787)
hp	−0.068***	−0.032**	−0.018
	(0.010)	(0.009)	(0.012)
wt		−3.878***	−3.167***
		(0.633)	(0.741)
cyl			−0.942
			(0.551)
N	32	32	32
R2	0.602	0.827	0.843
logLik	−87.619	−74.326	−72.738
AIC	181.239	156.652	155.477

*$p < .05$; **$p < .01$; ***$p < .001$.

Assume that we want to report the marginal effect of wt in Model (2). This can be done with another inline expression:

```
The marginal effect of `wt` in
Model (2) is
`r coef(model2)["wt"]`.
```

And we obtain the following:

The marginal effect of wt in Model (2) is −3.878.

If our data set changes, if we get more or fewer observations, then the text will always be consistent with the data.

Graphs

Let us complete this brief tour of literate programming of statistical texts with a graph (Figure 11.1). R offers several ways to create graphs. Here we use the ggplot2 library:

```
library(ggplot2)
ggplot(mtcars,aes(x=wt,y=mpg,
               lty=factor(cyl)))+
  geom_smooth(method="lm")+
  geom_point()
```

The example should illustrate that few commands can create a complex graph. The

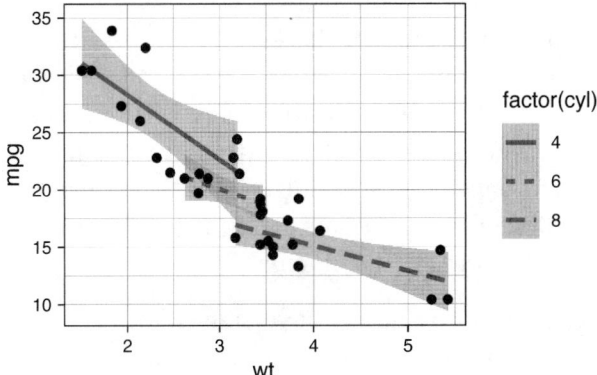

FIGURE 11.1

commands help us remembering what the graph really means and how its appearance could be changed. Should the underlying data change, the entire document, including the graph, can easily be updated.

Caching Results

Even for a fast computer, statistical analysis takes time. Redoing the entire analysis repeatedly when only a few words in the text have changed can be time-consuming. For a longer text, tools like `knitr` or `Sweave` have a built-in caching feature to speed up compilation. This feature is activated with a cache option:

```
```{r, cache=TRUE}
timeConsumingCalculation()
```
```

`knitr` and `Sweave` try to figure out when circumstances have changed, when the cache has become invalid and needs a (time-consuming) update. Often, `knitr` and `Sweave` are correct in their assessment. When they are wrong, caching can be disabled for some chunks and enabled for others. Alternatively, we could manually decide when to recalculate parts of our analysis; that is, we would do the (computationally) time-consuming analysis once and save the result. The next time, we would first test whether a file with the calculated results already exists. If it does not, we must generate it. If it exists, we will simply use the results that were calculated earlier.

```
if( file.exists(
    "timeConsumingResults.Rdata")) {
  load("timeConsumingResults.Rdata")
} else {
    ## file does not exist, hence
    ## we must create the file...
preciousData <-
do_the_time_consuming_calculation()
save(preciousData,
    file="timeConsumingResults.Rdata")
}
```

If ever we think the time-consuming calculation needs to be redone, we would simply delete the file `timeConsumingResults.Rdata` and compile again. The danger of such a procedure is that we might forget to recalculate the data when, for example, our prior data have changed.

VERSIONS

In the previous section we talked about literate programming that combines our statistical analysis and the text of our research. Now the statistical analysis and the text of our paper are in one file. This file will change. During our research, our statistical methods will change, and so will the text of the paper. We develop new ideas, we take new perspectives, we improve models to present our data, we polish our conclusions, new data comes in, etc.

While our paper keeps changing and our data keep growing, we have the following aims:

- We want to document the development of our project.
- We want to undo mistakes. Last week the perspective we took in our analysis had worked reasonably well. This week we have replaced this analysis with what we thought for a moment was a brilliant idea. Now we have changed our mind. Perhaps last week's approach was not so bad after all. We want to be able to return in a consistent way to prior states of our research.
- Perhaps even more importantly, we want to preserve versions we have given to others or submitted to a journal.

- We also want to allow concurrent edits. Many papers have more than a single author. We want to coordinate the work of several authors without constraining them. We want to make sure that changes to the paper by one author do not interfere with the work of another author. But even a single author might interfere with their own work if the author is working at different desks and at different machines. Changes to the paper made at one place by one person should not interfere with changes made at a different place or by a different person.

There are many solutions to the above problems. Some of these solutions are more efficient, others are less so:

- Manual versions of files: We could track versions of individual files manually. That is, we could have a file `paper_20210901.Rmd` to make clear that this file was created on a specific date. The version on the next day would be called `paper_20210902.Rmd`. Perhaps we could also add a time to the filename to distinguish different versions on the same day. Manual versions require a lot of discipline, create a lot of clutter on our hard disk, and do not solve the problem of concurrent edits.
- Snapshots: A variant of this approach involves file systems that can take snapshots (like `ZFS` or `Btrfs`). Snapshots on a file-system level can be stored in a very space efficient way. Snapshots can be a very useful second layer of security. However, snapshots are perhaps not the best primary method to document one's own work. Since automatic snapshots are taken even when no relevant progress was made, they create even more clutter. Furthermore, snapshots involve all files, regardless of whether they are important or unimportant. Snapshots do not help with concurrent edits of several people working on the same document, either.
- Cloud storage: Some cloud storage solutions offer a restricted snapshot capability. Many storage systems allow one to go back in time for at least a few days. Since this is just a restricted version of "real" snapshots, it suffers from the same drawbacks.
- Version control: "Version control" or "revision control" usually controls only a small number of really essential files. Often our raw data and our paper are sufficient. All other intermediate files and final outputs can be derived from these primary documents.

There are a number of version control systems, for example, `git`, `subversion`, `Mercurial`,... Here we use `git` as an illustration. `git` works with two types of repositories, remote and local. Remote repositories coordinate work with other people, whereas local repositories track local changes. Often we want both. Still, many advantages of version control can already be enjoyed with only a local repository. Remote repositories require a `git` server. Setting up such a server is not too complicated. Most academic institutions provide a `git` server for their researchers. There are also commercial providers of `git` servers.

If we use a front-end (like `RStudio`), the front-end would assist us in either setting up a local `git` repository or importing a remote repository if a project is already under version control at a different place.

- If we plan only a local repository, we create a local repository (`git --init`). This is done automatically by the front-end when we create a new project an enable support for `git`.
- If we plan to use a remote and a local repository, we create on the server side a bare remote repository (`git --init bare`). On the local side, we clone from the remote (`git clone <repository>`), where `<repository>` denotes the path to the repository, e.g., `/path/to/repo.git/` if the repository is on the same file system. If the repository is on a different file system (and a different machine), then `<repository>` could be something like `ssh://[user@]host.xz[:port]/path/to/repo.git/` or `https://host.xz[:port]/path/to/repo.git/`. Cloning from the remote creates a local repository and connects the local to the remote.

- Our local directory contains now a (hidden) subdirectory .git. This directory stores all the local versioning information. Next we populate the local directory with our raw data and with our paper. Let us assume that our paper is stored in our local directory (next to the .git subdirectory) as a file called paper.Rmd and our raw data are in a file called data.csv.

The command git add paper.Rmd data.csv adds the two files to the (local) repository. Alternatively, our front-end would allow us to stage or add the files to version control. To store our edits in the git database we use git commit. If we have access to a remote repository, we can now push the local edits to the remote repository with git push.

Having a remote repository allows us to exchange data with a second person or a second machine. So, at this second machine, we could (in a local repository that has the same remote) use the command git pull. All changes from the first repository then appear in the second repository.

Version control can help us to coordinate concurrent edits. Assume we have two people working on two different machines, A and B. Assume at machine A, we pull the current state from the repository, do some edits, commit our changes and push. At the same time, at machine B, somebody else (perhaps our coauthor) does the same. Let us illustrate the sequence of events with the help of the following table:

Machine A	Machine B
git pull	git pull
do some edits	*do some edits*
git commit	git commit
git push	
	git push

Here we assume that the user at the first machine, A, commits changes and pushes to the repository. A little while later, the user at machine B commits their changes and also wants to push to the repository. If both A and B have changed the same file, the second git push (at B) must fail; git push yields the following error message:

Error: failed to push some refs to . . . Updates were rejected because the remote contains work that you do not have locally . . . This is usually caused by another repository pushing to the same ref. You may want to first integrate the remote changes (e.g., 'git pull . . . ') before pushing again.

Indeed, the user at B is not aware of changes at A, so they have to pull the updated version before they push their own work.

Machine A	Machine B
	git pull

In executing git pull, B tries to merge the different edits automatically. This works well if the edits made at A are in a different part of the file than the edits made at B. After the successful git pull, we would push the merged files back to the repository:

Machine A	Machine B
	git push

If A and B edit the *same* part of the file in different ways, the merge will fail with an error message. If both authors rewrite the abstract, git cannot decide which version is the better one. A clear division of labor between coauthors is another element of good workflow. A clear division of labor avoids both authors trying to solve the same problem in different ways. If, nevertheless, git detects that labor has not been divided well and concurrent edits cannot be merged, git complains with a message similar to the following:

Auto-merging < . . . filename . . . > CONFLICT (content): Merge conflict in < . . . filename . . . > error: could not apply . . . Resolve all conflicts manually, mark them as resolved with "git add/rm ", then run "git rebase –continue". You can instead skip this commit: run "git rebase –skip". To abort and get back to the state before "git rebase", run "git rebase –abort".

There are a number of *mergetools*, which help to reconcile the conflicting edits in a transparent way. They all show the different versions of the same part of the file and allow the user to choose among these versions. The sequence would be as follows:

Machine A	Machine B
	`git mergetool`
	`git rebase --continue`
	`git push`

But, again, with a good division of labor, such a conflict would not arise.

This is only a very small subset of the functions offered by `git`. Another very useful set of functions concerns *branching*, that is, the possibility to create different versions of a project, for different purposes, and selectively merging the different versions back together.

CODING ISSUES

There are a number of excellent books on coding for different statistical languages. Long (2009) provided a very helpful introduction into workflow for `Stata`. Wickham and Grolemund (2017) and Gandrud (2020) are very useful books for `R`. In the current section, I can point out only a few issues.

Data Integrity

Information on storage media is bound to change (Panzer-Steindel, 2007). To ensure that we analyze the correct data, we use checksums. A *checksum* is a short block of data summarizing a long block of data. When the long block of data changes even in a very small detail, the checksum reflects this change. To ensure a file's integrity, it is, hence, sufficient to confirm the checksum's integrity. We could manually create checksums for our files, store them, and later compare the original checksums with the current checksums. Alternatively, we use a self-healing file system (like ZFS), which maintains these checksums for us.

The following command in `R` generates md5-checksums for all `csv` files in the directory `data` and saves these checksums in a file `md5sums.csv`.

```
write.csv(file="md5sums.csv",
    sapply(list.files(".","*.csv"),
        tools::md5sum))
```

If we later worry whether our raw data have changed, we can calculate the checksums again and compare with the checksums of the original data.

Robustness

Our code should work and generate the same results if it is executed on different computers, at different times, in different contexts. It would also be desirable that if the data change, our code still works and provides the appropriate results.

Randomness. Let us start with randomness as a first step to robustness. Many statistical procedures are based on pseudo-random numbers. Bootstraps, permutation tests, simulations, MCMC samples, etc., will, depending on the state of the random number generators, produce slightly different results. Getting different results each time would contradict reproducibility. To make sure that calculations with pseudo-random numbers always yield identical results, we set the seed of the random number generator to a fixed value before each calculation:

```
set.seed(1234)
```

Working with directories. When we read data or source code and when we write results, the files we read and write are stored on a file system. Most file systems represent files in a structure similar to a tree. Nodes of this tree are called *directories*. Consider a researcher who organizes one project in a directory called `project_A`. Such a project can have subdirectories. It is useful to have one subdirectory for the raw data. A directory `project_A/raw_data/` would contain, for example, files `01.csv`, `02.csv`, `03.csv`,..., which are the raw data of the project. The relevant literature could be in a directory `project_A/literature`, the derived data in `project_A/derived_data`, the paper in `project_A/paper`, etc. Our researcher might store all these directories in `/home/personA/research/`. This researcher could read the raw data with the help of absolute filenames as shown in Exhibit 11.1.

EXHIBIT 11.1

```
D01<-read.csv("/home/personA/research/project_A/raw_data/01.csv")
D02<-read.csv("/home/personA/research/project_A/raw_data/02.csv")
...
```

Assume we exchange files with a coauthor. On the coauthor's computer, the files are all in `C:\Users\personB\Projects\A\`. Any attempt to read file `01.csv` with the help of absolute filenames with the above commands from directories `/home/personA/research/project_A/` must fail. It would be very tedious if exchanging files always meant adjusting each and every command where directories are specified. This is why *relative* filenames and *working directories* are useful. The first researcher could use a working directory of `/home/personA/research/project_A/`, the second researcher would use a working directory `C:\Users\personB\Projects\A\`. The two researchers need only agree that the working directory for this project follows the same structure on both machines, that is, it contains subdirectories `raw_data`, `derived_data`, etc. All members of the project who use this structure would read the data using *relative* filenames as follows:

```
D01<-read.csv("raw_data/01.csv")
D02<-read.csv("raw_data/02.csv")
...
```

It remains to set the working directory. Some front-ends make the working directory part of the project. For other front-ends it is sufficient to put the *master* file, that is, the file with all the commands for the analysis into the working directory.

Documenting software versions. Earlier, I discussed how we control the versions of our own code. Still, versions of our software might change. Most of the time these changes do not affect our results, but sometimes they will. It is, therefore, useful to document in our code the version of the software we are using.

```
sessionInfo()$R.version$
    version.string
```

[1] "R version 4.2.0 (2022-04-22)"

Of course, libraries have versions, too. Here is one possibility to get an overview of the loaded packages:

```
paste(unlist(lapply(
    sessionInfo()$loadedOnly,
    function(x)
        paste(x$Package,x$Version))),
    collapse=", ")
```

If we include the output of this command in the printed version of our paper (perhaps in a footnote), then if ever one of the libraries should change in a way that affects our results, we understand why results changed and, if necessary, we can choose the right version of the package.

Transparent Code

Avoiding repetition. Statistical analysis often repeats itself. The same type of analysis is applied in the same way to different subgroups of the data or to different variables. Once the analysis seems to work for one situation (subset of the data, variables), it is tempting to copy and paste and adjust the code for each of the other situations. Copying and pasting have at least two disadvantages: One is: Copying and pasting and at the same time adjusting the code consistently is difficult. The second disadvantage is that each change in our analysis requires changing all copies. And, since our analysis develops, these changes will be frequent. In short, it is good practice to avoid repetition and, instead, write code that exploits the structure (Hunt & Thomas, 1999, p. 320).

To give a simple example, let us look at the `warpbreaks` data. The data set (which is built into `R`) gives the number of warp breaks per loom for different levels of tension (L, M, H) and for different types of wool (A and B). Assume we want to compare the two types of wool, A and B, for each of levels of tension

(`L`, `M`, `H`) separately. Compare the following two approaches: First, the redundant one, where we treat each case separately. Since there are three different levels of tensions, we write three different commands.

```
pL <- t.test(breaks ~ wool,
             data=warpbreaks,
             subset=tension=="L")$
                              p.value
pM <- t.test(breaks ~ wool,
             data=warpbreaks,
             subset=tension=="M")$
                              p.value
pH <- t.test(breaks ~ wool,
             data=warpbreaks,
             subset=tension=="H")$
                              p.value
huxtable(data.frame(tension=
          c("L","M","H"),
          p.value=c(pL,pM,pH)))
```

tension	p.value
L	0.0344
M	0.28
H	0.155

In this example there are three levels of tension, L, M, and H. In the code each level shows up four times. In this simple situation, we already have 12 opportunities to mix up the connection between levels and *p* values.

We can avoid these mistakes if we exploit the structure of the data. Here the `dplyr` library helps. We first group the data by `tension`, then we calculate the *p* value for each subgroup:

```
library(dplyr)
warpbreaks %>%
    group_by(tension) %>%
    summarise(p.value=
    t.test(breaks ~ wool)$
                      p.value) %>%
    huxtable
```

tension	p.value
L	0.0344
M	0.28
H	0.155

These commands solve the same problem, but with less redundancy.

In the `warpbreaks` example we repeat calculations for different values of a variable (here `tension`). We also often repeat the same calculation for different variables. Here, for example, we look at the data set `iris`. This data set contains five variables. One denotes `Species`, the other four are `Sepal.Length`, `Sepal.Width`, `Petal.Length`, and `Petal.Width`. Let us assume we are interested in the variances of the length and width variables. We could calculate the variances separately for each of the four variables:

```
Sepal.Length.Variance <-
             var(iris$Sepal.Length)
Sepal.Width.Variance  <-
             var(iris$Sepal.Width)
Petal.Length.Variance <-
             var(iris$Petal.Length)
Petal.Width.Variance  <-
             var(iris$Petal.Width)
huxtable(data.frame(name=c(
    "Petal.Length","Petal.Width",
    "Sepal.Length","Sepal.Width"),
    variance=c(
        Petal.Length.Variance,
        Petal.Width.Variance,
        Sepal.Length.Variance,
        Sepal.Width.Variance)))
```

name	variance
Petal.Length	3.12
Petal.Width	0.581
Sepal.Length	0.686
Sepal.Width	0.19

But, again, mistakes in such a calculation would easily go unnoticed. It is safer to pivot the `iris` data to "long" format (here we use `pivot_longer` from the `tidyr` library) and then group by variable names, so that we can calculate the variances for each group:

```
library(tidyr)
iris %>%
    pivot_longer(cols=matches(
            "Length|Width")) %>%
    group_by(name) %>%
    summarise(variance=
                var(value)) %>%
    huxtable
```

name	variance
Petal.Length	3.12
Petal.Width	0.581
Sepal.Length	0.686
Sepal.Width	0.19

This code is less repetitive. If there is a mistake, then the mistake will affect all results at once. We have a better chance to find the mistake.

Also note that we do not explicitly mention the variable names (`Petal.Length`, `Petal.Width`, `Sepal.Length` and `Sepal.Width`). Instead we use a pattern (`matches("Length|Width")`) to identify our variables. Using patterns becomes even more useful when the number of matching variables is large or when, at the time when we write the code, the exact names of the variables we want to include are not yet known.

Structure in models. In a similar way, we can exploit structure in our models. Previously, we calculated the three models `model1`, `model2`, and `model3`, one by one. Here is a different approach:

```
oneReg <- function(depVar,
    expVars = list("
    hp","hp + wt","hp + wt + cyl"))
    lapply(expVars, function(eVar)
        lm(paste(depVar," ~ ",eVar),
            data=mtcars)) %>%
    huxreg
oneReg("mpg")
```

	(1)	(2)	(3)
(Intercept)	30.099***	37.227***	38.752***
	(1.634)	(1.599)	(1.787)
hp	−0.068***	−0.032**	−0.018
	(0.010)	(0.009)	(0.012)
wt		−3.878***	−3.167***
		(0.633)	(0.741)
cyl			−0.942
			(0.551)
N	32	32	32
R2	0.602	0.827	0.843
logLik	−87.619	−74.326	−72.738
AIC	181.239	156.652	155.477

$^*p < .05;\ ^{**}p < .01;\ ^{***}p < .001$.

Once we have written the `oneReg` function, we could use it to create similar tables for different dependent variables:

```
oneReg("qsec")
...
```

Using functions. With more involved statistical analysis, functions help us to better understand the steps of this analysis. Let us assume that in the `iris` example we want (for the four variables `Petal.Length`, `Petal.Width`, `Sepal.Length` and `Sepal.Width`) to calculate the normalized interquartile range. If x_P is the P-percentile of x, then we define the normalized inter-quartile range as $(x_{.75} - x_{.25})/x_{.5}$. Our code can be read more easily if we define a function with a transparent name (`norm_interquartile_range` might be more transparent than `niqr`):

```
norm_interquartile_range <-
    function(x)
    (quantile(x,.75)-
    quantile(x,.25))/median(x)

iris %>%
    pivot_longer(cols=matches(
            "Length|Width")) %>%
    group_by(name) %>%
```

```
summarise(
    `norm. interquartile range`=
norm_interquartile_range(value)
) %>%
huxtable
```

name	norm. interquartile range
Petal.Length	0.805
Petal.Width	1.15
Sepal.Length	0.224
Sepal.Width	0.167

Even if we use this function only once, having a function with a name makes our code more transparent. If we plan to use the function multiple times, functions become even more attractive. If functions are used multiple times, they can help to find and to fix mistakes consistently.

CONCLUSION

In this chapter, I have summarized a few issues that are supposed to be helpful for our workflow. This is a personal view. Nevertheless, I hope that I have made a convincing case that an efficient workflow might reduce the time needed to document and organize a research project and might hopefully allow researchers to concentrate more on the fun aspects of research.

References

Barba, L. A. (2018). *Terminologies for reproducible research*. arXiv:1802.03311 [cs.DL]. https://doi.org/10.48550/arXiv.1802.03311

Buckheit, J. B., & Donoho, D. L. (1995). *WaveLab and reproducible research*. Tech Rep 474. Stanford University. https://doi.org/10.1007/978-1-4612-2544-7_5

Cacioppo, J. T., Kaplan, R. M., Krosnick, J. A., Olds, J. L., & Dean, H. (2015). *Social, behavioral, and economic sciences perspectives on robust and reliable science: Report of the Subcommittee on Replicability in Science Advisory Committee to the National Science Foundation Directorate for Social, Behavioral, and Economic Sciences*. https://www.nsf.gov/sbe/AC_Materials/SBE_Robust_and_Reliable_Research_Report.pdf

Camerer, C. F., Dreber, A., Forsell, E., Ho, T.-H., Huber, J., Johannesson, M., Kirchler, M., Almenberg, J., Altmejd, A., Chan, T., Heikensten, E., Holzmeister, F., Imai, T., Isaksson, S., Nave, G., Pfeiffer, T., Razen, M., & Wu, H. (2016). Evaluating replicability of laboratory experiments in economics. *Science, 351*(6280), 1433–1436. https://doi.org/10.1126/science.aaf0918

Camerer, C. F., Dreber, A., Holzmeister, F., Ho, T.-H., Huber, J., Johannesson, M., Kirchler, M., Nave, G., Nosek, B. A., Pfeiffer, T., Altmejd, A., Buttrick, N., Chan, T., Chen, Y., Forsell, E., Gampa, A., Heikensten, E., Hummer, L., Imai, T., . . . Wu, H. (2018). Evaluating the replicability of social science experiments in Nature and Science between 2010 and 2015. *Nature Human Behaviour, 2*(9), 637–644. https://doi.org/10.1038/s41562-018-0399-z

Chang, A. C., & Li, P. (2021). Is economics research replicable? Sixty published papers from thirteen journals say "often not." *Critical Finance Review, 11*(1), 185–206. https://doi.org/10.1561/104.00000053

Claerbout, J. F., & Karrenbach, M. (1992). Electronic documents give reproducible research a new meaning. [Society of Exploration Geophysicists.]. *SEG Technical Program Expanded Abstracts, 1992*, 601–604. https://doi.org/10.1190/1.1822162

Gandrud, C. (2020). *Reproducible research with R and RStudio* (3rd ed.). Chapman & Hall/CRC Press. https://doi.org/10.1201/9780429031854

Gelman, A., Vehtari, A., Simpson, D. P., Margossian, C., Carpenter, B., Yao, Y., Kennedy, L., Gabry, J. Burkner, P.-C., & Modrák, M. (2020). Bayesian workflow. arXiv:2011.01808 [stat.ME]. https://doi.org/10.48550/arXiv.2011.01808

Haghish, E. F. (2016). Markdoc: Literate programming in Stata. *The Stata Journal, 16*(4), 964–988. https://doi.org/10.1177/1536867X1601600409

Hermans, F., & Murphy-Hill, E. (2015). Enron's spreadsheets and related emails: A data set and analysis. In *2015 IEEE/ACM 37th IEEE International Conference on Software Engineering, 2*, 7–16. https://doi.org/10.1109/ICSE.2015.129

Herndon, T. C., Ash, M., & Pollin, R. (2014). Does high public debt consistently stifle economic growth? A critique of Reinhart and Rogoff. *Cambridge Journal of Economics, 38*(2), 257–279. https://doi.org/10.1093/cje/bet075

Hunt, A., & Thomas, D. (1999). *The pragmatic programmer: From journeyman to master*. Addison-Wesley.

John, L. K., Loewenstein, G., & Prelec, D. (2012). Measuring the prevalence of questionable research practices with incentives for truth telling. *Psychological Science, 23*(5), 524–532. https://doi.org/10.1177/0956797611430953

Kernighan, B. W., & Plauger, P. J. (1978). *The elements of programming style*. McGraw-Hill.

Knuth, D. E. (1992). *Literate programming*. Vol. 26. CSLI Lecture Notes. CSLI Publications. Stanford University.

Kulesz, D., & Wagner, S. (2018). Asheetoxy: A taxonomy for classifying negative spreadsheet-related phenomena. In *Proceedings of the 5th International Workshop on Software Engineering Methods in Spreadsheets*. arXiv:1808.10231 [cs.SE]. https://doi.org/10.48550/arXiv.1808.10231

Leisch, F. (2002). 'Sweave: Dynamic generation of statistical reports using literate data analysis,' In W. Härdle & B. Rönz (Eds.), *COMPSTAT—Proceedings in computational statistics* (575–580). Physica, Heidelberg. https://doi.org/10.1007/978-3-642-57489-4_89

Lenth, R. V., & Højsgaard, S. (2007). SASWeave: Literate programming using SAS. *Journal of Statistical Software, 19*(8), 1–20. https://doi.org/10.18637/jss.v019.i08

Long, J. S. (2009). *The workflow of data analysis using Stata*. Stata Press Books, wdaus. StataCorp LP. https://ideas.repec.org/b/tsj/spbook/wdaus.html

Munafò, M. R., Nosek, B. A., Bishop, D. V. M., Button, K. S., Chambers, C. D., du Sert, N. P., Simonsohn, U., Wagenmakers, E. J., Ware, J. J., & Ioannidis, J. P. A. (2017). A manifesto for reproducible science. *Nature Human Behaviour, 1*(1), 0021. https://doi.org/10.1038/s41562-016-0021

Nuijten, M. B., Hartgerink, C. H. J., van Assen, M. A. L. M., Epskamp, S., & Wicherts, J. M. (2016). The prevalence of statistical reporting errors in psychology (1985–2013). *Behavior Research Methods, 48*(4), 1205–1226. https://doi.org/10.3758/s13428-015-0664-2

Open Science Collaboration. (2015). Estimating the reproducibility of psychological science. *Science, 349*(6251). https://doi.org/10.1126/science.aac4716

Panzer-Steindel, B. (2007). *Data integrity*. CERN/IT. https://indico.cern.ch/event/13797/contributions/1362288/attachments/115080/163419/Dataintegrityv3.pdf

Plesser, H. E. (2018). Reproducibility vs. replicability: A brief history of a confused terminology. *Frontiers in Neuroinformatics, 11*(76), 76. https://doi.org/10.3389/fninf.2017.00076

Powell, S. G., Baker, K. R., & Lawson, B. (2008). A critical review of the literature on spreadsheet errors. *Decision Support Systems, 46*(1), 128–138. https://doi.org/10.1016/j.dss.2008.06.001

Reinhart, C. M., & Rogoff, K. S. (2010). Growth in a time of debt. *The American Economic Review, 100*(2), 573–578. https://doi.org/10.1257/aer.100.2.573

Rodríguez, G. (2017). Literate data analysis with Stata and Markdown. *The Stata Journal, 17*(3), 600–618. https://doi.org/10.1177/1536867X1701700304

Rossini, A., Maechler, M., Hornik, K., Heiberger, R. M., & Sparapani, R. (2001). *Emacs speaks statistics: A universal interface for statistical analysis*. UW Biostatistics Working Paper Series. Working Paper 173. https://biostats.bepress.com/uwbiostat/paper173

Silberzahn, R., Uhlmann, E. L., Martin, D. P., Anselmi, P., Aust, F., Awtrey, E., Bahník, Š., Bai, F., Bannard, C., Bonnier, E., Carlsson, R., Cheung, F., Christensen, G., Clay, R., Craig, M. A., Dalla Rosa, A., Dam, L., Evans, M. H., Flores Cervantes, I., ... Nosek, B. A. (2018). Many analysts, one data set: Making transparent how variations in analytic choices affect results. *Advances in Methods and Practices in Psychological Science, 1*(3), 337–356. https://doi.org/10.1177/2515245917747646

Simmons, J. P., Nelson, L. D., & Simonsohn, U. (2011). False-positive psychology: Undisclosed flexibility in data collection and analysis allows presenting anything as significant. *Psychological Science, 22*(11), 1359–1366. https://doi.org/10.1177/0956797611417632

Steegen, S., Tuerlinckx, F., Gelman, A., & Vanpaemel, W. (2016). Increasing transparency through a multiverse analysis. *Perspectives on Psychological Science, 11*(5), 702–712. https://doi.org/10.1177/1745691616658637

Stodden, V. (2011). Trust your science? Open your data and code. *Amstat News*, 21–22. https://magazine.amstat.org/blog/2011/07/01/trust-your-science/

Temple Lang, D. (2001, March 15-17). Embedding S in other languages and environments. In K. Hornik & F. Leisch (Eds.), *DSC 2001 Proceedings of the 2nd International Workshop on Distributed Statistical Computing*, Vienna, Austria. https://citeseerx.ist.psu.edu/viewdoc/download?doi=10.1.1.16.9303&rep=rep1&type=pdf

Veldkamp, C. L. S., Nuijten, M. B., Dominguez-Alvarez, L., van Assen, M. A. L. M., & Wicherts, J. M. (2014). Statistical reporting errors and collaboration on statistical analyses in psychological science. *PLOS ONE, 9*(12), e114876. https://doi.org/10.1371/journal.pone.0114876

Wicherts, J. M., Borsboom, D., Kats, J., & Molenaar, D. (2006). The poor availability of psychological research data for reanalysis. *American Psychologist, 61*(7), 726–728. https://doi.org/10.1037/0003-066X.61.7.726

Wickham, H., & Grolemund, G. (2017). *R for data science: Import, tidy, transform, visualize, and model data* (1st ed.). O'Reilly Media. https://r4ds.had.co.nz/

Xie, Y. (2015). *Dynamic documents with R and knitr* (2nd ed.). Chapman and Hall/CRC Press.

Xie, Y., Allaire, J. J., & Grolemund, G. (2018). *R Markdown: The definitive guide*. Chapman and Hall/CRC Press. https://doi.org/10.1201/9781138359444

Yale Law School Roundtable on Data and Code Sharing. (2010). Reproducible research—Addressing the need for data and code sharing in computational science. *Computing in Science & Engineering, 12*(05), 8–13. https://doi.org/10.1109/MCSE.2010.113

CHAPTER 12

OBTAINING AND EVALUATING RESEARCH FUNDING

Jonathan S. Comer and Amanda L. Sanchez

Psychology is a relatively young science compared with other established fields that have been applying the scientific method for centuries, such as biology, chemistry, and physics. Although we've seen tremendous advances in our basic understanding of the human mind and behavior, the majority of the work still lies ahead for psychological science. Given the number of fundamental and applied questions in psychology that remain unanswered, combined with the increasingly sophisticated and transformative technologies now available for measuring and analyzing psychological processes, this is an extraordinarily exciting time to be a psychological scientist. And yet, to repurpose the lyrics of the talented Rudy Clark, "It's gonna take money, a whole lotta spending money . . . to do it right."

Research is slow and purposeful (Kendall & Comer, 2013), and the most rigorous modern work typically requires substantial resources and expenditures. Team members need to be paid salaries, participants need to be compensated, modern equipment and technologies (e.g., computing devices, use of fMRI) are expensive, proper recruitment activities are not cheap, and data management and storage (particularly when biological specimens are involved) add further costs. Moreover, in this age of "team science" and big data, the field is witnessing an increasing number of collaborative projects with multiple principal investigators bringing complementary expertise, embarking on larger studies conducted in parallel across multiple sites. For example, the current Adolescent Brain Cognitive Development (ABCD) study brings together leading experts in neuroimaging, developmental science, mental health, substance use, cognitive science, and behavioral genetics, among other disciplines, to longitudinally study more than 10,000 children recruited across more than 20 research sites for a period of 10 years (Volkow et al., 2018). This unprecedented multisite project is poised to unlock many of the great mysteries of adolescent development, but with estimated costs of nearly half a billion dollars, it is also bringing an unprecedented price tag. Although the ABCD study is certainly an outlier when it comes to costs, the vast majority of psychological research, nonetheless, requires significant resources and expenditures.

There are rarely easy corners to cut to bring down research costs. Many cost-containment strategies introduce tradeoffs in project quality that, in turn, limit the conclusions that can be drawn. For example, it has become increasingly clear that convenient and inexpensive samples

---

Financial disclosures: Dr. Comer receives royalties from Macmillan Learning and an editorial stipend from the Association for Behavioral and Cognitive Therapies for work unrelated to the present chapter. Dr. Sanchez has no financial interests to declare.

https://doi.org/10.1037/0000318-012
APA Handbook of Research Methods in Psychology, Second Edition: Vol. 1. Foundations, Planning, Measures, and Psychometrics, H. Cooper (Editor-in-Chief)
Copyright © 2023 by the American Psychological Association. All rights reserved.

(e.g., undergraduates receiving course credit for participation) are rarely representative of the general population (Peterson & Merunka, 2014), and thus relying on convenience samples in order to reduce costs limits the generalizability of the research. In a similar vein, removing a control condition from a study design may reduce the number of subjects (and thus costs) needed, but it also reduces the internal validity of the work and compromises the extent to which the study can establish cause-and-effect relationships and/or rule out rival hypotheses (Comer & Kendall, 2013). In addition, reducing participant compensations would certainly cut down expenses, but insufficient incentives for participation will compromise recruitment and retention, and can reduce motivation in ways that reduce the integrity of the data collected. The list goes on.

For many, the importance of securing resources for research is further underscored by the value that research-intensive institutions place on external funding. Although there is certainly no perfect correlation between total grant funding and the quality, importance, and impact of a scholar's work, a reality of academia is that hiring, promotion, and tenure decisions often prioritize individual differences in external research funding and grant activity.

In sum, quality research is expensive to conduct, and external grant funding has become increasingly valued across academic institutions. Given the extent to which securing external funding has become a central part of the modern research enterprise, and given the link between research funding and a researcher's long-term success in many settings, it is surprising that doctoral training programs in psychology do not routinely incorporate focused training on securing and managing external grants and contracts. As a result, many early career researchers are entering the field at a disadvantage, lacking a clear understanding of the funding process and how to best navigate it.

This chapter aims to demystify the external funding process by providing an overview of decision points and procedures for obtaining and maintaining funding for research. We organize our chapter around several key aspects of the process, including choosing the right grant mechanism for a given project and understanding the grant evaluation process. Throughout, much of our discussion pays particular attention to grant mechanisms and procedures as they specifically relate to early-career scientists and/or scientists from backgrounds that have been underrepresented in the biomedical science workforce (e.g., Black and African American researchers, Hispanic and Latinx researchers, researchers with disabilities, among several other historically and currently underrepresented groups in the sciences). But first, we provide a brief overview of different sources of external funding, followed by a description of different categories of research costs.

SOURCES OF EXTERNAL FUNDING

There are many sources of external research funding. The two most common types of sources that award research grants to academic institutions are (a) federal and state government agencies, and (b) foundations and public charities.

Other funding sources include business and industry. Industry-funded research tends to prioritize studies that focus on products, processes, or activities that can be commercialized, or that can be used indirectly to shape or reshape policy and legal positions (Fabbri et al., 2018). Venture investors can be a source of research funding as well. For example, when the isolation of the COVID-19 pandemic increased mental health needs while reducing the accessibility of face-to-face care, venture investors poured over $1 billion into digital mental health projects (Jennings, 2021).

Some researchers are increasingly turning to crowdsourced funding strategies when applications to conventional funding sources are not successful. Crowdsourcing platforms such as Kickstarter, CitizenScience.gov, and Experiment.com are beyond the scope of this chapter, but they have funded a fair amount of psychological science in recent years. Students and junior investigators, in particular, have increasingly worked to crowdfund their research and have even been more successful at securing crowdsourced funding than senior investigators (Else, 2019). Crowdsourcing typically affords greater freedom from bureaucracies than traditional funding mechanisms.

Federal and State Government Agencies

Federal and state government agencies use governmental revenues (e.g., taxpayer dollars) to support grant funding for research examining a range of matters deemed to be in the public interest. Governments that make large investments in research and development recognize the links between such funding and the health and prosperity of their people, as well as the role of research in helping the government navigate societal challenges, gain competitive edges in the global marketplace, and foster an overall better future (Roback et al., 2011). Across countries, the United States is the largest spender on research and development, accounting for 25% of all global research and development spending (National Science Board and National Science Foundation, 2020). This research spending is spread across a very wide range of priority topics and projects. U.S. federal agencies that support the largest amounts of psychological research include the National Institutes of Health (NIH), the Department of Defense (DoD), the Department of Veterans Affairs, the National Science Foundation (NSF), and the Agency for Healthcare Research and Quality (AHRQ), among many other agencies.

Across these federal agencies, the NIH operates the largest annual budget for awarding grants to academic institutions. Each year, the NIH awards research funding to over 300,000 investigators at over 2,500 academic institutions. For fiscal year 2021, the United States House Appropriations Committee approved roughly $50 billion in federal spending for the NIH, an increase of $5.5 billion relative to fiscal year 2020 (U.S. House Appropriations Committee, 2020). At least $3 billion of this budget is to be spent on mental health research, and at least $3 billion is to be spent on child health and human development research. Within the National Institute of Mental Health (NIMH), roughly one in every seven reviewed proposals is funded (NIH, 2021, although specific success rates vary considerably across research topics and investigator levels.

Defense-related federal agencies have long served as a key source of funding for psychological science. For example, the DoD provides over $100 million each year for social and behavioral sciences research. The DoD's Minerva Research Initiative invests considerable funds each year in university-based research in the social, behavioral, and biomedical sciences for studies addressing topics of potential relevance to U.S. national security. The U.S. Army Research Institute for Behavioral and Social Sciences supports research that advances psychological and behavioral theory and practice that can be used to optimize individual soldier and army unit performance and readiness. The U.S. Defense Advanced Research Projects Agency (DARPA) invests in the development and evaluation of breakthrough technologies that may improve national security. Behavioral and social sciences research funded by DARPA has included research on artificial intelligence and human–machine interactions, digital connectivity and social influence, and complex drivers of social cooperation, instability, and resilience. DARPA offers a Young Faculty Award program for junior investigators and university faculty. Moreover, the DoD National Defense Science and Engineering Graduate (NDSEG) Fellowship Program awards hundreds of 3-year graduate fellowships to university-based students engaged in science and engineering research (including cognitive and behavioral science) relevant to national security.

Foundations and Public Charities

Foundations and public charities include nonprofit organizations that sponsor a broad range of research that aligns closely with programmatic priorities. These can include large, high-profile foundations that address a number of critical issues and priority areas in their granting programs (e.g., William T. Grant Foundation, Bill and

Melinda Gates Foundation), philanthropic organizations with more focused grant missions (e.g., the American Psychological Foundation [APF], Brain and Behavior Research Fund), and small family foundations with granting programs that typically address a single important mission (e.g., Klingenstein Third Generation Foundation).

Foundations and public charities are typically more agile than federal and state government funding sources. For example, they typically offer more rapid turnaround decisions on proposals because they involve fewer levels of review, and there are fewer restrictions on allowable costs relative to government grants. In addition, foundations and public charities are often quicker to respond to emerging issues and public health crises in their granting programs, as there are fewer regulations and fewer constraints placed on monies made available in a given year. It is also not uncommon for foundation grant proposal requirements to be relatively brief, compared with the much longer proposals typically required when seeking funding from a federal or state agency. At the same time, research grants from foundations and public charities tend to be much smaller than federal grants, and therefore less likely to cover all project and institutional costs. This latter factor can make grants from foundations and public charities less enticing to institutions, relative to federal funding.

CATEGORIES OF RESEARCH COSTS

Broadly speaking, the total costs in a research budget can be broken down into two categories: (a) direct costs, and (b) indirect costs (Table 12.1).

Direct Costs

Direct costs refer to all expenses that are specifically tied to a particular study. These are costs that can easily be identified as unique to a given project and will not be confused with expenditures for any other projects that might also be conducted at the same institution.

Salaries often make up a large portion of the direct costs budgeted for a given project. Importantly, only the portion of each team member's salary that directly corresponds to the amount of time they spend on the specific project can be included as a direct cost. This is easy to calculate for team members who are working exclusively on the project (i.e., those with no other responsibilities on any other projects or activities), as might be the case for a full-time project coordinator. Such individuals are said to be devoting "100% effort" to the project, and their full salaries can be budgeted as a direct cost. However, it is not uncommon for various team members to work across multiple studies or activities. For example, the principal investigator of a study may be a university professor who

TABLE 12.1

Categories of Research Costs

Category	Definition	Examples
Direct costs	Expenses that can easily be identified as unique to a given project	■ Project staff salaries ■ Project staff fringe benefits ■ Participant compensation ■ Project supplies ■ Project equipment ■ Project-related travel
Indirect costs[a]	Pooled institutional costs that are shared across projects and cannot be readily identified with an individual project	■ Office space ■ Electricity and heat ■ Computer services ■ Parking facilities ■ Security ■ Telephone lines

[a]Also called "overhead," "facilities and administrative costs," or "F&A."

spends about 8 hours per week directly working on the project, and then spends the rest of their professional time teaching two classes, mentoring several graduate students, and serving on various college and departmental committees. In this example, the principal investigator could budget 20% of their salary as a direct cost on the project (i.e., 8 hours/week corresponds to "20% effort" of a 40-hour workweek). Similarly, if a research assistant with a full-time position at the institution were splitting their professional time equally to work on two different funded projects (and had no other work responsibilities), they would be considered to be working at "50% effort" on each of the two projects, with half of their salary charged as a direct cost on the first project's budget and half of their salary charged as a direct cost on the second project's budget. As you probably guessed, an individual's salary structure gets increasingly complicated as a function of the number of funded projects to which they devote effort and draw salary.

Typically, standard fringe benefits for team members on a project are also an allowable direct cost. In the U.S., fringe benefits for university employees often include health insurance, paid time off, short- and long-term disability, and retirement plan contributions, among other perks. Universities charge standard rates for their employees' fringe benefits, broken down by different ranks of employees. For example, a given university may charge an additional 33% beyond salary for faculty members' fringe benefits and 41% beyond salary for administrative staff members' fringe benefits. Thus, if a faculty member at this university had $10,000 of their salary budgeted for a project, an additional $3,300 for fringe benefits (i.e., 33% of $10,000) would also be charged to the project as a direct cost. If an administrative staff member at this same university (e.g., a project coordinator) had $10,000 of their salary budgeted for a project, an additional $4,100 for fringe benefits (i.e., 41% of $10,000) would also be charged to the project as a direct cost.

Other direct costs might include participant compensations, travel, supplies, and equipment.

To qualify as direct costs, these expenses must be specifically and uniquely tied to the project. For example, travel would qualify as a direct cost only if it is specific to the project (e.g., travel to gather with project collaborators at a collaborating site for an in-person project-specific meeting; travel to attend a conference at which project results will be presented and disseminated). Equipment can qualify as a direct cost, but only if it is specific to the project. For example, one could not use direct costs of a research grant to buy an fMRI scanner for the institution at which the principal investigator works. But one would include project-specific fMRI usage charges (i.e., hourly costs to use the institution's fMRI scanner for the particular project).

Indirect Costs

Whereas direct costs refer to expenses tied specifically and uniquely to a particular research project, *indirect costs* refer to pooled institutional expenses that are shared across projects. Indirect costs—also referred to as "facilities and administrative costs" or "F&A"—cover the institution's general overhead expenses that are needed to house research. These costs include office space and building maintenance, electricity, heat and air conditioning, janitorial services, parking facilities, library operations, campus security, computer services, telephone lines, and so on. These overhead expenses cannot be readily disentangled across research projects. For example, it would be near impossible to calculate how much air conditioning one project is using versus another project, and it would be extraordinarily costly for a university to contract with separate janitorial staff for each research project.

Indirect costs that cover shared institutional expenses are typically assigned to projects as a percentage of the direct costs. The specific indirect cost rate for each institution is individually negotiated with the federal government, and at research-intensive institutions these indirect rates typically range from 45% to 65%. As an illustration, suppose a researcher submitting a grant is employed at an institution with a federally negotiated indirect cost rate of 50%, and suppose the funding agency to which they are applying allows for full recovery of indirect costs. In this scenario, for every $1 of direct costs in the budget, the researcher's university includes an additional $0.50 for indirect costs. Thus, if the project's direct costs come to $1 million, the university includes an additional $500,000 in the budget for the institution's indirect costs, and the total costs for this project are then $1.5 million.

Many federal agencies allow institutions to fully recover indirect costs on major project grants—that is, they allow institutions to include their full federally negotiated rates for indirect costs in the total costs of the award. However, educational and training grants often place much lower ceilings on the indirect rates that can be included. For example, training grants from the NIH for graduate students and postdoctoral fellows typically limit indirect charges to 8% of the direct costs, regardless of the receiving institution's federally negotiated indirect rate. Similarly, foundations and public charities commonly place limits on the amount of indirect costs that can be charged (e.g., ceiling = 5% of the direct costs), and many do not allow any indirect costs to be included. Accordingly, it is not uncommon for research-intensive institutions to prioritize federal grants that allow for full recovery of indirect costs over foundation grants when making hiring, promotion, and tenure decisions, given the importance of indirect costs in the operational budget of such institutions.

CHOOSING THE RIGHT GRANT PROGRAM OR MECHANISM FOR YOUR WORK

A critical first step in submitting a successful grant proposal is to identify a grant program or mechanism that closely aligns with the goals and scope of your proposed activities. We have seen many excellent grant proposals on important topics go unfunded simply because the investigators were knocking on the wrong door. Investigators should familiarize themselves with the types of projects that various agencies and foundations fund. For example, the Patient-Centered Outcomes Research Institute (PCORI) is a government-sponsored nonprofit organization that gives a very large amount of money to research that can help patients and families make informed health care decisions. A review of their large funding portfolio reveals that the majority of PCORI-funded clinical trials examine the performance of commonly used treatments delivered by routine care providers in frontline practices that are representative of typical care settings. Accordingly, PCORI would likely be a poor fit and misguided funding target for an investigator looking to develop a novel treatment in an experimental laboratory setting with members of their research team delivering the treatment.

The prepared investigator will carefully read through the organizational missions and latest research priorities of a range of funding agencies that may be relevant to their work. These research priorities are not kept secret—funding agencies and foundations typically post their missions and research priorities prominently on their websites. These priorities often reflect legal mandates or bylaw commitments on how allocated money is to be spent.

In addition to reviewing the overall missions and research priorities of various agencies, the prepared investigator will carefully read the details of specific funding opportunities that may be relevant. Investigators looking for U.S. government funding can use the public search portal at https://www.grants.gov to identify potentially relevant grant opportunities that are federally funded. At the time of this writing, a simple search with the keyword "research" on https://www.grants.gov returns over 2,000 results.

Within large funding agencies, such as the NIH, a wide variety of grant programs differentially focus on various topics of study, scopes of work, and investigator career stages. *Funding opportunity announcements* (FOAs) are posted documents in which a federal agency provides public notification of available funds for particular purposes and solicits applications for funding. The FOA clarifies the goals, objectives, eligibility requirements, and submission details associated with a particular funding opportunity. Federal grant applications must always be submitted in response to a specific FOA.

There are several types of FOAs. Many FOAs are broad funding announcements that are open for many years (called "parent announcements"). Parent announcements are often somewhat generic in nature (e.g., invitations for clinical trials; invitations for exploratory/pilot work) so that a wide variety of proposals will fit. In contrast to broad parent announcements, "requests for applications" (RFAs) are standing invitations for proposals that address a more narrowly defined area for which money has specifically been put aside (e.g., tools for identifying risk for suicide). Finally, "requests for proposals" (RFPs) are time-limited invitations (often only a single deadline) for proposals that address a narrowly defined area for which money has been allotted.

Most FOAs and grant mechanisms require several common core components in a submission, including a specific aims document, a research strategy narrative, and biosketch(es). The *specific aims* document is critical, as it briefly introduces the importance of a particular topic, identifies key gaps in knowledge, and convinces the reviewer of the urgency of a project's proposed solution(s). This is typically what reviewers see first, and thus it is an important opportunity to hook the reader and make a first impression. A brief series of aims for the project should be clearly delineated and accompanied by specific hypotheses. Next, the *research strategy* offers a somewhat longer, well-referenced narrative that spells out the background and significance of the proposed work (i.e., the scientific context of the work), the innovation of the proposed project (i.e., the novelty of the work), and a detailed account of the approach the investigator proposes to take to address the specific aims (i.e., the methods). Additionally, it is critical to communicate *who* will be conducting the study and what their specific qualifications are. That said, reviewers do not have time to review entire CVs for each member of the research team, so investigators provide biosketches for each key member of the study team. A *biosketch* is an abbreviated CV that briefly highlights a given study member's experiences and expertise and often includes a brief personal statement that describes why they are a strong fit for the study. Most major funding agencies require that biosketches follow very specific formatting guidelines that detail what information to include and in which order, how many publications can be included, among many other requirements.

Although specific RFAs and RFPs shift across time, parent announcements are relatively stable across several years. We now turn our attention to several major parent announcements and grant mechanisms that are used to fund research in the field. We focus here on NIH funding opportunities, as well as opportunities from some leading agencies and foundations that also fund psychological research, but the review is certainly not exhaustive. We organize our discussion around (a) awards and mechanisms that support training, career development, and/or diversity in the science workforce; (b) research project grants; (c) business technology and innovation grants; and (d) center grants and multiproject awards.

Awards and Mechanisms That Support Training, Career Development, and/or Diversity in the Science Workforce

There are a wide variety of FOAs and grant mechanisms developed to support training and career development. These grants typically focus on promoting the research trajectory of promising early-career researchers through a robust training plan, centered on a modest research project that sews together their training goals. These training and career development awards typically provide salary or stipend support as well as funds to support a structured training plan and project implementation. Given racial and ethnic disparities in the biomedical research workforce (Heggeness et al., 2016; Oh et al., 2015), as well as the critical importance of a diverse research workforce, many of these training awards and career development grant mechanisms are directly focused on improving the diversity of the field by enhancing the participation and persistence of individuals from underrepresented backgrounds in biomedical research.

NIH Fellowship and Training Grants

Classes of grant mechanisms at NIH are organized by different letters, and it is helpful for the investigator to familiarize themselves with the "alphabet soup" of NIH funding. With regard to NIH fellowship and training grants, individual fellowship mechanisms make up the "F" awards, institutional training awards (awarded to institutions, not individual researchers) make up the "T" awards, and career development grants make up the "K" awards.

Kirschstein-NRSA Individual Fellowships (F Awards).

At the NIH, there are a number of individual fellowship mechanisms (i.e., "F" awards) that differentially address various levels of investigators, including undergraduates, graduate students, postdoctoral investigators, and even a specific award for senior investigators. The most common F awards to which trainees apply are the Ruth L. Kirschstein National Research Service Awards (Kirschstein-NRSAs), which provide individual research training to candidates spanning pre- and postdoctoral training levels. As is common for fellowship awards, the primary focus of an NRSA is the scholar's training plan, rather than a research project. Although a research project is included in the NRSA, this research is there to primarily support the training plan with an applied research experience, rather than as a means to comprehensively answer a research question. Typically, the research at the center of a fellowship is seen as a pilot project or secondary data analysis that can lay the empirical foundation for a subsequent, larger project that will more adequately address the research question with greater rigor and statistical power. Moreover, training plans and research activities in a fellowship should directly connect to the candidate's stated future research goals and should provide foundational experiences and knowledge to help the candidate succeed in the long term. Importantly, NIH fellowships do not currently allow for the proposal of independent clinical trials. NRSAs include the predoctoral fellowship (F31), the postdoctoral fellowship (F32), and an award for senior fellows (F33).

The *F31 NRSA* is a training award for *pre*doctoral students enrolled in a PhD (or equivalent) program who are at the dissertation phase of training. The purpose of the F31 is to enable promising predoctoral graduate students to obtain individualized, mentored research training from faculty sponsors while conducting dissertation research. NIH offers two F31 programs—one that is available to all promising predoctoral students in PhD programs at the dissertation phase of training, and one used to enhance biomedical workforce diversity that is specifically for promising predoctoral students from backgrounds traditionally underrepresented in biomedical research. We discuss this latter program in a later section on grants for investigators from traditionally underrepresented backgrounds.

The main components of the F31 are the training plan, the dissertation project at the center of the training plan, and sponsor/consultant support. The training plan often includes traditional coursework but should also include tailored consultation with selected mentors that address gaps in the applicant's research skills and facilitate the applicant's potential to become a productive independent researcher. Successful F31 training plans usually involve a primary sponsor or two (usually the trainee's graduate mentor), as well as regular consultation from three or four additional experts with whom the applicant will meet regularly (e.g., biweekly or monthly) for directed readings and focused discussion. Other key experiences outlined in a successful training plan may include research experience and participation in the sponsor's laboratory, travel to visit with remote consultants and/or gain firsthand experience in their laboratory, intensive training workshops, selected conference attendance, secondary analyses on a sponsor or consultant's data set, and so on. The dissertation project should be well integrated with the proposed training plan and feasible to conduct within the proposed timeline and available resources. As with all fellowships, the research is included primarily as pilot work and as a training opportunity to merge the training goals with an applied research experience. F31 award budgets are composed of stipends, tuition and fees, and small, standard institutional allowance for health insurance, research supplies, equipment, books, and so on. The F31 stipend level is set by NIH and is standard across all awardees.

A common challenge for F31 candidates involves the consideration of *when* to submit their grant relative to their anticipated graduation date. Typical F31 awards provide somewhere between 18 months to 3 years of support (although they can provide up to 5 years of support). For F31 eligibility, candidates must have already identified their dissertation topic, and thus are typically already in the latter part of their graduate training with only a limited amount of time left in their program. In addition, the review process is lengthy (more on that later), and in reality, most submissions are not funded upon first submission. Accordingly, it is critical for the applicant to work far in advance with their sponsor to plot out a submission timeline that includes ample time for the review process, a resubmission cycle, and development of a training and project timeline can be completed prior to the applicant's desired graduation date.

The *F32 NRSA* is a training award for *post*doctoral trainees in the early phases of their postdoctoral training. The purpose of the F32 is to support the research training of promising early-career postdoctoral researchers under the guidance of faculty sponsors that commit to supporting the candidate in becoming an independent investigator. This postdoctoral fellowship is slightly different from that at the predoctoral level in that it is designed to support research training experiences in *new settings* or in *new areas of interest*. Therefore, the candidate must utilize their training and research plan to describe how they will acquire new skills and knowledge in new settings. Because of the focus on a new area of interest, the sponsoring institution is typically a site other than where the applicant already trained as a graduate student; however, it may be the same institution if the applicant clearly outlines opportunities for new research training. The applicant's proposed (new) sponsoring institution, rather than the applicant's current institution, actually submits the F32 NRSA application to NIH. Similar to the F31, the main components of the F32 include proposed training and research plans, including tailored sponsorship and consultation. Given the focus on training and acquiring new skills, it is important that the application materials outline strong mentorship, appropriate training and career development opportunities, and strong institutional support and commitment that will strengthen the individual's potential to develop into a productive independent researcher. The F32 award may provide up to 3 years of support for postdoctoral research training and may include a combination of support from institutional training grants and the individual fellowship award. F32 award budgets are composed of NIH-set stipends that increase with years of postdoctoral experience, tuition and fees, and an institutional allowance that is a bit larger than that allowed for the F31.

The *F33 NRSA* is a senior individual fellowship for established investigators with at least 7 years of postdoctoral research experience who are changing the direction of their research or wish to broaden their scientific background. Similar to the F32, the F33 focuses on the applicant's plans to acquire *new* research skills and expertise. The purpose of this award is to enable independent investigators to be able to take time (e.g., sabbatical) to receive focused training that broadens their scientific expertise in specific ways. F33 fellowship support usually does not exceed 2 years. As with the other NRSA mechanisms, the F33 applicant must select a sponsor or team of sponsors/consultants who will supervise and mentor their training in this new direction, and the main components are the proposed training plan and research activities. F33 award budgets are composed of stipends, tuition and fees, and a modest institutional allowance. The stipend amount for this senior fellowship varies across awardees and is commensurate with the base salary that the individual would have otherwise been paid by their institution.

Kirschstein-Institutional National Research Service Award (T32). The *T32* training grant provides support to *institutions* (not individual investigators) to fund programs at the graduate and postdoctoral levels that will enhance research training by providing high-quality, mentored research experiences. These programs help trainees develop the skills necessary for success in the next stage of their research training toward independent research careers. Once funded, the institution (not NIH) makes its own decisions each year about who to admit into their research training programs. Fellows typically participate in a T32 program for 2 to 3 years.

T32-funded programs are each designed with a particular focus on a specified shortage area (e.g., behavioral science research in HIV infection; neurobiological research in psychiatry; research training in the etiology, prevention, and treatment of adolescent substance use) and offer training and funding to multiple fellows each year across various labs at the awarded institution. Research training in a funded T32 program usually includes a combination of shared training experiences across all of the fellows in the program (e.g., weekly seminars in that cover relevant designs and methodologies, technologies, quantitative/computational approaches, and interpretation of data, and professional development skills such as communication, management, leadership, and teamwork), as well as individualized research training in a "home" lab led by one of the T32 mentors at the institution. Typically, a team of investigators with complementary expertise at an institution participate in the shared T32 program training efforts.

Institutions receive T32 funding for a set period of time, but these awards are often renewable when former trainees in the program are subsequently successful in securing their own research funding and/or research-focused positions. T32 funding supports trainees' stipends, tuition and fees, and training-related expenses. The T32 stipend level is set by NIH and is the same as fellowship support levels for other pre- and postdoctoral fellowship awardees. T32 programs will typically only accept trainees who have already demonstrated a clear commitment to a future career in research, and training activities are directly focused on opportunities to grow trainees' research skills and poise them for success in funding.

Career development awards.   At NIH, career development awards (i.e., "K" awards) are grant mechanisms that support research and career development training. Similar to the fellowships described earlier, these awards have a central focus on mentorship, training, and research, but unlike the awards described above, predoctoral trainees are not eligible, and the funding for the individual typically lasts 4 to 5 years. The expectation of these career awards is that across the funding period, the awardee will successfully transition from a highly promising early-career scientist conducting mentored research to the status of a fully independent scientist by the end of the award. K awards require the awardee to dedicate at least 75% of their professional effort and time to mentored career-development activities and research. As with the fellowships discussed previously, K award applicants must lay out a detailed training plan that includes a sponsor and a set of mentors/consultants, as well as a set of research activities that tangibly bring together the individual's training goals and can provide necessarily pilot data to lay the groundwork for a subsequent larger, project-based award.

Some leading K awards include the K01 Mentored Research Scientist Development Award, the K08 Mentored Clinical Scientist Research Career Development Award, and the K23 Mentored Patient-Oriented Research Career Development Award. Each of these awards provides funds for the investigator's salary and intensive training activities as well as some support for research activities. The *K01* is a mentored research scientist development award intended for early-career researchers or those who have had a break in their research career (e.g., due to illness or extraneous circumstances) who are not focusing on patient-oriented research. Given that the focus of the K01 is to foster and further the development of a research career that is not patient-oriented, the K01 is an appropriate mechanism for early-career scientists whose work focuses on *basic* science. The *K08* and the *K23* are similar mentored research awards for early-career researchers or who have had a break in their research career, but unlike the basic science focus on the K01, the K08 is for clinical scientists conducting translational research that applies basic science discoveries to health-related research, and the K23 is for clinical scientists conducting more applied patient-centered research that involves direct interaction with the participants. Applicants must hold a clinical doctoral degree to be eligible for the K08. The K23 further requires that the applicant has completed clinical training, as this mechanism is designed to encourage research-oriented clinicians to develop research skills needed to become independent investigators conducting patient-oriented research.

The *K99/R00* or the NIH Pathway to Independence Award is another mentored research award designed to support the successful transition from postdoctoral research fellowship to independent, tenure-track faculty position. The K99/R00 award is a transitional, two-phase funding mechanism. For the K99 phase, applicants propose 1 to 2 years of mentored postdoctoral training that will improve their candidacy for tenure-track faculty positions. The R00 phase then provides for up to 3 years of funding for independent (i.e., nonmentored) research. The R00 phase is of funding is not guaranteed—the applicant must achieve independence and secure a tenure-track position to be eligible for the second phase of funding. Only applicants in a mentored postdoctoral position are eligible to apply.

Unlike the mentored K01, K08, K23, and K99/R00 awards, the *K02* independent scientist award does not require a training or mentorship plan (but it does still require a career development plan). This mechanism enables newly independent scientists to concentrate on building their research careers and become successful candidates for additional independent research. Importantly, applicants for the K02 award need to have independent research support at the time the award is made, and although this mechanism provides salary support, unlike the other K awards, the K02 does not provide any research-related costs to the investigator.

NIH loan repayment programs. The NIH Loan Repayment Programs (LRPs) are a set of programs designed to support highly qualified early-career individuals and encourage them to engage in research careers. This mechanism specifically focuses on individuals with educational debt who may be more likely to leave research careers for higher paying private practice or industry careers. To be eligible for LRPs, candidates need to have loan debt equal to at least 20% of their annual salary and must conduct research for at least 20 hours per week. There are several types of LRPs depending on the type of work the investigator is conducting, including clinical research, pediatric research, and/or health disparities research. Unlike the career development awards, however, LRPs are not focused on a central research project, but rather a set of research activities that the applicant plans to pursue, and candidates can apply as mentored scientists or independent researchers. Awards are 2 years in length and are renewable for as long as the candidate qualifies. Currently, LRPs repay up to $50,000 per year of a researcher's qualified educational debt in exchange for the applicant's engagement in research activities.

Grants for Investigators From Traditionally Underrepresented Backgrounds

Research opportunities have not been equally available to all, and scientists from racial and ethnic minority backgrounds have been less likely to have their work funded (Does et al., 2018; Heggeness et al., 2016; Oh et al., 2015; Taffe & Gilpin, 2021). These disparities emerge early in training, narrowing the pipeline of research talent, and continue to expand across career stages. For example, Ginther and colleagues (2011) found that, even after controlling for applicants' educational backgrounds, previous grant success, and publication records, Black or African American applicants are 10% less likely than White applicants to be awarded NIH funding. Furthermore, only 2% of NIH-funded investigators have been Black or African American, and only 3% have been from Latinx backgrounds, despite these populations making up over 10% and 15%, respectively, of the U.S. population (Oh et al., 2015). In parallel, funded research has disproportionately sampled

White non-Hispanic populations. Reducing mental health disparities is impossible without investing time and resources in research by and for diverse communities (Oh et al., 2015).

Such disparities raise serious concerns about fairness, equal opportunity, and equity across scientists. Moreover, a diverse, representative research workforce is *essential* for fostering greater scientific innovation and discovery, ensuring that research addresses issues that are relevant to all communities, contributing to robust learning environments, and expanding the public trust (e.g., Oh et al., 2015). NIH has recognized issues related to racial equity within the organization and extramural funding mechanisms and has developed the UNITE initiative to address structural racism and promote racial equity.

Further recognizing the critical importance of a diverse research workforce, many training awards and career development grant mechanisms are directly focused on improving the diversity of the field by enhancing the participation and persistence of individuals from underrepresented backgrounds in biomedical research. NIH typically defines "underrepresented" individuals as those from particular racial or ethnic backgrounds (Black or African American, Hispanic or Latinx, American Indian or Alaska Native, Native Hawaiian and other Pacific Islander), as well as individuals with physical and/or mental disabilities. In addition, NIH considers individuals from socio-economically disadvantaged backgrounds to be underrepresented if they have experienced two or more of the following: experienced homelessness, were in the foster system, were eligible for free or reduced lunch, did not have caregivers who completed a bachelor's degree, received government aid, grew up in a designated rural area, or grew up in a designated low-income and health professional shortage area.

As noted earlier, the NIH offers a second F31 program that is specifically for promising predoctoral students from these underrepresented backgrounds. Specifically, the F31 Individual Predoctoral Fellowship to Promote Diversity is the same mechanism as the F31 NRSA parent mechanism and contains the same application requirements, with the additional requirement that the applicant must come from a background that meets one of the NIH definitions of underrepresented. Predoctoral graduate students from qualifying underrepresented backgrounds are also eligible for NIH's Mental Health Research Dissertation Grant to Enhance Workforce Diversity (i.e., the *R36*). The purpose of the R36 mechanism is to enhance the diversity of the research workforce by providing funding to underrepresented students to support the successful completion of the dissertation project and to enhance their overall research career preparedness. Unlike the F31, however, the R36 does not require a training plan component—the focus is entirely on completion of the doctoral research project. Further, given its primary focus on dissertation research rather than a detailed training plan, the R36 provides the fellow with greater funds that can be spent on dissertation research and related costs than does the F31.

In addition, all principal investigators with major NIH funding, regardless of whether they come from an underrepresented background, are eligible for *NIH Research Supplements to Promote Diversity*. These NIH research supplements provide additional financial support on top of existing grants to support the hiring of study personnel from underrepresented racial and ethnic minority groups, those with physical or mental disabilities, or those who have taken a career hiatus for family obligations. The individuals receiving the supplemental support can be qualifying high school students, undergraduates, postbaccalaureate assistants, graduate/doctoral students, postdoctoral fellows, or junior faculty. In the supplement application, the investigator focuses on the career goals, educational achievement, and potential for a career in research of the individual to be hired, as well as a proposed mentoring plan and how the individual's career development activities are linked to the already-funded research. Importantly, these research supplements do not undergo peer review, and, therefore, the application process is much quicker than for typical NIH grants.

Non-NIH Training Grants

Although we have focused on NIH grants in this section, there are many other sources of funding for training and career development. For example, the Graduate Research Fellowship Program (GRFP), awarded by the NSF, supports early graduate students with a $34,000 annual stipend for 3 years, as well as a $12,000 tuition/fee waiver (paid to the institution), to pursue research, training, and professional development opportunities. The American Psychological Association (APA) also offers a variety of grant opportunities for trainees. They include the APA Dissertation Research Awards, which provides $1,000 to $5,000 for the completion of dissertation research that reflects excellence in scientific psychology, and the APA Early Graduate Student Researcher Award, which provides $1,000 for excellence in basic, applied, or interdisciplinary research. In addition to these awards, a number of individual APA divisions offer funding opportunities for trainees, early-career investigators, and those from backgrounds underrepresented in psychological research. For example, the Society for the Advancement of Psychotherapy (APA Division 29) offers the Diversity Research Grant for Predoctoral Candidates, which provides $2,000 to support dissertation research for those from underrepresented backgrounds.

Many foundations also offer funding for trainees and early-career investigators. For example, the American Psychological Foundation (the philanthropic organization associated with APA) offers several grants, including APF/COGDOP Graduate Research Scholarships, which provide between $1,000 and $5,000 to assist with costs associated with master's thesis or doctoral dissertation research. The Elizabeth Munsterberg Koppitz Child Psychology Graduate Student Fellowship provides $25,000 to graduate students in clinical psychology to support their research and training.

Project-Focused Grant Mechanisms

In addition to grants focused on training, career development, and the promotion of diversity in the research workforce, there are a wide variety of project-focused FOAs and grant mechanisms. In fact, at NIH, project-focused grants (i.e., R awards) make up the largest category of their funding. Research project awards are those that focus on a discrete research project, and not on the training of the applicant. Although there are several types of research project awards, we focus here on the main and most highly sought-after research project grant (R01), as well as the NIH Small Grant Program (R03), the Exploratory/Development Research Grant Program (R21), and the NIH Clinical Trial Planning Grant Program (R34).

The *R01 grant* is for independent investigators proposing a discrete research project spanning 3 to 5 years. It is the original grant mechanism used by NIH and is the most prestigious NIH grant for independent investigators. While it is the most common research grant, it is also highly competitive. R01s can be investigator-initiated or submitted through a solicited RFA. The main components of the R01 application center on the research project itself, including its *significance* (how well the study addresses an important need in the field), *innovation* (how the study uses novel theoretical concepts or approaches to research), and *approach* (the overall strategy, methodology, and analyses of the proposed project). The investigators themselves are also an important aspect of the application in that the primary investigator and collaborators must be well suited for the particular project and demonstrate appropriate experience and complementary expertise. The research project must be in an area where the candidate can demonstrate specific expertise and competencies, so while the investigator does not necessarily need pilot data, they do need to demonstrate a very strong history of work in their area of interest. The usual maximum award budget for direct costs across the 3 to 5 years is $500,000 per year, but it can be increased with sufficient justification.

Many proposed research ideas are not ready for "the big test," and thus, given the very large size and scope of the R01, other, smaller grant mechanisms may be more appropriate targets.

The *R03 Small Grant Program* is a mechanism for investigators at different stages of their independent research careers. It provides support for small projects such as pilot or feasibility studies, preliminary data collection, secondary analysis of existing data, development of new research technology, or small, self-contained research projects. The research project must be able to be carried out in a short period of time with limited resources. The main components of the R03 grant applications are similar to that of the R01, but they are not expected to have the same level of detail. Instead, greater focus is placed on the conceptual framework and general approach, rather than on the specific methodological details. Additionally, pilot data are rarely provided for the R03 applications as their purpose is to create pilot data for lager studies. Whereas the R01 can be funded for up to 5 years, R03s are limited to 2 years of funding and can provide up to $50,000 per year of project support.

The *R21 Exploratory/Developmental Research Grant* is for independent investigators at any state of their research career who are interested in receiving support for the beginning stages of novel, innovative research projects. Whereas the R03 supports exploratory and developmental research and provides funding for early stages of research projects, R21s are usually for higher risk or more innovative study designs that have the potential to lead to the development of a new intervention or methodology that could impact the field of psychology. The main components of the R21 are similar to that of the R01; however, the project focus should be brief, exploratory, and novel. The funding award period is the same as the R03 but due to the novel nature of the R21 proposed studies, there is more project funding with the R21. Currently, NIH allows for up to $275,000 per year in direct costs for the R21.

The *R34 Clinical Trial Planning Grant* is for investigators at different stages in their career who are planning a larger scale R01 grant to fund a clinical trial. The R34 aids in the initial stages of an intervention study by supporting investigators as they collect preliminary data as a prerequisite to a larger scale intervention study. R34-funded research projects tend to focus on issues of feasibility, acceptability, and the safety of novel intervention approaches. Such projects provide early peer review for a clinical trial and support for the development of the essential elements for the larger scale clinical trial. Similar to the other project awards in the R-series, preliminary data are not required. Project periods range from 1 to 3 years with a budget of up to $100,000 per year in direct costs, sometimes up to $450,00 total.

A much wider range of studies and research activities are eligible for the *R34 Clinical Trial Planning Grant* than one might think. In 2014, NIH considerably broadened their definition of what constitutes a "clinical trial." The updated NIH definition of a clinical trial now includes all studies that prospectively assign human subjects to one or more interventions to examine the effects of the intervention(s) on biomedical or behavioral outcomes. Traditional clinical trials (e.g., randomized comparison of alternative treatment conditions in a clinical population) certainly meet this definition. But this updated clinical trial definition also now includes a much broader range of human subjects research, including more basic experimental studies with humans. For example, the broadened definition of a clinical trial now includes studies on healthy human subjects not seeking treatment, as well as uncontrolled studies that do not compare alternative conditions or include a randomized design and studies that assess mechanisms of action or engagement with services, rather than clinical outcomes. The broadened definition of what constitutes a clinical trial certainly widens the net of research activities that are eligible for R34 Clinical Trial Planning Grant, but clinical trials also come with very specific (and sometimes extensive) reporting requirements.

Beyond the R34 Clinical Trial Planning Grant, when applying for other project-focused grants, the applicant must be clear on whether their proposed research constitutes a clinical trial (as currently defined by NIH). If the proposed research does meet the broadened NIH definition of a clinical trial, they must be sure to submit their application in response to an FOA that is specifically designated as "Clinical Trial Required" or "Clinical Trial Optional." A proposal that meets the NIH definition of a clinical trial will not be considered if it has been submitted to an FOA that does not include one of these designations.

Business Technology and Innovation Grants

Although the grant mechanisms that we have focused on thus far have supported research activities in research institutions, NIH also has a set of research programs that support scientific and technological innovation either in the private sector or in collaboration between a small business and a research institution. For example, *Small Business Innovation Research Grants (SBIR: R43/R44)* support for-profit private organizations in the development of a novel idea or technology that has the potential to impact health care and medical science. The applicant proposes a research project on behalf of the for-profit business associated with the application. SBIRs support small businesses and encourage the private sector to engage in federal-level technology development. SBIRs are divided into two phases: the R43 supports the first phase of the research proposal focused on potential for commercialization, whereas the R44 supports the second phase of the research proposal focused on implementing the research project proposed in the first phase. Total funding for the first phase usually is up to $150,000, whereas the R44 provides up to $1,000,000 and is renewable. It is expected that investigators will subsequently initiate a third phase of activity focused on commercialization, but this stage cannot be supported by the SBIR.

The *Small Business Technology Transfer Grant (STTR: R41/R42)* is similar to the SBIR mechanism, but the STTR aims to promote *collaboration* between small business and research institutes in the development of scientific and technological innovations. Similar to the SBIR, there are multiple phases of study, with the first phase focused on feasibility (R41), the second phase focused on research project implementation (R42), and an expected third phase focused on commercialization that is not funded by the award.

Center Grants and Multiproject Awards

The NIH also offers multiproject and center funding in the form of Program Project/Center Grants, or *P awards*. The purpose of P awards is to encourage shared resources and support a system of research projects and activities that are directed toward a common research program goal. There is no specific dollar limit for these types of grants, unless specified by a funding announcement. P-funded projects typically involve the organized efforts and research activities of a relatively large number of research personnel who are each conducting smaller studies that address particular aspects of a larger objective. These projects are broadly focused and encourage interdisciplinary collaboration within the institution. Specific P awards include the Research Program Project Grant (P01), which funds long-term, multidisciplinary research programs, the Center Core Grants (P30), which provides funding for multidisciplinary research teams focusing on a common research area, and the Specialized Center Grant (P50), which supports a group of investigators focusing on a common research topic.

Several center-based awards have been developed to address workforce diversity and health disparities. The NIH National Institute on Minority Health and Health Disparities (NIMHD) leads scientific research to improve minority health and eliminate health disparities. This institute contains several mechanisms for programs to increase minority representation within research. NIMHD supports several multidisciplinary research centers focused on key topic areas in minority health and health disparities. These centers are designed to achieve greater scientific impact and effective resource utilization by focusing disparities research opportunities, streamlining infrastructure, enhancing multidisciplinary collaborations, and fostering deeper engagement among community, academic, and various other stakeholders. Specific center grant mechanisms include: the Specialized Centers of Excellence on Minority Health and Heath Disparities (U54), the Centers of Excellence Environmental Health Disparities research (P50), the Research Centers in Minority Institutions

(RCMI: U54), and the Transdisciplinary Collaborative Centers for Health Disparities Research (U54). Collectively, these multidisciplinary centers prioritize research that addresses mental health disparities, supports underrepresented investigators, and fosters community engaged work to enhance the impact.

LIFTING THE CURTAIN ON THE GRANT REVIEW PROCESS

For optimal grant-writing success, it is critical to understand how and by whom grants are evaluated. Although the process varies across funding agencies, organizations, and foundations, our present discussion focuses on the NIH grant review process.

After a grant proposal is submitted to NIH by the investigator's institution, it is received by the NIH Center for Scientific Review (CSR), which serves as the central receiving point for over 85,000 applications each year. The CSR receives the grant, confirms that the application is in compliance with all requirements, assigns a unique number to the application, and refers it for review. To preserve the integrity of the scientific review process, grants submitted to NIH must undergo two levels of peer review prior to funding. Separating the review into two levels ensures that the evaluation of each proposal's scientific merit is completed independently from subsequent funding considerations and decisions.

For each proposal, the first level of peer review is focused on evaluating the *scientific and technical merit* of the proposal. This level of review is completed by a Scientific Review Group (SRG, or study section), comprised of topic experts who are not employed by the federal government but are typically NIH-funded investigators themselves from various academic institutions. There are well over 100 SRGs reviewing NIH grants each year. Different SRGs specialize in the review of proposals for different content areas and/or investigator levels. Most SRGs will convene on a fixed schedule each year, in the presence of federal officials who themselves do not evaluate scientific merit, to review an assigned batch of proposals that were submitted to NIH in the previous cycle. Different reviewers rotate on and off each SRG across time.

In advance of each SRG meeting, the batch of proposals to be reviewed in that cycle are assigned to specific SRG members so that each proposal is assigned to three reviewers (i.e., Reviewer 1, 2, and 3). For each grant proposal, these three reviewers independently complete a detailed narrative review of the proposal and generate scores across structured dimensions of evaluation. For most NIH grants, these primary review dimensions include: *significance* (i.e., does the project address an important problem or a critical barrier to progress in the field?); *investigators* (i.e., do the investigators and team have the appropriate experience and expertise to successfully execute the project?); *innovation* (i.e., how novel is the project, and does it challenge and seek to shift current research or clinical practice paradigms?); *approach* (i.e., are the design, methods, and analyses appropriate to accomplish the aims of the project?); and *environment* (i.e., how strong is the research infrastructure and institutional support in the scientific environment in which the work is to be conducted?). In addition, reviewers of training and fellowship proposals evaluate the applicant's potential for training, their training plan, the quality of their sponsor(s) and consultants, and their institution's commitment to training. Further, reviewers of human subjects research evaluate the extent to which proposals provide adequate protections for human subjects and the extent to which the research includes women, children, and minorities.

In addition to providing independent narrative review summaries addressing each of the review criteria, each reviewer also independently assigns an overall impact score for each proposal, as well as numeric scores for each dimension so that it is clear how much the reviewer weighed various strengths and limitations. Reviewers assign scores ranging from 1 to 9, with lower numbers reflecting greater proposal strength, perceived impact, and a "higher score." Thus, a 1 reflects an "exceptional" score, a 5 reflects a "good" score, and a 9 reflects a "poor" score (Table 12.2).

TABLE 12.2

Scoring Guidelines for National Institutes of Health Grant Reviewers

Overall impact	High			Medium			Low		
Descriptor	"Exceptional"	"Outstanding"	"Excellent"	"Very Good"	"Good"	"Satisfactory"	"Fair"	"Marginal"	"Poor"
Score	1	2	3	4	5	6	7	8	9

When the SRG convenes (either in person or through video conference), a subset of the proposals for that cycle is triaged for full SRG discussion. Decisions about which proposals should be "discussed" at the SRG meeting are based on the overall scores independently given to each proposal by the three assigned reviewers. This allows the SRG to prioritize their time to only discussing proposals that show potential for funding. For each grant that is discussed, Reviewer 1 presents a brief summary of the proposal to the full SRG, along with the score they assigned it and a summary of what they perceived to be the proposal's strengths and weaknesses. Reviewer 2 and Reviewer 3 then follow with brief presentations to the full SRG of their scores and perceptions of the proposal's strengths and weaknesses. After these presentations, the three reviewers briefly discuss any areas of disagreement or clarifications, after which other members from the SRG can ask questions of the reviewers about the proposal and further discuss the proposal. After this discussion, each reviewer locks in and announces their final impact scores for the proposal, and then all of the members of the SRG additionally assign impact scores for the proposal.

A short period of time after a grant is reviewed by the SRG, the investigator receives a *summary statement*. This summary statement includes the narrative summaries of the proposal and individual scores prepared by each of the three primary reviewers, as well as an overall impact score that is equal to the mean of all of the impact scores assigned by the SRG members. For this overall impact score, the individual scores of each SRG member are weighted equally, whether or not they were one of the three primary reviewers. For proposals to most grant mechanisms, the overall impact score in the summary sheet is accompanied by a percentile score that ranks the application relative to the other applications that were reviewed by that SRG across the past year. This helps account for the possibility that some SRGs score more harshly than others by considering a priority/impact score relative to the other typical scores assigned by the same panel. So, for example, a percentile score of 16% means that the proposal's overall score was better than the scores of 84% of the other proposals reviewed across the past three meetings of that same SRG. If the proposal was not discussed by the SRG, the overall score will be "ND" (i.e., not discussed).

After this first scientific level of peer review conducted by the SRG, a second level of review is completed by specific institute advisory councils or boards. This *council review* makes recommendations to the institute on research priority areas and whether to fund a given proposal. The council is only presented with proposals to consider that were assigned very strong impact scores and percentile ranks. Members of these councils and boards are members of the scientific community and public representatives who are appointed and approved by the federal government to serve multiyear terms. It is not uncommon for the program officer to ask the investigator to submit supplementary information prior to Council review, such as a response to SRG reviews and or planned modifications to the proposal that will address SRG concerns. Such supplementary information can help the program officer present a stronger case to council for funding the proposal. Ultimately, the director of the funding institute incorporates the recommendations of Council and makes a final decision on each grant.

When a proposal receives strong scores and positive summaries but is not selected for funding, the investigator can resubmit a modified version of the unfunded proposal. Only one resubmission is allowed, and this resubmission must be submitted within 3 years of the initial proposal. The investigator will work closely with the program officer who oversaw the SRG process to consider how best to address the various concerns that were raised in the scientific review. The resubmission is accompanied by a one-page summary of the substantial additions, deletions, and modifications to the proposal. This resubmission should be reviewed by the same SRG that reviewed the initial submission, but given the gradual turnover across time on each SRG, it is unlikely there will be perfect roster overlap across the two review meetings. Although the investigator has up to 3 years to submit a revision, submitting sooner (rather than later) often minimizes the chances that the specific reviewers will change across review cycles.

The grant submission and review process is quite lengthy, lasting approximately 6 to 8 months from submission deadline to award notification (if the proposal is selected for funding). Typically, a proposal will not succeed on the first try and will need to be resubmitted with modifications. Furthermore, given that summary statements often arrive right before the next submission deadline, it is typically nearly impossible for the applicant to be able to adequately address SRG comments and prepare a responsive resubmission in time for the very next submission deadline. Accordingly, the applicant "loses" another 3 months of time because they have to wait until the following submission cycle deadline to submit their revised proposal.

CONCLUSION

In this chapter, we provided an overview of the necessities and benefits of external funding for supporting research, outlined the different sources of external funding and categories of research costs, provided an overview of specific mechanisms of grant funding that are differentially suited for various investigator levels and projects of various scopes, and outlined the major steps of grant review for NIH proposals.

The grant submission process can certainly be daunting and defeating at times. Given the amount of time it takes to develop, put together, and submit a grant proposal, it is of course very difficult to receive a score of "ND" or a score outside of the funding range, but it happens to all investigators from time to time. On a perhaps related note, the grant evaluation process is very much a human process, and reviewers and funding decisions do not always get it right. That said, in our experience, most strong psychology researchers ultimately get their work funded. But it does take preparation and hard work, a good dose of persistence, and some thick skin. After all, many of the most frequently funded researchers are also the very same researchers who receive the most rejections and unfunded proposals. The grounded investigator will savor the successes and will take what can be learned from disappointing outcomes, without getting overly distracted by the disappointments.

There are still many critical gaps in our understanding of the human mind and behavior, and rigorous research is rarely cheap. The good news is that federal agencies, private foundations, and various charities collectively provide a tremendous amount of financial support to fund psychological research. However, money can only bring the field so far. Even if there were unlimited funds, psychological discoveries and innovation can only be as strong as the pool of talented investigators participating. Although unacceptable disparities and inequities in research funding have been well documented and persist, there are now more funding mechanisms than ever specifically focused on increasing opportunities for researchers from underrepresented backgrounds and promoting overall equity in the field's research workforce. Moreover, new initiatives have been put in place to specifically assess and address disparities within NIH and the extramural funding process. The extent to which these funding mechanisms, along with other efforts, succeed in promoting a strong, inventive, and diverse research workforce will determine the extent to which psychological research will indeed make meaningful advances, discoveries, and innovations in the years to come.

References

Comer, J. S., & Kendall, P. C. (2013). *The Oxford handbook of research strategies for clinical psychology*. Oxford University Press. https://doi.org/10.1093/oxfordhb/9780199793549.001.0001

Does, S., Ellemers, N., Dovidio, J. F., Norman, J. B., Mentovich, A., van der Lee, R., & Goff, P. A. (2018). Implications of research staff demographics for psychological science. *American Psychologist, 73*(5), 639–650. https://doi.org/10.1037/amp0000199

Else, H. (2019). Crowdfunding research flips science's traditional reward model. *Nature*. Advance online publication. https://doi.org/10.1038/d41586-019-00104-1

Fabbri, A., Lai, A., Grundy, Q., & Bero, L. A. (2018). The influence of industry sponsorship on the research agenda: A scoping review. *American Journal of Public Health, 108*(11), e9–e16. https://doi.org/10.2105/AJPH.2018.304677

Ginther, D. K., Schaffer, W. T., Schnell, J., Masimore, B., Liu, F., Haak, L. L., & Kington, R. (2011). Race, ethnicity, and NIH research awards. *Science, 333*(6045), 1015–1019. https://doi.org/10.1126/science.1196783

Heggeness, M. L., Evans, L., Pohlhaus, J. R., & Mills, S. L. (2016). Measuring diversity of the National Institutes of Health-funded workforce. *Academic Medicine, 91*(8), 1164–1172. https://doi.org/10.1097/ACM.0000000000001209

Jennings, K. (2021). Venture funding for mental health startups hits record high as anxiety, depression skyrocket. *Forbes*. https://www.forbes.com/sites/katiejennings/2021/06/07/venture-funding-for-mental-health-startups-hits-record-high-as-anxiety-depression-skyrocket/?sh=6b5a43311165

Kendall, P. C., & Comer, J. S. (2013). Decades not days: The research enterprise in clinical psychology. In J. S. Comer & P. C. Kendall (Eds.), *The Oxford handbook of research strategies for clinical psychology* (pp. 437–441). Oxford University Press.

National Institutes of Health. (2021). *NIH budget and spending*. Retrieved on May 10, 2021, from https://report.nih.gov/funding/nih-budget-and-spending-data-past-fiscal-years/success-rates

National Science Board and National Science Foundation. (2020). Research and development: U.S. trends and international comparisons. *Science and Engineering Indicators 2020*. NSB-2020-3. https://ncses.nsf.gov/pubs/nsb20203/

Oh, S. S., Galanter, J., Thakur, N., Pino-Yanes, M., Barcelo, N. E., White, M. J., de Bruin, D. M., Greenblatt, R. M., Bibbins-Domingo, K., Wu, A. H. B., Borrell, L. N., Gunter, C., Powe, N. R., & Burchard, E. G. (2015). Diversity in clinical and biomedical research: A promise yet to be fulfilled. *PLOS Medicine, 12*(12), e1001918. https://doi.org/10.1371/journal.pmed.1001918

Peterson, R. A., & Merunka, D. R. (2014). Convenience samples of college students and research reproducibility. *Journal of Business Research, 67*(5), 1035–1041. https://doi.org/10.1016/j.jbusres.2013.08.010

Roback, K., Dalal, K., & Carlsson, P. (2011). Evaluation of health research: Measuring costs and socioeconomic effects. *International Journal of Preventive Medicine, 2*(4), 203–215.

Taffe, M. A., & Gilpin, N. W. (2021). Equity, diversity, and inclusion: Racial inequity in grant funding from the US National Institutes of Health. *eLife, 10*, e65697. https://doi.org/10.7554/eLife.65697

U.S. House Appropriations Committee. (2020). *Labor-HHS-Education: Fiscal year 2021 appropriations bill at-a-glance fact sheet*. Retrieved on May 10, 2021, from https://appropriations.house.gov/sites/democrats.appropriations.house.gov/files/Labor%2C%20Health%20and%20Human%20Services%2C%20Education%20FY21%20Fact%20Sheet.pdf

Volkow, N. D., Koob, G. F., Croyle, R. T., Bianchi, D. W., Gordon, J. A., Koroshetz, W. J., Pérez-Stable, E. J., Riley, W. T., Bloch, M. H., Conway, K., Deeds, B. G., Dowling, G. J., Grant, S., Howlett, K. D., Matochik, J. A., Morgan, G. D., Murray, M. M., Noronha, A., Spong, C. Y., . . . Weiss, S. R. B. (2018). The conception of the ABCD study: From substance use to a broad NIH collaboration. *Developmental Cognitive Neuroscience, 32*, 4–7. https://doi.org/10.1016/j.dcn.2017.10.002

Part III

MEASUREMENT METHODS

Section 1

BEHAVIOR OBSERVATION

CHAPTER 13

BEHAVIORAL OBSERVATION

Roger Bakeman and Vicenç Quera

Like the 18th-century historian William Douglass (1760), who wrote, "As an historian, every thing is in my province" (p. 230), the present-day behavioral scientist could say, "Everything I know and do begins with observing behavior." More conventionally, however, behavioral observation is simply and primarily about measurement—which is why you find the present chapter in *Part III: Measurement Methods* of this volume.

BEHAVIORAL OBSERVATION IS MEASUREMENT

Measurement, as you have learned from other chapters in Part III, is understood as the act of assigning numbers to things: persons, events, time intervals, and so forth. Measurement is inherently quantitative, which means that most chapters in this handbook are potentially relevant to users of observational measurement. For example, studies often are categorized either as correlational or experimental (contrast *Sampling Across People and Time* with *Designs Involving Experimental Manipulations*, Volume 2, Parts II and IV, this handbook). True, many experimental studies are performed in laboratories, and behavioral observations often are employed in field settings not involving manipulation. As a result, sometimes nonexperimental studies are referred to as "observational," as though observational were a synonym for correlational, and are assumed to occur outside laboratories. In fact, correlational studies can be performed in laboratories and experimental ones in the field—and behavioral observations can be employed for either type of study in either setting.

No matter the type of measurement, a key feature of any quantitative investigation is its design. As researchers plan an investigation and think forward to later data analysis, it is important at the outset to specify two key components: the basic *analytic units* and the *research factors*. Research factors usually are described as *between subjects* (e.g., gender with two levels, male and female) or *within subjects* (e.g., repeated observations in the same individuals at age 18, 24, and 30 months). Between-subjects analytic units are, for example, the individual participants, parent–child dyads, families, or other groups (often called *cases* in standard statistical packages, *subjects* in older literature, or simply basic *sampling units*), whose scores are organized by the between-subjects research factors. When repeated measures exist, additional analytic units, each identified with a level of a repeated measure, are nested within cases.

https://doi.org/10.1037/0000318-013
APA Handbook of Research Methods in Psychology, Second Edition: Vol. 1. Foundations, Planning, Measures, and Psychometrics, H. Cooper (Editor-in-Chief)
Copyright © 2023 by the American Psychological Association. All rights reserved.

OBSERVATIONAL SESSIONS ARE ANALYTIC UNITS

An *observational session* is a sequence of coded events for which continuity generally can be assumed (although either planned or unplanned breaks might occur during an observational session). For behavioral observation, sessions are equated with analytic units. Statistics and indexes derived from the coded data for an observational session constitute scores; scores from the various subjects and sessions are then organized by any between- and within-subjects factors and are analyzed subsequently using conventional statistical techniques as guided by the design of the study.

Speaking broadly, designs are of two types: single-subject (as described in Volume 2, Chapter 33, this handbook) and group. As noted in the previous paragraph, the factors of group designs may be between-subjects, within-subjects, or both. For more information about the analysis of group designs, see Volume 3, Chapters 1 to 24, this handbook (especially Chapters 8–10); for information about issues relevant for quantitative analysis generally, also see Chapters 33 to 38 of this volume. No matter what design is used, and regardless of whether scores are derived from behavioral observation or other measurement techniques, the basic psychometric properties of validity and reliability need to be established (see Chapters 33–38 of this volume; reliability issues unique to behavioral observation, particularly observer agreement, are discussed later in this chapter).

Many measurement methods are simple and efficient. What is a person's weight? Step on a scale. What is a person's age? Ask them. What is a person's self-esteem? Have the person rate several items on a 1-to-5 scale and then compute the average rating. In contrast, behavioral observation is often time-consuming. Observational sessions can vary from a few minutes to several hours, during which human observers need be present. Better (or worse), sessions can be recorded, which despite its advantages can take even more time as observers spend hours coding a few minutes of behavior. The data collected can be voluminous and their analysis seemingly intractable. Why bother with such a time-consuming method?

REASONS FOR USING OBSERVATIONAL MEASUREMENT

Several sorts of circumstances can lead an investigator to observational measurement, but three stand out. First, behavioral observation is useful when nonverbal organisms such as human infants, nonhuman primates, or other animals are being studied. We cannot ask them whether they strongly disagree or agree somewhat with a particular statement, nor can we ask them to fill out a daily diary saying how much they ate or drank or how much time they spent playing with their mother each day—only observational methods will work. And even when those we observe are verbal, we may nonetheless use observational methods when studying nonverbal behavior specifically. Not surprisingly, many early examples of behavioral observation are found in studies of animal behavior and infant development.

Second, investigators often choose behavioral observation because they want to assess naturally occurring behavior. The behavior could be observed in field or laboratory settings but presumably is "natural," reflecting the participant's proclivities and untutored repertoire and not something elicited, for example, by an experimenter's task. From this point of view, filling out a questionnaire is "unnatural" behavior; it only occurs in contrived, directed settings and is never spontaneous. Still, you might ask, how natural is observed behavior? Like observer effects in physics, doesn't behavior change when it is observed? Does awareness of being observed alter our behavior? The answer seems to be that we habituate rapidly to observation, perhaps more so than in earlier years now that security cameras are everywhere. For example, for Bakeman's dissertation research (Bakeman & Helmreich, 1975), marine scientists living in a space-station-like habitat 50 feet below the surface of Coral Bay in the Virgin Islands were on camera continuously, yet as they went about their work, awareness of the cameras seemingly disappeared within the first several minutes of their 2- to 3-week stay in the habitat.

Third, when investigators are interested in process—how things work and not just outcomes—observations capture behavior unfolding in time, which is essential to understanding process. A good example is Gottman's (1979) work on marital interaction, which predicted whether relationships would dissolve based on characterizations of moment-to-moment interaction sequences. One frequently asked process question concerns contingency. For example, when nurses reassure children undergoing a painful procedure, is children's distress lessened? Or, when children are distressed, do nurses reassure them more? Contingency analyses designed to answer questions like these may be one of the more common and useful applications of observational methods and is an application we return to later.

In sum, compared with other measurement methods (e.g., direct physical measurement or deriving a summary score from a set of rated items), observational measurement is often labor-intensive and time-consuming. Nonetheless, observational measurement is often the method of choice when nonverbal organisms are studied (or nonverbal behavior generally); when more natural, spontaneous, real-world behavior is of interest; and when processes and not outcomes are the focus (e.g., questions of contingency).

As detailed in subsequent sections of this chapter, behavioral observation requires some unique techniques. However, in common with other measurement methods, it produces scores attached to analytic units (i.e., sessions) that are organized by the within- and between-subjects factors of a group design or the within-subjects factors of a single-subject design. Consequently, if this chapter interests you, it is only a beginning; you should find at least some chapters in almost all parts of this three-volume handbook relevant to your interests and worth your attention. Longer treatments are also available: Bakeman and Gottman (1997) provided a thorough overview, Martin and Bateson (2007) emphasized animal and ethological studies, Yoder and Symons (2010) may be especially appealing to those concerned with typical and atypical development of infants and children, and Bakeman and Quera (2011) and Quera (2018) emphasized data analysis.

CODING SCHEMES: MEASURING INSTRUMENTS FOR OBSERVATION

Measurement requires a measuring instrument. Such instruments are often physical; clocks, thermometers, and rulers are just a few of many common examples. In contrast, a coding scheme—which consists of a list of codes (i.e., names, labels, or categories) for the behaviors of interest—is primarily conceptual. As rulers are to carpentry—a basic and essential measuring tool—coding schemes are to behavioral observation (although as we discuss, trained human observers are usually an integral part of the measuring apparatus).

As a conceptual matter, a coding scheme cannot escape its theoretical underpinnings—even if the investigator does not address these explicitly. Rulers say only that length is important. Coding schemes say these specific behaviors and particularly these distinctions are worth capturing; necessarily coding schemes reflect a theory about what is important and why. Bakeman and Gottman (1986, 1997) wrote that using someone else's coding scheme was like wearing someone else's underwear. In other words, the coding schemes you use should reflect your theories and not someone else's—and when you make the connections between your theories and codes explicit, you clarify how the data you collect can provide clear answers to the research questions that motivated your work in the first place.

Where then do coding schemes come from? Many investigators begin with coding schemes that others with similar interests and theories have used and then adapt them to their specific research questions. In any case, developing coding schemes is almost always an iterative process, a matter of successive refinement, and is greatly aided by working with video recordings. Pilot testing may reveal that codes that seemed important simply do not occur, or distinctions that seemed important cannot be reliably made (the solution is to lump the codes), or that the codes seem to miss important distinctions (the solution is to split original codes or define new ones). In its earlier stages especially, developing and refining coding schemes is qualitative research (see Volume 2, Chapters 1–15, this handbook).

Mutually Exclusive and Exhaustive Sets of Codes

In addition to content (i.e., the way codes fit your research questions), the structure of coding schemes can also contribute to their usefulness. Consider the three simple examples given in Figure 13.1. The first categorizes activity on the basis of Bakeman's dissertation research (Bakeman & Helmreich, 1975; as noted earlier, studying marine scientists living in a space-station-like habitat underwater); it is typical of coding schemes that seek to describe how individuals spend their day (time-budget information). The second categorizes infant states (Wolff, 1966), and the third categorizes children's play states (Parten, 1932).

Each of these three coding schemes consists of a set of mutually exclusive and exhaustive (ME&E) codes. This is a desirable and easily achieved property of coding schemes, one that often helps clarify our codes when under development and that usually simplifies subsequent recording and analysis. Still, when first developing lists of potential codes, we may note codes that logically can and probably will co-occur. This is hardly a problem and, in fact, is desired when research questions concern co-occurrence.

Perhaps the best solution is to assign the initial codes on our list to different sets of codes, each of which is ME&E in itself; this has several advantages we note shortly.

Of course, the codes within any single set can be made mutually exclusive by defining combinations (only A, only B, A+B), and any set of codes can be made exhaustive simply by adding a final none-of-the-above code. For example, if a set consisted of two codes, infant gazes at mother and mother gazes at infant, adding a third combination code, mutual gaze, would result in a mutually exclusive set, and adding a fourth nil code would make the set exhaustive. Alternatively, two sets each with two codes could be defined: mother gazes at infant or not, and infant gazes at mother or not. In this case, mutual gaze, instead of being an explicit code, could be determined later analytically.

Which is preferable: two sets with two codes each, or one set with four codes—or more generally, more sets with few if any combination codes, or fewer sets but some combination codes? This is primarily a matter of taste or personal preference—similar information can be derived from the data in either case—but especially when working with video records, there may be advantages to more versus fewer sets. Coders can make several passes, attending just to the codes in one set on each pass (e.g., first mother, then infant), which allows them to focus on just one aspect of behavior at a time. Moreover, different coders can be assigned different sets, which gives greater credibility to any patterns we detect later between codes in different sets.

We do not want to minimize the effort and hard work usually required to develop effective coding schemes—many hours of looking, thinking, defining, arguing, modifying, and refining can be involved—but if the result is well-structured (i.e., consists of several sets of ME&E codes, each of which characterizes a coherent dimension of interest), then subsequent recording, representing, and analysis of the observational data is almost always greatly facilitated.

To every rule, there is an exception. Imagine that we list five codes of interest, any of which

Activity	Infant state	Play state
1. Doing scientific work	1. Quiet alert	1. Unoccupied
2. At leisure	2. Crying	2. Onlooker
3. Eating	3. Fussy	3. Solitary play
4. Habitat-maintenance	4. REM sleep	4. Parallel play
5. Self-maintenance	5. Deep sleep	5. Associative play
6. Asleep		6. Cooperative play

FIGURE 13.1. Three examples of coding schemes; each consists of a set of mutually exclusive and exhaustive codes.

might co-occur. Should we define five sets each with two codes: the behavior of interest and its absence? Or should we simply list the five codes and ask observers to note the onset and offset times for each (assuming duration is wanted)? Either strategy offers the same analytic options, and thus it is a matter of taste. As with the fewer versus more combination codes question in the previous paragraph, a good rule is, whatever your observers find easiest to work with (and are reliable doing) is right.

Codes, which after all are just convenient labels, do not stand alone. The coding manual—which gives definitions for each code along with examples—is an important part of any observational research project and deserves careful attention. It will be drafted as coding schemes are being defined and thereafter stands as a reference when training coders; moreover, it documents your procedure and can be shared with other researchers.

Granularity: Micro to Macro Codes

One dimension worth considering when developing coding schemes is granularity. Codes can vary from micro to macro (or molecular to molar)—from detailed and fine-grained to relatively broad and coarse-grained. As always, the appropriate level of granularity is one that articulates well with your research concerns. For example, if you are more interested in moment-to-moment changes in expressed emotion than in global emotional state, you might opt to use the fine-grained facial action coding scheme developed by Paul Ekman (Ekman & Friesen, 1978), which relates different facial movements to their underlying muscles. A useful guideline is, if in doubt, define codes at a somewhat finer level of granularity than your research questions require (i.e., when in doubt split, don't lump). You can always analytically lump later but, to state the obvious, you cannot recover distinctions never made.

Concreteness: Physically to Socially Based Codes

Another dimension, not the same as granularity, is concreteness. Bakeman and Gottman (1986, 1997) suggested that coding schemes could be placed on an ordered continuum with one end anchored by physically based schemes and the other by socially based ones. More physically based codes reflect attributes that are easily seen, whereas more socially based codes rely on abstractions and require some inference (our apologies if any professional meta-physicians find this too simple).

An example of a physically based code might be infant crying, whereas an example of a more socially based code might be a child engaged in cooperative play. Some ethologists and behaviorists might regard the former as objective and the latter subjective (and so less scientific), but—again eliding matters that concern professional philosophers—we would say that the physically–socially based distinction may matter most when selecting and training observers. Do we regard them as detectors of things *really* there? Or more as cultural informants, able through experience to "see" the distinctions embodied in our coding schemes? To our mind, a more important question about coding schemes is whether we can train observers to be reliable, a matter to which we return later.

Examples often clarify. Figure 13.2 presents two additional coding schemes. The first categorizes the vocalizations of very young infants (simplified and adapted from Gros-Louis et al., 2006; see also Oller, 2000). It is a good example of a physically based coding scheme, so much

Infant vocalization	Maternal response
1. Vowels	1. Naming
2. Syllables (i.e., consonant–vowel transitions)	2. Questions
3. Babbling (a sequence of repeated syllables)	3. Acknowledgments
4. Other (e.g., cry, laugh, vegetative sounds)	4. Imitations
	5. Attributions
	6. Directives
	7. Play vocalizations

FIGURE 13.2. Two additional examples of coding schemes; the first is more physically based and the second more socially based. Adapted from "Mothers Provide Differential Feedback to Infants' Prelinguistic Sounds," by J. Gros-Louis, M. J. West, M. H. Goldstein, and A. P. King, 2006, *International Journal of Behavioral Development, 30*(6), pp. 511–512 (https://doi.org/10.1177/0165025406071914). Copyright 2006 by the International Society for the Study of Behavioural Development. Adapted with permission.

so that it is possible to automate its coding using sound spectrograph information. Computer coding—dispensing with human observers—has tantalized investigators for some time but remains mainly out of reach. True, computer scientists are attempting to automate the process, and some limited success has been achieved with automatic computer detection of Ekman-like facial action patterns (Cohn & Kanade, 2007), but the more socially based codes become, the more elusive any kind of computer automation seems. Consider the second coding scheme for maternal vocalizations (also adapted from Gros-Louis et al., 2006). It is difficult to see how this could be automated. For the foreseeable future at least, a human coder—a perceiver—likely will remain an essential part of behavioral observation.

Scales of Measurement and Coders Versus Raters

Finally, we present two examples of coding schemes—for measurement scales, not behavior—because they usefully foreshadow distinctions that become important when discussing codes and their analysis later. Most of us probably learned the classic S. S. Stevens (1946) scheme but not the more recent Cox and Donnelly (2011) one. Both of these two schemes distinguish between a *nominal* measurement scale or categorical level of measurement (the names assigned to the entities of interest have no natural order, like agreeable, extroverted, open) and an *ordinal* level of measurement (the integers assigned to entities can only be ranked or ordered, like strongly disagree, disagree, agree, strongly agree). But Cox and Donnelly added *binary* (just two labels are assigned to the entities of interest; e.g., male or female) and then distinguished between *integer* (i.e., whole numbers, often counts) and *continuous* (i.e., real numbers, allowing fractional values). In contrast, Stevens distinguished between *interval* (an increment anywhere on the scale involves the same amount of whatever is measured, but zero is arbitrary, like degrees Celsius) and *ratio* (every increment on the scale denotes an identical amount and zero indicates truly none of the quantity measured, like units of weight)—a distinction that matters little when selecting statistical techniques.

In practice, almost all observational measurement of interest to us will be binary, nominal, or ordinal, rarely integer or continuous—although the scores we derive from observational data (e.g., frequencies, rates, percentages, contingency indexes) will often be integer or continuous, a matter we return to later. (Note: *Continuous* is sometimes used to refer to scales that permit only integer values; to avoid muddling a useful distinction, the term seems best reserved for real-number scales.)

Many coding schemes are categorical, but some are ordinal, as when observers are asked to rate intervals or events on a 1-to-5 or 1-to-7 scale. Accordingly, we use the term *coders* for those asked to make categorical distinctions and *raters* for those asked to assign an ordinal number—and use the general term *observers* when referring to either coders or raters. Such usage is not universal but, in our view, preserves a useful distinction.

In sum, for behavioral observation to succeed, the investigator's toolbox should include well-designed, conceptually coherent, and pilot-tested coding schemes—these are the primary measuring instruments for behavioral observation. Often, but not always, each scheme reflects a dimension of interest and consists of a set of mutually exclusive and exhaustive codes.

RECORDING CODED DATA: FROM PENCIL AND PAPER TO DIGITAL

In the previous section, we argued that coding schemes are a conceptual matter, necessarily reflect your theoretical orientation, and work best when they mesh well with your research questions. In contrast, recording the data that result from applying those coding schemes (i.e., initial data collection) is a practical matter requiring physical materials ranging from simple pencil and paper to sophisticated electronic systems.

Live Observation Versus Recorded Behavior

Perhaps the first question to ask is, are coders (or raters) observing live or are they working with recordings (video–audio or just audio, once recorded on tape but now primarily digital)? Whenever feasible, we think recordings are preferable. First and most important, recorded behavior can be played and replayed—literally re-viewed—at various speeds, which greatly facilitates the observer's task. Second, only with recordings can we ask our observers to code different aspects in different passes; for example, coding a mother's behavior in one pass and her infant's in another. Third, recorded behavior facilitates checks on observers' reliability, both between observers who can be kept blind to the reliability check, and within observers when asked to code the same session later. Fourth, contemporary computer systems for capturing coded data work best with digital files. Finally, video–audio recording devices are relatively inexpensive; cost is not the factor it was in past decades.

Nonetheless, live observation may still be preferred in certain circumstances. In some settings (e.g., school classrooms), video–audio recording devices may be regarded as too intrusive, or for ethical or political reasons, permanent recordings may be unwelcome. And in some circumstances (e.g., observing animal behavior in the field) trained human observers may be able to detect behaviors that are unclear on recordings. Moreover, live observation is simpler; there is no need to purchase, learn about, or maintain video–audio recording devices.

Events and Intervals Are Primary Recording Units

Earlier, we defined measurement as assigning numbers to things. Given Stevens's (1946) and Cox and Donnelly's (2011) coding scheme for scales, we can now see that "numbers" should be expanded to include categories (i.e., nominal codes) and ranks (i.e., ordinal numbers representing position). Thus, behavioral observation almost always begins with categorical measurement: Codes are assigned to things (although ordinal measurement using ratings is another but less frequently used possibility). But to what "things" are codes or ratings assigned? The answer is this: to events (which may vary in duration) or to intervals (whose duration is fixed). These are the two primary recording units used for observational data.

Corresponding to the two primary recording units are two primary strategies for recording coded data: continuous and interval recording. As noted, the primary analytic unit for behavioral observation is a session. *Continuous recording* implies continuously alert observers, ready to code events when they do occur. In contrast, *interval recording* (also referred to as *time-sampling*; Altmann, 1974) requires that the session be segmented into fixed-length intervals and that observers assign a code or codes to each successive interval. The length of the interval may vary from study to study, but relatively brief intervals are fairly common (e.g., 10–15 seconds). In subsequent paragraphs, we discuss interval and continuous recording in greater detail and note advantages and disadvantages of each.

Interval recording. Arguably, interval recording is a limited technique, used more in the past than currently. Its merits are primarily practical: it can be easy and inexpensive to implement, but as a trade-off, data derived from interval recording may be less precise than data derived from other methods. Interval recording lends itself to pencil and paper or electronic tablet. All that is needed is a timing device so that interval boundaries can be identified, a lined paper tablet with columns added (rows represent successive intervals and columns are labeled with codes) or an electronic tablet suitably formatted, and a recording rule.

A common recording rule is to check the interval if a behavior occurs once or more within it; this is called *partial-interval* or *zero-one* sampling. Another possibility is *momentary* sampling—check only if the behavior is occurring at a defined instant, such as the beginning of the interval (although in practice this often is interpreted as check the behavior that predominated during the interval). Another less used possibility is *whole-interval* sampling—check only if the behavior occurs throughout the interval (see Altmann, 1974;

Suen & Ary, 1989). An example using infant state codes is shown in Figure 13.3; because each line is checked for only one of these ME&E codes, we can assume that momentary sampling was used.

As noted, with interval recording, summary statistics may be estimated only approximately. For example, with zero-one sampling, frequencies likely are underestimated (a check can indicate more than one occurrence in an interval), proportions are likely overestimated (a check does not mean the event occupied the entire interval), and sequences can be muddled (if more than one code is checked for an interval, which occurred first?)—and momentary and whole-interval sampling have other problems. There are possible fixes to these problems, but none seem completely satisfactory. As a result, unless approximate estimates are sufficient to answer your research questions and the practical advantages seem decisive, we usually recommend event and not interval recording whenever feasible.

Nonetheless, we recognize that interval recording has its partisans. Certainly interval recording seemed a good choice for Mel Konner studying mother–infant interaction among the !Kung in Botswana in the late 1960s and early 1970s (Bakeman et al., 1990; Konner, 1976). An electronic device delivered a click every 15 seconds to the observer's ear. Observers then noted which of several mother, infant, adult, and child behaviors had occurred since the last click. The remote location and the need for live observation in this era before inexpensive and reliable video made interval recording the method of choice.

A variant of interval recording could be termed *interrupted interval recording*, which is sometimes used in education and other settings. Coders observe for a fixed interval (e.g., 20 seconds) and then record for another fixed interval (e.g., 10 seconds). Such data are even less suitable for any sort of sequential analysis than ordinary interval recording, but as with standard interval recording, when approximate estimates are sufficient, simplicity of implementation may argue for even interrupted interval recording.

Continuous untimed event recording. Imagine that we ask observers to note whenever an event of interest occurs and record its code. What could be simpler? Like interval recording, simple event recording is limited but nonetheless sufficient to answer some research questions. The sequence of events is preserved, but no information concerning their duration is recorded. Thus we can report how often different types of events occurred and in what sequence, but we cannot report the average time different types of events lasted or how much of the session was devoted to different types of events.

Again, like interval recording, untimed-event recording lends itself to pencil and paper or simple electronics. Using a lined paper or electronic tablet, information identifying the session can be written at the top and then codes for each event noted on successive lines.

Two refinements are possible. First, even though event durations remain unrecorded, the start and stop times for the session can be recorded. Then, rates for the various events can be computed for each session and will be comparable across sessions that vary in length. Second, each event can be coded on more than one dimension using more than one set of ME&E codes, in effect cross-classifying the event and producing data appropriate for multidimensional contingency

	Infant code				
Interval	Alert	Cry	Fussy	REM	Sleep
1				√	
2				√	
3			√		
4	√				
5	√				
6	√				
7		√			
8		√			
9		√			
10				√	
...					

FIGURE 13.3. An example of interval recorded data for infant state.

tables. Such multievent data are formally identical with interval recorded data and could be collected using forms similar to the one shown in Figure 13.3, adding columns for additional ME&E sets. The only difference is, lines are associated with successive intervals for interval recording and with successive events for multi-event (but untimed) recording.

Recording simply the sequence of events, or sequences of cross-classified events, but ignoring the duration of those events, limits the information that can be derived from the coded data. If your research questions require nothing more than information about frequency (or rate), sequence, and possibly cross-classification, then the simplicity and low cost of untimed-event recording could cause you to adopt this approach.

Continuous timed-event recording. More useful and less limited data—data that offer more analytic options—result when not just events but their durations are recorded (i.e., their onset and offset times). In general, this is the approach we recommend. Of course, there is a price. Recording event onset and offset times is inevitably more complicated than either interval or untimed-event recording. The good news is, advances in technology in the past few decades have made timed-event recording simpler and more affordable than in the past. Continuous timed-event recording does not absolutely require computer technology, but nonetheless works best with it.

Let us begin by describing what is possible with current computer technology. Users can play one or more (synchronized) digital video–audio files using on-screen controls. The image (or images) can be paused and then played forward or backward at various speeds, displaying the current time (rounded to some fraction of a second, often a millisecond, but insofar as digital files preserve frames, accurate to the video frame—there are 29.97 per second per the National Television System Committee [NTSC] standard used in North America, much of South America, and Japan, and 25 per second per the Phase Alternating Line [PAL] standard used in most of Europe, the Middle East and North Africa, South Asia, and China). Typically, codes, their characteristics, and the recording method are defined initially. Then when a key is pressed on subsequent playback (or a code displayed on-screen is selected), a record of that code and the current time are shown on-screen and stored in an internal data file.

With such systems, the human observers do not need to worry about clerical details or keep track of time; the computer system attends to these tasks. If you make a mistake and want to add or delete a code or change a time, typically edits can be accomplished on-screen with minimal effort. The result is a file containing codes along with their onset and (optionally) offset times. Programs vary in their conventions and capabilities, but when sets of ME&E codes are defined, most systems automatically supply the offset time for a code when the onset time of another code in that set is selected; and when some codes are defined as *momentary* (i.e., occurring at a single point in time), meaning that only their frequency and not their duration is of concern, offset times are not required.

Some systems permit what we call *post hoc coding*—first you detect an event, and only afterward you code it. For example, when you think an event is beginning, hold down the space bar, and when it ends, release, which pauses play. You can then decide what the code should be, enter it, and restart play. Another advanced feature allows subsequent choices for an event to be determined by prior ones (one term for this is *lexical chaining*). For example, if you select *mother* for an event, a list of mother behavior codes would be displayed (e.g., talk, rock), whereas if you had selected *infant,* a list of infant codes would be displayed (e.g., cry, sleep). The next list thereafter, if any, could be determined by the particular mother or infant behavior selected, and so on, until the end of the lexical chain.

Although capabilities vary, computer systems of the sort just described free observers to concentrate on making judgments; clerical tasks are handled automatically and thus the possibility of clerical error is greatly reduced. Such systems can work with live observation or videotapes, but they are at their best with digital files. For those who have existing archives of video tape—an older recording medium now little used—the first step is digitation. With digital files, you can jump instantly to any point in the file; you can also ask that a particular episode be replayed repeatedly, and you can assemble lists of particular episodes that then can be played sequentially, ignoring other material. Such capabilities are useful for coding and training and for education purposes generally. (Four examples of such systems are Mangold International's INTERACT [see https://www.mangoldinternational.com]; Noldus Information Technology's The Observer [see https://www.noldus.com]; Max Planck Institute's ELAN [see https://archive.mpi.nl/tla/elan]; and University of Groningen's Mediacoder [see https://mediacoder.gmw.rug.nl/]; an internet search will quickly reveal others.)

Still, there is no need for investigators who require continuous timed-event recording to despair when budgets are limited. Digital files can be played with standard and free software on standard computers, or videotapes can be played on the usual tape playback devices. Codes and times then can be manually entered into, for example, a spreadsheet program running on its own computer or simply written on a paper tablet. Times can even be written when coding live; only pencil, paper, and a clock are required. Such low-tech approaches can be tedious and error-prone—and affordable. When used well, they can produce timed-event data that are indistinguishable from that collected with systems costing far more. Still, as our rich city cousin might say, it won't be as much fun.

Pencil-and-Paper Versus Electronic Methods

To summarize, once coding schemes are defined, refined, and piloted, and once observers are trained, you are ready to begin recording data. Derivation of summary measures and other data reduction comes later, but initial data collection (i.e., observational measurement) consists of observers assigning codes to either fixed time intervals or events. When codes are assigned to events, the events may be untimed, or onset and offset times may be recorded (or in some cases inferred). No matter whether the behavior is observed live or first recorded, any of these strategies (interval, untimed, or timed-event recording) could be used with anything from pencil, paper, and perhaps a timing device, to electronic tablets, to a high-end, bells-and-whistles computerized coding system. Nonetheless, as we first wrote in 1986 a bit humorously, pencil-and-paper methods have their advantages—they feel good in the hand, possess a satisfying physicality, rarely malfunction, and do not need batteries (Bakeman & Gottman, 1986).

Interval and untimed-event recording produce more limited, less rich, less precise data—data with fewer analytic options—than timed-event recording. At the same time, they can work satisfactorily with simple and inexpensive equipment, including pencil and paper or electronic tablets, observing either recorded material or live. In contrast, timed-event recording works best when video–audio recordings are used along with some electronic assistance. It is the usual trade-off: richer data, more analytic options, less tedious coding, fewer clerical errors, more tasks automated—as well as greater expense, longer learning times, and more resources devoted to maintenance. As always, the *right* recording system is the one that matches resources with needs, and when simpler, less precise data are sufficient to answer key research questions, simple and inexpensive may be best.

REPRESENTING OBSERVATIONAL DATA: THE CODE-UNIT GRID

Too often investigators take their data as collected and move directly to analysis, bypassing what can be an important step. This intervening step involves representing—literally, re-presenting—your data, by which we mean transforming the data-as-collected into a form more useful for subsequent analysis. As described in the previous section, when recording observational data initially, observer ease and accuracy are of primary importance. Therefore, it makes sense to design data collection procedures that work well for our observers; but analysis can be facilitated by how those data are represented subsequently, especially for timed-event recording.

When both preparing data for subsequent analysis and thinking about what those analyses should be, we have found it extremely helpful to organize observational data in one common underlying format (Bakeman, 2010). That underlying format is a grid, which is an ancient and useful organizing device. For observational data, rows represent codes and columns represent units (which are either intervals for interval recorded data, or events for untimed-event recorded data, or time units for timed-event recorded data). Thus, for interval and untimed-event data, recording and representational units are the same, whereas for timed-event data, recording and representational units differ: events for recording and time units for representing.

The time units for timed-event data are defined by the precision with which time was recorded. If seconds, each column of the grid represents a second; if tenths of a second, each column represents a tenth of a second; and so forth (see Figure 13.4). Computer programs may display multiple digits after the decimal point but, unless specialized equipment is used, claiming hundredth-of-a-second accuracy is dubious. Video recording is limited by the number of frames per second (a frame is 0.033 seconds for NTSC and 0.040 seconds for PAL), which allows claims of 10th of a second or somewhat greater, but not 100th-of-a-second, accuracy. Moreover, for most behavioral research questions, accuracy to the nearest second is almost always sufficient.

Understanding that investigators use different recording methods, as detailed in the previous section, yet also recognizing the advantages of representational standards, some years ago we defined conventions for observational data, which we called the Sequential Data Interchange Standard (SDIS) format (Bakeman & Quera, 1992). We defined five basic data types. As you might guess from the previous section, the two simplest were *event sequential data* and *interval sequential data*, which result from simple event and interval recording, respectively. *Multievent sequential data* result when events are cross-classified, as described earlier, and *timed-event sequential data* result from timed-event recording. A fifth type, *state sequential data*, is simply a variant of timed-event sequential data for which data entry is simplified if all codes can be assigned to ME&E sets. For simple examples, see Bakeman et al. (2005) and Bakeman and Quera (2011).

Once data are formatted per SDIS conventions, they can be analyzed with any general-purpose computer program that uses this standard, such as the Generalized Sequential Querier (GSEQ; Bakeman & Quera, 1995, 2009, 2011), a program we designed, not for initial data collection, but specifically for data analysis. Much of the power and usefulness of this program depends on representing observational data in terms of a universal code–unit grid, as just described.

Three advantages are noteworthy. First, representing observational data as a grid in which rows represent codes and columns represent successive events, intervals, or time units makes the application of standard frequency or contingency table statistics easy (the column is the tallying unit). Second, the grid representation makes data modification easy and easy to understand. New codes (i.e., rows in the grid) can be defined and formed from existing codes using standard logical operations (Bakeman et al., 2005; Bakeman & Quera, 1995, 2011). Third, the discrete time-unit view (i.e., segmenting time into successive discrete

Infant code	Second									
	1	2	3	4	5	6	7	8	9	10
Alert				■	■	■				
Cry							■	■	■	
Fussy			■							
REM	■	■								
Sleep										■

FIGURE 13.4. An example of a code-unit grid for timed-event recorded data with 1-second precision (i.e., times recorded to the nearest second).

time units defined by precision) of timed-event sequential data solves some, but not all, problems in gauging observer agreement, which is the topic of the next section.

OBSERVER AGREEMENT: EVENT BASED, TIME BASED, OR BOTH?

Observer agreement is often regarded as the sine qua non of observational measurement. Without it, we are left with individual narratives of the sort used in qualitative research (see Volume 2, Chapters 1 to 11, this handbook). Even so, a suitable level of agreement between two independent observers does not guarantee accuracy—two observers could share similar deviant views of the world—but it is widely regarded as an index of acceptable measurement. If test probes reveal that the records of two observers recorded independently do not agree (or an observer does not agree with a presumably accurate standard), the accuracy of any scores derived from data coded by those observers is uncertain; further observer training, modification of the coding scheme, or both are needed. On the other hand, when test probes reveal that observers' records substantially agree (or an observer agrees with a presumably accurate standard), we infer that our observers are adequately trained and regard the data they produce as trustworthy and reliable.

Classic Cohen's Kappa and Interval Recorded Data

Probably the most commonly used statistic of observer agreement is Cohen's kappa (1960), although as we explain shortly, it is most suited for interval recorded data. The classic Cohen's kappa characterizes agreement with respect to a set of ME&E codes while correcting for chance agreement. It assumes that things—demarcated units—are presented to a pair of observers, each of whom independently assigns a code to each unit. Each pair of observer decisions is tallied in a $K \times K$ table (also called an *agreement* or *confusion* matrix) where K is the number of codes in the ME&E set. For example, if 100 intervals were coded using the five infant state codes defined earlier, the agreement matrix might look like the one shown in Figure 13.5.

For this example, the two observers generally agreed (i.e., most tallies were on the diagonal); the most frequent confusion—when Observer 1 coded *alert* but Observer 2 coded *fussy*—occurred just three times. Kappa is computed by dividing chance-corrected observed agreement (i.e., the probability of observed agreement minus the probability of agreement expected by chance) by the maximum agreement not due to chance (i.e., 1 minus the probability of agreement expected by chance; see Bakeman & Gottman, 1997): $\kappa = (P_{obs} - P_{exp})/(1 - P_{exp})$. For this example, the value of kappa was .76.

Now, here is the problem. Cohen's kappa assumes that pairs of observers make decisions when presented with discrete units and that the number of decisions is the same as the number of units. This decision-making model fits interval-recorded data well but fits event-recorded data only when events are presented to observers as previously demarcated units, for example, as turns of talk in a transcript. Usually events are not prepackaged. Instead, with event recording, observers are asked to first segment the stream of behavior into events (i.e., detect the seams between events) and then code those segments. Because of errors of omission and commission—one observer detects events the other misses—usually the two observer's records will contain

Obs 1's codes	Obs 2's codes					Total
	Alert	Cry	Fussy	REM	Sleep	
Alert	26	2	3	0	0	31
Cry	2	27	1	0	0	30
Fussy	1	2	4	2	1	10
REM	0	0	1	17	1	19
Sleep	0	0	0	2	8	10
Total	29	31	9	21	10	100

FIGURE 13.5. Agreement matrix for two observers who independently coded 100 fixed-time intervals using the infant state coding scheme. For this example, Cohen's kappa = .76. Obs = observer.

different numbers of events and exactly how the records align is not always obvious. And when alignment is uncertain, how events should be paired and tallied in the agreement matrix is unclear.

Aligning Untimed Events When Observers Disagree

Aligning two observers' sequences of untimed events is problematic. Bakeman and Gottman (1997) wrote that especially when agreement is not high, alignment is difficult and cannot be accomplished without subjective judgment. Quera et al. (2007) developed an algorithm that determines the *optimal global alignment* between two event sequences. The algorithm is adopted from sequence alignment and comparison techniques that are routinely used by molecular biologists (Needleman & Wunsch, 1970). The task is to find an optimal alignment. The Needleman–Wunsch algorithm belongs to a broad class of methods known as *dynamic programming*, in which the solution for a specific subproblem can be derived from the solution for another, immediately preceding subproblem. It can be demonstrated that the method guarantees an optimal solution—that is, it finds the alignment with the highest possible number of agreements between sequences (Sankoff & Kruskal, 1983/1999, p. 48)—without being exhaustive—that is, it does not need to explore the almost astronomical number of all possible alignments (Galisson, 2000).

The way the algorithm works is relatively complex, but a simple example can at least show what results. Assume that two observers using the infant vocalization scheme described earlier recorded the two event sequences (S_1 and S_2) shown in Figure 13.6. The first observer coded 15 events and the second 14, but because of omission–commission errors, the optimal alignment shows 16. The 11 agreements are indicated with vertical bars and the two actual disagreements with two dots (i.e., a colon), but there were three additional errors: The algorithm estimated that Observer 1 missed one event that Observer 2 coded (indicated

Obs 1's codes	Obs 2's codes					Total
	Nil	Vowel	Syllable	Babble	Other	
Nil	–	0	1	0	0	1
Vowel	1	3	0	0	0	4
Syllable	1	0	4	0	0	5
Babble	0	0	0	3	0	3
Other	0	1	1	0	1	3
Total	2	4	6	3	1	16

```
Sequences:
 S1 = vvsbosbosvosbvs
 S2 = vsbssbsvsvobvs
Alignment:
 vvsbosb-osvosbvs
 |||:||  :|||  |||
 -vsbssbsvsvo-bvs
```

FIGURE 13.6. Alignment of two event sequences per our dynamic programming algorithm, and the resulting agreement matrix. For alignment, vertical bars indicate exact agreement, two dots (colon) disagreements, and hyphens events coded by one observer but not the other. For this example, alignment kappa = .60. Obs = observer.

with a hyphen in the top alignment line) and Observer 2 missed two events that Observer 1 coded (indicated with hyphens in the bottom alignment line).

The alignment then lets us tally paired observer decisions (using nil to indicate a missed event) and compute kappa, with two qualifications. First, because observers cannot both code nil, the resulting agreement matrix contains a logical (or structural) zero; as a consequence, the expected frequencies required by the kappa computation cannot be estimated with the usual formula for kappa but instead require an iterative proportional fitting (IPF) algorithm (see Bakeman & Robinson, 1994). Second, because Cohen's assumptions are not met, we should not call this Cohen's kappa; *alignment kappa* would be a better term (specifically, an event-based dynamic programming alignment kappa). For the simple example in Figure 13.6, we used our GSEQ program to determine the alignment and compute alignment kappa. For a real-world example with mother–infant interaction data, see Trenado et al. (2021).

Time-Unit and Event-Based Kappas for Timed-Event Data

The alignment algorithm solves the problem for untimed-event data but what of timed-event data? We have proposed two solutions. The first solution, which is the one presented by Bakeman and Gottman (1997), depends on the discrete view of time reflected in the code-time-unit grid described earlier. Assuming a discrete view of time and a code-time-unit grid like the one shown in Figure 13.4, agreement between successive pairs of time units can be tallied and kappa computed. As a variant, agreement could be tallied when codes for time units matched, if not exactly, then at least within a stated tolerance (e.g., 2 seconds). Because time units are tallied, the summary statistic should be called *time-unit kappa*, or *time-unit kappa with tolerance*, to distinguish it from the classic Cohen's kappa.

One aspect of time-unit kappa seems troublesome. With the classic Cohen model, the number of tallies represents the number of decisions each observer makes, whereas with time-unit kappa, the number of tallies represents the length of the session (e.g., when time units are seconds, a 5-minute session generates 300 tallies). With timed-event recording, observers are continuously looking for the seams between events, but how often they are making decisions is arguable, probably unknowable. One decision per seam seems too few—the observers are continuously alert—but one per time unit seems too many. Moreover, the number of tallies increases with the precision of the time unit (although multiplying all cells in an agreement matrix by the same factor does not change the value of kappa; see Bakeman & Gottman, 1997).

Thus the second solution is to align the events in the two observers' timed-event sequential data and compute an event-based kappa. Compared with tallying time units, tallying agreements and disagreements between aligned events probably underestimates the number of decisions observers actually make, but at least the number of tallies is closer to the number of events coded. Consequently, we modified our untimed-event alignment algorithm to work with timed-event sequential data and compared this algorithm with ones available in The Observer and INTERACT (Bakeman et al., 2009). Kappas with the different event-matching algorithms were not dramatically different; time-based and event-based kappas varied more.

In sum, we recommend as follows: When assessing observer agreement for interval-recorded data, use the classic Cohen's kappa. For untimed-event recorded data, use our event-matching algorithm, which allows for omission–commission errors, and report the event-based kappa. For timed-event data, compute and report both an event-based and a time-based kappa (with or without tolerance); their range likely captures the *true* value of kappa (both are computed by GSEQ). Moreover, examining individual cells of the kappa table provides observers with useful feedback. In the case of timed-event data, observers should examine agreement matrixes for both event-based and time-unit-based kappas. Each provides somewhat different but valuable information about disagreements, which can be useful as observers strive to improve their agreement.

Acceptable Values for Kappa

A value of .76 or .60, like those in Figures 13.5 and 13.6, may not seem like a particularly good level of agreement, which raises the question, what value of kappa is acceptable? Are their benchmarks for fair, good, and excellent? The simple answer is no: There is no single value for kappa that is universally acceptable, no benchmarks that can be universally applied (Bakeman et al., 1997; Bakeman & Quera, 2011)—even though it is possible to find articles that provide such benchmarks, mainly from the 1970s and 1980s, and later articles that cite them uncritically. But the correct answer is, it depends—primarily on the number of codes, but also on how variable code frequencies are (prevalence) and whether observer prevalence differs (bias).

Given a particular kappa table, Gardner (1995) developed equations to estimate how accurate observers would need to be to produce the kappa obtained, given the number of codes and their marginal distributions (i.e., taking into account possible prevalence and bias problems). Based on Gardner's equations, Bakeman (2022) developed a computer program that provides this estimate (KappaAcc). However, once estimated accuracy is computed, we need to decide what level is acceptable. Gardner characterized 80% as discouragingly low, "but possibly representative of the accuracy of classification for some social behavior or expressions of affect" (p. 347). For the examples in Figures 13.5 and 13.6, estimated accuracy was 90% and 82%. The 82% is a bit less than we might like, although still acceptable, but generally we think 85% or 90% accuracy are better targets.

Kappa With Rating Scales

As the title of Cohen's (1960) classic article indicates, kappa was initially intended as a coefficient of agreement for nominal scales. But kappa can also be used with ordinal scales. Each cell of the kappa table can be assigned a weight. The classic kappa results when cells on the diagonal are weighted 0 (agreements) and other cells are weighted 1 (disagreements). But different weights could be assigned (Cohen, 1968). This can be especially useful when rows represent, not nominal codes, but ordinal ratings. As an example, imagine that the rows and columns of Figure 13.5 represented ordinal 1-to-5 ratings instead of codes. We might then define disagreements of one scale point as agreements, weighting as 0 not just the cells on the diagonal but cells just off the diagonal as well. In this case, the classic kappa would remain the same (.76), but weighted kappa would be .89, and estimated accuracy 95% (weighted kappa computed with the KappaAcc program; Bakeman, 2022).

Observer Agreement During Data Collection and Data Analysis

Earlier we characterized observer agreement as the sine qua non of observational measurement. In the next section, we note that, with observational studies, often the data analyzed are not the data collected but are summary statistics derived from that data. Typically, the observational data collected are binary, nominal, or ordinal, but summary statistics analyzed are often integer or continuous. Thus, the typical observational research project proceeds in two phases, data collection and data analysis, each with different needs.

This section has emphasized kappa—and the kappa table—recognizing their importance in the data collection phase. For the typical project, once sessions have been recorded, data collection consists of observers coding or rating sessions. Some sessions—usually 15% to 20% or so—will be double coded, that is, independently coded by a second observer to assess observer agreement. Best practice is to keep observers unaware as to which sessions will be double coded and to space them randomly. Such double-coded sessions serve a second purpose, however, which is to guard against observer drift. After sessions have been double coded, primary observers, reliability observers, and investigators review disagreements, with the aim of keeping all calibrated. For this purpose, the kappa table is more useful than the value of kappa, pinpointing as it does specific disagreements (for further practical advice, see Bakeman & Goodman, 2020).

Intraclass correlation coefficient. A second agreement statistic, less emphasized here, is the intraclass correlation coefficient (ICC), a statistic that relies on continuous data and is similar to the analysis of variance. It can be used to assess the reliability of various scores derived from double-coded observational sessions (see Bakeman & Quera, 2011). It can also be used to assess the reliability of rating scale data (although this requires the assumption that the ordinal intervals are roughly equal).

In sum, kappa is useful when codes are categorical and for training observers and providing feedback during data collection, whereas the ICC and related statistics can be useful for rating scales and once data collection is complete and the focus has shifted to the various summary scores derived from the data collected. Hallgren (2012) provided a clear exposition of assessing interrater reliability using ICCs. Intraclass correlations can be easily computed using standard statistical software such as SPPS, or with Mangold's free ICC Calculator, http://www.raterreliability.com.

Krippendorff's alpha. A third agreement statistic that some investigators may find useful is Krippendroff's (2013) alpha. It is a conceptually similar, generalization of Cohen's kappa that is applicable to any number of coders, incomplete data, and binary, nominal, ordinal, and continuous scales of measurement. For two observers, its values are the same as Cohen's kappa.

Reporting Observer Agreement

Reporting levels of observer agreement, using any of the statistics described here, is an essential part of any research report involving observational methods, and human observers are usually an essential part of the measuring apparatus. As such, their characteristics—demographics and training—should be reported as well. This is not yet standard practice, but it should be.

ANALYZING OBSERVATIONAL DATA: SIMPLE STATISTICS

Perhaps more with behavioral observation than other measurement methods, the data collected initially are not analyzed directly. Intervening steps may be required with other methods—for example, producing a summary score from the items of a self-esteem questionnaire—but with observational data, producing summary scores and data reduction generally are almost always required. In the process, the usual categorical or binary measurements reflected in the data collected are transformed into scores for which, typically, integer or continuous measurement can be assumed. As with scores generally, so too with summary scores derived from behavioral observation, the first analytic step involves description, the results of which may limit subsequent analyses (as, e.g., when inappropriate distributions argue against analyses of variance). But what summary scores should be derived and described first?

It is useful to distinguish between simple statistics that do not take sequencing or contingency into account (described in this section) and contingency statistics that do take contingency into account (described in the section Analyzing Observational Data: Contingency Indexes). It makes sense to describe simple statistics first because, if their values are not appropriate, computation of some contingency statistics may be precluded or at best questionable. Simple statistics based on behavioral observation are relatively few in number, but, as you might expect, their interpretation depends on the data recording and representation methods used.

Seven Basic Statistics

In the following paragraphs, we describe seven basic statistics, note how data type affects their interpretation, and recommend which statistics are most useful for each data type.

Frequency. *Frequency* indicates how often. For event or timed-event data, it is the number of times an event occurred (i.e., was coded). For interval or multievent data, it is the number of bouts coded, that is, the number of times a code was checked without being checked for the previous interval or multievent; that is, if the same code occurred in successive intervals or multievents, one is added to its frequency count. As noted shortly, for interval and multievent data, duration gives the number of units checked.

Rate. *Rate* is the frequency per a specified amount of time and likewise indicates how often. Rate is preferable to frequency when sessions vary in length because it is comparable across sessions. Rates may be expressed per minute, per hour, or per any other time unit that makes sense. The session durations required to compute rate can be derived from the data for timed-event and interval data, but to compute rates for event or multievent data requires that session start and stop times be recorded explicitly.

Relative frequency. *Relative frequency* indicates proportionate use of codes. For all data types, it is a code's frequency, as just defined, divided by the sum of frequencies for all codes in a specified set, hence relative frequencies necessarily sum to 1. Alternatively, relative frequencies can be expressed as percentages summing to 100%.

For example, if we only coded mother vocalization, we might discover that 22% of a mother's vocalizations were coded *naming*. As discussed shortly, depending on your specific research questions relative frequency may or may not be a statistic you choose to analyze.

Duration. *Duration* indicates how long or how many. For timed-event data, duration indicates how much time during the session a particular code occurred. For simple event data, duration is the same as frequency. For interval or multievent data, duration indicates the number of intervals or multievents checked for a particular code; thus, duration may be a more useful summary statistic for these data types than frequency, which, as just noted, indicates the number of bouts.

Probability. *Probability* indicates likelihood. It can be expressed as either a proportion or a percentage. For timed-event data, it is duration divided by total session time, leading to statements like, "the baby was asleep for 46% of the session." For simple event data, it is the same as relative frequency. For interval or multievent data, it is duration divided by the total number of intervals or multievents, leading to statements like, solitary play was coded for 18% of the intervals.

Relative duration. *Relative duration* indicates proportionate use of time for timed-event data and of intervals or multievents for interval and multievent data. For all data types, it is a code's duration, as just defined, divided by the sum of durations for all codes; thus, it only makes sense when the codes specified form a single ME&E set. As with relative frequency, relative durations necessarily sum to 1 and can also be expressed as percentages summing to 100%. For example, when coding mother vocalizations, we might discover that 37% of the time when mother's vocalizations were occurring, they were coded *naming*. As with relative frequency, depending on your specific research questions, relative duration may or may not be a statistic you choose to analyze.

Mean bout duration. *Mean bout duration* indicates how long events last, on average, and makes sense primarily for timed-event data. It is duration divided by frequency, as just defined. When computed for interval or multievent data, it indicates the mean number of successive intervals or multievents checked for a particular code.

Recommended Statistics by Data Type

No matter whether your sessions are organized by a group or a single-subject design, we assume you will compute summary statistics for individual sessions (i.e., analytic units) and then subject those scores to further analyses. In the next few paragraphs, we discuss the simple summary statistics we think are most useful for each data type and, reversing our usual order, begin with timed-event data, which offers the most options.

For timed-event data, we think the most useful summary statistics indicate how often, how likely, and how long. Rate and probability are comparable across sessions (i.e., control for differences in session length) and therefore usually are preferable to frequency and duration. Mean bout duration provides useful description as well, but here you have a choice. These three statistics are not independent (mean bout length is duration divided by frequency), and thus you may present just two of them, or if you describe all three, be aware that any analyses are not independent. Finally, use relative frequency or duration only if clearly required by your research questions.

With timed-event data a key question is, should you use rate, probability, or both? These two statistics provide different, independent information about your codes; they may or may not be correlated. The answer is, it depends on your research question. For example, do you think that how often a mother corrects her child is important? Then use rate. Or, do you think that the amount of time (expressed as a proportion or percentage of the session) a mother corrects her child (or a child experiences being corrected) is important? Then use probability. Whichever you use (or both), always provide your readers with an explicit rationale for your choice; otherwise, they may think your decision was thoughtless.

For other data types, matters are simpler. For simple event data, we think the most useful summary statistics indicate how often and how likely—that is, frequency (or rate when sessions vary in length and start and stop times were recorded) and probability. Finally, for interval and multievent data, we think the most useful summary statistic indicates how likely—that is, how many intervals or multievents were checked for a particular code. With these data types, use other statistics only if clearly required by your research questions.

ANALYZING OBSERVATIONAL DATA: CONTINGENCY INDEXES

The summary statistics described in the previous section were called simple, but they could also be called one-dimensional because each statistic is computed for a single code. In contrast, the summary statistics described in this section could be called two-dimensional because they combine information about two codes, arranged in two-dimensional contingency tables. Still, the overall strategy is the same; summary statistics are computed for individual sessions followed by appropriate statistical analyses.

Statistics derived from two-dimensional tables are of three kinds. First are statistics for individual cells; these are primarily descriptive. Second are summary statistics for 2 × 2 tables; these indexes of contingency often turn out to be the most useful analytically. And third are summary indexes of independence and association for tables of varying dimensions such as Pearson chi-square and Cohen's kappa; because these are well-known or already discussed, we will not discuss them further here but instead focus on individual cell and 2 × 2 table statistics.

Statistics for Individual Cells

Statistics for the individual cells of a contingency table can be computed for tables of varying dimension but for illustrative purposes we give examples for the 2 × 2 table shown in Figure 13.7. The rows represent infant cry, columns represent mother soothe, and the total number of tallies is 100. This could be 100 events, or 100 intervals, or 100 time units, depending on data type. Usually for timed-event and often for interval or multievent

Given	Target		
	Soothe	No soothe	Total
Cry	13	11	24
No cry	21	55	76
Total	34	66	100

p(cry) = 24/200 = .24
p(soothe) = 34/100 = .34
p(cry|soothe) = 13/24 = .54

Odds ratio = (13/11)/(21/55) = 1.18/0.38 = 3.10
Log odds = 1.13
Yule's Q = .51

FIGURE 13.7. Determining the association between infant cry and maternal soothe: An example of a 2 × 2 table tallying 1-second time units and its associated statistics.

data, rows and columns are unlagged, that is, they represent concurrent time units, intervals, or events (i.e., Lag 0). For simple event data, columns usually are lagged (because all co-occurrences are zero); thus rows might represent Lag 0 and columns Lag 1, in which case the number of tallies would be one less than the number of simple events coded.

In the following paragraphs, we give definitions for the five most common cell statistics and provide numeric examples derived from the data in Figure 13.7. In these definitions, r specifies a row, c a column, f_{rc} the frequency count for a given cell, f_{r+} a row sum, f_{+c} a column sum, f_{++} the total number of tallies for the table, and p_i the simple probability for a row or column (e.g., $p_r = f_{r+} \div f_{++}$).

Observed joint frequency. The observed joint frequency is f_{rc}. The joint frequency for cry and soothe is 13.

Conditional probability. The *conditional probability* is the probability for the column (or target) behavior given the row (or given) behavior: $p(c|r) = f_{rc} \div f_{r+}$. The conditional probabilities in a row necessarily sum to 1. The probability of a mother soothe given an infant cry is .54 and of no soothe given infant cry is .46.

Expected frequency. The *expected frequency* is the frequency expected by chance given the simple probability for the column behavior and the frequency for the row behavior: $exp_{rc} = p_c \times f_{r+} = (f_{+c} \div f_{++}) \times f_{r+}$. The expected frequency for cry and soothe is 8.16, which is less than the observed value of 13.

Raw residual. The *raw residual* is the difference between observed and expected: $res_{rc} = f_{rc} - exp_{rc}$. The observed joint frequency for cry and soothe exceeds the expected value by 4.84 (13 – 8.16).

Adjusted residual. The *adjusted residual* is the raw residual divided by its estimated standard error: $z_{rc} = (f_{rc} - exp_{rc}) \div SE_{rc}$ where SE_{rc} = square root of $exp_{rc} \times (1 - p_c) \times (1 - p_r)$. The standard error is the square root of $8.16 \times .76 \times .66 = 2.02$, thus $z_{rc} = 4.84 \div 2.02 = 2.39$. If adjusted residuals were distributed normally we could say that the probability of a result this extreme by chance is less than .05 because 2.39 exceeds 1.96.

Of these statistics, perhaps the adjusted residual is the most useful. Values that are large and positive, or large and negative, indicate co-occurrences (or lagged associations) greater, or less, than expected by chance; a useful guideline is to pay attention to values greater than 3 absolute. Of the others, the conditional probability is useful descriptively but not analytically because its values are contaminated by its simple probabilities. For example, if cry occurs frequently, then values of soothe given cry are likely to be higher than if cry was not as frequent. In other words, the more frequently a code occurs, the more likely another code is to co-occur. The adjusted residual is a better candidate for subsequent analyses, but 2×2 contingency indexes as described in the next paragraph may be even better.

Contingency Indexes for 2 × 2 Tables

When research questions involve the contingency between two behaviors, one presumed antecedent and the other consequent (i.e., before and after, given and target, or row and column), tables of any dimensions can be reduced to a 2×2 table like the one shown in Figure 13.7. In this table, rows are labeled *given behavior*, *yes* or *no*, and columns are labeled *target behavior*, *yes* or *no*. This is advantageous because then the contingency between the presumed given and target behavior can be assessed with standard summary statistics for 2×2 tables. In the next several paragraphs, we provide definitions for five summary statistics typically defined but probably only one or two are needed. As is conventional, we label the cells of the 2×2 table as follows: $f_{11} = a$, $f_{12} = b$, $f_{21} = c$, $f_{22} = d$. Again, numeric examples are derived from the data in Figure 13.7.

Odds ratio. The *odds ratio* is a measure of effect size whose interpretation is straightforward and concrete: $OR = (a/b)/(c/d)$. It is useful descriptively and deserves to be used more by behavioral scientists (it is already widely used by epidemiologists). As the name implies, it is the ratio of two odds, derived from the top and bottom rows of a 2×2 table. For example, the odds of soothe to no soothe when crying are 13 to 11 or 1.18 to 1 and when not crying are 21 to 55 or 0.38 to 1, thus $OR = 1.18/0.38 = 3.10$. Concretely, this means that the likelihood (odds) of the mother soothing her infant are more than three times greater when her infant is crying than when not.

The odds ratio varies from 0 to infinity, with 1 indicating no effect. Values greater than 1 indicate that the target behavior (in column 1) is more likely in the presence of the given behavior (row 1) than its absence (row 2), whereas values less than 1 indicate that the target behavior (in column 1) is more likely in the absence of the given behavior (row 2) than its presence (row 1). If rows are reordered, the value of the odds ratio becomes its reciprocal (e.g., 0.67 becomes 1.5), thus—because we humans often find it easier to interpret numbers great than 1—values less than one can be avoided. Nonetheless—due to its concrete interpretation—the odds ratio is always useful descriptively.

Perhaps the best way to display its distribution in a given instance is with a box-and-whisker plot (Tukey, 1977). The box encloses 50% of the scores, the whiskers show the extent of scores that aren't extreme (1.5 times the interquartile range, as defined by Tukey), and any extreme scores are indicated with symbols. Because odds ratios can vary from 0 to infinity, distributions often are skewed, and the box-and-whisker plot can show how little or how much for a given instance (see Figure 13.8).

Qualitative terms, although arbitrary, are often helpful for interpretation and discussion. Expanding on benchmarks proposed by Haddock et al. (1998)—odds ratios close to 1.0 indicate *weak relationships*, whereas odds ratios over 3.0 or less than 0.33 indicate *strong relationships*—we have proposed that odds ratios between 1.25 and 2.00 (or 0.50–0.80) should be regarded as *weak*, and those between 2.00 and 3.00 (or 0.33–0.50) should be regarded as *moderate* (Bakeman & Quera, 2011). Thus, over half of the odds ratios portrayed in Figure 13.8 indicate moderate or strong associations.

Log odds. The *log odds* is the natural logarithm of the odds ratio: $LnOR = log_e OR$. For example, $log_e 3.10 = 1.13$ (i.e., $e^{1.13} = 3.10$, where $e = .2718\ldots$). It varies from negative to positive infinity, with zero indicating no effect and, compared with the odds ratio, its distributions are less likely to be skewed. However, it is expressed in difficult-to-interpret logarithmic units. It is sometimes recommended for use analytically (e.g., as values of a dependent variable in an ANOVA), but whether it is the best transformation or whether any transformation is even warranted, is something for individual investigators to determine.

Yule's Q. This index of effect size is a straightforward algebraic transform of the odds ratio: $Q = (ad - bc) / (ad + bc)$ (Bakeman et al., 2005). It is like the familiar correlation coefficient in two ways: it varies from -1 to $+1$ with 0 indicating no effect, and its units have no natural meaning. Thus its interpretation is not as concrete as the odds ratio.

Phi coefficient. The *phi coefficient* is a Pearson product-moment correlation coefficient computed for binary data. Like Yule's Q, it can vary from -1 to $+1$ but can only achieve its maximum value when $p_r = p_c = .5$, thus Yule's Q almost always seems preferable.

Risk difference. The *risk difference* is the difference between two conditional probabilities: $RD = a/(a + b) - c/(c + d)$, but an algebraic transformation—$RD = (ad - bc) / (ac + ad + bc + bd)$—shows its similarity to Yule's Q. If no cells are zero, values for the risk difference will correlate highly with but be slightly less than values for Yule's Q. However, if a cell is zero, the risk difference is the better index because it takes into account values in all cells. For example, if $b = 0$, Yule's Q = 1 no matter the $c:d$ odds, whereas $RD = .05$ if $c:d = 19:1$ and .95 if $c:d = 1:19$.

Which contingency index should you use, the odds ratio descriptively and the log odds analytically, or Yule's Q for both? It is probably a matter of taste. We think the odds ratio is more concretely descriptive, but Yule's Q may seem more natural to some, especially those schooled in correlation coefficients. Another consideration is computational vulnerability to zero cells. A large positive effect (column 1 behavior more

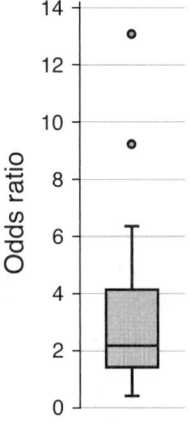

FIGURE 13.8. Box-and-whisker plot for odds ratios showing child's response to mother prompt for a novel word. The box includes scores from the 25th to the 75th percentile. The whiskers indicate the lowest and highest scores that are not extreme. Extreme scores, defined as any 1.5 times the interquartile range below the 25th or above the 75th percentile, are indicated with circles. Adapted from "How Parents Introduce New Words to Young Children: The Influence of Development and Developmental Disorders," by L. B. Adamson, R. Bakeman, and B. Brandon, 2015, *Infant Behavior and Development*, 39, pp. 148–158 (https://doi.org/10.1016/j.infbeh.2015.02.008). Copyright 2015 by Elsevier. Adapted with permission.

likely given row 1 behavior) occurs as *b* (or *c*) tends toward zero and a large negative effect (column 1 behavior less likely given row 1 behavior) occurs as *a* (or *d*) tends toward zero. If only one cell is zero, a large negative and a large positive effect is computed as −1 and +1 for Yule's Q, 0 and infinity for the odds ratio, and both undefined (log of 0, divide by 0) for the logs odds. Thus Yule's Q is not vulnerable to zero cells, the odds ratio is vulnerable only if *b* or *c* are zero (using the computational formula, *ad/bc*, for the odds ratio), and the log odds is vulnerable if any cell is zero—which leads Wickens (1989), among others, to advocate adding a small constant, typically 0.5, to each cell before computing a log odds. However, if a cell is zero, the risk difference should be used and not Yule's Q.

One circumstance is always fatal. If two or more cells are zero—which means that one or more row or column sums are zero—no contingency index can be computed and subsequent analyses would treat its value as missing. After all, if one of the behaviors does not occur, no contingency can be observed. Even when row or column sums are not zero but simply small, it may be wise to treat the value as missing. With few observations, there is little reason to have confidence in its value even when computation is technically possible. Our guideline is, if any row or column sum is less than 5, regard the value of the contingency index as missing, but some investigators may prefer a more stringent guideline.

Lag Sequential Analysis for Simple Event Data

Given simple event data and lagged contingency tables, either the adjusted residuals or the contingency indexes just described could be used for a lag sequential analysis. For example, if Figure 13.7 represented Lag 1 event data (given labeled Lag 0, target Lag 1, and tallying events and not time units), we could say that the probability of a soothe event following a cry event was .54, which is greater than the simple probability of soothe (.34). Moreover, the adjusted residual was 2.39 and the Yule's Q was .51, both positive. (For a more detailed description of event-based lag sequential analysis see Bakeman & Gottman, 1997, pp. 111–116.)

Time-Window Sequential Analysis for Timed-Event Data

Given timed-event data, traditional lag sequential analysis (using time units to indicate lags) does not work very well. Time-window sequential analysis (Bakeman, 2004; Bakeman et al., 2005; Yoder & Tapp, 2004) works better, allows more flexibility, and, incidentally, demonstrates the usefulness of the contingency indexes just described (e.g., Chorney et al., 2010). The generic question is, is the target behavior contingent on the given behavior. First, we define a window of opportunity or *time window* for the given behavior. For example, we might say for a behavior to be contingent, we need to see a response within 3 seconds; thus we would code the onset second of the given behavior and the following 2 seconds as a given window (assuming 1-second precision). Second, we code any second in which the target behavior starts as a target onset. Third, we tally time units for the session into a 2 × 2 table, and fourth, we compute a contingency index for the table (this can all be done with GSEQ).

For example, assume the tallies in Figure 13.7 represent 1-second time units, that *soothe* refers to the onset of verbal reassurance (it is probably better to imagine a behavior more quick and frequent than soothe for this example), and that *cry* refers to a cry window (e.g., within 3 seconds of a cry onset). Thus in 100 seconds there were 34 reassure episodes (onsets or bouts) and probably 8 episodes of infant cry (assuming the 24 seconds total divide into eight 3-second windows). For this example, reassure and cry appear associated. The likelihood that reassure would begin within 3 seconds of a cry starting was 3 times greater than at other times (and Yule's Q was .51). Descriptively, 38% (13 of 34) of reassure episodes began during cry windows although the windows accounted for 24% of the time. It only remains to compute such indexes for other sessions and use those scores in whatever analyses make sense given your design.

CONCLUSION

Behavioral observation is one of several measurement approaches available to investigators engaged in quantitative behavioral research. It is often the method of choice when nonverbal organisms are studied (or nonverbal behavior generally); when more natural, spontaneous, real-world behavior is of interest; and when processes and not outcomes are the focus (e.g., questions of contingency). Compared with other approaches, it is often labor-intensive and time-consuming.

Coding schemes—the basic measuring instrument of behavioral observation—need to be developed and observers trained in their reliable use, and the often-voluminous data initially collected need to be reduced to simple rates and probabilities or contingency indexes for later analyses. Behavior can be observed live or recorded for later viewing (and re-viewing). Observers either assign codes to predetermined time intervals (interval recording) or detect and code events in the stream of behavior (event recording), using instruments that vary from simple pencil and paper to sophisticated computer systems.

Coded data can be represented in a code-unit grid as interval, untimed-event or multievent, or timed-event data; the latter offers the most options but works best with electronic equipment. Behavioral observation can be used for experimental or nonexperimental studies, in laboratory or field settings, and with single-subject or group designs using between- or within-subjects variables. Summary scores derived from observational sessions can be subjected to any appropriate statistical approach from null-hypothesis testing to mathematical modeling (Rodgers, 2010).

References

Adamson, L. B., Bakeman, R., & Brandon, B. (2015). How parents introduce new words to young children: The influence of development and developmental disorders. *Infant Behavior and Development*, *39*, 148–158. https://doi.org/10.1016/j.infbeh.2015.02.008

Altmann, J. (1974). Observational study of behavior: Sampling methods. *Behaviour*, *49*(3-4), 227–266. https://doi.org/10.1163/156853974X00534

Bakeman, R. (2004). Sequential analysis. In M. Lewis-Beck, A. E. Bryman, & T. F. Liao (Eds.), *The SAGE encyclopedia of social science research methods* (Vol. 3, pp. 1024–1026). SAGE.

Bakeman, R. (2010). Reflections on measuring behavior: Time and the grid. In G. Walford, E. Tucker, & M. Viswanathan (Eds.), *The SAGE handbook of measurement* (pp. 221–238). SAGE. https://doi.org/10.4135/9781446268230.n12

Bakeman, R. (2022). KappaAcc: A program for assessing the adequacy of kappa. *Behavior Research Methods*. https://doi.org/10.3758/s13428-022-01836-1

Bakeman, R., Adamson, L. B., Konner, M., & Barr, R. G. (1990). !Kung infancy: The social context of object exploration. *Child Development*, *61*(3), 794–809. https://doi.org/10.2307/1130964

Bakeman, R., Deckner, D. F., & Quera, V. (2005). Analysis of behavioral streams. In D. M. Teti (Ed.), *Handbook of research methods in developmental science* (pp. 394–420). Blackwell. https://doi.org/10.1002/9780470756676.ch20

Bakeman, R., & Goodman, S. H. (2020). Interobserver reliability in clinical research: Current issues and discussion of how to establish best practices. *Journal of Abnormal Psychology*, *129*(1), 5–13. https://doi.org/10.1037/abn0000487

Bakeman, R., & Gottman, J. M. (1986). *Observing interaction: An introduction to sequential analysis*. Cambridge University Press.

Bakeman, R., & Gottman, J. M. (1997). *Observing interaction: An introduction to sequential analysis* (2nd ed.). Cambridge University Press. https://doi.org/10.1017/CBO9780511527685

Bakeman, R., & Helmreich, R. (1975). Cohesiveness and performance: Covariation and causality in an undersea environment. *Journal of Experimental Social Psychology*, *11*(5), 478–489. https://doi.org/10.1016/0022-1031(75)90050-5

Bakeman, R., McArthur, D., Quera, V., & Robinson, B. F. (1997). Detecting sequential patterns and determining their reliability with fallible observers. *Psychological Methods*, *2*(4), 357–370. https://doi.org/10.1037/1082-989X.2.4.357

Bakeman, R., & Quera, V. (1992). SDIS: A sequential data interchange standard. *Behavior Research Methods, Instruments, & Computers*, *24*(4), 554–559. https://doi.org/10.3758/BF03203604

Bakeman, R., & Quera, V. (1995). *Analyzing interaction: Sequential analysis with SDIS and GSEQ*. Cambridge University Press.

Bakeman, R., & Quera, V. (2009). *GSEQ 5* [Computer program]. Retrieved from Georgia State University website https://bakeman.gsucreate.org/gseq or https://www.mangold-international.com/en/products/software/gseq

Bakeman, R., & Quera, V. (2011). *Sequential analysis and observational methods for the behavioral sciences*. Cambridge University Press. https://doi.org/10.1017/CBO9781139017343

Bakeman, R., Quera, V., & Gnisci, A. (2009). Observer agreement for timed-event sequential data: A comparison of time-based and event-based algorithms. *Behavior Research Methods*, *41*(1), 137–147. https://doi.org/10.3758/BRM.41.1.137

Bakeman, R., & Robinson, B. F. (1994). *Understanding log-linear analysis with ILOG: An interactive approach*. Erlbaum.

Chorney, J. M., Garcia, A. M., Berlin, K. S., Bakeman, R., & Kain, Z. N. (2010). Time-window sequential analysis: An introduction for pediatric psychologists. *Journal of Pediatric Psychology*, *35*(10), 1061–1070. https://doi.org/10.1093/jpepsy/jsq022

Cohen, J. (1968). Weighted kappa: Nominal scale agreement with provision for scaled disagreement or partial credit. *Psychological Bulletin*, *70*(4), 213–220. https://doi.org/10.1037/h0026256

Cohen, J. A. (1960). A coefficient of agreement for nominal scales. *Educational and Psychological Measurement*, *20*(1), 37–46. https://doi.org/10.1177/001316446002000104

Cohn, J. F., & Kanade, T. (2007). Use of automated facial image analysis for measurement of emotion expression. In J. A. Coan & J. J. B. Allen (Eds.), *Oxford University Press Series in Affective Science: The handbook of emotion elicitation and assessment* (pp. 222–238). Oxford University Press.

Cox, D. R., & Donnelly, C. A. (2011). *Principles of applied statistics*. Cambridge University Press. https://doi.org/10.1017/CBO9781139005036

Douglass, W. (1760). *A summary, historical and political, of the first planting, progressive improvements, and present state of the British settlements in North-America* (Vol. 1). R. & J. Dodsley.

Ekman, P. W., & Friesen, W. (1978). *Facial action coding system: A technique for the measurement of facial movement*. Consulting Psychologist Press.

Galisson, F. (2000, August). *Introduction to computational sequence analysis*. Tutorial presented at the Eighth International Conference on Intelligent Systems for Molecular Biology, San Diego, CA, United States. https://www.iscb.org/ismb2000/tutorial_pdf/galisson4.pdf

Gardner, W. (1995). On the reliability of sequential data: Measurement, meaning, and correction. In J. M. Gottman (Ed.), *The analysis of change* (pp. 339–359). Erlbaum.

Gottman, J. M. (1979). *Marital interaction: Experimental investigations*. Academic Press.

Gros-Louis, J., West, M. J., Goldstein, M. H., & King, A. P. (2006). Mothers provide differential feedback to infants' prelinguistic sounds. *International Journal of Behavioral Development*, *30*(6), 509–516. https://doi.org/10.1177/0165025406071914

Haddock, C., Rindskopf, D., & Shadish, W. (1998). Using odds ratios as effect sizes for meta-analysis of dichotomous data: A primer on methods and issues. *Psychological Methods*, *3*(3), 339–353. https://doi.org/10.1037/1082-989X.3.3.339

Hallgren, K. A. (2012). Computing inter-rater reliability for observational data: An overview and tutorial. *Tutorials in Quantitative Methods for Psychology*, *8*(1), 23–34. https://doi.org/10.20982/tqmp.08.1.p023

Konner, M. J. (1976). Maternal care, infant behavior, and development among the !Kung. In R. B. DeVore (Ed.), *Kalahari hunter-gathers* (pp. 218–245). Harvard University Press.

Krippendorff, K. (2013). *Content analysis: An introduction to its methodology* (3rd ed.). SAGE.

Martin, P., & Bateson, P. (2007). *Measuring behaviour: An introductory guide* (3rd ed.). Cambridge University Press. https://doi.org/10.1017/CBO9780511810893

Needleman, S. B., & Wunsch, C. D. (1970). A general method applicable to the search for similarities in the amino acid sequence of two proteins. *Journal of Molecular Biology*, *48*(3), 443–453. https://doi.org/10.1016/0022-2836(70)90057-4

Oller, D. K. (2000). *The emergence of the speech capacity*. Erlbaum. https://doi.org/10.4324/9781410602565

Parten, M. B. (1932). Social participation among pre-school children. *Journal of Abnormal and Social Psychology*, *27*(3), 243–269. https://doi.org/10.1037/h0074524

Quera, V. (2018). Analysis of interaction sequences. In E. Brauner, M. Boos, & M. Kolbe (Eds.), *The Cambridge handbook of group interaction analysis* (pp. 295–322). Cambridge University Press. https://doi.org/10.1017/9781316286302.016

Quera, V., Bakeman, R., & Gnisci, A. (2007). Observer agreement for event sequences: Methods and software for sequence alignment and reliability estimates. *Behavior Research Methods*, *39*(1), 39–49. https://doi.org/10.3758/BF03192842

Rodgers, J. L. (2010). The epistemology of mathematical and statistical modeling: A quiet methodological revolution. *American Psychologist*, *65*(1), 1–12. https://doi.org/10.1037/a0018326

Sankoff, D., & Kruskal, J. (Eds.). (1999). *Time warps, string edits, and macromolecules: The theory and practice of sequence comparison.* CSLI. (Original work published 1983)

Stevens, S. S. (1946). On the theory of scales of measurement. *Science, 103*(2684), 677–680. https://doi.org/10.1126/science.103.2684.677

Suen, H. K., & Ary, D. (1989). *Analyzing quantitative behavioral data.* Erlbaum.

Trenado, R. M., Cerezo, M. A., Sierra-García, P., & Pons-Salvador, G. (2021). Sequential coding of maternal sensitivity: Application of nonlinear dynamic analyses and reliability. *Quality & Quantity, 55,* 827–844. https://doi.org/10.1007/s11135-020-01027-0

Tukey, J. (1977). *Exploratory data analysis.* Addison-Wesley.

Wickens, T. D. (1989). *Multiway contingency tables analysis for the social sciences.* Erlbaum.

Wolff, P. H. (1966). The causes, controls, and organization of behavior in the neonate. *Psychological Issues, 5*(1), 1–105.

Yoder, P., & Symons, F. (2010). *Observational measurement of behavior.* Springer.

Yoder, P. J., & Tapp, J. (2004). Empirical guidance for time-window sequential analysis of single cases. *Journal of Behavioral Education, 13*(4), 227–246. https://doi.org/10.1023/B:JOBE.0000044733.03220.a9

SECTION 2

SELF-REPORT

CHAPTER 14

QUESTION ORDER EFFECTS

Lisa Lee, Parvati Krishnamurty, and Struther Van Horn

A *question order effect* occurs when responses to an earlier question on a questionnaire affect responses to a later one. Because questionnaire designers must settle on some ordering of questions, question order effects are always a possibility. In this chapter, we review the literature on empirical studies of survey question order effects, discuss mechanisms and moderators of these effects, and provide guidance for questionnaire construction based on results of the studies.

Question order effects are sometimes categorized more generally as context effects because the prior question is thought to provide a context in which to view the subsequent question. However, strictly speaking, survey context is broader than question order and can involve instructions, letters, brochures, electronic media, and other materials presented as part of the survey. A question order effect is a special type of context effect. Question order effects can present serious problems when measuring change over time, whether in longitudinal surveys or in repeated cross-sectional surveys, or even when comparing the results of different cross-sectional surveys. Unless the question order is the same for each data collection, it is difficult to know whether change (or its absence) is due to real respondent change or to effects of question order.

Schuman and Presser (1981) presented the first extensive review of question order effects with a focus on studies of public opinion. They identified three basic kinds of question order effects: (a) unconditional question order effects, in which answers to the subsequent question are affected by having responded to the prior question but not necessarily affected by the response given on the prior question; (b) conditional question order effects, in which answers to the subsequent question depend on the response given to the prior question; and (c) associational question order effects, in which the correlation between two questions changes depending on which one is asked first. It should be noted that conditional question order effects and associational effects are two different ways of looking at the same phenomenon. Most often, conditional effects are expressed as differences in association.

Although Schuman and Presser (1981) did not provide a general framework for understanding and predicting question order effects, the increasing emphasis on psychology and surveys beginning in the early 1980s changed that. For the first time, the cognitive task of the respondent, rather than just the substance of the question, was given

---

The authors would like to thank Kenneth A. Rasinski, who was the lead author on the 2012 version of this chapter.

This chapter was authored by an employee or employees of the United States government as part of official duty and is considered to be in the public domain. Any views expressed herein do not necessarily represent the views of the United States government, and the author's participation in the work is not meant to serve as an official endorsement.

https://doi.org/10.1037/0000318-014
APA Handbook of Research Methods in Psychology, Second Edition: Vol. 1. Foundations, Planning, Measures, and Psychometrics, H. Cooper (Editor-in-Chief)

serious consideration. This breakthrough led to theories about the types of judgment required by a question and experimental work to test hypotheses about the psychology of the survey response process. The work of Tourangeau and his colleagues (Tourangeau, 1984; Tourangeau et al., 2000) extended psychological theory and research to survey response processes. They presented a model of psychological mechanisms likely to underlie survey responding. Their model emphasizes the cognitive tasks of the survey respondent—interpreting a question, retrieving relevant information from memory, forming a response, and reporting the response.

For question order effects, all of these tasks may come into play; explanations for question order effects could be based on tests of hypotheses generated from theories about how respondents process survey questions, rather than by post hoc explanations of observed phenomena. Based on the psychological mechanisms that underlie survey response, the context that precedes a question may affect how respondents *interpret* the question and *recall* relevant information. For example, a study on nutrition might ask respondents how often they eat five servings of fruits and vegetables each day. Preceding questions about specific fruits and vegetables they may have eaten in the prior week, and their consumption of canned and frozen fruits and vegetables, may influence respondents' interpretation of what counts (canned or frozen as well as fresh) and recall of how frequently they have eaten these foods in the past. This context can impact how respondents *form* their answer to the question. Remembering numerous instances of eating fruits and vegetables can lead respondents to judge themselves as frequent consumers. Further, knowledge about what is considered healthy eating may yield question order effects at the *reporting* or "editing" stage of the survey response process, where answers depend not on respondents' cognitive limitations but upon how they want to present themselves. Respondents may report a higher frequency in order to appear to eat healthily.

The most common methodology for studying question order effects is the randomized experiment conducted within a population-based survey. Typically, the experiments are embedded in longer questionnaires. Most of the time, the experiments have two conditions that study the effects of one or more earlier questions on the response(s) to one or more subsequent questions. Across experimental conditions, the specific questions that are presented and their order of presentation are experimentally varied, and respondents are assigned at random to one of the conditions. Researchers would test for differences in the responses to questions across conditions.

This chapter updates Schuman and Presser's (1981) review of question order effects in public opinion studies and includes a review of question order effects in other domains as well as a discussion of the psychological mechanisms underlying these effects. In addition to documenting, comparing, and contrasting mechanisms, we discuss findings on whether individual differences moderate context effects. An understanding of the mechanisms that underlie question order effects may provide insights about how to construct questionnaires that will diminish these effects and knowing which groups of individuals are more susceptible to them under some conditions may be useful in questionnaire construction. The more we can understand why question order effects occur, and for whom, the clearer it will be how best to ask questions in surveys and to interpret the potential effects of question order on the responses.

SOCIAL AND POLITICAL TOPICS

Social and political topics have frequently been examined for question order effects because such questions are often of a broad nature (e.g., "Do you favor or oppose the privatization of Social Security?"), potentially tapping into many different aspects of a particular respondent's attitudes, and attitudes themselves may fluctuate, especially on topics that the respondent has not thought much about.

Abortion

One of the major topics studied with regard to question order effects is abortion. A series of papers has examined discrepancies and possible explanations in the level of support that respondents express for a woman's right to an abortion. For example, the following two abortion questions have been the subject of intense scrutiny: (a) Do you think that it should be possible for a pregnant woman to obtain a legal abortion if she is married and does not want any more children? (b) Do you think it should be possible for a pregnant woman to obtain a legal abortion if there is a strong chance of a serious defect in the baby? The first question is also referred to as the *general* or *whole* question and the second question is referred to as the *specific* or *part* question.

The 1978 General Social Survey (GSS), conducted by the National Opinion Research Center (NORC), found 40.3% of respondents said "yes" to the general question. (The 1978 GSS actually had a seven-part question on approval of legal abortions, of which the questions on a defect in the baby and not wanting any more children were the first two questions.) Schuman et al. (1981), using the general question on abortion from the GSS, found significantly greater support for abortion, 58.4%, in a Survey Research Center (SRC) survey than the NORC survey demonstrated. A key methodological difference between the studies was that in the 1978 GSS, the general abortion question was immediately preceded by the specific question on abortion in the case of a defect in the unborn child, while the SRC survey asked only the general question. Another factor may have contributed to the differences between the 1978 GSS and the SRC study: in the 1978 GSS study, two questions on children appeared before the abortion questions. Smith (1983) found that support for abortion in the general case of not wanting any more children was lower when it followed the questions on children. He posited that a heightened focus on children reduced support for abortion (see Smith, 1983, for an additional study of the effects of the child questions).

To explore the differences between the 1978 GSS and the SRC findings, Schuman et al. (1981) conducted a split-ballot experiment in which both abortion questions were presented, with the order switched between ballots. They found that answers to the specific question did not differ significantly based on order. However, support for abortion in the general question exhibited a *contrast* effect; support was lower when it followed the specific question. These questions are described as having a *part-whole* relationship (Schuman & Presser, 1981) because the specific question on the child with a defect is considered to be contained within the general question on a woman's right in the case of not wanting more children. The respondent's answer to the part question is considered predictable based on their answer to the whole question. That is, someone who supports a woman's right in general to an abortion is likely to support that right in a specific case, such as when the child has a defect. However, the opposite may not be true; support for abortion in the specific case does not predict support in the general case. Schuman et al. (1981) suggested that it is possible that when asked about the specific case first, respondents take that scenario out of consideration (hence, they *subtract* it) when considering their level of support for abortion more generally. Thus, the specific-general question order yields less general support for abortion than the general-specific order.

Bishop et al. (1985) conducted experiments to attempt to replicate the Schuman et al. (1981) findings. In a split-ballot experiment, one version of the questionnaire included the two abortion questions presented by Schuman et al. (1981) and Smith (1978) in specific-general order. Another version asked these questions in general-specific order. Consistent with the SRC findings, responses to the specific question did not vary significantly across conditions. Responses to the general question showed an effect in the same direction as prior studies. Although Bishop et al. (1985) reported higher agreement with the general abortion question when it was asked before the specific question as compared to after it, the difference between the two conditions was not significant. Additionally, Bishop et al.'s (1985) experiment did not replicate findings of a question order effect with the general and specific abortion questions. Bishop et al. (1985) speculated that one contextual aspect of the experiment may have influenced the findings. For Bishop et al. (1985), the order of the abortion questions was preceded by two questions, one on welfare and one on the respondent's identification as a liberal, moderate, or conservative. In contrast, Schuman et al. (1981) preceded the abortion questions with questions about labor unions in one study and about the Soviet Union in another study. Thus, Bishop et al. (1985) suggested that the preceding context could have influenced responses to the abortion items by prompting respondents to approach the abortion items as questions on whether they have a liberal versus a conservative viewpoint.

To examine this, Bishop et al. (1985) conducted a second experiment. In addition to varying the order of the abortion questions, they also varied whether those questions immediately preceded or followed the questions on welfare and political self-identification. Further, they included an open-ended question after the general abortion question asking respondents why they felt a pregnant woman should or should not be able to obtain a legal abortion if she is married and does not want any more children. The order effect with the abortion questions was larger (but not significantly larger) when they appeared before the welfare and political self-identification questions as compared with after. To test the subtraction hypothesis, they examined reasons that respondents gave to the open-ended question following the general question. Results cast some doubt on a subtraction hypothesis and suggest instead an explanation based on *implicit contrast*. That is, when the general abortion question comes first, a woman's right to an abortion seems reasonable to support based on "freedom of choice." However, when the general abortion question comes second, after the birth defect question, the freedom of choice argument is no longer viewed as favorably.

Stark et al. (2020) examined the abortion questions in a cross-national look at 14 probability surveys in the United States and 11 other countries (Canada, Denmark, Germany, Iceland, Japan, the Netherlands, Norway, Portugal, Sweden, Taiwan, and the United Kingdom). Similar to Schuman and Presser (1981), the question order effect was found for both the U.S. survey samples and all countries except Japan, with support for the married woman who does not want any more children getting an abortion becoming significantly or marginally significantly reduced when that question was preceded by the birth defect question. In Japan, abortion was considered more acceptable for the birth defect question than for a married woman not wanting any more children; however, reversing the question order did not impact support for the married woman not wanting any more children.

Stark et al. (2020) also examined the subtraction order hypothesis, which would require respondents to consider birth defects as a more favorable reason for abortion than a married woman not wanting any more children, for the question order effect to occur. While this condition was met for 11 of the 14 samples, in three samples (Denmark, Norway, and Sweden), equal numbers of respondents were in favor of both reasons when each question was asked first. Despite the necessary condition not being met, question order effects were still observed in the three Scandinavian countries. These results, which are in alignment with Bishop et al. (1985), further cast doubt on the subtraction hypothesis.

The American and Communist Reporter Questions

The question order effects discussed above concern questions that have a *part-whole* relationship. A different phenomenon has been noted in questions that involve two competing parties. In these types of questions, an advantage/disadvantage or standard of judgment applied to one party might be considered to apply to the other party as well. A well-known example involves the following questions on what American and Communist reporters should be allowed to do: (a) Do you think a Communist country like Russia should let American newspaper reporters come in and send back to America the news as they see it? (b) Do you think the United States should let Communist newspaper reporters from other countries come in here and send back to their papers the news as they see it?

Hyman and Sheatsley (1950; cited in Schuman & Presser, 1981) found that people overwhelmingly supported allowing American reporters into Russia when this question was asked first (90%); support declined when this question was asked after the question on allowing Communist reporters into the United States (66%). When asked about Communist reporters first, support was low (36%); but after being asked about American reporters in Russia, support for letting in Communist reporters increased dramatically (73%). In their own replication, Schuman and Presser (1981) found similar results. They termed this a *part-part* effect because of the equal level of specificity of both questions and denoted it as a *consistency* effect because the response to the subsequent question moves in the direction of being consistent with the response to the prior question. This effect may occur because respondents tend to answer the first question in a way that favors the United States (whether in favor of American reporters or against Communist reporters), but they subsequently apply the norm of reciprocity in evaluating the second question in a way that is more consistent with their first answer (also called a norm of *even-handedness* by Schuman & Ludwig, 1983).

Klein et al. (2014) were able to replicate these results within a cross-cultural replicability study. For the U.S. studies, Russia was changed to North Korea, as a more modern target. For international countries, the target country was determined by researchers leading the individual studies, to ensure suitability. As the results did not vary for a lab versus online sample or for the U.S. versus an international sample; Klein et al. suggested that these replicability results are more dependent on the effect rather than reliant on the sample and setting.

Happiness

Some of the early research on question order effects concerned responses to questions on happiness. This research focused on two questions: a general question and a specific question on marital happiness. The questions were as follows:

1. Taken altogether, how would you say things are these days? Would you say you are very happy, pretty happy, or not too happy? (*general question*)
2. Taking things all together, how would you describe your marriage? Would you say that your marriage is very happy, pretty happy, or not too happy? (*specific question*)

Schuman and Presser (1981) found evidence for a contrast effect. When the general question followed the specific question, respondents were significantly less likely to report that they were very happy compared to when the question order was reversed. Specifically, 52.4% of respondents reported being generally very happy when the general question appeared first, while only 38.1% reported being very happy when the marital happiness question came first. Only the general question was subject to question order effects and not the specific question.

Sudman and Bradburn (1982) suggested the subtraction hypothesis as a mechanism to explain the contrast effect. According to this hypothesis, when the general question follows the specific question on marital happiness, respondents interpret the general question as asking about other aspects of the respondent's life and not their marriage. Another explanation is that when the general question on happiness follows the marital happiness question, respondents consider other domains in their life while answering the general question to avoid redundancy.

Smith (1982) reported experimental results for the 1980 General Social Survey in which he used the same questions on happiness but instead of a contrast effect, he found an *assimilation* effect, in which the context of the prior question was taken into consideration in answering the following question, leading to greater consistency in responses to the two questions. When the specific question on marital happiness preceded the general question, respondents were more likely to say that they were generally very happy. These results were similar to nonexperimental results reported in his earlier research (Smith, 1979). The assimilation effect seen here was fairly easy to explain. Since most people were happy in their marriages, the specific question primed them and made the information on their marital happiness cognitively accessible. Therefore, they included marital happiness in their assessment of general happiness.

Subsequent research (McClendon & O'Brien 1988b; Strack et al., 1988; Turner, 1984) has tried to replicate and reconcile the findings of these two early papers and find evidence to support various explanations for why the contrast effect or assimilation effect occurs. One reason for the apparently conflicting findings in these papers could be differences in the number of specific questions that preceded the general questions (Tourangeau & Rasinski, 1988). In Smith (1982), the happiness items were part of a series of five questions about satisfaction in different domains, whereas in Schuman and Presser (1981), there were no other questions on life satisfaction. When a series of specific questions preceded the general question, respondents may have thought they were expected to provide a summary judgment of their overall happiness when responding to the general question. This would have led to assimilation effects. On the other hand, when there was only one specific question, respondents may have excluded the specific domain in their judgment of overall happiness, which produced a contrast effect (Tourangeau & Rasinski, 1988).

McClendon and O'Brien (1988b) conducted an experiment to examine the role of cognitive accessibility in question order effects in an experiment with a general question on well-being and multiple specific questions. The questions were part of a split-ballot experiment included in a telephone survey on living in the greater Akron, Ohio, area; the specific domains included marriage, health, employment, neighborhood, and standard of living. The general question on well-being was placed either fourth or at the end of 11 questions on different domains. Analyses indicated that there were positive question order effects for domains such as marriage and health that were closer to the general question and negative effects for employment, which was farther away from the general question. The authors concluded that putting the specific questions before the general question increased the cognitive accessibility of those domains. The domains that were closer to the general question were accessed more recently and therefore showed stronger question order effects.

Another experiment conducted by Strack et al. (1988) investigated the effect of including an introduction to general happiness and happiness with dating questions to provide a common conversational context. The authors found that when the general question followed the specific question without the introduction, the correlation coefficient between the responses to the specific and general questions was significantly higher than with the introduction. They concluded that when the general and specific questions were presented in the same context, respondents excluded the information on dating while answering the general question. This is despite the fact that they had just accessed the information on dating to answer the prior question. Clearly, respondents thought they were expected to provide new information in the general question.

Schwarz, Strack, and Mai (1991) further explored the role of conversational context as a determinant of whether contrast or assimilation effects predominate. Their hypothesis was that when a specific question appeared before a general question in the same conversational context, then conversational norms applied and respondents tried to avoid redundancy, which would lead to a contrast effect. On the other hand, when the context appeared to be different, the placement of the specific marriage question before the general question increased the cognitive accessibility of the marriage domain, which would lead to an assimilation effect. When there were multiple preceding specific questions, the general question was also interpreted to be a summary judgment and an assimilation effect would be observed. Results generally supported their hypotheses. However, the expected contrast effect was observed only for unhappy respondents. Because this experiment used questions about satisfaction rather than happiness it was not a direct replication of the earlier studies.

Tourangeau et al. (1991) used happiness questions to test for the subtraction hypothesis. Their experiment had four conditions: (a) a general happiness question that asked the respondent to include their marriage in their consideration, (b) the standard general happiness/marital happiness sequence, (c) the standard marital happiness/general happiness sequence, and (d) a general happiness question that asked respondents to exclude their marriage from their considerations. They expected to see an assimilation effect in the general first (b) and the explicit inclusion conditions (d) and a contrast effect in the marital first (c) and explicit exclusion (a) conditions.

The condition where the general question came before the marital question showed a high correlation between the two questions and the conditions where the marital question appeared before the general question had a significantly lower correlation, giving some evidence of assimilation and contrast. However, the percentages of respondents who reported they were very happy were similar across the four conditions. Thus, they did not find the directional evidence that could lend support to the subtraction hypothesis.

To summarize, social and political topics have often been examined in question order effects research due to the broad nature and potential to tap into different aspects of respondent's attitudes. Social and political topics that have be widely researched include abortion, the American and Communist reporter questions (or questions that have two competing parties), and happiness. There are several considerations based on this research when looking at potential causes for question order effects. Research on both abortion and happiness questions have shown support for contrast effects, which is when a general question is followed by a specific question, and support is then lower, compared with when the question order is reversed. Research has also examined whether the opposite is true, that a subtraction effect may be present. The subtraction hypothesis occurs when respondent is asked about the specific case first, respondents take that scenario out of consideration (meaning, they subtract it) when considering their level of support for a more general topic. While early research did show support of the subtraction hypothesis, most recent research casts doubt on that being a primary reason we see question order effects, as these results are often not replicated. Assimilation effects should also be considered. An assimilation effect occurs when the context of the prior question was taken into consideration in answering the following question, which leads to greater consistency in response to the two questions. Finally, when looking at questions with two competing parties, such as the American Communist reporter questions, the norm of reciprocity (or norm of evenhandedness), should be considered. The norm of reciprocity occurs when a respondent evaluates a question in a way that is more consistent with their first answer.

HEALTH AND SAFETY STUDIES

Although many health-related surveys have been conducted, our search of the health literature turned up only a handful of question order experiments, and these were, for the most part, conducted after 2000. Using a telephone survey, Rimal and Real (2005) examined whether question order affected judgments about the perceived importance of skin cancer. They hypothesized that respondents who were more involved with the issue would be less likely to be influenced by prior health-related questions—including questions about other forms of cancer—than those who were less involved with the issue. Based on the elaboration-likelihood model of Petty and Cacioppo (1981), they hypothesized that involvement would result in central processing, in which respondents more carefully consider the question on skin cancer independently of the content of prior questions, which would make these respondents more immune from question order effects. Those less involved would engage in peripheral processing, in which readily available information from prior question context would play a larger role in responding, making question order effects more likely.

All respondents were asked to judge how important the issue of skin cancer was in their life. In the first condition, involvement questions were asked after the importance question; in the second condition, the involvement questions were asked before the importance question. Consistent with their hypothesis, when cognitive involvement (how much the respondent thought about skin cancer) was low, importance of skin cancer was rated as significantly greater when the question came first than when it came later. When cognitive involvement was high, there was no difference between question order conditions in importance ratings. Presumably, those respondents who had not thought much about skin cancer were engaging in a comparison of skin cancer with other health related questions on the survey.

In contrast to findings that respondents who are highly involved or judge an issue to be of high importance are less subject to question order effects, a study of perceptions of neighborhood safety suggests a contrary relationship between the salience of an issue and context effects (McClendon & O'Brien, 1988a). The authors predicted that perceptions of neighborhood safety would have a greater effect on neighborhood satisfaction when the safety question preceded rather than followed the neighborhood evaluation question. The authors found that this was the case, but only for Black respondents for whom safety was a more salient issue.

Self-reported health (SRH) questions are widely used to study health across a range of subject areas and populations. Some studies have looked at how the association between SRH and domain-specific health items changes depending on whether SRH precedes or follows these health items. Bowling and Windsor (2008) examined question order effects on two versions of a single self-rated health question (1) "How is your health in general? Would you say it was very good, good, fair, bad or very bad" and (2) "Would you say your health is excellent, very good, good, fair or poor?" This study used data from the English Longitudinal Study of Ageing (ELSA), a national in-person household survey of the population of Great Britain age 50 and older.

Two versions of the questionnaire were assigned at random to respondents. One version asked question (1) first followed by a series of specific health questions and then asked question (2). The second version asked question (2) first followed by a series of specific health questions and then asked question (1). In addition, to test the impact of including an extreme positive response category, half of the versions used "excellent" as the first choice and half used "very good." Regardless of the question ordering or the extremity of response options, respondents rated their health as slightly but significantly more positively when the question came at the end of the specific health questions than when it came at the beginning. This effect held even among patients who reported a long-standing illness. The authors suggested that respondents were excluding information about their specific health conditions when they made the overall judgment last (Bowling & Windsor, 2008).

In a study on question order effects for self-reported health measures, Garbarski et al. (2015) implemented a 2 × 2 between-subjects factorial experiment in an online panel survey to study the order of response options as well as the question order with the SRH question. The SRH question studied was similar to the general question studied by Bowling and Windsor (2008). The question was worded "Would you say your health in general is excellent, very good, good, fair, or poor?" In the experiment, the SRH question was asked either before or after domain-specific health items. On average, higher SRH is reported when SRH is presented before other health questions. When SRH is presented after the domain specific questions, there is increased correlation of SRH with these items. Among participants with the highest level of current health risks, SRH is worse when it is presented last versus first, particularly when SRH response options are ordered "excellent" to "poor." When

SRH is asked after domain specific items, an assimilation effect is observed for many items. The authors suggest presenting SRH before domain-specific health items in order to increase inter-survey comparability, since domain-specific health items will vary across surveys.

In a contingent valuation study, Kartman et al. (1996) used a telephone survey in Sweden to test question order effects on willingness to pay judgments of patients with reflex esophagitis. They found that a bid decision (i.e., a yes, definitely; yes, probably; no, definitely not; no, probably not; don't know decision) to pay an incremental amount to receive a superior hypothetical medication was not affected by the order in which scenarios explaining the superior compared to the inferior medication's properties were presented. Darker et al. (2007) also found no question order effects in belief elicitation to open-ended questions used in a theory of planned behavior study of walking as exercise.

Gold and Barclay (2006) found significant differences due to question order in correlations between judgments of one's own risk and of an adverse event occurring (e.g., "What is the chance that you will get into a car accident in the next year?") and judgments of the risk of others (e.g., "What is the chance the average person will get into a car accident in the next year?"). The correlations were lower when the own risk question came first, largely because respondents give answers that are idiosyncratic to their own experience, ignoring the larger context of events. However, when the "average person" question came first respondents were forced to take into account the larger context which drove up correlations between judgments of their own risk and that of the average person.

In a cross-linguistic study, Lee and Grant (2009) found question order effects when the SRH question was administered in Spanish but not in English. In an experiment conducted as part of the California Health Interview Survey (CHIS), they varied the position of the SRH question to either before or after a series of items on chronic conditions across Spanish- and English language interviews. In the Spanish language condition, respondents reported poorer overall health when they answered the SRH question before the specific questions on chronic conditions as compared to when they answered the SRH question after the questions on chronic conditions. No question order effect due to the placement of the SRH question was found in the English language interview. It is possible that there are differences in how respondents from different cultures may approach the task of determining their general health status. For some populations, the specific questions on chronic conditions may have a greater impact on how they evaluate their general health status than for other populations. The results of this study highlight the need to consider potential differences in question order effects due to cultural or linguistic characteristics within respondent subgroups, and consequently the impact of these characteristics on conclusions that could be drawn from the data.

Similar to the idea that specific health questions may help frame or anchor a more general health question for some respondents, a study by Rasinski et al. (2005) showed that prior questions designed to prime motivations to report honesty increased reporting of high-risk behaviors (in this case, excessive alcohol intake) among a group of college students. Students were given a self-administered questionnaire consisting of a set of health behavior questions about binge drinking and associated behaviors such as driving under the influence of alcohol or missing class because of hangovers. Half of the students at random were "primed" to report honestly using a nonconscious priming task. This task, a word matching exercise, preceded the health questionnaire, was in the same packet of materials, but was formatted to look like a separate task. Results showed that students primed with honesty-related words reported more alcohol-related behaviors than students in the neutral priming condition.

In summary, question order effects have been found in a variety of health studies. The size of the effect is mediated by the involvement of respondents, salience of the topic, and can be influenced by priming respondents. Questions on overall SRH are vulnerable to question order effects, but different studies have found contradictory effects, some finding higher SRH when the question is placed before domain specific questions and others finding higher SRH when it is placed at the end. To allow comparability across studies, it may be best to put the SRH question first. Yet, findings from one study suggest that differences in language and culture may yield differences in question order effects. The impact of language and culture in generating question order effects, not in only in health but other domains as well, is an area that requires further experimental study.

VIGNETTE RESEARCH

Vignettes have often been used in social science research to examine systematically the impact of specific characteristics on judgment. In this type of research, respondents are presented with vignettes, or scenarios, that describe a particular situation and are asked to make a judgment about each vignette. Versions of the vignette are created that include systematic variation among the characteristics of interest. Experimental comparison across respondents receiving different versions allows for the examination of the impact of each characteristic on judgments.

Auspurg and Jäckle (2012) examined whether the order in which characteristics are presented in a vignette affects judgments and the conditions under which order of the characteristics occur. They hypothesized that when vignettes vary in complexity, individual differences among respondents in cognitive ability, knowledge, certainty of their attitudes, will contribute to order effects for more complex vignettes. In a web survey, respondents were presented with vignettes that varied in the number and order in which characteristics were presented, and in number of judgments to be made about the vignettes. Their findings showed that the order in which characteristics are presented in vignettes, as well as the number of characteristics presented, can influence the conclusions that arise from the research. That is, order effects matter for vignettes. Further, knowledge and strength of attitude also mattered. Although effects of cognitive ability were not found, the respondents were all students, thus potentially narrowing the range of cognitive ability in the sample. Finally, the order of the vignette itself mattered too, with effects largest for vignettes presented earlier and later. The authors posited that a learning effect occurs as respondents become familiar with the characteristics, with effects of fatigue occurring toward the end.

MODE AND QUESTION ORDER EFFECTS

Surveys can be administered in a variety of modes, and many surveys are now multimode as response rates continue to decline (Olson et al., 2019) and costs of fielding traditional in-person and telephone surveys increase. Many of the question order effects experiments were done on interviewer administered surveys and these modes differ in many ways from self-administered surveys such as mail or web surveys. One difference between modes which may impact question order effects is that in mail and web surveys, respondents are not limited to progressing through the instrument sequentially but can go backwards and forwards while in interviewer-administered surveys like telephone and in-person interviews, this flexibility is not possible. With web surveys, respondents' ability to preview questions and navigate forward and backward through a survey is likely more limited than in mail surveys.

Some studies have found that question order effects vary by mode. Schwarz, Strack, Hippler, and Bishop (1991) found that in the telephone mode, German respondents were more likely to agree that Japanese imports to Germany should be limited than to agree that German imports to Japan should be limited when each of these questions was presented first. Further, as would be expected under a norm of reciprocity or even-handedness, support for limiting German imports to Japan increased when this question was asked after the question on limiting Japanese exports to Germany. However, in the self-administered mail mode they found that the question order effect was no longer present.

Schwarz and Hippler (1995) reported on a study conducted in Germany. Respondents were randomly assigned to a mail or telephone condition and were asked how much money they would be willing to donate to help suffering people in Russia (a prominent issue at the time of the survey). Two questions on taxes were also asked, which came either before or after the question about helping Russia. In the telephone condition, respondents were willing to donate less money to Russia if asked after the tax question. In the mail survey, donation amounts were low (compared with the lower donation in the telephone condition) in both question order conditions. They argued that the subsequent questions may have influenced answers to a preceding question because of the ability of respondents to skip ahead in the mail survey.

Bishop et al. (1988) found that question order effects apparent in their telephone surveys were eliminated in their mail surveys. A number of mode differences between mail and interview surveys may lead to differences in order effects. In the mail mode, effects such as acquiescence and social desirability biases may be less apparent because of the absence of an interviewer. Further, respondents have the ability to view the questions in any order which may lead to reduced effects of question order.

Ayidiya and McClendon (1990) extended this work using a split-ballot mail survey with the Communist-American reporter questions and the defect-in-child and woman's right abortion questions. Unlike the Bishop et al. (1988) findings, the results showed significant question order effects for the Communist reporter item and near significant effects for the American reporter item; these effects were in the same direction of consistency as in prior studies. That is, support for Communist reporters in America was higher when asked after the question on American reporters in Russia; support for American reporters in Russia was lower when asked after the question about Communist reporters in America. However, in accord with Bishop et al. (1988), no significant question order effects were found for the abortion questions. The absence of an interviewer-administered mode in this study prevents conclusions about effects of mode. However, the authors speculated that it is not the presence of an interviewer that prompts respondents to apply a norm of reciprocity or even-handedness with the reporter questions. Rather, respondents seem to have an internalized sense of even-handedness. Consistency effects continued to be observed with the American-Communist reporter items in the mail mode, however, with the abortion items, the contrast effect that is often found with these items was not observed. The mail mode of the survey appears to have attenuated the question order effect only for the abortion items.

An increasing number of self-administered surveys are now conducted online. The use of web surveys has grown rapidly not only due to the reduction in costs for data collection (Tourangeau et al., 2004) but also because web surveys have been shown to have good measurement properties, such as reducing social desirability issues (e.g., reading sensitive information in a self-administered setting rather than being administered by an interviewer) and web surveys can reduce cognitive burden by allowing respondents to re-read difficult questions (Tourangeau et al., 2013). Question order effects have been shown to be present in web surveys in a variety of topics, including college student surveys (see Bowman & Schuldt, 2014), self-rated health (see Garbarski et al., 2015), and political research (see Boukes & Morey, 2019).

Peytchev and Hill (2010) examined whether question order effects, as found in other modes, would also be present in mobile web surveys. Respondents were asked, "Do you think that authoritarian leaders like Iran's President Mahmoud Ahmadinejad should be invited to give speeches at U.S. universities?" They were then asked, "Do you think that democratic leaders like President Bill Clinton should be allowed to give speeches at universities in authoritarian regimes like Iran?" The authors found that question order effects were present in the mobile web survey. For half of the respondents, the order of the questions was reversed. For both groups, about 52% approved of President Ahmadinejad speaking in the United States (consistent with the high saliency of the issue at that time). Only 57% approved of Clinton speaking in authoritarian regimes when this question was presented after the question on Ahmadinejad, whereas 84% approved of Clinton speaking when it came first. With the transition of many surveys to the web mode, additional research that examines question order effects between web and other modes, and across devices in the web mode, will be informative for survey researchers.

Across experiments examining the impact of mode on question order effects, a consistent finding is that question order effects are observed in interviewer-administered or web modes, but not in the mail mode. This pattern in the findings across studies suggests that the ability to preview questions in the mail mode may lead to respondents' ability to examine each question in a fuller context. When they are no longer considering each question sequentially, as they do in an interviewer-administered or web format, question order effects are minimized. These studies make clear that mode can have a strong impact on whether question order effects are observed.

INDIVIDUAL DIFFERENCES AND THEIR IMPACT ON QUESTION ORDER EFFECTS

Question order effects may vary among subgroups. The studies described next examine how individual differences in age, education, strength of respondent attitudes or knowledge about the survey topic can moderate question order effects.

Age and Working Memory

The strength of question order effects may vary as a function of age because of declines in working memory capacity and speed of cognitive processing. As previously described, support for a woman's right to an abortion is higher when the question is presented before, as compared with after, the defect-in-child question. However, analysis of the data by respondent age showed a difference of 19.5% for younger respondents, but no question order effect for respondents age 65 and above (Schwarz, 2003). If older respondents are less able to remember the preceding question, that question will have less effect on responses to the subsequent question (Knauper et al., 2007). To test the memory hypothesis, Knauper et al. (2007) studied older adults with low and high working memory capacities and younger adults. An explanation based on working memory capacity would predict that older adults with high working memory should perform similarly to younger adults. As predicted, both younger respondents and older respondents with high working memory capacity showed a significant question order effect in the expected direction. The older adults with low working memory capacity showed no significant effects of question order.

Education/Cognitive Sophistication

In research on survey context or response effects, education level is often used as a proxy for cognitive sophistication and has been shown to interact with question order (e.g., Schuman & Ludwig, 1983). However, effects of education level may interact with other factors, such as attitudes about the survey topic. In examining their findings with the American-Communist reporter questions, Schuman and Presser (1981) noted that the question order effect is seen primarily in respondents with lower levels of education. They speculated that the college-educated respondents were likely already inclined to agree that Communist reporters should be allowed in the United States, and consequently asking this question second would not invoke a norm of reciprocity and question order should do little to affect response. However, in a follow-up study that included an item on how the respondent perceived Communism, Schuman and Presser found that antipathy towards Communism was more strongly associated with the question order effect than education level. The researchers also looked for effects of education level on order effects with the abortion questions and found no interactions between education and question order.

In other research, Schuman and Ludwig (1983) found effects of education level on question order, but they varied by question topic. In questions on trade restrictions between Japan and the United States, greater effects of question order were seen for respondents with lower levels of education. Respondents with lower levels of education were more likely than those with higher education levels to favor restrictions by the United States on Japan when that question came first and were more likely to favor trade restrictions by Japan when that question came second. However, an order effect by education level interaction was not seen for questions on political contributions by corporations and by labor unions. Schuman and Ludwig noted that such differing results suggest that explanations other than cognitive sophistication may also underlie the question order effect. For example, nationalistic tendencies may encourage order effects in some contexts (e.g., United States vs. Japan) but not in others (e.g., corporations vs. labor unions).

In a meta-analysis of the question order experiments in Schuman and Presser (1981), Narayan and Krosnick (1996) found that respondents with lower or medium levels of education showed greater question order effects than those with higher levels of education. Among the items examined were those that were explained in terms of a norm of reciprocity, such as the American and Communist reporter questions. Narayan and Krosnick proposed a different explanation based on satisficing behavior. Respondents who *satisfice* (i.e., apply minimal effort to the task at hand—see Krosnick, 1991) would not be likely to consider reciprocity when answering the first question compared to respondents who *optimize* their response behavior. For satisficers, the norm of reciprocity may not come to mind until presented with the second question, yielding a question order effect. In comparison, optimizers are more likely to consider the norm of reciprocity when presented with the first question and to apply this norm to both questions regardless of order. Other research (Narayan & Krosnick, 1996) has shown that satisficing is more prevalent among respondents with lower education because they are less able to meet the cognitive demands of a long or complicated survey.

Respondents with lower education may be more greatly influenced by the context that precedes a question because that context highlights information that is relevant to answering the later question. In a split-ballot telephone survey, Sigelman (1981) presented a question on presidential approval either before or after a series of questions on social and energy problems, energy costs, pollution, drugs and political corruption. Although he found no differences in presidential approval ratings by question order, a significant order effect was found for "opinionation," defined as the willingness to give an opinion about the president. Fewer respondents who received the presidential approval question early in the questionnaire ventured to give an evaluative response when compared with those who received the question after the series of questions on social topics. This tendency was pronounced for less educated respondents.

Although satisficing may be associated with education level, respondent interpretation of a task, as influenced by ordering of a question on record linkage, appears to impact the approach respondents decide to take to the survey. Eckman and Haas (2017) examined the impact of putting a question on consent to link data to records at the beginning versus the end of the survey and found effects of question order. Generally, consent rate to the linkage question is higher if the question is asked at the beginning but it was not known whether placement of the question would impact responses to the survey. Eckman and Haas found that, although not always significant, granting linkage consent in the beginning resulted in more measurement error. Respondents appeared to more likely to satisfice when the consent question came first, perhaps working under the assumption that their answers would be verified through linking to records.

The research suggests that question order effects can arise from satisficing behavior such that respondents with lower levels of education may be more likely to exhibit question order effects than respondents with higher levels of education due to differences in ability to meet the cognitive demands of the survey task. Other factors, however, may mediate the effect. Based on the findings we reviewed, question topic can sometimes play a role when the topic at hand is one that elicits stronger opinions that respondents have already formed. Yet, as will be discussed further, attitude crystallization is not always associated with diminished question order effects. The impact of respondent attitudes on question order effects is an area that requires further investigation.

Knowledge About Survey Topic

Some evidence suggests that the level of the respondent's knowledge about a topic may influence their susceptibility to question order effects. One study showed that question order effects about political topics are dependent on political knowledge. The third person effect is a phenomenon that has received much attention in communications research. This concept, first described by Davison (1983), is the common perception that media messages have a greater impact on others than on oneself. The effect, usually demonstrated by asking two questions, one about media effects on self and one about media effects on others, has been shown to be robust to question order (e.g., Gunther, 1995; Gunther & Hwa, 1996; Salwen & Driscoll, 1997). Price and Tewksbury (1996) examined question order under different levels of political knowledge. Respondents either received a single question about media effects on one's self, a single question about media effect on others or both questions in either order. The authors found a question order effect, but only when the data were examined within the context of the respondent's political knowledge. Higher political knowledge resulted in lower estimates of the media's effect on oneself, but only when the "self" question followed the "other" question. There was no effect of knowledge on ratings of self-impact when the "self" question preceded the "other" question. The joint effect of political knowledge and question order on third person effects require further examination to understand the circumstances under which the effects occur.

A study comparing consistency and framing explanations for context effects found that expressed interest in science could be moderated by the difficulty of science knowledge questions that preceded the interest question (Gaskell et al., 1995). Gaskell et al. (1995) tested whether it is the respondent's perception of their knowledge about science or their perception of what interest in science entails that influences context effects. They reasoned that a consistency effect would be demonstrated by an interaction between knowledge and question order such that respondents who answered questions correctly before they received the interest question (and regardless of whether they received the easy or difficult knowledge questions) would show a greater interest than those who answered the questions correctly after being asked about interest. A framing effect would be demonstrated by a main effect of test difficulty in the condition where the knowledge questions preceded the interest question, independent of test performance. According to this argument, a difficult test would frame "interest in science" as something more than just enjoying a casual exposure to stories about science from the media. In support of the framing hypothesis, the study found that respondents' interpretation of what it means to be interested in science, rather their perception of how knowledgeable they were about science, dictated question order effects.

Attitude Crystallization and Ambivalence

Schuman and Presser (1981) described a crystallized attitude as one that existed prior to measurement and that is stable across time. It would seem that question order effects may be less pronounced in respondents with more crystallized attitudes. Although the results of some studies suggest that question order effects are greatest in those with the weakest attitudes (e.g., Schuman et al., 1981; Wilson et al., 2008), a large-scale study found overall no evidence for a relationship between attitude strength and question order effects (Krosnick & Schuman, 1988).

Schuman et al. (1981) speculated whether the order effect may be influenced by ambivalence about the topic. In one of their Survey Research Center studies, they included the general and specific abortion items, separated by more than 50 items on other topics, and added a question about the respondent's ambivalence on abortion. The order effect was larger among those expressing ambivalence about abortion. In support of this result, Wilson et al. (2008) noted that question order does not affect the reported attitudes toward affirmative action among some groups whose views on affirmative action are likely to be less ambivalent. Both Blacks and liberals were found not to be subject to question order effects in the amount of support they showed for affirmative action programs for both racial minorities and women.

Krosnick and Schuman (1988) reported on experiments on question order effects with the defect-in-child and woman's right abortion questions and an experiment with questions on U.S. and Japanese import restrictions and assessed respondents' levels of attitude certainty about these topics. In one of the four abortion question experiments, they found that respondents with greater uncertainty about abortion were more likely to show the effect. However, in the other three experiments, respondents who were high and low in certainty about abortion showed similar question order effects. Further, the import restrictions questions also showed no relationship between attitude certainty and magnitude of context effects. They concluded that attitude certainty does not distinguish respondents who demonstrate question order effects and respondents who do not.

IMPLICATIONS OF THE STUDY OF QUESTION ORDER EFFECTS FOR QUESTIONNAIRE DESIGN

Our review of the literature gives a strong indication that question order effects do occur. While not every study demonstrated an effect, most of the research indicated that respondents do not approach each new question independently, clearing their minds of what came before. Within each stage of the survey response process, question order effects can arise. How respondents interpret a question can be influenced by the contextual information in preceding questions. This context will also affect the information that respondents recall and incorporate in their judgment/estimation processes, and it can even influence the response they choose to report. Further, respondent characteristics also play a role in the emergence of question order effects. Respondents will vary in the knowledge and attitudes they bring to a survey, as well as in characteristics such as age, educational attainment, and other factors that have shown a relationship to question order effects. They may also be subject to fatigue in survey responding and loss of motivation that can elicit question order effects.

The questionnaire designer is well-advised to keep potential impacts of question order in mind. However, questionnaire designers may wonder when it is necessary to worry about question order effects and what can be done to minimize them. We provide several recommendations that are informed by methodological research.

We begin with a discussion of the types of question order effects described by Schuman and Presser (1981). The first type, the unconditional context effect, occurs when answers to a subsequent question are affected not by the answer given to a prior question, but by the question's topical material. Research on context effects, a topic closely related to question order effects, has found that prior topic framing can have a substantial influence on responses to subsequent questions (Tourangeau & Rasinski, 1988; Tourangeau et al., 1989a, 1989b). Many topics, from major public policy issues (e.g., public assistance programs, gun control, abortion) to less far-reaching issues (e.g., satisfaction with a job training program, support for funding a local initiative) are complex and multidimensional by nature and can be viewed from many positions; these may fall prey to framing effects imposed by prior questions. For example, response to a survey question on increased funding for municipal services might be influenced by whether the prior questions frame the topic around government waste as opposed to the variety of services (e.g., emergency services, library, schools, parks) the city provides that would be jeopardized by lack of funding. Our general advice is to be aware of the potential of question influences in which the prior question is likely to affect the way in which the respondent thinks about the subsequent one—limiting or directing the way the respondent interprets the subsequent topic.

One approach to minimizing the potential effects of this type of question order effect is to separate the two questions within the survey. However, previous research has indicated that just separating two potentially reactive questions with other buffer questions may not solve the problem. Schuman et al. (1981) and Smith (1978) found that when abortion questions were asked in specific-general order, but the questions were separated by about 40 questions on topics not related to abortion, the question order effect was still present. Similarly, Schuman et al. (1983) found that when they presented the American reporter question first and the Communist reporter question second, with 17 neutral items intervening, question order effects were found even when separated by intervening questions. These findings suggest that a buffer may not suffice to reduce the effects of prior questions on the formulation of answers to a subsequent one. Another approach to this issue is to provide explicit instructions designed to separate the topics in the respondent's mind (Schwarz, Strack, & Mai, 1991), or to instruct respondents explicitly about what to take into account when answering the questions.

We have seen many examples of the second and third types of question order effects—conditional effects and correlational effects—in our review. Both effects occur when answers to the subsequent question depend on the response given to the prior question. As we have noted, under most circumstances, the two effects are an indication of the same kind of reactivity of respondents to questions. Different studies have given these effects different names, such as part-whole effects, part-part effects, invoking a norm of evenhandedness or of reciprocity, violating conversational norms, assimilation or carryover effects, contrast or backfire effects, and subtraction effects. The different names are attempts by researchers to give a psychological explanation for the effect. From a practical consideration, the questionnaire designer must be aware of situations where the juxtaposition of two questions is likely to set up a judgmental dependency.

There are different ways to avoid creating a judgmental dependency between questions. One is to omit one of the questions. In the case of part-whole effects, investigators must ask themselves if it is really necessary to have a global evaluation along with evaluation of parts. For example, if designing questions on satisfaction with a job training program, we could ask a general evaluate question only ("How satisfied were you with the training program?") or also include specific questions evaluating various aspects of the program ("How satisfied were you with the program content? With the instructor?"). We suggest that more useful information is obtained by asking carefully chosen specific questions and leaving out the general question entirely. The subjectivity of satisfaction ratings may be reduced even more by crafting specific questions that focus on objective behaviors ("Did the training program cover the content on the licensing exam? Did the program include hands-on training? Did the instructor provide written feedback on your performance?"). However, some researchers may be interested only in a general evaluation or may be interested in how the evaluation of specific components affects a general evaluation. In the latter case, the consensus from the literature is that if a general satisfaction question is included, it should be asked before the specific questions to avoid an impact of the specific questions on the general question.

Randomization of items is another way to minimize the effects of question order. Although this is logistically more difficult to do with mail surveys, computer-assisted interviewing and the prevalence of survey administration via the web mode makes it easier to randomize questions to reduce potential question order effects. We note that computer-assisted interviewing and self-administered web surveys also ease the process of carrying out split ballot experimentation to look for question order effects.

As our review indicates, many studies have observed that question order effects may be more prevalent based on individual differences such as social groups with different concerns, older or more poorly educated respondents, and those with less expertise in a content area compared with those with more expertise. It is difficult to give specific advice about questionnaire construction for each of these particular types of respondents and for individual and social difference groups that have yet to be tested for new and emerging topics to be addressed in surveys. The questionnaire designer should consider whether topics might interact with group characteristics such as age, educational attainment, or other demographics. For example, in a satisfaction survey that includes general-specific questions with a general population, in which subgroups such as older respondents are determined to be a small proportion of the population, then efforts to address potential question order effects and biased estimates might not be as necessary as in the case of a survey focusing on the older population. However, if the satisfaction survey yielded subgroup differences for older respondents, it may be important to consider whether the potential impact of cognitive differences by age could have yielded question order effects. Perhaps the most practical approach is to keep in mind that whatever one does to limit the effect of question order effects in general will limit them for specific subgroups.

Accordingly, the best advice for reducing question order effects is simply to follow best practices for survey questionnaire design (Schaeffer & Dykema, 2020). A well-designed survey includes clear questions, is engaging, and maintains a low level of burden. It accounts for the impact of characteristics of the survey population, including factors such as age, education level, cultural background, mode preference, and other considerations. Adhering to best practices for questionnaire design will help mitigate question order effects in many instances.

However, despite the use of best practices, it is difficult to completely avoid the possibility of question order effects. Questions cannot be separated from the context in which they appear. Yet, questionnaire designers can still be intentional in determining the context in which questions are presented and aware of the characteristics of questionnaires and respondents that can yield question order effects. We suggest that questionnaire designers do the following: First, review questionnaire topics and question order with potential question order effects in mind. Second, review characteristics of the population under study to identify potential subgroups that may be more subject to question order effects and consider whether subgroup differences may interact with survey findings. Third, identify ways to clarify and simplify the questionnaire and individual questions.

Finally, if a survey is to be fielded in multiple modes, an additional consideration is potential mode effects. Mixed-mode surveys are increasingly common (Olson et al., 2019), with respondents often presented with the choice to complete the survey via web first, followed by phone and/or mail survey options for nonrespondents. Given that mode differences will arise from differences in the response process and can interact with individual characteristics, there is the potential for question order effects by mode. When designing a survey across modes, it is important to consider how differences such as question length, presentation format (e.g., grouping of questions), aural versus visual presentation, and presence or absence of an interviewer may impact processing in ways that could produce question order effects.

In this chapter, we have reviewed the literature on question order effects in surveys and have attempted to give specific advice to researchers constructing questionnaires. Whether the questionnaire is for a population-based probability survey or a convenience sample, and whatever the scope or topic of the study, we hope that our survey of the literature and our recommendations are useful to help researchers collect the best data possible for their research purpose.

References

Auspurg, K., & Jäckle, A. (2012). *First equals most important? Order effects in vignette-based measurement* [working paper]. Institute for Social and Economic Research. https://www.iser.essex.ac.uk/research/publications/working-papers/iser/2012-01.pdf

Ayidiya, S. A., & McClendon, M. J. (1990). Response effects in mail surveys. *Public Opinion Quarterly*, 54(2), 229–247. https://doi.org/10.1086/269200

Bishop, G., Hippler, H.-J., Schwarz, N., & Strack, F. (1988). A comparison of response effects in self-administered and telephone surveys. In R. M. Groves, P. Biemer, L. Lyberg, J. T. Massey, W. L. Nicholls, & J. Waksberg (Eds.), *Telephone survey methodology* (pp. 321–340). Wiley.

Bishop, G. F., Oldendick, R. W., & Tuchfarber, A. J. (1985). The importance of replicating a failure to replicate: Order effects on abortion items. *Public Opinion Quarterly*, 49(1), 105–114. https://doi.org/10.1086/268904

Boukes, M., & Morey, A. C. (2019). Survey context effects and implications for validity: Measuring political discussion frequency in survey research. *Journal of Survey Statistics and Methodology*, 7(2), 201–226. https://doi.org/10.1093/jssam/smy008

Bowling, A., & Windsor, J. (2008). The effects of question order and response-choice on self-rated health status in the English Longitudinal Study of Ageing (ELSA). *Journal of Epidemiology and Community Health*, 62(1), 81–85. https://doi.org/10.1136/jech.2006.058214

Bowman, N. A., & Schuldt, J. P. (2014). Effects of item order and response options in college student surveys. *New Directions for Institutional Research*, 2014(161), 99–109. https://doi.org/10.1002/ir.20070

Darker, C. D., French, D. P., Longdon, S., Morris, K., & Eves, F. F. (2007). Are beliefs elicited biased by question order? A theory of planned behaviour belief elicitation study about walking in the UK general population. *British Journal of Health Psychology*, 12(1), 93–110. https://doi.org/10.1348/135910706X100458

Davison, W. P. (1983). The third person effect in communication. *Public Opinion Quarterly*, 47(1), 1–15. https://doi.org/10.1086/268763

Eckman, S., & Haas, G.-C. (2017). Does granting linkage consent in the beginning of the questionnaire affect data quality? *Journal of Survey Statistics and Methodology*, 5(4), 535–551. https://doi.org/10.1093/jssam/smx016

Garbarski, D., Schaeffer, N. C., & Dykema, J. (2015). The effects of response option order and question order on self-rated health. *Quality of Life Research*, 24(6), 1443–1453. https://doi.org/10.1007/s11136-014-0861-y

Gaskell, G. D., Wright, D. B., & O'Muircheartaigh, C. (1995). Context effects in the measurement of attitudes: A comparison of the consistency and framing explanations. *British Journal of Social Psychology*, 34(4), 383–393. https://doi.org/10.1111/j.2044-8309.1995.tb01072.x

Gold, R. S., & Barclay, A. (2006). Order of question presentation and correlation between judgments of comparative and own risk. *Psychological Reports*, 99(3), 794–798. https://doi.org/10.2466/PR0.99.3.794-798

Gunther, A. C. (1995). Overrating the X rating: The third person perception and support for censorship of pornography. *Journal of Communication*, 45(1), 27–38. https://doi.org/10.1111/j.1460-2466.1995.tb00712.x

Gunther, A. C., & Hwa, A. P. (1996). Public perceptions of television influence and opinions about censorship in Singapore. *International Journal of Public Opinion Research*, 8(3), 248–265. https://doi.org/10.1093/ijpor/8.3.248

Hyman, H. H., & Sheatsley, P. B. (1950). The current status of American public opinion. In J. C. Payne (Ed.), *The teaching of contemporary affairs* (pp. 11–34). National Education Association.

Kartman, B., Stålhammar, N.-O., & Johannesson, M. (1996). Valuation of health changes with the contingent valuation method: A test of scope and question order effects. *Health Economics*, 5(6), 531–541. https://doi.org/10.1002/(SICI)1099-1050(199611)5:6<531::AID-HEC235>3.0.CO;2-J

Klein, R. A., Ratliff, K. A., Vianello, M., Adams, R. B., Jr., Bahník, Š., Bernstein, M. J., Bocian, K., Brandt, M. J., Brooks, B., Brumbaugh, C. C., Cemalcilar, Z., Chandler, J., Cheong, W., Davis, W. E., Devos, T., Eisner, M., Frankowska, N., Furrow, D., Galliani, E. M., . . . Nosek, B. A. (2014). Investigating variation in replicability. *Social Psychology*, 45(3), 142–152. https://doi.org/10.1027/1864-9335/a000178

Knauper, B., Schwarz, N., Park, D., & Fritsch, A. (2007). The perils of interpreting age differences in attitude reports: Question order effects decrease with age. *Journal of Official Statistics*, 23(4), 515–528.

Krosnick, J. A. (1991). Response strategies for coping with the cognitive demands of attitude measures in surveys. *Applied Cognitive Psychology*, 5(3), 213–236. https://doi.org/10.1002/acp.2350050305

Krosnick, J. A., & Schuman, H. (1988). Attitude intensity, importance, and certainty and susceptibility to response effects. *Journal of Personality and Social Psychology*, 54(6), 940–952. https://doi.org/10.1037/0022-3514.54.6.940

Lee, S., & Grant, D. (2009). The effect of question order on self-rated general health status in a multilingual survey context. *American Journal of*

Epidemiology, 169(12), 1525–1530. https://doi.org/10.1093/aje/kwp070

McClendon, M. J., & O'Brien, D. J. (1988a). Explaining question order effects on the relationship between safety and neighborhood satisfaction. *Social Science Quarterly, 69*(3), 764–771.

McClendon, M. J., & O'Brien, D. J. (1988b). Question-order effects on the determinants of subjective well-being. *Public Opinion Quarterly, 52*(3), 351–364. https://doi.org/10.1086/269112

Narayan, S., & Krosnick, J. A. (1996). Education moderates some response effects in attitude measurement. *Public Opinion Quarterly, 60*(1), 58–88. https://doi.org/10.1086/297739

Olson, K., Smyth, J. D., Horwitz, R., Keeter, S., Lesser, V., Marken, S., & Associates. (2019). *Report of the AAPOR Task Force on Transitions From Telephone Surveys to Self-Administered and Mixed-Mode Surveys: Task Force Report*. American Association for Public Opinion Research.

Petty, R. E., & Cacioppo, J. T. (1981). *Attitudes and persuasion: Classic and contemporary approaches*. William C. Brown.

Peytchev, A., & Hill, C. A. (2010). Experiments in mobile web survey design: Similarities to other modes and unique considerations. *Social Science Computer Review, 28*(3), 319–335. https://doi.org/10.1177/0894439309353037

Price, V., & Tewksbury, D. (1996). Measuring the third person effect of news: The impact of question order, contrast and knowledge. *International Journal of Public Opinion Research, 8*(2), 120–141. https://doi.org/10.1093/ijpor/8.2.120

Rasinski, K. A., Visser, P. S., Zagatsky, M., & Rickett, E. (2005). Using non-conscious goal priming to improve the quality of self-report data. *Journal of Experimental Social Psychology, 41*(3), 321–327. https://doi.org/10.1016/j.jesp.2004.07.001

Rimal, R. N., & Real, K. (2005). Assessing the perceived importance of skin cancer: How question-order effects are influenced by issue involvement. *Health Education & Behavior, 32*(3), 398–412. https://doi.org/10.1177/1090198104272341

Salwen, M. B., & Driscoll, P. D. (1997). Consequences of the third person perception in support of press restrictions in the O. J. Simpson trial. *Journal of Communication, 47*(2), 60–78. https://doi.org/10.1111/j.1460-2466.1997.tb02706.x

Schaeffer, N. C., & Dykema, J. (2020). Advances in the science of asking questions. *Annual Review of Sociology, 46*(1), 37–60. https://doi.org/10.1146/annurev-soc-121919-054544

Schuman, H., Kalton, G., & Ludwig, J. (1983). Context and contiguity in survey questionnaires. *Public Opinion Quarterly, 47*(1), 112–115. https://doi.org/10.1086/268771

Schuman, H., & Ludwig, J. (1983). The norm of even-handedness in surveys as in life. *American Sociological Review, 48*(1), 112–120. https://doi.org/10.2307/2095149

Schuman, H., & Presser, S. (1981). *Questions and answers in attitude surveys*. Wiley.

Schuman, H., Presser, S., & Ludwig, J. (1981). Context effects on survey responses to questions about abortion. *Public Opinion Quarterly, 45*(2), 216–223. https://doi.org/10.1086/268652

Schwarz, N. (2003). Self-Reports in Consumer Research: The challenge of comparing cohorts and cultures. *The Journal of Consumer Research, 29*(4), 588–594. https://doi.org/10.1086/346253

Schwarz, N., & Hippler, H.-J. (1995). Subsequent questions may influence answers to preceding questions in mail surveys. *Public Opinion Quarterly, 59*(1), 93–97. https://doi.org/10.1086/269460

Schwarz, N., Strack, F., Hippler, H.-J., & Bishop, G. (1991). The impact of administration mode on response effects in survey measurement. *Applied Cognitive Psychology, 5*(3), 193–212. https://doi.org/10.1002/acp.2350050304

Schwarz, N., Strack, F., & Mai, H.-P. (1991). Assimilation and contrast effects in part-whole question sequences: A conversational logic analysis. *Public Opinion Quarterly, 55*(1), 3–23. https://doi.org/10.1086/269239

Sigelman, L. (1981). Question-order effects on presidential popularity. *Public Opinion Quarterly, 45*(2), 199–207. https://doi.org/10.1086/268650

Smith, T. (1982). *Conditional order effects*. General Social Survey Technical Report No. 33. NORC.

Smith, T. W. (1978). In search of house effects: A comparison of responses to various questions by different survey organizations. *Public Opinion Quarterly, 42*(4), 443–463. https://doi.org/10.1086/268473

Smith, T. W. (1979). Happiness: Time trends, seasonal variations, intersurvey differences, and other mysteries. *Social Psychology Quarterly, 42*(1), 18–30. https://doi.org/10.2307/3033870

Smith, T. W. (1983). *Children and abortions: An in question order* (General Social Survey Technical Report No. 42). NORC.

Stark, T. H., Silber, H., Krosnick, J. A., Blom, A. G., Aoyagi, M., Belchior, A., Bosnjak, M., Clement, S. L., John, M., Jónsdóttir, G. A., Lawson, K., Lynn, P., Martinsson, J., Shamshiri-Petersen, D., Tvinnereim, E., & Yu, R. R. (2020). Generalization of classic question order effects across cultures. *Sociological Methods & Research, 49*(3), 567–602. https://doi.org/10.1177/0049124117747304

Strack, F., Martin, L. L., & Schwarz, N. (1988). Priming and communication: The social determinants of information use in judgments of life-satisfaction. *European Journal of Social Psychology, 18*(5), 429–442. https://doi.org/10.1002/ejsp.2420180505

Sudman, S., & Bradburn, N. M. (1982). *Asking questions: A practical guide to questionnaire construction.* Jossey-Bass.

Tourangeau, R. (1984). Cognitive sciences and survey methods. In T. B. Jabine, M. L. Straf, J. M. Tanur, & R. Tourangeau (Eds.), *Cognitive aspects of survey methodology: Building a bridge between disciplines* (pp. 73–100). The National Academies Press. https://doi.org/10.17226/930

Tourangeau, R., Conrad, F. G., & Couper, M. P. (2013). *The science of web surveys.* Oxford University Press. https://doi.org/10.1093/acprof:oso/9780199747047.001.0001

Tourangeau, R., Couper, M. P., & Conrad, F. (2004). Spacing, position, and order: Interpretive heuristics for visual features of survey questions. *Public Opinion Quarterly, 68*(3), 368–393. https://doi.org/10.1093/poq/nfh035

Tourangeau, R., & Rasinski, K. A. (1988). Cognitive processes underlying context effects in attitude measurement. *Psychological Bulletin, 103*(3), 299–314. https://doi.org/10.1037/0033-2909.103.3.299

Tourangeau, R., Rasinski, K. A., & Bradburn, N. (1991). Measuring happiness in surveys: A test of the subtraction hypothesis. *Public Opinion Quarterly, 55*(2), 255–266. https://doi.org/10.1086/269256

Tourangeau, R., Rasinski, K. A., Bradburn, N., & D'Andrade, R. (1989a). Belief accessibility and context effects in attitude measurement. *Journal of Experimental Social Psychology, 25*(5), 401–421. https://doi.org/10.1016/0022-1031(89)90030-9

Tourangeau, R., Rasinski, K. A., Bradburn, N., & D'Andrade, R. (1989b). Carryover effects in attitude surveys. *Public Opinion Quarterly, 53*(4), 495–524. https://doi.org/10.1086/269169

Tourangeau, R., Rips, L. J., & Rasinski, K. (2000). *The psychology of survey response.* Cambridge University Press. https://doi.org/10.1017/CBO9780511819322

Turner, C. F. (1984). Why do surveys disagree? Some preliminary hypotheses and some disagreeable examples. In C. F. Turner & E. Martin (Eds.), *Surveying subjective phenomena* (Vol. 2, pp. 159–214). Russell Sage.

Wilson, D. C., Moore, D. W., McKay, P. F., & Avery, D. R. (2008). Affirmative action programs for women and minorities: Expressed support affected by question order. *Public Opinion Quarterly, 72*(3), 514–522. https://doi.org/10.1093/poq/nfn031

CHAPTER 15

INTERVIEWS AND INTERVIEWING TECHNIQUES

Anna Madill

A long-standing and useful definition of an *interview* is that it is a conversation with a purpose (Bingham & Moore, 1924). As this definition implies, interviewers and interviewees will draw on their everyday interactional competencies to do interviewing (Houtkoop-Steenstra, 1997). Even so, the limited empirical analyses available on interviews indicate that they involve a distinct *kind* of interaction. Interviews tend to be scheduled and conducted at a prearranged location, and the interviewee is usually offered some form of orientation to the task that prepares him or her for the potential strangeness of the interaction (Lee & Roth, 2004) and, sometimes, a financial incentive is offered. This strangeness allies interviews more with forms of institution talk than with ordinary conversation, in particular, the interview's question–answer format (Potter & Hepburn, 2005), tendency to favor interviewer neutrality (Antaki et al., 2000), and asymmetrical outcome agenda (Silverman, 1973). It may be that the most popular form—the semistructured interview—has greater similarity to ordinary conversation than most (Wooffitt & Widdicombe, 2006).

TYPES OF INTERVIEW

Interviews seem designed to tap lived experience, but there is a large variety of interviewing types. Differences are evident in terms of interviewing style; however, procedural differences are rooted more fundamentally in methodological approach. This encompasses different epistemologies (ways in which knowledge is conceptualized), ontologies (which includes different understandings of subjectivity), and axiologies (values and ethos; see also Chapter 1, this volume). Some interviewing methods offer a well-worked-out methodological framework in relation to such issues (e.g., Hollway & Jefferson, 2000), whereas for most, these remain implicit or vary according to the method of analysis the interviews serve. What is important, however, is that some consideration be given to the coherence between research questions, interview type, and method(s) of analysis.

A central procedural difference is the extent to which the interview is structured. The *semistructured* format is the most popular method of qualitative data collection and generation

---

I thank the participants on whose interviews I have drawn in this chapter. I extend my thanks also to the interviewers who contributed to these data sets and to the researchers who allowed me to comment on the discussions we have had about their interviewing experiences. Paragraphs describing interviewing types are adapted from "Qualitative Research and Its Place in Psychological Science," by A. Madill and B. Gough, 2008, *Psychological Methods, 13,* 254–271. Copyright 2008 by the American Psychological Association.

https://doi.org/10.1037/0000318-015
APA Handbook of Research Methods in Psychology, Second Edition: Vol. 1. Foundations, Planning, Measures, and Psychometrics, H. Cooper (Editor-in-Chief)
Copyright © 2023 by the American Psychological Association. All rights reserved.

in psychology (Madill, 2007). A schedule is prepared that contains open-ended questions and prompts that, prima facie, appear relevant to the research topic, although the interview is conducted with flexibility in the ordering of questions and the follow-up of unanticipated avenues that the participant raises (J. A. Smith, 1995). The *unstructured* interview uses a free-flowing conversational style in contrast to the *structured* interview, in which specific prepared questions are asked in a determined order. Both appear rare in the qualitative literature because qualitative researchers typically prefer to strike a balance between retaining interviewer control and approximating normal conversation (see Houtkoop-Steenstra, 2000, for research on the conduct of the structured, standardized, or survey interview).

Other types of interview include the *narrative* format, which, like the semistructured interview, uses nonleading, open questions. However, the narrative style prioritizes elicitation of personal stories with minimal researcher prompting (see Hollway & Jefferson, 2000, for a critique of the semistructured interview from a narrative perspective). *Biographical* interviews, by definition, focus on life history and may involve a narrative style. Moreover, inspired by the narrative style, the free-association narrative interview links the tradition of biographical interviewing with psychoanalytical theory. A central premise here is that participants will, unconsciously, provide important information about themselves that is then open to analytic interpretation by tracking the participant's chain of associations. Interpersonal process recall involves asking participants to make explicit their internal experiences during review of prior (usually video recorded) therapy sessions in which he or she took part, although this technique can be extended to other forms of recorded interactions. In the ethnographic interview, it is the participant's tacit and explicit knowledge as a member that is tapped.

INTERVIEWING DEVELOPMENT AND TECHNIQUES

The semistructured interview is the most popular interview format in psychological research, and many of the techniques used in semistructured interviewing are transferable to other interview formats. I therefore focus on the semistructured interview in discussing interviewing techniques and illustrate each identified technique with examples from my own corpus of transcribed semistructured interviews.[1] But first, I consider how one might go about developing a schedule for a semistructured interview.

Developing an Interview Schedule

Virtually all research interviewing will require preparation of an interview schedule that acts as a prompt for the interviewer. At the most basic, this may take the form of a topic guide that merely lists the themes or subjects about which the interviewee will be asked to comment. If a more detailed schedule is required, this will include fully worked out and carefully worded questions and prompts in what appears to be an appropriate order. The level of detail and flexibility of the question order will depend on the type of interview conducted. It is also worth considering whether the interview should start with the collection of structured demographic or other factual information that is necessary for describing the study participants and for contextualizing the findings (e.g., see situating the sample in Elliott et al., 1999).

A good approach to developing a schedule is to start by listing the kind of themes or content that should be covered in the interview to address the study research questions. This list then can be placed in an order that makes sense, although this order is likely to change if one is being appropriately responsive to the interviewee. Depending on the research, the interviews may have a fairly

---

[1]Each extract is identified first with the corpus from which it is drawn and second with the gender of the participant. The author (Anna Madill) is the interviewer unless otherwise stated. The three data corpora are as follows: quarry (interviews with residents living near an active stone quarry in rural England, research funded by the Minerals Industries Research Organisation), medic (interviews with medical students undertaking a year of study intercalating in psychology in a university in the North of England, research funded by the Higher Education Funding Council of England), and boundaries (interviews with counselors and psychotherapists in the United Kingdom on managing sexual boundaries in their professional practice, research funded by the British Association for Counselling and Psychotherapy).

straightforward temporal structure, for example, if they follow the timeline in the interviewee's life. In general, potentially more sensitive themes should, if possible, be placed later in the interview because the interviewee has then had time to settle into the interview and, hopefully, a rapport has been developed. If required and suitable for the interview format, these content themes can be developed into actual questions and prompts added. Finally, the interview schedule should be piloted to check both its acceptability and understandability to participants and its ability to generate relevant material for analysis. Many types of interviewing and approaches to research expect that the schedule will be revised continually throughout a study as data collection reveals the more and the less productive lines of questioning (Hollway & Jefferson, 2000). This process does not necessarily make earlier interviews redundant if they still contribute some useful information to the study.

Discussion now turns to interviewing techniques. As I show, although guidance can be offered to help generate a productive semistructured interview, no specific technique guarantees success. What catalyzes a rich and enlightening response with one interviewee at a certain juncture may misfire with another. The interviewer needs to be responsive to the ongoing interaction and, with experience, a good interviewer learns to draw on a range of strategies in flexible and contextually appropriate ways. I discuss and illustrate using extracts from my own corpus of transcribed semistructured interviews the following important considerations: nonleading questions, open questions, short questions, grounding in examples, prompts and follow-ups, silence, the not-knowing interviewer, formulations, interviewer self-disclosure, and challenging the interviewee.

Nonleading questions. A principal technique in semistructured interviewing is the asking of nonleading questions. *Nonleading questions* are interrogatives that avoid steering the interviewee toward a specific answer. The rationale for using nonleading questions is that the aim of the research interview is to solicit the interviewee's experiences and point of view and, conversely, to avoid merely reproducing the interviewer's assumptions and preconceptions. A common mistake is to ask a question that is leading in that it contains within it an either–or candidate answer, as I do, unfortunately, in the following extract (note that boldface is used to indicate the section of particular interest in each extract; I indicates *interviewer* and P indicates *participant*):

> Extract 1 (quarry, female participant)[2]
> I: **I'm with you. So he's been there since February and are you expecting it for a certain length of time or are you just going to see how it goes?**
> P: He is hoping that he can get it set up with other—he's already employed someone else. There's other staff out there and then he will just oversee it sort of fifty-fifty and then come home again.

Either–or questions are leading in that they delimit the scope of the interviewee's answer to a binary option—even if, as above, the interviewee refuses to be held to this. An appropriate nonleading question here would have been something like, "How do you see this situation panning out?"

Leading questions can take the form of a statement with tone of voice indicating that they are to be taken as interrogatives. In the following extract from the same interview, I produced two of this kind of leading question in a row:

> Extract 2 (quarry, female participant)
> I: **Yes it must be quite difficult him being away for three weeks out of four?**

---

[2]Transcription is light. Verbatim content is recorded with attention to general features of the talk that may impact the interpretation of that content: laughter ((laughs)); particular tone of voice ((smiley voice)); inaudible speech ((inaudible)); unclear content in double brackets with question mark, for example, ((To that end?)) yeah um; short untimed pauses (.); pauses timed in seconds (4); ? is upwards intonation indicating an interrogative; omitted names [town]; overlapping speech that does not constitute a new turn (I: Yes); speaker breaks off, for example, "Well so—but obviously"; the use of an ellipsis . . . at beginning or end of turn and (. . .) in the middle of a turn indicates truncated content.

P: Well two years ago it was two weeks out of four in Russia so.
I: Oh right so you're reasonably used to it?
P: Yes my dad was the same. He was an engineer and ended up six months in India, Kuwait, South Africa, Canada, and so on.

My first question is leading in that I offer an answer within the question itself: that "it is quite difficult." The interviewee responds by offering further contextualizing information, to which I again ask a question that itself contains an answer: that she is "reasonably used to it." This time she agrees explicitly and offers some further information. The contextualizing information is possibly useful, but the status as data of the "difficulty" and of being "used to it" is unclear because it came from the interviewer. Another problem with leading items is that immediate agreement in response to the interviewer must be treated with caution. The preference in conversation is for agreement, because agreement contributes to interactional ease (Pomerantz, 1984). A consensual first response may be followed by detail that suggests more ambivalence or even disagreement. In Extract 2, an appropriate, nonleading question would have been something like, "How do you feel about him being away for three weeks out of four?"

These are two passages in which my interviewing technique could have been better. Thankfully, most of the sequences offered in this chapter contain nonleading questions, as shown in Questions 1, 2, 3, and 5 in Extract 8 below.

Open—and closed—questions. An *open question* is an interrogative produced in a form that requires more than a simple "yes/no/don't know" answer. For example, open questions might start in any of the following ways: "Tell me about . . ." "To what extent . . ." or "In what ways . . ." Open questions are arguably the central technique of semistructured interviewing. Their purpose is to invite interviewees to provide an extended, on-topic answer, unconstrained as far as possible by the interviewer's assumptions, although this does not mean that open questions are not at times potentially leading (e.g., see Extracts 7 and 8). In Extract 3, the open question in the "tell me about" form catalyzes a rich narrative as intended.

Extract 3 (medic, female participant)
I: So can you tell me um about how you came to be doing a medical degree then ((laughs))?
P: Yeah it's a bit (.) of a strange story ((laughs)).
I: Okay.
P: I actually wanted to be a vet in the beginning (I: Hm mm) and I applied to um vet (.) to do veterinary medicine at university and I didn't get a place so I kind of had to re-think about what I wanted to do . . .

Open questions deliberately offer little guidance on the specific content or structure of the response. One drawback is that interviewees may be flummoxed by this and seek clarification on how to answer. So, although the participant in Extract 3 understands that my question invites a story, she still checks out whether a (probably extended) narrative is acceptable. As you will see in Extract 4, virtually the same question appears to wrong-foot another participant more dramatically. The participant's response indicates an interactional difficulty or misalignment, which may disrupt rapport and possibly tempt the interviewer to be more leading than desired.

Extract 4 (medic, female participant)
I: Okay ((laughs)) so can you tell me how you come to be doing a degree in medicine then?
P: Um why did I choose it?
I: Yes.
P: Um it's a long time ago ((laughs)) (.) um I think my strongest subjects are in sciences so and that's what my interest was . . .

The interviewer needs to judge when a participant is ready and able to provide an extended account on a particular topic. Extracts 3 and 4 are taken from early in the respective interviews and were preceded by a series of closed, demographic-style questions of fact that provided required information, were simple to answer, and were designed to ease participants into the interview situation. Even so, this open question was often responded to with a request for clarification, and the transcripts show that, actually, I often used a *why* question in the way suggested by the participant in Extract 4. There are, however, good reasons to avoid *why* questions in general, as I discuss in the section Grounding in Examples. An advantage of the "can you tell me" format is that it often provides better material for analysis because participants usually structure their answers in terms of what is important to them.

Another potential problem with open questions is that they can feel clumsy and can seem overly formalized. A common effect of inexperienced interviewing is the production of a short, shallow interview. In the anxiety of the moment, interviewers transform the interview schedule into a series of easy-to-articulate closed questions, sticking to the sequence of the questions in the schedule too rigidly and not following up novel aspects of the interviewee's contribution. This is shown in Extract 5, which is taken from a semistructured research interview conducted as part of an undergraduate project.

> Extract 5 (quarry, female interviewer, male participant)
>
> **I: And has there been any physical damage to your property or any of your possessions that you're aware of?**
> P: No no.
> **I: Do you think the quarry being so close by has affected house prices in the village?**
> P: (.) Erm no I don't think so. I don't think so. Well I suppose it might a little bit just where it is anyway cause it's a cold and bleak place anyway. It's foggy a lot (I: Mm). It isn't everybody's cup of tea like and we used to get really hard winters ((inaudible)) so cold and you just get snowed in for weeks on end sometimes.
> **I: Yeah so you think you think in comparison it's it's not so bad?**
> P: No no.
> **I: So you've never considered moving?**
> P: No no.

The interviewee appears rather reticent to speak and the series of closed questions probably contributed to the production of short answers structured to a high degree by the interviewer. Even so, Extract 5 illustrates how a closed question, the second in this extract, can be responded to with more than a yes/no/don't know answer. Although closed questions tend to be considered bad practice in semistructure interviewing, I think they do actually have their place. They can feel less awkward than some kinds of open questions, which is why inexperienced interviewers may fall back on them. More important, however, closed questions are often responded to in research interviews with the desirable, extended narrative without, for some participants, the anxiety of having to answer what might feel like a too-open question.

> Extract 6 (medic, female participant)
>
> **I: Have you ever been present when (.) a consultant or nurse or doctor has had to give any bad news to anybody?**
> P: Yeah yeah I have actually. Um, there was a man who had liver cancer and the doctor had to tell them um and that was also very surreal because (.) you can't you just can't believe that I'm there hearing (.) someone break this bad news to somebody and there wasn't much treatment that the patient could have so . . .

The participant in Extract 6 typically produces a yes (no–don't know) response to the closed question but goes on to provide a rich description of a relevant situation. Although I used a closed-question format, in not immediately coming in after "yeah, I have actually," I conveyed the impression of expecting additional material, which then was provided (see the section The Power of Silence).

As shown in Extract 7, a useful question to include toward the end of an interview is, "Is there anything you'd like to add?" This is a closed question but illustrates a further reason why, I believe, some kinds of closed question are appropriate in research interviews. Changing this into an open question would produce something like "What more would you like to add?" Ironically, to me, this sounds too directive and, like open questions in general, presents the assumption that there is indeed something further to add. I prefer the interactional delicacy of the closed format here and find that it does not stop participants producing rich material—even if at first the response is "no."

> Extract 7 (quarry, Participant 1 is female, Participant 2 is male)
>
> **I: Is there anything that I haven't covered that you'd like to add?**
>
> P1: I don't think so.
>
> P2: No I'd say it's got no impact on us at all.
>
> P1: Yes I mean I think the in-fill is a really good point and something that to think about.
>
> P2: Yes I think the in-fill and showing the artifacts that they've found down at the pub would would bring it out the closet a little bit I think. I think they've been and I've been in this industry so I know . . .

Extract 8 is discussed more fully in the next section, Short Questions—and One Question at a Time, but it is worth pointing out here that it offers a good example of how the wording of open questions has to be considered carefully to avoid being leading. In Extract 8 my question, "How did you work with it?" is a less leading open question than, for example, "Do you work with it therapeutically?," which is closed. Rephrasing simply as an open question, "How do you work with it therapeutically?" is possibly leading in assuming that the participant does in fact do this.

Short questions—and one question at a time. As I have become more experienced in research interviewing, I have become more comfortable asking shorter questions and, in general, saying less—and listening harder. Short questions can feel impolite, and rather direct, and a series of them can seem overly inquisitorial. Research interviewing is not an ordinary conversation, however, and, as long as there is good rapport, I think participants can find short questions helpful. In fact, in one pilot interview I conducted, my interviewee commented spontaneously to this effect. The following passage is from a research interview in which I deliberately practiced the short question technique [note that where content has been truncated midturn, this is indicated by (. . .)]:

> Extract 8 (boundaries, male participant)
>
> P: . . . I don't know what was in her mind or even half in her mind was was an unconscious sexual invitation. It might have been I don't know.
>
> **I: How did you work with it?**
>
> P: I think I just let it register (. . .) maybe if I think about it then maybe I was just afraid of my own reactions and wanted to put some kind of a ((inaudible word)).
>
> **I: How would you have dealt with it now?**
>
> P: Well in a dark street in downtown [name of town] I'm not sure I would stop (. . .) I'm not sure I would have done what I—I don't know I'd hope I ((inaudible phrase)).
>
> **I: And in what kind of way do you think?**
>
> P: Well you can't—if it happens in a session you can actually do it within the framework of the therapy (. . .) swung their legs and I just I tend to mostly dampen that out by not reinforcing it.
>
> **I: Okay. Do you work with it therapeutically?**

P: I can do yes I can do (. . .) I allow enough of my own responses and my relationship without crossing the boundary where it might become abusive.

I: How do you manage that?

P: I don't know ((laughing)) sometimes it's very—well I'll ask her if she's feeling uncomfortable (. . .) I might ask about her relationships and about her sexual needs you know. If it feels okay she will answer it.

A benefit of asking relatively brief questions is that it keeps the interview on task and avoids including possibly distracting or leading information (e.g., see the section Interviewer Self-Disclosure). Moreover, asking brief questions disciplines the interviewer to formulate one clearly worded question at a time. Asking long-winded questions that include several parts can overload the interviewee, and often it is only the final part of the question that is answered. Some of this kind of muddle is illustrated in Extract 9.

Extract 9 (boundaries, male participant)

I: There's actually now two things I want to follow up with you ((laughs)) (P: Go on yeah). **Your own use of supervision** (P: Yeah sure) **um and I want to follow up about intimacy of that** (P: Yeah sure). **I want to go back one step also about when um to continue a little bit more on the um counselors themselves** (P: Yes) **and where they are sexually. When you were um interviewing** (P: Yes) **potential counselors can you tell me how did you judge where that person was ((inaudible over-speaking))?**

P: ((Laughs)) It's appalling I mean it's like all interviewing procedures are very imperfect aren't they (. . .) but again it does suggest.

I: Having affairs?

P: With other—with other counselors.

I: With the counselors?

P: Yeah marriages breaking up and things (. . .) makes one wonder about you know how far people's boundaries are intact um yeah.

I: **How do you work with this in supervision** (P: Yeah) **because it's still ((inaudible over-speaking))**.

P: Yeah as a supervisee or a supervisor?

This passage was preceded by a series of fairly extended responses from the interviewee. To retain the flow of his answers I avoided interrupting and made a mental note of issues I wanted to follow up (see also the section Prompts and Follow-Up Questions). At the beginning of the extract, I list the issues, possibly as an aid to myself, in a rather muddled way and finally formulate a relevant question. I then have to remember to ask a question about the other issue I wanted to follow up—supervision—a bit later in the interview as indicated.

Grounding in examples. The purpose of a research interview is to generate material for analysis. A common mistake is to treat the interviewee as a kind of protosocial scientist by asking questions that require answers at a high level of conceptualization, particularly on issues that participants probably have not before thought about in this way (Potter & Hepburn, 2005). Such answers are of questionable value because they will too often consist of spontaneously produced lay theorizations and generalizations—unless, for good reasons, this is what is sought. A better strategy is to ask interviewees questions about their actual experiences and to request specific examples with detailed description. This is more likely to produce rich material that the researcher then analyses within a relevant, rigorous framework.

Extract 10 (boundaries, male participant)

P: . . . I think you know these three examples may be you know the extremes and extremes of how therapy was not managed very well. But these are the very same thing that went wrong in those relationships—go wrong or go well to various degrees in all relationships.

I: Okay can you give me an example then of maybe a process a similar kind of process in another therapy where you feel is very relevant to this management of the sexual boundary?

P: Well let's see. When patients have been referred and they attend for sexual dysfunction (. . .) for instance in my whole career I would occasionally be asked to assess women who were raped had been raped and I—they they never came back. And I think that that was which to do with with a a gender issue was also something about my particular approach to assessment . . .

Asking for specific examples from the interviewee's own experience has the benefit also of (almost always) ensuring that one is asking questions that the participant can actually answer. Had I followed this procedure, I would have avoided asking the participant in the following extract to speculate on things about which she could not know.

Extract 11 (boundaries, female participant)

I: Mm (2) do you think it might have been a difference in time that things have been more problematic for you in your personal life—that this particular client—that that the process with the client might have been difficult for you than it might?

P: Um (1) I think it might have been momentarily more difficult (. . .) I s—suspect in some ways it's a protection working with [client group] because it's a constant reminder that they they aren't there as partners.

I: And and I'm kind of struck that the kind of strength of that statement for you that your clients can't support your needs (P: Mm) **that—if that's a right interpretation of that—**(P: Mm) **and I'm wondering I'm wondering whether it might that might not be felt quite so strongly for some therapists in some situations do you think that's . . .?**

P: I think that's possibly and certainly I've a colleague who fell in love with a—(1) and I think she'd admit it fell in love with a male patient (. . .) and that it was a good ending and not see him again was very therapeutic.

I: Mm (1) f—for both of them do you think? ((laughs)) (P: Um) **I'm wondering about it's was sometimes more two ways?**

P: Possibly possibly I'm not so sure about (I: No) obviously.

I: Well yes you're talking a third third party here (P: Mm) . . .

In this extract, the participant provides a speculative answer to my question about how things might have been for her had circumstances been different—indeed, how would she know? She then does very well to provide a response to my question about other therapists by describing the experience of a colleague. However, she politely declines to speculate further when I ask about the client's perspective and I, at last, realize the inappropriateness of my line of questioning.

Perhaps surprisingly, it is usually good advice to avoid asking *why* questions. Interactionally, *why* questions may feel confrontational. Most important, however, people often have little knowledge about, or insight into, the reason for things or into what motivates them, and *why* questions too easily produce ad hoc rationalizations of questionable validity (see Hollway & Jefferson, 2000).

Extract 12 (medic, female participant)

P: Um well I did do a lot more work. [Person's name] did psychology as well and like I did a lot more work compared to him. He was really like I'll study the day before and.

I: ((Inaudible)) as you as well the same exams as you?

P: Yeah.

I: Right.

P: And he would like study maybe the next four and so like they almost feel better so.

I: Why do you think that was?

P: I dunno like he just (.) like he just probably (.) thought like you're not disciplined you know. Some people can do the work and some people don't.

I: Do you think it was to do with the subject matter because it was his first choice of degree and he'd already had a whole year of it before you came in and.

P: I suppose that's part of it . . .

In Extract 12, the participant indicates that she does not know the answer to my *why* question but, being helpful, goes on to offer a *probably* account. I go on to make the mistake of offering her a candidate answer, which she agrees is a possibility. The material produced, as in Extract 11, is therefore highly speculative and, because of this, probably difficult to analyze. I would have been much better asking her to describe her own study habits and, in relation to this, how her friend's strategy compared and how it made her feel about how she, herself, worked.

There are, of course, exceptions to the generally good advice of not asking *why* questions. Examples include research in which interviewees have been selected for their theoretical or professional knowledge and the study research questions require the tapping of this expertise. Another example is research that is interested in understanding the sense that people make of their experience when pushed to fall back on their stock of cultural common sense. For example, I helped design an interview schedule for a study exploring cultural differences in the understanding of somatic symptoms in pregnancy. The interview schedule contained questions in which participants were asked to ground their experiences in actual examples, but we considered it appropriate also to include some why questions to force a rationalization from, or at least an articulation of, the women's stock of cultural assumptions. Responses to *why* questions were not taken at face value but rather were analyzed for what they revealed about differences in the underlying assumptions of the two cultural groups studied.

Prompts and follow-up questions. A common mistake is sticking too rigidly to the interview schedule. This can produce a rather short, shallow interview. Good research interviewing requires active listening: monitoring constantly the links between what the interviewee is saying and the research schedule, noting which questions no longer need to be asked but also avenues needing to be explored in more detail through the use of prompts and follow-up questions. Prompts can be included in the interview schedule as they identify areas of prima facie interest, which, it is hoped, will be covered spontaneously by interviewees. If they are not covered by the interviewee, then the interviewer has a reminder in the schedule to ask.

Follow-up questions are developed during the interview by the interviewer to explore in more depth relevant, but unanticipated, information or direction in the talk. Follow-ups along the lines of "can you tell me more about" are usually productive and simple to use. Extract 13 offers an example of this format and also the technique of asking the interviewee to explain further their use of a specific word.

Extract 13 (boundaries, male participant)

P: . . . I mean look at the [name] guidelines for most of this can be savage and draconian in the sense of not just no relationships while you're working with somebody which is you know obvious but some will end up saying never and some say four years. Some of the guidelines say four years as you know and I mean that may be considered unduly prescriptive but.

I: Can I ask about (P: Yes) um you use the word draconian (P: Yes). Can you explain a little more to me?

P: Yeah yeah I suppose that seems to me to be unreasonably inhuman in terms of the kind of relationships . . .

In the following example, I start the interview by asking the first question in my interview schedule and then follow up with a question asking for more information about a novel aspect of the answer that is of research interest:

Extract 14 (medics, female participant)

I: You've had the whole cycle of a psychology degree. Can you tell me what your impression is about how this year has compared to what you've been used to in medicine?

P: Okay it's been quite different (. . .) it sounds silly but like seeing how normal students ((laughs)) kind of go about and like we're—like there's no lectures to go to what do we do and yeah. So I've found I've had a lot of time to myself.

I: How did you fill that time?

P: ((Laughs)) Well so—but obviously you're meant to study in that time but like I got a job . . .

Identifying aspects of the participant's answer that are relevant to the study but not on the interview schedule and formulating good follow-up questions to explore these areas in more depth are vital to a productive semistructured interview. It is almost inevitable that some novel areas are not explored fully during the interview, but it very frustrating to analyze an interview when tantalizing comments are passed by without further discussion. Good follow-up questions—presented at the right time—are, however, probably one of the most difficult aspects of research interviewing. Practice in phrasing short, open, nonleading questions is extremely helpful, as is familiarity with a few stock follow-up questions: "Can you tell me more about that?" "Can you give me an example of that?" "How did that make you feel?" and "What happened next?"

The Power of Silence

One important way in which the research interview tends to be different from ordinary conversation is that the deliberate aim of one interactant (the interviewer) is to facilitate the other's (the interviewee's) contribution. Ordinary conversation is usually more democratic in the sharing of the floor. Conversation analysis demonstrates that conversational turns can be considered usefully as consisting of turn construction units (TCUs; Liddicoat, 2007). Unless in storytelling mode or in certain institutional contexts, a speaker has the right to only one TCU before another speaker can take a turn, although, of course, there are strategies that can be employed to hold the floor, such as rushing on past the end of a TCU. Identification of a TCU is context specific, but they do have three central characteristics: TCUs complete an action (*do* something in talk, such as make a question); are grammatically complete (if not always grammatically correct); and, although of less import, the speaker's prosody makes them *sound* finished (Liddicoat, 2007).

Semistructured interviews are designed to encourage storytelling sequences from interviewees, as this usually provides a rich source of material for analysis. For example, the "can you tell me about" format prompts just such sequences. Another important technique for encouraging an extended contribution from the participant is for the interviewer to resist taking the floor at the end of an interviewee's TCU, even if the interviewee offers to hand this over through stopping and the use of body language, such as making eye contact. Not taking the floor at this point will leave a gap in the conversation, and this tends to feel awkward. Leaving a silence and using encouraging body language, such as a smile and a nod, or a simple acknowledging backchannel such as "hm mm" will encourage the interviewee to fill this silence with further material in a way that has not been led by the interviewer. This simple technique is particularly useful but does mean resisting the social pressure to speak, and this can take confidence and practice. In the following extract, I managed to leave a rather extreme 24 seconds of silence after the interviewee's TCU—an obvious handover point:

> Extract 15 (boundaries, female participant)
>
> I: Because this is something as a you know as a lay person ((smiley voice)) um you—could confla— possibly in my mind I had a conflation between um supervision and personal therapy which was very nicely kind of untangled a bit in in discussion with my colleagues so we thought it would be a thing to particularly ask about and.
>
> P: Well some people do run supervision like that and I think I'm not sure I think it's a very good idea personally um (24) I suppose there's a lot of themes on different levels aren't there about intrusion . . .

Working productively with silence can also take the form of avoiding rushing in to amend, re-ask, or add to a question but, instead, leaving time for the interviewee to think:

> Extract 16 (boundaries, male participant)
>
> I: Is there anything that we've not discussed that you think would be helpful to add?
>
> P: (16) I I suppose the the an aspect of this is um is to do with you know we we talked about this in in terms of therapy that's that's okay but of course you know there are there are these very same points apply within professional relationships . . .

Working with silence needs careful judgment, though, to avoid spoiling rapport—because silence is awkward socially. The following example occurred very early in an interview in which I was avoiding coming in too soon, having asked my first question. However, even though the silence was shorter than that tolerated much later in the interview (see Extract 15), the interviewee's response, in which she checks out the reason for my delay in speaking, suggests that I had left it too long and caused some misalignment.

> Extract 17 (boundaries, female participant)
>
> P: . . . sometimes people have got into a predicament and have had nowhere to go but I like the tone of your advert and thinking because I think it addressed an area that is quite important really (1) um (3) is that enough um yeah?
>
> I: And what is definition of sexual boundary can you work with.

Leaving silence, or responding to turn-completing TCUs with bland but encouraging backchannels (e.g., "hm mm"), can also help to avoid interrupting the interviewee. Interruptions can spoil rapport and lose the flow of the participant's associations, which may be useful for analysis (Hollway & Jefferson, 2000). With experience, one can make a mental note to return to a point later with a follow-up question (done, if badly, in Extract 9). Potentially worse than interruptions to ask a question are interruptions in which the interviewer attempts to finish the interviewee's turn—a type of exchange that is commonplace in ordinary conversation. In a research interview, finishing the interviewee's turn produces poor material for analysis because it is not clear whether it is the interviewee's perspective that is being captured, even if they subsequently agree with the statement.

> Extract 18 (quarry, female participant)
>
> P: . . . lets just say we've never been back for a meal cos we like to be leisurely and er.

I: And you've got other places that you can go.

P: Yes, that's right (I: Yes). You're quite right.

In this example, the interviewee hesitates in ending her statement but, rather than rushing in to finish it, I would have been much better leaving a silence and seeing where she went with this because the status of the material would then have been clear. Not all interviewees will agree with how the interviewer completes their turn, however, as in the following example from an interview conducted for an undergraduate project:

Extract 19 (quarry, female interviewer, Participant 1 is male, Participant 2 is female)

P1: And the wind generally blows from west to east (I: Mm) which is fine but now that they've built this great big bund what does the wind do because at one time it used to whistle across the village and carry on. Now it whistles across the village and hits the bund so.

I: And whistles all the way back.

P1: But no.

P2: Well no it it.

P1: On the other side of the bund.

P2: On the other s—somebody who used to live down [place name] er a farm down there they used to say . . .

A possible benefit of getting it wrong is that the interviewer can, as here, catalyze an extended, corrective narrative. Getting it wrong, however, demonstrates misunderstanding on the part of the interviewer, and in both Extract 18 and 19, mere silence would have been a better strategy.

The Not-Knowing Interviewer

The title of this section is derived from the therapeutic stance of the not-knowing therapist in which the client is seen as the principal author of the therapy dialogue (Anderson & Goolishian, 1988). In a very real sense, when generating interview data for analysis, the interviewer does not know in advance the content of the material that will be obtained. They may have a general idea of how it might go but good interviewing requires that the interviewer avoids influencing the material toward their own expectations, and the techniques discussed in this chapter can contribute to this general aim. It is therefore a good principle to approach a research interview with an extreme modesty as to one's understanding of the topic of investigation.

Taking a not-knowing stance does not remove the obligation to demonstrate expertise in the practice of interviewing. If taken seriously as an approach to interviewing, it does, however, predispose the interviewer to formulate good, probing questions that generate excellent material for analysis. So, for example, although I know what the word *draconian* (Extract 13) means, in taking a not-knowing approach, I did not take for granted that my understanding in that context was the same as that of my interviewee. In asking him to expand on his use of the word, I therefore generated more detailed information for analysis, which was central to my research interests.

Sometimes my use of a not-knowing stance is, possibly, a little less ingenious. In a series of interviews with counselors and psychotherapists about their professional practice, I found myself stressing my lay status. In one sense, I was using this in a genuine manner to catalyze detailed explanation of sophisticated professional knowledge. On the other hand, I have a doctorate in psychotherapy research, have supervised and examined several doctorates in clinical psychology, and have taught psychological disorders at the undergraduate level for a long time. Something else was probably going on here.

Extract 20 (boundaries, female participant)

I: Okay can I ask—as somebody who isn't a trained clinician or counselor or anything um what I I kinda have a query about which is the way that as s—taking a psychodynamic approach y—you do re—what it sounds like you do reinterpret the sexual feelings of of you may not—for this client in a similar way attraction in general um does does that mitigate against the the feeling of meeting the client as another person and just I'm slightly (1) can I have that clarified?

P: ((To that end?)) yeah um (1).

I: If if the the feelings of attraction are I mean kind of partly that kind of felt with meeting with for you the the the benefits of meeting with client also as a person that I don't know whether I'm interpreting er getting your meaning right and then I mean stepping back and reinterpreting that.

P: So you're thinking about as transference . . .

Aside from the fact that my question(s) are extremely inarticulate and far too long (even though the interviewee in this pilot commented that eventually the question was good at prompting her into a useful clarification), there was no need to preface this with a statement as to my lay status. My take on this type of sequence is that it demonstrates some of the power issues that are probably endemic to research interviewing. In drawing attention to a way in which I may have been considered to have lower status in this interaction, I was probably trying to throw off any implication that I was taking a dominant position as interviewer. Hence, I was being, possibly, overdeferential to my interviewee, to some extent communicating my feeling of vulnerability, and intimating to the interviewee to go gently on me. With growing experience, I used this self-deprecating strategy less as I conducted the interviews in this series. That is not to say that this particular technique is always to be avoided. It is useful, however, to reflect on what one might be doing in such situations in order to draw on strategies *knowingly* rather than defensively. Moreover, reflecting on why one was interacting in a particular way during an interview allows assessment of its impact on the data, potentially modifying one's approach in subsequent interviews, and provides possibly useful material for the analysis.

With certain participants, taking a fully not-knowing stance may be in some ways counterproductive. One of my doctoral students conducted interviews with male ex-prisoners about their use of illegal drugs in prison, and the interviewees used drug slang in their descriptions. Discussing this in a supervision meeting, we wondered if this told us something about how the interviewer, herself, was being positioned to some extent as an *insider* in these interviews because she was expected to understand these terms. Although she was familiar with most of the slang, she wondered if there was an element of testing out her expertise as well, and that her *knowing* response was important in terms of rapport, trust, and her credibility. So, although she did check out what was meant by some of the terms during the interviews, it seemed important to not appear overly naïve with these participants. It is important to be sensitive to such issues, and there will be contexts, such as this, in which it might be appropriate to ask interviewees to clarify or expand on some things specifically "for the tape" (see also the section Power and Vulnerability).

Interviewer Formulations

In conversation analytic research, a formulation is a summary of what has gone before in a discussion and, as such, exhibits an understanding of what has been talked about (Heritage & Watson, 1979). Formulations are common in ordinary conversation, and interviewers may find themselves using formulations spontaneously to summarize what the interviewee has just said. A potential benefit of a within-interview formulation is that it can allow the interviewer to check out their understanding, as I do in the following extract:

Extract 21 (boundaries, male participant)

P: . . . so just ask that how do you think things have been going recently

309

you know and see what emerges from that.

I: It seems to be if I can check this understanding out with you that the therapist or a counselor probably uses quite a lot of self knowledge about possibly what their boundaries vulnerab—particular boundary vulnerabilities are. Isn't there a role for personal therapy? A contribution?

P: Yeah I think there probably is but the troubling thing is . . .

In this extract, I produce a formulation by way of a summarized gloss of the interviewee's seeming meaning and state explicitly that I am doing so to check out my understanding. However, I leave no time for the interviewee to comment on this candidate understanding or, at least, he does not attempt to take the floor at the relevant point, and I immediately ask a further question. This is problematic for analysis in that I do not have confirmation of, or commentary on, this formulation. Even if the participant agreed with me, however, the status of this agreement would have been questionable because we know that agreements are preferred to disagreements in interaction. My advice would be to avoid the habit of providing formulations when conducting a research interview and, instead, use the other techniques discussed in this chapter to draw the interviewee out on points that could do with further exploration. Leave the analysis to a later stage—at which point one can consider the material generated in the context of the other research interviews and one's specific research questions.

Interviewer Self-Disclosure

Interviewing style can be usefully placed on a continuum from formal to informal (Schaeffer, 1991). A more informal interviewing style may deliberately mirror aspects of ordinary conversation and, in so doing, include elements of interviewer self-disclosure. In self-disclosing, the interviewer comments as an individual, takes a personalized stance, and possibly reveals information about themself. This can be contrasted to remaining in a more neutral, professionalized interviewing role. An informal interviewing style can increase the rapport between interviewer and interviewee and, hence, the potential openness of the participant (Houtkoop-Steenstra, 1997; Koole, 2003). The evidence suggests, however, that informal interviewing is also likely to increase the chance of interviewees responding in the way they think the interviewer wants (Antaki et al., 2002). This converging of opinion does not have to be sought actively by the interviewer. The odd, inadvertent leading question or encouraging body language at points in the interview can provide the context for the production of an agreeable, shared account. On the other hand, a certain professional formality on the part of the interviewer that avoids taking a stance may limit the chance of collusion. This is not to pretend, however, that total interviewer neutrality is possible, or probably always desirable (see the section Critique of Interviews as Data). Using the suggestions offered in this chapter, reflecting on the interactional impact of one's demeanor and questioning, and acknowledging that a research interview is different in many important respects to an ordinary conversation are probably good general approaches—not in terms of ensuring objectivity but in terms of facilitating the interviewee's account.

In the series of quarry interviews I conducted, I deliberately set out to undertake relatively informal, semistructured interviewing—and in so doing, to be open to self-disclosure. In the following extract, my self-disclosure may have contributed to rapport development, but otherwise probably adds little to generating useful information for analysis. The extract illustrates the possibility that overly informal interviewing can produce interviewer–interviewee consensus accounts.

Extract 22 (quarry, female participant)

P: . . . that's not just this village and I mean I've lived in a few and that's just the way it is. They just don't take kindly to change of any type.

I: I don't live in a village but I can kind of—in my little street there's a bit over the way that they are trying to develop and we've had petitions and you know ((laughs)) not in your backyard. They don't want the extra cars and the extra parking and.

P: No you don't you just want to keep exactly what you've got . . .

In another interview in this series, my informal style appears to set the context for a subtle change of role and the interviewee asks me a question. A bit later on, although my first self-disclosure in the sequence achieves a response, my second appears to derail the conversation and is responded to minimally by the interviewee. I attempt to salvage the situation, badly, and go on to ask two questions at the one time, appearing to realize rather late that my disclosure could be seen as irrelevant and possibly intrusive.

Extract 23 (quarry, female participant)

P: Did you come up the hill or along the flat?

I: I came in this direction ((pointing)).

P: Right well they come that way and then they turn left towards [village name] the bulk of them.

I: Right so the majority of them go towards [village name].

P: Twice as many go that way as come this way but you do get them coming up the dales from [other village name] and through.

I: You know I live in [city name] although I'd heard about you know bikers being a problem in [region name]

I hadn't really connected it cos I think it's so rural isn't it and then you know big bikes going fast I mean it's not quite what you associate.

P: And a lot of them now are mature men in their 40s and 50s who I think are having second childhood.

I: Yes I actually was introduced—a colleague of mine had a 50th birthday and introduced me to a friend of her's and erm a couple of weeks later she told me he'd been killed on his motorbike—again (I: Yes) yes ((laughs)). Oh mm erm okay so if you go back to—that that is relevant (P: Yes) ((laughter)). Thank you for the details of that. It gives me a little bit more about what you know what isn't a concern and what actually is and it's not not related to the quarry ((laughs)). So yeah erm can you tell me a little bit more about your quarry visit then and then how that visit made you think about you know coming and living out here.

My opinion now is that the safest strategy is to avoid interviewer self-disclosure. If remaining open to the possibility of interviewing toward the informal end of the spectrum and the likelihood of this including self-disclosures, disclosures need careful consideration and a lot of interviewing experience. For example, my self-disclosures in Extract 23 occurred in the context of a sensitive topic (violent and untimely deaths), which might, itself, have invited increased intimacy. With greater skill, I would have been more aware of this dynamic during the interview and avoided straying from role. I have not had the experience of being asked a personal question or for my own opinion during a research interviewer. However, these are always possibilities. A good strategy is to be clear with participants about the interview format before starting and, if asked for one's point of view, to say that you would rather leave that discussion until after the interview has ended.

Disagreeing With or Challenging the Interviewee

The interviewer's role is viewed, most often, as a professionally neutral one and, as my discussion of self-disclosure above reinforces, attempted neutrality is usually the safest option. However, conveying complete neutrality is difficult. The questions asked may imply a particular stance towards the topic, and characteristics, such as age, gender, or self-presentation like clothing, may be taken to indicate the interviewer has a predicable set of values. Engaging reflexively with interviewing as a means of generating data and considering the impact of the research context on the data obtained is key to working productively with such issues (see the section Critique of Interviews as Data). However, there may be times when the interviewer wishes, or is placed in the dilemma of needing, to disagree with or challenge the interviewee: that is, to take up explicitly a counter position.

In most interviews, it will be strictly outside the interviewer's remit to correct interviewees on presumed matters of fact even if the interviewer's opinion is sought as a perceived expert on the topic of the interview. A useful way of sidestepping such a request is to reiterate that currently you are focusing on the interviewee's opinion or account of an experience. Research on topics that may cover disturbing material (e.g., experiences in prison) or may touch on the participant's vulnerabilities (e.g., interviews about surviving cancer) make it essential ethically to provide interviewees with information about appropriate sources of support. Providing such information is essential partly because it is not appropriate for the interviewer to take on a dual role as quasi-counselor, even if they have the appropriate training (see the section Ethical Considerations). Situations that are potentially more problematic include points in an interview when the interviewer finds it difficult not to provide information pertinent to the discussion that appears to be at odds with what the participant is saying. The following extract, for example, illustrates how an otherwise appropriate not-knowing stance brought the interviewer into an awkward situation in that she asked a question to which she knew the interviewee's response was incorrect (unfortunately, the recording is poor, hence the inaudibles):

Extract 24 (quarry, female interviewer, female participant)

I: Hmm how much information have you received from the people at the quarry ((inaudible)) general areas ((inaudible)).

P: None ((laughs)).

I: **Um cos there's been some weekly ((inaudible)) newsletter there about all ((inaudible)) you know like cos there's a liaison committee and they meet sometimes. We've been told the—you had the biggest quarterly newsletter that people in the village get.**

P: Oh wait a minute this this is to do with [village name] parish council and um ((laughter)). Yeah yeah it's it's we've we've got um a quarry liaison officer . . .

The undergraduate student interviewer makes a good job of recovering this situation. The participant had been pretty vehement in her criticism of the quarry throughout the interview, and it would have been easy for the interviewer to have let this go for the sake of retaining rapport. However, bravely, she offers a gentle challenge to the interviewee's blanket statement "none," using the strategy of "we've been told" (two students were present during the interview), which allows the possibility that they have been incorrectly informed. Luckily, the interviewee, good humoredly, construes the problem as her own misunderstanding.

Challenges may be more deliberate and strategic. As part of my boundaries sequence of interviews, I took a calculated risk in questioning the position that appeared to be taken by one of the therapist participants. The highly mitigated way in which my challenge is made deliberately softens its force, but that it is indeed a challenge is, of course, not lost on my interviewee.

Extract 25 (boundaries, male participant)

I: As a lay person ((smiley voice)) (P: Yes) **which hopefully this might by enlightening me help dig a little deeper—is there—to me it feels appropriate to engage on a kind of human level as well as a therapeutic** level but um so that the communication of being affected by what the client has gone through may be appropriate. I'd just like you to expand a bit on that for me that by looking affected is that always inappropriate (P: No!) or is it.

P: No (I: Yeah) no of course not! (I: No). It is that's that's about a degree of kind of empathy (I: Yeah) and of understanding (I: Mm) and a kind of genuineness around with a warmth with the material that's being presented that I mean that should be part you know of a good working alliance (I: Right). But but er and and um there are kind of like the way like with the second patient. . . .

This sequence occurred quite late in the interview, and I would not have attempted such a question if I was not certain that a good level of rapport had been developed and that both the interviewee and I could tolerate and work productively with potential misalignment. The interviewee does not spare me, but neither does he abandon the interview, and the matter is clarified as being one of "degree." I, too, avoid taking this personally or being overly intimidated, although notice that I do work hard in my backchannels to demonstrate my realignment. I would certainly use the same technique again, but it is probably to be avoided until one has quite a lot of interviewing experience.

I am in the fortunate position of having interviewed rather pleasant and helpful individuals on topics in which, in the main, I have had little stake or have been on the whole sympathetic to the interviewee's point of view. This will not be case for all interviewing experiences. It is very likely that in some interviews, or in some interviewing studies, the interviewer meets with people who have, to them, repugnant opinions. An example might be the interviews that formed the basis of Wetherell and Potter's (1992) book *Mapping the Language of Racism*. The reader is directed to this book and to van den Berg et al. (2003) to see how the research interviews were undertaken, analyzed, and commented on.

INTERVIEWS: ADDITIONAL CONSIDERATIONS

There are many things to consider when preparing for and conducting research interviews over and above the techniques of interviewing. I discuss four important kinds of additional considerations in this section: design choice, ethics, recording and transcription, and being informed by the critique of interviews as data.

Design Choice

There are several decisions to be made about the design of an interview study. Main types of interview were discussed in the introductory section. I have been involved in interview studies that have differed in terms of the number of interviewees per interview and their characteristics, number and the characteristics of the interviewers, interview location, remote interviewing, image-led interviews, use of follow-up interviews, and the member check interview. Each of these is an important design consideration with practical implications and potential impact on the data.

Number of interviewees per interview and their characteristics. Defined purely in terms of there being more than one interviewee present, group interviewing can be viewed as a distinct form of data collection although, in theory, most interview styles may be used with a group. The terms *group interview* and *focus group* are often used interchangeably. However, the focus group might be considered a particular kind of group interview designed to elicit opinion about a product or topic, using particular terminology (e.g., moderator as opposed to interviewer), and originally was developed within in the field of market research (see Puchta & Potter, 2004, for research on the conduct of focus groups). Hence, I like to distinguish focus groups from a more generic kind of group interview that does not hold to the specific format and aims of the focus group but, nevertheless, contains more than one interviewee (Madill & Gough, 2008).

Interviews with more than one participant tend to be more difficult to organize because it means finding a time and location suitable for a number of different people. Participants also need to feel comfortable discussing the research topic with others, so attention needs to be paid to the group's makeup. For example, group interviews would have been inappropriate for the boundaries study because interviewee anonymity was exceptionally important for participants to feel safe describing what were at times painful struggles in their work.

Single-gender groups might be appropriate for some topics, and cultural issues may need to be taken into account. For example, in a study on organ donation, I and my master's student, Clare Hayward, arranged for Pakistani men and women living in the north of England to be interviewed in single-gender groups to avoid potential barriers to discussing body parts and medical issues in the presence of the opposite sex (and extended this strategy to our White Indigenous participants for methodological consistency; Hayward & Madill, 2003). In general, five to eight participants are ideal for a group research interview. This means recruiting more than eight people per group, however, with the expectation that fewer than those who confirm actually will attend.

In the quarry study, couples sometimes were interviewed together, and their children sometimes were present, although in this project none of the children contributed to the data. Interviewing couples together was productive in that passages of the interview became on-topic discussions between the couple. These points have the benefit of minimizing the contribution from the interviewer while obtaining positions, arguments, and debates of interest. One of my doctoral students, Victoria O'Key, arranged family interviews on the topic of food choice in which she hoped that the children would join the discussion (O'Key et al., 2009). Many did so and added interesting material, often challenging their parents' presentation of the family's eating habits.

The decision as to how many interviewees to include in an interview, who they should be, and what relationship they should have to one another should be guided by the study research questions and sensitivity to the topic and cultural traditions of participants. Having more than one participant in an interview can be helpful if participants are not likely to be inhibited from discussing the topic with others and in cases in which group debate might open up productively different points of view.

Number and characteristics of the interviewers. There may be good, practical reasons to have more than one interviewer employed in a study. The workload can be shared and the project can be completed faster, and fewer opportunities are lost because of interviewer unavailability. These are important considerations when working to tight deadlines.

Four interviewers were involved in generating the quarry interviews: myself and three undergraduate students who joined the study for their final-year research project and who received reimbursement of expenses to thank them for their contribution (Hugh-Jones & Madill, 2009; Madill, 2011). One of the students and I conducted interviews alone, whereas the other two students interviewed together, with one taking the lead in any particular interview. Although it is not the norm, benefits of the students interviewing together were that they were able to share transport to a fairly isolated location and it increased their safety collecting data off campus. (The other student and I let a responsible other person know where we had gone and when we were due back, which is a department stipulation for interview research.) I have conducted analysis of interviewing style in this corpus that shows that as the interviewer with the most research experience, I conducted interviews that tended to be longer and less formal and to include more follow-up questions and flexible use of the interview schedule. The impact of having two interviewers present is, however, unclear. Transcripts show that usually only the lead interviewer spoke during an interview, but at times, the other did ask a follow-up question or make a comment, and sometimes all who were present laughed together.

Five interviewers were involved in the boundaries project: three psychotherapy–counseling practitioners, one male and two female (all of whom also have academic posts); and two academic researchers, both female (one a sociologist and, myself, a psychologist; Martin et al., 2010). Each of us interviewed alone. As a team, we have discussed the possible impact of our lay and professional status in relation to the interviewees, who were all psychotherapy counseling practitioners. Our impression is that the participants may have spared the academic researchers some of the more difficult and intense material around their work with sexual boundaries with clients, possibly sensitive to our unfamiliarity working with such material. There was possibly more of a shared sense of struggle, use of a shared technical vocabulary, and trust that the more difficult material would be managed well emotionally during the interviews with another practitioner. On the other hand, in not assuming a shared experience or shared language, the academic interviewers may have asked the interviewees to explain in more detail their assumptions and frameworks for understanding. This is an extremely important point, as having, on the face of it, facets of shared experience and shared identity with interviewees—particularly if this coincides with the topic of the research—is not always helpful. These may facilitate access and the chance of initial rapport, but the interviewer must guard against assuming that they do indeed share understandings with their participants and ensure that important information is fully articulated and explored.

A project with multiple interviewers can generate rich data, particularly if the interviewers have relevantly variable characteristics that facilitate interviewees in engaging with different aspects of the research topic. This is interesting to consider when analyzing the material. There may also be good ethical reasons for providing a range of interviewers. For example, in the boundaries project, although the four main researchers were female, we gave our interviewees the choice of having a male interviewer. Sexual boundaries are a sensitive topic and, because gender is implicated, it was appropriate to orient to this in our interviewing strategy. In fact, one male participant did opt for a male interviewer, and one of our male colleagues conducted this interview.

Interview location. The location of a research interview can influence the way in which interviewer and interviewee relate and may exaggerate a power dynamic in one direction or another (see the section Power and Vulnerability). It is usual to offer interviewees a choice of location as part of facilitating their comfort and encouraging participation. However, the safety of the interviewer is an overriding consideration and, as mentioned, a minimal requirement should be that a responsible person knows where the interviewer has gone and when they are due back.

The quarry interviews all were conducted in interviewees' homes in a small village in the north of England. The role of interviewer in some respects was conflated with that of guest. Analysis of the overarching style of the interviewee contribution in this corpus of material suggests that, in general and as a group, interviewees responded to the interviewers as they would friends (as opposed to strangers or intimates such as a spouse), although none of the interviewers were known to participants before the study (Madill, 2011). It is possible that some of this friendliness reflected hospitality obligations. Victoria O'Key was not always made to feel welcome when interviewing in family homes, however, so it cannot be assumed that one will be treated like a guest in such situations.

In contrast, the medics' interviews were all conducted in my office at the university, and none of the participants took up my offer of the interview taking place elsewhere. I was also in a dual role to these students in that I taught one of their compulsory lecture courses, supervised some in their practical assignment, and marked (blind) subsequent exam scripts and reports. Because the interviews covered the experience of a year intercalating in psychology, there are sequences during which the students and I allude to our pedagogic relationship. This arose most clearly when some students mentioned, favorably, the course I taught them. At these points I tended to show embarrassed awareness that I might be perceived as having a degree of leverage over my participants by saying something like, "You don't have to say that." I am aware that I was quite persistent in my email invitations to attend interviews, and some students may have felt obliged to come given that I was one of their lecturers and assignment markers. (I also provided a small payment of £20 per interview.) There is some reassuring evidence, however, that the students felt they could act autonomously. In the first cohort, I had planned to conduct three interviews with each student; however, despite several emails, one did not reply to my invitation, or attend, the third interview. Moreover, the students were not reticent to use the interview as an opportunity to describe some of their disappointments with the psychology course.

The incipient power dynamic was in the opposite direction for me in the boundaries study. Here, I conducted one interview in a therapist's university office, two in consulting rooms at the interviewees' places of work, and one in the consulting room at the therapist's own home. These locations provided a strong cue for my lay status and bolstered my sense of the interviewees as high-status professionals (see the section The Not-Knowing Interviewer). Moreover, conducting three of these interviews in the interviewees' consulting rooms made for a rather strange dynamic. From my perspective, it probably contributed to a sense of vulnerability as the setting was suggestive, that on one level, I was there to receive therapy. On the other hand, as the interviewer it was my job to facilitate, listen, and ask questions on the intimate and charged topic of the therapists' experience of managing sexual boundaries in their work. I might surmise that the participants sensed a reversal of role in being invited to self-reveal within a setting in which this would otherwise be inappropriate. Added to this, the topic of the research was about boundaries, and the research team has discussed the possible parallel processes occurring as we, as interviewers, attempted to manage intimacy boundaries with our participants—which was entwined, for me, in complex ways with interview location.

Thus, some thought needs to be given to the location of the research interview in light of safety, comfort, appropriateness to the research topic, and acceptability to interviewees and impact on the data generated. Interview location, however, is never fully neutral. Keeping a research interviewing diary and reflecting on the possible impact on the data of interview location, for example, through awareness of how one felt interviewing in particular locations, which will include the impact of the kind of relationship catalyzed with participants, might inform the analysis of the data.

Remote interviews. It has become increasing important to consider forms of remote interviewing due to the COVID-19 pandemic. Remote interviewing includes using the telephone, email, and online platforms. Although widespread social distancing due to the pandemic is a relatively novel consideration for researchers, it can be considered also an opportunity to explore the benefits of remote interviewing. For example, I have been undertaking online interviews with development researchers and professionals from around the world (Madill et al., 2020) and have found it to be a highly effective and efficient process that I would now consider as a first, as opposed to expedient, option. I focus here on online interviews, but much of the following will be relevant also to telephone and possibly email interviews.

Some considerations are largely practical, such as, does the interviewee have online access and to one of the available platforms, such as Skype, Zoom, or Teams? I am glad to say that, although my project was particularly focused on low-to-medium income countries, all my interviewees in these regions had good access to Teams, although we sometimes switched to audio-only to improve the connection. Another consideration is what adaptations will increase the chance of online interviews being a rich and mutually rewarding process. Adaptations include securing, for participant ease, ethical approval to take consent verbally at the beginning of the audio-recording; spending time at the beginning to build rapport and to test for time delay, which might make it more likely you will accidentally interrupt each other; speaking slightly slower than usual; and keeping the interview relatively short and probably no longer than 1 hour. Benefits of remote interviewing include its global reach, flexibility (e.g., scheduling), inexpensiveness, and minimal risk (e.g., in terms of working alone). As with any form of interviewing, as an element of research rigor, it is useful to consider how remote interviewing may have impacted the data generated. This will depend to some extent on your research questions and contexts in which the interviewer and interviewee are situated.

Image-led interviews. There is increasing interest in visual methods in qualitative psychology (Reavey, 2021). Variants of the image-led interview can be found under labels such as *photo-elicitation* (Bates et al., 2017) and *photovoice* (Golden, 2020). Participants are either provided with or asked to bring images, often photographs, to interviews to facilitate data generation. There are choices also in how images are integrated into the interview; one relatively straightforward technique is to ask, "Can you tell me what this image means to you in relation to [topic of investigation]?"

Considerations include the extent to which participants will engage with images, particularly if asked to collect them in advance, if the data generated are compatible with the planned method of analysis, and whether or not the images themselves will be analyzed—and, if so, in what way. I have supervised several research projects using image-led interviews in which traditionally hard-to-reach demographics have been enthused about the activity and used their images to help convey meaningful experiences. This includes interviewees such as men with low income (Jestico, 2021), people with profound and enduring mental health challenges (P. Smith et al., 2021), and youth in recovery from substance addiction (Madill et al., 2019). Sometimes brought images are used by participants as a prompt to talk about an actual event or person. However, often images are used in highly symbolic ways, for example, as a metaphor for an ineffable experience or life theme. In addition, Duara et al. (2022) suggested that two key benefits of image-led interviews are that they can (a) facilitate participant agency and (b) have therapeutic value in supporting the opportunity to speak and for deep self-reflection.

Follow-up interviews. A single interview with each participant may be enough to furnish a study with appropriate and relevant information. Some research designs and research questions, however, require at least one follow-up interview. The free association, narrative, and interview method (Hollway & Jefferson, 2000) makes use of a double interview—two interviews about 1 week apart. The psychoanalytic framework of this method posits interviewer and interviewee as anxious, defended subjects and, hence, that the data generated will be shaped by such processes as transference and countertransference. The first interview allows the researcher to identify analytically interesting indicators of unconscious seepage: contradictions, avoidances, inconsistencies, and the way in which the interactants have been drawn together into a particular kind of relationship that has helped to cocreate the data, such as a mother–daughter dynamic. The second interview then allows the researcher to explore hunches about what this might mean in relation to the topic of research through a personalized interview with each participant, seeking further relevant information although, again, not taking responses at face value.

Follow-up interviews may be more straightforwardly connected to the topic of the research if it has a longitudinal facet. For example, I interviewed each of the intercalating medical students near the beginning of their psychology year and again toward the end. In the first interview, I was interested in their experience of medical training so far, and within this context, sought to learn about their decision to take a year of psychology. In the second interview, I tapped their actual experience of the year and any links they had made between psychology and their ongoing medical training.

Interviews may continue as an ongoing process. I had hoped to keep interviewing some of the intercalating medical students as they continued their medical training. I did not have enough resources, and although some of the students might have been interested in continuing, this kind of longitudinal study needs a lot of persistence and motivation on each side. One way to maintain such motivation is to engage in research such as memory work (e.g., Hamm, 2018), in which research interviews, or at least recorded discussions, are conducted as a continual, longitudinal process within a small, dedicated research group, each member of which has a stake in the result such that tasks, effort, and credit can be negotiated on a democratic and fair basis.

Member check interviews. A central purpose of member checking is to test the researcher's insights with participants. This lends itself to a follow-up interview with participants, even if the original research was not interview-based. Member checking can be used throughout a study in which findings are developed in an iterative cycle between researcher and participants. In cases in which the explicit purpose of a follow-up interview is a check on the validity of nearly final results, the process is probably better captured by the term "participant validation" (Lincoln & Guba, 1985). Participant validation, although applauded by many, is, I think, highly problematic, because good research from the perspective of the research community may not always be acceptable to participants. (Exceptions might be projects conducted with and for participants themselves, such as in the various forms of action research.) Participant validation therefore requires a sophisticated sensitivity to social and interactional context integrated with an appreciation of researcher and participant stake and investment in the results (e.g., Mays & Pope, 2000).

Follow-up contact with interviewees in the contexts discussed—the free association, narrative, and interview method; member checking; and participant validation—have different aims and can be positioned within different approaches to knowledge generation (epistemologies) and models of subjectivity (ontologies). Most of these complex issues are beyond the scope of this chapter, but it is important to be aware of such design choices, and the interested reader can follow up the references cited in the relevant sections. To offer an example, Madill and Sullivan (2018) explored the use of member check interviews as a strategy of knowledge exchange in the social sciences, in particular, how to manage different kinds of "difficult moments": participant ambivalence and participant challenge. They suggest three kinds of response to such moments are available to the interviewer. The first is to close down difficult moments by passing over or side-stepping them, or even reframing them in the interviewer's terms. The second is to explore difficult moments through open discussion without it, hopefully, turning into a dispute. The third response, which is subtly different, is for the interviewer to *reflect* on difficult moments with, or without, participants. Reflection might raise the possibility of new insights for the researcher (What might the difficult moment reveal about the researcher's blind spots?), insights for the participants (What might the difficult moment reveal about participants' blind spots?), and/or reflexive discovery (What does the difficult moment itself reveal about the phenomenon of research interest?).

Ethical Considerations

There are many ethical considerations pertinent to interviewing research, many of which I commented on in the previous section. Here, I cover some further issues that may be particularly relevant to interviewing studies—although, of course, the research must conform to the ethical guidelines of the professional organization or institutions to which the researchers are accountable. The issues covered here relate to informed consent, power and vulnerability, discredited participants, and interviewer experience.

Informed consent. The participant information sheet must give potential interviewees a good idea of what is involved if taking part in the research. This will include the general topics covered in the interview, where the interview might take place, how long it is expected to last, how it will be recorded, the ways in which participants' anonymity will be managed, and incentives offered. Some of these specifications already create problems for much interview research.

Although certain topics will be specified in an interview protocol, it is impossible to predict exactly what will be covered in anything but a highly structured interview. Moreover, although research questions can be stated, it is often difficult to know what will end up being the focus of analysis. The more exploratory forms of analysis, such as grounded theory (Strauss & Corbin, 1990/1998), will be led as far as possible by the data and thus open to revising the original research questions. To complicate matters, qualitative analysis is not likely to take, at some points at least, what the interviewee has said at face value but may offer, for example, a psycho-analytically informed interpretation (e.g., Hollway & Jefferson, 2000) or an account on the basis of a functional approach to language (e.g., Edwards & Potter, 1992).

Consent forms can become complicated if seeking consent for the use of material over and above anonymized quotes in reports of the research. Anonymization can be complex, too, with different media, and even with a transcript of the audio recording, it requires sensitivity to contextualizing details that might, when taken together, identify a participant to others in their profession (see, e.g., Extract 11, in which I omitted the type of client group with which this interviewee worked). It might be considered good practice to consider true informed consent in interview research to require two distinguishable stages: (a) consent to undertake and record the interview and (b) consent to use the material in research after the interview has been conducted and the content known, or even after the interviewee has seen a copy of the transcript and has had a chance to remove sections, if desired. It is also worth considering whether the topic of study makes relevant a statement demarking the limits of confidentiality. For example, we used the following statement in the boundaries study:

> The researchers are aware that sexual boundary violations with clients contravene the codes of ethics and practice to which practitioners adhere, and that for some of the team, their codes of ethics require that a serious breach of boundaries, particularly if there is potential future or actual harm to others, is reported. However, the focus of this study is on successful management of therapeutic boundaries; the interviewer will not ask you to provide information on actual breaches of sexual boundaries. Further, if the interviewer feels that the interview may be going that way, they will let you know, so that you have the opportunity to avoid disclosing details of sexual boundary violations that might require reporting to a professional body.

Whatever legitimate ethical position one takes on informed consent, an important stipulation is that participants know they can, and are able to, withdraw their material from the study. Beyond this, the extent to which the researcher facilitates participant control of their material is controversial, loaded with potentially competing interests (although I have never had a participant withdraw data), and not at all well worked out.

Power and vulnerability. Control over material raises the issue of power and vulnerability in interview studies. Early feminist work highlighted such issues but was possibly naïve in assuming that techniques and (researcher) sensitivity could equalize power differences between researcher and participant, particularly when both are women (e.g., Oakley, 1981). My own, certainly not unique, point of view is that interviewer and interviewee likely inhabit different epistemic communities, meaning that each can claim different kinds of knowledge, the most relevant contrast possibly being professional learning versus lived experience relevant to the topic of research. There will likely be differences also in the social positionings and identifications of interviewer and interviewee in terms of such categories as gender, race, class, age, educational background, sexual orientation, marital and parental status and so on, which may give some indication of incipient structural power differences. Given this, however, no specific form or direction of power should be assumed in any particular research interaction, and the operation of power is likely to fluctuate over the course of an interview and to be experienced in different ways by the interactants (see also Maryudi & Fisher, 2020). My experience is that interviewees have a lot of power in the research process. The researcher is reliant on their participation, and interviewees can decide not to attend an interview, can withdraw their data, and can use subtle strategies to make data collection an uncomfortable experience—for example, by being, often subtly, patronizing to the interviewer or derogatory about the value of research (e.g., see O'Key et al., 2009).

On the other hand, some kinds of interviewees may be considered particularly vulnerable if recruited specifically for relevant traumatic experiences (e.g., physical or mental health issues, problematic life experiences), although many different kinds of research topics will touch on sensitive issues for certain participants. When the research topic covers a personally sensitive area, the research interview may be experienced as a kind of protocounseling by some interviewees and the attention, rapport, and active listening of the interviewer may promote more intimate self-revelation than the interviewee had expected to give. This might generate good material for analysis but leave the interviewee feeling exposed. The interviewer needs to be aware that the research interview is not counseling and must take care not to stray into this (dual) role, even if they have relevant training. It is good practice to provide, as a matter of course, a list of appropriate support services for interviewees to contact if they wish after the interview. This should be given to all participants before interviewing commences to avoid the possibility of any one feeling shamed that they had been perceived as particularly vulnerable or needy.

Discredited participants. Another kind of interviewee worth discussing in terms of ethical practice is those who could be considered in some way discredited. By *discredited*, I mean individuals whose accounts and perspectives are, at the outset, vulnerable to being undermined or treated with particular skepticism for a variety of reasons. This might include those with mental health problems, those who might be considered to have repulsive or antisocial opinions, and those who are known to engage in criminal activities. Such interviewees are discredited to the extent that the researcher and research audience are prima facie willing to question the content of, or motivation behind, the participant's account or to be unsympathetic to their point of view. This may create a particular tension for the qualitative researcher as many, but certainly not all, qualitative approaches have a humanistic, participant-centered, or emancipatory ethos.

As mentioned, one of my doctoral students has interviewed male ex-prisoners about their use of illegal drugs in prison. In a supervision meeting, I raised the issue of not taking what was said always at face value and asking, for instance, what might be achieved for the participants in offering one kind of description instead of another at a certain points in the interview. My student queried whether I was suggesting this strategy in particular because of the nature of her interviewees. I had meant this as a generally good approach to analyzing qualitative data, but this led to an interesting discussion about the ways in which her participants may be vulnerable to discreditation. In subsequent meetings, we discussed markers in the data that might be used to speculate on possibly untold aspects of her participants' experience, for example, the men's use of distancing pronouns such as "they." Although our overall impression of the interviews was of the men's candor, we also discussed ways in which some of their descriptions may be open to less self-serving interpretations than offered or implied during interview. This is not to suggest that any objectively true version was to found, but to understand what might be being avoided in the men's accounts and to speculate on what this might mean.

Interviewer experience. The previous discussions revealed how my student felt accountable and loyal to her interviewees, and I have had similar feelings toward participants in my work. The experience of the interviewer is important to consider in terms of ethics: both the interviewer's *expertise* and *reaction* to the research. In particular, it is important to consider the relative sensitivity of the research topic and vulnerability of participants in relation to the expertise of the interviewer, frequency and intensity of research supervision, and opportunities for debriefing. For example, I consider it inappropriate for undergraduate students to interview participants who are under treatment for a psychological disorder or who are otherwise particularly vulnerable. Supervision should consider how the interviewer might be affected by the research, and reflection might be facilitated by keeping a research diary. Debriefing meetings after interviewing can help the researcher to work productively with his or her reaction as possibly revealing something about the topic of research. For example, we recorded our debriefing meetings as part of the boundaries project and view this material as a further layer of data collection. As alluded to earlier, these debriefs raised our awareness, among other things, of a possible parallel process in relation to boundaries operating in our interviewing experiences, which might be considered reflexively in our analysis as telling us something more about the phenomenon we were researching.

Recording and Transcription

As discussed in the section Ethical Considerations, permission must be granted by the interviewee for the mode of recording, with it being usual to audio-record research interviews. One participant in the boundaries project refused to be audio-recorded but agreed to the interviewer making written notes. This is not ideal, because a lot of detail is lost and the notes are already a glossed, preinterpreted version of the discussion. The research team decided that useful information could still be obtained from notes, however, particularly given that we had also several audio-recorded interviews in our corpus.

The state of the art in conversation analytic research is to work with video-recorded, naturalistic interactions, which may include interviews conducted as a matter of course in institutional settings, for example, between doctor and patient. Video-recording provides visual information about the setting, physically positioning, body language, actions, and movement of the participants. Such information may be important for many kinds of research, which might extend to some kinds of interviewing studies. For example, I am seeking to video-record follow-up interviews between researchers and their participants to understand in detail how these interactions get done and with what result. However, particularly in relation to sensitive research topics, participants may be reticent to be video-recorded, even though it is possible to obscure personal identity in video recordings. A graded consent form can be useful, which allows participants, if they wish, to consent to the use of video recordings for data analysis by the research team but for no other purpose.

To make recorded materials widely available, as increasingly expected, digital audio- or video-recording is necessary. Digital audio recorders are small, and recordings are downloaded easily onto a computer using the accompanying software. I would advise investing in an additional plug-in microphone for some dictation-style recorders. Even if they have a conference facility, the sound quality can be much improved, and this means many fewer inaudibles in the transcripts. I would also advise buying a digital recorder with a visual display of audio frequency because this is a good check that one is actually recording. Free downloads are available from the internet that allow short clips of material to be made for analysis and, with participant consent, presentation at conferences and workshops.

There is a convention that it is best to do one's own transcription. This may be a practical necessity if one has no research funding, usefully focuses the researcher on the detail of the text, and can be viewed as a stage of the analysis, particularly if ideas are noted down during the transcription process. My own opinion is that outsourcing at least some of the transcription can save valuable time for the analysis and take some of the stress out of the research process. Digital recording facilitates sending files for professional transcription. Many of these companies have an easy-to-use email drop-box to transfer the files. It is good practice to select a professional company that offers to sign a confidentiality statement that includes deleting all the material once transcription is complete. If not using a professional service, check out the experience of any individual who might be doing the transcription and discuss confidentiality issues with them. Inexperienced transcribers can misunderstand the task and tidy up or otherwise summarize the talk. I know of one who edited out the odd swear word that was used and other content to which she objected.

If transcription has been outsourced, it is always necessary to check each transcript carefully against the recording. This can take a long time, even with a relatively good transcript. Mark where the speech is inaudible and indicate the sections you are not quite sure that the transcript is right but is as close as you can get. Verbatim, word-for-word, transcription of the interview is probably necessary for most research projects and forms of analysis. After this, the level of detail depends on the kind of analysis undertaken. Conversation analysis requires some of the most detailed transcription and has developed excellent standardized transcription conventions (see Schlegoff, n.d.). Less detailed "Jefferson-lite" conventions may be quite appropriate for other forms of analysis (e.g., as here, but see Hugh-Jones & Madill, 2009). However, transcription is never a substitute for the actual recording, and I would recommend always referring back to the audio recording throughout an analysis.

A huge practical benefit of online interviewing (see the section Remote Interviews) is when the platform provides captioning. Although automatic captioning is not perfect, I have found it to be good enough to undertake a basic content/thematic analysis. In fact, the captioning capability has allowed me in the span of a few hours to undertake an interview with a participant in Nepal, Kenya, or Chile, among other countries, and complete an analysis appropriate for the purposes of my study along with relevant quotes. To get the best out of captions, check for online programs designed to clean up the formatting of caption documents such as Microsoft Stream transcript VTT file cleaner (https://amsglob0cdnstream13.azureedge.net/vttcleaner/CleanVTT.html).

Interestingly, I had the experience recently of doing quite of bit of initial analysis of an interview purely from the audio recording while I was waiting for the transcript. When I continued the analysis from the transcript, I found my attention drawn to different aspects of the interaction. The audio version had impressed on me the affability of the interaction through, most likely, the interactants' tone of voice and smoothness of communication. The transcript made more obvious differences of opinion between the interactants because the actual words used at points were, in and of themselves, much more hostile in implication than I had picked up in the audio recording. Neither analytic impression is more *true*. It was just interesting for me to experience so clearly the impact of working with the two media, and I have now an increased respect for the aspects of interaction possibly seen more clearly in transcript.

Critique of Interviews as Data

Conducting research using any form of interviewing should be informed by the growing critique in the social sciences of interviews as data. The essence of this critique is that interview data are contaminated by the research agenda. The researcher decides on the topic of the research, targets participants, designs the interview schedule, and coconstructs the interview discussion. A remedial approach is to use many of the techniques outlined in this chapter to limit the impact of the researcher on the material: open questions, nonleading questions, follow-up questions, and so on. Refining interviewing technique, however, does not tackle the more extended critique of interviews: that data coconstruction is endemic to research interviewing (and yet is often treated in analysis as if it were not) and that the interviewer's influence cannot be neutralized (and yet is often treated in analysis as if it were). Potter and Hepburn (2005) offered analysis of extracts from research interviews to substantiate this point of view. Their critique is based on a functional view of language as developed in discursive psychology (e.g., Edwards & Potter, 1992) in which the discussion generated in the interview is considered inseparable from the interview context in any meaningful way.

The strong critique of interviews as data, as illustrated by Potter and Hepburn (2005), argues for the use of naturally occurring data. These are interactions that would have occurred as they did whether or not the research had been undertaken. However, relevant interactions may be extremely difficult to obtain. Moreover, research questions often focus on understanding the meaning of experiences that need to be explored actively in a research interview, and many sophisticated methodologies have little issue with the validity of interview material per se (e.g., see Hollway, 2005; J. A. Smith et al., 2005). Hence, interview data are not completely undermined. The critique, however, challenges researchers to consider interview data in more complex ways and to work more reflectively and reflexively with interview material—to the benefit of interview research I am persuaded.

A middle ground might be to take critique seriously but to conceptualize interview data as still able to tell us something about the interviewee's life beyond the interview context. Analysis I conducted on the quarry corpus suggested that the interviewees interacted with the interviewers in a pattern similar to that typical between friends (but not strangers or intimates; Madill, 2011). This might be the beginning of evidencing that, in general, material generated in research interviews may be transferable to other kinds of identifiable contexts. A way of working that I think is productive is to always interrogate, in a reflexive manner, the possible impact of the interview context on the data generated. This should include consideration of why people agreed to be interviewed, how the research was presented to them, and how the interview might have triggered dilemmas for participants' self-presentation. For example, Siobhan Hugh-Jones and I forefronted in our analysis of the quarry data how the act of interviewing raised implicit challenges to the interviewees' place-identity, and we examined the ways in which participants managed this discursively during interview (Hugh-Jones & Madill, 2009). We also argued that our analysis had currency beyond the interview situation because a similar tacit challenge to participants' place-identity might also occur in other kinds of interaction.

CONCLUSION

In this chapter, I have described different types of interviewing; identified and illustrated in more detail the central techniques of research interviewing (particularly with regard to the semistructured format); and discussed in depth several additional considerations, such as design, ethics, recording, and transcription. I hope to have shown that interviewing research can be a rewarding endeavor. Good interviewing, however, is not easy, and in examining the central techniques, I have offered examples of where my own research interviewing could have been better. My technique has improved with practice, though, and my reminder to myself and to my students is that there is never the "perfect" interview, although there are definitely better and worse instances. I hope also to have shown that interviewing research is at an exciting methodological juncture in that we can no longer be unsophisticated about the status of interviews as data. Creative developments are required that allow interviews to be conducted and analyzed in ways that recognize their situated and coconstructed nature and at the same time are informative on the topic of the research.

References

Anderson, H., & Goolishian, H. A. (1988). Human systems as linguistic systems: Preliminary and evolving ideas about the implications for clinical theory. *Family Process*, 27(4), 371–393. https://doi.org/10.1111/j.1545-5300.1988.00371.x

Antaki, C., Houtkoop-Steenstra, H., & Rapley, M. (2000). "Brilliant. Next question.": High-grade assessment sequences in the completion of interactional units. *Research on Language and Social Interaction*, 33(3), 235–262. https://doi.org/10.1207/S15327973RLSI3303_1

Antaki, C., Young, N., & Finlay, M. (2002). Shaping client's answers: Departures from neutrality in care-staff interviews with people with a learning disability. *Disability & Society*, 17(4), 435–455. https://doi.org/10.1080/09687590220140368

Bates, E. A., McCann, J. J., Kaye, L. K., & Taylor, J. C. (2017). "Beyond words": A researcher's guide to using photo elicitation in psychology. *Qualitative Research in Psychology*, 14(4), 459–481. https://doi.org/10.1080/14780887.2017.1359352

Bingham, W., & Moore, B. (1924). *How to interview*. Harper & Row.

Duara, R., Hugh-Jones, S., & Madill, A. (2022). Photo-elicitation and time-lining to enhance the research interview: Exploring the quarterlife crisis of young adults in India and the UK. *Qualitative Research in Psychology*, 19(1), 131–154. https://doi.org/10.1080/14780887.2018.1545068

Edwards, D., & Potter, J. (1992). *Discursive psychology*. SAGE.

Elliott, R., Fischer, C. T., & Rennie, D. L. (1999). Evolving guidelines for publication of qualitative research studies in psychology and related fields. *British Journal of Clinical Psychology*, 38(3), 215–229. https://doi.org/10.1348/014466599162782

Golden, T. (2020). Reframing photovoice: Building on the method to develop more equitable and responsive research practices. *Qualitative Health Research*, 30(6), 960–972. https://doi.org/10.1177/1049732320905564

Hamm, R. (2018). Collective memory work: A method under the radar? *Other Education*, 7(2), 118–124.

Hayward, C., & Madill, A. (2003). The meanings of organ donation: Muslims of Pakistani origin and White English nationals living in North England. *Social Science & Medicine*, 57(3), 389–401. https://doi.org/10.1016/S0277-9536(02)00364-7

Heritage, J. C., & Watson, D. R. (1979). Formulations as conversational objects. In G. Psathas (Ed.), *Everyday language: Studies in ethnomethodology* (pp. 123–162). Irvington.

Hollway, W. (2005). Commentaries on Potter and Hepburn, "Qualitative interviews in psychology: Problems and possibilities." *Qualitative Research in Psychology*, 2(4), 312–314. https://doi.org/10.1191/1478088705qp046cm

Hollway, W., & Jefferson, A. (2000). *Doing qualitative research differently*. Sage. https://doi.org/10.4135/9781849209007

Houtkoop-Steenstra, H. (1997). Being friendly in survey interviews. *Journal of Pragmatics*, 28(5), 591–623. https://doi.org/10.1016/S0378-2166(97)00018-0

Houtkoop-Steenstra, H. (2000). *Interaction and the standardized survey interview: The living questionnaire*. Cambridge University Press. https://doi.org/10.1017/CBO9780511489457

Hugh-Jones, S., & Madill, A. (2009). The air's got to be far cleaner here: A discursive analysis of place-identity threat. *British Journal of Social Psychology*, 48(4), 601–624. https://doi.org/10.1348/014466608X390256

Jestico, M. (2021). *How low SES men negotiate and construct health practices* [Doctoral dissertation]. University of Leeds.

Koole, T. (2003). Affiliation and detachment in interviewer answer receipts. In H. van den Berg, M. Wetherell, & H. Houtkoop-Steenstra (Eds.), *Analyzing race talk: Multidisciplinary perspectives on the research interview* (pp. 178–199). Cambridge University Press.

Lee, Y.-J., & Roth, W.-M. (2004, January). Making a scientist: Discursive "doing" of identity and self-presentation during research interviews. *Forum: Qualitative Social Research* [Online journal], 5(1), Art. 12. https://doi.org/10.17169/fqs-5.1.655

Liddicoat, A. J. (2007). *An introduction to conversation analysis*. Continuum.

Lincoln, Y. S., & Guba, E. G. (1985). *Naturalistic inquiry*. Sage. https://doi.org/10.1016/0147-1767(85)90062-8

Madill, A. (2007). Survey of British Psychological Society Qualitative Methods in Psychology Section Members 2006. *British Psychological Society Qualitative Methods in Psychology Section Newsletter*, 3, 9–14.

Madill, A. (2011). Interaction in the semi-structured interview: A comparative analysis of the use of and response to indirect complaints. *Qualitative Research in Psychology*, 8(4), 333–353. https://doi.org/10.1080/14780880903521633

Madill, A., Cooke, P., Duara, R., Graber, R., Hugh-Jones, S., & Mirzoev, T. (2019). *The big picture: Preventing youth substance abuse in Assam. Dialogues: Wellbeing, lifespan perspectives and practices for sustainable communities*. International Conference Booklet, Assam, India. https://medicinehealth.leeds.ac.uk/dir-record/research-projects/1254/the-big-picture-preventing-youth-substance-abuse-in-assam

Madill, A., Courcher, K. T., Raghavan, R., Brown, B., Evans, A. A., Wilson, A. S., Taberner, S. J., Graber, R., Hugh-Jones, S. A., Cooke, P., Plastow, J. E., King, R., Colucci, E., Mirzoev, T., & Greene, O. (2020). *Mainstreaming global mental health: A praxis nexus approach*. EPSRC GCRF Challenge Cluster Seed-Funded Project (2020–21). https://gtr.ukri.org/projects?ref=EP%2FT023813%2F1

Madill, A., & Gough, B. (2008). Qualitative research and its place in psychological science. *Psychological Methods*, *13*(3), 254–271. https://doi.org/10.1037/a0013220

Madill, A., & Sullivan, P. (2018). Mirrors, portraits, and member checking: Managing difficult moments of knowledge exchange in the social sciences. *Qualitative Psychology*, *5*(3), 321–339. https://doi.org/10.1037/qup0000089

Martin, C., Godfrey, M., Meekums, B., & Madill, A. (2010). Staying on the straight and narrow. *Therapy Today*, *21*(5), 11–14.

Maryudi, A., & Fisher, M. (2020). The power in the interview: A practical guide for identifying the critical role of actor interests in environment research. *Forest and Society*, *4*(1), 142–150. https://doi.org/10.24259/fs.v4i1.9132

Mays, N., & Pope, C. (2000). Assessing quality in qualitative research. *British Medical Journal*, *320*(7226), 50–52. https://doi.org/10.1136/bmj.320.7226.50

Oakley, A. (1981). Interviewing women: A contradiction in terms. In H. Roberts (Ed.), *Doing feminist research* (pp. 30–61). Routledge & Keegan Paul.

O'Key, V., Hugh-Jones, S., & Madill, A. (2009). Recruiting and engaging with people in deprived locales: Interviewing families about their eating patterns. *Social Psychological Review*, *11*(20), 30–35.

Pomerantz, A. M. (1984). Agreeing and disagreeing with assessment: Some features of preferred/dispreferred turn shapes. In J. M. Atkinson & J. Heritage (Eds.), *Structures of social action: Studies in conversation analysis* (pp. 57–101). Cambridge University Press.

Potter, J., & Hepburn, A. (2005). Qualitative interviews in psychology: Problems and possibilities. *Qualitative Research in Psychology*, *2*(4), 281–307. https://doi.org/10.1191/1478088705qp045oa

Puchta, C., & Potter, J. (2004). *Focus group practice*. Sage. https://doi.org/10.4135/9781849209168

Reavey, P. (Ed.). (2021). *A handbook of visual methods in psychology: Using and interpreting images in qualitative research* (2nd ed.). Routledge.

Schaeffer, N. C. (1991). Conversation with a purpose—Or conversation? Interaction in the standardized interview. In P. P. Biemer, R. M. Groves, L. E. Lyberg, & N. A. Mathiowetz (Eds.), *Measurement errors in surveys* (pp. 367–391). Wiley.

Schlegoff, E. A. (n.d.) *Emanuel A. Schlegoff's home page: Transcription module*. Retrieved May 21, 2022, from https://www.sscnet.ucla.edu/soc/faculty/schegloff/TranscriptionProject/index.html

Silverman, D. (1973). Interview talk: Bringing off a research instrument. *Sociology*, *7*(1), 31–48. https://doi.org/10.1177/003803857300700103

Smith, J. A. (1995). Semi-structured interviewing and qualitative analysis. In J. A. Smith, R. Harré, & L. Van Langenhove (Eds.), *Rethinking methods in psychology* (pp. 10–26). Sage. https://doi.org/10.4135/9781446221792.n2

Smith, J. A., Hollway, W., & Mishler, E. G. (2005). Commentaries on Potter and Hepburn, "Qualitative interviews in psychology: Problems and possibilities." *Qualitative Research in Psychology*, *2*(4), 309–325. https://doi.org/10.1191/1478088705qp046cm

Smith, P., Simpson, L., & Madill, A. (2021). Service user experiences of a novel in-reach rehabilitation and recovery service for people with profound and enduring mental health challenges. *International Journal of Mental Health Nursing*, *30*(5), 1106–1116. https://doi.org/10.1111/inm.12861

Strauss, A., & Corbin, J. (1990/1998). *Basics of qualitative research*. Sage.

van den Berg, H., Wetherell, M., & Houtkoop-Steenstra, H. (Eds.). (2003). *Analyzing race talk: Multidisciplinary perspectives on the research interview*. Cambridge University Press.

Wetherell, M., & Potter, J. (1992). *Mapping the language of racism*. Sage.

Wooffitt, R., & Widdicombe, S. (2006). Interaction in interviews. In P. Drew, G. Raymond, & D. Weinberg (Eds.), *Talk and interaction in social research methods* (pp. 28–49). Sage. https://doi.org/10.4135/9781849209991.n3

CHAPTER 16

USING INTENSIVE LONGITUDINAL METHODS IN PSYCHOLOGICAL RESEARCH

Masumi Iida, Patrick E. Shrout, Jean-Philippe Laurenceau, and Niall Bolger

Intensive longitudinal methods typically involve densely spaced, repeated self-reports that aim to capture events, reflections, moods, pains, or interactions near the time they occur. Most modern intensive longitudinal methods and designs are systematic and often highly structured. Daily diaries, experience sampling methods, ecological momentary assessments, and real-time capture are some examples of intensive longitudinal designs. Two of the earliest examples of intensive longitudinal research date back to the early 1900s. *How Working Men Spend Their Time* (Bevans, 1913) tracked how individuals used their time with repeated survey design, and *Round About a Pound a Week* (Pember-Reeves, 1913) examined how poor middle-class families in London used their money through repeated interview visits.

Intensive longitudinal methods in psychological research build on the tradition of daily written accounts and the willingness of some persons to provide exquisite detail about their experiences on a daily basis for a specified period of time. The earliest intensive longitudinal study in psychological research that we know of is by Csikszentmihalyi, Larson, and Prescott (1977), who examined interpersonal contacts and interaction quality among adolescents.

They structured reporting forms and response intervals to make the information more systematic than free-form diaries of the literary tradition. Larson and Csikszentmihalyi (1983) called this methodology *experience sampling methods* (also called *ecological momentary assessment* [EMA]), and their method revolutionized modern psychological research by allowing investigators to capture daily experiences in the participants' own natural environment.

In the 4 decades since this first study, intensive longitudinal methods have been refined in many ways, most notably by embracing new technology for recording events. These types of longitudinal studies have become increasingly common in a variety of fields of psychology, including social (e.g., Iida et al., 2017; Rossignac-Milon et al., 2021), personality (e.g., Borghuis et al., 2020; Quintus et al., 2021), clinical (e.g., Cranford et al., 2010; Soriano et al., 2019), developmental (e.g., Ha et al., 2019; Seaton & Iida, 2019), organizational (e.g., Baethge et al., 2020; Hur et al., 2020), and health (e.g., Müller et al., 2019; Skaff et al., 2009) psychology. In fact, in the past 3 years, more than 250 journal articles per year have reported diary results. In addition, texts now focus explicitly on intensive longitudinal methods (Bolger & Laurenceau, 2013; Nezlek, 2012).

This work was partially supported by National Institute of Mental Health Grant R01-MH60366. We thank Lesa Hoffman for sharing details of her analyses, which allowed us to generate simulation data used in the Example 3 analysis.

https://doi.org/10.1037/0000318-016
APA Handbook of Research Methods in Psychology, Second Edition: Vol. 1. Foundations, Planning, Measures, and Psychometrics, H. Cooper (Editor-in-Chief)
Copyright © 2023 by the American Psychological Association. All rights reserved.

RESEARCH QUESTIONS USING INTENSIVE LONGITUDINAL METHODS

Proponents of intensive longitudinal methods point to the increased ecological validity of the data, which allows a bottom-up examination of psychological processes in the participants' daily environment. Because the reports are temporally close to the experience, they also greatly reduce retrospection bias that is associated with usual survey design. In addition to these methodological advantages, intensive longitudinal methods allow researchers to examine questions that are not amenable in more traditional study designs. These research questions can be broadly sorted into three major categories: (a) What are the average experiences of an individual, and how much do the experiences vary over time? (b) Is there systematic (e.g., linear, exponential) change in experiences across days, and do such trajectories differ across persons? and (c) What processes underlie a person's changes, and how do people differ from each other in these processes?

The first question often involves between-person comparisons of quantities that are summarized over time. The second and third questions have to do with descriptions and explanations of change within persons. They also allow a consideration of the sequencing of different behaviors. For example, an individual might seek social support when they experience a stressor, but not when life is going smoothly. To study the structural relation of support to distress, a researcher might compare distress levels following support receipt to levels on days when support was not available, adjusting for the severity of the stressor.

This within-persons approach is in stark contrast to cross-sectional survey designs that involve only between-persons comparisons. For example, coping researchers who use cross-sectional data might ask whether the people who use particular coping strategy also have lower levels of distress. The problem with this approach is that the within-individual associations of coping and distress are often not the same as between-individuals associations. Tennen et al. (2000) illustrated this problem with an example of the association between drinking behaviors and anxiety. Using daily diary methods, they showed that at the between-persons level, people who drink alcohol to cope with a stressor tend to exhibit higher level of anxiety. Drinking is associated with decreased anxiety (i.e., the within-person association is negative), which reinforces the behavior.

What Are the Average Experiences of an Individual, and How Much Do the Experiences Vary Over Time?

Many psychological phenomena operate as traits or relatively steady states. For instance, attitudes, health experiences, or distress are often stable over days, if not longer. Typically, psychological measures ask the respondent to summarize recent experience and attitudes into a single score, such as counts of alcoholic drinks in the past week or average level of a feeling. A typical example is the Dyadic Adjustment Scale (Spanier, 1976) measure of relationship satisfaction, which has respondents consider a statement such as "Describe the degree of happiness . . . of your relationship," with responses that range from 0 (*extremely unhappy*) to 6 (*perfect*). Respondents are given no advice on how to weigh degree of the satisfaction or how to overcome recency biases.

With intensive longitudinal methods, it is possible not only to consider how happy you are from *extremely unhappy* to *perfect* but also to consider how much you vary in relationship satisfaction from one time to the next. These questions are addressed by aggregating the repeated observations for each individual and calculating individual-specific means and variances. This has several advantages over a retrospective assessment at one point in time. In particular, the responses obtained by intensive longitudinal methods, such as daily questionnaires completed for a week, will minimize retrospective bias. Furthermore, because this approach allows for aggregation of responses, it will lead to a more valid and reliable measure.

The question of day-to-day variability often is overlooked by psychologists who are initially interested in stable traits of individuals. For example, many researchers are interested in ethnic identity as an individual difference that predicts cultural behavior, but Yip and Fuligni (2002) showed that the strength of ethnic identity varies in adolescents from day to day, depending on where they are and who they are with. For those who become interested in within-person variability, a descriptive analysis of day-to-day variation is a necessary step to see whether further analysis is warranted. Later in this chapter, we review methods that can be used to determine if the observed variation reflects reliable change or simply random noise.

What Is the Individual's Trajectory of Experiences Across Days, and How Do Trajectories Differ From Person to Person?

These questions are what Baltes and Nesselroade (1979) referred to as examinations of "intraindividual change and interindividual patterns . . . of intraindividual change" (p. 3). The first part of the question concerns the temporal structure underlying the intensive longitudinal data. If there is within-person variability in the outcome of interest, how much does the passage of time explain this variability? Descriptions of trends over time are often called *trajectories*. The simplest form of trajectory is that described by a linear model, one that has two parameters—an initial level and a slope for linear change. For instance, in a study of college students preparing for the Medical College Admission Test (MCAT), Bolger (1990) observed a linear increase in anxiety leading up to the examination. Although it is beyond the scope of this chapter, one may assume nonlinear change across days. For example, Boker and Laurenceau (2007) showed that relationship intimacy followed a cyclical pattern across the diary period and could be fit with a sinusoidal dynamic model that required only a few parameters for each person.

The question of interindividual differences captures whether there are between-person differences in trajectories. This is often the second step of a two-step process: (a) summarize each person's trajectory with a few parameters capturing a functional form of change over time, and (b) study the variation of those parameters across persons. For instance, in the example of the MCAT study by Bolger (1990), some participants may have showed sharp increases (i.e., slopes) in anxiety as they approached the exam day, whereas other participants showed very little increase in anxiety. The researchers can, then, try to explain what accounts for the differences in trajectories across days.

What Within-Person Process Underlies a Person's Changes, and How Do People Differ in This Process?

The final research question is the most challenging, but it is also the most interesting question that can be asked when using intensive longitudinal designs. Intensive longitudinal designs can determine the antecedents, correlates, predictors, and consequences of daily experiences. Most intensive longitudinal studies are concerned with this question. For example, Gleason et al. (2008) examined the consequences of social support receipt on mood and relationship intimacy.

Furthermore, intensive longitudinal designs allow for the examination of between-person differences in these processes, as in the case where some people may show stronger within-person processes than others. Lastly, we can examine what contributes to the between-person differences. For instance, Bolger and Zuckerman (1995) found that people who are high in neuroticism experienced more anxiety and depressed mood in response to interpersonal conflicts. The kinds of questions that can be asked of intensive longitudinal data continue to grow as new methodology develops. A recent example is the article by McNeish and Hamaker (2020) that describes two-level dynamic structural equation models that allow between-person differences in within-person autoregressive and residual variance parameters to be represented.

TYPES OF INTENSIVE LONGITUDINAL DESIGNS

Traditional intensive longitudinal designs can be classified into two broad categories: *time-based* and *event-based* protocols (e.g., Bolger et al., 2003). In the first, data collection is scheduled or sampled according to the passage of time, and in the second, data collection is triggered by some focal experience of the participant. In addition to the traditional designs, there are innovative new designs, such as device-contingent protocols. Recent developments in technology have allowed for designs in which participants are prompted by an electronic device on the basis of their physiological condition or surroundings.

Time-Based Designs

Time-based designs serve the purpose of investigating experiences as they unfold temporally. These designs include *fixed-interval* schedules, where participants report on their experiences or events at predetermined intervals, and *variable-interval* schedules, where signals prompt participants to report at either random intervals or some more complicated temporal-based pattern. In both schedules, time-based designs allow researchers to examine ongoing processes that occur over a certain period.

The most common design is a protocol in which participants answer a series of questions about their experiences and feelings at the same time each day, but researchers increasingly consider other time-based designs that involve several reports over the course of the day. The length of the interval between assessments should be informed by the nature of the research questions. In one of the daily diary studies, for example, adults with anxiety disorders and their spouses were asked to report on their relationship quality at the end of the day (Zaider et al., 2010). In a fixed-interval EMA study, participants reported on their intention to eat healthy food and actual food consumption five times a day because investigators were interested in within-day fluctuations of intention and behavior (Inauen et al., 2016).

One of the greatest challenges of fixed time-based design is deciding the suitable spacing between the assessments. We have already seen that intervals depend on the research questions, but there are other important considerations. Some processes (e.g., self-perceptions of personality traits) may not change as quickly as other processes (e.g., mood); the interval can be longer for slower processes, whereas shorter intervals may be more appropriate for processes that change quickly. Another issue is that the size of the effect can vary as a function of the length of time lag between predictor and outcome of interest (Cole & Maxwell, 2003; Gollob & Reichardt, 1987). For instance, in coping research, if an outcome (e.g., anxiety) is assessed a week or a month after the relevant coping takes place, researchers may fail to capture the effectiveness of that form of coping. Even after a general spacing of observations is chosen, investigators must consider the details of implementation. For example, a researcher might choose to obtain assessments at a specific time of the day (e.g., 8:00 a.m., noon, 4:00 p.m.), at a specific interval (every 3 waking hours, every evening), or in a time window when it is convenient for participants.

When considering the timing of fixed interval measurements, one must consider the prototypic pattern of change over time and to identify which components of change are of most interest. For example, if the investigators assess cortisol every 4 waking hours, the morning spike in cortisol (Cohen et al., 2006) will not be captured. It is also possible that an important event that occurs between assessments could be missed with longer intervals. In addition, accurate recall of events or experiences becomes challenging as the interval becomes longer, and the responses might be more susceptible to biases resulting from retrospective recall and current psychological state (Shiffman et al., 2008). On the other hand, shorter intervals introduce another set of problems. Investigators may miss some effects that take longer to manifest if assessments are collected at much shorter interval (e.g., daily) than what the process or phenomenon in question unfolds (e.g., week-to-week changes). Shorter intervals also increase participant burden; therefore, investigators may need to shorten the study period (e.g., from 4 weeks to 1 week).

The important message here is that the intervals should complement the processes that are being investigated. For example, retrospective bias may be less of a concern if investigators are interested in examining concrete, objective events (e.g., minutes exercised) rather than subjective, transient states (e.g., pain; see Redelmeier & Kahneman, 1996). Even with the increased uses of intensive longitudinal methodologies in psychological studies, the precise timings and dynamic processes of many phenomena are largely unknown because theory is often silent regarding the expected course of change over time and how long it takes for an X to influence a Y. Investigators who choose to use fixed-interval designs, however, must pick an interval before collecting any data. When the theory cannot inform how the processes or phenomenon unfold over time, Collins (2006) suggested choosing shorter intervals (e.g., hours) with the option of aggregating up to longer intervals (e.g., days).

In the variable-interval schedule, participants are asked to report their experiences at different times, and typically the participants do not know exactly when they will be asked for the next report. The investigator might use a beeper, pocket electronic organizer, cell phone, or smartphone to signal when reports should be given, and the timing of these signals might be genuinely random or based on a pattern that appears random to the participant. In some cases, designs might be a combination of the fixed- and variable-interval designs. For instance, some assessments may be signalled with random beeps throughout the day combined with an additional assessment at the end of the day. Signaling devices for variable-interval designs have changed with emerging technology. One of the earliest intensive longitudinal studies used an electronic paging device to transmit random beeps five to seven times per day, at which point adolescents would fill out a paper questionnaire about current activities (Csikszentmihalyi et al., 1977).

In recent years, researchers who use a variable-interval design tend to be interested in online assessment (e.g., How are you feeling right now?), and this type of design could minimize retrospective recall bias. It potentially allows for a random sampling of events, experiences, and behavior throughout the day. Many EMA studies fall into this category, where participants report whenever they are signaled (Shiffman et al., 2008). Variable-interval schedule may be suitable for processes that are sensitive to participant habits or expectations such that participants answer in a particular way because of the circumstances or locations (e.g., evening assessments usually provided in the bedroom before going to bed).

One of the disadvantages of this type of design is its reliance on a signaling device, which means that the device needs to be programmed to signal at certain times. It also requires participants to carry the signaling device. Some of the issues associated with this type of design are discussed in the section Intensive Longitudinal Method Design Issues, but the main shortcoming is that it could be disruptive to the participants' daily routines leading participants to avoid carrying the device. Because participants are signaled at an interval undisclosed to them, it may also increase participant burden.

A final consideration regarding time-based designs is whether the time points will be considered to be distinguishable in the analysis. When all participants are surveyed at equal intervals over a fixed survey period (e.g., the 2 weeks before an election), then time points can be considered to be *crossed* with person. If different people are measured at different times, however, perhaps because of an event-contingent design, then the time points will be *nested* within person. Nested designs do not allow interactions of specific time points with other predictors to be studied, as each person has a unique collection of time points. When interactions are of interest, investigators should consider using a crossed design.

Event-Based Designs

When researchers are interested in rare events, such as conflicts in happy couples or seizures among properly medicated epileptic patients, event-based designs (also known as *event-contingent* designs) are worth considering. Participants in this type of design will report every time an event meets the investigators' preestablished criterion. The most prototypical kind of design is the Rochester interaction record (Reis & Wheeler, 1991). In an early study using the Rochester interaction record, Wheeler et al. (1983) asked college students to provide information on every social interaction longer than 10 minutes or more. Event-based designs require investigators to give a clear definition of the event in which they are interested. The events may go unreported or missed if the participants have ambiguous understanding of the event. One way to reduce confusion and participant burden is to choose one class of event (e.g., social interactions with best friends only; Laurenceau et al., 1998). Another disadvantage of this design is that there is no way to assess compliance because it relies heavily on participants' ability to judge their situation.

Although we have presented time- and event-based designs as two separate categories, some studies have combined these two designs. For instance, adolescents were asked to report about their environment (e.g., who they were with) when they experienced self-destructive thoughts or behavior and when their handheld computer beeped randomly on a twice-daily schedule (Nock et al., 2009). These hybrid designs can markedly improve the study design, especially if the event is extremely rare, because researchers can collect daily data even if the event does not occur or goes unnoticed by the participants.

Device-Contingent Designs

In addition to traditional intensive longitudinal entries that require participants to stop and report on their behaviors and feelings, there are now ways to collect time-intensive data that bypass explicit participant self-report. Device-contingent designs have been made possible with the ubiquity of cell phones and other electronic devices. These devices often come with a set of inputs and outputs of sensory information, such as cameras, microphones, Bluetooth (for wireless networking of devices over short distance), accelerometers, and global positioning systems (GPS). The devices allow researchers to collect collateral information such as the location where the diaries are being filled out using GPS. In some cases these devices permit real-time data capture such as when participants wear a heart-rate monitor that is synced with a data collection device via Bluetooth.

Rather than consider the many potential device configurations, we will instead consider a particular example. Suppose one is interested in coping and feelings during times of stress. With a device configured with a heart-rate monitor, it is possible to prompt participants to report on their experiences and situations whenever their heart rate goes beyond 100 beats per minute for a sustained period of time and to collect additional information, such as a sound recording and visual record of the participant's environment. An advantage of this design is that the participants do not have to detect and report on particular events or situations (especially in an event-based design) because these devices trigger when sensors detect those events or situations. More important, this device configuration allows for the continuous monitoring of physiological data with little or no awareness on the part of the participant. The designs are increasingly becoming feasible. Intille, Rondoni, et al. (2003) developed a program called *context-aware experience sampling* that allows researchers to acquire feedback from participants only in particular situations detected by sensors attached to their mobile devices.

Intensive Longitudinal Method Design Issues

Although intensive longitudinal methods have important advantages over the traditional survey designs, there are some notable disadvantages as well. Some of these limitations can be minimized, but others are unavoidable. One practical concern is that most of the intensive longitudinal studies require a detailed training session with the participants to ensure that they understand the protocol (Reis & Gable, 2000). Also, for data reliability and validity, participants must be sufficiently motivated and committed to the study.

Intensive longitudinal methods are often used to capture the contexts and internal experiences of individuals as they unfold over time. To capture this richness, researchers are inclined to ask participants many questions as frequently as possible. As a consequence, a major obstacle for intensive longitudinal research is participant burden. There are three main aspects of burden: (a) length of the response task (e.g., 5- vs. 15-minute response task), (b) frequency of responses (e.g., every 2 waking hours), and (c) length of the study period (e.g., 9 weeks). Any one of these sources of burden can lead to subject noncompliance and attrition. The challenge for any investigator is to balance the information yield with burden management. Longer response tasks allow researchers to include more questions or in-depth questions but less frequent responses may be more desirable for data quality. Similarly, if the participants are instructed to respond frequently (e.g., every 2 waking hours or every time a physiological change triggers an entry request), researchers can closely monitor participants but perhaps at the expense of overall study length. Broderick et al. (2003) reported that using their EMA design, in which participants had to report at 10:00 a.m., 4:00 p.m., and 8:00 p.m., participant compliance significantly dropped after the first week. In most diary studies, response tasks are considerably shorter than cross-sectional surveys, and this presumably allows for the collection of more frequent responses or a longer diary period. Shortening protocols requires that researchers be selective about which questions to include. Shrout and Lane (2013) warned that protocols should not be shortened by relying on only one or two items per construct because this makes it difficult to distinguish reliable change from measurement error.

Like overall sample size, the number of repeated assessments in intensive longitudinal designs involves expenditure of resources, whether money or effort. Thus, a fundamental question is how to balance the number of subjects versus the number and length of assessments. Part of the answer to the question will come from issues of feasibility, that is, whether subjects are available and willing to submit to the study protocol.

Recruiting people to volunteer for studies that require long-term commitment is challenging. People commonly show initial interest but refuse to participate in the study once they hear the detailed explanation. Even if they agree to be part of the study, retaining these participants throughout the entire study period adds an additional layer of obstacles to researchers. These recruitment and retention issues might be magnified for minority participants (e.g., Black, Indigenous, people of color [BIPOC]). There is a high level of mistrust of the research process among Black, Indigenous, and Latinx populations stemming from historic violations by researchers (Ellard-Gray et al., 2015), and the sense of mistrust is amplified in the case of intensive longitudinal studies (E. Seaton, personal communication, July 20, 2020). Therefore, building a rapport with potential research participants prior to collecting data is a crucial first step to successfully carry out any intensive longitudinal studies, especially if researchers want to encourage participation from BIPOC.

The other part of the answer will come from considerations of the precision of statistical estimates from the study. If the intensive longitudinal study is being used to obtain reliable and valid measures of between-person differences, then subject sample size will dominate the design. If the study is being used to estimate the association between events and/or experiences that occur with-person, then the number of assessments will have to be sufficiently large to capture within-person variability in events and/or experiences of interest. We comment further about the statistical issues in the section titled Analysis of Intensive Longitudinal Data.

Another important issue is the degree to which the process of providing regular reports changes the subject's experience and behavior (also known as *measurement reactivity*; Barta et al., 2012). Intensive longitudinal methods are relatively new, and we know relatively little about how participation affects participants. What we do know from several studies is that participants' responses can change over time: For example, Iida et al. (2008, Study 1) found that participant reports of support provision increased over a 28-diary period across which no changes would be expected on average. Other effects, such as reactance and habituation, are possible, especially if the behavior is socially reactive. On the other hand, there is evidence that reactance does not pose a threat to the validity of diary questionnaires. For instance, Litt et al. (1998) found that participants were more aware of the monitored behavior, but the behavior itself was not reactive. In contrast, Shrout and his colleagues (2018) demonstrated the existence of initial elevation bias, which is a phenomenon that for the first few days of reporting participants tend to overestimate their reports, especially for negative mental states. These authors argued that of the many types of self-report research, intensive longitudinal study designs are the most immune to the bias, in that fast habituation leaves most later intensive longitudinal reports unbiased.

Reporting biases can also involve changes to participants' understanding of a particular construct, such as when the construct becomes more complex or the reports become less reliable over time. For example, repeated exposure to an IL questionnaire may affect encoding or retrieval of relevant information. For example, Iida and colleagues (2008) observed a surprising increase in support provision; as time passed, participants possibly included more behaviors that fell into the category of "social support," in part because these behaviors were made more accessible through the repeated exposure to questions about support. Although no study has directly examined this issue for intensive longitudinal studies, Thomas and Diener (1990) gave indirect evidence against increased complexity, at least for mood. They reported that the recall of mood did not differ following an intensive diary period.

Another potential effect is that completing the intensive longitudinal assessments may constrain participants' conceptualization of the domain to fit with those measured in the study. For example, a study of social support that asks about two kinds of support (e.g., emotional and instrumental) will make participants more aware of these kinds of supportive behaviors, but they might become less sensitive to other kinds of support. Lastly, there is some evidence that a certain kind of self-reflective process may have therapeutic effects (e.g., Pennebaker, 1997). These effects, however, have not been observed with quantitative ratings (e.g., Shrout et al., 2018).

An important limitation often listed for intensive longitudinal designs is that they produce only correlational data, and such data cannot be used to establish causal mechanisms. This limitation needs to be considered in the context of the broader research literature. Relative to cross-sectional surveys, intensive longitudinal studies allow effects to be ordered in time, and this data structure often can be used to test and reject causal predictions. Such data are rarely definitive, however, particularly because of the difficulty of establishing the correct time lags of causal effects. As Cole and Maxwell (2003) showed, an incorrect specification of the timing of the causal effect (e.g., how long it takes the aspirin to reduce headache pain and keep it reduced) will lead to biased and misleading causal estimates. Moreover, an appropriate temporal design, consideration of confounders, and estimation of theoretically driven within-person links better approximate the within-person comparisons that are at the heart of approaches to causal inference (Gelman & Hill, 2007). We conclude, thus, that relative to randomized experiments, intensive longitudinal studies are limited but relative to cross-sectional studies, intensive longitudinal studies can be a giant leap toward causal inference. In the future, we hope that researchers also will consider supplementing intensive longitudinal studies with experimental designs, if that is possible, to test causes and effects more definitively.

DIARY FORMAT AND TECHNOLOGY

Once investigators decide on the design of the intensive longitudinal study that is optimal for their research questions, they must make decisions about how to collect the data. Recent technological developments have changed the way participants report, and it is also possible to collect additional information, such as the location in which the participants make a diary entry,[1] or to integrate these reports with physiological measures. In this section, we review the three most commonly used diary formats: paper and pencil, brief telephone interviews, and electronic (e.g., internet-based diary, handheld computer, mobile phone) diary formats.

Paper-and-Pencil Format

Early intensive longitudinal studies tended to use paper-and-pencil format, and this format is still one of the most widely used. It remains a good option, especially when it is coupled with a device to check the compliance (e.g., Gershuny et al., 2020). In paper-and-pencil diary studies, participants are given packets, folders, or booklets of questionnaires, one for each diary entry, and they are instructed when to fill out and return the diary. In some studies, investigators instruct participants to return the diary every week (e.g., Bolger et al., 2000), whereas in other studies, they instruct participants to return the diary within 2 to 3 days (e.g., Impett et al., 2008, Study 2). Diary entries are similar to usual survey questionnaires, but they tend to be shorter to reduce participant burden. In general, there is little effort needed to adapt survey questions to a paper-and-pencil diary format. Another advantage of paper-and-pencil formats is that participants are familiar with the format, so it will be easier for them to fill it out. Paper-and-pencil diaries do not require complicated maintenance schedules, which is the case for some of the formats we will describe.

More and more researchers are moving away from the pencil-and-paper format because of its associated disadvantages. The main problem is participant forgetfulness with regard to compliance and diary completion. This could happen when participants fail to remember the time when they are supposed to fill out a diary entry (time-based study), or it could happen if they forget to bring the packet with them (both time- and event-based study). In either case, missed entries could lead to participants reconstructing their responses at later times or fabricating responses. Either occurrence could undermine the advantages of the intensive longitudinal study. To avoid these incidences, investigators can emphasize the importance of filling out entries at specified times and that participants will not be penalized for missed entries. Asking the participants whether they filled out the entry on time may be helpful as the question suggests that some entries may not be filled out on time. It also may be useful to train the participants to use implementation intentions (Gollwitzer, 1999), which involve if–then scripts, such as "If I go to brush my teeth at bedtime, then I will complete my diary."

The bigger issue with this format is that investigators cannot track the compliance of participants without further technology. In a intensive longitudinal study, compliance needs to be considered both in terms of number of entries and their validity. The first one is easy to assess, but the latter is impossible to evaluate without another kind of device that tracks the compliance. For example, Rafaeli et al. (2007) asked participants to report on the time of the diary entry, and they compared their responses with the information obtained from a separate computerized task. In another study, Maisel and Gable (2009) asked participants to put the entry in the envelope, seal the envelope, and stamp the date and time across the seal using an electronic stamp with a security-coded lock. Although these extra steps allow researchers to judge participant compliance, they do not ensure that participants follow the instructions. More certainty comes from using surreptitious time-stamp devices that record the time a paper diary is opened (e.g., Stone et al., 2002) or asking participants to wear wearable cameras (e.g., Gershuny et al., 2020),

---

[1] In this section, we use the term *diary* to refer to the repeated assessments in an intensive longitudinal studies. These assessments could be open-format responses, but most intensive longitudinal studies use quantitative questionnaires.

but such devices can increase the cost of a intensive longitudinal study considerably.

Another limitation of paper-and-pencil format is the burden of data entry. Although this is a problem with any survey study, the problem can be pronounced because of the volume of data that are collected by the participants. For instance, some of us were involved in a daily diary study with bar examinees and their partners (Iida et al., 2008, Study 2) that collected 44 days of diary from 303 couples. This means there were total of 26,664 (303 × 2 × 44) entries over the course of the study. During the data entry process, researchers must interpret ambiguous responses (e.g., overlapping circles on Likert-type scale responses). There may be an error during data entry process even if the responses are not ambiguous. With paper-and-pencil data records, we recommend that all of the data be entered twice by independent people, but we acknowledge that this can be costly and time-consuming.

Another shortcoming is that participants might make mistakes in responses. This could happen when participants do not understand the questions or when participants miss a section of the questionnaire. This limitation is, again, not limited to intensive longitudinal research, but it could lead to a larger problem because of the amount of data that are collected from one individual. This can be avoided if the researchers have participants come in on the first day of the study.

The final shortcoming of paper-and-pencil diaries is the potential breach of confidentiality. Because the previous responses may be viewed by others in their environment, participants may hesitate to be truthful in their responses. This problem could be avoided if the participants return the diary entries more frequently (e.g., Impett et al., 2008) or are asked to seal the envelope immediately after the completion (e.g., Maisel & Gable, 2009).

Since the first structured intensive longitudinal study, researchers have sought to overcome the limitations of paper-and-pencil formats by using pager signaling devices (Csikszentmihalyi et al., 1977), preprogrammed wristwatches (e.g., Litt et al., 1998), or phone calls (e.g., Morrison et al., 1999). Modern devices can be programmed to signal at certain times (fixed-interval schedule) or at random times (variable-interval schedule). These augmentations offer a remedy to one of the problems of paper-and-pencil format, which is participant forgetfulness. They also reduce the participant burden because they do not have to keep track of time or appropriate occasions to respond. On the other hand, these methods cannot be used for event-based sampling, and they involve additional expense.

On the one hand, the augmentation approach retains advantages of paper-and-pencil formats but adds the advantage of reminding people when to fill out the questionnaires. On the other hand, participant compliance cannot be estimated by this device alone, and the cumbersome data entry remains a challenge. In addition, augmentation approaches are intrusive at times. If they are preprogrammed to signal randomly, they could go off during important meetings. This can discourage participants from carrying the signaling device, and this would defeat the purpose of the intensive longitudinal approach.

Brief Telephone Interviews

Another common diary data collection method is to simply call the participant using a telephone (e.g., Almeida, 2005; Waldinger & Schulz, 2010). As we discuss later in the chapter, automatic telephone systems, such as interactive voice response (IVR), also can be used to collect data. In personal telephone diary designs, trained interviewers make brief calls to the participants; the timing of the calls is determined by fixed or variable interval schedules that are set by the investigator. This data collection modality is suitable for both open-ended questions (in which participants can freely respond to a question in their own words) and questionnaires with fixed responses. The conversations can be audio-taped, or the interviewer might simply be asked to take notes and complete forms.

Brief telephone interviews have a number of advantages over paper-and-pencil dairies. One is that they can be used with persons who are not literate or who have impairments, such as visual impairments, so long as they have access to a telephone. A second major advantage is that researchers can directly record compliance with the protocol. By actively engaging the participant, telephone interviews may help overcome participant forgetfulness and avoid any confusion about the diary protocols. In addition, researchers can allow for branching of questions (certain questions are asked depending on their previous responses), and presentation of items can be randomized to avoid habituation and boredom. If the participants provide invalid responses (out of range) or seem not to understand the questions, interviewers can correct and explain the questions. This feature of a telephone diary makes it suitable for older participants who may have trouble seeing the fonts on the paper-and-pencil diary. A key advantage of this procedure is that it involves personal interactions with the research team, and this can lead to more consistent participation and more engagement in any given interview.

Brief telephone designs also have a number of limitations. They are expensive to implement because they require hiring and training interviewers who are flexible when making calls and who are professional in their demeanor. Almeida (2005) used a survey research center, which has professional telephone interviewers, but this can be especially costly. Participants often are not available when the interviewer makes the call, and so repeated callbacks are needed. Unless interviewers enter data directly into a computer, the same data entry costs as paper-and-pencil methods will accrue. Confidentiality may be limited especially if participants take calls at home when other family members are around, and participants may not provide honest responses to sensitive questions. Response biases may operate and may be moderated by variables such as ethnicity, gender of the interviewer, or other people being in the vicinity when the call is taken. The convention for most studies is to use female interviewers (ideally matched for ethnic background) because they are thought to elicit better data, and this convention is used on the basis of studies of interviewer effects in face-to-face surveys (e.g., Kane & Macaulay, 1993).

Electronic Response Formats

Electronic formats began to be used in the late 1990s (e.g., Stone et al., 1998) and have grown to be the most common design in the past 2 decades. Uses of internet and computer devices increased in the 2 decades, which also increased the comfort of participants using these formats. There are many different kinds of electronic diary data collection, but we will focus on two broad formats: fixed schedule format and variable–ambulatory assessment.

Fixed schedule formats are often implemented in intensive longitudinal studies that ask participants to log into a secure website and access an online questionnaire (e.g., Impett et al., 2008, Study 3). In most studies, participants are given the access code (or user name) and password to identify their data and to ensure that only one set of responses is provided. Investigators can remind the participants of the scheduled times using email or phone-text messages. Some investigators provide participants with handheld devices, such as electronic personal organizers or pocket computers, which can be programmed with questions without connection to the internet. This approach was made feasible by Barrett and Feldman-Barrett (2001), who developed a free-ware diary program called ESP (Experience Sampling Program) with funding from the National Science Foundation. In recent years, most researchers ask their participants to use their own smartphones to go to a survey website and log in on a daily basis (e.g., Iida & Shapiro, 2019). Another way to implement fixed schedule surveys is to ask participants to use their own phones to call a number that is associated with automatic telephone systems. These might be IVR systems that ask questions and accept verbal responses, or they might require participants to answer a few questions using their touchtone telephone pad (see Cranford et al., 2010).

Electronic response formats share many of the advantages of personal telephone interviews, and they have additional advantages. For example, they provide time stamps (and date stamps) for responses, and these give direct measures of participant compliance. By examining when responses were entered, researchers can easily identify which entries were made on time and which were not. In addition, they often allow investigators to record how long participants took to respond, and this information may be relevant to data quality and respondent burden. For instance, if the participants take 3 hours to complete a diary entry that should only take 10 minutes to complete, researchers can take note. Alternatively, entries that take too short a time can be useful as well to pick up inattention.

One benefit of electronic response formats over many telephone interviews is that the responses can be easily uploaded onto the computer. This is especially true for some of the web-based questionnaires, which put participant responses in some accessible format, such as an Excel spreadsheet or SPSS data file. This feature of electronic formats eliminates errors associated with hand entry, and it allows researchers to ensure data accuracy. Electronic formats also avoid out-of-range responses because participants are constrained to choosing a response that is available. Finally, electronic data entry avoids the contamination of the data collection by response biases and interviewer effects.

There are some important limitations that are unique to electronic diaries. Most web survey programs (e.g., Qualtrics, SurveyMonkey) are not created for repeated designs, and depending on how the researchers create the surveys, participants may complete multiple entries in one sitting. This could create problems for researchers because researchers are left to figure out which entry is the valid entry for a given day. One way to avoid the problem is by asking the participants to explicitly report the time or date for the entry that they are responding at the beginning of every assessment. This would allow participants to specifically say that they are filling out a particular entry for a subsequent time point. Another strategy is to give specific instructions for missed entries, such as ignoring the missed assessments or giving them other formats to report on the missed entries. The researchers may also see multiple entries if the participants start an entry but not complete it for various reasons (e.g., technology failure, getting timed out). Other limitations of electronic diaries are similar to those of paper-and-pencil diaries; participants must understand the diary protocol, and formatting of the web-based questionnaires must be clear. Special care must be taken to ensure that participants do not fall into a response set in which they click on responses that happen to be in the same column. Nonresponse can be a problem, but devices can be programmed to ask the respondent to check data for completeness.[2] Moreover, IVR can be scheduled to call the participant if the responses are not made within the given time frame, and researchers can contact the participants if they do not make an entry on the diary website.

Variable schedule electronic formats differ from fixed schedule formats in that participants may be asked at any time to provide information about their experience. This design requires that participants always have near them a data-entry device, but with the rapidly growing number of smartphone owners around the world (Pew Research Center, 2019), this design is more feasible than ever. This type of format is often coupled with variable-interval schedule designs because researchers can schedule random and preprogrammed signaling via short message services (SMS).[3] Device-contingent designs also often use this format to collect data as well. Technological advances, such as context-aware experience sampling (Intille et al., 2003), also allow for other kind of data collection, such as physiological assessment combined with typical diary questionnaires, which assesses experiences and attitudes. For researchers who are interested in assessments of fluid and transient processes,

---

[2]Some web-based protocols can be programmed to require a response before the participant moves on, but this option often will be in violation of informed consent assurances that say that each response is voluntary.
[3]There may be an online survey application that would allow researchers to program both the survey and the reminders to be sent out to participants at schedule times. If the application does not provide such options, then the researchers can couple the survey application with a reminder application (e.g., SurveySignal, Constant Contact).

combination signaling and time-stamp responses reduce the likelihood of participant forgetfulness or retrospective recall bias.

Final Comments on Diary Format
Whichever diary format researchers choose, it is essential that careful pilot studies be carried out with participants who are drawn from the same population that will be the target of the full study. In our experience, these pilot studies almost always lead to a refinement (and improvement) of the protocol or procedure (to address the so-called "unknown unknowns"), and they help ensure that the methods are feasible with the specific population. For example, conducting a handheld computer diary study may not be ideal for older participants who have difficulty reading small text on the screen or who may lack dexterity to properly respond. Moreover, additional time and resources would be crucial for recruitment and retention of BIPOC participants.

ANALYSIS OF INTENSIVE LONGITUDINAL DATA

We consider data analysis issues related to the three questions that we posed previously: (a) What are the average experiences of an individual, and how much do the experiences vary from day to day? (b) What is the individual's trajectory of experiences across days, and how do trajectories differ by person? and (c) What process underlies a person's changes, and how do people differ in this process? Before addressing these substantive questions, we consider the important issue of measurement quality, particularly reliability and validity. To make these statistical considerations more concrete, we focus on two substantive examples, which we describe in the following sections.

Stress and Coping During Preparation for a Professional Licensing Exam (Bar Exam Data Set)
Several of us have been involved in a large survey of support and coping in intimate couples where one partner is a recent law school graduate who is preparing for the bar exam. As described in various places (Iida et al., 2008, Study 2; Shrout et al., 2018, Study 1), we asked both examinees and partners to complete daily paper-and-pencil questionnaires for 5 weeks before the bar exam days, the 2 days of the exam, and 1 week after the examination, for a total of 44 days. We asked them to report on their general mood, relationship feelings, support transactions, troublesome events, and coping strategies each evening.

Daily Affect and Blood Glucose Levels in Diabetic Patients (Diabetes Data Set)
Skaff et al. (2009) reported results from a daily diary study of 206 diabetic patients who completed diaries for 21 days and who provided morning blood samples using a glucometer so that blood glucose could be measured. We did not have access to the original data, but we simulated artificial data that show the same pattern of results as the published paper. Not only do we use these simulated data to illustrate methods of analysis, we also describe how simulation studies such as these can be useful when planning new studies.

Statistical Packages for Analysis for Intensive Longitudinal Data
There are various statistical packages for examining and modeling intensive longitudinal data. If researchers want to use a single package to both restructure and analyze the data, we recommend using comprehensive software, such as SAS, SPSS, and R. The data sets together with the syntax files for SPSS, SAS, and R can be downloaded from https://osf.io/8edwk/. If the data are already in a structure that is appropriate for a given analysis, then researchers might choose specialized packages, such as Mplus (Version 8; Muthén & Muthén, 2017) and HLM (Version 8; Raudenbush et al., 2019). For running intensive longitudinal data analyses using these specialized packages, please refer to the respective manuals for running these analyses. In this chapter, we analyzed example data sets using SAS (Version 9.4) and the reported estimates are from SAS output. The figures are created using the *ggplot2* package in R (Wickham, 2016).

Psychometric Analyses of Intensive Longitudinal Data

When reporting results from experiments or cross-sectional studies, it is considered standard good practice to report the reliability of measures and to present some evidence that they are valid. *Reliability* is typically defined as the tendency for measures to be replicated, whereas *validity* is defined as evidence that a measured quantity corresponds to the theoretical construct that is the focus of the research. Lane et al. provide details about reliability theory in Chapter 33 of this volume, and Grimm and Widaman give details about validity theory in Chapter 32.

Standard reliability designs typically focus on the reliability of between-person distinctions. The reliability coefficient is interpreted to be the proportion of observed measurement variation that can be attributed to true individual difference variation. The two most common approaches to estimating reliability in psychology are test–retest designs and internal consistency designs. Test–retest designs require the investigator to arrange to have second (retest) measurements taken on the same set of persons at another occasion but before the construct of interest has changed. Under classical test theory assumptions (Crocker & Algina, 1986), a simple Pearson correlation between the test and retest scores provides an estimate of the reliability coefficient. Internal consistency designs allow the investigator to estimate reliability at one measurement occasion assuming that the measure is composed of two or more items. Instead of replicating the whole measurement process, the internal consistency approach asks whether different items can be considered to be replications. The most common estimate of internal consistency reliability is Cronbach's alpha. Like test–retest reliability, it measures the quality of between-person differences.

Cranford et al. (2006) showed how the internal consistency approach can be extended to the analysis of the reliability of intensive longitudinal data using generalizability theory (GT; Cronbach et al., 1972). They pointed out that intensive longitudinal studies typically need separate reliability analyses to describe between-person differences and within-person change. The former is an extension of the usual approach of Cronbach's alpha, but it combines information from all diary days and all scale items into a summary score for each person. The reliability of change can be separately estimated whenever there are two or more items related to a concept included in each diary. For example, it will work if participants report in separate parts of the diary how (a) angry, (b) annoyed, and (c) resentful they feel. These replicate items allow the investigator to determine whether a participant really does have a high anger day or if some apparent daily variation might be caused by sloppy reporting.

To calculate the between-person reliability and the change reliability, the investigator uses a variance decomposition procedure that is available in most commercial statistical systems used by psychological researchers. Variation at the item level is broken into pieces attributable to Persons, Time, Items, Person × Item, Time × Item, and Person × Time. Shrout and Lane (2013) provided examples of syntax for calculating these effects and for combining them into the GT reliability coefficients of Cranford et al. (2006). These methods are illustrated in the next section.

Just as two versions of measurement reliability must be considered in intensive longitudinal studies, so too must we consider two versions of measurement validity. Self-report measures of fairly stable processes such as attachment style may show excellent patterns of validity in that they correlate highly with current relationship status and previous relationship difficulties, but such measures will not necessarily show validity when adapted to a daily diary research design. As Lane et al. (Chapter 33 of this volume) argue, a separate set of validity analyses are needed to describe how measures relate to other measures over time (rather than over people). Validity questions include face validity issues about whether participants agree that they can reflect on daily feelings related to stable self-constructs, convergent validity issues about whether daily variation in attachment feelings correlate with related constructs such as rejection sensitivity, and discriminant validity questions about whether the daily attachment measure can be shown to be distinct from (nonredundant with) related measures such as rejection sensitivity.

Multilevel Approaches to Intensive Longitudinal Data

Many psychological measures are designed to represent *usual* levels of attitudes, behavior, affect, motivation, and so on. Some versions of measures specify a time window to consider (e.g., in the past month), whereas others make no mention of time. For instance, the Dyadic Adjustment Scale (Spanier, 1976), a commonly used measure for relationship satisfaction, asks participants to report on various aspects of their relationships. To be specific, one of the items from the Dyadic Adjustment Scale asks the participants to "circle the dot which best describes the degree of happiness, all things considered, of your relationship" (p. 28). The response options are 0 (*extremely unhappy*) to 6 (*perfect*), with 3 (*happy*) as the midpoint. When responding, participants must mentally calculate and summarize their relationship over an unspecified amount of time, and this summary may be biased by the participant's current state or situation. In a intensive longitudinal study, we can avoid these mental calculations by asking participants to report on their relationship satisfaction every day. We can then compute an estimate of usual satisfaction by taking the average of the daily relationship satisfaction reports by each person. These averages can be kept separate for members of the couple, or they can be further averaged to represent a couple-level satisfaction value. In addition to the mean, the within-person variability can be derived by calculating the variance of the daily relationship satisfaction reports over days by each person. Calculating these descriptive statistics can be illuminating and can inform one about both degree and volatility of relationship satisfaction. These calculations eliminate the dependent time observations through the creation of between-person summaries of the daily experience.

More formal analysis of between- and within-person variation can be done using multilevel modeling (also known as hierarchical linear modeling, random regression modeling, and general mixed models), which is described in detail by Nezlek (see Volume 3, Chapter 11, this handbook). These methods retain the dependent data in the analysis (e.g., daily reports within person), but they explicitly model the structure of dependency in the data. A number of textbooks have been written about these methods (e.g., Raudenbush & Bryk, 2002; Singer & Willett, 2003), but the approach of Raudenbush and Bryk (2002) is particularly intuitive for analysis of intensive longitudinal data. In their language, the analysis of the repeated observations of each person is organized around a Level 1 equation, whereas the analysis of between-person differences is organized around Level 2 equations. The beauty of these models is that they both recognize some common structure to individual life experiences and allow the investigator to consider important individual differences in manifestations of this structure.

ANALYSIS EXAMPLE 1. WHAT ARE THE AVERAGE EXPERIENCES OF AN INDIVIDUAL, AND HOW MUCH DO THE EXPERIENCES VARY FROM DAY TO DAY?

The multilevel approach is well suited to address complicated questions such as one we posed at the beginning of the chapter: What are the average experiences of an individual, and how much do the experiences vary from day to day? As we illustrate in the example that follows, the question about the average experiences can be addressed by writing a simple Level 1 (within-person) model that essentially specifies a mean across diary days and nothing more. Level 2 (between-person) models allow the examination of individual differences such as gender and personality as well as dyadic variables such as time spent in the relationship. When we turn to questions about how the experiences vary from day to day, we build more complicated Level 1 models that describe how the participant's average experience is affected by such variables as time in the study, weekends, and even time-varying events such as conflicts or transient stressors. The participant-level experiences can then be summarized and analyzed using Level 2 models that compare time effects for males and females and so on. We illustrate the strengths of these methods in examples to follow.

Example Analysis Using the Bar Exam Data Set

Our first example uses the bar exam data set described in the previous section. In this example, we explore daily relationship satisfaction reported by the examinees and partners. Relationship satisfaction was measured with two items, "content" and "satisfied," and ratings were on a 5-point scale, ranging from 0 (*not at all*) to 4 (*extremely*). The form explicitly encouraged respondents to use midpoints, and, thus, 11 discrete rating values are possible. We first discuss how to structure intensive longitudinal data. Next, we provide a description of the patterns of data, and carry out a GT analysis of between-person reliability and reliability of change in satisfaction. Finally, we apply multilevel models to describe between-person differences in the context of the diary experience.

Preliminary steps. The first step of data analysis is restructuring the data set, and this step is particularly important to intensive longitudinal data set. In a cross-sectional study, data are structured such that each participant's responses are entered in a single row. Figure 16.1a shows an example of such data structure (wide format), in which each row represents the means of relationship satisfaction across 44 days (content 0 to content 43). So, the first person's average relationship satisfaction for the first day is 2, and this person's average satisfaction for the last day is 4. When conducting a intensive longitudinal data analysis, it is easier to structure the data where each row represents each person's daily responses (long format); therefore, each person is going to have as many rows as assessments (see Figure 16.1b). In our current example, each participant has 44 rows of data, which means our data set consists of 4,400 rows (44 days × 100 participants).

Figure 16.2 shows a graph of four participants' trajectories of the item "content" across days.

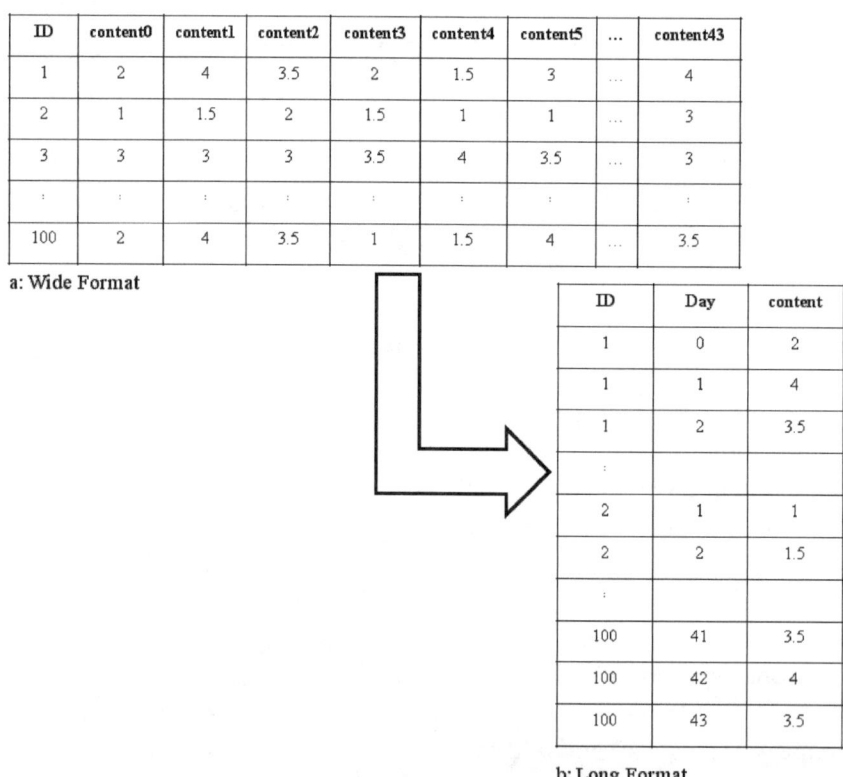

FIGURE 16.1. Data restructuring.

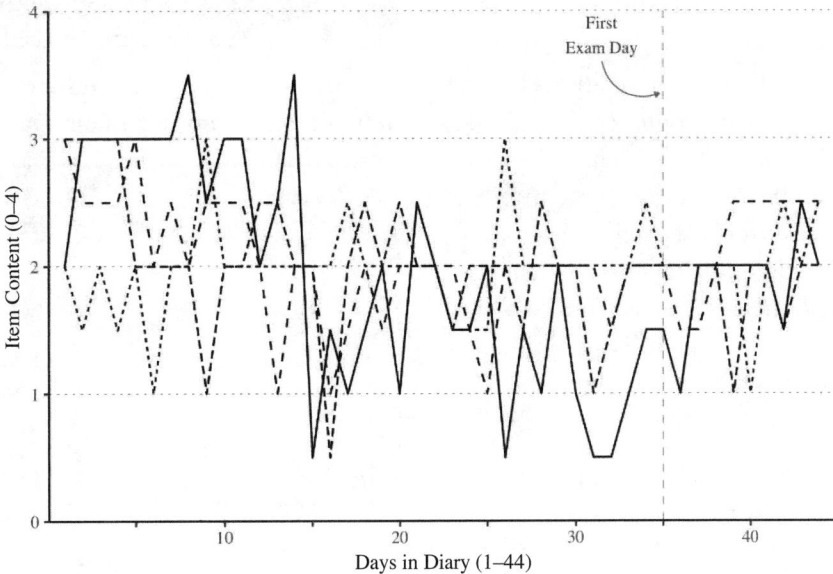

FIGURE 16.2. Trajectories of the item "content."

To illustrate within-person variability, we picked individuals whose average for relationship satisfaction during the diary period is 2 (*moderately*). One can see that all these participants reported higher satisfaction initially and then experienced some loss of satisfaction between Day 14 and Day 24. These are important examples of within-person change.

Figure 16.2 clearly shows that participants can differ both in level and in variability. The average score provides an efficient summary of the level and the sample variance provides a useful index of the stability of reports. When intensive longitudinal data are stacked (with person-time as the unit of analysis), one can use special software features such as AGGREGATE in SPSS or PROC MEANS in SAS to calculate subject-level summaries of the diary reports. The distribution of these subject mean and variance estimates can then be studied, by calculating the mean-of-means, the mean standard deviation (*SD*), and the variability of these subject-level summaries in terms of *SD*s and confidence bounds. When we do this using the examinees, we get a mean-of-means of 2.72 and an *SD* of these means of 0.84 with 5th and 95th percentiles of 1.28 and 3.99. For partners we find a mean-of-means of 2.73 and an *SD* of these means of 0.78 with 5th and 95th percentiles of 1.42 and 3.88, respectively. Within-person variance can be calculated in a similar manner. In this case, we find similar amounts of within-person variability for the members of the couple; the mean variances are 0.37 for both examinees and partners.

Once these summaries are computed, we can ask questions about their mutual associations. Is there evidence that variance of satisfaction is related to the level of satisfaction in the examinee and in the partner? Do examinees with high or low average satisfaction levels have partners with similar averages? Do members of the couple tend to have similar levels of volatility of daily satisfaction during the bar exam period? These questions can be approached with simple Pearson correlations of the within-person summaries. We find that there is a moderate relation between mean and variances ($r = -.29$ for examinees, and $r = -.35$ for partners). We do find substantial correlation between the mean satisfaction ratings of examinees and partners ($r = .60$), and we also find some evidence of correlation of volatility ($r = .30$).

Although these calculations are informative and easy to carry out, statisticians have suggested ways that they can be refined. The individual scores are a combination of signal and measurement error, but the above analysis treats the numbers as pure signal. Also, the simple procedure that we implemented would make use of all data, but some persons might miss a number of entries, whereas others will complete them all. This procedure does not take into account the number of days that are combined to create the summaries. Before we illustrate the multilevel statistical methods that address these issues, we first consider the question of how much error is apparent in the measurements. This requires applying the GT reliability methods of Cranford et al. (2006).

Reliability analyses using the GT approach. Unlike the analyses presented so far, and the multilevel analyses that follow, the GT analysis uses variation in the item scores rather than the scale scores. Although Lane et al. (Chapter 33, this volume) recommended that three or more items be used to measure important constructs, the bar exam study included only two daily items that addressed relationship satisfaction, "satisfied" and "content." On good days, both should get high scores, whereas on disappointing days both should get low scores. If the two items are discordant, the psychometric analysis concludes that error may be present.

The GT analysis states that the variability of the item scores across days and persons can be decomposed into the effects shown in Table 16.1: Person, Day, Item, Person × Day, Person × Item, Day × Item, and error. A special version of the data set was constructed in which each subject had two lines of data for each day, one with the response to "satisfied" and the other with the response to "content." These items were analyzed simultaneously using the VARCOMP procedure of SAS, which uses as a default the MIVQUE method, which allows us to use the data with missing observations.[4] Table 16.1 shows the results of the variance composition analysis for partner's relationship satisfaction.

In this example, three components explained most of the variability in these data. The first

TABLE 16.1

Results of G-Study—Examinee's Relationship Satisfaction From Bar Exam Data Set

Source of variance	Symbol	Variance estimates	%
Person	σ	0.689	58.7
Day	σ	0.007	0.6
Item	σ	0.013	1.1
Person × Day	σ	0.281	23.9
Person × Item	σ	0.020	1.7
Day × Item	σ	0.000	0.1
Error	σ	0.166	14.1
TOTAL		1.176	100.0

component is the variance due to person, the second component is the variance due to Person × Day, and third component is error variation. Variance due to person tells us that there were individual differences in the amount of relationship satisfaction the examinees reported, explaining more than half of the variation (58.7%). Variance due to Person × Day captures individual differences in change across the study period, meaning partners had different trajectories of relationship feelings across the study, and it explained slightly less than a quarter (23.9%) of the total variance. The third component is the variance due to error, which combines the random component and the variance due to Person × Day × Item, and it explained 14% of the variance.

Cranford et al. (2006) described how the estimates of the variance components can be compared to produce a number of different reliability coefficients. These make use of different variance components and consider the number of days (indexed by k) and the number of items (indexed by m). In this example, we focus on only two versions of reliability, the reliability of the overall mean of item responses across days (what Cranford et al., 2006, called R_{KF}),[5] and the reliability of day-to-day changes in scale scores (R_{change}). Both of these involve calculations of

---

[4] A similar procedure, VARCOMP, exists in SPSS. Examples of the syntax for both SAS and SPSS can be found in Chapter 33 of this volume.
[5] R_{KF} is named as such because it is the reliability of averages across K days for a set of fixed items. *Fixed items* mean that all participants answer the same set of items, as is the case in this example.

variance ratios, for which the numerator contains the variance of the presumed signal, either variance due to person and person by item or variance due to person by day, and the denominator contains the variance of signal plus variance due to error. According to classical test theory, the noise variation is reduced by the number of responses (m) that are averaged. This is where the impact of including additional items is most apparent.

The reliability of the average of m item scores across k days is excellent, as can be seen from the following calculation that uses Equation 4 of Cranford et al. (2006) with results in Table 16.1:

$$R_{KF} = \frac{\sigma^2_{PERSON} + ([\sigma^2_{PERSON*ITEM}]/m)}{[\sigma^2_{PERSON} + ([\sigma^2_{PERSON*ITEM}]/m) + (\sigma^2_{ERROR}/km)]}$$

$$= \frac{0.69 + (0.02/2)}{0.69 + (0.02/2) + [0.17/(44*2)]} = 0.99$$

(16.1)

The reliability of daily change is estimated using Equation 5 of Cranford et al. (2006) along with the numerical values in Table 16.1:

$$R_{Change} = \frac{\sigma^2_{PERSON*DAY}}{[\sigma^2_{PERSON*DAY} + (\sigma^2_{ERROR}/m)]}$$

$$= \frac{0.28}{0.28 + (0.17/2)} = 0.77 \quad (16.2)$$

This calculation suggests that about 77% of the variance of daily change is reliable variance. Although this level of reliability is often considered to be acceptable, we can note that if we had increased the number of items to, for example, $m = 4$ items, the reliability estimate (all other things being equal) would have been 0.87. In future studies, we should take note of the possibility of improving measurement.

Multilevel analyses of intensive longitudinal data. Assuming the psychometric analysis suggests that there is a reliable signal in the short diary forms of measures, it is appropriate to move to substantive analyses, which are best approached using the multilevel framework introduced earlier. In a typical intensive longitudinal design, Level 1 units are time or event-based observations within-persons, and Level 2 units are between-persons units. Thus, we say the Level 1 model reflects the within-person level and Level 2 the between-person level. In this chapter, we follow the multilevel notation used by Raudenbush and Bryk (2002), which distinguished the different levels rather than combining them into a reduced mixed form equation (for an alternative approach, see Fitzmaurice et al., 2004).

The simplest of the multilevel equations is called a *fully unconditional* model or an intercept-only model. For the current example with examinees, the relationship satisfaction of the ith examinee at the jth time (Y_{ij}) can be represented by two equations:

$$\text{Level 1: } Y_{ij} = \beta_{0i} + \varepsilon_{ij} \quad (16.3)$$

$$\text{Level 2: } \beta_{0i} = \gamma_{00} + u_{0i} \quad (16.4)$$

In the Level 1 equation, Y_{ij}, relationship satisfaction of examinee i on day j, is represented as a function of the average over time points for each person, β_{0i}, and ε_{ij}, the deviation of relationship satisfaction on day j from the examinee's intercept. The term ε_{ij} can also be understood as the within-person residual, and its variance is a parameter capturing within-person variance. The Level 2 equation models β_{0i}, the intercept for examinee i, as a function of grand mean, γ_{00}, and u_{0i}, the deviation of the examinee i from the grand mean. Thus, variance of u_{0i} captures the between-person variability of the average of relationship satisfaction across examinees in our data set. In multilevel modeling terms, γ_{00} is also known as a *fixed effect*, and u_{0i} is called a *random effect*. For partners, an identical model is estimated with partners' data replacing the examinees' data.

We can estimate this model using the MIXED procedure in SAS (syntax and partial output for examinees are available in Appendix 16.1) or other programs such as SPSS or HLM. When we do so, we get fixed effects of 2.72 for intercept for examinees and 2.73 for partners, which are identical to the estimates derived by taking the average of the averages. The variance of ε_{ij} is estimated to be 0.37 for examinees and 0.37 for partners, and the random effect of intercept is estimated to be 0.70 for examinees and 0.60 for partners. Note that the variance of the random effects from the unconditional model (0.70) is consistent with the between-person variability represented in the numerator of the formula for R_{KF} shown above. The value 0.70 is composed of the sum of overall person variance (0.689) plus one half of the person by item interaction (0.020).[6]

Assuming that the intercept estimates are normally distributed, we can estimate 95% prediction intervals by computing a standard deviation (the square root of the variance) for each group and using the usual symmetric interval of mean $\pm(1.96*SD)$. In our study the standard deviations are 0.84 for examinees and 0.77 for partners. Using these estimates, we can calculate intervals that includes 95% of estimates ($2.72 \pm 1.96 \times 0.84$ for examinees; $2.73 \pm 1.96 \times 0.773$ for partners), which is 4.36 and 1.08 for examinees and 4.24 and 1.21 for partners. The assumption of normality is not quite correct, evident by the fact that the upper bounds of the confidence intervals are out of range; however, they are an approximate representation of the *spread* of intercepts (i.e., means) in this sample.

We can build on this to look at simple between-person differences. In relationship research, we are often interested in gender differences, so we examine how daily level of intimacy varies by the gender of the participants. To examine the gender differences, we need to add gender as a predictor in the Level 2 question; thus, the model looks as follows:

Level 2: $\beta_{0i} = \gamma_{00} + \gamma_{01}(GENDER) + u_{0i}$ (16.5)

GENDER is a dummy variable that takes the value 0 for males and 1 for females. We do not find gender differences on the level of intimacy for either examinees or partners; γ_{01}(examinees) = -0.16, $SE = 0.17$; γ_{01}(partners) = 0.11, $SE = 0.16$. We can calculate 95% confidence bounds on these estimates, which are $[-0.49, 0.17]$ for examinees and $[-0.42, 0.20]$ for partners.

ANALYSIS EXAMPLE 2. EXAMINING CHANGES ACROSS TIME: WHAT IS THE INDIVIDUAL'S TRAJECTORY OF EXPERIENCES ACROSS DAYS, AND HOW DO TRAJECTORIES DIFFER FROM PERSON TO PERSON?

Once we know that there is sufficient within-person variance as evidenced by the variance of ε_{ij} in the previous model, the next simplest model is to examine whether passage of time explains the variance in outcome of interest, which in the current example is relationship satisfaction. Because these observations are ordered in time, this ordering may be relevant to one's analyses even if researchers have no direct interest in time. In most cases, responses from adjacent diary reports are more similar than reports farther apart. This idea is also known as the autoregressive effect. This could result if there is a change due to time. For instance, marital satisfaction tends to decline after the birth of the first child (e.g., Hackel & Ruble, 1992). Autoregressive effect is also possible due to the factors not related to time. For example, fatigue could be driven by extra demands at work due to an upcoming deadline.

Because we were able to examine the between-person variances of the intercept in the first research question, we can also estimate the between-person variances of trajectories. It is possible that some people show greater change compared with other people. If such between-person differences are observed, it is also possible to explain these differences. For example, people high in neuroticism may experience greater decline in marital satisfaction after the birth of the first child.

---

[6] Some programs, such as HLM, report an intraclass correlation from the multilevel model, and this is identical to R_{KF} for the fully unconditional model.

Example Analysis Using the Bar Exam Data Set

We continue to use the daily relationship satisfaction scale for this example analysis, but we focus on partners' report for this next example. Figure 16.3 shows the average of relationship satisfaction across participants for 44 days of the study, where Day 35 is the first day of the examination. On average, the marital satisfaction reported by partners steadily decreases as the examinees approach the examination and starts to increase right before the examination. Formal conclusion must be withheld until we estimate a statistical model, however, because the figure is a representation of mean satisfaction across participants for each day of the diary period, which ignores the within-person variability.

Modeling a linear trajectory. To formally test the within-person change in satisfaction, we must represent the multilevel model of individual change over time. We first start with the simplest model of trajectory. Equations 16.6 through 16.8 are often referred to as *individual growth models* (Singer & Willett, 2003, pp. 49–51).

$$\text{Level 1: } Y_{ij} = \beta_{0i} + \beta_{1i}(DAY0) + \varepsilon_{ij} \quad (16.6)$$

$$\text{Level 2: } \beta_{0i} = \gamma_{00} + u_{0i} \quad (16.7)$$

$$\text{Level 2: } \beta_{1i} = \gamma_{10} + u_{1i} \quad (16.8)$$

In the Level 1 equation, Y_{ij} represents satisfaction of partner i on Day j, and $DAY0$ is an indicator of the sequence of days, with the first day coded as 0. In the equation, satisfaction is modeled as a function of intercept, β_{0i}, which is the average satisfaction for partner i on Day 0, β_{1i}, which represents the linear change of satisfaction for each successive day, and ε_{ij}, the deviation of satisfaction on Day j from the partner's intercept after accounting for the linear effect of $DAY0$. The effects of day, in the current data set, is also a proxy variable for increased stressor because elapsed time also reflects the looming examination. The first Level 2 equation represents β_{0i}, the intercept for partner i on Day 0, as a function of γ_{00}, the mean of satisfaction on Day 0 after adjusting for linear change (a fixed effect), and u_{0i}, the deviation of the partner i from the mean (a random effect). The second Level 2 equation models β_{1i}, time slope for partner i, as a function of γ_{10}, fixed effect of the time slope, and u_{1i}, the deviation of the partner i from the average time slope (random effect of $DAY0$). In this model, because there are two random effects, we can ask whether they are correlated. When random effects are positively correlated, it implies that as initial level increases, the slope also increases (e.g., partners who have high initial level of satisfaction also increases more with each passage of day); negative correlation means that as the initial level increases, the slope

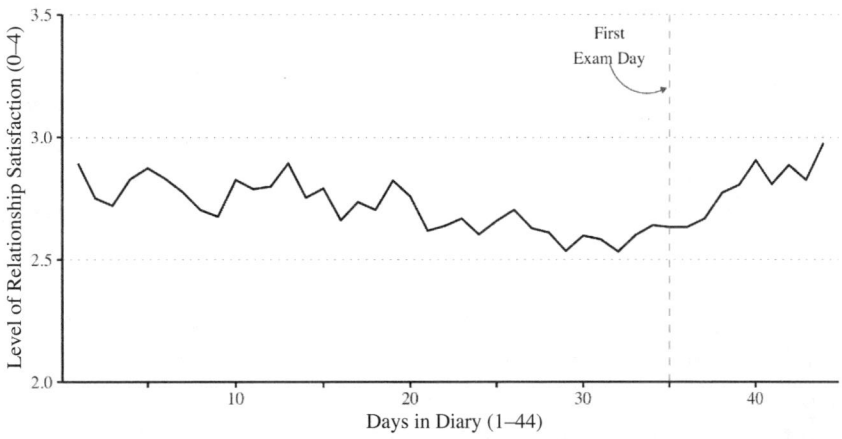

FIGURE 16.3. Trajectory of average relationship satisfaction for partners.

decreases (e.g., people who have high initial level of satisfaction show a decline in satisfaction across days).

Another important detail when modeling time is the specification of residual error structures (ε_{ij}), also known as the residual variance covariance matrix, because there is a statistical consequence for not specifying a proper structure (Greene & Hensher, 2007). In intensive longitudinal data, *residual error* refers to the unexplained variance associated with the particular day, and we expect errors to be correlated over time *within* people. There are several ways to structure the residual variance covariance matrix; however, we focus only on a first-order autoregressive residual (AR1) structure. In an AR1 model, the errors are structured as follows:

$$\begin{bmatrix} \sigma^2 & \sigma^2\rho & \sigma^2\rho^2 & \sigma^2\rho^3 & \cdots \\ \sigma^2\rho & \sigma^2 & \sigma^2\rho & \sigma^2\rho^2 & \cdots \\ \sigma^2\rho^2 & \sigma^2\rho & \sigma^2 & \sigma^2\rho & \cdots \\ \sigma^2\rho^3 & \sigma^2\rho^2 & \sigma^2\rho & \sigma^2 & \cdots \\ \vdots & \vdots & \vdots & \vdots & \ddots \end{bmatrix} \quad (16.9)$$

The autoregressive model is relatively efficient because it estimates only two parameters, σ and ρ. For those who are interested in other types of residual structures, please see Singer (1998).

In the example at hand, the fixed effects of the intercept is 2.76, which implies that the average relationship satisfaction on Day 0 (see Appendix 16.2). The fixed effect of *DAY0* is −0.001, which means that satisfaction decreases over the entire study period by approximately 0.001 unit each day, but in this case, the effect is not significant. The random effect of intercept is estimated to be 0.52, so if we take the square root of the estimate ($\sqrt{0.52} = 0.72$), it will give us the standard deviation of intercepts in our sample. Again, we can calculate the 95% prediction interval of intercepts, and we get 1.35 and 4.17. Similarly, the random effect of day is estimated to be 0.0001, which corresponds to a standard deviation of 0.01, and the 95% confidence interval of linear change is −0.02 and 0.02.

Thus far, we have not paid attention to the significance test of either fixed effects or random effects. The significance tests of fixed effects are tested by a *t*-test with degrees of freedom approximated by Satterthwaite estimates, which recognize that several different variances are being estimated from the same data (Raudenbush & Bryk, 2002). The significance tests of random effects are slightly more complex. The Wald *z*-test used to test random effects are known to be conservative, and methodologists recommend that differences in the deviance (−2 log likelihood, or −2LL) be used instead (Singer & Willett, 2003, pp. 116–117). In our example, the −2LL of full model is 7876.3, and the −2LL of the model without the random intercept is 8211.6. Therefore, the likelihood ratio difference is 335.3, and this value is significant at $p = .001$ level using the chi-square test with degree of freedom of 1. Similarly, the random effect of *DAY* is significant at $p = .001$ level, but remember that the fixed effect of *DAY* is not significant. In other words, there is no linear change in the relationship satisfaction *on average*, but there is significant variation around this effect, such that some people show a slight decline (−0.02 calculated in the preceding paragraph) yet other people show a slight increase (0.02) across the study period. The covariance between the random effects of intercept and effect of *DAY* are not significant. Because the random effects of intercept and *DAY* are significant, we know that there is systematic variation in these effects, which will be explored later.

Modeling a quadratic trajectory. The pattern in Figure 16.3 suggests a curvilinear trajectory of relationship satisfaction across days, so we will now test the quadratic effect of within-person change in satisfaction. The following equations capture the quadratic trajectory of satisfaction:

$$\text{Level 1: } y_{ij} = \beta_{0i} + \beta_{1i}(DAYc)_j$$
$$+ \beta_{2i}(DAYc^2)_j + \varepsilon_{ij} \quad (16.10)$$

$$\text{Level 2: } \beta_{0i} = \gamma_{00} + u_{0i} \quad (16.11)$$

$$\text{Level 2: } \beta_{1i} = \gamma_{10} + u_{1i} \quad (16.12)$$

$$\text{Level 2: } \beta_{2i} = \gamma_{20} \quad (16.13)$$

This model is similar to the prior set of equations but with an inclusion of the squared day effect in Level 1 equation and additional equation in Level 2. Another difference from the prior equation is that *DAYc* is now centered on the 15th day, which means that the 15th day is coded as 0, whereas *DAY0* was centered on the first day of the study in the linear trajectory model. The 15th day corresponds to 2 weeks before the examination. β_{2i} is the estimate for quadratic effect, and it is modeled as a function of γ_{20}, fixed effect of the quadratic effect. Because the model with quadratic random effects was unstable (random effect of *DAYc²*), we decided not to include u_{1i}, the deviation of the examinee *i* from the average quadratic effect.

Table 16.2 summarizes the results of this quadratic trajectory analysis. The interpretation of intercept changes from the previous model. Instead of representing the adjusted value on the first day, and it is now the adjusted average level of satisfaction on Day 15, which is 2.69. The estimate of day also changes from previous model, and this is the linear change of satisfaction on Day 15. Therefore, marital satisfaction is decreasing by 0.009 unit on Day 15. We also find that *DAYc²* is significant, which suggests that the satisfaction follows a quadratic pattern.

Moderation effects. We can explore how individuals vary in the linear and quadratic effects. This is especially useful when we have a theory about how to explain systematic individual differences. In our example, we chose relationship closeness as measured by the Inclusion of Others in the Self (IOS) scale (Aron et al., 1992) as a potential source of the individual differences (e.g., moderator). IOS is a single-item, pictorial measure of global relationship closeness ranging from 1 (*two circles are barely touching*) to 7 (*two circles are highly overlapped*). We thought that persons who included their partner as part of their self-concept would be more influenced by the partner's stressful bar exam experience. To examine the moderating effect of IOS, we ran a cross-level interaction model, where centered IOS (IOSc) was included as predictors in Level 2 equations. The Level 1 equation remained the same as prior model, and the Level 2 equations were as follows:

$$\text{Level 2: } \beta_{0i} = \gamma_{00} + \gamma_{01}(IOSc_i) + u_{0i} \quad (16.14)$$

$$\text{Level 2: } \beta_{1i} = \gamma_{10} + \gamma_{11}(IOSc_i) + u_{1i} \quad (16.15)$$

$$\text{Level 2: } \beta_{2i} = \gamma_{20} + \gamma_{21}(IOSc_i) \quad (16.16)$$

The first Level 2 equation models β_{0i}, the intercept for partner *i* on Day 0, as a function of γ_{00}, fixed effect of intercept; γ_{01}, fixed main effect of IOSc; and u_{0i}, the deviation of the partner *i* from the grand mean. In all of these models, IOSc was centered around 5.19, the mean in the sample. The second Level 2 equation models β_{1i}, the time slope for partner *i*, as a function of γ_{10}, fixed effect of the time slope; γ_{11}, fixed moderating

TABLE 16.2

Results of Analysis Examining Quadratic Change of Relationship Satisfaction

Effects		
Fixed effect	γ^a	**SE**
Intercept (level on day 10)	2.687*	0.076
DAYc (linear change)	−0.009*	0.002
DAYc² (quadratic change)	0.001*	0.0001
Random effect	τ	**LR**
Level 2 (between-person) intercept	0.568*	699.8
DAY (linear change)	0.001*	41.5
Intercept—day covariance	0.002†	2.8
Level 1 (within-person) autocorrelation	0.335*	442.7
Residual	0.3522ᵃ	NA

Note. LR = likelihood ratio; NA = not applicable.
ᵃThe model without Level 1 residual variance is implausible; therefore, the deviance difference cannot be calculated.
†$p < .10$. *$p < .001$.

effects of IOS of time on relationship satisfaction; and u_{1i}, the deviation of the partner i from the average time slope (random effect of $DAYc$). The third Level 2 equation models β_{2i}, the quadratic effect for partner i, as a function of γ_{20}, fixed effect of the quadratic effect; γ_{11}, fixed moderating effects of IOS of quadratic effect on relationship satisfaction.

We found that IOS is a significant between-person predictor of marital satisfaction levels such that people who are high on IOS tend to have higher levels of satisfaction on the 15th day of the study by 0.33 units ($\gamma_{01} = 0.33$, $SE = 0.05$). This, therefore, gives some evidence that IOS explains the variability (random effects) across participants in our sample. IOS was also a significant moderator of the quadratic effect ($\gamma_{03} = -0.0002$, $SE = 0.0001$), such that partners who were higher on IOS tended to show a smaller quadratic effect (Figure 16.4), which suggests that their daily marital satisfaction is less affected by the impact of the bar examination. As for the day effect, IOS does not moderate the effect ($\gamma_{02} = 0.002$, $SE = 0.0015$). In other words, IOS does not explain the variation in the effects of day across partners.

ANALYSIS EXAMPLE 3. PREDICTING CHANGE AND DAILY PROCESS: WHAT PROCESS UNDERLIES A PERSON'S CHANGES, AND HOW DO PEOPLE DIFFER IN THIS PROCESS?

Examining changes across time is interesting, but psychological researchers may be more interested in the predictors of the changes. Intensive longitudinal methods are a great way to model the proposed causal relationship as a temporal within-person process if the temporal measurement corresponds to when causes and effect take place. An intensive longitudinal design does not permit inferences as strong as that of experimental designs, however, because experimental conditions are experienced in temporal order, which leaves open the possibility of (a) carryover effects from the previous experiences; (b) order effects, in which the particular order of experiences moderates the effects of interest; or (c) expectancy effects, in which previous experience changes the meaning of subsequent experience.

Nevertheless, there are four ways in which intensive longitudinal methods can strengthen

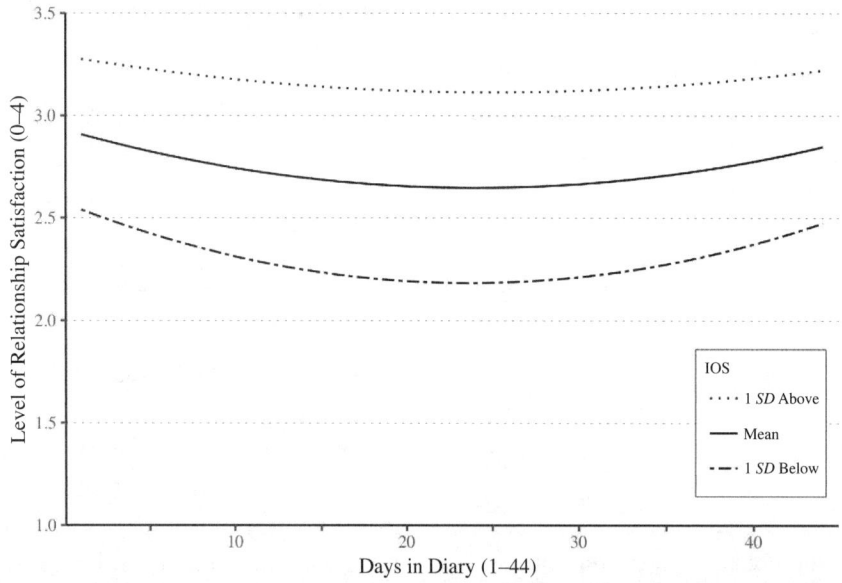

FIGURE 16.4. Quadratic effect of relationship satisfaction by Inclusion of Others in the Self (IOS) scale showing that higher IOS scores are associated with smaller quadratic effects than lower IOS scores.

causal inferences. First is that intensive longitudinal studies differentiate between-person and within-person associations. Many within-person variables collected in intensive longitudinal data, such as mood, vary both within and between persons. Within-person associations often are referred to as using the person as their own control, and it allows us to treat results as pertaining to the relationship between within-person changes in X and Y. In practical terms, we can differentiate two sources of variation by including each person's mean value of X. Second way to strengthen causal inference is by including elapsed time because there could be an effect of time even if that is not the main research questions. For example, if the study period were longer, participant boredom or habituation may affect the levels and interrelationships among variables. Third, analyses should accurately reflect the temporal structure of cause–effect relationships, which also includes having measurements at accurate times. Last, additional within-person confounding variables need to be taken into account as alternative explanations of a within-person link between Y and X. This could include lagged Y that could be acting as an alternative explanation of the relationships that one is examining.

Example Analysis Using Health Psychology Data

To illustrate how we can examine the process underlying how a person changes, we use the simulated health psychology data on the basis of the study by Skaff et al. (2009). In this data set, we have negative affect (NA) and waking blood glucose from 207 Type 2 diabetic patients for 21 days. As in the previous two examples, we use multilevel modeling to examine the association between prior day affects and waking blood glucose measure. Before we run any analysis, it is important to calculate means of negative and positive affect for each person, and they will be used to derive the within-person centered variable of negative affect, which in turn allows us to estimate the within-person effect. As described, this approach allows us to differentiate the within- and between-person associations. The within-person effects can be understood as the effects of the negative affect that is greater than the person's average.

The model is represented in the following equations:

$$\text{Level 1: } Y_{ij} = \beta_{0i} + \beta_{1i}(NA_{j-1} - MeanNA_i) + \varepsilon_{ij} \quad (16.17)$$

$$\text{Level 2: } \beta_{0i} = \gamma_{00} + \gamma_{01}(MeanNA)_i + u_{0i} \quad (16.18)$$

$$\text{Level 2: } \beta_{1i} = \gamma_{10} + u_{1i} \quad (16.19)$$

In the Level 1 equation, Y_{ij}, blood glucose of person i on day j, is modeled as a function of intercept, β_{0i} (the average blood glucose for person i), β_{1i} (within-person effect of NA from previous day), and ε_{ij} (the deviation of negative mood on Day j). The lagged effects of NA, β_{1i}, addresses the main research questions in this example—the within-person associations of previous day negative affect and waking blood glucose. In other words, when the participants experience negative affect more than they usually do, how much the blood glucose changes the following morning.

The Level 2 equation models β_{0i}, the intercept for person i, as a function of γ_{00}, fixed effects of intercept (grand mean of blood glucose); γ_{01}, between-person effect of mean negative affect (MeanNA) for person i; and u_{0i}, the deviation of the person i from the grand mean. The second Level 2 equation models β_{1i}, effect of NA for person i, as a function of γ_{10}, average effect of NA for all participants in this sample (fixed effect of NA), and u_{1i}, the deviation of the person i from the average effect of NA (random effect of NA).

Table 16.3 summarizes the results of the analyses examining affect and blood glucose. The fixed effect of the intercept is 4.90, which is the estimate of the average blood glucose. The fixed within-person effect of NA is 0.029, which means that when participants experience more negative affect than usual, their glucose increases by approximately 0.03 unit the following day.

TABLE 16.3

Results of Analysis Predicting Blood Glucose

Fixed effect	γ^a	SE
Intercept	4.900*	0.017
Negative affect (previous day)	0.029*	0.005
Mean negative affect (between-person)	0.088*	0.028

Random effect	τ	LR
Level 2 (between-person) intercept	0.058**	287.8
Negative affect (previous day)	0.001	0.0
Intercept—negative affect covariance	−0.001**	15.9
Level 1 (within-person) residual	0.029[a]	NA

Note. LR = likelihood ratio; NA = not applicable.
[a]The model without Level 1 residual variance is implausible; therefore, the deviance difference cannot be calculated.
*$p < .01$. **$p < .001$.

The between-person effect of mean negative affect is 0.088, which means that individuals who, on average, have high negative affect across the diary period tend to have higher waking blood glucose.

INTENSIVE LONGITUDINAL METHODS EXTENSIONS

Intensive longitudinal methods provide rich data on psychological processes as they unfold. The statistical analyses we have reviewed so far are only a starting point. More advanced methods are available in Bolger and Laurenceau (2013) and Mehl and Conner (2012) as well as in the current literature. In the next section, we mention some recent developments and speculate about future directions.

Dynamic Systems Models

One of the ways intensive longitudinal data can be analyzed is using dynamic systems models (see Volume 3, Chapter 16, this handbook). Dynamic systems, at their most general, are self-contained sets of elements that interact in complex, often nonlinear ways to form coherent patterns, with an underlying assumption that these systems regulate themselves over time. A key concept is that of stationary attractor points, representing a set of possible equilibrium states of the system. For psychological data, an attractor point can be thought of as a psychological state that a person tends to return to following a perturbation. When time trajectories of the system can be described by a sine or cosine function, it is useful to express the rate of acceleration of the function (second derivative) as a linear combination of the rate of change (first derivative) and level of the function (see Boker, 2001, for a detailed explanation). In their book *The Mathematics of Marriage: Dynamic Nonlinear Models*, Gottman et al. (2002) applied complex dynamic systems models to characterize marital interaction. When data are abundant and exhibit cyclical patterns of change, as is often the case for physiological data, dynamic models can be highly useful. Although currently small, the literature on dynamic models of intensive longitudinal data is likely to grow (e.g., Zee & Bolger, 2022). An application of dynamical systems modeling (second-order linear oscillator modeling) to dyadic intensive longitudinal data can be found in Boker and Laurenceau (2006, 2007).

Categorical Variables

In this chapter, we have focused on analysis for continuous outcomes; however, many of the variables that psychologists are interested in may be categorical or counts (e.g., whether support was received, whether a conflict occurred, number of alcoholic beverages consumed). For these types of outcomes, the analytic strategy described in this chapter will lead to misspecified models. Fortunately, however, a number of appropriate alternative methods can be considered, including nonlinear multilevel models and generalized estimating equations. These are readily available in most statistical packages, such as SAS (GLIMMIX, NLMIXED, and GENMOD procedures), SPSS, and the *nlme* package (Pinheiro et al., 2020) and the *gee* package (Carey, 2019) in R. For details on these types of multilevel analyses, please see Bolger and Laurenceau (2013) and Hox et al. (2017).

Multivariate Multilevel Analysis

Intensive longitudinal researchers typically ask participants to report on a variety of behaviors, feelings, and attitudes over time and are interested in how these processes operate in a multivariate system. For instance, Gleason et al. (2008) wondered how the costs of daily support on anxiety could be reconciled with the benefits of daily support on relationship closeness. In the context of multilevel analyses, they used a multivariate (multiple outcome) approach that has been described in detail by Raudenbush and Bryk (2002). This approach involves a treating the different outcomes as if they were repeated measures, that is, where each outcome is given its own data line. A special provision is needed, however, to recognize that each outcome has its own set of fixed and random effects. A more common approach is to treat the data as a multivariate system using structural equation modeling (e.g., McNeish & Hamaker, 2020; Preacher et al., 2010). Bollen and Curran (2004) proposed what they called ALT models that will be of special interest to researchers who have relatively few repeated time points.

Intensive Longitudinal Studies of Dyads, Families, and Groups

One of the fastest growing types of intensive longitudinal design is the multi-informant diary in which more than one person from a dyad (e.g., married couples), families (e.g., parents and eldest children), and groups (e.g., students in classrooms) participate in the study. In these types of data, there are at least two different sources of nonindependence: Observations are repeated within persons, and persons are nested within dyads, families, or groups. To account for both types of nonindependence, it is sometimes useful to use three-level multilevel models for groups greater than three people. For the smaller groups (dyads and three-member family groups with prespecified roles), a two-level multilevel model is sufficient in which the lowest level represents the multivariate repeated measurements mentioned in the previous section (Bolger & Laurenceau, 2013; Bolger & Shrout, 2007; Laurenceau & Bolger, 2005). Other books have been dedicated to analyses of nonindependent data (e.g., Kenny et al., 2006).

Simulation as a Tool for Intensive Longitudinal Researchers

When planning an intensive longitudinal study, how can one determine the necessary sample sizes of persons (N) and time points (t), and what is the trade-off between increasing either N or t? Many intensive longitudinal researchers first carry out a statistical simulation study, using software such as SAS or Mplus (Muthén & Muthén, 2017). These simulations can create data sets that are consistent with specific hypotheses, and analyses of these data sets can indicate to a researcher how small the standard errors are likely to get as the number of participants or time points increase. To carry out a simulation, one needs to go through six steps: (1) Write down a Level 1 statistical model for the within-subject responses, (2) write down a series of Level 2 statistical models that describe how the subjects differ in their within-subject process, (3) consult the literature or preliminary study to identify plausible effect sizes for the fixed effects, (4) consult the literature or a preliminary study to identify plausible values to represent variability of within-and between-subject processes, (5) write a program to simulate data according to the model from Steps 1 through 4, and (6) analyze the simulated data to determine how precise the results are. We have provided an example of simulated health data. Although we had access to an interesting published study (Skaff et al., 2009), we did not have access to the original data. From the published results and some personal communication with one of the authors, we were able to generate data that resembled daily glucose and mood patterns. We provide this simulation syntax as an example, which can be downloaded from https://osf.io/8edwk.

If one hopes to carry out intensive longitudinal studies with participants who have some rare condition, it may be difficult to recruit a sufficient number of subjects. Not only will statistical power be challenging in this case but also the usual inferential methods of multilevel models may be misleading. Much of the statistical theory for multilevel models assumes large samples. In cases such as this, simulation studies can be used to study the impact of sample size on both power and the usual control of Type I error. If small sample data are available, one could use simulation methods to carry out resampling studies of those data. For an example of a simulation-based power analysis for intensive longitudinal data, please see Bolger et al. (2013).

CONCLUSION

Although relatively new to psychology, intensive longitudinal study designs are changing the way psychologists think about psychological processes. They help survey researchers determine when retrospective memory is problematic, and on when it can be counted. When spaced over months, they can provide invaluable information about development in youth and adolescents. Intensive longitudinal accounts provide new sources of compelling data for health psychologists, and they allow stable individual differences to be distinguished from meaningful change. We predict that the number of intensive longitudinal studies will continue to increase in the literature.

In tandem, there are many ways that intensive longitudinal designs will continue to be refined. Technological advances, particularly in micro-recording devices, will open new doors for noninvasive measurement. Statistical methods will continue to be developed to deal with the complicated temporal patterns in nonstationary data. New methods for small samples and for complicated dependent data will be proposed. For those interested in making an impact on research methodology, the area of intensive longitudinal studies is very fruitful ground.

APPENDIX 16.1

Syntax for SAS
PROC MIXED covtest noclprint;
CLASS couple;
MODEL content = /s;
RANDOM int/SUBJECT = couple TYPE = vc;
RUN;

PARTIAL OUTPUT

Covariance Parameter Estimates

Cov parm	Subject	Estimate	Standard error	Z value	Pr > Z
Intercept	couple	0.6986	0.1005	6.95	< .0001
Residual		0.3706	0.007	993	46.37	< .0001

Solution for Fixed Effects

Effect	Estimate	Standard error	DF	t value	PR > |t|
Intercept	2.7189	0.08409	99	32.33	< .0001

APPENDIX 16.2

Syntax for SAS
PROC MIXED covtest noclprint DATA = dchap4;
CLASS couple day;
MODEL pcontent = day0/s;
RANDOM int day0/SUBJECT = couple TYPE = UN
REPEATED day/SUBJECT = couple TYPE = ar(1);
TITLE "Linear Trajectory Analysis - Partners";
RUN;

PARTIAL OUTPUT

Covariance Parameter Estimates

Cov rarm	Subject	Estimate	Standard error	Z value	Pr > Z
UN(1,1)	couple	0.5177	0.08232	6.29	< .0001
UN(2,1)	couple	0.000153	0.001163	0.13	0.8950
UN(2,2)	couple	0.000126	0.000032	3.94	< .0001
AR(1)	couple	0.3442	0.01592	21.63	< .0001
Residual		0.3581	0.009352	38.29	< .0001

Fit Statistics
–2 Res Log Likelihood 7876.3
AIC (smaller is better) 7886.3
AICC (smaller is better) 7886.3
BIC (smaller is better) 7899.3

Solution for Fixed Effects

Effect	Estimate	Standard error	DF	t value	Pr > |t|
Intercept	2.7588	0.07606	99	36.27	< .0001
day0	–0.00116	0.001492	99	–0.78	0.4402

References

Almeida, D. M. (2005). Resilience and vulnerability to daily stressors assessed via diary methods. *Current Directions in Psychological Science*, 14(2), 64–68. https://doi.org/10.1111/j.0963-7214.2005.00336.x

Aron, A., Aron, E. N., & Smollan, D. (1992). Inclusion of other in the self scale and the structure of interpersonal closeness. *Journal of Personality and Social Psychology*, 63(4), 596–612. https://doi.org/10.1037/0022-3514.63.4.596

Baethge, A., Vahle-Hinz, T., & Rigotti, T. (2020). Coworker support and its relationship to allostasis during a workday: A diary study on trajectories of heart rate variability during work. *Journal of Applied Psychology*, 105(5), 506–526. https://doi.org/10.1037/apl0000445

Baltes, P. B., & Nesselroade, J. R. (1979). History and rationale of longitudinal research. In J. R. Nesselroade & P. B. Baltes (Eds.), *Longitudinal research in the study of behavior and development* (pp. 1–39). Academic Press.

Barrett, L. F., & Feldman-Barrett, D. J. (2001). An introduction to computerized experience sampling in psychology. *Social Science Computer Review*, 19(2), 175–185. https://doi.org/10.1177/089443930101900204

Barta, W. D., Tennen, H., & Litt, M. D. (2012). Measurement reactivity in diary research. In M. R. Mehl & T. S. Conner (Eds.), *Handbook of research methods for studying daily life* (pp. 108–123). Guilford Press.

Bevans, G. E. (1913). *How workingmen spend their time* [Unpublished doctoral thesis]. Columbia University.

Boker, S. M. (2001). Differential models and "differential structural equation modeling of intraindividual variability." In L. M. Collins & A. G. Sayer (Eds.), *New methods for the analysis of change* (pp. 5–27). Oxford University Press. https://doi.org/10.1037/10409-001

Boker, S. M., & Laurenceau, J.-P. (2006). Dynamical systems modeling: An application to the regulation of intimacy and disclosure in marriage. In T. A. Walls & J. L. Schafer (Eds.), *Models for intensive longitudinal data* (pp. 195–218). Oxford University Press. https://doi.org/10.1093/acprof:oso/9780195173444.003.0009

Boker, S. M., & Laurenceau, J.-P. (2007). Coupled dynamics and mutually adaptive context. In T. D. Little, J. A. Bovaird, & N. A. Card (Eds.), *Modeling contextual effects in longitudinal studies* (pp. 299–324). Erlbaum.

Bolger, N. (1990). Coping as a personality process: A prospective study. *Journal of Personality and Social Psychology*, 59(3), 525–537. https://doi.org/10.1037/0022-3514.59.3.525

Bolger, N., Davis, A., & Rafaeli, E. (2003). Diary methods: Capturing life as it is lived. *Annual Review of Psychology*, 54, 579–616. https://doi.org/10.1146/annurev.psych.54.101601.145030

Bolger, N., & Laurenceau, J.-P. (2013). *Diary methods*. Guilford Press.

Bolger, N., Laurenceau, J.-P., & Stadler, G. (2013). Power analysis for intensive longitudinal measurement designs. In M. R. Mehl & T. Conner (Eds.), *Handbook of research methods for studying daily life* (pp. 283–301). Guilford Press.

Bolger, N., & Shrout, P. E. (2007). Accounting for statistical dependency in longitudinal data on dyads. In T. D. Little, J. A. Bovaird, & N. A. Card (Eds.), *Modeling contextual effects in longitudinal studies* (pp. 285–298). Erlbaum.

Bolger, N., & Zuckerman, A. (1995). A framework for studying personality in the stress process. *Journal of Personality and Social Psychology*, 69(5), 890–902. https://doi.org/10.1037/0022-3514.69.5.890

Bolger, N., Zuckerman, A., & Kessler, R. C. (2000). Invisible support and adjustment to stress. *Journal of Personality and Social Psychology*, 79(6), 953–961. https://doi.org/10.1037/0022-3514.79.6.953

Bollen, K. A., & Curran, P. J. (2004). Autoregressive Latent Trajectory (ALT) models: A synthesis of two traditions. *Sociological Methods & Research*, 32(3), 336–383. https://doi.org/10.1177/0049124103260222

Borghuis, J., Bleidorn, W., Sijtsma, K., Branje, S., Meeus, W. H. J., & Denissen, J. J. A. (2020). Longitudinal associations between trait neuroticism and negative daily experiences in adolescence. *Journal of Personality and Social Psychology*, 118(2), 348–363. https://doi.org/10.1037/pspp0000233

Broderick, J. E., Schwartz, J. E., Shiffman, S., Hufford, M. R., & Stone, A. A. (2003). Signaling does not adequately improve diary compliance. *Annals of Behavioral Medicine*, 26(2), 139–148. https://doi.org/10.1207/S15324796ABM2602_06

Butler, A. B., Grzywacz, J. G., Bass, B. L., & Linney, K. D. (2005). Extending the demands-control model: A daily diary study of job characteristics, work-family conflict and work-family facilitation. *Journal of Occupational and Organizational Psychology*, 78(2), 155–169. https://doi.org/10.1348/096317905X40097

Carey, V. (2019). *gee: Generalized estimation equation solver*. R package. https://cran.r-project.org/web/packages/gee/gee.pdf

Cohen, S., Schwartz, J. E., Epel, E., Kirschbaum, C., Sidney, S., & Seeman, T. (2006). Socioeconomic status, race, and diurnal cortisol decline in the Coronary Artery Risk Development in Young Adults (CARDIA) Study. *Psychosomatic Medicine*, 68(1), 41–50. https://doi.org/10.1097/01.psy.0000195967.51768.ea

Cole, D. A., & Maxwell, S. E. (2003). Testing mediational models with longitudinal data: Questions and tips in the use of structural equation modeling. *Journal of Abnormal Psychology*, 112(4), 558–577. https://doi.org/10.1037/0021-843X.112.4.558

Collins, L. M. (2006). Analysis of longitudinal data: The integration of theoretical model, temporal design, and statistical model. *Annual Review of Psychology*, 57, 505–528. https://doi.org/10.1146/annurev.psych.57.102904.190146

Cranford, J. A., Shrout, P. E., Iida, M., Rafaeli, E., Yip, T., & Bolger, N. (2006). A procedure for evaluating sensitivity to within-person change: Can mood measures in diary studies detect change reliably? *Personality and Social Psychology Bulletin*, 32(7), 917–929. https://doi.org/10.1177/0146167206287721

Cranford, J. A., Tennen, H., & Zucker, R. A. (2010). Feasibility of using interactive voice response to monitor daily drinking, moods, and relationship processes on a daily basis in alcoholic couples. *Alcoholism, Clinical and Experimental Research*, 34(3), 499–508. https://doi.org/10.1111/j.1530-0277.2009.01115.x

Crocker, L. M., & Algina, J. (1986). *Introduction to classical and modern test theory*. Holt, Rinehart, and Winston.

Cronbach, L. J., Gleser, G. C., Nanda, H., & Rajaratnam, N. (1972). *The dependability of behavioral measurements: Theory of generalizability for scores and profiles.* Wiley.

Csikszentmihalyi, M., Larson, R., & Prescott, S. (1977). The ecology of adolescent activity and experience. *Journal of Youth and Adolescence, 6*(3), 281–294. https://doi.org/10.1007/BF02138940

Ellard-Gray, A., Jeffrey, N. K., Choubak, M., & Crann, S. E. (2015). Finding the hidden participant: Solutions for recruiting hidden, hard-to-reach, and vulnerable populations. *International Journal of Qualitative Methods, 14*(5), 1–10. https://doi.org/10.1177/1609406915621420

Fitzmaurice, G. M., Laird, N. M., & Ware, J. H. (2004). *Applied longitudinal analysis.* Wiley-Interscience.

Gelman, A., & Hill, J. (2007). *Data analysis using regression and multilevel/hierarchical models.* Cambridge University Press.

Gershuny, J., Harms, T., Doherty, A., Thomas, E., Milton, K., Kelly, P., & Foster, C. (2020). Testing self-report time-use diaries against objective instruments in real time. *Sociological Methodology, 50*(1), 318–349. https://doi.org/10.1177/0081175019884591

Gleason, M. E. J., Iida, M., Shrout, P. E., & Bolger, N. (2008). Receiving support as a mixed blessing: Evidence for dual effects of support on psychological outcomes. *Journal of Personality and Social Psychology, 94*(5), 824–838. https://doi.org/10.1037/0022-3514.94.5.824

Gollob, H. F., & Reichardt, C. S. (1987). Taking account of time lags in causal models. *Child Development, 58*(1), 80–92. https://doi.org/10.2307/1130293

Gollwitzer, P. M. (1999). Implementation intentions—Strong effects of simple plans. *American Psychologist, 54*(7), 493–503. https://doi.org/10.1037/0003-066X.54.7.493

Gottman, J. M., Murray, J. D., Swanson, C. C., Tyson, R., & Swanson, K. R. (2002). *The mathematics of marriage: Dynamic nonlinear models.* MIT Press. https://doi.org/10.7551/mitpress/4499.001.0001

Greene, W. H., & Hensher, D. A. (2007). Heteroscedastic control for random coefficients and error components in mixed logit. *Transportation Research Part E, Logistics and Transportation Review, 43*(5), 610–623. https://doi.org/10.1016/j.tre.2006.02.001

Ha, T., van Roekel, E., Iida, M., Kornienko, O., Engels, R. C. M. E., & Kuntsche, E. (2019). Depressive symptoms amplify emotional reactivity to daily perceptions of peer rejection in adolescence. *Journal of Youth and Adolescence, 48*(11), 2152–2164. https://doi.org/10.1007/s10964-019-01146-4

Hackel, L. S., & Ruble, D. N. (1992). Changes in the marital relationship after the first baby is born: Predicting the impact of expectancy disconfirmation. *Journal of Personality and Social Psychology, 62*(6), 944–957. https://doi.org/10.1037/0022-3514.62.6.944

Hox, J. J., Moerbeek, M., & Van de Schoot, R. (2017). *Multilevel analysis: Techniques and applications.* Routledge. https://doi.org/10.4324/9781315650982

Hur, W. M., Shin, Y., & Moon, T. W. (2020). How does daily performance affect next-day emotional labor? The mediating roles of evening relaxation and next-morning positive affect. *Journal of Occupational Health Psychology, 25*(6), 410–425. https://doi.org/10.1037/ocp0000260

Iida, M., Gleason, M., Green-Rapaport, A. S., Bolger, N., & Shrout, P. E. (2017). The influence of daily coping on anxiety under examination stress: A model of interindividual differences in intraindividual change. *Personality and Social Psychology Bulletin, 43*(7), 907–923. https://doi.org/10.1177/0146167217700605

Iida, M., Seidman, G., Shrout, P. E., Fujita, K., & Bolger, N. (2008). Modeling support provision in intimate relationships. *Journal of personality and social psychology, 94*(3), 460–478. https://doi.org/10.1037/0022-3514.94.3.460

Iida, M., & Shapiro, A. (2019). Mindfulness and daily negative mood variation in romantic relationships. *Mindfulness, 10*(5), 933–942. https://doi.org/10.1007/s12671-018-1056-3

Impett, E. A., Strachman, A., Finkel, E. J., & Gable, S. L. (2008). Maintaining sexual desire in intimate relationships: The importance of approach goals. *Journal of Personality and Social Psychology, 94*(5), 808–823. https://doi.org/10.1037/0022-3514.94.5.808

Inauen, J., Shrout, P. E., Bolger, N., Stadler, G., & Scholz, U. (2016). Mind the gap? An intensive longitudinal study of between-person and within-person intention-behavior relations. *Annals of Behavioral Medicine, 50*(4), 516–522. https://doi.org/10.1007/s12160-016-9776-x

Intille, S. S., Rondoni, J., Kukla, C., Anacona, I., & Bao, L. (2003, April). *A context-aware experience sampling tool.* Paper presented at the CHI '03 Extended Abstracts on Human Factors in Computing Systems, Fort Lauderdale, FL, United States.

Kane, E. W., & Macaulay, L. J. (1993). Interviewer gender and gender attitudes. *Public Opinion Quarterly, 57*(1), 1–28. https://doi.org/10.1086/269352

Kenny, D. A., Kashy, D. A., & Cook, W. L. (2006). *Dyadic data analysis.* Guilford Press.

Larson, R., & Csikszentmihalyi, M. (1983). The experience sampling method. *New Directions for Methodology of Social and Behavioral Science, 15*, 41–56.

Laurenceau, J.-P., Barrett, L. F., & Pietromonaco, P. R. (1998). Intimacy as an interpersonal process: The importance of self-disclosure, partner disclosure, and perceived partner responsiveness in interpersonal exchanges. *Journal of Personality and Social Psychology, 74*(5), 1238–1251. https://doi.org/10.1037/0022-3514.74.5.1238

Laurenceau, J.-P., & Bolger, N. (2005). Using diary methods to study marital and family processes. *Journal of Family Psychology, 19*(1), 86–97. https://doi.org/10.1037/0893-3200.19.1.86

Litt, M. D., Cooney, N. L., & Morse, P. (1998). Ecological momentary assessment (EMA) with treated alcoholics: Methodological problems and potential solutions. *Health Psychology, 17*(1), 48–52. https://doi.org/10.1037/0278-6133.17.1.48

Maisel, N. C., & Gable, S. L. (2009). The paradox of received social support: The importance of responsiveness. *Psychological Science, 20*(8), 928–932. https://doi.org/10.1111/j.1467-9280.2009.02388.x

McNeish, D., & Hamaker, E. L. (2020). A primer on two-level dynamic structural equation models for intensive longitudinal data in Mplus. *Psychological Methods, 25*(5), 610–635. https://doi.org/10.1037/met0000250

Mehl, M. R., & Conner, T. S. (Eds.). (2012). *Handbook of research methods for studying daily life*. Guilford Press.

Morrison, D. M., Leigh, B. C., & Gillmore, M. R. (1999). Daily data collection: A comparison of three methods. *Journal of Sex Research, 36*(1), 76–81. https://doi.org/10.1080/00224499909551970

Müller, F., Hagedoorn, M., Soriano, E. C., Stephenson, E., Smink, A., Hoff, C., DeLongis, A., Laurenceau, J.-P., & Tuinman, M. A. (2019). Couples' catastrophizing and co-rumination: Dyadic diary study of patient fatigue after cancer. *Health Psychology, 38*(12), 1096–1106. https://doi.org/10.1037/hea0000803

Muthén, L. K., & Muthén, B. O. (2017). *Mplus user's guide* (8th ed.).

Nezlek, J. (2012). *Diary Methods for Social and Personality Psychology*. SAGE Publications. https://doi.org/10.4135/9781446287903

Nock, M. K., Prinstein, M. J., & Sterba, S. K. (2009). Revealing the form and function of self-injurious thoughts and behaviors: A real-time ecological assessment study among adolescents and young adults. *Journal of Abnormal Psychology, 118*(4), 816–827. https://doi.org/10.1037/a0016948

Pember-Reeves, M. (1913). *Round about a pound a week*. Bell.

Pennebaker, J. W. (1997). Writing about emotional experiences as a therapeutic process. *Psychological Science, 8*, 162–166. https://doi.org/10.1111/j.1467-9280.1997.tb00403.x

Pew Research Center. (2019, February 5). *Smartphone ownership is growing rapidly around the world, but not always equally*. https://www.pewresearch.org/global/2019/02/05/smartphone-ownership-is-growing-rapidly-around-the-world-but-not-always-equally/

Pinheiro, J., Bates, D., DebRoy, S., Sarkar, D., & R Core Team. (2020). _nlme: Linear and nonlinear mixed effects models_. R package version 3.1–144. https://CRAN.R-project.org/package=nlme

Preacher, K. J., Zyphur, M. J., & Zhang, Z. (2010). A general multilevel SEM framework for assessing multilevel mediation. *Psychological Methods, 15*(3), 209–233. https://doi.org/10.1037/a0020141

Quintus, M., Egloff, B., & Wrzus, C. (2021). Daily life processes predict long-term development in explicit and implicit representations of Big Five traits: Testing predictions from the TESSERA (Triggering situations, Expectancies, States and State Expressions, and ReActions) framework. *Journal of Personality and Social Psychology, 120*(4), 1049–1073. https://doi.org/10.1037/pspp0000361

Rafaeli, S., Ariel, Y., Joinson, A. N., McKenna, K. Y. M., Postmes, T., & Reips, U. D. (2007). Assessing interactivity in computer-mediated. *Oxford handbook of internet psychology* (pp. 71–88). Oxford University Press. https://doi.org/10.1093/oxfordhb/9780199561803.013.0006

Raudenbush, S. W., & Bryk, A. S. (2002). *Hierarchical linear models: Applications and data analysis methods* (2nd ed.). Sage.

Raudenbush, S. W., Bryk, A. S., Cheong, Y. F., & Congdon, R. (2019). *HLM 8 for Windows* [Computer software]. Scientific Software International.

Redelmeier, D. A., & Kahneman, D. (1996). Patients' memories of painful medical treatments: Real-time and retrospective evaluations of two minimally invasive procedures. *Pain, 66*(1), 3–8. https://doi.org/10.1016/0304-3959(96)02994-6

Reis, H. T., & Gable, S. L. (2000). Event-sampling and other methods for studying everyday experience. In H. T. Reis & C. M. Judd (Eds.), *Handbook of research methods in social and personality psychology* (pp. 190–222). Cambridge University Press.

Reis, H. T., & Wheeler, L. (1991). Studying social-interaction with the Rochester Interaction Record.

Rossignac-Milon, M., Bolger, N., Zee, K. S., Boothby, E. J., & Higgins, E. T. (2021). Merged minds: Generalized shared reality in dyadic relationships. *Journal of Personality and Social Psychology*, *120*(4), 882–911. https://doi.org/10.1037/pspi0000266

Seaton, E. K., & Iida, M. (2019). Racial discrimination and racial identity: Daily moderation among Black youth. *American Psychologist*, *74*(1), 117–127. https://doi.org/10.1037/amp0000367

Shiffman, S., Stone, A. A., & Hufford, M. R. (2008). Ecological momentary assessment. *Annual Review of Clinical Psychology*, *4*, 1–32. https://doi.org/10.1146/annurev.clinpsy.3.022806.091415

Shrout, P. E., & Lane, S. P. (2013). Psychometrics. In M. R. Mehl & T. S. Conner (Eds.), *Handbook of research methods for studying daily life* (pp. 302–320). Guilford Press.

Shrout, P. E., Stadler, G., Lane, S. P., McClure, M. J., Jackson, G. L., Clavél, F. D., Iida, M., Gleason, M. E. J., Xu, J. H., & Bolger, N. (2018). Initial elevation bias in subjective reports. *Proceedings of the National Academy of Sciences of the United States of America*, *115*(1), E15–E23. https://doi.org/10.1073/pnas.1712277115

Singer, J. D. (1998). Using SAS PROC MIXED to fit multilevel models, hierarchical models, and individual growth models. *Journal of Educational and Behavioral Statistics*, *23*, 323–355. https://doi.org/10.3102/10769986023004323

Singer, J. D., & Willett, J. B. (2003). *Applied longitudinal data analysis: Modeling change and event occurrence*. Oxford University Press. https://doi.org/10.1093/acprof:oso/9780195152968.001.0001

Skaff, M. M., Mullan, J. T., Almeida, D. M., Hoffman, L., Masharani, U., Mohr, D., & Fisher, L. (2009). Daily negative mood affects fasting glucose in type 2 diabetes. *Health Psychology*, *28*(3), 265–272. https://doi.org/10.1037/a0014429

Soriano, E. C., Perndorfer, C., Siegel, S. D., & Laurenceau, J. P. (2019). Threat sensitivity and fear of cancer recurrence: A daily diary study of reactivity and recovery as patients and spouses face the first mammogram post-diagnosis. *Journal of Psychosocial Oncology*, *37*(2), 131–144. https://doi.org/10.1080/07347332.2018.1535532

Spanier, G. B. (1976). Measuring dyadic adjustment: New scales for assessing the quality of marriage and similar dyads. *Journal of Marriage and the Family*, *38*(1), 15–28. https://doi.org/10.2307/350547

Stone, A. A., Schwartz, J. E., Neale, J. M., Shiffman, S., Marco, C. A., Hickcox, M., Paty, J., Porter, L. S., & Cruise, L. J. (1998). A comparison of coping assessed by ecological momentary assessment and retrospective recall. *Journal of Personality and Social Psychology*, *74*(6), 1670–1680. https://doi.org/10.1037/0022-3514.74.6.1670

Stone, A. A., Shiffman, S., Schwartz, J. E., Broderick, J. E., & Hufford, M. R. (2002). Patient non-compliance with paper diaries. *British Medical Journal*, *324*(7347), 1193–1194. https://doi.org/10.1136/bmj.324.7347.1193

Tennen, H., Affleck, G., Armeli, S., & Carney, M. A. (2000). A daily process approach to coping. Linking theory, research, and practice. *American Psychologist*, *55*(6), 626–636. https://doi.org/10.1037/0003-066X.55.6.626

Thomas, D. L., & Diener, E. (1990). Memory accuracy in the recall of emotions. *Journal of Personality and Social Psychology*, *59*(2), 291–297. https://doi.org/10.1037/0022-3514.59.2.291

Waldinger, R. J., & Schulz, M. S. (2010). What's love got to do with it? Social functioning, perceived health, and daily happiness in married octogenarians. *Psychology and Aging*, *25*(2), 422–431. https://doi.org/10.1037/a0019087

Wheeler, L., Reis, H., & Nezlek, J. (1983). Loneliness, social interaction, and sex roles. *Journal of Personality and Social Psychology*, *45*(4), 943–953. https://doi.org/10.1037/0022-3514.45.4.943

Wickham, H. (2016). *ggplot2: Elegant graphics for data analysis*. Springer-Verlag.

Yip, T., & Fuligni, A. J. (2002). Daily variation in ethnic identity, ethnic behaviors, and psychological well-being among American adolescents of Chinese descent. *Child Development*, *73*(5), 1557–1572. https://doi.org/10.1111/1467-8624.00490

Zaider, T. I., Heimberg, R. G., & Iida, M. (2010). Anxiety disorders and intimate relationships: A study of daily processes in couples. *Journal of Abnormal Psychology*, *119*(1), 163–173. https://doi.org/10.1037/a0018473

Zee, K. S., & Bolger, N. (2022). Physiological coregulation during social support discussions. *Emotion*. Advance online publication. https://doi.org/10.1037/emo0001107

CHAPTER 17

AUTOMATED ANALYSES OF NATURAL LANGUAGE IN PSYCHOLOGICAL RESEARCH

Laura K. Allen, Arthur C. Graesser, and Danielle S. McNamara

Research in psychology often relies on qualitative and quantitative assessments of natural language in order to better identify and understand the mechanisms underlying complex cognitive tasks (Dowell et al., 2019; Graesser & McNamara, 2011; Johns & Jamieson, 2018; Magliano & Graesser, 2012; Pennebaker et al., 2007; Yan et al., 2020). Essays, open-ended questions, think-aloud protocols, and interviews are often the most robust methods for gleaning detailed insights into individuals' thoughts. They are frequently collected throughout psychological fields, including applied research domains, such as education, discourse processes, cognitive science, social and personality psychology, forensics, and clinical psychology. Despite the wealth of information that can be gleaned from these responses, analyses often rely on time-intensive annotation and scoring on the part of human expert raters, which can hinder progress and deter researchers from collecting these sources of data.

In response to these methodological challenges, researchers and educators have turned to complementary fields in computer science and learning analytics that have made substantial progress in automating the analysis of natural language through natural language processing (NLP; Clark et al., 2013; Hirschberg & Manning, 2015; Jurafsky & Martin, 2008), as well as leveraging big data approaches more broadly (Griffiths, 2015; Jones, 2017). This interdisciplinary work has led to landmark advances in language learning (Kyle, 2021; Kyle & Crossley, 2018), education (Dowell et al., 2020; Litman, 2016; McNamara et al., 2017), discourse processes (McNamara et al., 2014), and automated analyses of discourse cohesion (Dascalu et al., 2018; Graesser & McNamara, 2011). Researchers now have a broad range of options to implement automated textual analyses by taking advantage of development packages with popular programming languages (e.g., spaCy in Python and R; NLTK in Python; tidytext in R) as well as freely available NLP software facilities that render accomplished programming knowledge unnecessary (e.g., Crossley, Kyle, et al., 2019; Kyle et al., 2018; McNamara et al., 2014).

This chapter provides an overview of current approaches to NLP and how they have been applied to research in the psychological domain. We first provide an overview of how NLP techniques are used to aid in the scoring of natural language responses. Second, we describe how

---

This research was supported in part by IES Grants R305A180261, R305A180144, and R305A190063 as well as the Office of Naval Research (Grants: N00014-17-1-2300, N00014-19-1-2424, N00014-20-1-2627). Opinions, conclusions, or recommendations do not necessarily reflect the view of the Department of Education, IES, or the Office of Naval Research.

https://doi.org/10.1037/0000318-017
APA Handbook of Research Methods in Psychology, Second Edition: Vol. 1. Foundations, Planning, Measures, and Psychometrics, H. Cooper (Editor-in-Chief)
Copyright © 2023 by the American Psychological Association. All rights reserved.

these same techniques can be used to infer psychological attributes from written responses, such as individual differences and learning processes. Third, we discuss how these analyses of natural language responses have been incorporated into intelligent tutoring systems (ITSs) that provide adaptive instruction to student users. Finally, we conclude with a brief discussion of more recently developed tools and approaches that examine multi-modal approaches to language analysis, with the inclusion of information related to timing, emotional states, and group dynamics.

NATURAL LANGUAGE PROCESSING AS A METHOD OF RESPONSE SCORING

The most common application of NLP to research has been in the automated scoring of written language. A variety of tasks in psychological domains rely on participants to generate written language responses, ranging from brief responses to longer essays. NLP techniques can be leveraged to provide scores on these written responses using features calculated at multiple dimensions of language. For example, NLP techniques can analyze characteristics of the words, sentences, and entire texts, including features related to a broad range of constructs including familiarity, complexity, cohesion, and semantics of language. These computational approaches have several advantages over human coding, which can be expensive and time-consuming. Compared with discourse analysis conducted by humans, computational approaches can provide instantaneous feedback, do not get fatigued, are reliable, and can provide greater detail on a wider number of dimensions (Hirschberg & Manning, 2015; McNamara et al., 2014). In the following sections, we provide examples of how NLP has been used in two different contexts: brief responses to prompts while reading and longer forms of writing (e.g., argumentative essays).

Automated Analyses of Short Natural Language Responses

Short natural language responses are commonly collected in psychological research. These responses may be answers to open-ended questions, contributions in dialogues or multiparty conversations, or think-aloud responses produced during complex tasks, such as reading or problem solving. Computational approaches have been leveraged to analyze these responses along a variety of dimensions, such as *accuracy, relevance, style, verbosity,* and *coherence*. Depending on the nature of the scoring task, the assessment of these verbal protocols can be simplistic (e.g., assessing the accuracy of students' responses on a short-answer test) or more complex (e.g., assessing students' use of strategies within a think-aloud task).

Constructed responses to texts have commonly been collected to examine cognitive processes underlying complex tasks such as reading or problem solving (Coté & Goldman, 1999; Denton et al., 2015; Magliano & Graesser, 2012; Magliano et al., 2011). There is substantial evidence that such constructed responses are sensitive to the processes involved in comprehending and learning new information (Magliano et al., 1999; Ozuru et al., 2004). For example, open-ended think-aloud protocols are assumed to capture a learner's thoughts and experiences while comprehending material and solving problems (K. A. Ericsson & Simon, 1984), whereas more targeted forms of constructed responses (e.g., self-explanation, question answering) have instructions that are intended to *modify* comprehension and learning (Magliano & Graesser, 2012; McNamara, 2004).

Although these responses have substantial value in the study of comprehension and learning, their use is substantially limited by the labor-intensive nature of protocol analysis (Magliano & Graesser, 2012). Thus, the past 2 decades have seen substantial advances in the application of NLP techniques to support the analyses of constructed responses (Allen et al., 2015; Landauer et al., 2007). These advances have been in the context of computer-based assessments of explanations and think-aloud protocols during reading comprehension (Gilliam et al., 2007; Magliano et al., 2011), the grading of short-answer questions (Leacock & Chodorow, 2003), and ITSs that require students to produce constructed responses during interactive conversations (Graesser, 2016; Graesser et al., 2020; McCarthy et al., 2020). These automated systems incorporate a variety of NLP tools and algorithms to assess the responses, and make inferences about student comprehension, learning, and problem solving.

As one example, Magliano and colleagues developed the Reading Strategy Assessment Tool (RSAT; Magliano et al., 2011), which asks students to produce open-ended responses to prompts that are intended to engender a think-aloud response or answer to questions designed to tap into comprehension levels (e.g., why and how questions related to a recently read sentence). RSAT uses simple computer algorithms to analyze responses for evidence of comprehension processes, such as paraphrasing, bridging inferences, and elaborative inferences. Assessments of RSAT (Magliano et al., 2011; Millis & Magliano, 2012) report that RSAT does a reasonable job predicting objective comprehension scores and discriminating comprehension strategies.

In the Magliano et al. (2011) study, college students read a set of texts and answered direct and indirect questions while interacting with RSAT. They then completed multiple measures of comprehension, including the Gates-MacGinitie reading test and experimenter-generated, open-ended comprehension assessments. Researchers first examined the correlations between RSAT's overall measure of text comprehension and participants' performance on the two comprehension measures. The RSAT scores were correlated with performance on both the Gates-MacGinitie reading test ($r = 0.52$) and the open-ended comprehension assessments ($r = 0.45$), suggesting that RSAT successfully detected comprehension processes based on participants' responses. Correlations between these RSAT strategy scores (i.e., paraphrasing, bridging, elaborating) and expert human raters' identification of such strategies varied between .46 and .70, indicating that RSAT successfully detected comprehension strategies based on the constructed responses. Students' RSAT strategy scores accounted for approximately 21% of the variance in performance on the open-ended comprehension test. Specifically, higher comprehension was positively related to the generation of bridging and elaborations but negatively associated with paraphrasing. Overall, this work suggests that NLP can be used to identify the use of strategies *during reading* and that those strategies are predictive of individuals' ability to learn from the text.

Automated Analyses of Essay Responses

Beyond the scoring of brief constructed responses, NLP techniques have also been applied to the automated scoring of essays. Indeed, automated essay scoring (AES) has now reached a level of accuracy that the scoring of many classes of essays is as accurate as expert human raters (Attali & Burstein, 2006; McNamara et al., 2015; Shermis et al., 2010; Yan et al., 2020). Typically, AES systems are trained on a corpus of essays that have been rated by expert human raters according to a rubric. The corpus is divided into two sets of essays: a training set (used to train a model) and a testing set (used to examine the extent to which the model generalizes to new essays). Machine learning algorithms are applied to optimally fit the essays in the training set. The developed model is then applied to the essays in the testing set and these scores are compared to the human raters' scores. An AES model is considered successful if the scores between the computer and humans are similarly aligned to the scores between humans.

Shermis et al. (2010) reviewed the performance of the three most successful AES systems: e-rater developed at Educational Testing Service (Attali & Burstein, 2006; Burstein, 2003), Intelligent Essay Assessor developed at Pearson Knowledge Technologies (Landauer et al., 2003), and IntelliMetric developed by Vantage Learning (Elliot, 2003; Rudner et al., 2006). These systems have reported exact agreements with raters as high as the mid-80s, adjacent agreements in the high mid-90s, and correlations as high as the mid-80s. Just as impressive, these performance measures are slightly higher than agreement between trained human raters.

The performance of these AES systems has been sufficiently impressive to scale them for use in educational applications. They have been used in a scoring process for high-stakes tests, such as the analytic writing assessment of the Graduate Management Admission Test (GMAT). The GMAT includes two 30-minute writing tasks to assess abilities related to critical thinking and communicating ideas. One task involves an analysis of an issue: Test takers receive an issue or opinion and are instructed to explain their point of view by citing relevant reasons or evidence. The second task is an analysis of an argument: Test takers read a brief argument, analyze the reasoning behind it, and critique the argument. The AESs are also used in electronic portfolio systems to help students improve writing by providing feedback on multiple features of their essays, similar to Criterion (Attali & Burstein, 2006) and MY Access (Elliot, 2003).

Although the practical use of AESs is undeniable, critics raise questions that challenge the ubiquitous use of these systems without some human expertise. Some critics voice concerns about aspects of writing that the AES systems are unlikely to capture, the ethics of using computers rather than teachers to teach writing, and differences in the criteria that humans versus the computers use to grade the essays (Calfee, 2000; P. F. Ericsson & Haswell, 2006). There is also a persistent third variable that robustly predicts essay scores, namely, the number of words in the essay. The incremental gain from computational algorithms beyond word count is often not reported or is unspectacular in some evaluations that have controlled for number of words. One barrier to overcoming this challenge is that human raters often base some aspects of their ratings on the number of words, and more words means more content, which results in better essays.

It is beyond the scope of this chapter to give a precise specification of the computational algorithms that have been implemented in AESs, particularly because some are proprietary or the published reports do not reflect the current systems. An edited volume by Shermis and Burstein (2003) provides detailed descriptions of many of the early systems to the extent that the corporations were comfortable in sharing the information. The e-rater AES (Attali & Burstein, 2006) scored essays on six areas of analysis aligned with human scoring criteria: errors in grammar, errors in word usage, errors in mechanics, style, inclusion of organizational segments (e.g., inclusion of a thesis statement or some evidence), and vocabulary content. The IntelliMetric AES (Elliot, 2003; Rudner et al., 2006) matched the words to a vocabulary of over 500,000 unique words, identified more than 500 linguistic and grammatical features that occur in the text, and analyzed this content through a word concept net, which examines similarities amongst words to determine their semantic meaning. These text characteristics were then associated with essays in each level of scoring rubric of the training corpus in order to discover which essay characteristics are most strongly diagnostic of each level.

The Intelligent Essay Assessor AES (Landauer et al., 2003) analyzed the words in the essay using latent semantic analysis (LSA; Landauer et al., 2007) and n-gram analyses (i.e., sequences of words, such as word pairs or triplets). The algorithm computes the similarity of the words and word sequences between the incoming essay and the essays associated with each level of the scoring rubric. LSA is an important method of computing the conceptual similarity between words, sentences, paragraphs, or essays because it considers implicit knowledge. LSA is a mathematical, statistical technique for representing knowledge about words and the world on the basis of a large corpus of texts that attempts to capture the knowledge of a typical test taker. The central intuition of LSA is that the meaning of a word, W, is reflected in the company of other words that surround the word in naturalistic documents (imagine 40,000 texts or 11 million words). Two words are similar in meaning to the extent that they share similar surrounding words. For example, the word "glass" will be highly associated with words of the same functional context, such as *cup, liquid, pour, shatter,* and *transparent*. These are not synonyms or antonyms that would occur in a dictionary but, rather, words that are likely to occur in the same documents as the word *glass*. LSA uses a statistical technique called singular value decomposition (SVD) to condense a very large corpus of texts to 100 to 500 statistical dimensions (Landauer et al., 2007).

More recently, computational methods have been developed to capture better words' contexts, with the assumption that words are embedded in contexts defined by surrounding words. Similar to LSA, Word2Vec represents words as vectors but uses two-layer neural networks (rather than SVD) to train models (Mikolov et al., 2013). Bidirectional Encoder Representations from Transformers (BERT) expands the window of words' contextual embeddings by using deep learning to generate multiple contextual representations for each word (Devlin et al., 2018). Semantic models such as these generally compute the conceptual similarity between text excerpts (e.g., word, clause, sentence, essay) as the geometric cosine (i.e., 0–1) between the values and weighted dimensions of the excerpts.

A holistic grade for an essay has some value to the writer as an overall index of writing quality. However, more specific feedback on different characteristics of writing provides more useful information to the student and instructor. Is there a problem with spelling, vocabulary, syntax, cohesion of the message, missing content, elements of style, and so on? The e-rater AES has provided this feedback on 12 features in support of *Criterion*, an electronic portfolio of the students' writing. The portfolio of writing samples can be collected over time for students or instructors to track progress. Similarly, the LSA modules in the Intelligent Essay Assessor have been used in a system called *Summary Street* (Franzke et al., 2005) that gives feedback to the student on the quality of their summaries of a text. Summary Street identifies sentences that have low LSA relevance scores with other sentences in the text and low scores with expected information in different content categories of an underlying content rubric. An ideal summary would cover the expected content and have sentences that relate to one another conceptually (see Botarleanu et al., 2021, and Crossley, Kim, et al., 2019, for recent summarization algorithms).

Burstein et al. (2003) developed an automated scoring technology for the Criterion system at Educational Testing Service (ETS) that identifies the extent to which an essay contains particular components of an essay. The targeted categories of the essay include the title, the introductory material, a thesis statement, main ideas with respect to the thesis, supporting ideas, conclusions, and irrelevant segments. Trained human judges can identify these sections with kappa agreement scores of approximately 0.80 (between 0.86 and 0.95 on three different essay prompts). Kappa scores correct for guessing, adjust for the distribution of decisions, and vary between 0 (chance) and 1.0 (perfect agreement). Kappa scores have an advantage over correlations, but in practice the performance metrics lead to identical conclusions in this line of research. The kappa scores between the computer algorithms and human raters are respectable, typically above .70.

In addition to kappa and correlations, researchers routinely collect recall, precision, and F-measure scores between the computer decision on specific observations and the decision of a human judge (or alternatively between one judge and another judge). A recall score for a computer system is the proportion of computer decisions that receive the same decision as a human on the occurrence of a particular language/discourse features in an observation. The precision score is the proportion of computer decisions that agree with a human. The F-measure is 2 * recall * precision/(recall + precision), essentially an average between recall and precision scores. Burstein et al. (2003) reported that the scores between computer and human were approximately the same for these three metrics and averaged .76, depending on various parameters and criteria. Agreement between pairs of human judges averaged .91. Although not perfect, these automated systems are clearly making significant progress in identifying components of essays. These categories are important to identify in order to give informative guidance on how students can improve writing.

This push towards more detailed feedback from AES systems has coincided with the development of automated writing evaluation (AWE) systems, which are intended to move beyond simply providing scores on students' essays. The purpose of AWE systems is to provide an opportunity for students to engage in writing practice and receive summative and formative feedback on their writing (Allen & Perret, 2016). These systems have been successfully integrated into a number of classroom environments and are commonly used in high-stakes writing assessments (Dikli, 2006). Although a substantial amount of research in this area still focuses on evaluating the accuracy of the automated scores (Warschauer & Ware, 2006; Yan et al., 2020), more recent research has also examined other aspects of writing, such as whether students can increase the quality of their essays after receiving system feedback (Roscoe et al., 2015) or whether they can more accurately monitor their own performance (Allen et al., 2015). A primary goal of computer-based writing systems should, therefore, be not only to provide accurate scores for students' performance but also to provide instruction and feedback that can help students to assess their own work more accurately.

Challenges in Automated Writing Evaluation

There are a number of methodological challenges that require attention for those who develop instructional systems designed to track and improve writing over time. One problem is that there are a limited number of standardized tests of writing achievement with norms that afford gauging progress over time. A second problem is that the available norm-referenced standardized tests, such as the Woodcock-Johnson or the Wechsler Individual Achievement Test, cover few writing skills and genres. A third problem is that the writing process is influenced by a number of factors associated with the pragmatic writing context, intended audience, writing prompts, time allotted for writing, mode of writing (handwriting vs. keyboard), choice of topics to write about, and characteristics of the writer (Graham & Perin, 2007).

The time-intensive nature of scoring written essays has traditionally limited teachers from giving a large number of writing assignments. This limitation can of course be circumvented by AES and AWE systems. There are also other methods other than the use of computers. For example, having students assess their own writing performance and development enhances writing skills (Andrade & Boulay, 2003; Graham & Perin, 2007; Ross et al., 1999). Teachers can also have students assess each other's writing. When learners are taught how to assess and provide feedback to their peers, their writing as well as their peers' writing improves (Cho et al., 2006; Graham & Perin, 2007).

Overview of NLP Assessment

Overall, this section illustrates the ways in which NLP techniques can be used to provide automated assessments of natural language across a variety of psychological and educational contexts. To illustrate the feasibility of these approaches, consider two students who are tasked with developing an opinion on whether uniforms should be required by schools. In this hypothetical task, the students would be asked to read multiple texts that provide information about this topic and would periodically be prompted to produce self-explanations of what they have just read. They would then be asked to provide a brief summary of their opinions on the issue. In this example, we have two primary sources of natural language that we can assess using NLP: the self-explanations and the summaries. Next, we illustrate a few ways that we may approach an NLP-based analysis of these self-explanations.

Consider the following excerpts from the self-explanations produced by the two students:

Student 1: I would never want anyone to tell me how to dress for school; that feels like such a violation of my freedom, and I like to be able to express myself creatively.

Student 2: I think this first passage is trying to indicate that one of the benefits of uniforms is that they can reduce perceptions of inequality. I wonder if the other passages will address the consequences as well.

In these two excerpts, we can see that the students are engaging in different types of text processing; Student 1 seems to be drawing on their own personal experiences when discussing the texts, whereas Student 2 is paraphrasing the purpose of the first text and engaging in metacognitive processing as they anticipate the content of the remaining texts. We may choose to characterize these self-explanations along multiple dimensions to assess these processing differences. Table 17.1 provides an example of some of the metrics that may be calculated (for this analysis we used all of the self-explanations the students produced, not just the excerpts given above) across two categories. We can see from Table 17.1 that NLP analyses can allow us to assess the self-explanations along multiple dimensions.

The descriptive indices indicate that Student 1 generated *more* words in their self-explanations overall, but Student 2 wrote longer words on average. This provides us with some basic information about their verbosity during the task as well as the lexical sophistication of the students. The RSAT indices follow from Magliano et al. (2011) and provide more nuanced information about the specific strategies the students were engaged in during reading. Here, we can see that Student 1 was engaged in more shallow processing of the text than Student 2, as they predominantly engaged in paraphrasing compared with bridging or elaboration. Importantly, the indices shown here are just a small subset of the indices that could be calculated for these self-explanations but are intended to illustrate the power of NLP to assess students' natural language from a more multidimensional perspective compared with more standard holistic scores.

TABLE 17.1

Example Natural Language Processing (NLP) Indices for the Assessment of Self-Explanations

NLP variable	Type of variable	Student 1	Student 2
Number of words	Descriptive	453.00	236.00
Mean letters per word	Descriptive	3.90	5.23
Number of paraphrases	Strategy use	6.00	3.00
Number of bridges	Strategy use	4.00	5.00
Number of elaborations	Strategy use	2.00	5.00

INFERRING PSYCHOLOGICAL ATTRIBUTES AND PROCESSES FROM NATURAL LANGUAGE

Thus far, we have focused on research that examines computational systems' accuracy in scoring individuals' constructed responses. However, there is a growing body of work that examines ways in which NLP techniques can be used to model aspects of individual writers and their behaviors. Such approaches could be used to provide more nuanced information about the contextual factors influencing discourse processing and production. Notably, research has begun to examine whether NLP techniques can be used to model individual differences based on the linguistic features of individuals' produced discourse (e.g., constructed responses, essays). For example, recent work suggests that the cohesion of individuals' constructed responses (e.g., self-explanations, think-aloud responses) during reading is indicative of the coherence of their mental representation (Allen et al., 2016a). For instance, Allen and colleagues (2016) reported that the cohesion of constructed responses was higher when readers were prompted to self-explain compared to paraphrase, and that the cohesion of students' constructed responses increased over the course of self-explanation instruction and practice. Thus, automated analyses of the cohesion of students' constructed responses provides a window into the coherence of readers' mental representations. In turn, we can predict that the individual is a better reader if they produce language that is cohesive and lexically sophisticated (Allen et al., 2016a).

This work has been extended to multiple-document comprehension contexts. Allen et al. (2021) asked participants to generate constructed responses while reading multiple documents and then write an essay to assess integration across documents. The cohesion of the constructed responses within the individual documents was negatively related to essay quality. By contrast, cohesion of the constructed responses across the documents was positively related to essay quality. Further, compared to thinking aloud, strategic instructions to either self-explain or evaluate sources enhanced across-document integration. As such, the NLP analyses of the cohesion of students' constructed responses provided both theoretical and practical insights into successful comprehension and learning processes and, in particular, strategic comprehension processes lending to more coherent mental representations of text.

Beyond individual differences, work has been conducted to examine emotions and other psychological states from written responses. One tool that has provided substantial advancements in the work in this domain is the Linguistic Inquiry and Word Count (LIWC) tool developed by Pennebaker et al. (2007). LIWC has been used to analyze a wide range of phenomena in psychology and education, far more than any other effort with automated systems. LIWC reports the percentage of words in a given text devoted to grammatical (e.g., "articles," "pronouns," "prepositions"), psychological (e.g., "emotions," "cognitive mechanisms," "social"), or content categories (e.g., "home," "occupation," "religion"). For example, "crying" and "grief" are words in the sad category, whereas "love" and "nice" are words that are assigned the positive emotion category. The mapping between words and word categories is not mutually exclusive because a word can map onto several categories. LIWC provides roughly 80 categories of words but also groups these word categories into broader dimensions, such as psychological constructs (e.g., causations, sadness) and personal constructs (e.g., work, religion). LIWC operates by analyzing a transcript of discourse and counting the number of words that belong to each category. A proportion score for each category is then computed by dividing the number of words in the discourse that belong to that category by the total number of words.

LIWC categories have been shown to be valid and reliable markers of a variety of psychologically meaningful constructs (Chung & Pennebaker, 2007; Pennebaker et al., 2003). The relative frequency of psychological words would obviously map onto relevant psychological constructs, and these references review such trends. However, the more counterintuitive finding that Pennebaker and his colleagues have documented is the role of the linguistic features of words. LIWC provides linguistic features that comprise function words, various types of pronouns, common and auxiliary verbs, different tenses, adverbs, conjunctions, negations, quantifiers, numbers, and swear words. Somewhat surprisingly, function words rather than the content words are diagnostic of many psychological states (Pennebaker, 2011). Function words are difficult for people to deliberately control and, thus, examining their use in text provides a nonreactive way to explore many social and personality processes.

Function word use has been linked to a wide range of individual differences. Function word use can vary as a function of sex, age, and social class (Pennebaker, 2011). For example, pronouns have been linked to psychological states such as depression and suicide in essays, natural conversations, and poetry (Rude et al., 2004; Stirman & Pennebaker, 2001). This work spurred research on language *style* (Pennebaker et al., 2003), represented by the use of function words across varied contexts. Language style has been linked to a number of factors, such as personality (Pennebaker, 2011) and emotional states (Tausczik & Pennebaker, 2010). More recently, researchers have examined how language styles dynamically shift during conversations. For example, Müller-Frommeyer and colleagues (2020) reported that language styles were significantly different in monologues compared with conversations and that this change was greater for conflict-based conversations compared with friendly conversations. Thus, NLP analyses have potential to reveal the nature of interactions in joint conversational contexts.

Inferring Emotions

One important application of LIWC and other similar tools has been the prediction of emotional states based on individuals' language. There are a number of different approaches to analyzing the affective content of text samples. One straightforward approach is to identify a small number of dimensions that underlie expressions of affect

(Samsonovich & Ascoli, 2006). This research was pioneered decades ago by Osgood and colleagues, who analyzed how people in different cultures rated the similarity of various emotion words (Osgood et al., 1975). His analyses converged on *evaluation* (i.e., good or bad), *potency* (i.e., strong or weak), and *activity* (i.e., active or passive) as the critical dimensions. These dimensions are aligned with valence and arousal, which are considered to be the fundamental dimensions of affective experience (Barrett et al., 2007; Russell, 2003).

A second approach is to conduct a more detailed lexical analysis of the text in order to identify words that are predictive of specific affective states of writers or speakers (Cohn et al., 2004; Crossley et al., 2017; Pennebaker et al., 2003). Other researchers have developed lexical databases that provide affective information for common words. For example, WordNet-Affect (Strapparava & Valitutti, 2004) is an extension of WordNet for affective content. Others have gone beyond the words and into a semantic analysis of the text. For example, Gill et al. (2008) analyzed blogs and reported that texts judged by humans as expressing fear and joy were semantically similar to emotional concept words (e.g., "phobia" and "terror" for "fear," but "delight" and "bliss" for "joy"). They used LSA (Landauer et al., 2007) and the hyperspace analogue to language model (Burgess et al., 1998) to automatically compute the semantic similarity between the texts and emotion keywords (e.g., "fear," "joy"). Although this method of semantically aligning text to emotional concept words showed some promise for fear and joy texts, it failed for texts conveying other emotions, such as anger and sadness. D'Mello and colleagues (2008, 2010) predicted student emotions using the language and discourse in tutorial dialogues with AutoTutor. They found that feedback, speech act categories (e.g., indirect hints), cohesion, negations, and other linguistic features successfully predicted student affect states that are frequent during tutoring, such as boredom, frustration, confusion, and engagement.

The fourth and most sophisticated approach to text-based affect sensing involves systems that construct affective models from a large corpora of world knowledge and apply these models to identify the affective tone in texts (Crossley et al., 2017; Pang & Lee, 2008; Wiebe et al., 2005). For example, the word "accident" is typically associated with an undesirable event so the presence of "accident" will increase the assigned negative valence of the sentence "I was held up from an accident on the freeway." This approach is sometimes called *sentiment analysis*, opinion extraction, or *subjectivity analysis* because it focuses on valence of a textual sample, rather than assigning the text to a particular emotion category (e.g., angry, sad).

Overview of NLP as a Tool of Modeling Psychological Processes

Overall, this section extends the section on assessment to reveal how NLP can be used to infer psychological and emotional states from natural language. We can illustrate these approaches by reconsidering Student 1 and Student 2 from the prior section. Above, we focused explicitly on assessments of the quality and types of strategies in which the students were engaged. However, we can also use NLP to infer the specific types of processes in which they are engaged as well as their emotional states during reading.

As shown in Table 17.2, the cohesion of the two students' self-explanations was quite varied. These indices indicated that the self-explanations generated by Student 2 were more cohesive than those written by Student 1, suggesting that

TABLE 17.2

Example Natural Language Processing (NLP) Indices for Inferring Psychological Processes and States From Self-Explanations

NLP variable	Type of variable	Student 1	Student 2
Number of connectives	Cohesion	10.00	15.00
Semantic overlap (LSA)	Cohesion	0.36	0.53
Positive words proportion	Emotion	0.53	0.21
Negative words proportion	Emotion	0.42	0.33

Note. LSA = latent semantic analysis.

Student 2 was potentially engaged in more integrative processes during reading, which has been linked to increased comprehension of the text information. On the other hand, Student 1 seemed to be engaged in more emotional processing of the text, which could have been linked to their focus on it related to their own life experiences. Thus, while this student was less likely to develop connections across the texts, they were more emotional, which could indicate that they were more motivated or engaged during the task. Overall, this example indicates that NLP techniques can be used to move beyond standardized assessments of natural language and provide context that is important to more fully understanding the learning process.

APPLICATION OF NLP TECHNIQUES TO INTELLIGENT TUTORING SYSTEMS

One common application of the work described above is to increase personalization and feedback delivery in educational technologies, such as ITSs. ITSs provide personalized learning through student modeling, which involves computational analyses that track the domain knowledge, strategies, and other psychological states of users (Chrysafiadi & Virvou, 2013; Woolf, 2009). ITSs adaptively respond to users by providing activities and feedback that are sensitive to these states and that advance instructional agendas. The interaction between the ITS and its users follows a large, if not an infinite number of alternative trajectories that attempt to fit constraints of both the student and the instructional goals. Thus, assessments of student responses are essential in any ITS. Such assessments are straightforward when the responses are selections among a fixed set of alternatives, as in the case of multiple-choice questions, true-false questions, ratings, or toggled decisions on a long list of possibilities. Challenges arise, however, when the student is prompted to input natural language within the ITS. In these circumstances, NLP techniques are required to provide scores and automated feedback to users on their responses.

A number of ITSs have been developed that process and respond to students using natural language. Examples include ITSPOKE (Litman et al., 2006), spoken conversational computer (Pon-Barry et al., 2004), tactical language and culture training system (L. W. Johnson & Valente, 2008), and Why-Atlas (VanLehn et al., 2007). In the following section, we describe three language-based ITSs to highlight work in this domain: AutoTutor (Graesser, 2016; Graesser, Lu et al., 2004), iSTART (McCarthy et al., 2020; McNamara et al., 2004), and the Writing Pal (Roscoe & McNamara, 2013).

AutoTutor

AutoTutor is an ITS that provides students with instruction on computer literacy, physics, critical thinking skills, and other technical topics by holding conversations in natural language (Graesser, 2016; Graesser et al., 2020; Graesser, Lu et al., 2004; Nye et al., 2014). AutoTutor shows learning gains of between 0.3 sigma (standard deviation units) and 0.8 sigma (Graesser, Jeon, & Dufty, 2008) compared with pretests or with a condition that has students read a textbook for an equivalent amount of time. The tutorial dialogues are organized around difficult questions and problems that require reasoning and explanations in the answers. For example, AutoTutor might ask, "If a lightweight car and a massive truck have a head-on collision, upon which vehicle is the impact force greater? Which vehicle undergoes the greater change in its motion, and why?" Such questions require the learner to construct approximately three to seven sentences and to exhibit reasoning in their responses.

When asked a question, students typically provide short answers during the first conversational turn, typically ranging from a few words to a couple of sentences. It takes a conversation to glean better insights into what the student knows even when the student has reasonable subject matter knowledge. The dialogue for one of these challenging questions consists of approximately 20 to 100 conversational turns between AutoTutor and the student. AutoTutor provides feedback based on the student's input (positive or neutral vs. negative feedback), pumps the student for more information ("What else?"), prompts the student to fill in missing words, gives the student hints, fills in missing information with assertions, corrects erroneous ideas and misconceptions, answers the student's questions, and summarizes answers. These responses are important dialogue moves of AutoTutor and lead to the eventually construction of a full answer to the question across the dialogue.

There are many different ways to score the performance of AutoTutor (Graesser et al., 2007, 2020; Jackson & Graesser, 2006; VanLehn et al., 2007). One method is to score the extent to which students' verbal contributions match good answers to the question (called *expectations*) versus bad answers (called *misconceptions*). Students receive higher scores to the extent that they express more of the expectations and fewer of the misconceptions in the tutorial dialogue. Scores of expectation coverage and misconceptions can be computed during the first student turn or after they have finished the conversational dialogue. Students rarely articulate the expectations perfectly because natural language is much too imprecise, fragmentary, vague, ungrammatical, and elliptical. Thus, AutoTutor has used a number of semantic match algorithms to evaluate the extent to the students' verbal responses match any given expectation (Graesser et al., 2020).

Another method of assessing student performance in AutoTutor is to analyze the number and type of dialogue moves by AutoTutor that were selected to extract information from the student during the evolution of the answer. The system periodically identifies a missing expectation during the course of the dialogue and posts the goal of covering the expectation. When an expectation is posted, AutoTutor attempts to induce the student to articulate it by generating hints and prompts that encourage the student to fill in words and propositions. Specific prompts and hints are generated that maximize the student's filling in this content and boosting the match score above threshold.

A student's level of performance in AutoTutor can be measured by computing the number of AutoTutor pumps, hints, and prompts it requires for the student to generate an answer to a question. This was assessed in an analysis of four dialogue move categories that attempt to cover the content of particular expectations: pumps, hints, prompts, and assertions (Jackson & Graesser, 2006). The proportion of dialogue moves in these categories should be sensitive to student knowledge of physics (as measured by a pretest of physics with multiple-choice questions similar to the Force Concept Inventory; Hestenes et al., 1992). There is a continuum from the student supplying information to the tutor supplying information as we move from pumps to hints to prompts to assertions. The correlations with student knowledge reflected this continuum perfectly, with correlations of .49, .24, −.19, and −.40. For students with more knowledge of physics, AutoTutor can get by with pumps and hints, thereby encouraging the student to articulate the expectations. For students with less knowledge of physics, AutoTutor needs to generate prompts that elicit specific words or to assert the correct information, thereby extracting knowledge piecemeal or merely telling the student the correct information.

These analyses of student verbal responses through AutoTutor support a number of claims. First, there are several automated algorithms that can score whether particular sentences are covered in verbal responses that evolve in conversational turns over the course of a conversation. Second, the computer scores for sentential content matches have a moderate but unspectacular level of accuracy, at least compared with the scoring of lengthy essays. There is less content in a sentence than an essay, so this second conclusion is quite expected. On the other hand, the scoring of verbal responses is extremely high when the expectation unit is a single word, intermediate when it is a sentence, and high when it is an essay. Third, the scoring of verbal responses with AutoTutor requires an analysis of expected content and an assessment of the extent to which verbal responses match the expected content. It is beyond the scope of AutoTutor to analyze content that is not on the radar of these expectations.

iSTART (Interactive Strategy Trainer for Automated Reading and Thinking)

iSTART (Levinstein et al., 2007; McNamara et al., 2004) is an ITS that helps high school, college, and adult literacy students learn and practice comprehension strategies to improve their comprehension of challenging expository text. iSTART has been shown to improve self-explanation quality, comprehension strategy use, and reading comprehension for readers from middle school through adulthood (Magliano et al., 2005; McCarthy et al., 2018; McNamara et al., 2007). iSTART is particularly effective in helping low knowledge and less skilled readers better understand challenging text.

iSTART includes modules for students to learn three macrostrategies: self-explanation (McNamara et al., 2017), question-asking (Ruseti et al., 2018), and summarization (Botarleanu et al., 2021; Crossley et al., 2019). Each module comprises brief lessons that provide the student with information on how to use the strategies, as well as microstrategies to facilitate students' application of the strategies. Students practice the strategies using natural language responses, such as generating self-explanations or summaries. A crucial aspect of iSTART's effectiveness is the feedback provided to students by a pedagogical agent as they type in responses to text using the comprehension strategies. Automated NLP algorithms detects the quality of the responses so that adaptive feedback can be provided to the student.

iSTART also includes two types of game-based practice (Jackson & McNamara, 2013). In generative games, students earn points for producing high-quality responses, such as explanations or summaries. In identification games, students read example responses to a text and earn points by correctly identifying which comprehension strategies were used in the examples. Students use their points to purchase customization features for students' avatars or to unlock new games. These "metagame" elements were designed to further enhance student motivation (Jackson & McNamara, 2013).

The core of iSTART is its focus on self-explaining challenging text using five empirically validated comprehension strategies: comprehension monitoring, paraphrasing, prediction, bridging, and elaboration. Comprehension monitoring is the reader's ability to assess their understanding of the text while reading. Paraphrasing is a restatement of the text in the reader's own words. Prediction is when a reader anticipates forthcoming information in a text either by making educated guesses or taking note of information that, if present, will aid in comprehension of a previous concept. Bridging is the act of drawing a connection between the current sentence to previous information in the text. Elaboration is using prior knowledge, either general or domain-specific, or logic to expand on the concepts in the text.

Several versions of the iSTART evaluation algorithm have been developed and assessed (McNamara et al., 2007). The ultimate goal was to develop an algorithm that was completely automated and did not rely on any human or hand-coded computations. The resulting algorithm uses a combination of both word-based approaches and semantic algorithms such as LSA (Landauer et al., 2007). Word-based approaches include a length criterion in which the student's explanation must exceed a specified number of content words that are in the text. The LSA-based approach relies on a set of benchmarks from the target text including the title of the passage, the words in the target sentence, and the words in the previous two sentences. The word-based algorithms provide feedback on shallow explanations (i.e., ones that are irrelevant or that repeat the target sentence). LSA augments the word-based algorithms by providing a deeper, qualitative assessment. More positive feedback is given for longer, more relevant explanations, whereas increased interactions and support are provided for shorter, less relevant explanations.

Students' self-explanations are assessed using a series of NLP algorithms. First, the response is screened for metacognitive and frozen expressions (e.g., "I don't understand what they are saying here," "I'm bored"). If the explanation is dominated by the frozen expressions and contains little other content, then the pedagogical agent responds directly to those statements using a pool of responses that are randomly chosen, "Please try to make a guess about what this means" or "Can you try to use one of the reading strategies? Maybe that will help your understanding." After the frozen statements are removed from the explanation, then the remainder of the explanation is analyzed using both word-based and LSA-based methods (McNamara et al., 2007). If the length of the explanation does not reach a particular threshold, T, relative to the length of the target text, then the student is asked to add more to the explanation. The agent might then say, "Could you add to your explanation? Try to explain how it relates to something you already know." If the explanation does not have sufficient overlap in words or semantically meaning to the target and surrounding text, then it is assessed as irrelevant.

The explanation is further assessed in terms of its similarity to the target text. If it is too close to the target text in terms of the total number of words and the number of overlapping content words, as in the example below, then it categorized as a repetition. A repetition might receive feedback such as, "Try adding some more information that explains what the sentence means." The goal is to induce the student to go beyond the sentence. Paraphrasing is an excellent and optimal way to start an explanation, but the goal is usually to induce the student to go beyond paraphrasing by bringing in prior text or outside knowledge to the explanation. In that case, the student would receive feedback such as, "It looks like you've reworded the sentence. Now can you explain it by thinking about what else you know?" Once the explanation passes the thresholds for length, relevance, and similarity, feedback is provided on its quality. Students are provided with qualitative feedback, such as, "That's pretty good" for a medium-quality explanation and "You're doing a great job!" for a higher quality explanation.

Lower quality explanations are just at the threshold and have little content that goes beyond the target text. They are provided with prompts and hints to help them use comprehension strategies.

iSTART can also adapt the difficulty of the texts that students read based on their performance in iSTART. When students' self-explanation quality is high, subsequent texts are more challenging, and vice versa, when self-explanation quality is low, subsequent text are adapted to students' ability levels (A. Johnson et al., 2017). Adapting the learning materials to the students' ability levels in iSTART leads to increased sense of learning (Watanabe et al., 2019) and leads to positive learning outcomes, specifically for less-skilled readers (McCarthy et al., 2018, 2020).

The accuracy of the iSTART evaluation algorithms has been assessed by computing linear equations based on a discriminate analysis of one data set and calculating its ability to predict human ratings for a variety of data sets (Boonthum et al., 2007; Jackson et al., 2010; McNamara et al., 2007; Millis et al., 2004). Across a number of evaluations, the iSTART algorithms have corresponded well to human ratings. McNamara et al. (2007) reported that algorithms corresponded highly with human evaluations of the self-explanations on two texts in the initial iSTART practice module; there was a 62% to 64% agreement between the algorithm and the human judgments ($r = .64 - .71$; $d' = 1.54 - 1.79$). The algorithms also successfully transferred to texts that were on a variety of science topics used in a classroom study that included 549 high school students who engaged in extended practice using iSTART across an academic year (Jackson et al., 2010). This study showed an $r = .66$ correlation between the human evaluations and iSTART's algorithms. This is remarkable given the variety of texts self-explained by the students in this study. Although this performance appears to be higher than AutoTutor, consider that the two systems target quite different information. iSTART assesses the quality of the student's self-explanation strategies whereas AutoTutor assesses the quality, depth, and accuracy of expected substantive content.

The analyses in this section support the claim that automated analyses are moderately successful in evaluating the quality of short verbal responses. A variety of algorithms have been used to compute semantic matches between student verbal responses and sentence expectations. Most of these algorithms are based on the overlap of content words and inferential content through LSA, but a few consider the order in which words are expressed and even deep symbolic analyses of the natural language. The performance of these computational analyses is moderately successful but not as impressive as automatic scoring of essays. We anticipate that future efforts will perform deeper analyses of the content with more sophisticated NLP.

Writing Pal

ITSs such as AutoTutor and iSTART focus on short, constructed responses. The Writing Pal is an ITS that has been developed as an extension to AWE systems that provide students with feedback on their writing. Specifically, the Writing Pal was designed to improve high school and college students' writing proficiency through explicit strategy instruction, deliberate practice, and automated feedback (Roscoe et al., 2014; Roscoe & McNamara, 2013). Contrary to the majority of computer-based writing systems (see Allen et al., 2016b, for a review), the Writing Pal strongly focuses on providing instruction and practice to use writing strategies in addition to providing opportunities to write essays with personalized feedback.

Strategy instruction in the Writing Pal system covers the three primary phases of the writing process: prewriting, drafting, and revising. In the system, these strategies are taught in the context of individual instructional modules that include Freewriting and Planning; Introduction Building, Body Building, and Conclusion Building; and Paraphrasing, Cohesion Building, and Revising. Each of these instructional modules contains multiple lesson videos, which are each narrated by an animated pedagogical agent. In these videos, the agent describes and provides examples of specific writing strategies. Once students have viewed the lesson videos, they can unlock mini-games that provide them with opportunities to practice the writing strategies in isolation before applying them in the context of a complete essay. In the Writing Pal, students can practice the strategies with identification mini-games, where they are asked to select the best answer to a particular question, or generative mini-games, where they produce natural language (typed) responses related to the strategies they are practicing.

An important component of the Writing Pal system is the AWE component (i.e., the essay practice component). This aspect of the Writing Pal contains a word processor in which students can write essays in response to a set of Scholastic Aptitude Test (SAT)–style prompts. Additionally, teachers have the option of adding their own prompts to the system. Once a student has completed an essay, it is submitted to the Writing Pal system for evaluation. As with other AES and AWE tools, the Writing Pal combines NLP and machine learning techniques to drive its automated feedback system and its adaptivity (Allen et al., 2016; McNamara et al., 2015). NLP techniques are used to assess students' essays across a variety of linguistic dimensions, such as the lexical sophistication or the organization of the essay. Once extracted, this information is used to drive essay scoring algorithms, which provide summative scores on a 6-point scale from *poor* to *great* similar to those used on the SAT rubrics (Roscoe et al., 2014). The formative feedback, on the other hand, provides information about strategies students can use to improve the quality of their essays. Formative feedback is an important component of writing development, as it provides knowledge about components of high-quality writing, as well as actionable recommendations on how to improve. The formative feedback in Writing Pal was developed with this in mind and provides recommendations that relate to multiple writing strategies. After they have read the feedback, students can revise their essays.

Students who have used the Writing Pal show significant improvements in writing skills, overall essay scores, and writing strategy knowledge

(Allen et al., 2015; Roscoe & McNamara, 2013). Receiving explicit writing strategy instruction helps students monitor their own strategy use and accuracy of their writing, which is beneficial when students need personalized writing feedback and their instructors are unavailable (Allen et al., 2015). The Writing Pal's success emphasizes the importance of individualized feedback for improving holistic writing quality.

THE FUTURE OF AUTOMATED LANGUAGE ANALYSES

This chapter surveyed the abundance of work that has been conducted on the automation of language analyses within the psychological domain. We know that language is an important construct in our understanding of a wide range of psychological and behavioral constructs; however, it is also highly complex, multimodal, and multi-dimensional (Allen et al., 2022; McNamara, 2021). Thus, the future of automated language analyses lies in the development of models that examine the complexity of language, considering language using multiple scales that range from examinations of word characteristics (e.g., the degree to which it is familiar, emotional, or abstract) to the organization of the discourse itself.

Such multidimensional analyses have the capacity to provide more nuanced information about the relations between language and psychological processes. For example, examination of languages at the word, sentence, and discourse level can provide more nuanced information about how certain experimental manipulations or individual differences influence discourse production and comprehension. Moreover, understanding and predicting human behavior calls for the integration of multiple sources of information from different modalities, such as gestures, eye movement, keystroke behaviors, and emotional responses. Thus, future research should not only consider the language being produced during psychological tasks but also consider other data sources that may be complementary. For instance, recent research has considered models that combine keystroke data with linguistic data (Allen et al., 2016), eye movements (Chukharev-Hudilainen et al., 2019), and click-stream data (Crossley et al., 2020). Multimodal work is likely to provide much more nuanced and robust understanding of discourse processes, cognition, and human behavior more broadly.

Overall, substantial progress has been made in our ability to provide automated assessments of natural language and discourse. This progress has been fueled by advances in computational power, statistical techniques, NLP tools, and theoretical understanding of discourse processes. These developments have undergirded techniques for scoring essays, analyzing characteristics of different types of writing, assessing text difficulty, assessing the accuracy, quality, and type of student contributions in tutoring systems, inferring psychological characteristics of speakers and writers, and detecting affective dimensions in discourse.

We expect that automated analyses of text and discourse will continue to grow and expand in the future. In this chapter, we have only covered a small slice of research at the intersections of computational modeling and psychology. Some colleagues will continue to have healthy skepticisms of the automated analyses of language and discourse. Others, however, will continue to discover how diverse aspects of psychological mechanisms can be captured using automated analyses of text and discourse. Both of these mindsets are needed to converge on automated assessments that most effectively and appropriately advance the field of psychology.

References

Allen, L. K., Creer, S. D., & Öncel, P. (2022). Natural language processing as a tool for learning analytics: Towards a multi-dimensional view of the learning process. In C. Lang, G. Siemens, A. F. Wise, D. Gašević, & A. Merceron (Eds.), *Handbook of learning analytics* (2nd ed., pp. 46–53). Society for Learning Analytics Research.

Allen, L. K., Jacovina, M. E., & McNamara, D. S. (2016a). Cohesive features of deep text comprehension processes. In J. Trueswell, A. Papafragou, D. Grodner, & D. Mirman (Eds.), *Proceedings of the 38th Annual Meeting of the Cognitive Science Society in Philadelphia, PA* (pp. 2681–2686). Cognitive Science Society.

Allen, L. K., Jacovina, M. E., & McNamara, D. S. (2016b). Computer-based writing instruction. In C. A. MacArthur, S. Graham, & J. Fitzgerald (Eds.), *Handbook of writing research* (2nd ed., pp. 316–329). Guilford Press.

Allen, L. K., Magliano, J. P., McCarthy, K. S., Sonia, A., Creer, S., & McNamara, D. S. (2021). In T. Fitch, C. Lamm, H. Leder, & K. Tessmar (Eds.), *Proceedings of the 43rd Annual Conference of the Cognitive Science Society* (pp. 931–937). Cognitive Science Society.

Allen, L. K., Mills, C., Jacovina, M. E., Crossley, S., D'Mello, S., & McNamara, D. S. (2016). Investigating boredom and engagement during writing using multiple sources of information: The essay, the writer, and keystrokes. *Proceedings of the 6th International Learning Analytics & Knowledge Conference* (pp. 114–123). ACM.

Allen, L. K., & Perret, C. A. (2016). Commercialized writing systems. In D. S. McNamara & S. A. Crossley (Eds.), *Adaptive educational technologies for literacy instruction* (pp. 145–162). Taylor & Francis, Routledge. https://doi.org/10.4324/9781315647500-11

Allen, L. K., Snow, E. L., & McNamara, D. S. (2015). Are you reading my mind? Modeling students' reading comprehension skills with Natural Language Processing techniques. *Proceedings of the International Learning Analytics & Knowledge Conference* (pp. 246–254). ACM.

Andrade, H. G., & Boulay, B. A. (2003). Role of Rubric-Referenced Self-Assessment in Learning to Write. *The Journal of Educational Research*, 97(1), 21–34. https://doi.org/10.1080/00220670309596625

Attali, Y., & Burstein, J. (2006). Automated essay scoring with e-rater R V.2. *The Journal of Technology, Learning, and Assessment*, 4(3), 1–30.

Barrett, L. F., Mesquita, B., Ochsner, K. N., & Gross, J. J. (2007). The experience of emotion. *Annual Review of Psychology*, 58(1), 373–403. https://doi.org/10.1146/annurev.psych.58.110405.085709

Boonthum, C., Levinstein, I., & McNamara, D. S. (2007). Evaluating self-explanations in iSTART: Word matching, latent semantic analysis, and topic models. In A. Kao & S. Poteet (Eds.), *Natural language processing and text mining* (pp. 91–106). Springer. https://doi.org/10.1007/978-1-84628-754-1_6

Botarleanu, R.-M., Dascalu, M., Allen, L. K., Crossley, S. A., & McNamara, D. S. (2021). Automated summary scoring with ReaderBench. In *International Conference on Intelligent Tutoring Systems (ITS 2021)*. Springer.

Burgess, C., Livesay, K., & Lund, K. (1998). Explorations in context space: Words, sentences, and discourse. *Discourse Processes*, 25(2–3), 211–257. https://doi.org/10.1080/01638539809545027

Burstein, J. (2003). The E-rater scoring engine: Automated essay scoring with natural language processing. In M. D. Shermis & J. C. Burstein (Eds.), *Automated essay scoring: A cross-disciplinary perspective* (pp. 113–121). Erlbaum.

Burstein, J., Marcu, D., & Knight, K. (2003). Finding the WRITE stuff: Automatic identification of discourse structure in student essays. *IEEE Intelligent Systems*, 18(1), 32–39. https://doi.org/10.1109/MIS.2003.1179191

Calfee, R. (2000). To grade or not to grade. *IEEE Intelligent Systems*, 15, 35–37.

Cho, K., Schunn, C. D., & Wilson, R. W. (2006). Validity and reliability of scaffolded peer assessment of writing from instructor and student perspectives. *Journal of Educational Psychology*, 98(4), 891–901. https://doi.org/10.1037/0022-0663.98.4.891

Chrysafiadi, K., & Virvou, M. (2013). Student modeling approaches: A literature review for the last decade. *Expert Systems with Applications*, 40(11), 4715–4729. https://doi.org/10.1016/j.eswa.2013.02.007

Chukharev-Hudilainen, E., Saricaoglu, A., Torrance, M., & Feng, H.-H. (2019). Combined deployable keystroke logging and eyetracking for investigating L2 writing fluency. *Studies in Second Language Acquisition*, 41(3), 583–604. https://doi.org/10.1017/S027226311900007X

Chung, C., & Pennebaker, J. (2007). The psychological functions of function words. In K. Fielder (Ed.), *Social communication* (pp. 343–359). Psychology Press.

Clark, A., Fox, C., & Lappin, S. (Eds.). (2013). *The handbook of computational linguistics and natural language processing*. John Wiley & Sons.

Cohn, M. A., Mehl, M. R., & Pennebaker, J. W. (2004). Linguistic markers of psychological change surrounding September 11, 2001. *Psychological Science*, 15(10), 687–693. https://doi.org/10.1111/j.0956-7976.2004.00741.x

Coté, N., & Goldman, S. R. (1999). Building representations of informational text: Evidence from children's think-aloud protocols. In H. van Oostendorp & S. R. Goldman (Eds.), *The construction of mental representations during reading* (pp. 169–193). Lawrence Erlbaum.

Crossley, S. A., Karumbaiah, S., Ocumpaugh, J., Labrum, M. J., & Baker, R. S. (2020). Predicting math identity through language and click-stream patterns in a blended learning mathematics program for elementary students. *Journal of Learning Analytics*, 7(1), 19–37. https://doi.org/10.18608/jla.2020.71.3

Crossley, S. A., Kim, M., Allen, L. K., & McNamara, D. S. (2019). Automated summarization evaluation (ASE) using natural language processing tools. In *Proceedings of the 20th International Conference of Artificial Intelligence in Education* (pp. 84–95). Lecture Notes in Computer Science, Vol. 11625. Springer.

Crossley, S. A., Kyle, K., & Dascalu, M. (2019). The Tool for the Automatic Analysis of Cohesion 2.0: Integrating semantic similarity and text overlap. *Behavior Research Methods, 51*(1), 14–27. https://doi.org/10.3758/s13428-018-1142-4

Crossley, S. A., Kyle, K., & McNamara, D. S. (2017). Sentiment Analysis and Social Cognition Engine (SEANCE): An automatic tool for sentiment, social cognition, and social-order analysis. *Behavior Research Methods, 49*(3), 803–821. https://doi.org/10.3758/s13428-016-0743-z

Dascalu, M., McNamara, D. S., Trausan-Matu, S., & Allen, L. K. (2018). Cohesion network analysis of CSCL participation. *Behavior Research Methods, 50*(2), 604–619. https://doi.org/10.3758/s13428-017-0888-4

Denton, C. A., Enos, M., York, M. J., Francis, D. J., Barnes, M. A., Kulesz, P. A., Fletcher, J. M., & Carter, S. (2015). Text-processing differences in adolescent adequate and poor comprehenders reading accessible and challenging narrative and informational text. *Reading Research Quarterly, 50*(4), 393–416. https://doi.org/10.1002/rrq.105

Devlin, J., Chang, M.-W., Lee, K., & Toutanova, K. (2018). Bert: Pretraining of deep bidirectional transformers for language understanding. *arXiv*, 1810.04805. https://doi.org/10.48550/arXiv.1810.04805

Dikli, S. (2006). An overview of automated scoring of essays. *The Journal of Technology, Learning, and Assessment, 5*(1), 1–35.

D'Mello, S. K., Craig, S. D., Witherspoon, A. W., McDaniel, B. T., & Graesser, A. C. (2008). Automatic detection of learner's affect from conversational cues. *User Modeling and User-Adapted Interaction, 18*(1–2), 45–80. https://doi.org/10.1007/s11257-007-9037-6

D'Mello, S. K., Graesser, A., & King, B. (2010). Toward spoken human-computer tutorial dialogues. *Human-Computer Interaction, 25*(4), 289–323. https://doi.org/10.1080/07370024.2010.499850

Dowell, N. M., Lin, Y., Godfrey, A., & Brooks, C. (2020). Exploring the relationship between emergent sociocognitive roles, collaborative problem-solving skills, and outcomes: A group communication analysis. *Journal of Learning Analytics, 7*(1), 38–57. https://doi.org/10.18608/jla.2020.71.4

Dowell, N. M. M., Nixon, T. M., & Graesser, A. C. (2019). Group communication analysis: A computational linguistics approach for detecting sociocognitive roles in multiparty interactions. *Behavior Research Methods, 51*(3), 1007–1041. https://doi.org/10.3758/s13428-018-1102-z

Elliott, S. (2003). IntelliMetric: From here to validity. In M. D. Shermis & J. Burstein (Eds.), *Automated essay scoring: A cross-disciplinary perspective* (pp. 71–86). Erlbaum.

Ericsson, K. A., & Simon, H. A. (1984). *Protocol analysis: Verbal reports as data*. MIT Press.

Ericsson, P. F., & Haswell, R. (Eds.). (2006). *Machine scoring of student essays: Truth and consequences*. Utah State University Press. https://doi.org/10.2307/j.ctt4cgq0p

Franzke, M., Kintsch, E., Caccamise, D., Johnson, N., & Dooley, S. (2005). Summary street: Computer support for comprehension and writing. *Journal of Educational Computing Research, 33*(1), 53–80. https://doi.org/10.2190/DH8F-QJWM-J457-FQVB

Gill, A., French, R., Gergle, D., & Oberlander, J. (2008). Identifying emotional characteristics from short blog texts. In B. C. Love, K. McRae & V. M. Sloutsky (Eds.), *Proceedings of the Annual Meeting of the Cognitive Science Society* (pp. 2237–2242). Cognitive Science Society.

Gilliam, S., Magliano, J. P., Millis, K. K., Levinstein, I., & Boonthum, C. (2007). Assessing the format of the presentation of text in developing a Reading Strategy Assessment Tool (R-SAT). *Behavior Research Methods, 39*(2), 199–204. https://doi.org/10.3758/BF03193148

Graesser, A. C. (2016). Conversations with AutoTutor help students learn. *International Journal of Artificial Intelligence in Education, 26*, 124–132.

Graesser, A. C., Hu, X., Rus, V., & Cai, Z. (2020). Conversation-based learning and assessment environments. In D. Yan, A. Rupp, & P. Foltz (Eds.), *Handbook of automated scoring: Theory into practice* (pp. 383–402). CRC Press/Taylor and Francis. https://doi.org/10.1201/9781351264808-21

Graesser, A. C., Jeon, M., & Dufty, D. (2008). Agent technologies designed to facilitate interactive knowledge construction. *Discourse Processes, 45*(4–5), 298–322. https://doi.org/10.1080/01638530802145395

Graesser, A. C., Lu, S., Jackson, G. T., Mitchell, H. H., Ventura, M., Olney, A., & Louwerse, M. M. (2004). AutoTutor: A tutor with dialogue in natural language. *Behavior Research Methods, Instruments, & Computers, 36*(2), 180–192. https://doi.org/10.3758/BF03195563

Graesser, A. C., & McNamara, D. S. (2011). Computational analyses of multilevel discourse comprehension. *Topics in Cognitive Science, 3*(2), 371–398. https://doi.org/10.1111/j.1756-8765.2010.01081.x

Graesser, A. C., Penumatsa, P., Ventura, M., Cai, Z., & Hu, X. (2007). Using LSA in AutoTutor: Learning through mixed initiative dialogue in natural language. In T. Landauer, D. McNamara, S. Dennis, & W. Kintsch (Eds.), *Handbook of latent semantic analysis* (pp. 243–262). Erlbaum.

Graham, S., & Perin, D. (2007). A meta-analysis of writing instruction for adolescent students. *Journal of Educational Psychology*, 99(3), 445–476. https://doi.org/10.1037/0022-0663.99.3.445

Griffiths, T. L. (2015). Manifesto for a new (computational) cognitive revolution. *Cognition*, 135, 21–23. https://doi.org/10.1016/j.cognition.2014.11.026

Hestenes, D., Wells, M., & Swackhamer, G. (1992). Force concept inventory. *The Physics Teacher*, 30(3), 141–158. https://doi.org/10.1119/1.2343497

Hirschberg, J., & Manning, C. D. (2015). Advances in natural language processing. *Science*, 349(6245), 261–266. https://doi.org/10.1126/science.aaa8685

Jackson, G. T., & Graesser, A. C. (2006). Applications of human tutorial dialog in AutoTutor: An intelligent tutoring system. *Revista Signos*, 39, 31–48.

Jackson, G. T., Guess, R. H., & McNamara, D. S. (2010). Assessing cognitively complex strategy use in an untrained domain. *Topics in Cognitive Science*, 2(1), 127–137. https://doi.org/10.1111/j.1756-8765.2009.01068.x

Jackson, G. T., & McNamara, D. S. (2013). Motivation and performance in a game-based intelligent tutoring system. *Journal of Educational Psychology*, 105(4), 1036–1049. https://doi.org/10.1037/a0032580

Johns, B. T., & Jamieson, R. K. (2018). A large-scale analysis of variance in written language. *Cognitive Science*, 42(4), 1360–1374. https://doi.org/10.1111/cogs.12583

Johnson, A., McCarthy, K. S., Kopp, K., Perret, C. A., & McNamara, D. S. (2017). Adaptive reading and writing instruction in iSTART and W-Pal. In Z. Markov & V. Rus (Eds.), *Proceedings of the 30th Annual Florida Artificial Intelligence Research Society International Conference (FLAIRS)* (pp. 561–566). AAAI Press.

Johnson, L. W., & Valente, A. (2008). Tactical language and culture training systems: Using artificial intelligence to teach foreign languages and cultures. *Proceedings of the Twentieth Conference on Innovative Applications of Artificial Intelligence*. AAAI Press.

Jones, M. N. (2017). *Big data in cognitive science*. Psychology Press: Taylor & Francis.

Jurafsky, D., & Martin, J. H. (2008). *Speech and language processing: An introduction to natural language processing, computational linguistics, and speech recognition*. Prentice-Hall.

Kyle, K. (2021). Natural language processing for learner corpus research. *International Journal of Learner Corpus Research*, 7(1), 1–16. https://doi.org/10.1075/ijlcr.00019.int

Kyle, K., Crossley, S., & Berger, C. (2018). The tool for the automatic analysis of lexical sophistication (TAALES): Version 2.0. *Behavior Research Methods*, 50(3), 1030–1046. https://doi.org/10.3758/s13428-017-0924-4

Kyle, K., & Crossley, S. A. (2018). Measuring syntactic complexity in L2 writing using fine-grained clausal and phrasal indices. *Modern Language Journal*, 102(2), 333–349. https://doi.org/10.1111/modl.12468

Landauer, T., McNamara, D. S., Dennis, S., & Kintsch, W. (Eds.). (2007). *Handbook of latent semantic analysis*. Erlbaum.

Landauer, T. K., Laham, D., & Foltz, P. W. (2003). Automatic essay assessment. *Assessment in Education: Principles, Policy & Practice*, 10(3), 295–308. https://doi.org/10.1080/0969594032000148154

Leacock, C., & Chodorow, M. (2003). C-rater: Automated scoring of short-answer questions. *Computers and the Humanities*, 37(4), 389–405. https://doi.org/10.1023/A:1025779619903

Levinstein, I. B., Boonthum, C., Pillarisetti, S. P., Bell, C., & McNamara, D. S. (2007). iSTART 2: Improvements for efficiency and effectiveness. *Behavior Research Methods*, 39(2), 224–232. https://doi.org/10.3758/BF03193151

Litman, D. (2016). Natural language processing for enhancing teaching and learning. *Proceedings of the AAAI Conference on Artificial Intelligence*, 30(1), 4170–4176. https://doi.org/10.1609/aaai.v30i1.9879

Litman, D. J., Rose, C. P., Forbes-Riley, K., VanLehn, K., Bhembe, D., & Silliman, S. (2006). Spoken versus typed human and computer dialogue tutoring. *International Journal of Artificial Intelligence in Education*, 16(2), 145–170.

Magliano, J. P., & Graesser, A. C. (2012). Computer-based assessment of student-constructed responses. *Behavior Research Methods*, 44(3), 608–621. https://doi.org/10.3758/s13428-012-0211-3

Magliano, J. P., Millis, K. K., The RSAT Development Team, Levinstein, I., & Boonthum, C. (2011). Assessing comprehension during reading with the Reading Strategy Assessment Tool (RSAT). *Metacognition and Learning*, 6, 131–154. https://doi.org/10.1007/s11409-010-9064-2

Magliano, J. P., Todaro, S., Millis, K. K., Wiemer-Hastings, K., Kim, H. J., & McNamara, D. S. (2005). Changes in reading strategies as a function of reading training: A comparison of live and computerized training. *Journal of Educational*

Computing Research, 32(2), 185–208. https://doi.org/10.2190/1LN8-7BQE-8TN0-M91L

Magliano, J. P., Trabasso, T., & Graesser, A. C. (1999). Strategic processing during comprehension. *Journal of Educational Psychology, 91*(4), 615–629. https://doi.org/10.1037/0022-0663.91.4.615

McCarthy, K. S., Likens, A. D., Johnson, A. M., Guerrero, T. A., & McNamara, D. S. (2018). Metacognitive overload! Positive and negative effects of metacognitive prompts in an intelligent tutoring system. *International Journal of Artificial Intelligence in Education, 28*(3), 420–438. https://doi.org/10.1007/s40593-018-0164-5

McCarthy, K. S., Watanabe, M., Dai, J., & McNamara, D. S. (2020). Personalized learning in iSTART: Past modifications and future design. *Journal of Research on Technology in Education, 52*(3), 301–321. https://doi.org/10.1080/15391523.2020.1716201

McNamara, D. S. (2004). SERT: Self-explanation reading training. *Discourse Processes, 38*(1), 1–30. https://doi.org/10.1207/s15326950dp3801_1

McNamara, D. S. (2017). Self-Explanation and Reading Strategy Training (SERT) Improves low-knowledge students' science course performance. *Discourse Processes, 54*(7), 479–492. https://doi.org/10.1080/0163853X.2015.1101328

McNamara, D. S. (2021). Chasing theory with technology: A quest to understand understanding. *Discourse Processes, 58*(5–6), 422–448. https://doi.org/10.1080/0163853X.2021.1917914

McNamara, D. S., Allen, L. K., Crossley, S. A., Dascalu, M., & Perret, C. A. (2017). Natural language processing and learning analytics. In G. Siemens & C. Lang (Eds.), *Handbook of learning analytics and educational data mining* (pp. 93–104). SOLAR. https://doi.org/10.18608/hla17.008

McNamara, D. S., Boonthum, C., Levinstein, I. B., & Millis, K. (2007). Evaluating self-explanations in iSTART: Comparing word-based and LSA algorithms. In T. Landauer, D. S. McNamara, S. Dennis, & W. Kintsch (Eds.), *Handbook of latent semantic analysis* (pp. 227–241). Erlbaum.

McNamara, D. S., Crossley, S. A., Roscoe, R. D., Allen, L. K., & Dai, J. (2015). Hierarchical classification approach to automated essay scoring. *Assessing Writing, 23*, 35–59. https://doi.org/10.1016/j.asw.2014.09.002

McNamara, D. S., Graesser, A. C., McCarthy, P., & Cai, Z. (2014). *Automated evaluation of text and discourse with Coh-Metrix*. Cambridge University Press. https://doi.org/10.1017/CBO9780511894664

McNamara, D. S., Levinstein, I. B., & Boonthum, C. (2004). iSTART: Interactive strategy training for active reading and thinking. *Behavior Research Methods, Instruments & Computers, 36*(2), 222–233. https://doi.org/10.3758/BF03195567

McNamara, D. S., O'Reilly, T., Rowe, M., Boonthum, C., & Levinstein, I. B. (2007). iSTART: A web-based tutor that teaches self-explanation and meta-cognitive reading strategies. In D. S. McNamara (Ed.), *Reading comprehension strategies: Theories, interventions, and technologies* (pp. 397–421). Erlbaum.

Mikolov, T., Sutskever, I., Chen, K., Corrado, G., & Dean, J. (2013). Distributed representations of words and phrases and their compositionally. In *Advances in Neural Information Processing Systems 26* (pp. 3111–3119). Curran Associates, Inc.

Millis, K., Kim, H. J., Todaro, S., Magliano, J. P., Wiemer-Hastings, K., & McNamara, D. S. (2004). Identifying reading strategies using latent semantic analysis: Comparing semantic benchmarks. *Behavior Research Methods, Instruments, & Computers, 36*(2), 213–221. https://doi.org/10.3758/BF03195566

Millis, K., & Magliano, J. (2012). Assessing comprehension processes during reading. In J. Sabatini, T. O'Reilly, & E. Albro (Eds.), *Reaching an understanding: Innovations in how we view reading assessment* (pp. 35–53). Rowman & Littlefield Education.

Müller-Frommeyer, L. C., Kauffeld, S., & Paxton, A. (2020). Beyond consistency: Contextual dependency of language style in monolog and conversation. *Cognitive Science, 44*(4), e12834. https://doi.org/10.1111/cogs.12834

Nye, B. D., Graesser, A. C., & Hu, X. (2014). AutoTutor and family: A review of 17 years of natural language tutoring. *International Journal of Artificial Intelligence in Education, 24*(4), 427–469. https://doi.org/10.1007/s40593-014-0029-5

Osgood, C. E., May, W. H., & Miron, M. (1975). *Cross-cultural universals of affective meaning*. University of Illinois Press.

Ozuru, Y., Best, R., & McNamara, D. S. (2004). Contribution of reading skill to learning from expository texts. In K. Forbus, D. Gentner, & T. Regier (Eds.), *Proceedings of the 26th Annual Cognitive Science Society* (pp. 1071–1076). Erlbaum.

Pang, B., & Lee, L. (2008). Opinion mining and sentiment analysis. *Foundations and Trends in Information Retrieval, 2*(1–2), 1–135. https://doi.org/10.1561/1500000011

Pennebaker, J. W. (2011). *The secret life of pronouns: What our words say about us*. Bloomsbury Press/Bloomsbury Publishing. https://doi.org/10.1016/S0262-4079(11)62167-2

Pennebaker, J. W., Booth, R. J., & Francis, M. E. (2007). Linguistic Inquiry and Word Count: LIWC 2007. Austin, TX: LIWC.net (https://www.liwc.net)

Pennebaker, J. W., Mehl, M. R., & Niederhoffer, K. G. (2003). Psychological aspects of natural language. use: Our words, our selves. *Annual Review of Psychology*, *54*(1), 547–577. https://doi.org/10.1146/annurev.psych.54.101601.145041

Pon-Barry, H., Clark, B., Schultz, K., Bratt, E. O., & Peters, S. (2004). Advantages of spoken language interaction in tutorial dialogue systems. In *Proceedings of the 7th International Conference on Intelligent Tutoring Systems* (pp. 390–400). Springer-Verlag.

Roscoe, R. D., Allen, L. K., Weston, J. L., Crossley, S. A., & McNamara, D. S. (2014). The Writing Pal intelligent tutoring system: Usability testing and development. *Computers and Composition*, *34*, 39–59. https://doi.org/10.1016/j.compcom.2014.09.002

Roscoe, R. D., & McNamara, D. S. (2013). Writing Pal: Feasibility of an intelligent writing strategy tutor in the high school classroom. *Journal of Educational Psychology*, *105*(4), 1010–1025. https://doi.org/10.1037/a0032340

Roscoe, R. D., Snow, E. L., Allen, L. K., & McNamara, D. S. (2015). Automated detection of essay revising patterns: Application for intelligent feedback in a writing tutor. *Technology, Instruction, Cognition, & Learning*, *10*(1), 59–79.

Ross, J. A., Rolheiser, C., & Hogaboam-Gray, A. (1999). Effects of self-evaluation training on narrative writing. *Assessing Writing*, *6*(1), 107–132. https://doi.org/10.1016/S1075-2935(99)00003-3

Rude, S. S., Gortner, E. M., & Pennebaker, J. W. (2004). Language use of depressed and depression-vulnerable college students. *Cognition and Emotion*, *18*(8), 1121–1133. https://doi.org/10.1080/02699930441000030

Rudner, L. M., Garcia, V., & Welch, C. (2006). An evaluation of the IntelliMetric essay scoring system. *The Journal of Technology, Learning, and Assessment*, *4*(4), 1–22.

Ruseti, S., Dascalu, M., Johnson, A. M., McNamara, D. S., Balyan, R., McCarthy, K. S., & Trausan-Matu, S. (2018). Scoring summaries using recurrent neural networks. In R. Nkambou, R. Azevedo, & J. Vassileva, (Eds.), *Proceedings of the 14th International Conference on Intelligent Tutoring Systems (ITS) in Montreal, Canada* (pp. 191–201). Springer.

Russell, J. A. (2003). Core affect and the psychological construction of emotion. *Psychological Review*, *110*(1), 145–172. https://doi.org/10.1037/0033-295X.110.1.145

Samsonovich, A., & Ascoli, G. (2006). Cognitive map dimensions of the human value system extracted from natural language. In B. Goertzel & P. Wang (Eds.), *Advances in artificial general intelligence: Concepts, architectures and algorithms* (pp. 111–124). IOS Press.

Shermis, M. D., & Burstein, J. (Eds.). (2003). *Automated essay scoring: A cross-disciplinary perspective*. Erlbaum.

Shermis, M. D., Burstein, J., Higgins, D., & Zechner, K. (2010). Automated essay scoring: Writing assessment and instruction. In E. Baker, B. McGaw, & N. S. Petersen (Eds.), *International encyclopedia of education* (3rd ed.). Elsevier. https://doi.org/10.1016/B978-0-08-044894-7.00233-5

Stirman, S. W., & Pennebaker, J. W. (2001). Word use in the poetry of suicidal and nonsuicidal poets. *Psychosomatic Medicine*, *63*(4), 517–522. https://doi.org/10.1097/00006842-200107000-00001

Strapparava, C., & Valitutti, A. (2004). *WordNet Affect: An affective extension of WordNet*. In *Proceedings of the Fourth International Conference on Language Resources and Evaluation* (pp. 1083–1086). European Language Resources Association.

Tausczik, Y. R., & Pennebaker, J. W. (2010). The psychological meaning of words: LIWC and computerized text analysis methods. *Journal of Language and Social Psychology*, *29*(1), 24–54. https://doi.org/10.1177/0261927X09351676

VanLehn, K., Graesser, A. C., Jackson, G. T., Jordan, P., Olney, A., & Rosé, C. P. (2007). When are tutorial dialogues more effective than reading? *Cognitive Science*, *31*(1), 3–62. https://doi.org/10.1080/03640210709336984

Warschauer, M., & Ware, P. (2006). Automated writing evaluation: Defining the classroom research agenda. *Language Teaching Research*, *10*(2), 157–180. https://doi.org/10.1191/1362168806lr190oa

Watanabe, M., McCarthy, K., & McNamara, D. S. (2019). Examining the effects of adaptive task selection on students' motivation in an intelligent tutoring system. In *Proceedings of the 9th International Conference on Learning Analytics and Knowledge* (pp. 161–162). SOLAR.

Wiebe, J., Wilson, T., & Cardie, C. (2005). Annotating expressions of opinions and emotions in language. *Language Resources and Evaluation*, *39*(2–3), 165–210. https://doi.org/10.1007/s10579-005-7880-9

Woolf, B. P. (2009). *Building intelligent interactive tutors*. Morgan Kaufmann Publishers.

Yan, D., Rupp, A. C., & Foltz, P. W. (Eds.). (2020). *Handbook of automated scoring: Theory into practice*. Chapman and Hall, CRC Press.

Section 3

PSYCHOLOGICAL TESTS

CHAPTER 18

OBJECTIVE TESTS AS INSTRUMENTS OF PSYCHOLOGICAL THEORY AND RESEARCH

David Watson

The goal of this chapter is to help researchers understand, create, and evaluate objective psychological tests. Its restricted focus, therefore, reflects the traditional psychometric differentiation between *objective* and *projective* tests (Loevinger, 1957), a distinction that some have questioned (e.g., Meyer & Kurtz, 2006). According to Loevinger (1957), the distinction between these two types of tests primarily "rests on item structure. Projective tests involve free response . . . whereas objective tests, in the sense that the term is used here, require in principle that every individual choose one of the stated alternatives for each item" (p. 648). Similarly, Meyer and Kurtz (2006) stated that

> the term *objective* typically refers to instruments in which the stimulus is an adjective, proposition, or question that is presented to a person who is required to indicate how accurately it describes his or her personality using a limited set of externally provided response options (true vs. false, yes vs. no, Likert scale, etc.). What is *objective* about such a procedure is that the psychologist administering the test does not need to rely on judgment to classify or interpret the test-taker's response; the intended response is clearly indicated and scored according to a pre-existing key. (p. 233)

CLASSIFYING OBJECTIVE TESTS

Ability Versus Nonability Tests

Objective tests can be further subdivided on a number of dimensions. One classic distinction is between *ability* and *nonability* tests (Anastasi & Urbina, 1997; Kaplan & Saccuzzo, 2009). These two types of tests differ markedly in terms of (a) how the target constructs typically are assessed and (b) their resultant susceptibility to faking.

For instance, it now is well established that work performance is significantly influenced by both ability and personality factors. More specifically, individuals who are smart and conscientious tend to be better employees (Roberts et al., 2007; Sackett & Walmsley, 2014; Schmidt et al., 2008). Psychologists typically assess intelligence by obtaining performance samples; for instance, respondents are asked to solve math problems, detect patterns, recall or complete sequences, and define the meaning of words. In the absence of cheating, this makes it virtually impossible to fake one's level of ability. In contrast, nonability tests assess thoughts, feelings, behaviors, and preferences. For instance, a typical conscientiousness scale asks respondents to indicate how reliable, dependable, and goal-oriented they are. It, therefore, is quite easy for respondents to misrepresent themselves as having attributes (e.g., dependability, goal motivation) that they actually do not possess, which creates problems when using these measures in high-stakes testing. This chapter discusses issues related to both types of tests, although the primary focus is on nonability tests.

Broad Versus Narrow Tests

Objective tests also can be classified according to their scope and breadth of coverage. In this regard, it now is clear that most important psychological domains (e.g., ability, personality, affect, psychopathology) are ordered hierarchically at multiple levels of abstraction or breadth (e.g., Markon et al., 2005; Schmidt & Hunter, 2004; Watson, 2005). For example, the broad higher order trait of conscientiousness can be decomposed into several distinct yet empirically correlated components, such as deliberation (i.e., conscientious individuals plan carefully before acting), dependability (i.e., conscientious individuals are reliable and responsible), and achievement striving (i.e., conscientious individuals are willing to work hard to achieve long-term goals; Markon et al., 2005; Watson et al., 2019). Similarly, in the domain of cognitive ability, the overarching dimension of g or general mental ability (Schmidt & Hunter, 2004; Spearman, 1904) can be decomposed into more specific abilities, such as verbal comprehension, perceptual reasoning, working memory, and processing speed (Benson et al., 2010; Bowden et al., 2006). In a related vein, Kotov et al. (2017) and others have proposed complex, multilevel hierarchical models of psychopathology. Issues related to both general and more specific measures are examined in this chapter.

PSYCHOMETRICS: A HISTORICAL OVERVIEW

To understand, create, and evaluate objective tests, it is necessary to examine basic concepts and principles of psychological measurement.

This topic can seem intimidating, in part because of the large number of potentially relevant concepts. Within the broad domain of validity, for instance, one encounters a confusing array of terms, including *concurrent validity*, *construct validity*, *content validity*, *criterion validity*, *discriminant validity*, *external validity*, *face validity*, *incremental validity*, and *predictive validity* (e.g., Anastasi & Urbina, 1997; Kaplan & Saccuzzo, 2009; Simms & Watson, 2007; Watson, 2006).

To place these concepts into a meaningful context, I outline the evolution of psychometric thinking over the last century. This thinking has revolved around the interplay of two core concepts—reliability and validity. *Reliability* can be defined as the consistency of scores that are obtained across repeated assessments (Anastasi & Urbina, 1997; Kaplan & Saccuzzo, 2009; Revelle & Condon, 2019; Watson, 2006). Reliability was the dominant concern among psychometricians and test developers during the first half of the 20th century, largely because it appeared to be a more straightforward and scientifically rigorous concept than validity. As I demonstrate subsequently, however, this apparent straightforwardness was deceptive; in fact, classical reliability theory was based on questionable assumptions that are unlikely to be fully met in many important areas of research. Moreover, it eventually was discovered that maximizing reliability (or, to put it more accurately, maximizing the value of conventional indicators of reliability) actually could be counterproductive and could lead to the creation of less informative measures (the "attenuation paradox"; see Loevinger, 1954, 1957); the nature of this paradox is explained in the section Reliability later in this chapter.

Consequently, reliability gradually lost its position of preeminence and was supplanted by validity as the conceptual centerpiece of measurement (although interest in reliability has resurged in the 21st century, as discussed in the section Reliability). In the current *Standards for Educational and Psychological Testing* (American Educational Research Association [AERA], American Psychological Association [APA], &

National Council on Measurement in Education [NCME], 2014), *validity* is defined as "the degree to which evidence and theory support the interpretations of test scores for proposed uses of tests. Validity is, therefore, the most fundamental consideration in developing and evaluating tests" (p. 11). Throughout most of the 20th century, psychometricians distinguished between several distinct types of validity, including content validity, criterion validity, and construct validity. For instance, the 1974 edition of the *Standards* stated,

> The kinds of validity depend upon the kinds of inferences one might wish to draw from test scores. Four interdependent kinds of inferential interpretation are traditionally described to summarize most test use: the *criterion-related* validities (*predictive* and *concurrent*); *content* validity; and *construct* validity. (pp. 25–26)

A major breakthrough occurred in the 1990s, however, when it was recognized that all other types of validity simply represent specific aspects of the all-encompassing process of construct validity (AERA, APA, & NCME, 1999, 2014; Messick, 1995). Thus, according to the current *Standards,* "Validity is a unitary concept. It is the degree to which all the accumulated evidence supports the intended interpretation of test scores for the proposed use" (AERA, APA, & NCME, 2014, pp. 13–14). Moreover, this expanded conceptualization of construct validity also subsumes all of the major types of reliability evidence, including both internal consistency and retest reliability. As Messick (1995) put it, "Construct validity is based on an integration of any evidence that bears on the interpretation or meaning of the test scores" (p. 742). Consequently, construct validity—a concept that originally was articulated by Cronbach and Meehl (1955)—has emerged as the central unifying principle in contemporary psychometrics.

Another crucial insight was the recognition that construct validity is not simply a process of evaluating the properties of an already developed test. Rather, it also serves as the basic principle for creating and refining new tests. Put differently, construct validity considerations should guide the entire process of scale creation. Loevinger (1957) originally articulated this view; many others subsequently have elaborated it (e.g., Clark & Watson, 1995, 2019; Messick, 1995; Simms & Watson, 2007; Watson, 2006). Loevinger (1957) divided the scale development and validation process into three basic phases: the substantive, the structural, and the external. The following discussion follows this framework.

SUBSTANTIVE VALIDITY: DEVELOPMENT OF THE INITIAL ITEM POOL

Literature Review

The substantive phase primarily addresses issues related to the traditional psychometric concept of content validity. It begins with a thorough review of the relevant literature to discover how others have attempted to conceptualize and measure the target construct under consideration. Initially, this review should include previous attempts to assess both the same construct and any closely related "near neighbor" concepts. Subsequently, the review should be broadened to encompass more tangentially related concepts to help define the conceptual boundaries of the target construct. Suppose, for instance, that one is interested in creating a new measure of guilt. One initially might focus on prior attempts to assess guilt and closely related affective states, such as shame and embarrassment. Eventually, however, a thorough review of the literature would reveal that a broad array of negative mood states (including guilt, shame, embarrassment, anxiety, depression, anger, and disgust) are strongly intercorrelated (Watson, 2005; Watson & Clark, 1984, 1992; Watson & Stanton, 2017), so that it is important to clarify the hypothesized relation between guilt and these other negative affects as well. In this way, a test developer can begin to create a predicted pattern of convergent and discriminant relations at the earliest stages of scale development (see Clark & Watson, 1995; Watson, 2006).

A comprehensive review of the literature is important for several reasons. First, it will explicate the nature and range of the content subsumed within the target construct. Second, it can help to identify possible problems in existing measures (e.g., confusing instructions, suboptimal response formats, poorly functioning item content) that then can be avoided. Finally—and most important—a thorough review will indicate whether the proposed new instrument is actually needed. If a good measure of the target construct already exists, why create another? The burden of proof is on the prospective test developer to articulate clearly how this new instrument represents a theoretical or empirical advance over existing measures; in the absence of such proof, there is no real justification for adding to the needless proliferation of assessment instruments.

Construct Conceptualization

Assuming that the test developer concludes that the new instrument actually is needed, the critical next step is to develop a precise and detailed conception of the target construct that will be the focus of assessment. Of course, test developers always have at least a sketchy understanding of what it is they are trying to measure. By itself, however, a vague conceptualization is insufficient and may create problems that reveal themselves in subsequent stages of the validation process. Unfortunately, many investigators fail to take the important next step of fleshing out the nature and scope of the target construct more precisely. Clark and Watson (1995, 2019) have recommended writing out a brief, formal description of the target construct, which can be useful in crystallizing one's conceptual model. An even better strategy would be to articulate a detailed measurement model that specifies both (a) the nature and scope of the overall construct and (b) all of the major hypothesized facets or subcomponents within it.

Suppose, for example, that a researcher is interested in developing a new measure of specific phobia. What is the appropriate range of content that should be included in this measure (for a discussion of this issue, see Watson, 2005, 2009b)? Moreover, what specific symptom dimensions might meaningfully emerge as subcomponents within this domain? The fifth edition of *Diagnostic and Statistical Manual of Mental Disorders* (DSM–5; American Psychiatric Association, 2013) formally recognizes four subtypes of specific phobia: animal, natural environment (e.g., storms, heights, water), blood–injection–injury, and situational (e.g., airplanes, elevators, enclosed spaces) fears. Does a review of the relevant literature support the value of this quadripartite scheme, or should an alternative measurement model be created? These types of issues all should be clearly addressed before creating the initial item pool.

Creation of the Initial Item Pool
Comprehensiveness and overinclusiveness.
Once the nature and scope of the content domain have been clarified, one can begin the actual task of item writing (see Clark & Watson, 1995, 2019, for a discussion of basic principles of good item writing). No data analytic technique can remedy significant deficiencies in the initial item pool; consequently, the creation of this pool is an absolutely critical stage in test development.

The basic goal is to sample systematically all content that potentially is relevant to the target construct. As Loevinger (1957) put it, "The items of the pool should be chosen so as to sample all possible contents which might comprise the putative trait according to all known alternative theories of the trait" (p. 659). Two key implications of this principle of overinclusiveness are that the initial item pool should (a) be broader and more inclusive than one's own theoretical view of the target construct and (b) include content that ultimately will be shown to be unrelated to this construct. The logic underlying this principle is simple: Subsequent analyses can identify weak, unrelated items that should be dropped, but they are powerless to detect relevant content that should have been included but was not. Thus, this principle of overinclusiveness ultimately serves the fundamental goal of *comprehensiveness*, which is a key consideration in establishing the content validity of a test (Haynes et al., 1995; Messick, 1995).

Representativeness. Another important consideration is *representativeness*, that is, the degree to which the item pool provides an adequate sample of each of the major content areas within the domain subsumed by the target construct (Clark & Watson, 1995; Haynes et al., 1995). To ensure that each important aspect of the construct is assessed adequately, some psychometricians recommend that formal, rational item groups be created to tap each major content area within a domain (see Simms & Watson, 2007; Watson, 2006). Hogan (1983; see also Hogan & Hogan, 1992) called these rational groupings "homogeneous item composites" (HICs).

For instance, the Inventory of Depression and Anxiety Symptoms (IDAS; Watson et al., 2007, 2008) is a multidimensional measure of mood and anxiety disorder symptoms. To assess symptoms of depression, the first step was the creation of an overinclusive pool of 117 items. In creating this item pool, the basic strategy was to include multiple markers—typically, a minimum of six items per target construct to ensure that any resulting factors are well defined—to assess all of the symptom dimensions that potentially could emerge in subsequent structural analyses. To ensure that sufficient markers were included for each potential dimension, the candidate items were rationally organized into 13 HICs, each of which contained eight to 14 items. Nine HICs corresponded to the basic symptom criteria for a major depressive episode (e.g., depressed mood, anhedonia/loss of interest, appetite disturbance). Four additional HICs tapped symptoms potentially relevant to the hopelessness subtype of depression (Abramson et al., 1989), the specific symptom features of melancholic depression (Joiner et al., 2005), angry and irritable mood (which can be an alternative expression of depressed mood in children and adolescents; APA, 2013), and markers of high energy and positive affect (which are negatively related to depressive symptoms; see Watson, 2009a). Finally, to help define the boundaries of this domain, seven additional HICs—containing six to 14 items—assessed various symptoms of anxiety (e.g., worry, panic, social anxiety).

It must be emphasized that the creation of rational HICs does not force a particular structure onto the items; rather, it simply ensures that hypothesized dimensions and scales have a reasonable opportunity to emerge in subsequent structural analyses. To illustrate this point, Table 18.1 presents the items from two of the final, factor analytically derived IDAS scales—dysphoria and lassitude—along with their initial HIC placements. As can be seen, each factor-based scale includes items from three or more of the original HICs; both scales contain items related to two or more symptom criteria for a major depressive episode (e.g., Lassitude contains items related to both sleep disturbance and fatigue/anergia). Clearly, organizing items into rational, content-based groups does not force them to define a single common scale.

TABLE 18.1

Final Scale Assignments and Initial HIC Placements of Selected IDAS Items

Final scale/item	Initial HIC placement
Dysphoria	
I felt depressed	Depressed mood (C1)
I had little interest in my usual hobbies or activities	Anhedonia (C2)
I felt fidgety, restless	Motor problems (C5)
I talked more slowly than usual	Motor problems (C5)
I felt inadequate	Worthlessness/guilt (C7)
I blamed myself for things	Worthlessness/guilt (C7)
I had trouble concentrating	Cognitive problems (C8)
I had trouble making up my mind	Cognitive problems (C8)
I felt discouraged about things	Hopelessness
I found myself worrying all the time	Worry
Lassitude	
I had trouble waking up in the morning	Sleep disturbance (C4)
I slept more than usual	Sleep disturbance (C4)
I felt exhausted	Fatigue/anergia (C6)
I felt drowsy, sleepy	Fatigue/anergia (C6)
It took a lot of effort to get me going	Fatigue/anergia (C6)
I felt much worse in the morning	Melancholic depression

Note. Numbers in parentheses indicate corresponding *Diagnostic and Statistical Manual of Mental Disorders* (5th ed.; American Psychiatric Association, 2013) symptom criteria for a major depressive episode. HIC = homogeneous item composite. IDAS = Inventory of Depression and Anxiety Symptoms.

Relevance. A final substantive consideration is *relevance* (Haynes et al., 1995; Messick, 1995), which is the requirement that all of the item content in the finished instrument should fall within the boundaries of the target construct. This requirement may seem incompatible with the earlier principle of overinclusiveness, but it is not. The principle of overinclusiveness simply stipulates that some marginally relevant content should be included in the initial item pool to clarify the boundaries of the construct. Subsequent psychometric analyses then can determine these limits and identify construct-irrelevant content that ultimately should be discarded. Relevance-related concerns arise when this inappropriate content is not discarded for some reason.

This property of content relevance may sound easy to attain in principle, but it often is more difficult to achieve in practice. One complicating factor is the dynamic nature of content validity (Haynes et al., 1995; Watson, 2006). As our understanding of the target construct evolves, content that previously was placed within the domain may now fall beyond its boundaries. An excellent example of this dynamic process can be seen in the assessment of anxiety and depression symptoms. Before the 1980s, most test developers failed to distinguish clearly between these constructs. Because of this, many older depression measures contain significant anxiety-related content and vice versa (Clark & Watson, 1991; Gotlib & Cane, 1989). This irrelevant content now is judged to highly problematic, given that it necessarily lessens the discriminant validity of these instruments.

Pilot Testing

At some point during the substantive phase—and before finalizing the initial item pool—many psychometricians strongly recommend that test developers pilot test their new instruments using methods such as cognitive interviews (Clark & Watson, 1995; Haynes et al., 1995; Lee, 2014; Simms & Watson, 2007). Pilot testing may involve a small amount of initial data collection, and it typically includes obtaining feedback from content experts and/or representatives of the target population (e.g., a group of trauma survivors for a proposed measure of posttraumatic growth). Pilot testing can be invaluable in identifying potential problems in the instructions and response format (e.g., confusing instructions, ambiguous response anchors) and in the items themselves (e.g., items that are unclear or can be interpreted in multiple ways). It also can identify significant gaps in the content coverage of the initial item pool (e.g., important content areas that should have been included but were not).

STRUCTURAL VALIDITY

Structural Fidelity

Structural fidelity is the basic principle underlying the structural phase of construct validation (Loevinger, 1957; see also Messick, 1995; Watson, 2006). This is the idea that the internal structure of the scale (i.e., the correlations among its component items) should be fully consistent with what is known about the internal organization of the underlying construct. In light of the fact that most constructs are posited to be homogeneous and internally consistent, this principle typically requires that the items in a test also should be homogeneous and internally consistent (although exceptions to this general rule are discussed in the section Reliability). Because of this, the structural phase also subsumes traditional forms of reliability evidence. Accordingly, the discussion of this stage will begin with an examination of the basic principles and methods of item selection and then turn to a consideration of major forms of reliability.

Methods of Item Selection

Classical test methods. After collecting data on the items in the initial pool, the next crucial step in the test construction process is to decide which of the items should be retained in the final scale(s). Several basic strategies can guide item selection. One strategy, criterion keying, is the focus of Volume 1, Chapter 18. Consequently, the following discussion is limited to methods based on some form of internal consistency analysis.

Currently, the most widely used item selection method is based on classical test theory and involves the use of factor analysis to identify groups of interrelated items (Clark & Watson, 1995, 2019; Floyd & Widaman, 1995). In the early stages of test construction, exploratory factor analysis (EFA) should be used to identify the underlying latent dimensions, which then can serve as a basis for creating the final scales (see also Clark & Watson, 1995, 2019; Simms & Watson, 2007); the resulting scales then can be refined using confirmatory factor analysis (CFA), where needed. Consistent with general guidelines in the broader factor analytic literature (see Fabrigar et al., 1999; Floyd & Widaman, 1995; D. W. Russell, 2002), principal factor analysis is recommended over principal components analysis as the initial extraction method in EFA.

Orthogonal (typically varimax) and oblique (e.g., promax, oblimin) rotations both offer unique advantages that are invaluable in identifying the optimal set of items, and it, therefore, is recommended that both be used in the item selection process (for discussions of different factor rotations, see Fabrigar et al., 1999; D. W. Russell, 2002). The chief advantage of oblique rotations (which allow the factors to be correlated) is that they model the associations among the factors; this, in turn, helps to identify potential discriminant validity problems in the resulting scales (i.e., strongly correlated factors likely will translate into strongly correlated scales). The primary advantage of orthogonal rotations (which constrain the factors to be uncorrelated) is that they are better at identifying "splitter" items, that is, items that have significant cross-loadings on two or more factors. Splitters tend to create discriminant validity problems (by increasing correlations among scales) and, therefore, are prime candidates for deletion.

This recommendation to use both oblique and orthogonal rotations may be surprising to some, particularly in light of the common misconception that orthogonal rotations should not be used when one is interested in assessing moderately to strongly correlated constructs (e.g., different subtypes of specific phobia, different facets of conscientiousness). Although this misconception seems intuitively compelling (how can uncorrelated factors validly capture correlated constructs?), the fact is that orthogonal rotations can be used to construct scales that are moderately to strongly correlated once simple unit weighting is employed. For instance, Watson and Clark (1999) used orthogonal varimax rotations to create the scales included in the expanded form of the Positive and Negative Affect Schedule (PANAS-X). Despite this strict reliance on orthogonal rotation, several of the resulting scales consistently show correlations of .50 and greater with one another (Watson, 2005; Watson & Clark, 1999). These substantial correlations reflect the fact that unit-weighted scales model the influence of nonzero cross-loadings on other factors.

In an EFA-based approach, the basic idea is to select items that load moderately to strongly on the target factor (typically, at least |.35| or greater when conducting a principal factor analysis) and have much lower loadings on all other factors (Clark & Watson, 1995, 2019; Simms & Watson, 2007). Regardless of the specific strategy that is used, the goal is to select items that are moderately correlated with one another (I subsequently discuss why one should avoid selecting strongly correlated items). Clark and Watson (1995, 2019) have recommended that the average interitem correlation generally should fall in the .15 to .50 range. This wide range is provided because the optimal value necessarily will vary with the generality versus specificity of the target construct. If one is measuring a relatively broad higher-order construct such as conscientiousness, a lower mean interitem correlation (e.g., a value in the .15–.30 range) likely will be optimal. In contrast, to measure a narrower construct such as deliberation, a higher mean correlation (e.g., in the .35–.50 range) likely will be needed. Again, the key principle is structural fidelity: The magnitude of the item intercorrelations should faithfully reflect the internal organization of the underlying construct.

Item response theory. Item response theory (IRT; Embretson, 1996; Reise et al., 2005;

Reise & Waller, 2009; Simms & Watson, 2007; Thomas, 2019) is increasingly being used in scale development (see Clark & Watson, 2019). IRT is based on the assumption that test responses reflect levels of an underlying trait and, moreover, that the relation between the response and the trait can be described for each item by a monotonically increasing function called an *item characteristic curve* (ICC). Individuals with higher levels of the trait have greater expected probabilities for answering the item in the keyed direction (e.g., quantitatively gifted individuals are more likely to get a math problem correct), and the ICC provides the precise values of these probabilities at each level of the trait.

In IRT, the emphasis is on identifying those items that are likely to be most informative for each individual respondent, given their level of the underlying trait. For instance, a challenging problem in calculus may provide useful information for an individual with a high level of quantitative ability (who may or may not be able to get it correct), but it will be useless if given to an individual with little facility in mathematics (because one knows in advance that they will get it wrong). From an IRT perspective, the optimal item to be administered next is one that the individual has a 50% probability of endorsing in the keyed direction—given what is known about that individual's trait level on the basis of their responses to previous items—because this conveys the maximum amount of new trait-relevant information for that person.

A variety of one-, two-, and three-parameter IRT models have been proposed (Reise & Waller, 2003). Of these, a two-parameter model—more specifically, one with parameters for item difficulty and item discrimination—has been applied most consistently in the literature (Clark & Watson, 2019; Simms & Watson, 2007). Item difficulty refers to the point along the trait continuum at which a given item has a 50% probability of being endorsed in the keyed direction. High difficulty values are associated with items that have low endorsement probabilities (i.e., that reflect higher levels of the trait). Discrimination reflects the degree of psychometric precision, or information, that is provided by the item.

In comparison with other item selection approaches, IRT offers two important advantages. First, it enables the test developer to determine the trait level at which a given item is maximally informative. This information, in turn, can be used to identify a set of items that yields precise, reliable assessment across the entire range of the trait. Put differently, IRT-based scales offer an improved ability to discriminate among individuals at the extreme ends of the trait distribution (e.g., among those both very high and very low in quantitative ability). Second, IRT methods allow one to estimate an individual's trait level without having to rely on a fixed, standard set of items. This property permits the development of computer-adaptive tests in which assessment is focused primarily on the subset of items that are maximally informative for each individual respondent (e.g., difficult items for quantitatively gifted individuals, easier items for those low in mathematical ability). Computer adaptive tests are extremely efficient and can yield the same amount of trait-relevant information using far fewer items than conventional measures (typically providing item savings of 50% or more; see Embretson, 1996; Reise & Waller, 2009).

IRT can be an extremely useful adjunct to other scale development methods, such as EFA. As a scale development technique, its main limitation is that it requires a good working knowledge of the basic underlying traits that need to be modeled. Put differently, it requires that one's measurement model already be reasonably well established. Consequently, IRT methods are most useful in those domains in which the basic constructs already are well known; conversely, it is less helpful in areas in which these constructs still need to be identified. Thus, EFA remains the basic method of choice for the early stages of assessment within a domain. Once the basic factors, scales, and constructs within the domain have been identified, they can be further refined using approaches such as CFA and IRT. Clark and Watson (2019) emphasized that IRT plays a particularly valuable role in the creation of short forms.

Finally, IRT can be used to assess differential item functioning (DIF; Thomas, 2019). Analyses of DIF can be invaluable in identifying items that are biased (i.e., perform differently) as a function of gender, race, age or other variables. For example, Teresi et al. (2009) performed DIF analyses of depression items as a function of gender. Most items performed similarly across women and men. However, the item "I felt like crying" demonstrated significant bias, such that women received higher scores given the same level of depression. Similarly, Thibodeau and Asmundson (2014) found that most depression symptoms behaved similarly across gender; however, an item assessing appetite change was biased, such that women obtained higher scores at the same level of depression. Even when significant bias was observed, it often was negligible in magnitude (e.g., Thibodeau & Asmundson, 2014). Nevertheless, replicated evidence of nonnegligible bias indicates that an item is problematic and needs to be handled differently across groups.

Sampling. This discussion of item bias highlights the importance of obtaining representative samples—that is, groups of participants who accurately reflect the ultimate target population of the instrument—at all stages of the scale development process. In the psychopathology literature, for instance, it long has been considered problematic to use college student samples to develop scales that are intended for use in clinical populations; in addition to their generally superior level of functioning, college students tend to differ from patients on a number of potentially important demographic variables (such as age). The general principle here is that one should not assume that the psychometric principles of an instrument are invariant across variables such as sex, age, and race/ethnicity. In this regard, Dong and Dumas (2020) recently reviewed the measurement invariance of personality measures (including scales assessing personality pathology) across cultures and ethnic groups (26 studies), gender (42 studies), and age (26 items). Their results demonstrated that personality measures were reasonably robust across gender and age but showed much less generalizability across ethnic and cultural groups.

Reliability

Overview. As noted earlier, reliability evidence is now subsumed within the all-encompassing concept of construct validity. There are two common methods for estimating reliability: internal consistency and test–retest reliability. Both of these methods—at least as they typically are employed—are better viewed as indicators of the consistency of measurement across various conditions rather than reliability per se. Indeed, they may either overestimate or underestimate the true level of reliability (as it is strictly defined) under various conditions.

To understand the material that follows, I summarize the central assumptions of classical reliability theory (Anastasi & Urbina, 1997; Kaplan & Saccuzzo, 2009; Revelle & Condon, 2019; Watson, 2006). According to the logic that originally was articulated by Spearman (1910), any observed score can be decomposed into two independent components: the true score and measurement error. The true score (e.g., the individual's true level of intelligence or conscientiousness) is assumed to be invariant and perfectly correlated across different assessment conditions. Conversely, measurement error is assumed to be entirely random; consequently, this component should fluctuate chaotically and be entirely uncorrelated across different assessment conditions. Within this framework, reliability can be defined as the ratio of true score variance to total (i.e., observed score) variance.

These assumptions further explain two important features of classical reliability theory. First, reliability and error were equated with consistency (i.e., the extent to which indicators of the construct are correlated across different assessments) and inconsistency (i.e., a lack of correlation across assessments), respectively. Accordingly, regardless of the specific method that is used, reliability estimates increase in magnitude as the assessed indicators of the construct (e.g., different items within a scale; different administrations of the same test over time; parallel forms of a test) become more highly interrelated. Second, reliability generally should increase as more and more indicators are aggregated together. This is because random errors are, by definition, uncorrelated across assessments and, therefore, they should increasingly cancel each other out as more observations are aggregated.

Internal consistency. Structural fidelity is the guiding consideration in evaluating the internal consistency of an objective test: The correlations among the items should faithfully parallel the internal organization of the underlying construct. Given that most constructs are posited to be homogeneous and internally consistent, the application of this principle typically means that the selected items also should be homogeneous and internally consistent. There are exceptions, however. These exceptions involve cases in which the items are designed to be causal (or formative) indicators (i.e., causal contributors to some cumulative index) rather than effect (or reflective) indicators (i.e., specific manifestations of a latent underlying construct; Bollen & Diamantopoulos, 2017; Smith & McCarthy, 1995; Watson, 2006). This commonly is the case in the measurement of stress and trauma. For example, Simms et al. (2002) created a severe exposures index (SEI) to assess combat-related trauma. The SEI consisted of three items: "come under small arms fire," "exposure to nerve gas," and "exposure to mustard gas or other blistering agents." In this case, there is no expectation or requirement that these items should be significantly intercorrelated—for instance, that individuals who came under small arms fire also were more likely to be exposed to nerve gas. Rather, these items simply are seen as causal/formative contributors that jointly create a cumulative index of combat-related trauma. It sometimes is unclear whether a given variable is a cause or an effect indicator. In such cases, statistical tests have been developed to help researchers make the appropriate decision (e.g., Bollen & Ting, 2000).

In most cases, however, the goal of assessment is to measure one thing (i.e., the target construct)—and only one thing—as precisely as possible. Unfortunately, many test developers and users continue to believe that item homogeneity can be established simply by demonstrating that a scale shows an acceptable level of internal consistency, as estimated by traditional indexes, such as K–R 20 (Kuder & Richardson, 1937) and coefficient alpha (Cronbach, 1951). Psychometricians, however, have long discouraged the practice of relying on these conventional reliability indexes to establish the homogeneity of a scale (Clark & Watson, 1995, 2019; Cortina, 1993; Revelle & Condon, 2019; Schmitt, 1996; Simms & Watson, 2007; Watson, 2006).

To understand this point, one must distinguish between internal consistency on the one hand and homogeneity or unidimensionality on the other. *Internal consistency* refers to the overall degree to which the items that make up the scale are interrelated, whereas *homogeneity* and *unidimensionality* indicate whether the items assess a single underlying factor or construct (Clark & Watson, 1995, 2019; Cortina, 1993; Schmitt, 1996; Simms & Watson, 2007; Watson, 2006). Thus, internal consistency is a necessary but not sufficient condition for homogeneity. Put differently, a scale cannot be homogeneous unless all of its items are related, but a scale can contain many interrelated items and still not be unidimensional. Because the goal of assessment typically is to measure a single construct systematically, the test developer ultimately should be interested in homogeneity, rather than internal consistency.

Unfortunately, K–R 20 and coefficient alpha are measures of internal consistency rather than homogeneity and so are of limited use in establishing the unidimensionality of a scale. Moreover, they are imperfect indicators of internal consistency because they actually are a function of two different parameters: (a) the number of scale items and (b) the average correlation among these items (Clark & Watson, 1995, 2019; Cortina, 1993; Cortina et al., 2020; Schmitt, 1996). That is, one can achieve a high coefficient alpha by having (a) many items, (b) highly correlated items, or (c) some combination of the two. This complicates matters because the number of items is irrelevant to the issue of internal consistency. In practical terms, this means that as the number of items becomes quite large, it is exceedingly easy to achieve a high coefficient alpha. In fact, Cortina (1993) suggested that coefficient alpha is virtually useless as an index of internal consistency for scales containing 40 or more items.

To complicate things further, a scale can have an acceptable mean interitem correlation and still not be homogeneous. This can occur when many high item correlations are averaged with many low ones (Cortina, 1993; Cortina et al., 2020; Schmitt, 1996). Cortina (1993), for instance, constructed an 18-item scale composed of two independent nine-item clusters. The items within each group were highly homogeneous and had an average interitem correlation of .50. These groups were created to be statistically independent of one another, such that items in different clusters were completely uncorrelated with each another. This scale was not unidimensional, but instead it reflected two uncorrelated factors. Nevertheless, it had a coefficient alpha of .85 and an average interitem correlation of .24.

Thus, one cannot ensure unidimensionality simply by focusing on the mean interitem correlation; it also is necessary to examine the distribution and range of these correlations. Consequently, the earlier guideline that the average interitem correlations should fall in the .15 to .50 range needs to be further explicated to state that virtually all of the individual interitem correlations should fall somewhere in the range of .15 to .50. Put differently, unidimensionality is achieved when almost all of the interitem correlations are moderate in magnitude and cluster around the mean level.

In practical terms, the easiest way to establish the homogeneity of a scale is to show that all of its items have a significant loading (e.g., a value of |.35| or higher; see Clark & Watson, 1995, 2019) on the first unrotated factor. This establishes that they all are indicators of the same underlying construct, that is, that they assess the same thing.

Schmitt (1996) advocated a different approach, recommending that test developers use CFA to test the fit of a single factor model. The focus here is somewhat different in that this CFA-based approach tests whether the items assess only one thing (i.e., that one can model the item correlations using only one latent dimension). Both approaches are informative, but it is important to realize that they provide somewhat different information about a test (for a discussion, see Clark & Watson, 2019).

The difference between these two approaches can be illustrated using a simple hierarchical example. Watson et al. (1988) created the higher order negative affect scale of the PANAS by selecting negative mood terms from different content groups. This scale includes four different indicators of fear (e.g., scared, afraid), two items assessing guilt (guilty, ashamed), two indicators of anger (irritable, hostile), and two indicators of distress (upset, distressed). The PANAS negative affect items all assess the same thing, given that they (a) are moderately to strongly intercorrelated and (b) all load significantly on the same general factor. They do not measure only one thing, however, in that they also assess specific content variance (viz., fear, guilt, anger, distress) beyond this overarching general factor. Thus, for example, a simple one-factor model cannot account for the strong observed correlation between afraid and scared; additional factors need to be specified to model this overlapping item content. More generally, measures of higher order constructs often contain at least some quasi-redundant item content and, therefore, do not neatly fit a simple one-factor model. Nevertheless, these scales are homogeneous in the sense that their items all measure the same thing (i.e., the target higher order construct) to a significant extent.

The attenuation paradox. This discussion has consistently emphasized that the interitem correlations should be moderate in magnitude. This may seem puzzling to some readers, given that estimates of internal consistency will increase as the average interitem correlation becomes higher. Obviously, therefore, one can maximize coefficient alpha by retaining items that are highly correlated with others in the pool. Is it not desirable, therefore, to maximize reliability by retaining highly intercorrelated items in the final scale?

No, it is not. This is the crux of the classic attenuation paradox in psychometrics: Increasing item correlations beyond a certain point actually will lessen the construct validity of a scale (see Boyle, 1991; Clark & Watson, 1995, 2019; Loevinger, 1954, 1957). This paradox occurs for two related reasons. First, strongly correlated items are highly redundant with one another. Once one of them is included in a scale, the others contribute virtually no incremental information. For example, an individual who endorses the item "I often feel uncomfortable at parties" almost certainly will also endorse the item "I usually feel uneasy at large social gatherings." Once one has asked the first item, there is no point in asking the second because the answer is evident. More generally, a scale will yield far more information—and, hence, be a more interesting and valid measure of a construct—if it contains clearly differentiated items that are only moderately correlated. Second, attempts to maximize internal consistency almost invariably produce scales that are quite narrow in content; if this content is narrower than the target construct, then the validity of the scale is compromised. Returning to the earlier example, a scale that simply contained a series of items assessing the level of discomfort at parties would lack comprehensiveness as a measure of social anxiety and, therefore, would not be a valid measure of this construct.

This discussion of the attenuation paradox should make clear that the goal of assessment is to maximize validity, not coefficient alpha. It was this realization, in fact, that eventually led psychometricians to embrace validity as the conceptual centerpiece of psychological measurement.

Alpha as an index of reliability. Conventional indexes such as coefficient alpha are best viewed as indicators of the consistency of measurement across various conditions, rather than reliability per se. Indeed, it is well established that alpha actually can either overestimate or underestimate the true level of reliability under different assessment conditions (Becker, 2000; Green, 2003; McCrae et al., 2011; McNeish, 2018; Osburn, 2000; Schmidt et al., 2003; Schmitt, 1996). Alpha will overestimate reliability when there are systematic errors of measurement (McNeish, 2018). Unlike random errors, systematic measurement errors are significantly correlated across different assessments. Consequently, they are misclassified as true score variance in classical reliability theory (which, as noted, equates true scores with consistency in measurement).

Two kinds of systematic errors are worth noting. The first are response biases, such as acquiescence and social desirability (see Watson & Tellegen, 2002; Watson & Vaidya, 2012). *Social desirability* refers to a tendency for respondents to distort their responses (either consciously or unconsciously) to make them more congruent with prevailing cultural norms (Paulhus & Reid, 1991; Watson & Vaidya, 2012). *Acquiescence* can be defined as "an individual-difference variable to agree or disagree with an item regardless of its content" (J. A. Russell, 1979, p. 346); in other words, acquiescence causes individuals to respond similarly to a wide range of item content. Both of these response biases can be expected to increase the magnitude of the interitem correlations, thereby spuriously raising coefficient alpha.

Transient error represents another potentially important type of systematic error that can be a problem when assessment is confined to a single occasion (Becker, 2000; Chmielewski & Watson, 2009; Green, 2003; Osburn, 2000; Schmidt et al., 2003). Transient error reflects the influence of time-limited processes, such as the current mood of the respondent. Generally speaking, transient errors can be expected to produce (a) inconsistency across different occasions but (b) consistent responses within the same assessment. For example, suppose that a respondent rates her job satisfaction on two different occasions. At the first assessment, she is happy and optimistic; however, at the time of the second testing, she is feeling down and discouraged. It is reasonable to expect that her current mood will distort her satisfaction ratings at least slightly, such that she reports being more satisfied with her job at Time 1 than at Time 2. Note, however, that these same mood effects should produce consistent within-occasion responses; that is, her Time 1 item ratings consistently should reflect greater satisfaction than her Time 2 responses. Consequently, transient errors will inflate values of coefficient alpha that are based on a single occasion.

Conversely, alpha underestimates the true reliability of a measure that is heterogeneous and multidimensional (Cho & Kim, 2015; Cronbach, 1951; Green & Yang, 2015; McNeish, 2018; Osburn, 2000; Schmitt, 1996). As noted, classical reliability theory equates inconsistency with measurement error. Sometimes, however, inconsistency reflects the heterogeneity of item content rather than error per se. This is a widespread problem that has long been recognized by psychometricians (Cronbach, 1951; McDonald, 1981), but it remains poorly understood by test developers and users.

The potential magnitude of this underestimation problem can be illustrated using a concrete example. For the purposes of this example, consider the fictitious construct of *anxious joy*, which can be defined as a state of nervous exhilaration. Two parallel forms of this imaginary concept were constructed using mood descriptors from the fear and joviality scales of the PANAS-X (Watson & Clark, 1999). Each form includes two fear and two joviality terms. Specifically, Form A consists of *afraid*, *shaky*, *joyful*, and *delighted*, whereas Form B contains *scared*, *nervous*, *happy*, and *cheerful*.

Table 18.2 presents item intercorrelation data for these two measures of anxious joy; these responses were obtained from large samples of undergraduate students at Southern Methodist University who rated their emotional experiences using one of six different time frames: moment (i.e., how they felt "right now"), today, past week, past few weeks, past month, and general (i.e., how they felt "on average"). Table 18.2 demonstrates that these measures are highly heterogeneous. Each scale consists of two item pairs that are

TABLE 18.2

Item Intercorrelations for Two Parallel Measures of "Anxious Joy" Across Different Time Instructions

Item intercorrelations	Moment	Today	Past week	Past few weeks	Past month	General
			Form A			
Afraid—shaky	.39	.40	.51	.45	.44	.37
Afraid—joyful	−.08	−.06	−.11	−.14	−.10	−.01
Afraid—delighted	−.01	−.01	−.09	−.06	−.02	.04
Shaky—joyful	−.13	−.12	−.13	−.08	−.09	−.05
Shaky—delighted	−.05	−.03	−.10	−.05	−.06	−.01
Joyful—delighted	.69	.67	.67	.64	.64	.64
Average interitem r	.14	.14	.13	.13	.14	.16
			Form B			
Scared—nervous	.58	.59	.60	.52	.49	.47
Scared—happy	−.17	−.08	−.13	−.17	−.18	−.07
Scared—cheerful	−.15	−.06	−.12	−.18	−.12	−.02
Nervous—happy	−.10	−.03	−.09	−.11	−.11	−.07
Nervous—cheerful	−.07	−.01	−.08	−.09	−.09	−.04
Happy—cheerful	.68	.75	.72	.67	.66	.67
Average interitem r	.13	.19	.15	.11	.11	.16

Note. $n = 1{,}027$ (moment); 1,007 (today); 1,278 (past week); 678 (past few weeks); 1,006 (past month); 1,657 (general).

slightly negatively correlated with one another. Thus, each scale clearly taps two underlying dimensions (i.e., anxiety and joy), not one. Consistent with this observation, the average interitem correlations are predictably low, ranging from only .11 to .19 across the various samples.

Given that these are short scales with low average interitem correlations, the coefficient alphas predictably are quite poor, ranging from only .31 to .48 across the various data sets (Table 18.3). If the assumptions of classical reliability are true—and if alpha is an accurate estimate of reliability—then these low alpha coefficients would place serious limits on the ability of these scales to correlate with other measures (i.e., given that unreliability reflects pure randomness, scale correlations cannot exceed their reliabilities). Clearly, however, this is not the case; indeed, Table 18.3 shows that these two parallel forms are highly correlated with one another, with coefficients ranging from .66 to .73 across the various data sets. Moreover, Table 18.3 further demonstrates that if one uses the traditional formula to "correct" these correlations for attenuation because of unreliability (Nunnally, 1978, Chapter 6)—with alpha as the estimate of reliability—the results are absurd, as the coefficients greatly exceed 1.00 in every sample. In this example, coefficient alpha obviously misspecifies measurement error and substantially underestimates the true reliability of these scales.

This discussion should not be taken to suggest that these anxious–joy scales are good measures or that heterogeneity is desirable in a test. The point, rather, is that although heterogeneity is problematic and highly undesirable, it is not the same thing as random measurement error. Because of this, coefficient alpha can substantially underestimate the reliability of multidimensional scales.

More generally, the consensus among psychometricians is that coefficient alpha is based on unrealistic assumptions that are unlikely to be met in typical research conditions; consequently, it should not be used to estimate reliability (Cho & Kim, 2015; Green & Yang, 2015; McDonald, 1981; McNeish, 2018; Osburn, 2000; Revelle & Condon, 2019). A number of alternative reliability coefficients have been proposed (see Cho & Kim, 2015; McNeish, 2018; Osburn, 2000; Revelle & Condon, 2019). Most of these alternatives use some form of structural equation modeling to explicate the factor structure of the measure (Cho & Kim, 2015). The most widely recommended—and most commonly used—alternative is coefficient omega (McDonald, 1999; Zinbarg et al., 2005). These proposed alternatives to alpha are based on more realistic assumptions that have a greater likelihood of being met in psychological research. Nevertheless, they do

TABLE 18.3

Coefficient Alphas and Scale Correlations for Two Parallel Measures of "Anxious Joy" Across Different Time Instructions

Scale/statistic	Moment	Today	Past week	Past few weeks	Past month	General
			Coefficient alphas			
Form A	.41	.41	.37	.37	.38	.45
Form B	.37	.48	.41	.31	.32	.41
			Scale correlations			
Uncorrected	.73	.72	.73	.70	.68	.66
"Corrected"	1.88	1.61	1.88	2.06	1.94	1.54

Note. n = 1,027 (moment); 1,007 (today); 1,278 (past week); 678 (past few weeks); 1,006 (past month); 1,657 (general). The "corrected" correlations were computed using the scale coefficient alphas to estimate the attenuating effects of unreliability.

not solve all of the problems associated with coefficient alpha. For example, if it is based on a single assessment, coefficient omega still misrepresents transient error as true score variance (Green & Yang, 2015).

Test–retest reliability. Classical reliability theory arose out of work on intelligence and related cognitive abilities (Spearman, 1910). Accordingly, it was assumed that basic dimensions of individual differences essentially are invariant over time, such that (a) the true score components were perfectly stable and (b) any observed change could be attributed to measurement error (Anastasi & Urbina, 1997; Kaplan & Saccuzzo, 2009; Watson, 2004). This assumption was incorporated into the concept of test–retest reliability, which is computed by correlating scores on the same test across two assessments separated by a specified time interval. Correlations that increasingly approach +1.00 indicate greater and greater reliability.

The temporal stability of psychological measures has been assessed using both (a) Pearson product–moment correlations and (b) intraclass correlations (Loas & Defélice, 2012; Santor et al., 1997). Pearson correlations are indicators of relative stability. That is, they assess the extent to which relative differences between individuals remain invariant over time. They are unaffected by the addition or subtraction of a constant, and, therefore, are relatively insensitive to mean-level change over time; for example, if the scores of every participant in a sample increased by exactly 2 points, it still would be possible to obtain a Pearson retest correlation of +1.00. In contrast, intraclass correlations are indicators of absolute stability. They are affected by changes in levels and, therefore, will only be +1.00 if there are no fluctuations in scores over time. I report Pearson correlations in my own work, as it seems more informative to model relative stability and mean-level change as two separate phenomena.

Temporal stability data can provide useful information about virtually any measure, regardless of the construct that is being assessed. Nevertheless, similar to internal consistency indexes, test–retest coefficients can misspecify reliability under many circumstances. For example, memory effects and practice effects significantly inflate cognitive ability scores when respondents are assessed multiple times (Lo et al., 2012; Scharfen et al., 2018); this temporal inconsistency typically is treated as measurement error and can lead to inaccurate estimates of reliability (Anastasi & Urbina, 1997).

The more general problem, however, is that retest correlations only represent clear, unambiguous indexes of reliability when it is reasonable to assume that there has been no actual change on the assessed variable, such that the underlying true score remains perfectly invariant. For many areas of psychological research, this assumption is unreasonable for one of two reasons. First, many important psychological constructs—for example, moods and emotions—are inherently unstable and are expected to fluctuate substantially over time. For instance, a broad range of evidence has established that the PANAS-X scales are sensitive to multiple influences. Scores on several of the negative mood scales are elevated during episodes of stress and show significant decreases during exercise; conversely, positive mood scores increase following exercise and in response to social interaction (Watson, 2000; Watson & Clark, 1999). The temporal instability of these scales is not problematic, and it is not reflective of measurement error. Indeed, these theoretically meaningful effects helped to establish the construct validity of these scales.

Second, even stable constructs may still show some true change that is not attributable to measurement error, particularly when the retest interval is quite lengthy. The personality literature provides an excellent illustration of this point. Various lines of evidence have established that personality traits are not static constructs; rather, they show meaningful change over time. Perhaps the most compelling evidence is that retest correlations for personality systematically decline as the elapsed time interval increases (e.g., Cattell, 1964a, 1964b; Roberts & DelVecchio, 2000). This finding is difficult to explain using the assumptions of classical reliability theory: If the underlying true scores are perfectly stable, and if errors are randomly distributed across assessments, then reliability estimates should be unaffected by the length of the retest interval (Watson, 2004). This finding makes perfect sense, however, if one assumes that true change is possible, because change is increasingly likely to occur across longer retest intervals (Anastasi & Urbina, 1997; Kaplan & Saccuzzo, 2009).

Cattell (1964a, 1964b) emphasized this point several decades ago, arguing for the importance of distinguishing between dependability and stability. Cattell et al. (1970) defined *dependability* as "the correlation between two administrations of the same test *when the lapse of time is insufficient for people themselves to change* with respect to what is being measured" (p. 30). In contrast, they defined *stability* as the correlation between two administrations of a test across a retest interval that is lengthy enough for true change to occur. This distinction is crucial: It makes it quite clear that dependability correlations provide an unambiguous index of reliability, whereas stability coefficients do not.

Dependability data can play a crucial role in the validation of trait measures (Chmielewski & Watson, 2009; Gnambs, 2014; Watson, 2004). My laboratory has conducted a number of dependability studies, examining data from a wide range of measures. These studies have yielded three important conclusions. First, there are no systematic differences between 2-week and 2-month retest coefficients, suggesting that both intervals can be used to establish the dependability of trait measures. Second, dependability is a consistent property of scales, such that some measures simply are more dependable than others. Third, even strongly correlated measures of the same construct can vary significantly in their dependability; for instance, some measures of neuroticism and negative affectivity consistently yield higher dependability coefficients than others (Chmielewski & Watson, 2009; Watson, 2004; Watson et al., 2015). These data demonstrate the importance of collecting dependability data as early as possible in the process of creating and validating trait measures.

EXTERNAL VALIDITY

Convergent Validity

In the final, external stage of construct validation, one moves beyond the test to examine how it relates to other variables. This external phase subsumes three basic considerations: convergent validity, discriminant validity, and criterion validity. The concept of *convergent validity* was formally introduced into psychometrics by Campbell and Fiske (1959). Convergent validity is assessed by examining the relations among different purported measures of the same construct (Anastasi & Urbina, 1997; Campbell & Fiske, 1959; Clark & Watson, 2019; Kaplan & Saccuzzo, 2009). This type of evidence obviously is crucial in the establishment of construct validity. If it can be shown that different indicators converge substantially, this significantly strengthens one's confidence that they actually do assess the target construct.

According to Campbell and Fiske (1959), these convergent correlations "should be significantly different from zero and sufficiently large to encourage further examination of validity" (p. 82). What does *sufficiently large* mean in this context? Campbell and Fiske were quite vague on this point, and their vagueness was entirely appropriate. In contrast to other types of construct validity evidence, one cannot offer simple guidelines for evaluating when convergent correlations are high enough to support the validity of a measure. This is because the expected magnitude of these correlations will vary dramatically as a function of various design features. The single most important factor is the nature of the different measures that are used to examine convergent validity. In their original formulation, Campbell and Fiske largely assumed that investigators would examine convergence across fundamentally different methods. In one analysis, for example, they examined the associations between trait scores assessed using (a) peer ratings versus (b) a word association task (Campbell & Fiske, 1959, Table 2). In another analysis, they investigated the convergence among free behavior, role-playing, and projective test scores (Campbell & Fiske, 1959, Table 8).

Over time, however, investigators began to interpret the concept of method much more loosely (indeed, some have even used retest correlations to assess convergent validity; e.g., Longley et al., 2005; Watson et al., 2007). For instance, contemporary researchers commonly establish convergent validity by reporting correlations among different self-report measures of the same target construct. This practice is not problematic. Clearly, however, it creates a situation that is very different from the one originally envisioned by Campbell and Fiske (1959). Most notably, convergent correlations will be—and should be—substantially higher when they are computed within the same basic method (e.g., between different self-report measures of conscientiousness) than when they are calculated across very different methods (e.g., between self-rated vs. teacher-rated conscientiousness). This, in turn, means that the same level of convergence might support construct validity in one context but challenge it in another. Suppose, for instance, that a researcher obtains a .40 correlation between two self-report measures of self-esteem. Given this moderate level of association, it would be difficult to argue that both of these instruments actually assess the same construct. In contrast, a .40 correlation between self and parent ratings of self-esteem would be far more encouraging and likely would enhance the construct validity of these measures.

Discriminant Validity

Discriminant validity is assessed by examining how a measure relates to purported indicators of other constructs (e.g., Anastasi & Urbina, 1997; Clark & Watson, 2019; Kaplan & Saccuzzo, 2009). Campbell and Fiske (1959) formally introduced this concept in the context of a multitrait–multimethod (MTMM) matrix. This type of matrix can be created whenever one assesses two or more constructs in at least two different ways. For interpretative purposes, the MTMM matrix can be decomposed into two basic subcomponents: (a) the monomethod triangles and (b) the heteromethod block. For instance, Watson et al. (2002) assessed six different traits (self-esteem, neuroticism, extraversion, openness, agreeableness, and conscientiousness) using two different methods (self-ratings and peer-ratings; see Watson et al., 2002, Table 2). One monomethod triangle contained all of the correlations among the self-ratings; the second included all of the associations among the peer-ratings. Finally, the heteromethod block contained all of the correlations between the self and peer ratings.

According to Campbell and Fiske (1959), an MTMM matrix yields three basic types of discriminant validity evidence (pp. 82–83). First, each of the convergent correlations should be higher than any of the other values in its row or column of the heteromethod block. For instance, self-rated self-esteem should correlate more strongly with peer-rated self-esteem than with peer-rated extraversion or peer-rated neuroticism. This type of evidence is particularly important in establishing that highly correlated constructs within multilevel hierarchical models are, in fact, empirically distinguishable from one another (e.g., Longley et al., 2005; Watson & Clark, 1992; Watson & Wu, 2005). Failure to achieve discriminant validity at this level signals a serious problem with either (a) one or more of the measures or (b) the construct itself.

One complication here is that the meaning of the word "higher" is ambiguous in this context. Some researchers interpret it rather loosely to mean simply that the convergent correlation must be descriptively higher than all of the other values in its row or column of the heteromethod block. For instance, if the convergent correlation is .50, and the highest relevant discriminant correlation is only .45, then it is assumed that this requirement is met.

It is better, however, to use the more stringent requirement that the convergent correlation must be significantly higher than all of the other values in its row or column of the heteromethod block. This requirement obviously is more difficult to meet; it also requires relatively large sample sizes to have sufficient statistical power to conduct these tests in a meaningful way. Nevertheless, the payoff is well worth it in terms of the resulting precision in the validity analyses. For instance, Watson et al. (2008) examined the convergent and discriminant validity of the 11 nonoverlapping IDAS scales in a sample of 605 outpatients. The convergent correlations ranged from .52 to .71, with a mean value of .62. Significance tests further revealed that these convergent correlations exceeded all of the other values in their row or column of the heteromethod block in 219 of 220 comparisons (99.5%). These results thereby provide substantial evidence of discriminant validity.

The second type of discriminant validity evidence is that the convergent correlations should exceed all of the corresponding values in the monomethod triangles. As Campbell and Fiske (1959) put it, a test should "correlate higher with an independent effort to measure the same trait than with measures designed to get at different traits which happen to employ the same method" (p. 83). For instance, self-rated self-esteem should correlate more strongly with peer-rated self-esteem that with self-rated extraversion or self-rated neuroticism.

This stronger test of discriminant validity is far more difficult to pass than the first; however, failure to achieve discriminant validity at this level is not necessarily catastrophic. A key consideration here is the true level of correlation among the underlying latent constructs. In this regard, it must be emphasized that—particularly within the context of hierarchical models—the most interesting tests of discriminant validity involve "near neighbor" constructs that are known to be strongly related. For example, Watson and Clark (1992) reported several MTMM matrixes to examine relations among measures of fear, sadness, guilt, and hostility. It is well established that these negative affects are strongly related, so it is hardly surprising that the monomethod triangles in these analyses included a number of substantial correlations. Of course, the presence of these strong monomethod correlations makes it difficult to pass this second test of discriminant validity, particularly when one uses very different methods (e.g., self vs. peer ratings) that can be expected to yield relatively modest convergent correlations.

The third and final consideration in discriminant validity is whether "the same pattern of trait interrelationship" can be identified "in all of the heterotrait triangles of both the monomethod and heteromethod blocks" (Campbell & Fiske, 1959, p. 83). The key issue here is the extent to which these heterotrait coefficients reflect (a) true trait interrelations versus (b) the complicating influence of method variance. If the pattern of associations remains relatively consistent across all of the heterotrait triangles (e.g., fear and sadness are strongly related in every case), then it is reasonable to conclude that these coefficients are accurate reflections of the true relations among the underlying constructs. Conversely, if the patterns show substantial differences across the triangles, then method variance likely is implicated. This type of evidence is best examined using CFA, which allows one to model simultaneously both construct-based and method-based factors (Byrne, 1994; Watson et al., 2002).

Criterion Validity

Criterion validity is assessed by relating a measure to important nontest variables. This type of evidence traditionally is further subdivided into concurrent validity (which involves relations with nontest criteria that are assessed at the same time as the measure) and predictive validity (which examines associations with criteria assessed at some point in the future; Anastasi & Urbina, 1997; Kaplan & Saccuzzo, 2009). Criterion validity evidence is important for two reasons. The first is purely pragmatic: Measures that have no established links to nontest variables likely will be of little interest to most researchers.

Second, criterion validity evidence is critically important in clarifying the inferences that can be drawn from test scores; it, therefore, plays a crucial role in establishing the construct validity of a measure. As an example, Watson and Clark (1993) described the development and validation of a personality scale. As part of this process, they provide a range of criterion validity evidence. Among other things, they found that high scores on this scale were associated with (a) heavier and more problematic use of alcohol, marijuana, and other drugs; (b) more casual sexual activity, including a greater number of different sex partners and more one-night stands; (c) lower levels of self-reported spirituality and religiosity; and (d) poorer grades in both high school and college (see also Clark & Watson, 1999). Without knowing anything else about this instrument, one already can make a reasonably good general guess about the type of trait it measures. In this case, the assessed trait is disinhibition, which "reflects broad individual differences in the tendency to behave in an undercontrolled versus overcontrolled manner" (Watson & Clark, 1993, p. 506). These behavioral correlates are quite consistent with this conceptualization and, therefore, enhance the construct validity of the test. In other instances, criterion data may be inconsistent with the current conceptualization of the construct (either because a predicted association was not found, or because an unexpected correlate has emerged); such inconsistencies indicate a significant problem that must be addressed.

CONCLUSION

This chapter has reviewed a large number of psychometric concepts. As emphasized at the beginning, however, all of these different types of evidence are now considered to be aspects of the more general process of construct validation. In other words, they all simply are pieces in the larger puzzle that is construct validity. This focus on construct validity has fundamentally changed our understanding of these concepts. Most notably, it now is clear that they need to be applied flexibly to match the theoretical specifications of the target construct. Put differently, the same set of psychometric data may enhance the validity of one measure but challenge the validity of another, depending on the nature of the target construct.

For instance, retest reliability is a crucial consideration if the goal of assessment is to measure a stable dimension, such as conscientiousness or intelligence. In this regard, recent studies of dependability have established that even strongly correlated measures of the same basic trait can contain substantially different levels of measurement error. Change, however, is to be expected—and instability is not inherently problematic—when one is assessing transient constructs, such as mood states. Similarly, although evidence of homogeneity is essential in establishing the construct validity of many measures, it is irrelevant when the goal of assessment is to create a cumulative index of traumatic experiences; here, there is no necessary expectation or requirement that different manifestations of trauma be interrelated. As a final example, a particular level of convergent validity may be encouraging in one context (e.g., between self-reported and supervisor-rated conscientiousness) but indicate significant problems in another (e.g., between two self-report measures of conscientiousness).

This emphasis on construct validity also underscores the need to develop clear, precise definitions of the key constructs in the target domain. This statement should not be misunderstood to mean that all of the important theoretical issues must be resolved before the start of scale development and data collection. Indeed, the scale development process offers a powerful mechanism for sorting through disputed issues and resolving them. As originally articulated by Loevinger (1957), the key point is to incorporate all of these alternative theoretical schemes into the initial item tool, so that they can be subjected to empirical scrutiny. Thus, psychological measurement involves a constant interplay between theoretical expectations and empirical data.

Objective psychological tests compare favorably with those created in other areas of science and medicine (Meyer et al., 2001) and represent a major success story within psychology. By adhering more closely to the principles articulated in this chapter, test developers can build on this tradition of success and create even better assessment instruments in the future.

References

Abramson, L. Y., Metalsky, G. L., & Alloy, L. B. (1989). Hopelessness depression: A theory based subtype of depression. *Psychological Review, 96*(2), 358–372. https://doi.org/10.1037/0033-295X.96.2.358

American Educational Research Association, American Psychological Association, & National Council on Measurement in Education. (1974). *Standards for educational and psychological testing*. American Psychological Association.

American Educational Research Association, American Psychological Association, & National Council on Measurement in Education. (1999). *Standards for educational and psychological testing*. American Educational Research Association.

American Educational Research Association, American Psychological Association, & National Council on Measurement in Education. (2014). *Standards for educational and psychological testing*. American Educational Research Association.

American Psychiatric Association. (2013). *Diagnostic and statistical manual of mental disorders* (5th ed.).

Anastasi, A., & Urbina, S. (1997). *Psychological testing* (7th ed.). Macmillan.

Becker, G. (2000). How important is transient error in estimating reliability? Going beyond simulation studies. *Psychological Methods*, 5(3), 370–379. https://doi.org/10.1037/1082-989X.5.3.370

Benson, N., Hulac, D. M., & Kranzler, J. H. (2010). Independent examination of the Wechsler Adult Intelligence Scale-Fourth Edition (WAIS-IV): What does the WAIS-IV measure? *Psychological Assessment*, 22(1), 121–130. https://doi.org/10.1037/a0017767

Bollen, K. A., & Diamantopoulos, A. (2017). In defense of causal-formative indicators: A minority report. *Psychological Methods*, 22(3), 581–596. https://doi.org/10.1037/met0000056

Bollen, K. A., & Ting, K. F. (2000). A tetrad test for causal indicators. *Psychological Methods*, 5(1), 3–22. https://doi.org/10.1037/1082-989X.5.1.3

Bowden, S. C., Weiss, L. G., Holdnack, J. A., & Lloyd, D. (2006). Age-related invariance of abilities measured with the Wechsler Adult Intelligence Scale—III. *Psychological Assessment*, 18(3), 334–339. https://doi.org/10.1037/1040-3590.18.3.334

Boyle, G. J. (1991). Does item homogeneity indicate internal consistency or item redundancy in psychometric scales? *Personality and Individual Differences*, 12(3), 291–294. https://doi.org/10.1016/0191-8869(91)90115-R

Byrne, B. M. (1994). *Structural equation modeling with EQS and EQS/Windows*. Sage.

Campbell, D. T., & Fiske, D. W. (1959). Convergent and discriminant validation by the multitrait-multimethod matrix. *Psychological Bulletin*, 56(2), 81–105. https://doi.org/10.1037/h0046016

Cattell, R. B. (1964a). Beyond validity and reliability: Some further concepts and coefficients for evaluating tests. *Journal of Experimental Education*, 33(2), 133–143. https://doi.org/10.1080/00220973.1964.11010865

Cattell, R. B. (1964b). Validity and reliability: A proposed more basic set of concepts. *Journal of Educational Psychology*, 55(1), 1–22. https://doi.org/10.1037/h0046462

Cattell, R. B., Eber, H. W., & Tatsuoka, M. M. (1970). *Handbook for the Sixteen Personality Factor Questionnaire (16PF)*. Institute for Personality and Ability Testing.

Chmielewski, M., & Watson, D. (2009). What is being assessed and why it matters: The impact of transient error on trait research. *Journal of Personality and Social Psychology*, 97(1), 186–202. https://doi.org/10.1037/a0015618

Cho, E., & Kim, S. (2015). Cronbach's coefficient alpha: Well known but poorly understood. *Organizational Research Methods*, 18(2), 207–230. https://doi.org/10.1177/1094428114555994

Clark, L. A., & Watson, D. (1991). Tripartite model of anxiety and depression: Psychometric evidence and taxonomic implications. *Journal of Abnormal Psychology*, 100(3), 316–336. https://doi.org/10.1037/0021-843X.100.3.316

Clark, L. A., & Watson, D. (1995). Constructing validity: Basic issues in objective scale development. *Psychological Assessment*, 7(3), 309–319. https://doi.org/10.1037/1040-3590.7.3.309

Clark, L. A., & Watson, D. (1999). Temperament: A new paradigm for personality. In L. Pervin & O. John (Eds.), *Handbook of personality* (2nd ed., pp. 399–423). Guilford Press.

Clark, L. A., & Watson, D. (2019). Constructing validity: New developments in creating objective measuring instruments. *Psychological Assessment*, 31(12), 1412–1427. https://doi.org/10.1037/pas0000626

Cortina, J. M. (1993). What is coefficient alpha? An examination of theory and applications. *Journal of Applied Psychology*, 78(1), 98–104. https://doi.org/10.1037/0021-9010.78.1.98

Cortina, J. M., Sheng, Z., Keener, S. K., Keeler, K. R., Grubb, L. K., Schmitt, N., Tonidandel, S., Summerville, K. M., Heggestad, E. D., & Banks, G. C. (2020). From alpha to omega and beyond! A look at the past, present, and (possible) future of psychometric soundness in the *Journal of Applied Psychology*. *Journal of Applied Psychology*, 105(12), 1351–1381. https://doi.org/10.1037/apl0000815

Cronbach, L. J. (1951). Coefficient alpha and the internal structure of tests. *Psychometrika*, 16(3), 297–334. https://doi.org/10.1007/BF02310555

Cronbach, L. J., & Meehl, P. E. (1955). Construct validity in psychological tests. *Psychological Bulletin*, *52*(4), 281–302. https://doi.org/10.1037/h0040957

Dong, Y., & Dumas, D. (2020). Are personality measures valid for different populations? A systematic review of measurement invariance across cultures, gender, and age. *Personality and Individual Differences*, *160*, 109956. https://doi.org/10.1016/j.paid.2020.109956

Embretson, S. E. (1996). The new rules of measurement. *Psychological Assessment*, *8*(4), 341–349. https://doi.org/10.1037/1040-3590.8.4.341

Fabrigar, L. R., Wegener, D. T., MacCallum, R. C., & Strahan, E. J. (1999). Evaluating the use of exploratory factor analysis in psychological research. *Psychological Methods*, *4*(3), 272–299. https://doi.org/10.1037/1082-989X.4.3.272

Floyd, F. J., & Widaman, K. F. (1995). Factor analysis in the development and refinement of clinical assessment instruments. *Psychological Assessment*, *7*(3), 286–299. https://doi.org/10.1037/1040-3590.7.3.286

Gnambs, T. (2014). A meta-analysis of dependability coefficients (test-retest reliabilities) for measures of the Big Five. *Journal of Research in Personality*, *52*, 20–28. https://doi.org/10.1016/j.jrp.2014.06.003

Gotlib, I. H., & Cane, D. B. (1989). Self-report assessment of depression and anxiety. In P. C. Kendall & D. Watson (Eds.), *Anxiety and depression: Distinctive and overlapping features* (pp. 131–169). Academic Press.

Green, S. B. (2003). A coefficient alpha for test-retest data. *Psychological Methods*, *8*(1), 88–101. https://doi.org/10.1037/1082-989X.8.1.88

Green, S. B., & Yang, Y. (2015). Evaluation of dimensionality in the assessment of internal consistency reliability: Coefficient alpha and omega coefficients. *Educational Measurement: Issues and Practice*, *34*(4), 14–20. https://doi.org/10.1111/emip.12100

Haynes, S. N., Richard, D. C. S., & Kubany, E. S. (1995). Content validity in psychological assessment: A functional approach to concepts and methods. *Psychological Assessment*, *7*(3), 238–247. https://doi.org/10.1037/1040-3590.7.3.238

Hogan, R. T. (1983). A socioanalytic theory of personality. In M. Page (Ed.), *Nebraska Symposium on Motivation* (Vol. 30, pp. 55–89). University of Nebraska Press.

Hogan, R. T., & Hogan, J. (1992). *Hogan Personality Inventory manual*. Hogan Assessment Systems.

Joiner, T. E., Jr., Walker, R. L., Pettit, J. W., Perez, M., & Cukrowicz, K. C. (2005). Evidence-based assessment of depression in adults. *Psychological Assessment*, *17*(3), 267–277. https://doi.org/10.1037/1040-3590.17.3.267

Kaplan, R. M., & Saccuzzo, D. P. (2009). *Psychological testing: Principles, applications, and issues* (7th ed.). Wadsworth.

Kotov, R., Krueger, R. F., Watson, D., Achenbach, T. M., Althoff, R. R., Bagby, R. M., Brown, T. A., Carpenter, W. T., Caspi, A., Clark, L. A., Eaton, N. R., Forbes, M. K., Forbush, K. T., Goldberg, D., Hasin, D., Hyman, S. E., Ivanova, M. Y., Lynam, D. R., Markon, K., . . . Zimmerman, M. (2017). The Hierarchical Taxonomy of Psychopathology (HiTOP): A dimensional alternative to traditional nosologies. *Journal of Abnormal Psychology*, *126*(4), 454–477. https://doi.org/10.1037/abn0000258

Kuder, G. F., & Richardson, M. W. (1937). The theory of the estimation of test reliability. *Psychometrika*, *2*(3), 151–160. https://doi.org/10.1007/BF02288391

Lee, J. (2014). Conducting cognitive interviews in cross-national settings. *Assessment*, *21*(2), 227–240. https://doi.org/10.1177/1073191112436671

Lo, A. H. Y., Humphreys, M., Byrne, G. J., & Pachana, N. A. (2012). Test-retest reliability and practice effects of the Wechsler Memory Scale-III. *Journal of Neuropsychology*, *6*(2), 212–231. https://doi.org/10.1111/j.1748-6653.2011.02023.x

Loas, G., & Defélice, E. (2012). Absolute and relative short-term stability of interpersonal dependency in suicide attempters. *The Journal of Nervous and Mental Disease*, *200*(10), 904–907. https://doi.org/10.1097/NMD.0b013e31826ba141

Loevinger, J. (1954). The attenuation paradox in test theory. *Psychological Bulletin*, *51*(5), 493–504. https://doi.org/10.1037/h0058543

Loevinger, J. (1957). Objective tests as instruments of psychological theory. *Psychological Reports*, *3*(3), 635–694. https://doi.org/10.2466/pr0.1957.3.3.635

Longley, S. L., Watson, D., & Noyes, R., Jr. (2005). Assessment of the hypochondriasis domain: The multidimensional inventory of hypochondriacal traits (MIHT). *Psychological Assessment*, *17*(1), 3–14. https://doi.org/10.1037/1040-3590.17.1.3

Markon, K. E., Krueger, R. F., & Watson, D. (2005). Delineating the structure of normal and abnormal personality: An integrative hierarchical approach. *Journal of Personality and Social Psychology*, *88*(1), 139–157. https://doi.org/10.1037/0022-3514.88.1.139

McCrae, R. R., Kurtz, J. E., Yamagata, S., & Terracciano, A. (2011). Internal consistency, retest reliability, and their implications for personality scale validity. *Personality and Social Psychology Review*, *15*(1), 28–50. https://doi.org/10.1177/1088868310366253

McDonald, R. P. (1981). The dimensionality of tests and items. *British Journal of Mathematical & Statistical Psychology*, *34*(1), 100–117. https://doi.org/10.1111/j.2044-8317.1981.tb00621.x

McDonald, R. P. (1999). *Test theory: A unified approach*. Lawrence Erlbaum.

McNeish, D. (2018). Thanks coefficient alpha, we'll take it from here. *Psychological Methods*, *23*(3), 412–433. https://doi.org/10.1037/met0000144

Messick, S. (1995). Validity of psychological assessment: Validation of inferences from persons' responses and performances as scientific inquiry into score meaning. *American Psychologist*, *50*(9), 741–749. https://doi.org/10.1037/0003-066X.50.9.741

Meyer, G. J., Finn, S. E., Eyde, L. D., Kay, G. G., Moreland, K. L., Dies, R. R., Eisman, E. J., Kubiszyn, T. W., & Reed, G. M. (2001). Psychological testing and psychological assessment. A review of evidence and issues. *American Psychologist*, *56*(2), 128–165. https://doi.org/10.1037/0003-066X.56.2.128

Meyer, G. J., & Kurtz, J. E. (2006). Advancing personality assessment terminology: Time to retire "objective" and "projective" as personality test descriptors. *Journal of Personality Assessment*, *87*(3), 223–225. https://doi.org/10.1207/s15327752jpa8703_01

Nunnally, J. C. (1978). *Psychometric theory* (2nd ed.). McGraw-Hill.

Osburn, H. G. (2000). Coefficient alpha and related internal consistency reliability coefficients. *Psychological Methods*, *5*(3), 343–355. https://doi.org/10.1037/1082-989X.5.3.343

Paulhus, D. L., & Reid, D. B. (1991). Enhancement and denial in socially desirable responding. *Journal of Personality and Social Psychology*, *60*(2), 307–317. https://doi.org/10.1037/0022-3514.60.2.307

Reise, S. P., Ainsworth, A. T., & Haviland, M. G. (2005). Item response theory: Fundamentals, applications, and promise in psychological research. *Current Directions in Psychological Science*, *14*(2), 95–101. https://doi.org/10.1111/j.0963-7214.2005.00342.x

Reise, S. P., & Waller, N. G. (2003). How many IRT parameters does it take to model psychopathology items? *Psychological Methods*, *8*(2), 164–184. https://doi.org/10.1037/1082-989X.8.2.164

Reise, S. P., & Waller, N. G. (2009). Item response theory in clinical measurement. *Annual Review of Clinical Psychology*, *5*, 27–48. https://doi.org/10.1146/annurev.clinpsy.032408.153553

Revelle, W., & Condon, D. M. (2019). Reliability from α to ω: A tutorial. *Psychological Assessment*, *31*(12), 1395–1411. https://doi.org/10.1037/pas0000754

Roberts, B. W., & DelVecchio, W. F. (2000). The rank-order consistency of personality traits from childhood to old age: A quantitative review of longitudinal studies. *Psychological Bulletin*, *126*(1), 3–25. https://doi.org/10.1037/0033-2909.126.1.3

Roberts, B. W., Kuncel, N. R., Shiner, R., Caspi, A., & Goldberg, L. R. (2007). The power of personality: The comparative validity of personality traits, socioeconomic status, and cognitive ability for predicting important life outcomes. *Perspectives on Psychological Science*, *2*(4), 313–345. https://doi.org/10.1111/j.1745-6916.2007.00047.x

Russell, D. W. (2002). In search of underlying dimensions: The use (and abuse) of factor analysis in *Personality and Social Psychology Bulletin*. *Personality and Social Psychology Bulletin*, *28*(12), 1629–1646. https://doi.org/10.1177/014616702237645

Russell, J. A. (1979). Affective space is bipolar. *Journal of Personality and Social Psychology*, *37*(3), 345–356. https://doi.org/10.1037/0022-3514.37.3.345

Sackett, P. R., & Walmsley, P. T. (2014). Which personality attributes are most important in the workplace? *Perspectives on Psychological Science*, *9*(5), 538–551. https://doi.org/10.1177/1745691614543972

Santor, D. A., Bagby, R. M., & Joffe, R. T. (1997). Evaluating stability and change in personality and depression. *Journal of Personality and Social Psychology*, *73*(6), 1354–1362. https://doi.org/10.1037/0022-3514.73.6.1354

Scharfen, J., Peters, J. M., & Holling, H. (2018). Retest effects in cognitive ability tests: A meta-analysis. *Intelligence*, *67*, 44–66. https://doi.org/10.1016/j.intell.2018.01.003

Schmidt, F. L., & Hunter, J. (2004). General mental ability in the world of work: Occupational attainment and job performance. *Journal of Personality and Social Psychology*, *86*(1), 162–173. https://doi.org/10.1037/0022-3514.86.1.162

Schmidt, F. L., Le, H., & Ilies, R. (2003). Beyond alpha: An empirical examination of the effects of different sources of measurement error on reliability estimates for measures of individual differences constructs. *Psychological Methods*, *8*(2), 206–224. https://doi.org/10.1037/1082-989X.8.2.206

Schmidt, F. L., Shaffer, J. A., & Oh, I.-S. (2008). Increased accuracy for range restriction corrections: Implications for the role of personality and general mental ability in job and training performance. *Personnel Psychology*, *61*(4), 827–868. https://doi.org/10.1111/j.1744-6570.2008.00132.x

Schmitt, N. (1996). Uses and abuses of coefficient alpha. *Psychological Assessment, 8*(4), 350–353. https://doi.org/10.1037/1040-3590.8.4.350

Simms, L. J., & Watson, D. (2007). The construct validation approach to personality scale construction. In R. W. Robins, R. C. Fraley, & R. F. Krueger (Eds.), *Handbook of research methods in personality psychology* (pp. 240–258). Guilford Press.

Simms, L. J., Watson, D., & Doebbeling, B. N. (2002). Confirmatory factor analyses of posttraumatic stress symptoms in deployed and nondeployed veterans of the Gulf War. *Journal of Abnormal Psychology, 111*(4), 637–647. https://doi.org/10.1037/0021-843X.111.4.637

Smith, G. T., & McCarthy, D. M. (1995). Methodological considerations in the refinement of clinical assessment instruments. *Psychological Assessment, 7*(3), 300–308. https://doi.org/10.1037/1040-3590.7.3.300

Spearman, C. (1904). "General intelligence," objectively determined and measured. *The American Journal of Psychology, 15*(2), 201–293. https://doi.org/10.2307/1412107

Spearman, C. (1910). Correlation calculated from faulty data. *British Journal of Psychology, 3*(3), 271–295. https://doi.org/10.1111/j.2044-8295.1910.tb00206.x

Teresi, J. A., Ocepek-Welikson, K., Kleinman, M., Eimicke, J. P., Crane, P. K., Jones, R. N., Lai, J. S., Choi, S. W., Hays, R. D., Reeve, B. B., Reise, S. P., Pilkonis, P. A., & Cella, D. (2009). Analysis of differential item functioning in the depression item bank from the Patient Reported Outcome Measurement Information System (PROMIS): An item response theory approach. *Psychological Science Quarterly, 51*(2), 148–180.

Thibodeau, M. A., & Asmundson, G. J. G. (2014). The PHQ-9 assesses depression similarly in men and women from the general population. *Personality and Individual Differences, 56*, 149–153. https://doi.org/10.1016/j.paid.2013.08.039

Thomas, M. L. (2019). Advances in applications of item response theory to clinical assessment. *Psychological Assessment, 31*(12), 1442–1455. https://doi.org/10.1037/pas0000597

Watson, D. (2000). *Mood and temperament*. Guilford Press.

Watson, D. (2004). Stability versus change, dependability versus error: Issues in the assessment of personality over time. *Journal of Research in Personality, 38*(4), 319–350. https://doi.org/10.1016/j.jrp.2004.03.001

Watson, D. (2005). Rethinking the mood and anxiety disorders: A quantitative hierarchical model for *DSM-V*. *Journal of Abnormal Psychology, 114*(4), 522–536. https://doi.org/10.1037/0021-843X.114.4.522

Watson, D. (2006). In search of construct validity: Using basic concepts and principles of psychological measurement to define child maltreatment. In M. Feerick, J. Knutson, P. Trickett, & S. Flanzer (Eds.), *Defining and classifying child abuse and neglect for research purposes* (pp. 199–230). Brookes.

Watson, D. (2009a). Differentiating the mood and anxiety disorders: A quadripartite model. *Annual Review of Clinical Psychology, 5*(1), 221–247. https://doi.org/10.1146/annurev.clinpsy.032408.153510

Watson, D. (2009b). Rethinking the anxiety disorders in *DSM-V* and beyond: Quantitative dimensional models of anxiety and related psychopathology. In J. Abramowitz, D. McKay, S. Taylor, & G. Asmundson (Eds.), *Current perspectives on the anxiety disorders: Implications for DSM-V and beyond* (pp. 275–302). Springer Press.

Watson, D., & Clark, L. A. (1984). Negative affectivity: The disposition to experience aversive emotional states. *Psychological Bulletin, 96*(3), 465–490. https://doi.org/10.1037/0033-2909.96.3.465

Watson, D., & Clark, L. A. (1992). Affects separable and inseparable: On the hierarchical arrangement of the negative affects. *Journal of Personality and Social Psychology, 62*(3), 489–505. https://doi.org/10.1037/0022-3514.62.3.489

Watson, D., & Clark, L. A. (1993). Behavioral disinhibition versus constraint: A dispositional perspective. In D. M. Wegner & J. W. Pennebaker (Eds.), *Handbook of mental control* (pp. 506–527). Prentice-Hall.

Watson, D., & Clark, L. A. (1999). *The PANAS-X: Manual for the positive and negative affect schedule—Expanded form* [Unpublished manuscript]. University of Iowa.

Watson, D., Clark, L. A., & Tellegen, A. (1988). Development and validation of brief measures of positive and negative affect: The PANAS scales. *Journal of Personality and Social Psychology, 54*(6), 1063–1070. https://doi.org/10.1037/0022-3514.54.6.1063

Watson, D., Nus, E., & Wu, K. D. (2019). Development and validation of the faceted inventory of the five-factor model (FI-FFM). *Assessment, 26*(1), 17–44. https://doi.org/10.1177/1073191117711022

Watson, D., O'Hara, M. W., Chmielewski, M., McDade-Montez, E. A., Koffel, E., Naragon, K., & Stuart, S. (2008). Further validation of the IDAS: Evidence of convergent, discriminant, criterion, and incremental validity. *Psychological Assessment, 20*(3), 248–259. https://doi.org/10.1037/a0012570

Watson, D., O'Hara, M. W., Simms, L. J., Kotov, R., Chmielewski, M., McDade-Montez, E. A., Gamez, W., & Stuart, S. (2007). Development and validation of the Inventory of Depression and Anxiety Symptoms (IDAS). *Psychological Assessment, 19*(3), 253–268. https://doi.org/10.1037/1040-3590.19.3.253

Watson, D., & Stanton, K. (2017). Emotion blends and mixed emotions in the hierarchical structure of affect. *Emotion Review, 9*(2), 99–104. https://doi.org/10.1177/1754073916639659

Watson, D., Stasik, S. M., Chmielewski, M., & Naragon-Gainey, K. (2015). Development and validation of the Temperament and Affectivity Inventory (TAI). *Assessment, 22*(5), 540–560. https://doi.org/10.1177/1073191114557943

Watson, D., Suls, J., & Haig, J. (2002). Global self-esteem in relation to structural models of personality and affectivity. *Journal of Personality and Social Psychology, 83*(1), 185–197. https://doi.org/10.1037/0022-3514.83.1.185

Watson, D., & Tellegen, A. (2002). Aggregation, acquiescence, and trait affectivity. *Journal of Research in Personality, 36*(6), 589–597. https://doi.org/10.1016/S0092-6566(02)00509-3

Watson, D., & Vaidya, J. (2012). Mood measurement: Current status and future directions. In J. A. Schinka & W. Velicer (Eds.), *Handbook of psychology: Research methods in psychology* (2nd ed., Vol. 2, pp. 369–394). Wiley.

Watson, D., & Wu, K. D. (2005). Development and validation of the Schedule of Compulsions, Obsessions, and Pathological Impulses (SCOPI). *Assessment, 12*(1), 50–65. https://doi.org/10.1177/1073191104271483

Zinbarg, R. E., Revelle, W., Yovel, I., & Li, W. (2005). Cronbach's α, Revelle's β, and McDonald's ω_H: Their relations with each other and two alternative conceptualizations of reliability. *Psychometrika, 70*(1), 123–133. https://doi.org/10.1007/s11336-003-0974-7

CHAPTER 19

NORM- AND CRITERION-REFERENCED TESTING

Kurt F. Geisinger

The distinction between norm- and criterion-referenced testing exists primarily within the realm of educational testing and, perhaps to a lesser extent, in industrial training. To understand this distinction, however, one must know something about the early days of psychological testing because it was the influence of psychological testing that shaped the early growth of educational testing. Both share much in common, as the associations representing these professions have jointly collaborated for over 50 years to develop professional standards in educational and psychological testing (American Educational Research Association [AERA], American Psychological Association [APA], & National Council on Measurement in Education [NCME], 2014).

This chapter begins with a brief history of psychological testing. This historical introduction is brief and is summarized by DuBois (1970) and, with respect to ability testing, by Thorndike and Lohman (1990). These references should be used by those wishing more information about the history of educational and psychological testing, the treatment of which is beyond the scope of this chapter. We begin the discussion of the history of psychological testing with a consideration of intelligence and then move to educational testing, which is the primary realm in which the norm- versus criterion-referenced testing distinction is made. Much of this history happened within 20 years, before and after, 1900. We then discuss the logic and methods (primarily basic psychometrics) of norm-referenced testing. A special focus of that section is on the validity of measurement (Chapter 35 in this volume provides a more thorough discussion of the topic). The procedures often used in developing norm-referenced measures are also discussed. That section concludes with some concerns about norm-referenced testing when assessing student learning in education today.

Criterion-referenced testing is described next. A brief historical overview details the beginning of this type of testing in the 1960s. The logic of criterion-referenced testing is addressed before some of the basic psychometrics for criterion-referenced testing is discussed. The setting of standards is particularly critical for criterion-referenced testing, and these procedures are mentioned as well. The use of criterion-referenced testing in the assessment of student achievement concludes this section.

The chapter concludes with a look at the similarities and differences between norm- and criterion-referenced testing.

https://doi.org/10.1037/0000318-019
APA Handbook of Research Methods in Psychology, Second Edition: Vol. 1. Foundations, Planning, Measures, and Psychometrics, H. Cooper (Editor-in-Chief)
Copyright © 2023 by the American Psychological Association. All rights reserved.

THE EARLY DAYS OF MODERN PSYCHOLOGICAL TESTING

At the beginning of the 20th century a number of highly interrelated and highly similar trends were occurring in education. This time period may be thought of as the birth of modern testing in psychology and education. In France, in reaction to students who were not succeeding in the earliest public education in the modern world, Binet had developed an approach to evaluate the intellectual ability of schoolchildren. This approach was related to the ability to solve problems both verbally and using what were called *performance measures*. This approach largely flew in the face of the work of others (e.g., Cattell, 1890) who at that time had been attempting to measure physical attributes as well as the ability to perceive, feel sensations, and other relatively pure psychological measures. It was thought that by such measuring, one could combine them to estimate the ability to succeed in school, at work, and the like. Cattell, an American, studied under the famed Wilhelm Wundt in Leipzig, earning his doctoral degree, and then worked as an assistant in Galton's anthropometric laboratory in England for 3 years. Cattell argued that the advancement of psychology depended upon a solid foundation of the measurement of human characteristics. A professor first at the University of Pennsylvania and later Columbia University, he developed batteries of tests, including measures of dynamometer pressure, rate of movement, sensation-areas, pressure causing pain, least noticeable differences in weight, reaction time to sound, time for naming colors, bisection of a 50-centimeter line, judgment of 10 seconds of time, and the number of letters one could repeat upon once hearing (DuBois, 1970). His more "elaborate measurements" (Cattell's words) involved sight, hearing, taste and smell, touch and temperature, sense of effort and movement, mental time, mental intensity (mostly dealing with sensations), and mental extensity (involving memory and perception). Mental extensity was used by Cattell operationally to mean the number of impressions that could be perceived at the same time, the number of successive impressions that could be repeated, and the rate at which simple perceptions fade from memory. These measures, recorded during the 1890s and early 1900s, represented what some have considered the state-of-the-art in mental measurements around the turn of that century (DuBois, 1970).

On the other side of the Atlantic, Binet (e.g., Binet & Simon, 1905b, 1905c) provided a basic description of his approach to understanding intellectual behavior, to measure it, and to diagnose what was then called *mental retardation*. His measures were so successful that the number of research studies using his measures had approached 800 within 20 years after he had begun this work.

Binet and Simon's (1905a) third paper actually provided a description of the techniques used to score and norm the measures that they had discussed in their previous paper (Thorndike & Lohman, 1990). Some elements of the procedures that they used to build their measures were also provided in this publication. Their 1908 paper expanded and reorganized the individually administered measures originally developed approximately 3 years earlier. Questions or test items were organized by the chronological age at which successful responses to a question might be expected, much as they are today on a number of measures.

To call Binet's work a major breakthrough in the assessment of intelligence would be an understatement. His work was quickly translated into English by a number of individuals: Goddard (1908), Yerkes et al. (1918), and Terman (1916), among others. Terman, who received his doctoral degree in the United States at about the time of Binet's work on intelligence and had performed a dissertation using his own test of intelligence, worked on this translation of the Binet measure after receiving a faculty appointment at Stanford University. While a number of measures already existed at that time, "The scale with the widest acceptance, however, turned out to be the Stanford Revision of the Binet-Simon Scale, published originally in 1916 by L. M. Terman and revised by Terman and Merrill in 1937 and again in 1960" (DuBois, 1970, p. 49).

The Stanford-Binet test was thought of as a standard against which many other tests of intelligence were compared. It was (and is) an individually administered test, typically where a psychologist assesses a child using a variety of verbal and performance tasks. In developing the test, Terman administered it to large numbers of children at all ages and collected and analyzed the data so that the median performance on the tests for all individuals at a given age was set to be an intelligence quotient of 100. These methods, described more fully in this chapter, represent an attempt to build a norm-referenced test, one in which the scores are associated with one's performance relative to the remainder of the group and are generally interpreted accordingly.

After his success with the Stanford-Binet, Terman, not insignificantly from the perspective of this chapter, helped to develop the Stanford Achievement Tests, measures of student learning still in use today. The Stanford Achievement Tests use essentially the same techniques that Terman used in setting scores for the Stanford-Binet intelligence tests, with one notable exception. Rather than norming the tests on each chronological age, as does the Stanford-Binet, the Stanford Achievement Tests were normed on academic grade levels. That is, students in each grade could determine how they compared with their classmates across the country. The test has continued to exist since it was first developed by Terman in 1926. The Stanford Achievement Tests measure developed academic skills such as reading comprehension, mathematical skills, and science knowledge across the 13 grade levels, from kindergarten to 12th grade. The Stanford Achievement Tests, currently published by Pearson Assessments, are group-administered, norm-referenced tests of academic achievement. (As such, these tests are similar to a number of other major published measures that have been used for widespread assessment of student achievement in a norm-referenced fashion: the California Achievement Tests, the Comprehensive Test of Basic Skills, the Iowa Tests [of Basic Skills and of Educational Development], and the Metropolitan Achievement Tests.)

Cattell's work was followed closely by that of one of his doctoral students, E. L. Thorndike, who earned his doctoral degree under Cattell in 1898 and who taught at Teacher's College, Columbia University for decades. Thorndike's dissertation used mazes to measure the intelligence of cats; Cattell urged Thorndike to apply the same principles to the assessment of schoolchildren. Approximately 20 years later, Thorndike developed one of the first group-administered tests of intelligence in 1919. At the same time, he was developing measures of intelligence, he was also concerned with the assessment of school achievement. Thorndike developed or worked with students to construct a great number of what we now consider tests of educational achievement. For example, in 1910 he developed a measure of handwriting for use with students in Grades 5 through 8. He differentiated examples of handwriting into different levels or score-points and had several examples of handwriting for each score point. To evaluate an individual student, a teacher had only to compare that student's handwriting to these examples. The exemplars each had scale values, and the one closest to the student's handwriting became that student's handwriting score. His student Hillegas (1912/2018) used similar methodology to develop a scale for evaluating English compositions, a method largely similar to what is used today, where student responses are compared to anchor papers so that a proper score along an operational scale can be assigned. Thorndike also was very interested in the process and assessment of reading and published "measures of reading words and sentences in 1914" (DuBois, 1970, p. 73). This volume set an early approach to the assessment of reading ability, albeit not at a deep comprehension level.

The early measurement of aptitudes, primarily intelligence, was seen as following a normal curve, or at least it was assumed that the distribution of these abilities was well represented by the normal curve. It appears that this assumption carried forward to early achievement and other tests. It can be seen in the section that follows how the psychometric and statistical procedures that psychometricians and other test developers followed in developing student achievement tests were the same ones as used in the development of ability tests. These procedures can be seen in what has been called classical psychometrics or, more recently, item-response theory (see Chapter 37 [on item-response theory], this volume), although the present chapter focuses primarily on the former. A standard normal ability distribution is commonly expected "in the absence of any strong a priori beliefs, a normal distribution is a good approximation to the usually encountered distributions of ability measures" (Hulin et al., 1982, p. 254). This approach to establishing an underlying distribution is important because it differs for criterion-referenced testing, as will be seen later in this chapter.

THE PSYCHOMETRICS OF NORM-REFERENCED TESTING

The normal curve is a statistical concept that has gained substantial acceptance in use in psychology and, in particular, in psychological and educational testing. A normal curve has a number of primary characteristics. It is ultimately a theoretical distribution, one that exists mathematically rather than as a law of nature. In mathematical usage, it is completely symmetrical. It is asymptotic, meaning that the end points of the curve never touch the axis; that is, it is always possible to have a small number of very extreme values, although the vast majority of scores are in the middle of the distribution. Quite importantly for psychologists, the normal curve has fixed proportions falling underneath specific sections of the curve. For example, there is always 34.13% of the curve (or in psychology, of the people in a distribution) falling between the mean of the distribution and one standard deviation above and one standard deviation below the mean. Knowing that a set of test scores follows a normal curve permits knowledgeable psychologists to interpret where a person falls in a given distribution of scores just by looking at the score that the person has achieved. Of course, it is rarely if ever that a distribution of actual test scores fits a normal curve exactly. Rather, if a frequency distribution or graph of actual test scores does not deviate from the theoretical normal distribution in a manner that exceeds chance, then we consider the curve to be essentially a normal distribution.

Magnusson (1967), in a commonly used textbook on classical test theory, described the assumption made in testing that scores follow a normal curve regularly. He stated,

> It was noticed long ago that, when human attributes are measured with objective measuring instruments which give the data on interval or ratio scales, the results are distributed approximately in accordance with the normal distribution. Such distributions are obtained for physical characteristics such as height, physiological characteristics such as temperature of human beings at rest, and performance variables such as hand strength, measured by means of a hand dynamometer . . .
>
> In view of such facts a fundamental assumption has been proposed for practical test construction, namely that if we could measure differences between individuals on an interval scale, we would obtain a normal distribution of individual scores. (p. 11)

Thus, many of those in the testing profession believed that the normal curve was essentially a given for the measurement of many human traits, including the learning of students in the schools. Therefore, a great number of tests were developed in ways that lead to distributions that approximated the normal curve. In other cases, transformations were made to the raw scores earned on a test that took any distribution of scores and reconstituted it as a normal curve using a monotonic, nonlinear transformation. The study of differential psychology accentuated this perception. Anastasi (1958), in a classic text on differential psychology, reported,

> It was the nineteenth-century Belgian statistician Adolph Quetelet who first applied normal probability theory to

the distribution of human characteristics. Quetelet noticed that certain human measurements, such as the heights and chest girths of many army conscripts, were distributed according to the bell-shaped probability curve. From the approximate applicability of this curve to human variability data, he theorized that such human variability occurred when nature aimed at an 'ideal' or norm . . . In somewhat different terms, it may be argued that people's heights, weights, or intelligence test performance depend upon a very large number of independent factors, so that the end result will be distributed according to the law of chance. (p. 28)

This work was later applied by Sir Francis Galton and his many students, which caused these approaches to be central in the statistical analysis of human characteristics.

The Fundamental Unit of Assessment— The Test Item

Much of test theory and practice emerges from the use of individual test items. Given the limitations of testing time in virtually all contexts, one must be extremely selective in terms of which items should be used to compose a given measure. Especially for what is often called *cognitive measurement* (tests of ability, achievement, performance, and competency) where questions have right and wrong answers, the test item is the fundamental unit of analysis. Of course, while by far the most common type of test item since about the 1930s is the multiple-choice test item, there are many other types of objectively and subjectively scored items. In addition to the multiple-choice test item, other objective test items are true-false items, matching items, and the like. Early in the history of testing, such items could be assessed using a template. Now they are typically either scored by a scanning machine that reads filled in bubbles on an answer sheet or by computer or one of a few handheld devices, such as a tablet, on which the test taker completes the assessment. The test is then scored electronically. Subjectively scored items include essays, short-answer essays, problems in mathematics where students must supply their own answer and sometimes show their work or computations, performance assessments that were especially popular in education in the 1980s, and other exercises in which those with expertise must use their judgment to assign a score to a response. So-called fill-in-the-blank questions bridge the gap, especially where scoring is virtually objective. Increasingly, essays and other written answers are being scored by computers using techniques of artificial intelligence, but such programs are almost always built to model human raters, weighting those aspects of the essay that human raters value (Elliot & Williamson, 2013; Shermis & Burstein, 2013).

Items such as multiple-choice items are most typically scored as 0 (for an incorrect answer) or 1 (for a correct answer). This scoring pattern is a principle upon which classical psychometrics is essentially based. The proportion of the population that answers a question correct is considered to be the variable, p, and the proportion that does not answer the item correctly, q. (For this example, those who have neither responded to the item nor answered it correctly are considered to be members of q, because they have not answered the question correctly.) In this instance, p and q together sum to 1.00, the total proportion of all the test takers. One can consider a single item as a mini-test whereby scores, 0 and 1, constitute a distribution. Those earning a 1 are at the top of this distribution and those scoring a 0, at the bottom. The variable p is also the mean of the distribution. If one sums all the 1's and the 0's and divides by the number of persons taking the test, one has calculated the mean, which also is p, the proportion of individuals answering the question correctly. The term p is also called the *item difficulty* of a question. France and Batchelder (2015) suggested that this term should be called *item easiness*, not *item difficulty*, because the higher the value, the easier the question. Nevertheless, it is almost certainly the most common index of item difficulty among item analysis procedures. In item-response theory, the b parameter relates to difficulty and the higher the number, unlike p in classical psychometrics, the harder the item is.

Many test construction texts suggested at one time that test developers select items with item difficulty values near .50 to maximize item variances. Because tests were mostly composed of multiple-choice test items, others suggested that guessing be factored into the ideal item difficulty value. To clarify this point, consider the following example. Assume we have a multiple-choice item with four options, one correct and three incorrect. Assume further that the item difficulty without guessing is .50, the ideal value as stated above. Now assume that those test takers who do not know the correct answer guess randomly. Thus, of the four options, each would be selected by a fourth of the remaining 50% of the test takers. It would, hence, be expected that the ideal item difficulty becomes .625, based upon the original .50 plus one fourth of the remaining .50 or .125. In practice, however, most test takers do not like taking tests where they only know about 50% of the items, and this approach to item selection is not commonly used in educational testing today. Nevertheless, unless the test has a very specialized use, the developers of norm-referenced tests rarely accept items shown to have very high or very low item difficulties.

Because the role of a norm-referenced test is to differentiate test takers in meaningful ways, the variance of an item is important as variances are used to demonstrate the degree to which individuals differ in their scores. In the case of proportions, the mean and the variance are integrally related to one another. The variance of a proportion is the proportion of those passing the items (or p) multiplied by the proportion of those failing the item (q). The variance of an item scored 1 (correct) or 0 (incorrect), therefore, is $p \times q$. This value is maximized when the passing proportion equals that of the failing proportion at .50 each. Similarly, there is no variance for an item when either everyone gets the item correct or incorrect. Items that are very difficult or very easy have minimal variance. For this and other reasons, such items are not typically placed on norm-referenced tests. Therefore, item variance of an item with a p value of .50 is .25, and the item variance of an easy item with a p value of .90 is .09. Thus, given that the role of a norm-referenced test is to differentiate people, items of relatively larger variance are needed. Moreover, as will be seen in upcoming sections, items need to correlate with other items for a test to be reliable using traditional definitions, and it is easier to correlate with an item (or a variable) if the variance is relatively larger.

A second general class of techniques in which items are evaluated relates to the degree to which the different items composing a test correlate with each other, or presumably measure aspects of the same or highly related aspects of the same construct. Therefore, a fundamental manner in which items are individually evaluated is the degree to which they correlate with one another. The typical manner in which such relationships are computed is by correlating the responses to an item with total test scores. Thus, for each test taker, they have either a 0 or a 1 for each individual item and then they have a continuous score (from 0 to the maximum, which equals the total number of items scored 0 or 1). Two such correlations are most common: the point-biserial and the biserial. These indices are known as *item discrimination indices*. While discrimination from a broader life perspective is a bad thing, item discrimination is perhaps the most valuable aspect of an item in a norm-referenced test, because it tells us the extent to which the item appears to validly differentiate people in a population according to the underlying construct.

The point-biserial is a standard Pearson product-moment correlation coefficient between a dichotomous variable (in this case the test item) and a continuous variable (in this case the total test score). It can be computed using normal correlation coefficient calculations or using specialized formulae that were developed in precomputer days. Essentially, both the point-biserial and the biserial (described below) correlations are based upon the notion that one expects the mean on a test to be higher for those answering a question correctly (and, thus, demonstrating knowledge of the underlying construct) relative to those failing the item. If such a difference is not found, then it seems that the item provides little information about the underlying construct.

The biserial correlation coefficient differs from the point-biserial correlation in that it is not a Pearsonian correlation coefficient and instead is essentially an adaptation of it based on certain assumptions. This index is based upon the already noted assumption that there is a normal distribution underlying most characteristics, including psychological characteristics. While most students who have taken even a single course in statistics know that the maximum absolute value of a Pearson correlation coefficient is 1.00 (or −1.00), not all recognize that correlations cannot reach those values unless the shapes of their distributions are identical (or mirror images in the case of −1.00). The fact that an item has only a dichotomous distribution and test scores typically have a more normal distribution greatly limits the maximum value of point-biserial correlations. The biserial index is essentially an adjustment of the point-biserial correlation that inflates the value from the perspective that the dichotomous distribution generated by a test item has an underlying normal distribution. A common caution regarding the biserial correlation is that one must believe that the distribution underlying construct assessed by the individual item is in fact normal or close to normal.

Both of the item discrimination indices, the point-biserial and the biserial, suffer from one negative aspect. These correlations are inevitably somewhat spuriously high. They are somewhat high because the item itself is part of the total test score; it contributes to the total test score. This is equivalent to measuring the length of your left leg and measuring your height overall. If we correlated these to variables, one would expect a high correlation coefficient, but one that is less than the perfect 1.00. For this reason, a correction formula was devised in which the effect of the item is removed from the test (Henrysson, 1963). In effect, this statistical adjustment estimates that the correlation is between one item and all the rest of the items composing the test or scale. Most software packages that perform item analysis provide this latter index rather than the point-biserial itself, but it is important to determine whether the package uses the correction or not. The spuriousness of the correlation coefficient is especially problematic when the number of items is relatively low. As the number of items increases, the effect of an individual item becomes minimized.

Internal Consistency Reliability

Reliability is more formally described in this volume in Chapter 33. However, one of the primary effects of selecting test items that correlate highly with total test score is that the internal consistency reliability of the test is increased. From the perspective of this chapter, we believe that the internal consistency reliability of a test is important generally for most tests, whether norm-referenced or criterion-referenced, but it is more critically important for norm-referenced tests. *Reliability* as traditionally defined is consistency of measurement. In the case of internal consistency, most typically and generically termed *coefficient alpha*, we have, for each test taker, multiple measures, one for each test item. Coefficient alpha provides an index of the degree to which these items provide similar assessments. Essentially, the coefficient is an index of the degree to which within-person variability (seen as $MS_{within\ persons}$) is large relative to between-person variability (seen as $MS_{between\ persons}$). In fact, this is the basis for a formula that is mathematically equivalent to coefficient alpha (Hoyt, 1941). To the extent that between-persons variability is large relative to within-persons validity, we can differentiate people easily and dependably. It has been defined in a number of ways. For example, the square root of alpha is the correlation between observed scores and true scores (Nunnally, 1978) and the average of all possible split-half correlations, a technique that has long since disappeared with the development of computers and scanning machines. And indeed, assessing individuals consistently is the nature and purpose of norm-referenced assessments! These coefficients, therefore, are critical when one is evaluating the value of norm-referenced tests. It is, therefore, incumbent upon any test developer to pretest the questions expected to supply a form of a norm-referenced tests minimally to see if they correlate highly with each other and, hence, serve to foster high internal consistency reliability. In recent decades, coefficient alpha has been faulted for the violation of a number of the assumptions upon which it is based (Green & Yang, 2009; McNeish, 2018; Trizano-Hermosilla & Alvarado, 2016). Flawed it is, but it continues to be used by virtually all test publishers and test users, and Cronbach's (1951) article introducing coefficient alpha remains one of the most highly cited articles in psychology.

Another measure of internal consistency reliability that avoids these violations is omega (as developed by McDonald, 1970, and clarified by him in 1999). One long problem with coefficient alpha is that users interpret it as a measure of unidimensionality; it is not. Omega is built on a factor model and is both a measure of the proportion of total variance that is true variance and a measure of unidimensionality. "Coefficient omega has been defined as the ratio of the variance due to the common attribute to the total variance of Y" (McDonald, 1999, p. 89), where Y is the sum of the common factor contributions of the items as well as the unique contributions of the items. Coefficient omega has found favor with psychometricians but has yet to have much of an impact on the practice of testing.

Popham and Husek (1969) demonstrated the case of an extremely successful criterion-referenced test. In this instance, the students prior to instruction all scored very low, near zero. At the conclusion of instruction, the students had all learned the material on the test and, therefore, scored very well, at or near 100%. Moreover, the consistency of students relative to each other was no longer in strict rank-ordered fashion: Those who had scored well on the pretest did not necessarily score as well on the posttest. In such a case, both test–retest and internal consistency reliability are poor. The former is low due to the change in rank ordering of the students.

The second, the focus of this brief discussion, because when all students score at or near the same score point, there is little or no between-subjects variability. How often such situations occur, of course, is an empirical matter, and certainly many teachers who expect all students to understand concepts that have been so clearly explicated in class end up being rather disappointed.

Norms and Norm Groups

One of the absolutely critical elements in norm-referenced testing, and that will be seen to be indirectly relevant to criterion-referenced testing, relates to norms themselves. Norms indicate the nature of the distribution of test scores. The key element in a norm-referenced test is that a person knows where they fall in a distribution of other, hopefully comparable test takers. Therefore, much work has been done in psychometrics, test development, and related disciplines to develop score scales that provide relevant information to the users of test scores. Much of this work relates to ways of assigning scores given various raw scores that individuals achieve on tests. From the perspective of test developers, it is critical to amass a large and representative norm group—with representative meaning that it needs to be representative of the group with which the test will ultimately be used. Typically, regarding development of a norm group, the larger that the norm group is, the better, but there is no easy solution if the norm group is not representative. From the perspective of a test user, it is critical to evaluate the membership of the group taking the test. When a potential test user is deciding whether to use a particular test, they must decide the extent to which the group on which the norms were established compares to the group for which the test is given. For this reason, the test standards (AERA, APA, & NCME, 2014) stress that test publishers need to portray their norm group accurately in the representative publications, such as the test user manuals. Norms can be international (uncommon), national, statewide, or local. All of these norms have their own uses;

the determination of the level of norms should depend upon their use.

Judging the appropriateness of a norm group is one of the most critical questions a potential test user can make about a test that he or she is considering using. One must make certain that the population on which the norms are based is comparable to that for which one hopes to assess, if one wishes the score interpretations to be valid and appropriate. This point is especially critical when the test is being used with special populations; racial and ethnic minority groups, individuals with disabilities, and English-language learners are among the groups most critical to review.

Some of the worst abuses of testing have occurred when tests are used with populations, especially for high-stakes uses, on which they have not been proportionately represented (see Geisinger, 1998, 2005). For example, when the Head Start program, a program aimed at the initial educational experiences of underserved children prior to their beginning their formal education, was initially evaluated, a test (the Peabody Picture Vocabulary Test) was used as part of the evaluation. This measure had been initially normed and validated using almost exclusively White children who were the children of college professors in one city in the United States. While the following statement is probably a bit of an overstatement, scores of the young children who took the test as part of the evaluation program were largely members of minority groups from relatively poor sections of a number of inner cities. In such a situation, one must question the appropriateness of test use. Another test, the Hiskey-Nebraska Test of Learning Aptitude was developed as a measure to be used with children who were hearing impaired. It was initially normed on a group of children who had normal hearing but were told to feign being deaf. The test was subsequently normed on a more appropriate group. Again, this first norming occurrence for the Hiskey-Nebraska happened some 60 years ago, and, hopefully, a study like this one would not be performed today. Nevertheless, the significance of these issues is such that they remain examples of what not to do. (These scenarios are also described in Geisinger, 2005.)

Achieving a representative norm sample is not always an easy task, especially if this sample must be acquired prior to the test being given in an operational form. Some testing programs collect normative data prior to a test being published; some intelligence tests, for example, compensate a large number of psychologists to assess children using a test that is being readied for publication. In such cases, the psychologists assessing children and adults are given prescriptions of exactly how many individuals of different types (by age, gender, racial and ethnic groups, geographical residence) so that they are assured of the overall apparent representativeness of their final sample. In many cases, tests attempt to replicate the population as found in the U.S. Census. For illustrative purposes, the Wechsler Intelligence Scale for Children, 5th edition (WISC-V) and the Minnesota Multiphasic Personality Inventory (3rd edition; MMPI-3) were both developed with normative samples that closely paralleled U.S. Census statistics (Ben-Porath & Tellegen, 2020; Wechsler, 2014), In other cases, publishers collect preliminary norms test data prior to a test being formally published and then enhance the data collection with the test's operational use. Reading and mathematics achievement tests given as part of statewide assessments under either the No Child Left Behind Act (NCLB) or the Elementary and Secondary Education Act (ESEA) are often normed in this fashion, even though their primary purpose is not as a norm-referenced test. A current practice followed by some test publishers is to develop norms in an ongoing, cumulative manner. Their samples tend to be very large, but they are not necessarily representative of the most appropriate population(s).

The same test can utilize numerous norms groups, norms data, and resultant norms tables to be employed by test users. Some tests have used different norms for males and females; these measures tend to be personality measures, vocational interest measures, and the like, although at one time some cognitive measures used gender-specific norms. Age-specific norms are used for most intelligence tests. Where state or regional differences exist, where scores differ largely for groups such as immigrants or English-language learners, or where disabilities are involved, it may make sense to use specialized norms.

The two key principles used in the evaluation of any normative data collection project are simple: We want samples to be as large as possible and representative of the population targeted. Any errors in sampling, whether random or systematic, can negatively affect the resultant norms.

> Cornell (1960) pointed out that sample statistics lack precision when: (a) the errors of random sampling are large, i.e., when there is a wide dispersion of the distribution of the sample about the population parameter, and (b) where there is a bias, e.g., when the mean of all such sample statistics and the parameter are not the same. (Angoff, 1971, p. 549)

While researchers often eschew systematic biases over randomly occurring errors, Angoff (1971) pointed out that small systematic biases may be preferable to large random errors. In general, the larger the random sample, the smaller the errors of random sampling. That part of sampling is clear. It is, of course, difficult to find a sample used to develop norms for a test that has not yet been made operational that has been assembled through truly random sampling; however, if the population is large and national, or even statewide, in focus, it may be satisfactory. Generally, for many kinds of samples, schools are selected to be representative or psychologists are hired to find individuals meeting various demographic characteristics; such samples may be large but are not really random. Random sampling sometimes is achieved when testing a population by spiraling test forms. *Spiraling* means that every nth test would contain specific common questions or the common test form in question. Stratified random sampling may be attempted to secure a representative sample that is somewhat smaller than it might be if it were collected solely through random sampling. With random sampling, errors of sampling can be known or estimated.

Often for convenience, cluster and quota samples are selected, and these may come with biases, known and unknown. Angoff (1971) provided perhaps the most comprehensive review of these methods and the biases that accompany them and other related issues, including ways to estimate standard errors. For example, schools are often invited to participate in the preoperational testing so that norms can be computed, but some of these schools decline to participate. Such decisions, while understandable from the perspective of instructional time, may nevertheless lead to biased norms. Angoff, therefore, suggested that when plans for norm samples are developed, they should include 2 to 3 times as many schools as are needed in the final sample.

Kolen (2006) pointed out that sometimes samples are highly specific if somewhat dated. His example of this situation is when the 2002 SAT was normed, the norms were from those students who took a similar form of the SAT in 1990. The population was a known, carefully described population, although one might question its appropriateness, especially if there were major changes in curricula or experiences between 1990 and 2002. As opposed to such a situation,

> the norm group used to set a score scale is chosen for convenience, such as when a scale is based on the group of individuals who happen to take a test at a particular time. However, in this case, the normative information incorporated into the score scale does little to help users meaningfully interpret test scores. (Kolen, 2006, p. 163)

Among the most important considerations in defining the norm sample for any test norming project is a careful and explicit definition of the population in question. Subsequently, the sample must be drawn with complete adherence to the rules drawn up for it, using random sampling whenever possible. When biases are present in drawing the sample, the norms may nevertheless be useful. "They may, in spite of their bias, represent a close enough approximation to the ideal for most purposes" (Angoff, 1971, p. 560). It is through the use of these norms that score interpretation within the group is made. Of course, the validity of the instrument must also always be considered, a statement that is omitted in discussions of norms.

Score Distributions

It is a given in psychometrics that raw scores (i.e., the number of correctly answered questions on a test) on a measure are essentially meaningless. There are several reasons for this statement. For one reason, the raw scores on different tests all follow a different distribution depending upon the number of questions, the manner in which different questions are scored (e.g., dichotomous, polytomous), the difficulty of the test questions, and the relationships (correlations) among those questions. For this reason, testing development professionals typically transform raw score distributions to those that are commonly known among psychologists and other test users.

One of the most common interpretative aids of any test score distribution is the percentile rank. This value tells the test taker and other users the percentage of the norm group that falls below that score. Thus, if a person receives a percentile rank score of 73, it denotes that he or she scored higher than 73% of the people in the norm group. This fact is an elementary but critical component of any test score, especially of a norm-referenced test score. In fact, in part, this single index is perhaps among the most critical interpretative factors basic to a norm-referenced score and is in some ways the essence of such scores. Such scores may carry this information whether or not there is a normal distribution underlying the score distribution. Few test reporting systems, however, rely simply on percentile ranks as their scoring system. Rather, they use scales that carry meaning to informed users, scales that can be developed through the use of score transformations.

There are two kinds of transformations, linear and nonlinear. Furthermore, in almost all cases, the transformations are done in a manner that leaves the ordering of scores as they are in the raw score distribution. Most commonly, the distribution is linear, and these are described briefly below. A *linear* transformation is simply one that changes the numbering of the distribution, but the shape of the raw score distribution is unchanged. The basis for any linear transformation is that there is a slope and intercept used to transform the original distribution from raw scores to a commonly used scale. There are numerous common scales that can be achieved through transformations.

The formula for linear transformations is simply

$$Y = [(X - \text{Mean}_x) \times (S_y/S_x)] + \text{Mean}_y$$

where X is the raw score for a score in question on the raw score distribution, Y is the transformed score, S_y is the standard deviation of the resultant transformed score distribution, S_x is the standard deviation of the raw score distribution, Mean_x is the mean of the scores on the raw score distribution, and Mean_y is the mean of the scores on the resultant distribution. As noted above, there are a number of distributions that are very commonly used. These may be found in Table 19.1.

The advantage of using a score that is commonly understood is that professionals seeing the score know something about how a person has done relative to the group of people for whom the test is intended and from whom a representative sample was presumably drawn to develop the norms tables. For example, a college admissions counselor at a selective institution would know

TABLE 19.1

Common Transformed Scales

Name of the distribution	Mean	Standard deviation
z-score	0.00	1.00
College Board scale (SAT)[a]	500	100
t-scores	50	10
IQ	100	15[b]
Stanine	9	2

[a]Used for SAT test scores, among others. [b]For older Stanford-Binet test scores, the standard deviation was 16 rather than 15.

the range of SAT scores that are likely to be acceptable under normal circumstances and even the lowest scores that might be accepted by a sought-after football recruit. Similarly, a school psychologist knows the scores on intelligence and educational tests that are likely to lead to special education placements, whether for gifted educational programs or those for needing other kinds of assistance. Of course, such scores also connote a sense of predictive validity—a sense of how well the student is likely to do in the proposed educational program. Such information can only be ascertained by validity studies that are beyond the scope of this chapter but are described elsewhere (see Chapter 35).

The transformations that were described above are all linear transformations. It is also possible to change the shape of the distribution. A common technique is what is called a *normalization transformation*. This transformation changes the shape of the distribution in a manner that permits a test score user to apply normal curve tables to the scores. How such a transformation is calculated is beyond the scope of this chapter, but that can be found in Angoff (1971, pp. 515–521) or Magnusson (1967, pp. 235–238). The bottom line is that the transformed scores approximate a normal distribution. While the primary advantage of conducting a normalization transformation is that the scores follow a normal distribution, there are other advantages as well. One additional advantage is that correlation coefficients representing the linear relationship between two variables are limited when the shapes of the distributions are not the same. By normalizing a distribution, one optimizes one's chance of maximizing the correlation between test scores that result from the test and other variables, such as criteria utilized in criterion-related validity studies.

Two other nonlinear transformations are often used, especially in school settings and/or with young children. These include age-equivalent and grade-equivalent score scales. Both were mentioned previously in this chapter in regard to the Stanford tests of ability and achievement. Each is described briefly next.

Age-equivalent scores differ from all of the scales previously presented. Measurement specialists and psychometricians employ scales based upon standard deviation units to make the case that the measurement is at the interval level of measurement rather than the ordinal. Age-equivalent scores, however, do not use standard deviation units in this way. Rather, these scales, which are most often used in conjunction with the ability testing of children, convey a sense of the age for which such results might be expected. Psychometricians, however, are not positive about this approach, which has been used in the schools and for communication with parents and other similar groups. The technique can perhaps be best understood by considering how age-equivalent scores are computed. First, a range of children across the age span with whom the test is intended to be used is assessed with the testing instrument. Second, children are grouped by their closest year of chronological age. (Sometimes finer demarcations are used, such as half-year or quarter-year gradations.) Then the median score for each age becomes that age. (Sometimes the mean is also used.) Imagine a 20-question test. If the children who are all grouped at age 7 achieve a median raw score of 14.0, then a raw score of 14.0 is seen as 7 years, 0 months of age on this scale. This procedure is followed for every age of interest in the population, and a smooth curve is drawn through the distribution using interpolation. Thus, the midpoint on the graph between ages 7 and 8 would be seen as the value representing 7 years, 6 months. Scores for each month can be interpolated from the graph (or table) in the same fashion. While age-equivalent scores were utilized early in the history of psychological testing (Angoff, 1971), there are too many disadvantages of this type of scale to continue their use, except perhaps in rare circumstances. Angoff (1971) presented these disadvantages in some depth. A few example would help the reader to decide to avoid these scores. In the norms chapters in the two subsequent editions of the classic *Educational Measurement* series, the topic of age-equivalent scores is barely touched. Grade-equivalent scores were addressed in the series by Peterson et al. (1989) but were only mentioned in Kolen (2006). First, the variation of performance around the line that is drawn may well vary throughout the age span of interest. In some cases, differences from the line may be rather extreme and yet the same difference from the line may be rather commonplace at another age. A second and perhaps more problematic concern emerges from scores of children who score much higher than or more poorly than their peers at a given age. Imagine an advanced 7-year-old child who scores the same as 10-year-olds. Such a finding does not mean that the child can think in the same manner as a child of 10. Anastasi and Urbina (1997) provided an example that an advanced 8-year-old may have a mental age of 10 years old, as may a developmentally delayed adult. That does not mean that their thinking ability is the same. Rather, it simply reflects how they scored on the test as a whole. Moreover, age- and grade-equivalent test scores are not well suited for statistical analysis because they are only an ordinal scale. Age-equivalent scores are only appropriate for children; it does not make sense to say that an individual who is 25 years old can answer questions equivalent to that of a 28-year-old. For these reasons, the use of age-equivalent scores has justifiably been reduced in recent years.

Grade-equivalent scores are similar to age-equivalent scores, except that rather than using the chronological age of children, their year in school is employed. Such scores continue to be used and psychometricians are only slightly less favorable to these scores than age-equivalent scores for similar reasons. Scores are provided for the year and month of schooling. A score of 6.4 would indicate that the student had scored equivalent to that of a sixth grader in their fourth month of the school year. These scores, too, are subject to misinterpretation. Imagine a fourth grader who earns a score on a mathematics test of 6.7. This score implies that the student has scored similarly to that of a sixth grader in their seventh month. However, there is much mathematics content that is covered during the students fourth, fifth, and sixth grades. It does not mean that the student has learned that material; it simply means that the child is much more advanced than a typical fourth grader.

Scales such as the age-equivalent and grade-equivalent scales must be seen as purely ordinal scales. Their use under normal circumstances should be avoided.

The Uses of Norm-Referenced Tests

Norm-referenced tests have many uses in psychology, education, and industry and continue to be widely used to this day. Their use in achievement testing has waned, however, in the assessment of student learning, as is described in the next section. During the 1980s, in virtually all states in the United States, schools administered norm-referenced achievement tests such as the California Achievement Tests, the Iowa Tests of Basic Skills, the Metropolitan Achievement Tests, or the Stanford Achievement Tests. All of these tests were carefully developed so that they did indeed measure content relevant to the grades in question across the United States, or at least across the states where these measures were used. These measures were provided by test publishers who developed the tests in ways to insure what was then called *content validity* and is now seen as *content-related evidence of validity*. The test developers provided information on how students compared to each other at each grade in terms of their achievement. They could also provide some information in terms of what students had learned. The use of these tests, while still prevalent and available, has declined substantially during the period of the 1990s when standards-based testing became the norm.

Norm-referenced tests are especially useful in situations where comparative decisions must be made about individuals. Indeed, the meaning of the scores comes in comparing scores to those from the fixed reference group. These situations generally involve the sorting of individuals into groups or a rank ordering and the selection of individuals for specific purposes or programs. Selection situations are perhaps the single instance of most positive use for norm-referenced tests. It was during World War I and World War II that a variety of mental and physical ability tests were used effectively to select and sort individuals for positions in the military that enabled the armed forces to work efficiently (e.g., Chapman, 1988). Choosing students for selective and highly selective colleges is another example of an effective use of psychological tests (Camara & Kimmel, 2005; Zwick, 2002). Personnel selection in industry has a long history of finding individuals with the skills to perform specific jobs.

The chapter on validity (see Chapter 35, this volume) includes much critical information about the use of tests in predictive situations. This information is only abstracted briefly here. In any predictive situation, one of the chief sources of information is related to the quality of the test to predict future performance, such as college or job success. These relationships are most commonly indexed as correlation coefficients between the predictive performance and some criterion of school or job performance. One can also imagine the use of the college admissions test as a 2 × 2 table, where the test is used to accept or reject candidates for admission. Similarly, students at the college can either succeed or fail. Therefore, those individuals who are selected and who succeed may be seen as the valid acceptances and those who are selected and fail out are false acceptances. We must then imagine how those who fail to be accepted would have done in college. Those who indeed would not have succeeded may be considered as valid rejections. Those who would have succeeded in spite of their lower test performance may be thought of as false rejections. Most colleges (and employers) wish to maximize the numbers of valid decisions. They are especially concerned about false acceptances, but false rejections are also costly. The seat filled by a student who is a false acceptance could well have been occupied by a false rejection!

Two factors that help institutions maximize their percentage of valid decisions and the effects of these factors, test validity and selection ratio, may be seen in the famous Taylor–Russell tables (Taylor & Russell, 1939). Test validity is characterized by a correlation coefficient; the higher the correlation coefficient, the better able we are to make valid decisions. Selection ratio is the proportion of candidates to be selected. The higher the selection ratio, the more candidates there are for the positions to be filled. What is clear is that when there are many candidates for every position, even a test of moderate validity can help make a great number of valid decisions. Likewise, if one needs to accept every candidate, the test can have only limited or no value. A third factor is also involved in the Taylor–Russell tables, the base rate of successful performance, that is, the proportion of candidates who would be successful even if no test were used. Clearly, the higher this percentage, the easier it is to fill one's class or employment positions with successful individuals. It is for reasons of selection ratio and base rate that colleges and employers work hard to recruit many applications.

Selection tests such as the SAT and ACT have provided useful information to colleges and universities making difficult admissions decisions, although it is always strongly recommended that such test scores not be used in isolation or even with a single fixed cutoff for admission. Most colleges and universities have recently halted the use of such measures or at least made them optional. There were several reasons for this decision, which has become national or virtually national. One reason was that test administrations became difficult in the COVID-19 pandemic; traditional group administrations were simply impossible. A second was that the differences between ethnic groups and other diversity groups (e.g., class, disability) became increasingly unacceptable at a time of the Black Lives Matter movement, a position widely accepted on college campuses. In fact, a court case in California State court ultimately prohibited the University of California system from using college admissions tests until 2025 (*Smith v. Regents of the University of California*, 2019). The case was also heavily influenced by the number of students with disabilities who were not able to receive the testing accommodations they needed in a timely way during the pandemic. Nevertheless, it remains to be seen whether college admissions tests will have a return to frequent use by higher educational institutions.

Similarly, there are a number of well-known measures that have been effectively used as part of admissions decisions for graduate and professional schools: the Graduate Record Examination (GRE) for admissions to many graduate school programs, the Law School Admission Test (LSAT) for admissions to law schools, the Medical College Admissions Test (MCAT) for medical colleges, and the Graduate Management Admission Test (GMAT) for admission to master of business administration (MBA) programs at business schools. These measures typically have a number of scales measuring verbal skills (primarily reading comprehension), mathematical skills and reasoning, and writing. In some of the more specialized tests, they also include subtests of science knowledge or reasoning and the like as well. All of these tests can perhaps best be thought of as measures of both ability and achievement; they are really measures of developed abilities, skills taught over years of schooling and not just through a quick training program intended to achieve success purely on the test. Much debate has occurred over their possible usefulness of short-term training programs to "coach" students to achieve success (e.g., Bond, 1989). Bond (1989) rightly identified the debate over the effects of coaching as both a scientific and a political debate. A number of his conclusions provide some information regarding this controversy. First, the more time one spends in a specialized training program, the more likely it is to have a positive effect. Second, the effects of most so-called coaching programs tend to be relatively minor, upwardly influencing scores by .10 to .20 standard deviations. Third, most of the largest gains that have been identified were found in studies that lacked a control group. Finally, where students have learned or relearned mathematical concepts but had not used them for a considerable period of time, the coaching may serve as something of a refresher and yield some positive effects. Nevertheless, Bond (1989) concluded that students would have to sift through information on their own to make decisions relative to their taking such courses or even purchasing a preparation book.

Norm-referenced tests are just as useful in personnel selection in industry as in college admissions, if not more so. This topic is largely beyond the scope of this chapter because the debate/discussion of norm-referenced versus criterion-referenced testing has largely occurred within the context of educational testing and, more specifically, the testing of student achievement. Nevertheless, tests do help in the selection of employees for a wide variety of positions. Just as in admissions testing, however, the biggest controversy in personnel selection relates to the fairness of tests in the personnel selection process. Specifically, in America questions arise frequently that tests have negative effects on racial minorities, language minorities, women, and other underserved groups. Within industrial psychology the controversy has been answered just as frequently, but it continues to raise its head in both the popular press and professional journals (e.g., De Soete et al., 2013; Roth et al., 2001).

Item Response Theory Approaches

Heretofore, this chapter has been written primarily from the perspective of classical psychometrics. Indices such as p values, point-biserial correlations, and internal consistency reliability coefficients such as coefficient alpha are important in classical psychometrics. Today, many educational tests are built on the basis of item response theory (IRT). (See Chapter 37, this volume, for an in-depth discussion of these models.) It needs to be stated in this chapter, however, that many large-scale educational and licensure tests such as statewide achievement tests use IRT rather than classical psychometrics to analyze their test data and achieve scores for test takers; nevertheless, all the principles provided heretofore are valid and appropriate. A variety of textbooks are available that describe the methods of IRT well; some of the better volumes are F. B. Baker and Kim (2017), De Ayala (2009), DeMars (2010), and Raykov and Marcoulides (2011).

There are a variety of IRT models, most often utilizing one, two or three parameters. If a one-parameter model is used, the parameter is "b," or *item difficulty*. If a two-parameter model is used, the parameters are "b" and "a," or *item discrimination*. Both of these values are analogous to the *p* value and point-biserial index already described. A common third parameter for large-scale tests is the "c" parameter, which is sometimes known as the *guessing parameter*, as this value provides an index of the likelihood that a test taker can get an item correct when they do not have sufficient knowledge to answer it from their knowledge base. It will be argued later in this chapter that while IRT procedures are appropriate for norm-referenced tests, in regard to criterion-reference while some IRT procedures such as the one-parameter model are clearly appropriate, others, such as those involving the "a" or discrimination index may be somewhat more questionable. The more parameters one estimates in IRT, the more test takers one needs to estimate the parameters.

Figure 19.1 provides two examples of the item characteristic curves that are representative of test taker performance in IRT. The x-axis provides a scaling of ability, the trait that underlies the tested characteristic. These values typically range from about –3.00 to about +3.00 in *z*-score terms.

The y-axis provides the probability of test takers getting an item correct. The origin, or 0 point, where the item characteristic curve crosses the y-axis, represents the proportion of examinees getting the item correct without appropriate knowledge, or, hence, the c parameter. The midpoint of the curve falling relative to the x-axis represents the difficulty of an item; that is, the further to the right the curve falls, the more difficult the item is because one needs a greater amount of ability to answer the questions correctly. The steepness of the curve represents the ability of the item to differentiate weaker test takers from stronger ones. The steepness may occur in specific portions of the curve where the discrimination of those who know the answer from those who do not is most intense.

THE ADVENT AND USES OF CRITERION-REFERENCED TESTING

Early in the 1960s, a small group of psychologists and educational psychologists began to advocate for a different kind of testing (e.g., Glaser, 1963;

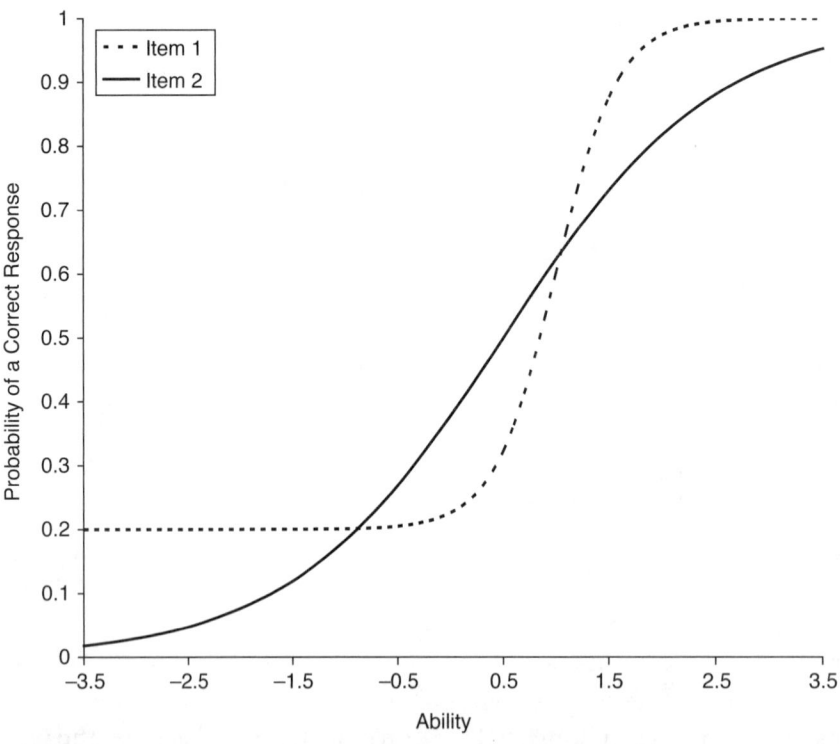

FIGURE 19.1. Item characteristic curves for two different assessment items.

Glaser & Kraus, 1962; Hammock, 1960). These individuals called for the construction and use of measures that did something different from norm-referenced, selection-type measures. Glaser (1963), for example, in the article often seen as the birth of criterion-referenced testing, called for a kind of measurement that we might now refer to as *authentic assessment*. It was an educational or achievement-type test that had more than content evidence of validity. The nature of this new kind of measurement was a concept that had not as then been developed. In Glaser's (1963) own terms, the character of this new kind of testing can best be understood by the following: "Achievement measurement can be defined as the assessment of criterion behavior; this involves the determination of the characteristics of student performance with respect to specific standards" (p. 519). Also, "measures which assess student achievement in terms of a criterion standard . . . provide information as to the degree of competence attained by a particular student which is independent of reference to the performance of others" (p. 520).

Millman (1974) defined the measures as tests that "provide information about the specific knowledge and skills of examinees and yield scores interpretable in terms of tasks or performances" (pp. 311–312). Millman (1974) also pointed out that the term *criterion* in *criterion-referenced testing* was confusing because it implied there was a criterion, as in a criterion-related validation study. Rather, the test is a criterion itself of evidence that learning had occurred.

Perhaps because of that confusion, a number of different names were utilized to refer to criterion-referenced tests over the years, although there are some differences among the implications for the different names as well. Ebel (1962) used the term *content-standard test scores*. Others later used terms such as *objectives-based testing*, *domain-referenced testing*, *mastery tests*, *edumetric tests*, and today's name of choice, *standards-based assessments*. This list is certainly not complete. (Nitko, 1980, provided what is certainly the most complete listing and explication of terms used for this type of test.)

The basic distinction between norm-referenced tests and criterion-referenced tests can perhaps be best seen with the following two examples:

A norm-referenced interpretation: On a 25-item, multiple-choice grammar test, Janet scored 16 of the items correctly. This score placed her performance at the 75 percentile of all fourth graders who took the examination in a nationally representative norm study.

A criterion-referenced interpretation: On a 25-item multiple-choice grammar test, Janet scored 16 of the items correctly. This score identified her performance as proficient. Her performance was substantially higher than the cut score for that category, and we are 92% confident that she belongs in this grouping. Had she answered three more items correctly, her score would have moved her to the Advanced Proficient category.

The aforementioned examples make no comparative reference to how other students performed on the test. These examples demonstrate Linn's (1994) characterization of criterion-referenced testing as "the essential idea that test results be interpreted in terms of a continuum of criterion performance that indicates what an individual can do" (p. 12). Essentially, the goal of criterion-referenced test use is to provide information that is readily able to be used by those guiding the instruction of students. A true criterion-referenced test would be one that provides elaborate direction to teachers and instructional supervisors and would permit such individuals to decide exactly what instruction a student needed next. The Gordon Commission (Gordon & Rajagopalan, 2016) called for tests that truly helped student learning and teacher testing. If tests truly met Linn's (1994) standard and the resultant data were readily available with great immediacy, such information would be able to provide the kind of information called for by the Gordon Commission.

To accomplish such tasks, however, a test needs to be built differently than a norm-referenced test. Rather than selecting test questions using p values (means) and item discrimination indices so that individual differences in scores are maximized, the test developer needs to write items very closely aligned to the curriculum in place and, to be sure, to the instruction that has been provided to students. The test needs to assess whether students have learned the critical concepts, often based on standards, in any instructional lesson or experience. So that such items could be developed, carefully written instructional specifications are needed. In fact, one of the leading proponents of criterion-referenced testing, James Popham (1994), stated that "the increased clarity attributed to criterion-referenced tests was derived from the test-item specifications that were generated in order to guide item writers. These specifications, in a very literal sense, operationalized what the test was intended to measure" (p. 16). Popham also identified a constant concern for developers of criterion-referenced tests, that one must find the correct and appropriate level of granularity. If one writes standards that are too narrow, then teachers are likely to teach to these narrow foci so that their students will succeed on the test; these foci will not generalize to the broader skill clusters that we hope to teach our students. If, on the other hand, one writes objectives that are too general, it becomes very difficult to decide what we need to measure. Popham (1994) described this situation as a dilemma that test developers of criterion-referenced tests must face.

Test items must be written carefully to address the standards and objectives of instruction. Numerous treatises have been written describing how test questions should be written for these tests (e.g., Davis & Diamond, 1974; Millman, 1980; Popham, 1980; Roid, 1984). I believe that the level of scrutiny required in terms of content validation is much more intense for a criterion-referenced educational achievement test than for a norm-referenced one, where items must meet statistical criteria to a greater extent. In fact, most educational tests used for statewide accountability purposes in the United States must have alignment studies performed. In such studies, individuals, typically teachers of the proper subject-matter and grade levels, review the items on the test and identify which content areas or statewide educational standards they are supposed to be assessing. The reviewers are blind to what content areas or standards the items were written to measure. When the reviewers have finished their work, psychometricians can assess the extent to which the test as a whole assesses what it is intended to measure. E. L. Baker (2016) and Linn (2003), among many others, identified a perception that the curriculum narrowed because of the use of tests as accountability criteria.

During the 1980s, criterion-referenced testing became exceedingly popular with a large number of states requiring minimum competency tests. These tests were based on the minimal expectations that those states held for all of their students and were, therefore, used, in some states, as graduation requirements, a matter that led to the Debra P. case in Florida (Madaus, 1983). In short, the state of Florida was concerned about the quality of its public educational system and, therefore, enacted laws requiring the administration and use of a minimum competency examination covering certain basic academic skills. This test was to be used as a requirement for high school graduation, that is, receipt of a diploma. While many students across the state passed the examination, a significant number failed, and the failing group included a disparate number or proportion of African American students. (For example, during one administration of the test, 25% of White students failed to pass one or more sections of the test; during that same administration, 78% of African Americans failed to pass at least one section of the test.) This class-action legal case, brought on the behalf of these African American students, challenged the right of the state to impose the passing of the examination as a requirement for the receipt of a high school diploma. From the perspective of the courts, the overriding legal issue for this case was whether the Florida could deprive public school students of the high school diplomas that they expected to receive on the basis of an examination. It became necessary to assess the degree to what was on the test covered subject matter not taught through the curriculum. The court of appeals in this case held that the state could not constitutionally deprive its students of diplomas unless it submitted proof of the curricular validity and instructional validity of the test. Curricular validity was determined on the basis of whether the curriculum required instruction to all students on the material covered by the examination. Instructional validity was determined on the basis of whether all students actually received the instruction on the test. Ho and Reardon (2012) have studied the continuing differences across ethnic groups based on criterion-referenced tests that provide students with ordinal categories of educational success.

One of the distinctions made by Linn (1994) about criterion-referenced testing is that while it is possible to develop norms for a test developed to be a criterion-referenced test; he believed, however, that it would rarely be possible to take a test built as a norm-referenced test and use it as a criterion-referenced test. Essentially, the manner in which a norm-referenced test is built simply would not permit such interpretations. Perhaps with the proper test construction procedures, this conclusion need not be the case, but it generally would be true.

In conclusion, Linn (1994), one of the paragons of educational testing, wrote that he considered Glaser's (1963) idea for criterion-referenced testing as one of the truly seminal ideas in educational testing. Perhaps it is not clear that criterion-referenced testing has achieved the goals Glaser and others originally desired. Criterion-referenced testing, however, especially in the current form of standards-based assessments, has taken on status of the primary way in which the educational achievement of students in the United States is measured especially for accountability. Moreover, techniques to ensure we have content evidence of validity such as alignment studies have helped close the gap between curriculum and testing, between instruction and assessment, and between state-mandated standards and the tests developed to assess whether they are being successfully taught and learned. The careful delineation of the content to be covered on an achievement test through its test specifications—for which a considerable attention is focused—is required; equally careful test construction procedures must meet the test specifications, and checks are made that the test questions are measuring the standards that drive both curriculum and instruction. Careful reviews by those not directly involved in the testing construction, including formal alignment studies, and the test-related procedures that have an impact on the quality of the test (e.g., standard setting) all characterize criterion-referenced testing in the early years of the 21st century. Fulmer (2011) provided an excellent summary of the statistics one should use to evaluate the extent to which a test is aligned with the intended curriculum. Squires (2012) provided a review of curriculum alignment studies conducted by school districts. Truly, good criterion-referenced tests can help a teacher, a school, a school system, and a state assess the extent to which their education is successful in helping students achieve the chosen standards of performance (Geisinger, 2021). Most licensure and certification tests, too, have become criterion-referenced tests in recent decades (Geisinger, 2020).

Psychometric Issues in Criterion-Referenced Testing

This section considers item difficulty, item discrimination, test reliability, validity and standard setting. Item difficulty indices have considerably less impact in true criterion referenced testing. After all, should not the vast majority of students who have been exposed to effective instruction be able to answer questions that are written to represent that instruction (rather than to spread out the performance of students)?

> It is important to distinguish between the difficulty of an item for a given student, which presumably is strictly a function of his (sic) experiences and his previous instruction (both formal and informal), and the normative concept of validity, which depends as well on who makes up the group of students whose responses provide the estimate of difficulty. (Harris, 1974, p. 101)

Item difficulty, therefore, a key index in norm-referenced testing, typically has far less impact for criterion-referenced testing. There are considerable changes when switching from using norm-referenced tests in terms of development and score interpretation to criterion-referenced tests. Bennett et al. (2012) presented a useful case study of a school system making these changes in Australia.

Variances of items, as described previously, are entirely dependent upon item difficulty and, thus, too, have much less impact in regard to criterion-referenced testing. Variances of test performance, too, are of somewhat less criticality; rather, key is the mastery status of test takers. In the early days of criterion-referenced testing, such states were mostly mastery and nonmastery. In today's standards-based examinations, especially under the No Child Left Behind Act of 2001, there are likely to be three to five ordinally arranged status levels. Harris (1974), after describing how one must construct test items to represent a domain of content carefully, actually made a remarkable statement for a psychometrician, "I conclude that the construction of the particular test should proceed without attention to response data" (p. 104). In particular, he argued that item-response data (e.g., item difficulty and discrimination) should not be used to decide if an item is placed on a test. He perceived the critical question as being how well a test can be used to sort students into groups, with each group qualitatively different in terms of their learning. He rightly argued that this question is really the validity argument. That is, if a test is able to identify those students who have learned the material in an instructional event from those who have not, it is a valid test. Clearly, the key question then is whether the test as a whole represents the content required by the standards, the curriculum, and the instruction in sequence; this question is an extreme one of content validity. Popham and Husek (1969) made some of the same points.

Berk (1980) provided a basic introduction to some item analysis techniques specifically for criterion-referenced tests. The techniques that Berk provided may be divided into (a) item-objective congruence, (b) item statistics, (c) item selection, and (d) item revision. In general, the item-objective congruence approaches involve judgment on the part of those knowledgeable about both objectives or standards on one hand and the test items on the other. These general techniques include the alignment studies now frequently used by states to assess the degree to which the high-stakes No Child Left Behind Act, also known as the Elementary and Secondary Education Act, examinations match the standards that the state has selected to assess. Such indices have preeminent value in the construction of most criterion-referenced tests.

The item statistics (Berk's second category) involve the comparisons of item performance, typically comparing those who have received instruction on the content covered by the test from those who have not. Such analyses can either be pre–post test comparisons of a single group or a contrast of two preexisting groups that differ in their instructional background. Essentially, such comparisons are contrasting those who are expected to have knowledge versus those who do not. A number of item analysis procedures analogous to those used in classical norm-referenced testing may also be provided. In fact, one possible analysis of items, for example, would perform traditional item analysis procedures using both students who have received instruction versus those who have not. Such analyses should identify those items that are most sensitive to instruction. Berk (1980) also suggested that test constructors also elicit informal student feedback about the questions.

Berk (1980) suggested that certain item analysis procedures be used in deciding whether or not to include item-objective congruence (more currently *item-standard congruence*), that is, item difficulty and discrimination. Congruence between item and the objective it is measuring is of paramount importance. Item difficulty and discrimination indices are mostly to be used to identify the extent to which the item helps the test differentiate masters from nonmasters. One can include pre- and postinstruction test takers in a single analysis to perform such an analysis. In some current statewide assessments, items are pretested on a single population and evaluated in terms of item–test discrimination; such analyses are exactly as used in norm-referenced testing, and it is not clear how that builds a truly criterion-referenced examination.

A final set of procedures described by Berk (1980) include those that help a test constructor to decide whether to revise an item. He provided the following general rules for identifying such items (and distractors within those items):

1. Each distractor should be selected by more students in the uninstructed group than in the instructed group.
2. At least a few uninstructed students should select each distractor.
3. No distractor should receive as many responses by the instructed group as the correct answer. (p. 70)

The reliability of criterion-referenced tests has been, at least in the early days of criterion-referenced testing, a somewhat controversial topic. Whereas norm-referenced tests are developed so that they differentiate individual test takers in terms of their level of achievement, criterion-referenced tests have a different purpose, and it is not clear that such indices are as relevant. Ultimately, as stated previously, it is not essential that a criterion-referenced test has variability, especially postinstructionally. Thus, at least according to Popham and Husek (1969), traditional indices of internal consistency are not appropriate. Berk (1984) classified the attempts to assess the reliability of criterion-referenced tests into three general approaches, two of which are relevant to this discussion: (a) the reliability or consistency of classification decisions, and (b) the more traditional reliability of test scores on criterion-referenced tests. However, Berk (1984) also stated that "the use of the term reliability coefficient to characterize the indices recommended for criterion-referenced tests is inappropriate" (p. 232). Classification accuracy is clearly the critical element of criterion-referenced examinations, which have as their primary purpose the sorting of test takers into the proper categories. Just as certainly, the closer the critical cut scores (i.e., passing scores or scores where one moves from one category of test taker to another) are to the median of the distribution, the more likely the decision consistency will be lower. Other reliability estimates use squared errors (e.g., Livingston, 1972), as they are in variance estimates, but rather than computing these values by subtracting a score from the mean and squaring it, they are subtracted from the relevant cut score and squared. One can imagine an analogue of the test–retest reliability coefficient where rather than using the difference between a score and the mean of the distribution in the formula, one uses the difference between that same score and the cut score. There have been criticisms, however, about these approaches (e.g., Hambleton & Novick, 1973).

The separation of students into groups based upon their performance has been one of the most studied topics in criterion-referenced tests. There is such a large variety of methods that they have been grouped into logical groupings of these methods. Several excellent books review these procedures (e.g., Cizek, 2001; Cizek & Bunch, 2007; Zieky et al., 2008). A few general principles are true of all methods, however. Some of these generalizations include the fact that all methods for setting cut scores are ultimately based upon judgment (Glass, 1978; Zieky et al., 2008). The nature of these judgments differs by class of method, as is mentioned below. Moreover, there is no true passing (or perfect) score for a test. Rather, different cut scores might be used for a test depending upon the population of students taking the test, upon the use to which the test scores are put, and so on. Finally, after any testing, there will be misclassifications of students into the incorrect groups. It is as hard to imagine a test that correctly classifies all students who take it (a criterion-referenced perspective) as it is to imagine a test where every student receives a test score that perfectly accurately estimates where they fall in the distribution of test takers (a norm-referenced perspective).

Initially, criterion-referenced tests divided students and trainees into two groups: passers and failures or masters and nonmasters. From a reliability perspective, it is more appropriate that we assess how similarly performing individuals are placed into groups. In many types of accountability testing, they have been broken into more achievement groups, often three to five such groups. Indices such as kappa are often used to assess the reliability of classification. Psychometric sophistication is needed to make these decisions and Dorans and his colleagues (2010) identified the impact of the exactitude of the test score scaling on making these decisions. Simply put, if the scale only provides 10 scores (e.g., 10, 20, 30, . . . 100), classifications will lose some of precision if there is more differentiated scoring. Diao and Sireci (2018) provided IRT approaches to assessing classification accuracy and consistency for such classification systems.

As previously noted, all techniques for setting passing scores involve judgment. The number of specific techniques or strategies for setting passing scores has easily reached 50 or more. The vast majority of these techniques, however, can be broken into two categories: techniques based upon the judgments of the test questions composing the test and techniques involving judgments about people. In the former, those knowledgeable about the nature review the test questions in a structured manner and use their knowledge and experience as well as their perceptions of the test to formulate judgments that permit those running the meeting to set proper cut scores. One common method is the Angoff method, a method that many people have modified to some extent. In this technique, judges define what a person just minimally in the status (e.g., just passing) would be like. After the judges reach some consensus, then the judges would independently decide, item by item, what proportion of these minimally passing students would get each item correct. Once each judge has reviewed all the items and assigned each a proportion, then discussion among the judges ensues, often followed by a second or subsequent round of ratings. After a particular round concludes, the average proportion of test items is selected as the passing score. This description is obviously overly simplified, and it represents just one of the many techniques that are based upon judgments of test items composing a test.

The importance of judges should be clear. Scholars have described how judges should be selected and trained to engage in these processes (e.g., Raymond & Reid, 2001). A difficult aspect of the above-named procedure is that the judges, typically teachers, are often not used to thinking about test items and the proportion of students at a particular level of achievement who would answer the item correctly. For this reason, in some cases, the items are arranged in terms of difficulty (as determined by the a priori collection of data) and then judges place bookmarks in the place where they believe the cuts should be made. These values are translated into the ability level of the examinees who would (just) get that last item correct. This technique is known as the Bookmark technique. Both the Angoff technique and the Bookmark technique have been mentioned only so that a flavor for how techniques where judges consider the test items is provided.

There are fewer techniques that consider the test takers rather than test items. Two mentioned are called the Borderline and the Contrasted Group approaches. In the former, knowledgeable judges such as teachers identify those students (without access to their performance on the test) whom they believe should just barely pass the test or perhaps who would have only a 50% chance of passing the test. Then when the actual test performance of these students has been gathered, the average can be made the passing score. Similarly, in the Contrasted Group approach, judges (i.e., teachers) identify those students who are clearly passers and those who are not. A passing score is selected that maximally differentiates these two groups. While teacher judgments about students are clearly within their normal practice, there are too many cases, such as in the case of licensure and certification tests, where such judgments are simply not practicable. There are dozens of different standard-setting methods, especially if one counts the multiple modifications of each method, and new methods continue to be advanced (e.g., Sondergeld et al., 2020).

Two aspects of test validity must be considered in regard to criterion-referenced tests. First, it should be clear that the level of test content coverage on a well-made, criterion-referenced test must be at least as high as on a well-made, norm-referenced test, and in most instances, it needs to be much higher. The detail that is needed in developing test specifications and in writing test questions to assess these specifications is reinforced by explicit procedures to check whether the items do measure those specifications independently. The second aspect relates to the validity of the passing score is that of the standard that has been set (Kane, 2001). Simply, if the standard is too high or too low, the decisions will be incorrect and, therefore, the use of the test scores less valid than optimal.

CONCLUSION

Norm-referenced testing has a long and successful history in regard to its usefulness in a wide variety of settings, especially those where selection decisions are made. Testing professionals, following the lead of those who first built intelligence tests, know how to build tests that differentiate individuals in meaningful ways. To do so in terms of students' academic achievement does not require that the content domain that is assessed is covered in a representative way; it does require that the test materials that are used on such tests are done so after considerable pretesting. Items must be selected that differentiate student examinees in a valid manner and that correlate highly with each other. We can do this validly and in ways that colleges making acceptance decisions and companies that are hiring make better decisions. The tests of subject-matter achievement that are associated with tests such as the SAT and the GRE actually predict the future success of students very well, as do the norm-referenced tests of ability or aptitude and developed academic skills. Norm-referenced tests are especially useful when there a limits to the number of people who can advance forward in a job search or admission to an educational program, such as a medical school or an honors program.

Criterion-referenced testing has a much shorter history. In one sense, criterion-referenced tests are simply tests whereby the tested domain is carefully mapped using test specifications and items are built to meet those test specifications. The test questions that are used should be sensitive to instruction; it is more important that they reflect student learning rather than differences among students. The item review procedures, rather than being dominated by empirical procedures in the manner of norm-referenced testing, are far more based on the judgment of educational professionals. As such, for measuring achievement in most contexts these tests have taken on the preeminent role. Nevertheless, the interplay of the two types of tests is constant and is more apparent than many in education may believe.

A serious issue in using criterion-referenced tests is the setting of passing scores, or cut scores. Norms can have real value here. Few states would wish to set passing scores on their academic tests so that every student failed or that a disproportionately small number of students passed the examination. It is common practice in many cut-score studies to inform the panel of judges, after they have recommended a passing score, the percentage of students who would pass the test were that passing score used. These judges often then have the opportunity to modify their recommended cut score based upon this information. In fact, it is quite common for a standard-setting meeting to have two or three waves of data collection with discussion and empirical data provided after each session.

Regardless of whether a test is a norm-referenced test or a criterion-referenced one, the validity of the examination is the key issue. The techniques to establish validity, however, may differ given the very different purposes of the tests.

References

American Educational Research Association, American Psychological Association, & National Council on Measurement in Education. (2014). *Standards for educational and psychological testing*. American Educational Research Association.

Anastasi, A. (1958). *Differential psychology: Individual and group differences in behavior* (3rd ed.). Macmillan.

Anastasi, A., & Urbina, S. (1997). *Psychological testing* (7th ed.). Prentice Hall/Pearson Education.

Angoff, W. H. (1971). Scales, norms, and equivalent scores. In R. L. Thorndike (Ed.), *Educational measurement* (2nd ed., pp. 508–600). American Council on Education.

Baker, E. L. (2016). Research to controversy in 10 decades. *Educational Researcher, 45*(2), 122–133. https://doi.org/10.3102/0013189X16639048

Baker, F. B., & Kim, S.-H. (2017). *The basics of item response theory using R*. Springer. https://doi.org/10.1007/978-3-319-54205-8

Bennett, J., Tognolini, J., & Pickering, S. (2012). Establishing and applying performance standards for curriculum-based examinations. *Assessment in Education: Principles, Policy & Practice, 19*(3), 321–339. https://doi.org/10.1080/0969594X.2011.614219

Ben-Porath, Y. S., & Tellegen, A. (2020). *Minnesota Multiphasic Personality Inventory-3 (MMPI-3). Technical manual*. University of Minnesota Press.

Berk, R. A. (1980). Item Analysis. In R. A. Berk (Ed.), *Criterion-referenced measurement: The state of the art* (pp. 49–79). Johns Hopkins University Press.

Berk, R. A. (1984). Selecting the index of reliability. In R. A. Berk (Ed.), *A guide to criterion-referenced test construction* (pp. 231–266). Johns Hopkins University Press.

Binet, A., & Simon, T. (1905a). Application of new methods of the diagnosis of the intellectual level among normal and subnormal children in institutions and in the primary schools. *L'Année Psychologique, 11*, 245–336. https://doi.org/10.3406/psy.1904.3676

Binet, A., & Simon, T. (1905b). New methods for the diagnosis of the intellectual level of subnormals. *L'Année Psychologique, 11*, 191–244. https://doi.org/10.3406/psy.1904.3675

Binet, A., & Simon, T. (1905c). Upon the necessity of establishing a scientific diagnosis of inferior states of intelligence. *L'Année Psychologique, 11*, 163–190. https://doi.org/10.3406/psy.1904.3674

Bond, L. (1989). The effects of special preparation programs on measures of scholastic ability. In R. L. Linn (Ed.), *Educational measurement* (3rd ed., pp. 429–444). American Council on Education/Macmillan.

Camara, W. G., & Kimmel, E. W. (Eds.). (2005). *Choosing students: Higher education admissions tools for the 21st century*. Erlbaum. https://doi.org/10.4324/9781410612533

Cattell, J. McK. (1890). Mental tests and measurements. *Mind, 15*(59), 373–381. https://www.jstor.org/stable/2247264

Chapman, P. D. (1988). *Schools as sorters: Lewis M. Terman, applied psychology, and the intelligence testing movement, 1890–1930*. New York University Press.

Cizek, G. J. (Ed.). (2001). *Setting performance standards: Concepts, methods and perspectives*. Erlbaum.

Cizek, G. J., & Bunch, M. B. (2007). *Standard setting: A guide to establishing and evaluating performance standards on tests*. Sage. https://doi.org/10.4135/9781412985918

Cornell, F. G. (1960). Sampling methods. In C. W. Harris (Ed.), *Encyclopedia of educational research* (3rd ed., pp. 1181–1183). Macmillan.

Cronbach, L. J. (1951). Coefficient alpha and the internal structure of tests. *Psychometrika, 16*(3), 297–334. https://doi.org/10.1007/BF02310555

Davis, F. B., & Diamond, J. J. (1974). The preparation of criterion-referenced tests. In C. W. Harris, M. C. Alkin, & W. J. Popham (Eds.), *Problems in criterion-referenced measurement* (pp. 116–138). Center for the Study of Evaluation, University of California.

De Ayala, R. J. (2009). *The theory and practice of item response theory*. Guilford Press.

DeMars, C. (2010). *Item response theory*. Oxford University Press. https://doi.org/10.1093/acprof:oso/9780195377033.001.0001

De Soete, B., Lievens, F., & Druart, C. (2013). Strategies for dealing with the diversity-validity dilemma in personnel selection: Where are we and where should we go? *Journal of Work and Organizational Psychology, 29*(1), 3–12. https://doi.org/10.5093/tr2013a2

Diao, H., & Sireci, S. G. (2018). Item response theory-based methods for estimating classification accuracy and consistency. *Journal of Applied Testing Technology, 19*(1), 20–25.

Dorans, N. J., Liang, L., & Puhan, G. (2010). *Aligning Scales of Certification Tests* (ETS Research Report #RR-10-07). https://onlinelibrary.wiley.com/doi/pdf/10.1002/j.2333-8504.2010.tb02214.x

DuBois, P. H. (1970). *A history of psychological testing*. Allyn & Bacon.

Ebel, R. L. (1962). Content standard test scores. *Educational and Psychological Measurement, 22*(1), 15–25. https://doi.org/10.1177/001316446202200103

Elliot, N., & Williamson, D. M. (2013). *Assessing Writing* special issue: Assessing writing with automated scoring systems. *Assessing Writing, 18*(1), 1–6. https://doi.org/10.1016/j.asw.2012.11.002

France, S. L., & Batchelder, W. H. (2015). Maximum likelihood item easiness models for test theory without an answer key. *Educational and Psychological Measurement, 75*(1), 57–77. https://doi.org/10.1177/0013164414527448

Fulmer, G. W. (2011). Estimating critical values for strength of alignment among curriculum, assessments, and instruction. *Journal of Educational and Behavioral Statistics*, *36*(3), 381–402. https://doi.org/10.3102/1076998610381397

Geisinger, K. F. (1998). Psychometric issues in test interpretation. In J. Sandoval, C. L. Frisby, K. F. Geisinger, J. D. Scheuneman, & J. Ramos Grenier (Eds.), *Test interpretation and diversity: Achieving equity in assessment* (pp. 17–30). American Psychological Association. https://doi.org/10.1037/10279-001

Geisinger, K. F. (2005). The testing industry, ethnic minorities, and individuals with disabilities. In R. P. Phelps (Ed.), *Defending standardized testing* (pp. 187–203). Erlbaum.

Geisinger, K. F. (2020). *The context for the proposed licensure test for psychologists* [Presidential address for Division 5 of the American Psychological Association]. Presented at the annual convention of the American Psychological Association, virtual.

Geisinger, K. F. (2021). The history of norm- and criterion-referenced testing. In B. F. Clauser & M. B. Bunch (Eds.), *The history of educational measurement: Key advancements, theory, policy, and practice* (pp. 42–64). Routledge.

Glaser, R. (1963). Instructional technology and the measurement of learning outcomes: Some questions. *American Psychologist*, *18*(8), 519–521. https://doi.org/10.1037/h0049294

Glaser, R., & Klaus, D. J. (1962). Proficiency measurement: Assessing human performance. In R. Gagné (Ed.), *Psychological principles in system development* (pp. 421–427). Holt, Rinehart & Winston.

Glass, G. V. (1978). Standards and criteria. *Journal of Educational Measurement*, *15*(4), 237–261. https://doi.org/10.1111/j.1745-3984.1978.tb00072.x

Goddard, H. H. (1908). The Binet and Simon tests of intellectual capacity. *The Training School*, *5*, 3–9.

Gordon, E. W., & Rajagopalan, K. (2016). *The testing and learning revolution: The future of assessment in education*. Palgrave Macmillan.

Green, S. B., & Yang, Y. (2009). Commentary on coefficient alpha: A cautionary tale. *Psychometrika*, *74*(1), 121–135. https://doi.org/10.1007/s11336-008-9098-4

Hambleton, R. K., & Novick, M. R. (1973). Toward an integration of theory and method for criterion-referenced tests. *Journal of Educational Measurement*, *10*(3), 159–170. https://doi.org/10.1111/j.1745-3984.1973.tb00793.x

Hammock, J. (1960). Criterion measures: Instruction vs. selection research. [Abstract]. *American Psychologist*, *15*, 435.

Harris, C. W. (1974). Some technical characteristics of mastery tests. In C. W. Harris, M. C. Alkin, & W. J. Popham (Eds.), *Problems in criterion-referenced measurement* (pp. 98–115). Center for the Study of Evaluation, UCLA.

Henrysson, S. (1963). Correction of item-total correlations in item analysis. *Psychometrika*, *28*(2), 211–218.

Hillegas, M. R. (2018). *A scale for the measurement of quality of English composition by young people* (Vol. 13). Forgotten Books. (Original work published 1912)

Ho, A. D., & Reardon, S. F. (2012). Estimating achievement gaps from test scores reported in ordinal "proficiency" categories. *Journal of Educational and Behavioral Statistics*, *37*(4), 489–517. https://doi.org/10.3102/1076998611411918

Hoyt, C. (1941). Test reliability estimated by analysis of variance. *Psychometrika*, *6*(3), 153–160. https://doi.org/10.1007/BF02289270

Hulin, C. L., Lissak, R. I., & Drasgow, F. (1982). Recovery of two- and three-parameter logistic item characteristic curves: A Monte Carlo study. *Applied Psychological Measurement*, *6*(3), 249–260. https://doi.org/10.1177/014662168200600301

Kane, M. T. (2001). So much remains the same: Conception and status of validation in setting standards. In G. J. Cizek (Ed.), *Setting performance standards: Concepts, methods and perspectives* (pp. 53–88). Erlbaum.

Kolen, M. J. (2006). Scaling and norming. In R. L. Brennan (Ed.), *Educational measurement* (4th ed., pp. 163–186). American Council on Education/Praeger.

Linn, R. L. (1994). Criterion-referenced measurement: A valuable perspective clouded by surplus meaning. *Educational Measurement: Issues and Practice*, *13*(4), 12–14. https://doi.org/10.1111/j.1745-3992.1994.tb00564.x

Linn, R. L. (2003). Accountability: Responsibility and Reasonable Expectations. *Educational Researcher*, *32*(7), 3–13. https://doi.org/10.3102/0013189X032007003

Livingston, S. A. (1972). Criterion-referenced applications of classical test theory. *Journal of Educational Measurement*, *9*(1), 13–26. https://doi.org/10.1111/j.1745-3984.1972.tb00756.x

Madaus, G. F. (Ed.). (1983). *The courts, validity, and minimum competency testing*. Kluver-Nijhoff. https://doi.org/10.1007/978-94-017-5364-7

Magnusson, D. (1967). *Test theory*. Addison-Wesley.

McDonald, R. P. (1970). The theoretical foundations of common factor analysis, principal factor analysis, and alpha factor analysis. *British Journal of Mathematical & Statistical Psychology*, *23*(1),

1–21. https://doi.org/10.1111/j.2044-8317.1970.tb00432.x

McDonald, R. P. (1999). *Test theory: A unified treatment*. Erlbaum.

McNeish, D. (2018). Thanks coefficient alpha, we'll take it from here. *Psychological Methods, 23*(3), 412–433. https://doi.org/10.1037/met0000144

Millman, J. (1974). Criterion-referenced testing. In W. J. Popham (Ed.), *Evaluation in education: Current applications* (pp. 309–397). McCutchan.

Millman, J. (1980). Individualizing test construction and administration by computer. In R. A. Berk (Ed.), *A guide to criterion-referenced test construction* (pp. 78–96). Johns Hopkins Press.

Nitko, A. J. (1980). Distinguishing the many varieties of criterion-referenced tests. *Review of Educational Research, 50*(3), 461–485. https://doi.org/10.3102/00346543050003461

No Child Left Behind Act of 2001, 20 U.S.C. § 6319 (2008).

Nunnally, J. C. (1978). *Psychometric theory*. McGraw-Hill.

Peterson, N. S., Kolen, M. J., & Hoover, H. D. (1989). Scaling, norming, and equating. In R. L. Linn (Ed.), *Educational measurement* (3rd ed., pp. 221–262). Macmillan.

Popham, W. J. (1980). Specifying the domain of content or behavior. In R. A. Berk (Ed.), *A guide to criterion-referenced test construction* (pp. 29–48). Johns Hopkins Press.

Popham, W. J. (1994). The instructional consequences of criterion-referenced clarity. *Educational Measurement: Issues and Practice, 13*(4), 15–18, 30. https://doi.org/10.1111/j.1745-3992.1994.tb00565.x

Popham, W. J., & Husek, T. R. (1969). Implications of criterion-referenced measurement. *Journal of Educational Measurement, 6*(1), 1–9. https://doi.org/10.1111/j.1745-3984.1969.tb00654.x

Raykov, T., & Marcoulides, A. (2011). *Introduction to psychometric theory*. Routledge. https://doi.org/10.4324/9780203841624

Raymond, M. R., & Reid, J. B. (2001). Who made thee a judge? Selecting and training participants for standard setting. In G. J. Cizek (Ed.), *Setting performance standards: Concepts, methods and perspectives* (pp. 119–157). Erlbaum.

Roid, G. H. (1984). Generating the test items. In R. A. Berk (Ed.), *A guide to criterion-referenced test construction* (pp. 49–77). Johns Hopkins Press.

Roth, P. L., Bevier, C. A., Bobko, P., Switcher, F. S., & Tyler, P. (2001). Ethnic group differences in cognitive ability in employment and educational settings: A meta-analysis. *Personnel Psychology, 54*(2), 297–330. https://doi.org/10.1111/j.1744-6570.2001.tb00094.x

Shermis, M. D., & Burstein, J. (Eds.). (2013). *Handbook of automated essay evaluation: Current applications and new directions*. Routledge/Taylor & Francis Group.

Smith v. Regents of the University of California, Docket No. RG19046222. (Cal. Super. Ct. Dec 10, 2019)

Sondergeld, T. A., Stone, G. A., & Kruse, L. M. (2020). Objective standard setting in educational assessment and decision making. *Educational Policy, 34*(3), 735–759. https://doi.org/10.1177/0895904818802115

Squires, D. (2012). Curriculum alignment: Research suggests that alignment can improve student achievement. *The Clearing House: A Journal of Educational Strategies, Issues and Ideas, 85*(4), 129–135. https://doi.org/10.1080/00098655.2012.657723

Taylor, H. C., & Russell, J. T. (1939). The relationship of validity coefficients to the practical effectiveness of tests in selection: Discussion and tables. *Journal of Applied Psychology, 23*, 565–578.

Terman, L. M. (1916). *The measurement of intelligence*. Houghton Mifflin.

Thorndike, R. M., & D. F. Lohman, D. F. (1990). *A century of ability testing*. Riverside.

Trizano-Hermosilla, I., & Alvarado, J. M. (2016). Best alternatives to Cronbach's Alpha reliability in realistic conditions: Congeneric and asymmetrical measurements. *Frontiers in Psychology, 7*(34), 1–8. https://doi.org/10.3389/fpsyg.2016.00769

Wechsler, D. (2014). *WISC-V: Technical and interpretive manual*. Pearson.

Yerkes, R. M., Bridges, J. W., & Hardwick, R. S. (1918). *A point scale for measuring ability*. Warwick & York.

Zieky, M. J., Perie, M., & Livingston, S. A. (2008). *Cutscores: A manual for setting standards of performance on educational and occupational tests*. Educational Testing Service.

Zwick, R. (2002). *Fair game? The use of standardized admissions tests in higher education*. RoutledgeFalmer.

CHAPTER 20

THE CURRENT STATUS OF "PROJECTIVE" "TESTS"

Robert E. McGrath, Alec Twibell, and Elizabeth J. Carroll

The term *projective tests* is often used to encompass a variety of procedures that allow the target individual to provide free-form responses to ambiguous stimuli. The participant's responses are thought to be sensitive to implicit processes and, consequently, may be somewhat resistant to efforts at misrepresentation.

This class of instruments has had a particularly checkered past. Due to concerns about honesty in responding to self-report measures, and the psychoanalytic belief that much of mental activity is resistant to self-observation, psychologists became enamored with the potential of projective instruments to circumvent misrepresentation by requiring responses to ambiguous stimuli, so that those responses were thought to be representative of the individual's style of engaging with the external world. The development of the Rorschach Inkblot Test (Rorschach, 1921/1942) preceded formal discussions of projective psychological tests, but its popularity in the United States was largely attributable to its presumed projective qualities. The Rorschach was soon joined by other instruments of similar ambiguity, including the Thematic Apperception Test (TAT; Morgan & Murray, 1935; Murray, 1943), the Rosenzweig (1978) Picture Frustration Study, and the Szondi Test (Deri, 1949). Even instruments developed for other purposes came to be used as indicators of projection, particularly the Bender Visual Motor Gestalt Test (Hutt, 1985). A 1959 survey found the three most commonly used psychological tests in clinical practice were projectives (Sundberg, 1961).

By the 1960s, though, the allure was fading for two reasons. One was the general critique of traditional personality assessment that emerged out of behaviorism. Mischel (1968) questioned whether the criterion-related validity of personality measures was sufficient to justify their use, while Goldfried and Kent (1972) criticized the practice of using latent constructs to account for associations between test behavior and behavioral outcomes.

The second factor was a psychometric critique of projective methods (e.g., Cronbach, 1949; Entwisle, 1972; Swensen, 1968). This critique has engendered an enduring negative perception of projective instruments in the scientific community. While surveys in the 1980s and 1990s found more than 75% of clinical doctoral programs required training in projective testing (Piotrowski & Keller, 1984; Piotrowski & Zalewski, 1993), a more recent summary indicates training in projective instruments has declined in both clinical doctoral and internship programs

We are grateful to Gregory Meyer for his comments on an earlier version of this chapter.
https://doi.org/10.1037/0000318-020
APA Handbook of Research Methods in Psychology, Second Edition: Vol. 1. Foundations, Planning, Measures, and Psychometrics, H. Cooper (Editor-in-Chief)
Copyright © 2023 by the American Psychological Association. All rights reserved.

(Piotrowski, 2015a), though this rate may have stabilized in recent years (Mihura et al., 2017). A recent attempt to generate a list of discredited psychological tests was largely dominated by projective instruments (Koocher et al., 2015). In contrast to what the publication record would suggest, training and use of the main projective instruments seems to have remained relatively stable outside the United States (Piotrowski, 2015b).

The remainder of this chapter summarizes the current status of projective instruments as scientific instruments. The first section offers a conceptual analysis of the nature of projective assessment. Drawing on discussions of projective assessment and comparisons with other psychological measurement methods, we suggest that the continuing use of the terms *projective* and *test* to refer to these instruments (e.g., Stedman et al., 2018) is problematic and probably should be discontinued.

Current evidence on each of three projective instruments—the Rorschach, TAT, and figure drawings—is also reviewed. Though other projective instruments are used in clinical assessment, particularly various forms of incomplete sentences blank (Rotter et al., 1992), these three techniques are the most extensively researched and effectively reflect the current status of projective instruments in general.

WHAT WE TALK ABOUT WHEN WE TALK ABOUT "PROJECTIVE" "TESTS"

Murray (1938) and L. K. Frank (1939) provided the seminal works on what is called the *projective hypothesis*. They proposed that free-format responding to ambiguous, or "culture-free" (Frank, p. 389), stimuli would encourage emergence of personal meanings and feelings. The labeling of certain instruments as *projective* also provided a clever phonetic contrast to *objective* measures such as rating scales that restrict the set of acceptable response alternatives.

The prototypical projective instrument demonstrates the following features:

1. Test stimuli are ambiguous in some important way. For example, the Rorschach Inkblot method presents the respondent with a fixed series of inkblots and the question "What might this be?" The TAT requires the respondent to create a story based on a picture in which people are engaged in unclear behavior.
2. Though some responses are incompatible with the instructions, for example, refusing to respond to a Rorschach card (in some instructional sets) or saying it is an inkblot, the number of acceptable responses to the stimuli is infinite. Traditional Rorschach practice even allows the individual to decide how many responses to make to each inkblot. The more recent Rorschach Performance Assessment System (R-PAS; Meyer et al., 2011), described below, limits the number of responses per card to four.
3. The use of ambiguous stimuli is intended to elicit idiosyncratic patterns of responding such as unusual percepts or justification for those percepts on the Rorschach or unusual story content or story structure on the TAT.
4. Because of their free response format, projective instruments often require individualized administration and specialized training in administration, scoring, and interpretation.

The Problem With Projection

The use of the term *projective* carries with it certain implications about the cognitive process that determines important test behavior, implications that have been questioned in recent years by individuals closely associated with the study of the Rorschach (e.g., Bornstein, 2007; Meyer & Kurtz, 2006). To understand why this shift has occurred, one must recognize there are at least three problems with calling these instruments *projective*.

The ambiguity of the term *projective*. The term *projective* has multiple connotations in the psychoanalytic literature from which it emerged. Freud (1896/1962) used the term first to refer to a specific defense mechanism characterized by the unconscious attribution of one's unacceptable feelings and wishes to some external object or individual. Later, though, he used the term in a more general sense to encompass any idiosyncratic construction of environmental stimuli (Freud, 1913/1990). It was this latter use of the term Murray (1938) referenced when he drew the connection between responding to psychological tests and psychoanalytic theory.

There is nothing uniquely Freudian about the general proposition that different people construe stimuli differently, that ambiguity in the stimulus field can contribute to individual differences in stimulus responding, and that those differences can reveal something important about the individual. Once that proposition is couched in terms of projection, however, it takes on an ambiguous psychoanalytic connotation.

Characterization of respondent behavior.
If the concept of projection is not necessary for understanding instruments such as the Rorschach, it is also clearly not sufficient. Based on prior attempts to define the scope of potentially interesting respondent behaviors to projective instruments (e.g., Basu, 2014; Exner, 1989; McGrath, 2008), as well as personal experience with these instruments, we suggest there are at least six sources of information that can be observed using a projective instrument (Table 20.1), though they tend to be of varying importance across instruments and respondents.

Thematic material refers to the degree to which responses contain language or phrasing that reflects certain attitudes or emotional states. This is the information source that comes closest to the concept of projection, in that respondents may respond to the stimuli in a manner reflecting issues of particular concern for them, but these concerns need not be unavailable to consciousness.

Exner (1989, 2003) argued that Rorschach was particularly interested in his instrument as a method for detecting perceptual idiosyncracies. This emphasis is evident in Rorschach's original instructional set, "What might this be?" It is also evident in his creation of the inquiry phase,

TABLE 20.1

Information Sources Available Through "Projective " "Tests"

Source	Examples
Thematic material	Morbid themes (R and T); stories that focus on achievement (T)
Perceptual idiosyncracies	Poor form quality (R); preoccupation with small details (R and T); omission of critical stimulus elements (R and T)
Extratest behavior	Card rotation (R); attempts to reject stimuli (R and T)
Self-descriptive statements	Indications of task-related discomfort or enjoyment (R and T)
Quality of thought	Illogical justification of percepts (R); tangentiality (R and T)
Quality of speech	Vocabulary, rhyming, or use of clang associations (R and T)

Note. R = Rorschach inkblot method variable; T = Thematic Apperception Test variable.

an important and distinctive element of Rorschach administration in which the respondent is asked to explain how each response was formulated. Though perceptual idiosyncrasies play a particularly central role in the Rorschach, they can be important for any instrument where the respondent is expected to respond to ambiguous stimulus materials. For example, clearly ignoring or distorting a central element of a TAT picture is sometimes taken as a reflection of a disordered perceptual style, perhaps suggestive of thought disorder, or of issues that are discomforting to the respondent, though Eron (1950) raised concerns about these interpretations.

Extratest behavior encompasses anything distinct from responses based on the instructional set, including the manner in which the person handles the physical stimuli or behaviors such as odd mannerisms and expressions of resistance. Of these, expressly self-descriptive statements are significant enough to mention as a distinct source of information. Because of its free-response format, the Rorschach or TAT gives the respondent license to make statements providing clues about cardinal traits or distinctive ways in which they understand themselves. This source of data provides a complementary perspective to the standardized approach to trait description offered by objective instruments. In practice, though, self-descriptive statements during administration of projective instruments are often restricted to the respondent's reactions to the instrument.

Quality of thought refers to the logic or reasonableness of the thought processes evidenced during the administration. Finally, *quality of speech* encompasses various factors associated with effectiveness of communication, including the length of responses, complexity and precision of the language used, and so forth. Considering the variety of types of information that can emerge during the administration of a so-called projective instrument, emphasizing the first has the potential to result in underestimation of the value of the others.

The role of ambiguity. Finally, it is worth speculating whether the emphasis on projection has led to misleading conclusions about the relationship between ambiguity and clinical usefulness, though the empirical basis for this point is thin. One of the corollaries of Frank's (1939) projective hypothesis was that greater ambiguity was associated with greater potential for projection. Perhaps the most extreme example of this proposition is Card 16 of the TAT, which is simply a white card for which the respondent is instructed to both imagine a picture and tell a story about that picture.

In fact, while there is some evidence that responding to Card 16 is related to creativity (Wakefield, 1986), clinicians find the stories are often less interesting than those provided in response to other cards (Groth-Marnat, 2009). Similarly, it turns out to be the case that Rorschach, who was something of an artist, touched up his original inkblots in a manner that made them more evocative of certain percepts (Exner, 2003); that is, he made them less ambiguous and more culture-bound than they were originally. They are less amorphous than, for example, the Holtzman Inkblot Technique (Holtzman et al., 1961). This difference may help explain why the latter has never been popular in clinical use despite much better psychometric qualities than the Rorschach. One may hypothesize that a moderate level of ambiguity is optimal, in that it challenges the respondent without overtaxing in a manner likely to result in disengagement from the task.

Implications

Taking these three arguments together, one can conclude that projection is not a necessary contributor to the clinical value of such instruments. These measures seem to be interesting not necessarily because they are *projective* but because they are *provocative*, and so elicit interesting behaviors from the respondent. This conclusion would imply value in retiring the term *projective tests* (Meyer & Kurtz, 2006), but then the question arises of the best alternative. Bornstein (2007) suggested calling them *stimulus-attribution tests*, suggesting the common thread is that the respondent is required to attribute meaning to the stimuli. McGrath and Carroll (2012) suggested *broadband implicit techniques*. This term was based in part on Fowler and Groat's (2008) proposal that projective instruments are consistent with other instruments that attempt to draw inferences about personal character without direct questioning such as the Implicit Association Test (Greenwald et al., 1998). However, where that instrument is limited in focus, providing no other information than how the individual associates two constructs, Table 20.1 demonstrates the popular projective instruments are broadband methods that potentially provide information across multiple channels. Because of its broadband nature, Weiner (1994) criticized the common practice of referring to the Rorschach as a *test*. In itself, the Rorschach is a method of data collection rather than the standard by which those data are judged, as is implied by the word *test*. For this reason, Weiner recommended referring to the Rorschach Inkblot *method*. His point is relevant to all the projective instruments, suggesting the term *test* should be generally avoided.

Despite these concerns, references to projective tests still appear widely in the literature. Stedman et al. (2018) suggested simply retaining the term *projective* for historical reasons. If precedent wins out over precision, however, it should be with the understanding that optimal applied use of projective measures requires using the totality of an individual's behavior during the administration. In this regard, the most important recent innovation in Rorschach methodology is the previously mentioned R-PAS (Meyer et al., 2011; see also Meyer & Mihura, 2020).

The emphasis on individual variation in responding to these instruments does create a challenge for projectives as psychometric instruments. The reliance on relatively ambiguous stimuli and/or instructions that allow for infinite diversity in responding creates a challenge in terms of meeting traditional standards for reliability and validity. This challenge will be addressed in the context of a general psychometric evaluation of the three most popular projectives.

THE PSYCHOMETRIC STATUS OF THE RORSCHACH

Of all projective instruments, the Rorschach inkblots remain the most popular in the assessment research literature. The continuing popularity of the Rorschach was founded in the success of Exner's (2003) Comprehensive System (CS), which brought uniformity in administration and scoring, normative data, and interpretation to the Rorschach. The R-PAS was subsequently developed to address limitations of the CS. This process included revising the CS's instructions for administration, choosing Rorschach variables for inclusion based on a history of good empirical support and gathering an international normative sample.

Before reviewing the evidence, which spans work gathered using both Exner's CS and R-PAS, the issue of generalizing findings from the former to the latter should be addressed. Administration instructions for the CS placed few limits on the number of responses per card. As a result, it was possible for the individual to generate too few responses for the results to be considered reliable (< 14), in which case the entire instrument was readministered. Rules for limiting length were more complex but allowed for protocols of 50 responses or more. Either of these procedures could result in cumbersome administrations, even though Exner (2003) concluded longer protocols were no more useful than shorter ones.

To address the issue of variation in responding, administration instructions were revised as part of the development of the R-PAS. The new R-Optimized instructions limit the protocol to 40 responses. As a result, some authors raised concerns that evidence gathered using the CS may not generalize to the R-PAS (e.g., Khadivi & Evans, 2012; Kivisto et al., 2013), especially as other differences exist in the two systems. More recently, summaries across multiple samples suggest the two forms of administration have little effect on Rorschach variable scores except for variables directly reflecting the number of responses, while R-Optimized tends to result in more efficient administration and less variability in the number of responses (Hosseininasab et al., 2019; Pianowski et al., 2021). That said, in the following sections we focus on results using the more defensible R-PAS but indicate when results came from the CS instead.

Reliability

Interrater reliability. Scoring of Rorschach variables involves two steps. The first has to do with the assignment of a series of codes to individual responses, the second with the aggregation of code results into variables. The first phase can be referred to as *response coding*, the second as *protocol scoring*. The latter is increasingly accomplished by entering response codes into software, reducing the importance of reliability in protocol scoring. On the other hand, interpretation is based largely on the R-PAS scores, so these represent the more important consideration in settings where scoring is still done by hand.

Response coding involves binary decisions about the presence or absence of a code, so the appropriate interrater reliability statistic is the kappa coefficient. Protocol scores are dimensional and so call for computation of the intraclass correlations (single measure). The R-PAS generates raw scores as well as scores adjusted for the overall complexity of the protocol, thought to be an indicator of engagement in the task (Ales et al., 2020). For the present purposes, we adopted the recommendation that reliability values of .60 or greater are acceptable for the reliability statistics commonly used in this literature, that is, coefficient alpha and the kappa coefficient (e.g., Cicchetti, 1994; Shrout, 1998). We note, however, that it can be difficult to achieve adequate values for kappa when the base rate for one outcome or the other is low. For example, Kivisalu et al. (2017) found acceptable kappa values for 40 of 62 R-PAS variables from 50 nonpatient protocols with a total of 1,168 responses. Using their results, we were able to compute the absolute differences between the base rate of each variable and .50, and correlate those differences with the corresponding kappa value. This correlation proved to be −.42; as expected, judgments of variables with more extreme base rates were less reliable. In contrast, Schneider et al. (2022) meta-analyzed intraclass correlation coefficients between raters across four samples. Out of 60 R-PAS variables, only one variable was associated with what should be considered a questionable reliability value (< .60).

Internal reliability. It would technically be possible to compute coefficient alpha or other indices of internal reliability for Rorschach codes if each card is treated as an observation and the presence-absence or frequency of each code on each card is treated as the outcome. An example of this approach is provided by Bornstein and Masling (2005), who found reliabilities of .61 to .62 for a measure of dependency. However, to our knowledge not a single study has evaluated the internal reliability of Rorschach variables in either the CS or R-PAS.

Test–retest reliability. The evaluation of test–retest reliability is particularly problematic for broadband measures such as the Rorschach. It requires setting the interval between administrations so there is a reasonable likelihood that the latent constructs underlying the scores remain consistent. While most R-PAS scores reflect constructs thought to be relatively stable, others focus on states of distress. As a result, studies examining the stability of an array of Rorschach variables are flawed. With this caveat in mind, a number of studies over the years have looked at temporal stability in various Rorschach variables, summarized in a meta-analysis conducted by Grønnerød (2003, 2006). He estimated that the mean 6-month correlation for Rorschach variables was > .70, with only three non-CS variables and one CS variable associated with correlations < .60. Sultan and Meyer (2009) provided evidence that temporal stability can be compromised if the number of responses is high or variable across records, providing further evidence that the R-Optimized administration should be preferred to the administration developed for the CS.

Validity

One approach to evaluating the validity of the Rorschach will be dispensed with quickly. Studies examining convergence between the Rorschach and a self-report indicator such as the Minnesota Multiphasic Personality Inventory (MMPI) have been disappointing, with little evidence of correlation between variables that seem to be measuring similar constructs (Meyer et al., 2017; Mihura et al., 2013). Several hypotheses have been suggested to explain this failure to converge (e.g., Meyer et al., 2000), the most compelling of which suggests that measures of different behavioral channels (McGrath, 2005) or methods of measurement (Bornstein, 2009) generally correlate more poorly than anticipated. For example, implicit measures correlate poorly with other psychological measures (Gawronski et al., 2007) and even with other types of implicit measures (e.g., Nosek et al., 2007; Ziegler et al., 2010).

A meta-analysis conducted by Mihura and colleagues (2013) examined the validity of each CS score, including diagnoses, intelligence test results, and observed behavior as criteria in addition to self-report as criteria. The authors concluded that the mean validity correlation for

30 variables was ≥ .21, while 35 had weak or limited supporting evidence. Variables with the strongest evidence reflected cognitive processes and perceptual styles, while rare variables such as food responses tended to demonstrate weaker validity. Czopp and Zeligman (2016) challenged some of the conclusions drawn in this meta-analysis, suggesting some of the research reviewed did not operationalize the variables in the same way as the CS, and as a result these variables may have been dismissed or restructured prematurely. Despite this concern that some potentially useful variables were poorly represented in the meta-analysis, this study played an important role in the subsequent development of R-PAS, influencing decisions about which CS variables to eliminate, what non-CS variables to add, and which variables merited modification (Meyer & Eblin, 2012). Table 20.2 lists variables with demonstrated validity according to the meta-analysis and changes made to variables in the R-PAS.

The R-PAS also introduced two innovations in Rorschach scoring. First, new normative samples were gathered for both adult and youth (Meyer et al., 2020; Viglione & Giromini, 2016) populations to address various problems with the CS norms. For example, the adult normative sample was collected across 17 countries to reflect the international popularity of the instrument. Scores are now standardized based on normative data to simplify the process of identifying extreme scores. In addition, as noted previously, a measure of complexity of responses is available as an indicator of engagement in the task, and standardized scores are generated both with and without adjustment for complexity.

The innovations described here make the R-PAS the most sophisticated instrument development program in the history of projective assessment. The focus on variables with existing empirical support, more representative normative samples, and consideration of engagement as a moderator all potentially contribute to the validity of the R-PAS. Unfortunately, research evaluating the success of these efforts at enhancing the validity of the Rorschach is limited, with Mihura et al. (2013) having provided the most comprehensive evidence base to date. This is perhaps the most important next step in the future of projective assessment.

Several studies have examined the incremental validity of the Rorschach. Dao et al. (2008) provided evidence that the Rorschach is a better predictor of psychosis than the MMPI, and the Rorschach has also shown superiority to the MMPI as a predictor of therapy outcome (Meyer, 2000). Though encouraging, this small literature is an insufficient basis for concluding the relatively demanding Rorschach provides sufficient incremental validity over other methods to justify its cost. Clearly, more research is needed on this topic before there is sufficient evidence of the Rorschach's clinical utility.

General Conclusions

Research has shown interrater reliability for Rorschach scoring is adequate for the majority of variables in their present form, though it is less than ideal for some variables that are rarely scored as positive. While the validity of the Rorschach in assessing multiple domains of functioning has long been accepted, the changes implemented with the introduction of the R-PAS creates the potential for a more psychometrically defensible instrument. That said, further research is needed to confirm this proposition. Furthermore, a great deal more research is needed to identify situations in which the Rorschach is worth using instead of or in addition to other more cost-effective techniques such as self-report. Certain situations intuitively appear to warrant its use. In particular, forensic evaluations often occur in contexts where self-misrepresentation is likely, and there is particular interest in the cognitive and perceptual constructs for which the Rorschach is a particularly useful gauge.

PSYCHOMETRIC STATUS OF THE TAT

The consistency in administration and scoring brought to the Rorschach by the CS and R-PAS is important if reliability results are to be assumed to be generalizable. Though Murray (1943) initially offered a prescribed administration procedure

TABLE 20.2

Strength of Validity Evidence for Rorschach Comprehensive System Variables

Domain	Supported	Little or no support	No evidence
Controls and situational distress	Human movement Experience actual[a] Sum of shading Inanimate movements Number of responses Lambda[a] Weighted sum of color[a] Diffuse shading Difference score Experienced stimulation[a]	Animal movement[b] Adjusted difference Score[b] Coping style (extratensive vs. introversive)[a]	Nonhuman Movement Coping style: pervasive[b] Coping style: ambitent[b]
Affective features	Achromatic color Form–color ratio Affective ratio Complexity ratio	White space[a] Pure color	Color projection[b] Constriction ratio
Interpersonal perception	Cooperative movement Whole, realistic Humans Texture Good human Representations Personal Poor human Representations	Aggressive movement Food[b] Isolation index[b] Active to passive ratio[a]	Interpersonal interest
Self-perception	Anatomy and X-ray Morbid Reflections Vista	Form dimension Egocentricity index[b]	
Information processing	Synthesized response[a] Organizational frequency[b] Vague response Perseveration[b]	Processing efficiency[b]	Aspiration ratio[b] Economy index
Cognitive mediation	Conventional form Distorted form Appropriate form Popular Unusual form Human movement, distorted form		White space distortion
Ideation	Critical special scores Critical special scores, severe		Human movement, formless[b]
Indices	Perceptual-thinking index Suicide constellation[a] Depression index[a] Coping deficit index	Hypervigilance index[a]	Intellectualization index Obsessive style index[b]

Note. Supported = mean $r \geq .15$ and fail-safe N (number of unpublished studies finding $r = .00$ needed to render the mean nonsignificant at .05) ≥ 10, and $p < .05$. Little support = mean $r < .15$ or fail-safe $N < 10$, and $p < .05$. No support = $p > .05$. No evidence = insufficient evidence to draw a conclusion. Adapted from "The Validity of Individual Rorschach Variables: Systematic Reviews and Meta-Analyses of the Comprehensive System," by J. L. Mihura, G. J. Meyer, N. Dumitrascu, and G. Bombel, 2013, *Psychological Bulletin, 139*(3), p. 570 (https://doi.org/10.1037/a0029406). Copyright 2013 by the American Psychological Association.
[a]Adjusted in R-PAS. [b]Omitted from R-PAS.

for the TAT, it involved administering 20 cards, which proved unwieldy in practice. Unfortunately, no commonly accepted alternative has emerged. Researchers continue to use different subsets of cards (e.g., Bram, 2014; Porcerelli et al., 2010), in most cases varying between four to six cards. Doctoral programs seem to offer little training in formal scoring of the TAT (Mihura et al., 2017), so that qualitative interpretations of uncertain validity likely remain the norm in applied settings. In addition, there are alternative apperceptive pictures developed for special populations, such as the Children's Apperception Test (Bellak & Bellak, 1949), as well as more narrowband picture sets intended to detect specific motivations (e.g., McClelland et al., 1953). There are even differences in whether the respondent delivers the story verbally or in writing, which should have significant effects on productivity. Any efforts to discuss expected reliability or validity of scores on the apperception technique in general, or the TAT in particular, are, therefore, problematic.

Only two scoring systems applicable to the TAT have received much research attention in recent years and so provide the most defensible basis for evaluating the TAT as a research tool. The more extensively studied is the Social Cognition and Object Relations Scale–Global Rating Method (SCORS-G; Stein et al., 2011; Westen, 1995). The original version of the instrument consisted of four scales, with multiple items for each dimension, but the SCORS-G involves giving a global 1–7 rating of level of maturity on eight dimensions of interpersonal functioning drawn from object relations theory: complexity of representation of people, affective quality of representations, emotional investment in relationships, emotional investment in values and moral standards, understanding of social causality, experience and management of aggressive impulses, self-esteem, and identity and coherence of self. Anchors are available for some response options. Though the SCORS-G is considered applicable to any self-revelatory narrative material, for example, reports of early memories, it is most commonly applied to TAT stories. A separate score is provided for each TAT response and then averaged to generate overall scores.

The second is the Defense Mechanism Manual (DMM; Cramer, 1991), which was developed specifically for use with the TAT and the Children's Apperception Test. It is intended to detect use of three defense mechanisms: denial, projection, and identification. Each of the defense mechanisms is evaluated on seven dimensions, with scoring criteria provided for each dimension on certain cards. Research with the DMM has focused on the TAT rather than the Children's Apperception Test.

Reliability

Reliability analyses for the two scoring systems have primarily focused on interrater reliability and, to a lesser extent, on internal reliability of scores across cards. Evidence for the interrater reliability of the SCORS-G is consistently supportive (e.g., Huprich & Greenberg, 2003; Pad et al., 2020). The same is true for the DMM, with one exception. Though some studies (e.g., Cramer, 2009; Porcerelli et al., 1998) have reported adequate interrater reliability for the Denial scale, others (Hibbard et al., 1994; Porcerelli et al., 2010) have reported interrater reliability estimates for the Denial scale below .60.

Evidence for the internal reliability of these scoring systems has been weaker. Hibbard et al. (1994) found the internal reliability of DMM scores across six cards for Denial and Identification were both < .60. Inslegers et al. (2012) similarly found consistently poor internal reliability across cards for the four original SCORS-G scales. Their study also involved administering six cards. Two responses have been offered to these concerns about internal reliability. Hibbard et al. (2001) examined internal reliability for the four original SCORS scales in samples where four, five, or 10 TAT cards were administered. They found reliability values were only consistently acceptable in the samples administered 10 cards, suggesting that the four to six cards typically used in TAT research may be insufficient to achieve reliable outcomes. An alternative perspective was offered by Schultheiss et al. (2008), who proposed that internal reliability analysis is irrelevant to the TAT because it is predicated on the invalid assumption that the cards are intended to represent interchangeable stimulus objects. Exner (1996) made a similar point about the Rorschach, suggesting that each card has unique properties that pull for its own distinctive types of responses. Of course, traditional psychometric considerations would suggest this variability in stimulus materials creates an obligation to administer more than four to five cards if the goal is to maximize the potential for generating test scores that demonstrate desirable levels of predictive validity.

Validity

Literature from multiple laboratories supports the validity of the SCORS-G scales as indicators of personality pathology and interpersonal functioning (e.g., Pad et al., 2020; Stein & Slavin-Mulford, 2018; Stein et al., 2018). However, given that the SCORS-G has particular relevance to personality pathology, Pad et al. (2020) found the SCORS-G had little incremental validity over self-report as an indicator of borderline and depressive personality disorder pathology.

The best evidence for the validity of the DMM comes from studies by Hibbard et al. (1994) and Porcerelli et al. (2010). The former found that undergraduates generated higher scores on identification (considered the most mature of the defenses evaluated) than psychiatric patients, and lower scores across the three defenses indicating primitive functioning. The latter similarly found that greater evidence of denial and projection in the stories was associated with lower ratings by clinician of defensive functioning. However, higher scores for identification were unrelated to clinician ratings. This represents a fairly limited evidence base for recommending these scores as sufficient measures of defensive functioning.

Murray (1943) originally intended the TAT as an indicator of the various motivations he referred to as *needs*, so it is worth noting that some evidence exists to support its use for that purpose. A meta-analytic review by Spangler (1992) concluded the TAT was a better predictor of achievement motivation than self-report measures. Entwisle (1972), however, raised the possibility that intelligence could account for the relationship. Research into the TAT as a predictor of the motivation for power, affiliation, and intimacy (McAdams, 1982; McClelland, 1965, 1975) has produced similar evidence of validity, though studies of incremental validity are almost nonexistent (More & Winch, 1956). It has also been used as a measure of problem-solving using the Personal Problem-Solving System–Revised (Ronan et al., 2008). This system has been validated in several studies, some of which have controlled for intelligence as a possible confound, but research on this topic has been absent in recent years.

General Conclusion

The evidence base supporting the TAT as a research tool is unfortunately sorely lacking. There is reasonable evidence that the most extensively researched scoring systems can generally achieve acceptable levels of interrater reliability. The evidence for internal reliability is weak, and it remains unclear whether better results are achievable through administration of more cards (though this will tend to create practical obstacles to use of the instrument) or whether internal reliability is an important consideration in apperceptive techniques. Though some intriguing evidence exists to support the validity of at least some TAT scales, a good deal more work would be needed, particularly on the topic of standardization of administration and incremental validity, before the TAT could be recommended as a strategy for collecting data rather than as a focus for research on its potential as a clinical instrument.

PSYCHOMETRIC STATUS OF FIGURE DRAWINGS

Figure drawings differ from most other projective techniques in that they depend on physical activity rather than verbal response. The information sources listed in Table 20.1 are still relevant, though some modifications are in order. Consistent elements of drawing style, such as the use of heavily elaborated lines, can be thought of as *themes*, in this case a theme often thought to be indicative of emotional issues. Unusual details, such as omitting windows from a house, are similar to the perceptual idiosyncracies found in TAT and Rorschach responding. The observation of extratest behavior and self-descriptive statements remains potentially useful, and the quality of thought and speech can also be evaluated if the administrator tests limits by asking questions about the drawings.

Several figure drawing techniques have drawn particular attention. The House-Tree-Person (H-T-P; Buck, 1948) calls for drawings of the three objects listed, each on a separate piece of paper. The Draw-A-Person test (DAP; Machover, 1949) requires drawing a person, then a person of the opposite sex. A more recent alternative is the Kinetic Family Drawing (KFD; Burns & Kaufman, 1972), which involves drawing a picture of one's family doing something.

Figure drawings remain popular clinical instruments. They are easily administered to almost any individual. They also involve a familiar task that helps reduce anxiety about the testing, particularly in children. At the same time, they have suffered the most radical decline in respectability of the three instruments discussed in this chapter. Early work relied heavily on a *sign approach*, where unusual drawing details were individually taken as evidence of a latent construct in a manner that relied heavily on psychoanalytic assumptions about the projection of unconscious conflicts onto ambiguous stimuli. This approach has been largely rejected (Joiner et al., 1996; Swensen, 1968), even by proponents of figure drawings as a clinical tool (e.g., Riethmiller & Handler, 1997).

Several systems have emerged for scoring elements of drawings. These consistently demonstrate excellent interrater reliability, but evidence for validity and incremental validity is questionable. Koppitz (1968) developed perhaps the most popular early scoring system for detecting emotional distress in the DAP. Research results, however, have not been encouraging (e.g., Pihl & Nimrod, 1976). In reviewing literature on the use of figure drawings, Swensen (1968) concluded holistic evaluations were more indicators of problems than scoring systems. For example, Tharinger and Stark (1990) found a holistic evaluation of four characteristics in DAP drawings (inhumanness, lack of agency, lack of well-being, and a hollow or stilted portrayal) was a better detector of emotional distress in children than the 30-item Koppitz system.

Naglieri et al.'s (1991) Draw-A-Person: Screening Procedure for Emotional Disturbance (DAP:SPED) has superseded the Koppitz scores as the most commonly studied scoring procedure. It consists of 55 criteria drawn from the DAP research literature that were expected to identify children with emotional difficulties. Though the authors reported strong interrater, internal reliability, and test–retest reliability, Wrightson and Saklofske (2000) questioned the temporal stability of scores over 23 to 27 weeks. Studies suggest correlations between DAP:SPED scores and various indicators of emotional difficulties are at best small, resulting in inadequate diagnostic accuracy (e.g., Crusco, 2013; Matto et al., 2005; McNeish & Naglieri, 1993; Naglieri & Pfeiffer, 1992; Wrightson & Saklofske, 2000). Given that the DAP:SPED requires even more judgments than the Koppitz criteria, an investigation of the incremental validity of the DAP:SPED over Tharinger and Stark's (1990) holistic evaluation would seem to be a useful topic for future research.

Various scoring systems have also been developed for using the DAP to estimate intelligence. As in the case of emotional distress, these methods tend to demonstrate good interrater reliability. However, evidence again tends to suggest at best small correlations between scores based on drawings and results from intelligence tests (e.g., Rehrig & Stromswold, 2018; Troncone et al., 2021).

At this point, no defensible standardized scoring system has emerged for the H-T-P. Though Burns and Kaufman (1972) offered guidelines for scoring the KFD, these are unsupported by any research. Various scoring systems were suggested in subsequent years. Though these systems demonstrate adequate interrater reliability, evidence that they can identify children with emotional difficulties is weak (Cummings, 1986; Knoff & Prout, 1985).

In contrast to the Rorschach, where research suggests an extensive scoring system is capable of generating valid information about a variety of psychological variables, the evidence is that simpler is generally better in the case of figure drawings. Evidence consistently suggests holistic evaluation of the drawing is a more useful indicator of emotional difficulties in children than complex scoring systems based on discrete drawing elements. This level of effort is also more justifiable given the limited validity of figure drawings as predictors of distress. The use of drawings to estimate intelligence is even more questionable and probably should be avoided even in clinical settings. There is no current basis for recommending the use of figure drawings as a research tool, and no evidence suggests the need for further development beyond the simple procedure suggested by Tharinger and Stark (1990). Future research might also look into whether increasing the number of pictures offers any increment in validity, but doing so undermines the simplicity that is one of the most attractive features of figure drawings as an icebreaker in clinical evaluation.

SUMMARY AND CONCLUSION

It is likely that projective techniques will continue to play an important role in clinical assessment. As Table 20.1 indicates, the potential array of sources of information resulting from administration of projective instruments can contribute to clinical understanding of the individual (e.g., Nakamura, 2012). As research tools, though, only the Rorschach in its most recent iteration in the R-PAS meets criteria for potential use as a research tool. One may expect continuing research to appear on broadband implicit techniques, and the Rorschach in particular, as clinical tools.

Though we have accepted continued use of the term *projectives* to refer to this class of instruments, our first important conclusion is that this must be understood as an anachronistic term. We hope that over time these will be increasingly accepted as a set of performance-based measures, founded on the assumption that provocative stimuli will encourage responding in a manner reflecting important features of the respondent. This perspective places these instruments in a category with commonly used research tools such as the Implicit Association Test. Conceptualizing the projective measures in this way allows one to draw several valuable conclusions about how they are best understood.

First, there is room yet for building a better mousetrap. The optimal projective technique would consistently use stimuli that are obscure enough to encourage individualized responding but evocative enough to engage the respondent. Second, the most successful performance-based measures of personality, those that are thought to demonstrate adequate fidelity, tend to demonstrate a clear intuitive connection to the implicit process they attempt to gauge. For example, bizarre responses to a Rorschach inkblot, TAT picture, or even a figure drawing task are likely to be accurate indicators either of significant pathology or active misrepresentation. The purely actuarial approach has largely failed as a means of identifying reliable relationships between behavior on projective instruments and psychological variables (McGrath, 2008). Even when intuitively reasonable relationships are demonstrated, however, cross-validation is essential.

Third, standardization in administration is important for any future program of research on these instruments. Thanks to the CS and the R-PAS, this goal has been achieved for the Rorschach. TAT administration on the other hand remains idiosyncratic. A review of research on the TAT suggests there are four cards that are used in almost every study on the instrument: cards 1, 3BM, 4, and 13MF. However, existing evidence suggests that adequate levels of internal reliability have only been achieved with administration of 10 cards. To our knowledge there is no research extant that evaluates this issue in administrations of seven to nine cards, so it is possible that adequate levels of reliability can be achieved with fewer than 10. The identification of a standard set of 10 cards to be used in any future work on the TAT (unless future research suggests seven to nine cards is sufficient) would be a valuable step forward.

Fourth, the association of projective instruments with other performance-based instruments has important implications for what has been a common strategy in the validation of projectives. Many studies have examined correlations between self-report measures and projective instruments over the years. We have limited our focus on such studies in this review. Research with implicit measures provides little evidence of convergence with self-report measures, and, in most cases, the latter are better predictors of important criteria than the former. However, there is also reasonable evidence that performance-based measures offer incremental validity over self-report in the prediction of such outcomes (Greenwald et al., 2009). Comparative studies that focus on correlations between projective methods and self-report measures rather than incremental validity of each over the other potentially result in underestimating the potential value of projectives.

With the possible exception of the Rorschach, projective instruments are likely to remain primarily instruments of clinical interest rather than research tools used for their measurement accuracy. We consider the R-PAS an important model for using research to steer the future of their applied use, and we hope those individuals who value their clinical contributions will continue to work towards a more empirically founded standard of practice.

References

Ales, F., Giromini, L., & Zennaro, A. (2020). Complexity and cognitive engagement in the Rorschach task: An eye-tracking study. *Journal of Personality Assessment, 102*(4), 538–550. https://doi.org/10.1080/00223891.2019.1575227

Basu, J. (2014). Psychologists' ambivalence toward ambiguity: Relocating the projective test debate for multiple interpretative hypotheses. *SIS Journal of Projective Psychology & Mental Health, 21*(1), 25–36.

Bellak, L., & Bellak, S. (1949). *The Children's Apperception Test.* C.P.S.

Bornstein, R. F. (2007). Toward a process-based framework for classifying personality tests: Comment on Meyer and Kurtz (2006). *Journal of Personality Assessment, 89*(2), 202–207. https://doi.org/10.1080/00223890701518776

Bornstein, R. F. (2009). Heisenberg, Kandinsky, and the heteromethod convergence problem: Lessons from within and beyond psychology. *Journal of Personality Assessment, 91*(1), 1–8. https://doi.org/10.1080/00223890802483235

Bornstein, R. F., & Masling, J. M. (2005). The Rorschach Oral Dependency Scale. In R. F. Bornstein & J. M. Masling (Eds.), *Scoring the Rorschach: Seven validated systems* (pp. 135–157). Erlbaum. https://doi.org/10.4324/9781410612526

Bram, A. D. (2014). Object relations, interpersonal functioning, and health in a nonclinical sample: Construct validation and norms for the TAT SCORS-G. *Psychoanalytic Psychology, 31*(3), 314–342. https://doi.org/10.1037/a0036286

Buck, J. N. (1948). The H-T-P technique, a qualitative and quantitative scoring manual. *Journal of Clinical Psychology, 4*(4), 317–396. https://doi.org/10.1002/1097-4679(194810)4:4<317::AID-JCLP2270040402>3.0.CO;2–6

Burns, R. C., & Kaufman, S. H. (1972). *Actions, styles and symbols in Kinetic Family Drawings (K-F-D): An interpretive manual.* Brunner-Routledge.

Cicchetti, D. V. (1994). Guidelines, criteria, and rules of thumb for evaluating normed and standardized assessment instruments in psychology. *Psychological Assessment, 6*(4), 284–290. https://doi.org/10.1037/1040-3590.6.4.284

Cramer, P. (1991). *The development of defense mechanisms: Theory, research and assessment.* Springer-Verlag. https://doi.org/10.1007/978-1-4613-9025-1

Cramer, P. (2009). The development of defense mechanisms from pre-adolescence to early adulthood: Do IQ and social class matter? A longitudinal study. *Journal of Research in Personality, 43*(3), 464–471. https://doi.org/10.1016/j.jrp.2009.01.021

Cronbach, L. J. (1949). Statistical methods applied to Rorschach scores; a review. *Psychological Bulletin*, *46*(5), 393–429. https://doi.org/10.1037/h0059467

Crusco, M. (2013). *Draw-A-Person: Screening procedure for emotional disturbance: An investigation of the sensitivity of this method to internalising and externalising behavioural problems identified by the Rutter Parent Questionnaire at age 7 in the 1958 National Child Development Study*. University of London.

Cummings, J. A. (1986). Projective drawings. In H. M. Knoff (Ed.), *The assessment of child and adolescent personality* (pp. 199–244). Guilford Press.

Czopp, S. T., & Zeligman, R. (2016). The Rorschach Comprehensive System (CS) psychometric validity of individual variables. *Journal of Personality Assessment*, *98*(4), 335–342. https://doi.org/10.1080/00223891.2015.1131162

Dao, T. K., Prevatt, F., & Horne, H. L. (2008). Differentiating psychotic patients from non-psychotic patients with the MMPI-2 and Rorschach. *Journal of Personality Assessment*, *90*(1), 93–101. https://doi.org/10.1080/00223890701693819

Deri, S. (1949). *Introduction to the Szondi test*. Grune & Stratton.

Entwisle, D. R. (1972). To dispel fantasies about fantasy-based measures of achievement motivation. *Psychological Bulletin*, *77*(6), 377–391. https://doi.org/10.1037/h0020021

Eron, L. D. (1950). A normative study of the Thematic Apperception Test. *Psychological Monographs: General and Applied*, *64*(9), i–48. https://doi.org/10.1037/h0093627

Exner, J. E., Jr. (1989). Searching for projection in the Rorschach. *Journal of Personality Assessment*, *53*(3), 520–536. https://doi.org/10.1207/s15327752jpa5303_9

Exner, J. E., Jr. (1996). Critical bits and the Rorschach response process. *Journal of Personality Assessment*, *67*(3), 464–477. https://doi.org/10.1207/s15327752jpa6703_3

Exner, J. E., Jr. (2003). *The Rorschach: A comprehensive system: Vol. 1. Basic foundations and principles of interpretation* (4th ed.). Wiley.

Fowler, J. C., & Groat, M. (2008). Personality assessment using implicit (projective) methods. In M. Hersen & A. M. Gross (Eds.), *Handbook of clinical psychology: Vol. 1. Adults* (pp. 475–494). Wiley.

Frank, L. K. (1939). Projective methods for the study of personality. *The Journal of Psychology*, *8*(2), 389–413. https://doi.org/10.1080/00223980.1939.9917671

Freud, S. (1962). Further remarks on the neuro-psychoses of defence. In J. Strachey (Ed.), *The standard edition of the complete psychological works of Sigmund Freud* (Vol. 3, pp. 159–188). Hogarth. (Original work published 1896)

Freud, S. (1990). *Totem and taboo: The standard edition*. W. W. Norton. (Original work published 1913)

Gawronski, B., LeBel, E. P., & Peters, K. R. (2007). What do implicit measures tell us?: Scrutinizing the validity of three commonplace assumptions. *Perspectives on Psychological Science*, *2*(2), 181–193. https://doi.org/10.1111/j.1745-6916.2007.00036.x

Goldfried, M. R., & Kent, R. N. (1972). Traditional versus behavioral personality assessment: A comparison of methodological and theoretical assumptions. *Psychological Bulletin*, *77*(6), 409–420. https://doi.org/10.1037/h0032714

Greenwald, A. G., McGhee, D. E., & Schwartz, J. L. (1998). Measuring individual differences in implicit cognition: The implicit association test. *Journal of Personality and Social Psychology*, *74*(6), 1464–1480. https://doi.org/10.1037/0022-3514.74.6.1464

Greenwald, A. G., Poehlman, T. A., Uhlmann, E. L., & Banaji, M. R. (2009). Understanding and using the Implicit Association Test: III. Meta-analysis of predictive validity. *Journal of Personality and Social Psychology*, *97*(1), 17–41. https://doi.org/10.1037/a0015575

Grønnerød, C. (2003). Temporal stability in the Rorschach method: A meta-analytic review. *Journal of Personality Assessment*, *80*(3), 272–293. https://doi.org/10.1207/S15327752JPA8003_06

Grønnerød, C. (2006). Reanalysis of the Grønnerød (2003) Rorschach temporal stability meta-analysis data set. *Journal of Personality Assessment*, *86*(2), 222–225. https://doi.org/10.1207/s15327752jpa8602_12

Groth-Marnat, G. (2009). *Handbook of psychological assessment* (5th ed.). Wiley.

Hibbard, S., Farmer, L., Wells, C., Difillipo, E., Barry, W., Korman, R., & Sloan, P. (1994). Validation of Cramer's Defense Mechanism Manual for the TAT. *Journal of Personality Assessment*, *63*(2), 197–210. https://doi.org/10.1207/s15327752jpa6302_1

Hibbard, S., Mitchell, D., & Porcerelli, J. (2001). Internal consistency of the object relations and social cognition scales for the Thematic Apperception Test. *Journal of Personality Assessment*, *77*(3), 408–419. https://doi.org/10.1207/S15327752JPA7703_03

Holtzman, W. H., Thorpe, J. S., Swartz, J. D., & Herron, E. W. (1961). *Inkblot perception and personality*. University of Texas Press.

Hosseininasab, A., Meyer, G. J., Viglione, D. J., Mihura, J. L., Berant, E., Resende, A. C., Reese, J., & Mohammadi, M. R. (2019). The effect of CS administration or an R-optimized alternative on R–PAS variables: A meta-analysis of findings from six studies. *Journal of Personality Assessment, 101*(2), 199–212. https://doi.org/10.1080/00223891.2017.1393430

Huprich, S. K., & Greenberg, R. P. (2003). Advances in the assessment of object relations in the 1990s. *Clinical Psychology Review, 23*(5), 665–698. https://doi.org/10.1016/S0272-7358(03)00072-2

Hutt, M. L. (1985). *The Hutt adaptation of the Bender-Gestalt Test: Rapid screening and intensive diagnosis* (4th ed.). Grune & Stratton.

Inslegers, R., Vanheule, S., Meganck, R., Debaere, V., Trenson, E., Desmet, M., & Roelstraete, B. (2012). The assessment of the social cognition and object relations scale on TAT and interview data. *Journal of Personality Assessment, 94*(4), 372–379. https://doi.org/10.1080/00223891.2012.662187

Joiner, T. E., Jr., Schmidt, K. L., & Barnett, J. (1996). Size, detail, and line heaviness in children's drawings as correlates of emotional distress: (More) negative evidence. *Journal of Personality Assessment, 67*(1), 127–141. https://doi.org/10.1207/s15327752jpa6701_10

Khadivi, A., & Evans, F. B. (2012). The brave new world of forensic Rorschach assessment: Comments on the Rorschach special section. *Psychological Injury and Law, 5*(2), 145–149. https://doi.org/10.1007/s12207-012-9134-7

Kivisalu, T. M., Lewey, J. H., Shaffer, T. W., & Canfield, M. L. (2017). Correction to: An investigation of interrater reliability for the Rorschach Performance Assessment System (R-PAS) in a nonpatient U.S. sample. *Journal of Personality Assessment, 99*(5), 558–560. https://doi.org/10.1080/00223891.2017.1325244

Kivisto, A. J., Gacono, C., & Medoff, D. (2013). Does the R-PAS meet standards for forensic use? Considerations with introducing a new Rorschach coding system. *Journal of Forensic Psychology Practice, 13*(5), 389–410. https://doi.org/10.1080/15228932.2013.838106

Knoff, H. M., & Prout, H. T. (1985). *The kinetic drawing system: Family and school*. Western Psychological Services.

Koocher, G. P., McMann, M. R., Stout, A. O., & Norcross, J. C. (2015). Discredited assessment and treatment methods used with children and adolescents: A Delphi poll. *Journal of Clinical Child and Adolescent Psychology, 44*(5), 722–729. https://doi.org/10.1080/15374416.2014.895941

Koppitz, E. M. (1968). *Psychological evaluation of children's human figure drawings*. Grune & Stratton.

Machover, K. (1949). *Personality projection in the drawing of the human figure*. Thomas.

Matto, H. C., Naglieri, J. A., & Claussen, C. (2005). Validity of the Draw-A-Person: Screening Procedure for Emotional Disturbance (DAP:SPED) in strength-based assessment. *Research on Social Work Practice, 15*(1), 41–46. https://doi.org/10.1177/1049731504269553

McAdams, D. P. (1982). Experiences of intimacy and power: Relationships between social motives and autobiographical memory. *Journal of Personality and Social Psychology, 42*(2), 292–302. https://doi.org/10.1037/0022-3514.42.2.292

McClelland, D. C. (1965). N achievement and entrepreneurship: A longitudinal study. *Journal of Personality and Social Psychology, 1*(4), 389–392. https://doi.org/10.1037/h0021956

McClelland, D. C. (1975). *Power: The inner experience*. Irvington.

McClelland, D. C., Atkinson, J. W., Clark, R. A., & Lowell, E. L. (1953). *The achievement motive*. Appleton-Century-Crofts. https://doi.org/10.1037/11144-000

McGrath, R. E. (2005). Conceptual complexity and construct validity. *Journal of Personality Assessment, 85*(2), 112–124. https://doi.org/10.1207/s15327752jpa8502_02

McGrath, R. E. (2008). The Rorschach in the context of performance-based personality assessment. *Journal of Personality Assessment, 90*(5), 465–475. https://doi.org/10.1080/00223890802248760

McGrath, R. E., & Carroll, E. J. (2012). The current status of "projective" "tests." In H. Cooper, P. M. Camic, D. L. Long, A. T. Panter, D. Rindskopf, & K. J. Sher (Eds.), *APA handbook of research methods in psychology: Vol. 1. Foundations, planning, measures, and psychometrics* (pp. 329–348). American Psychological Association. https://doi.org/10.1037/13619-018

McNeish, T. J., & Naglieri, J. A. (1993). Identification of individuals with serious emotional disturbance using the Draw-A Person: Screening Procedure for Emotional Disturbance. *The Journal of Special Education, 27*(1), 115–121. https://doi.org/10.1177/002246699302700108

Meyer, G. J. (2000). Incremental validity of the Rorschach Prognostic Rating Scale over the MMPI Ego Strength Scale and IQ. *Journal of Personality Assessment, 74*(3), 356–370. https://doi.org/10.1207/S15327752JPA7403_2

Meyer, G. J., & Eblin, J. J. (2012). An overview of the Rorschach Performance Assessment System (R-PAS).

Psychological Injury and Law, 5(2), 107–121. https://doi.org/10.1007/s12207-012-9130-y

Meyer, G. J., & Kurtz, J. E. (2006). Advancing personality assessment terminology: Time to retire "objective" and "projective" as personality test descriptors. *Journal of Personality Assessment*, 87(3), 223–225. https://doi.org/10.1207/s15327752jpa8703_01

Meyer, G. J., & Mihura, J. L. (2020). Performance-based techniques. In M. Sellbom & J. A. Suhr (Eds.), *The Cambridge handbook of clinical assessment and diagnosis* (pp. 278–290). Cambridge University Press.

Meyer, G. J., Riethmiller, R. J., Brooks, R. D., Benoit, W. A., & Handler, L. (2000). A replication of Rorschach and MMPI-2 convergent validity. *Journal of Personality Assessment*, 74(2), 175–215. https://doi.org/10.1207/S15327752JPA7402_3

Meyer, G. J., Viglione, D. J., & Mihura, J. L. (2017). Psychometric foundations of the Rorschach Performance Assessment System (R-PAS). In R. Erard & B. Evans (Eds.), *The Rorschach in multimethod forensic practice* (pp. 23–91). Routledge.

Meyer, G. J., Viglione, D. J., Mihura, J. L., Erard, R. E., & Erdberg, P. (2011). *Rorschach Performance Assessment System: Administration, coding, interpretation, and technical manual*. Rorschach Performance Assessment System.

Meyer, G. J., Viglione, D. J., Mihura, J. L., & Giromini, L. (2020, October 8). *2018 update to R-PAS transitional child and adolescent norms*. R-PAS. https://r-pas.org/UpdateYNorms.aspx

Mihura, J. L., Meyer, G. J., Dumitrascu, N., & Bombel, G. (2013). The validity of individual Rorschach variables: Systematic reviews and meta-analyses of the comprehensive system. *Psychological Bulletin*, 139(3), 548–605. https://doi.org/10.1037/a0029406

Mihura, J. L., Roy, M., & Graceffo, R. A. (2017). Psychological assessment training in clinical psychology doctoral programs. *Journal of Personality Assessment*, 99(2), 153–164. https://doi.org/10.1080/00223891.2016.1201978

Mischel, W. (1968). *Personality and assessment*. Wiley.

More, D. M., & Winch, R. F. (1956). Does TAT add information to interviews? Statistical analysis of the increment. *Journal of Clinical Psychology*, 12(4), 316–321. https://doi.org/10.1002/1097-4679(195610)12:4<316::AID-JCLP2270120403>3.0.CO;2-P

Morgan, C., & Murray, H. A. (1935). A method for investigating fantasies: The Thematic Apperception Test. *Archives of Neurology and Psychiatry*, 34(2), 289–306. https://doi.org/10.1001/archneurpsyc.1935.02250200049005

Murray, H. A. (1938). *Explorations in personality*. Oxford University Press.

Murray, H. A. (1943). *Manual for the Thematic Apperception Test*. Harvard University Press.

Naglieri, J. A., McNeish, T. J., & Bardos, A. N. (1991). *Draw A Person: Screening Procedure for Emotional Disturbance: Examiner's manual*. Pro-Ed.

Naglieri, J. A., & Pfeiffer, S. I. (1992). Performance of disruptive behavior disordered and normal samples on the Draw-A-Person: Screening Procedure for Emotional Disturbance. *Psychological Assessment*, 4(2), 156–159. https://doi.org/10.1037/1040-3590.4.2.156

Nakamura, N. (2012). Rorschach-based psychotherapy: Collaboration with a suicidal young woman. In S. E. Finn, C. T. Fischer, & L. Handler (Eds.), *Collaborative/therapeutic assessment: A casebook and guide* (pp. 269–290). Wiley.

Nosek, B. A., Greenwald, A. G., & Banaji, M. R. (2007). The Implicit Association Test at age 7: A methodological and conceptual review. In J. A. Bargh (Ed.), *Automatic processes in social thinking and behavior* (pp. 265–292). Psychology Press.

Pad, R. A., Huprich, S. K., & Porcerelli, J. (2020). Convergent and discriminant validity of self-report and performance-based assessment of object relations. *Journal of Personality Assessment*, 102(6), 858–865. https://doi.org/10.1080/00223891.2019.1625909

Pianowski, G., Meyer, G. J., de Villemor-Amaral, A. E., Zuanazzi, A. C., & do Nascimento, R. S. G. F. (2021). Does the Rorschach Performance Assessment System (R-PAS) differ from the Comprehensive System (CS) on variables relevant to interpretation? *Journal of Personality Assessment*, 103(1), 132–147. https://doi.org/10.1080/00223891.2019.1677678

Pihl, R., & Nimrod, G. (1976). The reliability and validity of the Draw-A-Person Test in IQ and personality assessment. *Journal of Clinical Psychology*, 32(2), 470–472. https://doi.org/10.1002/1097-4679(197604)32:2<470::AID-JCLP2270320257>3.0.CO;2-I

Piotrowski, C. (2015a). Clinical instruction on projective techniques in the USA: A review of academic training settings 1995–2014. *SIS Journal of Projective Psychology & Mental Health*, 22(2), 83–92.

Piotrowski, C. (2015b). Projective techniques usage worldwide: A review of applied settings 1995–2015. *Journal of the Indian Academy of Applied Psychology*, 41(3), 9–19.

Piotrowski, C., & Keller, J. W. (1984). Psychodiagnostic testing in APA-approved clinical psychology programs. *Professional Psychology, Research and Practice, 15*(3), 450–456. https://doi.org/10.1037/0735-7028.15.3.450

Piotrowski, C., & Zalewski, C. (1993). Training in psychodiagnostic testing in APA-approved PsyD and PhD clinical psychology programs. *Journal of Personality Assessment, 61*(2), 394–405. https://doi.org/10.1207/s15327752jpa6102_17

Porcerelli, J. H., Cogan, R., Kamoo, R., & Miller, K. (2010). Convergent validity of the Defense Mechanisms Manual and the Defensive Functioning Scale. *Journal of Personality Assessment, 92*(5), 432–438. https://doi.org/10.1080/00223891.2010.497421

Porcerelli, J. H., Thomas, S., Hibbard, S., & Cogan, R. (1998). Defense mechanisms development in children, adolescents, and late adolescents. *Journal of Personality Assessment, 71*(3), 411–420. https://doi.org/10.1207/s15327752jpa7103_9

Rehrig, G., & Stromswold, K. (2018). What does the DAP:IQ measure?: Drawing comparisons between drawing performance and developmental assessments. *The Journal of Genetic Psychology, 179*(1), 9–18. https://doi.org/10.1080/00221325.2017.1392281

Riethmiller, R. J., & Handler, L. (1997). Problematic methods and unwarranted conclusions in DAP research: Suggestions for improved research procedures. *Journal of Personality Assessment, 69*(3), 459–475. https://doi.org/10.1207/s15327752jpa6903_1

Ronan, G. F., Gibbs, M. S., Dreer, L. E., & Lombardo, J. A. (2008). Personal Problem-Solving System-Revised. In S. R. Jenkins (Ed.), *A handbook of clinical scoring systems for thematic apperceptive techniques* (pp. 181–207). Erlbaum.

Rorschach, H. (1942). *Psychodiagnostics: A diagnostic test based on perception*. Hans Huber. (Original work published 1921)

Rosenzweig, S. (1978). *Rosenzweig Picture-Frustration Study (P-F)* (rev. ed.). Psychological Assessment Resources.

Rotter, J. B., Lah, M. I., & Rafferty, J. E. (1992). *Manual: The Rotter Incomplete Sentences Blank: College form*. Psychological Corporation.

Schneider, A. M. de A., Bandeira, D. R., & Meyer, G. J. (2022). Rorschach Performance Assessment System (R-PAS) interrater reliability in a Brazilian adolescent sample and comparisons with three other studies. *Assessment, 29*(5), 859–871. https://doi.org/10.1177/1073191120973075

Schultheiss, O., Liening, S., & Schad, D. (2008). The reliability of a Picture Story Exercise measure of implicit motives: Estimates of internal consistency, retest reliability, and ipsative stability. *Journal of Research in Personality, 42*(6), 1560–1571. https://doi.org/10.1016/j.jrp.2008.07.008

Shrout, P. E. (1998). Measurement reliability and agreement in psychiatry. *Statistical Methods in Medical Research, 7*(3), 301–317. https://doi.org/10.1177/096228029800700306

Spangler, W. (1992). Validity of questionnaire and TAT measures of need for achievement: Two meta-analyses. *Psychological Bulletin, 112*(1), 140–154. https://doi.org/10.1037/0033-2909.112.1.140

Stedman, J. M., McGeary, C. A., & Essery, J. (2018). Current patterns of training in personality assessment during internship. *Journal of Clinical Psychology, 74*(3), 398–406. https://doi.org/10.1002/jclp.22496

Stein, M., Hilsenroth, M., Slavin-Mulford, J., & Pinsker, J. (2011). *Social Cognition and Object Relations Scale: Global Rating Method (SCORS-G)* (4th ed.) [Unpublished manuscript]. Massachusetts General Hospital and Harvard Medical School.

Stein, M. B., & Slavin-Mulford, J. (2018). *Social Cognition and Object Relations Scale: A comprehensive guide for clinicians and researchers*. Routledge.

Stein, M. B., Slavin-Mulford, J., Sinclair, S. J., Chung, W.-J., Roche, M., Denckla, C., & Blais, M. A. (2018). Extending the use of the SCORS–G composite ratings in assessing level of personality organization. *Journal of Personality Assessment, 100*(2), 166–175. https://doi.org/10.1080/00223891.2016.1195394

Sultan, S., & Meyer, G. J. (2009). Does productivity impact the stability of rorschach scores? *Journal of Personality Assessment, 91*(5), 480–493. https://doi.org/10.1080/00223890903088693

Sundberg, N. (1961). The practice of psychological testing in clinical services in the United States. *American Psychologist, 16*(2), 79–83. https://doi.org/10.1037/h0040647

Swensen, C. H. (1968). Empirical evaluations of human figure drawings: 1957–1966. *Psychological Bulletin, 70*(1), 20–44. https://doi.org/10.1037/h0026011

Tharinger, D. J., & Stark, K. (1990). A qualitative versus quantitative approach to evaluating the Draw-A-Person and Kinetic Family Drawings: A study of mood- and anxiety-disordered children. *Psychological Assessment, 2*(4), 365–375. https://doi.org/10.1037/1040-3590.2.4.365

Troncone, A., Chianese, A., Di Leva, A., Grasso, M., & Cascella, C. (2021). Validity of the Draw A Person: A quantitative scoring system (DAP:QSS) for clinically evaluating intelligence. *Child Psychiatry and Human Development, 52*(4), 728–738. https://doi.org/10.1007/s10578-020-01058-6

Viglione, D. J., & Giromini, L. (2016). The effects of using the International versus Comprehensive System Rorschach norms for children, adolescents, and adults. *Journal of Personality Assessment*, *98*(4), 391–397. https://doi.org/10.1080/00223891.2015.1136313

Wakefield, J. (1986). Creativity and the TAT blank card. *The Journal of Creative Behavior*, *20*(2), 127–133. https://doi.org/10.1002/j.2162-6057.1986.tb00427.x

Weiner, I. B. (1994). The Rorschach Inkblot Method (RIM) is not a test: Implications for theory and practice. *Journal of Personality Assessment*, *62*(3), 498–504. https://doi.org/10.1207/s15327752jpa6203_9

Westen, D. (1995). *Social cognition and object relations scale: Q-sort for projective stories (SCORS Q)* [Unpublished manuscript]. Department of Psychiatry, The Cambridge Hospital and Harvard Medical School.

Wrightson, L., & Saklofske, D. (2000). Validity and reliability of the Draw A Person: Screening Procedure for Emotional Disturbance with adolescent students. *Canadian Journal of School Psychology*, *16*(1), 95–102. https://doi.org/10.1177/082957350001600107

Ziegler, M., Schmukle, S., Egloff, B., & Bühner, M. (2010). Investigating measures of achievement motivation(s). *Journal of Individual Differences*, *31*(1), 15–21. https://doi.org/10.1027/1614-0001/a000002

CHAPTER 21

BRIEF INSTRUMENTS AND SHORT FORMS

Emily A. Atkinson, Carolyn M. Pearson Carter, Jessica L. Combs Rohr, and Gregory T. Smith

In this chapter, we consider psychological instruments to be those measures that are developed with the goal of brevity; some brief instruments are short forms of previously validated measures. The specific meaning of "brief" varies according to the needs and context of the assessment. In some cases, measures of three items may be desired and appropriate.[1] In other cases, researchers may seek to develop a 30-minute assessment to replace an existing 2-hour evaluation process. As we describe here, reasons for brevity include the need to measure multiple constructs in a single assessment, the need to save time, the need to save resources, or other practical considerations. The theme of our chapter is although most researchers have learned that longer measures tend to be more reliable and valid, that is not always true. Under the right conditions, brief measures can be as valid, or more valid, than longer measures of the same construct. We describe the (frequent) conditions under which this is likely to be true and provide guidance to researchers in the valid development of brief instruments. We also discuss procedures for developing reliable and valid shorter versions of existing measures.

The outline of the chapter is as follows. First, we briefly review the standard psychometric argument in favor of longer measures. We then observe that, as a result of this standard argument, many researchers' choices to use brief instruments or short forms are made grudgingly: Researchers tend to do so for practical reasons, even though they view themselves as potentially sacrificing important content coverage. We then make an argument for the opposite: Brief instruments that are developed with careful consideration of the need to include content prototypic of the construct can, in fact, be more valid than longer instruments. We thus observe that the pursuit of the practical is not inconsistent with the pursuit of validity; put differently, construction of brief tests can enhance both validity and practicality. We go on to address important issues in the construction of brief measures and limitations to the utility of brief measures. After providing examples of brief instruments for which there is good evidence of validity, we provide an overview for how to construct valid short forms of existing, longer measures. We then briefly consider item response theory (IRT) as an important vehicle for brief test construction.

---

[1] For the most part in this chapter, we use the term *item* to refer to an element of an assessment instrument. We do so for convenience of presentation; we do not intend to limit our discussion to questionnaires and questionnaire items. The principles we describe apply to any form of psychological assessment, including questionnaires, interviews, peer observations, behavioral observations, physiological assessments, and the like.

https://doi.org/10.1037/0000318-021
APA Handbook of Research Methods in Psychology, Second Edition: Vol. 1. Foundations, Planning, Measures, and Psychometrics, H. Cooper (Editor-in-Chief)
Copyright © 2023 by the American Psychological Association. All rights reserved.

PSYCHOMETRICS AND LONGER MEASURES

Psychological researchers are typically well aware of the test construction concept represented by the Spearman-Brown prophecy formula (SBPF; Spearman, 1910): Increasing the length of a test by adding parallel items (i.e., items assessing the same content, worded differently) will improve its reliability and, thus, its validity. The concept behind the SBPF is that there is an identified content domain of interest, and the items on a measure of that content domain are a random sample of all possible items. Under that assumption, if one were to add a certain number of additional items also sampled randomly from the content domain, the SBPF predicts the reliability of the new, longer measure. One version of the formula (Spearman, 1910) is

$$r_{ff} = \frac{k(r_{ss})}{1+(k-1)r_{ss}}$$

where r_{ss} refers to the reliability of the original (short) version of the measure, r_{ff} refers to the predicted reliability of the longer measure, and k is the factor by which the length of the measure is increased. Thus, if one had a measure with a reliability estimate of .75 and one doubled the measure length (using parallel items; k = 2), the formula would predict a reliability estimate for the new, longer measure of .86. And of course, such a change would mean a drop in the proportion of estimated error variance from .25 to .14. Subsequent advances in the form of generalizability theory (Cronbach et al., 1972) led to a removal of the requirement that items be strictly parallel; instead, items viewed simply as alternative indicators of the same construct (but without fully overlapping psychometric properties) could be included. One result of this advance is that it became even easier to add new items to measures.

In heavy part due to this seminal contribution by Spearman, psychological researchers have placed a strong emphasis on lengthy tests. It is, of course, important to develop measures that are as reliable as possible, that is, that they have the least possible error variance, and one way to approach that goal is to lengthen tests by adding additional items. Accordingly, when researchers use very brief measures, such as with two, three, or four items, they often do so with a sense that they are probably not representing the full content domain sufficiently and are, thus, sacrificing reliability.

Nevertheless, researchers often do decide to use brief measures, typically for practical reasons. Many psychological theories are multivariate. For example, risk researchers often propose models that involve the simultaneous operation of several risk factors, mediation of some risk factors by other risk factors, moderation effects, and the like. It is perhaps often the case that, as a practical matter, one cannot study such models by using lengthy tests for each construct in the model. In some cases, time constraints are paramount (participants are only available for a specified period of time, such as when children are studied during the course of the school day); in other cases, avoiding fatigue is important; and in still others, financial limitations preclude lengthy assessments. As researchers face the competing demands of reliable assessment and valid representation of complex models, they often make the choice to represent individual constructs with brief measures. At times, comprehensive coverage of a construct gives way to the need to represent multiple constructs in a single study. Many researchers view this choice as a regrettable necessity.

ON THE VALIDITY OF BRIEF INSTRUMENTS

In contrast to this perspective, we argue that researchers' devotion to lengthy tests is often not necessary and may actually lead to less valid assessment of target constructs. To introduce this argument, we note the relevance of the concepts of content validity (Cronbach & Meehl, 1955), construct representation (Embretson, 1998), and construct homogeneity (McGrath, 2005; Smith et al., 2009).

Content Validity

Haynes and colleagues (1995) presented a useful discussion of content validity and methods of content validation. We would like to emphasize two aspects of the content validation procedure that they described. The first concerns construct definition. It is well known that when a researcher develops a measure of a construct, they must define the construct in precise terms. As Haynes et al. noted, precise definitions include specifying both what content is included in the target construct and what content is excluded. Dixon and Johnston (2019), in the context of health psychology research, added the useful concept of discriminant construct validity. Perhaps in the past, in part due to the SBPF-based pressure to develop lengthier measures, researchers may have emphasized what to include more than they have emphasized what to exclude. We argue that consideration of what to exclude is every bit as important. There is a distinction between content that is prototypic of a target construct and content that is related to the target construct but actually representative of a different construct. To develop measures containing prototypic items, researchers must discriminate between these two types of items. Exclusion of related, nonprototypic content is an essential part of constructing a content valid instrument.

One possible example of inclusion of related, nonprototypic content was observed by Smith et al. (2003): On the Novelty Seeking scale of the Temperament and Character Inventory (Cloninger et al., 1991), one item appears to be prototypic of novelty seeking (the item refers to doing new things for fun or for the thrill) and another, which refers to the ability to convince others to believe something you know is untrue, seems not to be prototypic but may be a correlate of novelty seeking. The latter item does not seem to reflect the core content of novelty seeking. If the Smith et al. (2003) conjecture is correct, the inclusion of both items may increase estimates of internal consistency reliability but may lead to a test that includes content representing constructs related to, but separate from, novelty seeking.

This consideration is relevant to test length because (a) many lengthier tests include correlated but not prototypic content and (b) there is evidence that a construct's content domain can be represented with relatively few items. Ulrich (1985) showed that test validity does not increase with test length if the new items have even slightly different factor structures (or represent slightly different constructs). Additionally, Burisch (1997) demonstrated empirically that shortened scales can have improved convergent validity over longer scales when the shortened scales included only items that had been prescreened for content validity. A small set of items that has been judged to represent validly the target construct, that is, be prototypic of the target construct, can be combined to produce a more valid scale than a large set of items in which not all items are prototypic of the target construct. In fact, Burisch (1997) found that scales of two to four items had estimates of convergent validity that were at least as high, and often higher, than those of much lengthier scales.

A second contribution by Haynes et al. (1995) is the need for independent, quantitative evaluation of content validity. When trained experts conduct independent reviews of whether instrument content represents the target construct, and does not represent related constructs, researchers can have increased confidence in the fidelity of their measures. It is often advisable to have multiple, independent raters evaluate prospective content based on inclusionary and exclusionary criteria: One can then retain items that meet both sets of criteria, and one can report the rate of agreement among the experts. The combined focus on inclusionary and exclusionary criteria is likely to result in a smaller item pool composed of items that are more prototypic of the target construct. Further methodological advances by nursing researchers provide means of quantifying the necessity of items to reflect a content domain (the content validity ratio) and the relevance and clarity of items (the content validity index; see Zamanzadeh et al., 2015).

Construct Representation

Construct representation refers to the degree to which the tasks (e.g., items, observations) on an instrument validly represent the target construct (Embretson, 1998). This concept has often been used with respect to laboratory tasks, but the concept has more general application. To consider construct representation in a measure, one might think in terms of what percentage of the variance in response to an item reflects variance in the target construct, and what percentage reflects other factors instead. For example, in our eating expectancy inventory (a measure of a risk factor for eating disorders; Hohlstein et al., 1998), there is a scale understood to measure the tendency to eat to alleviate negative affect. The item "Eating seems to decrease my level of anxiety if I am feeling tense or stressed" may have good construct representation: Perhaps the bulk of the variance in responses to that item is related to variance in the target construct. In contrast, the item "Eating makes me feel loved," which is on the same scale, may not have as strong construct representation. It may well be that part of the variance in responses to that item does reflect variance in the target construct, while there are other sources of variance in response to that item not reflective of eating to alleviate negative affect. By including only items for which variance in item response is likely to be highly related to variance in the target construct, test developers can trim away unnecessary items and create scales that are both briefer and more valid.

The allure of ever more reliable tests has perhaps led researchers to write new items, and add new items, at the expense of careful consideration of whether each new item is truly prototypic of the target construct or at the expense of careful consideration of the degree to which variance in responses to the item represents variance in the target construct. It is true that when one adds items that are correlated to an existing item set, coefficient alpha estimates of reliability do go up. This can occur, however, even if the new items do not truly represent the target construct domain. The findings of Burisch (1997) and Ulrich (1985) suggest that the promise of increased reliability estimates is not necessarily realized as increased validity. Brief instruments can be more valid than lengthier instruments.

Construct Homogeneity

Another concept that may prove helpful for researchers as they seek to develop content-valid, brief measures is that of construct homogeneity. Several researchers have argued that scores on psychological measures should reflect variation along a single dimension, that is, variation on a definable, coherent, homogeneous psychological construct (Edwards, 2001; McGrath, 2005; Smith et al., 2009; Strauss & Smith, 2009). McGrath (2005) and Smith et al. (2009) provided several examples of scientific and measurement uncertainty that occur when a single score is used to reflect variation on several dimensions simultaneously.

Consider a single score on posttraumatic stress disorder (PTSD). Researchers have identified at least four different dimensions within that diagnosis. The fifth edition of the *Diagnostic and Statistical Manual of Mental Disorders* (*DSM-5*; American Psychiatric Association, 2013) currently recognizes four symptom clusters for PTSD including intrusions, avoidance, negative alterations in cognitions and mood, and alterations in arousal and reactivity, while several recent studies have identified five-, six-, and seven-factor models for the structure of PTSD (Armour et al., 2016). The four *DSM-5* symptom clusters are only modestly correlated with each other, and they do appear to refer to different experiences (Contractor et al., 2020). The same score on PTSD could be obtained by one person, high on alterations in arousal and reactivity and low on the other three dimensions, and another person, high on avoidance and low on the other three dimensions. Obviously, these two individuals are having very different psychological experiences, even though they would get the same score on the composite measure. Thus, a single score risks obscuring important differences in symptom profiles for different individuals. While a composite score on a broad measure of PTSD may provide valuable information related to presence and severity of symptoms, measures with scales assessing each symptom domain may be more valuable when treatment planning or assessing risk for specific dysfunction.

The pursuit of construct homogeneity can facilitate the development of brief psychological instruments. To the degree it is possible, researchers should seek to define constructs that are homogeneous. The process of refining construct definitions toward homogeneity is likely to result in exclusion of nonprototypic items. An initial attempt to define homogeneous constructs, together with careful consideration of content validity and construct representation, can help researchers develop measures that are both valid and brief.

We note three other considerations concerning the pursuit of constructs defined as homogeneous. The first is that understanding of homogeneity evolves over time: As scientific knowledge about a given construct advances, what was once thought to be a homogeneous construct can be discovered to have separable facets that operate differently. One example is in the measurement of impulsivity, where early views of a single dimension have evolved to the recognition that there are multiple traits that dispose individuals to impulsive action (Dick et al., 2010). The second is that some scales are not developed with the goal of measuring a single, homogeneous construct. For example, a measure of exposer to psychosocial stressors involves summing exposure to many different kinds of stressors that, themselves, are not necessarily related to each other. In this latter case, homogeneity of item content is not a goal and measure reliability cannot be assessed in terms of internal consistency among items.

The third consideration concerns the possibility of virtually infinite reduction in the scope of constructs to pursue complete homogeneity. With respect to PTSD, there are no doubt many different experiences of intrusions or alterations in arousal. If so, is it necessary to measure each different form of intrusion or alteration in arousal with its own scale? The obvious risks in parsing every construct into more and more homogeneous components are that (a) one may lose the essence of the construct by dividing it into ever more subcomponents and (b) every construct measure would require constant evaluation for further parsing, thus slowing scientific progress. We echo the argument offered by Strauss and Smith (2009) for a practical solution to this problem: One should parse constructs into lower level, (more) homogeneous facets to the degree that doing so is necessary for adequate explanation. In the case of PTSD, if intrusion symptoms place one at risk for outcome A and alterations in arousal symptoms do not, but instead place one at risk for outcome B, and if outcomes A and B are relevant to one's research, one should rely on the subscales rather than an overall PTSD scale. But if the two sets of symptoms play the same predictive role for one's purpose, one need not report their functions separately. Of course, to determine the value of reporting facet results separately, one must run preliminary analyses at the facet level. To do so using a brief instrument does require adequate representation of each facet. To extend this logic, if one suspects that different experiences of intrusions play different roles in functioning, one might well need to develop scales for facets of PTSD intrusions to test that hypothesis.

THE CREATION OF BRIEF INSTRUMENTS

First, and perhaps most important, nothing about the size of a scale alters the need to undergo careful and thorough scale construction and construct validation procedures. There is no basis for concluding that a brief measure needs less care in construction or less comprehensive validation. Other chapters have provided valuable guidance for many aspects of scale construction and validation (see Hayes & Embretson, 2012; Krosnick, 1999), as do other published articles (Clark & Watson, 2016; Smith et al., 2003) and books (Nunnally & Bernstein, 1994). Therefore, we will not review basic aspects of test construction here; instead, we focus on considerations specific to the construction of valid, brief instruments.

One of the challenges in developing a brief measure is to include content that is homogeneous but that is not simply a slight rephrasing of exactly the same content (Burisch, 1997; Loevinger, 1957). The degree to which two items are parallel measures of the same content domain, or instead (a) are substantively identical or (b) actually represent two different, correlated content domains, can only be evaluated by careful judgment. Mistakes are likely, and an iterative process involving repeated reexamination of item content and construct definition may prove useful. It is crucial that the nature of the judgment process be specified, the judgments evaluated empirically, and then empirical content validation procedures be applied on the item pool independently by experts (Dixon & Johnston, 2019; Haynes et al., 1995; Zamanzadeh et al., 2015).

Following item selection and empirical content validity procedures, corrected item-total correlations can be used to help further prune the measure. There is no agreed-on rule for the optimal magnitude of item intercorrelations: Recommendations vary from .15 to .50 and even higher. Most examinations of these recommendations observed the magnitude of the relationships between ordinal or semicontinuous items (Briggs & Cheek, 1986; Clark & Watson, 2016; Morey, 2003; Smith et al., 2003). These values reflect a balance between the concerns that items not be fully redundant and that they represent the same content domain. Of course, the optimal magnitude of interitem correlations is in part a function of the true breadth of the target construct. Moderately or very high item-total correlations do not prove construct homogeneity: An item can be correlated with the total while not reflecting the same construct, or two items can be substantively identical and so correlate very highly. On the other hand, if the item-total correlation is low, it is likely that the item does not reflect the target domain and should be excluded.

Item-total correlations are indeed helpful for building confidence that a judgment that an item represents the content domain was valid, but neither item-total correlations nor estimates of internal consistency (e.g., coefficients alpha and omega) speak to the important goal of unidimensionality (Clark & Watson, 2016; Dunn et al., 2014). There is an important difference between achieving strong internal consistency, which is reflected in coefficients α, ω, and interitem correlations, and construct homogeneity, which occurs when all items reflect a single underlying construct. One important tool for achieving the latter goal is factor analysis.

Factor analysis can be used to test hypotheses about the dimensional structure of an item set (Clark & Watson, 2016). For this analytic approach to be feasible, it is necessary to have a few items representing each possible dimension. For example, in order to test the competing hypotheses that an item set has one, two, or three underlying dimensions, one should have at least three items representing each of the three possible dimensions. There are two reasons for this recommendation. The first is definitional: A factor represents an underlying dimension of a construct. Although one may have only a single item reflecting a dimension in a given analysis, to make a convincing argument that the item references an underlying dimension, one would need ultimately to show shared variance among multiple items representing the same content domain. The second is statistical: A factor cannot be identified in confirmatory factor analysis, typically, without at least three items/indicators.

If a researcher suspects a single item represents a different dimension from the intended construct, the researcher can consider deleting the item. If, instead, the researcher wants to test the dimensionality hypothesis, writing two or more additional items parallel to the item in question may be necessary so that a comparative factor analysis can be conducted. Thus, the process of determining the dimensionality of an item set is likely to be an iterative one, consisting of content validity judgments, item deletion, item generation, and comparative factor analysis.

LIMITATIONS ON THE USE OF BRIEF INSTRUMENTS

There are also limitations on when brief instruments should be used. First, some target constructs simply require a large number of items, a large number of behavioral observations, or a lengthy interview for valid assessment. Second, when one seeks to assess a multidimensional construct, measuring each dimension reliably and validly is important (Smith et al., 2003); as a result, multidimensional measures often require greater length.

The Need for Lengthier Measures

There are a number of assessment circumstances in which brevity may not be appropriate. First, if a psychologist wants to observe a certain target behavior and determine the degree to which emission of the behavior is a function of external circumstances, it may well be necessary to construct a lengthy observation protocol. Second, constructs that involve a skill, and, thus, require items of graduated difficulty, may require lengthier assessments than other constructs. For example, the Wechsler Adult Intelligence Scale, 4th Edition (Wechsler, 2008) relies on 30 vocabulary items in order to facilitate discriminations at different levels of vocabulary skill. In fact, there may be many psychological constructs that are best assessed with a variety of items, each measuring a different intensity level of the construct: When that is true, it is necessary to beginning with a larger item pool is necessary. Third, researchers might well conclude that a small number of items (e.g., three to five) simply would not permit an adequate sampling of the content domain of a target construct and, thus, choose to construct a lengthier instrument.

The second circumstance under which lengthier measures may be necessary is when the goal is to assess a multidimensional construct. In some areas of psychological inquiry, such as the study of personality or the study of psychopathology, multidimensionality is the norm, not the exception. Concerning psychopathology, recall our earlier example of PTSD. It is now clear that, in order to validly assess this disorder, one must validly assess each of at least four symptom clusters. Most disorders described in the *DSM-5* are multidimensional in that they are composed of more than one cognitive, emotional, and behavioral domain (Clark et al., 2017). Concerning personality, virtually all comprehensive models of personality are hierarchical and multidimensional. For example, the NEO Personality Inventory Revised (NEO PI-R) version of the five-factor model (Costa & McCrae, 1992) includes five broad personality domains and six specific, homogeneous traits within each domain.

For many, if not most, purposes, valid assessment requires the separate assessment of each separate construct. In the example of PTSD, a single score simply averages across different constructs and, as noted earlier, may reflect different psychological experiences for different individuals. There are validated and distinct treatments for the four PTSD symptom clusters of intrusions, avoidance, negative alterations in cognitions and mood, and alterations in arousal and reactivity. For assessment to guide treatment effectively, it must validly assess each of the four symptom clusters.

Accordingly, assessment of multidimensional construct domains requires enough items, interview questions, or observations to represent each individual construct reliably and validly. The assessment of each individual construct could be done briefly, but the combination of several brief measures may not, itself, be brief. The use of brief measures to collapse across constructs within a construct domain is not usually advisable, because doing so can produce scores of unclear meaning, as in the example of PTSD.

SHORT FORMS

Next, we discuss short forms, that is, abbreviated versions of existing measures. There are two different types of short forms that should be discussed separately. The first type involves abbreviating an instrument to improve its validity by removing items that are not prototypic of the target construct; much of the preceding content of this chapter is relevant to this situation. The second type involves abbreviating a valid instrument strictly for practical reasons: In this latter case, researchers remove content valid, prototypic item content for the sake of efficiency. This latter situation is different from what we have discussed so far in this chapter; we, therefore, review procedures for shortening instruments that maintain reliability and validity as much as possible. In either case, reliable and valid short forms can be developed, providing that researchers take care to follow sound test construction and validation procedures.

Shortened measures have been a controversial topic since the early 20th century, when Doll (1917) created a short form of the Binet-Simon scale. Many original test developers have been highly critical of the development and use of short-form measurements (Levy, 1968; Wechsler, 1967). In fact, Wechsler (1967) advised those who felt there was not sufficient time for a full assessment to simply "find the time" (p. 37). Critics argued that the use of short forms is never or rarely justified and that their development often fails to resolve the trade-off between time saved and psychometric strength lost (Levy, 1968; Smith et al., 2000).

Nonetheless, researchers continue to develop short forms. Some of the reasons for their development include: to use for screening purposes; to fit a measure into a large multivariate study; to apply for use with children; and to reduce behavioral-observation time to save costs (Smith et al., 2000). In clinical settings today, there is pressure from health care providers to minimize assessment time and costs and, hence, to find quicker ways to measure constructs than was necessary in the past.

A short-form developer is attempting to measure a construct or answer a question that the original test developer concluded required a lengthier assessment (Smith et al., 2000). As a result, researchers must follow a set of methodological standards that lead to rigorous development and validation of useful short forms. The intent of this section is to provide guidance as to how to do so effectively. The guidelines mentioned here are most relevant for either classical test theory approaches, which rely on true-score theory (Zimmerman, 1975) or behavioral-assessment approaches (Haynes & Kaholokula, 2008). To begin, one can think of a short form as a new, alternate form of a measure; its reduced length and content coverage make it a different, alternative assessment to the original scale. It is, therefore, essential, as with any other measure, to establish independently the validity and reliability of the new, alternative measure. The short form must undergo the same validation process as did the original scale and meet the same standards of validity as are required for any other test.

We first briefly discuss the circumstance in which one shortens a measure with the goal of improving its homogeneity and construct representation, typically by removing nonprototypic item content. We then go on to discuss the classic conceptualization of short forms, which involves shortening valid scales and, thus, sacrificing validity for the benefit of time or cost savings.

Short Forms to Improve Validity

As we have discussed throughout this chapter, SBPF-based pressure to improve estimates of reliability can sometimes lead researchers to include items that measure content that is correlated with, but not prototypic of, the construct one intends to measure. This approach violates the assumption that all items are drawn from the same content domain and so can result in scales with compromised validity and even unclear meaning. When researchers judge this to be the case, they may choose to improve the content validity of the measure by removing nonprototypic content.

When researchers do make this judgment, we suggest they proceed in the following way. First, they should carefully define the nature of the target construct, with a particular emphasis on what content is not included in that construct (Dixon & Johnston, 2019). We recommend that the researchers approach the task with an eye toward construct homogeneity and construct representation: Each item should be evaluated in terms of whether it reflects the target construct, and researchers should consider how likely it is that variation in response to each item represents variation in the target construct.

Second, they should make formal, empirical judgments concerning the prototypicality of each item or each observation in the measure. If there is more than one researcher, they should do so independently and evaluate their rate of agreement statistically. If their agreement is good, they should resolve differences by discussion and, thus, arrive at a candidate set of items to be removed from the measure. If their agreement is not good, they should review their definitions, review their training, and train colleagues to make the new judgments. Once there are two sets of items (those to be maintained as prototypic and, thus, to be excluded), the researchers should train independent experts on the conceptual task, that is, by reviewing the concepts of construct homogeneity and construct representation; and on the substantive task, that is, the actual distinctions between prototypic and correlated content in this case. They should then have those experts provide quantitative content validity ratings for all items. Assuming agreement between the raters is good, and assuming the raters agree with the judgments of the researchers, the presumably few differences can be resolved by the researchers and items can be removed. At this point, the researchers have a draft of a new, shorter, presumably more valid measure.

We suggest that researchers view this draft as a new measure that requires investigation into its reliability and construct validity. Researchers should not rely on validity evidence for the original measure, because they found that measure wanting. Instead, they should follow standard validation procedures as described numerous times in the literature (Cronbach & Meehl, 1955; Landy, 1986; Loevinger, 1957; Messick, 1995; Smith, 2005; Strauss & Smith, 2009; see Chapter 35, this volume). We do not review the validation process here.

Short Forms That Involve the Removal of Valid Content

Of course, before one can develop a short form that involves removing valid content, one must have a good basis for believing that the original form does in fact have valid content, that is, adequate reliability and validity. It should have an established history of construct validation (Marsh et al., 2005; Smith et al., 2000). One should not attempt to abbreviate an instrument that has not been shown to measure what it purports to measure. If an original measure is not sufficiently validated, there is little reason to believe that a short form of that measure will fare better.

Among the findings researchers must demonstrate upon developing a short form of a valid measure are (a) that the short form preserves the content domain of the target construct; (b) that the short form preserves the factor structure if the construct domain was multidimensional; (c) that the shortened scale is reliable (or each scale or facet of a multidimensional measure is reliable); (d) that there is good evidence for the validity of the shortened scale on an independent sample and when the shortened scale is administered without the full, original scale; (e) that the shortened scale and the original scale have a high degree of agreement; (f) where appropriate, whether the short form provides acceptable classification rates; and (g) that the time savings justifies the loss of content. For additional considerations, the reader may wish to consult Smith et al. (2000). We consider each of these points in turn.

When choosing items to reduce the size of an instrument, it is important that items are chosen to cover adequately the content domain of the target behavior or construct. This process begins with a clear statement of the content domain measured by the original measure, and then a content validity analysis of the original scale's items. The content validity analysis might fruitfully address both whether each item represents the target construct and whether any pair of items is fully redundant (e.g., asks the same question with very slightly different wording). To remove one of two redundant items does not sacrifice representation of the construct's content domain.

The choices the researcher faces are more difficult after removal of redundant content. For example, researchers may seek to maintain representation of nonredundant items that are judged to represent the content domain. Retaining all nonredundant content may not often be possible; when it is not, researchers should be aware of which aspects of the content domain they have chosen to sacrifice. A related concern is that if one part of the content domain is removed, a remaining part of the domain may have greater influence on measure scores than it did in the original measure. Should this occur, there is a risk that the shortened measure has a slightly different meaning from the original measure.

Content validity analysis is fruitfully supplemented by examination of interitem correlations: If two items are both judged to represent the target content domain, responses to them should correlate moderately highly. If they do not, researchers should revisit their content validity analysis. Within whatever range of interitem and item-total correlations the researcher decides is optimal, and following consideration of content representation, researchers may choose to retain items with the highest item-total correlations. Doing so can facilitate removal of the weakest items without unduly sacrificing content coverage (Smith et al., 2000).

It is important to appreciate that if investigators fail at maintaining content coverage, then the new short form represents a different, perhaps more narrow, construct domain. Researchers and consumers of research should not assume that just because a short form has the same name as the original form, the short form measures the same construct. As we discuss further, it is necessary to demonstrate construct validity on the short form separately from what has been demonstrated on the original form.

If the original measure is multidimensional, as is the case when there are separate facets of a larger construct, the same content validity analyses should be completed at the unidimensional or facet level. Optimally, each separate content domain in the original measure will be represented by a short form of that domain. If, instead, it is necessary to abbreviate a measure so severely that one cannot represent each dimension of the original measure, it is important that researchers state directly that the shortened measure does not provide the information available from the original measure and is not a substitute for the original measure. Assuming that each dimension is represented briefly in the short form, researchers should demonstrate that the short form has the same factor structure as the original measure. We think it prudent not to assume that a factor structure is preserved after measure abbreviation and instead to test the factor structure empirically.

Shortening a measure does not lessen the need for reliable assessment. The SBPF predicts that a shorter measure will be less internally consistent, and indeed, researchers are often choosing to sacrifice reliability for brevity. But it is of course still true that low reliability means high error variance and a reduced probability of detecting relationships among variables that actually exist in the population. One guideline is to seek to maintain internal consistency reliability estimates of at least .70 for short forms (Smith et al., 2000). Anything less than .70 results in significant measurement problems due to random chance or error (Nunnally & Bernstein, 1994). Interestingly, researchers can use the SBPF in reverse to estimate the likely reliability of a shorter measure. Another possibility, for dichotomous items, is to experiment with use of Likert-type items that capture more variability per item (Smith & McCarthy, 1995). The idea behind this last suggestion is that if each item taps more variance in the target construct, fewer items may be necessary to measure the desired level of variability (Chomeya, 2010). Reliability analyses should be conducted using administration of the short form, separate from the longer, original form: Establishing the reliability of the short form as it will be used is important (Chomeya, 2010), though this does not necessarily apply to the exact ordering of individual items within a short form given that outcomes on personality measures are not significantly affected by item ordering (Schell & Oswald, 2013). In fact, shortened versions of longer personality measures may limit the impact of ordering effects (Steinberg, 1994).

Construct validation procedures should be applied to the short form, again separately from what has been done with the original measure. Neither researchers nor readers should assume that the body of validity evidence that exists for the long form necessarily applies to the short form. Instead, validation tests need to be conducted anew. Often, researchers extract a short form from a longer measure and then use data sets in which they had previously administered the longer measure to examine the validity of the short form. The economy of this approach is important, and it is likely true that validation evidence obtained in this way is informative; nevertheless, one must also demonstrate validity of the short form in new samples, when it is administered without the rest of the original measure. Readers need to know the performance of the measure when it is administered as it will be used in the future.

Most importantly, researchers and readers should not assume that the validity evidence of the original measure transfers automatically to the short form. The construct validation process is an ongoing one, and each new study provides evidence that pertains to the validity of the measures used in the study (Smith, 2005): Validity cannot be assumed. It is incumbent on researchers to demonstrate that a new short form has, for example, convergent and discriminant relationships with other, external measures as predicted by theory (Smith et al., 2000).

It is, of course, true that an important part of demonstrating the construct validity of a short form is to show that scores on the short form covary highly with scores on the original measure (Smith et al., 2000). This correlation can be spuriously inflated, however, when investigators calculate the correlation between the two forms on the basis of one test administration; that is, they extract a short form score from the same set of responses as provided the original measure score (Smith et al., 2000). When this is done, error variance in the responses to any of the short form items is completely reproduced in the long form and, thus, contributes to the correlation between the two (Smith et al., 2000). Also, systematic error effects on item responses, from neighboring items, will be present in both forms, thereby influencing the correlation between the two. And of course, the neighboring items will be different when the short form is administered separately, and that difference is not represented in such analyses.

The optimal method of controlling for these problems is to administer both the short form and the full-length form separately to the same participants (Smith et al., 2000). By giving both versions to participants, researchers reduce the likelihood of reporting biased estimates of correlations between the short and long forms and instead provide the best estimate of the overlap between the two forms. This often can be done during a single testing session, perhaps with filler questionnaires between the two forms. Alternatively, the two versions can be administered on separate occasions; when this is done, lack of perfect stability of what is measured over time introduces another source of disagreement between the two versions. In such a case, the correlation between the two forms can be compared to the test–retest correlation of the long form (Smith et al., 2000).

If one goal of a short form is to classify individuals accurately, investigators must assess classification using the short form on an independent sample. Of course, just as it is true that one should begin with a valid original measure, when classification is a goal, one should only develop short forms from longer measures that did classify with acceptable accuracy. To address classification accuracy, one set of tools researchers have available was described by Smith et al. (2000). One can use the SBPF to estimate the loss of reliability for given possible short forms, then apply a related formula to estimate loss of validity, and then use procedures described by Cliff (1987, p. 406) and Cohen and Cohen (1983, p. 39) to estimate classification accuracy given a certain validity level. If a certain necessary classification accuracy is to be achieved, researchers can use this procedure to decide if more items should be retained or if a short form is likely to perform adequately (Smith et al., 2000).

This is one a priori estimation procedure and is not a substitute for an independent, empirical test of a short form's accuracy. The tools provided by generalizability theory (Brennan, 1992; Cronbach et al., 1972) can also be quite helpful.

Generalizability theory enables one to estimate the proportion of variance in a measure that is due to differences among individuals. With that information plus average interitem correlations and item-total correlations, one has valuable information for choosing a short-form length that may provide validity evidence of the required magnitude.

The main purpose of developing a short form is to save valuable time or important resources. As Doppelt (1956) said, "a compromise must be made between economy of time and effort and accuracy of prediction" (p. 63). It is important for short-form authors to directly address this trade-off between assessment time and validity. Levy (1968) noted that "an equation must be found which defines a utility or cost function for the relationship between validity lost and time saved" (p. 415). Perhaps this goal can be approximated by applying the SBPF to estimate the likely loss of reliability and then, as noted in Smith et al. (2000), the likely loss in validity, for different length short forms. One can then consider the trade-offs between the advantage of certain time or resource savings and the cost of reduced validity. In short, the net value of short form development can be estimated quantitatively (Smith et al., 2000).

To summarize this section of the chapter, researchers can take a series of steps that will greatly enhance faith in the validity of short forms that they develop. These steps include careful consideration of content coverage, full dimensional representation, independent demonstration of reliability and validity, high covariation with the original scale, classification accuracy where appropriate, and demonstration of time or resource savings. If they take these steps, researchers will be in a strong position to argue that their short form is a reliable, valid alternative to a fuller, more comprehensive assessment (Smith et al., 2000).

ITEM RESPONSE THEORY AND TAILORED TESTING

So far in this chapter, we have assumed a classic true score theory approach to measurement. IRT is a very different approach that does not use true score theory: It focuses assessment on the item level in terms of discriminating among individuals at different intensity levels of the target construct. Applications of the technique prove quite useful when the goal is brief assessment. IRT is becoming increasingly well known across fields within psychology. Other chapters have provided valuable guidance for many aspects of scale construction and validation (see Hayes & Embretson, 2012; Krosnick, 1999). In this last section, we describe the procedure very briefly and point to its advantages for brevity.

For each item in a measure, a curve that describes the ability or intensity level at which the item maximally discriminates can be defined. These item characteristic curves (ICCs) are often S-shaped: The item maximally discriminates where the slope is the steepest (with ability or intensity level on the x-axis and item endorsement on the y-axis). Items differ with respect to the attribute intensity level at which they discriminate. Although IRT has historically been used most often in achievement assessment, its function is not limited to the assessment of such constructs. Imagine a scale measuring romantic jealousy. Positive endorsement of the item "I feel jealous when my significant other kisses a member of the opposite sex romantically" would probably be quite common; presumably, only people with very little jealousy would fail to endorse it. Thus, differential endorsement would probably differentiate among people at very low levels of jealousy. In contrast, the item "I feel jealous when my significant other talks to a member of the opposite sex" probably differentiates among individuals at much higher levels of jealousy. For every item, curves can be developed that describe the ability or intensity range at which the item will be maximally useful (see Figure 21.1 for example item characteristic curves for the above jealously measure).

ICCs can then be used in a tailored testing approach. One begins with some estimate of intensity of an attribute (perhaps a sample's average intensity level) and administers an item that maximally discriminates at that level. If the examinee endorses or passes the item, then an item that discriminates at a higher intensity

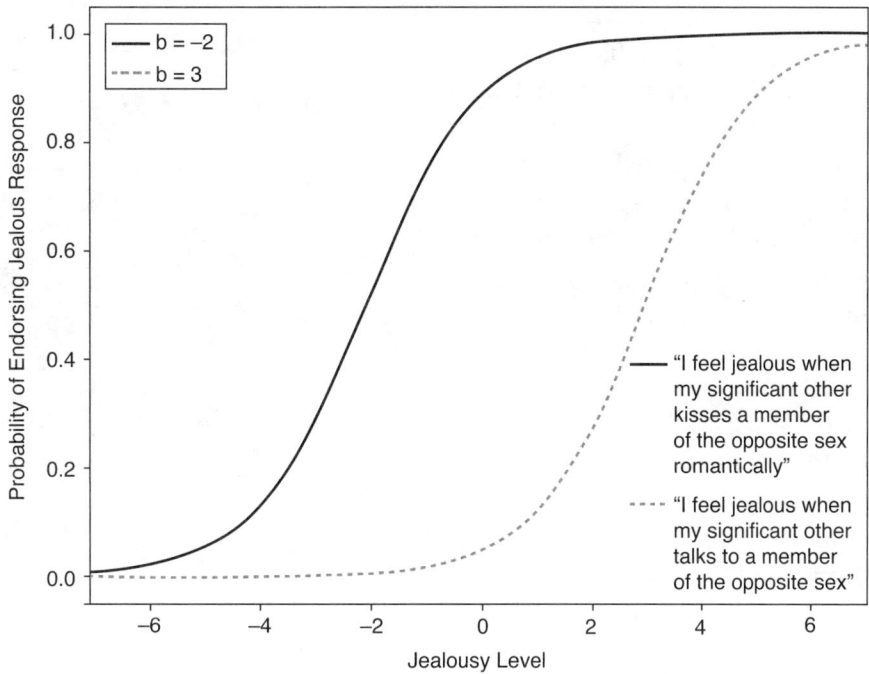

FIGURE 21.1. Item characteristic curves for a hypothetical measure of jealousy. b = the number of standard deviations away from the mean.

level is administered. If the examinee does not endorse or fails the first item, then an item that discriminates at a lower intensity level is administered instead. With the examinee's response to each new item, more information is available to estimate the examinee's intensity level of the attribute. Responses to each new item modify the estimate of attribute intensity, and the procedure continues until changes in the estimates from one item to the next become trivially small. When that occurs, one has a reliable estimate of attribute intensity for that examinee. Reliable estimates can be obtained with many fewer items than are typically used in traditional testing. Detailed discussion of the procedures involved is beyond our scope, but we do want to call attention to the technique as relevant to brief assessment.

SUMMARY AND CONCLUSION

Our intent in writing this chapter is to provide a perspective counter to the common emphasis on test length as a virtue for reliability and validity. The SBPF has perhaps been applied without sufficient consideration to one, key assumption underlying the formula: that all items are parallel, or at least alternative, reflections of the same content domain. To the degree that researchers either include the same item reworded slightly, or items reflecting different, though related constructs, longer tests do not necessarily bring increased validity. In fact, there is considerable evidence that carefully defined content domains can be assessed with relatively few items. We have drawn on existing psychometric theory to make this argument. In particular, we encourage researchers to give as much attention to exclusionary rules as to inclusionary rules as they select items, interview questions, or observational protocols. Attention to the concepts of content validity, construct representation, and construct homogeneity may facilitate researchers' efforts to develop brief, valid measures.

As a ready extension of this set of concerns, we have addressed procedures for the valid development of short forms of existing instruments. We do not argue against the development of short forms; rather, we emphasize the need to develop and independently validate short forms with the same rigor as is applied to any test. We also briefly discuss IRT. It is perhaps most often true that different items within an instrument assess the target construct at different levels of intensity (perhaps often as indicated by item endorsement rates in classic, true score theory approaches). IRT takes full advantage of this reality by developing curves that characterize the level of attribute intensity at which each item maximally discriminates. The information provided by ICCs leads readily to brief, accurate assessment.

In conclusion, the goal of any psychological assessment is to produce valid, accurate results. Lengthy tests are only useful insofar as they advance that goal, and test length is not as accurate an indicator of measure validity as has been presumed in the past. It is often quite possible to develop brief instruments that produce valid results.

References

American Psychiatric Association. (2013). *Diagnostic and statistical manual of mental disorders* (5th ed.). https://doi.org/10.1176/appi.books.9780890425596

Armour, C., Mullerová, J., & Elhai, J. D. (2016). A systematic literature review of PTSD's latent structure in the Diagnostic and Statistical Manual of Mental Disorders: DSM-IV to DSM-5. *Clinical Psychology Review, 44*, 60–74. https://doi.org/10.1016/j.cpr.2015.12.003

Brennan, R. L. (1992). Generalizability theory. *Educational Measurement: Issues and Practice, 11*(4), 27–34. https://doi.org/10.1111/j.1745-3992.1992.tb00260.x

Briggs, S. R., & Cheek, J. M. (1986). The role of factor analysis in the development and evaluation of personality scales. *Journal of Personality, 54*(1), 107–148. https://doi.org/10.1111/j.1467-6494.1986.tb00391.x

Burisch, M. (1997). Test length and validity revisited. *European Journal of Personality, 11*(4), 303–315. https://doi.org/10.1002/(SICI)1099-0984(199711)11:4<303::AID-PER292>3.0.CO;2-%23

Chomeya, R. (2010). Quality of psychology test between Likert scale 5 and 6 points. *Journal of Social Sciences, 6*(3), 399–403. https://doi.org/10.3844/jssp.2010.399.403

Clark, L. A., Cuthbert, B., Lewis-Fernández, R., Narrow, W. E., & Reed, G. M. (2017). Three approaches to understanding and classifying mental disorder: ICD-11, DSM-5, and the National Institute of Mental Health's Research Domain Criteria (RDoC). *Psychological Science in the Public Interest, 18*(2), 72–145. https://doi.org/10.1177/1529100617727266

Clark, L. A., & Watson, D. (2016). Constructing validity: Basic issues in objective scale development. In A. E. Kazdin (Ed.), *Methodological issues and strategies in clinical research* (pp. 187–203). American Psychological Association. https://doi.org/10.1037/14805-012

Cliff, N. (1987). *Analyzing multivariate data*. Harcourt Brace Jovanovich.

Cloninger, C. R., Przybeck, T. R., & Svrakic, D. M. (1991). The Tridimensional Personality Questionnaire: U.S. normative data. *Psychological Reports, 69*(3 Pt 1), 1047–1057. https://doi.org/10.2466/pr0.1991.69.3.1047

Cohen, J., & Cohen, P. (1983). *Applied multiple regression/correlation analysis for the behavior sciences* (2nd ed.). Erlbaum.

Contractor, A. A., Greene, T., Dolan, M., Weiss, N. H., & Armour, C. (2020). Relation between PTSD symptom clusters and positive memory characteristics: A network perspective. *Journal of Anxiety Disorders, 69*, 102157. https://doi.org/10.1016/j.janxdis.2019.102157

Costa, P. T., Jr., & McCrae, R. R. (1992). *Revised NEO Personality Inventory (NEO-PI-R) and NEO Five Factor Inventory (NEO-FFI) professional manual*. Psychological Assessment Resources.

Cronbach, L. J., Gleser, G. C., Nanda, H., & Rajaratnam, N. (1972). *The dependability of behavioral measurements: Theory of generalizability of scores and profiles*. Wiley.

Cronbach, L. J., & Meehl, P. E. (1955). Construct validity in psychological tests. *Psychological Bulletin, 52*(4), 281–302. https://doi.org/10.1037/h0040957

Dick, D. M., Smith, G., Olausson, P., Mitchell, S. H., Leeman, R. F., O'Malley, S. S., & Sher, K. (2010). Understanding the construct of impulsivity and its relationship to alcohol use disorders. *Addiction Biology, 15*(2), 217–226. https://doi.org/10.1111/j.1369-1600.2009.00190.x

Dixon, D., & Johnston, M. (2019). Content validity of measures of theoretical constructs in health psychology: Discriminant content validity is needed. *British Journal of Health Psychology, 24*(3), 477–484. https://doi.org/10.1111/bjhp.12373

Doll, E. A. (1917). A brief Binet-Simon scale. *The Psychological Clinic*, *11*(7), 197–211.

Doppelt, J. E. (1956). Estimating the full scale score on the Wechsler adult intelligence scale from scores on four subtests. *Journal of Consulting Psychology*, *20*(1), 63–66. https://doi.org/10.1037/h0044293

Dunn, T. J., Baguley, T., & Brunsden, V. (2014). From alpha to omega: A practical solution to the pervasive problem of internal consistency estimation. *British Journal of Psychology*, *105*(3), 399–412. https://doi.org/10.1111/bjop.12046

Edwards, J. R. (2001). Multidimensional constructs in organizational behavior research: An integrative analytical framework. *Organizational Research Methods*, *4*(2), 144–192. https://doi.org/10.1177/109442810142004

Embretson, S. E. (1998). A cognitive design system approach for generating valid tests: Approaches to abstract reasoning. *Psychological Methods*, *3*(3), 380–396. https://doi.org/10.1037/1082-989X.3.3.380

Hayes, H., & Embretson, S. E. (2012). Psychological measurement: Scaling and analysis. In H. Cooper, P. M. Camic, D. L. Long, A. T. Panter, D. Rindskopf, & K. J. Sher (Eds.), *APA handbook of research methods in psychology, Vol. 1. Foundations, planning, measures, and psychometrics* (pp. 163–179). American Psychological Association. https://doi.org/10.1037/13619-011

Haynes, S. N., & Kaholokula, J. K. (2008). *Behavioral assessment*. In M. Hersen & A. M. Gross (Eds.), *Handbook of clinical psychology: Vol. 1. Adults* (pp. 495–522). John Wiley & Sons.

Haynes, S. N., Richard, D. C. S., & Kubany, E. S. (1995). Content validity in psychological assessment: A functional approach to concepts and methods. *Psychological Assessment*, *7*(3), 238–247. https://doi.org/10.1037/1040-3590.7.3.238

Hohlstein, L. A., Smith, G. T., & Atlas, J. G. (1998). An application of expectancy theory to eating disorders: Development and validation of measures of eating and dieting expectancies. *Psychological Assessment*, *10*(1), 49–58. https://doi.org/10.1037/1040-3590.10.1.49

Krosnick, J. A. (1999). Maximizing measurement quality: Principles of good questionnaire design. In J. P. Robinson, P. R. Shaver, & L. S. Wrightsman (Eds.), *Measures of political attitudes*. Academic Press.

Landy, F. J. (1986). Stamp collecting versus science: Validation as hypothesis testing. *American Psychologist*, *41*(11), 1183–1192. https://doi.org/10.1037/0003-066X.41.11.1183

Levy, P. (1968). Short-form tests. A methodological review. *Psychological Bulletin*, *69*(6), 410–416. https://doi.org/10.1037/h0025736

Loevinger, J. (1957). Objective tests as instruments of psychological theory. *Psychological Reports*, *3*(Suppl. 3), 635–694. https://doi.org/10.2466/pr0.1957.3.3.635

Marsh, H. W., Ellis, L. A., Parada, R. H., Richards, G., & Heubeck, B. G. (2005). A short version of the Self Description Questionnaire II: Operationalizing criteria for short-form evaluation with new applications of confirmatory factor analyses. *Psychological Assessment*, *17*(1), 81–102. https://doi.org/10.1037/1040-3590.17.1.81

McGrath, R. E. (2005). Conceptual complexity and construct validity. *Journal of Personality Assessment*, *85*(2), 112–124. https://doi.org/10.1207/s15327752jpa8502_02

Messick, S. (1995). Validity of psychological assessment: Validation of inferences from persons' responses and performances as scientific inquiry into score meaning. *American Psychologist*, *50*(9), 741–749. https://doi.org/10.1037/0003-066X.50.9.741

Morey, L. C. (2003). Measuring personality and psychopathology. In J. A. Schinka, W. F. Velicer, & I. B. Weiner (Eds.), *Handbook of psychology: Vol. 2. Research methods in psychology* (pp. 377–405). John Wiley.

Nunnally, J. C., & Bernstein, I. H. (1994). *Psychometric theory*. McGraw-Hill.

Schell, K. L., & Oswald, F. L. (2013). Item grouping and item randomization in personality measurement. *Personality and Individual Differences*, *55*(3), 317–321. https://doi.org/10.1016/j.paid.2013.03.008

Smith, G. T. (2005). On construct validity: Issues of method and measurement. *Psychological Assessment*, *17*(4), 396–408. https://doi.org/10.1037/1040-3590.17.4.396

Smith, G. T., Fischer, S., & Fister, S. M. (2003). Incremental validity principles in test construction. *Psychological Assessment*, *15*(4), 467–477. https://doi.org/10.1037/1040-3590.15.4.467

Smith, G. T., & McCarthy, D. M. (1995). Methodological considerations in the refinement of clinical assessment instruments. *Psychological Assessment*, *7*(3), 300–308. https://doi.org/10.1037/1040-3590.7.3.300

Smith, G. T., McCarthy, D. M., & Anderson, K. G. (2000). On the sins of short-form development. *Psychological Assessment*, *12*(1), 102–111. https://doi.org/10.1037/1040-3590.12.1.102.

Note corrections to formulas provided in this paper: Same authors. *Psychological Assessment*, *16*(3), 340. https://doi.org/10.1037/1040-3590.16.3.340

Smith, G. T., McCarthy, D. M., & Zapolski, T. C. B. (2009). On the value of homogeneous constructs for construct validation, theory testing, and the description of psychopathology. *Psychological Assessment*, *21*(3), 272–284. https://doi.org/10.1037/a0016699

Spearman, C. (1910). Correlation calculated from faulty data. *British Journal of Psychology*, *3*(3), 271–295. https://doi.org/10.1111/j.2044-8295.1910.tb00206.x

Steinberg, L. (1994). Context and serial-order effects in personality measurement: Limits on the generality of measuring changes the measure. *Journal of Personality and Social Psychology*, *66*(2), 341–349. https://doi.org/10.1037/0022-3514.66.2.341

Strauss, M. E., & Smith, G. T. (2009). Construct validity: Advances in theory and methodology. *Annual Review of Clinical Psychology*, *5*(1), 1–25. https://doi.org/10.1146/annurev.clinpsy.032408.153639

Ulrich, R. (1985). Die Beziehung zwischen Testlange und Validitat fur nicht-parallele Aufgaben: Verschiedene Methoden der Validitatsmaximierung [The relationship of test length and validity for non-parallel items: Various methods of validity maximization]. *Zeitschrift für Differentielle und Diagnostische Psychologie*, *6*(2), 32–45.

Wechsler, D. (1967). *Manual for the Wechsler Preschool and Primary Scale of Intelligence*. Psychological Corporation.

Wechsler, D. (2008). *WAIS-IV administration and scoring manual*. The Psychological Corporation.

Zamanzadeh, V., Ghahramanian, A., Rassouli, M., Abbaszadeh, A., Alavi-Majd, H., & Nikanfar, A. R. (2015). Design and implementation content validity study: Development of an instrument for measuring patient-centered communication. *Journal of Caring Sciences*, *4*(2), 165–178. https://doi.org/10.15171/jcs.2015.017

Zimmerman, D. W. (1975). Two concepts of "True Score" in test theory. *Psychological Reports*, *36*(3), 795–805. https://doi.org/10.2466/pr0.1975.36.3.795

Section 4

Chronometric and Psychophysical Measures

CHAPTER 22

EYE MOVEMENTS, PUPILLOMETRY, AND COGNITIVE PROCESSES

Simon P. Liversedge, Sara V. Milledge, and Hazel I. Blythe

Moving our eyes is one of the most frequent behavioral activities that we engage in during our waking hours. Indeed, we typically move our eyes three to four times per second throughout much of our day. We even move our eyes while we sleep (although a discussion of this topic is beyond the scope of this chapter), and, on occasion, we keep moving our eyes during cognitive processing tasks even if the mind wanders. Because of the tight connection between the behavior of the eyes and activity in the brain, where we look and how long we look are good online measures of the various cognitive activities in which we engage when we perform a task. In reading, scene perception, and visual search, we continually make eye movements called *saccades*. Between the saccades, when static images are being processed, our eyes are relatively still in what are called *fixations*. It is during these fixations that we encode new information from the visual stimulus that we are processing. During saccades, cognitive processing continues in some tasks (e.g., lexical processing), whereas in others (e.g., mental rotation) research suggests there is a suspension of processing (Irwin, 1998). In this chapter, we review the basic properties of eye movements and how they relate to ongoing cognitive processing. In particular, we focus on eye movements during reading, scene perception, and visual search, and we briefly discuss pupillometry.

BACKGROUND INFORMATION ON EYE MOVEMENTS AND COGNITIVE PROCESSES

Before reviewing eye movements in reading, scene perception, and search, we first provide some background information. Our general strategy in this chapter is to give an up-to-date discussion of important issues, but we do not provide detailed citations to relevant work. Many of the points we make in the various sections are discussed in articles by Rayner (1998, 2009) and Kliegl et al. (2006); though, where appropriate, we have provided some more recent references.

Saccades

Saccades are rapid movements of the eyes with velocities as high as 500° per second. Sensitivity to visual input is markedly reduced during eye movements,[1] and we are functionally blind during

---

This chapter is an edited version of a chapter that was originally written by Keith Rayner and Reinhold Kliegl (Rayner & Kliegl, 2012). Overlap between the present chapter and the original represents the very significant contribution made by the original authors. Preparation of the chapter was supported by an ESRC grant (ES/R003386/1) to the first author.

[1]There is also some visual suppression just before and after a saccade.

https://doi.org/10.1037/0000318-022
APA Handbook of Research Methods in Psychology, Second Edition: Vol. 1. Foundations, Planning, Measures, and Psychometrics, H. Cooper (Editor-in-Chief)
Copyright © 2023 by the American Psychological Association. All rights reserved.

saccades. This phenomenon, *saccadic suppression*, historically was the topic of much debate, with some arguing for some type of central anaesthesia in which the neurons in the retina turn off during a saccade and others arguing that visual masking causes suppression. It now appears that we do not obtain new information during saccades because our eyes are moving so quickly across a relatively stable visual stimulus that only blur is perceived. Masking due to the information before and after the saccade results in our failing to perceive any blurring effect. Some suppression is found even when masking is eliminated, however, suggesting that there is also a central inhibitory contribution.

Plots of log peak velocity over log movement amplitude reveal a strikingly linear relationship, reflective of the ballistic nature of saccades. Thus, the velocity of a saccade is a monotonic function of how far the eyes move: A 2° saccade typical in reading takes about 30 ms, whereas a 5° saccade, more typical of scene perception, takes about 40 ms to 50 ms and a 10° saccade takes about 60 ms to 80 ms. The velocity rises during the saccade to a maximum that occurs slightly before the midpoint of the movement and then drops at a slower rate until the target location is reached. Saccades are motor movements that take time to plan and execute. *Saccade latency* refers to the amount of time needed to decide to make and initiate an eye movement to a new stimulus. Average saccade latency is in the order of 200 ms to 250 ms, and even under situations in which uncertainty is eliminated about where to move, it is at least 150 ms to 175 ms. Thus, the time involved in perceiving the new target location and actually getting the eyes moving is due to the need to send a command to the oculomotor system for the actual movement. There is a point of no return in that if the program to execute a saccade has reached a critical point, the saccade cannot be cancelled and is executed. During the time between when the command is given to the oculomotor system to execute the saccade and the actual movement, however, a second saccade can be programmed in parallel with the first.

Fixations and Fixational Movements

Fixations are the periods of time between saccades during which the eyes are relatively still and new information is obtained. The eyes are never really absolutely still, however, as there are three physiological categories of fixational movements: tremor, drift, and microsaccades. *Tremor* is characterized as 30 Hz to 100 Hz oscillatory behavior superimposed on other fixational movements; it is quite small and its exact nature is somewhat unclear, although it is believed to be related to perceptual activity and helps the nerve cells in the retina to keep firing. During fixation the eyes usually *drift* (i.e., make small, relatively slow movements) with a peak velocity smaller than 30-minute arc per second. *Microsaccades* are rapid movements with amplitudes shorter than 1° or 1.5°, usually occurring at a rate of 1 to 2 per second. For many years their functional role was in doubt mostly because they can be voluntarily suppressed (although they are not under voluntary control). Recent research, however, established their relevance both at the perceptual level and the level of spatial attention (for reviews, see Engbert, 2006, and Rolfs, 2009). Somewhat paradoxically, these fixational movements are a prerequisite of perception of letters, words, or other objects because stabilizing the visual input on the retina bleaches receptors and causes a perceptual "loss" of objects, leaving only the homogeneous background as percept. In most cognitive research, fixational movements are usually treated as *noise*, and various algorithms are used to smooth the oculomotor signal and associate time during these minor movements with temporally synchronous, usually longer duration, fixations.

Binocular Coordination of Eye Movements

The coordination of horizontal and vertical saccades is good, and it was long assumed that the two eyes move perfectly conjugately. It is now clear, however, that the movements of the *abducting* (temporally moving) eye are somewhat larger than the corresponding movements of the *adducting* (nasally moving) eye in simple scanning tasks. Reading research (Kirkby et al., 2008;

Nuthmann & Kliegl, 2009) demonstrated that up to 40% to 50% of the time the eyes may be fixating different letters of text and sometimes the lines of sight may be crossed or uncrossed. Interestingly, the amount of disparity tends to be greater in beginning readers than skilled readers.[2]

Eye Movements and Visual Acuity

We make saccades so frequently because of acuity limitations. When we look straight ahead, the visual field can be broadly divided into three areas: the fovea, parafovea, and periphery. Although acuity is very good in the fovea (the central 2° of vision), it is not nearly as good in the parafovea (which extends to 5° beyond the fovea around fixation), and it is even poorer in the periphery (the area beyond the parafovea). Thus, we make saccadic eye movements to allow light from the part of the stimulus that we want to see clearly fall directly onto the fovea. Properties of the stimulus in eccentric vision influence whether a saccade needs to be made to fixate it in order to identify it. Words in normal-size print can be identified more quickly and accurately when a saccade is made to fixate them. On the other hand, objects can often be identified in eccentric vision without a saccade.

Eye Movements and Attention

Although we often need to move our eyes to identify objects in a scene before us, it is also the case that we can move attention without moving our eyes (Posner, 1980). There is considerable evidence suggesting that attention is allocated to a given location in space prior to a saccade to that location, and that attention and saccades are obligatorily coupled. Although we can easily decouple the locus of attention and eye location in simple tasks, in more complex tasks, the link between the two is probably quite tight.

Measuring Eye Movements

Eye movements can be monitored in many ways, including (a) surface electrodes (which can be used to determine when the eyes move, but only very roughly where they move, e.g., which hemifield), (b) infrared corneal reflections, (c) video-based pupil monitoring, (d) infrared Purkinje image tracking, and (e) search coils attached to the surface of the eyes. There has been much discussion concerning the measurement, evaluation, and reporting of eye-movement data, but no measurement standards have been adopted, and many methodological issues remain unaddressed or unresolved. This may not necessarily be a bad thing, as most important findings have been replicated across different laboratories using the different methods.

EYE MOVEMENTS IN READING

Fixations and Saccades

The average fixation duration in reading is between approximately 200 ms and 225 ms, and the average saccade length is seven to nine letter spaces for skilled readers of English and other alphabetic writing systems.[3] However, these values are averages and there is considerable variability in both. Thus, fixation durations can be as short as 50 ms to 75 ms and as long as 500 ms to 600 ms (and on some occasions more, though this occurs infrequently). Saccade length can be as short as one letter space and as long as 15 to 20 letter spaces (or more), although such long saccades tend to occur after a regression (as readers typically move forward in the text past the point from which they originally launched the regression). Regressions (saccades that move backward in the text) occur about 10% to 15% of the time in skilled readers. Most regressions are to the immediately preceding word, although when comprehension difficulty occurs, longer

---

[2]Word frequency and case alternation affect fixation duration in reading (which we discuss in more detail in the following sections) but are not affected by fixation disparity. Thus, although researchers may need to worry about those rare situations in which the eyes are on different words, when both eyes are fixated within the same word robust effects like the frequency effect still emerge.
[3]Letter spaces are the appropriate indicator of how far the eyes move; regardless of the reading distance of the text (which modulates text size on the retina), eye movements extend the same number of letter spaces, not the same degree of visual angle.

regressions occur to points earlier in the text. Regressions are not well understood because it is difficult to control them experimentally (e.g., Inhoff et al., 2019). They need to be distinguished from return sweeps (right-to-left saccades from the end of one line to the beginning of the next). The first and last fixations on a line are typically five to seven letter spaces from the end of the line because about 80% of the text typically falls between the extreme fixations (Parker et al., 2019).

These average values can be influenced by text difficulty, reading skill, and characteristics of the writing system. Specifically, difficult text leads to longer fixations, shorter saccades, and more regressions. Typographical variables like font difficulty influence eye movements; more difficult to encode fonts yield longer fixations, shorter saccades, and more regressions (Slattery & Rayner, 2010). Beginning, less skilled, and dyslexic readers have longer fixations, shorter saccades, and more regressions than skilled readers (see Blythe, 2014). Chinese is a writing system that is visually and linguistically more dense than English, and Chinese readers are generally reported to have average fixations that are slightly longer and average saccade lengths that are shorter than those of readers of alphabetic writing systems because they typically move their eyes only two to three characters (which makes sense given the density of linguistic information in Chinese; Liversedge et al., 2016).

Different Measures of Fixation Time

Eye-movement data provide a good moment-to-moment indication of cognitive processes during reading and, thus, are sensitive to variables such as word length, frequency, and word predictability ("the big three"; Kliegl et al., 2006); these variables have strong influences on fixation times on a word. However, average fixation duration computed across all the fixations made during reading of a sentence is not a particularly informative measure with respect to the lexical properties of an individual word; it is a valuable global measure, but a number of local measures that can be computed for individual words, provide more informative estimates of moment-to-moment processing. The reason that average fixation duration is not particularly useful for capturing processing of individual words is related to two components of reading. First, readers skip words during reading; content words are fixated about 85% of the time, whereas function words are fixated about 35% of the time.[4] Function words are skipped more because they tend to be short and quite high in frequency. As word length increases, the probability of fixating the word increases. Words that are two to three letters are only fixated around 25% of the time, whereas words that are eight letters or more are almost always fixated. Second, longer words are often fixated more than once; that is, they are *refixated*. The joint problem of skipping and refixations led to the development of alternative local measures that capture fixation time and eye-movement behavior for an individual word or phrase. These measures are first fixation duration (the duration of the first fixation on a word), single fixation duration (when only one fixation is made on a word), and gaze duration (the sum of all fixations on a word before moving to another word). Recently, first fixation durations in multiple-fixation cases have been distinguished from the traditional definition to reduce the overlap with single-fixation durations for purposes of computational modeling. All of the measures are contingent on the word being fixated with a first-pass forward fixation.

If it were the case that readers fixated once and only once on each word, then average fixation duration on a word would be a more useful measure. Given, though, that many words are skipped and some words are refixated, it is much more informative to utilize the three measures just described, which provide a reasonable estimate of how long it takes to process each word. These measures are not perfect estimates as (a) preview information is obtained from a word before fixating

---

[4] The fact that words are skipped obviously means that readers do not invariably move forward in the text fixating each successive word in its canonical order. However, some type of inner speech code presumably aids the reader to maintain the correct word order.

it and (b) the processing of a given word can spill over to the next fixation. When regions of interest are larger than a single word, or effects have a more extensive time course, other measures like first-pass reading time, second-pass reading time, go-past time (the elapsed time from when a reader first enters a region until they move past it forward in the text), and total reading time are computed.

The Perceptual Span in Reading

How much information are we able to process and use during a fixation? Most readers have the impression that they can clearly see the entire line of text, even the entire page of text. This is an illusion, though, as research utilizing a gaze-contingent moving-window technique (McConkie & Rayner, 1975) has shown. The rationale with the moving-window technique is to vary how much information is available during a fixation and then determine how large the window of normal text has to be before readers read normally. Conversely, one can consider how small the window can be before there is disruption to reading. Thus, within the window area, text is normally displayed, but outside of the window, letters are replaced (with other letters, Xs, or a homogenous masking pattern).[5] Research using this paradigm has demonstrated that skilled readers of English and other alphabetic writing systems obtain useful information from an asymmetric region extending three to four character spaces to the left of fixation to about 14 to 15 character spaces to the right of fixation. Indeed, if readers have the fixated word and the word to the right of fixation available on a fixation (and all other letters are replaced with visually similar letters), they are not aware that the words outside of the window are not normal, and their reading speed decreases by only about 10%. Information from below the currently fixated line is not used, although if the task is visual search rather than reading, then information can be obtained below the currently fixated line (see Rayner, 2014, for a review of the moving-window technique). Finally, in moving-mask experiments (Rayner & Bertera, 1979), a mask moves in synchrony with the eyes covering the letters in the center of vision, making reading virtually impossible. This paradigm creates an artificial foveal scotoma that mimics patients with brain or retinal damage and effectively eliminates their use of foveal vision.

Characteristics of the writing system influence the perceptual span. When reading in languages like Japanese, Tibetan, Korean, and, especially, Chinese, which are more orthographically dense than alphabetic languages, readers have smaller perceptual spans (e.g., Choi & Koh, 2009; Wang et al., 2021). Thus, for readers of Chinese (which is typically read from left to right in mainland China), the perceptual span extends one character to the left of fixation to two to three characters to the right. In addition, for Hebrew, Urdu, and Arabic readers, the span is asymmetric and larger to the left of fixation because they read from right to left (e.g., Jordan et al., 2014; Paterson et al., 2014; Pollatsek et al., 1981). Also, text difficulty and reading skill influence the perceptual span: it is smaller when reading cognitively demanding text, and beginner and dyslexic readers have smaller spans than more skilled readers. Presumably, difficulty encoding the fixated word leads to a reduced perceptual span (Rayner et al., 2010). Older readers read more slowly than younger college-age readers, and their perceptual span is slightly smaller and less asymmetric than younger readers (Rayner et al., 2009a).

Preview Benefit in Reading

Research using another type of gaze-contingent display change technique, the boundary technique (Rayner, 1975), has revealed what kind of information is obtained from upcoming words to the right of fixation. An invisible boundary is located just to the left of a target word, and before the reader's eyes cross the boundary, there is typically

---

[5]In the most extreme situation, the window would contain only the fixated letter, thereby creating a situation in which the reader is literally forced to read letter by letter. In such a situation, normal readers' eye-movement data are very much like the eye-movement data of brain-damaged pure alexic or letter-by-letter readers (Rayner & Johnson, 2005).

a preview different from the target word. When the eyes cross the boundary, the preview is replaced by the target word. Readers are generally unaware of the identity of the preview and of the display change. Research using this technique has revealed that when readers have a valid preview of the word to the right of fixation, they spend less time fixating that word (following a saccade to it) than when they do not have a valid preview (i.e., another word or nonword or random string of letters initially occupied the target word location). The size of this *preview benefit* is typically 30 ms to 50 ms. Research has revealed that readers do not combine a literal visual representation of information across saccades; rather, abstract codes are used.

Information about abstract letter codes, letter position, and orthographic phonological codes is integrated across saccades (and serves as the basis of the preview benefit effect; see Schotter et al., 2012, for a review). Thus far, however, no reliable evidence has been reported for semantic preview benefit within English. That is, words that typically produce priming in a standard naming or lexical decision task (e.g., the prime word "tune" primes the target word "song") do not yield priming when the prime word is in parafoveal vision (with the target word presented as soon as the reader crosses the invisible boundary location). This result is probably because words in parafoveal vision are degraded sufficiently that readers cannot typically fully lexically identify them in order to process their meaning. There is also no evidence that morphological information is integrated across saccades in English.

Conversely, readers of Hebrew do integrate morphological information across saccades. Morphological information is more central to processing Hebrew than English, and the difference in findings presumably reflects this fact. Also, semantic preview benefit has been found for readers of Chinese and Korean (e.g., Yan et al., 2019; Yang et al., 2012). Moreover, semantic preview benefit has also been reported in German (e.g., Hohenstein & Kliegl, 2014) with it suggested that differences in the properties of orthography could drive why semantic preview benefit has been found in German but not reliably in English (i.e., the consistent capitalization of the first letter of nouns in German; Rayner & Schotter, 2014). It is also the case that the amount of preview benefit readers obtain varies as a function of the difficulty of the fixated word. If it is difficult to process, readers obtain little or no preview benefit from the word to the right of fixation. Conversely, if the fixated word is easy to process, readers obtain more preview benefit from the word to the right of fixation (though see Zhang et al., 2019, for a recent, powerful, investigation of this effect in Chinese). Also, preview benefit is larger within words than across words. A final issue concerns the spatial extent of preview benefit: Do readers obtain preview benefit from word $n + 2$? Although it is clear that readers generally obtain preview benefit from word $n + 1$ (the word to the right of fixation), it appears that readers typically do not get preview benefit from word $n + 2$. It may be that when word $n + 1$ is a very short word (two to three letters) that readers obtain preview benefit from word $n + 2$. It is also the case that when readers target their next saccade to word $n + 2$ that preview benefit is obtained. Moreover, there is evidence for $n + 2$ preview benefit in Chinese when word $n + 1$ is a high-frequency word (Yan et al., 2010; Yang et al., 2009).

Parafoveal-on-Foveal Effects

Do the characteristics of the word to the right of fixation influence the duration of the fixation on the currently fixated word? Such effects are referred to as *parafoveal-on-foveal effects*. Some studies have found that orthographic properties of the word to the right of fixation influence the duration of the current fixation. Other recent studies have suggested that the meaning of the word to the right of fixation can produce parafoveal-on-foveal effects. It would appear, though, that the frequency of the parafoveal word does not produce a parafoveal-on-foveal effect (Brothers et al., 2017), and there is no evidence of lexical parafoveal-on-foveal effects in analyses on the basis of select target words. Are parafoveal-on-foveal effects real, or are there other reasons why such effects sometimes appear in the eye-movement record? It has been demonstrated that some fixations in reading are mislocated because saccades are not perfectly accurate and do not land on the intended target; thus, some parafoveal-on-foveal effects may arise because of inaccurately targeted saccades. That is, some saccades that are meant to land on a given target word fall short of the target and land on the end of the previous word. In this scenario, however, attention is still allocated to the originally intended saccade target word such that processing of the target word influences the fixation on the previous word (e.g., Drieghe et al., 2008). We also note that reliable evidence for parafoveal-on-foveal effects from analyses of large eye-movement corpora (Kliegl, 2007) has been reported. Consequently, there seems to be converging agreement concerning the validity of orthographic parafoveal-on-foveal effects. There is, however, still controversy concerning lexical (and semantic) parafoveal-on-foveal effects (Drieghe, 2011).

The Control of Eye Movements

There are two component decisions to eye-movement control: *when* to move the eyes and *where* to move the eyes. These two decisions may be made somewhat independently: The decision of where to move next is largely driven by low-level (most often visual) properties of the text. The decision of when to move is driven by lexical properties of the fixated word (although models of eye movements in reading differ in the weight they give to lexical factors).

Where to move the eyes. For English and other alphabetic languages, where to move the eyes next is strongly influenced by low-level cues provided by word length and space information (see Rayner, 2009, for a review). Thus, saccade length is influenced by the length of the fixated word and the word to the right of fixation. If the word to the right of fixation is either very long or very short, the next saccade will be longer than when a medium-length word appears to the right of fixation. For example, if the 10 letter spaces to the right of the fixated word consist of a four- and a five-letter word (with a space between) or a single 10-letter word, the saccade will be longer in the latter case. If there is a short word (two to four letters) to the right of fixation, the next saccade will tend to be longer than when the next word is five to seven letters, largely because the short word would be skipped. The spaces between words (which demarcate how long words are) are, thus, used in targeting where the next saccade lands. When space information is removed, reading slows down considerably. Specifically, when spaces are removed or filled with irrelevant characters, reading slows down by as much as 30% to 50%. Of course, spaces between words are not present in all writing systems. Interestingly, some evidence within nonalphabetic writing systems suggests that even when interword spaces are orthographically illegal, they can be beneficial to reading (e.g., Bai et al., 2008; Winskel et al., 2009).

Landing position effects. Word spacing information in parafoveal vision leads to systematic tendencies with respect to where the eyes typically land. Readers' eyes tend to land halfway between the middle of a word and the beginning of that word; this is called the *preferred viewing location* (Rayner, 1979). It is generally argued that readers attempt to target the centre of words, but their saccades tend to fall short. When readers' eyes land at a nonoptimal position in a word, they are more likely to refixate that word. Where readers fixate in a word can be viewed not only as a landing site for that word but also as the launch site for the next saccade. Although the average landing position in a word lies between the beginning and the middle of a word, this position varies as a function of the prior launch site. Thus, if the launch site for a saccade landing on a target word is far from that word (say, eight to 10 letter spaces), the landing position will be shifted to the left. Likewise, if the distance is small (two to three letter spaces), the landing position is shifted to the right. Thus, the landing site distribution on a word depends on its launch site. Recently, Cutter et al. (2017, 2018) demonstrated that both the length of the fixated word as well as the length of the upcoming word jointly affect saccadic targeting, and that readers adapt their saccadic targeting to the length of the words in a sentence very rapidly.

Skipping effects. As noted, some words are skipped during reading. Two factors have a big impact on skipping: word length and contextual constraint (e.g., Drieghe, 2008; Rayner et al., 2011). First, the most important variable in skipping is word length: Short words are much more likely to be skipped than long words. When two to three short words occur in succession, there is a good chance that two of them will be skipped. Also, short words (e.g., "the") preceding a content word are often skipped (Zang et al., 2018, for similar effects in Chinese reading). In situations such as this, groups of words (e.g., three short words in succession and when an article precedes a content word) tend to be processed on a single fixation. Second, words that are highly constrained by the context are much more likely to be skipped than those that are not predictable, though whilst predictability influences how long readers look at a word and whether it is skipped, it does not influence where in the word the fixation lands (e.g., Rayner et al., 2001; with similar effects also present in other alphabetic languages, like Finnish, e.g., Vainio et al., 2009).

It is a mistake to think that if a word is skipped it is not processed. Fisher and Shebilske (1985) demonstrated this by examining the eye movements of readers on a passage of text. They then deleted all words from the passage that these readers had skipped and asked a second group of readers to read it. This group of readers had a hard time understanding the text. So, skipped words are processed. But when are they processed? Although somewhat controversial, some evidence suggests that when a word is skipped, it is processed on the fixation before or after the skip (or perhaps both).

When to move the eyes. It is clear that the ease or difficulty associated with processing the fixated word strongly influences when the eyes move. Thus, fixation time on a word is influenced by a host of lexical and linguistic variables including word frequency, word predictability, number of meanings, age of acquisition, phonological properties of words, and semantic relations between the fixated word and prior words. It is clear that variables assumed to have something to do with the ease or difficulty of processing a word can influence how long readers look at the word. Some variables have strong influences immediately when a word is fixated, whereas other variables seem to yield later occurring effects.

Perhaps the most compelling evidence that cognitive processing of the fixated word is driving the eyes through the text comes from experiments in which the fixated word either disappears or is masked after 50 ms to 60 ms (e.g., Rayner et al., 2003). Basically, these studies show that if readers are allowed to see the fixated word for 50 ms to 60 ms before it disappears, they read quite normally. This does not mean that words are completely processed in 50 ms to 60 ms but rather that this amount of time is sufficient for the processing system to encode the word. Interestingly, if the word to the right of fixation also disappears or is masked, then reading is disrupted; this quite strongly demonstrates that the availability of the word to the right of fixation is very important for parafoveal processing to occur in order that reading might proceed efficiently. More critically, when the fixated word disappears after 50 ms to 60 ms, how long the eyes remain in place is determined by the frequency of the word that disappeared: If it is a low-frequency word, the eyes remain in place longer. Thus, even though the word is no longer there, how long the eyes remain in place is determined by that word's frequency; this is compelling evidence for cognitive processing having a very strong influence on eye movements.

Lexical variables, thus, have strong and immediate effects on how long readers look at a word. Although other linguistic variables can have an influence on how soon readers move on in the text, it is generally the case that higher level linguistic variables have somewhat later effects, unless the variable "smacks you in the eye." So, for example, when readers fixate on a disambiguating word in a syntactic garden path sentence, there are increased fixation times on the word or a regression from the disambiguating word to earlier parts of the sentence. When readers encounter an anomalous word, they fixate on it longer, and the effect is quite immediate; when a word indicates an implausible but not truly anomalous event, an effect will be registered in the eye-movement record, but it is typically delayed slightly, appearing in later processing measures (see Rayner, 2009, and Clifton & Staub, 2011, for reviews). Readers also have longer fixations at the end of clauses and sentences, termed *wrap-up effects*, reflecting interpretation processes (e.g., Rayner & Morris, 1990).

Using eye movements to study sentence and discourse processing. In much of the foregoing discussion, the premise has largely been that lexical processing is the engine driving the eyes through the text. As we have also noted, however, there is good reason to believe that higher order comprehension processes influence eye movements, primarily when something does not make sense. In cases such as this, higher order comprehension processes can override the normal default situation in which lexical processing is driving the eyes, resulting in longer fixations, or regressions back to earlier parts of the text. It is quite interesting that eye-movement data have more or less become the gold standard in experiments dealing with sentence processing and syntactic ambiguity resolution. This is largely due to eye-tracking's precise temporal (and spatial) properties. In contrast, it is quite striking that there have not been nearly as many studies utilizing eye-movement data to examine online comprehension and discourse processing effects (see Rayner, 2009). Although there are increasing number of studies in which eye movements have been monitored to assess immediate comprehension in discourse processing (see Rayner et al., 2006), the number of such studies pales in comparison with the number of studies that used more gross reading time measures. Hopefully, the trend towards increasing numbers of researchers using eye-tracking methodology will continue into the future, and, if so, this approach will very likely develop current understanding of the moment-to-moment processes underlying discourse comprehension.

Models of Eye-Movement Control in Reading

Given the vast amount of information about eye movements during reading that has accumulated over the years, it is not surprising that a number of models of eye movements in reading have recently appeared (e.g., SWIFT, Engbert et al., 2005; E-Z Reader, Reichle et al., 1998; OB1-reader, Snell et al., 2018). Due to space limitations, other models are not discussed here. The models are all fully implemented, but they differ on a number of dimensions. In some of the models, the eyes are driven by lexical processing, whereas, in others, eye movements are largely viewed as being primarily influenced by oculomotor constraints. Some models allow for parallel processing of words, whereas, in others, lexical processing is serial so that the meaning of word $n + 1$ is not accessed until the lexical processing is complete (or nearly complete) for word n. E-Z Reader, SWIFT, and OB1-reader all predict how long readers look at words, which words they skip, and which words will most likely be refixated. They account for global aspects of eye movements in reading as well as more local processing characteristics. In addition, models have been be created to explain and simulate eye-movement behavior during reading within nonalphabetic languages (e.g., Chinese reading model; Li & Pollatsek, 2020). With careful experimentation and with the implementation of computational models that simulate eye movements during reading, great advances have been made in understanding eye movements in reading (and inferring the mental processes associated with reading).

EYE MOVEMENTS DURING SCENE PERCEPTION

The average fixation duration in scene perception tends to be longer than reading (approximately 300 ms, varying as a function of the task and scene characteristics). Average saccade size tends to be 4° to 5° (also varying with task and the nature of the scene). Whereas there is a well-defined task for readers, scene perception tasks are more variable. Common tasks include the requirement for subjects to look at the scene in anticipation of a memory test or to indicate whether a certain object is present in the scene. In the latter case, scene perception becomes very much a visual search task. The scan path of a viewer on a scene demonstrates that they do not fixate every part of the scene. Rather, most fixations tend to fall on the informative parts of the scene. Finally, the gist of a scene is understood very quickly, even before the eyes begin to move. The gist is thought to be acquired during the first fixation, allowing the viewer to orient subsequent fixations to interesting regions in the scene.

The Perceptual Span in Scene Perception

How much information can be obtained during fixation on a scene? Information is acquired over a wider range of the visual field in scene perception than reading. The best way to address this issue is via gaze-contingent paradigms, but very few such studies have been reported. In studies that have used the moving-window paradigm, scene information was presented normally within the window area around a fixation point, but the information outside of the window was degraded in a systematic way. These studies found that the functional field of view can consist of about half of the total scene regardless of the absolute size of the scene (at least for scenes up to $14.4° \times 18.8°$). There was also a serious deterioration in recognition of a scene when the window was limited to a small area (about $3.3° \times 3.3°$) on each fixation. Studies that used the moving-mask procedure found that the presence of a foveal mask influenced looking time, but it was not nearly as disruptive as in reading. Extrafoveal masks, where parafoveal and/or peripheral vision is degraded, decrease task accuracy and increase looking times on scenes (e.g., Nuthmann, 2014).

How close to the point of fixation does an object have to be for it to be recognized? Objects located within about $2.6°$ are generally recognized, but this depends to some extent on the characteristics of the object. Generally, the research suggests that the functional field of view only extends about $4°$ away from fixation and that qualitatively different information is acquired from the region within $1.5°$ around fixation than from regions further away. The size of the perceptual span in scene perception has not been defined as conclusively as it has in reading. It appears, though, that viewers typically gain useful information from a fairly wide region of the scene, again varying as a function of the scene and the task. Thus, the ease with which an object is identified may be related to its orientation, frequency within a scene context, and how well camouflaged it is. It is also likely that the ease of identifying a fixated object affects the extent of processing in eccentric vision.

Preview Benefit in Scenes

Viewers obtain preview benefit from objects that they have not yet fixated (with subsequent, direct fixations being approximately 100 ms shorter). Interestingly, viewers are rather insensitive to changes in scenes. In a series of experiments, while observers viewed a scene, changes were made during a saccade (when vision is suppressed). Remarkably, even though they were told that there would be changes, subjects were unaware of most of them, including changes involving the appearance and disappearance of large objects and objects changing colors (McConkie & Currie, 1996). Apparently low-level sensory information is not preserved from one fixation to the next. The lack of awareness of changes during saccades does not mean that there is no recollection of any visual details but, rather, that the likelihood of remembering visual information is highly dependent on the processing of that information.

Early theories of transsaccadic memory proposed that information is integrated across saccades in an integrative visual buffer (with properties like iconic memory). The experiments described thus far in the context of reading as well as nonreading experiments using relatively simply arrays demonstrated that this view is incorrect and that viewers do not integrate sensory information presented on separate fixations in a visual buffer. More recent work with more naturalistic scenes has arrived at the same conclusion, and evidence suggests that visuospatial working memory, which is thought to be at a higher level than a visual buffer, serves a primary role in integrating information across saccades (Van der Stigchel & Hollingworth, 2018). Thus, memory across saccades during scene perception appears to be due to higher level visual codes, which are abstracted from precise sensory representations, with visual short-term memory as the basis for integration.

Where Do Viewers Look in Scenes?

It has long been known that viewers' eyes are drawn to important aspects of the scene and that their goals in looking at the scene strongly influence their eye movements. Quite a bit of early research demonstrated that the eyes are quickly drawn to informative areas in a scene. It is also clear that the saliency of different parts of the scene influence what part of the scene is fixated. A large amount of empirical and computational research has recently been devoted to understanding the factors that govern fixation position in scenes, and much of this work revolves around how saliency (which is typically defined in terms of low-level components of the scene, such as contrast, color, intensity, brightness, and spatial frequency) influences where viewers look. It is relatively easy to control or manipulate such characteristics of scenes within experimental stimuli, but it is more complex to investigate the cognitive factors that influence where viewers look within scenes. More recent research examined the strong influence of factors such as memory and attention upon eye-movement behavior during scene perception (Castelhano & Krzyś, 2020; Henderson, 2017).

Are the eyes drawn to informative, unusual, or emotional parts of a scene? The evidence is somewhat uneven as some research indicates that the eyes are drawn to unusual parts of a scene, whereas other research suggests they are not. Early experiments found that the eyes move quickly to an object that is out of place in a scene. Unfortunately, these studies did not control physical distinctiveness well and, when it was controlled, the semantically inconsistent objects were not fixated earlier than consistent objects.

Recent experiments (Rayner et al., 2009b) with appropriate controls, however, have found that the eyes are drawn to unusual parts of a scene earlier than when the weird aspect was missing (although saccades to the unusual part of the scene are not instantaneous). More recently, the distinction has been drawn between semantic violations (what kinds of objects are likely to be found within a scene) and syntactic violations (where objects are likely to be located within a scene). The eyes move more quickly to objects within a scene that present either a semantic or a syntactic violation (Castelhano & Krzyś, 2020; Võ & Wolfe, 2015).

Dynamic scene perception. The vast majority of scene perception research has used static images as stimuli. Whilst there are a number of advantages to this approach (e.g., stimuli are relatively simple to generate, stimulus characteristics can be well-controlled or manipulated, and eye movements can be easily mapped onto the stimulus), there is a body of research that has focused upon the more naturalistic task of viewing dynamic scenes. Participants' eye movements are recorded as they watch videos on a screen (e.g., sports), or as they complete a real-life task while wearing a head-mounted eye tracker (e.g., making a sandwich). This work shows that viewers make anticipatory saccades that are guided by task demands reflecting cognitive control of eye movements during dynamic scene perception (Henderson, 2017).

When Do Viewers Move Their Eyes?

In contrast to reading, the variables that influence fixation durations during scene perception are less well understood. Given that attention precedes an eye movement to a new location within a scene, it follows that the eyes will move once information at the center of vision has been processed and a new fixation location has been chosen. The extraction of information at the fovea occurs fairly rapidly, and attention is then almost immediately directed to the periphery to choose a viable saccade target. Henderson and Pierce (2008) presented a visual mask at the beginning of eye fixations as viewers examined a scene. The duration of the mask was varied (with scene onset delays as short as 40 ms and as long as 1,200 ms), and the scene did not appear until the designated mask duration was exceeded. Then the scene appeared and remained visible until the viewer made a saccade. Scene onset delays took place on every 10th fixation. There was one population of fixations under direct control of the current scene, increasing in duration as the delay increased (e.g., responsive to the properties of the stimulus available during that fixation). A second population of fixations, however, was relatively constant across delay, with durations thought to be determined by a general oculomotor parameter that is not responsive to the current stimulus. Interestingly, the same two populations of fixations have been observed during reading as well (Nuthmann & Henderson, 2012). Rayner et al. (2009) masked the scene at certain points after the onset of each new fixation. It was found that viewers needed 150 ms to view the scene before the mask was not disruptive. This is much longer than the 50 ms to 60 ms needed in reading for the mask to not cause disruption and longer than one might predict given that the gist of a scene can be gleaned on the first fixation.

Cross-Cultural Effects in Scene Perception

Studies in this area have focused upon comparing Western and Eastern (typically Asian) cultures in their allocation of attention to scenes. Individualistic, Western cultures are thought to cause an analytical approach in their populations, causing participants to make the majority of their fixations on foreground objects within scenes. In contrast, more collectivistic Eastern cultures have a more holistic approach, resulting in a broader spread of attention across scenes with a higher proportion of fixations made on the background or context. The evidence in support of this cultural divide is mixed, and some studies have reported different patterns of eye movement behavior between cultures (e.g., Alotaibi et al., 2017; Chua et al., 2005), while others have not (e.g., Evans et al., 2009; Miellet et al., 2010).

Models of Eye-Movement Control in Scene Perception

A number of models of eye-movement control in scene perception have recently appeared. These models (Baddeley & Tatler, 2006; Itti & Koch, 2000, 2001; Parkhurst et al., 2002; Tatler et al., 2017) use the concept of a saliency map (Findlay & Walker, 1999) to model eye fixation locations in scenes. In this approach, bottom-up properties in a scene make explicit the locations of the most visually prominent regions of the scene. The models are basically used to derive predictions about the distribution of fixations on a given scene. Although these models can account for some of the variability in where viewers fixate in a scene, they are limited in that the assumption is that fixation locations are driven primarily by bottom-up factors; it is clear that higher level factors also come into play in determining where to look next in a scene (Torralba et al., 2006). More recent models have also begun to deal with when the eyes move in scene perception (Nuthmann et al., 2010; Tatler et al., 2017).

EYE MOVEMENTS AND VISUAL SEARCH

The majority of research on search has been done without measuring eye movements because it has often been assumed that they are not particularly important in understanding search. However, this attitude seems to be largely changing as many recent experiments have utilized eye movements to understand the process. Many of these studies deal with very low-level aspects of search and often focus on using the search task to uncover properties of the saccadic eye-movement system. It is becoming clear that eye-movement studies of visual search, like reading and scene perception, can provide important information on moment-to-moment processing in search. Here the focus will primarily be on research using eye movements to examine how viewers search through arrays to find specific targets. Fixation durations in search tend to be highly variable. Some studies report average fixation times as short as 180 ms, whereas others report averages on the order of 275 ms to 300 ms. This wide variability is probably due to the fact that the difficulty of the search array (or how dense or cluttered it is) and the nature of the search task strongly influence how long viewers pause with their eyes on average (see Rayner, 2009, for a review).

The Search Array Matters

Perhaps the most obvious thing about visual search is that the search array makes a big difference in how easy it is to find a target. When the array is cluttered or dense (with many objects or distractors), search is more costly than when the array is simple (or less dense), and eye movements typically reflect this fact. The number of fixations and fixation duration both increase as the array becomes more complicated, and the average saccade size decreases (e.g., Vlaskamp & Hooge, 2006). Also, the configuration of the search array affects the pattern of eye movements. In an array of objects arranged in an arc, fixations tend to fall between objects, progressively getting closer to the area where viewers think the target is located. On the other hand, in randomly arranged arrays, other factors such as color of the items and shape similarity to the target object influence the placement of fixations (see Rayner, 2009, for a review).

The Perceptual Span in Search

Studies using the moving-window technique as viewers searched through horizontally arranged letter strings for a specified target letter found that the size of the perceptual span varied as a function of the difficulty of the distractor letters. When the distractor letters were visually similar to the target letter, the size of the perceptual span was smaller than when the distractor letters were distinctly different from the target letter. The research suggests that there are two qualitatively different regions within the span: a decision region (where information about the presence or absence of a target is available) and a preview region (where some letter information is available but where information on the absence of a target is not available; e.g., Rayner & Fisher, 1987a, 1987b). Studies using moving windows and moving masks as viewers searched through a randomly arranged array of letters and digits for the presence of a target letter have also been conducted (e.g., Bertera & Rayner, 2000). Not surprisingly, the moving mask had a deleterious effect on search time and accuracy, and the larger the mask, the longer the search time, the more fixations were made, and the longer the fixations. Saccade size was affected by array size, but mask size had little effect. In the moving-window condition, search performance reached asymptote when the window was 5° (all letters and digits falling within 2.5° from the fixation point were visible with such a window size, but all other letters were masked).

Finally, other studies investigated the perceptual span via gaze-contingent multiresolution moving windows (e.g., Geisler et al., 2006). Within this paradigm, information outside the window is degraded in a manner that simulates resolution degradation (i.e., blurring) at various eccentricities from an observer's area of fixation. Eccentricity in degrees at which display resolution drops to one half of its value at the fixation point is termed ε_2. In a multiresolution display, the value of ε_2 controls the extent of blurring into the parafovea, such that the smaller the value of ε_2, the steeper the drop-off in resolution. Findings from these studies suggest that during any single fixation, when ε_2 is about 6°, the parafoveal blur imposed on a scene is not detectable. Thus, viewers do not notice that the scene has been artificially blurred. Consistent with other studies discussed here dealing with the use of information beyond the point of fixation, even when artificial blurring went undetected in eccentric vision, search performance was affected.

Preview Benefit

It is undoubtedly the case that viewers obtain preview benefit during search. Typically, studies of preview benefit in search provide a viewer with a preview of the search array (or part of the array) for a set period of time (e.g., 500 ms), or no preview in a control condition. Then the array is presented in its entirety. Generally, it is found that there are fewer fixations on previewed stimuli (and if they are fixated, for shorter durations) than in the control condition in which no preview of the array is provided (Rayner, 2009). Although studies of this type are interesting and suggestive of preview benefit, little research directly uses the types of gaze-contingent boundary paradigms that have been used in reading to study preview benefit in visual search (Pomplun et al., 2001). Perhaps the time is ripe to develop boundary paradigms (as used in reading research) to study preview benefit in visual search.

Where and When to Move the Eyes

Although there have been considerable efforts to determine the factors involved in deciding where and when to move the eyes in visual search, a clear answer to the issue remains elusive. Some have concluded that fixation durations in search are the result of a combination of preprogrammed saccades and fixations that are influenced by the fixated information. Others have suggested that the completion of foveal analysis is not necessarily the trigger for an eye movement, while others have suggested that it is. Still others have demonstrated that fixation position is an important predictor of the next saccade and influences both the fixation duration and selection of the next saccade target (see Rayner, 2009, for a review). Rayner (1995) suggested that the trigger to move the eyes in a search task is something like this: Is the target present in the decision area of the perceptual span? If it is not, a new saccade is programmed to move the eyes to a location that has not been examined. As with reading and scene perception, attention would move to the region targeted for the next saccade.

One issue over which there is general agreement is that the decision about where to fixate next and when to move the eyes is strongly influenced by the characteristics of the specific search task and the density of the visual array as well as viewer strategies (Clarke et al., 2019). It seems that parallels between visual search and scene perception are greater than with reading. In reading, linguistic processing is very central, whereas in scene perception and search it is almost always irrelevant. Additionally, the nature of visual processing is central to search and scene perception, while in reading, visual processes are generally considered to be involved predominantly in the earliest stages of reading. Thus, visual saliency, attentional allocation, and distraction all play an important role in directing fixations. Additionally, search for targets within visual search displays and scenes have different dimensions that are more variable than reading. For instance, with respect to search tasks, viewers may be asked to search for many different types of targets or may be asked to search for more than one target at the same time (dual target search; e.g., Stroud et al., 2012). Additionally, in search tasks, it is most often the case that in a proportion of trials a target will not be present, meaning that the participant has to decide when to abandon the search and make an absent decision. In turn, the nature of search allows for factors such as target prevalence and participant confidence to influence eye-movement behavior. For example, searching for a certain product on a grocery store shelf or searching for a person in a picture or for a tumor in an X-ray image may yield very different strategies than skimming text for a particular word. Unsurprisingly, eye movements will be quite different under these different circumstances. Although the task is generally much better defined in visual search than in scene perception, it is typically not as well specified as the task that is required in reading.

Models of Eye-Movement Control in Search

The most well-known model of eye-movement control related to visual search is that of Findlay and Walker (1999). This model focuses on saccade generation on the basis of parallel processing and competitive inhibition and, like many of the models of scene perception, relies heavily on the notion of a saliency map. Although the model is unquestionably interesting and very much tied to neurophysiological properties of the oculomotor system, it is not a fully implemented model. One fully implemented model is the target acquisition model of Zelinsky (2008). This model accounts for eye movements in search contexts ranging from fully realistic scenes to objects arranged in circular arrays to search for Os embedded in Qs (and vice versa). It can also account for manipulations such as set size, target eccentricity, and target-distractor similarity. It handles a number of important findings on eye movements and visual search. Comparisons of scan paths of the model to human viewers reveal that the model nicely mimics viewers' behavior, and it is difficult when presented with scan paths of the model and viewers to determine which is which. As impressive as the target acquisition model is with respect to simulating search behavior in terms of where the eyes go (and scan paths in finding targets), it does not provide an account of the determinants of when to move the eyes and, hence, it does not predict fixation durations in search. It also does not predict target absent trials (which is a difficult task for any search model). Hopefully, future instantiations of the model, alongside newly developed models, will lead to a better understanding of the mechanisms involved in accounting for how long the eyes pause in search. Clearly, given the centrality of saccades and fixations to human search, for models to be comprehensive, it is vital that they offer a mechanistic account of decision formation in respect to both when and where the eyes move.

A SUMMARY: EYE MOVEMENTS AND VISUAL COGNITION

Although there are obviously many differences between reading, scene perception, and visual search, we mention four important generalizations here. First, the perceptual span or functional field of view varies as a function of the task. The span is smaller in reading than in scene perception and visual search. As a result, fixations in scene perception tend to be longer and saccades are longer because more visual information is being processed on a fixation. Second, stimulus difficulty influences eye movements: (a) In reading, when the text becomes more difficult, fixations become longer and saccades are shorter; and (b) in scene perception and visual search, when the array is more difficult (crowded, cluttered, dense), fixations become longer and saccades become shorter. Third, the specific task (reading for comprehension vs. reading for gist, searching for a person in a scene vs. looking at the scene for a memory test) influences eye movements across the three tasks. Fourth, in all three tasks, it seems that viewers integrate visual information somewhat poorly across saccades, and what is most critical is that there is efficient processing of information on each fixation.

In the final section of this chapter, we briefly consider an experimental approach that involves the use of an eye-tracker for the acquisition of experimental data that does not involve recording saccadic eye movement—pupillometry.

PUPILLOMETRY

Pupillometry is an experimental method in which an eye tracker is used to acquire data regarding the moment-to-moment fluctuations in the size of a participant's pupil as they are engaged in a task. The pupil is the opening at the front of the eye through which light from objects in vision passes to fall on the retina. The human pupil is circular, and its size ranges from between approximately 1 mm and 9 mm with an average dilation of approximately 5 mm in ambient illumination (Beatty & Lucero-Wagoner, 2000). The pupil is reactive within approximately 200 ms, and its primary function is to regulate the amount of light entering the eye. When conditions are bright, the amount of light is reduced through the constriction of sphincter muscles that reduce the diameter of the pupil, and, conversely, under dim illumination conditions, dilator muscles cause the pupil to increase in diameter. Of course, if the size of the pupil were exclusively determined by light conditions, then as a behavioral measure, it would be of very limited value to experimental psychologists. Over centuries, however, observers found that pupil size was also influenced by psychological factors, and it is for this reason that researchers came to consider pupillary data as a potentially informative behavioral measure.

Early studies of pupillometry from the 1960s (e.g., Hess & Polt, 1960, 1964) showed that there was a relationship between pupil dilation and mental load, and later work demonstrated more generally that pupil size was related to arousal and task engagement. It is now established that pupil dilation in this regard has been associated with phasic activation in the locus coeruleus, a brain structure that plays a significant role in the control of the noradrenic system (Gilzenrat et al., 2010; Rajkowski et al., 1994). Pupillary movements associated with cognitive events are small (0.50 mm) and have little impact on visual performance. Furthermore, it is unclear whether these movements are actually functional. From the experimentalist's point of view, however, these movements are of interest as they offer an index of aspects of psychological process that does not require self-reporting from the participant (Beatty & Lucero-Wagoner, 2000). This is a property that is shared between pupillometric recordings and more standard saccadic oculomotor measures.

In relation to reading research, historically, pupillometric recordings have been used only infrequently to examine visual and linguistic processing. Carver (1971) undertook an early experiment to investigate whether pupillometric responses changed systematically in relation to text difficulty. Carver obtained no evidence to support this notion, however, methodological limitations may have contributed to this. Recently, the technique has been adopted more widely. For example, Shechter and Share (2021) reported mean and peak dilation and latency to peak dilation pupillometric indices (alongside speech onset times and pronunciation accuracy) from three experiments investigating oral and silent, longer and shorter, Hebrew word and pseudoword reading in adults and children. Unsurprisingly, speech onsets and accuracy were longer and reduced respectively for pseudowords relative to words. Interactive effects of lexical status and length also occurred. Most importantly, the pupillometric data also showed very complementary patterns of main effects and interactions with increased dilations under more cognitively demanding situations (longer relative to shorter stimuli and pseudowords relative to words). The authors concluded that the pupillometric data reflected cognitive effort during reading. Kuchinke et al. (2007) also investigated written word identification using pupillometry measures and a lexical decision task. In their experiment they manipulated lexical frequency and emotional valence, and they found robust increased pupillometric responses in relation to low-frequency words compared with high-frequency words (i.e., when processing was more effortful); however, emotional valence exhibited no influence. Pupillometric measurements have also been taken to assess mind wandering during natural reading. Franklin et al. (2013) used standard mind wandering probe techniques to assess whether readers were focused on task during reading. They found that prior to periods of mind wandering during reading, participants pupillary dilations were increased relative to comparable periods during which they remained on task. Again, Franklin et al. associated their findings with attentional allocation and cognitive effort in respect of ongoing cognitive processing.

Pupillometry has also been used to investigate cognitive processing effort during visual search and counting tasks. Porter et al. (2007) reported two experiments investigating visual search and target counting as pupillary responses were measured. During search, task difficulty was manipulated by varying the number and heterogeneity of visual distractors relative to targets. Consistent with the literature, they found that under more difficult search conditions pupil dilation was increased, once again, suggesting that increased task demands, attentional allocation and cognitive effort are tracked by increased pupil dilation. Interestingly, the magnitude of pupil dilation increased throughout each trial when participants were required to search for targets suggesting that more effort was being made as search was sustained. However, when participants were required to count targets, dilation was relatively high from the outset of the trial and this remained the case throughout until the trial was terminated. The authors argued that the counting task required a memory component (to ensure targets were not counted more than once) relative to search, and that this additional task component caused the increased cognitive load that resulted in the sustained pupil dilation throughout a trial.

Wright et al. (2013) reported an experiment in which they explored individual differences in participants' ability to detect an unexpected event as they undertook a primary task involving multiple-object tracking. They posited that the effort participants invested in engagement with the multiple-object tracking task might be indicative of the degree to which they might fail to detect an unexpected event. Further, they suggested that pupillometric responses might likely provide an index of the cognitive load associated with completion of the primary task (Wright et al., 2013). Consistent with these claims, the results showed a robust relationship between pupillary response, tracking load and response errors; however, pupillary responses were unrelated to whether participants did, or did not, detect the unexpected event. The results suggested that inattentional blindness (failure to detect an unexpected event) may be a phenomenon impervious to cognitive effort and load associated with a primary task.

Some research has also been conducted with regard to scene perception, showing that high-level visual processing of scenes leads to changes in pupil size. Naber and Nakayama (2013) found that when viewing natural scenes with or without a sun, presented either upright or inverted, participants' pupils constricted more to the onset of upright images, compared with inverted images. Also, the amplitudes of participants' pupil constriction to images containing a sun were larger compared with images not containing a sun (Experiment 1). As such, the researchers proposed that the processing of the abstract content of images, such as the interpretation associated with particular objects or conditions (e.g., the sun being present and the potential of damage to the retina due to high light levels), can lead to changes in pupil size. As image content processing requires higher level processing, the sun and scene inversion effects point to a high-level influence of scene perception on pupillary response. Overall, there is converging evidence from reading, visual search, and scene perception research that higher level (cognitive) processing seems to lead to changes in pupil size.

Beyond pupillometry research investigating reading, visual search, and scene perception, there has been work conducted to investigate a number of areas including perception, memory, decision making, and cognitive development. Space limitations preclude an extended discussion of this literature, but we direct the interested reader to several reviews (Hartmann & Fischer, 2014; Mathôt, 2018; Sirois & Brisson, 2014; van der Wel & van Steenbergen, 2018).

Before concluding our discussion of pupillometry research, given the nature of this chapter, we note several methodological issues that require consideration and attention if this approach is to be adopted. First, because the pupillometric state is very sensitive to fluctuations in luminance levels, care must be taken with respect to the preparation of stimuli across experimental conditions. Changes in the luminance characteristics of the stimuli, even if only very modest, can produce a pupillometric response and such pupillometric change may not necessarily be associated with the aspect of psychological processing that is under examination. Second, pupillometric responses can be controlled voluntarily to some extent. For example, if a participant imagines that they are engaged in a task with which a pupillary response is associated, then a pupillary response will occur. This means that a (nonnaïve) participant may be in a position to control their pupillary response and choose to present the response they wish throughout an experiment. Third, the stability of pupillary responses is reduced with fatigue, bringing into focus consideration of the duration of any experimental testing session. Fourth, after exposure to a visual stimulus, the pupil requires time to resume its baseline stability, meaning that intertrial intervals can be of importance. Finally, with respect to the physical recording of pupillary responses, with some eye trackers, the accuracy of pupillary dimensions may be affected by saccadic eye movements. To some degree, there is a systematic relation between the degree to which the pupil appears elliptical (rather than round) as the eyeball rotates. Researchers often work to avoid these issues by requiring a participant to maintain central fixation throughout recordings or by adopting methods of calibration and artefact removal with respect to recordings.

CONCLUSION

A great deal of knowledge has been gleaned from studies using eye movements to examine reading, scene perception, visual search, and other cognitive processing tasks. Research on eye movements during reading has advanced more rapidly and systematically than research on scene perception and visual search. This is probably due to the fact that stimulus characteristics (in reading, a limited set of letters make up words, whereas in scene perception the scene is not as constrained by stimulus properties) and the task (the task in reading and visual search is quite straightforward, but exactly what viewers do in scene perception is not as obvious) are more amenable to experimental manipulations in reading than scenes (especially) and search. Research on reading has significantly benefited from the use of the gaze-contingent paradigm. Although researchers in scene perception and visual search have been utilizing such paradigms recently, there are many issues in both domains where the paradigms could be effectively used. Another area where research on reading has been advanced over scene perception and visual search relates to the development of computational models to account for eye-movement data. Models of eye-movement control in reading tend to do a good job of accounting both for where readers look and how long they look at words. Models of eye-movement control in the domain of scene perception and visual search have largely focused on where viewers look to the exclusion of when they move their eyes, but the more recent controlled random-walk with inhibition for saccade planning (CRISP) model is a move in the right direction.[6]

Major advances have been made with respect to understanding eye movements in reading, scene perception, and visual search. More and more researchers are turning to eye-movement recording and data to examine important issues about how the brain and mind handles information in various tasks. Many brain-imaging techniques now enable researchers to record eye movements (although rather crudely). Attempts to simultaneously record eye movements and event-related potentials in reading (e.g., Degno & Liversedge, 2020) and other tasks look promising. Thus, the future looks bright with respect to the possibility of learning more about cognitive processing and how information is processed in the tasks described in this chapter via the use of eye movements.

References

Alotaibi, A., Underwood, G., & Smith, A. D. (2017). Cultural differences in attention: Eye movement evidence from a comparative visual search task. *Consciousness and Cognition*, 55, 254–265. https://doi.org/10.1016/j.concog.2017.09.002

Baddeley, R. J., & Tatler, B. W. (2006). High frequency edges (but not contrast) predict where we fixate: A Bayesian system identification analysis. *Vision Research*, 46(18), 2824–2833. https://doi.org/10.1016/j.visres.2006.02.024

Bai, X., Yan, G., Liversedge, S. P., Zang, C., & Rayner, K. (2008). Reading spaced and unspaced Chinese text: Evidence from eye movements. *Journal of Experimental Psychology: Human Perception and Performance*, 34(5), 1277–1287. https://doi.org/10.1037/0096-1523.34.5.1277

Beatty, J., & Lucero-Wagoner, B. (2000). The pupillary system. In J. T. Cacioppo, L. G. Tassinary, & G. G. Berntson (Eds.), *Handbook of psychophysiology* (pp. 142–162). Cambridge University Press.

Bertera, J. H., & Rayner, K. (2000). Eye movements and the span of the effective stimulus in visual search. *Perception & Psychophysics*, 62(3), 576–585. https://doi.org/10.3758/BF03212109

Blythe, H. I. (2014). Developmental changes in eye movements and visual information encoding associated with learning to read. *Current Directions in Psychological Science*, 23(3), 201–207. https://doi.org/10.1177/0963721414530145

Brothers, T., Hoversten, L. J., & Traxler, M. J. (2017). Looking back on reading ahead: No evidence

---

[6]There have been attempts to test the generalizability and limits of computational models developed for reading in the context of nonreading tasks like scene perception and visual search (Reichle et al., 2012; Trukenbrod & Engbert, 2007).

for lexical parafoveal-on-foveal effects. *Journal of Memory and Language, 96*, 9–22. https://doi.org/10.1016/j.jml.2017.04.001

Carver, R. P. (1971). Pupil dilation and its relationship to information processing during reading and listening. *Journal of Applied Psychology, 55*(2), 126–134. https://doi.org/10.1037/h0030664

Castelhano, M. S., & Krzyś, K. (2020). Rethinking space: A review of perception, attention, and memory in scene processing. *Annual Review of Vision Science, 6*(1), 563–586. https://doi.org/10.1146/annurev-vision-121219-081745

Choi, S. Y., & Koh, S. Y. (2009). The perceptual span during reading Korean sentences. *Korean Journal of Cognitive Science, 20*(4), 573–601. https://doi.org/10.19066/cogsci.2009.20.4.008

Chua, H. F., Boland, J. E., & Nisbett, R. E. (2005). Cultural variation in eye movements during scene perception. *Proceedings of the National Academy of Sciences of the United States of America, 102*(35), 12629–12633. https://doi.org/10.1073/pnas.0506162102

Clarke, A. D. F., Nowakowska, A., & Hunt, A. R. (2019). Seeing beyond salience and guidance: The role of bias and decision in visual search. *Vision, 3*(3), 46–62. https://doi.org/10.3390/vision3030046

Clifton, C., Jr., & Staub, A. (2011). Syntactic influences on eye movements in reading. In S. P. Liversedge, I. D. Gilchrist, & S. Everling (Eds.), *The Oxford handbook of eye movements* (pp. 895–909). Oxford University Press.

Cutter, M. G., Drieghe, D., & Liversedge, S. P. (2017). Reading sentences of uniform word length: Evidence for the adaptation of the preferred saccade length during reading. *Journal of Experimental Psychology: Human Perception and Performance, 43*(11), 1895–1911. https://doi.org/10.1037/xhp0000416

Cutter, M. G., Drieghe, D., & Liversedge, S. P. (2018). Reading sentences of uniform word length—II: Very rapid adaptation of the preferred saccade length. *Psychonomic Bulletin & Review, 25*(4), 1435–1440. https://doi.org/10.3758/s13423-018-1473-2

Degno, F., & Liversedge, S. P. (2020). Eye movements and fixation-related potentials in reading: A review. *Vision, 4*(1), 11. https://doi.org/10.3390/vision4010011

Drieghe, D. (2008). Foveal processing and word skipping during reading. *Psychonomic Bulletin & Review, 15*(4), 856–860. https://doi.org/10.3758/PBR.15.4.856

Drieghe, D. (2011). Parafoveal-on-foveal effects in eye movements during reading. In S. P. Liversedge, I. D. Gilchrist, & S. Everling (Eds.), *The Oxford handbook on eye movements* (pp. 839–855). Oxford University Press. https://doi.org/10.1093/oxfordhb/9780199539789.013.0046

Drieghe, D., Rayner, K., & Pollatsek, A. (2008). Mislocated fixations can account for parafoveal-on-foveal effects in eye movements during reading. *Quarterly Journal of Experimental Psychology, 61*(8), 1239–1249. https://doi.org/10.1080/17470210701467953

Engbert, R. (2006). Microsaccades: A microcosm for research on oculomotor control, attention, and visual perception. *Progress in Brain Research, 154*, 177–192. https://doi.org/10.1016/S0079-6123(06)54009-9

Engbert, R., Nuthmann, A., Richter, E. M., & Kliegl, R. (2005). SWIFT: A dynamical model of saccade generation during reading. *Psychological Review, 112*(4), 777–813. https://doi.org/10.1037/0033-295X.112.4.777

Evans, K., Rotello, C. M., Li, X., & Rayner, K. (2009). Scene perception and memory revealed by eye movements and receiver-operating characteristic analyses: Does a cultural difference truly exist? *Quarterly Journal of Experimental Psychology, 62*(2), 276–285. https://doi.org/10.1080/17470210802373720

Findlay, J. M., & Walker, R. (1999). A model of saccade generation based on parallel processing and competitive inhibition. *Behavioral and Brain Sciences, 22*(4), 661–674. https://doi.org/10.1017/S0140525X99002150

Fisher, D. F., & Shebilske, W. L. (1985). There is more that meets the eye than the eyemind assumption. In R. Groner, G. W. McConkie, & C. Menz (Eds.), *Eye movements and human information processing* (pp. 149–158). North Holland.

Franklin, M. S., Broadway, J. M., Mrazek, M. D., Smallwood, J., & Schooler, J. W. (2013). Window to the wandering mind: Pupillometry of spontaneous thought while reading. *Quarterly Journal of Experimental Psychology, 66*(12), 2289–2294. https://doi.org/10.1080/17470218.2013.858170

Geisler, W. S., Perry, J. S., & Najemnik, J. (2006). Visual search: The role of peripheral information measured using gaze-contingent displays. *Journal of Vision, 6*(9), 858–873. https://doi.org/10.1167/6.9.1

Gilzenrat, M. S., Nieuwenhuis, S., Jepma, M., & Cohen, J. D. (2010). Pupil diameter tracks changes in control state predicted by the adaptive gain theory of locus coeruleus function. *Cognitive, Affective & Behavioral Neuroscience, 10*(2), 252–269. https://doi.org/10.3758/CABN.10.2.252

Hartmann, M., & Fischer, M. H. (2014). Pupillometry: The eyes shed fresh light on the mind. *Current*

Biology, 24(7), R281–R282. https://doi.org/10.1016/j.cub.2014.02.028

Henderson, J. M. (2017). Gaze control as prediction. *Trends in Cognitive Sciences*, 21(1), 15–23. https://doi.org/10.1016/j.tics.2016.11.003

Henderson, J. M., & Pierce, G. L. (2008). Eye movements during scene viewing: Evidence for mixed control of fixation durations. *Psychonomic Bulletin & Review*, 15(3), 566–573. https://doi.org/10.3758/PBR.15.3.566

Hess, E. H., & Polt, J. M. (1960). Pupil size as related to interest value of visual stimuli. *Science*, 132(3423), 349–350. https://doi.org/10.1126/science.132.3423.349

Hess, E. H., & Polt, J. M. (1964). Pupil size in relation to mental activity during simple problem-solving. *Science*, 143(3611), 1190–1192. https://doi.org/10.1126/science.143.3611.1190

Hohenstein, S., & Kliegl, R. (2014). Semantic preview benefit during reading. *Journal of Experimental Psychology: Learning, Memory, and Cognition*, 40(1), 166–190. https://doi.org/10.1037/a0033670

Inhoff, A. W., Kim, A., & Radach, R. (2019). Regressions during reading. *Vision*, 3(3), 35. https://doi.org/10.3390/vision3030035

Irwin, D. E. (1998). Lexical processing during saccadic eye movements. *Cognitive Psychology*, 36(1), 1–27. https://doi.org/10.1006/cogp.1998.0682

Itti, L., & Koch, C. (2000). A saliency-based search mechanism for overt and covert shifts of visual attention. *Vision Research*, 40(10–12), 1489–1506. https://doi.org/10.1016/S0042-6989(99)00163-7

Itti, L., & Koch, C. (2001). Computational modelling of visual attention. *Nature Reviews Neuroscience*, 2(3), 194–203. https://doi.org/10.1038/35058500

Jordan, T. R., Almabruk, A. A. A., Gadalla, E. A., McGowan, V. A., White, S. J., Abedipour, L., & Paterson, K. B. (2014). Reading direction and the central perceptual span: Evidence from Arabic and English. *Psychonomic Bulletin & Review*, 21(2), 505–511. https://doi.org/10.3758/s13423-013-0510-4

Kirkby, J. A., Webster, L. A. D., Blythe, H. I., & Liversedge, S. P. (2008). Binocular coordination during reading and non-reading tasks. *Psychological Bulletin*, 134(5), 742–763. https://doi.org/10.1037/a0012979

Kliegl, R. (2007). Towards a perceptual-span theory of distributed processing in reading: A reply to Rayner, Pollatsek, Drieghe, Slattery, and Reichle (2007). *Journal of Experimental Psychology: General*, 136(3), 530–537. https://doi.org/10.1037/0096-3445.136.3.530

Kliegl, R., Nuthmann, A., & Engbert, R. (2006). Tracking the mind during reading: The influence of past, present, and future words on fixation durations. *Journal of Experimental Psychology: General*, 135(1), 12–35. https://doi.org/10.1037/0096-3445.135.1.12

Kuchinke, L., Võ, M. L. H., Hofmann, M., & Jacobs, A. M. (2007). Pupillary responses during lexical decisions vary with word frequency but not emotional valence. *International Journal of Psychophysiology*, 65(2), 132–140. https://doi.org/10.1016/j.ijpsycho.2007.04.004

Li, X., & Pollatsek, A. (2020). An integrated model of word processing and eye-movement control during Chinese reading. *Psychological Review*, 127(6), 1139–1162. https://doi.org/10.1037/rev0000248

Liversedge, S. P., Drieghe, D., Li, X., Yan, G., Bai, X., & Hyönä, J. (2016). Universality in eye movements and reading: A trilingual investigation. *Cognition*, 147, 1–20. https://doi.org/10.1016/j.cognition.2015.10.013

Mathôt, S. (2018). Pupillometry: Psychology, physiology, and function. *Journal of Cognition*, 1(1), 16. https://doi.org/10.5334/joc.18

McConkie, G. W., & Currie, C. B. (1996). Visual stability across saccades while viewing complex pictures. *Journal of Experimental Psychology: Human Perception and Performance*, 22(3), 563–581. https://doi.org/10.1037/0096-1523.22.3.563

McConkie, G. W., & Rayner, K. (1975). The span of the effective stimulus during a fixation in reading. *Perception & Psychophysics*, 17(6), 578–586. https://doi.org/10.3758/BF03203972

Miellet, S., Zhou, X., He, L., Rodger, H., & Caldara, R. (2010). Investigating cultural diversity for extrafoveal information use in visual scenes. *Journal of Vision*, 10(6), 21. https://doi.org/10.1167/10.6.21

Naber, M., & Nakayama, K. (2013). Pupil responses to high-level image content. *Journal of Vision*, 13(6), 7. https://doi.org/10.1167/13.6.7

Nuthmann, A. (2014). How do the regions of the visual field contribute to object search in real-world scenes? Evidence from eye movements. *Journal of Experimental Psychology: Human Perception and Performance*, 40(1), 342–360. https://doi.org/10.1037/a0033854

Nuthmann, A., & Henderson, J. M. (2012). Using CRISP to model global characteristics of fixation durations in scene viewing and reading with a common mechanism. *Visual Cognition*, 20(4–5), 457–494. https://doi.org/10.1080/13506285.2012.670142

Nuthmann, A., & Kliegl, R. (2009). An examination of binocular reading fixations based on sentence corpus data. *Journal of Vision*, *9*(5), 1–28. https://doi.org/10.1167/9.5.31

Nuthmann, A., Smith, T. J., Engbert, R., & Henderson, J. M. (2010). CRISP: A computational model of fixation durations in scene viewing. *Psychological Review*, *117*(2), 382–405. https://doi.org/10.1037/a0018924

Parker, A. J., Slattery, T. J., & Kirkby, J. A. (2019). Return-sweep saccades during reading in adults and children. *Vision Research*, *155*, 35–43. https://doi.org/10.1016/j.visres.2018.12.007

Parkhurst, D., Law, K., & Niebur, E. (2002). Modeling the role of salience in the allocation of overt visual attention. *Vision Research*, *42*(1), 107–123. https://doi.org/10.1016/S0042-6989(01)00250-4

Paterson, K. B., McGowan, V. A., White, S. J., Malik, S., Abedipour, L., & Jordan, T. R. (2014). Reading direction and the central perceptual span in Urdu and English. *PLOS ONE*, *9*(2), e88358. https://doi.org/10.1371/journal.pone.0088358

Pollatsek, A., Bolozky, S., Well, A. D., & Rayner, K. (1981). Asymmetries in the perceptual span for Israeli readers. *Brain and Language*, *14*(1), 174–180. https://doi.org/10.1016/0093-934X(81)90073-0

Pomplun, M., Reingold, E. M., & Shen, J. (2001). Investigating the visual span in comparative search: The effects of task difficulty and divided attention. *Cognition*, *81*(2), B57–B67. https://doi.org/10.1016/S0010-0277(01)00123-8

Porter, G., Troscianko, T., & Gilchrist, I. D. (2007). Effort during visual search and counting: Insights from pupillometry. *Quarterly Journal of Experimental Psychology*, *60*(2), 211–229. https://doi.org/10.1080/17470210600673818

Posner, M. I. (1980). Orienting of attention. *The Quarterly Journal of Experimental Psychology*, *32*(1), 3–25. https://doi.org/10.1080/00335558008248231

Rajkowski, J., Kubiak, P., & Aston-Jones, G. (1994). Locus coeruleus activity in monkey: Phasic and tonic changes are associated with altered vigilance. *Brain Research Bulletin*, *35*(5–6), 607–616. https://doi.org/10.1016/0361-9230(94)90175-9

Rayner, K. (1975). The perceptual span and peripheral cues during reading. *Cognitive Psychology*, *7*(1), 65–81. https://doi.org/10.1016/0010-0285(75)90005-5

Rayner, K. (1979). Eye guidance in reading: Fixation locations within words. *Perception*, *8*(1), 21–30. https://doi.org/10.1068/p080021

Rayner, K. (1995). Eye movements and cognitive processes in reading, visual search, and scene perception. In J. M. Findlay, R. Walker, & R. W. Kentridge (Eds.), *Eye movement research: Mechanisms, processes and applications* (pp. 3–22). North Holland. https://doi.org/10.1016/S0926-907X(05)80003-0

Rayner, K. (1998). Eye movements in reading and information processing: 20 years of research. *Psychological Bulletin*, *124*(3), 372–422. https://doi.org/10.1037/0033-2909.124.3.372

Rayner, K. (2009). Eye movements and attention in reading, scene perception, and visual search. *Quarterly Journal of Experimental Psychology*, *62*(8), 1457–1506. https://doi.org/10.1080/17470210902816461

Rayner, K. (2014). The gaze-contingent moving window in reading: Development and review. *Visual Cognition*, *22*(3–4), 242–258. https://doi.org/10.1080/13506285.2013.879084

Rayner, K., & Bertera, J. H. (1979). Reading without a fovea. *Science*, *206*(4417), 468–469. https://doi.org/10.1126/science.504987

Rayner, K., Binder, K. S., Ashby, J., & Pollatsek, A. (2001). Eye movement control in reading: Word predictability has little influence on initial landing positions in words. *Vision Research*, *41*(7), 943–954. https://doi.org/10.1016/S0042-6989(00)00310-2

Rayner, K., Castelhano, M. S., & Yang, J. (2009a). Eye movements and the perceptual span in older and younger readers. *Psychology and Aging*, *24*(3), 755–760. https://doi.org/10.1037/a0014300

Rayner, K., Castelhano, M. S., & Yang, J. (2009b). Eye movements when looking at unusual/weird scenes: Are there cultural differences? *Journal of Experimental Psychology: Learning, Memory, and Cognition*, *35*(1), 254–259. https://doi.org/10.1037/a0013508

Rayner, K., Chace, K. H., Slattery, T. J., & Ashby, J. (2006). Eye movements as reflections of comprehension processes in reading. *Scientific Studies of Reading*, *10*(3), 241–255. https://doi.org/10.1207/s1532799xssr1003_3

Rayner, K., & Fisher, D. L. (1987a). Eye movements and the perceptual span during visual search. In J. K. O'Regan & A. Levy-Schoen (Eds.), *Eye movements: From physiology to cognition* (pp. 293–302). North Holland. https://doi.org/10.1016/B978-0-444-70113-8.50045-X

Rayner, K., & Fisher, D. L. (1987b). Letter processing during eye fixations in visual search. *Perception & Psychophysics*, *42*(1), 87–100. https://doi.org/10.3758/BF03211517

Rayner, K., & Johnson, R. L. (2005). Letter-by-letter acquired dyslexia is due to the serial encoding of letters. *Psychological Science*, *16*(7), 530–534. https://doi.org/10.1111/j.0956-7976.2005.01570.x

Rayner, K., & Kliegl, R. (2012). Eye movements and cognitive processes. In H. Cooper, P. M. Camic,

D. L. Long, A. T. Panter, D. Rindskopf, & K. J. Sher (Eds.), *APA handbook of research methods in psychology: Vol. 1. Foundations, planning, measures, and psychometrics* (pp. 413–427). American Psychological Association. https://doi.org/10.1037/13619-022

Rayner, K., Liversedge, S. P., White, S. J., & Vergilino-Perez, D. (2003). Reading disappearing text: Cognitive control of eye movements. *Psychological Science*, *14*(4), 385–388. https://doi.org/10.1111/1467-9280.24483

Rayner, K., & Morris, R. K. (1990). Do eye movements reflect higher order processes in reading? In R. Groner, G. d'Ydewalle, & R. Parham (Eds.), *From eye to mind: Information acquisition in perception, search, and reading* (pp. 179–190). North-Holland.

Rayner, K., & Schotter, E. R. (2014). Semantic preview benefit in reading English: The effect of initial letter capitalization. *Journal of Experimental Psychology: Human Perception and Performance*, *40*(4), 1617–1628. https://doi.org/10.1037/a0036763

Rayner, K., Slattery, T. J., & Bélanger, N. N. (2010). Eye movements, the perceptual span, and reading speed. *Psychonomic Bulletin & Review*, *17*(6), 834–839. https://doi.org/10.3758/PBR.17.6.834

Rayner, K., Slattery, T. J., Drieghe, D., & Liversedge, S. P. (2011). Eye movements and word skipping during reading: Effects of word length and predictability. *Journal of Experimental Psychology: Human Perception and Performance*, *37*(2), 514–528. https://doi.org/10.1037/a0020990

Rayner, K., Smith, T. J., Malcolm, G. L., & Henderson, J. M. (2009). Eye movements and visual encoding during scene perception. *Psychological Science*, *20*(1), 6–10. https://doi.org/10.1111/j.1467-9280.2008.02243.x

Reichle, E. D., Pollatsek, A., Fisher, D. L., & Rayner, K. (1998). Toward a model of eye movement control in reading. *Psychological Review*, *105*(1), 125–157. https://doi.org/10.1037/0033-295X.105.1.125

Reichle, E. D., Pollatsek, A., & Rayner, K. (2012). Using E-Z Reader to simulate eye movements in nonreading tasks: A unified framework for understanding the eye-mind link. *Psychological Review*, *119*(1), 155–185. https://doi.org/10.1037/a0026473

Rolfs, M. (2009). Microsaccades: Small steps on a long way. *Vision Research*, *49*(20), 2415–2441. https://doi.org/10.1016/j.visres.2009.08.010

Schotter, E. R., Angele, B., & Rayner, K. (2012). Parafoveal processing in reading. *Attention, Perception & Psychophysics*, *74*(1), 5–35. https://doi.org/10.3758/s13414-011-0219-2

Shechter, A., & Share, D. L. (2021). Keeping an eye on effort: A pupillometric investigation of effort and effortlessness in visual word recognition. *Psychological Science*, *32*(1), 80–95. https://doi.org/10.1177/0956797620958638

Sirois, S., & Brisson, J. (2014). Pupillometry. *Wiley Interdisciplinary Reviews: Cognitive Science*, *5*(6), 679–692. https://doi.org/10.1002/wcs.1323

Slattery, T. J., & Rayner, K. (2010). The influence of text legibility on eye movements during reading. *Applied Cognitive Psychology*, *24*(8), 1129–1148. https://doi.org/10.1002/acp.1623

Snell, J., van Leipsig, S., Grainger, J., & Meeter, M. (2018). OB1-reader: A model of word recognition and eye movements in text reading. *Psychological Review*, *125*(6), 969–984. https://doi.org/10.1037/rev0000119

Stroud, M. J., Menneer, T., Cave, K. R., & Donnelly, N. (2012). Using the dual-target cost to explore the nature of search target representations. *Journal of Experimental Psychology: Human Perception and Performance*, *38*(1), 113–122. https://doi.org/10.1037/a0025887

Tatler, B. W., Brockmole, J. R., & Carpenter, R. H. (2017). LATEST: A model of saccadic decisions in space and time. *Psychological Review*, *124*(3), 267–300. https://doi.org/10.1037/rev0000054

Torralba, A., Oliva, A., Castelhano, M. S., & Henderson, J. M. (2006). Contextual guidance of eye movements and attention in real-world scenes: The role of global features in object search. *Psychological Review*, *113*(4), 766–786. https://doi.org/10.1037/0033-295X.113.4.766

Trukenbrod, H. A., & Engbert, R. (2007). Oculomotor control in a sequential search task. *Vision Research*, *47*(18), 2426–2443. https://doi.org/10.1016/j.visres.2007.05.010

Vainio, S., Hyönä, J., & Pajunen, A. (2009). Lexical predictability exerts robust effects on fixation duration, but not on initial landing position during reading. *Experimental Psychology*, *56*(1), 66–74. https://doi.org/10.1027/1618-3169.56.1.66

Van der Stigchel, S., & Hollingworth, A. (2018). Visuospatial working memory as a fundamental component of the eye movement system. *Current Directions in Psychological Science*, *27*(2), 136–143. https://doi.org/10.1177/0963721417741710

van der Wel, P., & van Steenbergen, H. (2018). Pupil dilation as an index of effort in cognitive control tasks: A review. *Psychonomic Bulletin & Review*, *25*(6), 2005–2015. https://doi.org/10.3758/s13423-018-1432-y

Vlaskamp, B. N. S., & Hooge, I. T. C. (2006). Crowding degrades saccadic search performance. *Vision*

Research, 46(3), 417–425. https://doi.org/10.1016/j.visres.2005.04.006

Võ, M. L.-H., & Wolfe, J. M. (2015). The role of memory for visual search in scenes. *Annals of the New York Academy of Sciences, 1339*(1), 72–81. https://doi.org/10.1111/nyas.12667

Wang, A., Yan, M., Wang, B., Jia, G., & Inhoff, A. W. (2021). The perceptual span in Tibetan reading. *Psychological Research, 85*(3), 1307–1316. https://doi.org/10.1007/s00426-020-01313-4

Winskel, H., Radach, R., & Luksaneeyanawin, S. (2009). Eye movements when reading spaced and unspaced Thai and English: A comparison of Thai-English bilinguals and English monolinguals. *Journal of Memory and Language, 61*(3), 339–351. https://doi.org/10.1016/j.jml.2009.07.002

Wright, T. J., Boot, W. R., & Morgan, C. S. (2013). Pupillary response predicts multiple object tracking load, error rate, and conscientiousness, but not inattentional blindness. *Acta Psychologica, 144*(1), 6–11. https://doi.org/10.1016/j.actpsy.2013.04.018

Yan, M., Kliegl, R., Shu, H., Pan, J., & Zhou, X. (2010). Parafoveal load of word N+1 modulates preprocessing effectiveness of word N+2 in Chinese reading. *Journal of Experimental Psychology: Human Perception and Performance, 36*(6), 1669–1676. https://doi.org/10.1037/a0019329

Yan, M., Wang, A., Song, H., & Kliegl, R. (2019). Parafoveal processing of phonology and semantics during the reading of Korean sentences. *Cognition, 193*, 104009. https://doi.org/10.1016/j.cognition.2019.104009

Yang, J., Wang, S., Tong, X., & Rayner, K. (2012). Semantic and plausibility effects on preview benefit during eye fixations in Chinese reading. *Reading and Writing, 25*(5), 1031–1052. https://doi.org/10.1007/s11145-010-9281-8

Yang, J., Wang, S., Xu, Y., & Rayner, K. (2009). Do Chinese readers obtain preview benefit from word n + 2? Evidence from eye movements. *Journal of Experimental Psychology: Human Perception and Performance, 35*(4), 1192–1204. https://doi.org/10.1037/a0013554

Zang, C., Zhang, M., Bai, X., Yan, G., Angele, B., & Liversedge, S. P. (2018). Skipping of the very-high-frequency structural particle de (的) in Chinese reading. *Quarterly Journal of Experimental Psychology, 71*(1), 1–10. https://doi.org/10.1080/17470218.2016.1272617

Zelinsky, G. J. (2008). A theory of eye movements during target acquisition. *Psychological Review, 115*(4), 787–835. https://doi.org/10.1037/a0013118

Zhang, M., Liversedge, S. P., Bai, X., Yan, G., & Zang, C. (2019). The influence of foveal lexical processing load on parafoveal preview and saccadic targeting during Chinese reading. *Journal of Experimental Psychology: Human Perception and Performance, 45*(6), 812–825. https://doi.org/10.1037/xhp0000644

CHAPTER 23

RESPONSE TIMES

Roger Ratcliff

Response times (RTs) typically measure the time from the presentation of a test stimulus to the response, for example, the time it takes to decide whether a test word was presented in a study list or not or whether a stimulus was dark or light. In many domains of psychology, RTs are used to measure the duration of mental processes; in others, they are ignored and only accuracy measures are reported. In every task, however, responses take time and any account of the processes involved in a task should account for RT. RTs vary from trial to trial and produce a distribution skewed to the right. In one sense, the skew of this distribution is easily explained—responses cannot be too fast (they run up against some minimum time), but there is no upper limit on how long they can take. This leads to two issues: How do we account for the shapes of RT distributions, and how do the shapes of RT distributions help constrain and test models? These issues have led to research in which empirical models for the shapes of RT distributions are used as summaries of data and to examine which parts of RT distributions change across experimental conditions.

One practical issue in using RT measures is how to handle outliers and contaminants. *Outliers* are responses outside of the normal spread of the RT distributions and can be random guesses (either fast or slow) or can result from a delay in processing, for example, a delay due to a moment's inattention. *Contaminants* are spurious responses that can appear anywhere in the RT distribution; thus, outliers are one kind of contaminant. Ratcliff and Tuerlinckx (2002) presented one theoretical approach to deal with contaminants within the framework of an explicit model of the decision process.

Long outliers, those that appear in the right tail of the RT distribution, are present in most data sets. These can affect estimates of mean RT moderately, sometimes enough to change significant effects into nonsignificant ones, and they also have serious effects on RT variance. A number of methods have been proposed to eliminate or reduce the impact of long outliers. No one method is best under all situations; however, there are best options if one knows how distribution shape changes across conditions.

Usually in psychology, when RTs are considered, the main concern has been with their means. However, if a theory of processing is proposed, even in a relatively weak form, predictions about the distributions of processing times can sometimes be derived. The even stronger claim is that, even if a theory is consistent with

---

This article was supported by NIA Grants R01-AG041176 and R01-AG057841.
https://doi.org/10.1037/0000318-023
APA Handbook of Research Methods in Psychology, Second Edition: Vol. 1. Foundations, Planning, Measures, and Psychometrics, H. Cooper (Editor-in-Chief)
Copyright © 2023 by the American Psychological Association. All rights reserved.

data at the level of mean RT, it might be highly inconsistent with the behavior of RT distributions (see Hacker, 1980; Heathcote et al., 1991; Hockley, 1984; Ratcliff & Murdock, 1976).

There are several questions about what happens to the shapes of RT distributions when mean RT increases. Quite different conclusions are reached if the increase is the result of the whole distribution of RTs slowing versus the longer RTs slowing more than the shorter RTs. For example, if the whole distribution shifts from one condition to another, then one might conclude that a process has been added. If, instead, the distribution spreads, then one might examine sequential sampling models that assume gradual accumulation of noisy information up to decision criteria (for a review of these models, see Ratcliff & Smith, 2004) in which the evidence-accumulation rate changes across experimental conditions.

In addition to RT distribution shapes, one must realize that all behavioral cognitive tasks provide both accuracy and RT measures. Sometimes examination of accuracy may suggest one effect, whereas examination of RT might suggest something different. For example, in several tasks in which the effects of aging on processing are examined, accuracy shows no decrement with age, whereas RT shows a large decrement (e.g., Ratcliff et al., 2010). To understand processing, explicit decision process models can be fit to data and then parameters, which reflect components of processing, and can be used to interpret the patterns of accuracy and RT.

In this chapter, I discuss how to deal with outlier RTs and different ways of representing RT distribution shape. I briefly describe fitting explicit RT distributions and then describe some remarkable invariances in RT distribution shape. Finally, I briefly discuss how processing models can account for distribution shape. But first, I discuss stability of RTs across a session.

STABILITY OF RTs ACROSS THE SESSION

Over the last few years, a great deal of effort has gone into making data openly available with a focus on replicability. This has been done without any clear cost–benefit criteria and analysis, such as whether there is increased replicability or whether there have been major empirical or theoretical advances based on open data. I believe a more important aim should be to produce high-quality data. High-quality data used to be a criterion on which an individual researcher was judged (there was considerable shame if results did not replicate), but with the increase in the number of articles being produced, it is hard to see the issue of data quality being addressed. Here I present one way of viewing RT data that exposes stability from trial to trial.

Ratcliff and Hendrickson (2021) tested Amazon Mechanical Turk subjects on a lexical decision task (Was this letter string a word or nonword?) and item recognition task (Was this word in the study list or was it new?) and two numerosity tasks. In the first two tasks, only about 10% of the subjects produced RTs that were unstable across the session; but, in the two numerosity tasks, about 45% produced unstable data. Unstable data were identified as fast guesses and/or systematic changes in the location and spread of the RT distribution over runs of trials. Figure 23.1 shows plots of each RT (with blocks of trials separated by vertical lines) for four of the subjects for the lexical decision task in Ratcliff and Hendrickson (this includes *word* and *nonword* responses from all stimulus categories for both correct and error responses). The first two subjects showed unstable data with RTs becoming mainly fast guesses halfway through the session (the horizontal dashed line is at 300 ms, and most RTs shorter than this are guesses). The third and fourth subjects show stable data. Combining all responses for the top two subjects will obviously produce distorted RT distributions with wider spreads than the stable nonguessing parts of the distributions. Also, error RTs would be much shorter than correct RTs (because of the greater proportion of errors being fast guesses). Distortions like these can affect hypothesis testing, reduce power, affect model fitting, and bias model comparison. It is likely that this happens much more than might be expected, and I have observed such behavior

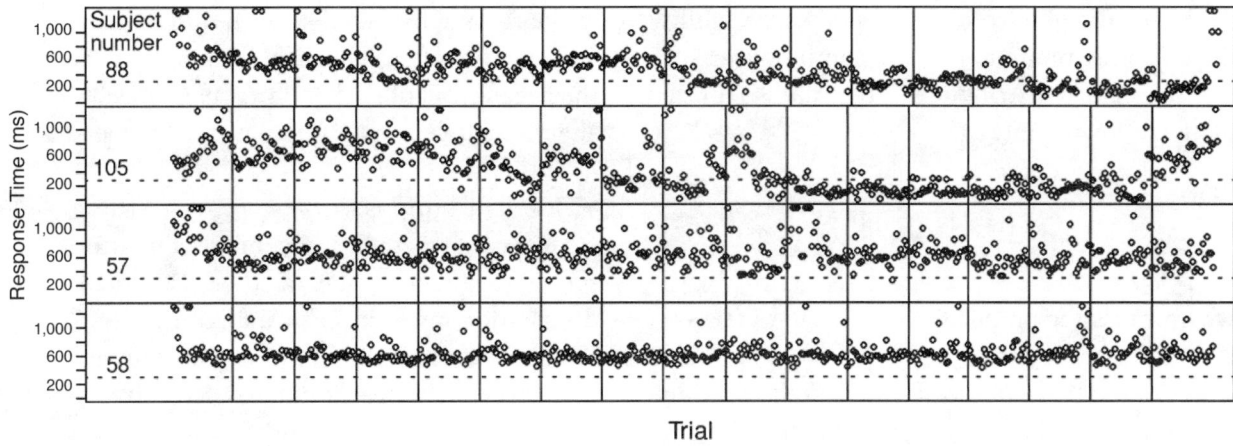

FIGURE 23.1. Plots of every response time (RT) across the session for the lexical decision task for four subjects in Ratcliff and Hendrickson (2021). The thin vertical lines represent blocks of trials, and the dashed horizontal line is at 300 ms and serves as an approximate way of identifying fast guesses (an RT below this is almost certainly a fast guess, RTs above but close to it may be fast guesses). Long RTs greater than 1,300 ms are replaced by 1,300 ms.

in up to half the subjects in published data sets. Ratcliff and Hendrickson presented data from published experiments from my laboratory that showed that the majority of subjects produced stable data (probably because they were individually monitored).

DENSITY, DISTRIBUTION, AND HAZARD RATE FUNCTIONS

There are three standard ways of representing distributions of responses: probability density functions, cumulative distribution functions, and hazard functions. The probability density function is the normalized version of the frequency distribution (Figure 23.2, left panel). A probability density function based on data involves dividing the RT scale into intervals, finding the number of observations in each interval (thus producing a histogram), and dividing these by the total number. The cumulative distribution (Figure 23.2, middle panel) provides the cumulative probability that a process has terminated as a function of time. A cumulative probability of 0.3 at some time means that 30% of responses have terminated by that time. The cumulative distribution function

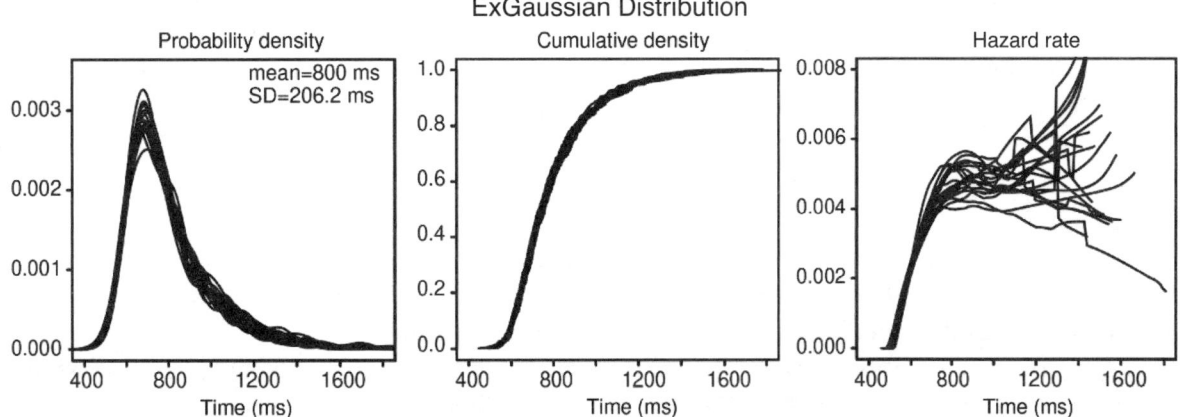

FIGURE 23.2. A probability density function, a cumulative density function, and a hazard function for the exGaussian distribution with 20 simulated distributions with 500 observations each and with Gaussian mean $\mu = 600$ ms and SD $\sigma = 50$ ms, and an exponential mean $\tau = 200$ ms.

at t is the sum of the probabilities in the probability density function up to t. In the continuous case (for theoretical distributions), the sum is replaced by the following integral:

$$F(t) = \int_0^t f(t') dt'$$

where $f(t)$ is the probability density and $F(t)$ is the cumulative distribution.

A close relative of the density and distribution functions is the hazard function (Figure 23.2, right panel). The hazard function is defined as $h(t) = f(t)/(1 - F(t))$ and it represents the likelihood that a process will terminate in the next instant of time given that the process has not yet terminated. For example, the exponential function ($f(t) = 1/\tau \exp(-t/\tau)$, where τ is the time constant, the time by which two thirds of the processes have terminated), has a constant hazard function. This means that the probability of terminating at any time does not depend on how long the process has been running (radioactive decay is an example of this; the probability of decay in the next instant of time is independent of how long the particle has been in existence). If the hazard function decreases over time, then the longer a process has been going, the more likely it is to terminate (e.g., old age in an animal population or in electronics). If the hazard function increases over time, then the longer a process has been going, the longer it is likely to go on (e.g., an increasing survival rate of infants with age in high-mortality situations).

The hazard function can serve as a signature to discriminate among models of different classes and so can be used to evaluate models that produce predictions for RT distributions (see Luce, 1986). The main limitation in using the hazard function to compare predictions to data is that often the part of the function that best discriminates between models is the part of the function in the right tail of the RT distribution corresponding to long RTs. The problem is that the tails of the distributions have few observations and so are less reliably estimated. Outliers can radically change the shape of the hazard function because they appear in the right tail. There has been little systematic examination of the effects of such outliers on the hazard function; therefore, serious use of it should include some examination of the effects of outliers.

RT distributions can also provide strong evidence that a condition contains a mixture of processes. Two well-separated peaks in the RT distribution might indicate a mixture of two separate processes. It might be, for example, that observed increases in mean RT might be the result of one, but not the other process slowing, or few responses in the faster process and more responses in the slower process.

Generally, when RTs are used as the dependent variable in testing a hypothesis, the way the RT distribution changes as a function of condition may lead to different conceptions of the processes under consideration. Thus, one must understand how RT distributions change as a function of condition when using RT measures.

THE EXGAUSSIAN AND INVERSE GAUSSIAN DISTRIBUTION FUNCTIONS

In order to illustrate how distribution shape is evaluated, how outliers affect measures of shape, and how outliers affect applications of models to data, I use two simple explicit distributions that have shapes similar to empirically observed RT distributions, the exGaussian and the inverse Gaussian. These distributions have also been used in simulations that examine the power of statistical tests under a variety of conditions and methods of data analysis. The exGaussian distribution (Hohle, 1965; Ratcliff, 1979; Ratcliff & Murdock, 1976; see applications in Ging-Jehli et al., 2021) has been widely used to summarize RT distribution shape; when the model fits experimental data reasonably well, then the behavior of the model parameters can be used to interpret how the distribution changes across experimental conditions. The inverse Gaussian is the distribution that is produced by a one boundary diffusion process (e.g., Burbeck & Luce, 1982; Ratcliff, 1978) and so is more process-based than the exGaussian.

For the exGaussian distribution, an RT from the distribution is the sum of a random value from a Gaussian (normal) distribution (mean μ and SD σ) and a random value from an exponential distribution (with mean τ). The density function is

$$f(t) = \frac{e^{-[(t-\mu)/\tau - \sigma^2/(2\tau^2)]}}{\tau\sqrt{2\pi}} \int_{-\infty}^{([(t-\mu)/\sigma] - \sigma/\tau)} e^{-y^2/2} \, dy$$

The mean of the distribution is μ + τ and the SD is $\sqrt{(\sigma^2 + \tau^2)}$.[1] When σ = 0, the distribution is a shifted exponential (starting at μ) and the mean is μ + τ, the SD is τ, and the median is μ + τlog$_e$(2). Thus Pearson's skewness (3[mean − median]/SD, see later) is 0.912. For the exGaussian, as σ increases, the skewness decreases.

The inverse Gaussian distribution is the distribution of finishing times in a one-boundary diffusion process. The density function (with the mean is θ + T_{er} and the SD is $\sqrt{(\theta^3/\lambda)}$) is

$$f(t) = \sqrt{\left(\frac{\lambda}{2\pi(t - T_{er})^3}\right)} e^{-\lambda(t - \theta - T_{er})^2/(2\theta^2(t - T_{er}))}$$

This function can be rewritten with diffusion model parameters with the transformation between the forms: θ = a/v and λ = a^2/s^2, where a is the boundary setting, v is drift rate (rate of evidence accumulation), T_{er} is the time offset of the distribution, which represents where in time the distribution begins to rise, and s is within trial SD (variability in the evidence accumulation process).

For both the exGaussian and inverse Gaussian functions, the probability density function rises quickly and then falls more slowly, like empirical RT distributions. Figure 23.2 illustrates the behavior of the probability density, the cumulative density, and the hazard function of the exGaussian distribution (the inverse Gaussian is very similar). The Gaussian mean is 600 ms, the Gaussian SD is 50 ms, and the exponential mean is 200 ms. In each panel, there are 20 distributions, each with 500 simulated observations per distribution. The cumulative density function is computed simply by sorting the data and producing cumulative counts at each RT. The probability density function and hazard functions use kernel estimation methods (Van Zandt, 2000). These essentially smooth the function at time t by averaging over data points around t.

Variability in the random samples of simulated data produces density functions and distribution functions that differ little across the different samples. However, most of the hazard functions show a rapid rise to a peak at around the mean RT, and then the function either rises, falls, or levels off. By 1,000 ms, it is difficult to see any regularity in the shape of the tail.

If either the exGaussian or the inverse Gaussian distribution is fit to RTs, the parameter estimates can be used to summarize RT distribution shape, and comparisons of parameter values across conditions can be used to summarize the changes in distributions over conditions. Visual inspection of RT distributions at the most macroscopic level shows three main features: the location at which the front edge of the distribution begins to rise, the rate of rise in the front edge, and the rate of fall in the tail, that is, about 3 degrees of freedom. Both the exGaussian and inverse Gaussian distributions have three parameters (3 degrees of freedom) with which to represent the whole distribution. The distribution that appears to be most useful is the exGaussian. Its three parameters capture the aspects of empirical distributions as noted above: the mean of the normal for the location of the fastest responses (and the mode), the SD of the normal for the rise of the front edge of the distribution, and the exponential parameter for the spread of the right tail.

The model parameters describe the shape of RT distributions; however, it is dangerous to assign meaning to them. In the exGaussian, one might speculate that the Gaussian represents one process and the exponential another. Attempts to identify processes in this way have not been fruitful. In contrast, the inverse Gaussian represents finishing times of a single boundary diffusion process. This has been considered to be a viable candidate for simple RT tasks (e.g., Burbeck & Luce, 1982; Luce, 1986; Smith, 1995; see applications to sleep deprivation, Ratcliff & Van Dongen, 2011, and to driving tasks, Ratcliff, 2015, and Ratcliff & Strayer, 2014), but would not be appropriate for two-choice tasks.

OUTLIER REACTION TIMES

Everyone who has used RT measures has realized that all the RTs that are collected do not come from the processes under consideration. One has only to observe subjects scratching themselves or checking a phone during the response period to be aware that there is likely to be bad data mixed in with the good. Even if one tests oneself, it is very apparent that sometimes a lapse of concentration produces a long RT. If outlier RTs were symmetric, so that a certain proportion of outlier RTs were long and another proportion short, with similar spread on either side, then there would be no bias except for a reduction in power. The mean would remain approximately constant, but the variance and other moments would be larger with outliers. Subjects in most cognitive paradigms, however, will mainly produce long outlier RTs unless they stop complying with the task instructions by producing random responses or fast guesses.

Short Outliers and Fast Guesses

Figure 23.1 shows examples of runs of fast guesses in data from the first two subjects. It is possible to identify many of these fast guesses by setting an upper RT cutoff at say 200, 250, and 300 ms and then examining accuracy. Fast guesses will produce chance or near chance performance for the faster responses. As the upper cutoff is increased, the point at which accuracy starts to rise above chance will show the point at which RTs begin to come from the processes involved in performing the task. Specifically, accuracy might be examined within a series of RT windows, say 200 ms to 250 ms, 250 ms to 300 ms, etc.

We find that most paid subjects do not fast guess, but some undergraduates from subject pools do when given the opportunity, especially at the end of the semester or when tested in very difficult (e.g., perceptual) experiments. Uncooperative subjects that fast guess usually would be able to leave the experiment earlier than if they tried to follow instructions. We have found that fast guessing can be discouraged to a large degree in subjects who are complying with the instructions by inserting a 1.5- or 2-second delay (with a message saying "TOO FAST") after very fast responses, for example, responses less than 250 ms in a fast perceptual task or less than 300 ms in a recognition memory or lexical decision task. This long delay eliminates the motivation for fast guesses. However, sometimes fast guessing may be optimal (Bogacz et al., 2006) or fast guessing may be a domain of study in its own right (Ollman, 1966). Most often, however, fast guessing is a nuisance that can be eliminated with this simple modification.

Long Outliers

Just one very long reaction time can completely change the pattern of means in an experiment. For example, suppose that 100 observations per condition are collected in an experiment and the process means are Condition A, 600 ms, and Condition B, 650 ms. Suppose in Condition A there are two outliers at 2.5 and 3.5 sec. The observed mean in Condition A will then be 648 ms, thus, masking the real 50-ms difference.

One method to deal with long outliers is to trim long RTs. To illustrate possible problems, I generated 96 random numbers from an exGaussian distribution with parameters $\mu = 500$ ms, $\sigma = 200$ ms, and $\tau = 200$ ms, values like those in observed recognition memory experiments. To these 96 RTs, four outlier RTs with values 4, 3, 2, and 1 s were added. The mean and SD were calculated for the RTs at cutoffs of 3,100, 2,100, and 1,100 ms. The means were 786, 754, 716, and 667 ms, and the SDs were 485, 361, 245, and 154 ms. The theoretical mean for this exGaussian distribution without outliers is 700 ms and the SD is 206 ms. With all of the RTs included, the mean was overestimated by 86 ms and the SD was over double the generating value (without outliers). By the 1,100-ms cutoff, the mean was 33 ms less than the generating value and the SD was 44 ms less than the generating value. These last two values at the 1,100-ms cutoff demonstrate an important problem with trimming, and that is in this case, 7 real RTs besides the outliers were removed, leading to a serious underestimation of both the mean and SD. The message is simple: In most sets of RT data, there are long RTs. Trimming data will remove many spurious RTs but will also remove long RTs that come from the processes under study.

Methods for Reducing the Impact of Long Outliers

Can we find a rule of thumb to maximize removal of the spurious RTs, yet minimize removal of real data? Ratcliff (1993) examined this question and found that every rule examined failed in some situations. The criterion that has been most often suggested involves trimming out data that falls some number of SDs outside the mean of that condition (e.g., 2 or 3 SDs). Any trimming or otherwise removing of data must be done completely independently of the hypotheses being tested. In addition, it is also reassuring if the trimming procedure does not remove significantly more data points from one condition than other conditions.

A diagnostic signal that outliers may be present in a condition of an experiment is the SD for the condition relative to those for other conditions. Suppose there are three conditions that are expected to have an increasing RT from first to last (e.g., 500, 600, and 700 ms). Suppose that the means are 520, 750, and 680 ms. Then it seems like the results disconfirm the prediction. However, examining the SDs in each condition may show that the conclusion is premature: If the SDs are 250, 500, and 285 ms, respectively, then it may be that outliers are responsible for the long mean RT in the middle condition. Trimming outliers may then produce the following set of results: 505, 602, and 678 ms, respectively with SDs 220, 249, and 277 ms, respectively. This pattern is more satisfactory because it shows monotonically increasing means and SDs.

Power of ANOVA and Outliers

There are several alternative methods for dealing with long outlier RTs in common use (besides trimming described above). First, the data can be Windsorized: Long RTs, instead of being trimmed out, can be replaced by RTs at some predetermined ceiling, for example, 3 SDs above the mean. This method makes the strong assumption that if there were no inattention (that produced the long outlier response), the process would have still produced a long RT. In general, I believe that this assumption is not justified in the RT domain. A second method involves use of medians. Typically, the median RT is computed for each subject in each condition and then these medians are used in an analysis of variance (for example). The advantage of medians is that they are relatively insensitive to outliers. This raises the question: If medians avoid the problem of outliers, then why is the median not used routinely instead of mean RT? The reason is that medians have higher variability than means. Simulations using medians showed that they rarely produce as much power as other methods. A third method involves transforming the RT data, by a log or inverse transformation. Both of these transformations reduce the impact of long RTs on the means.

Ratcliff (1993) performed a number of simulations that showed how these different methods influence the power of analysis of variance (ANOVA) to detect reliable differences. The methods affect power in different ways depending on how RT distributions change across conditions. Simulations were carried out with assumptions, first, that RT distributions spread with an increase in mean RT (as occurs with changes in memory strength or perceptual strength) or, second, that the distributions shifted with an increase in mean RT (as occurs with visual search when the order of search is controlled, Hockley, 1984). Simulations examined effects with and without outliers.

Results showed that no one method was optimal. If the difference in means between two conditions occurs because the RT distribution spreads with no change in the leading edge, and there are no outliers, then trimming reduces power as the cutoff is reduced. If there are outliers, then trimming increases power to a maximum as the cutoff is reduced, and then power decreases as more and more genuine RTs are eliminated (i.e., the data that are responsible for the difference in mean RTs). On the other hand, if the difference between two conditions is due to the distribution shifting with no change in the spread of the tail, then both with and without outliers, trimming increases power as more and more long RTs are eliminated (long RTs are more variable and so reduce power). Ratcliff (1993) reported results for log and inverse transformations, using medians, trimming the longest RT, trimming at some number of *SD*s above the mean, and Windsorizing. One method that seemed to give high power for studies with and without outliers and with distributions both spreading and shifting was the inverse transformation.

The prescription that we follow in dealing with outlier RTs in analyzing data is as follows: In a new experimental paradigm, we analyze the data in several different ways. We look at the results without trimming, we trim at several values, and we calculate medians. If all of these measures tell us the same thing, then we proceed to other experiments with the measure derived from trimming at some reasonable point (if the mean is 700 ms and *SD* is 300 ms, a cutoff of between 1,500 and 2,000 ms will probably work well). This value is determined independently of the hypothesis being tested. What we want to see (if the means calculated from the raw data are noisy) is order coming out of variability as the RT cutoff is reduced. We also want to see that the median tells us the same thing as the trimmed mean. If the measures do not agree, then there may be problems. It may be that there are no real trends in the data (statistical tests will usually confirm this by not producing significance at any cutoff or with medians). The results that are collected from the different cutoffs, transformations, and medians may then point the way towards a better design. But, in all of these analyses, one should not experiment with different methods on marginal data to try to find one that produces a significant effect to report. Such an effect may be spurious. The most important outcome is to report results that replicate.

FITTING REACTION TIME DISTRIBUTIONS

Here, I describe two methods for fitting models of RT distributions to empirical data (Heathcote et al., 2002; Ratcliff & Murdock, 1976; Ratcliff & Tuerlinckx, 2002; Van Zandt, 2000, 2002). The best is maximum likelihood; the estimates are best in the sense that variability in the estimates of the parameters is smaller than any other unbiased estimate. In this method, each RT is put into the expression for probability density to find the probability density for that RT (e.g., in the equation for the exGaussian). Then, the densities for all the RTs are multiplied, and this product is called the *likelihood*. If $f(t_i)$ is the density for the ith RT, then $L = \pi_i f(t_i)$ is the likelihood. The parameter values of the model are adjusted to find those that maximize the likelihood. In practice, because the product of many likelihoods can be small, the logarithm of each likelihood is taken and minus the sum of the log-likelihoods ($-\log(ab) = -\log(a) - \log(b)$ so the log of products is the sum of logs) is minimized as a function of model parameters. This works because the logarithm of a function is monotonically related to the function so the parameter values that maximize the function are those that minimize minus the log of the function. Minimization can be done by standard function minimization routines.

One problem with the maximum likelihood method for most distributions that are used to model RT is that a single short outlier RT can distort the whole fit. For example, the inverse Gaussian cannot produce a RT less than T_{er}. This means that if a RT is very short, T_{er} must be adjusted to be less than that RT in order to produce a probability density. Short RTs can be trimmed, but then the value of T_{er} will be partly determined by the value of the cutoff. This means that the estimate will be the choice of the person fitting the model.

One way to mitigate this problem is to use quantile RTs instead of individual RTs. *Quantile* RTs are the times at which some quantile proportion of processes have terminated. The proportion of responses between the quantile RTs is used to compute either a chi-square or a G-square goodness of fit statistic (see Ratcliff & Smith, 2004). If we use the .05, .15, . . . , .95 quantile RTs, then .05 probability mass lies outside the .05 and .95 quantiles and .1 probability mass lies between the quantiles. These probability masses are multiplied by the number of observations to give the observed frequencies. The quantile RTs can be used with the theoretical cumulative density function to compute the probability mass between the quantile RTs and these are multiplied by the number of observations to give the expected values. Then, a chi-square or G-square goodness of fit measure can be computed and model parameters can be adjusted to find its minimum. The observed probability masses (p_i) for the example above are .05, .1, .1, . . . , .05, and if the expected probability masses are π_i, then the chi-square statistic is $\chi^2 = N\Sigma(p_i - \pi_i)^2/\pi_i$ (where N is the number of observations) and $G^2 = 2N\Sigma p_i \ln(p_i/\pi_i)$. I have found that minimizing chi-square and minimizing G-square produce almost the same parameter estimates (Ratcliff & Childers, 2015). This is not surprising because they are asymptotically equivalent (Jeffreys, 1961, pp. 196–197). (See also the use of Kolmogorov-Smirnov statistic, Voss & Voss, 2007.)

The use of quantiles has the major advantage that a few short RTs (e.g., less than 10% if the lowest quantile used is the .1 quantile) will not distort the fit. Along with some judicious trimming of short RTs (e.g., much shorter than a possible response based on processing the stimulus and not guessing), this avoids problems with short outliers. In addition, some trimming of long RTs (e.g., at, say, 2 seconds if the mean RT is 600 ms) along with the use of quantiles will reduce the effect of long outliers. Sometimes, especially within a process modeling framework, it is possible to model contaminant responses, either as delays in processing (Ratcliff & Tuerlinckx, 2002) or as random guesses (Ratcliff & Van Dongen, 2009; Vandekerckhove & Tuerlinckx, 2007), depending on the task and experimental manipulations.

Monte Carlo Methods

In order to see how well a fitting method recovers parameter values, we run Monte Carlo simulations. In these, we generate simulated data from the model with the same numbers of observations as in real data and then fit the model to the simulated data. Then, we repeat this, say 100 times, that is, 100 Monte Carlo simulations, and compute the mean parameter values and the *SD* in the parameter values. The values of the mean provide a way of looking at bias in the parameter estimates; that is, does the fitting method produce fits that systematically differ from the values that were used to generate the simulated data? The values of the *SD*s provide estimates of variability in the parameter estimates based on the sample size and these can be used to compare the efficiency of different estimation methods. In addition, the *SD*s provide estimates of variability for statistical tests on parameter values across conditions and also provide estimates that allow comparison with individual differences to see if individual difference studies can be sensibly conducted. Finally, correlations between parameter values across the Monte Carlo trials can be used to examine tradeoffs across parameters. The way to interpret such tradeoffs is if one or more data points (e.g., quantile RTs) were extra high by chance, then the model may compensate for this by moving one parameter higher and another parameter (or more) may also move higher or lower to also compensate. These correlations can also be used to decide whether differences in parameter values might be the result of real differences or tradeoffs. Ratcliff and Tuerlinckx (2002, Figure 5) presented a detailed discussion, Ratcliff and Murdock (1976) provided theoretical estimates of *SD*s in exGaussian parameter values, and Wagenmakers et al. (2004) discussed such Monte Carlo methods in detail. Standard properties of estimators are presented in Ratcliff and Tuerlinckx (2002, Appendix A).

REPRESENTING DISTRIBUTION SHAPE: RT QUANTILES

In the previous section, I indicated that quantile RTs can be used in fitting a model to data; here I show how they can be used to display distribution shape. The quantiles of an RT distribution are the times at which some proportion of the processes have terminated. In Figure 23.2, middle panel, the 0.2 quantile RT is obtained by drawing a horizontal line from 0.2 on the y-axis to intersect the cumulative distribution function; the quantile RT is the RT on the x-axis where the two intersect. Quantiles of a RT distribution can be used as a summary of the distribution as is shown in Figure 23.3, left panel. The circles connected with the jagged line show a frequency polygon, which is a histogram with the top of the bars replaced by the circles. On the x-axis, the arrows show RT quantiles. Because there is a probability mass of .2 between the .1, .3, .5, .7, and .9 quantiles, and .1 outside of each of two extreme values, rectangles with these areas can be constructed between and outside the quantiles. The further apart the quantiles are, the lower the height of the rectangle. The .005 and .995 quantiles are used to mark the extremes of the distribution because they provide relatively stable estimators of the fastest and slowest RTs. Because each of the rectangles has an area of .2 (with the remaining .2 shared between the two extremes), all of the information about distribution shape is carried by the spacing between the quantiles. As can be seen, the equal-area histogram captures the overall shape of the distribution, that is, its location, spread, and skewness, as well as the frequency polygon does. This correspondence works for RT distributions with as few as 5 quantiles because RT distributions are usually regular with a fast rise and a slower fall in the right tail.

Ratcliff (2001) presented plots of quantiles against the response proportion for the condition as a way of showing how they jointly change as a function of the independent variable. Figure 23.3 right panel shows a plot, termed a *quantile-probability plot*, in which the RT quantiles for each condition are plotted vertically with the response proportion for the condition providing the value on the x-axis. If the probability of a correct response for a stimulus condition is p, the quantiles of the distribution of correct responses are plotted in a vertical column against p on the x-axis and the quantiles of the distribution of errors are plotted against $1 - p$. In the figure, this correspondence is illustrated by the double-ended arrows connecting pairs of conditions. This means that correct responses appear (usually) on the right of the .5 point on the x-axis and errors appear on the left. In plots of this kind, the outermost pair of distributions in the figure are the errors and correct RTs for

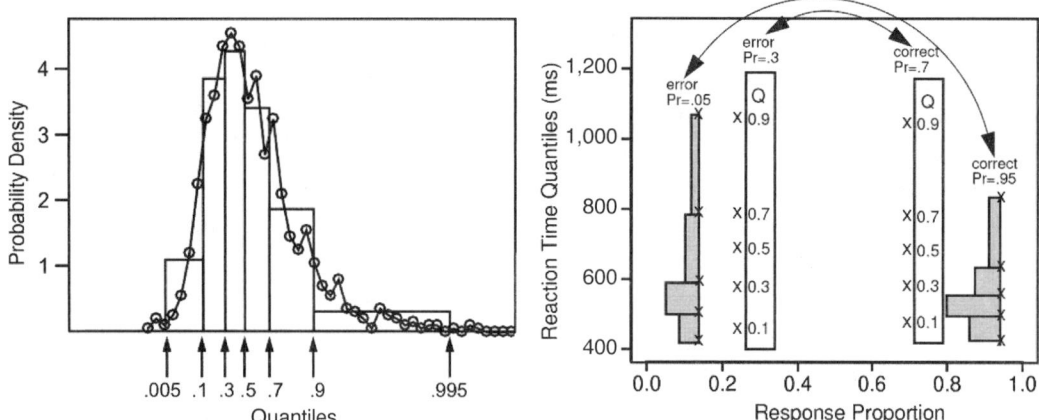

FIGURE 23.3. Histograms and quantile probability plots. The left panel shows a response time (RT) distribution as a frequency polygon, along with a quantile RT distribution with equal area rectangles drawn between the .1, .3, .5, .7, and .9 quantile RTs and rectangles with half the area outside the .1 and .9 quantile RTs. The right panel shows a quantile probability plot with the proportion of responses for that condition on the x-axis and quantile RTs plotted as x's on the y-axis. Equal areas rectangles are drawn between two of the sets of the quantiles to illustrate how to interpret an RT distribution shape in the plot (these are comparable to the distribution in the top panel).

the easiest stimulus condition and the innermost pair are the errors and correct RTs for the most difficult stimulus condition. This example is for cases in which correct responses can be combined across the two choices, for example, bright responses to bright stimuli combined with dark responses to dark stimuli; in other cases they cannot be combined in this way and separate plots are needed for the two response types, for example, words and nonwords in lexical decision (Ratcliff et al., 2004; Figure 23.4).

When one becomes familiar with the plot, one can see the way RT distributions change over conditions. For example, in Figure 23.3, right panel, going from right to left, the leading edge (lower "x," .1 quantile RT) increases a little, but the tail (top "x," .9 quantile RT) increases from around 850 ms to 1,080 ms. This means that the RT distribution shifts only a little, but spreads out a lot more. Comparing the extreme right and left quantiles (correct response proportion 0.95 and error proportion 0.05), error responses have a longer tail than correct responses, but the leading edges are about the same. These quantile probability plots can contain both the data and the predictions (e.g., Figure 23.4) and, hence, provide a useful way of examining the joint fit of accuracy and correct and error RT distributions of a model to data (Ratcliff & Smith, 2004).

Averaging Over Subjects

In many situations in cognitive psychology, materials are difficult to construct or a limited number are available. With patient populations, it may not be possible to collect more than a relatively few observations (e.g., 15 minutes' worth of data). For example, in text processing research it can be extremely difficult to construct paragraphs with the required structure while controlling potentially confounding variables; in clinical research there may be relatively few words associated with, for example, anxiety, and in semantic memory research there may be a limited number of typical members of a category or highly associated pairs of items. In these situations, it may be impossible to get more than 30 or 40 observations per subject per condition.

Averaging quantiles over subjects provides a way of grouping data when the number of observations is small. Note that just combining the RTs from the different subjects does not work. For example, if RTs were combined from two subjects that had narrow distributions that were well separated (e.g., with means at 500 ms and 800 ms), then the resulting distribution would be bimodal and would not reflect the shape of either individual distribution.

A major advantage of using quantile RTs to represent distribution shape is that they can be averaged over subjects to give a reasonable representation of average quantiles and, hence, the distribution of the average subject. There are two methods of doing this. One is to simply average quantiles. The second is to produce "Vincentiles" (Ratcliff, 1979; after Vincent, 1912; see also Estes, 1956) in which mean RTs between quantiles are computed and then averaged over subjects. In fitting models to data, we always use quantiles and not Vincentiles for the simple reason that quantiles can be computed from a model more easily that Vincentiles. Either the model is simulated to give a cumulative distribution function and then the quantile can be computed by interpolation (Ratcliff & Smith, 2004; Ratcliff & Starns, 2009; Usher & McClelland, 2001), or the data quantile RT can be entered into the computation for the cumulative distribution function and the predicted cumulative probability can be obtained (to be used in a chi-square or G-square fitting method; Ratcliff & Tuerlinckx, 2002). Visually, in the second panel of Figure 23.2, a straight line is projected up from the quantile RT on the x-axis and the value on the y-axis where it intersects the cumulative density function is the cumulative probability. If Vincentiles were to be used, the model cumulative distribution function would have to be integrated between the quantile RTs, which would add a much larger computational load to the fitting program.

A number of exact results have been obtained for Vincent averaging (Thomas & Ross, 1980). Thomas and Ross (1980) described conditions under which the Vincent average distribution belongs to the same family as the individual

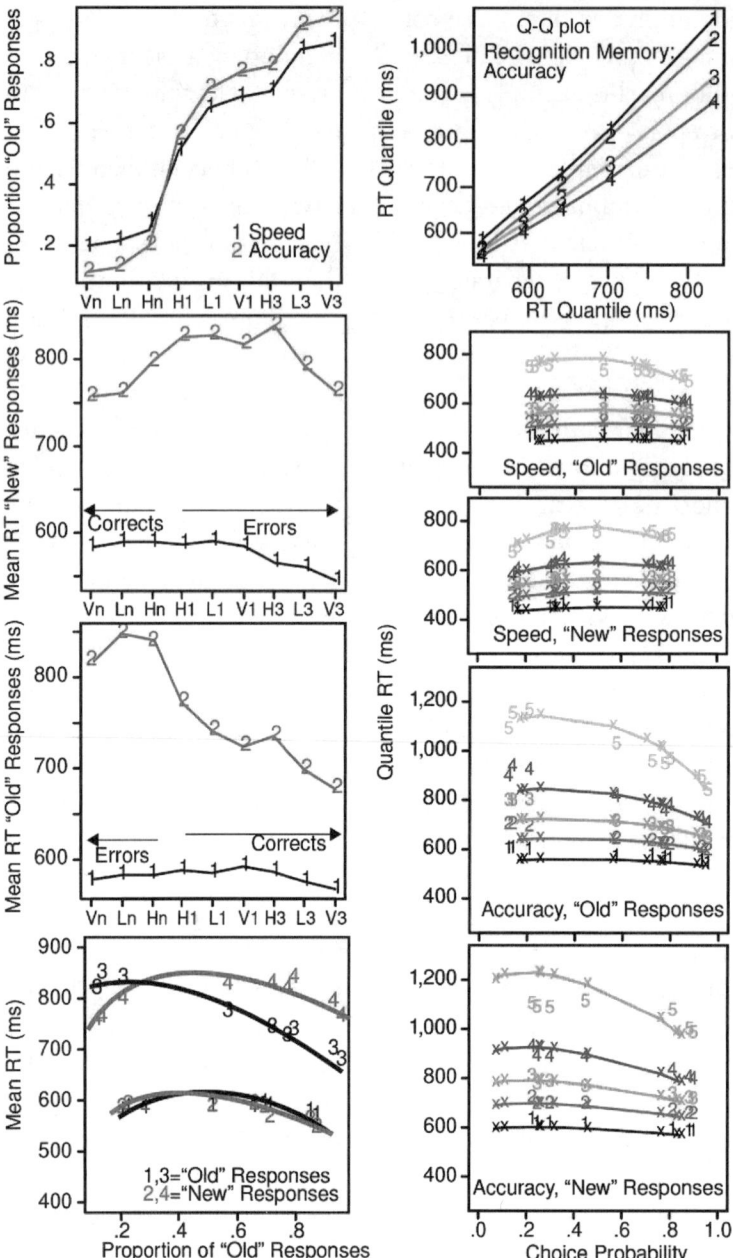

FIGURE 23.4. Plots of accuracy, mean response time (RT), and RT quantiles. The left column plots accuracy and mean RT against the independent variable (H, L, and V are high, low, and very low word frequency; 3, 1, and n are words presented 3 times, 1 time, and new words) for the recognition memory experiment from Ratcliff et al. (2004) with a speed/accuracy manipulation. The top left plot shows the proportion of responses, the second and third plots show mean RT, and the fourth plot shows a plot of mean RT against response proportions for each condition. The top right plot shows a Q-Q plot for the accuracy condition with quantiles for four conditions that spanned fastest to slowest plotted against the quantiles for the one of the other conditions. The four lower right plots show quantile-probability functions with the numbers for the empirical quantile RTs, and the x's and lines are for diffusion model fits. Data from Ratcliff et al. (2004); see for details.

distributions (this is true for the exponential, Weibull, and logistic distributions) and when the parameters from the Vincent average are averages of the parameters from the individual distributions. They showed that for the individual distributions to belong to the same family, a plot of quantiles for one subject versus quantiles for another subject (Q-Q plot) will be linear (Tukey, 1977). Figure 23.4 (top right panel) shows one example of a linear Q-Q plot from data from Ratcliff et al. (2004).

In the process of fitting theoretical distribution functions to experimental data, it usually becomes necessary to obtain an average of the parameter values across subjects in order to make some statements about group trends. There are two main ways to do this. First is to average the data across subjects in some way, then fit the model and use those parameters as the summary. Second is to fit the model to each individual subject's data, then to average the individual's parameters to provide the group parameters. In fitting the diffusion model to data, we have performed this comparison a number of times. In almost all of the cases, the parameters of the model fit to group data are close (within 2 standard errors) to the average of the parameter values from fits to individual subjects (Ratcliff et al., 2010). To date, this is a practical result and not theoretically exact, and it applies for the diffusion model, although we do not know about other models.

MEASURES OF DISTRIBUTION SHAPE

The question that is of interest in this section is how to obtain information about distribution shape from real RT data. Distribution shape can be defined in several different ways. Probably the most reasonable and least theory-bound is given by Mosteller and Tukey (1977, Chapter 1). They defined *shape* as what is left when location (position of the distribution) and scale (spread of the distribution) are eliminated, that is, the distribution is normalized. A probability density function is not sufficient to define shape as defined by Mosteller and Tukey (1977, Chapter 1); for example, their Figure 4 shows that the family of beta density functions have the same mathematical form but differ widely in shape. However, because RT distributions have roughly the same shape (skewed to the right), and some probability density functions that have been proposed as models of the RT distribution fit reasonably well, the ways that the parameters in these models change across conditions in the probability density function provides a reasonable way of describing how shape changes over conditions (e.g., for the exGaussian distribution).

Skewness

Everyone who has taken an introductory statistics course is familiar with the mean, SD, and variance of a set of scores. The mean represents the location of the distribution and the SD the spread or scale of the distribution. Introductory statistics books sometimes discuss skewness and kurtosis as measures of distribution shape. These are based on the moments of the distribution. For example, the kth moment can be written as $\mu_k = \int_{-\infty}^{\infty}(t - \mu_1)^k f(t)dt$. Then skewness is defined as $Sk_\mu = \mu_3/s^3$ and kurtosis is defined as $\kappa = \mu_4/s^4$ (where s^2 is μ_2, the variance, and μ_1 is the mean). It can be demonstrated mathematically that if all the moments of the distribution are known, then the shape of the distribution is completely determined.

There are serious problems, however, with using moments as measures of distribution shape (Ratcliff, 1979). First, the contributions to the third and fourth moments come from relatively far in the tail of the distribution (see Ratcliff, 1979, Figure 6, which was reprinted from Pearson, 1963). This means that these moments are sensitive to parts of the distribution that do not correspond to what we see as distribution shape by visual inspection. Second, the higher moments have very large standard errors associated with them. This means that many more observations are needed to obtain reasonable estimates (with low standard errors) than are usually collected in RT experiments (e.g., tens of thousands). Third, outlier RTs can affect the size of moments from the variance on up very severely, to the extent that if there are a few extreme reaction times, the higher moments essentially reflect these long RTs. The problem becomes critical if some of the outlier RTs are from processes other than the process being examined (e.g., a second retrieval attempt or worse, a head scratch or a moment's distraction). Then, the higher moments are measuring outlier RTs and these outliers are not of any interest in examining distribution shape. Better measures of distribution shape are Pearson's second skewness measure and the quartile coefficient of skewness. Pearson's second skewness measure is $Sk_p = 3(\text{mean}-\text{median})/SD$ and quartile skewness is defined by $Sk_q = (Q_3 - 2Q_2 + Q_1)/(Q_3 - Q_1)$.

Ratcliff (1993) performed a set of simulation studies that compared the behavior of these different measures of skewness across different random samples of data from the same distribution. Results showed that Pearson's second skewness measure and quantile skewness correlated highly and neither correlated with skewness from the third moment. Practically, what one sees in visually examining a distribution corresponds to Pearson's second skewness measure and the quartile coefficient of skewness.

RELATIONSHIPS AMONG DEPENDENT VARIABLES

As previously discussed, quantile probability plots provide one way to show the relationships among accuracy and correct and error RT distributions. If one has not examined the relationships, then they can be quite startling and require explanation. Here I work through one example (Ratcliff et al., 2015) with data from Ratcliff et al. (2004). The top left panel of Figure 23.4 shows plots of the probability of "old" responses as they varied across conditions with different lines for speed and accuracy instructions. The second row shows plots of mean RTs for correct responses and errors for "new" responses, and the third shows them for "old" responses (the data are averaged over subjects). These plots show regular behavior of accuracy and mean RT but it is difficult to see relationships between the variables. The bottom row shows latency-probability plots in which mean RT is plotted against the choice proportion. These directly lay out the relationships among choice probabilities and mean RTs as a function of the experimental conditions (word frequency, whether a test word was studied or not, number of presentations, and speed vs. accuracy instructions). The top two lines for each latency–probability plot represent responses under accuracy instructions, and the bottom two responses under speed instructions. The black lines represent "old" responses, and the gray lines represent "new" responses. What is compelling from the latency–probability plots is that the points all fall on very regular, inverted U-shaped functions. With these functions, it is easy to see how mean RT changes with accuracy. It is also easy to see whether mean RTs for correct responses are faster or slower than mean RTs for errors, a relationship that provides a crucial test of decision-making models. The lower four right panels of Figure 23.4 show quantile–probability plots corresponding to the latency–probability functions in the bottom left panel. These show relatively small changes in the 0.1 quantile RTs, with most of the change in mean from a spreading of the tail. The lines in the plot are from average fits of the diffusion model to the average data. The Q-Q plot in the top right panel can be constructed by taking the vertical quantile RTs in the lower right plots and plotting one against another. These are relatively linear, which shows that the RT distributions all have roughly the same shape. Diffusion models produce this shape invariance.

Diffusion Models

There are several different kinds of diffusion decision models that account for distribution shape in two-choice tasks. These diffusion models (Ratcliff, 1978; Usher & McClelland, 2001; reviews in Forstmann et al., 2016; Ratcliff & McKoon, 2008; Ratcliff et al., 2016) provide an account of how accuracy and the shapes of RT distributions change across experimental conditions that manipulate both difficulty and speed/accuracy criterion settings. The models assume the accumulation of noisy evidence towards decision criteria for each alternative response. The models provide the following accounts of RT distributions for two-choice decisions. First, most empirical RT distributions have an approximately exponential tail, which leads to a flat hazard function in the extreme right tail. Diffusion models automatically produce this behavior. Second, RT distributions spread out to the right as mean RT increases with difficulty with only a small shift in the distribution. This is a strong prediction of diffusion models. Third, as speed/accuracy settings are altered (by, for example, instructions), RT distributions shift and spread. Again, this is a strong prediction of the models. Fourth, RT distribution shape is approximately invariant under all of these manipulations and diffusion models produce this kind of invariance. Fifth, diffusion models produce increasing hazard functions or functions that increase to a peak and then decrease a little (Ratcliff et al., 1999); patterns that are observed in most two-choice data. In sum, most observed behaviors of RT distributions are captured almost automatically by diffusion models of the decision process. Methods of fitting the model to data can be found in Ratcliff and Tuerlinckx (2002) and Ratcliff and Childers (2015), and computer packages to fit the model are described in Voss and Voss (2007, 2008) and Wiecki et al. (2013). All these methods deal with outlier and contaminant RTs by explicitly modeling them and extracting estimates of the proportions of contaminants.

Explicit Distribution Functions

Some of the earliest attempts to model the shape of RT distributions started with an assumed distribution and attempted to work back from fits of the distribution to empirical data and then to the processes underlying the task. For example, McGill (1963) voiced the hope that the shape of the RT distribution would serve as a signature that would help identify the underlying processes. It seems that the strong version of this hope has not been realized; rather, RT distributions are critical in testing models but cannot be used to unambiguously identify processes.

There are several practical problems with working back from fits of the theoretical functions to the mechanisms. First, the theoretical distributions that are chosen for fitting have often been selected for mathematical tractability rather than for a description of theoretical mechanisms. Second, the method depends critically on comparison of different goodness-of-fit measures for the different distributions considered. These goodness-of-fit measures may interact with outlier problems that were discussed before, that is, a particular distribution may fit data better than another distribution because it better fits the combination of regular RTs and outliers that may not come from the processes under consideration. Third, there is a major problem of mimicking: It is certainly possible to produce distributions of much the same shape from many different processing assumptions. It is my opinion that the shape of RT distributions alone usually does not provide enough constraints to specify the underlying processing mechanisms. However, RT distribution shape provides the strongest constraints on process models that attempt to account for RT distribution shape for correct and error responses as well as accuracy.

In some cases, however, it may be possible to work back from distributions to processes. For example, if there were bimodality in the RT distribution, then this would strongly imply that there was a mixture of two component processes. However, the shapes of the two component distributions would not specify the components underlying those subprocesses.

The exGaussian has been used in many applications to summarize the shape of RT distributions (e.g., Balota & Spieler, 1999; Ging-Jehli et al., 2021; Hacker, 1980; Heathcote et al., 1991; Hockley, 1984; Ratcliff, 1979; Ratcliff & Murdock, 1976; Yap et al., 2008). The advantage of using this distribution is that the parameter τ provides an estimate of the fall in the tail relative to the rise of the distribution (which is represented by σ). From a more theoretical perspective, Matzke and Wagenmakers (2009) used the diffusion model to generate predictions and showed that if the diffusion model were correct, then the way diffusion model parameters change does not correspond to the way the exGaussian parameters change, for example, a change in drift rate does not correspond to a change in one exGaussian parameter.

CONCLUSION

This chapter discussed a number of issues, both practical and theoretical, that revolve around knowing the shape of RT distributions and how distributions change across conditions. From a theoretical perspective, I described methods of fitting distributions and summarizing distributions, with quantiles or explicit distributions, methods of averaging distributions over subjects, and covariances among model parameters. A practical consideration in most research using RT measures is how to identify and deal with outlier RTs. It is clear that methods are available to deal with outliers that can increase the power of an experiment substantially.

Probably the most important empirical lesson that can be taken from the discussion presented here is that someone using RT measures needs to know how their RTs are distributed and how the RT distributions change over conditions. Knowing about RT distribution can lead to insights about processing that are not available from mean RT alone.

References

Balota, D. A., & Spieler, D. H. (1999). Word frequency, repetition, and lexicality effects in word recognition tasks: Beyond measures of central tendency. *Journal of Experimental Psychology: General*, 128(1), 32–55. https://doi.org/10.1037/0096-3445.128.1.32

Bogacz, R., Brown, E., Moehlis, J., Holmes, P., & Cohen, J. D. (2006). The physics of optimal decision making: A formal analysis of models of performance in two-alternative forced-choice tasks. *Psychological Review*, 113(4), 700–765. https://doi.org/10.1037/0033-295X.113.4.700

Burbeck, S. L., & Luce, R. D. (1982). Evidence from auditory simple reaction times for both change and level detectors. *Perception & Psychophysics*, 32(2), 117–133. https://doi.org/10.3758/BF03204271

Estes, W. K. (1956). The problem of inference from curves based on group data. *Psychological Bulletin*, 53(2), 134–140. https://doi.org/10.1037/h0045156

Forstmann, B. U., Ratcliff, R., & Wagenmakers, E.-J. (2016). Sequential sampling models in cognitive neuroscience: Advantages, applications, and extensions. *Annual Review of Psychology*, 67(1), 641–666. https://doi.org/10.1146/annurev-psych-122414-033645

Ging-Jehli, N. R., Ratcliff, R., & Arnold, L. E. (2021). Improving neurocognitive testing using computational psychiatry—A systematic review for ADHD. *Psychological Bulletin*, 147(2), 169–231. https://doi.org/10.1037/bul0000319

Hacker, M. J. (1980). Speed and accuracy of recency judgments for events in short-term memory. *Journal of Experimental Psychology: Learning, Memory, and Cognition*, 6(6), 651–675.

Heathcote, A., Brown, S., & Mewhort, D. J. K. (2002). Quantile maximum likelihood estimation of response time distributions. *Psychonomic Bulletin and Review*, 9(2), 394–401.

Heathcote, A., Popiel, S. J., & Mewhort, D. J. K. (1991). Analysis of response time distributions: An example using the Stroop task. *Psychological Bulletin*, 109(2), 340–347. https://doi.org/10.1037/0033-2909.109.2.340

Hockley, W. E. (1984). Analysis of response time distributions in the study of cognitive processes. *Journal of Experimental Psychology: Learning, Memory, and Cognition*, 10(4), 598–615. https://doi.org/10.1037/0278-7393.10.4.598

Hohle, R. H. (1965). Inferred components of reaction times as a function of foreperiod duration. *Journal of Experimental Psychology*, 69(4), 382–386. https://doi.org/10.1037/h0021740

Jeffreys, H. (1961). *Theory of probability* (3rd ed.). Oxford University Press.

Luce, R. D. (1986). *Response times*. Oxford University Press.

Matzke, D., & Wagenmakers, E.-J. (2009). Psychological interpretation of the ex-Gaussian and shifted Wald parameters: A diffusion model analysis. *Psychonomic Bulletin & Review*, 16(5), 798–817. https://doi.org/10.3758/PBR.16.5.798

McGill, W. J. (1963). Stochastic latency mechanisms. In R. D. Luce, R. R. Bush, & E. Galanter (Eds.), *Handbook of mathematical psychology* (pp. 309–360). John Wiley and Sons.

Mosteller, F., & Tukey, J. W. (1977). *Data analysis and regression*. Addison-Wesley.

Ollman, R. T. (1966). Fast guesses in choice reaction time. *Psychonomic Science*, 6(4), 155–156. https://doi.org/10.3758/BF03328004

Pearson, E. S. (1963). Some problems arising in approximating to probability distributions, using moments. *Biometrika*, *50*(1-2), 95–112. https://doi.org/10.1093/biomet/50.1-2.95

Ratcliff, R. (1978). A theory of memory retrieval. *Psychological Review*, *85*(2), 59–108. https://doi.org/10.1037/0033-295X.85.2.59

Ratcliff, R. (1979). Group reaction time distributions and an analysis of distribution statistics. *Psychological Bulletin*, *86*(3), 446–461. https://doi.org/10.1037/0033-2909.86.3.446

Ratcliff, R. (1993). Methods for dealing with reaction time outliers. *Psychological Bulletin*, *114*(3), 510–532. https://doi.org/10.1037/0033-2909.114.3.510

Ratcliff, R. (2001). Diffusion and random walk processes. In J. D. Wright (Ed.), *International encyclopedia of the social and behavioral sciences* (Vol. 6, pp. 3668–3673). Elsevier.

Ratcliff, R. (2015). Modeling one-choice and two-choice driving tasks. *Attention, Perception & Psychophysics*, *77*(6), 2134–2144. https://doi.org/10.3758/s13414-015-0911-8

Ratcliff, R., & Childers, R. (2015). Individual differences and fitting methods for the two-choice diffusion model. *Decision*, *2*(4), 237–279. https://doi.org/10.1037/dec0000030

Ratcliff, R., & Hendrickson, A. T. (2021). Do data from mechanical Turk subjects replicate accuracy, response time, and diffusion modeling results? *Behavior Research Methods*, *53*, 2302–2325. https://doi.org/10.3758/s13428-021-01573-x

Ratcliff, R., & McKoon, G. (2008). The diffusion decision model: Theory and data for two-choice decision tasks. *Neural Computation*, *20*(4), 873–922. https://doi.org/10.1162/neco.2008.12-06-420

Ratcliff, R., & Murdock, B. B., Jr. (1976). Retrieval processes in recognition memory. *Psychological Review*, *83*(3), 190–214. https://doi.org/10.1037/0033-295X.83.3.190

Ratcliff, R., & Smith, P. L. (2004). A comparison of sequential sampling models for two-choice reaction time. *Psychological Review*, *111*(2), 333–367. https://doi.org/10.1037/0033-295X.111.2.333

Ratcliff, R., Smith, P. L., Brown, S. D., & McKoon, G. (2016). Diffusion decision model: Current issues and history. *Trends in Cognitive Sciences*, *20*(4), 260–281. https://doi.org/10.1016/j.tics.2016.01.007

Ratcliff, R., Smith, P. L., & McKoon, G. (2015). Modeling regularities in response time and accuracy data with the diffusion model. *Current Directions in Psychological Science*, *24*(6), 458–470. https://doi.org/10.1177/0963721415596228

Ratcliff, R., & Starns, J. J. (2009). Modeling confidence and response time in recognition memory. *Psychological Review*, *116*(1), 59–83. https://doi.org/10.1037/a0014086

Ratcliff, R., & Strayer, D. (2014). Modeling simple driving tasks with a one-boundary diffusion model. *Psychonomic Bulletin & Review*, *21*(3), 577–589. https://doi.org/10.3758/s13423-013-0541-x

Ratcliff, R., Thapar, A., Gomez, P., & McKoon, G. (2004). A diffusion model analysis of the effects of aging in the lexical-decision task. *Psychology and Aging*, *19*(2), 278–289. https://doi.org/10.1037/0882-7974.19.2.278

Ratcliff, R., Thapar, A., & McKoon, G. (2004). A diffusion model analysis of the effects of aging on recognition memory. *Journal of Memory and Language*, *50*(4), 408–424. https://doi.org/10.1016/j.jml.2003.11.002

Ratcliff, R., Thapar, A., & McKoon, G. (2010). Individual differences, aging, and IQ in two-choice tasks. *Cognitive Psychology*, *60*(3), 127–157. https://doi.org/10.1016/j.cogpsych.2009.09.001

Ratcliff, R., & Tuerlinckx, F. (2002). Estimating parameters of the diffusion model: Approaches to dealing with contaminant reaction times and parameter variability. *Psychonomic Bulletin & Review*, *9*(3), 438–481. https://doi.org/10.3758/BF03196302

Ratcliff, R., & Van Dongen, H. P. A. (2009). Sleep deprivation affects multiple distinct cognitive processes. *Psychonomic Bulletin & Review*, *16*(4), 742–751. https://doi.org/10.3758/PBR.16.4.742

Ratcliff, R., & Van Dongen, H. P. A. (2011). Diffusion model for one-choice reaction-time tasks and the cognitive effects of sleep deprivation. *Proceedings of the National Academy of Sciences of the United States of America*, *108*(27), 11285–11290. https://doi.org/10.1073/pnas.1100483108

Ratcliff, R., Van Zandt, T., & McKoon, G. (1999). Connectionist and diffusion models of reaction time. *Psychological Review*, *106*(2), 261–300. https://doi.org/10.1037/0033-295X.106.2.261

Smith, P. L. (1995). Psychophysically principled models of visual simple reaction time. *Psychological Review*, *102*(3), 567–593. https://doi.org/10.1037/0033-295X.102.3.567

Thomas, E. A. C., & Ross, B. H. (1980). On appropriate procedures for combining probability distributions within the same family. *Journal of Mathematical Psychology*, *21*(2), 136–152. https://doi.org/10.1016/0022-2496(80)90003-6

Tukey, J. W. (1977). *Exploratory data analysis*. Addison-Wesley.

Usher, M., & McClelland, J. L. (2001). The time course of perceptual choice: The leaky, competing accumulator model. *Psychological Review*, *108*(3), 550–592. https://doi.org/10.1037/0033-295X.108.3.550

Vandekerckhove, J., & Tuerlinckx, F. (2007). Fitting the Ratcliff diffusion model to experimental data. *Psychonomic Bulletin & Review*, *14*(6), 1011–1026. https://doi.org/10.3758/bf03193087

Van Zandt, T. (2000). ROC curves and confidence judgements in recognition memory. *Journal of Experimental Psychology: Learning, Memory, and Cognition*, *26*(3), 582–600. https://doi.org/10.1037/0278-7393.26.3.582

Van Zandt, T. (2002). Analysis of response time distributions. In J. T. Wixted (Vol. Ed.) & H. Pashler (Series Ed.), *Stevens' handbook of experimental psychology: Vol. 4. Methodology in experimental psychology* (3rd. ed., pp. 461–516). Wiley Press. https://doi.org/10.1002/0471214426.pas0412

Vincent, S. B. (1912). The function of the viborissae in the behavior of the white rat. *Behavioral Monographs*, *1*.

Voss, A., & Voss, J. (2007). Fast-dm: A free program for efficient diffusion model analysis. *Behavior Research Methods*, *39*(4), 767–775. https://doi.org/10.3758/BF03192967

Voss, A., & Voss, J. (2008). A fast numerical algorithm for the estimation of diffusion-model parameters. *Journal of Mathematical Psychology*, *52*(1), 1–9. https://doi.org/10.1016/j.jmp.2007.09.005

Wagenmakers, E.-J., Ratcliff, R., Gomez, P., & Iverson, G. J. (2004). Assessing model mimicry using the parametric bootstrap. *Journal of Mathematical Psychology*, *48*(1), 28–50. https://doi.org/10.1016/j.jmp.2003.11.004

Wiecki, T. V., Sofer, I., & Frank, M. J. (2013). HDDM: Hierarchical Bayesian estimation of the Drift-Diffusion Model in Python. *Frontiers in Neuroinformatics*, *7*, 14. https://doi.org/10.3389/fninf.2013.00014

Yap, M. J., Balota, D. A., Tse, C.-S., & Besner, D. (2008). On the additive effects of stimulus quality and word frequency in lexical decision: Evidence for opposing interactive influences revealed by RT distributional analyses. *Journal of Experimental Psychology: Learning, Memory, and Cognition*, *34*(3), 495–513. https://doi.org/10.1037/0278-7393.34.3.495

CHAPTER 24

PSYCHOPHYSICS: CONCEPTS, METHODS, AND FRONTIERS

Allie C. Hexley, Takuma Morimoto, and Manuel Spitschan

WHAT IS PSYCHOPHYSICS?

Fundamental to the human experience is sensing and perceiving properties of the environment. In natural language, *sensing* generally refers to the processing of physical stimuli and patterns in our environment and the extraction of relevant information. As psychologists, we want to understand these processes systematically and scientifically. How can we quantify the quality or magnitude of a percept, and how can we meaningfully compare percepts between different individuals or from different environments? While we can easily measure physical phenomena, such as the weight of an object in grams using the appropriate instruments (e.g., a scale), the measurement of perceptual phenomena is nontrivial. The set of methods in psychological science that concern the measurement of sensory and perceptual phenomena through behavior is called *psychophysics*. The goal of psychophysics is to quantitatively characterize the relationship between the physical properties of a stimulus—such as the radiance, spatial frequency content, or motion velocity for a visual stimulus, or the amplitude, pitch, or spatial location for an auditory stimulus—and our associated percept.

Psychophysical methods have a long history in psychological science. A major milestone is the formalization of psychophysics of Gustav Theodor Fechner (1801–1887) in the 1860s, though the study of perception, of course, does not start in the 19th century but has a much longer history (Wade, 1998). Since then, psychophysical methods have contributed to discovering numerous fundamental rules that appear to govern our sensory and perceptual processes. Psychophysical experiments can take many forms, yet a common denominator is usually the precise and parametric control of stimuli along one or multiple physical dimensions.

As such, experiments are intimately linked to the technology available for stimulus control. In particular, the arrival of computers and displays in the 1960s and 1970s stimulated psychophysical research. For example, modern computer graphics methods have dramatically increased the ability to control visual stimuli and make them more naturalistic. Furthermore, while the traditional paradigm for psychophysical experiments is a laboratory setting, online experiments have facilitated the collection of psychophysical data from hundreds or thousands of participants

---

A.C.H. is supported by funding received under the European Union's Horizon 2020 research and innovation programme under the Marie Skłodowska-Curie Grant Agreement N° 765911 (RealVision). T.M. is supported by the Wellcome Trust (Sir Henry Wellcome Fellowship to T.M.; Wellcome Trust 218657/Z/19/Z) and Pembroke College, University of Oxford (Junior Research Fellowship to T.M.). M.S. is supported by the Wellcome Trust (Sir Henry Wellcome Fellowship to M.S.; Wellcome Trust 204686/Z/16/Z).

https://doi.org/10.1037/0000318-024
APA Handbook of Research Methods in Psychology, Second Edition: Vol. 1. Foundations, Planning, Measures, and Psychometrics, H. Cooper (Editor-in-Chief)
Copyright © 2023 by the American Psychological Association. All rights reserved.

in more recent years. Psychophysics is very much alive and indeed provides valuable insights into human sensory and perceptual processing.

The psychophysical literature is immense. It is hopeful and naïve at best and impossible at worst to attempt to summarize it or give a coherent definition for it within the scope of a single book chapter. Therefore, we do not engage with the premise of psychophysics in this chapter: Sensation and perception are indeed objectively measurable, which has been extensively detailed elsewhere (Box 24.1, Further Reading, for pointers at the end of the chapter). We provide a pragmatic approach to psychophysics. First, we discuss why psychophysics is useful and present examples from the published literature of psychophysics "in action." We then examine and discuss the ingredients of a psychophysical experiment: the measure, the stimulus, the observer, the task, the method, and the analysis. Finally, we discuss the current frontiers of psychophysical experimentation.

At the outset, we note that our approach to psychophysics is fundamentally one focused around visual psychophysics (as our backgrounds are all rooted in vision science). We, therefore, primarily discuss examples from vision and visual perception. The key ideas we discuss, however, are applicable across all perceptual mechanisms, including, for example, audition, somatosensation, taste perception, and multisensory perception.

WHY IS PSYCHOPHYSICS USEFUL?

At the core of psychophysics is the measurement and characterization of human sensory and perceptual responses to external stimuli. Psychophysical methods are useful for psychological science for a variety of reasons: (a) to quantify and put bounds on human sensation and perception, (b) as a tool to predict underlying sensory and perceptual mechanisms, (c) to inform neural underpinnings, and (d) as a tool to guide ergonomic and "human-centric" design.

Psychophysics as a Tool to Quantify and Put Bounds on Human Sensation and Perception

Psychophysical measurements help us understand the properties and limitations of human sensation and perception. One of the operative units of analysis of psychophysics is the concept of the threshold: the minimum level of a physical stimulus at which a specific perceptual performance level occurs. Threshold measurements allow us to quantify the bounds of our perception. In many cases, psychophysics allows us to characterize when physically distinguishable stimuli are perceptually indistinguishable. For example, color discrimination thresholds tell us the amount of physical difference that needs to exist between two different colors for them

---

BOX 24.1

Further Reading on Psychophysical Theory

The primary aim of this chapter is to provide an overview of psychophysics as a tool, and we have, therefore, left out theoretical details. Here, we point the reader to some further reading.

- **Kingdom and Prins (2016)** provide a detailed description of psychophysical methods and theory. The associated Palamedes toolbox (https://www.palamedestoolbox.org/) provides a set of MATLAB functions to implement various useful functions, including fitting psychometric function and adaptive staircase procedures.
- **Gescheider (1997)** wrote a classic text on introducing the fundamentals of classical psychophysical methods.
- **Green and Swets (1974)** provide an authoritative overview of signal detection theory.
- **Morgan, Melmoth, and Solomon (2013)** provide a general discussion regarding class A observation applied to threshold-level stimuli and Class B observation for suprathreshold-level stimuli.
- **Read (2015)** discusses the place of psychophysics in contemporary neuroscience, with a specific focus on binocular stereopsis.
- **Treutwein (1995)** discusses adaptive methods in psychophysics, and **Treutwein and Strasburger (1999)** discuss fitting psychometric functions.
- **Wichmann and Hill (2001a)** and **Wichmann and Hill (2001b)** dive deep into psychometric function fitting and doing inference on them.

to be reliably distinguished as separate colors. Importantly, psychophysical methods are also at the basis of many vision and hearing examinations in a clinical context (Johnson, 2013).

Psychophysics as a Tool to Predict Underlying Sensory and Perceptual Mechanisms

In addition to describing and characterizing performance, psychophysical measurements can also uncover underlying sensory and perceptual mechanisms or classes of mechanisms when designed carefully. One specific tool that allows for this is adaptation, also termed the "psychophysicist's electrode" (Frisby, 1980). The logic underlying adaptation is as follows. An observer is repeatedly exposed to a specific stimulus, the adapting stimulus. If this exposure modifies performance on a given task (but not another), this means that the adapting stimulus has affected a mechanism underlying this specific task. In other words, "if it adapts, it's there" (Webster, 2015, page 547). A particular example in which adaptation has been used to uncover specific mechanisms is color adaptation: Exposure to an adapting sinusoidal stimulus modulating along one dimension of color space modifies performance along that dimension but not along others (Krauskopf et al., 1982).

Psychophysics Helps Inform Neurophysiological Underpinnings

While psychophysics fundamentally provides a behavioral output, psychophysical data can inform the underlying neurophysiological processes that ultimately govern behavior and performance (even though these are important in their own right). In many ways, neurophysiological data describing a specific neural response to a physical stimulus are more compelling when supported by psychophysical data.

Psychophysics as a Tool to Guide Ergonomic and "Human-Centric" Design

In addition to these basic uses of psychophysical measurement techniques, which ultimately help develop our mechanistic understanding of how the brain processes information from the external world, psychophysics also generates knowledge that is immediately useful in the world, and there are many examples of this in our day-to-day life. For example, computer monitors have only three independent primary colors—red (R), green (G), and blue (B)—because human color vision is three-dimensional, owing to the trichromatic retina comprising three classes of cones: long (L), medium (M), and short (S). Therefore, additional primaries would carry no further color information for the observer to exploit. Knowledge of the trichromatic nature of human color vision, therefore, directly informs display color reproduction design. When you look for it, you notice that many aspects of design in the human environment are ultimately guided by psychophysical data, such as the choice of specific warning signals and colors and the development of JPEG and MP3 standards for image and sound compression, respectively.

WHAT ARE THE INGREDIENTS OF A PSYCHOPHYSICS EXPERIMENT?

The preceding section has, hopefully, illustrated the benefits of psychophysics and convinced the reader that psychophysics is still very much a valuable tool in psychological science today. This section provides an outline of the key considerations an experimenter has to make when designing a psychophysics experiment. Following a modified framework from Kingdom and Prins (2016), we break this down into the "six ingredients" of a psychophysics experiment: the measure, stimulus, the observer, the task, the method, and the analysis.

Measure

The first thing to consider when designing a psychophysical experiment is what it is that we are trying to measure. Any model parameters estimated from psychophysical data can be taken as a psychophysical measure. The exact measure of interest is inherently tied to the psychophysical experimental design. We do not unpack all possible measures one could draw from psychophysical data but rather highlight a few common ones and how one may determine an appropriate measure for their data. One clear dichotomy to emphasize when considering which measure to use is whether the measure is of a *threshold* or some *suprathreshold* metric.

A pervasive psychophysical measure, the threshold quantifies the limits of our perceptual ability—for example, the threshold for detecting a stimulus embedded in noise or the absolute threshold of vision. Thresholds are points along a specific physical dimension for which particular levels of psychophysical performance are defined. Sensitivity, defined as the reciprocal of the threshold, is another commonly used measure. The *sensitivity index, d'* (dee-prime), is the standardized psychophysical measure for sensitivity (Box 24.2, Signal Detection Theory).

Thresholds can be further subdivided into *detection thresholds* and *discrimination thresholds*. Detection thresholds refer to the minimum level of a stimulus required for sensing the presence of the stimulus, such as detecting the absolute threshold of vision. Discrimination thresholds refer to the minimum difference between two stimuli required for the observer to be able to distinguish the two stimuli as different from each other, such as the minimum color difference between two stimuli required for the two to be perceived as different colors. The *just-noticeable difference* (JND) is a measure of the difference in physical stimulus intensity required for a difference to be perceived, while the *point of subjective equality* (PSE) is a measure of the physical stimulus range over which the two stimuli are perceived to be identical to each other.

Suprathreshold experiments are primarily focused on measuring perceptual performance above threshold level, for example, measuring the perceived loudness over a wide range of sound amplitudes, rather than looking for the amplitudes at which a sound can be detected or discriminated from another. Suprathreshold measures tend to be a *sensory scale*, relating the physical stimulus magnitude to the perceived magnitude. This relationship is typically characterized by Stevens' power law (Box 24.3, Classical Psychophysical Laws; Box 24.4, Psychophysics From A to Z), and the measure would be the constants that describe the mathematical relationship between the physical and perceived magnitude specific to the given modality.

Stimulus

A fundamental requirement for a psychophysical experiment is to be able to control something in the environment in a given modality and present it to an observer in some systematic fashion. This "something" is called the *stimulus* (pl. *stimuli*). Usually, stimuli are defined along some physical dimension that can be characterized using physical measurements such that they have a "ground truth" value, and stimuli are parametrized along this specific physical dimension. For example, we can present and modulate the radiance or the spectral content (i.e., the wavelength composition) of light using well-defined physical measurements and use these as stimuli to understand our perception of brightness and color. A key principle of stimulus design is *stimulus reduction* (Koenderink, 1999), that is, reducing the rather complex visual world into parametrizable components.

In practice, this control and parametrization of stimuli cannot be achieved using everyday objects but requires dedicated apparatus for it. Prior to the advent of personal computers, which allow for the relatively easy generation of perceptual stimuli with a good amount of user control, psychophysical experiments were generally performed with custom-made equipment tailored to fit the needs of the stimulus and investigation in question.

Generally, psychophysical experiments with their high demands on stimulus control are performed in laboratory suites in which other aspects that might interfere with the presentation of stimuli—such as room illumination or glare from windows that can interfere with the presentation of visual stimuli on a display—can be minimized. These conditions lend themselves to restrictive viewing conditions (Koenderink, 1999) to ensure that truly only one parameter,

BOX 24.2

Signal Detection Theory

Signal detection theory is the model underlying the perceptual decision-making process, that is, what drives an observer to report "seeing" a stimulus on a yes–no task. Perceptual mechanisms are inherently noisy, hence, the sigmoid nature of the psychometric function. Let's unpack that: The sigmoid shape of the psychometric function tells us that there are some stimulus intensities for which the observer detects somewhere between 0% and 100% of the stimuli presentations. For example, if an observer is asked to report whether they saw a flash of light at a certain stimulus intensity, they will report seeing the flash on only half of the occasions the flash was presented. This is due to the inherent noise in the visual system. Perhaps the observer was capable of seeing the flash on all of those instances but simply blinked or looked away and missed the flash. Or perhaps the observer was anticipating the flash and so reported seeing it when, in fact, nothing was presented. Signal detection theory provides a framework for dealing with the noisy perceptual signals that drive perceptual decisions and, thus, performance in psychophysical tasks.

We can model perceptual mechanisms as having some internal perceptual response that exists in the absence of any external stimulus of a particular modality; we call this the *internal noise distribution*. We model this noise as a Gaussian probability density function, with a mean, μ, and a standard deviation, σ. We can also model the internal perceptual response that exists in the presence of an external stimulus as a Gaussian probability density function with the same standard deviation as the noise but a higher σ and with a higher mean response μ_{s+n}. We call this the *signal-plus-noise distribution*.

These two distributions inevitably overlap. We can quantify the separation between them using the *sensitivity index*, d' (pronounced dee-prime), defined as

$$d' = \frac{(\mu_{Signal+Noise} - \mu_{Noise})}{\sigma}$$

The sensitivity index, d', is simply a standardized measure of our stimulus intensity: the separation between the signal-plus-noise and noise reported in terms of the standard deviation of the internal noise distributions. As the stimulus intensity increases, d' increases, and correspondingly so too does the observer's likelihood to report seeing a stimulus when it is shown. Thus, the signal detection theory model explains why the psychometric function has a sigmoid shape—it is simply the shape of the Gaussian cumulative density function.

One can see that the overlapping Gaussian model leads to a central issue in signal detection theory: Where does the observer set their criteria for detection, and how can we, the experimenter, tell? The arbitrary placement of criterion by the observer is known as *response bias*. On a yes–no task, one can use the *hit rate* (the proportion of correct detections on a trial where the stimulus is presented) and the *false alarm rate* (the proportion of detections on a trial where the stimulus is absent) to calculate d' and response bias, c, independently from each other as

$$d' = z(Hit\ rate) - z(False\ alarm\ rate)$$

$$c = \frac{z(Hit\ rate) - z(False\ alarm\ rate)}{2}$$

These equations (for derivations, see Green & Swets, 1974; Macmillan & Creelman, 1991, 2005) only hold if the *equal-variance assumption* holds: that is, if the variance of the signal-plus-noise distribution and noise distribution really can be modelled as the same, as we assumed in our signal detection theory model. To check whether the equal variance assumption holds, one can plot a *receiver operating characteristics* (ROC) *curve*, which plots hit rate against false alarm rate. When the equal variance assumption holds, ROC curves will be symmetrical. An asymmetrical ROC tells us the equal variance assumptions fails, and sensitivity cannot be easily disentangled from response bias in this case. To vary the hit rate and false alarm rate in practice, one can ask the observer to give a confidence rating alongside their yes–no response in a yes–no task, with each confidence level having its own hit rate and false alarm rate that can be plotted along the ROC curve. Alternatively, one could vary the payoffs for the observer, to encourage more liberal observers to become more conservative and vice versa. It is worth emphasizing that alternative force choice tasks are not susceptible to response bias by design and are, thus, often preferred to yes–no tasks, which require an additional response bias analysis as described above.

> **BOX 24.3**
>
> ## Classical Psychophysical Laws
>
> Weber's law expresses the relationship between background intensity (I) and the minimum intensity change that can be detected (the just-noticeable difference) (ΔI) mathematically as
>
> $$\Delta I / I = k$$
>
> where k is some constant dependent on the specific modality. Fechner's law expands on Weber's law by relating the sensation, φ, to the stimulus magnitude, S, through the following logarithmic relationship:
>
> $$\varphi = k \log(S)$$
>
> where again, the constant k is dependent on the modality. The mathematically savvy reader may notice that Weber's law is simply the derivative of Fechner's law. Thus the two laws are really one and the same and often referred to collectively as the *Weber–Fechner law*. The Weber–Fechner law is a key principle in psychophysics as it allows us to link the physical stimulus magnitude to perceptual sensation.
>
> At suprathreshold levels, Steven's power law is used instead to equate the magnitude of the perceived sensation, φ, to the magnitude of the physical stimuli, S, as such
>
> $$\varphi = kS^a$$
>
> where k and a are both constants dependent on the specific modality.

the one under investigation, of the physical world is changed between trials and across an experiment while minimizing possible behavioral confounders, such as head movement (controlled by a chin rest and bite bar) or eye movement (controlled by instructions and conjoint eye movement registration).

In visual psychophysics, we distinguish between *Newtonian* (free) viewing conditions and *Maxwellian* viewing conditions. In Maxwellian viewing conditions, stimuli are imaged in high-contrast directly onto the pupil of the observer, requiring special focusing optics. The majority of contemporary psychophysicists use Newtonian (free) viewing conditions with computer monitors to display visual stimuli and manipulate their properties.

Psychophysical data can be collected in museums (Martin, 2014), in extreme environments (Willmann et al., 2010), and during Guinness World Record attempts (Todor, 1975). Additionally, online experiments have recently opened new means for psychophysical data collection (Sauter et al., 2020), they but present problems for stimulus calibration and precise control. When presented online, visual stimuli are not calibrated in size, luminance, color, and timing and, therefore, may not yield high-quality results. Workarounds have been proposed to address some aspects of this, for example, using a common object such as a credit card for calibrating size and distance (Li et al., 2020) or using perceptual calibration techniques for display linearization (Xiao et al., 2011). Another promising way to deliver stimuli (including in remote experiments) may be using consumer-grade virtual reality (VR) sets (Scarfe & Glennerster, 2019).

A key task of the psychophysicist is to ensure that stimuli are calibrated. *Calibration* refers to the practice of ensuring that the physical dimensions one hopes to manipulate and control in a psychophysical experiment are indeed under full control. This is to ensure that aspects of psychophysical performance can be uniquely ascribed to the psychophysical observer and to rule out any confounding artifacts.

For computer-controlled monitors, this involves the measurement of the light emitted from the monitors using a spectroradiometer or colorimeter (Brainard et al., 2002) and using these physical measurements to inform which parameters need to be used to produce a specific stimulus of known characteristics. Spatial and temporal characterization is another necessary step of monitory calibration. The exact nature of calibration depends on the modality. For instance, in visual psychophysics, calibration is focused on characterizing the spectral, spatial, and temporal content of the light and often performed using specialized physical equipment to measure the physical properties of the light. In auditory psychophysics, however, calibration is often done perceptually: using experienced observers to match the perceived loudness of two sounds that differ in a different physical attribute of interest, such as pitch. Developing confidence in the physical characteristics of the stimulus, whether through

BOX 24.4

Psychophysics From A to Z

Alternative forced choice (AFC). A bias-free task where the observers are presented with more than two intervals. One of the intervals includes a stimulus, and the observer must respond in which interval the stimulus was presented. The expression *2AFC*, in which stimulus is presented in one of two intervals, is commonly used.

Absolute threshold. Minimum level of stimulus intensity required for detection, for example, the minimum number of photons required for seeing or the minimum amplitude of an auditory stimulus required for hearing.

Adaptation. A neural process to alter the sensitivity of a sensory system after exposure to a certain physical stimulus.

Contrast. The ratio between lowest and highest stimulus magnitude along a specific physical dimension. For example, lightness contrast is often expressed as a ratio between the darkest and brightest light levels.

Criterion (SDT). An observer's internal threshold of whether or not to respond "yes" on a given trial. This is often placed by the observer unconsciously and may change as they first start out on a new task before settling.

d' (SDT). In SDT the separation between the signal-plus-noise and noise distributions reported in terms of the standard deviation of the internal noise distribution $d' = \mu s + n - \mu n/\sigma$.

Category scaling. A method to rate a suprathreshold stimulus by choosing one of the fixed number of categories on which the stimulus falls.

Difference scaling. A method to rate the perceptual difference of stimulus pairs. In a difference scaling task, participants are presented a pair of stimulus pairs and asked to select which pair has a larger perceptual difference.

Discrimination threshold. Minimum difference in intensity between two stimuli along a given physical dimension required for the observer to be able to identify the two stimuli as different from one another, for example, the minimum number of photons required for one light to be perceived as brighter than a second light.

Equal-variance assumption (SDT). Assumption that noise and noise + signal are distributed as normal distributions with equal variance.

False alarm rate (SDT). On a catch trial when the stimulus is not presented, but the observer responds that they detected the stimulus, the result is a false alarm. The false alarm rate is the proportion of false alarms in the total number of catch trials.

Hit rate (SDT). In a trial when the stimulus is presented and the observer responds correctly, it is referred to as a *hit*. The hit rate is the proportion of hits among the total number of trials in which the stimulus was presented.

Interval judgements. A process to decide the magnitude of difference of a pair of stimuli.

Just noticeable difference (JND). Minimum physical difference of a pair of stimuli that can be perceptually discriminated.

Magnitude estimation. Method to quantify the perceptual strengths of a physical stimulus by directly asking participants to assign numerical estimate to the stimulus.

Maximum likelihood conjoint measurement (MLCM). A suprathreshold probabilistic measurement to estimate perceptual scale that explains how two (or more) dimensions of physical stimuli interact and influence a perceptual judgement. Each trial typically consists of a presentation of a pair of stimulus, and participants are asked to make a comparative judgement (e.g., which is heavier) for all possible stimulus pairs multiple times.

Maximum likelihood different scaling (MLDS). A suprathreshold probabilistic measurement to estimate a perceptual scale along a continuous physical dimension based on perceptual judgements regarding difference.

Measure. Process to quantify the magnitude of a physical or perceptual quantity.

Method. Logistic framework to collect data systematically during an experiment.

Observer. Person who participates in an experiment and provides subjective responses.

Ordinal judgements. A process to decide the order of two stimuli according to some dimension. In psychophysics, this would be perceptual strength.

Ordinal perceptual scale. A scale to describe the ranking of a set of stimulus that vary in physical strengths.

Pairwise comparisons. Method to estimate subjective difference or rank among a set of physical stimuli based on paired comparison. Participants are normally asked to make a comparative judgement for every possible pair of stimuli.

Point of subjective equality (PSE). When discriminating a comparison stimulus from a standard stimulus, the stimulus magnitude of the comparison stimulus that is judged to be perceptually equal to that of the standard stimulus.

Psychometric function. Describes the relationship between the stimulus strength and the probability of the observer's ability to detect or discriminate the stimulus.

Rank order. An order across more than two stimuli along a given dimension.

Response bias. The variation in criterion settings between observers.

Receiver operating characteristics (ROC) **curve** (SDT). A plot of hit rate against false alarm rate. An ROC curve can be used to check the equal variance assumption: A symmetrical ROC curve tells us the equal variance assumption holds while an asymmetric ROC curve tells us the equal variance assumption has been violated.

(continues)

> **BOX 24.4**
>
> **Psychophysics From A to Z** (*Continued*)
>
> **Scaling**. A measurement to develop a ruler that describes a mapping between physical stimuli along a continuous physical dimension and associated subjective sensation or perception.
> **Scaling function**. A mathematical function to describe a relationship between physical strengths of a stimulus and corresponding perceptual responses.
> **Sensitivity**. The inverse of the threshold (1/threshold).
> **Signal detection theory** (SDT). A framework for uncovering thresholds in a system with inherent internal noise and dealing with confounds such as response bias.
> **Stimulus**. A physical phenomenon that elicits a neural, sensory, or perceptual response (e.g., sound, light).
> **Stimulus magnitude**. A physical strength of an experimental stimulus. Perceptual output is normally measured over a range of stimulus magnitude.
> **Stimulus reduction**. A process to compress the features of complex stimuli, such as ones observed in the real world, into a set of experimentally tractable parameters.
> **Suprathreshold**. Stimulus that is comfortably above threshold, that is, easily distinguishable.
> **Task**. An action or a judgement that a participant is asked to make in a single experimental trial.
> **Yes–no task**. Task in which the observer responds "yes" or "no" to indicate whether they observed the stimulus or an aspect of it presented in a given trial.
>
> *Note.* Specific concepts related to the signal detection theory framework are marked by (SDT) in parentheses.

physical or perceptual calibration, is a key and nontrivial aspect of psychophysical stimulus design and development.

Just as with the measure, we often distinguish between stimuli at threshold and suprathreshold stimuli. Threshold stimuli are those that are supposed to be difficult to detect and distinguish. Suprathreshold stimuli are those that are above a given psychophysical threshold.

Observer

If the goal of psychophysics is to relate external phenomenon to perceptual experiences, then in addition to our calibrated, well-defined physical stimulus, we clearly also need an observer to sense the stimulus and report their perceptual experience. The observer is, thus, the participant in the psychophysical experiment, whose performance and perception are studied (in contrast with the "experimenter" who runs the experiment). In this chapter, we focus on psychophysics when the observer is human, but, in principle, all organisms with overt behavior—or indeed, computational algorithms—can be psychophysical observers.

Just as one needs to consider the characteristics of their stimuli, one must also consider the characteristics of their observer. For instance, in visual psychophysics, the experimenter needs to know if their observers have normal visual acuity and typically whether or not they have a color vision deficiency. Comparing results in color matching tasks between trichromats and dichromats without knowing the observer's color deficiency status would lead to confusing results. Additionally, the experimenter can often choose to manipulate the state of the observer for their experimental advantage.

A commonly used example of such observer state manipulation is adaptation, and a psychophysical experiment often begins with an adaptation procedure. The precise nature of this procedure depends on the research question studied. In studies of human vision, a common procedure is dark adaptation. During dark adaptation, an observer is in the dark, with no light available. The idea behind dark adaptation is to sensitize the rods, the retinal photoreceptors sensitive to dim light (in contrast to the cones, which are active in daylight) and, thereby, remove any lingering "photic history" effects due to the slow recovery of rods. Adaptation to the background, that is, presentation of a neutral stimulus in the absence of a task-related stimulus, is often performed to ensure that stimuli are indeed well-defined in contrast.

Generally, a distinction is made between naïve and trained observers. The term *naïve* here is used in its technical sense, as in not knowing the purpose of an experiment or the hypotheses it tests. In practice, every psychophysical experimenter is typically an observer in their own experiment at least once, to test it and make sure it runs smoothly. In psychophysics, self-testing and self-experimentation has a long history, with many authors describing themselves as "experienced psychophysical observers" and reporting their own data in experiments. This is not least because many psychophysical experiments are very demanding and time-consuming (and frankly, not often the most exciting way to spend a few hours of your day).

In threshold psychophysics, experienced observers may be preferred to naïve observers, as threshold psychophysics aim to test the limits of sensation. There is typically, as with any psychological experiment, an initial period in which performance on psychophysics tasks improves before reaching peak performance, that is, the threshold level. Experienced observers may require less time to reach such a peak performance than naïve observers. Participants who have never participated in a psychophysical experiment (or quite often, every participant) may benefit from a set of practice trials at the start of the experiment, which simulates the task without leading to archival data.

Unlike most psychological experiments, psychophysical experiments have typically relied on collecting large volumes of data from a very small number of observers. The use of study designs with small samples has a long history and a prominent place in current practice (Smith & Little, 2018). This is often supported by the desire to use experienced observers who require minimal instruction and no further external motivation, as discussed above. A different paradigm is the use of a large number of observers with fewer trials collected per participant. While these are often impractical or hard-to-resource in the laboratory, they provide valuable insights into individual differences (Mollon et al., 2017).

The use of online experiments and online recruitment platforms such as Prolific or Pavlovia has facilitated accessing larger numbers of observers with fewer resources (time spent with and recruiting participants, participant payments for in-laboratory visits). It is, however, imperative to consider the data ethics surrounding the use of these platforms, which may sometimes be labor markets rather than participant pools (Fort et al., 2011; Moss et al., 2020).

Task

Just as the visual world is reduced into parametrizable and controllable dimensions, visual behavior is also reduced in a psychophysical experiment. Rather than allowing "natural" and uncontrollable behavioral responses to visual stimuli, in a psychophysical experiment, behavior is subject to a specific task that the participant performs. Broadly speaking, a task is any type of behavior that the observer is asked to perform in response to a certain stimulus presentation protocol. There are many different psychophysical tasks, and which to choose is often dictated by the research question asked. As with stimuli and measure, the appropriate task also often depends on whether the experiment is at threshold or suprathreshold levels.

A classic task is a *yes–no* task in which the stimulus is either presented or not on a given trial, and the participant is asked to indicate (e.g., using a button-press) whether or not they sensed the stimulus in that trial. Yes–no tasks are commonly used in high-threshold theory psychological experiments but are susceptible to response bias in low-threshold theory psychophysical experiments (Box 24.2. Signal Detection Theory). To control for response bias in yes–no tasks, experimenters often collect confidence ratings alongside the observer's response or often avoid such tasks altogether in preference for a bias-free task—an *alternative forced-choice* (AFC) *task*.

In AFC tasks, the observer is presented with multiple spatial locations simultaneously or multiple temporal intervals successively, one of locations or intervals will always contain the stimulus while the others do not, and the observer must respond in which location or interval the stimulus was present. The most common AFC tasks are *two-alternative forced-choice tasks* (2AFC) where two intervals are presented in either distinct spatial locations or successively in time during a single trial, and only one of these intervals contains the stimulus. As long as the stimulus presentation interval is randomized, AFC tasks are inherently free from response bias.

AFC tasks are commonly used for threshold measures. For instance, one might present a Gabor stimulus in one interval and not the other when measuring contrast sensitivity thresholds. AFC tasks are also a popular choice for suprathreshold measurements, where they are often referred to as *pairwise comparison tasks*. In a classic pairwise comparison task, observers are shown stimuli in pairs and asked to rate which stimulus is say brighter, more translucent, or louder. Such judgements are called *ordinal judgements* as the observer's task is to respond with which order these stimuli fall in on the perceptual scale. Ordinal judgements may also be made in *rank order* tasks, where the observer is shown more than two stimuli at once and asked to rank them along the perceptual dimension.

Recently, AFC *difference scaling* tasks have been used instead of classical pairwise comparisons, where the observer is presented with two pairs of stimuli and asked which of the two pairs has the biggest perceptual difference (Maloney & Yang, 2003). Such *interval judgements* allow the experimenter to extract not only the *ordinal perceptual scale* but a full perceptual *difference scale*.

Suprathreshold stimuli can also be characterized using *category scaling*, one of the oldest psychophysical tasks. Observers are asked to assign stimuli, of a known physical stimulus magnitude, to one of a discrete and finite number of categories. For example, one may be asked to assign chili peppers (with known varying degrees of capsaicin) into one of five categories, with 1 being the least spicy, and 5 the spiciest. Category scaling is limited in that only a set number of categories are used to quantify the perceptual experience, which may not accurately capture the full range of the perceptual experience. For instance, in the chili pepper example, there may be a wide range of spice levels within the least spicy group, which may be perceptually distinct: information that is lost through category scaling.

Magnitude estimation tasks can be used instead of category scaling, where the observer is asked to assign any number to quantify the stimulus, thus opening up the range of possible numerical values the observer can assign to a particular physical stimulus. For example, the experimenter may give the participant a slight electric shock and ask them to put a number to the pain induced by the shock. The experimenter often provides an arbitrary reference value, for example, deliver a shock of 10V and tell the participant that they have been given a shock of level 5. When delivering a shock of 20V, the participant will then freely assign a number to that shock level, in reference to the level 5 shock they received before. Different participants will give different numbers for different levels. For example, one participant may rate the 20V shock a 5.5, while another may rate it a 7, and a third a 20. While the numerical scales assigned differs between participants, scale values are usually repeatable and robust within a participant (there are some stimuli, however, where participants always struggle to ascribe reliably meaningful magnitude values).

Method

While we refer to the *task* as what happens on a single experimental trial, we call the *method* the way that the entire psychophysical experiment is organized and how stimulus levels are chosen and how this choice might depend on previous decisions made by the participant. We distinguish between "adaptive" and "nonadaptive" or "fixed" procedures. Broadly speaking, in adaptive methods, namely, the method of adjustment or staircases, stimulus levels on a given trial are informed by previous decisions. In nonadaptive procedures, namely, the method of constant stimuli or the method of limits, a fixed set of stimuli or stimulus comparisons are shown to the participant.

Method of constant stimuli. In the method of constant stimuli, stimuli at different magnitudes are presented in randomized order, and the participant is asked to perform the task, such as a 2AFC task detecting a sound in one of two intervals presented successively on each presentation interval. The magnitude of the stimulus should range between the level at which the participant can never detect the stimulus and the level at which participants can easily detect (i.e., a 100% detection rate), with stimuli ideally being spread to induce even detection rates between these extremes. This method is a classic and reliable psychophysical method. One challenge with the method of constant stimuli is knowing a priori the appropriate range of stimulus magnitudes to set. Experiments run using the method of constant stimuli also tend to be time-consuming.

Method of limits. In the method of limits, the stimulus magnitude is increased or decreased on subsequent trials until a threshold level is reached. Two stimulus presentation series are typically used: an ascending series in which the starting stimulus magnitude is way below threshold and the stimulus magnitude is increased over subsequent trials until threshold is reached, and a descending series where the starting stimulus magnitude is way above threshold and decreased over subsequent presentations until threshold level is reached. Typically, participants complete both series multiple times, and the threshold is taken as the average of the threshold estimate obtained in each series.

The method of limits tends to be quite quick for data collection, but there are two types of error associated with this method. First, because participants are exposed to similar stimuli many times, they could get used to stimuli (error of habituation). Second, because stimuli intensity gradually changes, some participants might predict when the stimuli will become visible even when they do not see the stimuli (response bias). Careful instruction partially helps suppression of these two sources of errors, though the method of limits is often regarded as being a less accurate measure of thresholds than other methods.

Method of adjustment. The method of adjustment gives participants control of the magnitude of stimulus. For example, when measuring absolute thresholds, participants are asked to change the stimulus intensity until they can just detect the stimulus. Trials end when a participant makes a satisfactory match. The initial point of stimulus magnitude is randomized to minimize the error of habituation.

This conceptually simple method is efficient and has the advantage that it requires participants to engage actively in the experiment. It can also often be quicker than requiring the participant to view multiple stimulus magnitudes that are above or below threshold (though this depends on the individual participant; for the more hesitant observers, a time limit may be introduced to encourage them to not spend too long making a match).

Staircase method. The staircase method is an adaptive variation of the method of limits. Over subsequent trials, the stimulus magnitude is updated according to participants' response in a previous trial. In the simple-up down staircase, the stimulus magnitude in the current trial increases by a predefined step size if the participant makes a mistake in the previous trial, and the magnitude decreases when the participant makes a correct response. This procedure continues until the predefined number of reversals (i.e., transition from incremental stream to decremental stream or vice versa) are recorded. Threshold estimates are obtained by averaging the stimulus magnitude across a certain number of reversals (for instance, if the staircase is allowed to reverse 12 times, the last four reversals may be averaged to find the threshold).

Adaptive versions of the staircase method have offered improvements on the classic staircase design. In adaptive staircases, the step size can change over trials, allowing the staircase to settle (or converge) quicker, improving efficiency (Kontsevich & Tyler, 1999; Watson & Pelli, 1983). The next stimulus magnitude presentation is estimated from adaptive staircases based on the history of participants' responses during the experiment and aims to present a stimulus magnitude around the estimated threshold that supports the efficient convergence of the staircase. The idea behind this approach is to make use of the history of observer responses containing rich amounts of information about participants' sensitivity.

Analysis

The final stage in a psychophysical experiment is the analysis. To extract the relevant measure of observer perceptual performance to a specific physical stimulus on a given task and experimental method, one needs to apply the appropriate analysis. The choice of stimulus, task, and method is intimately linked to the choice of analytic procedure applied to psychophysical data. Importantly, different psychophysical experimental designs (to extract different measures) require different analyses. Kingdom and Prins (2016) reviewed the major classes of psychophysical experiments and provide a toolbox to analyze psychophysical data in MATLAB, and Knoblauch and Maloney (2012) provided a textbook and toolbox on how to analyze psychophysical data in R. Here, we only touch upon a few basic, theoretical analysis concepts. Just as we distinguish between threshold and suprathreshold measures and stimuli, so do analysis techniques distinguish between extracting threshold and suprathreshold measures.

In threshold experiments, the fundamental representation of psychophysical data in detection and discrimination is the *psychometric function*. The psychometric function relates the underlying stimulus dimension that is changed in a psychophysical experiment—for example, brightness of a light or the contrast of stimulus—to the performance of the psychophysical observer (typically plotted as the proportion of correct detections or discriminations). Sensory mechanisms are inherently noisy: meaning that the same level of the physical stimulus may sometimes induce a perceptual response and sometimes may not. Due to this inherent internal noise, the psychometric function has a sigmoid shape, rather than a simple step-function shape that it would take if the observer's sensory system were not subject to internal noise (see Box 24.2. Signal Detection Theory). We do not detail methods for fitting a psychometric function to psychophysical data here but refer the reader to the MATLAB and R toolboxes developed and published by Prins and Kingdom (2018) and Knoblauch and Maloney (2012), respectively, for tools with which to do this.

Psychometric functions are the fundamental analysis method in threshold experiments, yet the sigmoid shape of the psychometric function poses an obvious problem for measuring thresholds—what point on the psychometric function does one take as the threshold? By convention, thresholds are taken as the 50% correct level, though this is an arbitrary choice made by the experimenter.

Further, when dealing with threshold experiment analysis, one must consider how the observer sets their internal threshold for detection and discrimination. In the Task section, we described the two types of tasks for threshold experiments: yes–no tasks and alternative-forced choice tasks. In a yes–no task, the observer must (typically unconsciously) decide a certain level of internal sensory system response to ascribe to detection or discrimination, such that anytime the observer experiences an internal response greater than that level they respond that they can detect or discriminate the stimulus, and any response below that threshold they respond seeing nothing. Different observers will have different internal thresholds for responding yes or no, known as *response bias*. Thus, if a yes–no task is used, response bias must be separated from sensitivity during analysis. Signal detection theory provides a framework for modeling such inherently noisy sensory mechanisms and untangling thresholds from response bias (see Box 24.2. Signal Detection Theory). By design, alternative-forced choice tasks are criterion bias–free, and, thus, response bias does not need to be untangled during analysis. There may still be, for example, attentional biases, but these are compensated for by randomizing the stimulus presentation interval.

When adaptive methods are applied, psychometric functions do not necessarily need to be used for threshold analysis. For example, in experiments that use staircases, one may simply take the threshold to be the average of the last few reversal points. In method of adjustment experiments, one typically just takes the threshold to be the point set by the observer: the observer typically completes the experiment at least twice, once starting above threshold and once below such that the threshold is taken as the average of the two settings made when approaching the threshold from opposing directions.

For suprathreshold measures, the appropriate analysis method is usually determined based on a combination of the task and the stimulus. Again, different tasks require different analysis methods, and we do not detail individual analysis techniques here but outline the basic principles. Magnitude estimation tasks and category scaling are typically analyzed by fitting a *scaling function,* typically in the form of Steven's power law, to the relationship between the physical stimulus value and the assigned perceptual magnitude value.

In suprathreshold AFC pairwise comparison tasks, the experimenter uses *difference scaling* to extract the difference measure of interest. A multitude of difference scaling approaches exist, and the appropriate difference scaling analysis to use depends on both the physical properties of the stimulus and the type of pairwise comparison task. Classically, for ordinal judgements, Thurstonian scaling (using Thurstone's law of comparative judgement) was applied for difference scaling analysis. Thurstonian scaling is useful in that it can be used for complex stimuli whose physical characteristics are multidimensional and difficult to parameterize, such as judgements on the attractiveness of a painting. Thurstonian scaling can also be used to analyze interval (difference) judgements, though stochastic methods developed specifically for interval judgements—namely *maximum likelihood difference scaling* (MLDS) (Maloney & Yang, 2003), extending similar but nonstochastic methods first developed by Schneider et al. (1974) and Schneider (1980)—are better suited for deriving suprathreshold difference scales.

Further, in suprathreshold tasks where two or more physical dimensions contribute to a single perceptual dimension, for example, scattering and absorption properties of a material both affect the perception of translucency (Chadwick et al., 2018); *maximum likelihood conjoint measurement* (MLCM) can be applied to pairwise comparison judgements to quantify the interaction between the multiple physical continua to the perceptual scale (Ho et al., 2008; Knoblauch & Maloney, 2012, Chapter 8).

In both threshold and suprathreshold experiments, reaction time measurements can also be fed into the analysis of the psychophysical data. Reaction times contain information about how easy or difficult the observer found a particular detection or comparison, with reaction times being quicker when a stimulus is much above threshold, and, thus, the detection or decision is easier to make and slower when closer to threshold. One of the advantages of using reaction times is that they can be applied to almost any stimulus (including tasks probing other neural mechanisms such as working memory or attention). Reaction time analysis depends on the specific experimental design and is not further detailed here.

FRONTIERS OF PSYCHOPHYSICS

Psychophysics has a long past, and it is here to stay—not least because it is one of the only ways to learn about how we (and other organisms) sense, perceive, and make sense of the world around us. Importantly, the way we do psychophysics is, in many cases strongly constrained by the technology that is available to display stimuli, structure the task and procedure, and analyze data. As a consequence, the use of psychophysical methods is far from stagnant and indeed is a field with a high drive for innovation.

In the following sections, we highlight some developments at the frontiers of psychophysics. Our examples are from the fields of vision. We identify a series of "sites of innovation" that are not specific to the visual modality, namely, (a) more precise stimulus control; (b) more realistic, naturalistic, and immersive stimuli; (c) development of input-computable models; and (d) developments towards more open psychophysics (in the "open scholarship" sense).

More Precise Stimulus Control

Historically, the introduction of computer equipment allowing for the presentation of near-arbitrary stimuli revolutionized the ability to run psychophysical experiments. In the visual domain, the computer display has become a key piece of psychophysical apparatus, allowing for the display of arbitrary stimulus patterns and subsequent collection of responses in an integrated fashion.

We noted earlier that we could use RGB monitors to display a wide range of colors visible to humans because human vision is trichromatic. While conventional three-primary-color monitors only allow for the precise production of the signals of three photoreceptor classes, matched to the number of cone classes in the retina, we now know that in addition to the low-light sensitive rods, there is another class of photoreceptors in the human retina. The intrinsically photosensitive retinal ganglion cells (ipRGCs), which are known to be involved in driving nonvisual responses to light, such as circadian rhythms, sleep–wake control, mood, pupil size, and alertness, express the short-wavelength-sensitive photopigment melanopsin and encode environmental light intensity independent of the cones and rods (but also receive synaptic input from cones and rods) (Do, 2019; Lucas et al., 2014; Provencio et al., 2000; Spitschan, 2019). Conventional three-primary color displays do not allow for the reproduction and control of rod and ipRGC signals, requiring at least five photoreceptor classes (Hexley et al., 2021). Generating stimuli that stimulate only one photoreceptor class (while producing no signal in another set of classes) is done using the method of silent substitution (Estévez & Spekreijse, 1982; Spitschan & Woelders, 2018). In practice, this often requires the development of custom stimulation systems or displays (Bayer et al., 2015; Cao et al., 2015; Hexley et al., 2020; Pokorny et al., 2004).

Over the past 30 years, technology has been developed and become available to image the retina at high resolution, resolving single photoreceptors at the cellular level (Roorda & Williams, 1999). Referred to as "adaptive optics," these techniques allow us to compensate for the optical imperfections of the eye that would otherwise render the imaging of the cones and rods at single-cell resolution impossible. More recently, adaptive optics retinal imaging has been combined with psychophysical techniques to deliver stimuli to single photoreceptors (Harmening & Sincich, 2019). This allows for examination of the sensitivity of single cones (Bruce et al., 2015), spatial integration (Schmidt et al., 2018), and their contributions to the perception of color (Harmening et al., 2014; Tuten et al., 2017).

More Realistic, Naturalistic, and Immersive Stimuli

The increase in computing power with time has made realistic rendering of visual stimuli, along with the ability to parametrize them, widely accessible. Photorealistic rendering engines allow for the simulation of optical interactions between and within objects under complex illumination, producing compelling images that can be used in psychophysical experiments. In the visual domain, the use of photorealistic stimuli that can be manipulated and parametrized is key to understanding aspects of high-level perception. There are many examples where computer graphics have been used to provide insight into our perception of materials (e.g., translucency, Fleming & Bülthoff, 2005). While the use of naturalistic stimuli allows for generating data that are more ecologically valid, their use may limit the ability to build models "from parts" that can be synthetically modulated (Rust & Movshon, 2005). Importantly, naturalistic stimuli require means to capture naturally occurring scenes in a calibrated fashion (see Morimoto et al., 2019, for an approach for capturing hyperspectral light fields).

Parallel and in lockstep with the development of more advanced computer graphics techniques, virtual reality (VR) and augmented reality (AR) techniques now enable the presentation of stimuli in a more realistic fashion. Head-mounted VR displays have been on the consumer market for a while and have proven to be an invaluable tool for research. Indeed, VR is one area in which psychophysical methods indeed help with the development of novel displays (Scarfe & Glennerster, 2019). Similarly, AR allows for the mixing of on-the-fly parametric stimulus control with concurrent viewing of the natural world (Hassani & Murdoch, 2019; Murdoch, 2020).

Towards Input-Computable Models

A core component of psychophysics is modeling human data using various classes of psychophysical models of varying structure and nature. These models go well beyond simply analyzing the data but seek to provide evidence for the computations that the brain performs in solving a specific psychophysical task to gain mechanistic understanding (Pugh & Andersen, 2008). In vision, modeling psychophysical data has a long history. A contemporary approach to modeling of psychophysical data is the development of image-computable models. Image-computable models require an input image—such as a stimulus seen by the visual system—and produce an output. This is encapsulated in the phrase "pixels in, estimates out" (Burge, 202, p. 493). For low-level vision, the ISETBio model framework (Cottaris et al., 2019) enables the modeling of retinal signals based on spectral radiance images. Finally, artificial neural network models can be used to constrain psychophysical models (Saxe et al., 2021).

Open Psychophysics

The use of open-source software in psychophysics has a long history, with some core software to run psychophysical experiments, such as the Psychophysics Toolbox (Brainard, 1997; Pelli, 1997) and PsychoPy (J. Peirce et al., 2019; J. W. Peirce, 2007, 2009), being available as an open-source tool from the start. More recently, principles of open scholarship have been adopted in psychology, a field which has been said to be in a "reproducibility crisis." As many journals and funders now require data to be open and available, the sharing of psychophysical data will also become more common, thereby facilitating meta-analytic approaches to synthesize evidence (see Baker et al., 2018, for an example).

CONCLUSION

Psychophysics has a large history, and psychophysical measurements continue to be an integral part of sensory and perception science. Recent developments in stimulus control and how experiments are run have provided innovative impulses in the study of how we see and perceive the world around us.

References

Baker, D. H., Lygo, F. A., Meese, T. S., & Georgeson, M. A. (2018). Binocular summation revisited: Beyond √2. *Psychological Bulletin*, 144(11), 1186–1199. https://doi.org/10.1037/bul0000163

Bayer, F. S., Paulun, V. C., Weiss, D., & Gegenfurtner, K. R. (2015). A tetrachromatic display for the spatiotemporal control of rod and cone stimulation. *Journal of Vision*, 15(11), 15. https://doi.org/10.1167/15.11.15

Brainard, D. H. (1997). The psychophysics toolbox. *Spatial Vision*, 10(4), 433–436. https://doi.org/10.1163/156856897X00357

Brainard, D. H., Pelli, D., & Robson, T. (2002). Display characterization. In J. Hornak (Ed.), *Encyclopedia of imaging science and technology* (pp. 172–188). Wiley. https://doi.org/10.1002/0471443395.img011

Bruce, K. S., Harmening, W. M., Langston, B. R., Tuten, W. S., Roorda, A., & Sincich, L. C. (2015). Normal perceptual sensitivity arising from weakly reflective cone photoreceptors. *Investigative Ophthalmology & Visual Science*, 56(8), 4431–4438. https://doi.org/10.1167/iovs.15-16547

Burge, J. (2020). Image-computable ideal observers for tasks with natural stimuli. *Annual Review of Vision Science*, 6(1), 491–517. https://doi.org/10.1146/annurev-vision-030320-041134

Cao, D., Nicandro, N., & Barrionuevo, P. A. (2015). A five-primary photostimulator suitable for studying intrinsically photosensitive retinal ganglion cell functions in humans. *Journal of Vision*, 15(1), 27. https://doi.org/10.1167/15.1.27

Chadwick, A. C., Cox, G., Smithson, H. E., & Kentridge, R. W. (2018). Beyond scattering and absorption: Perceptual unmixing of translucent liquids. *Journal of Vision*, 18(11), 18. https://doi.org/10.1167/18.11.18

Cottaris, N. P., Jiang, H., Ding, X., Wandell, B. A., & Brainard, D. H. (2019). A computational-observer model of spatial contrast sensitivity: Effects of wave-front-based optics, cone-mosaic structure, and inference engine. *Journal of Vision*, 19(4), 8. https://doi.org/10.1167/19.4.8

Do, M. T. H. (2019). Melanopsin and the Intrinsically Photosensitive Retinal Ganglion Cells: Biophysics to Behavior. *Neuron*, 104(2), 205–226. https://doi.org/10.1016/j.neuron.2019.07.016

Estévez, O., & Spekreijse, H. (1982). The "silent substitution" method in visual research. *Vision Research*, 22(6), 681–691. https://doi.org/10.1016/0042-6989(82)90104-3

Fleming, R. W., & Bülthoff, H. H. (2005). Low-Level Image Cues in the Perception of Translucent Materials. *ACM Transactions on Applied Perception*, 2(3), 346–382. https://doi.org/10.1145/1077399.1077409

Fort, K., Adda, G., & Cohen, K. B. (2011). Amazon Mechanical Turk: Gold mine or coal mine? *Computational Linguistics*, 37(2), 413–420. https://doi.org/10.1162/COLI_a_00057

Frisby, J. P. (1980). *Seeing: Illusion, brain, and mind*. Oxford University Press.

Gescheider, G. A. (1997). *Psychophysics: The fundamentals* (3rd ed.). L. Erlbaum Associates.

Green, D. M., & Swets, J. A. (1974). *Signal detection theory and psychophysics*. R. E. Krieger Pub. Co.

Harmening, W. M., & Sincich, L. C. (2019). Adaptive optics for photoreceptor-targeted psychophysics. In J. Bille (Ed.), *High-resolution imaging in microscopy and ophthalmology* (pp. 359–375). Springer. https://doi.org/10.1007/978-3-030-16638-0_17

Harmening, W. M., Tuten, W. S., Roorda, A., & Sincich, L. C. (2014). Mapping the perceptual grain of the human retina. *The Journal of Neuroscience*, 34(16), 5667–5677. https://doi.org/10.1523/JNEUROSCI.5191-13.2014

Hassani, N., & Murdoch, M. J. (2019). Investigating color appearance in optical see-through augmented reality. *Color Research and Application*, 44(4), 492–507. https://doi.org/10.1002/col.22380

Hexley, A. C., Morimoto, T., Smithson, H. E., & Spitschan, M. (2021). Beyond colour gamuts: Novel metrics for the reproduction of photoreceptor signals. *bioRxiv*. Advance online publication. https://doi.org/10.1101/2021.02.27.433203

Hexley, A. C., Yöntem, A. O., Spitschan, M., Smithson, H. E., & Mantiuk, R. (2020). Demonstrating a multi-primary high dynamic range display system for vision experiments. *Journal of the Optical Society of America. A, Optics, Image Science, and Vision*, 37(4), A271–A284. https://doi.org/10.1364/JOSAA.384022

Ho, Y. X., Landy, M. S., & Maloney, L. T. (2008). Conjoint measurement of gloss and surface texture. *Psychological Science*, 19(2), 196–204. https://doi.org/10.1111/j.1467-9280.2008.02067.x

Johnson, C. A. (2013). Psychophysical factors that have been applied to clinical perimetry. *Vision Research*, 90, 25–31. https://doi.org/10.1016/j.visres.2013.07.005

Kingdom, F. A. A., & Prins, N. (2016). *Psychophysics: A practical introduction* (2nd ed.). Elsevier/Academic Press.

Knoblauch, K., & Maloney, L. T. (2012). *Modeling psychophysical data in R*. Springer. https://doi.org/10.1007/978-1-4614-4475-6

Koenderink, J. J. (1999). Virtual psychophysics. *Perception*, 28(6), 669–674. https://doi.org/10.1068/p2806ed

Kontsevich, L. L., & Tyler, C. W. (1999). Bayesian adaptive estimation of psychometric slope and threshold. *Vision Research*, 39(16), 2729–2737. https://doi.org/10.1016/S0042-6989(98)00285-5

Krauskopf, J., Williams, D. R., & Heeley, D. W. (1982). Cardinal directions of color space. *Vision Research*, 22(9), 1123–1131. https://doi.org/10.1016/0042-6989(82)90077-3

Li, Q., Joo, S. J., Yeatman, J. D., & Reinecke, K. (2020). Controlling for participants' viewing distance in large-scale, psychophysical online experiments using a virtual chinrest. *Scientific Reports*, 10(1), 904. https://doi.org/10.1038/s41598-019-57204-1

Lucas, R. J., Peirson, S. N., Berson, D. M., Brown, T. M., Cooper, H. M., Czeisler, C. A., Figueiro, M. G., Gamlin, P. D., Lockley, S. W., O'Hagan, J. B., Price, L. L., Provencio, I., Skene, D. J., & Brainard, G. C. (2014). Measuring and using light in the melanopsin age. *Trends in Neurosciences*, 37(1), 1–9. https://doi.org/10.1016/j.tins.2013.10.004

Macmillan, N. A., & Creelman, C. D. (1991). *Detection theory: A user's guide*. Cambridge University Press.

Macmillan, N. A., & Creelman, C. D. (2005). *Detection theory: A user's guide* (2nd ed.). Lawrence Erlbaum Associates.

Maloney, L. T., & Yang, J. N. (2003). Maximum likelihood difference scaling. *Journal of Vision*, 3(8), 573–585. https://doi.org/10.1167/3.8.5

Martin, C. (2014). Making colour in the mind. *Lancet Neurology*, 13(10), 975. https://doi.org/10.1016/S1474-4422(14)70147-4

Mollon, J. D., Bosten, J. M., Peterzell, D. H., & Webster, M. A. (2017). Individual differences in visual science: What can be learned and what is good experimental practice? *Vision Research*, 141, 4–15. https://doi.org/10.1016/j.visres.2017.11.001

Morgan, M. J., Melmoth, D., & Solomon, J. A. (2013). Linking hypotheses underlying Class A and Class B methods. *Visual Neuroscience*, 30(5-6), 197–206. https://doi.org/10.1017/S095252381300045X

Morimoto, T., Kishigami, S., Linhares, J. M. M., Nascimento, S. M. C., & Smithson, H. E. (2019). Hyperspectral environmental illumination maps: Characterizing directional spectral variation in natural environments. *Optics Express*, *27*(22), 32277–32293. https://doi.org/10.1364/OE.27.032277

Moss, A. J., Rosenzweig, C., Robinson, J., & Litman, L. (2020). *Is it ethical to use mechanical Turk for behavioral research?* Relevant data from a representative survey of MTurk participants and wages. PsyArXiv Preprints. https://doi.org/10.31234/osf.io/jbc9d

Murdoch, M. J. (2020). Brightness matching in optical see-through augmented reality. *Journal of the Optical Society of America. A, Optics, Image Science, and Vision*, *37*(12), 1927–1936. https://doi.org/10.1364/JOSAA.398931

Peirce, J., Gray, J. R., Simpson, S., MacAskill, M., Höchenberger, R., Sogo, H., Kastman, E., & Lindeløv, J. K. (2019). PsychoPy2: Experiments in behavior made easy. *Behavior Research Methods*, *51*(1), 195–203. https://doi.org/10.3758/s13428-018-01193-y

Peirce, J. W. (2007). PsychoPy—Psychophysics software in Python. *Journal of Neuroscience Methods*, *162*(1-2), 8–13. https://doi.org/10.1016/j.jneumeth.2006.11.017

Peirce, J. W. (2009). Generating stimuli for neuroscience using PsychoPy. *Frontiers in Neuroinformatics*, *2*, https://doi.org/10.3389/neuro.11.010.2008

Pelli, D. G. (1997). The VideoToolbox software for visual psychophysics: Transforming numbers into movies. *Spatial Vision*, *10*(4), 437–442. https://doi.org/10.1163/156856897X00366

Pokorny, J., Smithson, H., & Quinlan, J. (2004). Photostimulator allowing independent control of rods and the three cone types. *Visual Neuroscience*, *21*(3), 263–267. https://doi.org/10.1017/S0952523804213207

Prins, N., & Kingdom, F. A. A. (2018). Applying the model-comparison approach to test specific research hypotheses in psychophysical research using the Palamedes toolbox. *Frontiers in Psychology*, *9*, 1250. https://doi.org/10.3389/fpsyg.2018.01250

Provencio, I., Rodriguez, I. R., Jiang, G., Hayes, W. P., Moreira, E. F., & Rollag, M. D. (2000). A novel human opsin in the inner retina. *The Journal of Neuroscience*, *20*(2), 600–605. https://doi.org/10.1523/JNEUROSCI.20-02-00600.2000

Pugh, E. N., Jr., & Andersen, O. S. (2008). Models and mechanistic insight. *The Journal of General Physiology*, *131*(6), 515–519. https://doi.org/10.1085/jgp.200810041

Read, J. C. (2015). The place of human psychophysics in modern neuroscience. *Neuroscience*, *296*, 116–129. https://doi.org/10.1016/j.neuroscience.2014.05.036

Roorda, A., & Williams, D. R. (1999). The arrangement of the three cone classes in the living human eye. *Nature*, *397*(6719), 520–522. https://doi.org/10.1038/17383

Rust, N. C., & Movshon, J. A. (2005). In praise of artifice. *Nature Neuroscience*, *8*(12), 1647–1650. https://doi.org/10.1038/nn1606

Sauter, M., Draschkow, D., & Mack, W. (2020). Building, hosting and recruiting: A brief introduction to running behavioral experiments online. *Brain Sciences*, *10*(4), 251. https://doi.org/10.3390/brainsci10040251

Saxe, A., Nelli, S., & Summerfield, C. (2021). If deep learning is the answer, what is the question? *Nature Reviews Neuroscience*, *22*(1), 55–67. https://doi.org/10.1038/s41583-020-00395-8

Scarfe, P., & Glennerster, A. (2019). The science behind virtual reality displays. *Annual Review of Vision Science*, *5*(1), 529–547. https://doi.org/10.1146/annurev-vision-091718-014942

Schmidt, B. P., Sabesan, R., Tuten, W. S., Neitz, J., & Roorda, A. (2018). Sensations from a single M-cone depend on the activity of surrounding S-cones. *Scientific Reports*, *8*(1), 8561. https://doi.org/10.1038/s41598-018-26754-1

Schneider, B. (1980). Individual loudness functions determined from direct comparisons of loudness intervals. *Perception & Psychophysics*, *28*(6), 493–503. https://doi.org/10.3758/BF03198817

Schneider, B., Parker, S., & Stein, D. (1974). The measurement of loudness using direct comparisons of sensory intervals. *Journal of Mathematical Psychology*, *11*(3), 259–273. https://doi.org/10.1016/0022-2496(74)90022-4

Smith, P. L., & Little, D. R. (2018). Small is beautiful: In defense of the small-N design. *Psychonomic Bulletin & Review*, *25*(6), 2083–2101. https://doi.org/10.3758/s13423-018-1451-8

Spitschan, M. (2019). Melanopsin contributions to non-visual and visual function. *Current Opinion in Behavioral Sciences*, *30*, 67–72. https://doi.org/10.1016/j.cobeha.2019.06.004

Spitschan, M., & Woelders, T. (2018). The method of silent substitution for examining melanopsin contributions to pupil control. *Frontiers in Neurology*, *9*, 941. https://doi.org/10.3389/fneur.2018.00941

Todor, J. I. (1975). Changes in depth perception during a non-stop walk of 302 1/4 miles. *Perceptual and Motor Skills*, *40*(3), 762. https://doi.org/10.2466/pms.1975.40.3.762

Treutwein, B. (1995). Adaptive psychophysical procedures. *Vision Research*, *35*(17), 2503–2522. https://doi.org/10.1016/0042-6989(95)00016-X

Treutwein, B., & Strasburger, H. (1999). Fitting the psychometric function. *Perception & Psychophysics*, 61(1), 87–106. https://doi.org/10.3758/BF03211951

Tuten, W. S., Harmening, W. M., Sabesan, R., Roorda, A., & Sincich, L. C. (2017). Spatiochromatic interactions between individual cone photoreceptors in the human retina. *The Journal of Neuroscience*, 37(39), 9498–9509. https://doi.org/10.1523/JNEUROSCI.0529-17.2017

Wade, N. J. (1998). *A natural history of vision*. MIT Press.

Watson, A. B., & Pelli, D. G. (1983). QUEST: A Bayesian adaptive psychometric method. *Perception & Psychophysics*, 33(2), 113–120. https://doi.org/10.3758/BF03202828

Webster, M. A. (2015). Visual adaptation. *Annual Review of Vision Science*, 1(1), 547–567. https://doi.org/10.1146/annurev-vision-082114-035509

Wichmann, F. A., & Hill, N. J. (2001a). The psychometric function: I. Fitting, sampling, and goodness of fit. *Perception & Psychophysics*, 63(8), 1293–1313. https://doi.org/10.3758/BF03194544

Wichmann, F. A., & Hill, N. J. (2001b). The psychometric function: II. Bootstrap-based confidence intervals and sampling. *Perception & Psychophysics*, 63(8), 1314–1329. https://doi.org/10.3758/BF03194545

Willmann, G., Ivanov, I. V., Fischer, M. D., Lahiri, S., Pokharel, R. K., Werner, A., & Khurana, T. S. (2010). Effects on colour discrimination during long term exposure to high altitudes on Mt Everest. *The British Journal of Ophthalmology*, 94(10), 1393–1397. https://doi.org/10.1136/bjo.2009.178491

Xiao, K., Fu, C., Karatzas, D., & Wuerger, S. (2011). Visual gamma correction for LCD displays. *Displays*, 32(1), 17–23. https://doi.org/10.1016/j.displa.2010.09.003

# SECTION 5

MEASURES IN PSYCHOPHYSIOLOGY

CHAPTER 25

THE PERIMETRIC PHYSIOLOGICAL MEASUREMENT OF PSYCHOLOGICAL CONSTRUCTS

Louis G. Tassinary, Ursula Hess, Luis M. Carcoba, and Joseph M. Orr

For well over a century, the noninvasive recording of perimetric[1] physiological activity has enriched our understanding of embodied and embedded psychological processes. For the past 3 decades, such measures have, in addition, afforded the necessary context for interpreting the significance of direct measures of neural activity. In this chapter, we review the state of the art on the psychophysiological measurement of activity in the muscular, sudomotor, and cardiovascular systems.

The scientific roots of modern psychophysiology as well as cognitive, social, and affective neuroscience can be traced directly back to the second volume of Gustav Fechner's famous *Elemente der Psychophysik* (1860), with pre-echoes earlier in the 19th century (see Tassinary et al., 1989b), and even as far back as the 18th and 17th centuries (see Geen & Tassinary, 2002). In this seminal volume, Fechner explored conceptually the functional relationship between the intensity of the sensation and the magnitude of brain activity, albeit limited by nascent empirical tools and methods. In seeking the elemental nature of consciousness, Wundt (1897) elaborated on these speculations, postulating that the contents of consciousness were divided into objective contents (sensations) and subjective contents (simple feelings). These simple feelings or affective elements differed significantly from sensations because they explicitly represented the psychological response to sensations, and they were characterized as forming a single interconnected manifold defined by the dimensions of pleasantness–unpleasantness, tension–relaxation, and excitation–inhibition. There was intense debate throughout the early years of the 20th century regarding such formulations, ultimately ending in a theoretical cul-de-sac (see Gardiner et al., 1937). Yet this framework, related but distinct from the one proposed independently by Carl Lange (1885) and William James (1884), fostered the use of perimetric physiological measures in psychological experiments because it explicitly linked specific changes in physiological function with each of the three dimensions of feeling. Wundt (1904) minimized such relationships, stating that observable processes "are merely indications and not in the slightest degree proofs. Where introspection does not show univocally the existence of a definite feeling, such a feeling can naturally not be deduced from objective events, no matter how numerous they may be" (p. 272). Nonetheless, the James–Lange theory spurred research on perimetric physiological

---

[1]The use of the term *perimetric* is admittedly novel in this context. The term *peripheral* is far more common. We choose this particular term to both emphasize the generally acknowledged embedded and embodied character of many psychological constructs and to avoid the pejorative connotations of *peripheral*.

https://doi.org/10.1037/0000318-025
APA Handbook of Research Methods in Psychology, Second Edition: Vol. 1. Foundations, Planning, Measures, and Psychometrics, H. Cooper (Editor-in-Chief)
Copyright © 2023 by the American Psychological Association. All rights reserved.

measures of psychological states and processes, rationalized the search for lawful relationships between psychological constructs and physiological activity, and established the goal of finding invariant psychophysiological signatures. The methods, analyses, instruments, and theories have become vastly more sophisticated over the past century, yet the fundamental quest remains remarkably unchanged (see Cacioppo et al., 2017).

Despite the dizzying array of technological advances, the use of traditional perimetric psychophysiological measures continues to play a critical role in the interpretation of brain activity and overt behavior. To paraphrase the pioneering neuroscientist Roger W. Sperry (1952) the fundamental anatomical plan and working principles of the nervous system are understandable only by acknowledging that its principal function is the coordinated control of the body.

INFERENTIAL CHALLENGES

Our ability to measure and decipher a wide array of physiological events at multiple temporal and spatial scales expands almost daily and has enabled the routine measurement not only of brain activity but also of simultaneous activity throughout the entire nervous system, both within and between individuals (e.g., hyperscanning: see Czeszumski, 2020; Montague, 2002). The search for unobtrusive ambulatory monitoring also continues unabated (Darrow, 1934; Poh et al., 2010) and more recently has led to advances in healthcare through wearable monitoring systems used, for example, for cardiac monitoring generally (Sana et al., 2020) and for elder care specifically (Stavropoulos et al., 2020). The interpretation of such measurements continues to spark controversy, however, regarding not only the simple reliability and validity of such measurements but, importantely, their precise psychological significance.

Physiological changes are the product of an organism's ongoing adaptation to its environment, reflecting a large number of processes, only some of which are related to a given experimental manipulation. Put differently, observed changes in physiology, as with behavior, are routinely polysemous. For example, equivalent increases in heart rate (HR) may be due to sympathetic activation, parasympathetic withdrawal, or coactivation (Berntson et al., 2017), each of which implies different psychological antecedents. Physiological measures are inherently multiply determined and psychological processes nearly always manifest in more than one measure.

Cacioppo and Tassinary (1990) distinguished four types of relations characterized as quadrants within the bivariate space defined by dimensions of specificity and generality. *Specificity* refers to the coupling between an empirical measurement and a theoretical process, the extent to which the presence or degree of a particular response unequivocally indicates the process in question (high specificity) or reflects the vagaries of many processes (low specificity) (cf. the schemapiric bond; Stevens, 1968). *Generality* refers to the extent to which such relations are context bound, varying between context-dependent (low generality) to context-independent (high generality). Context-dependent multiply determined relations are referred to as *outcomes*. If it can be established that the measure has sufficient generality, the measure is a *concomitant*. If it can be shown that—at least within a particular measurement context—the measure is specific, it is a *marker*. And, if the measure is both specific and context independent, it is an *invariant*. The value of this taxonomy lies principally in its ability to simultaneously highlight inferential limitations and guide future research.

To illustrate, an outcome relation precludes the absence of a specific response being used to infer the absence of a specific psychological state. For example, it has been known for more than 2 decades that incipient brow furrowing detected via facial electromyography can be associated with anger (e.g., Dimberg & Öhman, 1996); however, the lack of such activity does not support the inference that the person is not angry. Similarly, the presence of increased muscle activity in the brow region does not unequivocally indicate anger. It may, for example, be due to increased mental effort (Pope & Smith, 1994), glare (Berman et al., 1994), or even photophobia (Stringham et al., 2003). More recently, the muscle activation primarily responsible for this observed electromyographic activity has even been characterized as the muscle of "empathy and determination" (Hwang, 2017). The primary means to avoid erroneous inferences is via creative experimental design, namely, the nuanced control of independent variables coupled tightly to careful multivariate measurement, always building upon the foundation of prior research and guided by explicit theory.

GENERAL ISSUES

When attempting to infer psychological states or processes on the basis of observed physiological events, a small set of issues always demand explicit attention, issues that remain the bane of the psychophysiologist. They are baselines, ambient noise, and artifacts. In addition, given the disconsolate setting of the typical laboratory, creating a participant-centric experience is important.

Baselines

Physiological data tend to be characterized by significant variability, both within and between individuals. Resting HR, for example, can vary between 40 beats per minute for a marathon runner and more than 100 beats per minute for an obese individual with a history of smoking. And the spontaneous recall of significant events (e.g., a forgotten appointment) may affect physiological responses across a series of trials. As a result, it is common in most research reports to find the analysis of responses "corrected" in some manner using baseline data. Such corrections range from quite sophisticated (e.g., longitudinal data analysis; see Singer & Willett, 2003) to deceptively simple (i.e., difference scores; see Edwards, 2001). In the latter case, measurements are taken during resting or pretrial periods (baselines), allowing subsequent measurements during experimental trials to be expressed as the difference between the data recorded in response to the stimulus or situation and that recorded during the baseline(s). This correction, however, presupposes that the participant is quiescent during the recorded baseline. In reality, participants are often somewhat stressed when first entering a psychophysiology laboratory. Unfamiliarity with the procedures and the environment also sometimes lead to increased vigilance. Over time these effects typically diminish. Yet, if resting baselines are taken before adaptation, the baseline measurements may be higher than trial levels late in the experiment. Alternatively, if the resting period lasts too long, participants may show relaxation levels that are considerably lower than during normal alertness, thereby inflating difference scores. And if the intertrial intervals are too brief to allow the aftermath of the prior stimulus to dissipate, the carryover effects undermine the presumed stability of the baseline. It is advisable, therefore, to allow sufficient time for participants both to become familiar with the laboratory environment and to recover between trials as well as to create an atmosphere that enables a relaxed attentive state.

A more sophisticated real-time procedure involves the use of a closed-loop procedure in which the onset of a trial is predicated on an immediately prior quiescent baseline (McHugo & Lanzetta, 1983). Tassinary and Cacioppo (2000) pointed out that such a requirement may inadvertently shape the participants reactions in ways both undesirable and unknowable. When increased sensitivity is needed in a complex within-subjects design; however, such a procedure may be advisable (e.g., Ehrlich et al., 2019).

In short, the choice of baseline depends on the specifics of the experimental procedure and the characteristics of the research participants. It is, therefore, critical to consider carefully the implications of this choice for the validity of the data-based inferences regarding psychological states and processes (see Fishel et al., 2007).

Ambient Noise

The ubiquitous bioamplifiers used in psychophysiological research nearly always involve bipolar sensor placements and employ differential amplification. The theory behind such measurement techniques is that any electrical activity common to both sensors is *noise* and any activity unique to a particular sensor is considered *signal*. Filters applied subsequent to the detection and preamplification stages are then used to restrict more precisely the activity passed on to the final amplification stage to the particular physiological signal of interest. Stray noise or unwanted signals can affect either of the two bipolar sensors differently, however, and, hence, would not be rejected as noise but rather allowed to pass as signal by the amplifier. Said differently, in certain situations, ambient noise or interlopers can masquerade as signal. Common sources of noise are transformers, fluorescent lights, heaters, nearby electrical power lines, other physiological events, and, in rare cases, even local radio stations.

Best practices require minimizing noise to the extent possible by identifying and removing sources of interference. If the source can neither be removed nor shielded, it should simply be moved as far as possible from the participant and any cables connected to the participant. For example, unshielded extension or power cords should be replaced with well-shielded cables. Fluorescent lights or halogen lamps emit more noise than light-emitting diode (LED) lights and, if problematic, may need to be replaced. The interference caused by endogenous sources (e.g., electrical potentials originating from the heart interfering with the recording of muscle activity) is typically addressed through both a priori sensor placement and filter selection and a posteriori data processing.

Artifacts

Any movement, regardless of its cause, may lead to observed activity. Forceful movements such as sneezing are usually readily discernible as large synchronized activity across multiple recording channels. Smaller yet stereotyped movements such as blinking and swallowing are similarly discernible. Yet, some movements, such as licking or scratching (i.e., adaptors; Ekman & Friesen, 1969), may generate activity that masquerades as signal. Because the appearance of these movements in the recording is likely fleeting and difficult to characterize or predict, a video record is an essential supplement, allowing the researcher to detect such interlopers and scrub the record accordingly. The ratio of the duration of the trial to the duration of the artifact is typically the primary determinant for whether the trial in question should be rejected entirely or just the artifact can be excised from the data. Whatever the decision, one must keep a record of the number of times such artifacts occur as their frequency may be coupled with particular experimental conditions or participant characteristics. As with ambient noise, best practices suggest redesigning the experimental protocol, when possible, to reduce the likelihood of artifacts. Unlike ambient noise, the likelihood of artifacts cannot be determined a priori and typically requires careful pilot testing.

Participant Considerations

In contrast to many experiments in psychology that focus exclusively on overt behavior, psychophysiological experiments nearly always require the physical attachment of sensors to a person's body. Such attachments routinely involve skin preparation (e.g., cleaning and mild abrasion) as well as the use of gels or pastes to bridge between the surface of the sensor and skin, although "dry" sensor technology has advanced significantly (see Roy et al., 1993). Not surprisingly, some participants will be allergic to particular adhesives, particular soaps, or astringents or particular gels or pastes, all used when attaching sensors. Some participants will likely be uncomfortable with the degree of physical touching involved. And when recording from areas on the face, the presence of facial hair or makeup can be problematic. Finally, a few participants may feel uncomfortable in a situation in which they are literally connected to the recording equipment and unable to move freely. For these reasons and others it is very important for the experimenter to establish a good rapport with each participant as early as possible.

Overall, a participant must understand that they can freely communicate with the experimenter throughout the experiment, and the protocol should not unnecessarily undermine a participant's perceived sense of control. A simple way to achieve the goal of unfettered communication is via an intercom system coupled with video surveillance. This can be achieved by grouping the trial sequence into relatively short blocks, the initiation of which is controlled by the participant. Successful psychological experiments involving physiological monitoring require that each research participant be both well informed with respect to the recording environment they encounter and allowed to maintain a modicum of perceived control. All of this can be achieved with comfortable, supportive furniture and a pleasant interior design (cf. Kweon et al., 2007), combined with a protocol that minimizes both the psychological and physiological sequelae associated with long, sometime monotonous experiences.

In the following pages, we briefly review and contextualize a highly selected set of traditional measures of cardiovascular, sudomotor, and muscular activity, measures that have become part of the routine armamentarium of experimental psychology. Most of the issues touched on in this review are discussed in depth in recent handbooks (e.g., Cacioppo et al., 2017), textbooks (e.g., Andreassi, 2006), technical monographs (e.g., Stern et al., 2001), seminal treatises (e.g., Martin & Venables, 1980), chapters on setting up a laboratory (e.g., Curtin et al., 2007), and relevant committee reports (e.g., Boucsein et al., 2012; Fridlund & Cacioppo, 1986; Shapiro et al., 1996).

CARDIOVASCULAR ACTIVITY

For well over two millennia the relationship between the mind and the blood has been discussed and debated. Recalling the allegory of Cupid and Psyche, the great physicians of antiquity recognized the diagnostic value of the pulse. For example, a quickening pulse in the presence of a hidden and forbidden love object was believed to be diagnostic of lovesickness (Mesulam & Perry, 1972). An accurate understanding of the mechanism of circulation, however, was not realized until the early 17th century by English physician William Harvey, and not until the 18th century was a physical mechanism proposed to explain the relationship between emotional states and cardiac reactivity (see Thayer & Lane, 2009).

Important technological advances at the turn of the 19th century greatly aided the measure of pulse rate; specifically, the invention of the electrocardiogram (ECG) by the Dutch physiologist Willem Einthoven in 1901 (Fisch, 2000), which built upon earlier work demonstrating that the heart's electrical activity could be monitored noninvasively (Sykes, 1987). Such technological advances were exploited by early psychophysiologists to explore empirically the correspondences between psychological states and physiological activity and were met with mixed success (cf. Ax, 1953; Darrow, 1929a, 1929b). More recent work has focused on sophisticated indices of the neural control of the heart, with continuing special attention to reactivity (e.g., Obrist et al., 1978) and variability (e.g., Berntson et al., 1997).

Anatomy and Physiology

The cardiovascular system comprises a central pump (the heart) and an intricate system of vessels distributed through the body. Its primary function is to provide a continuous adequate supply of oxygen and nutrients and to eliminate carbon dioxide and waste products.

The heart is a cone-shaped organ located in the medial cavity of the thorax between the lungs. The myocardium or cardiac muscle performs the pumping function and has a thin inner tissue layer called the *endocardium* covering the wall of the cardiac chambers. There are four chambers in the heart, the right and left atria, and the right and left ventricles. During a normal cardiac cycle, deoxygenated blood enters the right atrium via the superior vena cava, the inferior vena cava, and the coronary sinus (transporting blood from the myocardium). Simultaneously, oxygenated blood enters the left atrium from four pulmonary veins. Blood from the right atrium enters the right ventricle through the right atrioventricular (tricuspid) valve and is pumped through the pulmonary semilunar valve out to the lungs (pulmonary circuit). The left ventricle receives blood from the left atrium via the left atrioventricular (bicuspid or mitral) valve and is pumped through the aortic semilunar valve out to the rest of the body (systemic circuit). Put simply, the heart is essentially two hearts—a left heart in the systemic circuit and a right heart in the pulmonary circuit. With each heat beat, the systemic circuit supplies oxygenated blood to all the organs of the body via the systemic circuit, whereas the pulmonary circuit takes deoxygenated blood from the heart to the lungs.

The arterial system comprises three subgroups that vary by size and function. The elastic arteries are the biggest, conducting blood from the heart to medium-size muscular arteries responsible for supplying the major organs with oxygenated blood. The arterioles are the smallest, responsible for the intraorgan transfer of blood, and are the primary proximal mechanism involved in regulating both local blood flow and systemic blood pressure (BP). The capillaries, the smallest of all vessels, are primarily involved in the diffusion of gases and nutrient to and from surrounding tissues.

The venous system comprises distinct subgroups, all of which, with one notable exception (i.e., the hepatic portal vein), conduct blood to the heart. Superficial veins course close to the skin and have no corresponding arteries, whereas deep veins course well below the surface and corresponding arteries. Systemic veins service the tissues of the body and deliver deoxygenated blood to the heart whereas pulmonary veins deliver oxygenated blood to the heart from the lungs. All these vessels have the same three layers characteristic of all blood vessels, yet they are thinner, and the lumens are significantly larger than in their corresponding arteries. Veins are very compliant and hold up to 65% of the blood supply, acting as blood reservoirs.

Neural Control

The heart has an intrinsic rhythm controlled by self-generated electrical impulses in the sinoatrial (SA) node. The brain, however, exerts a powerful modulatory influence on both the heart and vascular activity. Such control includes changes that originate at different levels of the central nervous system and that are affected primarily via either the sympathetic or parasympathetic branches of the autonomic nervous systems. Some of the main brain control centers are located in the medulla. For example, the cardioacceleratory center, when activated, produces a positive chronotropic effect (i.e., a decrease in heart period or increase in heart rate) and increases the tone of the muscular tunica of the blood vessels. Information from this center is conducted via sympathetic pathways reaching the SA node, where the release of norepinephrine causes a direct stimulation of the cells of the node. The medullary cardio-inhibitory center has the opposite function—its activation produces negative chronotropic effects. This center is mediated primarily by parasympathetic fibers traveling via the vagus nerve. Other brain centers affecting autonomic control of heart and blood vessels are the limbic system and the cerebral cortex that, via efferent and afferent fibers, communicate with the amygdala. The amygdala, in turn, can modulate medullar centers resulting in both parasympathetic suppression and sympathetic activation generating a large positive chronotropic effect. The hypothalamus also plays an important role through its influence on autonomic and sensory responsiveness (Lumb & Lovick, 1993).

Recent evidence reveals differences between genders in responses to the cardiovascular system's autonomic nervous control, with men showing increased and decreased activity of the sympathetic and parasympathetic nervous system activity respectively, during both basal and dynamic conditions (Pothineni et al., 2016). This differential activity results in a lower baseline heart rate for men compared with women (Koenig & Thayer, 2016; Zafar et al., 2020), as well as higher hypertension rates due to increased vascular resistance (Joyner et al., 2016). Although gender-related differences in electrocardiographic measures, such as a shorter PR interval and QRS duration, lower ECG voltage, and longer QT interval in women (James et al., 2007; Macfarlane, 2018), are not new, recent studies emphasize the hormonal and genetic mechanisms involved in these differences (Boese et al., 2017; Regitz-Zagrosek & Kararigas, 2017).

A different level of control exerted via the autonomic nervous system derives from a series of broadly distributed sensory receptors throughout the body (Secomb, 2008). The three main classes of receptors are chemical, pressure, and tension. *Chemoreceptors* are located in the medulla oblongata, in the carotid bodies and in the aortic arch. These receptors detect changes in blood pH, low oxygen pressure, and levels of carbon dioxide (CO_2). Stimulation of chemoreceptors activate compensatory changes at the respiratory and cardiovascular system levels. *Baroreceptors* are pressure sensors located in the internal carotid arteries and in the aorta. Their function is regulated by a special negative feedback circuit. These receptors have cells that under normal conditions are continually firing and sending inhibitory signals to the cardiac centers in the medulla via the *nucleus tractus solitarius*. A detected decrease in blood pressure triggers a reduction in their rate of firing, allowing the medullary cardiac centers to send excitatory signals to the heart, leading to a consequent decrease in heart period and a resulting increase in BP. Once BP is normalized, these receptors resume their normal activity. *Proprioceptors* are distributed in muscles and joints. They sense changes in movement and spatial orientation of the body and respond to length modification on muscle and tendons. In the heart, these receptors react to the changes in size of the cardiac chambers. During physical activity, many of these receptors are activated, resulting in the recruitment of sympathetic mechanisms (Mittelstaedt, 1998).

Measurement

Cardiovascular measures such as HR and BP have been employed since the early days of psychophysiology (Ax, 1953; Elliott, 1969, 1974; Graham & Clifton, 1966; McGinn et al., 1964; Scott, 1930). A considerable number of indices of different aspects of cardiovascular functioning can be derived and have been used in psychological research. Standard psychophysiological measurement procedures include the ECG for the assessment of HR or heart period, the finger pulse plethysmograph for the assessment of pulse volume as well as sometimes pulse rate, impedance cardiography for the assessment of cardiac output measures, and the measurement of BP. We now briefly discuss each of these procedures. Of the various measures of cardiovascular activity that can be derived, HR, HR variability (HRV), and BP are described in some detail and illustrated with research examples.

Electrocardiogram. The ECG measures the electrical activity of the heart. During normal contractions the entire myocardium behaves as a single coherent system. As detailed, the heart cycle begins with a signal at the SA node, the pacemaker tissue located in the right atrium of the heart, which generates the sinus rhythm. This impulse leads to a depolarization of the atria, which unfolds as the P-wave in the ECG. The depolarization of the ventricles unfolds as the QRS complex, and the T inflection indicates the repolarization of the ventricles. The total time from initiation of the impulse by the SA node to depolarization of the last ventricular muscle cell is about 0.3 to 0.4 seconds. The entire sequence of complete contraction and relaxation of the heart chambers is known as the *cardiac cycle*.

The time for one complete heart cycle, usually measured from one R-wave to the next and expressed in milliseconds, is the heart period or interbeat interval (IBI). HR is expressed in beats per second and is related to IBI as follows: HR = 60,000/IBI. Berntson et al. (1993) advocated the use of IBI because changes in heart period are linearly related to autonomic activity over a wide range of baseline values, whereas the relation between autonomic activity and HR is decidedly nonlinear.

Sensors. For laboratory measurements, disposable adhesive silver/silver chloride (Ag/AgCl) sensors are typically used. Several different placements are possible. The standard placements are as follows: (a) Lead I on the left and right wrists on the inside of the arms, with the positive lead on the left arm; (b) Lead II on the right arm and left ankle, with the positive lead on the left ankle; and (c) Lead III on the left wrist and left ankle, with the positive lead on the ankle. The preparation of the skin surface typically requires, at most, a mild rub with an astringent and the sensors themselves are available in a wide variety of sizes and materials.

Because the arm and leg placements are quite sensitive to movement artifact, a modified Lead II placement is often used where the sensors are placed on the torso. In this case, the right sensor is placed under the right sternum and the left sensor under the left ribcage. When body hair makes the sternum placement impractical, the equivalent location on the back can also be used. When clothing hinders the attachment of a sensor to the lower ribcage, an ankle placement can be used, still leaving the arm free.

Traditional metrics. HR and IBI have been used routinely as dependent measures in the study of emotion (e.g., Ax, 1953; Lang et al., 2000), motivation (e.g., Elliott, 1969, 1974; Fowles, 1988), and attention (e.g., Cook & Turpin, 1997; Graham & Clifton, 1966; Verschuere et al., 2004). Tonic HR has also been used as an individual difference measure—for example, as a correlate of antisocial behavior in children and adolescents (see, Ortiz & Raine, 2004). Because the heart is innervated by both sympathetic and parasympathetic branches of the autonomic nervous system, the interpretation of simple indexes such as HR can be challenging. As mentioned, quite distinct patterns of autonomic activation may lead to similar observed changes in HR and vice versa (Berntson et al., 1993). Hence, HR is often assessed in the context of other measures to improve its diagnostic utility. For example, when HR is used to assess task engagement and perceptions of ability, the additional use of BP measures has proven useful (Wright & Kirby, 2001).

An example: Attention or affect? The concealed information or guilty knowledge test (GKT) was originally developed by Lykken (1959) and under laboratory conditions has been found to be very accurate (Iacono, 2010). The test is based on the fact that an item of unique significance to the perpetrator (e.g., an iPhone that was used to break a window), but not to an innocent person, will elicit a skin conductance response in the former but not the latter. Verschuere et al. (2004) addressed whether this response is due to an emotional defense reaction (Sokolov, 1963) or to an orientation reaction (see Lynn, 1966). Because HR has been found to decelerate during orientation but accelerate during defense (Cook & Turpin, 1997; Graham & Clifton, 1966), HR was recorded while each participant enacted only one of two mock crimes. Pictures related to both crimes were then presented, and HR and electrodermal activity (EDA) were measured concurrently. As expected, participants showed enhanced electrodermal response to pictures of the crime they had committed compared with pictures of the crime they had not. Importantly, this reaction was accompanied by HR deceleration, suggesting that the pictures linked to their specific crime elicited greater attention from the perpetrators in contradistinction to a negative emotional response.

Heart rate variability. In addition to HR and IBI, the ECG can also be used to derive measures of heart rate variability (HRV). This measure is largely influenced by vagal tone and has been used as an individual difference measure of behavioral impulsivity (Lacey & Lacey, 1958) and self-regulation (Stephens et al., 1975) as well as of emotional dispositions such as hostility (Sloan et al., 1994) and trait worry (Brosschot et al., 2007). It has also been employed to assess states such as attention (Porges & Raskin, 1969), mental load (Kalsbeek & Ettema, 1963), and executive function (Hansen et al., 2003).

The theoretical underpinnings of the psychophysiological utility of HRV, both evolutionary and neurophysiological, have been articulated in the polyvagal theory proposed by Porges (1995). Polyvagal theory proposes that with respect to the heart, vagal egress supports the mobilization behaviors of fight and flight, whereas vagal ingress supports spontaneous social engagement behaviors. More specifically, the theory notes that in addition to the phylogenetically older unmyelinated branch involved primarily in visceral homeostasis (e.g., digestion), the mammalian vagus nerve has a myelinated branch, which can rapidly regulate cardiac output (via modulated inhibition) to foster engagement and disengagement with the environment. The myelinated branch is further neuroanatomically linked to the brain regions that regulate social engagement via facial expression and vocalization and is, thus, characterized as the *smart vagus*. Generally, a high degree of vagal tone (i.e., the degree to which HRV is controlled by the smart vagus) has been shown to be positively associated with good psychological, physiological (e.g., Ruiz-Padial et al., 2003), and sexual (e.g., Brody & Preut, 2003) functioning.

Quantification. A number of different procedures can be used to derive HRV from both the temporal and the frequency domains (see Task Force of the European Society of Cardiology and the North American Society of Pacing and Electrophysiology [Task Force], 1996). For time domain measures, intervals between successive normal complexes are determined. Specifically, each QRS complex is first detected and an array of IBIs is created. Analysis in the frequency domain involves the decomposition of the ECG into its frequency components using techniques such as the fast Fourier transform (FFT) or autoregressive modeling. In addition, Porges and Bohrer (1990) developed a propriety hybrid method, the moving polynomial method.

A simple time domain measure, which provides accurate estimates under conditions of normal breathing (e.g., Hayano et al., 1991) and allows editing of spurious heart beats (Salo et al., 2001), is the standard deviation of all IBIs in an epoch. Another common method is to calculate the square root of the mean-squared differences of successive IBIs. A common frequency domain measure is based on decomposing the time series using the FFT. The high frequency (HF) band (0.15–0.4 Hz) is used as an index of parasympathetic activity, whereas the low frequency (LF) band (0.05–0.15 Hz) represents mixed influences. The choice of measure depends on several considerations. Even though the simple time domain measures have been shown to be adequate estimates of parasympathetic activity for typical experimental contexts, there are also good reasons to consider frequency-based measures if more detailed analyses are required (see Berntson et al., 1997).

Because HRV is derived from a time series, the length of the epoch is of importance. For frequency domain measures, the Task Force (1996) recommends a length 10 times the wavelength of the lowest frequency of interest. This translates into 1-minute epochs for the HF and 2-minute epochs for the LF band. Time domain measures should be based on at least 5-minute epochs.

Artifact control. As HRV is derived from the R–R interval of the ECG, the quality of the measure depends on the quality of the original ECG signal. One problem is that because most measures of HRV depend on an intact time series, artifacts cannot be simply deleted from the signal. The case of spurious R-wave detections (i.e., by mistaking a T-wave for an R-wave) can be addressed by summing the two short periods that were created by the spurious detection. Missing R-waves need to be replaced. This can be done by interpolating between the adjacent R–R intervals or by splitting the spuriously long interval in half.

The riddle of respiration. Respiratory sinus arrhythmia (RSA) refers to the observation that HR accelerates during inspiration and decelerates during expiration. This pattern was first observed by Hales (1733) in horses and Ludwig (1847) in dogs. Based on a wide variety of studies involving both chemical and surgical interventions, it is now well established that RSA is determined largely by vagal parasympathetic activity (see Berntson et al., 1997).

The HRV measures discussed above do not include controls for respiration. Yet, the issue of control of respiration is a controversial one (for contrasting views, see Denver et al., 2007; Grossman & Taylor, 2007). Denver at al. (2007) noted that the central issue is whether respiration is causal for HRV or whether HRV and respiratory frequency are parallel outputs of a common cardiopulmonary oscillator. In the latter case, control for respiration would not be necessary, possibly even counterproductive.

An example: Emotion regulation. As mentioned, HRV (specifically vagal tone) has been proposed as a global index of healthy functioning. Based on this hypothesis, Ruiz-Padial et al. (2003) predicted that individuals with high vagal tone would show a pattern of highly differentiated affect-modulated startle reflexes when viewing pleasant, neutral, and unpleasant images, whereas those with low vagal tone would show evidence of attenuated affective modulation.

Female participants were presented with affect-laden stimuli of varying durations, and their affective state was appraised by recording the amplitude of the startle blink response to a brief acoustic stimulus during viewing. In such paradigms, the eye-blink startle reflex, on average, is routinely observed to be potentiated when participants view negative images and reduced when participants view positive images compared with neutral images. As predicted, however, this pattern was clearly evident for participants with high vagal tone, yet it was conspicuously absent for those with low HRV.

An example: Cortical flexibility. The neurovisceral integration model (Thayer et al., 2009) proposes that individual differences in vagally mediated heart rate variability (vmHRV) may relate to differences in prefrontal cortex activity. Colzato et al. (2018) measured resting state HRV in 90 students. Participants then performed a task-switching paradigm. As predicted, higher resting-state HRV (indexed both by time domain and frequency domain measures) was associated with smaller switch costs (i.e., greater flexibility).

Blood pressure. Because of its relative ease of measurement, BP was a popular measure in the early days of psychophysiological research and was used to investigate a variety of constructs such as deception (Mager, 1931) and emotion (Landis, 1926; Scott, 1930) as well as to characterize individual differences (see McGinn et al., 1964). The difficulties associated with continuous noninvasive BP measurement and the relative obtrusiveness of the measure, however, pose challenges. BP measurement remains nonetheless a basic tool in the assessment of cardiovascular reactions. Typical domains in which BP is assessed include stress (e.g., Obrist et al., 1978; Taylor et al., 2010), perceived threat (e.g., Blascovich et al., 2001; Manuck et al., 1978), and mental effort (see Wright & Kirby, 2001).

Traditional methods. There are several ways to measure BP. The best known is the *auscultatory* method, which relies on the use of a sphygmomanometer. The procedure typically involves placing an inflatable cuff around the upper arm and a stethoscope is placed over the brachial artery. The cuff is inflated until the arterial blood flow is cut off and then the pressure is slowly released. When the blood first begins to flow again, an audible sound is generated by the ensuing turbulence. As more pressure is released, the sound intensity and quality changes, eventually disappearing. The pressure level at which the first sound is heard corresponds to the pressure in the arterial system during heart systole or contraction; the pressure level at which the sound disappears corresponds to the pressure in the arterial system during heart diastole or relaxation. Although the time-honored method is still valid and continues to have diagnostic clinical value, the intermittent nature and the obtrusiveness of the procedure limit its psychophysiological utility in the laboratory.

Several automated BP measurement devices are available, however, that do not require continual human intervention. These devices are based either on the auscultatory method or on the oscillometric method. For the latter method, the cuff is first inflated to a pressure in excess of the systolic arterial pressure and then pressure is reduced to below diastolic pressure. At this point blood flows, but the blood flow is restricted. Under these conditions the cuff pressure oscillates in synchrony with the cyclic expansion and contraction of the brachial artery. From these oscillations it is possible to compute both systolic BP (SP) and diastolic BP (DP).

The advantage of such automated measures is that they can be taken several times within the framework of an experiment without interrupting the procedure. The inflation and deflation of the cuff, however, is a salient stimulus, which may affect reactions. Continuous BP measurement is also possible with devices that use either tonometric or vascular unloading methods and may be designed for use on either the finger or wrist (see Stern et al., 2001). In all cases the BP measurement remains obtrusive to some degree and over time may become uncomfortable or otherwise disruptive.

Quantification. BP is typically expressed in millimeters of mercury pressure (mmHg) and reflects the amount of pressure on the blood vessel walls during the cardiac cycle. SP is the peak pressure in the arteries and occurs when the ventricles are contracting, near the end of the cardiac cycle. DP is the minimum pressure in the arteries and occurs near the beginning of the cardiac cycle when the ventricles are filling with blood. Pulse pressure is approximated by subtracting DP from SP. Mean arterial pressure is a weighted average of both DP and SP, approximated by adding DP to .33 pulse pressure. The simple unweighted arithmetic mean more closely approximates the true mean arterial pressure at very high HRs because of changes in the morphology of the actual pressure pulse.

An example: Evaluative threat. Performing a task in the presence of others often results in an improvement compared with performing it alone (Zajonc, 1965). This effect is moderated, however, by how well the task is learned. When task outcomes are uncertain, then the presence of an audience (e.g., evaluative threat) can interfere with performance (e.g., Kamarck et al., 1990). Allen et al. (1991) tested this notion by asking women to perform a stressful task first in the laboratory with only the experimenter present and then 2 weeks later at home either again in the presence of just the experimenter or with the additional presence of either a female friend or a pet dog. The pet dog was chosen because a dog was considered to be a supportive other who—unlike the friend—would likely not pose an evaluative threat. Skin conductance reactions, pulse rate, and BP were assessed. In the home setting, the presence of a friend was associated with larger task-related skin conductance reactions and SP changes than in the neutral control conditions (i.e., neither friend nor pet present), whereas the presence of a pet was associated with smaller such changes. Task performance was also poorer in the friend present condition. This study illustrates that the perceived nature of the other in terms of evaluative threat can either exacerbate or ameliorate task-induced stress.

Plethysmography. Blood volume, pulse volume, and pulse rate can be detected using plethysmography—a technique used to measure volumetric changes. *Blood volume* refers to slow or tonic changes of volume in a limb, whereas pulse volume refers to rapid or phasic changes and is usually assessed on the finger. The finger-clip photoplethysmograph is commonly used in psychophysiological research. This is a photometric technique that exploits the fact that when an infrared light shines through in vivo tissue, the amount of absorption of the light depends on the amount of blood in the blood vessels. In psychophysiological research, the amplitude change from the lowest to the highest volume is usually measured, and the time between amplitude peaks can be used to estimate IBIs. The advantage of this measurement is that, unlike the recording of a traditional ECG, participants will not have to move clothing as the sensor is affixed to the finger.

Research comparing ECG and photoplethysmograph-derived IBIs, however, suggests that although the two measures correlate well at rest, they can become uncoupled during task performance (e.g., Giardino et al., 2002). In addition, it is difficult to compare absolute values both between and within participants because variation in skin characteristics influences the measure (Jennings et al., 1980), and pulse volume estimates have been found to be unreliable when derived over multiple sessions (e.g., Speckenbach & Gerber, 1999). The use of this convenient measure, therefore, must be carefully considered in each experimental context.

Wearable cardiac sensors and HR apps on smartphones or smart watches also tend to rely on photoplethysmograph-derived IBIs and, hence, suffer from similar problems (Carpenter & Frontera, 2016). Additional problems are movement artifact, for example, when wearing a wrist device while running, or the condition of the skin, which can affect reflection. Nonetheless, such devices are discussed as useful adjuncts in cardiac monitoring (Carpenter & Frontera, 2016).

Impedance cardiography. The amount of blood in the aorta changes during the cardiac cycle, resulting in corresponding changes in electrical impedance measured across the chest, with lower impedance values indicating greater blood volume. Impedance cardiography allows the calculation of a variety of hemodynamic parameters, in particular an estimate of *stroke volume*—the volume of blood pumped by the heart with each beat. Because cardiac output equals HR times stroke volume, the combination of ECG and impedance cardiography permits the noninvasive estimate of this parameter as well. For additional measures derived from impedance cardiography and more detail on the technique, see Sherwood (1993) or Sherwood et al. (1990).

Measures derived from impedance cardiography have been used prominently in social psychophysiological investigations of threat and challenge responses to stressors (e.g., Blascovich et al., 2003; Tomaka et al., 1993) and research on loneliness (e.g., Cacioppo & Hawkley, 2009; Cacioppo et al., 2002; Hawkley et al., 2003).

SUDOMOTOR ACTIVITY

The measurement of electrical changes in the human skin caused by sudomotor activity is a robust psychophysiological technique used routinely over the past century to track the intensive aspects of emotion and attention across a wide variety of situations (Dawson et al., 1990; Knezevic & Bajada, 1985; Venables & Christie, 1980). It has been used as well in some controversial contexts, such as forensic lie detection and Dianetic auditing.

The initial development of techniques to measure the electrical conductivity of skin occurred in France during the last decades of the 19th century with the work of Romain Vigoroux (1879). Vigoroux's work was not the first to detect electrical surface activity, yet he appears to have been the first to recognize that the electrical activity observed in previous experiments and considered merely an "electric disturbance" was actually an expression of changes in the skin's electrical conductivity (Ho et al., 1994). Additional work by Charles Féré and Ivan Romanovish Tarchanoff in the following decade further clarified the nature of this phenomenon. By passing a small electrical current between two sensors placed on the surface of the skin, Féré (1888) observed changes in skin resistance when an individual was presented with evocative stimuli. Tarchanoff (1890), however, measured endogenous changes in electrical potential between two sensors placed on the surface of the skin and attributed the observed variations to changes in the secretory activity of sweat glands (Neumann & Blanton, 1970).

The significance of these discoveries for psychophysiology was not generally recognized, however, until the renowned Swiss psychologist Carl Jung reported on the results of word association experiments using such techniques in *Studies in Word Association* (1906/1918). In the following year he expanded his examination on the topic in a seminal publication that explored the "value of the so-called 'psycho-physical galvanic reflex' as a recorder of psychical changes in connection with sensory and psychical stimuli . . . [and] . . . its normal and pathological variations" (Peterson & Jung, 1907, p. 154). Such explorations have profitably continued for more than a century, with implications for our embodied understanding of emotion and attention already acknowledged by the 1950s (see Woodworth & Schlosberg, 1954).

Anatomy and Physiology

The skin is composed of two layers: the epidermis and dermis. The uppermost layer, the *epidermis*, constitutes the cellular part of the skin and is a very thin structure (Forslind et al., 1997). Because of its peculiar organization, however, the structure of the epidermis provides the key to understanding the electrical properties of the skin. The epidermis comprises five sublayers of closely packed cells: the stratum corneum, lucidum, granulosum, spinosum, and germinativum, names that reflect either their function or their appearance. The *stratum corneum* or "horny layer" is the superficial layer composed of thin, flat, dead cells filled with protein keratin that are continually being sloughed off and replaced by new dead cells. This layer not only is an important barrier against heat, chemicals, light, and microorganisms but also provides a significant pathway for ion conductance, thus contributing significantly to the electrical properties of the skin (Edelberg, 1977). The other layers constitute essentially a "cell factory," with new cells originating in the deepest layer, the *stratum germinature*. The *dermis*, the second layer of the skin, is located below the epidermis and is formed principally of elastic and fibrous connective tissue. This layer contains loops of capillary blood vessels, terminal receptors of sensory nerves, coiled tubes of sweat glands, and sebaceous glands. Ducts from sweat glands pass through the dermis and epidermis as spiral canals and open onto the skin surface.

Two kinds of sweat glands exist in the human body, eccrine and apocrine. The phylogenetically newer eccrine sweat glands—found only in primates—occur in nearly all regions of the skin, yet they are most numerous in the soles, palms, and scalp. This poses a problem for wearable devices that measure EDA at the wrist.

In contrast, the phylogenetically older apocrine sweat glands are far less numerous and are located primarily in the axilla and perianal areas. It is the eccrine system that forms the proximal basis for nearly all psychophysiological measurement. As mentioned, gland ducts traverse the dermis and the epidermis, opening onto the surface of the skin. When active, these ducts fill with sweat, with consequent variations in conductivity (Jacob & Francone, 1982). The resistance of a given gland duct to the passage of an applied current is inversely proportional to the amount of sweat in the duct. To understand observed changes in overall conductivity across thousands of gland ducts, it is useful to conceptualize the sweat glands as variable resistors wired in parallel. Overall conductance, therefore, is quite simply the sum of all the individual conductances.

Neural Control

Sweating is a normal physiological reaction, having both thermoregulatory and psychogenic antecedents. Psychogenic sweating tends to be more pronounced in areas like the palms and soles, whereas thermoregulatory sweating is a more generalized response (Darrow, 1933; Edelberg, 1972), and distinct mechanisms of neural control appear to be involved (Shibasaki et al., 2006; Wang, 1964). Specifically, thermoregulatory sweating is a complex system controlled primarily by the hypothalamus via unmyelinated postganglionic sympathetic C-fibers and are activated by acetylcholine sympathetic cholinergic pathways. Even though parasympathetic modulation is also mediated by acetylcholine, the general parasympathetic influence on sudomotor function is imperceptible (Illigens & Gibbons, 2009). Afferent pathways from the peripheral thermoreceptors in the skin connect to the central thermoregulatory center of the hypothalamus where the information is integrated with information arriving from other brain areas involved with fluid regulation (Boulant, 1981). Efferent pathways descend ipsilaterally via the brainstem, medulla, and mediolateral spinal cord, and then preganglionic sympathetic fibers relay to paravertebral sympathetic ganglia where unmyelinated postganglionic efferent fibers innervate the sweat glands (Boucsein, 2012; Nagai et al., 2004). Additional regulation exists at the spinal level possibly via reflex circuits (Ogawa, 1981).

The brain systems involved in psychogenic sweating are those associated with emotional and cognitive processes. The most important areas are the premotor cortex and its connections with the basal ganglia, the sensorimotor cortex, and the anterior cingulate cortex (Neafsey, 1991), all of which are implicated in the control of emotional experience and the arousal mechanisms involved in attention (Vetrugno et al., 2003). Other important structures that play a role in the psychogenic sweating are the hypothalamus, hippocampus, and amygdala via their role in motivation (Dawson et al., 1990) and the reticular formation via its role in vigilance (Roy et al., 1993).

Using functional magnetic resonance imaging, Critchley et al. (2000) concluded that the brain areas implicated in emotion and attention are differentially involved in the generation and representation of psychogenic sweating. Additional evidence has suggested that such sweating is related to fear-induced activation of the amygdala (Cheng et al., 2006; Phelps et al., 2001).

Measurement

Using the terminology discussed in this chapter, the recording of sudomotor activity via of the measurement of electrodermal changes is a prototypical example of an outcome relation. That is, EDA is influenced by a variety of factors and can originate from multiple regions of the brain, making it quite risky to impart particular psychological significance to any observed activity. Not unlike reaction time, however, its egalitarian sensitivity and relative ease of use make it an ideal dependent measure, whether alone or in combination with other measures, when carefully incorporated into a well-designed experiment. An excellent example of such a partnership is the GKT used for lie detection (Lykken, 1959; see also Lykken, 1998). It has been observed repeatedly that phasic EDA is observed following the presentation of novel relevant (i.e., significant) stimuli (Öhman, 1979), yet such activity is mute with respect to the precise nature of the significance. The GKT is predicated on the presence of information that would be significant only for the perpetrator (i.e., a specific item used in a crime or some salient object at a crime scene). The goal is to properly construct a multiple-choice test, which embeds the significant item among other plausible items. The guilty person is expected to show consistent EDA to the significant items but not to the plausible alternatives, whereas none of the alternatives should be of significance to an innocent person. The exploitation of significance also undergirds the use of EDA in discrimination classical conditioning (Grings & Dawson, 1973).

Recording Technique

In the introduction to their proposal for the standardization of electrodermal measurement, Lykken and Venables (1971) famously noted the usefulness of EDA "in spite of being frequently abused by measurement techniques which range from the arbitrary to the positively weird" (p. 656). Lykken and Venables's insistence on standardized procedures did bear fruit, however, and standard procedures are now the norm and not the exception in psychophysiological laboratories. Although there remain a variety of valid options in particular contexts (i.e., skin potential, skin resistance, and skin impedance; see Boucsein, 2012), the use of skin conductance is ubiquitous.

Sensors. Because of the need to record accurately slow changes in the conductivity of the skin, nonpolarizing Ag/AgCl sensors are highly recommended. Because of the differential distribution of the eccrine sweat glands, sensors are nearly always placed on the palmar surfaces of either the hand or foot. The hands are preferred when working with adults (but see Carpenter et al., 1999), but for small children and infants, the foot may be the better choice. Commonly used placements on the hand are either the thenar and hypothenar eminences or the medial and distal phalanges of the index and ring finger. Because the conductive properties of the skin are being measured, best practices suggest that skin should not be abraded before sensor placement. The standard recommendation is simply to ask the participants to wash their hands with a neutral soap.

The guidelines published by the Society for Psychophysiological Research (Boucsein et al., 2012; Fowles et al., 1981) suggest a sensor surface area of 1 cm^2, but 10 mm diameter circular sensors are commercially available and are, in most cases, sufficient. It is not uncommon to find commercial ECG or electroencephalography (EEG) gels used as conducting media, yet, because these media are designed explicitly to reduce resistance, they will affect measurements, especially in longer duration experiments (see Boucsein, 2012). Hence, a neutral conducting medium is generally recommended, although recent developments involving flexible, dry Ag/AgCl electrodes have been very promising (see Posada-Quintero & Chon, 2020, for a general review). In the past, such media were not commercially available and had to be compounded in-house (see Dormire & Carpenter, 2002; Fowles et al., 1981). Although relatively easy, such compounding is sometimes unnecessary because neutral media are presently available in some markets (e.g., EC33; Grass Technologies, United States).

Traditional metrics. Skin conductance can be either assessed tonically, as skin conductance level (SCL), or phasically, as skin conductance response (SCR). Event-related reactions occur in a window of 1 second to 4 seconds after event onset. They also occur spontaneously—so-called nonspecific skin conductance responses (NS-SCRs). A number of possible metrics can be derived from the recorded waveform (Table 25.1). Of these, the frequency of NS-SCRs, the SCL, and the electronic response skin conductance responses (ER-SCR) amplitude are among the more commonly used.

An example: Prejudice. Dotsch and Wigboldus (2008) hypothesized that prejudicial behavior toward outgroup members in social interactions results from nonconscious automatic categorization processes. Specifically, the authors predicted that implicitly held negative attitudes toward, but not explicit stereotypes of, Moroccans would be related to the avoidance behavior shown by Dutch participants. SCL was used as a measure of basic affective responding based on its association with amygdala activation. It was predicted that the relation between implicit prejudice and behavior would be mediated by SCL. Participants were placed into an immersive virtual environment in which they encountered European- and Moroccan-appearing avatars. Avoidance was operationalized as the distance that the participants kept from the avatars. Implicit prejudice was measured using a single target implicit association test (see Bluemke & Friese, 2008; de Liver et al., 2007). Participants high in implicit prejudice kept a larger distance between themselves and the avatar and showed larger SCLs. Explicit stereotype did not predict distance and SCL. As predicted by the authors, the effect of implicit prejudice on distance was fully mediated by SCL. The authors concluded that this finding provided evidence for the automatic activation of a previously learned prejudice that is accompanied by a basic affective reaction—that is, an activation resulting in an aversive, uncontrolled behavioral reaction toward the target.

An example: Task engagement. Nonspecific skin conductance activity has been found to vary with task engagement or more generally the effortful allocation of resources to a task (see Dawson et al., 1990). Pecchinenda and Smith (1996) hypothesized that when coping potential—the perceived ability to deal with a task—is high, participants should stay engaged in a task but when coping potential

TABLE 25.1

Electrodermal Measures, Definitions, and Typical Values

Measure	Definition	Typical values
Skin conductance level (SCL)	Tonic level of electrical conductivity of skin	2–20 µS
Change in SCL	Gradual changes in SCL measured at two or more points in time	1–3 µS
Frequency of NS-SCRs	Number of SCRs in absence of an identifiable eliciting stimulus	1–3/min
ER-SCR amplitude	Phasic increase in conductance shortly following stimulus onset	0.2–1.0 µS
ER-SCR latency	Temporal interval between stimulus onset and SCR initiation	1–3 s
ER-SCR rise time	Temporal interval between SCR initiation and SCR peak	1–3 s
ER-SCR half recovery time	Temporal interval between SCR peak and point of 50% recovery of SCR amplitude	2–10 s
ER-SCR habituation (trials to habituation)	Number of stimulus presentations before two or three trials with no response	2–8 stimulus presentations
ER-SCR habituation (slope)	Rate of change of ER-SCR amplitude	0.01–0.5 µS per trial

Note. ER-SCR = event-related skin conductance response; NS-SCR = nonspecific skin conductance response. Adapted from *Principles of Psychophysiology: Physical, Social, and Inferential Elements* (p. 304), by J. T. Cacioppo and L. G. Tassinary (Eds.), 1990, Cambridge University Press. Copyright 1990 by Cambridge University Press. Adapted with permission.

is low, participants should disengage from the task. They gave participants a series of anagram tasks. Task difficulty was manipulated by varying both the difficulty of the anagrams and the available solution time. Participants reported that their coping potential was lower when the task was more difficult. Within trials, nonspecific skin conductance activity was initially high in all conditions. In the most difficult condition, however, it decreased significantly by the end of the trial, suggesting that participants gave up. In support of the initial hypothesis, NS-SCRs were positively correlated within subjects with self-reports of coping potential and with actual time to solution.

MUSCULAR ACTIVITY

The history of muscle physiology can be traced back to the 4th century B.C.E., when Aristotle provided clear descriptions of coordinated motor acts (e.g., locomotion and the importance of the mechanism of flexion) in his books *De Motu Animalium* and *De Incessu Animalium*. It was not until the early 19th century, however, that a sensitive instrument for measuring small electric currents was invented (i.e., the galvanometer). In 1833, Carlo Matteucci used such a device to demonstrate an electrical potential between an excised frog's nerve and its damaged muscle. Du-Bois Reymond, a student of the renowned physiologist Johannes Müller, built on Matteucci's then-recent publication, eventually publishing the results of an extensive series of investigations on the electrical basis of muscular contraction as well as providing the first in vivo evidence of electrical activity in human muscles during voluntary contraction (see Basmajian & Deluca, 1985). The foundations of modern electromyography were finally laid in the 1930s with publications of Adrian and Bronk (1929), Jacobson (1927), and Lindsley (1935) and the introduction of the differential amplifier (Mathews, 1934).

Detecting myoelectric signals using surface sensors remained difficult throughout the 19th and early 20th centuries. Electrically stimulating a muscle cutaneously was considerably simpler, however. Perhaps best known for this work was Guillaume Duchenne de Boulogne, who used this technique in the mid-19th century to investigate the dynamics and function of the human facial muscles in vivo (Duchenne, 1862/1990). Not surprisingly, Charles Darwin corresponded with Duchenne to evaluate his own observations about facial expressions and emotion (Cuthbertson, 1990).

Darwin's interest in muscular action was based upon his belief that many behaviors were in part inherited. He focused his inquiry on the expression of emotions in man and animals to buttress this belief and presaged contemporary studies of the patterns of muscle contractions and facial actions that are undetectable to the naked eye with his conclusion that "whenever the same state of mind is induced, however feebly, there is a tendency through the force of habit and association for the same movements to be performed, though they may not be of the least use" (Darwin, 1872/1873, p. 281).

The somatic elements of William James's (1884) theory of emotions and the various motor theories of thinking prevalent at the turn of the century (e.g., Washburn, 1916) further fueled interest in objective measures of subtle or fleeting muscle contractions. Among the more creative procedures used to magnify tiny muscular contractions were sensitive pneumatic systems used to record finger movements during conflict situations (Luria, 1932) as well as elaborate lever-based systems to record subtle tongue movements during thinking (Thorson, 1925). Sensitive and specific noninvasive recordings, however, awaited the development of metal surface sensors, vacuum tube amplifiers, and the cathode-ray oscilloscope early in the 20th century to enable the pioneering work of Edmund Jacobson (1927, 1932) on electrical measurements of muscle activity during imagery. The results of these studies and others (e.g., R. C. Davis, 1938) demonstrated that electromyographic (EMG) activity evoked by psychologically relevant tasks (e.g., recall a poem) were minute and highly localized, and often occurred in the part of the body that one would use had the task called for an overt response.

Anatomy and Physiology

Fundamentally, muscle is a tissue that both generates and transmits force. Striated muscle, in particular, is a hierarchical material made up of a very large number of parallel fibers whose diameters are orders of magnitude smaller than a millimeter and yet may be up to several centimeters in length. The term *striated* comes from the fact these fibers are actually bundles of thinner structures, known as *fibrils*, which have repeating cross-striations throughout their length known as *Z-lines* or *Z-bands*. Each striated muscle is innervated by a single motor nerve whose cell bodies are located primarily in the anterior horn of the spinal cord or, in the case of the muscles of the head, in the cranial nerves of the brain stem. All behavior—that is, all actions of the striated muscles regardless of the brain processes involved—result from neural signals traveling along these motor nerves. For this reason, the set of lower motor nerves has been designated the final common pathway (Sherrington, 1906/1923). The most elementary functional unit within the final common pathway, referred to as the *motor unit*, comprises the motoneuron cell body, its axon, its axon fibrils, and the individual muscle fibers innervated by these axon fibrils.

The depolarization of a motoneuron results in the quantal release of acetylcholine at the motor end plates. The activating neurotransmitter acetylcholine is quickly metabolized by the enzyme acetylcholinesterase so that continuous efferent discharges are required for continued propagation of muscle action potentials (MAPs) and fiber contraction. Nonetheless, the transient excitatory potential within a motor end plate can lead to a brief (e.g., 1 ms) depolarization of the resting membrane potential of the muscle cell and a MAP that is propagated bidirectionally across the muscle fiber with constant velocity and undiminished amplitude. The MAP travels rapidly along the surface of the fiber and flows into the muscle fiber itself via a system of T-tubules, thus ensuring that the contraction (known as a *twitch*) involves the entire fiber. The physiochemical mechanism responsible for the twitch involves a complex yet well-characterized self-regulating calcium-dependent interaction between the actin and myosin molecules.

The initial force of contraction produced by a muscle is attributable to small motoneurons discharging intermittently and then discharging more frequently. Stronger muscle contractions are attributable to the depolarization of increasingly large motoneurons within the motoneuron pool concurrent with increases in the firing rates of the smaller motoneurons already active. As muscle contraction approaches maximal levels, further increases in force are attributable primarily to the entire pool of motoneurons firing more rapidly. This cascade of processes appears to be regulated by unidimensional increases in the aggregate neural input to the motoneuronal pool, a process referred to as "common drive" (Brown, 2000; Deluca & Erim, 1994).

A small portion of the changing electromagnetic field confederated with these processes passes through the extracellular fluids to the skin, and it is these voltage fluctuations that constitute the major portion of the surface EMG signal. The voltage changes that are detected in surface EMG recording do not emanate from a single MAP but rather from MAPs traveling across many muscle fibers within a motor unit (i.e., motor unit action potential, or MUAP) and, more typically, from MAPs traveling across numerous motor fibers because of the activation of multiple motor units. Thus, the EMG does not provide a direct measure of tension, muscular contraction, or movement but rather the electrical activity associated with these events. More specifically, the surface EMG signal represents the ensemble electromagnetic field detectable at the surface of the skin at a given moment in time. Reliable, valid, and sensitive information about the aggregate actions (or inactions) of motoneuron pools across time, however, can nonetheless be obtained by careful attention to the elements of surface EMG recording and analysis (see Tassinary et al., 2017).

Neural Control

Our understanding of the neural control of movement has undergone rapid development over the past 2 decades, and although an even better understanding is still needed (Graziano et al., 2002; Nordin et al., 2017), traditional notions remain useful. In simple classical terms, the initiation of a discrete voluntary movement begins in the motor association premotor area of the frontal lobes and continues to the primary motor area located in the precentral gyrus and the anterior bank of the central sulcus. At this point, the upper motor neurons send signals to the brainstem and spinal cord via the corticobulbar and corticospinal pathways. Below these areas, the descending fibers from the upper motor neurons synapse with lower motor neurons, and the axons from these neurons innervate the striated musculature. The signals traversing this pathway are modulated via a wide variety of structures, including the cerebellum, reticular formation, and basal nuclei, structures that enable coordination, regulate muscle tone, and support the planning and execution of movements. The complexity of the reentrant circuits and corticocortical connections, combined with subcortical control structures involving both reflexes and central pattern generators, complicates the classical story considerably (see Solodkin et al., 2007).

Measurement

Electromyography. Electromyographic signals are small in two ways: They have low voltage and low current. An amplifier supplies both voltage gain (turning low into high voltages), which can be controlled by the investigator, and current gain, a function of the ratio of the input and output impedances of the amplifier. Electromyographic signals are amplified using differential amplifiers wherein the difference signal between two sensors (with respect to a third ground electrode) is amplified and carried through the signal processing chain. Any bioelectrical or extraneous electrical signal that is common to both electrodes (the common-mode signal) is, therefore, attenuated. The most commonly used method of recording EMG signals is one in which sensor pairs are aligned parallel to the course of the muscle fibers and is referred to as bipolar. This alignment, coupled with the high common-mode rejection capability of modern differential amplifiers, produces a relatively sensitive and selective recording of the activity of the underlying muscle groups (Basmajian & Deluca, 1985).

Sensors. Surface EMG electrodes can be attached to the skin in a variety of ways, but the most common is via double-sided adhesive collars. A highly conductive medium (paste or gel) is routinely used between skin and the detection surface although "active" electrodes typically forgo the conductive medium through the use of sophisticated materials and proximal microelectronics (e.g., Murphy et al., 2020). With traditional "passive" electrodes the medium serves to stabilize the interface between the skin and each detection surface by minimizing movement artifacts (i.e., by establishing an elastic connection between the detection surface and the skin), reducing inter-electrode impedances (i.e., by forming a highly conductive pathway across the hornified layers of the skin), and stabilizing the hydration and conductivity of the skin surface.

The designated site on the skin surface is usually cleaned to remove dirt and oil and typically abraded gently to lower intersensor impedances. The electrodes are then commonly affixed in a bipolar configuration according to a system for the accurate placement of such electrode pairs over the muscle(s) of interest (e.g., Tassinary et al., 1989a). The proximity of the ground electrode to the EMG sites being monitored is less important than the impedance of the skin–ground contact to help minimize extraneous electrical noise in the EMG recording. Consequently, care and reflection can and should be used to ensure a stable and low-impedance connection to ground. Finally, to avoid obstructing movement resulting from the attachment of surface electrodes, thought should be given to the orientation of electrode collars and wires. Electrode wires, for instance, should be draped and secured to minimize distraction, annoyance, or obstruction of movement or vision.

Signal conditioning. Some filtering of the raw EMG signal is necessary to increase the signal-to-noise ratio, decrease 50/60 Hz or ECG/EEG artifact, and reduce crosstalk. The primary energy in the bipolar recorded surface EMG signal lies between approximately 10 Hz and 200 Hz (van Boxtel et al., 1984). Between 10 Hz and 30 Hz, this power is due primarily to the firing rates of motor units; beyond 30 Hz, it is due to the shapes of the aggregated motor unit action potentials (Basmajian & Deluca, 1985). Attenuating the high frequencies in the EMG signal (e.g., using 500-Hz low-pass filters) reduces amplifier noise but rounds peaks of the detected motor unit action potentials. Retaining sharp signal peaks may be important for waveform or spectral analysis but is less critical for obtaining overall estimates of muscle tension. Attenuating the low frequencies (e.g., using 90-Hz high-pass filters) reduces 50/60 Hz noise from AC power lines, EEG and ECG artifacts, and, to some extent, crosstalk (because of the intervening tissue's preferential transmission of low frequencies) but, unfortunately, also eliminates a significant and sizable portion of the EMG signal. Use of an overly restricted EMG signal passband may result in inaccurate appraisal of the level and form of EMG activity or in a failure to detect small changes in the level of EMG activity. Hence, selection of an EMG detection passband must proceed based on susceptibility to artifact, presence of extraneous electrical noise at the source and high frequency noise internal to the amplifier, consideration of the amplitude of the EMG signals to be detected, need to minimize crosstalk, and variations across conditions in muscular fatigue. A passband from 10 Hz to 500 Hz is satisfactory for most psychophysiological recording situations (van Boxtel, 2001); if low-frequency artifact and crosstalk are problematic, then a 20 Hz or 30 Hz high-pass filter may be used. The investigator should realize one consequence of this selection is that weak signals from the target muscle may also be attenuated.

The most common signal conditioning technique used is smoothing, a term often confused with integration. True *integration* is the temporal summation or accumulation of EMG activity, whereas *smoothing* typically refers to performing integration with a built-in signal decay and is accomplished either by low-pass analog filtering or some type of digital signal averaging. Because the total energy in the EMG signal in any epoch of time is roughly equivalent to the rectified and smoothed EMG response, considerable economy in terms of data acquisition and signal processing can be achieved by rectification and smoothing before digitization when frequency components of the raw signal are not of interest.

Signal representation. Electromyographic activity unfolds over time, and, like many other psychophysiological responses, the complexity of the raw signal necessitates data reduction. Whether represented in the time, amplitude, or frequency domains, the first step involves the conversion of the digitized signal to a descriptive (e.g., physiological) unit of measurement.

Most psychophysiological research using EMG has focused on some variation of EMG signal amplitude as the dependent variable. Simple averaging of the raw EMG amplitudes is uninformative, however, because the nature of the signal ensures that the average expected value is 0. Counting or averaging the peaks in the EMG signal, or tallying its directional changes or zero crossings, are relatively easy methods to implement and are useful for gauging differences in EMG activity provided a sufficiently high sampling rate is used. As discussed, muscles consist of large numbers of homogeneous units, generating similarly sized action potentials recruited at similar levels of effort. Consequently, increments in the level of effort are generally found to be more accurately reflected in an integral-based measure rather than in a frequency-based measure. EMG signals consisting of low rates of widely varying spikes (e.g., those generated by small numbers of recruited motor units or closely spaced differential electrodes), however, generate poorly fused and noisy integrals, whereas the zero-crossing counts may reflect more accurately the level of effort (Loeb & Gans, 1986, Chapter 17).

The phrase *integrated EMG* has been used in this research to refer to the output of several different quantification techniques. Two of the most common parameters in contemporary research are the arithmetic average of the rectified and smoothed EMG signal and the root-mean-square of the raw EMG signal. Both processing techniques transform the EMG voltage-time function into a waveform that is nonnegative and bounded in time and amplitude. The moment-by-moment amplitude of this function represents an estimate of the total energy of the signal across time, the mean amplitude of this voltage-time function represents the average level of electrical energy emanating from the underlying muscle region(s) during a given recording epoch, and the integral of this function (e.g., the sum of the amplitudes) represents the total electrical activity (i.e., the size of the response) emanating from the underlying muscle region(s) during the recording epoch.

Facial EMG. The most common use of surface EMG measurement in psychophysiological settings is to record transient affective reactions linked to facial expressions. Such expressions, however, can also be assessed by naïve observer ratings as well as by objective coding systems. Observer ratings typically require a relatively large number of observers, and the interrater reliability can be quite variable depending on the specific rating task (Rosenthal, 2005). The systematic coding of facial expressions (i.e., Facial Action Coding System [FACS]; Ekman & Friesen, 1978) requires highly trained observers or an automated system (e.g., Cohn et al., 1999; Zeng et al., 2009). FACS provides a complete assessment of observable facial movements but is restricted to the measurement of observable facial behavior. The specific advantages of facial EMG by contrast are its high spatial and temporal resolution combined with its ability to track incipient facial reactions too subtle or fleeting to result in visible changes (Tassinary & Cacioppo, 1992).

Facial EMG has been used for the assessment of affective states in a large number of contexts and has become an accepted index of affective reactions to a variety of emotive visual (e.g., W. J. Davis et al., 1995; Larsen et al., 2003), auditory (e.g., Dimberg, 1990), gustatory (e.g., Hu et al., 1999), and olfactory (e.g., Jäncke & Kaufmann, 1994) stimuli; emotional faces (e.g., Dimberg, 1982; Dimberg & Öhman, 1996; Hess et al., 1988), real (e.g., Hess & Bourgeois, 2010) or virtual (e.g., Mojzisch et al., 2006); interaction partners; and nicotine (e.g., Robinson et al., 2007) and other drugs (e.g., Newton et al., 1997). It has also become an accepted index of attitudes toward others (e.g., Brown et al., 2006; Dambrun et al., 2003) and oneself (e.g., Buck et al., 2004) in adults and in children (e.g., Armstrong et al., 2007) using supra- as well as subliminal stimuli (e.g., Arndt et al., 2001).

For certain questions, facial EMG measures of affect have been found to be more reliable and revealing than self-report measures, making this method specifically attractive (e.g., Hazlett & Hazlett, 1999; Vanman et al., 1997; see also below). In addition, facial EMG has been used to assess attention (e.g., Cohen et al., 1992) and fatigue (e.g., Veldhuizen et al., 2003).

An example: Prejudice. Vanman et al. (2004) employed facial EMG as a measure of prejudice. Specifically, they measured EMG at the zygomaticus major (smile) and corrugator supercilii (frown) sites to assess White university students' positive and negative affective reactions to pictures of Black and White individuals. In a separate task on a different day, the same university students were asked to choose the best of three applicants (two were White and one was Black) for a prestigious teaching fellowship. White individuals who showed less zygomaticus major activity when looking at photos of Black individuals were found to be more likely to show a bias against selecting a Black applicant. Interestingly, the implicit attitude task (Greenwald et al., 1998)—an implicit measure of racial bias—did not predict selection bias. Furthermore, motivation to control prejudice influenced the implicit attitude task but not the EMG measure, suggesting that facial EMG can be used as a sensitive measure of implicit prejudice related to overt discrimination.

Reflex probe. Another popular use of facial EMG is for the assessment of the potentiation of eyeblinks in reaction to a startling sound (see Blumenthal & Franklin, 2009). Ample research has demonstrated that the startle eyeblink reflex to a sudden acoustic probe is modulated by the individual's emotional state (e.g., Bradley et al., 2006). Theoretically, when an individual is exposed to an unpleasant stimulus, the relevant subcortical aversive system circuitry is activated, leading to the augmentation of defensive reflexes such as the eye blink reflex. Because appetitive and aversive—defensive states are opponent states, the opposite effect can be observed when the individual is exposed to pleasant stimuli. Lesion and blockade studies support a key mediational role of the central nucleus of the amygdala for startle potentiation. (e.g., Hitchcock & Davis, 1986). Additional research has also demonstrated that reflex modulation is a complex function of vigilance and the valence of an expected event (Sege et al., 2014).

Benning et al. (2004) obtained a pattern opposite to that for the eye blink reflex for the reflexive contraction of the postauricular muscle, which serves to pull the ear back and up (Bérzin & Fortinguerra, 1993). The postauricular reflex (PAR) can be observed in response to nonstartling sounds as well. This reflexive reaction to a sound is augmented when individuals are exposed to pleasant stimuli and a reduced one when exposed to unpleasant stimuli.

An example: Approach and avoid. Hess, Adams, and Kleck (2007) explored people's reaction to male and female anger and happiness expressions. Specifically, they tested a prediction on the basis of the functional equivalence hypothesis (Hess, Sabourin, & Kleck, 2007), which postulates that facial expressive behavior and morphological cues to dominance and affiliation are similar in their effects on emotional attributions. They noted that the cues linked to perceived dominance (e.g., square jaw, heavy eyebrows, high forehead) are more typical for men, and men are generally perceived as more dominant than are women. In contrast, baby-facedness, a facial aspect more closely linked to perceived affiliation, is more common in women. This leads to the hypothesis that anger in men should be seen as more threatening because of the double association with dominance of both anger and male features. Likewise, because of the double association of happiness and female features, smiling women should be perceived as more appetitive. Hess, Sabourin, and Kleck (2007) measured both eye blink startle and the PAR while participants were viewing happy and angry expressions shown by men and women. Overall, the PAR was potentiated during happy expressions and inhibited during anger expressions, and, as predicted, this pattern was more clearly found for female expressers. Also as predicted, eye blink startle was potentiated during viewing of angry faces and inhibited during viewing of happy faces only for expressions shown by men.

Summary. Surface EMG has a high temporal and spatial resolution and, thus, allows the measurement of fleeting and subtle movements. Facial EMG is an ideal tool for the real-time measurement of emotional and cognitive processes. Studies like those by Vanman et al. (2004) and Hess, Sabourin, and Kleck (2007) pointed to its use as an implicit measure that is not easily influenced by voluntary action—not because participants can't smile or blink voluntarily but simply because they are neither aware nor capable of micromanagement of nascent movements. The use of EMG does typically require, however, that the researcher can specify in advance which of a few muscles will be of interest in a given context.

Video-based. Until recently, EMG was the primary method for obtaining accurate information about movement timing and amplitude. Advances in video-based coding of movements, including marker and markerless motion capture and automated classification of movement, allow for alternatives to EMG (e.g., Teitelebaum et al., 2004).

In the last decade, several automated classifiers for facial affect recognition have become commercially available. A recent review by Dupré et al. (2020) concluded that, while these automated facial recognition systems tend to be as good as—and sometimes even better than—human observers, when it comes to posed expressions, they are less efficient for natural spontaneous expressions. In this test both human observers and automated systems produced single labels that best fit the expressions shown. Facial EMG by contrast provides very detailed information about single muscle sites. As such, the two approaches are not truly comparable. For some limited use—for example, to assess whether people show a positive or negative facial reaction to a stimulus—one could use an automated facial recognition system instead of measuring zygomaticus major and corrugator supercilii activity. Automated facial recognition systems however, just like human observers, rely only on visible information. For some uses, for example, the assessment of facial mimicry, which typically is a more subtle expressive signal (Hess, 2021), this could be a limitation. Nonetheless, in a recent study Kastendieck and colleagues (2021) were able to use an automated facial recognition system for this purpose. Eye blink rate may also be reliably measured with automated video analysis methods (Chen & Epps, 2014).

Eye movements. While eye movement measurement in psychology is typically done with camera-based eye tracking (see Chapter 22 for a review of eye tracking), measurements of eye movement via EEG, EMG, or electrooculography (EOG) remains popular for brain- or human–computer interface (BCI/HCI) applications (Majaranta & Bulling, 2014). The EOG involves the recording of changes in electrical potentials from eye movements and eye blinks. The eyes have an electrical charge with a positive potential at the cornea and a negative potential at the retina that changes when the eyes move or blink (Berg & Scherg, 1991). These changes are readily measured with electrodes placed above and below the eye (capturing blinks and vertical eye movements) and just lateral to the outer canthus of the left and right eyes (capturing horizontal eye movements). While eye movements, and especially eye blinks, are routinely treated as artifacts to be removed or corrected (Hoffmann & Falkenstein, 2008), there are practical uses for eye blink and other eye movement data. One use of eye blink measurement is probing the startle reflex, reviewed previously (see Reflex Probe); another use for eye blink measurements in calculating spontaneous eye blink rate (sEBR), also referred to as endogenous eye blinks. It has been known for at about a century that spontaneous eye blink rates are related to psychological constructs (see Stern et al., 1984, for a review). Resting eye blink rate has also been used for decades as a marker of striatal dopamine function in neurological and psychiatric studies (Karson, 1983), and there has been more recent interest in using eye blink rate to indirectly relate dopamine function and behavior (Jongkees & Colzato, 2016). Low sEBR has been found to be associated with learning from punishment, although high sEBR is not associated with learning from reward. Nevertheless, high EBR has been shown to positively correlate with effort individuals are willing to expend for reward (Pas et al., 2014). Reliable sEBR measurements can be obtained within a period of 5 minutes where participants are resting and gazing at a point on a nearby wall. EOG data are typically preprocessed with bandpass filters to reduce noise (e.g., 0.01–10 Hz) and counted manually or automatically by algorithms that detect amplitude changes of greater than 100 μV with durations less than 500 milliseconds (Barbato et al., 2000; Colzato et al., 2008).

Pupillometry. The dilation and contraction of the pupil are under autonomic control by a pair of smooth muscles (i.e., iris dilator muscle and iris sphincter muscle), acting in opposition to one another (see Beatty & Lucero-Wagoner, 2000). The sphincter muscle contracts the pupil in a spherical motion, and the dilator muscles widen the pupil by pulling the iris outward. The dilation of the pupil is under control of the sympathetic nervous system and relies on the neurotransmitter norepinephrine; when sympathetic activity is high, for example, in the fight-or-flight reflex. The iris sphincter muscle regulates pupillary constriction (miosis) and accommodation via parasympathetic innervation through the short ciliary nerves from the Edinger-Westphal nucleus of cranial nerve III. Joint function is mainly a result of sympathetic innervation, and both the sympathetic and parasympathetic systems work in antagonism regulating pupillary aperture (Bloom et al., 2020; McDougal & Gamlin, 2015).

In psychological research, pupil dilation is often used as a marker of physiological arousal, or more specifically, sympathetic activation (Bradley et al., 2008). Pupil dilation has been associated with several different conditions, such as emotional arousal, both positive and negative (e.g., Henderson et al., 2018; decision making, de Gee et al., 2014; attentional expectancy, Wierda et al., 2012). During decision making, pupil dilation has specifically been related to surprise, that is an error in the prediction of uncertainty rather that uncertainty or reward prediction itself (Preuschoff et al., 2011). In addition, findings suggest that mental effort is reliably indexed by pupil dilation (Van Der Wel & Van Steenbergen, 2018), which has led to increased use of pupil dilation in studies of human–computer interaction (Iqbal et al., 2004).

As pupillometry is covered elsewhere in this volume (Chapter 22), we will just briefly mention a few critical aspects here. Pupil contraction and dilation are routinely measured with commercially available eye tracking systems that typically rely on infrared cameras that must be calibrated to the individual participant. Recent developments on the judicious use of facial landmarks, however, have allowed changes in pupil dilation to be reliably detected even from low-quality webcams (Samara et al., 2017). Independent of the technology, however, it is important to recognize that pupil dilation is strongly affected by changes in luminance and, thus, the illumination of the experiment room must be controlled, and the use of isoluminant stimuli is highly recommended (Van Der Wel & Van Steenbergen, 2018). A recent careful and thorough replication of the germinal papers by Hess on pupillary dilation as a measure of interest (de Winter et al., 2021) reinforces the critical importance of luminance control in pupillometric studies.

CONCLUSION

It has become customary in the cognitive and social sciences to view perimetric physiological measures in the same way as reaction time—namely, as an index, or an observable correlate of some aggregate property of a psychological process, and not as a response computed explicitly by a psychological process. This assumption affords such measures their great potential to illuminate putative mechanisms (Pylyshyn, 1980). Psychophysiological measures, thus, play a major role in efforts to understand the mind–brain as both an embodied and embedded phenomenon. Their applied utility continues to expand, most recently making significant inroads into the burgeoning fields of game research (Yannakakis et al., 2016) and human–computer interaction (Cowley et al., 2016). Coupled with advances in signal acquisition and analysis, we predict that these traditional measures will be increasingly incorporated into sophisticated theoretical frameworks on the basis of our evolving understanding of the myriad coalitions formed between organisms and their environment.

References

Adrian, E. D., & Bronk, D. W. (1929). The discharge of impulses in motor nerve fibres: Part II. The frequency of discharge in reflex and voluntary contractions. *The Journal of Physiology*, 67(2), i3–i151. https://doi.org/10.1113/jphysiol.1929.sp002557

Allen, K. M., Blascovich, J., Tomaka, J., & Kelsey, R. M. (1991). Presence of human friends and pet dogs as moderators of autonomic responses to stress in women. *Journal of Personality and Social Psychology*, 61(4), 582–589. https://doi.org/10.1037/0022-3514.61.4.582

Andreassi, J. L. (2006). *Psychophysiology: Human behavior and response* (4th ed.). Erlbaum.

Armstrong, J. E., Hutchinson, I., Laing, D. G., & Jinks, A. L. (2007). Facial electromyography: Responses of children to odor and taste stimuli. *Chemical Senses*, 32(6), 611–621. https://doi.org/10.1093/chemse/bjm029

Arndt, J., Allen, J. J. B., & Greenberg, J. (2001). Traces of terror: Subliminal death primes and facial electromyographic indices of affect. *Motivation and Emotion*, 25(3), 253–277. https://doi.org/10.1023/A:1012276524327

Ax, A. F. (1953). The physiological differentiation between fear and anger in humans. *Psychosomatic Medicine*, 15(5), 433–442. https://doi.org/10.1097/00006842-195309000-00007

Barbato, G., Ficca, G., Muscettola, G., Fichele, M., Beatrice, M., & Rinaldi, F. (2000). Diurnal variation in spontaneous eye-blink rate. *Psychiatry Research*, 93(2), 145–151. https://doi.org/10.1016/S0165-1781(00)00108-6

Basmajian, J. V., & Deluca, C. J. (1985). *Muscles alive: Their functions revealed by electromyography* (5th ed.). Williams & Wilkins.

Beatty, J., & Lucero-Wagoner, B. (2000). The pupillary system. In J. T. Cacioppo, L. G. Tassinary, & G. G. Berntson (Eds.), *Handbook of psychophysiology* (pp. 142–162). Cambridge University Press.

Benning, S. D., Patrick, C. J., & Lang, A. R. (2004). Emotional modulation of the post-auricular reflex. *Psychophysiology*, *41*(3), 426–432. https://doi.org/10.1111/j.1469-8986.00160.x

Berg, P., & Scherg, M. (1991). Dipole models of eye movements and blinks. *Electroencephalography and Clinical Neurophysiology*, *79*(1), 36–44. https://doi.org/10.1016/0013-4694(91)90154-V

Berman, S. M., Bullimore, M. A., Jacobs, R. J., Bailey, I. L., & Gandhi, N. (1994). An objective measure of discomfort glare. *Journal of the Illuminating Engineering Society*, *23*(2), 40–49. https://doi.org/10.1080/00994480.1994.10748079

Berntson, G. G., Bigger, J. T., Jr., Eckberg, D. L., Grossman, P., Kaufmann, P. G., Malik, M., Nagaraja, H. N., Porges, S. W., Saul, J. P., Stone, P. H., & van der Molen, M. W. (1997). Heart rate variability: Origins, methods, and interpretive caveats. *Psychophysiology*, *34*(6), 623–648. https://doi.org/10.1111/j.1469-8986.1997.tb02140.x

Berntson, G. G., Cacioppo, J. T., & Quigley, K. S. (1993). Cardiac psychophysiology and autonomic space in humans: Empirical perspectives and conceptual implications. *Psychological Bulletin*, *114*(2), 296–322. https://doi.org/10.1037/0033-2909.114.2.296

Berntson, G. G., Quigley, K. S., Norman, G. J., & Lozano, D. L. (2017). Cardiovascular Psychophysiology. In J. T. Cacioppo, L. G. Tassinary, & G. G. Berntson (Eds.), *Handbook of psychophysiology* (4th ed., pp. 183–216). Cambridge University Press.

Bérzin, F., & Fortinguerra, C. R. (1993). EMG study of the anterior, superior and posterior auricular muscles in man. *Anatomischer Anzeiger*, *175*(2), 195–197. https://doi.org/10.1016/S0940-9602(11)80182-2

Blascovich, J., Mendes, W. B., Tomaka, J., Salomon, K., & Seery, M. (2003). The robust nature of the biopsychosocial model challenge and threat: A reply to Wright and Kirby. *Personality and Social Psychology Review*, *7*(3), 234–243. https://doi.org/10.1207/S15327957PSPR0703_03

Blascovich, J., Spencer, S. J., Quinn, D., & Steele, C. (2001). African Americans and high blood pressure: The role of stereotype threat. *Psychological Science*, *12*(3), 225–229. https://doi.org/10.1111/1467-9280.00340

Bloom, J., Motlagh, M., & Czyz, C. N. (2020). *Anatomy, head and neck, eye iris sphincter muscle*. StatPearls Publishing.

Bluemke, M., & Friese, M. (2008). Reliability and validity of the Single-Target IAT (ST-IAT): Assessing automatic affect towards multiple attitude objects. *European Journal of Social Psychology*, *38*(6), 977–997. https://doi.org/10.1002/ejsp.487

Blumenthal, T. D., & Franklin, J. C. (2009). The startle eyeblink response. In E. Harmon-Jones & J. S. Beer (Eds.), *Methods in social neuroscience* (pp. 92–117). Guilford Press.

Boese, A. C., Kim, S. C., Yin, K.-J., Lee, J.-P., & Hamblin, M. H. (2017). Sex differences in vascular physiology and pathophysiology: Estrogen and androgen signaling in health and disease. *American Journal of Physiology. Heart and Circulatory Physiology*, *313*(3), H524–H545. https://doi.org/10.1152/ajpheart.00217.2016

Boucsein, W. (2012). *Electrodermal activity* (2nd ed.). Springer Nature. https://doi.org/10.1007/978-1-4614-1126-0

Boucsein, W., Fowles, D. C., Grimnes, S., Ben-Shakhar, G., Roth, W. T., Dawson, M. E., Filion, D. L., & the Society for Psychophysiological Research Ad Hoc Committee on Electrodermal Measures. (2012). Publication recommendations for electrodermal measurements. *Psychophysiology*, *49*(8), 1017–1034. https://doi.org/10.1111/j.1469-8986.2012.01384.x

Boulant, J. A. (1981). Hypothalamic mechanisms in thermoregulation. *Federation Proceedings*, *40*(14), 2843–2850.

Bradley, M. M., Codispoti, M., & Lang, P. J. (2006). A multi-process account of startle modulation during affective perception. *Psychophysiology*, *43*(5), 486–497. https://doi.org/10.1111/j.1469-8986.2006.00412.x

Bradley, M. M., Miccoli, L., Escrig, M. A., & Lang, P. J. (2008). The pupil as a measure of emotional arousal and autonomic activation. *Psychophysiology*, *45*(4), 602–607. https://doi.org/10.1111/j.1469-8986.2008.00654.x

Brody, S., & Preut, R. (2003). Vaginal intercourse frequency and heart rate variability. *Journal of Sex & Marital Therapy*, *29*(5), 371–380. https://doi.org/10.1080/00926230390224747

Brosschot, J. F., Van Dijk, E., & Thayer, J. F. (2007). Daily worry is related to low heart rate variability during waking and the subsequent nocturnal sleep period. *International Journal of Psychophysiology*, *63*(1), 39–47. https://doi.org/10.1016/j.ijpsycho.2006.07.016

Brown, L. M., Bradley, M. M., & Lang, P. J. (2006). Affective reactions to pictures of ingroup and outgroup members. *Biological Psychology, 71*(3), 303–311. https://doi.org/10.1016/j.biopsycho.2005.06.003

Brown, P. (2000). Cortical drives to human muscle: The Piper and related rhythms. *Progress in Neurobiology, 60*(1), 97–108. https://doi.org/10.1016/S0301-0082(99)00029-5

Buck, S. M., Hillman, C. H., Evans, E. M., & Janelle, C. M. (2004). Emotional responses to pictures of oneself in healthy college age females. *Motivation and Emotion, 28*(3), 279–295. https://doi.org/10.1023/B:MOEM.0000040155.79452.23

Cacioppo, J. T., & Hawkley, L. C. (2009). Loneliness. In M. R. Leary & R. H. Hoyle (Eds.), *Handbook of individual differences in social behavior* (pp. 227–240). Guilford Press.

Cacioppo, J. T., Hawkley, L. C., Crawford, L. E., Ernst, J. M., Burleson, M. H., Kowalewski, R. B., Malarkey, W. B., Van Cauter, E., & Berntson, G. G. (2002). Loneliness and health: Potential mechanisms. *Psychosomatic Medicine, 64*(3), 407–417. https://doi.org/10.1097/00006842-200205000-00005

Cacioppo, J. T., & Tassinary, L. G. (Eds.). (1990). *Principles of psychophysiology: Physical, social, and inferential elements*. Cambridge University Press.

Cacioppo, J. T., Tassinary, L. G., & Berntson, G. G. (Eds.). (2017). *The handbook of psychophysiology* (4th ed.). Cambridge University Press.

Carpenter, A., & Frontera, A. (2016). Smart-watches: A potential challenger to the implantable loop recorder? *Europace, 18*(6), 791–793. https://doi.org/10.1093/europace/euv427

Carpenter, J. S., Andrykowski, M. A., Freedman, R. R., & Munn, R. (1999). Feasibility and psychometrics of an ambulatory hot flash monitoring device. *Menopause, 6*(3), 209–215. https://doi.org/10.1097/00042192-199906030-00006

Chen, S., & Epps, J. (2014). Efficient and robust pupil size and blink estimation from near-field video sequences for human-machine interaction. *IEEE Transactions on Cybernetics, 44*(12), 2356–2367. https://doi.org/10.1109/TCYB.2014.2306916

Cheng, D. T., Knight, D. C., Smith, C. N., & Helmstetter, F. J. (2006). Human amygdala activity during the expression of fear responses. *Behavioral Neuroscience, 120*(6), 1187–1195. https://doi.org/10.1037/0735-7044.120.5.1187

Cohen, B. H., Davidson, R. J., Senulis, J. A., Saron, C. D., & Weisman, D. R. (1992). Muscle tension patterns during auditory attention. *Biological Psychology, 33*(2-3), 133–156. https://doi.org/10.1016/0301-0511(92)90028-S

Cohn, J. F., Zlochower, A. J., Lien, J., & Kanade, T. (1999). Automated face analysis by feature point tracking has high concurrent validity with manual FACS coding. *Psychophysiology, 36*(1), 35–43. https://doi.org/10.1017/S0048577299971184

Colzato, L. S., Jongkees, B. J., de Wit, M., van der Molen, M. J. W., & Steenbergen, L. (2018). Variable heart rate and a flexible mind: Higher resting-state heart rate variability predicts better task-switching. *Cognitive, Affective & Behavioral Neuroscience, 18*(4), 730–738. https://doi.org/10.3758/s13415-018-0600-x

Colzato, L. S., Slagter, H. A., Spapé, M. M. A., & Hommel, B. (2008). Blinks of the eye predict blinks of the mind. *Neuropsychologia, 46*(13), 3179–3183. https://doi.org/10.1016/j.neuropsychologia.2008.07.006

Cook, E. W., & Turpin, G. (1997). Differentiating orienting, startle and defense responses: The role of affect and its implications for psychopathology. In P. J. Lang, R. F. Simons, & M. T. Balaban (Eds.), *Attention and orienting: Sensory and motivational processes* (pp. 137–164). Erlbaum.

Cowley, B., Filetti, M., Lukander, K., Torniainen, J., Henelius, A., Ahonen, L., Barral, O., Kosunen, I., Valtonen, T., Huotilainen, M., Ravaja, N., & Jacuzzi, G. (2016). The psychophysiology primer: A guide to methods and a broad review with a focus on human–computer interaction. *Foundations and Trends in Human-Computer Interaction, 9*(3-4), 151–308. https://doi.org/10.1561/1100000065

Critchley, H. D., Elliott, R., Mathias, C. J., & Dolan, R. J. (2000). Neural activity relating to generation and representation of galvanic skin conductance responses: A functional magnetic resonance imaging study. *The Journal of Neuroscience, 20*(8), 3033–3040. https://doi.org/10.1523/JNEUROSCI.20-08-03033.2000

Curtin, J. J., Lozano, D. L., & Allen, J. J. B. (2007). The psychophysiology laboratory. In J. A. Coan & J. J. B. Allen (Eds.), *Handbook of emotion elicitation and assessment* (pp. 398–425). Series in affective science. Oxford University Press.

Cuthbertson, R. A. (1990). The highly original Dr. Duchenne. In R. A. Cuthbertson (Ed.), *The mechanism of human facial expression* (pp. 225–241). Cambridge University Press. https://doi.org/10.1017/CBO9780511752841.024

Czeszumski, A., Eustergerling, S., Lang, A., Menrath, D., Gerstenberger, M., Schuberth, S., Schreiber, F., Rendon, Z. Z., & König, P. (2020). Hyperscanning: A valid method to study neural inter-brain underpinnings of social interaction. *Frontiers in Human Neuroscience, 14,* 39. https://doi.org/10.3389/fnhum.2020.00039

Dambrun, M., Després, G., & Guimond, S. (2003). On the multifaceted nature of prejudice: Psychophysiological responses to ingroup and out-group ethnic stimuli. *Current Research in Social Psychology*, *8*(14), 200–204.

Darrow, C. W. (1929a). Differences in the physiological reactions to sensory and ideational stimuli. *Psychological Bulletin*, *26*(4), 185–201. https://doi.org/10.1037/h0074053

Darrow, C. W. (1929b). Electrical and circulatory responses to brief sensory and ideational stimuli. *Journal of Experimental Psychology*, *12*(4), 267–300. https://doi.org/10.1037/h0064070

Darrow, C. W. (1933). Functional significance of the galvanic skin reflex and perspiration on the back and palms of the hands. *Psychological Bulletin*, *30*, 712.

Darrow, C. W. (1934). The reflexohmeter (pocket type). *The Journal of General Psychology*, *10*(1), 238–239. https://doi.org/10.1080/00221309.1934.9917731

Darwin, C. (1873). *The expression of the emotions in man and animals*. Appleton. (Original work published 1872)

Davis, R. C. (1938). The relation of muscle action potentials to difficulty and frustration. *Journal of Experimental Psychology*, *23*(2), 141–158. https://doi.org/10.1037/h0059544

Davis, W. J., Rahman, M. A., Smith, L. J., Burns, A., Senecal, L., McArthur, D., Halpern, J. A., Perlmutter, A., Sickels, W., & Wagner, W. (1995). Properties of human affect induced by static color slides (IAPS): Dimensional, categorical and electromyographic analysis. *Biological Psychology*, *41*(3), 229–253. https://doi.org/10.1016/0301-0511(95)05141-4

Dawson, M. E., Schell, A. M., & Filion, D. L. (1990). The electrodermal system. In J. T. Cacioppo & L. G. Tassinary (Eds.), *Principles of psychophysiology: Physical, social, and inferential elements* (pp. 295–324). Cambridge University Press.

de Gee, J. W., Knapen, T., & Donner, T. H. (2014). Decision-related pupil dilation reflects upcoming choice and individual bias. *Proceedings of the National Academy of Sciences of the United States of America*, *111*(5), E618–E625. https://doi.org/10.1073/pnas.1317557111

de Liver, Y., Wigboldus, D., & van der Pligt, J. (2007). Positive and negative associations underlying ambivalent attitudes: Evidence from implicit measures. *Journal of Experimental Social Psychology*, *43*(2), 319–326. https://doi.org/10.1016/j.jesp.2006.02.012

De Luca, C. J., & Erim, Z. (1994). Common drive of motor units in regulation of muscle force. *Trends in Neurosciences*, *17*(7), 299–305. https://doi.org/10.1016/0166-2236(94)90064-7

Denver, J. W., Reed, S. F., & Porges, S. W. (2007). Methodological issues in the quantification of respiratory sinus arrhythmia. *Biological Psychology*, *74*(2), 286–294. https://doi.org/10.1016/j.biopsycho.2005.09.005

de Winter, J. C. F., Petermeijer, S. M., Kooijman, L., & Dodou, D. (2021). Replicating five pupillometry studies of Eckhard Hess. *International Journal of Psychophysiology*, *165*, 145–205. https://doi.org/10.1016/j.ijpsycho.2021.03.003

Dimberg, U. (1982). Facial reactions to facial expressions. *Psychophysiology*, *19*(6), 643–647. https://doi.org/10.1111/j.1469-8986.1982.tb02516.x

Dimberg, U. (1990). Perceived unpleasantness and facial reactions to auditory stimuli. *Scandinavian Journal of Psychology*, *31*(1), 70–75. https://doi.org/10.1111/j.1467-9450.1990.tb00804.x

Dimberg, U., & Öhman, A. (1996). Behold the wrath: Psychophysiological responses to facial stimuli. *Motivation and Emotion*, *20*(2), 149–182. https://doi.org/10.1007/BF02253869

Dormire, S. L., & Carpenter, J. S. (2002). An alternative to Unibase/glycol as an effective nonhydrating electrolyte medium for the measurement of electrodermal activity. *Psychophysiology*, *39*(4), 423–426. https://doi.org/10.1111/1469-8986.3940423

Dotsch, R., & Wigboldus, D. H. R. (2008). Virtual prejudice. *Journal of Experimental Social Psychology*, *44*(4), 1194–1198. https://doi.org/10.1016/j.jesp.2008.03.003

Duchenne, G. B. (1990). *The mechanism of human facial expression* (R. A. Cuthbertson, Ed. & Trans.). Cambridge University Press. (Original work published 1862) https://doi.org/10.1017/CBO9780511752841

Dupré, D., Krumhuber, E. G., Küster, D., & McKeown, G. J. (2020). A performance comparison of eight commercially available automatic classifiers for facial affect recognition. *PLOS ONE*, *15*(4), e0231968. https://doi.org/10.1371/journal.pone.0231968

Edelberg, R. (1972). Electrical activity of the skin: Its measurements and uses in psychophysiology. In N. S. Greenfield & R. A. Sternbach (Eds.), *Handbook of psychophysiology* (pp. 367–418). Holt.

Edelberg, R. (1977). Relation of electrical properties of skin to structure and physiologic state. *The Journal of Investigative Dermatology*, *69*(3), 324–327. https://doi.org/10.1111/1523-1747.ep12507771

Edwards, J. R. (2001). Ten difference score myths. *Organizational Research Methods*, *4*(3), 265–287. https://doi.org/10.1177/109442810143005

Ehrlich, S. K., Agres, K. R., Guan, C., & Cheng, G. (2019). A closed-loop, music-based brain-computer interface for emotion mediation. *PLOS ONE*, *14*(3), e0213516. https://doi.org/10.1371/journal.pone.0213516

Ekman, P., & Friesen, W. V. (1969). The repertoire of nonverbal behavior: Categories, origins, usage, and coding. *Semiotica*, *1*(1), 49–98. https://doi.org/10.1515/semi.1969.1.1.49

Ekman, P., & Friesen, W. V. (1978). *The facial action coding system: A technique for the measurement of facial movement*. Consulting Psychologists Press.

Elliott, R. (1974). The motivational significance of heart rate. In P. A. Obrist, A. H. Black, J. Brener, & L. V. DiCara (Eds.), *Cardiovascular psychophysiology* (pp. 505–537). Aldine.

Elliott, R. (1969). Tonic heart rate: Experiments on the effects of collative variables lead to a hypothesis about its motivational significance. *Journal of Personality and Social Psychology*, *12*(3), 211–228. https://doi.org/10.1037/h0027630

Fechner, G. (1860). *Elemente der Psychophysik*. Breitkopf & Härtel.

Féré, C. (1888). Note sur les modifications de la résistance électrique sous l'influence des excitations sensorielles et des emotions [Note on the modification of electrical resistance under the effects of sensory stimulation and emotional excitement]. *Comptes Rendus des Seances de la Societe de Biologie*, *5*, 217–219.

Fisch, C. (2000). Centennial of the string galvanometer and the electrocardiogram. *Journal of the American College of Cardiology*, *36*(6), 1737–1745. https://doi.org/10.1016/S0735-1097(00)00976-1

Fishel, S. R., Muth, E. R., & Hoover, A. W. (2007). Establishing appropriate physiological baseline procedures for real-time physiological measurement. *Journal of Cognitive Engineering and Decision Making*, *1*(3), 286–308. https://doi.org/10.1518/155534307X255636

Forslind, B., Lindberg, M., Roomans, G. M., Pallon, J., & Werner-Linde, Y. (1997). Aspects on the physiology of human skin: Studies using particle probe analysis. *Microscopy Research and Technique*, *38*(4), 373–386. https://doi.org/10.1002/(SICI)1097-0029(19970815)38:4<373::AID-JEMT5>3.0.CO;2-K

Fowles, D. C. (1988). Psychophysiology and psychopathology: A motivational approach. *Psychophysiology*, *25*(4), 373–391. https://doi.org/10.1111/j.1469-8986.1988.tb01873.x

Fowles, D. C., Christie, M. J., Edelberg, R., Grings, W. W., Lykken, D. T., & Venables, P. H. (1981). Publication recommendation for electrodermal measurements. *Psychophysiology*, *18*(3), 232–239. https://doi.org/10.1111/j.1469-8986.1981.tb03024.x

Fridlund, A. J., & Cacioppo, J. T. (1986). Guidelines for human electromyographic research. *Psychophysiology*, *23*(5), 567–589. https://doi.org/10.1111/j.1469-8986.1986.tb00676.x

Gardiner, H. M., Metcalf, R. C., & Beebe-Center, J. G. (1937). *Feeling and emotion: A history of theories*. American Book Company. https://doi.org/10.1037/10763-000

Geen, T. R., & Tassinary, L. G. (2002). The mechanization of emotional expression in John Bulwer's "Pathomyotomia" (1649). *The American Journal of Psychology*, *115*(2), 275–299. https://doi.org/10.2307/1423439

Giardino, N. D., Lehrer, P. M., & Edelberg, R. (2002). Comparison of finger plethysmograph to ECG in the measurement of heart rate variability. *Psychophysiology*, *39*(2), 246–253. https://doi.org/10.1111/1469-8986.3920246

Graham, F. K., & Clifton, R. K. (1966). Heart-rate change as a component of the orienting response. *Psychological Bulletin*, *65*(5), 305–320. https://doi.org/10.1037/h0023258

Graziano, M. S. A., Taylor, C. S. R., & Moore, T. (2002). Complex movements evoked by microstimulation of precentral cortex. *Neuron*, *34*(5), 841–851. https://doi.org/10.1016/S0896-6273(02)00698-0

Greenwald, A. G., McGhee, D. E., & Schwartz, J. L. K. (1998). Measuring individual differences in implicit cognition: The implicit association test. *Journal of Personality and Social Psychology*, *74*(6), 1464–1480. https://doi.org/10.1037/0022-3514.74.6.1464

Grings, W. W., & Dawson, M. E. (1973). Complex variables in conditioning. In W. F. Prokasy & D. C. Raskin (Eds.), *Electrodermal activity in psychological research* (pp. 203–254). Academic Press. https://doi.org/10.1016/B978-0-12-565950-5.50009-0

Grossman, P., & Taylor, E. W. (2007). Toward understanding respiratory sinus arrhythmia: Relations to cardiac vagal tone, evolution and biobehavioral functions. *Biological Psychology*, *74*(2), 263–285. https://doi.org/10.1016/j.biopsycho.2005.11.014

Hales, S. (1733). *Statical essays: Containing haemastaticks*. Universität Lausanne.

Hansen, A. L., Johnsen, B. H., & Thayer, J. F. (2003). Vagal influence on working memory and attention. *International Journal of Psychophysiology*,

48(3), 263–274. https://doi.org/10.1016/S0167-8760(03)00073-4

Hawkley, L. C., Burleson, M. H., Berntson, G. G., & Cacioppo, J. T. (2003). Loneliness in everyday life: Cardiovascular activity, psychosocial context, and health behaviors. *Journal of Personality and Social Psychology*, 85(1), 105–120. https://doi.org/10.1037/0022-3514.85.1.105

Hayano, J., Sakakibara, Y., Yamada, A., Yamada, M., Mukai, S., Fujinami, T., Yokoyama, K., Watanabe, Y., & Takata, K. (1991). Accuracy of assessment of cardiac vagal tone by heart rate variability in normal subjects. *The American Journal of Cardiology*, 67(2), 199–204. https://doi.org/10.1016/0002-9149(91)90445-Q

Hazlett, R. L., & Hazlett, S. Y. (1999). Emotional response to television commercials: Facial EMG vs. self-report. *Journal of Advertising Research*, 39(2), 7–23.

Henderson, R. R., Bradley, M. M., & Lang, P. J. (2018). Emotional imagery and pupil diameter. *Psychophysiology*, 55(6), e13050. https://doi.org/10.1111/psyp.13050

Hess, U. (2021). Who to whom and why: The social nature of emotional mimicry. *Psychophysiology*, 58(1), e13675. https://doi.org/10.1111/psyp.13675

Hess, U., Adams, R. B., Jr., & Kleck, R. E. (2007). When two do the same it might not mean the same: The perception of emotional expressions shown by men and women. In U. Hess & P. Philippot (Eds.), *Group dynamics and emotional expression* (pp. 33–50). Cambridge University Press. https://doi.org/10.1017/CBO9780511499838.003

Hess, U., & Bourgeois, P. (2010). You smile—I smile: Emotion expression in social interaction. *Biological Psychology*, 84(3), 514–520. https://doi.org/10.1016/j.biopsycho.2009.11.001

Hess, U., Kappas, A., McHugo, G. J., Kleck, R. E., & Lanzetta, J. T. (1988). An analysis of the encoding and decoding of spontaneous and posed smiles: The use of facial electromyography. *Journal of Nonverbal Behavior*, 13(2), 121–137. https://doi.org/10.1007/BF00990794

Hess, U., Sabourin, G., & Kleck, R. E. (2007). Post-auricular and eyeblink startle responses to facial expressions. *Psychophysiology*, 44(3), 431–435. https://doi.org/10.1111/j.1469-8986.2007.00516.x

Hitchcock, J. M., & Davis, M. (1986). Lesions of the amygdala, but not of the cerebellum or red nucleus, block conditioned fear as measured with the potentiated startle paradigm. *Behavioral Neuroscience*, 100(1), 11–22.

Ho, M. W., Popp, F. A., & Warnke, U. (Eds.). (1994). *Bioelectrodynamics and biocommunication*. World Scientific. https://doi.org/10.1142/2267

Hoffmann, S., & Falkenstein, M. (2008). The correction of eye blink artefacts in the EEG: A comparison of two prominent methods. *PLOS ONE*, 3(8), e3004. https://doi.org/10.1371/journal.pone.0003004

Hu, S., Player, K. A., Mcchesney, K. A., Dalistan, M. D., Tyner, C. A., & Scozzafava, J. E. (1999). Facial EMG as an indicator of palatability in humans. *Physiology & Behavior*, 68(1-2), 31–35. https://doi.org/10.1016/S0031-9384(99)00143-2

Hwang, K. (2017). Corrugator: Muscle of Empathy and Determination. *The Journal of Craniofacial Surgery*, 28(1), 3. https://doi.org/10.1097/SCS.0000000000003013

Iacono, W. G. (2010). Psychophysiological detection of deception and guilty knowledge. In J. L. Skeem, K. S. Douglas, & S. O. Lilienfeld (Eds.), *Psychological science in the courtroom: Controversies and consensus* (pp. 224–241). Guilford Press.

Illigens, B. M., & Gibbons, C. H. (2009). Sweat testing to evaluate autonomic function. *Clinical Autonomic Research*, 19(2), 79–87. https://doi.org/10.1007/s10286-008-0506-8

Iqbal, S. T., Zheng, X. S., & Bailey, B. P. (2004). Task-evoked pupillary response to mental workload in human-computer interaction. In *CHI '04 Extended abstracts on human factors in computing systems*, 1477–1480. https://doi.org/10.1145/985921.986094

Jacob, S. W., & Francone, C. A. (Eds.). (1982). *Structure and function of man* (2nd ed.). Saunders.

Jacobson, E. (1927). Action currents from muscular contractions during conscious processes. *Science*, 66(1713), 403.

Jacobson, E. (1932). Electrophysiology of mental activities. *The American Journal of Psychology*, 44(4), 677–694. https://doi.org/10.2307/1414531

James, A. F., Choisy, S. C., & Hancox, J. C. (2007). Recent advances in understanding sex differences in cardiac repolarization. *Progress in Biophysics and Molecular Biology*, 94(3), 265–319. https://doi.org/10.1016/j.pbiomolbio.2005.05.010

James, W. (1884). What is an emotion? *Mind*, os-IX(34), 188–205. https://doi.org/10.1093/mind/os-IX.34.188

Jäncke, L., & Kaufmann, N. (1994). Facial EMG responses to odors in solitude and with an audience. *Chemical Senses*, 19(2), 99–111. https://doi.org/10.1093/chemse/19.2.99

Jennings, J. R., Tahmoush, A. J., & Redmond, D. P. (1980). Non-invasive measurement of peripheral vascular activity. In I. Martin & P. H. Venables (Eds.), *Techniques in psychophysiology* (pp. 69–137). Wiley.

Jongkees, B. J., & Colzato, L. S. (2016). Spontaneous eye blink rate as predictor of dopamine-related cognitive function-A review. *Neuroscience and Biobehavioral Reviews, 71,* 58–82. https://doi.org/10.1016/j.neubiorev.2016.08.020

Joyner, M. J., Wallin, B. G., & Charkoudian, N. (2016). Sex differences and blood pressure regulation in humans. *Experimental Physiology, 101*(3), 349–355. https://doi.org/10.1113/EP085146

Jung, C. G. (1918). *Studies in word association* (M. D. Eder, Trans.). William Heinemann. (Original work published 1906)

Kalsbeek, J. W. H., & Ettema, J. H. (1963). Scored irregularity of the heart pattern and the measurement of perceptual or mental load. *Ergonomics, 6,* 306–307.

Kamarck, T. W., Manuck, S. B., & Jennings, J. R. (1990). Social support reduces cardiovascular reactivity to psychological challenge: A laboratory model. *Psychosomatic Medicine, 52*(1), 42–58. https://doi.org/10.1097/00006842-199001000-00004

Karson, C. N. (1983). Spontaneous eye-blink rates and dopaminergic systems. *Brain: A Journal of Neurology, 106*(3), 643–653. https://doi.org/10.1093/brain/106.3.643

Kastendieck, T., Mauersberger, H., Blaison, C., Ghalib, J., & Hess, U. (2021). Laughing at funerals and frowning at weddings: Top-down influences of context-driven social judgments on emotional mimicry. *Acta Psychologica, 212,* 103195. https://doi.org/10.1016/j.actpsy.2020.103195

Knezevic, W., & Bajada, S. (1985). Peripheral autonomic surface potential. A quantitative technique for recording sympathetic conduction in man. *Journal of the Neurological Sciences, 67*(2), 239–251. https://doi.org/10.1016/0022-510X(85)90120-0

Koenig, J., & Thayer, J. F. (2016). Sex differences in healthy human heart rate variability: A meta-analysis. *Neuroscience and Biobehavioral Reviews, 64,* 288–310. https://doi.org/10.1016/j.neubiorev.2016.03.007

Kweon, B., Ulrich, R. S., Walker, V., & Tassinary, L. G. (2007). Anger and stress: The role of art posters in an office setting. *Environment and Behavior, 40*(3), 355–381. https://doi.org/10.1177/0013916506298797

Lacey, J. I., & Lacey, B. C. (1958). Verification and extension of the principle of autonomic response-stereotypy. *The American Journal of Psychology, 71*(1), 50–73. https://doi.org/10.2307/1419197

Landis, C. (1926). Studies of emotional reactions. V. Severe emotional upset. *Journal of Comparative Psychology, 6*(3), 221–242. https://doi.org/10.1037/h0071773

Lang, P. J., Davis, M., & Öhman, A. (2000). Fear and anxiety: Animal models and human cognitive psychophysiology. *Journal of Affective Disorders, 61*(3), 137–159. https://doi.org/10.1016/S0165-0327(00)00343-8

Lange, C. G. (1885). *Om Sindsbevægelser* [The mechanisms of the emotions: A psychophysiological study]. Kronar.

Larsen, J. T., Norris, C. J., & Cacioppo, J. T. (2003). Effects of positive and negative affect on electromyographic activity over zygomaticus major and corrugator supercilii. *Psychophysiology, 40*(5), 776–785. https://doi.org/10.1111/1469-8986.00078

Lindsley, D. B. (1935). Electrical activity of human motor units during voluntary contraction. *The American Journal of Physiology, 114*(1), 90–99. https://doi.org/10.1152/ajplegacy.1935.114.1.90

Loeb, G. E., & Gans, C. (1986). *Electromyography for experimentalists.* University of Chicago Press.

Ludwig, C. (1847). Beiträge zur Kenntniss des Einflusses der Respirationsbewegungen auf den Blutlauf im Aortensysteme [Contribution to the knowledge of the influence of respiratory movements on the blood flow in the aortic system]. *Archiv für Anatomie, Physiologie und wissenschaftliche Medicin,* 242-57.

Lumb, B. M., & Lovick, T. A. (1993). The rostral hypothalamus: An area for the integration of autonomic and sensory responsiveness. *Journal of Neurophysiology, 70*(4), 1570–1577. https://doi.org/10.1152/jn.1993.70.4.1570

Luria, A. R. (1932). *The nature of human conflicts.* Liveright.

Lykken, D. T. (1959). The GSR in the detection of guilt. *Journal of Applied Psychology, 43*(6), 385–388. https://doi.org/10.1037/h0046060

Lykken, D. T. (1998). *A tremor in the blood: Uses and abuses of the lie detector.* Plenum Press.

Lykken, D. T., & Venables, P. H. (1971). Direct measurement of skin conductance: A proposal for standardization. *Psychophysiology, 8*(5), 656–672. https://doi.org/10.1111/j.1469-8986.1971.tb00501.x

Lynn, R. (1966). *Attention, arousal, and the orientation reaction.* Pergamon.

Macfarlane, P. W. (2018). The influence of age and sex on the electrocardiogram. *Sex-Specific Analysis of Cardiovascular Function, 1065,* 93–106. https://doi.org/10.1007/978-3-319-77932-4_6

Mager, H. (1931). Deception: A study in forensic psychology. *Journal of Abnormal and Social Psychology, 26*(2), 183–198. https://doi.org/10.1037/h0074408

Majaranta, P., & Bulling, A. (2014). Eye tracking and eye-based human-computer interaction.

In S. Fairclough & K. Gilleade (Eds.), *Advances in physiological computing* (pp. 39–65). Springer. https://doi.org/10.1007/978-1-4471-6392-3_3

Manuck, S. B., Harvey, A. H., Lechleiter, S. L., & Neal, S. K. (1978). Effects of coping on blood pressure responses to threat of aversive stimulation. *Psychophysiology*, *15*(6), 544–549. https://doi.org/10.1111/j.1469-8986.1978.tb03107.x

Martin, I., & Venables, P. H. (Eds.). (1980). *Techniques in psychophysiology*. John Wiley.

Mathews, B. H. C. (1934). A special purpose amplifier. *The Journal of Physiology*, *81*, 28.

McDougal, D. H., & Gamlin, P. D. (2015). Autonomic control of the eye. *Comprehensive Physiology*, *5*(1), 439–473.

McGinn, N. F., Harburg, E., Julius, S., & McLeod, J. M. (1964). Psychological correlates of blood pressure. *Psychological Bulletin*, *61*(3), 209–219. https://doi.org/10.1037/h0043509

McHugo, G., & Lanzetta, J. T. (1983). Methodological decisions in social psychophysiology. In J. T. Cacioppo & R. E. Petty (Eds.), *Social psychophysiology: A sourcebook* (pp. 630–665). Guilford Press.

Mesulam, M. M., & Perry, J. (1972). The diagnosis of love-sickness: Experimental psychophysiology without the polygraph. *Psychophysiology*, *9*(5), 546–551. https://doi.org/10.1111/j.1469-8986.1972.tb01810.x

Mittelstaedt, H. (1998). Origin and processing of postural information. *Neuroscience and Biobehavioral Reviews*, *22*(4), 473–478. https://doi.org/10.1016/S0149-7634(97)00032-8

Mojzisch, A., Schilbach, L., Helmert, J. R., Pannasch, S., Velichkovsky, B. M., & Vogeley, K. (2006). The effects of self-involvement on attention, arousal, and facial expression during social interaction with virtual others: A psychophysiological study. *Social Neuroscience*, *1*(3-4), 184–195. https://doi.org/10.1080/17470910600985621

Montague, P. R., Berns, G. S., Cohen, J. D., McClure, S. M., Pagnoni, G., Dhamala, M., Wiest, M. C., Karpov, I., King, R. D., Apple, N., & Fisher, R. E. (2002). Hyperscanning: Simultaneous fMRI during linked social interactions. *NeuroImage*, *16*(4), 1159–1164. https://doi.org/10.1006/nimg.2002.1150

Murphy, B. B., Mulcahey, P. J., Driscoll, N., Richardson, A. G., Robbins, G. T., Apollo, N. V., Maleski, K., Lucas, T. H., Gogotsi, Y., Dillingham, T., & Vitale, F. (2020). A gel-free $Ti_3C_2T_x$-based electrode array for high-density, high-resolution surface electromyography. *Advanced Materials Technologies*, *5*(8), 2000325. https://doi.org/10.1002/admt.202000325

Nagai, Y., Critchley, H. D., Featherstone, E., Trimble, M. R., & Dolan, R. J. (2004). Activity in ventromedial prefrontal cortex covaries with sympathetic skin conductance level: A physiological account of a "default mode" of brain function. *NeuroImage*, *22*(1), 243–251. https://doi.org/10.1016/j.neuroimage.2004.01.019

Neafsey, E. J. (1991). Prefrontal cortical control of the autonomic control in the rat: Anatomical and electrophysiological observations. *Progress in Brain Research*, *85*, 147–166. https://doi.org/10.1016/S0079-6123(08)62679-5

Neumann, E., & Blanton, R. (1970). The early history of electrodermal research. *Psychophysiology*, *6*(4), 453–475. https://doi.org/10.1111/j.1469-8986.1970.tb01755.x

Newton, T. F., Khalsa-Denison, M. E., & Gawin, F. H. (1997). The face of craving? Facial muscle EMG and reported craving in abstinent and non-abstinent cocaine users. *Psychiatry Research*, *73*(1-2), 115–118. https://doi.org/10.1016/S0165-1781(97)00115-7

Nordin, A. D., Rymer, W. Z., Biewener, A. A., Schwartz, A. B., Chen, D., & Horak, F. B. (2017). Biomechanics and neural control of movement, 20 years later: What have we learned and what has changed? *Journal of Neuroengineering and Rehabilitation*, *14*(1), 91–101. https://doi.org/10.1186/s12984-017-0298-y

Obrist, P. A., Gaebelein, C. J., Teller, E. S., Langer, A. W., Grignolo, A., Light, K. C., & McCubbin, J. A. (1978). The relationship among heart rate, carotid dP/dt, and blood pressure in humans as a function of the type of stress. *Psychophysiology*, *15*(2), 102–115. https://doi.org/10.1111/j.1469-8986.1978.tb01344.x

Ogawa, T. (1981). Dermatomal inhibition of sweating by skin pressure. In Z. Szelenyi & M. Szekely (Eds.), *Advances in physiological sciences: Vol. 32. Contribution to thermal physiology* (pp. 413–415). Akademiai Kiado. https://doi.org/10.1016/B978-0-08-027354-9.50084-3

Öhman, A. (1979). The orientation response, attention, and learning: An information-processing perspective. In H. D. Kimmel, E. H. van Olst, & J. F. Orlebeke (Eds.), *The orienting reflex in humans* (pp. 443–471). Erlbaum.

Ortiz, J., & Raine, A. (2004). Heart rate level and antisocial behavior in children and adolescents: A meta-analysis. *Journal of the American Academy of Child & Adolescent Psychiatry*, *43*(2), 154–162. https://doi.org/10.1097/00004583-200402000-00010

Pas, P., Custers, R., Bijleveld, E., & Vink, M. (2014). Effort responses to suboptimal reward cues are related to striatal dopaminergic functioning.

[Original Paper]. *Motivation and Emotion*, *38*(6), 759–770. https://doi.org/10.1007/s11031-014-9434-1

Pecchinenda, A., & Smith, C. A. (1996). The affective significance of skin-conductance activity during a difficult problem-solving task. *Cognition and Emotion*, *10*(5), 481–504. https://doi.org/10.1080/026999396380123

Peterson, F., & Jung, C. G. (1907). Psycho-physical investigations with the galvanometer and pneumograph in normal and insane individuals (from the Psychiatric Clinic of the University of Zürich). *Brain: A Journal of Neurology*, *30*, 153–218. https://doi.org/10.1093/brain/30.2.153

Phelps, E. A., O'Connor, K. J., Gatenby, J. C., Gore, J. C., Grillon, C., & Davis, M. (2001). Activation of the left amygdala to a cognitive representation of fear. *Nature Neuroscience*, *4*(4), 437–441. https://doi.org/10.1038/86110

Poh, M. Z., Swenson, N. C., & Picard, R. W. (2010). A wearable sensor for unobtrusive, long-term assessment of electrodermal activity. *IEEE Transactions on Biomedical Engineering*, *57*(5), 1243–1252. https://doi.org/10.1109/TBME.2009.2038487

Pope, L. K., & Smith, C. A. (1994). On the distinct meanings of smiles and frowns. *Cognition and Emotion*, *8*(1), 65–72. https://doi.org/10.1080/02699939408408929

Porges, S. W. (1995). Orienting in a defensive world: Mammalian modifications of our evolutionary heritage. A polyvagal theory. *Psychophysiology*, *32*(4), 301–318. https://doi.org/10.1111/j.1469-8986.1995.tb01213.x

Porges, S. W., & Bohrer, R. E. (1990). The analysis of periodic processes in psychophysiological research. In J. T. Cacioppo & L. G. Tassinary (Eds.), *Principles of psychophysiology: Physical, social, and inferential elements* (pp. 708–753). Cambridge University Press.

Porges, S. W., & Raskin, D. C. (1969). Respiratory and heart rate components of attention. *Journal of Experimental Psychology*, *81*(3), 497–503. https://doi.org/10.1037/h0027921

Posada-Quintero, H. F., & Chon, K. H. (2020). Innovations in electrodermal activity data collection and signal processing: A systematic review. *Sensors (Basel)*, *20*(2), 479–497. https://doi.org/10.3390/s20020479

Pothineni, N. V., Shirazi, L. F., & Mehta, J. L. (2016). Gender differences in autonomic control of the cardiovascular system. *Current Pharmaceutical Design*, *22*(25), 3829–3834. https://doi.org/10.2174/1381612822666160518125810

Preuschoff, K., 't Hart, B. M., & Einhäuser, W. (2011). Pupil dilation signals surprise: Evidence for noradrenaline's role in decision making. *Frontiers in Neuroscience*, *5*(115), 115. https://doi.org/10.3389/fnins.2011.00115

Pylyshyn, Z. (1980). Computation and cognition: Issues in the foundation of cognitive science. *Behavioral and Brain Sciences*, *3*(1), 111–132. https://doi.org/10.1017/S0140525X00002053

Regitz-Zagrosek, V., & Kararigas, G. (2017). Mechanistic pathways of sex differences in cardiovascular disease. *Physiological Reviews*, *97*(1), 1–37. https://doi.org/10.1152/physrev.00021.2015

Robinson, J. D., Cinciripini, P. M., Carter, B. L., Lam, C. Y., & Wetter, D. W. (2007). Facial EMG as an index of affective response to nicotine. *Experimental and Clinical Psychopharmacology*, *15*(4), 390–399. https://doi.org/10.1037/1064-1297.15.4.390

Rosenthal, R. (2005). Conducting judgment studies: Some methodological issues. In J. A. Harrigan, R. Rosenthal, & K. R. Scherer (Eds.), *The new handbook of methods in nonverbal behavior research* (pp. 199–234). Oxford University Press.

Roy, J. C., Sequeira, H., & Delerm, B. (1993). Neural Control of Neurodermal Activity: Spinal and Reticular Mechanisms. In J. C. Roy, W. Boucsein, D. C. Fowles, & J. H. Gruzelier (Eds.), *Progress in electrodermal research* (pp. 73–92). Plenum Press. https://doi.org/10.1007/978-1-4615-2864-7_7

Ruiz-Padial, E., Sollers, J. J., III, Vila, J., & Thayer, J. F. (2003). The rhythm of the heart in the blink of an eye: Emotion-modulated startle magnitude covaries with heart rate variability. *Psychophysiology*, *40*(2), 306–313. https://doi.org/10.1111/1469-8986.00032

Salo, M. A., Huikuri, H. V., & Seppänen, T. (2001). Ectopic beats in heart rate variability analysis: Effects of editing on time and frequency domain measures. *Annals of Noninvasive Electrocardiology*, *6*(1), 5–17. https://doi.org/10.1111/j.1542-474X.2001.tb00080.x

Samara, A., Galway, L., Bond, R., & Wang, H. (2017). Tracking and evaluation of pupil dilation via facial point marker analysis. In *2017 IEEE International Conference on Bioinformatics and Biomedicine (BIBM)*, pp. 2037–2043.

Sana, F., Isselbacher, E. M., Singh, J. P., Heist, E. K., Pathik, B., & Armoundas, A. A. (2020). Wearable devices for ambulatory cardiac monitoring: JACC state-of-the-art review. *Journal of the American College of Cardiology*, *75*(13), 1582–1592. https://doi.org/10.1016/j.jacc.2020.01.046

Scott, J. C. (1930). Systolic blood-pressure fluctuations with sex, anger and fear. *Journal of Comparative Psychology*, *10*(2), 97–114. https://doi.org/10.1037/h0073671

Secomb, T. W. (2008). Theoretical models for regulation of blood flow. *Microcirculation*, *15*(8), 765–775. https://doi.org/10.1080/10739680802350112

Sege, C. T., Bradley, M. M., & Lang, P. J. (2014). Startle modulation during emotional anticipation and perception. *Psychophysiology*, *51*(10), 977–981. https://doi.org/10.1111/psyp.12244

Shapiro, D., Jamner, L. D., Lane, J. D., Light, K. C., Myrtek, M., Sawada, Y., Steptoe, A., & the Society for Psychophysical Research. (1996). Blood pressure publication guidelines. *Psychophysiology*, *33*(1), 1–12. https://doi.org/10.1111/j.1469-8986.1996.tb02103.x

Sherrington, C. S. (1923). *The integrative actions of the nervous system*. Yale University Press. (Original work published 1906) https://doi.org/10.1097/00005053-192306000-00038

Sherwood, A. (1993). Use of impedance cardiography in cardiovascular reactivity research. In J. J. Blascovich & E. S. Katkin (Eds.), *Cardiovascular reactivity to psychological stress and disease* (pp. 157–199). American Psychological Association. https://doi.org/10.1037/10125-007

Sherwood, A., Allen, M. T., Fahrenberg, J., Kelsey, R. M., Lovallo, W. R., & van Doornen, L. J. (1990). Methodological guidelines for impedance cardiography. *Psychophysiology*, *27*(1), 1–23. https://doi.org/10.1111/j.1469-8986.1990.tb02171.x

Shibasaki, M., Wilson, T. E., & Crandall, C. G. (2006). Neural control and mechanisms of eccrine sweating during heat stress and exercise. *Journal of Applied Physiology*, *100*(5), 1692–1701. https://doi.org/10.1152/japplphysiol.01124.2005

Singer, J. D., & Willett, J. B. (2003). *Applied longitudinal data analysis: Modeling change and event occurrence*. Oxford University Press. https://doi.org/10.1093/acprof:oso/9780195152968.001.0001

Sloan, R. P., Shapiro, P. A., Bigger, J. T., Jr., Bagiella, E., Steinman, R. C., & Gorman, J. M. (1994). Cardiac autonomic control and hostility in healthy subjects. *The American Journal of Cardiology*, *74*(3), 298–300. https://doi.org/10.1016/0002-9149(94)90382-4

Sokolov, E. N. (1963). *Perception and the conditioned reflex*. Macmillan.

Solodkin, A., Hlustik, P., & Buccino, G. (2007). The anatomy and physiology of the motor system in humans. In J. T. Cacioppo, L. G. Tassinary, & G. G. Berntson (Eds.), *Handbook of psychophysiology* (3rd ed., pp. 507–539). Cambridge University Press. https://doi.org/10.1017/CBO9780511546396.022

Speckenbach, U., & Gerber, W. D. (1999). Reliability of infrared plethysmography in BVP biofeedback therapy and the relevance for clinical application. *Applied Psychophysiology and Biofeedback*, *24*(4), 261–265. https://doi.org/10.1023/A:1022286930738

Sperry, R. (1952). Neurology and the mind-brain problem. *American Scientist*, *40*(2), 291–312.

Stavropoulos, T. G., Papastergiou, A., Mpaltadoros, L., Nikolopoulos, S., & Kompatsiaris, I. (2020). IoT wearable sensors and devices in elderly care: A literature review. *Sensors*, *20*(10), 2826. https://doi.org/10.3390/s20102826

Stephens, J. H., Harris, A. H., Brady, J. V., & Shaffer, J. W. (1975). Psychological and physiological variables associated with large magnitude voluntary heart rate changes. *Psychophysiology*, *12*(4), 381–387. https://doi.org/10.1111/j.1469-8986.1975.tb00006.x

Stern, J. A., Walrath, L. C., & Goldstein, R. (1984). The endogenous eyeblink. *Psychophysiology*, *21*(1), 22–33. https://doi.org/10.1111/j.1469-8986.1984.tb02312.x

Stern, R. M., Ray, W. J., & Quigley, K. S. (2001). *Psychophysiological recording*. Oxford University Press.

Stevens, S. S. (1968). Measurement, statistics, and the schemapiric view. Like the faces of Janus, science looks two ways—Toward schematics and empirics. *Science*, *161*(3844), 849–856. https://doi.org/10.1126/science.161.3844.849

Stringham, J. M., Fuld, K., & Wenzel, A. J. (2003). Action spectrum for photophobia. *Journal of the Optical Society of America*, *20*(10), 1852–1858. https://doi.org/10.1364/JOSAA.20.001852

Sykes, A. H. (1987). A D Waller and the electrocardiogram, 1887. *British Medical Journal*, *294*(6584), 1396–1398. https://doi.org/10.1136/bmj.294.6584.1396

Tarchanoff, I. (1890). Über die galvanischen Erscheinungen an der Haut des Menschen bei Reizung der Sinnesorgane und bei verschiedenen Formen der psychischen Tätigkeit [On the galvanic aspect of the human skin in response to stimulation of sense organs and with different forms of psychological activity]. Pflügers Archiv für die gesamte. *Physiologie*, *46*, 46–55.

Task Force of the European Society of Cardiology and the North American Society of Pacing and Electrophysiology. (1996). Heart rate variability: Standards of measurement, physiological interpretation and clinical use. *Circulation*, *93*(5), 1043–1065. https://doi.org/10.1161/01.CIR.93.5.1043

Tassinary, L. G., & Cacioppo, J. T. (1992). Unobservable facial actions and emotion. *Psychological Science*, *3*(1), 28–33. https://doi.org/10.1111/j.1467-9280.1992.tb00252.x

Tassinary, L. G., & Cacioppo, J. T. (2000). The skeletomotor system: Surface electromyography. In J. T. Cacioppo, L. G. Tassinary, & G. G. Berntson (Eds.), *Handbook of psychophysiology* (2nd ed., pp. 163–199). Cambridge University Press.

Tassinary, L. G., Cacioppo, J. T., & Geen, T. R. (1989a). A psychometric study of surface electrode placements for facial electromyographic recording: I. The brow and cheek muscle regions. *Psychophysiology*, 26(1), 1–16. https://doi.org/10.1111/j.1469-8986.1989.tb03125.x

Tassinary, L. G., Cacioppo, J. T., & Vanman, E. J. (2017). The somatic system. In J. T. Cacioppo, L. G. Tassinary, & G. G. Berntson (Eds.), *Handbook of psychophysiology* (4th ed., pp. 151–182). Cambridge University Press.

Tassinary, L. G., Geen, T. R., Cacioppo, J. T., & Swartzbaugh, R. (1989b). Born of animal magnetism: 150 years of psycho-physiology. *Psychophysiology*, 26(6), 713–715. https://doi.org/10.1111/j.1469-8986.1989.tb03178.x

Taylor, S. E., Seeman, T. E., Eisenberger, N. I., Kozanian, T. A., Moore, A. N., & Moons, W. G. (2010). Effects of a supportive or an unsupportive audience on biological and psychological responses to stress. *Journal of Personality and Social Psychology*, 98(1), 47–56. https://doi.org/10.1037/a0016563

Teitelbaum, O., Benton, T., Shah, P. K., Prince, A., Kelly, J. L., & Teitelbaum, P. (2004). Eshkol-Wachman movement notation in diagnosis: The early detection of Asperger's syndrome. *Proceedings of the National Academy of Sciences of the United States of America*, 101(32), 11909–11914. https://doi.org/10.1073/pnas.0403919101

Thayer, J. F., Hansen, A. L., Saus-Rose, E., & Johnsen, B. H. (2009). Heart rate variability, prefrontal neural function, and cognitive performance: The neurovisceral integration perspective on self-regulation, adaptation, and health. *Annals of Behavioral Medicine*, 37(2), 141–153. https://doi.org/10.1007/s12160-009-9101-z

Thayer, J. F., & Lane, R. D. (2009). Claude Bernard and the heart-brain connection: Further elaboration of a model of neurovisceral integration. *Neuroscience and Biobehavioral Reviews*, 33(2), 81–88. https://doi.org/10.1016/j.neubiorev.2008.08.004

Thorson, A. M. (1925). The relation of tongue movements to internal speech. *Journal of Experimental Psychology*, 8(1), 1–32. https://doi.org/10.1037/h0073795

Tomaka, J., Blascovich, J., Kelsey, R. M., & Leitten, C. L. (1993). Subjective, physiological, and behavioral effects of threat and challenge appraisal. *Journal of Personality and Social Psychology*, 65(2), 248–260. https://doi.org/10.1037/0022-3514.65.2.248

van Boxtel, A. (2001). Optimal signal bandwidth for the recording of surface EMG activity of facial, jaw, oral, and neck muscles. *Psychophysiology*, 38(1), 22–34. https://doi.org/10.1111/1469-8986.3810022

van Boxtel, A., Goudswaard, P., & Schomaker, L. R. (1984). Amplitude and bandwidth of the frontalis surface EMG: Effects of electrode parameters. *Psychophysiology*, 21(6), 699–707. https://doi.org/10.1111/j.1469-8986.1984.tb00260.x

van der Wel, P., & van Steenbergen, H. (2018). Pupil dilation as an index of effort in cognitive control tasks: A review. *Psychonomic Bulletin & Review*, 25(6), 2005–2015. https://doi.org/10.3758/s13423-018-1432-y

Vanman, E. J., Paul, B. Y., Ito, T. A., & Miller, N. (1997). The modern face of prejudice and structural features that moderate the effect of cooperation on affect. *Journal of Personality and Social Psychology*, 73(5), 941–959. https://doi.org/10.1037/0022-3514.73.5.941

Vanman, E. J., Saltz, J. L., Nathan, L. R., & Warren, J. A. (2004). Racial discrimination by low-prejudiced Whites. Facial movements as implicit measures of attitudes related to behavior. *Psychological Science*, 15(11), 711–714. https://doi.org/10.1111/j.0956-7976.2004.00746.x

Veldhuizen, I. J. T., Gaillard, A. W. K., & de Vries, J. (2003). The influence of mental fatigue on facial EMG activity during a simulated workday. *Biological Psychology*, 63(1), 59–78. https://doi.org/10.1016/S0301-0511(03)00025-5

Venables, P. H., & Christie, M. J. (1980). Electrodermal activity. In I. Martin & P. H. Venables (Eds.), *Techniques in psychophysiology* (pp. 3–67). Wiley.

Verschuere, B., Crombez, G., De Clercq, A., & Koster, E. H. W. (2004). Autonomic and behavioral responding to concealed information: Differentiating orienting and defensive responses. *Psychophysiology*, 41(3), 461–466. https://doi.org/10.1111/j.1469-8986.00167.x

Vetrugno, R., Liguori, R., Cortelli, P., & Montagna, P. (2003). Sympathetic skin response: Basic mechanisms and clinical applications. *Clinical Autonomic Research*, 13(4), 256–270. https://doi.org/10.1007/s10286-003-0107-5

Vigoroux, R. (1879). Sur la röle de la resistance electrique des tissus dans l'electrodiagnostique [On the role of the electrical resistance of tissues on electrodiagnostics]. *Comptes Rendus des Seances de la Societe de Biologie*, 31, 336–339.

Wang, G. H. (1964). *The neural control of sweating*. University of Wisconsin Press.

Washburn, M. F. (1916). *Movement and imagery: Outlines of a motor theory of the complexer mental processes*. Houghton Mifflin. https://doi.org/10.1037/11575-000

Wierda, S. M., van Rijn, H., Taatgen, N. A., & Martens, S. (2012). Pupil dilation deconvolution reveals the dynamics of attention at high temporal resolution. *Proceedings of the National Academy of Sciences of the United States of America*, *109*(22), 8456–8460. https://doi.org/10.1073/pnas.1201858109

Woodworth, R. S., & Schlosberg, H. (1954). *Experimental psychology* (Rev. ed.). Holt.

Wright, R. A., & Kirby, L. D. (2001). Effort determination of cardiovascular response: An integrative analysis with applications in social psychology. In M. P. Zanna (Ed.), *Advances in experimental social psychology* (Vol. 33, pp. 255–307). Academic Press. https://doi.org/10.1016/S0065-2601(01)80007-1

Wundt, W. (1897). *Outlines of psychology*. Wilhelm Engelmann. https://doi.org/10.1037/12908-000

Wundt, W. (1904). *Principles of physiological psychology*. Swan Sonnenschein.

Yannakakis, G. N., Martinez, H. P., & Garbarino, M. (2016). Psychophysiology in games. In K. Karpouzis & G. Yannakakis (Eds.), *Emotion in games: Socio-affective computing* (Vol. 4, pp. 119–137). Springer. https://doi.org/10.1007/978-3-319-41316-7_7

Zafar, U., Rahman, S. U., Hamid, N., & Salman, H. (2020). Assessment of gender differences in autonomic nervous control of the cardiovascular system. *The Journal of the Pakistan Medical Association*, *70*(9), 1554–1558. https://doi.org/10.5455/JPMA.27702

Zajonc, R. B. (1965). Social facilitation. *Science*, *149*(3681), 269–274. https://doi.org/10.1126/science.149.3681.269

Zeng, Z., Pantic, M., Roisman, G. I., & Huang, T. S. (2009). A survey of affect recognition methods: Audio, visual, and spontaneous expressions. *IEEE Transactions on Pattern Analysis and Machine Intelligence*, *31*(1), 39–58. https://doi.org/10.1109/TPAMI.2008.52

CHAPTER 26

SALIVARY HORMONE ASSAYS

Linda Becker, Nicolas Rohleder, and Oliver C. Schultheiss

Hormones can be assayed from blood, urine, spinal fluid, hair, and saliva samples, among other sources. Because measuring hormones in saliva is the easiest and least stressful method for participants, it is often the method of choice for psychologists. In this chapter, which represents a revised and updated version of an earlier chapter by Schultheiss et al. (2012),[1] we give an overview about the assessment of hormones from saliva samples. We first describe which hormones can be assessed in saliva and typical research questions that are addressed in biobehavioral research. Furthermore, we provide an overview of quality criteria that should be considered when choosing an analysis method. Next, we discuss how hormones can be assessed and how to deal with saliva samples. Additionally, we provide a screening questionnaire with which the most important confounding variables can be assessed. In closing, we make suggestions about how to analyze data obtained with hormone assays, how to report hormone data in research journals, and how to implement open science practices in behavioral endocrinological research.

HORMONES IN BIOBEHAVIORAL RESEARCH

Many questions in biobehavioral research focus on the interrelationships between hormones, brain functioning, human experience, and behavior.

Hormones are messenger molecules that are released by specialized neurons in the brain and by glands in the body. Free-circulating hormones in the blood stream or in the interstitial fluid interact through positive and negative feedback loops with other parts of the body and with the brain, where they can affect neural processing. This can result in behavioral changes that are related with changes in emotional and cognitive processes. Therefore, the assessment of hormones is particularly interesting for researchers from different domains such as clinical, motivational, health, or cognitive psychology and neuroscience.

Generally, two broad classes of hormonal effects on physiology and behavior can be distinguished. *Organizational effects* are lasting effects that hormones exert on the organism, thus changing its shape and functional properties in various ways. Organizational hormone effects often occur during development or when significant hormonal changes take place, such as during puberty. For instance, the development of the female and male body morphology is largely under hormonal control during fetal development, and deviations from typical gendered body morphology are frequently the result of deviations in hormone production, enzymatic conversion, or receptor action. Although direct endocrine assessment (e.g., through amniocentesis or umbilical cord blood analysis

---

[1]We thank Maika Rawolle and Anja Schiepe-Tiska for contributing to the first version of this chapter.

https://doi.org/10.1037/0000318-026
APA Handbook of Research Methods in Psychology, Second Edition: Vol. 1. Foundations, Planning, Measures, and Psychometrics, H. Cooper (Editor-in-Chief)
Copyright © 2023 by the American Psychological Association. All rights reserved.

for pre- and perinatal effects as well as repeated blood or saliva assessment during puberty) provides some limited insights in the role of organizational effects of hormones on human development, such effects are currently more typically assayed from bone-growth patterns that integrate hormonal action over longer stretches of time, albeit with less endocrine specificity (e.g., Köllner et al., 2019; Manning et al., 2014). In contrast to organizational effects, *activational effects* are those effects that hormones exert temporarily without producing lasting changes in the brain or the body.

The relationship between hormones and behavior is *bidirectional*. Hormones can have a facilitating or deteriorating effect on cognition and behavior, such as when high levels of testosterone increase aggressive responses in a game setting (Geniole et al., 2019), or high levels of cortisol decrease memory performance (Becker & Rohleder, 2019; Het et al., 2005). Such hormone-behavior effects can be most conclusively demonstrated through experimental manipulation of hormone levels (e.g., through stress tasks that induce the release of stress hormones such as cortisol; Becker et al., 2019; Kirschbaum et al., 1993). An alternative to an experimental manipulation with the intention to alter hormone levels is the direct application of hormones via oral drugs or nasal sprays and the investigation of their effects on psychological (e.g., behavioral, emotional, or cognitive) processes, such as decreased memory performance after hydrocortisone administration (e.g., Wolf, 2019). However, while oral hormone administration is a widely used and accepted method in experimental studies (e.g., Geniole et al., 2019; Wolf, 2009), other methods, such as the nasal application of oxytocin, have been questioned, and the presence of results supporting this method has been attributed to publication bias (Lane et al., 2016). Conversely, the situational outcome of a person's behavior as well as the stimuli and events impinging on the person can influence current hormone levels; for example, individuals who win or lose experimentally manipulated contests show characteristic gonadal steroid changes (Oxford et al., 2017; Vongas et al., 2020). These are all examples of studies that investigated acute effects of hormones on behavior or vice versa in experimental laboratory settings.

Another frequent research topic is the investigation of the hormone systems themselves and their circadian secretion patterns. Secretion of most hormones follows a circadian rhythm (e.g., for cortisol: an increase after waking and a decline throughout the day until bedtime). Several measures can be obtained from the diurnal course such as, for cortisol, the awakening response, the diurnal slope, or the area under the daytime curve as a measure for average cortisol exposure (Adam & Kumari, 2009). Altered diurnal secretion patterns have been found in psychopathology (e.g., flatter diurnal cortisol and testosterone slopes have been found in depression; Adam et al., 2017).

One issue of concern to biobehavioral researchers who want to use endocrine measures is how easy or difficult it is to assess a particular hormone. This depends primarily on the biochemical properties of the hormone. One class of hormones are *steroid hormones*, which are synthesized from cholesterol. The most important steroid hormones are glucocorticoids (e.g., the stress hormone cortisol), mineralocorticoids (e.g., aldosterone), and sex hormones (e.g., testosterone, estradiol, progesterone). Steroid hormones are highly stable, and in their free bioactive form (i.e., not bound to larger proteins) they can pass through cell membranes, leading to roughly similar levels of the free fraction of a hormone across body fluid compartments. More importantly, they can also pass the blood-brain barrier and thus affect neural processing directly. Therefore, concentrations of steroid hormone levels in saliva are usually proportional to hormone levels in the blood. However, as most steroids are bound to transport proteins in blood, only the free fraction (about 10% of cortisol, for example) can be measured in saliva. For this reason, and because saliva sampling is much easier and relatively stress-free for research participants than the collection of blood samples, salivary hormone assessment has become the method of choice among psychoneuroendocrinologists working with human populations (Schultheiss & Stanton, 2009;

Strahler et al., 2017). Another class of hormones are *peptide hormones*, which are short protein molecules composed of a small number of amino acids. Important peptide hormones are insulin, arginine-vasopressin, adrenocorticotropic hormone, norepinephrine (Ne), and oxytocin. In contrast to steroid hormones, peptide hormones are not liposoluble and are large structures by molecular standards and therefore do not easily pass through cell membranes. As a consequence, peptide hormones can be measured only in the medium or body compartment into which they have been released or actively transported. Importantly, in many cases peptide hormone concentrations measured in the body do not accurately reflect peptide hormone concentrations in the brain, because they are released by different hypothalamic neuron populations. Furthermore, peptide hormones break down easily, and special precautions are necessary to stabilize their molecular structure after sampling. Some ways of measuring peptide hormone levels indirectly through the assessment of enzymes (that are related to hormones) from saliva have been suggested. One example is the assessment of salivary α-amylase (sAA) as an indicator for sympathetic nervous system (SNS) activity, which is associated with the fight-or-flight stress response. sAA and blood Ne responses to stimulation (both are released when the SNS is activated) are highly correlated (Nater & Rohleder, 2009). However, although sAA is an established and suitable marker for stress reactivity, researchers must be methodologically well informed when measuring sAA and aware that sAA mainly reflects SNS *reactivity*—and that it is not necessarily a suitable measure for absolute SNS *activity* (Bosch et al., 2011; Rohleder & Nater, 2009). Another class of substances that are not considered hormones but that can also be obtained from saliva and are also of interest for psychologists, are *markers of inflammation* (e.g., interleukins, C-reactive protein, tumor necrosis factor-α, immunoglobulin-A). However, the validity and reliability of using such salivary markers in psychological research still need further investigation before these markers can actually be recommended (Engeland et al., 2019; Slavish et al., 2015). Table 26.1 provides an overview of relevant hormones and hormone-related substances that can be assessed in saliva, their psychological correlates and effects, and references that discuss the validity of saliva assays and their main area of application for each marker.

QUALITY CRITERIA

Hormone assays have to meet a number of quality criteria. Assays must demonstrate validity, which is assessed through accuracy, sensitivity, and specificity. They also must demonstrate reliability, which is assessed through precision. We briefly discuss each of these concepts in the following paragraphs (for a thorough discussion of hormone assay validation, see O'Fegan, 2000).

Accuracy is the ability of the assay to measure the true analyte concentration in a sample. Accuracy is determined by including control samples with known analyte concentrations in the assay and comparing the amount of analyte estimated by the assay with the actual amount added. The result is expressed as the percentage of the actual amount that is recovered by the assay. Recovery coefficients between 90% and 110% reflect good accuracy.

Sensitivity is the lowest concentration of an analyte that can be distinguished from a sample containing no analyte. Sensitivity is often derived by calculating the lower limit of detection, which refers to a signal obtained from a sample with zero analyte (B0) minus 3 times the standard deviation (*SD*). Values outside this range are considered as measurements that can be validly differentiated from zero. Only values that are at least 3 *SD* units above B0 are interpreted as nonzero concentrations.

Specificity refers to the ability of an assay to maximize detection of the targeted analyte and minimize detection of other analytes. Specificity is often established by measuring the degree to which an assay produces measurements different from zero for nontargeted analytes (e.g., in the case of a cortisol assay, measurements greater than zero for related steroid hormones such as aldosterone). Cross-reactivity with nontargeted

TABLE 26.1

Hormones and Other Markers That Can Be Assayed in Saliva

Marker	Psychological functions	References
α-amylase	Marker of sympathetic nervous system activation; related with blood NE stress responses	Bosch et al., 2011; Nater & Rohleder, 2009; Rohleder & Nater, 2009
Cortisol	Indicates activation of the hypothalamus–pituitary–adrenal axis (e.g., during stress); associated with cognitive processes (memory, executive functions)	Hellhammer et al., 2009; Smyth et al., 2013
C-reactive protein	Inflammatory marker; associated with the risk for cardiovascular disease	Christodoulides et al., 2005; Slavish et al., 2015
Dehydroepiandrosterone (DHEA)	Biomarker of aging and development; associated with mood, well-being, and cognitive processes (e.g., memory and attention)	Kamin & Kertes, 2017; Wolkowitz & Reus, 2003
Estradiol	Enhances libido; involved in social dominance and sexual behavior; associated with cognitive processes (e.g., verbal ability, memory) and emotional processes	Riad-Fahmy et al., 1987; Toffoletto et al., 2014
Interleukins (e.g., IL-1, IL-6, IL-10)	Inflammatory markers; associated with the acute stress response and long-term health	Slavish et al., 2015
Oxytocin	Supports prosocial behavior and social cognition (e.g., social memory and social decision making); associated with pair bonding and parental behavior	Lane et al., 2016; Martins et al., 2020; McCullough et al., 2013
Progesterone	Decreases libido (particularly in men); anxiolytic; associated with affiliation motivation; associated with cognitive and emotional processes	Riad-Fahmy et al., 1987; Toffoletto et al., 2014
Testosterone	Associated with aggressive behavior and social dominance; enhances libido; supports sexual behavior; associated with cognitive performance (e.g., memory, executive functions, spatial performance)	Carré et al., 2017; van Anders et al., 2014

analytes is estimated by dividing the measured, apparent concentration of the target analyte by the amount of nontargeted analyte added, multiplied by 100.

Precision is the degree of agreement between test results repeatedly and independently obtained under stable conditions. Precision is typically reported in terms of the coefficient of variation (*CV*), which is calculated as the mean of replicate measurements of a given sample, divided by the standard deviation of the measurements, multiplied by 100. The *intra-assay CV* refers to the average of the *CV*s of all duplicate samples (i.e., when the sample is assayed twice). The *inter-assay CV* is calculated from the between-assay mean and *SD* of a control sample (e.g., a saliva pool) included in all assays. Intra- and interassay *CV*s < 10% are considered to indicate good precision.

HOW CAN HORMONES BE ASSESSED?

Assays are procedures for determining the presence and amount of a substance in a biological sample, such as hormone concentrations in saliva samples. For the assessment of hormones, a variety of assays are available. In many laboratories, *immunoassays* are used. The mechanism behind this procedure is the binding of antibodies to antigens. *Antibodies* are produced by an organism's immune system to bind in a precise way to specific substances, or *antigens*. For instance, an immunoassay for cortisol contains antibodies that specifically bind to cortisol. From the number of bound molecules, the concentration can be quantified. One of the oldest and still most precise immunoassays is the *radioimmunoassay* (RIA). In RIAs, a fixed quantity of hormone molecules with radioactive labels (also called *tracer*;

e.g., radioiodine [125-I]) is added to the assay. The tracer molecules compete with the hormones contained in samples for antibody binding. After a fixed incubation time, all excess tracer and sample are discarded, and only the antibody-bound molecules (both with and without the radioactive label) are retained. The bound radioactivity is then measured. If a higher signal from the radioactive substance is detected, there is more tracer-labeled hormone and less natural sample hormone present. Conversely, if a lower signal is detected, then more natural hormone is present. Quantification is carried out using a standard curve that is generated using samples with a known concentration of the analyte. From this, a regression equation can be derived; that is, a formula that allows estimating the amount of hormone present in a given sample from the strength of the signal detected in the tube (see Schultheiss & Stanton, 2009, for more details on this procedure). Although RIAs are widely considered the most valid and direct way of assessing hormones by means of immunoassays, they are increasingly being replaced, because of the drawbacks of running a radioisotope laboratory. Common nonradioactive alternatives are *enzymatic immunoassays* (EIAs) and *enzyme-linked immunosorbent assays* (ELISAs; Lequin, 2005). Both EIAs and ELISAs operate according to the same principles as RIAs, except that the tracer signal is based on enzyme-labeled antigens and antibodies, leading, for instance, to differences in sample coloration or luminescence that can be quantified according to the same principles as described above for RIA. The drawbacks of EIAs/ELISAs, in comparison with RIAs, are the complexity of the assay protocols and the relatively lower accuracy and sensitivity (Schultheiss et al., 2019; Welker et al., 2016). An alternative method, which is often considered as the gold standard for salivary hormone assays, is (ultra-) high-pressure *liquid chromatography* (LC), combined with *mass spectrometry* (MS). LC-MS systems include four main components, a chromatograph, an ionizer, a mass analyzer, and a detector. In the LC component of the system, the analytes are separated by their chemical and physical properties according to chromatographical properties (i.e., with respect to their stationary and a mobile phases). These separated analytes then enter the MS interface, where they become ionized. The ionized molecules enter the mass analyzer, the part of the system in which they are analyzed with respect to their mass and charge. The molecules are accelerated in a vacuum through an electromagnetic field toward a detector. Only ions with a specific, predefined mass-to-charge ratio can pass the detector, enabling measurement with high specificity (see Schultheiss et al., 2019, for a detailed description of this method). The use of LC-MS systems has become popular in a growing number of laboratories, because this technique demonstrates high levels of specificity and is argued to be free of many of the limitations of immunoassays, such as cross-reactivity (Welker et al., 2016). In several studies, the assessment of different hormones from saliva samples with RIA, EIA/ELISA, or LC-MS has been compared. For example, for salivary testosterone, EIA/ELISA assays fail to capture the typical difference between male and female samples revealed by LC-MS, and correlations between LC-MS and EIA/ELISA measurements were disappointingly low, particularly in the female (low) range of concentrations (Prasad et al., 2019; Welker et al., 2016). RIAs appear to provide more valid measurements vis-à-vis LC-MS (Schultheiss et al., 2019).

DESIGNING THE STUDY AND SCREENING PARTICIPANTS

High-quality hormone assessment starts with careful planning and study design. Hormone levels are associated with many factors, of which psychological variables are particularly important in biobehavioral research. To tease out the effects of interests (i.e., relationships between hormones and psychological variables), it is almost always necessary to control for or hold constant other influences on hormone levels. The most important factors are age and gender, which should always be recorded and controlled for in psychoneuroendocrinological research. Furthermore, as outlined earlier, for most hormones, strong circadian fluctuations can be found (Liening et al., 2010). Therefore, we recommend to control for time of day and, if possible, to avoid collecting samples in the morning, when the variations are strongest and hormone release is closest to its physiological maximum. Furthermore, it is important to control for menstrual-cycle changes in hormonal levels for female participants. For instance, progesterone levels are low in the first half of the cycle and rise in the second half (e.g., Gangestad et al., 2016; Hampson, 2020). Several procedures to assess menstrual-cycle stage have been suggested. At least, the day of the beginning of the last cycle as well as the cycle length should be assessed. However, because of strong intrapersonal variations (Hampson, 2020), the start of the next cycle after saliva collection should be verified by the participant, and cycle stage should be determined by counting backward from the beginning of the subsequent cycle (Gangestad et al., 2016). Moreover, the use of hormonal contraceptives can alter hormone levels, and therefore, it is recommended to exclude women who take hormonal contraceptives, if possible, or otherwise to control for this factor. Further important factors that should be considered are the reproductive status (e.g., many hormonal systems operate differently in prepubertal children than in adults in their reproductive years), and the use of further medications (other than hormonal contraceptives) that alter hormone levels or endocrine responses (e.g., glucocorticoid-containing medication). We strongly recommend to include a screening questionnaire in behavioral endocrinology studies that covers the most important factors that can influence circulating hormone levels. We provide an example in Table 26.2. If children are included, stages of development (e.g., Tanner stage) should be additionally assessed. Finally, date and start time of each session should routinely be noted for each participant to control for diurnal variations in hormone levels and seasonality (e.g., androgens are highest in autumn; Stanton et al., 2011).

On the day of sample collection, participants should be instructed to refrain from eating at least 2 hours before saliva collection to avoid contaminants like blood or residues from meals ending up in the samples. For the same reasons, participants should not brush their teeth within the 2 hours before sample collection. Furthermore, on arrival, participants should rinse their mouths with water. Collection of the first sample should start no earlier than 5 minutes after rinsing to avoid dilution of saliva samples with water. Moreover, participants should refrain from excessive physical activity at least 2 hours prior to the first saliva sample.

The number of saliva samples that should be collected in a study strongly depends on the research question and the study design. If a researcher is interested in using hormone levels as a dependent variable (e.g., to assess the question "Does performing a neuropsychological test lead to an increase in cortisol levels"; Becker et al., 2020), at least two samples are needed to address the research question meaningfully: one baseline sample and at least one sample that is taken after the procedure at the timepoint of the expected peak in the hormonal level. However, if the goal is to measure a precise time course, more samples may be required (e.g., to assess the question "What is the precise time course of sAA and cortisol levels during and after a resistance training?"; Becker et al., 2020). The baseline sample should be collected immediately before the intervention. Placement of the postintervention samples depends on the dynamics of salivary hormone changes and the properties of the intervention (e.g., the type of the stressor). For testosterone and cortisol, the peak of the highest concentration can be expected approximately 20 to 30 minutes after the end of the intervention (e.g., the stressor; Goodman et al., 2017). Markers that are associated with the activation of the SNS, such as sAA, typically peak immediately after the end of the intervention (e.g., the stressor). Samples taken more than 45 minutes after the end of the intervention are less likely to yield detectable effects of an experimental manipulation but are usually used to assess recovery of the hormonal response. In many studies, more than one postintervention sample is collected.

TABLE 26.2

Screening Questionnaire for Use in Studies With Hormone Assessments

Variable	Question
Age	Please enter your age (in years).
Gender	Please enter your gender (male, female, other [please specify]).
Weight	Please enter your weight (in customary unit [e.g., pounds]).
Height	Please enter your height (in customary unit [e.g., inches]).
Menstrual cycle (women only)	What was the date on which your last menstrual period started? What is the average duration of your menstrual cycle (in days)? How much does your menstrual-cycle length typically vary (0 to 1 day, 2 to 3 days, 4 days or more) (By "menstrual cycle" we mean the time from the start of one menstrual period to the start of the next.)
Menopause (women only)	Have you entered menopause? If so, at what age approximately?
Oral infections, oral lacerations, oral bleeding	Have you experienced any oral bleeding, oral lacerations, or oral infections over the past day?
Physical activity	Did you engage in any intense physical activity during the last 2 hours (e.g., sports, cycling, running). If yes, please specify.
Caffeine consumption	How many hours ago has it been since you consumed caffeine (contained in coffee, tea, soda, chocolate)?
Food consumption	Did you consume any food or beverages (except water) during the last 2 hours? If yes, please specify.
Smoking	Do you smoke? If yes, when did you have your last cigarette (in hours)? How many cigarettes do you smoke a day?
Alcohol consumption	How many hours ago has it been since you consumed an alcoholic beverage?
Drugs	Do you use any recreational drugs (e.g., marijuana, Ecstasy, speed, cocaine)? If yes, please specify (which type, how often, time of last consumption).
Anabolic steroids	Do you take anabolic steroids?
Hormonal contraceptives (women only)	Do you currently take hormonal contraceptives (i.e., the "pill" or a patch)? If yes, please specify (name). Do you take the pill continuously? If applicable, in which intake phase are you currently (intake or pill break)?
Medication	Are you currently on any kind of medication(s) (prescription or nonprescription)? If yes, please provide the name of the prescription(s).
Endocrine disorders	Do you have a diagnosed endocrine disorder? If yes, please name the disorder.
Further disorders	Do you have any further diagnosed disorders (psychiatric or physical)? If yes, please name the disorder.
Relationship status	Are your currently involved in a steady relationship?
Handedness	Please indicate the hand (left or right) you typically use in activities such as writing, brushing your teeth, holding a glass, etc.
Sleep	What time did you wake up today? How many hours did you sleep last night?

We recommend to collect more than one post-intervention sample if the exact time course is not known in advance. However, it should be kept in mind that hormone assays are associated with costs that should be calculated in advance. In our experience, the following rule of thumb works reasonably well when calculating the cost of a hormone assay: For each sample and each hormone assessed in duplicate, costs of approximately $15 can be expected. Thus, if a researcher wants to collect three samples each from 100 participants and would like to have them assayed for cortisol and testosterone, the research budget should include $9,000 for the hormone assays (3 samples × 100 participants × 2 hormones × $15). These costs should be considered while planning and designing study and applying for funding.

COLLECTING, PROCESSING, AND ASSAYING SALIVA SAMPLES

A further key point for high-quality hormone assessment is the collection and processing of the samples that will later be assayed for hormone concentrations. The goal of the saliva-collection stage is to collect high-quality samples (i.e., samples free of contaminants). Several methods for collecting saliva have been introduced and evaluated. Some methods have aimed at stimulating saliva flow and speeding up the collection process (e.g., through the use of chewing gum, citric acid, or Parafilm®); others have attempted to combine this with a reduction of the embarrassment of letting spit drool out of one's mouth (e.g., through collecting saliva with the use of cotton or polyester rolls that participants chew on). As the overview of saliva collection methods provided in Table 26.3 indicates, very few methods can be recommended for the assessment of salivary hormones. The method that is least likely to produce interference through the collection process is having participants spit directly into collection tubes (e.g., 50-mL centrifugation tubes), perhaps with the aid of a plastic straw through which saliva can flow into the tube (i.e., passive drooling). The only drawback of this method is that it can take some participants a long time to collect a sufficient quantity of saliva. Possibly the only viable alternative to the passive drool method is the use of Parafilm® as a stimulant, which has been proven suitable for the assessment of cortisol, testosterone, progesterone, and estradiol (Dlugash & Schultheiss, 2021). However, this method has been validated only for use of RIA, and its validity for the assessment with EIA/ELISA or LC-MS remains to be tested. For a long time (and also in the previous version of this chapter), the use of sugarless chewing gum was recommended; new findings suggest that this recommendation is no longer tenable (Schultheiss, 2013; van Anders, 2010). Other stimulants (e.g., citric acid, cotton, or polyester rolls) are also not recommended, because they fail to provide consistently interference-free measurements for more than one target hormone.

However, the choice of collection device also depends on the hormones that are intended to be measured. In particular for cortisol and sAA, the use of polyester or cotton rolls does not pose any of the above problems (Rohleder & Nater, 2009). Especially, for sAA, polyester rolls lead to a uniform stimulation of saliva flow, and therefore the impact of flow rate on amylase concentrations is reduced (Rohleder et al., 2006). Therefore, the use of polyester rolls is recommended for sAA collection.

The amount of saliva to be collected for each sample depends on the number and type of assays to be performed on them later. For EIA/ELISA, lower volumes are needed than for RIA. For EIA/ELISA, a total volume of 1 mL is sufficient for the analysis of several analytes. For RIA, a sample volume of 1 mL is sufficient if one hormone will be measured only, but the amount collected needs to be increased if more hormones are to be assayed. We recommend obtaining information about how much saliva will be needed for each hormone assessment, adding up the volumes and adding 1 mL to account for sample attrition during saliva processing to calculate the target sample volume for testosterone assessment

TABLE 26.3

Overview and Evaluation of Saliva Collection Methods

Collection method	Recommendation
Passive drooling into plastic collection tube (can be aided by plastic straw)	Recommended; produces no interference; potential drawback: some participants may take several minutes to collect a sample (Schultheiss, 2013)
Parafilm®	Recommended; has been validated for the assessment of cortisol, testosterone, progesterone, and estradiol for RIA (Dlugash & Schultheiss, 2021)
Sugared or sugarless chewing gum	Not recommended; increases testosterone, estradiol (van Anders, 2010), and progesterone levels (Schultheiss, 2013)
Cotton or polyester rolls (salivettes)	Recommended if only one specific hormone is to be measured for that the device has been optimized (e.g., cortisol). Not recommended if other hormones than the one for which it was optimized should be assessed or different hormones should be assayed from one sample
Citric acid (crystals or powder)	Not recommended; alters pH value of samples, which may later interfere with pH-critical immunoassays (Dlugash & Schultheiss, 2021)

via RIA. For cortisol and sAA assessment via EIA/ELISA, lower volumes are sufficient (e.g., 200 μL to assess both in duplicate). In our experience, it is easy to collect as much as 5 mL within 5 minutes, which easily accommodates the assessment of three or four hormonal parameters per sample in RIAs. To ensure that participants collect a sufficient amount of saliva, we recommend to mark the collection tubes at the targeted volume and instruct participants to fill the tube to the mark (see Schultheiss & Stanton, 2009, for further details).

After saliva sample-collection, all samples should be sealed and frozen immediately. We recommend storage at −80 °C if storage for several weeks or months is intended. For shorter times, storage in regular −20 °C chest freezers will suffice to preserve salivary hormone concentrations (Toone et al., 2013). When using polyester rolls for the assessment of sAA and cortisol, it is not necessary to proceed as strictly, because these molecules remain stable at room temperature for several weeks within this collection device.

The next step is preparation of the samples for the actual assay. Several procedures have been suggested. We recommend the following: First, all samples should be thawed and refrozen three times. This procedure helps to break down the long molecule chains that make saliva sticky and viscous and turn the chains into a more watery, and thus more precisely pipettable, fluid. If necessary, this step can be sped up by freezing and thawing through the use of dry ice and a warm water bath. After the third freeze-thaw cycle, the samples should be centrifuged for 10 minutes at $1,000-2,000 \times g$ in a refrigerated centrifuge to push all coarse content to the bottom of the tube (note that centrifugation may add bias, e.g., lower testosterone levels, after centrifugation; Durdiaková et al., 2013) to the assessment of some hormones). After centrifugation, the supernatant (i.e., the watery part of the sample that stays on top after centrifugation) of each sample is transferred to aliquot tube(s) or deepwell plates (e.g., 5-mL, 2-mL, or 1.5-mL tubes or 96 × 1-mL deepwell plates). Care must be taken to avoid stirring up and transferring the detritus at the bottom of the tube during transfer. For this reason, we recommend centrifuging and aspirating only small batches of tubes (≤ 12) at a time or to use a pipetting robot, which can pipette faster and with less error than humans. After aliquoting, samples can be assayed or refrozen for later assaying. Note that the coarse and watery components of saliva tend to mingle again after long waits between centrifugation and sample transfer to aliquots. Therefore, repeating the centrifugation procedure may become necessary.

There are several ways to get saliva samples assayed for hormone concentration. If the researcher's university does not have an endocrinology lab whose services can be used or that at least provides researchers with an opportunity to run their assays, the set-up of a dedicated salivary hormone laboratory may be an option. The bare bones of such a lab include sufficient bench and storage space. Depending on the equipment and the assay method, the price tag for a sufficiently equipped laboratory starts at about $50,000. Furthermore, running costs for resources such as technical staff should be included in the cost calculation. A further option is to have saliva sample analysis conducted by commercial assay labs that specialize in salivary hormone measurement. We strongly recommend that researchers not simply trust the claims these labs are making, but actually test their validity before and after sending off the samples. A thorough understanding of the quality parameters (i.e., specificity, sensitivity, accuracy, and precision, which we described in the section Quality Criteria) of good endocrine measurement is essential for this testing. A simple way to select a good assay service is to compare the claims of the assay provider with the published literature. Good assay services offer assays that cover the range of hormone concentrations typically observed in salivary hormones and also report quality data. Finally, customers of commercial assay services should expect to receive a complete set of data that include not only the mean hormone level and *CV* for each sample but also the values for each individual measurement (for verification of the intra-assay *CV*), the values for standard pools used across assays (for verification of interassay *CVs*), and the complete data on the standard curve, including the zero-concentration calibrator (see Schultheiss & Stanton, 2009, for further recommendations).

DATA ANALYSIS AND RESEARCH REPORT WRITING

Once the raw data from the assays have been collected, they need to be processed to arrive at estimates of the actual sample hormone concentrations. Schultheiss and Stanton (2009) offered a guided tour through the steps of data processing, and Nix and Wild (2000) provided an excellent in-depth treatment of the ins and outs of assay data processing. We next concentrate on data analytic strategies and presentation of the findings.

In general, the same rules and best practices for analyzing and reporting other kinds of data also apply to hormone measures. Most important is transparency; that is, all analysis steps (including reasons for and number of exclusions of participants) should be reported. Hormone data distributions should be examined for skewness and, if necessary, transformed to bring them closer to a normal distribution. For cortisol and sAA data, applying a natural-logarithm transformation is suitable in most cases. If outliers are present in the data and they cannot be accommodated through standard data transformations, analyses should be run and reported with and without them.

As discussed previously, almost all hormone measures are influenced by factors such as age, gender, and time of day (see Table 26.2). The influence of such factors needs to be controlled for in the data analyses, if it was not controlled in the study itself (e.g., by testing only female participants of the same age and menstrual-cycle stage). If these potentially confounding factors should be considered in the statistical analysis, regression analysis in general and analysis of covariance (ANCOVA) as a specific instantiation of this analytical approach can be used. With the use of an ANCOVA, the effect of the hormone of interest on the criterion measure is tested after such outside influencing factors have been held constant. Keep in mind, however, that the ANCOVA approach is valid only if the covariates exert only main effects on the criterion and do not significantly interact with the hormone in question (see Schultheiss & Stanton, 2009, for a discussion of how to deal with covariates for pre- and post-intervention designs).

Reporting the results of hormone assays involves describing the method of assessment and its quality in the methods section and reporting the actual findings in the results section. The method description should include the exact type and make of the assay; a short summary of the sample processing and sample assay protocol, and a statement of the main quality control parameters of the assay (see Table 26.4 for two examples).

Reporting of findings should include descriptive data about the hormone levels observed in the sample and their relationship to major confounding variables. Researchers who want to publish their findings in psychology and psychoendocrinology journals should follow the guidelines of the American Psychological Association Task Force on Statistical Inference (Wilkinson & APA Task Force on Statistical Inference, 1999) and allow readers to evaluate the suitability of the statistical procedures used and inferences made, given the shape of the data (e.g., by using line or bar graphs with error bars in the case of repeated-measures designs or scatter plots with fitted regression lines in the case of correlations).

In recent years, a debate about reproducibility in science has started and is changing the way we are doing research (Baker, 2015). This debate has also included findings and practices in behavioral endocrinology. Schultheiss and Mehta (2019) gave a comprehensive overview about this development in social neuroendocrinology and provided recommendations for conducting transparent and reproducible science. We agree with these recommendations and will emphasize the main points: (1) Preregister your study and hypotheses, (2) run power analyses, (3) make your raw data and analysis scripts available, and (4) use well-validated methods. Furthermore, we recommend running replication studies of your own and other researchers' work.

TABLE 26.4
Two Examples for Description of the Methods in an Article for Two Scenarios

Step	Examples
Saliva collection	(1) For each of the salivary samples, participants collected up to 7.5 mL unstimulated saliva in a sterile polypropylene vial.
	(2) Saliva was collected by means of polyester rolls ([product name], [company name]). Participants were instructed to keep the polyester roll in their mouth for at least 1 minute and to move it back and forth, but not to chew on it.
Storage	(1) Participants sealed the vials immediately after each collection. The experimenter placed the vials in frozen storage (−20 °C) after each experimental session.
	(2) Saliva samples were stored in the participants fridge or freezer for approximately 1–2 weeks until they were given back to the experimenters and stored at −30 °C.
Sample processing in the laboratory	(1) Samples were freed from mucopolysaccharides and other residuals by three freeze–thaw cycles, followed by centrifugation for 10 minutes at 3,000 rpm. All standards and controls were diluted with water (resulting analytic ranges: 5–400 pg/mL for testosterone; 0.51–19.50 pg/mL for estradiol; 5–400 pg/mL for progesterone; 0.5–25 ng/mL for cortisol).
	(2) For analysis, the polyester rolls were thawed at room temperature and were centrifuged at $2,000 \times g$ and 20 °C for 10 minutes immediately before analysis.
Laboratory analysis	(1) Salivary hormones were determined by solid-phase 125-I radioimmunoassays ([assay name], [company name]), using assay protocols previously validated for use with saliva [references]. Lower limits of detection (B0—$3 \times SD$) were 3.02 pg/mL for testosterone, 0.60 pg/mL for estradiol, 1.04 pg/mL for progesterone, and 0.06 ng/ml for cortisol. Low and high control samples were included in each assay ([product name], [company name]; 20 and 100 pg/mL for testosterone; 1.23 and 3 pg/mL for estradiol; 27 and 101 ng/mL for progesterone; 1.5 and 3.5 ng/ml for cortisol). Average recovery values for low and high controls were 107% and 94% for testosterone; 128% and 131% for estradiol; 54% and 72% for progesterone; 89% and 88% for cortisol. Median intra-assay CVs were 10.94% for testosterone; 21.86% for estradiol; 8.91% for progesterone; 4.59% for cortisol.
	(2) Salivary cortisol concentrations were determined in duplicate using enzyme-linked immunosorbent assays (ELISA, ([assay name], [company name]). Intra- and interassay coefficients of variation were below 10%.
Statistical analysis	(1) Visual histogram inspection and Shapiro-Wilks tests indicated that hormone values deviated from normal distributions. We therefore subjected progesterone, estradiol, and cortisol to log transformations and testosterone to a square-root transformation, after adding a constant of 1, and used these transformed scores in all inferential statistical procedures. Descriptive statistics are given for untransformed values.
	(2) The total diurnal cortisol output was calculated as area under the curve with respect to ground (AUCg). Because of positive skewness, AUCg values were transformed by means of the natural logarithm prior to further statistical analysis.

Note. Data from Oxford et al. (2017) and Pretscher et al. (2021): (1) Assessment of multiple hormones by means of radioimmunoassay (RIA), (2) cortisol assessment using enzymatic immunoassays/enzyme-linked immunosorbent assays (EIA/ELISA).

CONCLUSION

To summarize, the assessment of hormones from saliva samples is of broad interest in many fields in biobehavioral research. The areas of application are diverse, and saliva sample collection is straightforward. However, the measured hormone concentration depends on the data collection procedure and the sensitivity and specificity of the analysis method. Furthermore, the study should be well planned, and confounding factors should be identified and controlled. Researchers should adhere to the rules of good scientific practice throughout the research process and use open-science practices. In this chapter, we have provided a comprehensive overview of the most important steps, which is a good starting point. Nevertheless, we recommend newcomers to seek support from experienced researchers. We believe that linking psychology with endocrinology paves the way for fruitful interdisciplinary work in the behavioral, cognitive, and health sciences.

References

Adam, E. K., & Kumari, M. (2009). Assessing salivary cortisol in large-scale, epidemiological research. *Psychoneuroendocrinology, 34*(10), 1423–1436. https://doi.org/10.1016/j.psyneuen.2009.06.011

Adam, E. K., Quinn, M. E., Tavernier, R., McQuillan, M. T., Dahlke, K. A., & Gilbert, K. E. (2017). Diurnal cortisol slopes and mental and physical health outcomes: A systematic review and meta-analysis. *Psychoneuroendocrinology, 83*, 25–41. https://doi.org/10.1016/j.psyneuen.2017.05.018

Baker, M. (2015). Reproducibility crisis: Blame it on the antibodies. *Nature, 521*(7552), 274–276. https://doi.org/10.1038/521274a

Becker, L., & Rohleder, N. (2019). Time course of the physiological stress response to an acute stressor and its associations with the primacy and recency effect of the serial position curve. *PLOS ONE, 14*(5), e0213883. https://doi.org/10.1371/journal.pone.0213883

Becker, L., Schade, U., & Rohleder, N. (2019). Evaluation of the socially evaluated cold-pressor group test (SECPT-G) in the general population. *PeerJ, 7*, e7521. https://doi.org/10.7717/peerj.7521

Becker, L., Schade, U., & Rohleder, N. (2020). Activation of the hypothalamic-pituitary adrenal axis in response to a verbal fluency task and associations with task performance. *PLOS ONE, 15*(4), e0227721. https://doi.org/10.1371/journal.pone.0227721

Becker, L., Semmlinger, L., & Rohleder, N. (2021). Resistance training as an acute stressor in healthy young men: Associations with heart rate variability, alpha-amylase, and cortisol levels. *Stress, 24*(3), 318–330. https://doi.org/10.1080/10253890.2020.1799193

Bosch, J. A., Veerman, E. C. I., de Geus, E. J., & Proctor, G. B. (2011). α-Amylase as a reliable and convenient measure of sympathetic activity: Don't start salivating just yet! *Psychoneuroendocrinology, 36*(4), 449–453. https://doi.org/10.1016/j.psyneuen.2010.12.019

Carré, J. M., Ruddick, E. L., Moreau, B. J. P., & Bird, B. M. (2017). Testosterone and human aggression. In P. Sturmey (Ed.), *The Wiley handbook of violence and aggression: Vol. 1. Definition, conception, and development*. John Wiley & Sons. https://doi.org/10.1002/9781119057574.whbva020

Christodoulides, N., Mohanty, S., Miller, C. S., Langub, M. C., Floriano, P. N., Dharshan, P., Ali, M. F., Bernard, B., Romanovicz, D., Anslyn, E., Fox, P. C., & McDevitt, J. T. (2005). Application of microchip assay system for the measurement of C-reactive protein in human saliva. *Lab on a Chip, 5*(3), 261–269. https://doi.org/10.1039/b414194f

Dlugash, G., & Schultheiss, O. C. (2021). Suitability of saliva stimulants for valid assessment of steroid hormones via radioimmunoassay. *Psychoneuroendocrinology, 127*, 105175. https://doi.org/10.1016/j.psyneuen.2021.105175

Durdiaková, J., Fábryová, H., Koborová, I., Ostatníková, D., & Celec, P. (2013). The effects of saliva collection, handling and storage on salivary testosterone measurement. *Steroids, 78*(14), 1325–1331. https://doi.org/10.1016/j.steroids.2013.09.002

Engeland, C. G., Bosch, J. A., & Rohleder, N. (2019). Salivary biomarkers in psychoneuroimmunology. *Current Opinion in Behavioral Sciences, 28*, 58–65. https://doi.org/10.1016/j.cobeha.2019.01.007

Gangestad, S. W., Haselton, M. G., Welling, L. L. M., Gildersleeve, K., Pillsworth, E. G., Burriss, R. P., Larson, C. M., & Puts, D. A. (2016). How valid are assessments of conception probability in ovulatory cycle research? Evaluations, recommendations, and theoretical implications. *Evolution and Human Behavior, 37*(2), 85–96. https://doi.org/10.1016/j.evolhumbehav.2015.09.001

Geniole, S. N., Procyshyn, T. L., Marley, N., Ortiz, T. L., Bird, B. M., Marcellus, A. L., Welker, K. M., Bonin, P. L., Goldfarb, B., Watson, N. V., & Carré, J. M. (2019). Using a psychopharmacogenetic approach to identify the pathways through which—and the people for whom—testosterone promotes aggression. *Psychological Science, 30*(4), 481–494. https://doi.org/10.1177/0956797619826970

Goodman, W. K., Janson, J., & Wolf, J. M. (2017). Meta-analytical assessment of the effects of protocol variations on cortisol responses to the Trier Social Stress Test. *Psychoneuroendocrinology, 80*, 26–35. https://doi.org/10.1016/j.psyneuen.2017.02.030

Hampson, E. (2020). A brief guide to the menstrual cycle and oral contraceptive use for researchers in behavioral endocrinology. *Hormones and Behavior, 119*, 104655. https://doi.org/10.1016/j.yhbeh.2019.104655

Hellhammer, D. H., Wüst, S., & Kudielka, B. M. (2009). Salivary cortisol as a biomarker in stress research. *Psychoneuroendocrinology, 34*(2), 163–171. https://doi.org/10.1016/j.psyneuen.2008.10.026

Het, S., Ramlow, G., & Wolf, O. T. (2005). A meta-analytic review of the effects of acute cortisol administration on human memory. *Psychoneuroendocrinology, 30*(8), 771–784. https://doi.org/10.1016/j.psyneuen.2005.03.005

Kamin, H. S., & Kertes, D. A. (2017). Cortisol and DHEA in development and psychopathology. *Hormones and Behavior, 89*, 69–85. https://doi.org/10.1016/j.yhbeh.2016.11.018

Kirschbaum, C., Pirke, K.-M., & Hellhammer, D. H. (1993). The 'Trier Social Stress Test'—A tool for investigating psychobiological stress responses in a laboratory setting. *Neuropsychobiology, 28*(1-2), 76–81. https://doi.org/10.1159/000119004

Köllner, M. G., Janson, K. T., & Bleck, K. (2019). The social biopsychology of implicit motive development. In O. C. Schultheiss & P. H. Mehta (Eds.), *Routledge international handbook of social neuroendocrinology* (pp. 568–585). Routledge.

Lane, A., Luminet, O., Nave, G., & Mikolajczak, M. (2016). Is there a publication bias in behavioural intranasal oxytocin research on humans? Opening the file drawer of one laboratory. *Journal of Neuroendocrinology, 28*(4). https://doi.org/10.1111/jne.12384

Lequin, R. M. (2005). Enzyme immunoassay (EIA)/enzyme-linked immunosorbent assay (ELISA). *Clinical Chemistry, 51*(12), 2415–2418. https://doi.org/10.1373/clinchem.2005.051532

Liening, S. H., Stanton, S. J., Saini, E. K., & Schultheiss, O. C. (2010). Salivary testosterone, cortisol, and progesterone: Two-week stability, interhormone correlations, and effects of time of day, menstrual cycle, and oral contraceptive use on steroid hormone levels. *Physiology & Behavior, 99*(1), 8–16. https://doi.org/10.1016/j.physbeh.2009.10.001

Manning, J., Kilduff, L., Cook, C., Crewther, B., & Fink, B. (2014). Digit ratio (2D:4D): A biomarker for prenatal sex steroids and adult sex steroids in challenge situations. *Frontiers in Endocrinology, 5*, 9. https://doi.org/10.3389/fendo.2014.00009

Martins, D., Gabay, A. S., Mehta, M., & Paloyelis, Y. (2020). Salivary and plasmatic oxytocin are not reliable trait markers of the physiology of the oxytocin system in humans. *eLife, 9*, e62456. https://doi.org/10.7554/eLife.62456

McCullough, M. E., Churchland, P. S., & Mendez, A. J. (2013). Problems with measuring peripheral oxytocin: Can the data on oxytocin and human behavior be trusted? *Neuroscience and Biobehavioral Reviews, 37*(8), 1485–1492. https://doi.org/10.1016/j.neubiorev.2013.04.018

Nater, U. M., & Rohleder, N. (2009). Salivary alpha-amylase as a non-invasive biomarker for the sympathetic nervous system: Current state of research. *Psychoneuroendocrinology, 34*(4), 486–496. https://doi.org/10.1016/j.psyneuen.2009.01.014

Nix, B., & Wild, D. (2000). Data processing. In J. P. Gosling (Ed.), *The Practical Approach series. Immunoassays: A practical approach* (pp. 239–261). Oxford University Press.

O'Fegan, P. (2000). Validation. In J. P. Gosling (Ed.), *The Practical Approach series. Immunoassays: A practical approach* (pp. 211–238). Oxford University Press.

Oxford, J. K., Tiedtke, J. M., Ossmann, A., Özbe, D., & Schultheiss, O. C. (2017). Endocrine and aggressive responses to competition are moderated by contest outcome, gender, individual versus team competition, and implicit motives. *PLOS ONE, 12*(7), e0181610. https://doi.org/10.1371/journal.pone.0181610

Prasad, S., Lassetter, B., Welker, K. M., & Mehta, P. H. (2019). Unstable correspondence between salivary testosterone measured with enzyme immunoassays and tandem mass spectrometry. *Psychoneuroendocrinology, 109*, 104373. https://doi.org/10.1016/j.psyneuen.2019.104373

Pretscher, A., Kauzner, S., Rohleder, N., & Becker, L. (2021). Associations between social burden, perceived stress, and diurnal cortisol profiles in older adults: Implications for cognitive aging. *European Journal of Ageing, 18*(4), 575–590. https://doi.org/10.1007/s10433-021-00616-8

Riad-Fahmy, D., Read, G. F., Walker, R. F., Walker, S. M., & Griffiths, K. (1987). Determination of ovarian steroid hormone levels in saliva. An overview. *The Journal of Reproductive Medicine, 32*(4), 254–272.

Rohleder, N., & Nater, U. M. (2009). Determinants of salivary α-amylase in humans and methodological considerations. *Psychoneuroendocrinology, 34*(4), 469–485. https://doi.org/10.1016/j.psyneuen.2008.12.004

Rohleder, N., Wolf, J. M., Maldonado, E. F., & Kirschbaum, C. (2006). The psychosocial stress-induced increase in salivary alpha-amylase is independent of saliva flow rate. *Psychophysiology, 43*(6), 645–652. https://doi.org/10.1111/j.1469-8986.2006.00457.x

Schultheiss, O. C. (2013). Effects of sugarless chewing gum as a stimulant on progesterone, cortisol, and testosterone concentrations assessed in saliva. *International Journal of Psychophysiology, 87*(1), 111–114. https://doi.org/10.1016/j.ijpsycho.2012.11.012

Schultheiss, O. C., Dlugash, G., & Mehta, P. H. (2019). Hormone measurement in social neuroendocrinology: A comparison of immunoassay and mass spectrometry methods. In O. C. Schultheiss & P. H. Mehta (Eds.), *Routledge international handbook of social neuroendocrinology* (pp. 26–40). Routledge.

Schultheiss, O. C., & Mehta, P. H. (2019). Reproducibility in social neuroendocrinology: Past, present, and future. In O. C. Schultheiss & P. H. Mehta (Eds.), *Routledge international handbook of social neuroendocrinology* (pp. 41–64). Routledge.

Schultheiss, O. C., Schiepe-Tiska, A., & Rawolle, M. (2012). Hormone assays. In H. Cooper, P. M. Camic,

D. L. Long, A. T. Panter, D. Rindskopf, & K. J. Sher (Eds.), *Handbook of research methods in psychology* (Vol. 1: Foundations, planning, measures, and psychometrics, pp. 489–500). American Psychological Association. https://doi.org/10.1037/13619-026

Schultheiss, O. C., & Stanton, S. J. (2009). Assessment of salivary hormones. In E. Harmon-Jones & J. S. Beer (Eds.), *Methods in social neuroscience* (pp. 17–44). Guilford Press.

Slavish, D. C., Graham-Engeland, J. E., Smyth, J. M., & Engeland, C. G. (2015). Salivary markers of inflammation in response to acute stress. *Brain, Behavior, and Immunity, 44*, 253–269. https://doi.org/10.1016/j.bbi.2014.08.008

Smyth, N., Hucklebridge, F., Thorn, L., Evans, P., & Clow, A. (2013). Salivary cortisol as a biomarker in social science research. *Social and Personality Psychology Compass, 7*(9), 605–625. https://doi.org/10.1111/spc3.12057

Stanton, S. J., Mullette-Gillman, O. A., & Huettel, S. A. (2011). Seasonal variation of salivary testosterone in men, normally cycling women, and women using hormonal contraceptives. *Physiology & Behavior, 104*(5), 804–808. https://doi.org/10.1016/j.physbeh.2011.07.009

Strahler, J., Skoluda, N., Kappert, M. B., & Nater, U. M. (2017). Simultaneous measurement of salivary cortisol and alpha-amylase: Application and recommendations. *Neuroscience and Biobehavioral Reviews, 83*, 657–677. https://doi.org/10.1016/j.neubiorev.2017.08.015

Toffoletto, S., Lanzenberger, R., Gingnell, M., Sundström-Poromaa, I., & Comasco, E. (2014). Emotional and cognitive functional imaging of estrogen and progesterone effects in the female human brain: A systematic review. *Psychoneuroendocrinology, 50*, 28–52. https://doi.org/10.1016/j.psyneuen.2014.07.025

Toone, R. J., Peacock, O. J., Smith, A. A., Thompson, D., Drawer, S., Cook, C., & Stokes, K. A. (2013). Measurement of steroid hormones in saliva: Effects of sample storage condition. *Scandinavian Journal of Clinical and Laboratory Investigation, 73*(8), 615–621. https://doi.org/10.3109/00365513.2013.835862

van Anders, S. M. (2010). Chewing gum has large effects on salivary testosterone, estradiol, and secretory immunoglobulin A assays in women and men. *Psychoneuroendocrinology, 35*(2), 305–309. https://doi.org/10.1016/j.psyneuen.2009.06.009

van Anders, S. M., Goldey, K. L., & Bell, S. N. (2014). Measurement of testosterone in human sexuality research: Methodological considerations. *Archives of Sexual Behavior, 43*(2), 231–250. https://doi.org/10.1007/s10508-013-0123-z

Vongas, J. G., Al Hajj, R., & Fiset, J. (2020). Leader emergence and affective empathy: A dynamic test of the dual-hormone hypothesis. *PLOS ONE, 15*(12), e0244548. https://doi.org/10.1371/journal.pone.0244548

Welker, K. M., Lassetter, B., Brandes, C. M., Prasad, S., Koop, D. R., & Mehta, P. H. (2016). A comparison of salivary testosterone measurement using immunoassays and tandem mass spectrometry. *Psychoneuroendocrinology, 71*, 180–188. https://doi.org/10.1016/j.psyneuen.2016.05.022

Wilkinson, L., & Task Force on Statistical Inference, American Psychological Association, Science Directorate. (1999). Statistical methods in psychology journals: Guidelines and explanations. *American Psychologist, 54*(8), 594–604. https://doi.org/10.1037/0003-066X.54.8.594

Wolf, O. T. (2009). Stress and memory in humans: Twelve years of progress? *Brain Research, 1293*, 142–154. https://doi.org/10.1016/j.brainres.2009.04.013

Wolf, O. T. (2019). The impact of psychosocial stress on cognition. In O. C. Schultheiss & P. H. Mehta (Eds.), *Routledge international handbook of social neuroendocrinology* (pp. 441–453). Routledge.

Wolkowitz, O. M., & Reus, V. I. (2003). Dehydroepiandrosterone in psychoneuroendocrinology. In O. M. Wolkowitz & A. J. Rothschild (Eds.), *Psychoneuroendocrinology: The scientific basis of clinical practice* (pp. 205–242). American Psychiatric Publishing, Inc.

Section 6

MEASURES IN NEUROSCIENCE

CHAPTER 27

ELECTRO- AND MAGNETOENCEPHALOGRAPHIC METHODS IN PSYCHOLOGY

Eddie Harmon-Jones, David M. Amodio, Philip A. Gable, and Suzanne Dikker

Electroencephalography (EEG) refers to the recording of electrical brain activity from the human scalp. This method of measurement was discovered by Hans Berger in the late 1920s in experiments in which two sponges were soaked in saline and were then connected to a differential amplifier (Berger, 1929). EEG measurement techniques have advanced considerably since that time, and they now represent one of the most common methods for measuring brain function in studies of basic psychological and motor processes and in studies of psychological and motor dysfunction. Magnetoencephalography (MEG) is a more recent invention, first reported by Cohen (1968). MEG is not as widely used as EEG for multiple reasons: It is less affordable, requires a more elaborate setup (including a magnetically shielded room), and is high-maintenance (sensors need to be kept at very low temperatures by way of helium, which needs to be replaced at set intervals).

EEG and MEG both make it possible to record neural activity noninvasively with a high temporal resolution (on the order of milliseconds), but EEG and MEG signals differ in crucial ways, and thus they are complementary tools. The observed EEG/MEG signal, which is recorded at the human scalp, stems from electrical voltages (EEG) and their corresponding magnetic fields (MEG) generated inside the brain.

Electrical activity that is associated with neurons comes from action potentials and postsynaptic potentials. Action potentials are composed of a rapid series of electrochemical changes that run from the beginning of the axon at the cell body to the axon terminals where neurotransmitters are released. Postsynaptic potentials occur when the neurotransmitters bind to receptors on the membrane of the postsynaptic cell. This binding causes ion channels to open or close and it leads to a graded change in the electrical potential across the cell membrane. While (invasive) single-unit recordings allow the assessment of action potentials, EEG/MEG primarily capture postsynaptic potentials.

EEG/MEG signals are thought to primarily reflect the summation of postsynaptic potentials rather than action potentials because of the timing of action potentials and the physical arrangement of axons. That is, unless the neurons fire within microseconds of each other, action potentials in different axons will typically cancel each other out. If one neuron fires shortly after another one, then the current at a given location will flow into one axon at the same time that it flows out of another one; thus, they cancel each other out and produce a much smaller signal at the electrode. Although the duration of an action potential is approximately 1 ms, the duration of postsynaptic

https://doi.org/10.1037/0000318-027
APA Handbook of Research Methods in Psychology, Second Edition: Vol. 1. Foundations, Planning, Measures, and Psychometrics, H. Cooper (Editor-in-Chief)
Copyright © 2023 by the American Psychological Association. All rights reserved.

potentials is much longer, often tens or hundreds of milliseconds. Postsynaptic potentials are also mostly confined to dendrites and cell bodies and occur instantaneously rather than traveling down the axon at a fixed rate. These factors allow postsynaptic potentials to summate rather than to cancel, which results in voltage changes that have larger amplitudes and can be recorded on the cortical surface or at the scalp. Hence, EEG signals are most likely the result of postsynaptic potentials, which have a slower time course and are more likely to be synchronous and summate than presynaptic potentials. Recent models suggest that action potentials may also contribute to the EEG/MEG signal, but likely only if they are very tightly coupled between local populations of 10K to 50K neurons (Gross, 2019; Murakami & Okada, 2006).

EEG/MEG activity recorded outside the scalp is the result of the activity of populations of neurons. This activity can be recorded on the scalp surface because the tissue between the neurons and the scalp acts as a volume conductor. The activity generated by one neuron is small; thus, the activity that is recorded at the scalp is the integrated activity of numerous neurons that are active synchronously. Moreover, for activity to be recorded at the scalp, the electromagnetic fields that are generated by each neuron must be oriented in such a way that their effects accumulate. That is, the neurons must be arranged in an open as opposed to a closed field. In an open field, the neurons' dendrites are all oriented on one side of the structure, whereas their axons all depart from the other side. Open fields are present where neurons are organized in layers, as in most of the cortex, parts of the thalamus, the cerebellum, and other structures, as opposed to closed fields which characterize structures such as the amygdala and hippocampus.

The raw EEG/MEG signal is a complex waveform that can be analyzed in the temporal domain or frequency domain. Processing of the temporal aspect is typically done with event-related designs and analyses (Bartholow & Amodio, 2009). Event-related potentials (ERPs) in EEG do not always straightforwardly map onto event-related fields (ERFs) in MEG (e.g., Pylkkänen & Marantz, 2003). This is due to the inherent differences in the signals. First, MEG is more sensitive to superficial brain activity (i.e., activity originating from cortex located closer to the skull) than EEG because electrical fields are less subject to decay. In addition, MEG selectively measures brain activity stemming from cortical sulci, where the dendrites of pyramidal cortical neurons are oriented tangentially with respect to the surface of the scalp. The EEG signal, in contrast, picks up activity from both sulci and gyri, although it is dominated by gyral activity (from neurons that are radially oriented to the scalp surface). This is because electrical and magnetic fields are oriented perpendicular to each other (Sutherling et al., 1988). Importantly, magnetic fields are less distorted by skull tissue than electrical signals, rendering the source of the MEG signal better interpretable than the source of the EEG signal. Still, source localization in both techniques is complicated by the inverse problem, and the spatial resolution is nowhere near hemodynamic techniques such as functional magnetic resonance imaging (fMRI).

In this chapter, we present a few examples of frequency analyses of EEG/MEG, in which frequency is specified in hertz or cycles per second. For more comprehensive EEG/MEG primers and discussions about issues and best practice around EEG/MEG preprocessing and analysis, see Pernet et al. (2020), Hari and Puce (2017), and Puce and Hämäläinen (2017).

EEG/MEG RECORDING

MEG requires an elaborate recording setup. Because the brain's magnetic fields are very small, the participant's head rests on a dewar containing superconducting MEG sensors and liquid helium to keep them at the correct temperature.

To offset magnetic noise interference from the environment (e.g., elevators, subways), MEG systems are located inside a magnetically shielded room (two layers of mu metal of a few millimeters' thickness each). Inside the room, the participant is either reclining or sitting upright during the recording. Systems vary with respect to the number of channels. For example, a typical "160-channel" MEG system may have 157 axial gradiometers located near the scalp to measure brain activity, three orthogonally oriented (reference) magnetometers located in the dewar but away from the brain to measure and reduce external noise offline, and 32 open positions for stimulus triggers, eye-tracker data, auditory signals, and vocalization information from the microphone inside the chamber.

To allow for a reconstruction of the head location inside the dewar and subsequent coregistration with a structural MRI scan of the participant's brain, marker coils and electrodes as well as three fiducial locations (the nasion, and the left and right preauricular points) are recorded before the participant enters the MEG. Additionally, the shape of the participant's head may be registered using a 3D laser scanning system.

In contemporary psychological lab research, EEG is recorded from 32, 64, 128, or more electrodes that are often mounted in a stretch-lycra electrode cap. Caps are relatively easy to position on a participant's head, and they include electrodes positioned over the entire scalp surface. Caps can utilize wet electrodes in which sponges around the electrodes are soaked in a saline solution or a conductive gel is placed inside the electrode. Dry electrode systems use electrodes coated in gold, silver, or nickel, and place electrodes directly on the head, without any conductive solution. Wet electrode systems remain the gold standard for clinical and research EEG recording due to their low impedance and higher signal quality. However, dry electrode recordings may have benefits when high impedance levels are tolerable, at-home recording is preferred, or when recording for long periods when a conductance solution might dry out (Hinrichs et al., 2020). Wet electrodes are often made of tin or silver and silver chloride; the latter are nonpolarizable but are typically much more expensive. Most modern EEG amplifiers with high input impedance utilize very low electrode currents. Thus, polarizable electrodes (tin) can often be used to record the typical range of electrical frequencies that are of interest in psychology experiments without distortion. However, for frequencies less than 0.1 Hz, nonpolarizable electrodes are recommended (see Polich & Lawson, 1985).

Another distinction commonly seen among electrode systems is whether they have active or passive electrodes. An active electrode system has a small preamplification unit directly attached to the conductive metal in the electrode. This allows the EEG signal to be immediately amplified before additional noise can be introduced while the signal is transmitted from the electrode to the main amplifier unit, which is often 1 meter away. Passive electrodes do not have the preamplification unit at the electrode. As compared to passive electrodes, active electrodes minimize noise introduced during signal transmission, tolerate high impedance recording, and reduce participant preparation time. However, passive electrodes are generally less expensive, can be used inside an MRI machine, and have a lower profile to benefit transcranial magnetic stimulation over the cap.

The electrode placements are typically based on the 10–20 system (Jasper, 1958), which was subsequently extended to a 10% electrode system (Chatrian et al., 1988) and beyond. The naming convention for electrode positions is as follows. The first letter of the name of the electrode refers to the brain region over which the electrode sits. Thus, Fp refers to frontal pole, F refers to frontal region, C to central region, P to parietal region, T to temporal region, and O to occipital region. Electrodes in between these regions are often designated by using two letters, such as FC for frontal-central. After the letter is a number, as in F3, or another letter, as in FZ. Odd numbers designate sites on the left side of the head and even numbers designate sites on the right side of the head. Numbers increase as distance from the middle of the head increases, so F7 is farther from the midline than F3. Z is used to designate the midline, which goes from the front to the back of the head. Figure 27.1 illustrates a modern multichannel system based on the 10–20 system. Caps often contain a ground electrode, which is connected to the iso-ground of the amplifier and assists in reducing electrical noise. Eye movements, recorded using an electrooculogram (EOG),

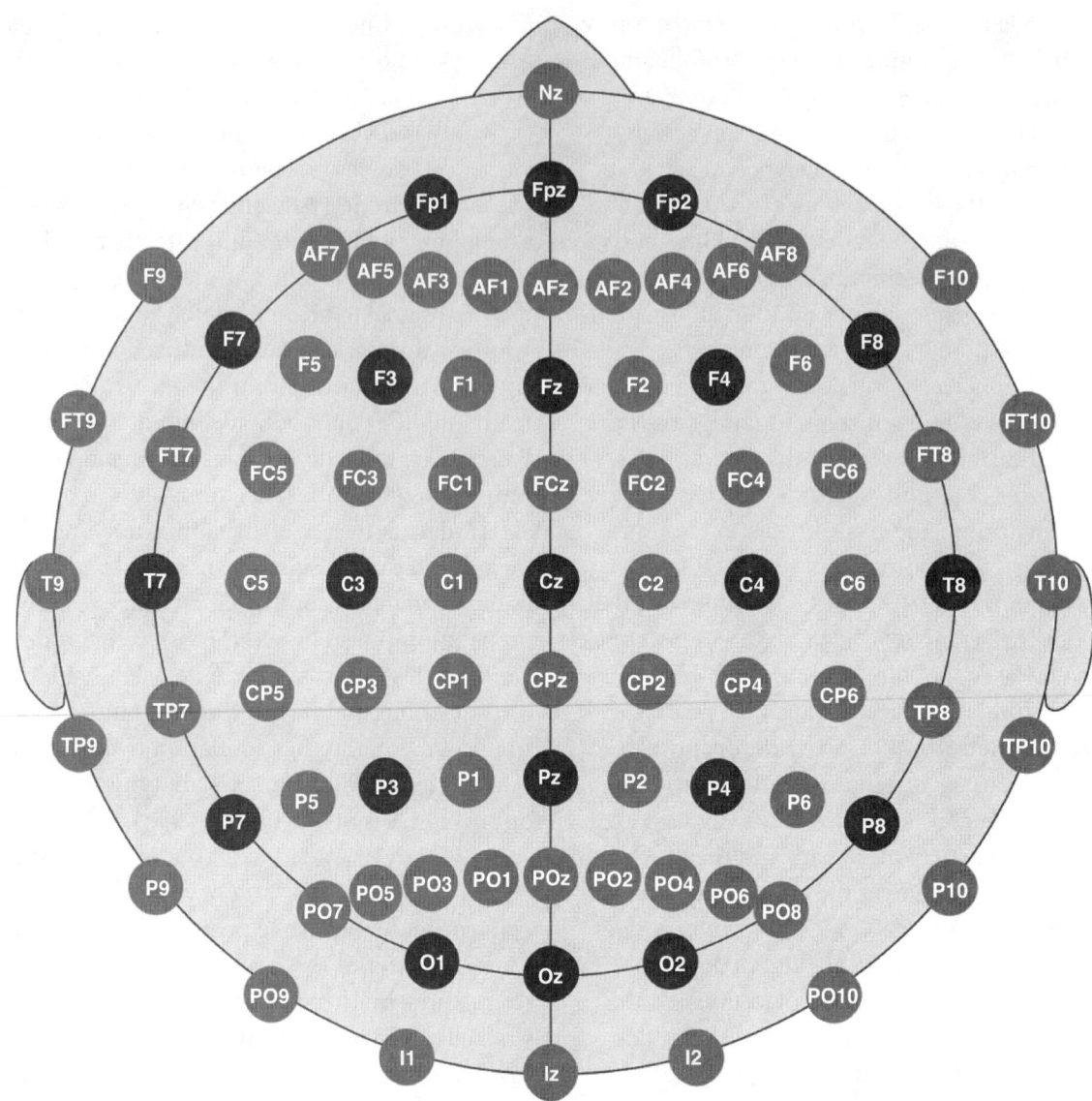

FIGURE 27.1. Electrode layout and labels commonly used in electroencephalography recording. The figure shows the top of the head, with the triangle at the top representing the nose. The electrodes displayed in black are the original 10–20 electrodes.

are also recorded to facilitate artifact scoring of the EEG. EOG can be recorded from the supra- and suborbits of the eyes, to assess vertical eye movements, and from the left and right outer canthus, to assess horizontal eye movements. Additional electrodes are often placed on earlobes so that offline, digitally derived references can be computed. See the section titled Offline Data Processing: EEG-Specific Referencing for a more complete discussion of reference electrodes.

When using gel-based electrode systems, sites where electrodes will be placed must be abraded (i.e., exfoliated) and cleaned to reduce electrode impedances, typically to under 5,000 Ω. Mild skin abrasion removes dead skin cells and oils that impede electrical conductance. Conductive gel is used as a medium between the scalp and electrodes. EEG, EOG, and other signals are then amplified with bioamplifiers.

For EEG/MEG frequency analyses, the raw signals are often bandpass filtered online (e.g., 0.1 Hz to 100 or 200 Hz) because the frequencies of interest tend to fall within a relatively narrow frequency band (e.g., between 1 Hz and 40 Hz). Online 60-Hz notch filters (in the United States; 50 Hz in Europe) may also be used to further reduce electrical noise from alternating current (AC) sources, such as lamps and computers.

The raw EEG/MEG signals are digitized onto a computer at a sampling rate greater than twice the highest frequency of interest. For example, if one is only interested in frequencies below 40 Hz, then a minimum 80 samples should be recorded per second. This sampling rate is necessary because of the Nyquist theorem, which states that reliable reconstruction of a continuous signal from its samples is possible if the signal is of limited bands and if it is sampled at a rate that is a least twice the actual signal bandwidth. If this sampling condition is not met, then frequencies will overlap; that is, frequencies above half the sampling rate will be reconstructed as frequencies below half the sampling rate. This distortion is called *aliasing* because the reconstructed signal is said to be an alias of the original signal. Given the power and large storage capacity of modern computers, however, sampling rates well above the Nyquist frequency are typically used, allowing for high-fidelity digital representations of analog signals.

PREPARING THE PARTICIPANT

Most EEG/MEG protocols require the researcher to spend several minutes to an hour preparing the participant for data collection; the time required depends on the type (dry, sponge-based, gel-based, active, or passive electrodes) and number of electrodes used. Thus, we offer a few comments regarding the behavior of the researcher. When talking with participants, we avoid using words such as *electricity*, *electrodes*, *needles*, or anything that sounds painful. Instead, we say, "I am going to be putting a cap on your head to measure brain activity." We also train our experimenters to adopt the mindset of a person who has done this *very routine procedure* many times. We work with them so that they appear confident and do not cause the participant to worry about the procedure. For example, mistakes may be made during the attachment procedure, but we avoid announcing them to the participant because they can often be corrected easily. We also recommend that researchers avoid being too friendly because this can alter the mood of the participants in ways that may influence their behavior in the experiment. In general, researchers working with participants should be encouraged to adopt a professional mindset and demeanor, as well as a professional appearance (e.g., by wearing a lab coat).

Once all of the materials needed for data collection are ready (e.g., electrodes, adhesive collars, conductive gel), the participant is brought into the experiment room. For MEG recordings, participants are asked to arrive at the lab without any metal objects or materials (e.g., mascara, piercings) attached to their bodies. Once in the lab, they are asked to empty their pockets and remove any glasses, jewelry, shoes, belts, and underwire bras.

With passive EEG systems, electrical impedance of the scalp will need to be brought under 5,000 Ω; higher impedance (up to 50,000 Ω) is acceptable when using active electrode systems, due to the higher signal-to-noise ratio of the active electrode systems. To assist in reducing impedance, we ask participants to brush their hair vigorously for about 5 minutes with a stiff-bristled brush, which aids in exfoliating the scalp. For example, we tell participants, "Be sure to press the brush hard against your scalp as you brush. It helps with the attachment process. I will tell you when you can stop."

Once they are finished brushing their scalp, participants are told that we are going to use an exfoliant to clean some areas of their skin and use rubbing alcohol to remove the exfoliant. We clean their forehead, earlobes, temples, and above and below the eyes with a mildly abrasive cleaning solution (e.g., pumice-based gel) and gauze pad. We follow the cleaning by wiping the areas with alcohol, which assists in removing the cleaning solution but also assists with further cleaning of the area.

Because most labs now use EEG caps instead of single electrodes to collect EEG data, we will describe the capping procedure. We first use a metric tape to measure the length from the *nasion* (a point just below the eyebrows where there is an indentation at the top of the nose) to the *inion* (bump on skull over the occipital region at the back of head). Then, 10% of this total distance (in centimeters) is calculated and measured up from the nasion. We mark this spot on the forehead with a wax pencil and explain this by saying, "I am going to make a mark on your forehead with a wax pencil. It will wipe right off." This mark will aid cap placement. Cap size is determined by measuring the distance around the participant's head, crossing the marks on the forehead and the inion. Caps often come in various adult and child sizes. The experimenter aligns the Fp1 and Fp2 electrodes with the wax pencil marking on the forehead. The cap is then stretched toward the back of the participant's head and down. Having the participant hold the cap in place on the forehead helps get the cap over the head. After the cap is straightened so that the mid-line electrodes align with the midline of the head, the distance from the nasion to the inion should be remeasured to ensure that Cz is halfway between these sites. If it is not, adjust the cap so that it is. Cz is centered horizontally by measuring from the preauricular indention in front of each ear; the indention can be found by having participants open their mouths and then feeling for the indention.

After attaching the cap's connectors to the main amplifier unit, electrodes are often attached to each earlobe or mastoid because one of these sites is often used as a reference site and the other is recorded as a separate channel so that off-line rereferencing of the average of the ears or mastoids can be performed (online averaging of ears is not recommended; see the section Offline Data Processing: EEG-Specific Referencing). The electrodes are attached by placing an adhesive collar on the flat side and sticking it on the ear. Additional adhesive collars may be placed on top of the electrode to ensure that the electrode remains attached. If using gel-based electrodes, fill sensors with conductive gel but do not overfill; that is, avoid having gel run between two sensors or outside the adhesive collar, because this will cause measurement problems (e.g., a conductive bridge between sensors) or interfere with the adhesion of the collar. Next, abrade the ground electrode site with the blunt tip of a wooden cotton swab or the blunt tip of a large-gauge needle, and apply gel with a syringe. We demonstrate to participants how we do this by making a motion with the syringe and blunt tip on their hands so that they know what to expect. We then say, "I am going to put gel into each sensor." Impedances should be below 5,000 Ω for passive electrode systems (Kappenman & Luck, 2010). Active electrodes systems permit measuring EEG with moderate impedances (< 50,000 Ω with similar results; Laszlo et al., 2014; Mathewson et al., 2017), but dry electrode systems with higher impedance have increased noise and reduced statistical power (Mathewson et al., 2017). Finally, a chinstrap for the cap is positioned comfortably under the participant's chin to ensure that the cap stays in place. Eye movements are often measured in EEG/MEG research so that procedures can later be taken to remove eye movements from the data or to correct the data from these movements (see the section Eye Movement Artifacts).

In addition to ensuring that the recording conditions are optimal, it is equally important to ensure that the participant is in a state of mind that is desired for the research question. For instance, if the study concerns personality characteristics or individual differences, it is important that characteristics of the situation not be so intense as to overwhelm potential individual differences of interest. Along these lines, we avoid making participants self-conscious by, for example, covering the computer monitor until it is ready to be used because a black-screened computer monitor can act as a mirror. Similarly, video cameras are best hidden to avoid the arousal of excessive self-consciousness.

Artifacts

Artifacts, whether of biological or nonbiological origin, are best dealt with by taking preventative measures. When they do occur, procedures exist to reduce their effects on EEG/MEG measurements.

Muscle artifact. Muscle artifact (electromyography [EMG]) typically comprises electrical signals that cycle at higher frequencies than EEG/MEG signals of interest. EMG is typically greater than 40 Hz, although some EMG may blend in with the lower frequencies, so it is advisable to limit muscle artifacts by instructing the participants to limit their muscle movements. If muscle artifacts do appear in studies in which muscle movements should not occur, the artifacts can be removed during the data-processing stage. Often, this is done manually, through visual inspection and exclusion by someone trained in EEG scoring.

In some experiments, particularly those that evoke emotion, muscle artifacts cannot be avoided. That is, if an intense amount of fear is evoked, the facial muscles of the participant will move and create muscle artifact in the data, particularly in frontal and temporal regions. Removing these muscle movements is not advisable because the removal process would also exclude signals of interest related to emotion. One way to handle the EMG that may contaminate the EEG is to measure facial EMG directly and then use the facial EMG responses (in EMG frequency ranges, such as 50–250 Hz) in covariance analyses. This analysis would indicate whether any observed effects for EEG were related to EMG responses or whether statistical adjustment may be needed to reveal effects. Similarly, one can obtain EMG frequencies from the scalp electrode sites, rather than facial muscle sites, and use these EMG frequencies in covariance analyses (see Coan et al., 2001, for examples). These issues have been investigated extensively in recent research (e.g., McMenamin et al., 2009).

Eye movement artifacts. The eyeball is polarized, with a dipole running from the cornea to the retina, and the relatively large voltage changes from eye movements are recorded in EEG/MEG (especially near the eyes). These measurements are referred to as *electro-oculograms* (EOG). Electrodes are affixed to the face using double-sided adhesive collars. For measuring vertical eye movements (e.g., caused by eye blinks), one electrode is placed 10% of the inion–nasion distance above the pupil and another is placed 10% of the inion–nasion distance below the pupil.

These two electrodes are referenced to each other. For measuring horizontal eye movements, one electrode is placed on the right temple and another is placed on the left temple (referenced to each other). Because the EOG signal is relatively large, impedances up to 10,000 Ω are acceptable, and thus less face abrasion may be needed. In lieu of EOG electrodes, eye-tracking setups are often used in conjunction with MEG, which makes it possible to later regress out eye movements and blinks.

Eye-movement artifacts are also best dealt with in advance of EEG recording. That is, training participants to limit eye movements during EEG recording is recommended. Researchers must not encourage participants to control their blinking, because blinks and spontaneous eye movements are controlled by several brain systems in a highly automatic fashion (e.g., Brodal, 1992), and the instruction to suppress these systems may act as a secondary task, creating distraction and cognitive load (see Verleger, 1991, for a discussion).

Participants will inevitably blink, and these blinks will influence the EEG data, particularly in the frontal electrodes. Therefore, epochs containing blinks can be removed from the EEG, but this procedure can cause significant amounts of data loss. Because blink rate has been related to psychological and physiological processes (Taylor et al., 1999; Stern et al., 1984), this approach may remove data relevant to the psychological phenomena being studied. As such, it is preferable to correct blink artifact via a computer algorithm (Gratton et al., 1983; Semlitsch et al., 1986). These algorithms often rely on regression techniques, but other techniques involving principal or independent component analyses (ICA) have been recommended (e.g., Joyce et al., 2004; Wallstrom et al., 2004). In the regression approaches to EOG correction, the actual EEG time-series is regressed on the EOG time-series, and the resulting residual time-series represents a new EEG from which the influence of the ocular activity is statistically removed. Then, eye-movement, artifact-corrected EEG data may be processed as would EEG data without EOG artifacts. This latter procedure has the advantage of not losing data, but it can sometimes introduce another source of artifact as the regression subtracts, and may overcorrect the EEG data. ICA is a source-blind separation technique that breaks a signal into components whether the sources are independent or not (Delorme et al., 2007). Once the artifact components are identified, the signal can be reconstructed without the component considered artifact. ICA can be more useful than linear regression because it can extract more than just ocular artifacts, such as those occurring from bad electrodes or head muscle movement (Curham & Allen, 2021).

Nonbiological artifacts. Nonbiological artifacts are those that typically involve external electrical noise coming from elevator motors, electric lights, computers, or almost anything running electricity nearby the subject. Again, prevention is the best defense against such artifacts. Good grounding is perhaps the simplest and most cost-effective way to reduce the external noise sources. In contrast to MEG, which, as described above, requires a fully magnetically shielded room, full electrical shielding is not usually necessary with modern EEG amplifiers. Still, it is important to remove or repair any poorly shielded electrical equipment. It is also helpful to limit the use of power outlets in the EEG recording chamber and to use direct-current (DC) lamps if possible. High electrode impedances or a faulty ground connection can also increase AC noise (e.g., 60 Hz). Electrodes need to be carefully washed after each use to prevent corrosion and to assist in prevention of artifacts. When electrical noise is present, it can be dealt with through filtering of the signal; that is, 60-Hz activity can be removed with an online filter or after the data are collected.

In MEG, nonbiological artifacts are often removed by comparing the MEG data recorded from the participant with an "empty room" recording (without the participant). This allows for the removal from the data of a spatial subspace that is assumed to stem from noise sources, and it can also help attenuate the impact of eye-related and cardiac artifacts (Puce & Hämäläinen, 2017).

OFFLINE DATA PROCESSING: EEG-SPECIFIC REFERENCING

In contrast to MEG, EEG signals are often re-referenced. The issue of referencing is the subject of some debate (Allen et al., 2004; Davidson et al., 2000; Hagemann, 2004; Nunez & Srinivasan, 2006). All bioelectrical measurements reflect the difference in activity between at least two sites. In EEG research, one site is typically placed on the scalp, whereas the other site may be on the scalp or on a nonscalp area, such as an earlobe or nose tip. Researchers strive to obtain measures that reflect activity in particular brain regions; thus, they often search for a relatively inactive reference, such as the earlobe. There are no "inactive sites," however; all sites near the scalp reflect some EEG activity because of volume conduction. To address this issue when 64 or more electrodes are used, some researchers suggest using an average reference composed of the average of activity at all recorded EEG sites. The average reference should approximate an inactive reference if a sufficiently large array of electrodes is placed in a spherical arrangement around the head. That is, activity generated from dipoles will be positive at one site and negative at a site 180 degrees opposite to this site. Thus, the sum across sites should approach zero with a representative sample of the sphere. Electrodes are not placed under the head; thus, this assumption is rarely met. Moreover, use of smaller montages of electrodes causes more residual activity in the average reference.

Other researchers have recommended the use of linked earlobes as a reference because of the relatively low EEG activity in the earlobes and because linking the earlobes should theoretically center the reference on the head, making the determination of lateralized activity more accurate. Linking the ears into one reference electrode has been questioned (Katznelson, 1981), however, because it can produce a low-resistance shunt between the two sides of the head, reducing any asymmetries that are observed at the scalp. Research, however, has suggested that physically linking the ears does not alter the observed EEG asymmetries (Gonzalez Andino et al., 1990). Some EEG researchers have suggested that the original idea was ill conceived because electrode impedances will be higher than the internal resistance within the head. Hence, linked earlobes do not provide a shunt that is lower in resistance than what is present inside the head (Davidson et al., 2000). Physically linking the ears is inappropriate for another reason. When the ears are linked before input into the amplifier, variations in the impedances of the left and right electrodes will change the spatial location of the reference and potentially alter the magnitude and direction of any observed differences in left versus right EEG activity (Davidson et al., 2000). This does not happen when creating an averaged ears reference offline, after the data have been collected, because most contemporary amplifiers have very high input impedances (around 100 kΩ) and variations in electrode impedances of several thousand ohms will have a tiny effect on the observed voltage. To create an offline linked or averaged ears reference, the collected EEG data need to be actively referenced online to one of the ears or some other location (e.g., Cz). Then, electrical signals need to be collected from the other ear when the active reference is one ear, or both ears, in the case of a Cz reference. Offline, the data are re-referenced to the average of the two ears.

Which reference should be used? From the perspective of psychological construct validity, use and comparison of different reference schemes in each study might be advisable (see Coan & Allen, 2003, for an example). A significant interaction involving reference factor would indicate that the EEG–psychological variable relation is moderated by the reference. If such research is conducted over several years, EEG researchers may establish good psychological construct validity of the particular EEG measure.

From the perspective of neurophysiological construct validity, selecting a particular reference in advance might be advisable, considering the advantages and disadvantages of each method for the EEG measurement construct. For example, in research on asymmetrical frontal cortical activity and emotion and motivation, Hagemann (2004) recommended against using the average reference if only limited head coverage was used, as in the 10–20 system. He indicated that the average reference may cause increased anterior alpha activity; averaging of the whole head can inflate anterior alpha because anterior regions have much lower alpha power than posterior regions. Thus, the offline average of earlobes may be more appropriate. Although this reference shows some alpha activity and, thus, is not inactive, it may yield better signal-to-noise ratio for anterior sites than the average (whole head) reference.

Current-source density (CSD) is a transformation that obtains a "reference-free" representation of the EEG signal. Specifically, the scalp-Laplacian at an electrode compares the potential at one electrode to an average of the electrodes around it, using spherical spline interpolation (Delorme & Makeig, 2004). CSD has advantages in that it accounts for the spherical nature of the scalp and the uneven placement of electrodes. In addition, CSD can address volume conduction differences resulting from signals emerging from different brain regions being conducted through different types of tissue (Curham & Allen, 2021). Comparisons of resting data across different reference montages revealed that only the CSD transformation ensures occipital alpha caused by eyes closed is not reflected in frontal regions (Smith et al., 2017).

In EEG, electrode positions rarely shift during the experiment. In MEG, in contrast, because the sensors are not attached to the scalp but rather located inside a fixed dewar, the person's head may have moved during the experiment. Such shifts can be corrected using the information from the head coil and fiducial information mentioned above. In addition, researchers have started using headcases designed to minimize shifts in head positions inside scanners. For example, S. S. Meyer, Bonaiuto, et al. (2017) designed flexible, subject-specific cases that can be used to stabilize and (re)position the head both during and between scanning sessions.

Obtaining the Frequencies of the EEG/MEG Signal

Several steps are involved in transforming EEG/MEG signals into indices that are used in data analyses. We will illustrate this analysis with EEG, but similar principles apply to MEG. First, a signal is collected in the time-domain and is then converted to a frequency-domain representation, usually in the form of a power spectrum. The spectrum, which collapses data across time, summarizes which frequencies are present (see Figure 27.2 for an illustration). Spectral analysis involves examining the frequency composition of short windows of time (epochs), often 1 or 2 seconds each. The spectra are averaged across many epochs. Epochs of 1 or 2 seconds are used to meet an assumption underlying the Fourier transform, which is the method used to derive power spectra. The Fourier transform assumes a periodic signal—one that repeats at a uniformly spaced interval. Any periodic signal can be decomposed into a series of sine and cosine functions of various frequencies, with the function for each frequency beginning at its own particular phase. EEG signals are not exactly periodic because the repetition of features is not precisely spaced at uniform intervals. The use of short epochs allows one to analyze small segments of data that will have features that repeat in a highly similar fashion at other points in the waveform.

In EEG research, epochs are often overlapped. This is done to prevent a problem that occurs with

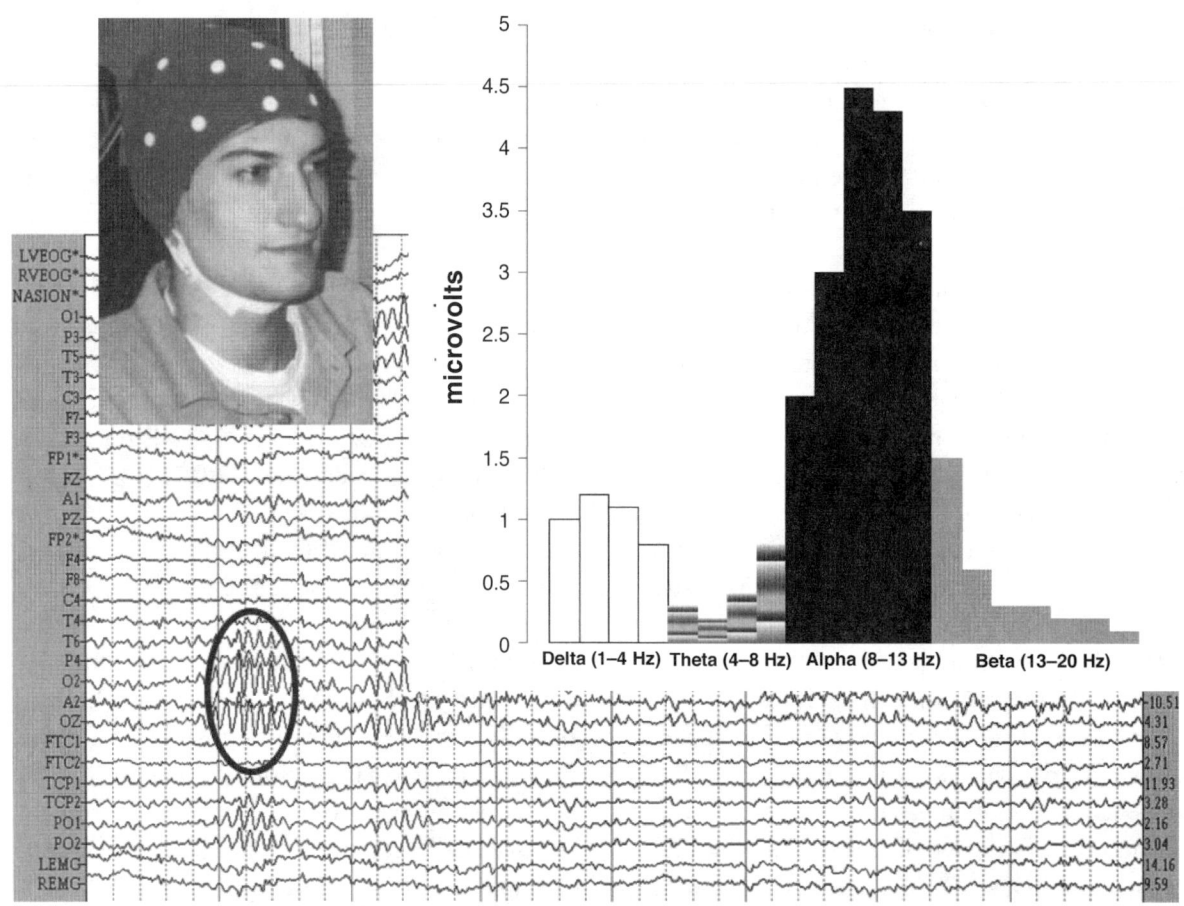

FIGURE 27.2. The background displays raw electroencephalography (EEG), and the circled portion is an example of a prominent alpha burst obtained over the occipital region when a subject's eyes are closed. The picture in the upper right displays the results of a fast Fourier transform at one electrode. The picture in the upper left displays David Amodio wearing an EEG cap.

windowing, a necessary part of the EEG data processing. Windowing, as with a Hamming window, is used to avoid creating artifactual frequencies in the resultant power spectra. Windowing tapers the power of signals in an epoch toward the endpoints of the epoch, reducing the endpoints to near-zero values so that discontinuities will not occur if copies of the epochs are placed immediately before or after the epoch. This assists in meeting the Fourier assumption that the epoch repeats infinitely both forward and backward in time. Fourier methods introduce spurious frequencies if windowing is not used to prevent discontinuities in the signal. Windowing prevents discontinuity, but also prevents data near the ends of the epoch from being fully represented in the power spectrum. Overlapping epochs provides a solution to this problem because data minimally weighted at the end of one epoch will be weighted more heavily in subsequent epochs.

Most signal processing programs use a fast Fourier transform (FFT). The FFT requires that the epochs to be analyzed have data points that are a power of 2 (e.g., 128, 256, 512, or 1,048 data points). The FFT produces two spectra, a power spectrum and a phase spectrum. The power spectrum reflects the power in the signal at each frequency from direct current (DC) to the Nyquist frequency, with a spectral value every $1/T$ points, where T is the length of the epoch analyzed. The phase spectrum presents the phase of the waveform at each interval $1/T$. Often, analyses focus only on the power spectrum. The FFT of each epoch produces a power spectrum, and the average of the obtained power values is used in analyses. Further reduction is accomplished by summarizing data within conventionally defined frequency bands.

Time-Frequency Analysis

Frequency analyses based on windows limit the frequency analyses to a single time frame. As such, they do not capture the change in frequencies over time. In contrast, ERP analyses examine changes over time, but collapse across frequency. Time-frequency analyses capture the change in power across time and frequency.

The earliest method used for time-frequency analysis was the short-time Fourier transform (STFT). The STFT breaks up the signal into small windows of time and conducts a Fourier analysis on each window to deconstruct the frequencies which exist in that segment. The resulting output of an STFT provides the power and phase of the signal at each point in time. To apply an STFT, the researchers must determine the length and shape of the window that will be applied. However, this becomes a tradeoff between the resolution of time or frequency. Known as the uncertainty principal, if the length of the window increases in time, then the time resolution decreases but the frequency resolution increases, and vice versa (Cohen, 1995).

Related to the STFT is a wavelet transform. In the wavelet transform, the signals are decomposed into small waves according to a wavelet function, with the Morlet wavelet being one most frequently applied to EEG analysis. The advantage of the wavelet transform is that it takes into account the time-frequency tradeoff that comes with windowing. The reduced interference distributions (RIDs) is another method that applies a kernel function to determine time-frequency resolution. The binomial kernel is the one most commonly applied to EEG signal. RIDs allow high resolution of both time and frequency in the EEG signal, which aids in parsing out EEG components. For more on these analyses, see Aviyente (2022) and Cohen (2014).

Frequency Bands of Interest

Past discussions of EEG/MEG frequency bands have suggested that there are five bands with relationships to psychological and behavioral outcomes. These bands are delta (1–4 Hz), theta (4–8 Hz), alpha (8–13 Hz), beta (13–20 Hz), and gamma (> 20 Hz). Many of the psychological and behavioral correlates of these frequency bands that are mentioned in past reviews were based on visual inspection of the frequency bands and not on mathematical derivations of the frequencies of interest, as is now commonly done with spectral analyses. Recent research with these more precise and accurate methods of measuring EEG/MEG frequencies has questioned some earlier conclusions, although much of the work is relatively recent and as yet has not been incorporated into psychology (Pernet et al., 2020). For example, simulation work suggests that, in order to arrive at a more accurate characterization of the frequency component of the electrophysiological signal, the aperiodic (1/f-like) component should be taken into account in addition to periodic features (Donoghue et al., 2020). Moreover, the extent to which these bands are discrete from each other or differ as a function of scalp region has not been examined in a rigorous statistical fashion. Finally, research has suggested that the frequency bands below 20 Hz are highly and positively correlated (Davidson et al., 1990; Harmon-Jones & Allen, 1998). Consequently, we review research that has focused on alpha power in relation to emotive processing, as it has attracted much attention from psychologists, perhaps in part because it accounts for a large percentage of the adult EEG. For MEG, we review research in the frequency domain in relation to music, speech, and language comprehension (see Dikker et al., 2020, for a review of MEG language research).

Research Examples

Now, we briefly review a few studies that illustrate how these frequency bands have been used in psychological research.

Frontal alpha asymmetry. Several studies have examined differences in left and right frontal cortical activity in relationship to emotional and motivational processes (Coan & Allen, 2004; Harmon-Jones et al., 2010). In this research, alpha power has been used because it appears to be inversely related to cortical activity according to studies using a variety of methods, such as positron emission tomography (PET; Cook et al., 1998) and fMRI (Goldman et al., 2002). Moreover, behavioral tasks that are presumed to activate a particular brain region have been shown to cause alpha power suppression in that region (e.g., Davidson et al., 1990).

Power within the alpha frequency range is obtained using the methods described in the previous section. Alpha power values are often log transformed for all sites to normalize the distributions. Then, in the research that is reviewed in this section, asymmetry indexes (natural log right minus natural log left alpha power) are computed for all homologous sites, such as F3 and F4 or P3 and P4. Because alpha power is inversely related to cortical activity, higher scores on the asymmetry indexes indicate greater relative left-hemispheric activity.

A large portion of the frontal EEG alpha-power asymmetry literature on individual differences has examined relations between personality and resting baseline asymmetry. In these studies, resting asymmetry is utilized as a stable index of an individual's dispositional style across situations. For example, resting EEG asymmetry appears to relate to social behavior. In one study, EEG data recorded from infants at 9 months old were used to predict social wariness at 4 years old (Henderson et al., 2001). Negative emotionality, as reported by the infants' mothers, predicted social wariness in infants who displayed relatively greater right-frontal activity. This relationship was not found in infants who displayed relatively greater left-frontal activity (Henderson et al., 2001). Another study found that socially anxious preschool children exhibited increased right frontal activity compared with their peers (Fox et al., 1995).

The largest body of literature examining relations with resting EEG asymmetry stems from the research on emotion. Greater relative left- and greater relative right-frontal activity have been found to relate to individual differences in dispositional positive and negative affect, respectively (Tomarken et al., 1992). Individuals with stable relative left-frontal activity report greater positive affect to positive films, whereas individuals with stable relative right-frontal activity report greater negative affect to negative films (Wheeler et al., 1993). The positive affect–left versus negative affect–right frontal asymmetry has been referred to as the *affective-valence* hypothesis of frontal asymmetry.

Other research suggested that affective valence does not explain the relation between emotive traits and asymmetric frontal activity and that approach–withdrawal motivational direction may provide a more accurate explanation of this relation (Harmon-Jones, 2003). For example, Harmon-Jones and Allen (1997) compared resting frontal asymmetry to behavioral withdrawal–approach sensitivities, as measured by the Behavioral Inhibition System/Behavioral Activation System (BIS/BAS) scales (Carver & White, 1994). They found that higher left-frontal cortical activity during a resting baseline period related to higher trait-approach motivation scores. Sutton and Davidson (1997) replicated this effect and found that asymmetrical frontal activity was more strongly related to approach–withdrawal motivation than positive and negative affectivity (as measured with the Positive and Negative Affect Schedule; Watson et al., 1988). Other research has extended these findings linking left-frontal asymmetry to BAS to other domains of self-regulation linked to approach motivation, including individual differences in emotional approach coping (Master et al., 2009), promotion focus (Amodio et al., 2004), and egalitarian social motivation (Amodio, 2010).

Additional research examining relations between resting frontal asymmetry and psychopathology has also supported the role of motivational direction. Depression, for example, has been characterized by a general lack of approach motivation and decreased positive affect. Research has shown that higher scores on the Beck Depression Inventory (Beck et al., 1961) relate to greater relative right-frontal cortical activity at resting baseline (Schaffer et al., 1983). Further studies support the relation, showing that depression relates to trait-level, increased right-frontal activity or reduced left-frontal activity (Allen et al., 1993; Henriques & Davidson, 1990, 1991). Other examples come from research on bipolar disorder; increased relative right-frontal activity at resting baseline has been observed in bipolar depression (Allen et al., 1993), whereas increased relative left-frontal activity at resting baseline has been observed in mania (Kano et al., 1992).

The evidence that most strongly challenges the affective-valence hypothesis comes from research on anger. Most studies examining relations between frontal asymmetry and emotion have confounded valence and motivational direction, for example, because most of the negative affects that have been examined are withdrawal-oriented (e.g., fear, disgust). Anger, however, is an approach-oriented negative emotion (Carver & Harmon-Jones, 2009) that appears to relate to relatively greater left-frontal resting cortical activity rather than relatively greater right-frontal cortical activity (Harmon-Jones, 2004). For example, Harmon-Jones and Allen (1998) assessed dispositional anger using the Buss and Perry (1992) Aggression Questionnaire and then measured resting alpha power asymmetries over the whole head. Trait anger correlated positively with left-frontal activity and negatively with right-frontal activity (Harmon-Jones & Allen, 1998). These findings support the *motivational direction* model of frontal asymmetry, which proposes that approach motivation relates to relatively greater left- than right-frontal activity, whereas withdrawal motivation relates to relatively greater right- than left-frontal activity (Harmon-Jones, 2004).

Although resting baseline frontal asymmetries predict certain dispositional styles and psychopathologies, there have been failures to replicate some of the resting baseline asymmetry and affective trait relations (see Coan & Allen, 2004, for a review). This may be because asymmetrical frontal cortical activity is also sensitive to state manipulations (e.g., Hagemann et al., 1998; Reid et al., 1998). In fact, approximately half of the variance in baseline resting measurements is associated with state rather than trait variance (Hagemann et al., 2002). Variance in resting EEG has even been found to be caused by time of day and time of year, such that relative right-frontal activity is greatest during fall mornings (Peterson & Harmon-Jones, 2009). This latter finding fits with other work suggesting that (a) seasonal variations influence mood such that autumn is associated with more depression than other seasons and (b) circadian variations influence the release of the stress hormone, cortisol, such that mornings are associated with greater cortisol. These factors need to be considered in EEG asymmetry research.

Several studies have revealed asymmetric alpha power activations during the experience of emotive states. For instance, newborn infants evidenced greater relative left-hemispheric activation (suppression of alpha power) in response to a sucrose solution placed on the tongue, whereas they evidenced greater relative right-hemispheric activation in response to a water solution, which elicited a disgust facial expression (Fox & Davidson, 1986).

Other experiments have examined the effect of manipulated facial expressions of emotion on asymmetric frontal alpha power. In one experiment, participants made expressions of disgust, fear, anger, joy, and sadness while EEG was recorded. Relatively less left- than right-frontal activity was found during facial expressions of withdrawal-oriented emotions (disgust, fear) compared with approach-oriented emotions (joy, anger; Coan et al., 2001).

Experiments on asymmetric alpha power have also examined more complex emotions such as guilt. Manipulated feelings of guilt, as a result of feedback informing low-prejudice participants that they had responded with racial bias, were found to cause a reduction in relative left-frontal cortical activity, and greater reductions were correlated with greater self-reported guilt but not with other negative emotions (Amodio et al., 2007).

To further compare the affective-valence (positive–negative) model with the motivational direction (approach–withdrawal) model of asymmetric frontal cortical activity, experiments were conducted in which anger was manipulated. For example, Harmon-Jones and Sigelman (2001) manipulated state anger by leading participants to believe that another participant (ostensibly in the next room) had insulted them on the basis of an essay that they wrote on an important social issue. EEG activity recorded immediately following the insult revealed an increase in left-frontal activation compared with individuals in the no-insult condition (Harmon-Jones & Sigelman, 2001). This increase in left-frontal activation related to an increase in self-reported anger and aggressive behavior, which was not the case in the no-insult condition (Harmon-Jones & Sigelman, 2001). Subsequent studies have conceptually replicated these effects demonstrating that increases in state self-reported anger (and jealousy) relate to greater relative left-frontal activation after social rejection (Harmon-Jones et al., 2009; Peterson et al., 2011). Additional research has found that manipulating sympathy before an angering event reduces the left-frontal activation that is caused by anger (Harmon-Jones et al., 2004). Other research has revealed that it is specifically the approach-motivational character of anger that increases relative left-frontal activation (Harmon-Jones et al., 2003, 2006).

Motivation often involves body movements and postures, so it may come as no surprise that body postures antithetical to approach motivation would reduce patterns of neural activity that are associated with approach motivation. When individuals were in a supine body posture and angered, they did not respond with an increase in relative left-frontal cortical activity that is typically observed during anger (Harmon-Jones & Peterson, 2009). These results may have important implications for research using neuroimaging methods that require individuals to be in a supine position during experiments.

In the above studies, anger and approach motivation were manipulated and EEG was assessed. To more firmly establish the causal role of relative left-frontal activity in aggressive motivation, a study was conducted in which asymmetrical frontal cortical activity was manipulated, and the effects of this manipulation on aggression was measured (Peterson et al., 2008). In this experiment, participants made either left-hand or right-hand contractions for four periods of 45 seconds. The contractions caused contralateral activation of the motor cortex and prefrontal cortex (i.e., right-hand contractions caused greater relative left activation and vice versa). Participants were then insulted by another ostensible participant. Following the insult, participants played a reaction-time game against the insulting participant. Participants were told that they would be able to administer a blast of white noise (and could decide the length and intensity of the noise blast) to the other participant if they responded faster to the stimulus than did the other participant. Individuals who made right-hand contractions were significantly more aggressive during the game than individuals who made left-hand contractions, and the degree of relative left-frontal activation correlated with aggression in the right-hand contraction condition (Peterson et al., 2008).

The motivational direction model can also be compared with the affective-valence model by examining positive affects that differ in motivational intensity. Some positive affects are more strongly associated with approach motivation than others. According to the motivational direction model, positive affects that are higher in approach motivational intensity should evoke greater relative left-frontal activation than positive affects that are lower in approach motivational intensity. To test these ideas, participants were asked to recall and write about one of three things: (a) a neutral day; (b) a time when something positive happened to them that they did not cause, such as a surprise gift from a friend; or (c) a goal they were committed to achieving. The second condition was designed to manipulate positive affect that was low in approach motivation. The third condition was designed to manipulate positive affect that was higher in approach motivation. Past research suggested that this third condition increases positive affect (Harmon-Jones & Harmon-Jones, 2002; Taylor & Gollwitzer, 1995). Results from the experiment revealed greater self-reported positive affect in the two positive affect conditions relative to the neutral condition. More important, greater relative left-frontal cortical activity was found in the approach-oriented positive affect condition compared with the neutral condition and the low-approach positive affect condition (Harmon-Jones et al., 2008).

Research has also examined the role of individual differences in responses to state manipulations. For example, the BAS dysregulation theory posits that individuals with bipolar disorder are extremely sensitive to reward and failure cues, so that they show "an excessive increase in BAS activity in response to BAS activation-relevant events (e.g., reward incentives, goal striving) and an excessive decrease in BAS activity in response to BAS deactivation-relevant events (e.g., definite failure)" (Nusslock et al., 2007, p. 105). Given that the left-frontal cortical region is associated with approach motivation, it was predicted and confirmed that individuals with bipolar disorder would show increased left-frontal activation in response to goal-striving (Harmon-Jones et al., 2002).

Another study examined how hypomanic and depressive traits affected frontal asymmetry in response to an anger-inducing event (Harmon-Jones et al., 2002). Research on hypomania has suggested the involvement of increased BAS activity, whereas depression may be associated with decreased BAS activity. In support of these ideas, proneness toward hypomania related to an increase in left-frontal activation and proneness toward depression related to a decrease in left-frontal activation in response to an anger-inducing event (Harmon-Jones et al., 2002).

Research has also been conducted on normal populations. Gable and Harmon-Jones (2008) examined individual differences in response to appetitive stimuli. They found that self-reported time since last eating and reported liking for dessert related to greater relative left-frontal activation during viewing of desirable food pictures (Gable & Harmon-Jones, 2008; see also Harmon-Jones & Gable, 2009).

The research on asymmetrical frontal cortical activity has shed light on a number of questions of interest to psychologists. Indeed, of the EEG frequency research to date within psychology, research on EEG asymmetry is the most prevalent.

Other Analyses of Interest

Other EEG frequency research is of interest to psychologists, and we briefly review some of this exciting work in this section.

Relations among frequency bands. Recent research has suggested that the ratio between resting-state frontal theta and beta activity might shed light on important psychological processes. For example, increased theta–beta ratio has been observed in children with attention-deficit/hyperactivity disorder (Barry et al., 2003). Other research has revealed that increased theta–beta ratios are associated with disadvantageous decision-making strategies on the Iowa gambling task (Schutter & van Honk, 2005). Scientists have suggested that slower-frequency waves such as delta and theta are associated with subcortical brain regions involved in affective processes (Knyazev & Slobodskaya, 2003), whereas faster-frequency waves such as beta are associated with thalamo-cortical- and cortico-cortical-level activations that may be involved in cognitive control processes (Pfurtscheller & Lopes da Silva, 1999).

Event-related desynchronization. Event-related desynchronization (ERD) is a measurement of the time-locked average power associated with the desynchronization of alpha rhythms. It is measured using ERP designs, which are described in Bartholow and Amodio (2009). That is, across multiple experimental events, an average is taken within the same stimulus condition. The time window is usually 1 second in length, and the amount of desynchronization is examined over 100-ms bins within the 1-second window. We have examined alpha ERD in an experiment in which participants viewed photographs of attractive desserts or neutral items. Results indicated that relatively greater left-frontal activity, as measured by ERD, occurred during the first second of viewing of the photograph (Gable & Harmon-Jones, 2008). Moreover, this effect appeared to peak at 400 ms.

Coherence. Coherence and other types of connectivity analyses can be used to evaluate the degree to which signals (within a given frequency) that are measured at two distinct sensor locations are linearly related to one another. High coherence implies that amplitudes at a given frequency are correlated across EEG samples. Moreover, there tends to be a constant phase angle (or time lag) between the two signals. Research has suggested that high EEG coherence occurs between scalp regions that are connected by known white-matter tracts (Thatcher et al., 1986). For instance, during right-hand contractions, individuals with greater trait-approach motivational tendencies show greater EEG alpha power coherence between the left motor cortex and left-frontal region than do individuals with lower trait-approach motivational tendencies (Peterson & Harmon-Jones, 2008). Perhaps the appetitive processes associated with trait approach motivation and activation of the left-frontal cortical region require close connectivity with the motor cortex.

Similarly, phase synchrony in gamma band (30–80 Hz) EEG has been used to investigate various cognitive phenomena such as selective attention and working memory (Fell et al., 2003) and in understanding clinical problems such as schizophrenia (e.g., Lee et al., 2003).

Studies using MEG suggest that a language network comprising inferior frontal and temporal cortex is supported by different patterns of oscillatory activity. For example, Granger causality analysis suggests that alpha activity may support the transfer of information from temporal to frontal regions, whereas beta activity is likely to support frontal to temporal information flow (Schoffelen et al., 2017). Intertrial phase-locking-value analysis comparing neural oscillations to expected versus unexpected sentence-final words further showed synchronized beta and low-gamma oscillations between the two regions (Mamashli et al., 2019), as well as cross-frequency connectivity between gamma power within the left prefrontal region and alpha power within the left temporal region (Wang et al., 2018).

Neuroscientists have also begun to apply coherence and other connectivity metrics to investigate the extent to which neural oscillations become coupled between participants (e.g., Burgess, 2013), both in dyads (Dumas et al., 2010) and groups (Dikker et al., 2017). In this research, such analyses in combination with so-called "hyperscanning" setups (simultaneously recording from multiple EEG or MEG devices), have allowed researchers to ask how interbrain coupling might relate to socially relevant factors such as affect, social closeness, joint attention, joint action, and linguistic communication (Czeszumski et al., 2020).

Due to the relatively young nature of the field of hyperscanning, much remains to be explored about the role of interbrain coupling in social communication. In contrast, there is a much richer literature, especially in MEG, using intrabrain coupling and stimulus-brain coupling to investigate the role of oscillations in how the human brain analyzes social stimuli with a temporal structure, in particular music and speech. Specifically, neural oscillations synchronize to the temporal regularities of music (Doelling & Poeppel, 2015) and speech (Luo & Poeppel, 2007). In speech, low-frequency neural oscillations in the theta and delta range synchronize to the speech envelope (linked to syllables and phrases), and gamma oscillations track the fine-grained temporal dynamics associated with phonetic features. This particular set of findings has led to the hypothesis that neural oscillations help define the temporal boundaries between linguistic items within the continuous acoustic signal (Giraud & Poeppel, 2012), as such supporting speech parsing and, consequently, language comprehension. This model is corroborated by findings showing an increase in brain-to-speech coupling for intelligible speech (e.g., Peelle et al., 2013). Delta and gamma oscillations further synchronize to more "abstract" language features, such as lexical and grammatical properties (Kösem et al., 2016; L. Meyer, Henry, et al., 2017). Importantly, the strength and precision of the synchronization is linked to language comprehension (Kösem et al., 2018), for example, in multitalker settings, where neural oscillations are found to synchronize to the dynamics of the attended speaker (the so-called "cocktail party effect"; Rimmele et al., 2015).

ADVANTAGES AND DISADVANTAGES OF EEG/MEG METHODS

We hope that we have conveyed some advantages of using EEG methods in our brief review. In addition to these advantages, EEG methods are relatively inexpensive compared with other neuroimaging methods. For instance, time on an fMRI scanner averages approximately $500 per hour (as of April 2021), and the scanner typically costs around $5 million to set up. The hourly rate that is charged to researchers assists in covering the maintenance contracts and salaries of the support personnel. In contrast, most EEG researchers have their own equipment, which costs less than $100,000. In this situation, no hourly fees are charged, and maintenance contracts rarely exceed $3,000 per year. EEG caps need to be replaced approximately once per year (depending on use), and they cost between $300 and $2,000, depending on the number and type of electrodes. There are also other regular expenses for conducting gel, adhesive collars, and sterilizing solution, but these costs are relatively minimal.

In relation to PET and fMRI, MEG/EEG provides better temporal resolution but poorer spatial resolution. EEG measures electrical activations instantaneously, at sub-millisecond resolution. However, EEG is less capable of giving precise information regarding the anatomical origin of the electrical signals. In contrast, PET and fMRI have better spatial resolution but poorer temporal resolution. Ultimately, both PET and fMRI rely on metabolism and blood flow to brain areas that have been recently involved in neuronal activity, although other changes affect fMRI such as oxygen consumption and blood volume changes. Because both PET and fMRI measure blood flow rather than neuronal activity, the activations are not in real time with neuronal activations but rather are blood responses to neuronal responses. Thus, there is a biological limit on the time resolution of the response, such that even in the best measurement systems, the peak blood flow response occurs 6 to 9 seconds after stimulus onset (Reiman et al., 2000). However, there are suggestions that experimental methods can be designed to detect stimulus condition differences as early as 2 seconds (Bell-Gowan et al., 2003). Finally, PET and EEG permit measurement of tonic (e.g., resting, baseline) activity as well as phasic (e.g., in response to a state manipulation) activity, whereas fMRI permits measurement of phasic but not tonic activity.

Spatial and temporal resolution comparisons are often made between EEG, MEG, fMRI, and PET, but rarely do researchers consider that these methods may provide different information about neural activity. For instance, correlations between EEG alpha power and fMRI or PET measures are only of moderate magnitude, suggesting that the two measures are not assessing exactly the same signals or activations. Moreover, EEG measures are selective measures of current source activity, often corresponding to small subsets of total synaptic action in tissue volumes and largely independent of action potentials, as discussed. By contrast, hemodynamic and metabolic measures are believed to increase with action potential firing rates (Nunez & Silberstein, 2000). Consider, for example, cortical stellate cells. They occupy roughly spherical volumes and, as such, their associated synaptic sources provide a closed field structure. Thus, these stellate cells are electrically invisible to EEG sensors. Although stellate cells constitute only about 15% of the neural population of neocortex (Braitenberg & Schuz, 1991; Wilson et al., 1994), they contribute disproportionately to cortical metabolic activity because of their higher firing frequencies of action potentials (Connors & Gutnick, 1990). Thus, they appear as large signals in fMRI and PET. On the other hand, strong EEG signals can appear while weak metabolic activity occurs. EEG can be large if only a few percent of neurons in each cortical column are synchronously active, provided a large-scale synchrony among different columns produces a large dipole in which individual columns tend to be phase locked in particular frequencies. Because, in this scenario, the majority of neurons in each intracolumn population are relatively inactive, minimal metabolic activity is produced. Consequential dissociations between electrical and metabolic measures have been found in studies of epilepsy (e.g., Olson et al., 1990). For example, in one study of children with lateralized epileptic spikes (measured with EEG), regional glucose metabolism that was measured with PET was not lateralized, suggesting that "metabolic changes associated with interictal spiking cannot be demonstrated with PET with 18F-fluorodeoxyglucose" (Van Bogaert et al., 1998, p. 123).

Methodologically, fMRI and EEG differ in an important way, particularly for research on motivational processes. Typically, fMRI studies require participants to lie flat on their backs while brain images are collected. In contrast, EEG studies often have participants in upright, sitting positions. Given the connection between body posture and motivation (Riskind & Gotay, 1982), we should expect that lying in a supine position may decrease approach motivation, as this position is often antithetical to approaching goals. In line with these ideas, EEG research has suggested that these body postures influence regional brain activity, with a supine posture leading to relatively less left-frontal cortical activation in response to approach motivation manipulations (Harmon-Jones & Peterson, 2009). Moreover, simply leaning forward causes greater relative left-frontal activity (as measured by EEG) than lying in a supine position (Price & Harmon-Jones, 2011).

CONCLUSION

As we have described in this chapter, EEG and MEG measures of neural activity provide an important method for testing psychological theories and hypotheses. Among the most exciting new developments in EEG/MEG that are awaiting applications in psychological studies is the examination of distributed patterns of activation. Many psychological processes likely involve widely distributed networks of brain dynamics and most past work in EEG, MEG, fMRI, and PET has failed to examine the dynamics of brain activations as they unfold on the order of milliseconds. Given the exquisite temporal resolution of EEG and MEG, it will be the method of choice in addressing these questions. When brain operations are viewed as a "combination of quasi-local processes allowed by functional segregation and global processes facilitated by functional integration" (Nunez & Silberstein, 2000, p. 93), the importance of EEG and MEG methods, in conjunction with other neurobiological methods, in addressing important psychological questions will be obvious.

References

Allen, J. J., Iacono, W. G., Depue, R. A., & Arbisi, P. (1993). Regional electroencephalographic asymmetries in bipolar seasonal affective disorder before and after exposure to bright light. *Biological*

Psychiatry, 33(8-9), 642–646. https://doi.org/10.1016/0006-3223(93)90104-L

Allen, J. J. B., Coan, J. A., & Nazarian, M. (2004). Issues and assumptions on the road from raw signals to metrics of frontal EEG asymmetry in emotion. *Biological Psychology, 67,* 183–218. https://doi.org/10.1016/j.biopsycho.2004.03.007

Amodio, D. M. (2010). Coordinated roles of motivation and perception in the regulation of intergroup responses: Frontal cortical asymmetry effects on the P2 event-related potential and behavior. *Journal of Cognitive Neuroscience, 22*(11), 2609–2617. https://doi.org/10.1162/jocn.2009.21395

Amodio, D. M., Devine, P. G., & Harmon-Jones, E. (2007). A dynamic model of guilt: Implications for motivation and self-regulation in the context of prejudice. *Psychological Science, 18*(6), 524–530. https://doi.org/10.1111/j.1467-9280.2007.01933.x

Amodio, D. M., Shah, J. Y., Sigelman, J., Brazy, P. C., & Harmon-Jones, E. (2004). Implicit regulatory focus associated with resting frontal cortical asymmetry. *Journal of Experimental Social Psychology, 40*(2), 225–232. https://doi.org/10.1016/S0022-1031(03)00100-8

Aviyente, S. (2022). Time-frequency decomposition methods for event-related potential analysis. In P. Gable, M. Miller, & E. Bernat (Eds.), *The Oxford handbook of EEG frequency* (pp. 65–87). Oxford University Press.

Barry, R. J., Clarke, A. R., & Johnstone, S. J. (2003). A review of electrophysiology in attention-deficit/hyperactivity disorder: I. Qualitative and quantitative electroencephalography. *Clinical Neurophysiology, 114*(2), 171–183. https://doi.org/10.1016/S1388-2457(02)00362-0

Bartholow, B. D., & Amodio, D. M. (2009). Using event-related brain potentials in social psychological research: A brief review and tutorial. In E. Harmon-Jones & J. Beer (Eds.), *Methods in social neuroscience* (pp. 198–232). Guilford Press.

Beck, A. T., Ward, C. H., Mendelson, M., Mock, J., & Erbaugh, J. (1961). An inventory for measuring depression. *Archives of General Psychiatry, 4*(6), 561–571. https://doi.org/10.1001/archpsyc.1961.01710120031004

Bellgowan, P. S., Saad, Z. S., & Bandettini, P. A. (2003). Understanding neural system dynamics through task modulation and measurement of functional MRI amplitude, latency, and width. *Proceedings of the National Academy of Sciences of the United States of America, 100*(3), 1415–1419. https://doi.org/10.1073/pnas.0337747100

Berger, H. (1929). Electroencephalogram in humans. *Archiv für Psychiatrie und Nervenkrankheiten, 87*(1), 527–570. https://doi.org/10.1007/BF01797193

Braitenberg, V., & Schuz, A. (1991). *Anatomy of the cortex. Statistics and geometry.* Springer-Verlag. https://doi.org/10.1007/978-3-662-02728-8

Brodal, P. (1992). *The central nervous system.* Oxford University Press.

Burgess, A. P. (2013). On the interpretation of synchronization in EEG hyperscanning studies: A cautionary note. *Frontiers in Human Neuroscience, 7,* 881. https://doi.org/10.3389/fnhum.2013.00881

Buss, A. H., & Perry, M. (1992). The aggression questionnaire. *Journal of Personality and Social Psychology, 63*(3), 452–459. https://doi.org/10.1037/0022-3514.63.3.452

Carver, C. S., & Harmon-Jones, E. (2009). Anger is an approach-related affect: Evidence and implications. *Psychological Bulletin, 135*(2), 183–204. https://doi.org/10.1037/a0013965

Carver, C. S., & White, T. L. (1994). Behavioral inhibition, behavioral activation, and affective responses to impending reward and punishment: The BIS/BAS scales. *Journal of Personality and Social Psychology, 67*(2), 319–333. https://doi.org/10.1037/0022-3514.67.2.319

Chatrian, G. E., Lettich, E., & Nelson, P. L. (1988). Modified nomenclature for the "10%" electrode system. *Journal of Clinical Neurophysiology, 5*(2), 183–186. https://doi.org/10.1097/00004691-198804000-00005

Coan, J. A., & Allen, J. J. B. (2003). Frontal EEG asymmetry and the behavioral activation and inhibition systems. *Psychophysiology, 40*(1), 106–114. https://doi.org/10.1111/1469-8986.00011

Coan, J. A., & Allen, J. J. B. (2004). Frontal EEG asymmetry as a moderator and mediator of emotion. *Biological Psychology, 67,* 7–50. https://doi.org/10.1016/j.biopsycho.2004.03.002

Coan, J. A., Allen, J. J. B., & Harmon-Jones, E. (2001). Voluntary facial expression and hemispheric asymmetry over the frontal cortex. *Psychophysiology, 38*(6), 912–925. https://doi.org/10.1111/1469-8986.3860912

Cohen, D. (1968). Magnetoencephalography: Evidence of magnetic fields produced by alpha-rhythm currents. *Science, 161*(3843), 784–786. https://doi.org/10.1126/science.161.3843.784

Cohen, L. (1995). *Time-frequency analysis* (Vol. 778). Prentice Hall.

Cohen, X. M. (2014). *Analyzing neural time series data.* MIT Press. https://doi.org/10.7551/mitpress/9609.001.0001

Connors, B. W., & Gutnick, M. J. (1990). Intrinsic firing patterns of diverse neocortical neurons. *Trends in Neurosciences, 13*(3), 99–104. https://doi.org/10.1016/0166-2236(90)90185-D

Cook, I. A., O'Hara, R., Uijtdehaage, S. H. J., Mandelkern, M., & Leuchter, A. F. (1998). Assessing the accuracy of topographic EEG mapping for determining local brain function. *Electroencephalography and Clinical Neurophysiology*, *107*(6), 408–414. https://doi.org/10.1016/S0013-4694(98)00092-3

Curham, K. J., & Allen, J. J. B. (2021). Logic behind EEG frequency analysis: Basic electricity and assumptions. In P. Gable, M. Miller, & E. Bernat (Eds.), *The Oxford handbook of EEG frequency*. Oxford University Press.

Czeszumski, A., Eustergerling, S., Lang, A., Menrath, D., Gerstenberger, M., Schuberth, S., Schreiber, F., Rendon, Z. Z., & König, P. (2020). Hyperscanning: A valid method to study neural inter-brain underpinnings of social interaction. *Frontiers in Human Neuroscience*, *14*, 39. https://doi.org/10.3389/fnhum.2020.00039

Davidson, R. J., Chapman, J. P., Chapman, L. J., & Henriques, J. B. (1990). Asymmetrical brain electrical activity discriminates between psychometrically-matched verbal and spatial cognitive tasks. *Psychophysiology*, *27*(5), 528–543. https://doi.org/10.1111/j.1469-8986.1990.tb01970.x

Davidson, R. J., Jackson, D. C., & Larson, C. L. (2000). Human electroencephalography. In J. T. Cacioppo, L. G. Tassinary, & G. G. Berntson (Eds.), *Handbook of psychophysiology* (2nd ed., pp. 27–52). Cambridge University Press.

Delorme, A., & Makeig, S. (2004). EEGLAB: An open source toolbox for analysis of single-trial EEG dynamics including independent component analysis. *Journal of Neuroscience Methods*, *134*(1), 9–21. https://doi.org/10.1016/j.jneumeth.2003.10.009

Delorme, A., Sejnowski, T., & Makeig, S. (2007). Enhanced detection of artifacts in EEG data using higher-order statistics and independent component analysis. *NeuroImage*, *34*(4), 1443–1449. https://doi.org/10.1016/j.neuroimage.2006.11.004

Dikker, S., Assaneo, M. F., Gwilliams, L., Wang, L., & Kösem, A. (2020). Magnetoencephalography and Language. *Neuroimaging Clinics*, *30*(2), 229–238. https://doi.org/10.1016/j.nic.2020.01.004

Dikker, S., Wan, L., Davidesco, I., Kaggen, L., Oostrik, M., McClintock, J., Rowland, J., Michalareas, G., Van Bavel, J. J., Ding, M., & Poeppel, D. (2017). Brain-to-brain synchrony tracks real-world dynamic group interactions in the classroom. *Current Biology*, *27*(9), 1375–1380. https://doi.org/10.1016/j.cub.2017.04.002

Doelling, K. B., & Poeppel, D. (2015). Cortical entrainment to music and its modulation by expertise. *Proceedings of the National Academy of Sciences of the United States of America*, *112*(45), E6233–E6242. https://doi.org/10.1073/pnas.1508431112

Donoghue, T., Haller, M., Peterson, E. J., Varma, P., Sebastian, P., Gao, R., Noto, T., Lara, A. H., Wallis, J. D., Knight, R. T., Shestyuk, A., & Voytek, B. (2020). Parameterizing neural power spectra into periodic and aperiodic components. *Nature Neuroscience*, *23*(12), 1655–1665. https://doi.org/10.1038/s41593-020-00744-x

Dumas, G., Nadel, J., Soussignan, R., Martinerie, J., & Garnero, L. (2010). Inter-brain synchronization during social interaction. *PLOS ONE*, *5*(8), e12166. https://doi.org/10.1371/journal.pone.0012166

Fell, J., Fernández, G., Klaver, P., Elger, C. E., & Fries, P. (2003). Is synchronized neuronal gamma activity relevant for selective attention? *Brain Research Reviews*, *42*(3), 265–272. https://doi.org/10.1016/S0165-0173(03)00178-4

Fox, N. A., & Davidson, R. J. (1986). Taste-elicited changes in facial signs of emotion and the asymmetry of brain electrical activity in human newborns. *Neuropsychologia*, *24*(3), 417–422. https://doi.org/10.1016/0028-3932(86)90028-X

Fox, N. A., Rubin, K. H., Calkins, S. D., Marshall, T. R., Coplan, R. J., Porges, S. W., Long, J. M., & Stewart, S. (1995). Frontal activation asymmetry and social competence at four years of age. *Child Development*, *66*(6), 1770–1784. https://doi.org/10.2307/1131909

Gable, P., & Harmon-Jones, E. (2008). Relative left frontal activation to appetitive stimuli: Considering the role of individual differences. *Psychophysiology*, *45*(2), 275–278. https://doi.org/10.1111/j.1469-8986.2007.00627.x

Giraud, A. L., & Poeppel, D. (2012). Cortical oscillations and speech processing: Emerging computational principles and operations. *Nature Neuroscience*, *15*(4), 511–517. https://doi.org/10.1038/nn.3063

Goldman, R. I., Stern, J. M., Engel, J., Jr., & Cohen, M. S. (2002). Simultaneous EEG and fMRI of the alpha rhythm. *Neuroreport*, *13*(18), 2487–2492. https://doi.org/10.1097/00001756-200212200-00022

Gonzalez Andino, S. L., Pascual Marqui, R. D., Valdes Sosa, P. A., Biscay Lirio, R., Machado, C., Diaz, G., Figueredo Rodriguez, P., & Castro Torrez, C. (1990). Brain electrical field measurements unaffected by linked earlobes reference. *Electroencephalography and Clinical Neurophysiology*, *75*(3), 155–160. https://doi.org/10.1016/0013-4694(90)90169-K

Gratton, G., Coles, M. G. H., & Donchin, E. (1983). A new method for off-line removal of ocular artifact. *Electroencephalography and Clinical Neurophysiology*, *55*(4), 468–484. https://doi.org/10.1016/0013-4694(83)90135-9

Gross, J. (2019). Magnetoencephalography in cognitive neuroscience: A primer. *Neuron*, *104*(2), 189–204. https://doi.org/10.1016/j.neuron.2019.07.001

Hagemann, D. (2004). Individual differences in anterior EEG asymmetry: Methodological problems and solutions. *Biological Psychology*, *67*(1-2), 157–182. https://doi.org/10.1016/j.biopsycho.2004.03.006

Hagemann, D., & Naumann, E. (2001). The effects of ocular artifacts on (lateralized) broadband power in the EEG. *Clinical Neurophysiology*, *112*(2), 215–231. https://doi.org/10.1016/S1388-2457(00)00541-1

Hagemann, D., Naumann, E., Becker, G., Maier, S., & Bartussek, D. (1998). Frontal brain asymmetry and affective style: A conceptual replication. *Psychophysiology*, *35*(4), 372–388. https://doi.org/10.1111/1469-8986.3540372

Hagemann, D., Naumann, E., Thayer, J. F., & Bartussek, D. (2002). Does resting electroencephalograph asymmetry reflect a trait? An application of latent state–trait theory. *Journal of Personality and Social Psychology*, *82*, 619–641. https://doi.org/10.1037/0022-3514.82.4.619

Hari, R., & Puce, A. (2017). *MEG-EEG primer*. Oxford University Press. https://doi.org/10.1093/med/9780190497774.001.0001

Harmon-Jones, E. (2003). Clarifying the emotive functions of asymmetrical frontal cortical activity. *Psychophysiology*, *40*(6), 838–848. https://doi.org/10.1111/1469-8986.00121

Harmon-Jones, E. (2004). Contributions from research on anger and cognitive dissonance to understanding the motivational functions of asymmetrical frontal brain activity. *Biological Psychology*, *67*(1-2), 51–76. https://doi.org/10.1016/j.biopsycho.2004.03.003

Harmon-Jones, E., Abramson, L. Y., Sigelman, J., Bohlig, A., Hogan, M. E., & Harmon-Jones, C. (2002). Proneness to hypomania/mania symptoms or depression symptoms and asymmetrical frontal cortical responses to an anger-evoking event. *Journal of Personality and Social Psychology*, *82*(4), 610–618. https://doi.org/10.1037/0022-3514.82.4.610

Harmon-Jones, E., & Allen, J. J. B. (1997). Behavioral activation sensitivity and resting frontal EEG asymmetry: Covariation of putative indicators related to risk for mood disorders. *Journal of Abnormal Psychology*, *106*(1), 159–163. https://doi.org/10.1037/0021-843X.106.1.159

Harmon-Jones, E., & Allen, J. J. B. (1998). Anger and frontal brain activity: EEG asymmetry consistent with approach motivation despite negative affective valence. *Journal of Personality and Social Psychology*, *74*(5), 1310–1316. https://doi.org/10.1037/0022-3514.74.5.1310

Harmon-Jones, E., & Gable, P. A. (2009). Neural activity underlying the effect of approach-motivated positive affect on narrowed attention. *Psychological Science*, *20*(4), 406–409. https://doi.org/10.1111/j.1467-9280.2009.02302.x

Harmon-Jones, E., Gable, P. A., & Peterson, C. K. (2010). The role of asymmetric frontal cortical activity in emotion-related phenomena: A review and update. *Biological Psychology*, *84*, 451–462. https://doi.org/10.1016/j.biopsycho.2009.08.010

Harmon-Jones, E., & Harmon-Jones, C. (2002). Testing the action-based model of cognitive dissonance: The effect of action-orientation on post-decisional attitudes. *Personality and Social Psychology Bulletin*, *28*(6), 711–723. https://doi.org/10.1177/0146167202289001

Harmon-Jones, E., Harmon-Jones, C., Fearn, M., Sigelman, J. D., & Johnson, P. (2008). Left frontal cortical activation and spreading of alternatives: Tests of the action-based model of dissonance. *Journal of Personality and Social Psychology*, *94*, 1–15. https://doi.org/10.1037/0022-3514.94.1.1

Harmon-Jones, E., Lueck, L., Fearn, M., & Harmon-Jones, C. (2006). The effect of personal relevance and approach-related action expectation on relative left frontal cortical activity. *Psychological Science*, *17*(5), 434–440. https://doi.org/10.1111/j.1467-9280.2006.01724.x

Harmon-Jones, E., & Peterson, C. K. (2009). Supine body position reduces neural response to anger evocation. *Psychological Science*, *20*(10), 1209–1210. https://doi.org/10.1111/j.1467-9280.2009.02416.x

Harmon-Jones, E., Peterson, C. K., & Harris, C. R. (2009). Jealousy: Novel methods and neural correlates. *Emotion*, *9*(1), 113–117. https://doi.org/10.1037/a0014117

Harmon-Jones, E., & Sigelman, J. (2001). State anger and prefrontal brain activity: Evidence that insult-related relative left-prefrontal activation is associated with experienced anger and aggression. *Journal of Personality and Social Psychology*, *80*(5), 797–803. https://doi.org/10.1037/0022-3514.80.5.797

Harmon-Jones, E., Sigelman, J., Bohlig, A., & Harmon-Jones, C. (2003). Anger, coping, and frontal cortical activity: The effect of coping potential on anger-induced left frontal activity. *Cognition and Emotion*, *17*(1), 1–24. https://doi.org/10.1080/02699930302278

Harmon-Jones, E., Vaughn-Scott, K., Mohr, S., Sigelman, J., & Harmon-Jones, C. (2004). The effect of manipulated sympathy and anger on left and right frontal cortical activity. *Emotion*, *4*(1), 95–101. https://doi.org/10.1037/1528-3542.4.1.95

Henderson, H. A., Fox, N. A., & Rubin, K. H. (2001). Temperamental contributions to social behavior: The moderating roles of frontal EEG asymmetry and gender. *Journal of the American Academy of Child & Adolescent Psychiatry, 40*(1), 68–74. https://doi.org/10.1097/00004583-200101000-00018

Henriques, J. B., & Davidson, R. J. (1990). Regional brain electrical asymmetries discriminate between previously depressed and healthy control subjects. *Journal of Abnormal Psychology, 99*(1), 22–31. https://doi.org/10.1037/0021-843X.99.1.22

Henriques, J. B., & Davidson, R. J. (1991). Left frontal hypoactivation in depression. *Journal of Abnormal Psychology, 100*(4), 535–545. https://doi.org/10.1037/0021-843X.100.4.535

Hinrichs, H., Scholz, M., Baum, A. K., Kam, J. W. Y., Knight, R. T., & Heinze, H. J. (2020). Comparison between a wireless dry electrode EEG system with a conventional wired wet electrode EEG system for clinical applications. *Scientific Reports, 10*(1), 5218. https://doi.org/10.1038/s41598-020-62154-0

Jasper, H. H. (1958). The ten-twenty electrode system of the International Federation. *Electroencephalography and Clinical Neurophysiology, 10*, 371–375.

Joyce, C. A., Gorodnitsky, I. F., & Kutas, M. (2004). Automatic removal of eye movement and blink artifacts from EEG data using blind component separation. *Psychophysiology, 41*(2), 313–325. https://doi.org/10.1111/j.1469-8986.2003.00141.x

Kano, K., Nakamura, M., Matsuoka, T., Iida, H., & Nakajima, T. (1992). The topographical features of EEGs in patients with affective disorders. *Electroencephalography and Clinical Neurophysiology, 83*(2), 124–129. https://doi.org/10.1016/0013-4694(92)90025-D

Kappenman, E. S., & Luck, S. J. (2010). The effects of electrode impedance on data quality and statistical significance in ERP recordings. *Psychophysiology, 47*(5), 888–904. https://doi.org/10.1111/j.1469-8986.2010.01009.x

Katznelson, R. D. (1981). Increased accuracy of EEG scalp localization by measurement of current source density using a Laplacian derivation. *Electroencephalography and Clinical Neurophysiology, 51*, 45.

Knyazev, G. G., & Slobodskaya, H. R. (2003). Personality trait of behavioral inhibition is associated with oscillatory systems reciprocal relationships. *International Journal of Psychophysiology, 48*(3), 247–261. https://doi.org/10.1016/S0167-8760(03)00072-2

Kösem, A., Basirat, A., Azizi, L., & van Wassenhove, V. (2016). High-frequency neural activity predicts word parsing in ambiguous speech streams. *Journal of Neurophysiology, 116*(6), 2497–2512. https://doi.org/10.1152/jn.00074.2016

Kösem, A., Bosker, H. R., Takashima, A., Meyer, A., Jensen, O., & Hagoort, P. (2018). Neural entrainment determines the words we hear. *Current Biology, 28*(18), 2867–2875. https://doi.org/10.1016/j.cub.2018.07.023

Laszlo, S., Ruiz-Blondet, M., Khalifian, N., Chu, F., & Jin, Z. (2014). A direct comparison of active and passive amplification electrodes in the same amplifier system. *Journal of Neuroscience Methods, 235*, 298–307. https://doi.org/10.1016/j.jneumeth.2014.05.012

Lee, K. H., Williams, L. M., Breakspear, M., & Gordon, E. (2003). Synchronous gamma activity: A review and contribution to an integrative neuroscience model of schizophrenia. *Brain Research. Brain Research Reviews, 41*(1), 57–78. https://doi.org/10.1016/S0165-0173(02)00220-5

Luo, H., & Poeppel, D. (2007). Phase patterns of neuronal responses reliably discriminate speech in human auditory cortex. *Neuron, 54*(6), 1001–1010. https://doi.org/10.1016/j.neuron.2007.06.004

Mamashli, F., Khan, S., Obleser, J., Friederici, A. D., & Maess, B. (2019). Oscillatory dynamics of cortical functional connections in semantic prediction. *Human Brain Mapping, 40*(6), 1856–1866. https://doi.org/10.1002/hbm.24495

Master, S. L., Amodio, D. M., Stanton, A. L., Yee, C. M., Hilmert, C. J., & Taylor, S. E. (2009). Neurobiological correlates of coping through emotional approach. *Brain, Behavior, and Immunity, 23*(1), 27–35. https://doi.org/10.1016/j.bbi.2008.04.007

Mathewson, K. E., Harrison, T. J. L., & Kizuk, S. A. D. (2017). High and dry? Comparing active dry EEG electrodes to active and passive wet electrodes. *Psychophysiology, 54*(1), 74–82. https://doi.org/10.1111/psyp.12536

McMenamin, B. W., Shackman, A. J., Maxwell, J. S., Greischar, L. L., & Davidson, R. J. (2009). Validation of regression-based myogenic correction techniques for scalp and source-localized EEG. *Psychophysiology, 46*(3), 578–592. https://doi.org/10.1111/j.1469-8986.2009.00787.x

Meyer, L., Henry, M. J., Gaston, P., Schmuck, N., & Friederici, A. D. (2017). Linguistic bias modulates interpretation of speech via neural delta-band oscillations. *Cerebral Cortex (New York, N.Y.), 27*(9), 4293–4302. https://doi.org/10.1093/cercor/bhw228

Meyer, S. S., Bonaiuto, J., Lim, M., Rossiter, H., Waters, S., Bradbury, D., Bestmann, S., Brookes, M., Callaghan, M. F., Weiskopf, N., & Barnes, G. R. (2017). Flexible head-casts for high spatial precision MEG. *Journal of Neuroscience Methods, 276*, 38–45. https://doi.org/10.1016/j.jneumeth.2016.11.009

Murakami, S., & Okada, Y. (2006). Contributions of principal neocortical neurons to magnetoencephalography and electroencephalography signals. *The Journal of Physiology, 575*(3), 925–936. https://doi.org/10.1113/jphysiol.2006.105379

Nunez, P. L., & Silberstein, R. B. (2000). On the relationship of synaptic activity to macroscopic measurements: Does co-registration of EEG with fMRI make sense? *Brain Topography, 13*(2), 79–96. https://doi.org/10.1023/A:1026683200895

Nunez, P. L., & Srinivasan, R. (2006). *Electric fields of the brain: The neurophysics of EEG* (2nd ed.). Oxford University Press. https://doi.org/10.1093/acprof:oso/9780195050387.001.0001

Nusslock, R., Abramson, L. Y., Harmon-Jones, E., Alloy, L. B., & Hogan, M. E. (2007). A goal-striving life event and the onset of hypomanic and depressive episodes and symptoms: Perspective from the behavioral approach system (BAS) dysregulation theory. *Journal of Abnormal Psychology, 116*(1), 105–115. https://doi.org/10.1037/0021-843X.116.1.105

Olson, D. M., Chugani, H. T., Shewmon, D. A., Phelps, M. E., & Peacock, W. J. (1990). Electrocorticographic confirmation of focal positron emission tomographic abnormalities in children with intractable epilepsy. *Epilepsia, 31*(6), 731–739. https://doi.org/10.1111/j.1528-1157.1990.tb05514.x

Peelle, J. E., Gross, J., & Davis, M. H. (2013). Phase-locked responses to speech in human auditory cortex are enhanced during comprehension. *Cerebral Cortex, 23*(6), 1378–1387. https://doi.org/10.1093/cercor/bhs118

Pernet, C., Garrido, M. I., Gramfort, A., Maurits, N., Michel, C. M., Pang, E., Salmelin, R., Schoffelen, J. M., Valdes-Sosa, P. A., & Puce, A. (2020). Issues and recommendations from the OHBM COBIDAS MEEG committee for reproducible EEG and MEG research. *Nature Neuroscience, 23*(12), 1473–1483. https://doi.org/10.1038/s41593-020-00709-0

Peterson, C. K., Gravens, L. C., & Harmon-Jones, E. (2011). Asymmetric frontal cortical activity and negative affective responses to ostracism. *Social Cognitive and Affective Neuroscience, 6*(3), 277–285. https://doi.org/10.1093/scan/nsq027

Peterson, C. K., & Harmon-Jones, E. (2008). Proneness to hypomania predicts EEG coherence between left motor cortex and left prefrontal cortex. *Biological Psychology, 78*, 216–219. https://doi.org/10.1016/j.biopsycho.2008.01.011

Peterson, C. K., & Harmon-Jones, E. (2009). Circadian and seasonal variability of resting frontal EEG asymmetry. *Biological Psychology, 80*(3), 315–320. https://doi.org/10.1016/j.biopsycho.2008.11.002

Peterson, C. K., Shackman, A. J., & Harmon-Jones, E. (2008). The role of asymmetrical frontal cortical activity in aggression. *Psychophysiology, 45*(1), 86–92. 10.1111/j.1469-8986.2007.00597.x

Pfurtscheller, G., & Lopes da Silva, F. H. (1999). Event-related EEG/MEG synchronization and desynchronization: Basic principles. *Clinical Neurophysiology, 110*(11), 1842–1857. https://doi.org/10.1016/S1388-2457(99)00141-8

Polich, J., & Lawson, D. (1985). Event-related potential paradigms using tin electrodes. *The American Journal of EEG Technology, 25*(3), 187–192. https://doi.org/10.1080/00029238.1985.11080171

Price, T. F., & Harmon-Jones, E. (2011). Approach motivational body postures lean toward left frontal brain activity. *Psychophysiology, 48*(5), 718–722. https://doi.org/10.1111/j.1469-8986.2010.01127.x

Puce, A., & Hämäläinen, M. S. (2017). A review of issues related to data acquisition and analysis in EEG/MEG studies. *Brain Sciences, 7*(6), 58. https://doi.org/10.3390/brainsci7060058

Pylkkänen, L., & Marantz, A. (2003). Tracking the time course of word recognition with MEG. *Trends in Cognitive Sciences, 7*(5), 187–189. https://doi.org/10.1016/S1364-6613(03)00092-5

Reid, S. A., Duke, L. M., & Allen, J. J. B. (1998). Resting frontal electroencephalographic asymmetry in depression: Inconsistencies suggest the need to identify mediating factors. *Psychophysiology, 35*(4), 389–404. https://doi.org/10.1111/1469-8986.3540389

Reiman, E. M., Lane, R. D., Van Petten, C., & Bandettini, P. A. (2000). Positron emission tomography and functional magnetic resonance imaging. In J. T. Cacioppo, L. G. Tassinary, & G. G. Berntson (Eds.), *Handbook of psychophysiology* (2nd ed., pp. 85–118). Cambridge University Press.

Rimmele, J. M., Zion Golumbic, E., Schröger, E., & Poeppel, D. (2015). The effects of selective attention and speech acoustics on neural speech-tracking in a multi-talker scene. *Cortex, 68*, 144–154. https://doi.org/10.1016/j.cortex.2014.12.014

Riskind, J. H., & Gotay, C. C. (1982). Physical posture: Could it have regulatory or feedback effects on motivation and emotion? *Motivation and Emotion, 6*(3), 273–298. https://doi.org/10.1007/BF00992249

Schaffer, C. E., Davidson, R. J., & Saron, C. (1983). Frontal and parietal electroencephalogram asymmetry in depressed and nondepressed subjects. *Biological Psychiatry, 18*(7), 753–762.

Schoffelen, J. M., Hultén, A., Lam, N., Marquand, A. F., Uddén, J., & Hagoort, P. (2017). Frequency-specific directed interactions in the human brain network for language. *Proceedings of the National Academy of Sciences of the United States of America, 114*(30), 8083–8088. https://doi.org/10.1073/pnas.1703155114

Schutter, D. J. L. G., & van Honk, J. (2005). Electrophysiological ratio markers for the balance between reward and punishment. *Cognitive Brain Research*, 24, 685–690. https://doi.org/10.1016/j.cogbrainres.2005.04.002

Semlitsch, H. V., Anderer, P., Schuster, P., & Presslich, O. (1986). A solution for reliable and valid reduction of ocular artifacts, applied to the P300 ERP. *Psychophysiology*, 23(6), 695–703. https://doi.org/10.1111/j.1469-8986.1986.tb00696.x

Smith, E. E., Reznik, S. J., Stewart, J. L., & Allen, J. J. (2017). Assessing and conceptualizing frontal EEG asymmetry: An updated primer on recording, processing, analyzing, and interpreting frontal alpha asymmetry. *International Journal of Psychophysiology*, 111, 98–114. https://doi.org/10.1016/j.ijpsycho.2016.11.005

Stern, J. A., Walrath, L. C., & Goldstein, R. (1984). The endogenous eyeblink. *Psychophysiology*, 21(1), 22–33. https://doi.org/10.1111/j.1469-8986.1984.tb02312.x

Sutherling, W. W., Crandall, P. H., Darcey, T. M., Becker, D. P., Levesque, M. F., & Barth, D. S. (1988). The magnetic and electric fields agree with intracranial localizations of somatosensory cortex. *Neurology*, 38(11), 1705–1714. https://doi.org/10.1212/WNL.38.11.1705

Sutton, S. K., & Davidson, R. J. (1997). Prefrontal brain asymmetry: A biological substrate of the behavioral approach and inhibition systems. *Psychological Science*, 8(3), 204–210. https://doi.org/10.1111/j.1467-9280.1997.tb00413.x

Taylor, J. R., Elsworth, J. D., Lawrence, M. S., Sladek, J. R., Jr., Roth, R. H., & Redmond, D. E., Jr. (1999). Spontaneous blink rates correlate with dopamine levels in the caudate nucleus of MPTP-treated monkeys. *Experimental Neurology*, 158(1), 214–220. https://doi.org/10.1006/exnr.1999.7093

Taylor, S. E., & Gollwitzer, P. M. (1995). Effects of mindset on positive illusions. *Journal of Personality and Social Psychology*, 69(2), 213–226. https://doi.org/10.1037/0022-3514.69.2.213

Thatcher, R. W., Krause, P. J., & Hrybyk, M. (1986). Cortico-cortical associations and EEG coherence: A two-compartmental model. *Electroencephalography and Clinical Neurophysiology*, 64(2), 123–143. https://doi.org/10.1016/0013-4694(86)90107-0

Tomarken, A. J., Davidson, R. J., Wheeler, R. E., & Doss, R. C. (1992). Individual differences in anterior brain asymmetry and fundamental dimensions of emotion. *Journal of Personality and Social Psychology*, 62(4), 676–687. https://doi.org/10.1037/0022-3514.62.4.676

Van Bogaert, P., Wikler, D., Damhaut, P., Szliwowski, H. B., & Goldman, S. (1998). Cerebral glucose metabolism and centrotemporal spikes. *Epilepsy Research*, 29, 123–127. https://doi.org/10.1016/S0920-1211(97)00072-7

Verleger, R. (1991). The instruction to refrain from blinking affects auditory P3 and N1 amplitudes. *Electroencephalography and Clinical Neurophysiology*, 78(3), 240–251. https://doi.org/10.1016/0013-4694(91)90039-7

Wallstrom, G. L., Kass, R. E., Miller, A., Cohn, J. F., & Fox, N. A. (2004). Automatic correction of ocular artifacts in the EEG: A comparison of regression-based and component-based methods. *International Journal of Psychophysiology*, 53(2), 105–119. https://doi.org/10.1016/j.ijpsycho.2004.03.007

Wang, L., Hagoort, P., & Jensen, O. (2018). Language prediction is reflected by coupling between frontal gamma and posterior alpha oscillations. *Journal of Cognitive Neuroscience*, 30(3), 432–447. https://doi.org/10.1162/jocn_a_01190

Watson, D., Clark, L. A., & Tellegen, A. (1988). Development and validation of brief measures of positive and negative affect: The PANAS scales. *Journal of Personality and Social Psychology*, 54(6), 1063–1070. https://doi.org/10.1037/0022-3514.54.6.1063

Wheeler, R. E., Davidson, R. J., & Tomarken, A. J. (1993). Frontal brain asymmetry and emotional reactivity: A biological substrate of affective style. *Psychophysiology*, 30(1), 82–89. https://doi.org/10.1111/j.1469-8986.1993.tb03207.x

Wilson, F. A., Ó'Scalaidhe, S. P., & Goldman-Rakic, P. S. (1994). Functional synergism between putative gamma-aminobutyrate-containing neurons and pyramidal neurons in prefrontal cortex. *Proceedings of the National Academy of Sciences of the United States of America*, 91(9), 4009–4013. https://doi.org/10.1073/pnas.91.9.4009

CHAPTER 28

EVENT-RELATED POTENTIALS

Steven J. Luck

Event-related potentials (ERPs) are electrical *potentials* (voltages) generated by the brain that are *related* to specific internal or external *events* (e.g., stimuli, responses, decisions). They can be recorded safely and painlessly from almost any group of research participants, and they can provide information about a broad range of sensory, cognitive, social, and affective processes. Consequently, the ERP technique has become a common tool in almost all areas of psychological research, and it is important for students and researchers to develop the vocabulary and conceptual background needed to read and evaluate ERP studies. This chapter is designed to provide you with this background information so that you can be an informed consumer of ERP studies in your own area of interest. A brief video-based online course covers much of this same material (Luck, 2020). More detailed works are available if you would like to learn more or would like to conduct your own ERP experiments (Cohen, 2014; Luck, 2014; Luck & Kappenman, 2012).

The ERP waveform that we obtain from scalp electrodes consists of a set of positive- and negative-going *peaks* or *waves* that reflect a set of underlying *components* in the brain. We begin this chapter by looking at how one of these components—the face-related N170 wave— has been used to address issues ranging from perception and attention to typical and atypical development. We will then take a tour of the major ERP components, which will provide you with both a vocabulary for discussing ERPs and a sense of the topics that are commonly explored with ERPs. The next sections describe how ERPs are generated in the brain and how the neural generator site of a given ERP can be localized. This is followed by a discussion of the basic methodological issues involved in recording and analyzing ERPs, using a study of impaired cognition in patients with schizophrenia as a concrete example. The chapter ends with a set of questions to ask when reading and evaluating an ERP study.

Example: The N170 Component and Face Processing

Figure 28.1 shows the results of an experiment focusing on the N170 component, a negative-going wave over visual cortex that typically peaks around 170 ms after stimulus onset. In a typical N170 paradigm, photographs of faces and various types of nonface objects are briefly flashed on a computer monitor while the participants passively view the stimuli. In the ERP waveforms shown in Figure 28.1A, the *x*-axis represents time (in milliseconds) and the *y*-axis represents the magnitude

---

Preparation of this chapter was supported by National Institute of Mental Health Grants R01MH076226, R01MH065034, R01MH087450, and R25MH080794.

https://doi.org/10.1037/0000318-028
APA Handbook of Research Methods in Psychology, Second Edition: Vol. 1. Foundations, Planning, Measures, and Psychometrics, H. Cooper (Editor-in-Chief)
Copyright © 2023 by the American Psychological Association. All rights reserved.

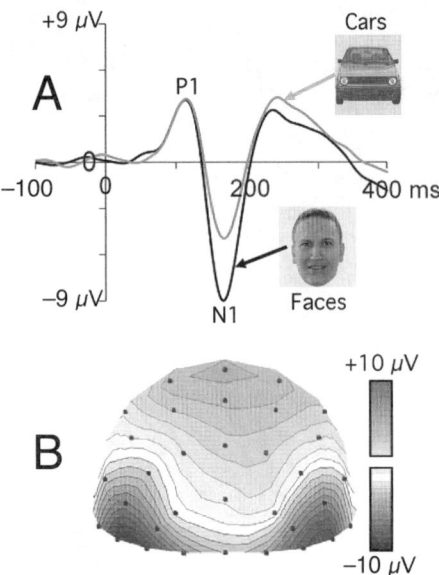

FIGURE 28.1. Example N170 experiment, including ERP waveforms elicited by cars and faces and recorded at an occipito-temporal electrode site (A) and the scalp distribution of the voltage in the N170 latency range (B). Adapted from *The Oxford Handbook of Event-Related Potential Components* (p. 117), by S. J. Luck & E. S. Kappenman (Eds.), 2012, Oxford University Press. Copyright 2012 by Oxford University Press. Adapted with permission. Face image from "Confused Male Face Png Free" by transparentpng.com (https://www.transparentpng.com/details/confused-male-face-free-_32776.html). CC BY 4.0.

of the neural response (in microvolts [μV]). Time zero is stimulus onset. In the scalp map shown in Figure 28.1B, the shading indicates the voltage measured at each electrode site during the time period of the N170 (with interpolated values between the individual electrode sites).

In the early days of ERP research, waveforms were plotted with negative upward and positive downward (largely because of historical accident). Most researchers now use the more common Cartesian convention of plotting positive upward, but this is not universal, so it is important to check which convention is used in a given ERP waveform plot. The waveforms in this chapter are all plotted with positive upward.

The N170 component is larger when the eliciting stimulus is a face compared with when the stimulus is a nonface object such as an automobile (see the review by Rossion & Jacques, 2012). The difference between faces and nonface objects begins approximately 150 ms after the onset of the stimulus; this simple fact allows us to conclude that the human brain is able to distinguish between faces and other objects within 150 ms. The scalp distribution helps us to know that this is the same component that is observed in similar studies of the N170, and it suggests that the N170 generator lies in visual cortex (but note that the active region of cortex may not be directly underneath the electrodes where the voltage is maximal).

The N170 component has been used to address many interesting questions about how faces are processed in the brain. For example, some studies have asked whether face processing is automatic by testing whether the face-elicited N170 is smaller when the faces are ignored. The results of these experiments indicate that face processing is at least partially automatic (Carmel & Bentin, 2002) but can be modulated by attention under some conditions (e.g., when the faces are somewhat difficult to perceive; Sreenivasan et al., 2009). Other studies have used the N170 to ask whether faces are processed in a specialized face module or whether the same neural process is also used when people process other sorts of complex stimuli for which they have extensive expertise. Consistent with a key role for expertise, these studies have shown that bird experts exhibit an enhanced N170 in response to birds, dog experts exhibit an enhanced N170 in response to dogs, and fingerprint experts exhibit an enhanced N170 in response to fingerprints (Busey & Vanderkolk, 2005; Tanaka & Curran, 2001). Developmental studies have used N170 to track the development of face processing, showing that face-specific processing is present early in infancy but becomes faster and more sophisticated over development (Coch & Gullick, 2012). Given the broad evidence for impaired face processing in children with autism compared with typically developing children, researchers initially hoped that the N170 component could be used as a biomarker for this disorder (Jeste & Nelson, 2009). However, meta-analyses have failed to find a consistent reduction in face-elicited N170 amplitude in autistic individuals (Feuerriegel et al., 2015; Kang et al., 2018). By contrast, people with schizophrenia—who also experience impaired face processing—reliably exhibit reduced face-elicit N170 amplitudes (Feuerriegel et al., 2015).

This brief review of N170 research makes several important points. First, it shows that ERPs can be used to address important questions across a wide range of basic science and clinical domains. Second, it illustrates the precise temporal resolution of the technique. ERPs reflect ongoing brain activity with no delay, and an ERP effect observed at 150 ms reflects neural processing that occurred at 150 ms. Consequently, ERPs are especially useful for answering questions about the timing of mental processes. Sometimes this timing information is used explicitly, by asking whether two conditions or groups differ in the timing of a given neural response (just as one might ask whether response time differs across conditions or groups). In other cases, the timing information is used to ask whether a given experimental manipulation influences sensory activity that occurs shortly after stimulus onset or higher level cognitive processes that occur hundreds of milliseconds later. For example, ERPs have been used to ask whether attentional manipulations influence early sensory processes or whether they instead influence postperceptual memory and decision processes (Luck & Hillyard, 2000). More broadly speaking, ERPs are commonly used to determine which specific cognitive processes are influenced by a given experimental manipulation. For example, response times (RTs) are slowed when people perform two tasks at the same time compared with when they perform a single task, and ERPs have been used to show that this does not reflect a delay in discriminating the identity of the stimuli (Luck, 1998) but instead it reflects a slowing in determining which response is appropriate for the stimulus (Osman & Moore, 1993). ERPs can also be used to assess the anticipatory processes that occur before a stimulus (Brunia et al., 2012) and the performance monitoring processes that occur during and after a behavioral response (Gehring et al., 2012).

A third important point is that the high temporal resolution of the ERP technique is accompanied by relatively low spatial resolution. The topographic map of the N170 component shown in Figure 28.1B is very coarse compared with the maps of face-related brain activity provided by functional magnetic resonance imaging (fMRI). Moreover, Figure 28.1B shows a map of voltage on the scalp, not the distribution of brain activity. For reasons that will be detailed later in this chapter, it is difficult to determine which brain areas produce the scalp voltages and converging evidence (e.g., lesion data) is usually necessary to know with certainty the neuroanatomical origins of a given ERP effect. For example, several converging sources of evidence indicate that the N170 is generated along the ventral surface of the brain near the border between the occipital and temporal lobes (Rossion & Jacques, 2012), but it is difficult to be certain that this is the source of the effect in most individual N170 experiments. Thus, ERPs are usually most appropriate for answering questions about timing rather than questions about specific brain regions (although there are some exceptions to this generalization).

A fourth key attribute of ERPs is that they can be used to "covertly" monitor mental activity in the absence of a behavioral response. For example, the N170 can be used to assess the ability of preverbal infants to discriminate between different types of faces (e.g., male vs. female faces). Similarly, dissociations between ERP activity and behavioral responses can sometimes be informative. For example, ERPs have been used to show that stimuli that cannot be reported (because of inattention or subliminal presentation) have been processed to the point of activating semantic information (Luck et al., 1996) and premotor response codes (Dehaene et al., 1998).

In addition to knowing what kinds of issues can be readily explored with ERPs, it is also useful to know what kinds of issues are *not* easily studied with this technique. As will be discussed in detail later, ERPs are extracted from the electroencephalogram (EEG) by averaging together many trials, using a discrete event such as the onset of a stimulus as a time-locking point. ERPs are typically not useful in situations that make it difficult to perform this averaging process. For example, the mental process must be time-locked to a discrete, observable event (e.g., a stimulus or a response). In addition, tens or hundreds of trials must typically be averaged together for each condition, and some experimental paradigms do not permit large numbers of repetitions. ERPs also tend to be most sensitive to processes that unfold over a period of 2 seconds or less, and slower processes are difficult to see in ERPs (e.g., long-term memory consolidation). Finally, ERPs are not usually appropriate for answering neuroanatomical questions.

A final implication of the N170 example is that ERP studies usually focus on specific ERP components. To use ERPs, it is important to learn about the major components because the components are tools that can be used to address many interesting questions. Moreover, a component that reflects one type of process might be very useful for studying other processes. For example, deficits in executive control resulting from aging and from prefrontal lesions have been studied by examining how the impaired control leads to changes in sensory ERP activity (Chao & Knight, 1997). Similarly, language-related ERP components have been used to study how attention influences perception (Luck et al., 1996) and ERP components related to motor preparation have been used to study syntactic processes (van Turennout et al., 1998). Thus, it is important to acquire a basic vocabulary of the major ERP components.

First, however, it is important to ask what is meant by the term *ERP component*. An ERP component can be defined, at least approximately, as a voltage deflection that is produced when a specific neural process occurs in a specific brain region. Dozens of components will be elicited by a stimulus in a given task, and the different components sum together to produce the observed ERP waveform. Unfortunately, it can be difficult to isolate the individual components, and there is no one-to-one relationship between the observable peaks in the scalp waveform and the underlying components. For example, the voltage recorded at 170 ms does not reflect a single face-selective N170 component but instead reflects the sum of at least 10 different components that are active at 170 ms. ERP researchers have developed a number of methods for isolating individual components from the observed waveform, but this is still a constant challenge in ERP research (for detailed discussions, see Kappenman & Luck, 2012; Luck, 2014, Chapter 2).

A BRIEF OVERVIEW OF THE MAJOR ERP COMPONENTS

This section covers the major ERP components, providing both a vocabulary for understanding ERP research and an overview of the breadth of research areas in which ERPs have been used. ERP components can be divided into three main categories: (a) *exogenous* sensory components that are obligatorily triggered by the presence of a stimulus (but may be modulated to some degree by top-down processes); (b) *endogenous* components, which reflect neural processes that are entirely task-dependent; and (c) *motor* components that necessarily accompany the preparation and execution of a given motor responses. Here we will be able to describe only a subset of the components in these classes. For a comprehensive treatment, see Luck and Kappenman (2012).

Naming Conventions

Before discussing individual components, it is necessary to say a few words about the naming conventions for ERP components. Unfortunately, the naming can be confusing for ERP novices. The most common convention is to begin with a P or N to indicate that the component is positive-going or negative-going, respectively. This is then followed by a number indicating the peak latency of the waveform (e.g., *N400* for a negative-going component peaking at 400 ms) or the ordinal position of the peak within the waveform (e.g., *P2* for the second major positive-going peak). These two conventions seem as if they are purely descriptive and theory-free, but they are not usually used this way. For example, the term *P300* was coined because this component was positive and peaked at approximately 300 ms when it was first discovered (Sutton et al., 1965). In most studies, however, the same functional brain activity typically peaks between 350 and 600 ms but is still often labeled P300. The use of a number that represents the ordinal position of the component in the waveform (e.g., P3 instead of P300) can also be confusing. For example, the P3 component is typically the third positive peak at occipital sites but the second positive peak at frontal sites (but is called P3 at all these sites because it is a single component that extends broadly across the scalp). Even the N and P can be confusing because a component may be positive at some scalp sites and negative at others.

Although these conventions for naming ERP components can be confusing to novices, experts usually have no trouble understanding exactly what is meant by these names. This is just like the problem of learning words in natural languages: two words that mean different things may sound exactly the same (*homophones*); two different words may have the same meaning (*synonyms*); and a given word may be used either literally or metaphorically. When you encounter a component name, you should do the same thing you do to disambiguate words in a natural language: Use the context to interpret the name, and don't take it too literally.

ERP components are sometimes given more functional names, such as the *syntactic positive shift* (which is observed when the participant detects a syntactic error in a sentence) or the *error-related negativity* (which is observed when the participant makes an obviously incorrect behavioral response). These names are often easier to remember, but they can become problematic when subsequent research shows that the same component can be observed under other conditions. For example, some investigators have argued that the error-related negativity is not directly related to the commission of an error and is present (although smaller) even when the correct response is made (Yeung et al., 2004).

Exogenous Sensory ERP Components

Figure 28.2 shows the typical ERP components evoked by the presentation of an auditory stimulus (see review by Pratt, 2012). If the stimulus has a sudden onset (such as a click), a distinctive set of peaks can be seen over the first 10 ms that reflect the flow of information from the cochlea through the brainstem and into the thalamus. These *auditory brainstem responses* (ABRs) are typically labeled with Roman numerals (Waves I–VI). They are highly automatic and can be used to assess the integrity of the auditory pathways. The ABRs are followed by the *midlatency responses* (MLRs) between 10 and 60 ms, which reflect the flow of information through the thalamus and into auditory cortex. The MLRs are influenced both by sensory factors (e.g., age-related hearing decline) and cognitive factors (e.g., attention). The MLRs are followed by the *long-latency responses*, which typically begin with the P50 (P1), N100 (N1), and P160 (P2). The phrase *long-latency response* is a bit confusing because these are relatively short latencies compared with high-level cognitive components, such as P3 and N400. However, the transmission of information along the auditory pathway is very fast, and 100 ms is a relatively long latency from the perspective of auditory sensory processing. The long-latency auditory responses can be strongly influenced by high-level factors, such as attention and arousal.

The midlatency and long-latency auditory responses become much smaller when the interval between successive stimuli decreases, with refractory periods that may exceed 1,000 ms (this is true for sensory components in other modalities as well). Moreover, the ERP elicited by one stimulus may not be finished before the next stimulus begins when the interval between stimuli is short, which can also confound the results of an experiment. Thus, when evaluating an ERP study, it is important to assess whether a difference between groups or conditions might be confounded by differences in the inter-stimulus interval.

When visual stimuli are presented, the initial ERP response does not begin until approximately

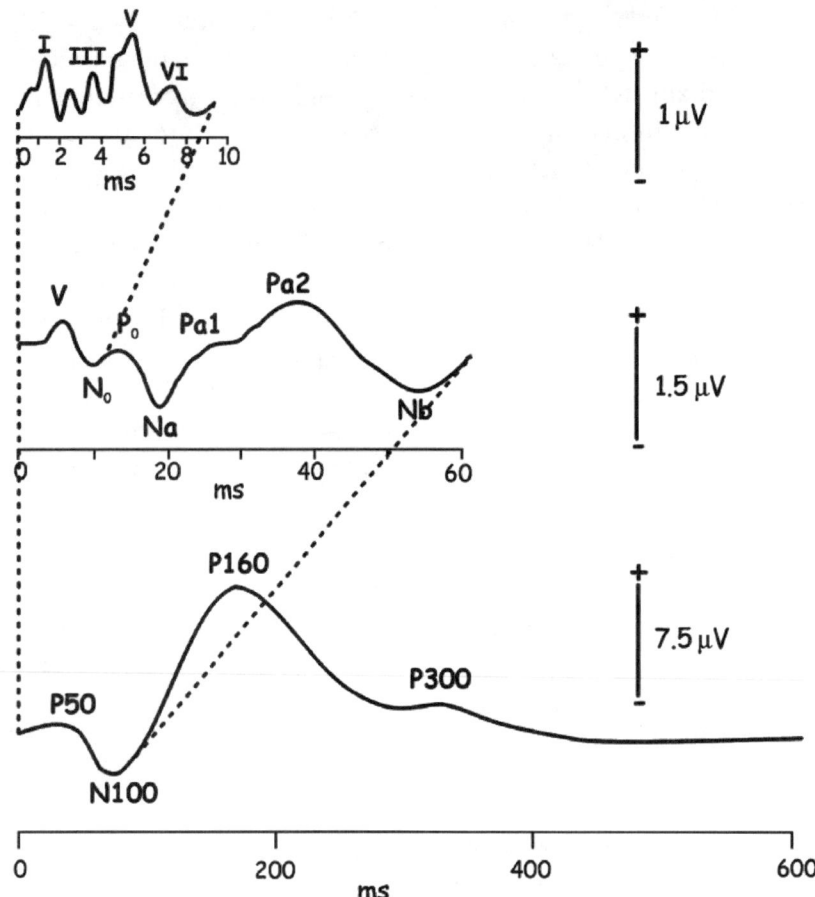

FIGURE 28.2. Typical sequence of auditory sensory components. The waveform elicited by a click stimulus is shown over different time ranges with different filter settings to highlight the auditory brainstem responses (top), the midlatency responses (middle), and the long-latency responses (bottom). Adapted from *The Oxford Handbook of Event-Related Potential Components* (p. 91), by S. J. Luck and E. S. Kappenman (Eds.), 2012, Oxford University Press. Copyright 2012 by Oxford University Press. Adapted with permission.

50 ms poststimulus. This greater onset latency for visual relative to auditory stimuli is a result of the relatively long period of time required by the retina to accumulate enough photons to produce a reliable response. The typical scalp ERP waveform for a visual stimulus is shown in Figure 28.3. The waveforms are shown for the most common ERP paradigm, the *oddball paradigm*. In this paradigm (which is similar to the *continuous performance task*), two classes of stimuli are used, a frequently occurring *standard* stimulus and an infrequently occurring *oddball* stimulus. For example, 80% of the stimuli might be the letter X and 20% might be the letter O. Each stimulus is presented briefly (e.g., 100–200 ms), and the interval between successive stimulus onsets is typically 1,000 ms to 2,000 ms. Participants typically count or make a manual response to the oddball stimuli.

The initial sensory response is usually the same for the standards and the oddballs. It begins with the *C1* wave, which is generated in early areas of visual cortex and is negative for upper-field stimuli and positive for lower-field stimuli (Ales et al., 2010; Clark et al., 1994). The C1 wave is strongly influenced by sensory factors but is not usually influenced by the task. The C1 wave is followed by the P1 wave, which is generated in higher-level areas of visual

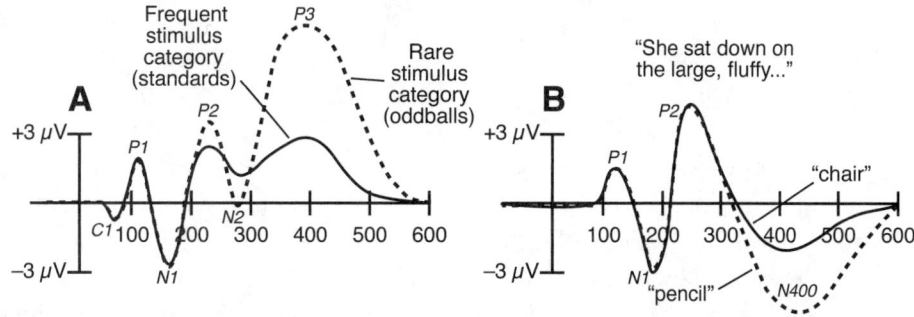

FIGURE 28.3. (A) Typical event-related potential (ERP) waveforms elicited by standards and oddballs at a posterior electrode site in a visual oddball paradigm. (B) ERPs elicited by the last word of a sentence that is either semantically congruent ("chair") or incongruent ("pencil") with the preceding context.

cortex and is influenced by sensory factors, attention, and arousal (Di Russo et al., 2003; Hillyard et al., 1998). The P1 is followed by the N1 wave, which consists of several distinct subcomponents. That is, several different brain areas produce negative voltages in the same approximate time range, which sum together to produce the overall N1 voltage. The N1 complex includes the N170 component described earlier. It also includes a subcomponent that is present when the participant attempts to discriminate the identity of the stimulus rather than merely detecting the presence of a stimulus (Vogel & Luck, 2000). These N1 subcomponents are also influenced by attention (Hillyard et al., 1998). Distinct sensory responses are also produced by somatosensory, olfactory, and gustatory stimuli, as reviewed by Pratt (2012).

The P3 Family of Components

The most common endogenous ERP component is the P3 or P300 wave (reviewed by Polich, 2012). As illustrated in Figure 28.3A, the most distinctive property of the P3 wave is that it is much larger for infrequently occurring stimulus categories than for frequently occurring stimulus categories. It is most often observed in the oddball paradigm, in which the oddball stimuli elicit a larger P3 than the standard stimuli. Two distinctly different P3 components can be observed. The most common is called *P3b*, and it is sensitive to *task-defined* probability. That is, it is larger for improbable stimuli only when the task requires sorting the stimuli in a way that makes a given stimulus category improbable. Imagine, for example, that the stimuli are the letters A, B, C, D, and E, each with a probability of .2. If the task requires pressing a left-hand button for C and a right-hand button for A, B, D, and E, the task imposes a probability of .2 for the stimulus that requires the left-hand response (the C) and a probability of .8 for the stimuli that require a right-hand response (A, B, D, and E). As a result, the P3b component will be much larger for the "C" category than for the "non-C" category even though the probability of a C is equal to the probability of any other individual letter (Kappenman, Farrens, et al., 2021). This dependence on the task-defined category means that task-irrelevant stimuli generate very little P3b activity, and probability along task-irrelevant dimensions does not influence P3b amplitude. For example, if 10% of the stimuli are red and 90% are blue, red and blue stimuli will elicit equivalent P3b responses if color is not relevant for the task.

Because P3b amplitude depends on task-defined probability, the difference in amplitude between the oddball and standard stimuli cannot occur until the brain has begun to determine the category of a given stimulus. As a result, factors that influence the time required to perceive and categorize a stimulus strongly influence the onset and peak latency of the P3b, and P3b latency is often tightly tied to RT (for examples, see Luck, 1998; Luck & Hillyard, 1990). However, RT is often influenced by postcategorization factors, such as the complexity of the stimulus-response mapping, and P3b latency sometimes varies independently of RT (Kutas et al., 1977). Thus, P3b latency can be used to distinguish between pre- and postcategorization processes (but see Verleger, 1997, for a different perspective).

A different P3 subcomponent—called either *P3a* or the *novelty P3*—is elicited by highly distinctive improbable stimuli, even when the task does not require discrimination of these stimuli. For example, if participants are required to count the Xs in a stream of Xs and Os, and photographs of distinctive scenes are occasionally presented, the scenes will elicit a P3a component. The P3a component has a frontal scalp distribution and is reduced in individuals with lesions of prefrontal cortex, whereas the P3b component is largest over central and parietal electrodes and is reduced in individuals with lesions near the temporal-parietal junction.

The N2 Family of Components

Several anatomically and functionally distinct components contribute to the overall N2 wave (see the review by Folstein & Van Petten, 2008). Like the P3b, the N2c subcomponent of the N2 complex is typically larger for infrequent stimulus categories. This component appears to reflect the actual process of categorizing the stimulus (whereas the P3b reflects a process that follows stimulus categorization). The N2c is present for both auditory and visual stimuli, but with quite different scalp distributions.

When auditory stimuli are used, the oddballs also elicit a component that was originally called *N2a* but is now called the *mismatch negativity* or *MMN* (see the review by Näätänen & Kreegipuu, 2012). Unlike the N2c and P3b components, the MMN is enhanced for rare stimuli even if the stimuli are task irrelevant. In a typical MMN study, a sequence of low- and high-pitched tones is presented while the participant reads a book. If the pitch difference is discriminable, and one of the two pitches is less probable than the other, then the oddball pitch will elicit an enhanced negative voltage peaking around 200 ms at anterior electrode sites. This MMN is very useful for determining whether the auditory system can distinguish between different stimulus categories, especially in participants who cannot easily respond behaviorally to indicate the category of a stimulus. For example, the MMN can be used to determine whether infants of a given age can differentiate between two phonemic categories (Coch & Gullick, 2012). The MMN is largely specific for auditory stimuli (Kenemans et al., 2003).

In the visual domain, the *N2pc* component can be used to track the allocation of spatial attention (Luck, 2012). The pc in N2pc stands for "posterior contralateral" because the N2pc is observed over posterior scalp sites contralateral to the location of an object that is being attended. As participants shift attention from one side of the display to the other, the N2pc shifts from one hemisphere to the other. In addition, the timing of the N2pc can be used to track how long it takes an individual to find a task-relevant object and shift attention to it. When the attended item must be stored in working memory over a delay interval, a sustained voltage is observed over the delay interval (Luria et al., 2016). This *contralateral delay activity* is strongly correlated with individual differences in working memory capacity.

An *anterior* N2 component can be observed at frontal and central electrode sites. This component appears to be sensitive to the mismatch between an expectation and a stimulus, and it is often seen when participants are asked to compare sequentially presented stimuli and the two stimuli mismatch. It is also observed on incompatible trials in the Eriksen flankers task and in the Stroop task; in these situations, the mismatch is between two elements of a single stimulus array (Folstein & Van Petten, 2008). Yeung et al. (2004) proposed that this component reflects the operation of a conflict detection system and that this same system is also responsible for the error-related negativity (ERN; for a review, see Gehring et al., 2012). That is, the ERN occurs when the conflict is so great that an incorrect response occurs. By this account, the anterior N2 and the ERN are actually the same component.

Language-Related ERP Components

Several ERP components have been discovered that are related to language comprehension (see the review by Swaab et al., 2012). The most widely used language-related component is the N400, which is typically observed for words that are semantically, lexically, or associatively unrelated to preceding words, phrases, or sentences. As shown in Figure 28.3B, for example, the last word of a sentence will elicit a large N400 if its meaning is incongruous with the rest of the sentence (as in "She sat down on the large, fluffy pencil"). The N400 can also be seen with simple word pairs that vary in their degree of relatedness. For example, the word "table" will elicit a larger N400 in "bicycle-table" than in "chair-table."

The N400 is specific to semantic incongruity. For example, syntactic anomalies instead produce a P600 component (sometimes called the *syntactic positive shift*). For example, a larger P600 would be elicited by the word "were" in the syntactically incorrect sentence "The dog were barking" than in the syntactically correct sentence "The dogs were barking." Syntactic anomalies may also produce a *left anterior negativity* (LAN) 300 to 500 ms after the anomalous word. For example, the LAN is observed when the participant is expecting a word in one syntactic category but instead sees or hears a word in a different category (as in the last word of the sentence "He went outside to take a walking"). The LAN is also larger for words that play a primarily syntactic role (e.g., articles, prepositions) than for words that have strong semantic content (e.g., nouns and verbs).

Memory-Related ERP Components

As with language, several ERP components have been identified that are related to memory. In working memory paradigms, sustained activity can be observed during the retention interval at frontal electrode sites and—when lateralized visual stimuli are used—over the posterior contralateral electrode sites (Luria et al., 2016). In long-term memory paradigms, separate ERPs components have been identified that operate during the encoding and retrieval phases of the task. Encoding-related ERPs are often studied by taking the ERPs that were recorded during the encoding phase and sorting them according to whether a given item was later remembered. Any difference in the ERP between stimuli that were later remembered and stimuli that were later forgotten is called a *Dm* (difference because of memory) or a *subsequent memory effect* (see the review by Wilding & Ranganath, 2012). In most cases, the Dm contains a broad positivity from approximately 400 ms to 800 ms over centroparietal electrode sites. It may also contain left anterior activity, however, and the details of the scalp distribution depend on whether the stimuli were words or pictures and on the instructions given to the participants. Thus, the Dm is not a single component but instead reflects many different processes that can influence whether a stimulus is later remembered. Other ERP components are observed at the time of memory retrieval.

Emotion-Related ERP Components

ERP studies of emotion have typically used emotion-inducing pictures as stimuli. The emotional content of the stimuli influences many of the components that have already been described. For example, the P1, N1/N170, N2, and P3 components may all be increased for emotion-inducing stimuli relative to neutral stimuli (see the review by Hajcak et al., 2012). Two emotion-related components have been studied particularly intensively. First, the *early posterior negativity* is a negative potential over visual cortex in the N2 latency range that is enhanced for emotion-inducing stimuli, particularly those with a positive valence. This component is thought to reflect the recruitment of additional perceptual processing for emotion-inducing stimuli. The early posterior negativity may include contributions from the attention-related N2pc component, which is automatically elicited by emotion-inducing stimuli (Kappenman, Geddert, et al., 2021; Kappenman et al., 2015). Second, the *late positive potential* is a positive voltage that typically has the same onset time and scalp distribution as the P3b wave (i.e., onset around 300 ms and parietal maximum). It may extend for many hundreds of milliseconds and may become more centrally distributed over time. The initial portion may actually consist of an enlarged P3b component, reflecting an effect of the intrinsic task relevance of emotion-inducing stimuli. Interestingly, the amplitude of the late positive potential is correlated with subjective arousal ratings for the stimuli, suggesting that it may reflect subjective emotional experience.

Response-Related ERP Components

If one creates averaged ERP waveforms time-locked to a motor response rather than time-locked to a stimulus, it is possible to see ERP components reflecting the processes that lead up to the response. If a participant is asked to make self-paced responses every few seconds, a large negative voltage is observed over motor cortex that builds up gradually over a period of several hundred milliseconds. This is called the *Bereitschaftspotential* (pronounced in English as *buh-RIGHT-shafts-potential*) or *readiness potential* (see the review by Brunia et al., 2012). This component is also present when participants are presented with stimuli and asked to make speeded responses. A portion of the readiness potential is larger over the hemisphere contralateral to the response than over the ipsilateral hemisphere, and the difference in voltage between the two hemispheres can be used to isolate the response-specific activity. This difference is called the *lateralized readiness potential* (LRP), and it has been widely used to study the processes that are involved in selecting an appropriate response following an imperative stimulus (see the review by Smulders & Miller, 2012).

ERP Components in Special Populations

The discussion of ERP components up to this point has focused on studies of healthy young adults. However, ERPs have also been widely used to study typical and atypical development across infancy and childhood (Coch & Gullick, 2012), to study healthy aging and dementia (Friedman, 2012), and to study a variety of psychological disorders, including schizophrenia (O'Donnell et al., 2012) and affective disorders (Bruder et al., 2012). In the context of infants and young children, ERPs are particularly useful because these individuals have relatively poor control over their behavior, and the ERPs can reveal mental processes that are difficult to assess behaviorally. ERPs are relatively well tolerated in infants and young children, for whom fMRI is not usually a realistic option. In the domain of aging, ERPs are useful for determining whether the overall slowing of responses reflects slowing in specific processes (e.g., perceptual vs. motor processes). In the context of mental health disorders, ERPs can be useful in determining exactly which processes are impaired (by determining which components are changed). In addition, ERPs can potentially be used as biomarkers to define specific treatment targets and assess the effectiveness of new treatments (Javitt et al., 2008; Luck et al., 2011). Moreover, many human ERP components have animal homologues (Woodman, 2012), creating opportunities for translating between animal and human research.

MULTIVARIATE PATTERN ANALYSIS (DECODING)

Although most ERP research focuses on specific ERP components, some research instead uses *component-independent experimental designs* to simply ask whether and when the brain activity differs between groups or conditions (see Chapter 4 in Luck, 2014). This general idea has recently been extended by marrying it with the *multivariate pattern analysis* approach developed in the fMRI literature (Norman et al., 2006). Rather than examining the *magnitude* of the neural response, this approach focuses on the *pattern* of brain activity (across voxels in fMRI, across electrode sites in ERPs) to see if it is possible to *decode* what a person is seeing, thinking, or doing from the pattern of activity.

For example, whereas early fMRI research asked whether the magnitude of activity in the fusiform face area was greater for faces than for non-face stimuli (Kanwisher et al., 1997), decoding methods ask whether the pattern of activity within this area can be used to decode which specific face is currently being viewed

(Anzellotti et al., 2014; Axelrod & Yovel, 2015). Similarly, in ERP research, it is possible to ask whether the pattern of voltage across the scalp at a given moment in time can be used to decode which of several faces is being perceived (Nemrodov et al., 2016). Although the superior spatial resolution of fMRI allows decoding to be performed separately in different brain areas, the superior temporal resolution of ERPs allows decoding to be performed separately at each moment in time following stimulus onset.

Figure 28.4 shows an example from the study of Bae (2021), in which participants saw a sequence of faces (500-ms duration) and performed a working memory task. There were 16 different face images, factorially combining four different people with four different emotional expressions (neutral, fearful, happy, and angry). In the analysis shown in Figure 28.4B, a machine learning algorithm was trained to decode which person was being perceived, independent of what emotion was being expressed, on the basis of the distribution of voltage over the scalp at each time point. New test data were then presented, and the algorithm guessed which of the four face identities produced those data, making it possible to compute *decoding accuracy* (the proportion of test cases that were correctly classified).

The decoding accuracy rose sharply shortly after stimulus onset, just as the face information was reaching the cerebral cortex, and remained above chance while the information was being maintained in working memory. This is quite remarkable: The voltages were generated in the brain but recorded on the surface of the scalp, and yet the measured signals contained enough information to determine which of four faces was being perceived and maintained in working memory, independent of what emotion the faces are expressing. A separate analysis showed that the emotion could be decoded independent of which face was expressing that emotion. The decoding of face identity and emotional expression were far from perfect, and required averaging together many trials, so this method is not suitable for practical applications such as brain–computer interfaces or lie detection. However, this general approach—which can be applied to

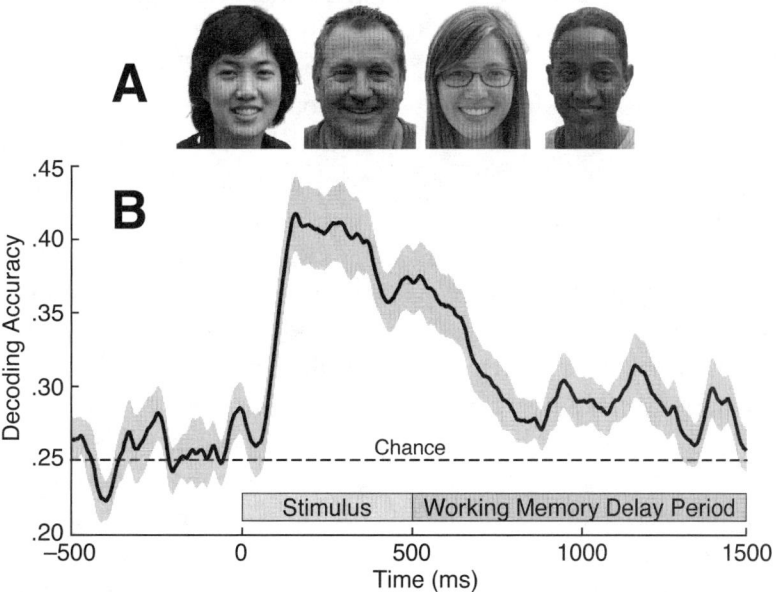

FIGURE 28.4. ERP decoding. (A) Examples of four different face identities (not the actual faces used in the study). CC0 1.0 Universal (CC0 1.0). In the public domain. (B) Decoding accuracy at each point in time relative to face onset, defined as the proportion of test cases that were accurately classified. There were four faces, so chance was 1 in 4 (25%).

many kinds of stimuli beyond faces (Grootswagers et al., 2017)—is quite useful for understanding how the brain works (Hebart & Baker, 2018) and for determining how neurological and psychological disorders alter brain function (Bae et al., 2020).

NEURAL ORIGINS OF ERPs

In almost all cases, ERPs originate as postsynaptic potentials (PSPs), which occur during neurotransmission when the binding of neurotransmitters to receptors changes the flow of ions across the cell membrane (see the review by Jackson & Bolger, 2014). ERPs are not associated with action potentials except for a few of the very earliest, sub-cortical sensory responses. When PSPs occur at the same time in large numbers of similarly oriented neurons, they summate and are conducted at nearly the speed of light through the brain, meninges, skull, and scalp. Thus, ERPs provide a direct, instantaneous, millisecond-resolution measure of neurotransmission-mediated neural activity. This contrasts with the blood oxygen level–dependent (BOLD) signal in fMRI, which reflects a delayed secondary consequence of neural activity. Moreover, the close link to neurotransmission make ERPs potentially valuable as biomarkers in studies of pharmacological treatments (Luck et al., 2011).

ERP Generation

When a PSP occurs within a single neuron, it creates a tiny electrical dipole (an oriented flow of current), which as shown as the dashed arrow in Figure 28.5. Measureable ERPs can be recorded at the scalp only when the dipoles from many thousands of similarly oriented neurons sum together. If the orientations of the neurons in a given region are not similar to each other, the dipoles will cancel out and will be impossible to detect at a distant electrode. The main neurons that have this property are the pyramidal cells of the cerebral cortex, which are the main input-output cells of the cortex. That is, these cells are oriented perpendicular to the cortical surface, and their dipoles add together rather than canceling out. Consequently, scalp-recorded

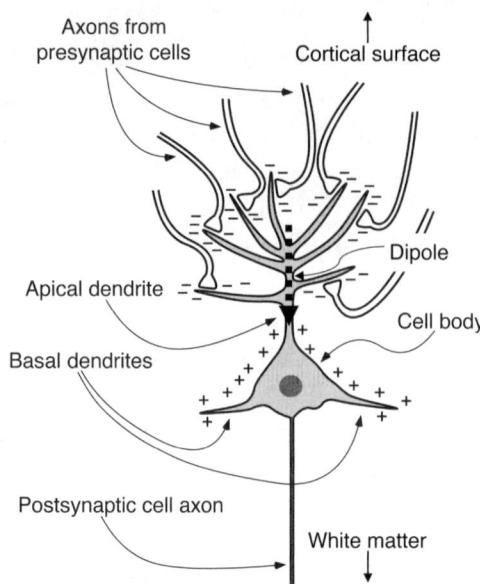

FIGURE 28.5. Electrical field resulting from a postsynaptic potential in a cortical pyramidal neuron. In this example, an excitatory neurotransmitter is released on the apical dendrites, leading to a net negativity in that region and a net positivity near the cell body. The combination of negative and positive creates a current dipole (indicated by the dashed arrow).

ERPs almost always reflect neurotransmission that occurs in these cortical pyramidal cells. Nonlaminar structures such as the basal ganglia do not typically generate ERPs that can be recorded from the scalp, nor do interneurons within the cortex. Thus, only a fraction of brain activity leads to detectable ERP activity on the scalp.

ERP components can be either positive or negative at a given electrode site. The polarity depends on a combination of at least four factors: (a) the orientation of the neurons with respect to the recording electrode, (b) the location of the reference electrode, (c) the part of the cell in which the neurotransmission is occurring (the apical dendrites or the basal dendrites), and (d) whether the neurotransmission is excitatory or inhibitory. If three of these factors were known, then the fourth could be inferred from the polarity of the ERP component. One almost never knows three of these factors, however, so it is usually impossible to draw strong conclusions from the polarity of an ERP component.

When the dipoles from many individual neurons sum together, the summed activity can be represented as a single *equivalent-current dipole* (represented by the small arrows inside the heads in Figure 28.6). For the rest of this chapter, the term *dipole* will refer to these equivalent-current dipoles.

The voltage recorded on the surface of the scalp will be positive on one side of the dipole and negative on the other, with a single line of zero voltage separating the positive and negative sides (see Figure 28.6A). The voltage field spreads out through the conductive medium of the brain, and the high resistance of the skull and the low resistance of the overlying scalp lead to further spatial blurring. Thus, the voltage for a single dipole will be broadly distributed over the surface of the scalp, especially for ERPs that are generated in relatively deep cortical structures. This can be seen in the more diffuse voltage distribution for the relatively deep dipole in Figure 28.6B compared with the relatively superficial dipole in Figure 28.6A.

Electrical dipoles are always accompanied by magnetic fields, but the skull is transparent to magnetism, leading to less blurring of the magnetic fields. Consequently, it is sometimes advantageous to record the magnetic signal (the magnetoencephalogram [MEG]) rather than—or in addition to—the electrical signal (the EEG). However, MEG recordings require extremely expensive equipment and are much less common than EEG recordings.

ERP Localization

When a single dipole is present, the observed scalp distribution can be used to estimate the location and orientation of the dipole with good accuracy unless the dipole is relatively deep in the brain or the data are noisy (for an overview of ERP localization techniques, see Luck, 2014, Chapter 14). When multiple dipoles are simultaneously active, they simply sum together. That is, the voltage distribution for two dipoles will simply be the sum of the two individual distributions. For example, Figure 28.6C shows the same dipole as in Figure 28.6A plus another dipole, and clear voltage foci can be seen over each dipole. Some precision is lost when localizing two simultaneous dipoles, but localization can still be reasonably accurate as long as the dipoles are relatively far apart and the noise level is low. However, it can be difficult to separately localize two dipoles that are similar in orientation and fall within several centimeters of each other. For example, the scalp distribution for the two dipoles in Figure 28.6D is nearly identical to the distribution of the single dipole in Figure 28.6A. As more and more simultaneous dipoles are added, it becomes more and more difficult to determine how many dipoles are present and to localize them, especially when the data are noisy. Under these conditions, a set of estimated dipole locations that matches the observed scalp distribution can be quite far from the actual locations. Even with

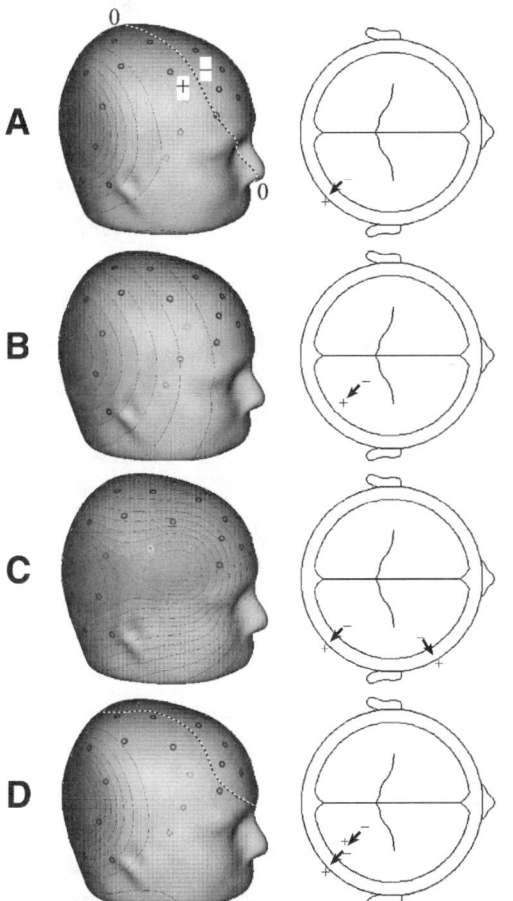

FIGURE 28.6. Scalp distributions (left) produced by different dipole configurations (right). Courtesy of Jesse Bengson.

only one or two dipoles, localization accuracy may be poor unless hundreds of trials have been averaged together to minimize noise in the data.

The number of dipoles is very large in most experiments, and localizing ERPs solely on the basis of the observed scalp distribution becomes difficult or impossible. Formally speaking, the number of internal generator configurations that could explain an observed voltage distribution is infinite (Helmholtz, 1853). In other words, there is no unique solution to the problem of determining the internal generators solely on the basis of the observed scalp distribution. The only way to localize ERPs in this case is to add external constraints, and this is how existing procedures for localizing ERPs solve the non-uniqueness problem. For example, one approach chooses the solution that best minimizes sudden changes from one patch of cortex to the next (Pascual-Marqui et al., 2002). Although constraints such as this produce a unique solution, they do not necessarily produce the correct solution. Thus, you should be cautious when evaluating studies in which the conclusions rely heavily on mathematical localization procedures, especially when the data are noisy.

EXAMPLE: IMPAIRED COGNITION IN SCHIZOPHRENIA

This section provides a somewhat more detailed discussion of a specific experiment in which ERPs were used to study impaired cognition in schizophrenia (Luck et al., 2009). This will both show how ERPs can be used to isolate specific cognitive processes and provide a concrete example that will be used in the following sections, which focus on the technical details that one must understand to read and evaluate ERP studies.

Schizophrenia involves impairments in a variety of basic cognitive processes, and a common finding is that RTs are slowed in people with schizophrenia when they perform simple sensorimotor tasks. The goal of our example experiment was to ask which particular cognitive processes are slowed in schizophrenia. That is, are RTs slowed because of an impairment in perceptual processes, in decision processes, or in response processes? ERPs are ideally suited for answering this question because they provide a direct means of measuring the timing of the processes that occur between a stimulus and a response. On the basis of prior research, we hypothesized that the slowing of RTs in schizophrenia in simple tasks does not result from slowed perception or decision processes, but instead results from an impairment in the process of determining which response is appropriate once the stimulus has been perceived and categorized (the *response selection* process).

To test this hypothesis, we recorded ERPs from 20 individuals with schizophrenia and 20 healthy control participants in a modified oddball task (Luck et al., 2009). In each 5-minute block of trials, a sequence of letters and digits was presented at fixation. One stimulus was presented every 1,300 ms to 1,500 ms, and participants made a button-press response for each stimulus, pressing with one hand for letters and with the other hand for digits. One of these two categories was rare (20%) and the other was frequent (80%) in any given trial block. The category probabilities and response hands were counterbalanced across trial blocks.

This design allowed us to isolate specific ERP components by means of *difference waves*, in which the ERP waveform elicited by one trial type is subtracted from the ERP waveform elicited by another trial type (much like difference images in fMRI studies). Difference waves are valuable because they isolate neural processes that are differentially active for two trial types, separating these processes from the many concurrently active brain processes that do not differentiate between these trial types. In the current study, difference waves were used to isolate the P3 wave (subtracting frequent trials from rare trials) and the LRP (by subtracting ipsilateral electrode sites from contralateral electrode sites, relative to the responding hand). The P3 difference wave reflects the time course of stimulus categorization (e.g., determining whether the current stimulus falls into the rare or frequent category), whereas the LRP difference wave reflects the time course of response selection following stimulus categorization (e.g., determining whether the left button or right button is the appropriate response for the current stimulus). We found that RTs were slowed by approximately 60 ms in patients compared with control participants, and the question was whether this reflects a slowing of perception and categorization (which would be seen in the P3 difference wave) or whether it reflects a slowing of postcategorization response selection processes (which would be seen in the LRP difference wave).

Figure 28.7 shows the P3 difference waves (rare minus frequent) and the LRP difference waves (contralateral minus ipsilateral for the frequent stimulus category) overlaid for patients and control participants. These are *grand average* waveforms, meaning that average waveforms were first computed across trials for each participant, and then these waveforms were averaged together to visualize the data. In the grand average waveforms, the P3 wave was virtually indistinguishable for patients versus controls (although the preceding N2 was diminished in the patients). In contrast, the LRP was delayed by 75 ms in onset time and diminished by 50% in amplitude for patients versus controls. Moreover, the degree of amplitude reduction across patients was significantly correlated with the degree of RT slowing. Thus, for a relatively simple perceptual task, the slowed RTs exhibited by the schizophrenia patients appear to result primarily from a slowing of response selection (as evidenced by the later and smaller LRP) rather than a slowing of perception or categorization (as evidenced by no slowing or reduction of the P3).

ERP RECORDING AND ANALYSIS

Recording the Electroencephalogram

We now turn to the recording and analysis methods that you need to know to understand published ERP studies, using the schizophrenia experiment as an example. A recording session begins by placing electrodes on the scalp, with a conductive gel or liquid between the electrode and the skin to make a stable electrical connection. The electrical potential (voltage) can then be recorded from each electrode, resulting in a separate waveform from each electrode, with time on the *x*-axis and voltage on the *y*-axis (see Figure 28.8B). This waveform will be a mixture of actual brain activity, artifactual electrical potentials produced outside of the brain (by the skin, the eyes, the muscles, etc.), and induced electrical activity from external sources (e.g., video monitors) that are picked up by the head, electrodes, or electrode wires. Studies that do not adequately control these sources of noise may have poor statistical power.

The impact of the noise on the data can be evaluated by examining the prestimulus baseline period in the waveforms. As a rule of thumb, the differences between groups and conditions owing to noise during the baseline period should be small relative to the poststimulus differences. In Figure 28.7, for example, the waveforms include a 200-ms prestimulus baseline period, and although the waveforms are not perfectly flat during this prestimulus period, the differences between patients and controls during this period are much smaller than the P3 and LRP deflections. You should be cautious if a paper reports

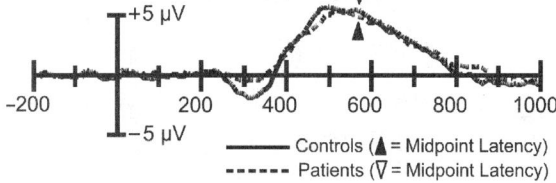

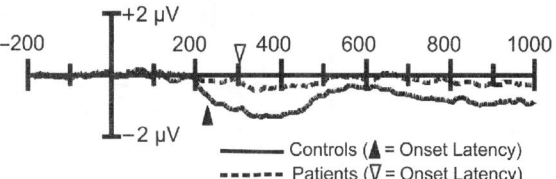

FIGURE 28.7. The P3 was isolated by constructing rare-minus-frequent difference waves at the Pz electrode site (top), and the lateralized readiness potential was isolated by constructing contralateral-minus-ipsilateral difference waves at the C3 and C4 electrode sites (bottom). Triangles show mean latency values. Figure created on the basis of data from Luck et al. (2009).

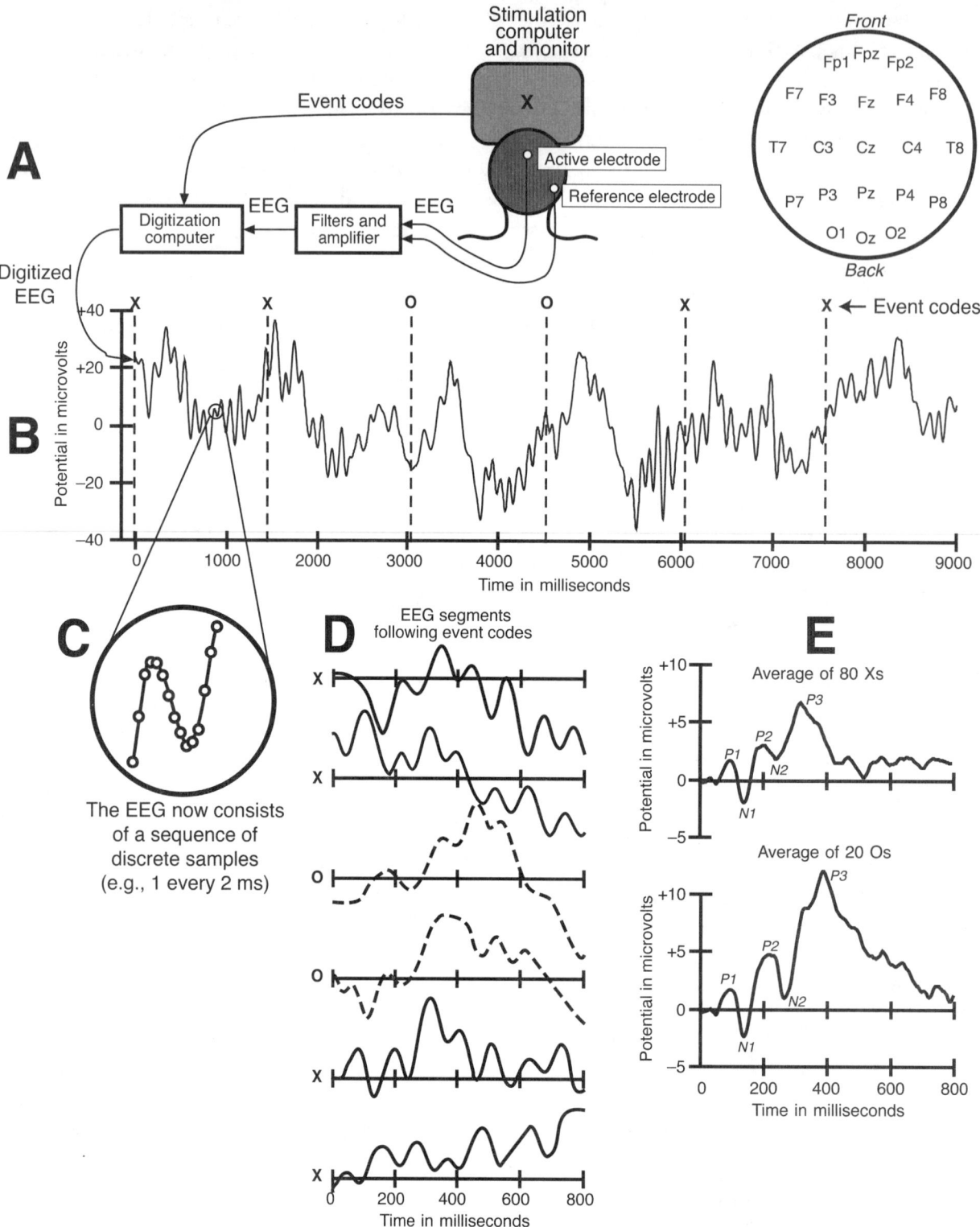

FIGURE 28.8. Illustration of the procedures used to measure the electroencephalogram (EEG) and construct averaged event-related potential waveforms in a typical visual oddball paradigm.

significant differences between conditions or groups in some poststimulus interval when there are differences of comparable magnitude in the prestimulus interval (unless the statistical test was one of a small number preregistered analyses). In general, ERP data sets are so rich that there are many opportunities for noise to produce significant effects, so you should treat statistical significance as only a first step in determining whether an effect is believable (see Luck & Gaspelin, 2017, for an extensive discussion).

The EEG is quite small (usually under 100 microvolts [μV]), so the signal from each electrode is usually amplified by 1,000 to 100,000 times (an amplifier *gain* of 5,000 was used in the experiment shown in Figure 28.7). The continuous EEG voltage signal is then turned into a series of discrete digital values for storage in a computer. In most experiments, the voltage is sampled from each channel at a rate of between 200 and 1,000 evenly spaced samples per second (Hz; see Figure 28.8C). In the experiment shown in Figure 28.7, the EEG was sampled at 500 Hz (1 sample every 2 ms). In addition, filters are usually used to remove very slow voltage changes (< 0.01–0.1 Hz) and very fast voltage changes (>15–100 Hz), because scalp-recorded voltages in these frequency ranges are likely to be noise from nonneural sources. Frequencies below 0.1 Hz and above 18.5 Hz were filtered from the waveforms shown in Figure 28.7. Filters can dramatically distort the time course of an ERP waveform and can induce artifactual oscillations when the low cutoff is greater than approximately 0.5 Hz or when the high cutoff is less than approximately 10 Hz (Luck, 2014; Tanner et al., 2015), so caution is necessary when extreme filters are used.

The EEG is typically recorded from multiple electrodes distributed across the scalp. As shown in Figure 28.8A, each electrode name begins with one to two letters denoting a general brain region (Fp for frontal pole, F for frontal lobe, C for central sulcus, P for parietal lobe, O for occipital lobe, T for temporal lobe). The letters are followed by a number that reflects the distance from the midline (1 is close to the midline; 5 is far from the midline). Odd numbers are used for the left hemisphere and even numbers are used for the right, with z for zero when the electrode is on the midline. Thus, F3 lies over frontal cortex to the left of midline, Fz lies over frontal cortex on the mid-line, and F4 lies over frontal cortex to the right of midline. Different studies use very different numbers of electrodes. For some studies, almost all of the relevant information can be obtained from five to six electrodes; for others, as many as 256 electrodes are needed. Although it might be tempting to assume that more is better, it is actually more difficult to ensure that high-quality data are being recorded when the number of electrodes is large. That is, increasing the number of electrodes increases the probability of one or more bad connections, and it difficult for the experimenter to monitor the EEG and detect problems during the recording when the number of electrodes is large. Moreover, methods for rapidly applying large numbers of electrodes may lead to poorer signal quality and lower statistical power (Kappenman & Luck, 2010). An intermediate number of electrodes (10–64) is best for most studies. Only 13 scalp sites were used in the study shown in Figure 28.7. Because ERPs are spatially blurred by the skull, it is very unlikely that an effect will be missed because of insufficient sampling of the scalp unless the number of electrodes is very small.

It is important to note that *voltage* is the *potential* for electrical charges to move between two locations, and the EEG is therefore measured as the voltage between two electrodes. One is called the *active* electrode, and the other is called the *reference* electrode, and a single reference electrode is typically used for all of the scalp electrodes. The reference is often placed at a location such as the earlobe, the *mastoid process* (a bony protrusion behind the ear), or the tip of the nose. These sites are sometimes thought to be electrically neutral, with all of the brain activity originating from the active electrode. This is a misconception, however, and there is no electrically neutral location. Thus, it is important to realize that the voltage attributed to a given site is really the potential between two sites, and brain activity at both the active and reference sites contributes to the recorded signal. Thus, when reading the method section of a published ERP study, it is important to see what reference site was used. The average of the left and right earlobes was used in the study shown in Figure 28.7.

Artifact Rejection and Correction

Several common artifacts are picked up by the EEG electrodes and require special treatment. The most common artifacts arise from the eyes but propagate widely across the scalp. When the eyes blink, a large voltage deflection is observed over the front of the head. This artifact is usually much larger than the ERP signals. Moreover, eyeblinks are sometimes systematically triggered by tasks and may vary across groups or conditions, yielding a systematic distortion of the data. In addition, large potentials are produced by eye movements, and these potentials can confound experiments that use large or lateralized stimuli, especially when the stimulus duration is long enough for the participants to make eye movements (> 200 ms). In many ERP experiments, the participants are instructed to maintain fixation on a central point and to minimize eyeblinks. Most participants cannot avoid blinking entirely, and they may be unable to avoid making eye movements toward lateralized stimuli. Thus, trials containing blinks, eye movements, or other artifacts are often excluded from the averaged ERP waveforms. In the study shown in Figure 28.7, for example, three patients and two controls were excluded from the final analysis because more than 50% of trials were rejected (mainly because of blinks). In the remaining participants, an average of 23% of trials was rejected.

The rejection of trials containing eyeblinks has two shortcomings. First, a fairly large number of trials may need to be rejected, thus reducing number of trials remaining in the averaged ERP waveforms. Second, the mental effort involved in suppressing eyeblinks may impair task performance (Ochoa & Polich, 2000). Fortunately, methods have been developed to estimate the artifactual activity and subtract it out, leaving artifact-free EEG data that can be included in the averaged ERP waveforms. These methods are not perfect, but the best current methods (independent component analysis, Jung et al., 2000; and second-order blind identification, Tang, 2010) work quite well for blinks and moderately well for eye movements. Note, however, that these methods cannot correct for the change in sensory input that occurs when the eyes blink or move.

Extracting Averaged ERPs From the EEG

ERPs are, by definition, related to *events* such as stimuli and responses, so it is necessary to include *event codes* in the EEG recordings that mark when these events happened (Figure 28.8A). These event codes are then used as a time-locking point to extract segments of the EEG surrounding each event.

To illustrate this, Figure 28.8 shows the EEG recorded over a 9-second period in an oddball task with infrequent X stimuli (20%) and frequent O stimuli (80%). The broken lines show the event codes for the stimuli. Figure 28.8D shows 800-ms segments of EEG following each of these event codes. Stimulus onset is time zero. There is quite a bit of variability in the EEG waveforms from trial to trial, and this variability largely reflects the fact that the EEG reflects the sum of many different sources of electrical activity in the brain, many of which are not involved in processing the stimulus. To extract the activity that is related to stimulus processing and eliminate unrelated activity, the EEG segments following each X are averaged together into one waveform, and the EEG segments following each O are averaged together into a different waveform (Figure 28.8E). Any brain activity that is unrelated to the stimulus will be positive at a given latency on some trials and negative at that latency on other trials, and if many trials are averaged together, these voltages will cancel each other out and approach zero. However, any brain activity that is consistently elicited by the stimulus—with approximately the same voltage at a given latency from trial to trial—will remain in the average. Thus, by averaging together many trials of the same type, the brain activity that is consistently time-locked to the stimulus across trials can be extracted from other sources of voltage (including EEG activity that is unrelated to the stimulus and nonneural sources of electrical noise). Other types of events can also be used as the time-locking point in the averaging process (e.g., button-press responses, vocalizations, saccadic eye movements, electromyographic activity).

How many trials must be averaged together? That depends on several factors, including the size of the ERP response of interest, the amplitude of the unrelated EEG activity, and the amplitude of nonneural activity. For large components, such as the P3 wave, very clear results can usually be obtained by averaging together 10 to 30 trials. For smaller components, such as the P1 wave, it is usually necessary to average together 100 to 500 trials for each trial type to see reliable differences between groups or conditions. Of course, the number of trials that is required to observe a significant difference will also depend on the number of participants and the magnitude of the difference between conditions. Also, as discussed, looking at the prestimulus baseline period in the ERP waveforms can be useful in evaluating whether enough trials were averaged together to minimize noise. In the experiment shown in Figure 28.7, each participant received 256 oddball stimuli and 1,024 standard stimuli. This is more trials than would be typical for a P3 study, but it was appropriate given that we were also looking at the much smaller LRP and that we anticipated rejecting a large percentage of trials because of eyeblinks.

Although the averaging procedure can be extremely useful in extracting consistent brain responses from the EEG, it is based on a key assumption that is not always valid. Specifically, averaging the EEG segments across trials will work well only if the timing of the neural response is the same across trials. Figure 28.9A shows an example of several single trials in which the latency varies substantially from trial to trial. The average across these trials begins at the onset time of the earliest single trials and ends at the offset time of the latest single trials, and the peak amplitude of the average is much smaller than the peak amplitude of the individual trials. Figure 28.9B shows an example with less variability in latency, resulting in an average that is less broad and has a greater peak amplitude. Thus, if the averaged ERPs are compared for two conditions in which the single-trial ERPs are of equivalent amplitude, but one condition has greater latency variability, the difference in the peak amplitudes of the averaged waveforms might lead to the incorrect conclusions that these conditions differ in the magnitude of the ERP response when in fact they differ in the timing of the response.

This can be a significant problem, especially when a patient group is compared with a control group, because the patient group might appear to have a smaller amplitude as a result of greater variability in timing. There are several ways to address this problem (Luck, 2014). The simplest is to measure the amplitude of an ERP component as the mean voltage over a broad time range rather than as the peak voltage, taking advantage of the fact that the mean amplitude is not influenced by latency variability (with one exception, described in the next paragraph).

Figure 28.9C shows a situation that is even more problematic. In this example, each stimulus elicits a sequence of two sinusoidal oscillations. The first oscillation is phase-locked to the stimulus (e.g., the oscillation starts at the same part of the sine wave on each trial), and this oscillation is captured well in the averaged waveform. The second oscillation, however, varies in phase from trial to trial. Consequently, even though the oscillation occurs in the same general time range on each trial, the voltage at a given time point is positive on some trials and negative on other trials, leading to nearly complete cancellation in the averaged waveform. Using mean amplitude to quantify the amplitude of the response in the averaged waveform does not work in this example because the single-trial waveform has both positive and negative parts; mean amplitude is effective in the face of latency or phase variability only for monophasic ERPs.

There is, however, a solution that works for oscillations such as those shown in Figure 28.9C.

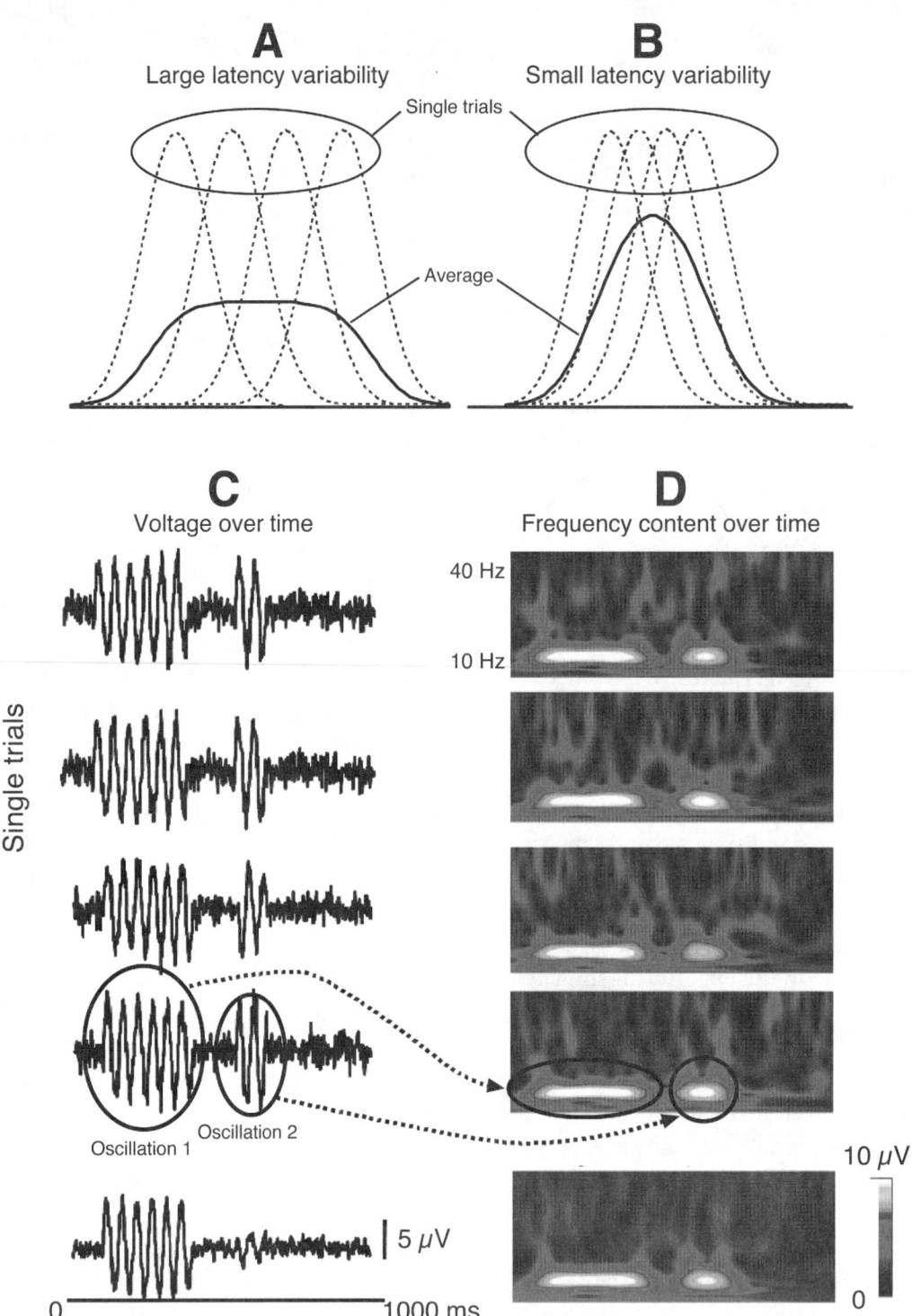

FIGURE 28.9. Illustration of the effects of latency and phase variability on averaged event-related potentials. With a monophasic component, like the P3 wave, a large amount of latency variability in the individual trials leads to a broad averaged waveform with a reduced peak amplitude (A), and reduced latency variability leads to a narrower averaged waveform with a larger peak amplitude (B). When an oscillation is elicited by the stimulus, it will remain in the average if the phase is constant from trial to trial but will virtually disappear from the average if the phase varies randomly (C). The problem of phase variability can be addressed by first converting each single trial into the frequency domain and then averaging across trials (D). The second oscillation remains in this time-frequency average, even though it was largely lost in the conventional average. Adapted from *The Oxford Handbook of Event-Related Potential Components* (p. 33), by S. J. Luck and E. S. Kappenman (Eds.), 2012, Oxford University Press. Copyright 2012 by Oxford University Press. Adapted with permission.

As shown in Figure 28.9D, it is possible to convert the data into a *time-frequency* representation on each trial, which quantifies the power present in different frequency bands at each point in time. The power of a frequency band is represented independently of its phase. Consequently, when the time-frequency representations are averaged across trials, the phase variation does not cause cancellation of the power. These time-frequency analyses have become quite popular because they can reveal brain activity that is lost by conventional averaging (Bastiaansen et al., 2012; Cohen, 2014). Although this approach is extremely useful, the results are often overinterpreted. The main problem is that nonoscillating brain activity also produces power in time-frequency analyses, and it can be quite difficult to distinguish between true oscillations and transient, nonoscillating activity. Thus, one should be cautious when a study makes claims about oscillations from time-frequency analyses. That is, these analyses reveal real neural activity that would be obscured by conventional averaging, but they do not always prove that the neural activity consists of bona fide oscillations.

Quantification of Component Magnitude and Timing

The most common way to quantify the magnitude and timing of a given ERP component is to measure the amplitude and latency of the peak value within some time window. For example, to measure the peak of the P3 wave in the data shown in Figure 28.7, one would define a measurement window (e.g., 400–700 ms) and find the most positive point in that window. Peak amplitude would be the voltage at this point, and peak latency would be defined as the time of this point (it is also possible to search for negative peaks). This was the only realistic approach to measuring ERPs before the advent of inexpensive computers, when a ruler was the only available means of quantifying the waveform. This approach is still used in many studies, but it has several drawbacks. First, there is nothing special about the point at which the waveform reaches an extreme value, and the peak does not represent the magnitude or timing of the entire component. Second, because peak measures are based on extremes, they tend to be sensitive to noise. Third, peak measures are not linear, so the peak in an average waveform will not be the same as the average of the peaks from the individual trials. This makes peak amplitude highly sensitive to trial-to-trial latency variability, and it can also result in grand averages that are not representative of the waveforms from the individual participants. Fourth, peak measures can be greatly influenced by overlapping ERP components, making it difficult to know whether a given effect truly reflects the component of interest.

Because of these limitations, other methods for quantifying ERP amplitudes and latencies have been developed. For measuring the magnitude of a component, it is possible to simply measure the mean voltage over a given time window. This captures all or most of a component, not just the most extreme value, and it is less sensitive to noise than peak amplitude. In addition, mean amplitude is a linear measure, so the mean voltage measured from the waveforms on multiple single trials and then averaged together will be equal to the mean voltage measured from the averaged waveform, and trial-to-trial latency variability will have no effect on the measured amplitude (for monophasic components). Thus, mean amplitude is almost always superior to peak amplitude as a measure of the magnitude of a component.

Statistical Analysis

In most ERP experiments, an averaged ERP waveform is calculated at each electrode site for each subject in each condition. The amplitude or latency of a component of interest is then measured in each one of these waveforms, and these measured values are then entered into a statistical analysis just like any other variable. Thus, the statistical analysis of ERP data is not usually very different from the analysis of traditional behavioral measures.

One issue, however, is important to consider when reading published ERP studies. Specifically, ERP experiments provide extremely rich data sets, usually consisting of several gigabytes of data.

This can lead to both the implicit and explicit use of many statistical comparisons per study, which can dramatically increase the probability of a Type I error (i.e., concluding that a difference is real when it was actually a result of sampling error or measurement error). The explicit use of multiple comparisons arises when, for example, separate statistical analyses are reported for several different components. The implicit use of multiple comparisons occurs when researchers conduct many different analyses and then report only a subset (mainly those that yielded significant results). A related problem occurs when researchers first look at the waveforms and then decide on the time windows to be used for quantifying component amplitudes and latencies. If a time window is chosen because the difference between conditions is greatest in that time window, then this biases the results in favor of statistical significance, even if the difference was caused by noise. An analogous problem arises in studies using a large number of electrode sites, when the sites with the largest differences between conditions are chosen for the statistical analyses. With enough electrode sites, it is almost always possible to find a statistically significant difference between two groups or two conditions at a few electrode sites simply because of random noise. Thus, one should be suspicious if unusual, idiosyncratic, and unjustified electrode sites or measurement windows are selected for the statistical analyses (Luck & Gaspelin, 2017).

A second important statistical issue in the analysis of ERP data arises because nearby electrodes are almost always more correlated with each other than distant electrodes. When an electrode site is entered as a within-subjects factor in an analysis of variance (ANOVA), this produces heterogeneity of covariance, which increases the Type I error rate. That is, the actual probability of falsely rejecting the null hypothesis is higher than indicated by the p value. This problem can be addressed in several ways (see Luck, 2014, Chapter 10), but the most common approach is to use the Greenhouse-Geisser epsilon correction, which produces an adjusted p value that more closely reflects the actual probability of a Type I error. Other factors can also produce heterogeneity of covariance, so this adjustment is used even when electrode site is not entered into the ANOVA.

CONCLUSION

The ERP technique is extremely valuable for answering questions about the processes that lead up to and follow a behavioral response, providing information that cannot be obtained from any other noninvasive technique. In addition, ERPs are useful for evaluating cognitive and affective processes in individuals who cannot easily perform complex tasks, and they can be used to reveal processes that are not evident in overt behavior. Moreover, ERPs can be useful in evaluating pharmacological interventions because they reflect the PSPs generated during neurotransmission. However, technical problems can make it difficult for a study to reach a strong conclusion, and there are several questions you should consider when evaluating an ERP study:

1. Are there substantial voltage deflections during the prestimulus baseline period? If so, then the noise level may have been too high or the number of trials averaged together may have been too low, and the reported differences between groups or conditions may be spurious.
2. Could differences in interstimulus interval confound a comparison between conditions or groups, either because of changes in sensory responsiveness or overlapping activity from the previous trial?
3. What reference site was used? It is important to remember that the voltage at a given electrode reflects the potential between that site and the reference electrode, and that an ERP may be generated quite far from the scalp site where the effect was observed.
4. What were the filter settings? Extreme filter settings can cause large temporal distortions and artificial oscillations. Be especially cautious if the cutoff for low frequencies is greater than 0.1 Hz.
5. If artifact rejection was used, how many trials were rejected per participant? If artifact

correction was used, might blinks or eye movements have changed the sensory input in a manner that confounded the experiment?

6. How many trials were averaged together for each condition? For large components such as P3 and N400, this should typically be 10 to 50. For small components such as P1 and N1, this should typically be 100 to 500.
7. Might differences in peak amplitudes in the averaged ERP waveforms be a result of differences in latency variability rather than true differences in the magnitude of the single-trial ERP responses?
8. Does the study imply that the generator source of a given effect is known with certainty? If so, is this well justified?
9. Does the study conclude that oscillations were present in a given frequency band simply because a time-frequency analysis indicated that significant power was present in that frequency band? Even transient, nonoscillating brain responses can produce such effects.
10. Could changes in the ERP waveform that are attributed to changes in a specific ERP component actually be a result of changes in some other overlapping component?
11. Were peak measures used to quantify the magnitude and timing of an ERP component? If so, then this may have reduced the accuracy and statistical power of the study, or it may be sensitive to differences in latency variability across groups or conditions.
12. Were unusual, idiosyncratic, and unjustified measurement windows and electrode sites chosen for the statistical analysis? If so, the results may be spurious, and a replication may be necessary for the conclusions to be believable.

References

Ales, J. M., Yates, J. L., & Norcia, A. M. (2010). V1 is not uniquely identified by polarity reversals of responses to upper and lower visual field stimuli. *NeuroImage*, *52*(4), 1401–1409. https://doi.org/10.1016/j.neuroimage.2010.05.016

Anzellotti, S., Fairhall, S. L., & Caramazza, A. (2014). Decoding representations of face identity that are tolerant to rotation. *Cerebral Cortex*, *24*(8), 1988–1995. https://doi.org/10.1093/cercor/bht046

Axelrod, V., & Yovel, G. (2015). Successful decoding of famous faces in the fusiform face area. *PLOS ONE*, *10*(2), e0117126. https://doi.org/10.1371/journal.pone.0117126

Bae, G. Y. (2021). The time course of face representations during perception and working memory maintenance. *Cerebral Cortex Communications*, *2*(1), tgaa093. https://doi.org/10.1093/texcom/tgaa093

Bae, G. Y., Leonard, C. J., Hahn, B., Gold, J. M., & Luck, S. J. (2020). Assessing the information content of ERP signals in schizophrenia using multivariate decoding methods. *NeuroImage: Clinical*, *25*, 102179. https://doi.org/10.1016/j.nicl.2020.102179

Bastiaansen, M., Mazaheri, A., & Jensen, O. (2012). Beyond ERPs: Oscillatory neuronal dynamics. In S. J. Luck & E. S. Kappenman (Eds.), *The Oxford handbook of event-related potential components* (pp. 31–49). Oxford University Press.

Bruder, G. E., Kayser, J., & Tenke, C. E. (2012). Event-related brain potentials in depression: Clinical, cognitive, and neurophysiologic implications. In S. J. Luck & E. S. Kappenman (Eds.), *The Oxford handbook of event-related potential components* (pp. 563–595). Oxford University Press.

Brunia, C. H. M., van Boxtel, G. J. M., & Böcker, K. B. E. (2012). Negative slow waves as indices of anticipation: The *Bereitschaftspotential*, the contingent negative variation, and the stimulus preceding negativity. In S. J. Luck & E. S. Kappenman (Eds.), *The Oxford handbook of event-related potential components* (pp. 189–207). Oxford University Press.

Busey, T. A., & Vanderkolk, J. R. (2005). Behavioral and electrophysiological evidence for configural processing in fingerprint experts. *Vision Research*, *45*(4), 431–448. https://doi.org/10.1016/j.visres.2004.08.021

Carmel, D., & Bentin, S. (2002). Domain specificity versus expertise: Factors influencing distinct processing of faces. *Cognition*, *83*(1), 1–29. https://doi.org/10.1016/S0010-0277(01)00162-7

Chao, L. L., & Knight, R. T. (1997). Prefrontal deficits in attention and inhibitory control with aging. *Cerebral Cortex*, *7*(1), 63–69. https://doi.org/10.1093/cercor/7.1.63

Clark, V. P., Fan, S., & Hillyard, S. A. (1994). Identification of early visual evoked potential generators by retinotopic and topographic analyses. *Human Brain Mapping*, *2*(3), 170–187. https://doi.org/10.1002/hbm.460020306

Coch, D., & Gullick, M. (2012). Event-related potentials and development. In S. J. Luck & E. S. Kappenman (Eds.), *The Oxford handbook of event-related potential components* (pp. 475–511). Oxford University Press.

Cohen, M. X. (2014). *Analyzing neural time series data: Theory and practice*. MIT Press. https://doi.org/10.7551/mitpress/9609.001.0001

Dehaene, S., Naccache, L., Le Clec'H, G., Koechlin, E., Mueller, M., Dehaene-Lambertz, G., van de Moortele, P. F., & Le Bihan, D. (1998). Imaging unconscious semantic priming. *Nature*, 395(6702), 597–600. https://doi.org/10.1038/26967

Di Russo, F., Martínez, A., & Hillyard, S. A. (2003). Source analysis of event-related cortical activity during visuo-spatial attention. *Cerebral Cortex*, 13(5), 486–499. https://doi.org/10.1093/cercor/13.5.486

Feuerriegel, D., Churches, O., Hofmann, J., & Keage, H. A. D. (2015). The N170 and face perception in psychiatric and neurological disorders: A systematic review. *Clinical Neurophysiology*, 126(6), 1141–1158. https://doi.org/10.1016/j.clinph.2014.09.015

Folstein, J. R., & Van Petten, C. (2008). Influence of cognitive control and mismatch on the N2 component of the ERP: A review. *Psychophysiology*, 45(1), 152–170.

Friedman, D. (2012). The components of aging. In S. J. Luck & E. S. Kappenman (Eds.), *The Oxford handbook of event-related potential components* (pp. 513–535). Oxford University Press.

Gehring, W. J., Liu, Y., Orr, J. M., & Carp, J. (2012). The error-related negativity (ERN/Ne). In S. J. Luck & E. S. Kappenman (Eds.), *The Oxford handbook of event-related potential components* (pp. 231–292). Oxford University Press.

Grootswagers, T., Wardle, S. G., & Carlson, T. A. (2017). Decoding dynamic brain patterns from evoked responses: A tutorial on multivariate pattern analysis applied to time series neuroimaging data. *Journal of Cognitive Neuroscience*, 29(4), 677–697. https://doi.org/10.1162/jocn_a_01068

Hajcak, G., Wienberg, A., MacNamara, A., & Foti, D. (2012). ERPs and the study of emotion. In S. J. Luck & E. S. Kappenman (Eds.), *The Oxford handbook of event-related potential components* (pp. 441–472). Oxford University Press.

Hebart, M. N., & Baker, C. I. (2018). Deconstructing multivariate decoding for the study of brain function. *NeuroImage*, 180(Pt. A), 4–18. https://doi.org/10.1016/j.neuroimage.2017.08.005

Helmholtz, H. (1853). Ueber einige Gesetze der Vertheilung elektrischer Ströme in körperlichen Leitern mit Anwendung auf die thierisch-elektrischen Versuche [On laws of the distribution of electric currents in bodily conductors with application to electrical experiments in animals]. *Annalen Der Physik Und Chemie*, 89, 211–233, 354–377.

Hillyard, S. A., Vogel, E. K., & Luck, S. J. (1998). Sensory gain control (amplification) as a mechanism of selective attention: Electrophysiological and neuroimaging evidence. *Philosophical Transactions of the Royal Society of London: Series B, Biological Sciences*, 353(1373), 1257–1270. https://doi.org/10.1098/rstb.1998.0281

Jackson, A. F., & Bolger, D. J. (2014). The neurophysiological bases of EEG and EEG measurement: A review for the rest of us. *Psychophysiology*, 51(11), 1061–1071. https://doi.org/10.1111/psyp.12283

Javitt, D. C., Spencer, K. M., Thaker, G. K., Winterer, G., & Hajós, M. (2008). Neurophysiological biomarkers for drug development in schizophrenia. *Nature Reviews: Drug Discovery*, 7(1), 68–83. https://doi.org/10.1038/nrd2463

Jeste, S. S., & Nelson, C. A., III. (2009). Event related potentials in the understanding of autism spectrum disorders: An analytical review. *Journal of Autism and Developmental Disorders*, 39(3), 495–510. https://doi.org/10.1007/s10803-008-0652-9

Jung, T. P., Makeig, S., Humphries, C., Lee, T. W., McKeown, M. J., Iragui, V., & Sejnowski, T. J. (2000). Removing electroencephalographic artifacts by blind source separation. *Psychophysiology*, 37(2), 163–178. https://doi.org/10.1111/1469-8986.3720163

Kang, E., Keifer, C. M., Levy, E. J., Foss-Feig, J. H., McPartland, J. C., & Lerner, M. D. (2018). Atypicality of the N170 event-related potential in autism spectrum disorder: A meta-analysis. *Biological Psychiatry: Cognitive Neuroscience and Neuroimaging*, 3(8), 657–666. https://doi.org/10.1016/j.bpsc.2017.11.003

Kanwisher, N., McDermott, J., & Chun, M. M. (1997). The fusiform face area: A module in human extrastriate cortex specialized for face perception. *The Journal of Neuroscience*, 17(11), 4302–4311. https://doi.org/10.1523/JNEUROSCI.17-11-04302.1997

Kappenman, E. S., Farrens, J. L., Zhang, W., Stewart, A. X., & Luck, S. J. (2021). ERP CORE: An open resource for human event-related potential research. *NeuroImage*, 225, 117465. https://doi.org/10.1016/j.neuroimage.2020.117465

Kappenman, E. S., Geddert, R., Farrens, J. L., McDonald, J. J., & Hajcak, G. (2021). Recoiling from threat: Anxiety is related to heightened suppression of threat, not increased attention to threat. *Clinical Psychological Science*, *9*(3), 434–448. https://doi.org/10.1177/2167702620961074

Kappenman, E. S., & Luck, S. J. (2010). The effects of electrode impedance on data quality and statistical significance in ERP recordings. *Psychophysiology*, *47*(5), 888–904. https://doi.org/10.1111/j.1469-8986.2010.01009.x

Kappenman, E. S., & Luck, S. J. (2012). ERP components: The ups and downs of brainwave recordings. In S. J. Luck & E. S. Kappenman (Eds.), *The Oxford handbook of event-related potential components* (pp. 3–30). Oxford University Press.

Kappenman, E. S., MacNamara, A., & Proudfit, G. H. (2015). Electrocortical evidence for rapid allocation of attention to threat in the dot-probe task. *Social Cognitive and Affective Neuroscience*, *10*(4), 577–583. https://doi.org/10.1093/scan/nsu098

Kenemans, J. L., Jong, T. G., & Verbaten, M. N. (2003). Detection of visual change: Mismatch or rareness? *Neuroreport*, *14*(9), 1239–1242. https://doi.org/10.1097/00001756-200307010-00010

Kutas, M., McCarthy, G., & Donchin, E. (1977). Augmenting mental chronometry: The P300 as a measure of stimulus evaluation time. *Science*, *197*(4305), 792–795. https://doi.org/10.1126/science.887923

Luck, S. J. (1998). Sources of dual-task interference: Evidence from human electrophysiology. *Psychological Science*, *9*(3), 223–227. https://doi.org/10.1111/1467-9280.00043

Luck, S. J. (2012). Electrophysiological correlates of the focusing of attention within complex visual scenes: N2pc and related ERP components. In S. J. Luck & E. S. Kappenman (Eds.), *The Oxford handbook of event-related potential components* (pp. 329–360). Oxford University Press.

Luck, S. J. (2014). *An introduction to the event-related potential technique* (2nd ed.). MIT Press.

Luck, S. J. (2020). *Introduction to ERPs*. https://courses.erpinfo.org/courses/Intro-to-ERPs

Luck, S. J., & Gaspelin, N. (2017). How to get statistically significant effects in any ERP experiment (and why you shouldn't). *Psychophysiology*, *54*(1), 146–157. https://doi.org/10.1111/psyp.12639

Luck, S. J., & Hillyard, S. A. (1990). Electrophysiological evidence for parallel and serial processing during visual search. *Perception & Psychophysics*, *48*(6), 603–617. https://doi.org/10.3758/BF03211606

Luck, S. J., & Hillyard, S. A. (2000). The operation of selective attention at multiple stages of processing: Evidence from human and monkey electrophysiology. In M. S. Gazzaniga (Ed.), *The new cognitive neurosciences* (pp. 687–700). MIT Press.

Luck, S. J., & Kappenman, E. S. (2012). *The Oxford handbook of event-related potential components*. Oxford University Press.

Luck, S. J., Kappenman, E. S., Fuller, R. L., Robinson, B., Summerfelt, A., & Gold, J. M. (2009). Impaired response selection in schizophrenia: Evidence from the P3 wave and the lateralized readiness potential. *Psychophysiology*, *46*(4), 776–786. https://doi.org/10.1111/j.1469-8986.2009.00817.x

Luck, S. J., Mathalon, D. H., O'Donnell, B. F., Hämäläinen, M. S., Spencer, K. M., Javitt, D. C., & Ulhaaus, P. F. (2011). A roadmap for the development and validation of ERP biomarkers in schizophrenia research. *Biological Psychiatry*, *70*, 28–34. https://doi.org/10.1016/j.biopsych.2010.09.021

Luck, S. J., Vogel, E. K., & Shapiro, K. L. (1996). Word meanings can be accessed but not reported during the attentional blink. *Nature*, *383*(6601), 616–618. https://doi.org/10.1038/383616a0

Luria, R., Balaban, H., Awh, E., & Vogel, E. K. (2016). The contralateral delay activity as a neural measure of visual working memory. *Neuroscience and Biobehavioral Reviews*, *62*, 100–108. https://doi.org/10.1016/j.neubiorev.2016.01.003

Näätänen, R., & Kreegipuu, K. (2012). The mismatch negativity (MMN). In S. J. Luck & E. S. Kappenman (Eds.), *The Oxford handbook of event-related potential components* (pp. 143–157). Oxford University Press.

Nemrodov, D., Niemeier, M., Mok, J. N. Y., & Nestor, A. (2016). The time course of individual face recognition: A pattern analysis of ERP signals. *NeuroImage*, *132*, 469–476. https://doi.org/10.1016/j.neuroimage.2016.03.006

Norman, K. A., Polyn, S. M., Detre, G. J., & Haxby, J. V. (2006). Beyond mind-reading: Multi-voxel pattern analysis of fMRI data. *Trends in Cognitive Sciences*, *10*(9), 424–430. https://doi.org/10.1016/j.tics.2006.07.005

O'Donnell, B. F., Salisbury, D. F., Niznikiewicz, M., Brenner, C., & Vohs, J. L. (2012). Abnormalities of event-related potential components in schizophrenia. In S. J. Luck & E. S. Kappenman (Eds.), *The Oxford handbook of event-related potential components* (pp. 537–562). Oxford University Press.

Ochoa, C. J., & Polich, J. (2000). P300 and blink instructions. *Clinical Neurophysiology*, *111*(1), 93–98. https://doi.org/10.1016/S1388-2457(99)00209-6

Osman, A., & Moore, C. M. (1993). The locus of dual-task interference: Psychological refractory effects on movement-related brain potentials. *Journal of Experimental Psychology: Human Perception and Performance*, *19*(6), 1292–1312. https://doi.org/10.1037/0096-1523.19.6.1292

Pascual-Marqui, R. D., Esslen, M., Kochi, K., & Lehmann, D. (2002). Functional imaging with low-resolution brain electromagnetic tomography (LORETA): A review. *Methods and Findings in Experimental and Clinical Pharmacology, 24*(Suppl. C), 91–95.

Polich, J. (2012). Neuropsychology of P300. In S. J. Luck & E. S. Kappenman (Eds.), *The Oxford handbook of event-related potential components* (pp. 159–188). Oxford University Press.

Pratt, H. (2012). Sensory ERP components. In S. J. Luck & E. S. Kappenman (Eds.), *The Oxford handbook of event-related potential components* (pp. 89–114). Oxford University Press.

Rossion, B., & Jacques, C. (2012). The N170: Understanding the time course of face perception in the human brain. In S. J. Luck & E. S. Kappenman (Eds.), *The Oxford handbook of event-related potential components* (pp. 115–141). Oxford University Press.

Smulders, F. T. Y., & Miller, J. O. (2012). The lateralized readiness potential. In S. J. Luck & E. S. Kappenman (Eds.), *The Oxford handbook of event-related potential components* (pp. 209–229). Oxford University Press.

Sreenivasan, K. K., Goldstein, J. M., Lustig, A. G., Rivas, L. R., & Jha, A. P. (2009). Attention to faces modulates early face processing during low but not high face discriminability. *Attention, Perception & Psychophysics, 71*(4), 837–846. https://doi.org/10.3758/APP.71.4.837

Sutton, S., Braren, M., Zubin, J., & John, E. R. (1965). Evoked-potential correlates of stimulus uncertainty. *Science, 150*(3700), 1187–1188. https://doi.org/10.1126/science.150.3700.1187

Swaab, T. Y., Ledoux, K., Camblin, C. C., & Boudewyn, M. (2012). Language-related ERP components. In S. J. Luck & E. S. Kappenman (Eds.), *The Oxford handbook of event-related potential components* (pp. 397–439). Oxford University Press.

Tanaka, J. W., & Curran, T. (2001). A neural basis for expert object recognition. *Psychological Science, 12*(1), 43–47. https://doi.org/10.1111/1467-9280.00308

Tang, A. (2010). Applications of second order blind identification to high-density EEG-based brain imaging: A review. In L. Zhang, B.-L. Lu, & J. Kwok (Eds.), *Advances in neural networks—ISNN 2010* (pp. 368–377). Springer. https://doi.org/10.1007/978-3-642-13318-3_46

Tanner, D., Morgan-Short, K., & Luck, S. J. (2015). How inappropriate high-pass filters can produce artifactual effects and incorrect conclusions in ERP studies of language and cognition. *Psychophysiology, 52*(8), 997–1009. https://doi.org/10.1111/psyp.12437

Turennout, M., Hagoort, P., & Brown, C. M. (1998). Brain activity during speaking: From syntax to phonology in 40 milliseconds. *Science, 280*(5363), 572–574. https://doi.org/10.1126/science.280.5363.572

Verleger, R. (1997). On the utility of P3 latency as an index of mental chronometry. *Psychophysiology, 34*(2), 131–156. https://doi.org/10.1111/j.1469-8986.1997.tb02125.x

Vogel, E. K., & Luck, S. J. (2000). The visual N1 component as an index of a discrimination process. *Psychophysiology, 37*(2), 190–203. https://doi.org/10.1111/1469-8986.3720190

Wilding, E. L., & Ranganath, C. (2012). Electrophysiological correlates of episodic memory processes. In S. J. Luck & E. S. Kappenman (Eds.), *The Oxford handbook of event-related potential components* (pp. 373–395). Oxford University Press.

Woodman, G. F. (2012). Homologues of human ERP components in nonhuman primates. In S. J. Luck & E. S. Kappenman (Eds.), *The Oxford handbook of event-related potential components* (pp. 611–625). Oxford University Press.

Yeung, N., Botvinick, M. M., & Cohen, J. D. (2004). The neural basis of error detection: Conflict monitoring and the error-related negativity. *Psychological Review, 111*(4), 931–959. https://doi.org/10.1037/0033-295X.111.4.931

CHAPTER 29

FUNCTIONAL NEUROIMAGING

Megan T. deBettencourt, Wilma A. Bainbridge, and Monica D. Rosenberg

Functional neuroimaging enables us to peer inside human brains and explore the complex activity that underlies human cognition. In this chapter, our goal is to provide an introduction to multiple imaging techniques that are indispensable for human psychology and cognitive neuroscience (Figure 29.1), including functional magnetic resonance imaging (fMRI), functional near-infrared spectroscopy (fNIRS), and positron emission tomography (PET). These techniques have empowered researchers to investigate human brain activity. Findings from these techniques have revealed important insights into the human brain, from how we see and perceive visual information in the world, to how we remember and recall information, to the processes involved in making decisions. Over many decades, researchers have gained extraordinary knowledge on the neural signals that underlie functional neuroimaging and have also established best practices integral to conducting high-quality research with reproducible results.

FUNCTIONAL MAGNETIC RESONANCE IMAGING

fMRI is a noninvasive method that measures fluctuations in brain activity from one moment to the next. In that way, it is fundamentally different from structural MRIs of a shoulder, knee, or even a brain. Structural MRI produces a static, three-dimensional (3D) picture of anatomy. In contrast, fMRI measures brain dynamics via an indirect proxy of brain activity, using a hemodynamic signal of blood flow. This signal is known as *blood oxygen-level-dependent* or BOLD. The BOLD signal relies on two principles. First, active areas of the brain receive an excess supply of oxygenated blood. Second, oxygenated and deoxygenated blood have different magnetic susceptibilities. Therefore, by tracking the flow of oxygenated blood, that is, the BOLD signal, fMRI can identify areas of the brain that are most active. This generates a 3D snapshot of brain activity that is extremely spatially precise. Just as points in a two-dimensional (2D) picture are referred to as pixels, points in the 3D brain volume are referred to as *voxels*. However, the BOLD signal has relatively poor temporal resolution, with a sluggish hemodynamic response function that peaks roughly 6 to 8 seconds following neural activity. In addition, there are many sources of fMRI data noise that can further obscure the signal, including scanner noise and artifacts from the participants in your study. Knowing the advantages and disadvantages of fMRI is very important as you consider developing and designing an experiment.

https://doi.org/10.1037/0000318-029
APA Handbook of Research Methods in Psychology, Second Edition: Vol. 1. Foundations, Planning, Measures, and Psychometrics, H. Cooper (Editor-in-Chief)
Copyright © 2023 by the American Psychological Association. All rights reserved.

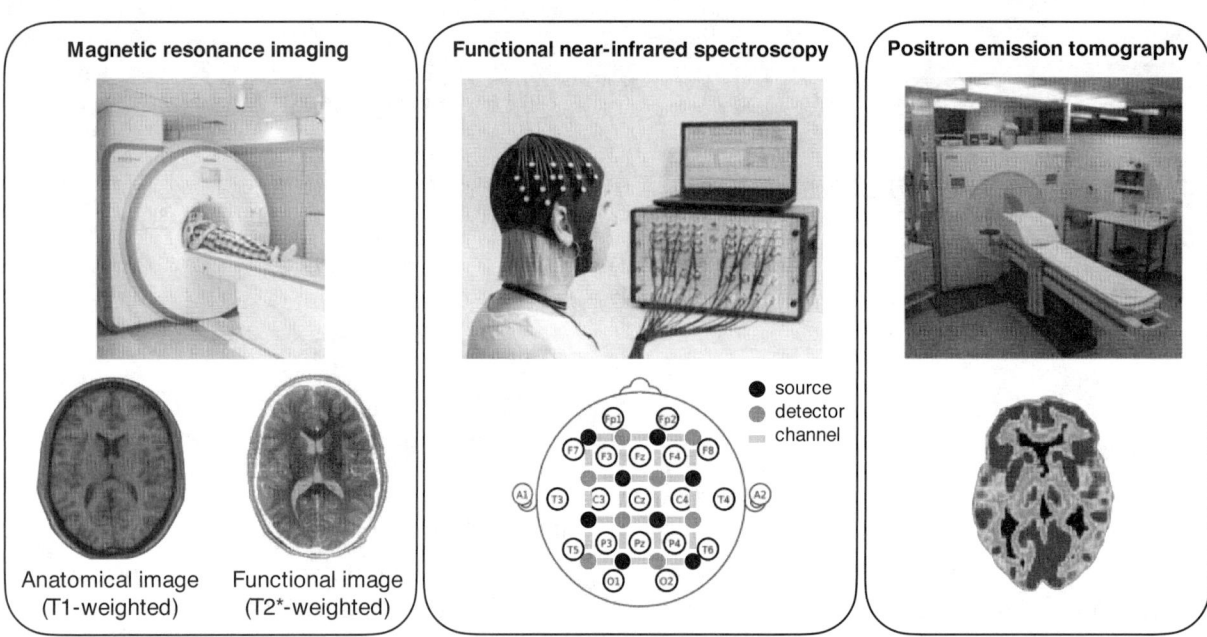

FIGURE 29.1. Magnetic resonance imaging (MRI), functional near-infrared spectroscopy (fNIRS), and positron emission tomography (PET) systems and their representative brain images. All images are public domain or creative commons: MRI machine (CC BY-SA 4.0); anatomical image (visualized in an MRI viewer from scratch; copyright 1993–2009 Louis Collins, McConnell Brain Imaging Centre, Montreal Neurological Institute, McGill University); functional image (CC BY-SA 3.0); fNIRS (CC BY-SA 4.0); electroencephalography cap (adapted for the fNIRS figure; in the public domain); PET scanner (in the public domain); PET brain image (in the public domain).

Scan Parameters

The first step when embarking on an fMRI study is deciding on certain scan parameters to help you collect high-quality data. These parameters are also informed by the specific goals of your study. If you want to acquire images quickly, you compromise on the resolution of the images. Conversely, if you want very high-resolution images, you must acquire the images less frequently. That is, you must trade off whether you want to sample rapidly (high temporal resolution) or densely (high spatial resolution). Finally, if you are only interested in data from a particular part of the brain, you can collect fewer slices more quickly and more densely. That is, you can achieve high temporal and high spatial resolution by sacrificing brain coverage. Essentially, you need to determine which images should be acquired of the brain, with what frequency, in what order, and at what resolution.

In order to construct a 3D image of brain activity, fMRI acquires a series of 2D images (or slices). The slice prescription (where the images will be acquired) will be largely determined by whether you are interested in distributed activity from the whole brain or whether you are interested in a particular brain area. Another decision is the acquisition orientation, or angle at which these images are acquired. When performing a whole-brain scan, the most common orientation is to obtain axial slices of the brain, parallel to the shoulders. These slices are often oriented to align along the plane that intersects the anterior commissure and the posterior commissure in the brain (called the AC-PC plane), using a sagittal (side) view. This plane is used because these anatomical landmarks exist in almost everyone and are visible to the eye from a single anatomical scan, without any preprocessing. However, when examining a specific region of the brain, it may make sense to orient the slices differently. For example, studies interested in the hippocampus typically orient slices perpendicular to its long axis, acquiring coronal slices of the brain, somewhat parallel to the face. The acquisition orientation you select may also vary based on the resolution of your voxels. Many common scanning protocols will use cubic voxels, with equal in-plane resolution (e.g., 3 × 3 mm) and slice thickness (3 mm). But some protocols may use a different slice thickness, especially if there is a particular plane along which the experimenter wants higher resolution.

The temporal resolution is also a key factor to consider when designing an fMRI experiment. You will need to set a repetition time (TR), which refers to the length of time between brain volumes. A shorter TR allows the experimenter to collect brain volumes more rapidly, but a longer TR also can permit higher resolution images and may result in a clearer image (referred to as a high *signal-to-noise ratio* or SNR). Another measure of time to consider is the echo time (TE), or the time between the excitation pulse, a radiofrequency (RF) signal, and the sampling of the subsequent MR signal detected by the RF coils. Functional MRI scans generally have longer TE and TR times and are known as T2*-weighted images because of the underlying MR physics. In these images, white matter appears dark gray, and cerebrospinal fluid appears light. This contrast is best able to capture changes over time in the BOLD signal. Usually at the beginning or end of an fMRI session, you will also collect an anatomical brain scan of the subject. This scan is structural (as opposed to functional scans, like BOLD T2* scans) and is intended to give a high-resolution picture of the brain anatomy for that subject. These anatomical MRI scans generally have short TE and TR times (called T1-weighted), and white matter appears light while the cerebrospinal fluid appears dark.

There are several other parameters you may consider when designing your fMRI study. The scanning protocol will include a flip angle, which is the amount of rotation induced by the RF pulse of the scanner and relates to image contrast. You will also need to determine the slice order of acquisition. A common choice is interleaved, meaning that all odd number slices are acquired and then even number slices are acquired (or vice versa). This helps to reduce artifacts that can be induced across slices, although it is possible to instead select a consecutive ascending or descending order. You will also choose the pulse sequence, which for fMRI is most commonly an echo planar image (EPI). Depending on the scanning facility, you may also have the option to choose among different head coils that have different numbers of channels for creating an MR image. A higher number of channels tends to improve the SNR but may be worse at imaging subcortical structures. Currently, the most common head coil in use has 32 channels, though 12-channel and 64-channel head coils are also common. Finally, it is important to consider the magnetic field strength of your MRI machine. These are measured in Tesla (T), and generally a higher field strength improves SNR as well as temporal and spatial resolution. For research purposes, 3T scanners are most common, but 1.5T are also often used as well as ultra-high field 7T scanners. With higher magnetic field strength, some participants may feel some side effects, including dizziness when moving through the stronger gradient of the scanner.

This list of parameters may sound daunting, but there are some commonly used scanning protocols across the field that are saved at most scanning institutions. As of 2021, a common fMRI sequence for a whole-brain scan is a T2* EPI sequence with interleaved acquisition, with approximately 2- to 3-mm cubic voxels, 33 axial slices parallel to the AC-PC line, and a TR of 2 seconds. The most common anatomical MRI scan is a T1 magnetization-prepared rapid gradient-echo (MPRAGE) sequence with 1-mm cubic voxels. When collecting data for an fMRI study, make sure to note the exact parameters you use in your methodology section (refer to Poldrack et al., 2008, for a useful guide on how to report fMRI data in a manuscript). However, the scanning protocol conventions and recommendations will also likely change with developments in the field.

Two main innovations are making headway in fMRI image quality. First, multiband fMRI uses special sequences that acquire data from multiple slices simultaneously (the number of parallel acquisitions is defined by a multiband acceleration factor, which usually ranges from 2 to 6), which speeds up the time it takes to acquire an entire brain volume. This can allow for increased spatial and/or temporal resolution. However, multiband can also introduce artifacts into a scan and can reduce SNR. A second emerging method is multi-echo fMRI, which collects images at multiple TEs for each brain volume. This allows researchers to compare or combine data across different echoes (as they are sensitive to different tissue types) and may help reduce noise in the data.

Complementing innovations in fMRI data collection, many MRI systems now permit collecting simultaneous information during a scan from other sensors. Many will include physiological sensors that can record heart rate and respiration, factors that can influence blood-flow measures of fMRI. Some scanning facilities also have the capability of recording electroencephalography (EEG) simultaneously with fMRI. This enables analytical methods that combine the high temporal resolution of EEG with the high spatial resolution of fMRI. Some MRI scanners also have eye-trackers to record eye position during the fMRI scan. This can allow researchers to ensure that participants are centrally fixating, as eye movements may be confounded with the conditions of interest (Voss et al., 2017). Conversely, researchers may be interested in examining the influence of eye movements on brain activity and behavior (Liu et al., 2017). When an MRI does *not* have an eye-tracker, it may still be possible to determine the eye position (Frey et al., 2021). However, the experimenter may want to consider asking participants to centrally fixate during tasks to minimize the influence of eye movements.

Practical Considerations for Scans

In addition to the technical considerations of the scanning protocol, there are a number of practical considerations related to participant safety and comfort to keep in mind while you plan your fMRI study. First, you want to make sure your participant is eligible to participate based on the guidelines of the imaging center. Common contraindications for participating in an MRI study include metal implants (e.g., pacemakers; a comprehensive list can be found online, including at MRIsafety.com). You also want to ensure that subjects are prepared for participating in the study by removing any metal jewelry or accessories. This is because an MRI machine is a giant magnet that is always on (even when a scan is not being conducted), so any metal near the scanner could get pulled into the scanner and injure a participant or damage the scanner. This is perhaps the largest risk with MRI scanning, and a key focus of your training will be on ensuring you are vigilant about keeping ferromagnetic metals outside of the MRI scanning room. MRI scanners can also be very loud (reaching up to 110 decibels), so it is important to offer your subjects hearing protection, usually ear plugs and/or noise-cancelling headphones.

As the experimenter, you want to ensure that participants are comfortable upon entering the scanner bore and throughout your study, by checking in with them frequently. This will help reduce the (nonzero) probability that participants might fall asleep and also can reduce motion confounds as participants may fidget when they are uncomfortable. Generally, each "run" (a continuous period of fMRI data collection) should aim to be under 10 minutes long, so that the experimenter can check in with the participant and keep them motivated to perform the tasks well. Ideally, tasks should have participants actively engaged, either making behavioral responses in a task or watching and/or listening to a highly engaging stimulus (like a movie). Behavioral responses allow you to ensure participants are alert and performing the task and can also serve as useful measures for fMRI analyses. You should also design your run order with fatigue in mind, by placing the highest priority runs first and ensuring that different conditions of interest are self-contained within each run. In total, you should try to ensure that the total time in the scanner is under 100 minutes (including all functional and anatomical data collection), to minimize discomfort and fatigue.

Preprocessing

After designing and collecting data for a study, there are important steps that must occur before starting the analyses. These critical preprocessing steps can remove the impact of potential confounds on your data and can improve the power of your eventual analyses for detecting differences in brain activity (Figure 29.2). Most of these preprocessing steps can be accomplished with sophisticated fMRI toolboxes that handle preprocessing, analyses, and data visualization, such as FSL (https://fsl.fmrib.ox.ac.uk/fsl/fslwiki/; Jenkinson et al., 2012), SPM (https://www.fil.ion.ucl.ac.uk/spm/; Penny et al., 2011), AFNI (https://afni.nimh.nih.gov/; Cox, 1996), BrainVoyager (https://www.brainvoyager.com/; Goebel, 2012), and FreeSurfer (https://surfer.nmr.mgh.harvard.edu/; Fischl, 2012). Newer preprocessing-focused tools, such as fMRIprep (https://fmriprep.org/; Esteban et al., 2019) and Nipype (https://nipype.readthedocs.io/en/latest/; Gorgolewski et al., 2011), further standardize these methods and ensure that they are reproducible. However, it is still important to understand when, how, and why to preprocess your data.

Some of the preprocessing steps deal with fundamental aspects of fMRI data collection. For example, the entire brain volume is not measured simultaneously. Rather, fMRI is collected using 2D slices that are then assembled to create a 3D brain volume. Therefore, slice-timing correction adjusts the data to reflect the order and the offset between different slices. In addition, unwarping can reduce the influence of subtle differences (or inhomogeneities) throughout the magnetic field of the scanner. To apply this unwarping step, you need to collect a separate scan that can calculate distortions in the brain image caused by these inhomogeneities. This unwarping procedure can be especially important when you are interested in areas of the brain that are prone to distortions and signal dropout, such as the anterior temporal lobe, orbitofrontal cortex, and other brain regions near sinus and ear cavities. Also, fMRI is especially prone to "scanner drift," which refers to slow temporal changes in the BOLD response over time. To remove the influence of scanner drift, you can apply high pass temporal filtering. However, it is important to consider your experimental design to ensure that applying a high pass filter does not remove any important signal. Another approach for reducing the influence of scanner drift is collecting and discarding a few brain volumes at the start of each run.

Other preprocessing steps help improve your analyses by reducing the influences of confounds. Motion confounds are particularly prominent and pernicious in fMRI studies. Human subjects who are completing lengthy experiments may

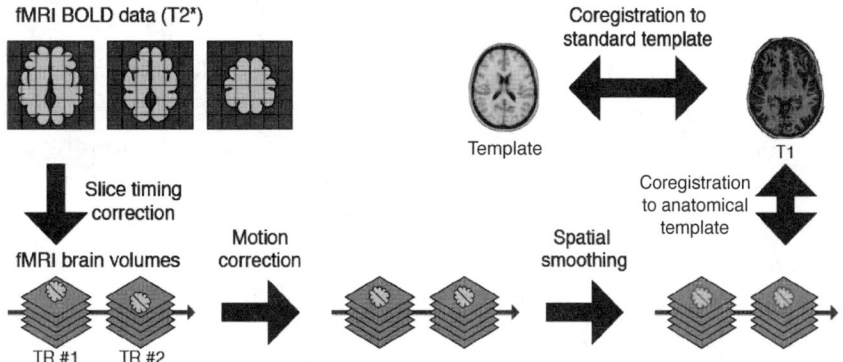

FIGURE 29.2.   Preprocessing functional magnetic resonance imaging (fMRI) data. There are many steps involved in preprocessing fMRI blood oxygen-level-dependent (BOLD) data prior to analyzing it, some of which we have depicted here. We have depicted axial slices of BOLD fMRI data, which are preprocessed and then coregistered to anatomical and standard templates.

shift or tilt their head. If you do not account for these movements, this can lead your data to be misaligned across the fMRI session. The first and best way to minimize the influence of motion artifacts on your data is to try to prevent them in the first place, by ensuring that subjects are comfortable with cushions and pillows around their head. There are also newer techniques involving printing a 3D case specially contoured for a subject's head in advance of the scan. These headcases can be an especially powerful way to minimize motion and displacement within as well as across sessions (Power et al., 2019) when you want to scan the same subject multiple times (although these benefits are debated; Jolly et al., 2020). You can also apply motion correction, which estimates the level of head motion in the scan, allowing you to later factor out those motion parameters (see the section on fMRI analyses). Finally, you can apply spatial smoothing techniques, typically a 3D Gaussian filter, that reduces differences between adjacent voxels and can increase SNR.

When you collect BOLD fMRI activity in a 3D box, it is not necessarily evident which voxels correspond to which brain areas. Coregistration aligns your fMRI data with anatomical regions. There are two steps in this process. First, you align your fMRI scan with an anatomical (T1) MRI scan from the same subject. This is important because an anatomical MRI scan from the same subject provides insight into brain regions by measuring a different magnetic signal with higher spatial resolution. By coregistering a subject's functional data to a subject's anatomical data, you relate BOLD activity from a specific voxel to a particular brain region. This step requires linear coregistration, because the brains that generated these functional and anatomical images are the same. Second, you may align your subject's brain with an anatomical template, known as group, common, or standard space. These templates may be generated from many individuals or many scans of the same individual to create a general reference space. Two prominent templates are the Talairach (Lancaster et al., 2000; Talairach & Tournoux, 1988) and Montreal Neuro-logical Institute (MNI; McGill Centre for Integrative Neuroscience) atlases. This step requires non-linear coregistration, because there are individual differences across individuals' brains. Generally, fMRI papers will display results in these standardized templates, using volume-based representations, although sometimes data are also depicted as surface-based representations. Surface representations provide better insight into how activity maps onto cortical folds and are especially popular for studies investigating visual cortical representations. Surface alignment is conducted by "inflating" the individual's brain image and the anatomical template into spheres that are then matched based on anatomical landmarks. Surface alignment has been shown to result in less noisy and more spatially accurate signal (e.g., Jo et al., 2007), but volume-based alignment may be better for analyzing subcortical regions.

fMRI Analyses

Once you preprocess your data, it is time to consider how you will analyze them. In this section, we will briefly describe common analysis approaches. In this chapter, we will largely focus on univariate analyses that rely upon the general linear model. This framework has been incredibly powerful within fMRI for revealing which brain areas are active during an enormous variety of tasks. More advanced analyses, including multivariate approaches, are covered in more detail in Chapter 32, this volume, "Neuroimaging Analysis Methods."

General linear model. To extract "brain signals" for relevant conditions of interest, you will likely find yourself relying upon a general linear model (GLM). The goal is to find the best fit that relates our set of independent variables to our dependent variable, using a multiple linear regression model defined by:

$$y = \beta_1 x_1 + \beta_2 x_2 + \beta_3 x_3 \ldots + \varepsilon$$

For fMRI studies, the dependent variable (y) is the BOLD time series data that you measured for a specific voxel across an entire scan. The independent variables ($x_1, x_2, x_3, \ldots$) are also called predictors or regressors, which include your conditions of interest (e.g., tasks or stimuli). For example, a regressor could correspond to moments when a certain stimulus was on the screen. The goal is to find the coefficients or slopes (β_1, β_2, β_3, . . .), that is, the beta values, that correspond to the contribution of each regressor to the measured BOLD data. Beta values account for the relationship between the independent variables (conditions) and dependent variables (measured BOLD data). The final intercept term (the residual) reflects the remaining unexplained variance, or the noise in the signal.

When implementing a GLM in fMRI studies, there will be multiple independent variables that also vary over the time course of the scan. In addition to your conditions of interest, you will commonly include covariates and nuisance regressors. These may be independent variables that are not your main conditions of interest but that may nonetheless influence your data. Covariates are commonly behavioral measures that the experimenter wishes to examine that may not be specific to a task or stimulus. For example, reaction time (RT) on each trial may be included as a regressor to assess the relationship of RT (which could reflect confidence or engagement) to the brain signal. Very common nuisance regressors are head motion measures, which are usually outputted by motion correction algorithms as six values: displacement (x, y, z) and rotations (pitch, roll, yaw) in three dimensions. If you record physiological data, heart rate or respiration measures may be other regressors. By including these nuisance regressors, you can remove the influence of these measures from your beta and covariate estimates.

Finally, we also know that the BOLD signal reflects a slow hemodynamic response. Therefore, our GLM also convolves each regressor (x) with the hemodynamic response function (HRF). In other words, the regressor for a condition will not just predict high signal during that condition and low signal during other conditions, it will instead predict a signal matching the shape of the HRF that emerges when that condition is present (Figure 29.3). In the end, we will obtain a beta value for each voxel for each regressor. That is,

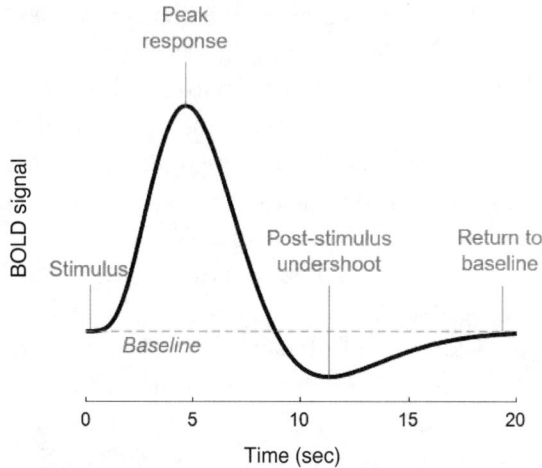

FIGURE 29.3. The hemodynamic response function (HRF), reflecting the slow change in blood oxygenation when neurons are active in a given voxel in the brain. After observing a stimulus, it takes several seconds for the signal to peak. This signal then undershoots the baseline before eventually returning to the baseline blood oxygen-level-dependent (BOLD) signal.

the output of a GLM creates a map of how well the data measured at each location reflect the predicted signal from a given regressor.

There are multiple levels to GLM analyses within an fMRI study. We first examine responses within each run of each participant. Next, we often aggregate across multiple runs from the same participant. Analyses at the level of individual participants are considered first-level analyses. Functional MRI analyses also often rely upon second-level analyses, which examine the results across a group of participants. Second-level analyses can use t tests, analyses of variance (ANOVAs), or other related nonparametric tests to compare the coefficients of different voxels for different conditions. These tests can be conducted as a fixed-effects analysis, for which beta values are compared across both runs and participants (i.e., not accounting for variance within individual participants). These sorts of analyses tend to have higher statistical power and are well suited for experiments with few subjects, but the results may not generalize beyond the current sample. Alternatively, tests can be conducted as a random-effects analysis, for which the participant is included as a random intercept in the GLM, allowing for results that are more likely to generalize beyond the sample.

After performing a GLM analysis, the spatial resolution of fMRI offers enormous opportunities for exploring activity across the brain. Some fMRI studies are interested in voxel activity throughout the entire brain, without a specific region central to the research question, in what is referred to as a whole-brain analysis. Whole-brain analyses allow us to have a full view of the patterns and interactions across the brain during a specific cognitive process. You could examine univariate effects across the brain, by applying statistical tests (e.g., t-test, ANOVA) to every voxel separately and then visualizing the resulting statistics (e.g., t statistic, F statistic) on a brain map after applying a threshold based on the significance of the effect (p value) at each voxel. You could also examine multivariate differences across the whole brain by including all voxels in a multivoxel pattern classifier (Haxby et al., 2001; Norman et al., 2006). Or you can use searchlight analyses that look at local patterns within small cubes or spheres of voxels that is iteratively roved throughout the brain (Etzel et al., 2013; Kriegeskorte et al., 2006). However, the broad view offered by whole-brain analyses comes with challenges, because you must correct your statistical analyses for an enormous number of comparisons in order to avoid false positive results, which may instead lead to false negatives (i.e., missed effects).

Region of interest analyses. In contrast to whole brain analyses, many other fMRI studies are interested in specific brain regions, motivating region-of-interest (ROI) analyses. ROIs can be defined either structurally (based on brain anatomy) or functionally (based on fMRI responses). It is important to be cautious in how one selects an ROI to avoid double-dipping—that is, using the same data to define a ROI and test an effect (Kriegeskorte et al., 2009). There are four main ways in which ROIs are commonly defined.

First, anatomical ROIs are defined within participants, based on specific landmarks in the brain. This approach is especially common for subcortical anatomical structures like the hippocampus, because region boundaries can be easily labeled by a trained human eye (Insausti et al., 1998). These segmentations are traditionally conducted by hand on a high-resolution anatomical MRI of each participant, by a researcher drawing the outline of the ROI in each slice on their computer using a mouse or tablet pen. Recently, new computational tools have allowed for automatic segmentation of anatomical landmarks (e.g., Yushkevich et al., 2015). However, manual segmentation may be preferred when high accuracy is desired, or when looking at smaller or more noise-prone regions for which there exist fewer automatic tools.

Second, atlas-based ROIs are defined using standardized atlases or templates. Rather than using an individual participant's anatomical landmarks, atlas-based ROIs are defined from standard template brains that exist in a common space (e.g., MNI, Talairach). After coregistering a participant's MRI data with a standard template, atlas-based ROIs can be applied to the participant's fMRI data to examine activity. This approach is most common with larger anatomical structures which do not necessitate the precision of manual segmentation, such as the parahippocampal cortex. Atlas-based ROIs are relatively quick and easy to apply and are largely automated. However, they assume that participants will have relatively similar anatomy captured by this template, and so will not be as sensitive to subtle individual anatomical differences.

A third method for defining an ROI is using a probabilistic map (e.g., Julian et al., 2012). This method uses an external set of data from separate participants to determine the ROI. Rather than using anatomical landmarks or templates, these maps can be defined functionally. For example, a map could reflect voxels that activated across a majority of participants when they viewed a specific class of stimuli, such as faces (Coutanche et al., 2011). Probabilistic maps can also be derived from meta-analytic data sets of fMRI results such as NeuroSynth (https://neurosynth.org/; Yarkoni et al., 2011). These resources reveal which voxel coordinates are commonly reported in studies investigating a particular topic. Probabilistic maps are data-driven and require few anatomical assumptions. However, like atlas-based ROIs, probabilistic ROIs assume similar anatomical organization across individuals.

Finally, ROIs can be determined functionally within each individual participant. The first step to defining functional ROIs is localizing voxels in individual participants based on fMRI activity. Most commonly, participants will engage in separate localizer scans to identify the brain areas that respond to a certain type of stimuli. For example, visual experiments may have participants engage in a retinotopic localizer, where participants view flashing bars of different orientations and eccentricities that elicit strong responses from the visual cortex. Alternatively, experiments may have participants engage in a category-specific localizer, where participants view images belonging to different categories (e.g., faces, scenes, objects) that elicit strong responses in category-selective areas of the ventral temporal cortex. You can use the data from these localizer tasks to define voxels that are sensitive to specific contrasts, such as horizontal versus vertical bars to identify early visual cortex, or faces versus scenes to identify the fusiform face area (Kanwisher et al., 1997) and parahippocampal place area (Epstein & Kanwisher, 1998). Then, you can examine the responses of these functionally defined ROIs during separate task runs. An advantage of functional ROIs is that they adapt to the idiosyncrasies present in each person's brain and find the voxels with the strongest responses for the specific stimuli. However, functional localizers take time in the scanner, it may be challenging to localize a given region for everyone, and the definitions can require subjective decisions about which voxels to include.

Task-Based fMRI

When participants enter an MRI scanner, they often perform one or more psychological tasks so that experimenters can observe BOLD signal changes related to the task. In contrast to behavioral experiments conducted outside of a scanner, fMRI experiments need to be designed with the sluggish hemodynamic response in mind. There are three main types of task scans (Figure 29.4).

Slow event-related design. In slow event-related tasks, a single trial is presented each 8 to 20 seconds. In other words, there is sufficient time to account for the hemodynamic response to each trial. This allows you to more completely and separately measure the BOLD response for each trial, with relatively little interference from nearby trials. The advantage of this design is that it results in incredibly clear signal for each trial. However, this design limits the number of trials that can be presented and is relatively inefficient in terms of time. In addition, the long delay from trial to trial may cause participant boredom, fatigue, or disengagement.

Block design. In block design tasks, multiple trials of the same condition are presented in rapid succession within what is referred to as a "block." A delay of 4 to 8 seconds is introduced between different blocks. The goal is to measure a BOLD response for the condition of the block, not from individual trials within the block. One common example is showing blocks of face, scene, or object images to identify brain regions sensitive to each stimulus category. The advantage of this design is that it results in a robust signal, as multiple similar trials in succession generate a strong BOLD response. Also, block designs may be more engaging for participants as individual trials appear more rapidly (e.g., 1–2 seconds per stimulus). However, this design limits the ability to resolve information from a specific trial.

Rapid event-related design. In rapid event-related tasks, individual trials are presented more rapidly (every 2–5 seconds). Trials may belong to different conditions, randomly or pseudo-randomly ordered within each run, rather than blocked. There exist useful tools for pseudo-randomization, including Optseq (https://surfer.nmr.mgh.harvard.edu/optseq/; Dale, 1999). While the hemodynamic response is not able to return to baseline during this brief period of time, you can derive the condition-related response based on the sequence of conditions because, in general, the hemodynamic response to two consecutive trials combines linearly. Therefore, you will still be able to derive a signal that likely

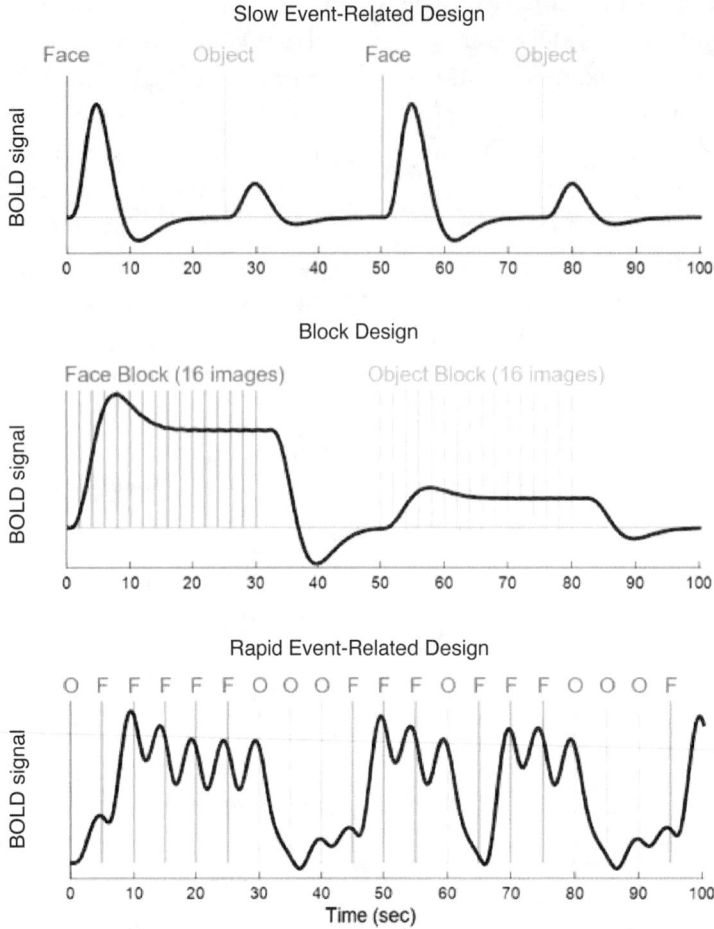

FIGURE 29.4. Given the slow hemodynamic response function, the experimenter can select different experimental design types based on a desire for clear signal versus a desire for high numbers of trials. Shown here are examples of how the blood oxygen-level-dependent (BOLD) signal would fluctuate in a face-selective voxel (with some signal to objects) during a slow event-related design, block design, and rapid event-related design of intermixed face and object stimuli.

relates to each condition, even though they are not sufficiently separated in time to independently measure the response of each trial. A key advantage is that rapid event-related designs are extremely efficient because runs can include many trials. In addition, it is the most engaging for participants because stimuli and conditions are constantly changing. However, this design will not yield the cleanest signal and is the most susceptible to noise.

Although experimental tasks are not limited to these three different experimental design types, these illustrate the difficult trade-off of wanting to maximize the SNR in the BOLD signal but also wanting to maximize the statistical power and the participant engagement with the experiment. In general, the design of an fMRI experiment requires a balancing of competing interests. You want accurate signal measurements for each trial (block designs, slow event-related designs), but you also want a time-efficient experiment with many trials per condition (rapid event-related designs). Functional MRI is also still a relatively limited resource; it is expensive, and researchers often have limited time with the scanner. Thus, the experimenter may be limited in the number of participants they can feasibly scan, as well as the number of trials they can have a single participant undergo. The norms of statistical power are continuously shifting in the field. About a decade ago, a common sample size for a single study was 12 to 16 participants. Now, a common sample size is 20 to 40 participants, but this is still understood to be less than ideal, and standards are continuing to increase over time. With significant government funding, some groups have begun collecting massive data sets from hundreds, thousands, and even tens and hundreds of thousands of participants and making these data open to other scientists. Other groups have begun collecting "deep" data sets that include many scan sessions from a few individuals. Your goal should be to maximize the statistical power by ensuring you collect the highest quality data and that each of your participants is continuously engaged in the task.

When designing the experiment, there are also some general decisions that you will need to make and other factors that you should keep in mind. It is important to ensure that your stimulus conditions differ *only* in your variable(s) of interest. Otherwise, confounding variables may emerge that can explain differences in fMRI activity. For example, stimulus factors such as object size (Bainbridge & Oliva, 2015) and how memorable a stimulus is (Bainbridge & Rissman, 2018) may explain some previous results. It is almost always useful to determine certain time periods that you will use as a baseline, during which participants will be performing no task at all. The BOLD signal is analyzed as a relative signal, calculated as a contrast between an experimental condition versus the baseline or as a contrast of two experimental conditions. You will also need to choose your response method—will participants press buttons, move a joystick, move their eyes, speak into a microphone, etc.? If participants make different responses to different trial types, it can be challenging to discern whether the brain responses reflect the processes of interest or the motor responses. In many cases, you can counterbalance the button responses across runs or across participants to help solve this problem. Alternatively, you can design the motor responses such that they do not correlate with the conditions of interest. Another common issue is if two conditions are preceded by separate instructions on the screen—will activity differences reflect the different conditions or the different visual features of the instructions? One solution is to introduce a random jitter (a random delay, 1–5 seconds) between the instructions and the trial. This helps ensure that the BOLD signal to the instructions will be separable from the trial. In addition, adding jitter between trials can make it easier to estimate the BOLD response to individual trials (e.g., Bainbridge et al., 2021).

Resting-State fMRI

Traditional fMRI studies follow a relatively stereotyped series of steps: researchers formulate a question, develop a task battery, collect and analyze data, share results in conference presentations and publications, and move on to the next study. Task development almost always requires multiple rounds of pilot testing to ensure that performance is satisfactory and that effects of interest are observed behaviorally in the target participant population. The process can take several months or more, especially for studies involving special participant populations and/or complex multimodal data collection techniques. It is increasingly popular, however, for experimenters to collect functional data while participants are not performing any task at all—that is, while they are simply resting in the scanner. During so-called resting-state scans, participants are typically instructed to lie still and relax. Although some studies *only* collect resting-state data, most studies that do collect rest data collect a combination of task and rest scans.

Our discussion so far has focused on relating BOLD signals to mental processes evoked by task manipulations and/or observed in behavior. So why do researchers collect data during rest, a cognitive state in which ongoing mental processes are unknown and unconstrained? Several factors have contributed to the popularity of resting-state fMRI. First and foremost, there is growing interest in research questions that can be answered with task-free data. For example, how does resting-state functional brain organization predict individual differences in cognitive abilities or behavior, vary as a function of clinical status, and change across the lifespan? Second, resting-state data are relatively easy to collect, compare across participant populations, and share across sites. Unlike task data, there is no need to program or pilot tasks, titrate task difficulty to different groups (e.g., children and adults; patients and controls) or control for potential performance differences between them, or harmonize task parameters and share timing information across labs. Finally, there is a growing expectation in the cognitive neuroscience community that fMRI data sets will be analyzed by multiple groups to answer multiple research questions (a form of "green science"; Rosenberg et al., 2018). Adding resting-state data to an fMRI study can increase its utility for answering a range of psychological and neuroscientific questions. For example, including rest runs in an fMRI study that was originally designed to measure emotion regulation could increase the utility of the data set for answering scientific questions unrelated to emotion. Funders, too, recognize resting-state data's flexibility and potential for providing relatively easy-to-collect brain-based biomarkers of disease and disorder. Three of today's most widely used publicly available big data fMRI samples include a significant amount of rest data: The Human Connectome Project ($N = 1,200$ younger adults; Barch et al., 2013), Adolescent Brain Cognitive Development Study ($N = 11,875$ children; Casey et al., 2018), and UK Biobank (planned $N = 100,000$ older adults; Miller et al., 2016). These big data collection efforts include 60, 20 and 6 minutes of resting-state data and 60, 33, and 4 minutes of task data, respectively.

Data collection. Just as with task data, there is no single, universal approach to collecting resting-state data, although the field is converging on some consensus recommendations. During resting-state runs, experimenters ask participants to either keep their eyes closed or open. Although eyes-closed rest is easier for participants because they can rest their eyes, it is not ideal for experimenters for that same reason: Participants can get *so* relaxed that they fall asleep, potentially increasing head motion and decreasing compliance for the rest of the scan session. A participant falling asleep can add extra time required to wake the participant, and also introduce extra preprocessing challenges as the head position may differ between runs collected before and after the reset. During eyes-open rest, the more common approach, participants are instructed to look at a fixation cross in the center of the screen. The fixation cross is preferably presented on a gray or black background as it can be uncomfortable to stare at a white or brightly colored screen. Compliance may be assessed with eye-tracking if a device is available. Eye-tracking data can be recorded for later analysis, or the camera may simply be turned on so the experimenter can monitor wakefulness during the scan. Before the scan starts, participants are also repeatedly and emphatically reminded to hold as still as possible because head motion is particularly problematic for resting-state data analyses. Careful attention to participant comfort and head padding at the start of the scan session can go a long way in reducing head motion. Mock-scanner training prior to scanning can help familiarize participants with the scan environment and reduce motion. Beyond information about keeping eyes open and remaining still, researchers typically keep instructions to a minimum. They may ask participants to relax, let their minds wander, and/or to not think of anything in particular. More detailed instructions are typically avoided to help make rest scans as natural and task-free as possible.

An important consideration when collecting resting-state data is how much data to collect. Although in the early days of resting-state data collection, studies often included a short 5-minute rest scan at the end of fMRI sessions, there is growing evidence that this is insufficient to provide reliable estimates of resting-state brain networks (Noble et al., 2019). Instead, as with task data, the more data the better, and recent studies include 20 minutes or more of rest data per individual. Placement of the resting-state scan(s) in the MRI session should also be carefully considered. Rest runs at or near the end of long sessions can suffer from increased head motion as participants grow tired or uncomfortable.

Collecting rest data after cognitive tasks may also lead to concerns that the rest data are influenced by the preceding task states (Tambini et al., 2010). Thus, it is preferable to collect rest data at or near the start of a scan session if possible.

Preprocessing. Some preprocessing steps differ between resting-state and task data. Data are often bandpass-filtered to retain signal fluctuations of interest in the range of approximately .01 to .1 Hz. Because head motion is of particular concern, high-motion frames (i.e., TRs or whole-brain volumes) are frequently censored, or scrubbed, from the time series. In addition, some resting-state preprocessing pipelines include global signal regression (GSR), in which the mean signal from the whole brain is included as a regressor of no interest. Work has shown that GSR helps minimize confounds associated with head motion (Ciric et al., 2017). However, its application is debated because it can result in "false positive" anticorrelations between activity time-courses in different brain regions (Murphy & Fox, 2017).

Data analysis. How can resting-state data be analyzed given that they lack task conditions required for the GLM analyses introduced earlier? A common approach is functional connectivity analysis, which measures the statistical dependence between the BOLD signal in spatially distinct brain regions. Studies investigating functional connectivity have characterized a number of large-scale brain networks, including the default-mode network and frontoparietal networks, made up of distributed sets of brain regions whose activity is correlated during tasks and at rest (Finn et al., 2015). Functional connectivity is related to—but not redundant with—structural brain connectivity measured with diffusion imaging (Honey et al., 2009).

Functional connectivity can be measured in many different ways. One common measure is temporal correlation. Regions whose activity time-courses are highly correlated are considered strongly functionally connected, whereas regions whose activity time-courses are out of sync are considered weakly functionally connected. A positive functional connection indicates that two regions' activity time-courses increase and decrease together, whereas a negative functional connection indicates that activity in one region increases when activity in the other decreases and vice versa (with the GSR-related caveat noted above). Static functional connectivity characterizes relationships between an entire BOLD signal time series, such as a whole run or scan session, while dynamic functional connectivity measures changing functional connections and/or networks over time within runs. Seed-based functional connectivity approaches relate the BOLD signal in a specific region of interest with all other regions (i.e., voxels or pre-defined ROIs) in the brain. Atlas-based approaches, also known as whole-brain functional connectivity, relate BOLD signal time-courses in all pairs of regions in a brain atlas. Brain atlases "parcellate" the brain into several hundred regions, or nodes, based on anatomical or functional boundaries. Common atlases include the Harvard-Oxford anatomical atlas (Makris et al., 2006) and the Yeo functional atlas (Yeo et al., 2011). Atlas selection should be based on a study's particular research question and participant population. A benefit of using a common, publicly available atlas is the ability to directly compare functional connectivity patterns and network organization across participants as well as across studies from different research groups. It is also theoretically possible to calculate whole-brain functional connectivity by relating the time-course of every voxel with every other voxel, although this is extremely computationally challenging and may be unnecessary in practice. Finally, data-driven approaches such as independent component analysis can be applied to resting-state data to decompose the BOLD signal into independent functional networks.

Naturalistic Task fMRI

Carefully designed psychological tasks effectively target specific mental processes, whereas the unconstrained resting state is useful for exploring functional brain organization in the absence of an explicit external task. If a goal of fMRI research is to understand the mind, however, it is interesting to consider the fact that we do not actually spend much of our daily lives performing constrained tasks or quietly staring at a blank screen. Can we use fMRI to study the mind as it operates in more naturalistic settings?

Naturalistic tasks, such as watching movies and listening to stories or music, have gained traction as a way to study cognitive, attentional, emotional, and social processes in complex environments. In a typical naturalistic task, participants are asked to watch or listen to a stimulus naturally. Stimuli can be auditory, visual, or both, and are most commonly selected from existing movies, television shows, podcasts, or online video clips. Examples include an excerpt from the film *The Good, The Bad, and The Ugly* (Hasson et al., 2004) and the first episode of the BBC television show *Sherlock* (Chen et al., 2017). There are also examples of naturalistic stimuli special-made for fMRI studies, such an audio-narrated story written to evoke varying degrees of suspicion from different participants (Finn et al., 2018) and an abstract, narrative-free animated short film without scene cuts designed to reduce head motion in developmental fMRI studies (*Inscapes*; Vanderwal et al., 2015). Naturalistic task runs may last longer than typical controlled task or rest runs, as stimuli may be more subjectively engaging and mid-stimulus run breaks may disrupt narratives. Researchers may collect concurrent eye-tracking or physiological data to measure attention and arousal. Naturalistic tasks may also encompass participant-generated naturalistic behavior, like describing memories verbally. They can also be interactive, game-like tasks that require participant input during the stimulus, such as ratings of engagement, or choices to influence the story. As when designing a controlled task, it is important to consider your primary research questions when selecting a naturalistic stimulus. Is it important that the stimulus contains a narrative? Social or emotional content? Information that will be interpreted in the same or different ways across individuals?

Data analysis. Unlike participants in most controlled psychological tasks, participants in naturalistic tasks are perceiving the same input at the same time. Although researchers typically randomize stimulus orders and task conditions to avoid potential confounds associated with order and time-on-task, intersubject correlation (ISC) analyses take advantage of this unique feature of naturalistic tasks to ask how participants' brain activity is synchronized by the stimulus. Temporal ISC measures the correlation between different participants' BOLD signal time series in the same brain region. Higher ISC indicates that activity in that brain region is stimulus-driven and consistent across individuals (Nastase et al., 2019). Temporal ISC can be measured by correlating time series between pairs of participants or by correlating one participant's time series with the mean time-series of the rest of the sample. It can be performed at the voxel level (which is computationally intensive and sensitive to spatial alignment across individuals) or the node level (which is less computationally intensive and sensitive to spatial alignment but also less spatially precise). Temporal ISC has revealed, for example, that different brain regions are sensitive to information at different time scales. Whereas primary auditory cortex is sensitive to high-frequency auditory signals—responding reliably across individuals to a story played in both the forward and reverse directions—association cortices including frontal and parietal regions are sensitive to higher level narrative content, responding reliably across individuals to intact stories but not stories whose paragraphs were presented out of order (Hasson et al., 2015).

Other forms of ISC are also commonly applied to naturalistic task data. Like dynamic functional connectivity, dynamic ISC characterizes relationships between subsets of a time series. In particular, dynamic ISC asks how across-participant synchrony varies during a naturalistic stimulus. Dynamic ISC analyses have shown that ISC is higher during more engaging moments of movies and stories (Song et al., 2021). Spatial ISC asks how voxel-wise patterns of activity are similar across individuals at particular moments of time (Chen et al., 2017; Koch et al., 2020). Intersubject functional correlation (sometimes called intersubject functional connectivity) relates the time series of one brain region from one participant to the time series of all other brain regions from other participants and can be used to map stimulus-driven functional brain networks. Intersubject representational similarity analysis asks whether individuals who are more similar in terms of a behavior of interest—such as their interpretation of an ambiguous narrative—show more synchronous patterns of fMRI responses (Finn et al., 2020). Finally, intrasubject correlation analyses measure relationships between activity in the same person's brain over repeated exposures to a naturalistic stimulus or between two related naturalistic task conditions. For example, researchers used intrasubject correlation to discover that individuals show similar patterns of brain activity when watching a television show and later recalling the same episode (Chen et al., 2017). These and other analytic techniques have begun allowing fMRI researchers to analyze data collected during complex, uncontrolled naturalistic tasks and begin characterizing the mind "in the wild."

Real-Time fMRI

Most fMRI studies involve designing the experiment, collecting the data, and then analyzing the data after the fact. On the other hand, there are many research groups that are pushing the boundaries on how rapidly we can process and return feedback on fMRI data (Stoeckel et al., 2014; Sulzer et al., 2013; Watanabe et al., 2017). These real-time fMRI studies describe an entire range of studies in which experimenters reveal BOLD activity to the human participants (e.g., providing a readout of a particular ROI) or leverage BOLD activity to directly manipulate tasks. These studies allow experimenters to engage dynamically with ongoing brain activity and patterns.

Real-time fMRI data analysis.
Real-time fMRI encompasses many, if not most, forms of fMRI analysis. However, the critical difference is that all preprocessing and data analysis must occur during the experiment in under a few seconds, rather than in the days, weeks, months, or even years after data collection. This may involve selecting a subset of the preprocessing steps that are absolutely necessary for the goals of the study. An increasing number of fMRI packages support real-time fMRI analysis (including AFNI, Turbo-BrainVoyager and BrainIAK); however, the analysis pipeline may still require extensive customization depending on the goals of your study. After minimally preprocessing the data (e.g., temporal filtering, spatial smoothing), you can use univariate or multivariate analyses to analyze the data. For example, you could examine the univariate BOLD signal in an anatomical or functional ROI (deCharms et al., 2005), analyze the BOLD signal patterns across an ROI using multivariate analyses (LaConte, 2011), or analyze functional connectivity between multiple brain regions in real time (Ramot et al., 2017; Scheinost et al., 2020). These techniques require extensive planning ahead of time, which can be challenging, but is also an important way to effectively "preregister" your hypotheses.

Types of feedback.
After analyzing fMRI data in real time, it is then necessary to decide what to do with this information. There are a wide range of ways of providing neurofeedback or leveraging real-time fMRI data analysis for the goals of your study. You could use the real-time data analysis to provide simple motion feedback, to encourage participants to stay still. Or you could use real-time data analysis to provide a window into the activity of a particular brain region (e.g., early visual cortex), and encourage participants to regulate the activity or patterns of activity within this ROI (Shibata et al., 2011). Finally, monitoring fMRI data in real time can be used to modify the experiment, either adaptively updating the task difficulty (deBettencourt et al., 2015, 2019) or triggering stimulus onsets contingent to brain activity (Chew et al., 2019). In sum, real-time fMRI encompasses a wide range of research that can powerfully link brain patterns with behavior and explore cognitive plasticity.

Considerations for fMRI Analyses

fMRI data are a form of noisy, temporally correlated big data shaped by multiple experimenter decisions. Thus, there are many common pitfalls when analyzing such complex data.

Even when answering a singular question, fMRI analyses often necessitate multiple experimental tests, across multiple ROIs, networks, searchlights, or voxels. Because of these multiple tests, the false positive rate becomes greatly inflated. Consider the alpha level of 0.05 generally accepted in the field at the current moment. A p value of 0.05 essentially means that there is only a 5% probability that we would have observed an effect this extreme by chance. This is not a bad probability for a single test, but in fMRI, we may conduct statistical tests in each of the approximately 100,000+ voxels in the brain. Just by chance, 5,000 voxels would show a significant effect by this threshold. Thus, in order to account for the high number of statistical tests performed with fMRI data, we must perform multiple comparisons correction on our data. The most stringent method is Bonferroni correction, which divides the acceptable alpha-level by the number of tests conducted. However, this is extremely stringent; for a whole brain analysis with 100,000 voxels, the corresponding threshold would be $p < 10^{-7}$! A more common and less conservative method is false discovery rate correction, which controls for the false positive rate only within the voxels that claim an effect (resulting in a corrected q value). Also common is cluster-threshold correction, which leverages the spatial dependencies present in fMRI data. Essentially, if many adjacent voxels show an effect, this is more likely to be a true effect (versus if the effect is only observed in a single voxel in isolation). Cluster-threshold correction will calculate a minimum cluster size required for an effect to be considered significant.

Functional MRI analyses are also extremely complicated, which can lead you to running (and re-running) many similar analyses. Thus, one easy pitfall in this scenario is double-dipping. As described earlier, double-dipping refers to using data to localize an effect and then using the same data to test the reliability of the effect (Kriegeskorte et al., 2009). This will drastically artificially inflate your effect of interest, which is why it is important to identify ROIs using *independent* localizers that use different stimuli and occur on different runs. Functional MRI data also have high temporal autocorrelations—the signal on two consecutive trials is more likely to be similar than the signal on two different runs. This is due to a combination of the slow timecourse of the BOLD signal, changes in participant engagement and movement over time, and scanner drift over time. Thus, it is also important to ensure any effects that you observe are distinct from scan time. For example, you could use odd-numbered runs to identify an effect, and then test that the effect replicates using even-numbered runs. Splitting the data in this way is more appropriate than looking at the first half versus the last half of runs within each scan.

FUNCTIONAL NEAR-INFRARED SPECTROSCOPY

fNIRS (Figure 29.1) is a noninvasive neuroimaging technique that uses near-infrared light (650–950 nm) to measure changes in blood oxygen concentration (Pinti et al., 2020). Like fMRI, fNIRS measures blood oxygenation as a proxy for neural activity and thus is also sensitive to the hemodynamic response. Data are collected on the scalp using optodes, or sources that emit near-infrared light and detectors that measure the reflected (or backscattered) light that travels an elliptical path from the source. Sources and detectors are typically spaced about 2 to 4 cm apart. To reach a detector, light must travel through the skull, scalp, cerebrospinal fluid, and brain tissue. In the process, it is attenuated due to scatter and absorption. Whereas skin, bone, and brain tissue do not absorb much near-infrared light, oxygenated hemoglobin (oxy-Hb or HbO_2) and deoxygenated hemoglobin (deoxy-Hb or HbR) in the blood absorb different wavelengths of light in the near-infrared range. Therefore, changes in the relative concentration of oxygenated and deoxygenated hemoglobin affect—and can be estimated from—the degree of light attenuation between source and detector. Like fMRI, fNIRS detects relative changes in blood oxygenation but does not provide a measure of absolute baseline concentrations of oxygenated and deoxygenated hemoglobin.

fNIRS offers a number of advantages over fMRI. It is easier to collect, as data collection is performed with a NIRS cap rather than an MRI scanner and does not require volunteers to lie down or remain perfectly still. Like an EEG cap, the NIRS cap can be worn in a lab setting as volunteers perform cognitive or naturalistic tasks or rest at a computer screen. NIRS systems can also be portable, meaning that data can be collected as participants engage in real-world behaviors like exploring an environment or interacting with other people. NIRS is also less expensive than MRI, with systems costing between tens and hundreds of thousands of dollars compared with millions of dollars for MRI systems. Finally, while MRI has safety risks with any ferromagnetic metallic objects, NIRS does not have these safety risks, allowing it to be used with individuals with metallic implants. These advantages make fNIRS particularly well suited for studying many different participant populations, including infants, young children, and patients. Work using fNIRS has revealed, for example, that infants use adult-like top-down feedback neural strategies to modulate sensory information during learning (Emberson et al., 2015).

When considering the appropriate neuroimaging modality to use to answer a particular research question, it is important to keep in mind some limitations of fNIRS. First, fNIRS can be used to study hemodynamic signals near the brain's outer surface, but not those in deeper brain structures. This is because light emitted from a source only travels a short distance—about half the distance between the source and detector—into the brain before reaching a detector. Increasing the source-detector separation allows light to travel further into the brain before being registered. However, this also results in less light reaching the detector in the first place and thus a relatively low SNR (Pinti et al., 2020). One way to mitigate this issue is to pair short-separation and long-separation channels by placing one detector very close to a source (on the order of millimeters) and one detector farther away (on the order of centimeters). The light that travels from the source to the *closer* detector will only penetrate the skull and thus its attenuation will reflect non-neuronal signal. The light that reaches the *farther* detector, on the other hand, will travel through brain tissue and thus will reflect both neuronal and non-neuronal signal. Subtracting the short channel signal from the long channel signal can serve as a form of denoising to increase SNR (Brigadoi & Cooper, 2015; Gagnon et al., 2014). Another drawback of fNIRS compared with fMRI is its lower spatial resolution and lack of information about anatomical structures. Recognizing the pros and cons of each modality, ongoing work compares fNIRS and fMRI data collected at different times—as well as simultaneously—to inform our understanding of relationships between cognitive processes, neural activity, and hemodynamic responses (Scarapicchia et al., 2017).

POSITRON EMISSION TOMOGRAPHY

PET (Figure 29.1) is another imaging technique that measures brain function, though unlike the other techniques we have mentioned, it is minimally invasive. It measures brain function by measuring the presence of radioactive isotopes that rapidly decay. First, participants are injected with safe levels of radioactive isotopes (e.g., ^{15}O), and then they are asked to perform different tasks. The PET scan localizes where in the brain the radioactive isotopes end up during each task by comparing different conditions. This provides a measure of blood flow to different regions within the brain, which is used as an indirect measure of neural activity. In that way, this technique is similar to fMRI which also measures blood flow within the brain. However, PET has an even poorer temporal resolution than fMRI. PET data requires similar preprocessing to fMRI, in that it needs to be transformed to a standard brain template. Unlike fMRI, you may need to normalize for global flow rate differences. Generally, you can examine findings at each location (pixel/voxel) using the procedures for whole brain analyses. Since fMRI has grown in popularity, there have been fewer studies using PET. However, PET may still provide certain benefits, for example, it may be specifically beneficial for measuring brain metabolism in patient populations (e.g., for identifying β-amyloid plaques, a biomarker of Alzheimer's disease) or for measuring specific neurotransmitters or receptors (e.g., dopamine D1 and D2 receptors).

Prior to the advent of fMRI, PET provided a window into the brain activity of healthy human participants. Many seminal findings in PET were later replicated using fMRI. For example, PET provided some of the first evidence of the default mode network, by demonstrating that certain brain areas were more active during rest (Raichle et al., 2001). In addition, PET was used to reveal the neural underpinnings of spatial working memory (Jonides et al., 1993) and dissociate different subcomponents of working memory (Courtney et al., 1996).

A key initial advantage of PET is the ability to measure brain function in action deep within the brain. Researchers also claim it may be less sensitive to small movements than fMRI. However, there are many drawbacks of PET that may contribute to the fact that it is relatively rare these days. First, PET is invasive in that it requires injecting radioactive tracers into human participants. This approach limits the participant pool, as participants may not be able to repeatedly participate in studies. In addition, this reliance on radioactive tracers makes the temporal resolution extremely limited, even more so than the hemodynamic response function of fMRI. In addition, PET is relatively expensive and may be cost prohibitive for certain research.

Every couple of decades there are new techniques that revolutionize the field of functional neuroimaging. These techniques will build upon advances from the past, from PET, fMRI, and fNIRS. It is exciting to consider how future technologies will enable researchers to directly and noninvasively measure neural activity with spatial and temporal precision.

COMMON PITFALLS IN NEUROIMAGING ANALYSIS

These neuroimaging methods of fMRI, fNIRS, and PET share some important considerations when designing experiments and analyzing data. Traditionally, a large portion of psychology studies have been hypothesis-driven, in that an experiment is designed to test a specific question, often culminating in a small number of statistical comparisons (or even just one!) defined a priori (i.e., in advance) to test the existence of an effect related to this question. Some neuroimaging studies may differ from this traditional pipeline. Neuroimaging studies may be data-driven, asking where in the brain an effect may be found, or what information may be decoded for a given area. These studies may rely on several post-hoc (i.e., after the fact) analyses, decided upon once specific patterns are identified in the brain. Both hypothesis-driven and data-driven research are essential to science; the former can isolate and test specific questions, while the latter can help generate new questions. However, when conducting a more exploratory or data-driven experiment, it is important to be cautious about the sorts of statistical tests that we perform, and the inferences that we make.

Another common error that many neuroimaging researchers may make is reverse inference (Poldrack, 2011). Many studies will culminate in a map of brain activity as a final result. We are often tempted to make strong inferences about the underlying cognitive processes based on where we see activation; for example, if we see activity in the amygdala, we may hypothesize that the task engaged emotional processing. This is called reverse inference because we are inferring the underlying process from the result (using the result to lead to the mechanism), rather than perturbing a specific process to see how it influences brain activity (using a mechanism to lead to the result). Generally, a specific region of the brain will be responsible for multiple cognitive processes. We should be cautious when interpreting activity in brain regions outside our tested questions or hypotheses and be clear when some ideas are strongly indicated by the data versus when they suggest interesting hypotheses for future research.

Ensuring Robust, Reproducible Results

With all functional neuroimaging methods, it is critical to ensure that your results are robust and reproducible. This helps reduce the likelihood of bugs in complicated analyses and avoid these common pitfalls. You can facilitate reproducibility by sharing your data and code on open-data websites such as the Open Science Framework (https://osf.io/) or OpenNeuro (https://openneuro.org/) and ensuring it is in a legible format to share with your colleagues, collaborators, and the broader field. There have been ongoing efforts to standardize how we organize data, for example the Brain Imaging Data Structure (BIDS) format. These efforts help ensure that all of the many files (e.g., different functional and anatomical scans, different GLM analyses, different behavioral files) are similarly organized across people, labs, and institutions. This is also helpful to democratize functional neuroimaging research, to allow multiple researchers access to valuable and expensive data that has already been collected. There are numerous open data repositories that you can explore and use to analyze data from thousands of participants, even before you start on the ambitious path of collecting your own data (Poldrack & Gorgolewski, 2014). For example, the Human Connectome Project (HCP; Van Essen et al., 2013) includes fMRI data from hundreds of adults. In addition, the Adolescent Brain Cognitive Development (ABCD) Study will eventually include fMRI data from thousands of children scanned over ten years (Casey et al., 2018). Other data repositories include data from dozens or hundreds of scan sessions from a small number of individuals (e.g., Poldrack et al., 2015). It is important to keep in mind ethical considerations as you analyze, and also as you eventually share your data with the wider scientific world. For example, it is important to deidentify shared data by removing any personally identifying information (name, birthdate) and removing facial information from the brain scans (e.g., by including skull-stripping as a step during your preprocessing).

CONCLUSION

Functional neuroimaging encompasses multiple powerful techniques that enable researchers to peer into the human brain. As you embark on using fMRI, fNIRS, and PET, there are numerous important considerations about how to collect, analyze, and interpret your results. It is important to consider your goals as well as the nature of these signals while you are designing an experiment and deciding on data acquisition. It is also critical to collect high-quality data, to take care to minimize artifacts, and to process the data in line with state-of-the-art recommendations. There are also many sophisticated ways to analyze these high-dimensional data, including with general linear models that take into account the underlying nature of the hemodynamic response as well as functional connectivity analyses that capture complex dependencies in networks across the brain. We are also exploring more naturalistic tasks that can provide a powerful bridge between highly controlled psychological tasks and the real world. Finally, we have developed sophisticated tools to engage with brain dynamics as they occur and provide neurofeedback based on real-time brain activity. For all of these approaches and techniques, it is important to keep in mind common pitfalls and to prioritize conducting replicable, reproducible science. We hope to have provided you a comprehensive overview of functional neuroimaging, that can help you as you embark on your own studies. From three neuroimaging researchers to another, bon voyage!

References

Bainbridge, W. A., Hall, E. H., & Baker, C. I. (2021). Distinct representational structure and localization for visual encoding and recall during visual imagery. *Cerebral Cortex*, 31(4), 1898–1913. https://doi.org/10.1093/cercor/bhaa329

Bainbridge, W. A., & Oliva, A. (2015). Interaction envelope: Local spatial representations of objects at all scales in scene-selective regions. *NeuroImage*, 122, 408–416. https://doi.org/10.1016/j.neuroimage.2015.07.066

Bainbridge, W. A., & Rissman, J. (2018). Dissociating neural markers of stimulus memorability and subjective recognition during episodic retrieval. *Scientific Reports*, 8(1), 8679. https://doi.org/10.1038/s41598-018-26467-5

Barch, D. M., Burgess, G. C., Harms, M. P., Petersen, S. E., Schlaggar, B. L., Corbetta, M., Glasser, M. F., Curtiss, S., Dixit, S., Feldt, C., Nolan, D.,

Bryant, E., Hartley, T., Footer, O., Bjork, J. M., Poldrack, R., Smith, S., Johansen-Berg, H., Snyder, A. Z., Van Essen, D. C., & the WU-Minn HCP Consortium. (2013). Function in the human connectome: Task-fMRI and individual differences in behavior. *NeuroImage*, *80*, 169–189. https://doi.org/10.1016/j.neuroimage.2013.05.033

Brigadoi, S., & Cooper, R. J. (2015). How short is short? Optimum source-detector distance for short-separation channels in functional near-infrared spectroscopy. *Neurophotonics*, *2*(2), 025005. https://doi.org/10.1117/1.NPh.2.2.025005

Casey, B. J., Cannonier, T., Conley, M. I., Cohen, A. O., Barch, D. M., Heitzeg, M. M., Soules, M. E., Teslovich, T., Dellarco, D. V., Garavan, H., Orr, C. A., Wager, T. D., Banich, M. T., Speer, N. K., Sutherland, M. T., Riedel, M. C., Dick, A. S., Bjork, J. M., Thomas, K. M., . . . the ABCD Imaging Acquisition Workgroup. (2018). The Adolescent Brain Cognitive Development (ABCD) study: Imaging acquisition across 21 sites. *Developmental Cognitive Neuroscience*, *32*, 43–54. https://doi.org/10.1016/j.dcn.2018.03.001

Chen, J., Leong, Y. C., Honey, C. J., Yong, C. H., Norman, K. A., & Hasson, U. (2017). Shared memories reveal shared structure in neural activity across individuals. *Nature Neuroscience*, *20*(1), 115–125. https://doi.org/10.1038/nn.4450

Chew, B., Hauser, T. U., Papoutsi, M., Magerkurth, J., Dolan, R. J., & Rutledge, R. B. (2019). Endogenous fluctuations in the dopaminergic midbrain drive behavioral choice variability. *Proceedings of the National Academy of Sciences of the United States of America*, *116*(37), 18732–18737. https://doi.org/10.1073/pnas.1900872116

Ciric, R., Wolf, D. H., Power, J. D., Roalf, D. R., Baum, G. L., Ruparel, K., Shinohara, R. T., Elliott, M. A., Eickhoff, S. B., Davatzikos, C., Gur, R. C., Gur, R. E., Bassett, D. S., & Satterthwaite, T. D. (2017). Benchmarking of participant-level confound regression strategies for the control of motion artifact in studies of functional connectivity. *NeuroImage*, *154*, 174–187. https://doi.org/10.1016/j.neuroimage.2017.03.020

Courtney, S. M., Ungerleider, L. G., Keil, K., & Haxby, J. V. (1996). Object and spatial visual working memory activate separate neural systems in human cortex. *Cerebral Cortex*, *6*(1), 39–49. https://doi.org/10.1093/cercor/6.1.39

Coutanche, M. N., Thompson-Schill, S. L., & Schultz, R. T. (2011). Multi-voxel pattern analysis of fMRI data predicts clinical symptom severity. *NeuroImage*, *57*(1), 113–123. https://doi.org/10.1016/j.neuroimage.2011.04.016

Cox, R. W. (1996). AFNI: Software for analysis and visualization of functional magnetic resonance neuroimages. *Computers and Biomedical Research*, *29*(3), 162–173. https://doi.org/10.1006/cbmr.1996.0014

Dale, A. M. (1999). Optimal experimental design for event-related fMRI. *Human Brain Mapping*, *8*(2-3), 109–114. https://doi.org/10.1002/(SICI)1097-0193(1999)8:2/3<109::AID-HBM7>3.0.CO;2-W

deBettencourt, M. T., Cohen, J. D., Lee, R. F., Norman, K. A., & Turk-Browne, N. B. (2015). Closed-loop training of attention with real-time brain imaging. *Nature Neuroscience*, *18*(3), 470–475. https://doi.org/10.1038/nn.3940

deBettencourt, M. T., Turk-Browne, N. B., & Norman, K. A. (2019). Neurofeedback helps to reveal a relationship between context reinstatement and memory retrieval. *NeuroImage*, *200*, 292–301. https://doi.org/10.1016/j.neuroimage.2019.06.001

deCharms, R. C., Maeda, F., Glover, G. H., Ludlow, D., Pauly, J. M., Soneji, D., Gabrieli, J. D. E., & Mackey, S. C. (2005). Control over brain activation and pain learned by using real-time functional MRI. *Proceedings of the National Academy of Sciences of the United States of America*, *102*(51), 18626–18631. https://doi.org/10.1073/pnas.0505210102

Emberson, L. L., Richards, J. E., & Aslin, R. N. (2015). Top-down modulation in the infant brain: Learning-induced expectations rapidly affect the sensory cortex at 6 months. *Proceedings of the National Academy of Sciences of the United States of America*, *112*(31), 9585–9590. https://doi.org/10.1073/pnas.1510343112

Epstein, R., & Kanwisher, N. (1998). A cortical representation of the local visual environment. *Nature*, *392*(6676), 598–601. https://doi.org/10.1038/33402

Esteban, O., Markiewicz, C. J., Blair, R. W., Moodie, C. A., Isik, A. I., Erramuzpe, A., Kent, J. D., Goncalves, M., DuPre, E., Snyder, M., Oya, H., Ghosh, S. S., Wright, J., Durnez, J., Poldrack, R. A., & Gorgolewski, K. J. (2019). fMRIPrep: A robust preprocessing pipeline for functional MRI. *Nature Methods*, *16*(1), 111–116. https://doi.org/10.1038/s41592-018-0235-4

Etzel, J. A., Zacks, J. M., & Braver, T. S. (2013). Searchlight analysis: Promise, pitfalls, and potential. *NeuroImage*, *78*, 261–269. https://doi.org/10.1016/j.neuroimage.2013.03.041

Finn, E. S., Corlett, P. R., Chen, G., Bandettini, P. A., & Constable, R. T. (2018). Trait paranoia shapes inter-subject synchrony in brain activity during an ambiguous social narrative. *Nature Communications*, *9*(1), 2043. https://doi.org/10.1038/s41467-018-04387-2

Finn, E. S., Glerean, E., Khojandi, A. Y., Nielson, D., Molfese, P. J., Handwerker, D. A., & Bandettini, P. A. (2020). Idiosynchrony: From shared responses to individual differences during naturalistic neuroimaging. *NeuroImage, 215*, 116828. https://doi.org/10.1016/j.neuroimage.2020.116828

Finn, E. S., Shen, X., Scheinost, D., Rosenberg, M. D., Huang, J., Chun, M. M., Papademetris, X., & Constable, R. T. (2015). Functional connectome fingerprinting: Identifying individuals using patterns of brain connectivity. *Nature Neuroscience, 18*(11), 1664–1671. https://doi.org/10.1038/nn.4135

Fischl, B. (2012). FreeSurfer. *NeuroImage, 62*(2), 774–781. https://doi.org/10.1016/j.neuroimage.2012.01.021

Frey, M., Nau, M., & Doeller, C. F. (2021). Magnetic resonance-based eye tracking using deep neural networks. *Nature Neuroscience, 24*, 1772–1778. https://doi.org/10.1038/s41593-021-00947-w

Gagnon, L., Yücel, M. A., Boas, D. A., & Cooper, R. J. (2014). Further improvement in reducing superficial contamination in NIRS using double short separation measurements. *NeuroImage, 85*(Pt. 1), 127–135. https://doi.org/10.1016/j.neuroimage.2013.01.073

Goebel, R. (2012). BrainVoyager—Past, present, future. *NeuroImage, 62*(2), 748–756. https://doi.org/10.1016/j.neuroimage.2012.01.083

Gorgolewski, K., Burns, C. D., Madison, C., Clark, D., Halchenko, Y. O., Waskom, M. L., & Ghosh, S. S. (2011). Nipype: A flexible, lightweight and extensible neuroimaging data processing framework in python. *Frontiers in Neuroinformatics, 5*, 13. https://doi.org/10.3389/fninf.2011.00013

Hasson, U., Chen, J., & Honey, C. J. (2015). Hierarchical process memory: Memory as an integral component of information processing. *Trends in Cognitive Sciences, 19*(6), 304–313. https://doi.org/10.1016/j.tics.2015.04.006

Hasson, U., Nir, Y., Levy, I., Fuhrmann, G., & Malach, R. (2004). Intersubject synchronization of cortical activity during natural vision. *Science, 303*(5664), 1634–1640. https://doi.org/10.1126/science.1089506

Haxby, J. V., Gobbini, M. I., Furey, M. L., Ishai, A., Schouten, J. L., & Pietrini, P. (2001). Distributed and overlapping representations of faces and objects in ventral temporal cortex. *Science, 293*(5539), 2425–2430. https://doi.org/10.1126/science.1063736

Honey, C. J., Sporns, O., Cammoun, L., Gigandet, X., Thiran, J. P., Meuli, R., & Hagmann, P. (2009). Predicting human resting-state functional connectivity from structural connectivity. *Proceedings of the National Academy of Sciences of the United States of America, 106*(6), 2035–2040. https://doi.org/10.1073/pnas.0811168106

Insausti, R., Juottonen, K., Soininen, H., Insausti, A. M., Partanen, K., Vainio, P., Laakso, M. P., & Pitkänen, A. (1998). MR volumetric analysis of the human entorhinal, perirhinal, and temporopolar cortices. *AJNR American Journal of Neuroradiology, 19*(4), 659–671.

Jenkinson, M., Beckmann, C. F., Behrens, T. E. J., Woolrich, M. W., & Smith, S. M. (2012). FSL. *NeuroImage, 62*(2), 782–790. https://doi.org/10.1016/j.neuroimage.2011.09.015

Jo, H. J., Lee, J.-M., Kim, J.-H., Shin, Y.-W., Kim, I.-Y., Kwon, J. S., & Kim, S. I. (2007). Spatial accuracy of fMRI activation influenced by volume- and surface-based spatial smoothing techniques. *NeuroImage, 34*(2), 550–564. https://doi.org/10.1016/j.neuroimage.2006.09.047

Jolly, E., Sadhukha, S., & Chang, L. J. (2020). Custom-molded headcases have limited efficacy in reducing head motion during naturalistic fMRI experiments. *NeuroImage, 222*, 117207. https://doi.org/10.1016/j.neuroimage.2020.117207

Jonides, J., Smith, E. E., Koeppe, R. A., Awh, E., Minoshima, S., & Mintun, M. A. (1993). Spatial working memory in humans as revealed by PET. *Nature, 363*(6430), 623–625. https://doi.org/10.1038/363623a0

Julian, J. B., Fedorenko, E., Webster, J., & Kanwisher, N. (2012). An algorithmic method for functionally defining regions of interest in the ventral visual pathway. *NeuroImage, 60*(4), 2357–2364. https://doi.org/10.1016/j.neuroimage.2012.02.055

Kanwisher, N., McDermott, J., & Chun, M. M. (1997). The fusiform face area: A module in human extrastriate cortex specialized for face perception. *Journal of Neuroscience, 17*(11), 4302–4311. https://doi.org/10.1523/JNEUROSCI.17-11-04302.1997

Koch, G. E., Paulus, J. P., & Coutanche, M. N. (2020). Neural patterns are more similar across individuals during successful memory encoding than during failed memory encoding. *Cerebral Cortex, 30*(7), 3872–3883. https://doi.org/10.1093/cercor/bhaa003

Kriegeskorte, N., Goebel, R., & Bandettini, P. (2006). Information-based functional brain mapping. *Proceedings of the National Academy of Sciences of the United States of America, 103*(10), 3863–3868. https://doi.org/10.1073/pnas.0600244103

Kriegeskorte, N., Simmons, W. K., Bellgowan, P. S. F., & Baker, C. I. (2009). Circular analysis in systems neuroscience: The dangers of double dipping. *Nature Neuroscience, 12*(5), 535–540. https://doi.org/10.1038/nn.2303

LaConte, S. M. (2011). Decoding fMRI brain states in real-time. *NeuroImage, 56*(2), 440–454. https://doi.org/10.1016/j.neuroimage.2010.06.052

Lancaster, J. L., Woldorff, M. G., Parsons, L. M., Liotti, M., Freitas, C. S., Rainey, L., Kochunov, P. V., Nickerson, D., Mikiten, S. A., & Fox, P. T.

(2000). Automated Talairach atlas labels for functional brain mapping. *Human Brain Mapping*, *10*(3), 120–131. https://doi.org/10.1002/1097-0193(200007)10:3<120::AID-HBM30>3.0.CO;2-8

Liu, Z.-X., Shen, K., Olsen, R. K., & Ryan, J. D. (2017). Visual sampling predicts hippocampal activity. *The Journal of Neuroscience*, *37*(3), 599–609. https://doi.org/10.1523/JNEUROSCI.2610-16.2016

Makris, N., Goldstein, J. M., Kennedy, D., Hodge, S. M., Caviness, V. S., Faraone, S. V., Tsuang, M. T., & Seidman, L. J. (2006). Decreased volume of left and total anterior insular lobule in schizophrenia. *Schizophrenia Research*, *83*(2-3), 155–171. https://doi.org/10.1016/j.schres.2005.11.020

McGill Centre for Integrative Neuroscience. (n.d.). *Atlases*. https://mcin.ca/research/neuroimaging-methods/atlases/

Miller, K. L., Alfaro-Almagro, F., Bangerter, N. K., Thomas, D. L., Yacoub, E., Xu, J., Bartsch, A. J., Jbabdi, S., Sotiropoulos, S. N., Andersson, J. L. R., Griffanti, L., Douaud, G., Okell, T. W., Weale, P., Dragonu, I., Garratt, S., Hudson, S., Collins, R., Jenkinson, M., . . . Smith, S. M. (2016). Multimodal population brain imaging in the UK Biobank prospective epidemiological study. *Nature Neuroscience*, *19*(11), 1523–1536. https://doi.org/10.1038/nn.4393

Murphy, K., & Fox, M. D. (2017). Towards a consensus regarding global signal regression for resting state functional connectivity MRI. *NeuroImage*, *154*, 169–173. https://doi.org/10.1016/j.neuroimage.2016.11.052

Nastase, S. A., Gazzola, V., Hasson, U., & Keysers, C. (2019). Measuring shared responses across subjects using intersubject correlation. *Social Cognitive and Affective Neuroscience*, *14*(6), 667–685. https://doi.org/10.1093/scan/nsz037

Noble, S., Scheinost, D., & Constable, R. T. (2019). A decade of test-retest reliability of functional connectivity: A systematic review and meta-analysis. *NeuroImage*, *203*, 116157. https://doi.org/10.1016/j.neuroimage.2019.116157

Norman, K. A., Polyn, S. M., Detre, G. J., & Haxby, J. V. (2006). Beyond mind-reading: Multi-voxel pattern analysis of fMRI data. *Trends in Cognitive Sciences*, *10*(9), 424–430. https://doi.org/10.1016/j.tics.2006.07.005

Penny, W. D., Friston, K. J., Ashburner, J. T., Kiebel, S. J., & Nichols, T. E. (2011). *Statistical parametric mapping: The analysis of functional brain images*. Elsevier.

Pinti, P., Tachtsidis, I., Hamilton, A., Hirsch, J., Aichelburg, C., Gilbert, S., & Burgess, P. W. (2020). The present and future use of functional near-infrared spectroscopy (fNIRS) for cognitive neuroscience. *Annals of the New York Academy of Sciences*, *1464*(1), 5–29. https://doi.org/10.1111/nyas.13948

Poldrack, R. A. (2011). Inferring mental states from neuroimaging data: From reverse inference to large-scale decoding. *Neuron*, *72*(5), 692–697. https://doi.org/10.1016/j.neuron.2011.11.001

Poldrack, R. A., Fletcher, P. C., Henson, R. N., Worsley, K. J., Brett, M., & Nichols, T. E. (2008). Guidelines for reporting an fMRI study. *NeuroImage*, *40*(2), 409–414. https://doi.org/10.1016/j.neuroimage.2007.11.048

Poldrack, R. A., & Gorgolewski, K. J. (2014). Making big data open: Data sharing in neuroimaging. *Nature Neuroscience*, *17*(11), 1510–1517. https://doi.org/10.1038/nn.3818

Poldrack, R. A., Laumann, T. O., Koyejo, O., Gregory, B., Hover, A., Chen, M.-Y., Gorgolewski, K. J., Luci, J., Joo, S. J., Boyd, R. L., Hunicke-Smith, S., Simpson, Z. B., Caven, T., Sochat, V., Shine, J. M., Gordon, E., Snyder, A. Z., Adeyemo, B., Petersen, S. E., . . . Mumford, J. A. (2015). Long-term neural and physiological phenotyping of a single human. *Nature Communications*, *6*(1), 8885. https://doi.org/10.1038/ncomms9885

Power, J. D., Silver, B. M., Silverman, M. R., Ajodan, E. L., Bos, D. J., & Jones, R. M. (2019). Customized head molds reduce motion during resting state fMRI scans. *NeuroImage*, *189*, 141–149. https://doi.org/10.1016/j.neuroimage.2019.01.016

Raichle, M. E., MacLeod, A. M., Snyder, A. Z., Powers, W. J., Gusnard, D. A., & Shulman, G. L. (2001). A default mode of brain function. *Proceedings of the National Academy of Sciences of the United States of America*, *98*(2), 676–682. https://doi.org/10.1073/pnas.98.2.676

Ramot, M., Kimmich, S., Gonzalez-Castillo, J., Roopchansingh, V., Popal, H., White, E., Gotts, S. J., & Martin, A. (2017). Direct modulation of aberrant brain network connectivity through real-time neurofeedback. *eLife*, *6*, e28974. https://doi.org/10.7554/eLife.28974

Rosenberg, M. D., Casey, B. J., & Holmes, A. J. (2018). Prediction complements explanation in understanding the developing brain. *Nature Communications*, *9*(1), 589. https://doi.org/10.1038/s41467-018-02887-9

Scarapicchia, V., Brown, C., Mayo, C., & Gawryluk, J. R. (2017). Functional magnetic resonance imaging and functional near-infrared spectroscopy: Insights from combined recording studies. *Frontiers in Human Neuroscience*, *11*, 419. https://doi.org/10.3389/fnhum.2017.00419

Scheinost, D., Hsu, T. W., Avery, E. W., Hampson, M., Constable, R. T., Chun, M. M., & Rosenberg, M. D.

(2020). Connectome-based neurofeedback: A pilot study to improve sustained attention. *NeuroImage, 212*, 116684. https://doi.org/10.1016/j.neuroimage.2020.116684

Shibata, K., Watanabe, T., Sasaki, Y., & Kawato, M. (2011). Perceptual learning incepted by decoded fMRI neurofeedback without stimulus presentation. *Science, 334*(6061), 1413–1415. https://doi.org/10.1126/science.1212003

Song, H., Finn, E. S., & Rosenberg, M. D. (2021). Neural signatures of attentional engagement during narratives and its consequences for event memory. *Proceedings of the National Academy of Sciences of the United States of America, 118*(33), e2021905118. https://doi.org/10.1073/pnas.2021905118

Stoeckel, L. E., Garrison, K. A., Ghosh, S., Wighton, P., Hanlon, C. A., Gilman, J. M., Greer, S., Turk-Browne, N. B., deBettencourt, M. T., Scheinost, D., Craddock, C., Thompson, T., Calderon, V., Bauer, C. C., George, M., Breiter, H. C., Whitfield-Gabrieli, S., Gabrieli, J. D., LaConte, S. M., . . . Evins, A. E. (2014). Optimizing real time fMRI neurofeedback for therapeutic discovery and development. *NeuroImage: Clinical, 5*, 245–255. https://doi.org/10.1016/j.nicl.2014.07.002

Sulzer, J., Haller, S., Scharnowski, F., Weiskopf, N., Birbaumer, N., Blefari, M. L., Bruehl, A. B., Cohen, L. G., DeCharms, R. C., Gassert, R., Goebel, R., Herwig, U., LaConte, S., Linden, D., Luft, A., Seifritz, E., & Sitaram, R. (2013). Real-time fMRI neurofeedback: Progress and challenges. *NeuroImage, 76*, 386–399. https://doi.org/10.1016/j.neuroimage.2013.03.033

Talairach J., & Tournoux P. (1988). *Co-planar stereotaxic atlas of the human brain*. Thieme Medical Publishers.

Tambini, A., Ketz, N., & Davachi, L. (2010). Enhanced brain correlations during rest are related to memory for recent experiences. *Neuron, 65*(2), 280–290. https://doi.org/10.1016/j.neuron.2010.01.001

Van Essen, D. C., Smith, S. M., Barch, D. M., Behrens, T. E. J., Yacoub, E., Ugurbil, K., & the WU-Minn HCP Consortium. (2013). The WU-Minn Human Connectome Project: An overview. *NeuroImage, 80*, 62–79. https://doi.org/10.1016/j.neuroimage.2013.05.041

Vanderwal, T., Kelly, C., Eilbott, J., Mayes, L. C., & Castellanos, F. X. (2015). Inscapes: A movie paradigm to improve compliance in functional magnetic resonance imaging. *NeuroImage, 122*, 222–232. https://doi.org/10.1016/j.neuroimage.2015.07.069

Voss, J. L., Bridge, D. J., Cohen, N. J., & Walker, J. A. (2017). A closer look at the hippocampus and memory. *Trends in Cognitive Sciences, 21*(8), 577–588. https://doi.org/10.1016/j.tics.2017.05.008

Watanabe, T., Sasaki, Y., Shibata, K., & Kawato, M. (2017). Advances in fMRI real-time neurofeedback. *Trends in Cognitive Sciences, 21*(12), 997–1010. https://doi.org/10.1016/j.tics.2017.09.010

Yarkoni, T., Poldrack, R. A., Nichols, T. E., Van Essen, D. C., & Wager, T. D. (2011). Large-scale automated synthesis of human functional neuroimaging data. *Nature Methods, 8*(8), 665–670. https://doi.org/10.1038/nmeth.1635

Yeo, B. T. T., Krienen, F. M., Sepulcre, J., Sabuncu, M. R., Lashkari, D., Hollinshead, M., Roffman, J. L., Smoller, J. W., Zöllei, L., Polimeni, J. R., Fischl, B., Liu, H., & Buckner, R. L. (2011). The organization of the human cerebral cortex estimated by intrinsic functional connectivity. *Journal of Neurophysiology, 106*(3), 1125–1165. https://doi.org/10.1152/jn.00338.2011

Yushkevich, P. A., Pluta, J. B., Wang, H., Xie, L., Ding, S.-L., Gertje, E. C., Mancuso, L., Kliot, D., Das, S. R., & Wolk, D. A. (2015). Automated volumetry and regional thickness analysis of hippocampal subfields and medial temporal cortical structures in mild cognitive impairment. *Human Brain Mapping, 36*(1), 258–287. https://doi.org/10.1002/hbm.22627

CHAPTER 30

NONINVASIVE STIMULATION OF THE CEREBRAL CORTEX

Dennis J. L. G. Schutter

Transcranial magnetic and electric current stimulation are noninvasive brain stimulation (NBS) techniques that are used to study the relation between neurophysiology and behavior by influencing nerve cells with electric currents. This chapter provides an overview of brain stimulation techniques that are progressively finding their way into modern social and affective neuroscientific research. The main part of the chapter describes the basic principles, paradigms, and contributions of NBS to study the neural mechanisms of motivation, emotion, and social cognition. In addition, critical analyses of safety, strengths, and limitations of NBS technology and current developments in the field are provided. The final part of this chapter gives a brief summary and some concluding remarks on the role of NBS in understanding the workings of the social brain.

TRANSCRANIAL MAGNETIC STIMULATION

Credited with the discovery of a physical phenomenon called *electromagnetic induction*, Michael Faraday (1791–1867) can be considered the founding father of modern transcranial magnetic stimulation (TMS). He was the first to show that when a conductor is placed inside a rapidly varying magnetic field, an electric current will be created in the conductor. In other words, time varying magnetic fields can be used to induce electric currents in conductive materials such as nerve cells. Even though the main principle of TMS was discovered in 1820, it was not until 1985 that the human cerebral cortex was successfully stimulated by applying magnetic pulses in a noninvasive and painless manner (Barker et al., 1985). When the stored energy in the capacitors connected to the coil is released via an electronic switch (thyristor), an electric current starts to flow through the coil, generating a strong but short (~200 ms) magnetic field (i.e., Ørsted's law). In accordance with Faraday's law of electromagnetic induction, the magnetic field will cause a secondary electric current in neurons. This secondary current gives rise to a transmembrane potential; when this potential is strong enough, neurons will depolarize and produce action potentials (Pitcher et al., 2021; Wassermann et al., 2008). Figure 30.1 shows the basic circuitry underlying TMS. Figure 30.2 illustrates the principle of electromagnetic induction and current flows necessary for stimulating nerve cells (Hallett, 2007).

The magnetic field strength is highest directly under the coil and is usually on the order of 1 to 3 Tesla. However, the direct effects of TMS

Dennis J. L. G. Schutter was supported by an Innovational Research Grant (VI.C.181.005) from the Netherlands Organization for Scientific Research. The author reports no conflict of interest.
https://doi.org/10.1037/0000318-030
APA Handbook of Research Methods in Psychology, Second Edition: Vol. 1. Foundations, Planning, Measures, and Psychometrics, H. Cooper (Editor-in-Chief)
Copyright © 2023 by the American Psychological Association. All rights reserved.

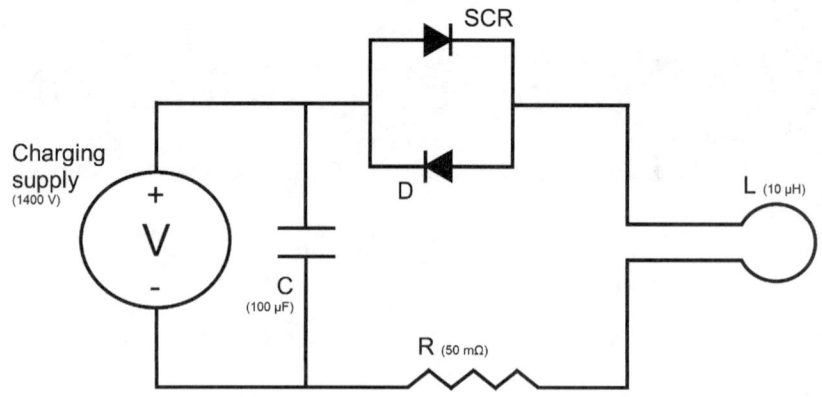

FIGURE 30.1. Biphasic pulse circuit. C = capacitor, D = diode, L = induction (coil), R = resistor, SCR = silicon-controlled rectifier, V = power supply.

are confined to the superficial parts of the brain that face the cranium (i.e., cerebral and cerebellar cortex) because the strength of the magnetic field decays exponentially with distance (Hallett, 2007). The spatial resolution of the magnetic pulse for effective stimulation, which shares an inverse relation with maximal magnetic field strength, can be in the order of several squared centimeters. The circular and eight-shaped coil types are most commonly used in research and clinical applications. As can be seen from Figure 30.3, the distribution of the magnetic field depends on coil type. The use of a particular coil for targeting the brain involves a tradeoff between focality and depth of stimulation.

Single-Pulse Magnetic Stimulation

The intensity of the magnetic pulse that is needed to excite nerve tissue depends on scalp-cortex distance and physiological properties of the

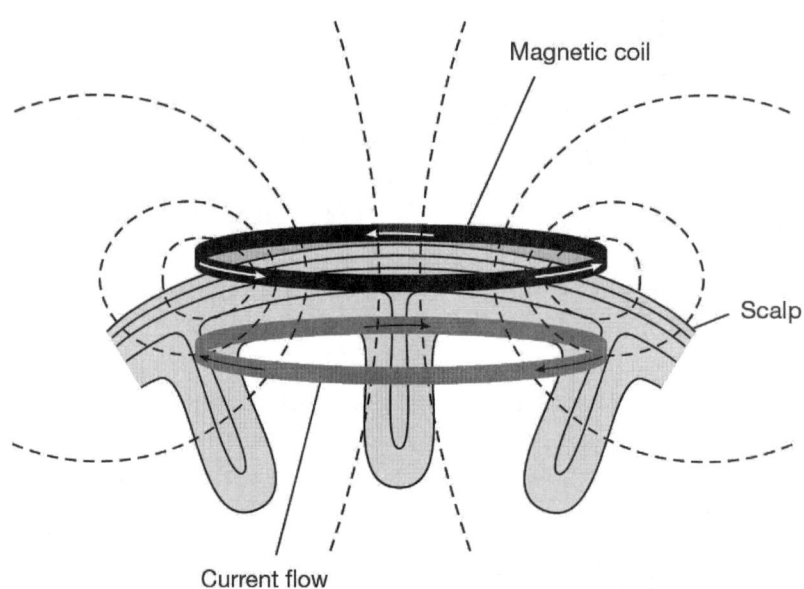

FIGURE 30.2. Magnetic and electric current flows in the brain. From "Transcranial Magnetic Stimulation and the Human Brain," by M. Hallett, 2000, *Nature*, *406*, p. 147 (https://doi.org/10.1038/35018000). Copyright 2000 by Macmillan Publishers Ltd. Reprinted with permission.

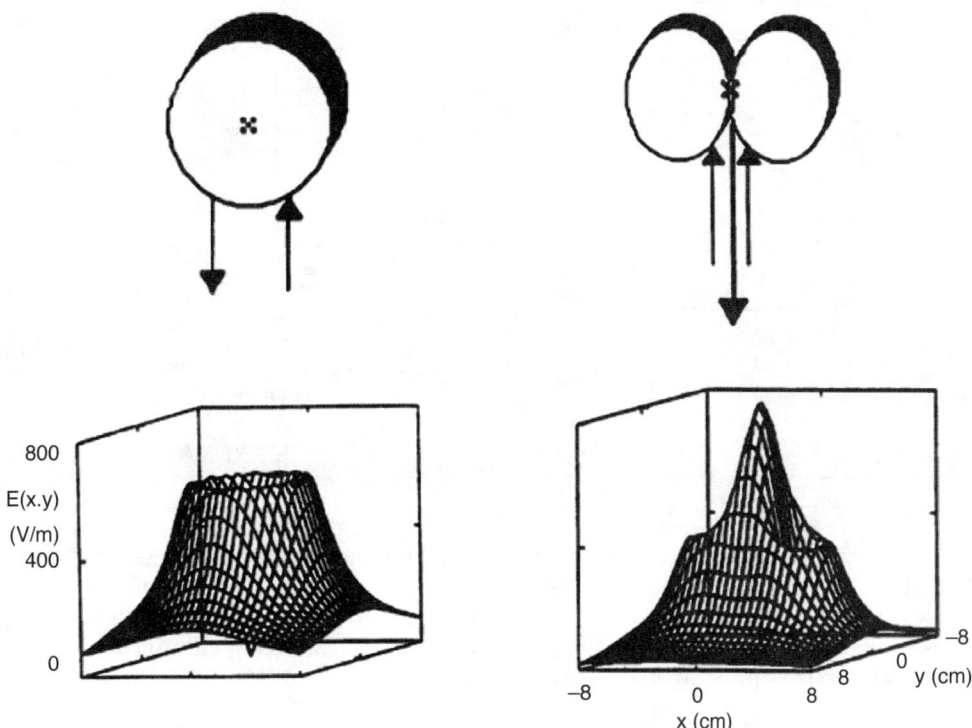

FIGURE 30.3. Electric field distribution of a standard circular (left) and eight-shaped coil (right). The induced electric field of the circular coil (mean diameter: 66.5 mm) is at its maximum at the outer radius of the copper windings, whereas the induced electric field of the eight-shaped coil (mean diameter: 73 mm) is at its maximum (i.e., sum of both fields) at the intersection of the two smaller coils. Adapted from "Transcranial Magnetic Stimulation: A Primer," by M. Hallett, 2007, *Neuron*, 55, p. 188. Copyright 2007 by Elsevier; and adapted from "Effects of Coil Design on Delivery of Focal Magnetic Stimulation: Technical Considerations," by L. G. Cohen, B. J. Roth, J. Nilsson, N. Dang, M. Panizza, S. Bandinelli, W. Friauf, and M. Hallett, 1990, *Electroencephalography and Clinical Neurophysiology*, 75(4), pp. 351 and 353 (https://doi.org/10.1016/0013-4694(90)90113-x). Copyright 1990 by Elsevier. Adapted with permission.

stimulated tissue. When controlled for distance, the magnetic field strength that is required for activating neuronal populations provides a direct index of cortical excitability of that particular population of cells, and it likely reflects excitability of axonal fibers of neurons and excitatory and inhibitory interneurons that act on these neurons (Moll et al., 1999). For example, in line with frontal lateralization theories of motivation, asymmetries in left- and right-cortical excitability have been associated with differences in approach and avoidance-related motivational tendencies (Schutter, Hofman, & Van Honk, 2008). Interestingly, the opposite asymmetry has been found in non-medicated patients suffering from major depressive disorder (Bajbouj et al., 2006; Cotovio et al., 2022).

On the macroscopic level, neural excitability is the weighted sum of inhibitory and excitatory processes in the cortex and can be measured by studying the amplitude of the motor-evoked potential (MEP) recorded from different finger muscles following suprathreshold stimulation of the motor cortex (Figure 30.4a). Moreover, when a single suprathreshold TMS pulse targeting the primary motor cortex is preceded by voluntary contralateral muscle contraction, the MEP will be followed by a transient silencing of muscle activity, called the cortical silent period (CSP; Figure 30.4b). This interruption of muscle activity to single-pulse suprathreshold TMS to the motor cortex provides an index of intracortical inhibitory processes. Pharmacological

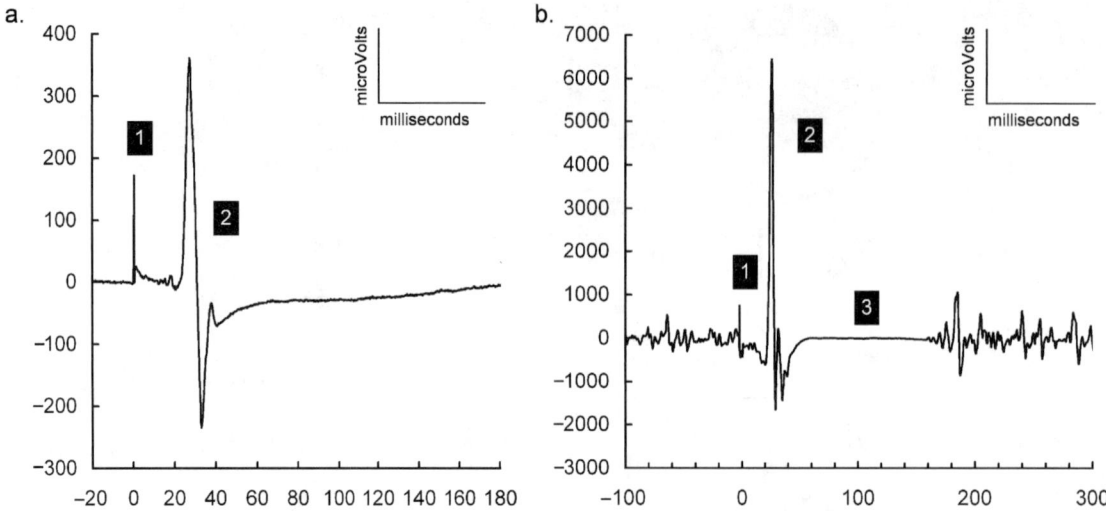

FIGURE 30.4. Motor-evoked potential (MEP) recorded from abductor pollicis brevis (APB) to contralateral suprathreshold single-pulse transcranial magnetic stimulation (TMS) over the primary motor cortex (a). MEP followed by a cortical silent period (CSP) recorded from APB contralateral suprathreshold single pulse TMS over the primary motor cortex during voluntary muscle contraction (b). 1 = TMS pulse artifact; 2 = MEP amplitude; 3 = CSP.

manipulation studies have shown that inhibitory γ-aminobutyric acid (GABA) interneurons are responsible for the CSP (Cantello et al., 1992).

Single-pulse TMS, for instance, has been used to establish the role of emotional saliency on the interrelation between perception and action in a direct way. In a study by Hajcak et al. (2007), increased-baseline-controlled MEP amplitudes were found in response to the presentation of highly arousing scenes that were selected from the International Affective Picture System (IAPS). Evidence in further support of evolutionary views on the relation between threat signals and action readiness (Öhman, 1986) was obtained in another study that showed significant MEP amplitude increases in response to viewing fearful as compared with happy and neutral facial expressions (Schutter, Hofman, & Van Honk, 2008). The latter finding provides direct evidence for motor cortex involvement in brain circuits that are devoted to threat and action preparation (Davis & Whalen, 2001). Furthermore, anticipatory anxiety has a facilitating effect on MEP amplitude, providing evidence for relations among worrying, anxiety, action preparedness, and frontal cortex excitability (Oathes et al., 2008).

In addition to the study of local excitability levels, single-pulse TMS can also be used to study connectivity between the cerebral hemispheres. Signal transfer between the hemispheres is based on a cortical mechanism of excitatory transcallosal fibers targeting inhibitory interneurons on the contralateral hemisphere and is known as transcallosal inhibition (TCI). TCI can be demonstrated by the suppression of voluntary muscle activity in the ipsilateral hand to a unilateral magnetic pulse, called the *ipsilateral silent period* (iSP). This inhibitory process starts between 30 ms and 40 ms in response to a contralateral magnetic pulse over the primary motor cortex (Figure 30.5). For example, abnormalities in TCI as evidenced by a relatively long iSP have been observed in children with attention-deficit/hyperactivity disorder (ADHD; Buchmann et al., 2003). Emotion dysregulation, impulsivity, and motor hyperactivity observed in ADHD may find its origins in suboptimal development of interhemispheric interactions and possible delayed brain maturation as shown by reduced transcallosal inhibition. The developmental aspect of TCI was further illustrated in a study by Ciechanski et al. (2017), who demonstrated that TCI increases with age. In sum, single-pulse TMS can be used to study direct emotion and motivation in relation to

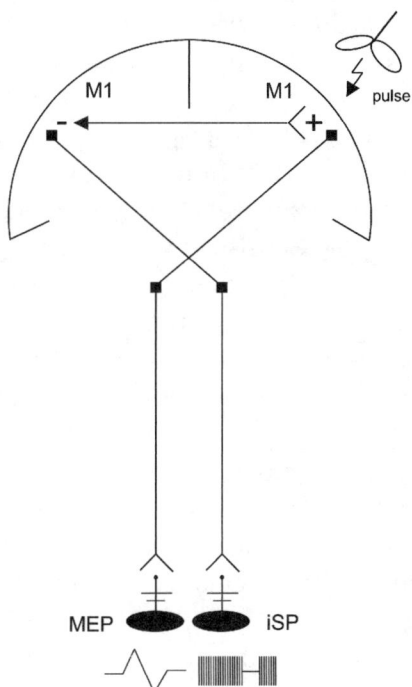

FIGURE 30.5. Single-pulse transcranial magnetic stimulation and transcallosal inhibition. – = inhibitory projections; iSP = ipsilateral silent period; M1 = primary motor cortex. Adapted from *Methods in Social Neuroscience* (p. 248), by E. Harmon-Jones and J. S. Beer (Eds.), 2009, Guilford Press. Copyright 2009 by Guilford Press. Adapted with permission.

cortical excitability levels, and functional interhemispheric connectivity.

Paired-Pulse Magnetic Stimulation

Cortical excitability is considered a general term for the responsivity of neurons to suprathreshold single-pulse TMS, whereas paired-pulse TMS provides additional physiological information on inhibitory and excitatory processes that underlie excitability levels of the cerebral cortex (Wassermann et al., 2008).

In a typical paired-pulse TMS paradigm, a low-intensity conditioning pulse is preceded by a suprathreshold test pulse to the primary motor cortex. When the interval between the two pulses is between 1 and 6 ms, the test pulse MEP will be smaller compared with the test MEP pulse without the preceding conditioning pulse. This phenomenon is known as *intracortical inhibition* (ICI) and reflects GABA-ergic activity of cortical interneurons (Ziemann, 2004).

If the low-intensity conditioning pulse is preceded 8 to 30 ms by the test pulse, then the test MEP amplitude will be larger than the test MEP amplitude without the conditioning pulse. This phenomenon is referred to as *intracortical facilitation* (ICF; Chen et al., 1998) and is associated with excitatory-related processes in the cortex (Ziemann, 2004). Typically, the degree of ICI and ICF are presented as the ratio between the unconditioned and conditioned test MEP amplitude.

As mentioned, paired-pulse TMS can provide indirect information on GABA-mediated inhibitory and glutamate-mediated excitatory processes in the cortex. Using paired pulse, TMS associations between reduced ICI of the frontal cortex and neuroticism have been established (Wassermann et al., 2001). Reduced GABA-ergic inhibitory tone causing higher levels of neural excitability in the frontal cortex may provide a neurophysiological proxy for elevated vigilance and feelings of anxiety. Notably, drug agents that act as GABA agonists have been effective in reducing feelings of anxiety (Breier & Paul, 1990), which suggests that the working mechanisms of anxiolytic drugs may involve changes in GABA-ergic function on the level of the cerebral cortex as evidenced by paired-pulse TMS (Wassermann et al., 2001).

Furthermore, deficits in GABA neurotransmission have been found in treatment-resistant major depressive disorder (MDD; Levinson et al., 2010). In this study, unmedicated MDD patients and medicated euthymic patients with a history of MDD were compared with healthy participants and tested on ICI with paired-pulse TMS. Patients with treatment-resistant MDD had lower ICI in the left primary motor cortex compared with medicated and healthy volunteers. Together with the significantly elevated motor threshold in the left primary motor cortex, these findings indicate that left-frontal cortex hypoexcitability is part of the pathophysiology associated with treatment-resistant MDD (Bajbouj et al., 2006). Interestingly, this observation concurs with the proposed relation between underactivation of the left frontal cortex and the chronic absence of approach-related behavior seen in MDD patients.

Even though slightly different from single-pulse TMS, paired-pulse TMS can also be deployed to measure TCI (Ferbert et al., 1992). In the paired-pulse TMS variant, the MEP amplitude to a single unilateral pulse is compared with the MEP amplitude to a unilateral magnetic (test) pulse that is preceded by a contralateral magnetic (conditioning) pulse. When the test pulse is given ~10 ms after the conditioning pulse, a significant reduction in MEP size of the test response can be observed as compared with when the test pulse is not preceded by the contralateral conditioning pulse. Figure 30.6 shows a schematic illustration of how TCI can be evoked in a paired-pulse TMS setup.

For example, interhemispheric connectivity between left- and right-frontal cortex correlates with an aggressive personality style (Hofman & Schutter, 2009). Consistent with their proposal that an aggressive personality style is associated with asymmetry in the frontal cortex, higher levels of left-to-right TCI were correlated with a more aggressive personality style. In addition, increased left-to-right, together with reduced right-to-left, TCI was associated with an attentional bias for angry faces. These findings provide a neurophysiological foundation for frontal asymmetry models of emotion and motivation (Schutter & Harmon-Jones, 2013). Interestingly, alcohol consumption decreases TCI, illustrating the loss of functional integrity of the frontal cortex in the context of lowered behavioral inhibition and control (Hoppenbrouwers et al., 2010).

In sum, paired-pulse TMS paradigms can be used to investigate unique aspects of cortical physiology in vivo and contribute to our understanding of how intracortical physiology and interhemispheric connectivity relate to emotion, motivation, and its disorders.

Repetitive Magnetic Stimulation

The effects of a single or short train of TMS pulses are transient in nature, and the duration of the effects is usually very short. However, when single pulses are applied at a particular frequency for an extended period of time (e.g., ≥ 10 minutes), the effects can easily outlast the stimulation period. This repetitive TMS (rTMS) approach provides researchers with a time window for examining rTMS-related effects on the level of emotion and motivation. Intensity and frequency of stimulation determine whether rTMS reduces or increases cortical excitability in the stimulated area. Repetitive stimulation between 0–1 Hz, called *slow-frequency* rTMS, reduces cortical excitability, whereas repetitive stimulation at frequencies of ≥ 5 Hz, termed *fast-frequency* rTMS, increases cortical excitability (Wassermann & Lisanby, 2001). The physiological working

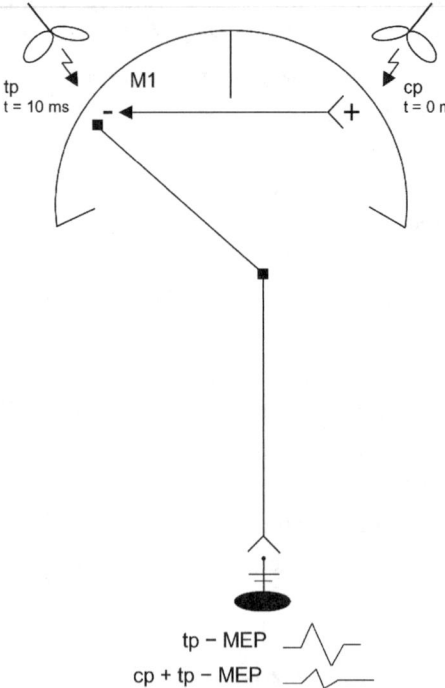

FIGURE 30.6. Paired-pulse transcranial magnetic stimulation and transcallosal inhibition. − = inhibitory projections; M1 = primary motor cortex; cp = conditioning pulse (t = 0 ms); tp = test pulse (t = ~10 ms); MEP = motor-evoked potential. Adapted from "Transcranial Magnetic Simulation," by D. J. L. G. Schutter, in E. Harmon-Jones and J. S. Beer (Eds.), *Methods in Social Neuroscience* (p. 247), 2009, Guilford Press. Copyright 2009 by Guilford Press. Adapted with permission.

mechanisms are still unclear, but slow-frequency rTMS may lower the resting state potential of neurons, producing a state of neuronal hyperpolarization, whereas fast-frequency rTMS may increase the resting state potential of neurons, causing a state of neuronal depolarization (Pascual-Leone et al., 1998). This is somewhat comparable to the long-term depression and long-term potentiation models involving electrical stimulation of the hippocampus in animals (Hoogendam et al., 2010). In addition, the effects of slow- and fast-frequency rTMS on cortical excitability may also depend on the modulation of GABA-ergic activity (Khedr et al., 2007). The effects of rTMS on behavior, however, are likely to depend on the current excitability state of the brain as well as the type of mental process that is being investigated (Silvanto et al., 2008).

Intensity of rTMS is another important parameter that contributes to its effects on the brain. Stimulation intensity is usually established by establishing the lowest threshold for eliciting small finger movements by applying single-pulse TMS to the hand area of the motor cortex (i.e., the motor threshold). Studies have shown that low-intensity (subthreshold) rTMS mainly affects underlying tissues, whereas high-intensity (suprathreshold) produces both local and distal effects (Ilmoniemi et al., 1997; Speer et al., 2003).

In social neuroscience, rTMS has been used to investigate frontal lateralization models in emotion, motivation, and decision making. From an evolutionary perspective, a fine-tuned balance between approach- and avoidance-related responses to rewards and punishments is crucial for survival and signifies psychobiological well-being (Davidson, 1984). This view argues against the affective-valence model, which is among the primary cortical-centered theories in the social neurosciences, and proposes that the left prefrontal cortex (PFC) subserves approach-related positive emotions, whereas the right PFC subserves avoidance-related negative emotions (Harmon-Jones, 2003). There is increasing debate on the positive-negative valence dimension in this model, however, because experimental findings from electroencephalography (EEG) research indicate that the left PFC is involved in the processing of anger and aggression (Harmon-Jones, 2003). This alternative model of motivational direction suggests that approach-related emotion (with its prototype, anger) is processed by the left PFC, whereas avoidance-related emotion (with its prototype, fear) is processed by the right PFC (van Honk & Schutter, 2006b). In an offline, slow-frequency (inhibitory) rTMS design employing an affective response task, vigilant and avoidant attentional responses to angry facial expressions were observed after right and left PFC slow-frequency rTMS, respectively (d'Alfonso et al., 2000). Slow-frequency rTMS to the left PFC resulted in (fearful) avoidance of angry faces because of a shift in dominant processing to the right PFC (van Honk & Schutter, 2006b). Inhibitory rTMS to the right PFC, on the other hand, resulted in vigilant, approach-related responses to angry faces, pointing at dominant left-PFC processing. In a follow-up study, reductions in vigilant attention to fearful faces were observed after slow-frequency rTMS over the right PFC in a sham-controlled study (van Honk et al., 2002). Moreover, interleaved rTMS-EEG demonstrated that these reductions in fear responsivity were likely to be anxiolytically mediated and that the locally inhibitory effects of right-PFC rTMS actually produce left-PFC excitation (Schutter et al., 2001). Finally, in an off-line, sham-controlled, slow-frequency subthreshold rTMS to the left and right PFC of healthy volunteers, significant reductions in the processing of anger occurred exclusively after left PFC rTMS, whereas the processing of happiness remained unaffected (van Honk & Schutter, 2006a).

The field of neuroeconomics has recently tackled PFC laterality of risk-taking behaviors by way of sophisticated experimental paradigms using rTMS (Fehr & Camerer, 2007). Increased risky decision making was demonstrated in an experiment applying slow-frequency rTMS to study the right PFC (Knoch, Gianotti, et al., 2006). Twenty-seven healthy subjects received 15 minutes of 1-Hz rTMS (100% MT), after which participants played a risk task in which the probability of either getting a reward or punishment was determined by the ratio of pink-to-blue boxes displayed during each trial. Significant reductions were observed for the percentage choices of the low-risk prospect in right ($n = 9$) compared with left ($n = 9$) and sham ($n = 9$) rTMS. According to Knoch, Gianotti, et al. (2006), the right, and not the left, PFC are involved in actively inhibiting attractive options (i.e., high reward probability). Interestingly, the laterality findings are also in agreement with idea that the right PFC is associated with avoidance-related motivation and punishment sensitivity. Even though the authors propose that the effects were due to local disruption of right PFC function, providing causal evidence for right PFC involvement in the inhibitory cognitive regulation of risk taking, a shift in frontal cortical asymmetry to more approach-related motivation (reward) and reduced avoidance-related motivation (punishment) provides an explanation as well (Schutter, de Weijer, et al., 2008).

In another study, slow-frequency rTMS was used to examine the involvement of the right PFC in reciprocal fairness (Knoch, Pascual-Leone, et al., 2006). Reciprocal fairness is linked to the moral standard that implies that, for instance, social behavior is reciprocated with kindness, whereas antisocial behavior is reciprocated with hostility (Rabin, 1993). Following right-PFC rTMS in comparison to both left PFC and sham rTMS, healthy volunteers accepted more unfair offers despite suffering personal financial loss (Knoch, Pascual-Leone, et al., 2006). The results suggest that the right PFC plays an important role in accepting unfair monetary offers. These findings build upon earlier rTMS findings that established a link between the right PFC and strategic decision making (van 't Wout et al., 2005).

In sum, the rTMS paradigm can be used to modulate the cerebral cortex and to address issues concerning the relation between cortical areas and their associated functions.

Safety

TMS is a noninvasive way to convey electric charges into the brain by way of a magnetic field that can elicit adverse events, of which the induction of an accidental seizure is considered to be the most serious one. Potential risk factors are a family history of epilepsy, certain types of medication that lower cortical excitability levels, brain trauma, metal inside the cranium, and exposure to fast-frequency rTMS at high intensities. General safety guidelines were introduced in 1998 and amended in 2009 and 2020 by the International Federation of Clinical Neurophysiology (Rossi et al., 2021). TMS has been around for 25 years, and it is estimated that, around the world, tens of thousands of subjects have participated in research. Reports on accidental seizures have been extremely rare. In fact, slow-frequency rTMS is increasingly being used to treat epilepsy by reducing cortical excitability in the epileptic foci (Santiago-Rodríguez et al., 2008). Some evidence suggests that rTMS exhibits neuroprotective and anti-inflammatory effects (Medina-Fernández, Luque, et al., 2017).

Sham Stimulation

A sham stimulation condition is routinely included in rTMS experiments for subject blinding purposes as well as to control for intrinsic procedural and time-related effects on the variable(s) of interest. An often-used method for sham stimulation is to tilt the stimulation coil 45 to 90 degrees, so presumably, the magnetic field does not reach the cortical target tissues. More recently, sham coils have been used that look identical to real coils but have an aluminum plate inside the housing of the coil that prevents the magnetic pulse from reaching the cortical surface. Even newer sham coils make use of additional electrodes that apply small electric pulses to the scalp that exactly mimic the scalp sensations, making it impossible to distinguish real from "fake" rTMS (Arana et al., 2008).[1]

---

[1] Even weak currents can have physiological effects on the brain (see also the section Transcranial Direct Current Stimulation later in this chapter), which could compromise the true sham concept.

Spatial Resolution and Localization

The surface area with the highest intensity that is covered by TMS depends to a great extent on the configuration of the coil (see Figure 30.3) and is usually in the order of several square centimeters.

Furthermore, the exponential decay of the magnetic field does not allow stimulation of deep brain regions that are critically involved in emotion and motivation, such as the ventral striatum and amygdala. Even if the magnetic field was strong enough to reach deep brain regions, the large drop in focality that is associated with the large field would become a substantial problem in localizing functions at greater depths. Interestingly, local effects induced by suprathreshold TMS usually give rise to distal effects and are caused by signal propagation from the stimulated area to interconnected regions. Ilmoniemi et al. (1997) were among the first to successfully combine single-pulse TMS with EEG recordings. They showed increases in electrophysiological activity over the right primary motor cortex starting approximately 20 ms after stimulation of the left primary motor cortex. The distal pattern of activation originates from nerve impulses that (via white-matter fibers of the corpus callosum) activate the contralateral site. On the basis of paired-pulse TMS research, it has been suggested that the EEG activity is a correlate of transcallosal inhibition of the ipsilateral cortex. These trans-synaptic effects provide a physiological basis for studying interconnected networks in the brain. Using this methodology, breakdown of cortico–cortical connectivity, for instance, has been demonstrated to correlate with the loss of consciousness (Ferrarelli et al., 2010). Other neuroimaging modalities, including positron emission tomography, have shown distributed effects in cortical and subcortical brain regions in response to rTMS over the frontal cortex (Speer et al., 2003).

The MEP recorded from hand muscles is the most common, although indirect, method for assessing cortical excitability. Even though epidural stimulation and recordings studies suggest that the effects of TMS have a cortical basis, subcortical and spinal contributions to the MEP cannot be excluded (Di Lazzaro et al., 2010). Furthermore, results found for the primary motor cortex cannot simply be generalized to other cortical areas that do not share the same underlying neural architectonics. Combined single-pulse TMS-EEG studies have found that TMS-evoked electric potentials over the primary motor cortex correlate to TMS-evoked electric potentials over the PFC (Kähkönen et al., 2005). Additional paired-pulse TMS-EEG research on intracortical inhibition have yielded comparable electrophysiological results for the primary motor cortex and PFC (Fitzgerald et al., 2009). In addition, a positive relation has been observed between the motor threshold of the primary motor cortex and phosphene threshold of the primary visual cortex (Deblieck et al., 2008). Nowadays, TMS and EEG are increasingly combined in multimodal fashion to study the effects of magnetic pulse on cortical physiology and its associated functions (Esposito et al., 2020). Single and paired-pulse TMS pulses, for example, evoke brain potentials, like the N100, that are directly coupled to intracortical GABAerigc inhibitory processes (Premoli et al., 2018). Interleaved TMS-EEG still faces technical challenges, however, which include how to deal with muscle, auditory, and somatosensory artifacts that contaminate the first 100 to 150 ms of the EEG trace. Fortunately, increasing numbers of research groups are starting to combine TMS and EEG technology and currently are working out ways to optimize the recordings and unravel the exact functional relations between EEG and cortical physiology (for a review, see Esposito et al., 2020).

In sum, while the physiological workings of the primary motor cortex may provide valuable information concerning the physiology of other cortical areas, interleaving TMS and EEG has made considerable progress in understanding the cortical correlates of behavior.

Developments in the Field

A TMS paradigm called *theta burst stimulation* (TBS) has proven highly effective in modulating neuronal excitability (Huang et al., 2005). Intermittent theta burst (iTBS) is a 3-minute excitatory protocol approved by the U.S. Food and Drug Administration that administers 20 patterned 5-Hz trains of three pulses at 50 Hz with an intertrain interval of 10 seconds. In contrast, continuous TBS or cTBS is a 40-second inhibitory protocol that applies 5-Hz trains with each train containing three pulses at 50 Hz with an intertrain interval of 1 second. TBS is a fast procedure that is capable of producing reliable and long-lasting (> 60 minutes) effects on cortical physiology and appears more effective than the traditional rTMS paradigms. Administration of cTBS to the right inferior frontal cortex lessens inhibitory control and the ability to override distracting information during decision making in healthy volunteers (Chung et al., 2017).

In addition to refining the stimulation paradigms, researchers focus on the development of the Hesed (H)-coil that can stimulate deep brain structures. Studies have shown that the H-coil is able to activate cortical tissue at a distance of 5 to 6 cm (Zangen et al., 2005). Despite holding great promise in targeting deep brain structures, optimizing the spatial resolution of the H-coil is currently the major challenge in targeting isolated areas. The use of anatomic magnetic resonance imaging (MRI) scans to calculate the distribution of the magnetically induced electric fields in the brain is increasingly used to further improve the usability and reliability of TMS in research. Last, in addition to the traditional focus on the frontal cortex with respect to cognitive and emotive processes associated with social behavior, rTMS to the parietal cortex as well as the cerebellum has been successfully applied to examine contributions of these areas in the neural architecture of motivation and emotion (Mulckhuyse et al., 2017; Schutter, 2020). In sum, despite the relatively short career of TMS in neurology and social neurosciences, its contributions have already been substantial in providing unique as well as novel insights into the workings of the human brain.

TRANSCRANIAL DIRECT CURRENT STIMULATION

In transcranial direct-current stimulation (tDCS), a current generator is used to deliver a constant, one-directional flow of electric current between two water-soaked sponge electrodes (Priori, 2003). The electrode size typically ranges from 20 to 35 cm^2 and conductive gel is used to reduce the impedance between the electrode and scalp (Nitsche et al., 2008). The intensity of the administered current typically lies between 0.5 mA and 2.0 mA (Wagner et al., 2007). Even though the scalp and skull act as a large shunt, studies have demonstrated that a small but significant part of the weak current underlying the electrodes actually reaches the cortical surface (Nitsche et al., 2008; Wagner et al., 2007). In a series of studies, Priori et al. (1998) showed that weak electric currents (< 0.5 mA) applied between two scalp electrodes targeting cortical motor regions yielded changes in MEP amplitude in response to single-pulse TMS.

The biophysical principle underlying tDCS involves the polarization of nerve tissue. Because of the low intensity and the fact that the injected current does not vary in time, tDCS, unlike TMS, cannot induce transmembrane potentials that are strong enough to cause action potentials in the underlying tissue. Instead, tDCS influences spontaneous firing rates through the modulation of cortical excitability levels (Nitsche et al., 2008). Importantly, the direction of the current flow has differential effects on cortical excitability. The positively charged anode (+) electrode depolarizes neurons and enhances excitability, whereas the negatively charged cathode (−) electrode hyperpolarizes neurons and decreases excitability levels in the cortical tissue underneath the electrode (Priori, 2003). Notably, increasing or decreasing cortical excitability does necessarily equate with better or worse functionality, respectively, as evidenced by seemingly paradoxical impairments following anodal tDCS and improvement of function following cathodal tDCS (Hsu et al., 2016).

The modulation of firing probability of inhibitory interneurons in the superficial parts (layer 2) of the cerebral cortex is a possible mechanism for the changes in cortical excitability. In vitro studies suggest that tDCS sorts effects on ion channels that are in line with the upregulation (i.e., depolarization) or downregulation (i.e., hyperpolarization) of resting-state potentials (Nitsche et al., 2008). Even though the effects of tDCS are transient, studies of the time course of tDCS effects have shown that sessions of 15 minutes of continuous tDCS can induce aftereffects that can last up to 1 hour (Priori, 2003). However, the neural effects of tDCS have been challenged. A recent double-blind, placebo-controlled study did not find evidence for effects of 2 mA anodal tDCS on neural excitability in the motor cortex as evaluated with TMS (Jonker et al., 2020). Low intensity of the currents, shunting of scalp and skull, and the presence of cerebrospinal fluid are among the reasons why tDCS is not likely to produce any meaningful effects—or, at most, will produce highly variable results. While it is true that the effects of tDCS are often small and show considerable interindividual variability, systematic evaluation of the available evidence shows that tDCS can induce significant neurophysiological and behavioral effects (Filmer et al., 2020; Figure 30.7).

For example, the role of the right PFC in fairness behavior during simultaneous social interactions in a large experimental group ($n = 64$) was examined using cathodal tDCS (Knoch et al., 2008). The cathode electrode (35 cm²) was placed over right dorsolateral PFC and the reference electrode (35 cm²) over the left orbit to reduce cortical excitability of the right PFC. A constant current of 1.5 mA intensity was started 4 minutes before the onset of the fairness game and lasted until termination of the game (~10 minutes). During sham tDCS, only 30 seconds of real stimulation was applied at the onset of stimulation. Subjects who received cathodal ($n = 30$) tDCS to the right PFC were less likely to punish unfair behavior compared with sham tDCS ($n = 34$). In other words, during right PFC cathodal tDCS, subjects were more prone to accept smaller rewards during unfair offers rather than to reject the offer and receive no reward at all. In an additional study, the role of the left and right PFC in decision making was investigated by using a cathodal–anodal tDCS montage (electrode size: 35 cm², intensity: 2 mA) in 36 healthy participants (Fecteau et al., 2007). Percentage of risky decision making was examined during anodal–right cathodal tDCS ($n = 12$), left cathodal–right anodal tDCS ($n = 12$), and sham tDCS ($n = 12$) over the PFC. During left cathodal–right anodal tDCS, subjects displayed significant reductions in risky decision making as compared with left anodal–right cathodal tDCS and sham tDCS.

According to Knoch et al. (2008), these findings stress the importance of the interhemispheric balance across the PFC in decision making. Interestingly, the findings are also partially in line with the frontal lateralization model of motivation and emotion. The lateralization model predicts that the left cathodal–right anodal tDCS-induced shift in cortical asymmetry to the right PFC increases the sensitivity to punishment and risk aversion.

Finally, in a randomized, sham-controlled experiment, the effects of tDCS to the PFC on reward processing and decision making in relation to food craving were investigated in 23 healthy participants (Fregni et al., 2008). Electrodes (35 cm²) were attached over the left and right PFC and a constant current was applied for 20 minutes at an intensity of 2 mA. The experiment consisted of three different treatments: (a) anodal left–cathodal right, (b) cathodal left–anodal right, and (c) sham tDCS. The significant increase in food craving that was observed after sham tDCS was not present after right anodal–left cathodal tDCS. Furthermore, following right anodal–left cathodal tDCS, participants fixated less frequently on food-related pictures and participants consumed

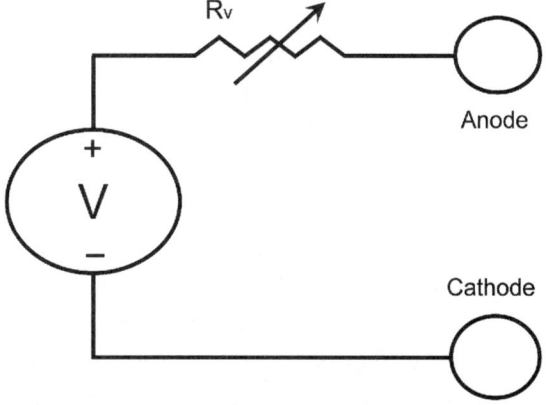

FIGURE 30.7. Electric current stimulation circuit. V = power supply, Rv = variable resistor.

less food after receiving right anodal–left cathodal tDCS and left anodal–right cathodal tDCS as compared with sham tDCS. These findings suggest that tDCS applied over the frontal cortex can influence food craving and, arguably, the cortical structures that are involved in appetite control, reward sensitivity, and decision making. In sum, the first series of studies demonstrate the feasibility of applying weak electric currents to the scalp to address social neuroscientific issues by in vivo manipulation of the human brain in a transient fashion.

Safety

Transcranial electric stimulation has been associated with three potential sources of damage: (a) generation of electrochemical toxins, (b) tissue heating, and (c) excitotoxicity. Because the electrodes in tDCS do not make direct contact with the brain's surface, generation of electrochemical toxins are limited to the skin. Furthermore, chemical reactions at the electrode–skin interface can be minimized by using nonmetallic, water-soaked sponge electrodes. Nonetheless, anecdotal reports of skin irritation following repeated daily tDCS strongly suggest that subjects with skin disease or a history of skin disease should not participate. Heating of nerve tissue as a result of dissipation may be an additional source of damage during electric stimulation. Several experiments have shown that tDCS (current density 0.029 mA/cm^2) that is applied for up to 13 minutes does not cause heating effects under the electrodes (Nitsche & Paulus, 2000). Finally, *excitotoxicity*, which is the phenomenon of calcium influx causing a disruption of the electrolytic balance in the nerve tissue that is due to overdriven neurons, is not considered a hazard for tDCS. Even though tDCS is able to increase spontaneous firing rates that remain within the physiological range, tDCS cannot induce action potentials in neurons that are not active (Nitsche et al., 2008). Thousands of participants have undergone tDCS worldwide and, except for itching under the electrodes and a few reported cases of headache, nausea and small skin burns, no serious negative side effects have been observed.

Sham Stimulation

Similar to rTMS experiments, sham tDCS is routinely performed for subject blinding and to control for possible confounding effects of the procedure. Because tDCS uses weak electric currents and does not produce sound clicks as in TMS, participants in general are not able to distinguish real from fake tDCS. To mimic the itching sensation that is often reported during the first 30 seconds following stimulation onset, researchers usually apply 30 seconds of real stimulation in the sham condition as well. This procedure makes it difficult to discern real from "fake" stimulation.

Spatial Resolution and Localization

The low spatial resolution that is associated with tDCS resulting from the relatively large electrode (20–35 cm^2) should be considered a limitation, particularly in cortical mapping studies.

Reducing electrode size is one way to improve the focality of stimulation, but the noninvasive character and nature of stimulation (i.e., electricity) will limit the degree of spatial resolution that is attainable with the modification of electrode sizes. Additionally, similar to TMS, the direct effects of tDCS are mainly confined to the superficial tissues that face the cranium. Indirect effects on distal interconnected structures can be expected when higher intensities are used. For example, unilateral anodal tDCS induces changes in cortical excitability of both ipsilateral and contralateral motor cortex (Vines et al., 2008).

In contrast to TMS, in which stimulation intensity is determined by individual thresholds to overcome individual differences in scalp–cortex distance and cortical excitability, participants in tDCS experiments usually get a fixed dose of electric stimulation. Without additional anatomical data, the exact amount of injected current that reaches the cortical surface and whether the amount is sufficient to elicit local and possibly distal effects cannot be known. Furthermore, individual differences in cortical physiology may yield different effects of tDCS in the brain using fixed parameters. The use of TMS in determining the intensity to excite cortical neurons may have

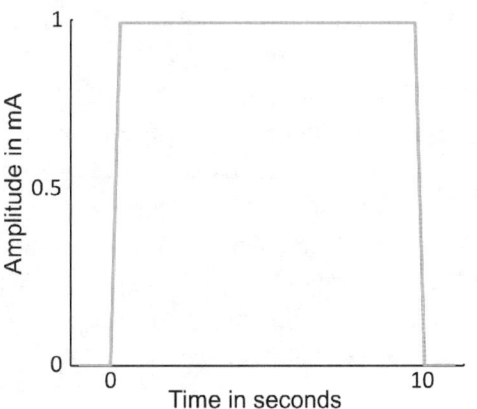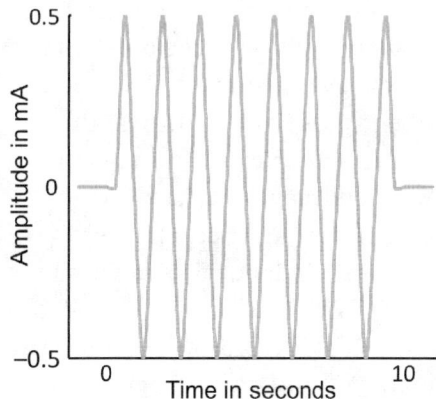

FIGURE 30.8. Wave form of constant direct current and 0.8-Hz alternating current stimulation.

some additional value in guiding the proper intensity needed for effective tDCS in forthcoming research. The use of neuroimaging techniques will become necessary to more fully capture the tDCS-related changes in distributed brain circuits.

A notable feature of tDCS is the fact that the anode–cathode electrode montage allows for the simultaneous modulation of two cortical sites. Research questions involving the modulation of cortical asymmetries and hemispheric interactions may benefit from dual-site stimulation. The reference electrode is not inert. As discussed, tDCS involves an electric current that flows between two electrodes and, depending on its direction, the electrodes function either as an anode or cathode. In short, cephalic references may have an effect on cortical physiology as well. One way to overcome possible reference effects is by increasing the size of the electrode, thereby reducing the current density and its effects on physiology. A montage with a 4 × 1 ring setup, which involves a central electrode surrounded by four return electrodes arranged in a circle around the central electrode, not only improves focality of the electric field but also reduces potential effects of the return electrodes (DaSilva et al., 2015). Finally, the use of noncephalic references (i.e., shoulder) is another way of minimizing the possible confounding effects of the reference electrode. One should be careful in applying noncephalic electrode montages (e.g., frontal electrode with reference attached to the leg) that can potentially cause stimulation of the brain stem or heart (Nitsche et al., 2008).

Developments in the Field

Rather than applying a constant unidirectional current as in tDCS, electric stimulation can also be applied in an alternating fashion according to a predefined frequency (Figure 30.8). Transcranial alternating current stimulation (tACS) has its roots in the idea that local and distal oscillations reflect the synchronization of large populations of neurons and constitute an important organizing principle of brain functions (Schutter, 2014).

This opens new exciting possibilities in the field of noninvasive neuromodulation of the cortex by mimicking natural brain oscillations (Kanai et al., 2008).[2] Because current direction is constantly changing during tACS, polarization of cortical tissue is unlikely. Thus, one of the mechanisms by which tACS reaches its effects may be through the induction of a rhythm or by way of amplification of an existing dominant rhythm by phase-locking neuronal activity (Zaghi et al., 2010). An increasing number of experiments have now replicated prior studies by showing that the application of low-intensity, alternating

---

[2]Repetitive TMS can also be viewed as a form of oscillatory stimulation of the cerebral cortex.

currents to the scalp can manipulate cortical physiology and alter cognitive behavior in humans (Schutter & Wischnewski, 2016).

While meta-analyses have confirmed the feasibility of using weak electric currents in studying cognitive and emotive behavior, current studies focus on increasing effect sizes and reducing the high interindividual variability in susceptibility to tDCS and tACS across individuals. Examples of research are the search for neural state dependent factors (e.g., presence of particular brain rhythms) and electric field modeling with realistic head models. Ultimately, the working mechanisms of tDCS and tACS resides in our understanding of brain physiology and the processes that govern behavior.

In sum, even though electric current stimulation research in the field of cognitive and affective neuroscience is still in its infancy, the noninvasive manipulation of the cerebral cortex with weak electric currents offers a unique approach to study the neurological correlates of cognition and emotion.

CONCLUSION

NBS provides a unique means to study the mind–brain relation in a relatively direct fashion by way of intervention and allows for a more causal approach in linking functions with the underlying neural representations in spatial as well as temporal domains of information processing (Schutter et al., 2004).

In addition to the modulation of cortical circuits and functionally connected networks, NBS is used to study inhibitory and excitatory properties of the cerebral cortex and functional connectivity in vivo. Moreover, results from basic social neuroscientific experiments extend our knowledge on the workings of the social brain and provide a rationale for modulating cortical excitability and subsequent affective processes to treat psychiatric disorders with NBS stimulation techniques.

On a final, critical note, the workings of complex affective behavior may not be unraveled on the basis of decomposition approaches, for the assumption of a one-to-one relation between the function and the localization of its underlying neural representations may be false. Although NBS stimulation cannot account for the explanatory gap between neurophysiological dynamics and how subjective experiences arise from such functions of the brain, these new and innovative techniques can identify and locate certain psychoneural entities or at least key nodes within the greater whole by means of true causal analyses (Schutter et al., 2004).

References

Arana, A. B., Borckardt, J. J., Ricci, R., Anderson, B., Li, X., Linder, K. J., Long, J., Sackeim, H. A., & George, M. S. (2008). Focal electrical stimulation as a sham control for repetitive transcranial magnetic stimulation: Does it truly mimic the cutaneous sensation and pain of active prefrontal repetitive transcranial magnetic stimulation? *Brain Stimulation*, *1*(1), 44–51. https://doi.org/10.1016/j.brs.2007.08.006

Bajbouj, M., Lisanby, S. H., Lang, U. E., Danker-Hopfe, H., Heuser, I., & Neu, P. (2006). Evidence for impaired cortical inhibition in patients with unipolar major depression. *Biological Psychiatry*, *59*(5), 395–400. https://doi.org/10.1016/j.biopsych.2005.07.036

Barker, A. T., Jalinous, R., & Freeston, I. L. (1985). Non-invasive magnetic stimulation of human motor cortex. *The Lancet*, *325*(8437), 1106–1107. https://doi.org/10.1016/S0140-6736(85)92413-4

Breier, A., & Paul, S. M. (1990). The $GABA_A$/benzodiazepine receptor: Implications for the molecular basis of anxiety. *Journal of Psychiatric Research*, *24*(Suppl. 2), 91–104. https://doi.org/10.1016/0022-3956(90)90040-W

Buchmann, J., Wolters, A., Haessler, F., Bohne, S., Nordbeck, R., & Kunesch, E. (2003). Disturbed transcallosally mediated motor inhibition in children with attention deficit hyperactivity disorder (ADHD). *Clinical Neurophysiology*, *114*(11), 2036–2042. https://doi.org/10.1016/S1388-2457(03)00208-6

Cantello, R., Gianelli, M., Civardi, C., & Mutani, R. (1992). Magnetic brain stimulation: The silent period after the motor evoked potential. *Neurology*, *42*(10), 1951–1959. https://doi.org/10.1212/WNL.42.10.1951

Chen, R., Tam, A., Bütefisch, C., Corwell, B., Ziemann, U., Rothwell, J. C., & Cohen, L. G. (1998). Intracortical inhibition and facilitation in different representations of the human motor cortex. *Journal of Neurophysiology*, *80*(6), 2870–2881. https://doi.org/10.1152/jn.1998.80.6.2870

Chung, H. K., Sjöström, T., Lee, H. J., Lu, Y. T., Tsuo, F. Y., Chen, T. S., Chang, C. F., Juan, C. H., Kuo, W. J., & Huang, C. Y. (2017). Why do irrelevant alternatives matter? An fMRI-TMS study of context-dependent preferences. *The Journal of Neuroscience*, 37(48), 11647–11661. https://doi.org/10.1523/JNEUROSCI.2307-16.2017

Ciechanski, P., Zewdie, E., & Kirton, A. (2017). Developmental profile of motor cortex transcallosal inhibition in children and adolescents. *Journal of Neurophysiology*, 118(1), 140–148. https://doi.org/10.1152/jn.00076.2017

Cohen, L. G., Roth, B. J., Nilsson, J., Dang, N., Panizza, M., Bandinelli, S., Friauf, W., & Hallett, M. (1990). Effects of coil design on delivery of focal magnetic stimulation: Technical considerations. *Electroencephalography and Clinical Neurophysiology*, 75(4), 350–357. https://doi.org/10.1016/0013-4694(90)90113-x

Cotovio, G., Rodrigues da Silva, D., Real Lage, E., Seybert, C., & Oliveira-Maia, A. J. (2022). Hemispheric asymmetry of motor cortex excitability in mood disorders: Evidence from a systematic review and meta-analysis. *Clinical Neurophysiology*, 137, 25–37. https://doi.org/10.1016/j.clinph.2022.01.137

d'Alfonso, A. A. L., van Honk, J., Hermans, E., Postma, A., & de Haan, E. H. F. (2000). Laterality effects in selective attention to threat after repetitive transcranial magnetic stimulation at the prefrontal cortex in female subjects. *Neuroscience Letters*, 280(3), 195–198. https://doi.org/10.1016/S0304-3940(00)00781-3

DaSilva, A. F., Truong, D. Q., DosSantos, M. F., Toback, R. L., Datta, A., & Bikson, M. (2015). State-of-art neuroanatomical target analysis of high-definition and conventional tDCS montages used for migraine and pain control. *Frontiers in Neuroanatomy*, 9, 89. https://doi.org/10.3389/fnana.2015.00089

Davidson, R. J. (1984). Affect, cognition, and hemispheric specialization. In C. E. Izard, J. Kagan, & R. B. Zajonc (Eds.), *Emotion, cognition, and behavior* (pp. 320–365). Cambridge University Press.

Davis, M., & Whalen, P. J. (2001). The amygdala: Vigilance and emotion. *Molecular Psychiatry*, 6(1), 13–34. https://doi.org/10.1038/sj.mp.4000812

Deblieck, C., Thompson, B., Iacoboni, M., & Wu, A. D. (2008). Correlation between motor and phosphene thresholds: A transcranial magnetic stimulation study. *Human Brain Mapping*, 29(6), 662–670. https://doi.org/10.1002/hbm.20427

Di Lazzaro, V., Profice, P., Pilato, F., Dileone, M., Oliviero, A., & Ziemann, U. (2010). The effects of motor cortex rTMS on corticospinal descending activity. *Clinical Neurophysiology*, 121(4), 464–473. https://doi.org/10.1016/j.clinph.2009.11.007

Esposito, R., Bortoletto, M., & Miniussi, C. (2020). Integrating TMS, EEG, and MRI as an approach for studying brain connectivity. *The Neuroscientist*, 26(5-6), 471–486. https://doi.org/10.1177/1073858420916452

Fecteau, S., Knoch, D., Fregni, F., Sultani, N., Boggio, P., & Pascual-Leone, A. (2007). Diminishing risk-taking behavior by modulating activity in the prefrontal cortex: A direct current stimulation study. *The Journal of Neuroscience*, 27(46), 12500–12505. https://doi.org/10.1523/JNEUROSCI.3283-07.2007

Fehr, E., & Camerer, C. F. (2007). Social neuroeconomics: The neural circuitry of social preferences. *Trends in Cognitive Sciences*, 11, 419–427. https://doi.org/10.1016/j.tics.2007.09.002

Ferbert, A., Priori, A., Rothwell, J. C., Day, B. L., Colebatch, J. G., & Marsden, C. D. (1992). Interhemispheric inhibition of the human motor cortex. *The Journal of Physiology*, 453(1), 525–546. https://doi.org/10.1113/jphysiol.1992.sp019243

Ferrarelli, F., Massimini, M., Sarasso, S., Casali, A., Riedner, B. A., Angelini, G., Tononi, G., & Pearce, R. A. (2010). Breakdown in cortical effective connectivity during midazolam-induced loss of consciousness. *Proceedings of the National Academy of Sciences of the United States of America*, 107(6), 2681–2686. https://doi.org/10.1073/pnas.0913008107

Filmer, H. L., Mattingley, J. B., & Dux, P. E. (2020). Modulating brain activity and behaviour with tDCS: Rumours of its death have been greatly exaggerated. *Cortex*, 123, 141–151. https://doi.org/10.1016/j.cortex.2019.10.006

Fitzgerald, P. B., Maller, J. J., Hoy, K., Farzan, F., & Daskalakis, Z. J. (2009). GABA and cortical inhibition in motor and non-motor regions using combined TMS-EEG: A time analysis. *Clinical Neurophysiology*, 120(9), 1706–1710. https://doi.org/10.1016/j.clinph.2009.06.019

Fregni, F., Orsati, F., Pedrosa, W., Fecteau, S., Tome, F. A., Nitsche, M. A., Mecca, T., Macedo, E. C., Pascual-Leone, A., & Boggio, P. S. (2008). Transcranial direct current stimulation of the prefrontal cortex modulates the desire for specific foods. *Appetite*, 51(1), 34–41. https://doi.org/10.1016/j.appet.2007.09.016

Hajcak, G., Molnar, C., George, M. S., Bolger, K., Koola, J., & Nahas, Z. (2007). Emotion facilitates action: A transcranial magnetic stimulation study of motor cortex excitability during picture viewing. *Psychophysiology*, 44(1), 91–97. https://doi.org/10.1111/j.1469-8986.2006.00487.x

Hallett, M. (2000). Transcranial magnetic stimulation and the human brain. *Nature, 406,* 147–150. https://doi.org/10.1038/35018000

Hallett, M. (2007). Transcranial magnetic stimulation: A primer. *Neuron, 55*(2), 187–199. https://doi.org/10.1016/j.neuron.2007.06.026

Harmon-Jones, E. (2003). Early Career Award. Clarifying the emotive functions of asymmetrical frontal cortical activity. *Psychophysiology, 40*(6), 838–848. https://doi.org/10.1111/1469-8986.00121

Harmon-Jones, E., & Beer, J. S. (Eds.). (2009). *Methods in social neuroscience.* Guilford Press.

Hofman, D., & Schutter, D. J. L. G. (2009). Inside the wire: Aggression and functional interhemispheric connectivity in the human brain. *Psychophysiology, 46,* 1054–1058. https://doi.org/10.1111/j.1469-8986.2009.00849.x

Hoogendam, J. M., Ramakers, G. M. J., & Di Lazzaro, V. (2010). Physiology of repetitive transcranial magnetic stimulation of the human brain. *Brain Stimulation, 3*(2), 95–118. https://doi.org/10.1016/j.brs.2009.10.005

Hoppenbrouwers, S. S., Hofman, D., & Schutter, D. J. L. G. (2010). Alcohol breaks down interhemispheric inhibition in females but not in males: Alcohol and frontal connectivity. *Psychopharmacology, 208*(3), 469–474. https://doi.org/10.1007/s00213-009-1747-5

Hsu, T. Y., Juan, C. H., & Tseng, P. (2016). Individual differences and state-dependent responses in transcranial direct current stimulation. *Frontiers in Human Neuroscience, 10,* 643. https://doi.org/10.3389/fnhum.2016.00643

Huang, Y. Z., Edwards, M. J., Rounis, E., Bhatia, K. P., & Rothwell, J. C. (2005). Theta burst stimulation of the human motor cortex. *Neuron, 45*(2), 201–206. https://doi.org/10.1016/j.neuron.2004.12.033

Ilmoniemi, R. J., Virtanen, J., Ruohonen, J., Karhu, J., Aronen, H. J., Näätänen, R., & Katila, T. (1997). Neuronal responses to magnetic stimulation reveal cortical reactivity and connectivity. *NeuroReport, 8*(16), 3537–3540. https://doi.org/10.1097/00001756-199711100-00024

Jonker, Z. D., Gaiser, C., Tulen, J. H. M., Ribbers, G. M., Frens, M. A., & Selles, R. W. (2020). No effect of anodal tDCS on motor cortical excitability and no evidence for responders in a large double-blind placebo-controlled trial. *Brain Stimulation, 14*(1), 100–109. https://doi.org/10.1016/j.brs.2020.11.005

Kähkönen, S., Komssi, S., Wilenius, J., & Ilmoniemi, R. J. (2005). Prefrontal TMS produces smaller EEG responses than motor-cortex TMS: Implications for rTMS treatment in depression. *Psychopharmacology, 181*(1), 16–20. https://doi.org/10.1007/s00213-005-2197-3

Kanai, R., Chaieb, L., Antal, A., Walsh, V., & Paulus, W. (2008). Frequency-dependent electrical stimulation of the visual cortex. *Current Biology, 18*(23), 1839–1843. https://doi.org/10.1016/j.cub.2008.10.027

Khedr, E. M., Rothwell, J. C., Ahmed, M. A., Shawky, O. A., & Farouk, M. (2007). Modulation of motor cortical excitability following rapid-rate transcranial magnetic stimulation. *Clinical Neurophysiology, 118*(1), 140–145. https://doi.org/10.1016/j.clinph.2006.09.006

Knoch, D., Gianotti, L. R., Pascual-Leone, A., Treyer, V., Regard, M., Hohmann, M., & Brugger, P. (2006). Disruption of right prefrontal cortex by low-frequency repetitive transcranial magnetic stimulation induces risk-taking behavior. *The Journal of Neuroscience, 26*(24), 6469–6472. https://doi.org/10.1523/JNEUROSCI.0804-06.2006

Knoch, D., Nitsche, M. A., Fischbacher, U., Eisenegger, C., Pascual-Leone, A., & Fehr, E. (2008). Studying the neurobiology of social interaction with transcranial direct current stimulation—The example of punishing unfairness. *Cerebral Cortex, 18*(9), 1987–1990. https://doi.org/10.1093/cercor/bhm237

Knoch, D., Pascual-Leone, A., Meyer, K., Treyer, V., & Fehr, E. (2006). Diminishing reciprocal fairness by disrupting the right prefrontal cortex. *Science, 314*(5800), 829–832. https://doi.org/10.1126/science.1129156

Levinson, A. J., Fitzgerald, P. B., Favalli, G., Blumberger, D. M., Daigle, M., & Daskalakis, Z. J. (2010). Evidence of cortical inhibitory deficits in major depressive disorder. *Biological Psychiatry, 67*(5), 458–464. https://doi.org/10.1016/j.biopsych.2009.09.025

Medina-Fernández, F. J., Luque, E., Aguilar-Luque, M., Agüera, E., Feijóo, M., García-Maceira, F. I., Escribano, B. M., Pascual-Leone, Á., Drucker-Colín, R., & Túnez, I. (2017). Transcranial magnetic stimulation modifies astrocytosis, cell density and lipopolysaccharide levels in experimental autoimmune encephalomyelitis. *Life Sciences, 169,* 20–26. https://doi.org/10.1016/j.lfs.2016.11.011

Moll, G. H., Heinrich, H., Wischer, S., Tergau, F., Paulus, W., & Rothenberger, A. (1999). Motor system excitability in healthy children: Developmental aspects from transcranial magnetic stimulation. *Electroencephalography and Clinical Neurophysiology Supplement, 51,* 243–249.

Mulckhuyse, M., Engelmann, J. B., Schutter, D. J. L. G., & Roelofs, K. (2017). Right posterior parietal cortex is involved in disengaging from threat: A 1-Hz rTMS study. *Social Cognitive and Affective Neuroscience, 12*(11), 1814–1822. https://doi.org/10.1093/scan/nsx111

Nitsche, M. A., Cohen, L. G., Wassermann, E. M., Priori, A., Lang, N., Antal, A., Paulus, W., Hummel, F., Boggio, P. S., Fregni, F., & Pascual-Leone, A. (2008). Transcranial direct current stimulation: State of the art 2008. *Brain Stimulation*, *1*(3), 206–223. https://doi.org/10.1016/j.brs.2008.06.004

Nitsche, M. A., & Paulus, W. (2000). Excitability changes induced in the human motor cortex by weak transcranial direct current stimulation. *The Journal of Physiology*, *527*(3), 633–639. https://doi.org/10.1111/j.1469-7793.2000.t01-1-00633.x

Oathes, D. J., Bruce, J. M., & Nitschke, J. B. (2008). Worry facilitates corticospinal motor response to transcranial magnetic stimulation. *Depression and Anxiety*, *25*(11), 969–976. https://doi.org/10.1002/da.20445

Öhman, A. (1986). Face the beast and fear the face: Animal and social fears as prototypes for evolutionary analyses of emotion. *Psychophysiology*, *23*(2), 123–145. https://doi.org/10.1111/j.1469-8986.1986.tb00608.x

Pascual-Leone, A., Tormos, J. M., Keenan, J., Tarazona, F., Cañete, C., & Catalá, M. D. (1998). Study and modulation of human cortical excitability with transcranial magnetic stimulation. *Journal of Clinical Neurophysiology*, *15*(4), 333–343. https://doi.org/10.1097/00004691-199807000-00005

Pitcher, D., Parkin, B., & Walsh, V. (2021). Transcranial magnetic stimulation and the understanding of behavior. *Annual Review of Psychology*, *72*(1), 97–121. https://doi.org/10.1146/annurev-psych-081120-013144

Premoli, I., Király, J., Müller-Dahlhaus, F., Zipser, C. M., Rossini, P., Zrenner, C., Ziemann, U., & Belardinelli, P. (2018). Short-interval and long-interval intracortical inhibition of TMS-evoked EEG potentials. *Brain Stimulation*, *11*(4), 818–827. https://doi.org/10.1016/j.brs.2018.03.008

Priori, A. (2003). Brain polarization in humans: A reappraisal of an old tool for prolonged noninvasive modulation of brain excitability. *Clinical Neurophysiology*, *114*(4), 589–595. https://doi.org/10.1016/S1388-2457(02)00437-6

Priori, A., Berardelli, A., Rona, S., Accornero, N., & Manfredi, M. (1998). Polarization of the human motor cortex through the scalp. *Neuroreport*, *9*(10), 2257–2260. https://doi.org/10.1097/00001756-199807130-00020

Rabin, M. (1993). Incorporating fairness into game theory and economics. *The American Economic Review*, *83*(5), 1281–1302.

Rossi, S., Antal, A., Bestmann, S., Bikson, M., Brewer, C., Brockmöller, J., Carpenter, L. L., Cincotta, M., Chen, R., Daskalakis, J. D., Di Lazzaro, V., Fox, M. D., George, M. S., Gilbert, D., Kimiskidis, V. K., Koch, G., Ilmoniemi, R. J., Lefaucheur, J. P., Leocani, L., . . . Hallett, M. (2021). Safety and recommendations for TMS use in healthy subjects and patient populations, with updates on training, ethical and regulatory issues: Expert guidelines. *Clinical Neurophysiology*, *132*(1), 269–306. https://doi.org/10.1016/j.clinph.2020.10.003

Santiago-Rodríguez, E., Cárdenas-Morales, L., Harmony, T., Fernández-Bouzas, A., Porras-Kattz, E., & Hernández, A. (2008). Repetitive transcranial magnetic stimulation decreases the number of seizures in patients with focal neocortical epilepsy. *Seizure*, *17*(8), 677–683. https://doi.org/10.1016/j.seizure.2008.04.005

Schutter, D. J. L. G. (2009). Transcranial magnetic stimulation. In E. Harmon-Jones & J. S. Beer (Eds.), *Methods in social neuroscience* (pp. 233–258). Guilford Press.

Schutter, D. J. L. G. (2014). Syncing your brain: Electric currents to enhance cognition. *Trends in Cognitive Sciences*, *18*(7), 331–333. https://doi.org/10.1016/j.tics.2014.02.011

Schutter, D. J. L. G. (2020). *The cerebellum in emotions and psychopathology*. Taylor & Francis. https://doi.org/10.4324/9781315145082

Schutter, D. J. L. G., de Weijer, A. D., Meuwese, J. D., Morgan, B., & van Honk, J. (2008). Interrelations between motivational stance, cortical excitability, and the frontal electroencephalogram asymmetry of emotion: A transcranial magnetic stimulation study. *Human Brain Mapping*, *29*(5), 574–580. https://doi.org/10.1002/hbm.20417

Schutter, D. J. L. G., & Harmon-Jones, E. (2013). The corpus callosum: A commissural road to anger and aggression. *Neuroscience and Biobehavioral Reviews*, *37*(10 Pt. 2), 2481–2488. https://doi.org/10.1016/j.neubiorev.2013.07.013

Schutter, D. J. L. G., Hofman, D., & Van Honk, J. (2008). Fearful faces selectively increase corticospinal motor tract excitability: A transcranial magnetic stimulation study. *Psychophysiology*, *45*(3), 345–348. https://doi.org/10.1111/j.1469-8986.2007.00635.x

Schutter, D. J. L. G., van Honk, J., d'Alfonso, A. A. L., Postma, A., & de Haan, E. H. F. (2001). Effects of slow rTMS at the right dorsolateral prefrontal cortex on EEG asymmetry and mood. *Neuroreport*, *12*(3), 445–447. https://doi.org/10.1097/00001756-200103050-00005

Schutter, D. J. L. G., van Honk, J., & Panksepp, J. (2004). Introducing transcranial magnetic stimulation (TMS) and its property of causal inference in investigating brain-function relationships. *Synthese*, *141*(2), 155–173. https://doi.org/10.1023/B:SYNT.0000042951.25087.16

Schutter, D. J. L. G., & Wischnewski, M. (2016). A meta-analytic study of exogenous oscillatory electric potentials in neuroenhancement. *Neuropsychologia*, *86*, 110–118. https://doi.org/10.1016/j.neuropsychologia.2016.04.011

Silvanto, J., Muggleton, N., & Walsh, V. (2008). State-dependency in brain stimulation studies of perception and cognition. *Trends in Cognitive Sciences*, *12*(12), 447–454. https://doi.org/10.1016/j.tics.2008.09.004

Speer, A. M., Willis, M. W., Herscovitch, P., Daube-Witherspoon, M., Shelton, J. R., Benson, B. E., Post, R. M., & Wassermann, E. M. (2003). Intensity-dependent regional cerebral blood flow during 1-Hz repetitive transcranial magnetic stimulation (rTMS) in healthy volunteers studied with H215O positron emission tomography: II. Effects of prefrontal cortex rTMS. *Biological Psychiatry*, *54*(8), 826–832. https://doi.org/10.1016/S0006-3223(03)00324-X

Thut, G., & Miniussi, C. (2009). New insights into rhythmic brain activity from TMS-EEG studies. *Trends in Cognitive Sciences*, *13*(4), 182–189. https://doi.org/10.1016/j.tics.2009.01.004

van Honk, J., & Schutter, D. J. L. G. (2006a). From affective valence to motivational direction: The frontal asymmetry of emotion revised. *Psychological Science*, *17*(11), 963–965. https://doi.org/10.1111/j.1467-9280.2006.01813.x

van Honk, J., & Schutter, D. J. L. G. (2006b). Unmasking feigned sanity: A neurobiological model of emotion processing in primary psychopathy. *Cognitive Neuropsychiatry*, *11*(3), 285–306. https://doi.org/10.1080/13546800500233728

van Honk, J., Schutter, D. J. L. G., d'Alfonso, A. A. L., Kessels, R. P. C., & de Haan, E. H. F. (2002). 1 hz rTMS over the right prefrontal cortex reduces vigilant attention to unmasked but not to masked fearful faces. *Biological Psychiatry*, *52*(4), 312–317. https://doi.org/10.1016/S0006-3223(02)01346-X

van 't Wout, M., Kahn, R. S., Sanfey, A. G., & Aleman, A. (2005). Repetitive transcranial magnetic stimulation over the right dorsolateral prefrontal cortex affects strategic decision-making. *NeuroReport*, *16*(16), 1849–1852. https://doi.org/10.1097/01.wnr.0000183907.08149.14

Vines, B. W., Cerruti, C., & Schlaug, G. (2008). Dual-hemisphere tDCS facilitates greater improvements for healthy subjects' non-dominant hand compared to uni-hemisphere stimulation. *BMC Neuroscience*, *9*(1), 103. https://doi.org/10.1186/1471-2202-9-103

Wagner, T., Valero-Cabre, A., & Pascual-Leone, A. (2007). Noninvasive human brain stimulation. *Annual Review of Biomedical Engineering*, *9*(1), 527–565. https://doi.org/10.1146/annurev.bioeng.9.061206.133100

Wassermann, E. M., Epstein, C. M., Ziemann, U., Walsh, V., Paus, T., & Lisanby, S. (2008). *The Oxford handbook of transcranial stimulation*. Oxford University Press.

Wassermann, E. M., Greenberg, B. D., Nguyen, M. B., & Murphy, D. L. (2001). Motor cortex excitability correlates with an anxiety-related personality trait. *Biological Psychiatry*, *50*(5), 377–382. https://doi.org/10.1016/S0006-3223(01)01210-0

Wassermann, E. M., & Lisanby, S. H. (2001). Therapeutic application of repetitive transcranial magnetic stimulation: A review. *Clinical Neurophysiology*, *112*(8), 1367–1377. https://doi.org/10.1016/S1388-2457(01)00585-5

Zaghi, S., Acar, M., Hultgren, B., Boggio, P. S., & Fregni, F. (2010). Noninvasive brain stimulation with low-intensity electrical currents: Putative mechanisms of action for direct and alternating current stimulation. *The Neuroscientist*, *16*(3), 285–307. https://doi.org/10.1177/1073858409336227

Zangen, A., Roth, Y., Voller, B., & Hallett, M. (2005). Transcranial magnetic stimulation of deep brain regions: Evidence for efficacy of the H-coil. *Clinical Neurophysiology*, *116*(4), 775–779. https://doi.org/10.1016/j.clinph.2004.11.008

Ziemann, U. (2004). TMS and drugs. *Clinical Neurophysiology*, *115*(8), 1717–1729. https://doi.org/10.1016/j.clinph.2004.03.006

CHAPTER 31

COMBINED NEUROIMAGING METHODS

Marius Moisa and Christian C. Ruff

The scientific study of cognition and emotion has been fundamentally transformed by the advent of techniques for functional neuroimaging and neuromodulation. The methods that have gained the most popularity among psychologists are functional magnetic resonance imaging (fMRI), electroencephalography (EEG), magnetoencephalography (MEG), and noninvasive brain stimulation (NIBS) techniques such as transcranial magnetic stimulation (TMS) and transcranial electric current stimulation (tES). Development of these techniques has made possible the study of cognitive processes and emotional states not only via their expression in behavior but also by inspecting or manipulating the associated brain activity. Numerous psychological constructs—such as perception, attention, memory, language, emotional states, decision making, and so on—are now investigated in terms of the associated brain activity, and the novelty and worth of this work has been acknowledged by high public interest. The perceived increase in explanatory power that comes with the use of these techniques has led to the foundation of specialized learned societies for cognitive neuroscience, affective neuroscience, decision neuroscience, and social neuroscience. Moreover, other sciences that study human behavior (e.g., economics) have also introduced neuroimaging into their field.

As exciting and promising as findings of brain-behavior relations are, their ultimate worth depends crucially on properties of the research methods with which they are derived. As described in several preceding chapters (see Chapters 27–30 of this volume), each neuroimaging or neuromodulation method can only capture, or influence, specific aspects of brain activity. Thus, it remains difficult to give one overarching explanation of how, for example, the act of reading this printed word is instantiated in our brains. Few would doubt that this mental act should depend on a well-defined set of neural processes, but researchers using either MEG or fMRI might give somewhat different accounts of what this set includes, simply because these techniques focus on different aspects of brain function (e.g., event-related potential [ERP] components and fMRI activations). This raises the question as to what common "true" brain state may underlie these method-specific observations.

This chapter presents an overview of methodological developments that attempt to deal with this fundamental problem. All of these developments focus on combinations of existing methods from the present armory of cognitive neuroscientists, an approach often referred to as *multimodal imaging*. Three such combinations are described and discussed: fMRI–EEG/MEG,

https://doi.org/10.1037/0000318-031
APA Handbook of Research Methods in Psychology, Second Edition: Vol. 1. Foundations, Planning, Measures, and Psychometrics, H. Cooper (Editor-in-Chief)
Copyright © 2023 by the American Psychological Association. All rights reserved.

NIBS-EEG, and NIBS-fMRI. These approaches allow researchers to capitalize on complementary strengths of two methods, thereby gaining a more complete picture of neural processing and reducing uncertainties associated with the use of each method in isolation. Of course, this does not come for free: Multimodal imaging techniques are technically and conceptually more complicated than the use of each single method. Standardized solutions, however, are increasingly established and can be employed by the community in an increasingly routine fashion. Ambitious work attempts to combine even three types of neuroimaging methods concurrently (Fehér et al., 2017; Peters et al., 2020); however, this is even more technically challenging and beyond the scope of this chapter.

The chapter begins with a brief description of the basic mechanisms of action for EEG/MEG, fMRI, and NIBS. Because detailed accounts of these methods are given in the preceding chapters (see Chapters 27–30, this volume), this section outlines only the strengths and shortcomings of each technique to motivate their multimodal combination.

We then describe the three multimodal combinations in detail in separate sections. The sections start with the general rationale of each approach, give a brief outline of technical considerations, and discuss the unique insights that can be gained with the particular methodical combination by means of illustrative studies.

USES AND LIMITATIONS OF SINGLE NEUROIMAGING METHODS

Electroencephalography and Magnetoencephalography

EEG and MEG are somewhat related methods in that both measure electrical activity in the brain noninvasively via signals recorded outside the head. Both methods rely on the fact that neuronal activity is associated with weak electric currents in the brain tissue (for detailed mechanisms see Chapter 27). EEG can detect these currents as weak electric potentials at the scalp via a set of electrodes mounted on the skin. MEG, in contrast, measures changes in magnetic fields associated with these currents.

Although the signals measured by MEG and EEG index somewhat different types of neural activity, both techniques occupy a largely similar niche in research on brain–behavior relations. Both methods measure neural activity directly via associated electric signals and can index neural activity with millisecond precision. Averaging EEG/MEG signal epochs following repetitions of one type of experimental event yields an event-related potential (ERP)/event-related field (ERF) that visualizes the typical time course of neural processing associated with a mental event. Both types of signals, thus, prove information about neural changes during different temporal stages of processing (for examples, see Chapter 27).

A further strength of EEG and MEG is that the acquired data are highly multidimensional and can reveal many different aspects of neural dynamics. For instance, both methods allow researchers to study changes in neural oscillations in different frequency bands (e.g., delta: 1–4 Hz; theta: 4–8 Hz; alpha: 8–13 Hz; beta: 13–30 Hz; and gamma: > 30 Hz). Changes in the power spectral density of each frequency band can be averaged for comparable experimental episodes to reveal systematic changes in oscillatory activity that are time-locked to experimentally induced mental events (for details, see Chapter 27). Moreover, advanced analysis methods (e.g., debiased weighted phase lag index, Vinck et al., 2011) can show if the oscillatory activity at a specific frequency band is synchronized between different remote areas. This coherence in the activity between two specific areas is thought to reflect information transfer/communication between these areas during a particular mental process (Polanía et al., 2014; Siegel et al., 2008).

The strengths of EEG and MEG for brain-behavior research are complemented by equally salient weaknesses. For instance, the underlying biophysics result in EEG being most sensitive to neural activity in the neocortex, as firing of subcortical cell assemblies is not usually associated with clearly detectable electric potentials at the scalp (this problem is somewhat less severe for magnetic field changes measured by MEG; see Chapter 27). Perhaps even more critically, it is usually difficult to determine the anatomical location of a cortical source for a particular ERP or ERF or for a change in oscillatory power, as infinite theoretical solutions exist that may result in a particular arrangement of electric scalp potentials or magnetic fields. Solutions to this *inverse problem* (of determining what precise intracranial sources produce observed signals outside the head) can be provided by mathematical approaches (e.g., Laufs et al., 2008; Michel & Brunet, 2019). Nevertheless, there always remains a degree of uncertainty about the neuroanatomical origin of observed EEG/MEG signals. Finally, it may be critical that both methods are sensitive to the firing of only specific cell types and, thus, may index different types of neural activity: EEG signals are thought to mainly reflect activity of pyramidal cells that are perpendicular to the scalp, on the crown of cortical gyri, whereas MEG signals may be most sensitive to pyramidal cells located in the sulci, tangential to the scalp (Nunez & Srinivasan, 2006).

In sum, EEG and MEG offer psychologists good ways to study the precise temporal aspects of cortical processing associated with experimental tasks. The data are multidimensional and provide several different approaches to cortical dynamics that are associated with mental states. These methods do not allow strong inferences about the neuroanatomical structures that show changes in neural activity. They also cannot reliably measure activity in many brain areas that are of interest to psychologists (for instance, various subcortical areas relevant for emotion processing and memory).

Functional Magnetic Resonance Imaging

fMRI measures neural activity only indirectly via associated changes in blood oxygenation (a detailed account of the relevant physics and physiology is given in Chapter 29 of this volume). The major strength of fMRI is that it can visualize neural activity (indirectly via its metabolic consequences) throughout the whole brain with good spatial resolution (around 2–3 mm^3 at present, but less than 1 mm^3 is possible on high-field scanners; see Chapter 29 of this volume). The high spatial resolution and the ability to measure blood oxygenation level-dependent (BOLD) activity for all regions of the brain with equal sensitivity make fMRI arguably the current gold standard for testing hypotheses about brain–behavior relations in humans (Poldrack & Farah, 2015).

The strengths of fMRI are fully complementary to those of EEG/MEG, and the same can be said of its weaknesses. For instance, the temporal resolution of fMRI is relatively modest. The hemodynamic response to a discrete neural event is temporally sluggish, peaking at around 4 to 7 seconds after the relevant neural activity and returning to baseline several seconds later. Further complicating matters, standard fMRI sequences covering the full cortex can only sample this hemodynamic response with a temporal resolution of 2 to 3 seconds. Although standardized deconvolution procedures can nevertheless resolve neural events that are spaced within approximately 2 seconds of one another (for details, see Chapter 29 of this volume), it is very difficult to use fMRI to make inferences about different temporal stages of processing during a trial. fMRI data, thus, normally only present a temporally averaged snapshot of neural activity associated with a mental event rather than a detailed account of associated neural dynamics (but see, e.g., Valdés-Sosa et al., 2005, for an overview of mathematical modeling procedures to infer neural dynamics underlying BOLD time series).

Use of the hemodynamic response to infer neural processing is complicated not only with respect to temporal resolution but also regarding the question of which aspect of neural activity is causing the measured signals. The relation between BOLD increases and neural activity is intensely debated. Issues that appear most relevant for researchers of brain–behavior relations include whether BOLD increases reflect mostly spiking output of neural populations or synaptic input and local processing within an area, whether BOLD increases reflect only activity of neurons or also of glial cells, whether neural inhibition of an area produces BOLD signal increases or decreases, and whether BOLD signal increases linearly with neural activity (for detailed discussion, see Hall et al., 2016). Answers to all of these questions will be important for the interpretation of fMRI results and for establishing links between the fMRI and the EEG/MEG literatures.

Noninvasive Brain Stimulation

Both EEG/MEG and fMRI are purely correlative methods, revealing which electrical or blood flow changes in the brain are associated with experimental manipulations of psychological processes. Such correlative data have greatly advanced our understanding of brain-behavior relations, but they leave doubt as to whether the observed brain activity is causally necessary for the observed behavior. Moreover, many neuroimaging findings leave open questions as to which aspect of the experimental situation may have triggered electrical or hemodynamic activity. In principle, only some of the observed brain activations may relate to performance of the experimental task, whereas others may reflect changes in task-correlated psychological or physiological context factors (e.g., arousal).

These shortcomings have triggered great interest in the use of NIBS techniques, allowing tests of whether and how focal manipulation of neural activity in specific regions of the brain can affect behavior in experimental situations. In this chapter, we address the two most popular of these techniques, namely, transcranial magnetic stimulation (TMS) and transcranial electric stimulation (tES). TMS and tES are somewhat related methods in that both are modulating the activity of the targeted areas. TMS works by electromagnetic induction, while tES works by direct electric current flow (for details, see Chapter 30). For TMS, an encased copper coil (often consisting of two loops put together in a figure-8 form) is connected to a set of capacitors that store a large electrical charge. For each TMS pulse, this charge is released via an electric switch that shorts the charged elements through the TMS coil, leading to a strong current (several thousand amperes) passing rapidly (in less than 1 ms) through the coil. The current is associated with a magnetic field that falls off exponentially with increasing distance from the coil, but it can permeate head tissue without attenuation. If the coil is placed tangentially on the scalp, overlying a cortical region of interest, the magnetic flux (rate of change of the magnetic field) associated with each pulse electromagnetically induces a current in the underlying conductive neural tissue. This current elicits action potentials in neurons with appropriate orientations relative to the electric current (for a more detailed description of the biophysics of TMS and necessary apparatus, see Chapter 30 of this volume and Wassermann et al., 2008).

For tES, two rubber electrodes are placed on the head and an electric potential is set up between them so that an electric current flows between the anode (+, positive charge) and cathode (−, negative charge). These currents are weak (usually around 1–2 mA) and, thus, do not directly elicit action potentials, but they change neuronal excitability. That is, neurons under the anode are depolarized and, thus, triggering of action potentials is facilitated, while neurons under the cathode electrode are hyperpolarized and, thus, triggering of action potentials is inhibited (for more details, see Chapter 30 of this volume and Knotkova et al., 2019). The most common type of tES is transcranial direct current simulation (tDCS) where the potential and current is constant, but more specialized tES protocols have also been set up. One example is transcranial alternating current stimulation (tACS), for which an oscillatory current is applied at a specific frequency, usually informed by EEG results, to modulate the amplitude and/or phase of oscillatory activity in this specific frequency in the targeted area (for more details, see Herrmann et al., 2013). The neural effects of this protocol are currently under investigation, and there are promising demonstrations that it can be used to test the functional relevance of cortical oscillatory activity for cognition (Antal & Paulus, 2013; Herrmann et al., 2016; Polanía et al., 2018; Yavari et al., 2018).

Both tES and TMS can be applied online, during a specific behavioral task. For example, the neural activity induced by TMS can be used to mask or disrupt the neural processing necessary for an experimental task. Importantly, TMS has excellent temporal resolution (in the order of milliseconds up to tens of milliseconds) and pulses applied during different temporal stages of task performance can reveal the involvement of the stimulated region for each specific phase (see Walsh & Pascual-Leone, 2003). In contrast, tES has a much lower temporal resolution (in the order of seconds to tens of seconds, because tES starts to be effective after a few seconds) and, thus, cannot be used to investigate the stimulation effects on a specific task phase. Alternatively, both TMS and tES can be used in an offline manner before task performance. This leads to changes in the excitability of the stimulated region that persist for a limited time beyond the stimulation period, from a few minutes until a couple of hours depending on the stimulation parameters (for details, see Chapter 30 in this volume).

Another difference between TMS and tES is the focality of the stimulation and the ease with which certain areas can be stimulated. TMS is rather focal (the induced electric field is maximum right beneath the center of the TMS coil and falls off exponentially with increasing distance from the center of the coil). In contrast, tES is not very focal—the electric field is the strongest under the electrodes but does expand to areas between the electrodes. Frontal areas (i.e., orbital frontal cortex and dorsolateral prefrontal cortex), however, are difficult to target with TMS due to the peripheral stimulation (e.g., muscle twitches that yield a great discomfort for the participants), but these areas can be targeted more easily with tES.

A unique strength of NIBS compared with other neuroimaging methods is that it allows truly causal evidence for the necessity of neural processing in the stimulated brain region for task performance. In that respect, NIBS may be closely related to neuropsychological studies of deficits in patients with brain lesions but can overcome many of the shortcomings of the lesion approach: It can be used to modulate activity in the brains of healthy people, who unlike patients do not suffer from possible side effects of clinical states, such as neural reorganization, medication, and so on. Moreover, all effects of NIBS are fully reversible and can be studied on a within-subject basis by comparing each participant during and after the NIBS intervention with themselves during a matched control condition.

Like all other neuroimaging methods, NIBS methods have shortcomings. At present, both TMS and tES can only be used to target brain areas on the outer cortical convexity. Many subcortical and medial brain regions are located too far from the scalp to be reached by magnetic and electric fields produced by TMS and tES, respectively. Another critical point is that the mechanism of action of NIBS is still not fully understood. It is currently debated as to which types of neurons are most prone to be stimulated by NIBS, how exactly the artificial modulation of activity induced by NIBS interferes with ongoing cortical activity that is relevant for behavior, and how the effects of NIBS may depend on the current functional state of the tissue (see Chapter 30 of this volume and Wassermann et al., 2008; Polanía et al., 2018). Finally, NIBS studies by themselves provide no information as to whether observed behavioral changes are due only to manipulation of neural processing in the region directly underneath the TMS coil or tES electrodes or whether effects on remote brain areas interconnected with the stimulation site may also contribute.

In sum, any researcher who uses EEG/MEG, fMRI, and NIBS to study brain-behavior relations will only be able to focus on specific aspects of neural function (e.g., timing, neurophysiology, anatomical origin, cortical vs. subcortical regions, causality), while being partially blind to other aspects. Luckily, it appears that the weaknesses of one method are usually the strength of another, motivating the combination of neuroimaging techniques to overcome many of these limitations. In the next sections, three such combinations are discussed in detail, touching on both the conceptual and technical considerations associated with each.

Electroencephalography/ Magnetoencephalography and Functional Magnetic Resonance Imaging

fMRI can provide detailed information about where in the brain neural processing increases during task performance, whereas EEG/MEG can reveal the timing and cortical dynamics of these effects. Hence, recording both types of signals during performance of the same task and combining their information may give a spatiotemporal perspective on cortical processes associated with the task. This logic has been successfully used in several studies, as described in the upcoming section Sequential Combination of EEG/MEG and fMRI. There are also, however, more subtle methodological reasons for why EEG/MEG–fMRI combinations may be informative.

The biophysics and neurophysiology of electrical neural activity (as measured with MEG/EEG) and the BOLD response (as measured with fMRI) suggest that neural activations detected with either of these methods may not always correspond to those found in the other (Nunez & Srinivasan, 2006). Parts of the observed signals may be truly specific to either method because of each technique's unique sensitivity for certain types of neural activity, insensitivity for others, and method-specific artifacts (Debener et al., 2006). Measuring both EEG/MEG and fMRI during performance of the same task may, thus, "separate the wheat from the chaff," identifying the types of neural activity that leave a trace in both modalities concurrently. Such shared neural markers can refine our understanding of the signals detected by both methods, resolve uncertainties about the spatial origin and temporal characteristics of the constituting neural processes, and provide strong evidence for a distinct brain state associated with behavior. Thus, now that many reliable effects have been documented with each method used in isolation, establishing correspondences between neural signatures of cognitive processes in MEG/EEG and fMRI may be a crucial next step for cognitive neuroscience. Such data fusion requires either sequential, offline combinations of the two methods, or online parallel acquisition of data in both modalities. Both of these approaches have advantages and disadvantages.

Sequential combination of EEG/MEG and fMRI. From a technical perspective, sequential combinations of EEG/MEG and fMRI are straightforward. No special apparatus is needed other than the devices used for either method alone. The same participants take part in the same experiment twice, once in the MR scanner and once in the EEG/MEG setup. This allows individual combination of fMRI data and the corresponding ERP/ERF scalp maps and, hence, information on both timing and spatial localization of neural activity associated with the behavioral task.

The biggest challenge for offline combinations of EEG/MEG and fMRI may be the experimental design, as it is crucial that the experiment is exactly replicated in the two different contexts. For instance, MR scanners are usually noisy and vibrate, and participants lie in a supine position, whereas EEG/MEG setups usually require complete silence and that participants sit upright. Moreover, differences in psychological state between experiments (e.g., learning effects, fluctuations of fatigue across sessions, or different levels of task performance) may affect results. Careful counterbalancing and close matching of all relevant context factors across sessions may, thus, be essential.

Offline combinations of EEG/MEG and fMRI have traditionally been used for modeling cortical sources of the observed ERPs. Peak fMRI activations are taken to indicate likely candidates for cortical generators of electrophysiological activity, and these regions are used as informed guesses when trying to localize observed ERPs by means of fMRI-informed mathematical algorithms (e.g., Dale et al., 2000; Horwitz & Poeppel, 2002; Nguyen et al., 2016). One of the first studies to use this approach was conducted by Heinze et al. (1994), who used positron emission tomography (PET; see Chapter 29 of this volume) rather than fMRI to identify brain regions in visual cortex that showed higher metabolic activity during attention to one hemifield of a display versus the other. Such attention-responsive regions were found in the contralateral extrastriate cortex in the fusiform gyri. ERPs recorded in the same participants revealed significant modulations at the scalp contralateral to the side of attention at 80 ms to 130 ms after stimulus onset. A dipole-fit model suggested that the extrastriate regions identified with PET were indeed likely generators of the ERPs identified with EEG. Fusing PET and EEG data, thus, demonstrated that effects of spatial attention in extrastriate visual cortex presumably arise at an early stage of stimulus processing (80 ms–130 ms after stimulus onset). Following this initial study, subsequent fMRI-EEG (Martínez et al., 1999) and fMRI–EEG/MEG (Noesselt et al., 2002) studies further demonstrated that BOLD activity increases in striate visual cortex during spatial attention reflect delayed (emerging 140 ms after stimulus onset) and, hence, presumably reentrant neural activity. In another example, Pfabigan et al. (2014) aimed to identify the link between putative electrophysiological markers of reward processing (the P300) and BOLD activity in reward-related brain areas during anticipatory monetary gains and losses. The participants performed a monetary incentive delay task in which they were cued to win or lose money during separate fMRI and EEG sessions. The P300 amplitude positively correlated with the change in BOLD activity in the ventral striatum. As this relationship was observed during both gain and loss anticipation, the authors concluded that these neural mechanisms reflect more general motivational processing rather than a specific reward-related process. All of these combined multimodal neuroimaging studies reveal a spatiotemporal profile of neural activity that could not have been derived with any method alone.

Concurrent combination of EEG and fMRI.
A unique strength of EEG and MEG is that both methods can visualize dynamic and spontaneous aspects of neural activity with millisecond temporal resolution. These signal properties are lost when EEG/MEG is combined with fMRI in an offline fashion, as corresponding stimulus-locked episodes have to be averaged to yield typical responses to events (e.g., ERPs/ERFs and average BOLD responses, respectively). For this reason, increasing effort has been directed at recording EEG signals inside the scanner bore during fMRI. Such online EEG-fMRI allows researchers to relate metabolic changes throughout the brain with those aspects of electrical brain activity that are hard to control experimentally and that are variable over time.

Online combination with fMRI is not possible for MEG because it relies on recording weak magnetic field changes (in the range of femtotesla [fT]). This is incompatible with the strong static magnetic fields (at present 3–7 tesla in human scanners), switching gradients, and radio-frequency (RF) pulses inside an MR scanner. By contrast, EEG electrodes and cables can be introduced in the MR environment, but this combination is quite complicated and requires considerable methodical expertise. A comprehensive discussion of technical problems arising in this context is beyond the scope of this chapter, but interested readers can consult several reviews (e.g., Abreu et al., 2018; Herrmann & Debener, 2008; Huster et al., 2012; Jorge et al., 2014; Laufs et al., 2008; Mulert & Lemieux, 2010; Ritter & Villringer, 2006). The following paragraphs give a brief overview of the dedicated EEG hardware and procedures for a successfully concurrent combination with fMRI.

From a hardware point of view, all the EEG equipment used inside the scanner room must be nonferromagnetic and MR-compatible EEG electrodes must be used. Furthermore, the EEG amplifier should have sufficient bandwidth to capture the full range of the scanner artifact, with enough sensitivity for detecting the small fluctuations in the EEG signal.

The MR scanner interacts dynamically with the EEG equipment. For example, the MR might induce currents or heating in the EEG electrodes that may lead to electrical stimulation and even tissue damage. Several standardized procedures have been established for minimizing the participant risks associated with the interactions of fMRI and EEG equipment (for safety details, see Laufs, 2012; Laufs et al., 2008; Mulert &

Lemieux, 2010). Additionally, the interactions of the magnetic field changes and RF pulses with EEG equipment affect recorded EEG signals. This so-called *scanner artifact* can be avoided if the acquisition of EEG and fMRI data is interleaved in temporal gaps between adjacent MR volumes (e.g., Bonmassar et al., 2001). This approach, however, cannot provide EEG signal types that need to be identified in longer periods of data acquisition (e.g., oscillatory activity). Thus, most of the current studies record EEG concurrently with fMRI and attempt to exclude the scanner artifact by using filtering and correction routines that rely on knowledge about temporal and spatial characteristics of the expected artifacts. More problematic to remove is the *ballistocardiac artifact* due to the participant's heartbeat as it is less periodic and stable and less distinct from the EEG signals (e.g., Herrmann & Debener, 2008). For more details on these standard hardware, data acquisition, and corrections routines see Abreu et al., 2018; Laufs, 2012; and Ritter & Villringer, 2006.

A final technical consideration concerns data analysis. The most common approaches are *asymmetrical*, that is, change in BOLD activity is used to inform the analysis of EEG data and vice versa. However, such simplified analyses can be biased because not all neural processes that generate one type of signal may also induce responses detected by the other method (Debener et al., 2006). Thus, *symmetrical* strategies are recommended that explicitly attempt to model how neural activity translates into the effects measured by both methods (e.g., Daunizeau et al., 2010).

From a conceptual perspective, the major advantage of acquiring EEG concurrently with fMRI lies in the ability to study spontaneous neural events that are not under direct experimental control but that can be defined via their EEG signatures. This strategy has been a major motivation driving development of concurrent EEG-fMRI because of clinical interest in the neuroanatomical basis of ictal (during seizure) and interictal (between seizures) epileptic activity (for an overview, see Mulert & Lemieux, 2010).

Such pathological abnormalities in electrical brain activity occur spontaneously and are of very brief duration, so that concurrent recording of fMRI may be essential for determining the individual cortical sites where these effects originate. Although tremendous progress has been made in this respect, it has also become clear that BOLD increases are detected not only at the cortical loci where discharges are triggered but also at remote brain sites affected by spreading neural activity. This is due to the temporally sluggish nature of the BOLD signal, leading to integration of neural activity over much longer time frames than EEG signals. Hence, concurrent EEG-fMRI does not measure brain activity with the same temporal resolution as EEG alone. Rather, the method enables researchers to use temporal profiles and dynamics of EEG effects to define different brain states and to investigate with fMRI which brain regions show correlated changes in metabolic activity (Ritter & Villringer, 2006).

This very logic has also been employed in sleep studies in which different stages of sleep are usually defined via characteristic waveforms in the EEG (e.g., delta waves, sleep spindles). Concurrent measurements with fMRI have focused on the cortical origins of these waveforms and have used the online EEG information to define different sleep states that are then further investigated with fMRI. For instance, Mitra et al. (2016) tested for possible reciprocal cortical–hippocampal communication thought to underlie the consolidation of declarative memories. They used EEG recordings to determine epochs of both wake states and slow-wave sleep (SWS), as well as concurrent resting-state fMRI to analyze the temporal lags in BOLD signals between regions to infer the net propagation of slow network activity (< 0.1 Hz). The results show that the direction of activity propagation is state dependent: Specifically, during the wake state, the cortical resting state networks (RSN) respond later than the hippocampus, whereas during SWS, activity in most RSNs precedes that in the hippocampus. This pattern of results could hardly have been reached without simultaneous recording of EEG and fMRI.

Spontaneous brain activity not only is relevant for research on epilepsy and sleep but is also being investigated in basic cognitive and affective neuroscience. For instance, a classic finding from the EEG literature is that the power of neuronal oscillations in particular frequency bands (e.g., alpha over occipital electrodes) can directly relate to the participant's vigilance state. Endogenous fluctuations of such neural activity can be behaviorally relevant. For instance, the degree of lateralized suppression of alpha activity over occipital electrodes, immediately before visual stimulus presentation, can predict whether the stimulus is detected (Thut et al., 2006). Characterizing which cortical regions generate cortical oscillations may, thus, inform neural models of cognition and behavior. Such questions are best answered with concurrent EEG–fMRI, and several studies have addressed this issue (e.g., Hanslmayr et al., 2011; Scheeringa et al., 2011).

A final advantage of combined EEG–fMRI recordings is that this combination allows researchers to use information contained in trial-to-trial variability in ERPs (Bayer et al., 2018) or cortical oscillations (Hanslmayr et al., 2011; Scheeringa et al., 2011). This approach also defines variation of a brain state by means of EEG data; however, now this state is time-locked to stimulus presentation on each experimental trial. Variability in EEG signatures across trials is assumed to relate to dynamic changes in functional contributions of cortical regions; these regions can be identified by analyzing the simultaneously recorded fMRI data for BOLD changes covarying with the EEG components across trials. For instance, Hanslmayr et al. (2011) investigated the neural mechanisms that underlie the role of different frequency bands for long-term memory encoding. During concurrent EEG-fMRI, the participants had to remember and subsequently recall a list of displayed words. During recall, the authors observed for remembered versus forgotten words an increase in theta frequency with a concomitant decrease in the beta frequency. Analyses of the fMRI data and source localization of the EEG findings showed that for remembered versus forgotten words, the left inferior prefrontal cortex (IFG) exhibited increased BOLD activity and was also the source of the observed decrease in the beta frequency band. Importantly, trial-by-trial correlations between EEG power and BOLD signals showed that beta power correlated negatively with BOLD activity in the IFG. The authors, therefore, could conclude that beta oscillations in the IFG reflect semantic memory encoding processes. This pattern of results further motivated the authors to test the causal role of beta band oscillatory activity during memory formation by means of TMS applied over IFG (see the upcoming section Sequential Combination of NIBS and EEG).

In sum, combinations of EEG and fMRI allow researchers to characterize neural activity with the temporal precision of EEG and the spatial resolution of fMRI. Both methods, however, do not necessarily index the same types of neural activity; combined measurements are nevertheless able to reveal distinct brain states expressed jointly in both imaging modalities. Combining EEG and fMRI enhances our understanding of the origins of EEG and BOLD signals, and our understanding of the relation between brain activity and cognition, emotion, and behavior.

Noninvasive Brain Stimulation and Functional Magnetic Resonance Imaging

Noninvasive brain stimulation occupies a distinct niche among the tools available to cognitive neuroscientists. It is one of the few methods that demonstrates the causal necessity of neural activity in a brain region for a given mental function. Nevertheless, the use of NIBS can greatly benefit from combination with correlative neuroimaging methods such as fMRI. For instance, purely behavioral NIBS studies usually do not provide information on the neural mechanisms that mediate stimulation-induced changes in behavior (but see Harris et al., 2008; Silvanto et al., 2008). Conversely, NIBS can add an interesting causal dimension to neuroimaging studies of functional brain responses because it can be used to modulate directly neural function in one area and visualize the effects of this intervention on activity throughout the brain (see the upcoming section Concurrent Combination of NIBS and fMRI).

As NIBS can have immediate, short-term, and long-lasting effects on brain function, these methods can be combined with fMRI either sequentially or concurrently.

Sequential combination of NIBS and fMRI. Sequential use of NIBS and fMRI requires no special hardware other than a conventional TMS/tES setup and an fMRI scanner. No major technical problems need to be addressed for this methodical combination. The only point to note is that the NIBS setup should be located in the vicinity of the MR scanner, so that the time between NIBS application and fMRI can be standardized and kept to a minimum. This may be essential for some studies, as the neural effects of offline NIBS protocols only last for a limited amount of time.

Many purely behavioral NIBS studies have combined this technique with fMRI to determine stimulation sites for NIBS by means of individual fMRI activations or anatomical scans. Only a few regions in the human brain can be identified with certainty on the basis of TMS effects alone. One example of such a region is the hand area in the primary motor cortex, which produces measurable motor-evoked potentials (MEPs) in hand muscles when stimulated with TMS (Rothwell et al., 1987). Another example is retinotopic visual cortex, in which TMS can lead to the perception of brief, spatially circumscribed flashes of light (so-called phosphenes; Marg & Rudiak, 1994). Crucially, none of the above-mentioned cortical areas can be identified with tES. Furthermore, for regions in the association cortex, finding the appropriate stimulation site can be more complicated. One popular strategy is to acquire anatomical MR images for each participant and define the cortical stimulation site in these images on the basis of neuroanatomical criteria (e.g., via the individual patterns of sulci and gyri). Many brain regions in the association cortex show large variability in their position, however, and can only be defined properly by patterns of neural responsiveness to specific stimuli. For such regions, fMRI can be used in each participant before TMS to determine the individual stimulation sites for the TMS experiment (so called "functional localizer" of the stimulation site). The optimal scalp position for TMS coil placement over an anatomically or functionally defined region can then be determined with commercially available stereotactic procedures.

As an example for this approach, Li et al. (2019) investigated the temporal dynamics of activity in two different visual areas (V1 and V3b) during perceptual contour integration. The participants had to indicate if a contour presented in a Gabor field was displayed in the upper left or lower right visual field. fMRI data were analyzed in terms of retinotopic mapping to localize the two visual areas for each participant individually. These visual areas were then targeted with TMS applied at different onsets with respect to the task onset. The earliest time window for which behavioral performance was impaired by TMS was 100 ms for V3b and 130 ms for V1, indicating that feedback from V3b to V1 is necessary for contour integration. These results provide evidence that the fine-grained contour detection in V1/V2 is preceded by initial coarse template detection in the higher visual areas, such as V3b, and that this recurrent mechanism is causally relevant for contour integration.

For localization of the areas targeted by tES, most researchers use coordinates based on previous group fMRI analyses rather than specific individual coordinates. For example, Hu et al. (2017) used this approach to investigate altruistic behavior. Initial fMRI results showed that activity in dorsolateral prefrontal cortex (DLPFC) was positively associated with self-interested behavior, while activity in DLPFC and inferior parietal lobe (IPL) was negatively associated with other-interested behavior. Informed by these fMRI results, the authors employed tDCS to test the causal role of these specific areas during altruistic behavior. Indeed, tDCS over DLPFC affected both self- and other-interested behavior, whereas tDCS over IPL selectively affected only other-interested behavior, arguing for a clear neural separation in how these two motivational tendencies are implemented in the brain.

A diametrically opposite way to combine both methods is to acquire fMRI immediately following application of NIBS to better understand the cortical processes that bring about TMS effects on behavior. This multimodal combination relies crucially on the finding that specific types of NIBS protocols lead to changes in cortical excitability that outlast the duration of the stimulation by periods of minutes to hours (e.g., Huang et al., 2005; Nitsche & Paulus, 2001; Nyffeler et al., 2009). Such protocols are often used to study causal contributions of a stimulated region to behavior, with the advantage that behavioral measurements are conducted after the NIBS and, hence, in the absence of stimulation and their side effects (e.g., auditory stimulation for TMS and peripheral stimulation at the scalp, for both TMS and tES). It is essential for such approaches to know—or to be able to estimate—how long the neural effects of stimulation persist. This has been most convincingly characterized for both rTMS and tES over motor cortex, using MEPs triggered by single TMS pulses as probes of excitability changes for different time points following the initial stimulation (e.g., Huang et al., 2005; Nitsche & Paulus, 2001). For regions outside the motor cortex, however, combinations of NIBS with offline fMRI (or PET) can be essential for providing information on the nature and duration of NIBS-elicited changes in neural activity, both in the stimulated region and for interconnected brain areas (Alekseichuk et al., 2016; Eisenegger et al., 2008; Keeser et al., 2011; Pleger et al., 2006; Polanía et al., 2011; Rounis et al., 2006; Siebner et al., 2001).

As an example for this approach, Hill et al. (2017) used an offline rTMS protocol (see Huang et al., 2005) and fMRI to investigate the functional contribution of the right temporal parietal junction (rTPJ) to strategic social behavior. rTMS was applied over rTPJ, a key area of the so-called mentalizing network (Schurz et al., 2014), and fMRI was acquired immediately afterward, during a competitive game played by the participant inside the scanner against another human opponent. In this strategic thinking game, mentalizing-related processes are essential to correctly infer the strategy of the opponent. Disrupting the neural excitability in the rTPJ by means of rTMS reduced the behavioral mentalizing-related computations as well as the neural representation of these computations in the stimulated rTPJ. Importantly, Hill et al. (2017) showed that disruption of these computations in rTPJ was accompanied by decreased functional connectivity between the rTPJ and dorsal medial prefrontal cortex, another area thought to play a key role for updating the representation of other's actions in relation to one's own behavior. The rTMS also disrupted the computation-related functional connectivity between the stimulated rTPJ and ventro-medial prefrontal cortex, a key region for value representation. Taken together, this study shows that the ability to integrate opponent beliefs into strategic choice causally relies on neural computations that are instantiated in rTPJ and that draw on functional interactions with valuation and mentalizing networks. Only the sequential combination of rTMS and fMRI made it possible to obtain this finding.

Finally, efforts have been made to combine NIBS with other MRI methods, such as MRI spectroscopy and diffusion tensor imaging (DTI). NIBS-MRI spectroscopy allows measuring NIBS-induced changes in relative concentrations of neurotransmitters such as glutamate and GABA (e.g., Bachtiar et al., 2018; Dyke et al., 2017; Hone-Blanchet et al., 2016), while NIBS-DTI allows tests of how NIBS-induced modulatory effects on behavior and/or functional connectivity depend on the structural integrity of particular anatomical pathways (e.g., Bachtiar et al., 2018; Boorman et al., 2007; Schintu et al., 2021). These combinations, thus, allow further validation and optimization of new NIBS protocols and can fully characterize the link between behavior, functional brain activity, and anatomical brain pathways.

Concurrent combination of NIBS and fMRI. The online combination of NIBS with fMRI proves to be crucial for understanding the physiological underpinnings of NIBS as well as the neural effects underlying NIBS-induced effects on behavior. In particular for TMS, for which a cardinal strength is its good temporal resolution, concurrent TMS and fMRI allows researchers to interfere selectively with neural processing during specific trials in an experiment or even during different temporal epochs of task performance on a given trial. Harnessing these features of TMS requires specific online protocols that apply one or several pulses during task performance. Such protocols are increasingly popular in studying the neural basis of perception and cognition, and they can provide unique information when combined with concurrent neuroimaging measures such as fMRI. Before discussing some applications of concurrent NIBS-fMRI in detail, the technical requirements for both concurrent TMS-fMRI and tES-fMRI are briefly discussed (for a more detailed description, see Bestmann et al., 2008; Meinzer et al., 2014; Saiote et al., 2013; Wassermann et al., 2008).

Starting in the late 1990s, a few pioneering groups developed special apparatus and procedures that have become the benchmark for concurrent TMS-fMRI (e.g., Baudewig et al., 2000; Bohning et al., 1998). For example, inside the MR scanner, only nonferromagnetic TMS coils can be used, coils that are solidly encased to withstand vibrations due to Lorentz forces generated by interaction of the magnetic fields of the TMS pulse and the scanner. Mechanical holding devices can further minimize these vibrations while allowing for flexible coil positioning over a particular target (e.g., Moisa et al., 2009). The TMS stimulator is ferromagnetic and has to be located outside the scanner room or in a shielded encasing. Thus, the TMS coil needs a cable of appropriate length that has to be connected to the stimulator through specific RF filters to prevent transmission of RF noise from the stimulator into the scanner room.

If the TMS pulses are applied at the same time as RF pulses used for fMRI, the image volumes recorded subsequently are distorted (Bestmann et al., 2008). Thus, it is crucial to coordinate the timing of TMS pulse application with the fMRI acquisition. This can be achieved by applying the TMS pulses during small temporal gaps introduced between two consecutive fMRI volumes. Alternatively, the TMS pulses can be applied during no gradients or RF pulses periods, for example, during signal readout. This will lead to complete loss of signal for specific slices that can be replaced by appropriate signal estimates.

In recent years, several new methodological developments have further improved different aspects of the concurrent TMS-fMRI setup. For example, TMS-compatible MR receive coils have been developed, which allow signal-to-noise ratios at the stimulation site that are up to 5 times larger than when TMS is combined with conventional MR-head coils (Navarro de Lara et al., 2015). Moreover, real-time neuronavigation of the TMS coil inside the MR scanner has been shown to be feasible, as well as real-time motion feedback that allows participants to correct for head movements with respect to the TMS coil (Woletz et al., 2019).

Although less technically challenging, similar hardware and software solutions are required for concurrent tES with fMRI. For example, MR-compatible tES electrodes have to be fed inside the scanner through cables of appropriate length and connected through specific RF filters to the tES stimulator located outside the scanner room. In general, the impact of tES stimulation on the fMRI image quality is minimal (see Moisa et al., 2016) and, thus, no special requirements have to be considered when tES application is coordinated with the fMRI acquisition. Importantly, several manufacturers are now offering standard hardware-software solutions for concurrent NIBS-fMRI.

So why undergo the effort to apply NIBS concurrently with fMRI? One basic motivation is to find out how NIBS affects neural processing throughout the brain. Knowledge about this can be essential in developing and optimizing NIBS protocols to influence brain activity whether it is for clinical contexts or for neurophysiological research. The unique contribution of concurrent NIBS-fMRI is that it can visualize the immediate, short-term impact of NIBS on brain activity, whereas sequential NIBS-fMRI can only reveal medium-term compensatory changes in neural processing in the aftermath of NIBS. The concurrent combination is, thus, essential for researchers who want to evaluate the effectiveness of TMS protocols to stimulate immediately the targeted brain area. Moreover, concurrent NIBS-fMRI allows researchers to use NIBS as controlled experimental inputs into the stimulated brain regions to study context-dependent changes in neural excitability of the stimulated tissue. This strategy has been used, for instance, to evaluate the effects of anticonvulsant pharmacological agents on cortical excitability (e.g., Li et al., 2010).

Assessing the neurophysiological effects of NIBS might arguably be of peripheral interest to most psychologists and cognitive neuroscientists. Studies of brain-behavior relations can also benefit from the use of concurrent NIBS-fMRI, however, because this method allows direct study of causal functional interactions between different areas of interconnected brain networks. Inducing a brief change in activity of one node of a brain network, by means of NIBS, should influence activity specifically in interconnected brain regions that are currently receptive for incoming neural signals from the stimulated region. Hence, using fMRI to measure neural activity throughout the brain during TMS can help us to identify interconnected brain regions that are influenced in their function by neural signals from a stimulated site. This approach, thus, increases the explanatory power of fMRI by adding a causal approach to the study of functional networks in the human brain.

For example, Feredoes et al. (2011) used concurrent TMS-fMRI to test the role of DLPFC during visual working memory (WM). It was unclear if DLPFC enhances neural maintenance of memory targets or suppresses processing of irrelevant information, that is, distractors. To test this, three 11-Hz TMS pulses were applied at either high or low intensity, as control, while the participants performed a visual delayed recognition paradigm in which they had to remember a target (faces or houses), in the presence or absence of external distractors from the opposite category (e.g., for face targets the distractors were houses). Thus, the targets and distractors were neurally represented in distinct posterior cortical areas. High-intensity TMS over DLPFC increased the activity in the parietal regions representing the current memory targets, only in the presence and not in the absence of distractors. Importantly, the stimulation did not affect the activity in regions representing distractors. This clearly suggests that control signals from DLPFC propagate in a top-down fashion to posterior target–representing regions to overcome the distraction during WM maintenance.

In another example, Violante et al. (2017) investigated the causal role of theta-band oscillatory synchronization between regions within the frontoparietal network during WM. The authors applied theta-tACS to the middle frontal gyrus and inferior parietal lobule either in a synchronous or desynchronous fashion (i.e., with 0° or 180° relative phase lag), while the participants performed a 1- and 2-back WM task or a pure motor-reaction control task. A first behavioral experiment showed that externally induced synchronization (i.e., 0° relative phase) improved WM performance only when cognitive demands were high, that is, during the 2-back task but not during the 1-back or motor control tasks. Importantly, a second concurrent tACS-fMRI experiment showed that tACS modulated the brain activity and connectivity in a phase and task dependent manner. Specifically, synchronous tACS during the WM task increased parietal activity, and this change in activity correlated with behavioral performance. Furthermore, functional connectivity results indicate that the relative phase of frontoparietal stimulation influences information flow within specific pathways in the involved brain network. These studies illustrate how NIBS and fMRI can provide evidence for the causal role of functional interactions in brain networks for cognitive performance.

The use of concurrent NIBS-fMRI in cognitive neuroscience is relatively new, and many important properties of the method are just being established. For instance, crucial recent findings showed that remote BOLD changes caused by NIBS change with experimental manipulations of context, such as levels of visual stimulation, motor performance, or tactile stimulation (reviewed in Bergmann et al., 2016; Bestmann et al., 2008; Driver et al., 2009; Ghobadi-Azbari et al., 2021; Saiote et al., 2013). Such findings provide evidence for flexible changes in the functional impact of stimulated areas on interconnected brain regions. Adaptive changes in effective connectivity may be a fundamental property of neural processing in brain networks, which has been suggested by neuroimaging studies employing sophisticated analyses of statistical dependencies between activity time courses in different brain areas (Valdés-Sosa et al., 2005). The recent concurrent NIBS-fMRI findings now confirm this notion and add a directed and causal dimension to existing analysis methods for purely correlative neuroimaging data.

A final important set of findings concerns the functional significance of remote activity changes resulting from NIBS. If NIBS is used to interfere with behavior, then concurrent fMRI can be used to study which short-term neural effects across the brain, remote from the stimulation site, may underlie the observed behavioral changes. For example, Hermiller et al. (2020) investigated the neural substrates of rhythmic neural activity in the theta-band in the hippocampus during memory processing. Brief volleys of theta-burst TMS were applied over a parietal cortex site identified to be connected to hippocampus, and the change in neural activity in hippocampus was assessed with concurrent fMRI while the participants evaluated visual scenes. After each TMS-fMRI session, the participants performed a memory recollection task of the visual scenes. This revealed that the theta-burst TMS increased both the activity in hippocampus during scene encoding and the subsequent memory recollection. These behavioral and neural effects were specific to theta-burst stimulation over parietal cortex, as no such effects were observed when TMS was delivered over a control stimulation site or at a different frequency. This shows that concurrent TMS-fMRI can visualize how distributed brain areas coordinate their activity to enable performance of specific cognitive tasks.

Noninvasive Brain Stimulation and Electroencephalography

Brain-behavior questions motivating the combination of NIBS and EEG are similar to those driving combination of NIBS and fMRI. The focus of both approaches is on somewhat different aspects of neural activity, however. For instance, NIBS-EEG allows a focus on the timing and the dynamics of NIBS effects on neural function rather than on the detailed neuroanatomy of implicated brain networks (as for fMRI). In principle, EEG can be used in many different ways to further specify the effects of TMS on neural activity. Some of these approaches relate to different analysis methods for EEG data (e.g., in terms of ERPs, oscillations in different frequency bands, or synchronization and desynchronization, see Chapter 28). Others relate to the principle that, as for fMRI, EEG can be combined with NIBS either sequentially or simultaneously.

Sequential combination of NIBS and EEG.
Applying NIBS to influence cognition and behavior requires some prior knowledge, or assumptions, about the neural process that is to be influenced by NIBS. As outlined in the previous section, the brain regions to be stimulated are often determined by means of fMRI data acquired before stimulation. Following a similar logic, EEG signals recorded before NIBS experiments can be a powerful tool to derive the parameters of the stimulation protocol (i.e., number, frequency, and temporal pattern of TMS pulses or the frequency of the tACS) that should be applied to manipulate task-related neural processing. NIBS protocols can be tailored on the basis of several different aspects of EEG data, for example, timing of ERP components or changes in neural oscillations in different frequency bands or synchronization and desynchronization.

For instance, Hanslmayr et al. (2011) showed in an initial combined EEG–fMRI study that the beta-band activity in the inferior prefrontal cortex (IFG) is decreased during long-term memory encoding (see the section Concurrent Combination of EEG and fMRI). Based on these initial results, the authors tested the causal role of beta band oscillatory activity in IFG by means of TMS (Hanslmayr et al., 2014). Application of TMS pulses at 18.7 Hz, to entrain the endogenous beta oscillations in the IFG, indeed impaired memory encoding, compared to TMS delivered at two other control frequencies and to sham stimulation. Concurrent EEG recordings (see the Simultaneous

Combination of NIBS and EEG section) showed that the beta-band TMS entrainment triggered a sustained beta oscillatory "echo" in the stimulated IFG that correlated with the memory impairments. Thus, this set of studies illustrates how a multimodal combination of methods can fully characterize the neural substrates of a specific behavioral feature.

In another example study, Polanía et al. (2014) used EEG recordings to identified electrophysiological markers that underlie value-based decision making. The participants performed value-based choices requiring them to indicate which of two displayed food items they preferred to eat. The consistency of value-based choices was defined as the consistency of the decision outcome with initial ratings of the food choices. This measure correlated with the strength of gamma-band coherence between electrodes over medial-prefrontal and parietal cortex, only during value-based choices and not during a control perceptual task on the same stimuli. Based on these EEG results, the same authors tested in a consecutive brain stimulation study if the medial-prefrontal–parietal coherence is indeed causally necessary for value-based decisions (Polanía et al., 2015). They applied a tACS protocol specifically designed to interfere with gamma-band oscillatory functional communication between medial-prefrontal and parietal cortex. This disrupted value-based choice consistency, while leaving performance of the perceptual-control task unaffected, thereby demonstrating that the gamma-band coherence is causally required for stable value-based choices. These studies show that information derived from prior EEG experiments can be used to determine the stimulation sites and to tailor the temporal dynamics of NIBS protocols to influence optimally corresponding cognition and behavior.

NIBS and EEG can be combined sequentially to investigate medium-term effects of offline NIBS protocols. As discussed previously, such stimulation protocols are applied over an extended time to produce neural (and behavioral) effects that outlast the stimulation period. Any effects of such NIBS on spontaneous neural oscillations or ERPs can then be studied with subsequently recorded EEG (in analogy to how fMRI can be used to identify regions showing BOLD changes following NIBS). Studies using such approaches have yielded somewhat divergent results, depending on the precise stimulation site and NIBS protocol (for reviews, see Thut & Pascual-Leone, 2010; Veniero et al., 2015). But most studies have demonstrated that this strategy can be used to validate and optimize the capability of NIBS protocols to influence brain function.

In terms of technical setup, application of NIBS following EEG is straightforward and does not require any special hardware or software on top of that needed for use of either method alone. Measuring EEG following NIBS is somewhat more complicated, as electrode setup and measurement preparation for an EEG session with standard equipment can often take longer than the after-effects of conventional NIBS protocols. Those researchers interested in this specific combination, thus, prepare EEG measurements before applying NIBS, using a special setup of EEG-compatible electrodes (see the next section for details).

Simultaneous combination of NIBS and EEG. TMS and EEG operate on similar time scales, rendering concurrent combinations of these techniques well suited to investigate neural and behavioral effects of TMS with millisecond temporal resolution. Efforts to apply TMS during EEG were, thus started, in the late 1980s (Cracco et al., 1989; Ilmoniemi et al., 1997), only a few years after the groundbreaking technical developments that enabled TMS in humans (Barker et al., 1985). The greatest problem in combining TMS and EEG online are the severe artifacts introduced in the EEG, resulting from the strong currents, mechanical vibration, and peripheral nerve stimulations associated with each TMS pulse. Many of these artifacts can be successfully prevented or corrected, however.

Conventional TMS stimulators and coils can be used for combination with EEG. The contact between the TMS coil and EEG electrodes has to be kept to a minimum, to prevent artifacts triggered by the coil vibrations. Special TMS-compatible

EEG electrodes and TMS-compatible amplifiers should be employed. Some of such amplifiers have dedicated electronics that block the induced currents during TMS pulses. Other types of amplifiers record the EEG signal continuously. However, artifact correction routines are required, for example, subtraction of a generic template of the position-specific TMS artifact.

Other types of artifacts can be reduced with appropriate procedures. For instance, possible TMS-induced polarization of the stimulated EEG electrodes can be removed by fitting exponential functions to the data. Artifacts due to unspecific TMS effects, such as sound and tactile scalp sensation, can be removed by comparison with appropriate control conditions (e.g., the same TMS protocol during rest or a different task). Artifacts due to TMS-triggered peripheral nerve stimulation can be prevented by choosing the appropriate coil orientation, while possible artifacts due to TMS induced eye blinks can be monitored due by means of eye tracking devices or dedicated electrodes. (For further details on apparatus and artifacts removal procedures, see Farzan et al., 2016; Ilmoniemi & Kičić, 2010; Veniero et al., 2009.)

In the last few years, great effort was invested into the online combination of EEG with tES, in particular with tACS. It seems, however, that achieving successful concurrent tES-EEG is still difficult and the field is awaiting development of standard, easy-to-implement procedures. One possibility is to place the tES electrodes directly under the EEG cap. Another is to use dedicated caps for online tES-EEG with a single set of electrodes used for both EEG and tES stimulation. For both setups, the EEG gel has to have the right viscosity in order to avoid leaking and, thus, bridging between the tES and EEG electrodes, while at the same time assuring good contact between the tES electrodes and the scalp. A high-resolution analog-to-digital converter (i.e., 24 bits) should be employed in order to avoid the saturation of the amplifier due to the magnitude of the tES artifact (for details, see Fehér and Morishima, 2016). Importantly, pioneering work (Helfrich et al., 2014) showed that tACS stimulation artifacts could be removed successfully from the EEG signals by following a two-way procedure. First, an artifact template, comprising several adjacent artifacts, has to be subtracted from every artifact segment (by means of a moving average approach that is similarly used in online EEG-fMRI artifact removal). The remaining residual artifacts can be further removed by means of an independent component analysis approach. For a detailed description of all available methods for artifact removal, see Kasten & Herrmann, 2019.

The section on NIBS-fMRI introduced the notion that NIBS to one brain area can affect neural processing in interconnected areas and that such remote effects of NIBS can be used to study directly effective connectivity in brain networks. A similar logic has been applied by TMS-EEG studies since the early days of this technique (e.g., Ilmoniemi et al., 1997; Komssi et al., 2002). Such studies focus on the spread of cortical activity from the stimulated site to other regions, with a particular interest in temporal properties of such network interactions. Several studies have now used this approach to demonstrate differences in effective connectivity of cortical networks between different contexts, such as different sleep stages (Massimini et al., 2005) or different states of consciousness induced by pharmacological agents (Ferrarelli et al., 2010). All of these studies illustrate how concurrent TMS-EEG provides an interesting research tool to directly trigger and assess the dynamic spread of neural activity in cortical networks.

Concurrent TMS-EEG can also be used to examine how manipulations of processing in one region (via TMS) can change ERPs or oscillations originating in specific interconnected brain regions during task performance. Any such effects reflect dynamic functional interactions between both sets of brain areas during task performance, not unlike effects observed in corresponding TMS-fMRI studies (see the previous section). The unique strength of concurrent TMS-EEG in this context is the excellent temporal resolution with which such interactions can be assessed. A major weakness, however, is the uncertainty about the anatomical origin of signals observed in the EEG data (see also the section on EEG-fMRI). Concurrent TMS-EEG is, thus, perhaps best suited for investigating remote influences on those ERP components, or cortical oscillations, which are well understood with respect to their cortical origin.

For example, concurrent TMS-EEG was used to investigate how TMS applied over the frontal or parietal cortex during visual attention tasks may influence neural processing in remote parieto-occipital areas, both with respect to ERPs (Fuggetta et al., 2006; Morishima et al., 2009; Taylor et al., 2007) and anticipatory alpha rhythms (Capotosto et al., 2009). All of these studies illustrate how concurrent TMS-EEG can reveal the cortical dynamics of functional interactions among remote but interconnected brain areas underlying task performance.

Furthermore, the online combination of NIBS and EEG showed that the external application of NIBS can entrain the ongoing oscillatory brain activity through phase-locking. For example, Thut et al. (2012) applied TMS bursts at alpha-frequency over the parietal cortex concurrently with EEG recordings while the participants were at rest. The frequency and the site of the stimulation were selected based on MEG results that showed that alpha-band oscillatory activity is triggered specifically in the parietal cortex during a visual-spatial attention task. TMS at the alpha-frequency leaded to progressive enhancement, that is, increased enhancement with the number of pulses in the TMS burst, of the oscillatory activity in the targeted alpha-frequency. The authors further show that the TMS interacted directly with the ongoing activity through phase locking. Importantly the oscillatory enhancement was frequency- and coil-orientation-specific (i.e., present only when the coil was oriented perpendicular to the targeted gyrus), as these effects were absent when the TMS pulses were delivered arrhythmically within one burst or when the same α-frequency stimulation was applied for a different coil orientation (i.e., parallel to the targeted gyrus). In another example using tES, tACS at 10 Hz alpha-frequency was applied concurrently with EEG recordings while the participants performed a visual oddball paradigm where they had to indicate if the stimuli were of target- or a standard-color (Helfrich et al., 2014). The tACS electrodes were placed over the Cz and Oz positions of the international 10/20 system, such that the induced electric field was maximum in the medial occipital and parieto-occipital. The tACS increased the target detection performance, and this behavioral change was accompanied by an increase in oscillatory power in the alpha band in the parieto-occipital cortex. These studies illustrate how the concurrent combination of NIBS with EEG can reveal entrainment of the oscillatory activity in a frequency-specific manner and how this combination can further facilitate the understanding of the functional role of oscillatory activity for specific cognitive functions.

In a slightly different approach, Ozdemir et al. (2020) used concurrent TMS-EEG to induce controlled perturbations in a specific brain network, and to characterize the propagation of neural activity (so-called TMS-evoked potentials) at the network level with millisecond resolution. The stimulation sites targeting the default mode network and the dorsal attention network were determined based on maps of resting state networks determined in a large sample of 1,000 individuals. Neural activity triggered by TMS targeting each of these specific networks was not restricted to the stimulation site but rather propagated to functionally connected distal areas within the same network. Moreover, these TMS-induced cortical responses were highly reproducible across sessions that were spaced 1 month apart. Importantly, the specificity of TMS propagation across these two networks was related to individual differences in cognitive abilities as measured by IQ scores. Thus, the measures of brain dynamics across distant regions assessed with the online combination of TMS with EEG appears functionally relevant for cognition.

CONCLUSION

There has been rapid growth in the use of neuroimaging methods to study the brain basis of human perception, cognition, emotion, and behavior.

The most popular methods (EEG/MEG, fMRI, and NIBS) differ strongly in their sensitivity to different aspects of neural activity. Moreover, each method has its unique profile of strengths and weaknesses for making inferences about brain-behavior relations. No single method presently available represents the ideal tool for investigating, for all brain regions, whether specific temporal patterns of neural activity are causally necessary for a mental state of interest. For this reason, different neuroimaging methods are increasingly combined in a single study to obtain optimal results in terms of explanatory power and, hence, a more complete picture of the neural processes underlying behavior.

The three combinations most frequently employed at present are EEG-fMRI, NIBS-fMRI, and NIBS-EEG. Studies using any of these combinations have the potential to elucidate the relative sensitivity of EEG, fMRI, and NIBS to different types of neural activity. Even more important for psychologists, these methodological combinations can reveal distinct brain states relating to behavior that could not be assessed with either neuroimaging method alone. For example, EEG combined with fMRI can characterize spatio-temporal neural processes (brain regions that generate specific patterns of ERPs or neural oscillations), whereas NIBS combined with fMRI or EEG can demonstrate causal functional interactions among remote but interconnected brain regions. Such largely unexplored aspects of neural function may play a central role during the next few decades of research on brain–behavior relations. Sequential combinations of two neuroimaging methods are technically straightforward and possible to implement with standard setup and procedures for both techniques. Simultaneous combinations, by contrast, require special hardware and software for safe and reliable combination and are used by only a few laboratories at present. But the history of technological developments in neuroimaging suggests that the community at large may soon employ multimodal methods to enhance our understanding of how brain activity enables perception, cognition, emotion, and behavior.

References

Abreu, R., Leal, A., & Figueiredo, P. (2018). EEG-informed fMRI: A review of data analysis methods. *Frontiers in Human Neuroscience*, 12, 29. https://doi.org/10.3389/fnhum.2018.00029

Alekseichuk, I., Diers, K., Paulus, W., & Antal, A. (2016). Transcranial electrical stimulation of the occipital cortex during visual perception modifies the magnitude of BOLD activity: A combined tES-fMRI approach. *NeuroImage*, 140, 110–117. https://doi.org/10.1016/j.neuroimage.2015.11.034

Antal, A., & Paulus, W. (2013). Transcranial alternating current stimulation (tACS). *Frontiers in Human Neuroscience*, 7, 317. https://doi.org/10.3389/fnhum.2013.00317

Bachtiar, V., Johnstone, A., Berrington, A., Lemke, C., Johansen-Berg, H., Emir, U., & Stagg, C. J. (2018). Modulating regional motor cortical excitability with noninvasive brain stimulation results in neurochemical changes in bilateral motor cortices. *The Journal of Neuroscience*, 38(33), 7327–7336. https://doi.org/10.1523/JNEUROSCI.2853-17.2018

Barker, A. T., Jalinous, R., & Freeston, I. L. (1985). Non-invasive magnetic stimulation of human motor cortex. *Lancet*, 1(8437), 1106–1107. https://doi.org/10.1016/S0140-6736(85)92413-4

Baudewig, J., Paulus, W., & Frahm, J. (2000). Artifacts caused by transcranial magnetic stimulation coils and EEG electrodes in T(2)*-weighted echo-planar imaging. *Magnetic Resonance Imaging*, 18(4), 479–484. https://doi.org/10.1016/S0730-725X(00)00122-3

Bayer, M., Rubens, M. T., & Johnstone, T. (2018). Simultaneous EEG-fMRI reveals attention-dependent coupling of early face processing with a distributed cortical network. *Biological Psychology*, 132, 133–142. https://doi.org/10.1016/j.biopsycho.2017.12.002

Bergmann, T. O., Karabanov, A., Hartwigsen, G., Thielscher, A., & Siebner, H. R. (2016). Combining non-invasive transcranial brain stimulation with neuroimaging and electrophysiology: Current approaches and future perspectives. *NeuroImage*, 140, 4–19. https://doi.org/10.1016/j.neuroimage.2016.02.012

Bestmann, S., Ruff, C. C., Blankenburg, F., Weiskopf, N., Driver, J., & Rothwell, J. C. (2008). Mapping causal interregional influences with concurrent TMS-fMRI. *Experimental Brain Research*, 191(4), 383–402. https://doi.org/10.1007/s00221-008-1601-8

Bohning, D. E., Shastri, A., Nahas, Z., Lorberbaum, J. P., Andersen, S. W., Dannels, W. R., Haxthausen, E. U., Vincent, D. J., & George, M. S. (1998).

Echoplanar BOLD fMRI of brain activation induced by concurrent transcranial magnetic stimulation. *Investigative Radiology*, 33(6), 336–340. https://doi.org/10.1097/00004424-199806000-00004

Bonmassar, G., Schwartz, D. P., Liu, A. K., Kwong, K. K., Dale, A. M., & Belliveau, J. W. (2001). Spatiotemporal brain imaging of visual-evoked activity using interleaved EEG and fMRI recordings. *NeuroImage*, 13(6 Pt. 1), 1035–1043. https://doi.org/10.1006/nimg.2001.0754

Boorman, E. D., O'Shea, J., Sebastian, C., Rushworth, M. F. S., & Johansen-Berg, H. (2007). Individual differences in white-matter microstructure reflect variation in functional connectivity during choice. *Current Biology*, 17(16), 1426–1431. https://doi.org/10.1016/j.cub.2007.07.040

Capotosto, P., Babiloni, C., Romani, G. L., & Corbetta, M. (2009). Frontoparietal cortex controls spatial attention through modulation of anticipatory alpha rhythms. *The Journal of Neuroscience*, 29(18), 5863–5872. https://doi.org/10.1523/JNEUROSCI.0539-09.2009

Cracco, R. Q., Amassian, V. E., Maccabee, P. J., & Cracco, J. B. (1989). Comparison of human transcallosal responses evoked by magnetic coil and electrical stimulation. *Electroencephalography and Clinical Neurophysiology*, 74(6), 417–424. https://doi.org/10.1016/0168-5597(89)90030-0

Dale, A. M., Liu, A. K., Fischl, B. R., Buckner, R. L., Belliveau, J. W., Lewine, J. D., & Halgren, E. (2000). Dynamic statistical parametric mapping: Combining fMRI and MEG for high-resolution imaging of cortical activity. *Neuron*, 26(1), 55–67. https://doi.org/10.1016/S0896-6273(00)81138-1

Daunizeau, J., Laufs, H., & Friston, K. J. (2010). EEG–fMRI information fusion: Biophysics and data analysis. In C. Mulert & L. Lemieux (Eds.), *EEG–fMRI: Physiological basis, technique, and applications* (pp. 511–526). Springer.

Debener, S., Ullsperger, M., Siegel, M., & Engel, A. K. (2006). Single-trial EEG-fMRI reveals the dynamics of cognitive function. *Trends in Cognitive Sciences*, 10(12), 558–563. https://doi.org/10.1016/j.tics.2006.09.010

Driver, J., Blankenburg, F., Bestmann, S., Vanduffel, W., & Ruff, C. C. (2009). Concurrent brain-stimulation and neuroimaging for studies of cognition. *Trends in Cognitive Sciences*, 13, 319–327. https://doi.org/10.1016/j.tics.2009.04.007

Dyke, K., Pépés, S. E., Chen, C., Kim, S., Sigurdsson, H. P., Draper, A., Husain, M., Nachev, P., Gowland, P. A., Morris, P. G., & Jackson, S. R. (2017). Comparing GABA-dependent physiological measures of inhibition with proton magnetic resonance spectroscopy measurement of GABA using ultra-high-field MRI. *NeuroImage*, 152, 360–370. https://doi.org/10.1016/j.neuroimage.2017.03.011

Eisenegger, C., Treyer, V., Fehr, E., & Knoch, D. (2008). Time-course of "off-line" prefrontal rTMS effects—a PET study. *NeuroImage*, 42, 379–384. https://doi.org/10.1016/j.neuroimage.2008.04.172

Farzan, F., Vernet, M., Shafi, M. M. D., Rotenberg, A., Daskalakis, Z. J., & Pascual-Leone, A. (2016). Characterizing and modulating brain circuitry through transcranial magnetic stimulation combined with electroencephalography. *Frontiers in Neural Circuits*, 10, 73. https://doi.org/10.3389/fncir.2016.00073

Fehér, K. D., & Morishima, Y. (2016). Concurrent electroencephalography recording during transcranial alternating current stimulation (tACS). *Journal of Visualized Experiments*, 2016, 107, e53527. https://doi.org/10.3791/53527

Fehér, K. D., Nakataki, M., & Morishima, Y. (2017). Phase-dependent modulation of signal transmission in cortical networks through tACS-induced neural oscillations. *Frontiers in Human Neuroscience*, 11, 471. https://doi.org/10.3389/fnhum.2017.00471

Feredoes, E., Heinen, K., Weiskopf, N., Ruff, C., & Driver, J. (2011). Causal evidence for frontal involvement in memory target maintenance by posterior brain areas during distracter interference of visual working memory. *Proceedings of the National Academy of Sciences of the United States of America*, 108(42), 17510–17515. https://doi.org/10.1073/pnas.1106439108

Ferrarelli, F., Massimini, M., Sarasso, S., Casali, A., Riedner, B. A., Angelini, G., Tononi, G., & Pearce, R. A. (2010). Breakdown in cortical effective connectivity during midazolam-induced loss of consciousness. *Proceedings of the National Academy of Sciences of the United States of America*, 107(6), 2681–2686. https://doi.org/10.1073/pnas.0913008107

Fuggetta, G., Pavone, E. F., Walsh, V., Kiss, M., & Eimer, M. (2006). Cortico-cortical interactions in spatial attention: A combined ERP/TMS study. *Journal of Neurophysiology*, 95(5), 3277–3280. https://doi.org/10.1152/jn.01273.2005

Ghobadi-Azbari, P., Jamil, A., Yavari, F., Esmaeilpour, Z., Malmir, N., Mahdavifar-Khayati, R., Soleimani, G., Cha, Y. H., Shereen, A. D., Nitsche, M. A., Bikson, M., & Ekhtiari, H. (2021). fMRI and transcranial electrical stimulation (tES): A systematic review of parameter space and outcomes. *Progress in Neuro-Psychopharmacology & Biological Psychiatry*, 107, 110149. https://doi.org/10.1016/j.pnpbp.2020.110149

Hall, C. N., Howarth, C., Kurth-Nelson, Z., & Mishra, A. (2016). Interpreting BOLD: Towards a dialogue between cognitive and cellular neuroscience. *Philosophical Transactions of the Royal Society of London: Series B. Biological Sciences, 371*(1705). https://doi.org/10.1098/rstb.2015.0348

Hanslmayr, S., Matuschek, J., & Fellner, M. C. (2014). Entrainment of prefrontal beta oscillations induces an endogenous echo and impairs memory formation. *Current Biology, 24*(8), 904–909. https://doi.org/10.1016/j.cub.2014.03.007

Hanslmayr, S., Volberg, G., Wimber, M., Raabe, M., Greenlee, M. W., & Bäuml, K. H. T. (2011). The relationship between brain oscillations and BOLD signal during memory formation: A combined EEG-fMRI study. *The Journal of Neuroscience, 31*(44), 15674–15680. https://doi.org/10.1523/JNEUROSCI.3140-11.2011

Harris, J. A., Clifford, C. W. G., & Miniussi, C. (2008). The functional effect of transcranial magnetic stimulation: Signal suppression or neural noise generation? *Journal of Cognitive Neuroscience, 20*(4), 734–740. https://doi.org/10.1162/jocn.2008.20048

Heinze, H. J., Mangun, G. R., Burchert, W., Hinrichs, H., Scholz, M., Münte, T. F., Gös, A., Scherg, M., Johannes, S., Hundeshagen, H., Gazzaniga, M. S., & Hillyard, S. A. (1994). Combined spatial and temporal imaging of brain activity during visual selective attention in humans. *Nature, 372*(6506), 543–546. https://doi.org/10.1038/372543a0

Helfrich, R. F., Schneider, T. R., Rach, S., Trautmann-Lengsfeld, S. A., Engel, A. K., & Herrmann, C. S. (2014). Entrainment of brain oscillations by transcranial alternating current stimulation. *Current Biology, 24*(3), 333–339. https://doi.org/10.1016/j.cub.2013.12.041

Hermiller, M. S., Chen, Y. F., Parrish, T. B., & Voss, J. L. (2020). Evidence for immediate enhancement of hippocampal memory encoding by network-targeted theta-burst stimulation during concurrent fMRI. *The Journal of Neuroscience, 40*(37), 7155–7168. https://doi.org/10.1523/JNEUROSCI.0486-20.2020

Herrmann, C. S., & Debener, S. (2008). Simultaneous recording of EEG and BOLD responses: A historical perspective. *International Journal of Psychophysiology, 67*(3), 161–168. https://doi.org/10.1016/j.ijpsycho.2007.06.006

Herrmann, C. S., Rach, S., Neuling, T., & Strüber, D. (2013). Transcranial alternating current stimulation: A review of the underlying mechanisms and modulation of cognitive processes. *Frontiers in Human Neuroscience, 7*, 279. https://doi.org/10.3389/fnhum.2013.00279

Herrmann, C. S., Strüber, D., Helfrich, R. F., & Engel, A. K. (2016). EEG oscillations: From correlation to causality. *International Journal of Psychophysiology, 103*, 12–21. https://doi.org/10.1016/j.ijpsycho.2015.02.003

Hill, C. A., Suzuki, S., Polania, R., Moisa, M., O'Doherty, J. P., & Ruff, C. C. (2017). A causal account of the brain network computations underlying strategic social behavior. *Nature Neuroscience, 20*(8), 1142–1149. https://doi.org/10.1038/nn.4602

Hone-Blanchet, A., Edden, R. A., & Fecteau, S. (2016). Online effects of transcranial direct current stimulation in real time on human prefrontal and striatal metabolites. *Biological Psychiatry, 80*(6), 432–438. https://doi.org/10.1016/j.biopsych.2015.11.008

Horwitz, B., & Poeppel, D. (2002). How can EEG/MEG and fMRI/PET data be combined? *Human Brain Mapping, 17*(1), 1–3. https://doi.org/10.1002/hbm.10057

Hu, J., Li, Y., Yin, Y., Blue, P. R., Yu, H., & Zhou, X. (2017). How do self-interest and other-need interact in the brain to determine altruistic behavior? *NeuroImage, 157*, 598–611. https://doi.org/10.1016/j.neuroimage.2017.06.040

Huang, Y. Z., Edwards, M. J., Rounis, E., Bhatia, K. P., & Rothwell, J. C. (2005). Theta burst stimulation of the human motor cortex. *Neuron, 45*(2), 201–206. https://doi.org/10.1016/j.neuron.2004.12.033

Huster, R. J., Debener, S., Eichele, T., & Herrmann, C. S. (2012). Methods for simultaneous EEG-fMRI: An introductory review. *The Journal of Neuroscience, 32*(18), 6053–6060. https://doi.org/10.1523/JNEUROSCI.0447-12.2012

Ilmoniemi, R. J., & Kičić, D. (2010). Methodology for combined TMS and EEG. *Brain Topography, 22*(4), 233–248. https://doi.org/10.1007/s10548-009-0123-4

Ilmoniemi, R. J., Virtanen, J., Ruohonen, J., Karhu, J., Aronen, H. J., Näätänen, R., & Katila, T. (1997). Neuronal responses to magnetic stimulation reveal cortical reactivity and connectivity. *Neuroreport, 8*(16), 3537–3540. https://doi.org/10.1097/00001756-199711100-00024

Jorge, J., van der Zwaag, W., & Figueiredo, P. (2014). EEG-fMRI integration for the study of human brain function. *NeuroImage, 102*(Pt. 1), 24–34. https://doi.org/10.1016/j.neuroimage.2013.05.114

Kasten, F. H., & Herrmann, C. S. (2019). Recovering brain dynamics during concurrent tACS-M/EEG: An overview of analysis approaches and their methodological and interpretational pitfalls. *Brain Topography, 32*(6), 1013–1019. https://doi.org/10.1007/s10548-019-00727-7

Keeser, D., Meindl, T., Bor, J., Palm, U., Pogarell, O., Mulert, C., Brunelin, J., Möller, H. J., Reiser, M., & Padberg, F. (2011). Prefrontal transcranial direct current stimulation changes connectivity of resting-state networks during fMRI. *The Journal of Neuroscience*, *31*(43), 15284–15293. https://doi.org/10.1523/JNEUROSCI.0542-11.2011

Knotkova, H., Nitsche, M. A., Bikson, M., & Woods, A. J. (Eds.). (2019). *Practical guide to transcranial direct current stimulation*. Springer International Publishing.

Komssi, S., Aronen, H. J., Huttunen, J., Kesäniemi, M., Soinne, L., Nikouline, V. V., Ollikainen, M., Roine, R. O., Karhu, J., Savolainen, S., & Ilmoniemi, R. J. (2002). Ipsi- and contralateral EEG reactions to transcranial magnetic stimulation. *Clinical Neurophysiology*, *113*(2), 175–184. https://doi.org/10.1016/S1388-2457(01)00721-0

Laufs, H. (2012). A personalized history of EEG-fMRI integration. *NeuroImage*, *62*(2), 1056–1067. https://doi.org/10.1016/j.neuroimage.2012.01.039

Laufs, H., Daunizeau, J., Carmichael, D. W., & Kleinschmidt, A. (2008). Recent advances in recording electrophysiological data simultaneously with magnetic resonance imaging. *NeuroImage*, *40*(2), 515–528. https://doi.org/10.1016/j.neuroimage.2007.11.039

Li, X., Ricci, R., Large, C. H., Anderson, B., Nahas, Z., Bohning, D. E., & George, M. S. (2010). Interleaved transcranial magnetic stimulation and fMRI suggests that lamotrigine and valproic acid have different effects on corticolimbic activity. *Psychopharmacology*, *209*(3), 233–244. https://doi.org/10.1007/s00213-010-1786-y

Li, Y., Wang, Y., & Li, S. (2019). Recurrent processing of contour integration in the human visual cortex as revealed by fMRI-guided TMS. *Cerebral Cortex*, *29*(1), 17–26. https://doi.org/10.1093/cercor/bhx296

Marg, E., & Rudiak, D. (1994). Phosphenes induced by magnetic stimulation over the occipital brain: Description and probable site of stimulation. *Optometry and Vision Science*, *71*(5), 301–311. https://doi.org/10.1097/00006324-199405000-00001

Martínez, A., Anllo-Vento, L., Sereno, M. I., Frank, L. R., Buxton, R. B., Dubowitz, D. J., Wong, E. C., Hinrichs, H., Heinze, H. J., & Hillyard, S. A. (1999). Involvement of striate and extrastriate visual cortical areas in spatial attention. *Nature Neuroscience*, *2*(4), 364–369. https://doi.org/10.1038/7274

Massimini, M., Ferrarelli, F., Huber, R., Esser, S. K., Singh, H., & Tononi, G. (2005). Breakdown of cortical effective connectivity during sleep. *Science*, *309*(5744), 2228–2232. https://doi.org/10.1126/science.1117256

Meinzer, M., Lindenberg, R., Darkow, R., Ulm, L., Copland, D., & Flöel, A. (2014). Transcranial direct current stimulation and simultaneous functional magnetic resonance imaging. *Journal of Visualized Experiments*, *2014*(86), 51730. https://doi.org/10.3791/51730

Michel, C. M., & Brunet, D. (2019). EEG source imaging: A practical review of the analysis steps. *Frontiers in Neurology*, *10*, 325. https://doi.org/10.3389/fneur.2019.00325

Mitra, A., Snyder, A. Z., Hacker, C. D., Pahwa, M., Tagliazucchi, E., Laufs, H., Leuthardt, E. C., & Raichle, M. E. (2016). Human cortical-hippocampal dialogue in wake and slow-wave sleep. *Proceedings of the National Academy of Sciences of the United States of America*, *113*(44), E6868–E6876. https://doi.org/10.1073/pnas.1607289113

Moisa, M., Pohmann, R., Ewald, L., & Thielscher, A. (2009). New coil positioning method for interleaved transcranial magnetic stimulation (TMS)/functional MRI (fMRI) and its validation in a motor cortex study. *Journal of Magnetic Resonance Imaging*, *29*(1), 189–197. https://doi.org/10.1002/jmri.21611

Moisa M., Polania R., Grueschow, M., & Ruff, C. C. (2016). Brain network mechanisms underlying motor enhancement by transcranial entrainment of gamma oscillations. *Journal of Neuroscience*, *36*(47), 12053–12065. https://doi.org/10.1523/JNEUROSCI.2044-16.2016

Morishima, Y., Akaishi, R., Yamada, Y., Okuda, J., Toma, K., & Sakai, K. (2009). Task-specific signal transmission from prefrontal cortex in visual selective attention. *Nature Neuroscience*, *12*(1), 85–91. https://doi.org/10.1038/nn.2237

Mulert, C., & Lemieux, L. (Eds.). (2010). *EEG–fMRI*. Springer. https://doi.org/10.1007/978-3-540-87919-0

Navarro de Lara, L. I., Tik, M., Woletz, M., Frass-Kriegl, R., Moser, E., Laistler, E., & Windischberger, C. (2017). High-sensitivity TMS/fMRI of the human motor cortex using a dedicated multichannel MR coil. *NeuroImage*, *150*, 262–269. https://doi.org/10.1016/j.neuroimage.2017.02.062

Navarro de Lara, L. I., Windischberger, C., Kuehne, A., Woletz, M., Sieg, J., Bestmann, S., Weiskopf, N., Strasser, B., Moser, E., & Laistler, E. (2015). A novel coil array for combined TMS/fMRI experiments at 3 T. *Magnetic Resonance in Medicine*, *74*(5), 1492–1501. https://doi.org/10.1002/mrm.25535

Nguyen, T., Potter, T., Nguyen, T., Karmonik, C., Grossman, R., & Zhang, Y. (2016). EEG source imaging guided by spatiotemporal specific fMRI: Toward an understanding of dynamic cognitive processes. *Neural Plasticity*, *2016*, 4182483. https://doi.org/10.1155/2016/4182483

Nitsche, M. A., & Paulus, W. (2001). Sustained excitability elevations induced by transcranial DC motor cortex stimulation in humans. *Neurology*, *57*(10), 1899–1901. https://doi.org/10.1212/WNL.57.10.1899

Noesselt, T., Hillyard, S. A., Woldorff, M. G., Schoenfeld, A., Hagner, T., Jäncke, L., Tempelmann, C., Hinrichs, H., & Heinze, H.-J. (2002). Delayed striate cortical activation during spatial attention. *Neuron*, *35*(3), 575–587. https://doi.org/10.1016/S0896-6273(02)00781-X

Nunez, P. L., & Srinivasan, R. (2006). *Electric fields of the brain: The neurophysics of EEG* (2nd ed.). Oxford University Press. https://doi.org/10.1093/acprof:oso/9780195050387.001.0001

Nyffeler, T., Cazzoli, D., Hess, C. W., & Müri, R. M. (2009). One session of repeated parietal theta burst stimulation trains induces long-lasting improvement of visual neglect. *Stroke*, *40*(8), 2791–2796. https://doi.org/10.1161/STROKEAHA.109.552323

Ozdemir, R. A., Tadayon, E., Boucher, P., Momi, D., Karakhanyan, K. A., Fox, M. D., Halko, M. A., Pascual-Leone, A., Shafi, M. M., & Santarnecchi, E. (2020). Individualized perturbation of the human connectome reveals reproducible biomarkers of network dynamics relevant to cognition. *Proceedings of the National Academy of Sciences of the United States of America*, *117*(14), 8115–8125. https://doi.org/10.1073/pnas.1911240117

Peters, J. C., Reithler, J., Graaf, T. A., Schuhmann, T., Goebel, R., & Sack, A. T. (2020). Concurrent human TMS-EEG-fMRI enables monitoring of oscillatory brain state-dependent gating of cortico-subcortical network activity. *Communications Biology*, *3*(1), 40. https://doi.org/10.1038/s42003-020-0764-0

Pfabigan, D. M., Seidel, E. M., Sladky, R., Hahn, A., Paul, K., Grahl, A., Küblböck, M., Kraus, C., Hummer, A., Kranz, G. S., Windischberger, C., Lanzenberger, R., & Lamm, C. (2014). P300 amplitude variation is related to ventral striatum BOLD response during gain and loss anticipation: An EEG and fMRI experiment. *NeuroImage*, *96*, 12–21. https://doi.org/10.1016/j.neuroimage.2014.03.077

Pleger, B., Blankenburg, F., Bestmann, S., Ruff, C. C., Wiech, K., Stephan, K. E., Friston, K. J., & Dolan, R. J. (2006). Repetitive transcranial magnetic stimulation-induced changes in sensorimotor coupling parallel improvements of somatosensation in humans. *The Journal of Neuroscience*, *26*(7), 1945–1952. https://doi.org/10.1523/JNEUROSCI.4097-05.2006

Polanía, R., Krajbich, I., Grueschow, M., & Ruff, C. C. (2014). Neural oscillations and synchronization differentially support evidence accumulation in perceptual and value-based decision making. *Neuron*, *82*(3), 709–720. https://doi.org/10.1016/j.neuron.2014.03.014

Polanía, R., Moisa, M., Opitz, A., Grueschow, M., & Ruff, C. C. (2015). The precision of value-based choices depends causally on fronto-parietal phase coupling. *Nature Communications*, *6*(1), 8090. https://doi.org/10.1038/ncomms9090

Polanía, R., Nitsche, M. A., & Paulus, W. (2011). Modulating functional connectivity patterns and topological functional organization of the human brain with transcranial direct current stimulation. *Human Brain Mapping*, *32*(8), 1236–1249. https://doi.org/10.1002/hbm.21104

Polanía, R., Nitsche, M. A., & Ruff, C. C. (2018). Studying and modifying brain function with non-invasive brain stimulation. *Nature Neuroscience*, *21*(2), 174–187. https://doi.org/10.1038/s41593-017-0054-4

Poldrack, R. A., & Farah, M. J. (2015). Progress and challenges in probing the human brain. *Nature*, *526*(7573), 371–379. https://doi.org/10.1038/nature15692

Ritter, P., & Villringer, A. (2006). Simultaneous EEG-fMRI. *Neuroscience and Biobehavioral Reviews*, *30*(6), 823–838. https://doi.org/10.1016/j.neubiorev.2006.06.008

Rothwell, J. C., Thompson, P. D., Day, B. L., Dick, J. P., Kachi, T., Cowan, J. M., & Marsden, C. D. (1987). Motor cortex stimulation in intact man. 1. General characteristics of EMG responses in different muscles. *Brain: A Journal of Neurology*, *110*(Pt. 5), 1173–1190. https://doi.org/10.1093/brain/110.5.1173

Rounis, E., Stephan, K. E., Lee, L., Siebner, H. R., Pesenti, A., Friston, K. J., Rothwell, J. C., & Frackowiak, R. S. (2006). Acute changes in fronto-parietal activity after repetitive transcranial magnetic stimulation over the dorsolateral prefrontal cortex in a cued reaction time task. *The Journal of Neuroscience*, *26*(38), 9629–9638. https://doi.org/10.1523/JNEUROSCI.2657-06.2006

Saiote, C., Turi, Z., Paulus, W., & Antal, A. (2013). Combining functional magnetic resonance imaging with transcranial electrical stimulation. *Frontiers in Human Neuroscience*, *7*, 435. https://doi.org/10.3389/fnhum.2013.00435

Scheeringa, R., Fries, P., Petersson, K. M., Oostenveld, R., Grothe, I., Norris, D. G., Hagoort, P., & Bastiaansen, M. C. M. (2011). Neuronal dynamics underlying high- and low-frequency EEG oscillations contribute independently to the human BOLD signal.

Neuron, 69(3), 572–583. https://doi.org/10.1016/j.neuron.2010.11.044

Schintu, S., Cunningham, C. A., Freedberg, M., Taylor, P., Gotts, S. J., Shomstein, S., & Wassermann, E. M. (2021). Callosal anisotropy predicts attentional network changes after parietal inhibitory stimulation. NeuroImage, 226, 117559. https://doi.org/10.1016/j.neuroimage.2020.117559

Schurz, M., Radua, J., Aichhorn, M., Richlan, F., & Perner, J. (2014). Fractionating theory of mind: A meta-analysis of functional brain imaging studies. Neuroscience and Biobehavioral Reviews, 42, 9–34. https://doi.org/10.1016/j.neubiorev.2014.01.009

Siebner, H. R., Takano, B., Peinemann, A., Schwaiger, M., Conrad, B., & Drzezga, A. (2001). Continuous transcranial magnetic stimulation during positron emission tomography: A suitable tool for imaging regional excitability of the human cortex. NeuroImage, 14(4), 883–890. https://doi.org/10.1006/nimg.2001.0889

Siegel, M., Donner, T. H., Oostenveld, R., Fries, P., & Engel, A. K. (2008). Neuronal synchronization along the dorsal visual pathway reflects the focus of spatial attention. Neuron, 60(4), 709–719. https://doi.org/10.1016/j.neuron.2008.09.010

Silvanto, J., Muggleton, N., & Walsh, V. (2008). State-dependency in brain stimulation studies of perception and cognition. Trends in Cognitive Sciences, 12(12), 447–454. https://doi.org/10.1016/j.tics.2008.09.004

Taylor, P. C., Nobre, A. C., & Rushworth, M. F. (2007). FEF TMS affects visual cortical activity. Cerebral Cortex, 17(2), 391–399. https://doi.org/10.1093/cercor/bhj156

Thut, G., Miniussi, C., & Gross, J. (2012). The functional importance of rhythmic activity in the brain. Current Biology, 22(16), R658–R663. https://doi.org/10.1016/j.cub.2012.06.061

Thut, G., Nietzel A., Brandt S. A., & Pascual-Leone, A. (2006). Alpha-band electroencephalographic activity over occipital cortex indexes visuospatial attention bias and predicts visual target detection. Journal of Neuroscience, 26(37), 9494–9502. https://doi.org/10.1523/JNEUROSCI.0875-06.2006

Thut, G., & Pascual-Leone, A. (2010). A review of combined TMS-EEG studies to characterize lasting effects of repetitive TMS and assess their usefulness in cognitive and clinical neuroscience. Brain Topography, 22(4), 219–232. https://doi.org/10.1007/s10548-009-0115-4

Valdés-Sosa, P. A., Kötter, R., & Friston, K. J. (2005). Introduction: Multimodal neuroimaging of brain connectivity. Philosophical Transactions of the Royal Society of London: Series B. Biological Sciences, 360(1457), 865–867. https://doi.org/10.1098/rstb.2005.1655

Veniero, D., Bortoletto, M., & Miniussi, C. (2009). TMS-EEG co-registration: On TMS-induced artifact. Clinical Neurophysiology, 120(7), 1392–1399. https://doi.org/10.1016/j.clinph.2009.04.023

Veniero, D., Vossen, A., Gross, J., & Thut, G. (2015). Lasting EEG/MEG aftereffects of rhythmic transcranial brain stimulation: Level of control over oscillatory network activity. Frontiers in Cellular Neuroscience, 9, 477. https://doi.org/10.3389/fncel.2015.00477

Vinck, M., Oostenveld, R., van Wingerden, M., Battaglia, F., & Pennartz, C. M. (2011). An improved index of phase-synchronization for electrophysiological data in the presence of volume-conduction, noise and sample-size bias. NeuroImage, 55(4), 1548–1565. https://doi.org/10.1016/j.neuroimage.2011.01.055

Violent, I. R., Li, L. M., Carmichael, D. W., Lorenz, R., Leech, R., Hampshire, A., Rothwell, J. C., & Sharp, D. J. (2017). Externally induced frontoparietal synchronization modulates network dynamics and enhances working memory performance. eLife, 6, e22001. https://doi.org/10.7554/eLife.22001

Walsh, V., & Pascual-Leone, A. (2003). Neurochronometrics of mind: Transcranial magnetic stimulation in cognitive science. MIT Press.

Wassermann, E. M., Epstein, C. M., & Ziemann, U. (2008). The Oxford handbook of transcranial stimulation. Oxford University Press.

Woletz, M., Tik, M., Pratapa, N., Prinčič, M., Schuler, A., & Windischberger, C. (2019). Real-time neuronavigation feedback in concurrent TMS-fMRI. Brain Stimulation, 12(2), 574–575. https://doi.org/10.1016/j.brs.2018.12.904

Yavari, F., Jamil, A., Mosayebi Samani, M., Vidor, L. P., & Nitsche, M. A. (2018). Basic and functional effects of transcranial Electrical Stimulation (tES)-An introduction. Neuroscience and Biobehavioral Reviews, 85, 81–92. https://doi.org/10.1016/j.neubiorev.2017.06.015

CHAPTER 32

NEUROIMAGING ANALYSIS METHODS

Yanyu Xiong and Sharlene D. Newman

Magnetic resonance imaging (MRI), first used for clinical imaging in the early 1980s, has become an important tool for both clinical assessment and research of human brain functioning. Almost a decade later, in the early 1990s the first functional MRI (fMRI) results were presented (Belliveau et al., 1991). Since then, there have been dramatic advances in the way in which MRI data are analyzed over the past 30 years. In this chapter, we provide an overview of a subset of analytical techniques most widely used in functional and structural MRI data analyses.

THE GENERAL LINEAR MODEL (MASS UNIVARIATE MODEL)

The most widely used approach to identify activated brain regions via experimental manipulation is the massive univariate analysis under the framework of the general linear model (GLM; Friston et al., 1991; Friston, Holmes, et al., 1994; Worsley et al., 2002). The GLM models brain responses in each voxel independently as a linear combination of different fixed effects and a random error. The prevalence of the GLM method is due to its flexibility in incorporating different experimental designs at both the individual and group level analyses, and the easy estimation and interpretability of parameters. These conveniences, however, are obtained at the expense of relatively more restricted model assumptions, such as independent voxels, uncorrelated time points, and constant error variance (Lazar, 2008).

Consider the time series of voxel i, the model of its blood oxygenation level dependent (BOLD) response: Y_i is $Y_i = X\beta_i + \varepsilon_i$. X is a design matrix of the predictor functions with the columns corresponding to experimental conditions and covariates (e.g., low-frequency signals, the global mean of brain activation, motion parameters, and physiological factors). β_i is a vector of unknown coefficients describing the effects of the predictors, and ε_i is the stochastic part of the model, which is assumed to have a multivariate Gaussian distribution.

Under the model assumptions, the parameter coefficients can be estimated using the ordinary least squares (OLS) method. The estimation process minimizes the sum of squared errors between the observed and predicted BOLD responses. The estimator is unbiased with a minimum variance based on the Gauss-Markov theorem (Ashby, 2011). In practice, researchers often need to use jittered interstimulus intervals so that the sampling points can be appropriately modeled to obtain more accurate estimates of each parameter (Serences, 2004).

Statistical Inferences Based on β

Most research fMRI studies are designed to compare two or more experimental conditions or groups of participants. This can easily be done with the GLM using t statistics. The t distribution can be approximated by the z distribution with mean 0 and variance 1, so both t- and z-statistic parametric maps can be constructed.

F tests are more appropriate when comparing multiple experimental conditions. In this case, more than one contrast needs to be tested and the null hypotheses related to multiple conditions are set as 0s simultaneously. The null hypothesis is $H_0: \beta_1 = \beta_2 \ldots \beta_n = 0$, and the alternative hypothesis is $H_1: \beta_1 \neq 0 \text{ or } \beta_2 \neq 0 \ldots \text{ or } \beta_n \neq 0$, that is, the null hypothesis can be rejected if any of the parameters is nonzero.

Multiple Comparison Issue

As the voxel-wise GLM approach involves multiple hypothesis testing, the number of tests could reach the scale of several hundred thousand (Eddy et al., 1999). In a whole-brain analysis, if 100,000 voxels are tested with the Type I error rate at .05 and all the voxels are assumed to be independent, the total number of false positives will be inflated to $100,000 \times .05 = 5,000$. This alarming rate of false positives was more strikingly demonstrated by the Bennett team, who reported brain activation of a dead salmon exposed to a standard human task (Bennett et al., 2009). To gauge the overall false positives in multiple testing, the probability of at least one false positive in any voxel, called *family-wise error rate* (FWE), is often controlled at a specific level, for instance, $\alpha_E = .05$, which means 95 out of 100 data sets contain 0 false positives. However, how to set the threshold for each test to control the FWE is another issue that researchers need to tackle in practice. Below we discuss three common methods (Ashby, 2011; Bowman et al., 2007; Lazar, 2016; Nichols & Hayasaka, 2003; Perrin, 2013; Polzehl & Tabelow, 2019; Woolrich et al., 2016).

The most straightforward correction method is Bonferroni correction, which, although easy to implement, is incredibly stringent, as the voxel-wise alpha threshold needs to be set as $\frac{\alpha_E}{\# \text{ of tests}}$. The more tests are performed, the more stringent the significance statistic threshold will be. Such a conservative criterion inflates the false negative rate (Type II error) as the neighboring voxels are inherently correlated in space and time (Lazar, 2016; Perrin, 2013). To avoid overcorrection, one solution is the region-of-interest (ROI) analysis, which reduces the number of tests by both averaging across voxels in a specified region and selecting a limited number of regions (Ashby, 2011; Bowman et al., 2007).

The second correction method is based on the Gaussian random field theory (GRFT), which was first applied by Worsley et al. (1992, 1996) to address the multiple comparison issue in neuroimaging. It assumes that the smoothness of the data is sufficient and can be derived from the residuals. The independent unit called *RESEL* in a volume with equivalent smoothness is created based on the full width at half maximum parameter of the noise. Both the number of RESELs and the z values influence the corrected p value of each voxel. If the number of RESELs increases, such as in a large volume or with less smoothed data, or if the z value is low, then it will lead to a more stringent threshold.

The third most widely used correction method is false discovery rate (FDR), which controls the proportion of false positives among all the rejected null hypotheses under a threshold q (Benjamini & Yosef, 1995). Because this proportion is a random variable with an unknown value for an individual experiment, it is the expected value of the proportion that is controlled. The FDR approach is a more general and less restrictive correction because some fraction of false positives is acceptable. In fMRI statistical analysis, the p values of each voxel are first ranked in ascending order. Then the largest ith p value for which $p_i \leq q\frac{i}{N}$ is found (Genovese et al., 2002). All the null hypotheses satisfying the inequality equation are rejected. The two extreme cases of FDR correspond to the Bonferroni method and no correction respectively. If $q = .05$ is set as the risk of Type I error and $i = 1$, $p_i = \frac{.05}{N}$, then it is the same as the Bonferroni correction. When $i = N$, $p_i = .05$, no hypothesis testing is corrected.

Modeling the Hemodynamic Response

A large repertoire of proposed linear models assume that the BOLD response can be modeled with a convolution of the neural activation function and the hemodynamic response function, as it does not directly reflect the spiking activity of individual neurons, but is associated with the fluctuation of local field potentials from an ensemble of cells (Logothetis, 2003; Logothetis et al., 2001; Ogawa et al., 1990). These models vary in their degree of accuracy, complexity, and flexibility in modeling the hemodynamic response (Boynton et al., 1996; Calhoun et al., 2004; Dale, 1999; Friston, Jezzard, & Turner, 1994; Glover, 1999; Worsley et al., 2002).

The simplest models of the hemodynamic response function (HRF) are the Poisson model with λ as the only parameter to control its shape (Friston, Jezzard, & Turner, 1994) and two gamma probability density functions proposed by Worsley and Friston (1995). However, one limitation of the above models is that the HRF shape is assumed to be independent of brain regions and subjects (Aguirre et al., 1998; Huettel et al., 2001; Richter & Richter, 2003; Schacter et al., 1997). Ignoring the HRF variability by applying the same function to all voxels and all subjects may result in either bias in data analysis or difficulties in identifying the effects. Some alternative models using basis functions offer more flexibility to model these differences, but the optimization procedure for parameter estimation can still be used within the framework of the GLM (Calhoun et al., 2004; Dale, 1999; Friston, Fletcher, et al., 1998; Josephs et al., 1997). For detailed information on these models, readers are directed to Woolrich et al. (2016), Ashby (2011), and Zhang et al. (2016).

Although the aforementioned models assume that the BOLD response is a linear, time-invariant system, there are increasing reports that this assumption only holds under restricted conditions when the duration of experimental stimuli is greater than 3 seconds (Boynton et al., 1996). If the stimuli are shorter than 1 second, the BOLD responses to two simultaneously presented stimuli are not equal to the sum of the responses to each stimulus (Vazquez & Noll, 1998). For the fast event-related paradigm, the events spaced with interstimulus intervals shorter than 2 seconds may lead to nonlinear BOLD responses (Dale & Buckner, 1997; Wager et al., 2005). Several models have attempted to account for the nonlinearity of the BOLD response by including the nonlinearity in neural activation and vascular response (Boynton et al., 1996; Buxton et al., 1998; Wager et al., 2005; Zheng et al., 2002). The most well-known models are the biophysical balloon model proposed by Buxton et al. (1998), which directly describes the nonlinear relationship between the changes in the BOLD response, blood volume, and the amount of deoxyhemoglobin using the biomechanical function of the blood vessels as a swelling balloon, and the linear model with the second-order nonlinear Volterra series (Friston, Josephs, et al., 1998). For readers who want to get more mathematical details about these models, please see Ashby (2011) and Zhang et al. (2016).

Dealing With Temporal Autocorrelation

fMRI data are naturally autocorrelated due to the presence of multiple noise sources, such as the instability of magnetic field, thermal noise, motion, physiological effects, and spontaneous neural activity. Underestimating the variation introduced by this noise will generate spurious effects, which will possibly lead to biased conclusions. One approach to deal with the temporal autocorrelation is to model the noise explicitly, such as adding some nuisance regressors like motion and physiological factors in the GLM. Apparently, one limitation of this method is the constrained Gaussian distribution model assumption of the error term, especially when the autocorrelation contributed by physiological factors is much smaller than random noise (Friston et al., 1995).

Another strategy is to temporally smooth the data and the design matrix with a smoothing kernel similar to the HRF (Friston et al., 1995; Worsley & Friston, 1995). The rationale is that fMRI data are inherently smoother than the hemodynamic response function. The convolution of the smoothing kernel with the fMRI time series temporally low-pass filters the data and takes out the high-frequency noise, thereby, enhancing the variance of the low-frequency signal relative to noise. A more widely used method is called *prewhitening* (Bullmore et al., 1996; Friston, Josephs, et al., 2000; Woolrich et al., 2001, 2016), which removes the temporal correlation in the data and the resulting power spectrum of the residuals resembles white noise with approximately equal power across frequencies. A number of other models have also been used to derive the temporal correlation structure of fMRI data, such as spatial regularization of autocorrelation estimates (Gautama & Van Hulle, 2004) and the Bayesian-based models (Penny et al., 2003; Woolrich et al., 2004).

Resources

Several software tools are available to implement GLM analysis of fMRI data. The standard software packages include SPM12 and CONN toolbox based on MATLAB (The MathWorks, Inc., Natick, MA); FEAT software tool (https://fsl.fmrib.ox.ac.uk/fsl/fslwiki/FEAT) as part of FSL (FMRIB's Software Library); Analyses of Functional Neuroimages (AFNI) as a freely distributed package of C programs; BrainVoyager of Brain Innovation B.V. (Maastricht, The Netherlands) and the nlme package of R (https://cran.r-project.org/web/packages/nlme/index.html). Python-based workflow Nipype is another useful interface to integrate the analysis from multiple neuroimaging software.

For readers who prefer to learn the GLM analysis with demonstrations, some high-quality online tutorials are also available, such as the Principles of fMRI course on Coursera (https://www.coursera.org/learn/functional-mri), the training courses of SPM (https://www.fil.ion.ucl.ac.uk/spm/course/), FSL (https://fsl.fmrib.ox.ac.uk/fslcourse/), AFNI tutorials (https://afni.nimh.nih.gov/pub/dist/doc/htmldoc/educational/bootcamp_recordings.html), and the Brain Book by Andrew Jahn (https://andysbrainbook.readthedocs.io/en/latest/).

MULTIVARIATE MODELS

In addition to the model-based GLM approach, model-free multivariate techniques, such as independent component analysis (ICA; McKeown et al., 1998, 2003) and principal components analysis (PCA; Friston et al., 1993), can also be applied to fMRI data. The GLM diverges from the multivariate approaches in terms of the assumptions of the spatiotemporal characteristics of fMRI signals (Hyvärinen & Oja, 2000). The GLM assumes (a) that the observed data follow a priori distribution (e.g., the Gaussian distribution), (b) the BOLD responses to repeated presentation of a stimulus are the same across an experiment, and (c) the signals of different voxels are independent. ICA, on the other hand, does not require these assumptions (Hyvärinen & Oja, 2000). PCA requires the assumption of a multivariate Gaussian distribution though, it takes the spatial relationship among voxels into account.

Independent Component Analysis

There are two types of independent component analysis commonly used in the fMRI literature: standard and probabilistic approaches.

Standard independent component analysis. ICA arises from the cocktail party problem of unmixing the sound signals collected in each microphone in a noisy room. It aims to extract the voices of individual speakers by treating each mixed signal as a weighted linear combination of its components. With the two fundamental assumptions that the components are non-Gaussian distributed and mutually independent, the method can better characterize vast types of signals in nature. This approach has gained popularity in neuroimaging research due to its ability to extract brain network features from the entire spatiotemporal fMRI data. The technique has been widely used in investigating resting-state networks in healthy populations and patients with neurological disorders (Calhoun & Adali, 2012; Rosazza & Minati, 2011; Smith et al., 2013), task-related networks (Calhoun et al., 2008; Kim et al., 2011; Xiong & Newman, 2021; Xu et al., 2013), and artifact removal (Griffanti et al., 2014; Pruim et al., 2015). Meanwhile, ICA allows for the specification of the structure of sparsity, which is an inherent feature of brain networks.

ICA can be classified as temporal ICA (Biswal & Ulmer, 1999) and spatial ICA (McKeown et al., 1998). Put in the context of functional neuroimaging, *temporal* ICA models each voxel as a linear combination of independent time series. The weights associated with each time series carry the spatial information, that is, voxel locations. For *spatial* ICA, the brain activation pattern at each time point is a linear mixture of functionally independent neural networks. Each spatial map is associated with a time series, which contains the weights (or contribution) of the networks at individual repetition time RTs.

ICA models the input data as the product of a mixing matrix and several independent components. To derive these components from observations, we need an unmixing matrix W. In practice, before the application of ICA, the input data need to be whitened, so the variance-covariance matrix of the data is transformed into an identity matrix. Theoretically speaking, whitening is very essential to decorrelate the data so that its shape before any stretching and sheering transformations can be recovered. Thus, estimation of the unmixing matrix is simplified to a problem of rotating the whitened data to the initial coordinates.

There are several estimation algorithms in the current ICA literature, which differ in the procedure of either maximizing the statistical independence or the non-Gaussianity of the components using higher order statistical moments like kurtosis, but similar in terms of their goals and final solution (Hyvärinen et al., 2001). Readers are directed to the detailed discussions of these algorithms by Bell and Sejnowski (1995), Ashby (2011), and Hyvärinen (1999).

Probabilistic independent component analysis. The aforementioned noise-free ICA model, though easier to implement, has two inherent limitations. One is that without a noise component in the model, the variance of the data is assumed to be completely captured by the estimated source components and their mixing weights. The number of underlying sources needs to fit exactly the number of time points. The other is that all of the detected differences in BOLD signals have to be treated as "real effects" and no direct statistical testing techniques can be employed to test research hypotheses. Beckmann and Smith (2004) adjusted the standard model by adding a Gaussian noise term with the mean equal to 0 and variance equal to $\sigma^2\Sigma$. This probabilistic model allows the mixing matrix to be nonsquare and the covariance structure of the noise to vary in different tissue types. The estimation procedure of the unmixing matrix can be performed in a similar way as the noise-free ICA, but the noise needs to be removed when restoring the components using the maximum likelihood approach. Moreover, the significance testing can be performed following the standard statistical testing procedure under the assumption that each component is a weighted linear combination of Gaussian distributions. In recent years, the application of ICA in fMRI data analysis has also developed to utilize the sparsity feature of the components to improve the detection power, estimation accuracy, and computing efficiency of the algorithms (Boukouvalas et al., 2017; Wang et al., 2013).

For readers who are interested in learning the detailed information of other algorithms to estimate the unmixing matrix (e.g., maximum likelihood approach), please refer to Ashby (2011) and Eloyan (2016). There is also a rich repertoire of variants of the classical ICA method, such as adaptive ICA (Hong et al., 2005), semi-blind ICA (Calhoun et al., 2005), parallel ICA (Meda et al., 2012), and nonlinear ICA (Bi et al., 2018).

Resources. Multiple software packages have included ICA as a module in their analysis pipeline for different purposes (e.g., network reconstruction and artifact removal). GIFT, as a versatile extension of SPM, not only supports different ICA algorithms at both the single-subject and group level but also implements temporal ICA. The ICA module of CONN selects the FastICA to extract spatially independent components (https://web.conn-toolbox.org/fmri-methods/connectivity-measures/networks-voxel-level). Different from both previous packages, the MELODIC module (https://web.mit.edu/fsl_v5.0.10/fsl/doc/wiki/MELODIC.html) of the FMRIB software library (FSL) implements probabilistic ICA with statistical significance assigned to the decomposed spatial components. Fusion ICA (FIT) is a MATLAB toolbox, which goes beyond the single modality by extracting the shared information. It supports the joint ICA, parallel ICA and CCA-joint ICA methods.

Principal Components Analysis

PCA is often used for dimension reduction and artifact removal in fMRI research. Different from ICA, it assumes a multivariate Gaussian distribution and represents data as a linear combination of orthogonal spatiotemporal components (Friston et al., 1993). The projection of the data onto each orthogonal direction accounts for most variability in that direction within the projected space (Hotelling, 1933). The components are ranked in descending order in terms of the amount of variance explained.

The standard PCA algorithm includes three steps. First, the data matrix is demeaned by subtracting the average of all voxels in each column from each entry in the corresponding column. Second, the eigenvalues and eigenvectors are derived from the variance-covariance matrix using the singular value decomposition (SVD). The eigenvalues are equal to the variance of the data specified by the eigenvector in that direction, and larger eigenvalues indicate greater variance. Third, the data are projected onto each of the principal axes by matrix multiplication of the mean-centered data with the eigenvectors. Dimension reduction can be performed at this stage by only including a subset of the first few eigenmaps as a sufficient approximation of the data.

Conceptually, by diagonalizing the covariance matrix, PCA decorrelates the data and removes some "redundant" information so that data can be represented in a much lower-dimensional space. This dimension reduction feature has been used in a number of fMRI studies (Andersen & Rayens, 2004; Barnathan et al., 2011; Hansen et al., 1999). Under the assumption that task-related BOLD responses should show greater variability than noise due to the modulation of the corresponding cognitive processes (Ashby, 2011), PCA has also proved to be useful in removing motion, cardiac, and respiratory artifacts (Mandelkow et al., 2010; Muschelli et al., 2014).

The application of PCA to extract the functional networks is rather limited, however, as neurobiological data usually violate its assumptions that the signals are spatiotemporally independent and follow the Gaussian distribution. A number of computational algorithms have been developed to address the above limitations, such as nonlinear functional PCA, which includes a second-order term in its nonlinear function to account for the nonadditive dependency between components (Friston et al., 1999; Friston, Phillips, et al., 2000), and Kernel PCA, which integrates temporal patterns of voxels obtained from the univariate analysis into PCA (Thirion & Faugeras, 2003). Compared with the standard PCA, these approaches show increased sensitivity to detect the signal variation modulated by different experimental tasks.

Resources PCA is supported by nearly all mainstream data analysis software like R, MATLAB, and Python. It is often implemented together with ICA in neuroimaging packages to reduce the data dimensions at both subject and group levels to facilitate the blind source separation processes of ICA. These packages include GIFT, CONN toolbox, BrainVoyager, MELODIC of FSL

(FMRIB's software library), GitHub resources Brain Imaging Analysis Kit (BrainIAK), and mapca. PCA has also been combined with the multivariate least-square multiple regression to estimate the hemodynamic response associated with a particular functional network or test the experimental manipulations. The constrained PCA is supported by fMRI-CPCA (extension of SPM: https://www.nitrc.org/projects/fmricpca).

For readers who are interested in other online tutorials and resources, some links that may be helpful include the Principles of fMRI 2 course on Coursera (https://www.coursera.org/lecture/functional-mri-2/module-17-multivariate-decomposition-methods-q26Uu) and the Brains, Minds, and Machines Summer Course (https://cbmm.mit.edu/learning-hub/tutorials/computational-tutorial/dimensionality-reduction-i).

Multivoxel Pattern Analysis

The past 20 years have seen an explosion of fMRI research using another multivariate approach, multivoxel pattern analysis (MVPA), to determine how a cognitive state is encoded in brain activity (Bauer & Just, 2015; Haynes & Rees, 2006; Lewis-Peacock & Norman, 2013; Mason & Just, 2020; Norman et al., 2006; Weaverdyck et al., 2020). MVPA reverses the inferential logic of the conventional univariate approaches by focusing more on the information contained in the spatially distributed pattern of activity across multiple voxels, rather than only those voxels showing significant responses to the stimuli (Haxby et al., 2001; Haynes & Rees, 2006; Kamitani & Tong, 2005; Mitchell et al., 2004; Pereira et al., 2009). It offers the novel possibilities of discovering the idiosyncratic neural representations of information across individuals and how the representations dynamically change in the brain.

Compared with the univariate approaches, MVPA has greater sensitivity to detecting the presence of a cognitive state (Haynes & Rees, 2006; Lewis-Peacock & Norman, 2013). First, the univariate approaches only identify the voxels that show significant responses to the stimuli, thus, losing the information contained in those subthreshold voxels. By contrast, MVPA takes each voxel as an information source, which contributes to the overall response with different weights and extracts joint information across voxels even when individual voxels do not carry this information. Second, the conventional GLM approach may fail to distinguish experimental conditions of similar response magnitude, but MVPA can capture the distinct activity patterns between the two conditions, which may convey functional meaning hidden from researchers. Third, to achieve a better signal-to-noise ratio, the univariate approaches use spatial smoothing to average the responses of multiple voxels, resulting in the loss of fine-grained spatial information. MVPA, on the other hand, does not involve specific spatial smoothing at the level of individual analysis; thereby, it is believed to probe the activity patterns revealed at a finer spatial scale. Nevertheless, several studies have also found that smoothing does not decrease the prediction accuracy of MVPA in the brain regions where signals are correlated and smooth, but the degree of the improvement depends on the columnar configurations of different regions and individual differences (Op de Beeck, 2010; Gardumi et al., 2016; Hendriks et al., 2017; Mandelkow et al., 2017). Lastly, the univariate approaches assume that the responses to the same condition across trials do not change during the experiment, regardless of the instrument-related and psychological factors, while each sample of MVPA could be represented as a single point in multidimensional voxel space. The variation across different trials or time points could be characterized by the extent to which the samples cluster together. MVPA, therefore, provides methods to investigate the dynamic changes of the functional state in the brain with a much higher temporal resolution. A variety of approaches can be employed to capture the representation patterns, such as the discrete (e.g., binary classifier) and continuous classifier metrics (e.g., the distance from the classification hyperplane and correlation with the prototypical pattern). They differ in their ability to capture the representation information at the trial level (Anzellotti & Coutanche, 2018).

Decoding analyses. MVPA involves two broad categories of methods: decoding analyses (including classification and regression) (Haxby et al., 2001; Kamitani & Tong, 2005) and representational similarity analysis (RSA; Kriegeskorte et al., 2008a, 2008b). Neural decoding, as an opposite processing of encoding stimulus features in the neural system, is related to making predictions of the stimulus features with brain activity. Decoding analyses model a nonlinear relationship between the input space and feature space and a linear relationship between the feature space and activity space (Naselaris et al., 2011). The methods try to find the weights of each feature that maximize the difference in the activity patterns of different conditions. Although the features are discrete for pattern classification (e.g., human, animal) and continuous for regression (e.g., how angry a person is), both methods aim to predict experimental conditions based on the corresponding neural activation pattern with similar analytic procedures.

The first important step of the decoding analysis involves feature selection. Constraining the number of voxels reduces the data dimensions and is advantageous to achieve optimal classification results (Aberg & Wessberg, 2008; Sayres et al., 2005). The most commonly used feature-selection approaches in the present literature include the region-of-interest method (Chadwick et al., 2010; Haxby et al., 2001; Serences et al., 2009); the "searchlight" method (Kriegeskorte et al., 2006; Woolgar et al., 2016); the independent feature-selection only in the training set, which is originally separated out to perform the k-fold cross-validation of the decoding analysis (Weaverdyck et al., 2020); and the dimension reduction methods such as PCA and ICA to preserve the ideal proportion of variance in the data in terms of a few informative features. After feature-selection, each brain activity pattern is labelled according to its corresponding experimental condition. The hemodynamic lag needs to be accounted for in the labeling process (Lewis-Peacock & Norman, 2013; Norman et al., 2006).

Pattern classification of MVPA includes two steps. First, the data set is split into training and test sets. The classifier function is trained with the training set by optimizing the weights of each contributing voxel to maximize the difference between classes. After the classifier function learns the mapping relationship between the activity pattern and the corresponding class, the test data set is used to assess how accurately the classifier function can distinguish new samples of different classes. The accuracy level indicates the extent to which the multivoxel activity patterns carry the information of classes.

MVPA has imported several machine learning techniques to extract the multivoxel pattern information in a high-dimensional voxel space (Hastie et al., 2009). Two linear classification methods are commonly used in fMRI studies: (a) linear support vector machine (SVM) and (b) linear discriminant analysis (LDA) (Carlson et al., 2003; Cox & Savoy, 2003; Hastie et al., 2009; Misaki et al., 2010; Pereira et al., 2009). Both try to find a hyperplane in the activity space, which can best discriminate between the activity related to different categories. Linear discriminant analysis, in addition to the common assumption that the activity space and feature space are linearly mapped, is more stringent for assuming Gaussian distribution and equal variance of the responses across categories (Mahmoudi et al., 2012). It attempts to maximize the between-category variance in relation to the within-category variance (Weaverdyck et al., 2020). SVM, on the other hand, does not require any distribution assumption and tries to find a boundary separating the samples of different categories with maximum margin. Readers are encouraged to seek other resources for technical explanations (e.g., Hastie et al., 2009; Mahmoudi et al., 2012).

Some MVPA studies have used nonlinear classifiers such as nonlinear SVM and neural networks to perform decoding analysis (Cox & Savoy, 2003; Davatzikos et al., 2005; McNorgan et al., 2020). Though very powerful for identifying the mapping relationship between activity patterns and classes, nonlinear classifiers also have some unresolved limitations, such as an overfitting problem with reduced generalizability in new data sets, only marginal performance gain over the linear classifiers and greater difficulties in interpreting the mapping (Cox & Savoy, 2003; Kamitani & Tong, 2005; Naselaris et al., 2011; Norman et al., 2006).

Representational similarity analysis. Another branch of MVPA is RSA (Kriegeskorte et al., 2008a, 2008b), which calculates the similarity (e.g., Person correlation) of the activity patterns associated with each pair of experimental conditions and constructs a symmetric similarity matrix of all the conditions. Kriegeskorte et al. (2008a) used a representational dissimilarity matrix (RDM), which is a correlation distance matrix with each cell calculated as 1-correlation. As RDM abstracts from the first-order isomorphism that directly maps the stimuli with their neural responses, it is called a *second-order isomorphism*. This level of abstraction, compared with the pattern-classification-based techniques, offers the RSA approach greater flexibility in terms of the number of voxels selected in analysis and linking the neural representation with the behavioral patterns and computational modeling (Chikazoe et al., 2014; Nastase et al., 2017). Meanwhile, various within- and between-subjects hypothesis tests can be conducted on the RDMs with the standard procedure of nonparametric tests. Apart from correlation, other similarity metrics, such as Euclidean distance, Mahalanobis distance, and classification accuracies, can also be used to record the dissimilarity structure of the activity patterns. The correlation distance is more sensitive to the activation level of the experimental conditions compared with Euclidean and Mahalanobis distances but is more resilient to the mean and variance of the dissimilarities (Walther et al., 2016).

RSA involves four analytic steps. The first step is to obtain the activity patterns either based on the predicted BOLD response in each voxel by fitting a mass univariate or other spatiotemporal patterns. Second, a single-activity pattern for each experimental condition is calculated by averaging across trials and runs. These condition-specific activity patterns are then compared with each other in terms of the Pearson correlation distance. Each RDM of brain responses to different conditions is constructed with each cell corresponding to a pair-wise Pearson correlation distance. Likewise, the RDM models can also be constructed based on the information processing theories or other psychophysiological measures from subjects, like response time, pupil dilation, etc. (Kiani et al., 2007; Kriegeskorte et al., 2008a; O'Hearn et al., 2020; Visser et al., 2015). The third step is to compare the neural RDMs with the RDM models with only the upper or lower triangles of the matrices because they are symmetric. Although similar techniques like dissimilarity correlation distance and Euclidean distance can be used, Kriegeskorte et al. (2008a) suggested using Spearman correlation distance for matrices at different scales. The final step is the statistical testing of the RDM correlation. Because the correlation for each pair of conditions cannot justify the independence of activity patterns across conditions, the nonparametric permutation tests are often recommended. Assuming that all conditions evoke the same response pattern, the condition labels are shuffled in each RDM matrix by interchanging the rows and columns many times (e.g., 1,000–10,000 times). Each permutation generates a new correlation coefficient after comparing the two randomized RDM matrices. The test correlation is then tested against the distribution of these correlations under the null hypothesis that the two RDMs are not related.

Resources. For the implementation of MVPA, there are currently several software packages available including MATLAB toolboxes CosMoMVPA; RSA toolbox; the Decoding Toolbox; Pattern Recognition for Neuroimaging Toolbox (PRoNTo); Princeton MVPA Toolbox; and Python-based packages Nilearn (https://nilearn.github.io), PyMVPA, and Neuropredict.

For readers interested in more general online tutorials of machine learning in neuroimaging analysis, please check the Neurohackademy lecture series (https://neurohackademy.org/course/introduction-to-machine-learning/).

NETWORK ANALYSES

Over the past 2 decades, network analysis of brain activity has flourished because of the rapid development in the theories of applied mathematics, statistical physics, and complex systems (for reviews, see Bassett & Sporns, 2017; Cribben & Fiecas, 2016; Fornito, 2016; Ginestet et al., 2016). Brain function as a product of the interactions among multiple brain regions highlights the importance of a network perspective to advance our understanding of its underlying biological and systematic mechanisms. Although brain networks could be characterized at the microscale, mesoscale, and macroscale levels, limited by the space of the present section, our discussions focus on the macroscale connectomics, that is, the system level instead of the neuron and neuronal circuitry levels. For a more comprehensive introduction to the latter two levels, readers are encouraged to check the textbook by Fornito et al. (2016).

The Basics of Network Analysis

The most fundamental network analysis applied in the field of functional and structural MRI arises from graph theory (Bollobás & Riordan, 2004; Szabó et al., 2002; Xu & Hero, 2013). Brain system can be represented by a graph G of nodes ($V(G)$) and edges ($E(G)$) (Ginestet et al., 2016). Each node can be defined based on its internal homogeneity, external heterogeneity, or its spatial relations with other nodes (Fornito et al., 2013). There are four ways that have been frequently used in the literature to define a node, including the voxel-based, atlas-based, ROI-based, and data-driven approaches (Fornito, 2016; Ginestet et al., 2016; see the review of Stanley et al., 2013).

The voxel-based method constructs a network using each voxel as a node. For the atlas-based approach, the whole brain is parcellated into spatially discrete regions based on either the sulcal and gyral landmarks (e.g., automated anatomical labeling; Tzourio-Mazoyer et al., 2002) or probabilistic maps, and each region is taken as a node in the graph. In recent years, the boundary between the atlas-based and data-driven approaches has become blurry due to more advanced methodologies employed in the resting-state fMRI analysis to parcellate the brain into finer divisions of cortical areas (Cohen et al., 2008; Gordon et al., 2016; Schaefer et al., 2018; Wig et al., 2014; Xu et al., 2016; Yeo et al., 2011; and see the review of Abdedayem et al., 2020). These recent maps yield more reliable and neurobiologically meaningful parcellations of cortical areas. The ROI method is a hypothesis-driven approach to defining the nodes for both task and resting-state fMRI (Andrews-Hanna et al., 2010; Cocchi et al., 2014; Fornito et al., 2012). The benefits of this approach lie in its increased power to detect the connectivity features in a specific set of brain regions relevant to the research interest (Crossley et al., 2013; Dosenbach et al., 2010). One drawback of this approach is that it is not appropriate for exploratory analysis without strong assumptions of the cortical areas involved.

Edges represent the connections between each pair of nodes. The strength of the connections is represented by the cell values of a connectivity matrix. The edges can be quantified in multiple ways depending on the type of data (e.g., fMRI or diffusion MRI) and the nature of the nodes. For fMRI, the edge indicates statistical dependence between nodes (Fornito et al., 2016).

Network Metrics

Network analysis is performed on a matrix representation of the nodes and edges $G = (V, E)$. In the context of graph theory, the matrix is called an *adjacency matrix*. The matrix is *binary* if the cell values are 1 when the edges are present and 0 otherwise. A *weighted adjacency matrix* contains cell values within a range indicating the connection strength. The connectivity matrix can also be classified as directed and undirected matrices. An *undirected matrix* is symmetric like a correlation matrix, in which the correlation between node *i* and *j* is the same as the correlation between *j* and *i*, that is $G_{ij} = G_{ji}$. If $G_{ij} \neq G_{ji}$, the adjacency matrix is *directed*.

To utilize the analytic tools of network analysis and remove spurious connections, the first step of network analysis often involves thresholding (van den Heuvel et al., 2017; van Wijk et al., 2010). Absolute thresholding is based on researchers' prior knowledge or the mass-univariate tests of all edges in a network. Proportional thresholding selects the same proportion of connections relative to the total connections across individuals to keep a constant network density (Achard & Bullmore, 2007; van den Heuvel et al., 2008), In practice, one should test the robustness of the experimental results across a range of thresholds (Fornito et al., 2016). The next step is to decide on graph metrics used to perform the network analysis. The current literature offers a plethora of choices. For more comprehensive and technical information on these metrics, readers are referred to Kolaczyk (2009), Rubinov and Sporns (2010), and Fornito et al. (2016). The following section briefly discusses the four most commonly used descriptive metrics: degree distribution, clustering coefficient, modularity, and characteristic path length.

The *degree* of a node refers to the number of edges in a graph linked to this node. It is a measure of the extent to which the node is connected to other nodes within the network. The aggregate degrees of all the nodes in a graph form a *degree distribution*, which has been found to follow the power-law distribution (scale-free distribution) in many areas of science including brain networks (Achard et al., 2006; Barabási & Albert, 1999; Fornito et al., 2010; Kolaczyk, 2009; van den Heuvel et al., 2008). The power-law distribution is highly skewed, heterogeneous, and heavy-tailed. The probabilities of finding high-degree nodes are higher than random graphs, but the majority of the nodes have a low degree. Research shows that the best fit of the degree distribution could be approximated by an exponentially truncated power law, which holds important implications for the roles of the highly connected brain regions (hubs) in functional segregation and integration (Crossley et al., 2013; Power et al., 2013; van den Heuvel et al., 2012; van den Heuvel & Sporns, 2011).

Clustering coefficient, as a measure of local information flow, is defined as the ratio between the pair number of connected nodes in the neighborhood of a node and the total number of pairs of neighbors that the node has. This is equivalent to the ratio of closed triangles linked to the node and the total number of all possible closed triangles in its neighborhood (Fornito et al., 2016; Rubinov & Sporns, 2010; Watts & Strogatz, 1998). The node-wise clustering coefficient can be averaged across the nodes to derive the mean clustering coefficient of the whole graph and is bounded between 0 and 1, with 0 indicating a graph lack of clustering and 1 suggesting a fully connected graph. Clustering coefficient and shortest path length are frequently taken as two crucial attributes of the small-worldness organization of a network.

To resolve the trade-off between efficiency and wiring costs when performing cognitive functions, the human brain network does not process the information in a linear fashion. Instead, the nodes of the network are organized in a hierarchical modular manner with each module performing specialized functions, and the processing is coordinated and integrated at a supra-modular level. A *module* is a cluster of nodes that are more densely connected with each other than with the nodes outside of the cluster (Rubinov & Sporns, 2010). It serves as a relatively self-contained and independent processing component within the neural system to enhance the flexibility and resilience of the whole network to dysfunctions. Module detection (also called community detection) is an important research topic on modularity. There are many algorithms available (Fortunato, 2010) and the most commonly used is the modularity index Q proposed by Newman and Girvan (2004). For a binary, undirected network, it quantifies the mean difference between the observed degree of intramodular connectivity and the expected degree estimated based on an ensemble of random networks (null model) with the same degree of distribution (Leicht & Newman, 2008; Rubinov & Sporns, 2011). If Q is 0, it suggests that the partition of the modular structure does not differ from the null model. A negative Q indicates that the network does not have a modular structure.

An extensive search for the maximum modularity across all possible partitions of a network can yield the highest modularity index Q, but this approach is computationally prohibitive for large networks (Fortunato, 2010). Among the different algorithms proposed to tackle the issue (Guimerà et al., 2004; Leicht & Newman, 2008; Newman, 2006; Newman & Girvan, 2004), the Louvian algorithm gains more currency in recent studies due to its high efficiency, flexibility at different levels of partitioning, and high accuracy based on simulation studies (Blondel et al., 2008). The power of modularity analysis lies not only in the decomposition of the brain network into hierarchical modular communities but also in the identification of the nodal roles in intra- and intermodular connectivity (Guimerà & Amaral, 2005). The nodes more closely connected to the nodes in the same module may mainly contribute to the specialized function and act as provincial hubs, while the nodes with a more even distribution across different modules may play a core role in integrating information between distinct modules as connector hubs.

Path length is another important metric of network analysis closely related to the efficiency and cost of a graph. A shorter path length indicates that a graph is more integrated with efficient information flow within the network. Characteristic path length refers to the average shortest path length between all pairs of nodes in the network (Rubinov & Sporns, 2010; Watts & Strogatz, 1998). The inverse of the characteristic path is global efficiency, which is tied to the small-worldness organization characterized by highly clustered modules compounded by a few random long-distance connections (Bassett et al., 2010; Bullmore & Sporns, 2012; Latora & Marchiori, 2003). Brain networks generally show short paths connecting nodes both within and between modules to minimize wiring costs on the one hand, but some long-range costly links between disparate brain regions to facilitate information transfer on the other hand.

All graph metrics discussed so far only offer descriptive information of the typological properties of a graph. It is difficult to conclude that the global efficiency of a graph 0.18 is high or low without comparing it to a benchmark. In the context of statistical inferences, an ideal benchmark should be a random graph matching the empirical graph on all properties except for the one of interest. The difference between the two graphs determines whether the global efficiency is higher or lower than expected by chance. Because graphs differ in multiple dimensions, in practice, the random graph is generated to match some basic graph properties such as size (number of nodes), density (mean network degree), and degree distribution. There are two ways of generating the null networks—generative null models and connection rewiring. Readers can refer to Fornito et al. (2016), Zalesky et al. (2010) and Zalesky, Cocchi, et al. (2012) for detailed technical discussions of the two approaches.

Analogous to the multivariate approaches applied to the BOLD responses as discussed in the previous section, some multivariate approaches can also be applied to connectivity data. A variety of machine learning techniques are gaining the favor of researchers in recent years, and the graph measures are incorporated into the algorithms to extract features that can assist in classifying, diagnosing, and predicting brain disorders such as schizophrenia (Kim et al., 2016), autism (Tolan & Isik, 2018), Alzheimer's disease (Prasad et al., 2015), and Parkinson's disease (Kazeminejad et al., 2017).

Functional and Effective Connectivity

The most commonly used approaches to examine connectivity can be classified into two types—functional and effective connectivity analysis. *Functional connectivity analysis* attempts to quantify the interactions between brain regions using Pearson correlation between each pair of time series. Since the Pearson correlation only identifies the linear association between time courses and cannot preclude the possible mediating effect from a third source, the partial correlation, which removes the effect of the mediator, can be used. However, both Pearson correlation and partial correlation suffer from the limitations of the linear assumption and are subject to spurious connections (Zalesky, Fornito, & Bullmore, 2012). Some more complex metrics are proposed to construct the edges, such as mutual information (Kraskov et al., 2004; Paninski, 2003; Salvador et al., 2005), which characterizes the nonlinear dependency in terms of the marginal probability density and joint probability density of the two signals.

If functional connectivity characterizes the statistical dependency between distinct brain areas, *effective connectivity* assesses the influence of one neural system on the other (Friston, 2011). This research field has spurred strong interest in the (f)MRI community as cortical connections are predominantly bidirectional, and information propagation will shed light on the mechanisms underlying the spatiotemporal reconfiguration of the brain in response to both external and internal changes (Daunizeau et al., 2011; Friston et al., 2013; Roebroeck et al., 2005). However, researchers have not reached a consensus regarding the equivalence between "effective" and "causal," as causal relationship can only be observed at the neural level (Zarghami & Friston, 2020). Effective connectivity in the context of (f)MRI suffers from a similar inverse problem as EEG because the BOLD response needs to be mapped back to the unobserved level of neural activity to account for causality. For the several methods proposed to measure effective connectivity, each method differs in the extent to which they address the issue of causality. The most popular approaches include dynamic causal modeling (Daunizeau et al., 2011; Friston et al., 2003), structural equation modeling (Büchel et al., 1999; McLntosh & Gonzalez-Lima, 1994), and Granger causality (Deshpande et al., 2008; Granger, 1969). Readers interested in the technical details of the methods are directed to the review by Friston (2011).

Resources

Multiple standard software packages support brain connectivity analysis, such as the SPM-based cPPI (https://www.nitrc.org/projects/cppi_toolbox/), gPPI (https://www.nitrc.org/projects/gppi), and CONN toolboxes, FreeSurfer-based FSFAST version 6.0 toolbox (https://surfer.nmr.mgh.harvard.edu/fswiki/FsFastTutorialV6.0), and AFNI-based FATCAT toolbox (https://afni.nimh.nih.gov/pub/dist/doc/htmldoc/FATCAT/FATCAT_All.html). There is also a number of stand-alone packages built upon different program languages. This incomplete list includes MATLAB Brain Connectivity Toolbox, Graph Theory GLM Toolbox, GraphVar, REST, Python Brain Modulyzer, C-PAC, and Connectome workbench.

Readers who are interested in obtaining the conceptual and mathematical understanding of brain connectivity analysis are also encouraged to refer to the online tutorials, such as Center for Brains, Minds and Machines tutorials (https://www.youtube.com/watch?v=i3NpKY5tcQA), Organization for Human Brain Mapping courses (https://www.pathlms.com/ohbm/courses), and Andy's Brain Book by Andrew Jahn (https://andysbrainbook.readthedocs.io/en/latest/FunctionalConnectivity/CONN_ShortCourse/CONN_AppendixA_GraphTheory.html).

CONCLUSION

The (f)MRI analysis landscape is changing rapidly, therefore, this chapter is in no way a comprehensive review of all analytical techniques. We have described the most widely used methods in the current research field, and we listed website addresses of some useful software in Table 32.1 to provide convenient references for future researchers to conduct their (f)MRI data analyses.

TABLE 32.1

List of Main Software Used in (f)MRI Data Analyses

Software	Type	Website
SPM12	Comprehensive	https://www.fil.ion.ucl.ac.uk/spm/software/spm12/
FSL	Comprehensive	https://fsl.fmrib.ox.ac.uk/fsl/fslwiki/FEAT
AFNI	Comprehensive	https://afni.nimh.nih.gov/
BrainVoyager	Comprehensive	https://www.brainvoyager.com/
FreeSurfer	Comprehensive	https://surfer.nmr.mgh.harvard.edu/
Nipype	Comprehensive	https://nipype.readthedocs.io/en/latest/
CONN toolbox	GLM; ICA; PCA; Network	https://web.conn-toolbox.org/home/
GIFT	ICA; PCA	https://trendscenter.org/software/gift/
FIT	ICA	https://trendscenter.org/software/fit/
mapca	PCA	https://github.com/ME-ICA/mapca
BrainIAK	PCA; MVPA	https://brainiak.org/
CosMoMVPA	MVPA	https://cosmomvpa.org/
RSA toolbox	MVPA	https://github.com/rsagroup/rsatoolbox/
Decoding Toolbox	MVPA	https://sites.google.com/site/tdtdecodingtoolbox/home/
Princeton MVPA Toolbox	MVPA	https://pni.princeton.edu/pni-software-tools/mvpa-toolbox
PRoNTo	MVPA	http://www.mlnl.cs.ucl.ac.uk/pronto/
PyMVPA	MVPA	http://www.pymvpa.org
Neuropredict	MVPA	https://github.com/raamana/neuropredict/
Brain Connectivity Toolbox	Network	https://www.nitrc.org/projects/bct
Graph Theory GLM Toolbox	Network	https://www.nitrc.org/docman/?group_id=802
GraphVar	Network	https://www.nitrc.org/projects/graphvar/
REST	Network	https://www.nitrc.org/projects/rest/
Brain Modulyzer	Network	https://github.com/sugeerth/BrainModulyzer
C-PAC	Network	https://fcp-indi.github.io/docs/latest/user/index
Connectome workbench	Network	https://www.humanconnectome.org/software/connectome-workbench

References

Abdedayem, F., Kallel, F., Chaabane, M., Ben Hamida, A., & Sellami, L. (2020). fMRI imaging based human brain parcellation methods: A review. *2020 International Conference on Advanced Technologies for Signal and Image Processing, ATSIP 2020*, 1–5. https://doi.org/10.1109/ATSIP49331.2020.9231946

Aberg, M. B., & Wessberg, J. (2008). An evolutionary approach to the identification of informative voxel clusters for brain state discrimination. *IEEE Journal of Selected Topics in Signal Processing*, 2(6), 919–928. https://doi.org/10.1109/JSTSP.2008.2007788

Achard, S., & Bullmore, E. (2007). Efficiency and cost of economical brain functional networks. *PLOS Computational Biology*, 3(2), e17. https://doi.org/10.1371/journal.pcbi.0030017

Achard, S., Salvador, R., Whitcher, B., Suckling, J., & Bullmore, E. (2006). A resilient, low-frequency, small-world human brain functional network with highly connected association cortical hubs. *The Journal of Neuroscience: The Official Journal of the Society for Neuroscience*, 26(1), 63–72. https://doi.org/10.1523/JNEUROSCI.3874-05.2006

Aguirre, G. K., Zarahn, E., & D'esposito, M. (1998). The variability of human, BOLD hemodynamic responses. *NeuroImage*, 8(4), 360–369. https://doi.org/10.1006/nimg.1998.0369

Andersen, A. H., & Rayens, W. S. (2004). Structure-seeking multilinear methods for the analysis of fMRI data. *NeuroImage*, 22(2), 728–739. https://doi.org/10.1016/j.neuroimage.2004.02.026

Andrews-Hanna, J. R., Reidler, J. S., Sepulcre, J., Poulin, R., & Buckner, R. L. (2010). Functional-anatomic fractionation of the brain's default network. *Neuron*, 65(4), 550–562. https://doi.org/10.1016/j.neuron.2010.02.005

Anzellotti, S., & Coutanche, M. N. (2018). Beyond functional connectivity: Investigating networks of multivariate representations. *Trends in Cognitive Sciences*, 22(3), 258–269. https://doi.org/10.1016/j.tics.2017.12.002

Ashby, F. G. (2011). *Statistical analysis of fMRI data*. MIT press. https://doi.org/10.7551/mitpress/8764.001.0001

Barabási, A.-L., & Albert, R. (1999). Emergence of scaling in random networks. *Science*, *286*(5439), 509–512. https://doi.org/10.1126/science.286.5439.509

Barnathan, M., Megalooikonomou, V., Faloutsos, C., Faro, S., & Mohamed, F. B. (2011). TWave: High-order analysis of functional MRI. *NeuroImage*, *58*(2), 537–548. https://doi.org/10.1016/j.neuroimage.2011.06.043

Bassett, D. S., Greenfield, D. L., Meyer-Lindenberg, A., Weinberger, D. R., Moore, S. W., & Bullmore, E. T. (2010). Efficient physical embedding of topologically complex information processing networks in brains and computer circuits. *PLOS Computational Biology*, *6*(4), e1000748. https://doi.org/10.1371/journal.pcbi.1000748

Bassett, D. S., & Sporns, O. (2017). Network neuroscience. *Nature Neuroscience*, *20*(3), 353–364. https://doi.org/10.1038/nn.4502

Bauer, A. J., & Just, M. A. (2015). Monitoring the growth of the neural representations of new animal concepts. *Human Brain Mapping*, *36*(8), 3213–3226. https://doi.org/10.1002/hbm.22842

Beckmann, C. F., & Smith, S. M. (2004). Probabilistic independent component analysis for functional magnetic resonance imaging. *IEEE Transactions on Medical Imaging*, *23*(2), 137–152. https://doi.org/10.1109/TMI.2003.822821

Bell, A. J., & Sejnowski, T. J. (1995). An information-maximization approach to blind separation and blind deconvolution. *Neural Computation*, *7*(6), 1129–1159. https://doi.org/10.1162/neco.1995.7.6.1129

Belliveau, J. W., Kennedy, D. N., Jr., McKinstry, R. C., Buchbinder, B. R., Weisskoff, R. M., Cohen, M. S., Vevea, J. M., Brady, T. J., & Rosen, B. R. (1991). Functional mapping of the human visual cortex by magnetic resonance imaging. *Science*, *254*(5032), 716–719. https://doi.org/10.1126/science.1948051

Benjamini, Y., & Yosef, H. (1995). Controlling the false discovery rate : A practical and powerful approach to multiple testing. *Journal of the Royal Statistical Society: Series B. Methodological*, *57*(1), 289–300. https://doi.org/10.1111/j.2517-6161.1995.tb02031.x

Bennett, C. M., Baird, A. A., Miller, M. B., & Wolford, G. L. (2009). Neural correlates of interspecies perspective taking in the post-mortem Atlantic Salmon: An argument for multiple comparisons correction. *NeuroImage*, *47*, S125. https://doi.org/10.1016/S1053-8119(09)71202-9

Bi, X. A., Sun, Q., Zhao, J., Xu, Q., & Wang, L. (2018). Non-linear ICA analysis of resting-state fMRI in mild cognitive impairment. *Frontiers in Neuroscience*, *12*, 413. https://doi.org/10.3389/fnins.2018.00413

Biswal, B. B., & Ulmer, J. L. (1999). Blind source separation of multiple signal sources of fMRI data sets using independent component analysis. *Journal of Computer Assisted Tomography*, *23*(2), 265–271. https://doi.org/10.1097/00004728-199903000-00016

Blondel, V. D., Guillaume, J., Lambiotte, R., & Lefebvre, E. (2008). Fast unfolding of communities in large networks. *Journal of Statistical Mechanics*, *10*(10), P10008. Advance online publication. https://doi.org/10.1088/1742-5468/2008/10/P10008

Bollobás, B., & Riordan, O. (2004). The diameter of a scale-free random graph. *Combinatorica*, *24*(1), 5–34. https://doi.org/10.1007/s00493-004-0002-2

Boukouvalas, Z., Levin-Schwartz, Y., & Adali, T. (2017). Enhancing ICA performance by exploiting sparsity: Application to FMRI analysis. *IEEE International Conference on Acoustics, Speech and Signal Processing*, 2532–2536. https://doi.org/10.1109/ICASSP.2017.7952613

Bowman, F. D., Guo, Y., & Derado, G. (2007). Statistical approaches to functional neuroimaging data. *Neuroimaging Clinics of North America*, *17*(4), 441–458, viii. https://doi.org/10.1016/j.nic.2007.09.002

Boynton, G. M., Engel, S. A., Glover, G. H., & Heeger, D. J. (1996). Linear systems analysis of functional magnetic resonance imaging in human V1. *The Journal of Neuroscience*, *16*(13), 4207–4221. https://doi.org/10.1523/JNEUROSCI.16-13-04207.1996

Büchel, C., Coull, J. T., & Friston, K. J. (1999). The predictive value of changes in effective connectivity for human learning. *Science*, *283*(5407), 1538–1541. https://doi.org/10.1126/science.283.5407.1538

Bullmore, E., Brammer, M., Williams, S. C. R., Rabe-Hesketh, S., Janot, N., David, A., Mellers, J., Howard, R., & Sham, P. (1996). Statistical methods of estimation and inference for functional MR image analysis. *Magnetic Resonance in Medicine*, *35*(2), 261–277. https://doi.org/10.1002/mrm.1910350219

Bullmore, E., & Sporns, O. (2012). The economy of brain network organization. *Nature Reviews Neuroscience*, *13*(5), 336–349. https://doi.org/10.1038/nrn3214

Buxton, R. B., Wong, E. C., & Frank, L. R. (1998). Dynamics of blood flow and oxygenation changes during brain activation: The balloon model. *Magnetic Resonance in Medicine, 39*(6), 855–864. https://doi.org/10.1002/mrm.1910390602

Calhoun, V. D., & Adali, T. (2012). Multisubject independent component analysis of fMRI: A decade of intrinsic networks, default mode, and neurodiagnostic discovery. *IEEE Reviews in Biomedical Engineering, 5*, 60–73. https://doi.org/10.1109/RBME.2012.2211076

Calhoun, V. D., Adali, T., Stevens, M. C., Kiehl, K. A., & Pekar, J. J. (2005). Semi-blind ICA of fMRI: A method for utilizing hypothesis-derived time courses in a spatial ICA analysis. *NeuroImage, 25*(2), 527–538. https://doi.org/10.1016/j.neuroimage.2004.12.012

Calhoun, V. D., Kiehl, K. A., & Pearlson, G. D. (2008). Modulation of temporally coherent brain networks estimated using ICA at rest and during cognitive tasks. *Human Brain Mapping, 29*(7), 828–838. https://doi.org/10.1002/hbm.20581

Calhoun, V. D., Stevens, M. C., Pearlson, G. D., & Kiehl, K. A. (2004). fMRI analysis with the general linear model: Removal of latency-induced amplitude bias by incorporation of hemodynamic derivative terms. *NeuroImage, 22*(1), 252–257. https://doi.org/10.1016/j.neuroimage.2003.12.029

Carlson, T. A., Schrater, P., & He, S. (2003). Patterns of activity in the categorical representations of objects. *Journal of Cognitive Neuroscience, 15*(5), 704–717. https://doi.org/10.1162/jocn.2003.15.5.704

Chadwick, M. J., Hassabis, D., Weiskopf, N., & Maguire, E. A. (2010). Decoding individual episodic memory traces in the human hippocampus. *Current Biology, 20*(6), 544–547. https://doi.org/10.1016/j.cub.2010.01.053

Chikazoe, J., Lee, D. H., Kriegeskorte, N., & Anderson, A. K. (2014). Population coding of affect across stimuli, modalities and individuals. *Nature Neuroscience, 17*(8), 1114–1122. https://doi.org/10.1038/nn.3749

Cocchi, L., Halford, G. S., Zalesky, A., Harding, I. H., Ramm, B. J., Cutmore, T., Shum, D. H. K., & Mattingley, J. B. (2014). Complexity in relational processing predicts changes in functional brain network dynamics. *Cerebral Cortex, 24*(9), 2283–2296. https://doi.org/10.1093/cercor/bht075

Cohen, A. L., Fair, D. A., Dosenbach, N. U. F., Miezin, F. M., Dierker, D., Van Essen, D. C., Schlaggar, B. L., & Petersen, S. E. (2008). Defining functional areas in individual human brains using resting functional connectivity MRI. *NeuroImage, 41*(1), 45–57. https://doi.org/10.1016/j.neuroimage.2008.01.066

Cox, D. D., & Savoy, R. L. (2003). Functional magnetic resonance imaging (fMRI) "brain reading": Detecting and classifying distributed patterns of fMRI activity in human visual cortex. *NeuroImage, 19*(2 Pt 1), 261–270. https://doi.org/10.1016/S1053-8119(03)00049-1

Cribben, I., & Fiecas, M. (2016). Functional connectivity analyses for fMRI data. In H. Ombao, M. Lindquist, W. Thompson, & J. Aston (Eds.), *Handbook of neuroimaging data analysis* (pp. 369–397). CRC Press. https://doi.org/10.1201/9781315373652

Crossley, N. A., Mechelli, A., Vértes, P. E., Winton-Brown, T. T., Patel, A. X., Ginestet, C. E., McGuire, P., & Bullmore, E. T. (2013). Cognitive relevance of the community structure of the human brain functional coactivation network. *Proceedings of the National Academy of Sciences of the United States of America, 110*(28), 11583–11588. https://doi.org/10.1073/pnas.1220826110

Dale, A. M. (1999). Optimal experimental design for event-related fMRI. *Human Brain Mapping, 8*(2-3), 109–114. https://doi.org/10.1002/(SICI)1097-0193(1999)8:2/3<109::AID-HBM7>3.0.CO;2-W

Dale, A. M., & Buckner, R. L. (1997). Selective averaging of individual trials using fMRI. *NeuroImage, 5*, 329–340. https://doi.org/10.1002/(SICI)1097-0193(1997)5:5<329::AID-HBM1>3.0.CO;2-5

Daunizeau, J., David, O., & Stephan, K. E. (2011). Dynamic causal modelling: A critical review of the biophysical and statistical foundations. *NeuroImage, 58*(2), 312–322. https://doi.org/10.1016/j.neuroimage.2009.11.062

Davatzikos, C., Ruparel, K., Fan, Y., Shen, D. G., Acharyya, M., Loughead, J. W., Gur, R. C., & Langleben, D. D. (2005). Classifying spatial patterns of brain activity with machine learning methods: Application to lie detection. *NeuroImage, 28*(3), 663–668. https://doi.org/10.1016/j.neuroimage.2005.08.009

Deshpande, G., Hu, X., Stilla, R., & Sathian, K. (2008). Effective connectivity during haptic perception: A study using Granger causality analysis of functional magnetic resonance imaging data. *NeuroImage, 40*(4), 1807–1814. https://doi.org/10.1016/j.neuroimage.2008.01.044

Dosenbach, N. U. F., Nardos, B., Cohen, A. L., Fair, D. A., Power, J. D., Church, J. A., Nelson, S. M., Wig, G. S., Vogel, A. C., Lessov-Schlaggar, C. N., Barnes, K. A., Dubis, J. W., Feczko, E., Coalson, R. S., Pruett, J. R., Jr., Barch, D. M., Petersen, S. E., & Schlaggar, B. L. (2010). Prediction of individual brain maturity using fMRI. *Science, 329*(5997), 1358–1361. https://doi.org/10.1126/science.1194144

Eddy, W. F., Fitzgerald, M., Genovese, C., Lazar, N., Mockus, A., Welling, J., Eddy, W. F., Fitzgerald, M.,

Genovese, C., Lazar, N., Mockus, A., & Welling, J. (1999). The challenge of functional magnetic resonance imaging. *Journal of Computational and Graphical Statistics*, *8*(3), 545–558. https://doi.org/10.2307/1390875

Eloyan, A. (2016). Multivariate decompositions in brain imaging. In H. Ombao, M. Lindquist, W. Thompson, & J. Aston (Eds.), *Handbook of neuroimaging data analysis* (pp. 439–458). Chapman and Hall/CRC. https://doi.org/10.1201/9781315373652

Fornito, A., Harrison, B. J., Zalesky, A., & Simons, J. S. (2012). Competitive and cooperative dynamics of large-scale brain functional networks supporting recollection. *Proceedings of the National Academy of Sciences of the United States of America*, *109*(31), 12788–12793. https://doi.org/10.1073/pnas.1204185109

Fornito, A., Zalesky, A., & Breakspear, M. (2013). Graph analysis of the human connectome: Promise, progress, and pitfalls. *NeuroImage*, *80*, 426–444. https://doi.org/10.1016/j.neuroimage.2013.04.087

Fornito, A., Zalesky, A., & Bullmore, E. (2016). *Fundamentals of brain network analysis*. Elsevier Science & Technology. https://doi.org/10.1016/c2012-0-06036-x

Fornito, A., Zalesky, A., & Bullmore, E. T. (2010). Network scaling effects in graph analytic studies of human resting-state FMRI data. *Frontiers in Systems Neuroscience*, *4*, 22. https://doi.org/10.3389/fnsys.2010.00022

Fortunato, S. (2010). Community detection in graphs. *Physics Reports*, *486*(3-5), 75–174. https://doi.org/10.1016/j.physrep.2009.11.002

Friston, K., Moran, R., & Seth, A. K. (2013). Analysing connectivity with Granger causality and dynamic causal modelling. *Current Opinion in Neurobiology*, *23*(2), 172–178. https://doi.org/10.1016/j.conb.2012.11.010

Friston, K., Phillips, J., Chawla, D., & Büchel, C. (1999). Revealing interactions among brain systems with nonlinear PCA. *Human Brain Mapping*, *8*(2-3), 92–97. https://doi.org/10.1002/(SICI)1097-0193(1999)8:2/3<92::AID-HBM4>3.0.CO;2-#

Friston, K., Phillips, J., Chawla, D., & Büchel, C. (2000). Nonlinear PCA: Characterizing interactions between modes of brain activity. *Philosophical Transactions of the Royal Society of London: Series B. Biological Sciences*, *355*(1393), 135–146. https://doi.org/10.1098/rstb.2000.0554

Friston, K. J. (2011). Functional and effective connectivity: A review. *Brain Connectivity*, *1*(1), 13–36. https://doi.org/10.1089/brain.2011.0008

Friston, K. J., Fletcher, P., Josephs, O., Holmes, A., Rugg, M. D., & Turner, R. (1998). Event-related fMRI: Characterizing differential responses. *NeuroImage*, *7*(1), 30–40. https://doi.org/10.1006/nimg.1997.0306

Friston, K. J., Frith, C. D., Liddle, P. F., & Frackowiak, R. S. J. (1991). Comparing functional (PET) images: The assessment of significant change. *Journal of Cerebral Blood Flow and Metabolism*, *11*(4), 690–699. https://doi.org/10.1038/jcbfm.1991.122

Friston, K. J., Frith, C. D., Liddle, P. F., & Frackowiak, R. S. J. (1993). Functional connectivity: The principal-component analysis of large (PET) data sets. *Journal of Cerebral Blood Flow and Metabolism*, *13*(1), 5–14. https://doi.org/10.1038/jcbfm.1993.4

Friston, K. J., Harrison, L., & Penny, W. (2003). Dynamic causal modelling. *NeuroImage*, *19*(4), 1273–1302. https://doi.org/10.1016/S1053-8119(03)00202-7

Friston, K. J., Holmes, A. P., Poline, J. B., Grasby, P. J., Williams, S. C. R., Frackowiak, R. S. J., & Turner, R. (1995). Analysis of fMRI time-series revisited. *NeuroImage*, *2*(1), 45–53. https://doi.org/10.1006/nimg.1995.1007

Friston, K. J., Holmes, A. P., Worsley, K. J., Poline, J.-P., Frith, C. D., & Frackowiak, R. S. J. (1994). Statistical parametric maps in functional imaging: A general linear approach. *Human Brain Mapping*, *2*(4), 189–210. https://doi.org/10.1002/hbm.460020402

Friston, K. J., Jezzard, P., & Turner, R. (1994). Analysis of functional MRI time-series. *Human Brain Mapping*, *1*(2), 153–171. https://doi.org/10.1002/hbm.460010207

Friston, K. J., Josephs, O., Rees, G., & Turner, R. (1998). Nonlinear event-related responses in fMRI. *Magnetic Resonance in Medicine*, *39*(1), 41–52. https://doi.org/10.1002/mrm.1910390109

Friston, K. J., Josephs, O., Zarahn, E., Holmes, A. P., Rouquette, S., & Poline, J. (2000). To smooth or not to smooth? Bias and efficiency in fMRI time-series analysis. *NeuroImage*, *12*(2), 196–208. https://doi.org/10.1006/nimg.2000.0609

Gardumi, A., Ivanov, D., Hausfeld, L., Valente, G., Formisano, E., & Uludağ, K. (2016). The effect of spatial resolution on decoding accuracy in fMRI multivariate pattern analysis. *NeuroImage*, *132*, 32–42. https://doi.org/10.1016/j.neuroimage.2016.02.033

Gautama, T., & Van Hulle, M. M. (2004). Optimal spatial regularisation of autocorrelation estimates in fMRI analysis. *NeuroImage*, *23*(3), 1203–1216. https://doi.org/10.1016/j.neuroimage.2004.07.048

Genovese, C. R., Lazar, N. A., & Nichols, T. (2002). Thresholding of statistical maps in functional neuroimaging using the false discovery rate. *NeuroImage*, *15*(4), 870–878. https://doi.org/10.1006/nimg.2001.1037

Ginestet, C. E., Kramer, M., & Kolaczyk, E. D. (2016). Network analysis. In H. Ombao, M. Lindquist, W. Thompson, & J. Aston (Eds.), *Handbook of neuroimaging data analysis* (pp. 441–465). Chapman and Hall/CRC. https://doi.org/10.1201/9781315373652

Glover, G. H. (1999). Deconvolution of impulse response in event-related BOLD fMRI. *NeuroImage*, *9*(4), 416–429. https://doi.org/10.1006/nimg.1998.0419

Gordon, E. M., Laumann, T. O., Adeyemo, B., Huckins, J. F., Kelley, W. M., & Petersen, S. E. (2016). Generation and evaluation of a cortical area parcellation from resting-state correlations. *Cerebral Cortex*, *26*(1), 288–303. https://doi.org/10.1093/cercor/bhu239

Granger, C. J. W. (1969). Investigating causal relations by econometric models and cross-spectral methods. *Econometrica*, *37*(3), 424–438. https://doi.org/10.2307/1912791

Griffanti, L., Salimi-Khorshidi, G., Beckmann, C. F., Auerbach, E. J., Douaud, G., Sexton, C. E., Zsoldos, E., Ebmeier, K. P., Filippini, N., Mackay, C. E., Moeller, S., Xu, J., Yacoub, E., Baselli, G., Ugurbil, K., Miller, K. L., & Smith, S. M. (2014). ICA-based artefact removal and accelerated fMRI acquisition for improved resting state network imaging. *NeuroImage*, *95*, 232–247. https://doi.org/10.1016/j.neuroimage.2014.03.034

Guimerà, R., & Amaral, L. A. N. (2005). Functional cartography of complex metabolic networks. *Nature*, *433*(7028), 895–900. https://doi.org/10.1038/nature03288

Guimerà, R., Sales-Pardo, M., & Amaral, L. A. N. (2004). Modularity from fluctuations in random graphs and complex networks. *Physical Review*, *70*(2 Pt 2), 025101. https://doi.org/10.1103/physreve.70.025101

Hansen, L. K., Larsen, J., Nielsen, F. Å., Strother, S. C., Rostrup, E., Savoy, R., Lange, N., Sidtis, J., Svarer, C., & Paulson, O. B. (1999). Generalizable patterns in neuroimaging: How many principal components? *NeuroImage*, *9*(5), 534–544. https://doi.org/10.1006/nimg.1998.0425

Hastie, T., Tibshirani, R., & Friedman, J. (2009). *The elements of statistical learning: Data mining, inference, and prediction*. Springer. https://doi.org/10.1007/978-0-387-84858-7

Haxby, J. V., Gobbini, M. I., Furey, M. L., Ishai, A., Schouten, J. L., & Pietrini, P. (2001). Distributed and overlapping representations of faces and objects in ventral temporal cortex. *Science*, *293*(5539), 2425–2430. https://doi.org/10.1126/science.1063736

Haynes, J. D., & Rees, G. (2006). Decoding mental states from brain activity in humans. *Nature Reviews Neuroscience*, *7*(7), 523–534. https://doi.org/10.1038/nrn1931

Hendriks, M. H. A., Daniels, N., Pegado, F., & Op de Beeck, H. P. (2017). The effect of spatial smoothing on representational similarity in a simple motor paradigm. *Frontiers in Neurology*, *8*, 222. https://doi.org/10.3389/fneur.2017.00222

Hong, B., Pearlson, G. D., & Calhoun, V. D. (2005). Source density-driven independent component analysis approach for fMRI data. *Human Brain Mapping*, *25*(3), 297–307. https://doi.org/10.1002/hbm.20100

Hotelling, H. (1933). Analysis of a complex of statistical variables into principal components. *Journal of Educational Psychology*, *24*(6), 417–441. https://doi.org/10.1037/h0071325

Huettel, S. A., Singerman, J. D., & McCarthy, G. (2001). The effects of aging upon the hemodynamic response measured by functional MRI. *NeuroImage*, *13*(1), 161–175. https://doi.org/10.1006/nimg.2000.0675

Hyvärinen, A. (1999). Fast and robust fixed-point algorithms for independent component analysis. *IEEE Transactions on Neural Networks*, *10*(3), 626–634. https://doi.org/10.1109/72.761722

Hyvärinen, A., Karhunen, J., & Oja, E. (2001). *Independent component analysis*. John Wiley & Sons. https://doi.org/10.1002/0471221317

Hyvärinen, A., & Oja, E. (2000). Independent component analysis: Algorithms and applications. *Neural Networks*, *13*(4-5), 411–430. https://doi.org/10.1016/S0893-6080(00)00026-5

Josephs, O., Turner, R., & Friston, K. (1997). Event-related fMRI. *Human Brain Mapping*, *5*(4), 243–248. https://doi.org/10.1002/(SICI)1097-0193(1997)5:4<243::AID-HBM7>3.0.CO;2-3

Kamitani, Y., & Tong, F. (2005). Decoding the visual and subjective contents of the human brain. *Nature Neuroscience*, *8*(5), 679–685. https://doi.org/10.1038/nn1444

Kazeminejad, A., Golbabaei, S., & Soltanian-Zadeh, H. (2017). Graph theoretical metrics and machine learning for diagnosis of Parkinson's disease using rs-fMRI. *Artificial Intelligence and Signal Processing Conference (AISP)*, 134–139. https://doi.org/10.1109/aisp.2017.8324124

Kiani, R., Esteky, H., Mirpour, K., & Tanaka, K. (2007). Object category structure in response patterns of neuronal population in monkey inferior temporal cortex. *Journal of Neurophysiology, 97*(6), 4296–4309. https://doi.org/10.1152/jn.00024.2007

Kim, J., Calhoun, V. D., Shim, E., & Lee, J. H. (2016). Deep neural network with weight sparsity control and pre-training extracts hierarchical features and enhances classification performance: Evidence from whole-brain resting-state functional connectivity patterns of schizophrenia. *NeuroImage, 124*(Pt A), 127–146. https://doi.org/10.1016/j.neuroimage.2015.05.018

Kim, K. K., Karunanayaka, P., Privitera, M. D., Holland, S. K., & Szaflarski, J. P. (2011). Semantic association investigated with functional MRI and independent component analysis. *Epilepsy & Behavior, 20*(4), 613–622. https://doi.org/10.1016/j.yebeh.2010.11.010

Kolaczyk, E. (2009). *Statistical analysis of network data: Methods and models*. Springer-Verlag. https://doi.org/10.1007/978-0-387-88146-1

Kraskov, A., Stögbauer, H., & Grassberger, P. (2004). Estimating mutual information. *Physical Review E, 69*(6), 066138. https://doi.org/10.1103/physreve.69.066138

Kriegeskorte, N., Goebel, R., & Bandettini, P. (2006). Information-based functional brain mapping. *Proceedings of the National Academy of Sciences of the United States of America, 103*(10), 3863–3868. https://doi.org/10.1073/pnas.0600244103

Kriegeskorte, N., Mur, M., & Bandettini, P. (2008a). Representational similarity analysis: Connecting the branches of systems neuroscience. *Frontiers in Systems Neuroscience, 2*, 4. https://doi.org/10.3389/neuro.06.004.2008

Kriegeskorte, N., Mur, M., Ruff, D. A., Kiani, R., Bodurka, J., Esteky, H., Tanaka, K., & Bandettini, P. A. (2008b). Matching categorical object representations in inferior temporal cortex of man and monkey. *Neuron, 60*(6), 1126–1141. https://doi.org/10.1016/j.neuron.2008.10.043

Latora, V., & Marchiori, M. (2003). Economic small-world behavior in weighted networks. *European Physical Journal. B, Condensed Matter and Complex Systems, 32*(2), 249–263. https://doi.org/10.1140/epjb/e2003-00095-5

Lazar, N. (2008). *The statistical analysis of functional MRI data*. Springer Science & Business Media. https://doi.org/10.1111/j.1467-985x.2009.00624_6.x

Lazar, N. (2016). Corrections for multiplicity in functional neuroimaging data. In H. Ombao, M. Lindquist, W. Thompson, & J. Aston (Eds.), *Handbook of neuroimaging data analysis* (pp. 395–408). https://doi.org/10.1201/9781315373652

Leicht, E. A., & Newman, M. E. J. (2008). Community structure in directed networks. *Physical Review Letters, 100*(11), 118703. https://doi.org/10.1103/PhysRevLett.100.118703

Lewis-Peacock, J. A., & Norman, K. A. (2013). Multi-voxel pattern analysis of fMRI data. In M. S. Gazzaniga & G. R. Mangun (Eds.), *The cognitive neurosciences* (4th ed., pp. 911–920). MIT Press.

Logothetis, N. K. (2003). The underpinnings of the BOLD functional magnetic resonance imaging signal. *The Journal of Neuroscience, 23*(10), 3963–3971. https://doi.org/10.1523/JNEUROSCI.23-10-03963.2003

Logothetis, N. K., Pauls, J., Augath, M., Trinath, T., & Oeltermann, A. (2001). Neurophysiological investigation of the basis of the fMRI signal. *Nature, 412*(6843), 150–157. https://doi.org/10.1038/35084005

Mahmoudi, A., Takerkart, S., Regragui, F., Boussaoud, D., & Brovelli, A. (2012). Multivoxel pattern analysis for FMRI data: A review. *Computational and Mathematical Methods in Medicine, 2012*, 961257. Advance online publication. https://doi.org/10.1155/2012/961257

Mandelkow, H., Brandeis, D., & Boesiger, P. (2010). Good practices in EEG-MRI: The utility of retrospective synchronization and PCA for the removal of MRI gradient artefacts. *NeuroImage, 49*(3), 2287–2303. https://doi.org/10.1016/j.neuroimage.2009.10.050

Mandelkow, H., de Zwart, J. A., & Duyn, J. H. (2017). Effects of spatial fMRI resolution on the classification of naturalistic movies. *NeuroImage, 162*, 45–55. https://doi.org/10.1016/j.neuroimage.2017.08.053

Mason, R. A., & Just, M. A. (2020). Neural representations of procedural knowledge. *Psychological Science, 31*(6), 729–740 https://doi.org/10.1177/0956797620916806

McKeown, M. J., Hansen, L. K., & Sejnowsk, T. J. (2003). Independent component analysis of functional MRI: What is signal and what is noise? *Current Opinion in Neurobiology, 13*(5), 620–629. https://doi.org/10.1016/j.conb.2003.09.012

McKeown, M. J., Makeig, S., Brown, G. G., Jung, T. P., Kindermann, S. S., Bell, A. J., & Sejnowski, T. J. (1998). Analysis of fMRI data by blind separation into independent spatial components. *Human Brain Mapping, 6*(3), 160–188. https://doi.org/10.1002/(SICI)1097-0193(1998)6:3<160::AID-HBM5>3.0.CO;2-1

McLntosh, A. R., & Gonzalez-Lima, F. (1994). Structural equation modeling and its application to network analysis in functional brain imaging. *Human Brain Mapping, 2*(1-2), 2–22. https://doi.org/10.1002/hbm.460020104

McNorgan, C., Smith, G. J., & Edwards, E. S. (2020). Integrating functional connectivity and MVPA through a multiple constraint network analysis. *NeuroImage, 208,* 116412. https://doi.org/10.1016/j.neuroimage.2019.116412

Meda, S. A., Narayanan, B., Liu, J., Perrone-Bizzozero, N. I., Stevens, M. C., Calhoun, V. D., Glahn, D. C., Shen, L., Risacher, S. L., Saykin, A. J., & Pearlson, G. D. (2012). A large scale multivariate parallel ICA method reveals novel imaging-genetic relationships for Alzheimer's disease in the ADNI cohort. *NeuroImage, 60*(3), 1608–1621. https://doi.org/10.1016/j.neuroimage.2011.12.076

Misaki, M., Kim, Y., Bandettini, P. A., & Kriegeskorte, N. (2010). Comparison of multivariate classifiers and response normalizations for pattern-information fMRI. *NeuroImage, 53*(1), 103–118. https://doi.org/10.1016/j.neuroimage.2010.05.051

Mitchell, T. M., Hutchinson, R., Niculescu, R. S., Pereira, F., Wang, X., Just, M., & Newman, S. (2004). Learning to decode cognitive states from brain images. *Machine Learning, 57*(1), 145–175. https://doi.org/10.1023/B:MACH.0000035475.85309.1b

Muschelli, J., Nebel, M. B., Caffo, B. S., Barber, A. D., Pekar, J. J., & Mostofsky, S. H. (2014). Reduction of motion-related artifacts in resting state fMRI using aCompCor. *NeuroImage, 96,* 22–35. https://doi.org/10.1016/j.neuroimage.2014.03.028

Naselaris, T., Kay, K. N., Nishimoto, S., & Gallant, J. L. (2011). Encoding and decoding in fMRI. *NeuroImage, 56*(2), 400–410. https://doi.org/10.1016/j.neuroimage.2010.07.073

Nastase, S. A., Connolly, A. C., Oosterhof, N. N., Halchenko, Y. O., Guntupalli, J. S., Visconti di Oleggio Castello, M., Gors, J., Gobbini, M. I., & Haxby, J. V. (2017). Attention selectively reshapes the geometry of distributed semantic representation. *Cerebral Cortex, 27*(8), 4277–4291. https://doi.org/10.1093/cercor/bhx138

Newman, M. E. J. (2006). Modularity and community structure in networks. *Proceedings of the National Academy of Sciences of the United States of America, 103*(23), 8577–8582. https://doi.org/10.1073/pnas.0601602103

Newman, M. E. J., & Girvan, M. (2004). Finding and evaluating community structure in networks. *Physical Review, 69*(2), 026113. https://doi.org/10.1103/physreve.69.026113

Nichols, T., & Hayasaka, S. (2003). Controlling the familywise error rate in functional neuroimaging: A comparative review. *Statistical Methods in Medical Research, 12*(5), 419–446. https://doi.org/10.1191/0962280203sm341ra

Norman, K. A., Polyn, S. M., Detre, G. J., & Haxby, J. V. (2006). Beyond mind-reading: Multi-voxel pattern analysis of fMRI data. *Trends in Cognitive Sciences, 10*(9), 424–430. https://doi.org/10.1016/j.tics.2006.07.005

O'Hearn, K., Larsen, B., Fedor, J., Luna, B., & Lynn, A. (2020). Representational similarity analysis reveals atypical age-related changes in brain regions supporting face and car recognition in autism. *NeuroImage, 209,* 116322. https://doi.org/10.1016/j.neuroimage.2019.116322

Ogawa, S., Lee, T.-M., Nayak, A. S., & Glynn, P. (1990). Oxygenation-sensitive contrast in magnetic resonance image of rodent brain at high magnetic fields. *Magnetic Resonance in Medicine, 14*(1), 68–78. https://doi.org/10.1002/mrm.1910140108

Op de Beeck, H. P. (2010). Against hyperacuity in brain reading: Spatial smoothing does not hurt multivariate fMRI analyses? *NeuroImage, 49*(3), 1943–1948. https://doi.org/10.1016/j.neuroimage.2009.02.047

Paninski, L. (2003). Estimation of entropy and mutual information. *Neural Computation, 15*(6), 1191–1253. https://doi.org/10.1162/089976603321780272

Penny, W., Kiebel, S., & Friston, K. (2003). Variational Bayesian inference for fMRI time series. *NeuroImage, 19*(3), 727–741. https://doi.org/10.1016/S1053-8119(03)00071-5

Pereira, F., Mitchell, T., & Botvinick, M. (2009). Machine learning classifiers and fMRI: A tutorial overview. *NeuroImage, 45*(1 Suppl.), S199–S209. https://doi.org/10.1016/j.neuroimage.2008.11.007

Perrin, V. (2013). *MRI techniques.* John Wiley & Sons. https://doi.org/10.1002/9781118761281

Polzehl, J., & Tabelow, K. (2019). *Magnetic resonance brain imaging.* Springer International Publishing. https://doi.org/10.1007/978-3-030-29184-6

Power, J. D., Schlaggar, B. L., Lessov-Schlaggar, C. N., & Petersen, S. E. (2013). Evidence for hubs in human functional brain networks. *Neuron, 79*(4), 798–813. https://doi.org/10.1016/j.neuron.2013.07.035

Prasad, G., Joshi, S. H., Nir, T. M., Toga, A. W., & Thompson, P. M. (2015). Brain connectivity and novel network measures for Alzheimer's disease classification. *Neurobiology of Aging, 36*(S1), S121–S131. https://doi.org/10.1016/j.neurobiolaging.2014.04.037

Pruim, R. H. R., Mennes, M., van Rooij, D., Llera, A., Buitelaar, J. K., & Beckmann, C. F. (2015). ICA-AROMA: A robust ICA-based strategy for removing motion artifacts from fMRI data. *NeuroImage, 112,* 267–277. https://doi.org/10.1016/j.neuroimage.2015.02.064

Richter, W., & Richter, M. (2003). The shape of the fMRI BOLD response in children and adults changes systematically with age. *NeuroImage*, *20*(2), 1122–1131. https://doi.org/10.1016/S1053-8119(03)00347-1

Roebroeck, A., Formisano, E., & Goebel, R. (2005). Mapping directed influence over the brain using Granger causality and fMRI. *NeuroImage*, *25*(1), 230–242. https://doi.org/10.1016/j.neuroimage.2004.11.017

Rosazza, C., & Minati, L. (2011). Resting-state brain networks: Literature review and clinical applications. *Neurological Sciences*, *32*(5), 773–785. https://doi.org/10.1007/s10072-011-0636-y

Rubinov, M., & Sporns, O. (2010). Complex network measures of brain connectivity: Uses and interpretations. *NeuroImage*, *52*(3), 1059–1069. https://doi.org/10.1016/j.neuroimage.2009.10.003

Rubinov, M., & Sporns, O. (2011). Weight-conserving characterization of complex functional brain networks. *NeuroImage*, *56*(4), 2068–2079. https://doi.org/10.1016/j.neuroimage.2011.03.069

Salvador, R., Suckling, J., Schwarzbauer, C., & Bullmore, E. (2005). Undirected graphs of frequency-dependent functional connectivity in whole brain networks. *Philosophical Transactions of the Royal Society of London: Series B. Biological Sciences*, *360*(1457), 937–946. https://doi.org/10.1098/rstb.2005.1645

Sayres, R., Ress, D., & Grill-Spector, K. (2005). Identifying distributed object representations in human extrastriate visual cortex. In *Proceedings of the 18th International Conference on Neural Information Processing Systems* (pp. 1169–1176). MIT Press.

Schacter, D. L., Buckner, R. L., Koutstaal, W., Dale, A. M., & Rosen, B. R. (1997). Late onset of anterior prefrontal activity during true and false recognition: An event-related fMRI study. *NeuroImage*, *6*(4), 259–269. https://doi.org/10.1006/nimg.1997.0305

Schaefer, A., Kong, R., Gordon, E. M., Laumann, T. O., Zuo, X.-N., Holmes, A. J., Eickhoff, S. B., & Yeo, B. T. T. (2018). Local-global parcellation of the human cerebral cortex from intrinsic functional connectivity MRI. *Cerebral Cortex*, *28*(9), 3095–3114. https://doi.org/10.1093/cercor/bhx179

Serences, J. T. (2004). A comparison of methods for characterizing the event-related BOLD timeseries in rapid fMRI. *NeuroImage*, *21*(4), 1690–1700. https://doi.org/10.1016/j.neuroimage.2003.12.021

Serences, J. T., Ester, E. F., Vogel, E. K., & Awh, E. (2009). Stimulus-specific delay activity in human primary visual cortex. *Psychological Science*, *20*(2), 207–214. https://doi.org/10.1111/j.1467-9280.2009.02276.x

Smith, S. M., Vidaurre, D., Beckmann, C. F., Glasser, M. F., Jenkinson, M., Miller, K. L., Nichols, T. E., Robinson, E. C., Salimi-Khorshidi, G., Woolrich, M. W., Barch, D. M., Uğurbil, K., & Van Essen, D. C. (2013). Functional connectomics from resting-state fMRI. *Trends in Cognitive Sciences*, *17*(12), 666–682. https://doi.org/10.1016/j.tics.2013.09.016

Stanley, M. L., Moussa, M. N., Paolini, B. M., Lyday, R. G., Burdette, J. H., & Laurienti, P. J. (2013). Defining nodes in complex brain networks. *Frontiers in Computational Neuroscience*, *7*, 169. https://doi.org/10.3389/fncom.2013.00169

Szabó, G., Alava, M., & Kertész, J. (2002). Shortest paths and load scaling in scale-free trees. *Physical Review E*, *66*(2), 026101. https://doi.org/10.1103/physreve.66.026101

Thirion, B., & Faugeras, O. (2003). Dynamical components analysis of fMRI data through kernel PCA. *NeuroImage*, *20*(1), 34–49. https://doi.org/10.1016/S1053-8119(03)00316-1

Tolan, E., & Isik, Z. (2018l). Graph theory based classification of brain connectivity network for autism spectrum disorder. In *International Conference on Bioinformatics and Biomedical Engineering* (pp. 520–530). Springer, Cham. https://doi.org/10.1007/978-3-319-78723-7_45

Tzourio-Mazoyer, N., Landeau, B., Papathanassiou, D., Crivello, F., Etard, O., Delcroix, N., Mazoyer, B., & Joliot, M. (2002). Automated anatomical labeling of activations in SPM using a macroscopic anatomical parcellation of the MNI MRI single-subject brain. *NeuroImage*, *15*(1), 273–289. https://doi.org/10.1006/nimg.2001.0978

van den Heuvel, M. P., de Lange, S. C., Zalesky, A., Seguin, C., Yeo, B. T. T., & Schmidt, R. (2017). Proportional thresholding in resting-state fMRI functional connectivity networks and consequences for patient-control connectome studies: Issues and recommendations. *NeuroImage*, *152*, 437–449. https://doi.org/10.1016/j.neuroimage.2017.02.005

van den Heuvel, M. P., Kahn, R. S., Goñi, J., & Sporns, O. (2012). High-cost, high-capacity backbone for global brain communication. *Proceedings of the National Academy of Sciences of the United States of America*, *109*(28), 11372–11377. https://doi.org/10.1073/pnas.1203593109

van den Heuvel, M. P., & Sporns, O. (2011). Rich-club organization of the human connectome. *The Journal of Neuroscience*, *31*(44), 15775–15786. https://doi.org/10.1523/JNEUROSCI.3539-11.2011

van den Heuvel, M. P., Stam, C. J., Boersma, M., & Hulshoff Pol, H. E. (2008). Small-world and scale-free organization of voxel-based resting-state functional connectivity in the human brain. *NeuroImage*, *43*(3), 528–539. https://doi.org/10.1016/j.neuroimage.2008.08.010

van Wijk, B. C. M., Stam, C. J., & Daffertshofer, A. (2010). Comparing brain networks of different size and connectivity density using graph theory. *PLOS ONE*, *5*(10), e13701. https://doi.org/10.1371/journal.pone.0013701

Vazquez, A. L., & Noll, D. C. (1998). Nonlinear aspects of the BOLD response in functional MRI. *NeuroImage*, *7*(2), 108–118. https://doi.org/10.1006/nimg.1997.0316

Visser, R. M., Kunze, A. E., Westhoff, B., Scholte, H. S., & Kindt, M. (2015). Representational similarity analysis offers a preview of the noradrenergic modulation of long-term fear memory at the time of encoding. *Psychoneuroendocrinology*, *55*, 8–20. https://doi.org/10.1016/j.psyneuen.2015.01.021

Wager, T. D., Vazquez, A., Hernandez, L., & Noll, D. C. (2005). Accounting for nonlinear BOLD effects in fMRI: Parameter estimates and a model for prediction in rapid event-related studies. *NeuroImage*, *25*(1), 206–218. https://doi.org/10.1016/j.neuroimage.2004.11.008

Walther, A., Nili, H., Ejaz, N., Alink, A., Kriegeskorte, N., & Diedrichsen, J. (2016). Reliability of dissimilarity measures for multi-voxel pattern analysis. *NeuroImage*, *137*, 188–200. https://doi.org/10.1016/j.neuroimage.2015.12.012

Wang, N., Zeng, W., & Chen, L. (2013). SACICA: A sparse approximation coefficient-based ICA model for functional magnetic resonance imaging data analysis. *Journal of Neuroscience Methods*, *216*(1), 49–61. https://doi.org/10.1016/j.jneumeth.2013.03.014

Watts, D. J., & Strogatz, S. H. (1998). Collective dynamics of 'small-world' networks. *Nature*, *393*(6684), 440–442. https://doi.org/10.1038/30918

Weaverdyck, M. E., Lieberman, M. D., & Parkinson, C. (2020). Tools of the Trade Multivoxel pattern analysis in fMRI: A practical introduction for social and affective neuroscientists. *Social Cognitive and Affective Neuroscience*, *15*(4), 487–509. https://doi.org/10.1093/scan/nsaa057

Wig, G. S., Laumann, T. O., & Petersen, S. E. (2014). An approach for parcellating human cortical areas using resting-state correlations. *NeuroImage*, *93*(Pt 2), 276–291. https://doi.org/10.1016/j.neuroimage.2013.07.035

Woolgar, A., Jackson, J., & Duncan, J. (2016). Coding of visual, auditory, rule, and response information in the brain: 10 years of multivoxel pattern analysis. *Journal of Cognitive Neuroscience*, *28*(10), 1433–1454. https://doi.org/10.1162/jocn_a_00981

Woolrich, M. W., Beckmann, C. F., Nichols, T. E., & Smith, S. M. (2016). Statistical analysis of fMRI data. In M. Filippi (Ed.), *fMRI techniques and protocols* (2nd ed., pp. 182–239). Humana Press. https://doi.org/10.1007/978-1-4939-5611-1_7

Woolrich, M. W., Behrens, T. E. J., & Smith, S. M. (2004). Constrained linear basis sets for HRF modelling using Variational Bayes. *NeuroImage*, *21*(4), 1748–1761. https://doi.org/10.1016/j.neuroimage.2003.12.024

Woolrich, M. W., Ripley, B. D., Brady, M., & Smith, S. M. (2001). Temporal autocorrelation in univariate linear modeling of FMRI data. *NeuroImage*, *14*(6), 1370–1386. https://doi.org/10.1006/nimg.2001.0931

Worsley, K. J., Evans, A. C., Marrett, S., & Neelin, P. (1992). A three-dimensional statistical analysis for CBF activation studies in human brain. *Journal of Cerebral Blood Flow and Metabolism*, *12*(6), 900–918. https://doi.org/10.1038/jcbfm.1992.127

Worsley, K. J., & Friston, K. J. (1995). Analysis of fMRI time-series revisited—Again. *NeuroImage*, *2*(3), 173–181. https://doi.org/10.1006/nimg.1995.1023

Worsley, K. J., Liao, C. H., Aston, J., Petre, V., Duncan, G. H., Morales, F., & Evans, A. C. (2002). A general statistical analysis for fMRI data. *NeuroImage*, *15*(1), 1–15. https://doi.org/10.1006/nimg.2001.0933

Worsley, K. J., Marrett, S., Neelin, P., Vandal, A. C., Friston, K. J., & Evans, A. C. (1996). A unified statistical approach for determining significant signals in images of cerebral activation. *Human Brain Mapping*, *4*(1), 58–73 https://doi.org/10.1002/(SICI)1097-0193(1996)4:1<58::AID-HBM4>3.0.CO;2-O

Xiong, Y., & Newman, S. (2021). Both activation and deactivation of functional networks support increased sentence processing costs. *NeuroImage*, *225*, 117475. https://doi.org/10.1016/j.neuroimage.2020.117475

Xu, J., Zhang, S., Calhoun, V. D., Monterosso, J., Li, C. S., Worhunsky, P. D., Stevens, M., Pearlson, G. D., & Potenza, M. N. (2013). Task-related concurrent but opposite modulations of overlapping functional networks as revealed by spatial ICA. *NeuroImage*, *79*, 62–71. https://doi.org/10.1016/j.neuroimage.2013.04.038

Xu, K. S., & Hero, A. O. (2013). Dynamic stochastic blockmodels: Statistical models for time-evolving networks. In A. M. Greenberg, W. G. Kennedy, & N. D. Bos (Eds.), *Social computing, behavioral-cultural modeling and prediction* (pp. 201–210). Springer. https://doi.org/10.1007/978-3-642-37210-0_22

Xu, T., Opitz, A., Craddock, R. C., Wright, M. J., Zuo, X. N., & Milham, M. P. (2016). Assessing variations in areal organization for the intrinsic brain: From fingerprints to reliability. *Cerebral Cortex*, *26*(11), 4192–4211. https://doi.org/10.1093/cercor/bhw241

Yeo, B. T. T., Krienen, F. M., Sepulcre, J., Sabuncu, M. R., Lashkari, D., Hollinshead, M., Roffman, J. L., Smoller, J. W., Zöllei, L., Polimeni, J. R., Fischl, B., Liu, H., & Buckner, R. L. (2011). The organization of the human cerebral cortex estimated by intrinsic functional connectivity. *Journal of Neurophysiology*, *106*(3), 1125–1165. https://doi.org/10.1152/jn.00338.2011

Zalesky, A., Cocchi, L., Fornito, A., Murray, M. M., & Bullmore, E. (2012). Connectivity differences in brain networks. *NeuroImage*, *60*(2), 1055–1062. https://doi.org/10.1016/j.neuroimage.2012.01.068

Zalesky, A., Fornito, A., & Bullmore, E. (2012). On the use of correlation as a measure of network connectivity. *NeuroImage*, *60*(4), 2096–2106. https://doi.org/10.1016/j.neuroimage.2012.02.001

Zalesky, A., Fornito, A., & Bullmore, E. T. (2010). Network-based statistic: Identifying differences in brain networks. *NeuroImage*, *53*(4), 1197–1207. https://doi.org/10.1016/j.neuroimage.2010.06.041

Zarghami, T. S., & Friston, K. J. (2020). Dynamic effective connectivity. *NeuroImage*, *207*, 116453. https://doi.org/10.1016/j.neuroimage.2019.116453

Zhang, T., Shen, H., & Li, F. (2016). Linear and non-linear models for time series. In H. Ombao, M. Lindquist, W. Thompson, & J. Aston (Eds.), *Handbook of neuroimaging data analysis* (pp. 309–328). CRC Press. https://doi.org/10.1201/9781315373652

Zheng, Y., Martindale, J., Johnston, D., Jones, M., Berwick, J., & Mayhew, J. (2002). A model of the hemodynamic response and oxygen delivery to brain. *NeuroImage*, *16*(3 Pt 1), 617–637. https://doi.org/10.1006/nimg.2002.1078

Part IV
PSYCHOMETRICS

CHAPTER 33

RELIABILITY

Sean P. Lane, Elizabeth N. Aslinger, and Patrick E. Shrout

One of the first principles in research design is that measures should be selected that are reliable. *Reliability* is defined as the reproducibility of measurements, and this is the degree to which a measure produces the same values when applied repeatedly to a person or process that has not changed. This quality is observed when there are no or few random contaminations to the measure. If reliability is compromised, then the validity of the measure will also be compromised. *Validity* is defined as the degree to which a measure corresponds to the theoretical construct of interest. The more a measure is contaminated by measurement error, the less useful it is likely to be, and, hence, establishing reliability is usually considered to be the first step in ascertaining measurement quality.

In this chapter, we review the basics for reliability theory and show why it is important to quantify the degree of reliability of a measure. We provide a summary of ways to improve measurement reliability, with a special emphasis on statistical approaches. The bulk of the chapter is concerned with designs and procedures for estimating reliability of ratings and for self-report measures constructed from items. We conclude with suggestions for steps to take to assess and report reliability in research studies.

RELIABILITY FROM THE PERSPECTIVE OF CLASSICAL TEST THEORY

To help make the theory of reliability concrete, we start with a few examples of ratings and self-report measurements. Suppose 10 nominations for an award have been collected, and three judges are asked to independently rate the importance of the nominees' contributions using a 9-point ordinal scale. In addition, suppose they make binary judgments of whether participants should be considered for an award. Table 33.1 shows an example of data from such a design. We constructed this example to illustrate one judge that tends to use higher numbers (Judge 1) and another that tends to use lower numbers (Judge 3). How reliable is a randomly selected rating or judgment? How reliable is the average of the three ratings?

In a second scenario, suppose that 100 subjects are asked to report how much they agree with six different statements about gun control and gun rights. Endorsement of each item is collected on a 7-point ordinal scale. As illustrated with the hypothetical example in Table 33.2, the statements that define the attitude items might vary in extremity, and, therefore, the average endorsements might vary considerably from item

https://doi.org/10.1037/0000318-033
APA Handbook of Research Methods in Psychology, Second Edition: Vol. 1. Foundations, Planning, Measures, and Psychometrics, H. Cooper (Editor-in-Chief)
Copyright © 2023 by the American Psychological Association. All rights reserved.

TABLE 33.1

Example of Simulated Data for Three Judges Rating 10 Nominees for an Award

Nominee	Judge 1	Judge 2	Judge 3	Mean for nominee	SD for nominee
1	9 [1]	9 [1]	5 [0]	7.67 [.67]	2.31 [.47]
2	8 [0]	7 [1]	6 [1]	7.00 [.67]	1.00 [.47]
3	7 [0]	5 [0]	4 [0]	5.33 [.00]	1.53 [.00]
4	5 [0]	3 [0]	2 [0]	3.33 [.00]	1.53 [.00]
5	6 [0]	5 [0]	2 [0]	4.33 [.00]	2.08 [.00]
6	4 [0]	1 [0]	1 [0]	2.00 [.00]	1.73 [.00]
7	5 [0]	4 [0]	2 [0]	3.67 [.00]	1.53 [.00]
8	4 [0]	1 [0]	1 [0]	2.00 [.00]	1.73 [.00]
9	8 [1]	8 [1]	5 [1]	7.00 [1.0]	1.73 [.00]
10	6 [0]	5 [0]	3 [0]	4.67 [.00]	1.53 [.00]
Judge mean	6.20 [.20]	4.80 [.30]	3.10 [.20]		
Judge SD	1.75 [.40]	2.70 [.46]	1.79 [.40]		

Note. The first value is a quantitative rating of the importance of the nominee's contribution on a 1-to-9 scale. In brackets is a binary indicator of whether the person is recommended for an award (1) or not recommended (0). Means and standard deviations (SD) correspond to importance scores.

TABLE 33.2

Example of Simulated Responses by 100 Participants Rating Agreement to Six Items About Gun Control on a 1-to-7 Scale

Participant	Item 1	Item 2	Item 3	Item 4	Item 5	Item 6	Mean for participant	SD[a] of participant responses
1	5	6	2	5	5	7	5.00	1.67
2	4	5	1	4	6	6	4.33	1.86
3	6	5	3	6	4	7	5.17	1.47
4	1	2	1	1	3	2	1.67	0.82
5	4	4	1	3	6	6	4.00	1.90
6	3	4	1	3	4	5	3.33	1.37
7	4	5	1	4	5	5	4.00	1.55
...[b]	...	...	...	...	...	...	...	...
99	5	3	3	6	5	7	4.83	1.60
100	4	3	1	4	5	5	3.67	1.51
Item mean	3.94	3.77	1.34	3.74	4.78	5.75		
Item SD[a]	1.04	1.14	0.62	1.13	1.32	1.13		

[a]Sample standard deviations (SD). [b]Lines 8 through 98 of the data are not shown here.

to item. For example, on average participants do not tend to endorse Item 3 very highly, whereas they do endorse Item 6 rather highly. How reliable is a measure based on a response to a single statement? How reliable is the average of all six responses? Can the attitude be reliably assessed with a smaller set of items than six?

Whatever the measurement procedure, we represent the numerical score by a variable X. When an individual i has been measured by a procedure j, we write the measure as X_{ij}. X can represent quantitative values or binary (0, 1) values. Individuals are sampled from a specific population, and we are interested in both the mean and variance of X over various individuals.

According to *classical test theory* (e.g., Crocker & Algina, 1986; Lord & Novick, 1968), the overall variation in X might be influenced by error variation as well as true differences between persons. Returning to the example in Table 33.1, suppose 30 experts were available and each was asked to rate one of the 10 nominees. In this case, the ratings in the three judge columns would all be from different raters, and it is conceivable that the raters themselves might differ in how they use the rating scale. Some might tend to use somewhat lower scores, and others might tend to use higher scores. If raters differ in how they use the rating scale across all nominees, then the variation of X in each column will be larger than if we use the same rater to make all the ratings in that column. In the former case, a nominee would benefit (randomly) from having a positive rater, while they would be penalized if assigned a tough-minded rater, and this random benefit/penalty would add variance to the ratings. In the latter case, the tendency of the rater to be impressed or skeptical would be applied to all the X values. The absolute values of the ratings would be affected by the choice of raters, but the relative ordering of nominees would not be affected by selecting a single rater. However, even a single rater might have lapses in judgment or might be distracted for a given rating. If that rater provided replicate measures, they might not give the same ratings to the same nominee. In this example the ratings could be affected by three different components: (a) the qualifications of the nominee, (b) the skepticism or rating style of the rater, and (c) random measurement error. We initially collapse the latter two random components into a generic error variable.

The top portion of Figure 33.1 shows a path model for a measurement X. The model shows the true individual difference, T, and the random error, E, influencing a single measurement of X. Classical test theory envisions a possibly infinite number of replicate measurements, and the bottom portion of Figure 33.1 shows three such possible replications. In fact, the value of T_i is defined simply as the population average of replicate measurements for person i, which is sometimes written as $E(X_i) = T_i$. It is not observed, but it is well defined, and T_i is, therefore, called a *latent variable*.

The variance of X, σ_X^2, describes how much the observed measurements differ from person to person in the population being studied, whereas the variance of T, σ_T^2, describes how much the

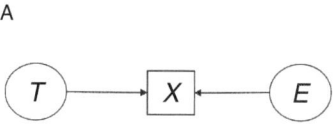

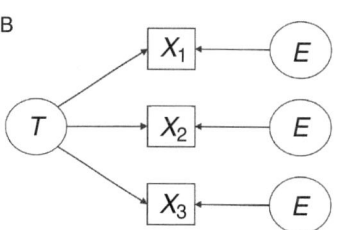

FIGURE 33.1. Path model depicting the different components of a measured variable, X, as true score, T, and error, E (Model A). Path model depicting the true score, T, of an underlying latent variable, as measured by three replicate measures X_1, X_2, and X_3 (Model B). In classical test theory, each replicate measure is assumed to have equal error variance, although this assumption can be relaxed.

true features of persons vary in the population. In some populations σ_T^2 might be relatively small, while in other populations the variance might be large. Small variance implies that the measurement distinction is subtle in the population, while large variation implies the opposite. In populations with small overall true score variation in X, any measurement error may be quite serious, leading to low values of reliability.

Classical test theory defines *error* to be the difference between X_i and T_i, and, therefore, errors are independent of the value of T_i. This allows us to decompose σ_X^2 into two components, $\sigma_X^2 = \sigma_T^2 + \sigma_E^2$, where σ_T^2 is variance due to systematic differences between persons, and σ_E^2 is variance due to measurement noise. This equation shows that random measurement noise increases the total measurement variation. If measurement errors can be eliminated, then the error variance, σ_E^2, goes to 0 and the total variance of X shrinks to σ_T^2. If errors dominate the measurement, then the majority of σ_X^2 may be attributable to σ_E^2, even if there is systematic variation between persons that is of interest. The reliability coefficient, R_X, is defined as the ratio of the population parameters, σ_T^2 and σ_X^2.

$$R_X = \frac{\sigma_T^2}{\sigma_X^2} = \frac{\sigma_T^2}{\sigma_T^2 + \sigma_E^2} \qquad (33.1)$$

R_X provides a quantitative measure of how reliable the measure X is. It varies from 0 (X is due entirely to unsystematic random processes) to 1 (X is due entirely to systematic individual differences). It can be thought of as the proportion of σ_X^2 that represents genuine, replicable differences in subjects.

From Equation 33.1, we can make three important points. First, because it is a function of population variances, the reliability of a specific measurement procedure can never be globally established. R_X needs to be estimated anew each time an investigator moves from one population (e.g., men, women, college students, community members, industrial workers, retired persons) to another. One should not claim that a measure "is reliable" on the basis of previous studies unless those studies were of the same subject population. Second, the reliability of a measure can be improved by either reducing error variation or by shifting to a population with more true score variation. Third, the classic definition of reliability assumes constant error variance across replicate measures. When we consider ways to obtain estimates of R_X we have to consider whether that assumption is reasonable. A common challenge to that assumption is when the measurement method cannot accommodate the potential range of the T, leading to floor or ceiling patterns in the distribution of X. This occurs, for example, if an achievement test is too difficult or too easy for the population being studied. In such cases, the measure will be less reliable than when it is applied to a population where there is no restriction of range.

Spearman (1910) showed that if one is interested in the correlation of T and another variable Y, but only has X to represent T, then the correlation will be too small by a factor of the square root of R_X. If both X and Y are measured with error, and one is interested in the correlation of T_X and T_Y, then ρ_{XY}, the correlation of X and Y, will equal

$$\rho_{XY} = \rho_{T_X T_Y} \sqrt{R_X R_Y} \qquad (33.2)$$

For example, if both X and Y have reliabilities of 0.70, then a true correlation of 0.30, which Cohen (1988) called "medium" in size, would on average be estimated to be 0.21, which is by convention called "small." This is called the *attenuation effect of unreliability* (Cochran, 1968).

The consequences of unreliable measurement are even more pernicious in multivariate analyses. For example, Hoyle and Kenny (1999) examined the impact of measurement error on inferences about mediation processes. Suppose one believes that the effect of X on Y is completely explained by an intervening variable, M. Baron and Kenny (1986) famously described how the mediation analysis involves two separate regression equations. The mediator variable, M, is regressed on X, and the outcome variable, Y, is simultaneously regressed on X and M. If M is measured with error, then the estimate of the path M→Y will be too small, and the indirect mediation path will also be too small. If X is measured with error, then the path X→M will be too small, but the effect of M→Y might be too large because of incomplete adjustment for X. Ledgerwood and Shrout (2011) have additionally shown that even structural equation modeling approaches, used to adjust for unreliability in such mediating processes, are associated with tradeoffs in precision despite improvement in accuracy. In other words, the pattern and inferences of mediation results can be obscured in complicated ways by the measurement error. In some cases, complete mediation might be claimed when other important processes need to be considered, and, in other cases, the researchers might fail to detect the mediated path even though the process is truly mediated.

How do we evaluate different values of R_X? If we know that a measure truly has a reliability of .50, then we know that only half of its variance is systematic. That may not be what we hope for, but it might be good enough for some preliminary studies. For more definitive studies, we should aim to have reliability above .80. To provide some interpretive guidelines, Shrout (1998) recommended the following characterizations of reliability values: .00 to .10, *virtually no reliability*; .11 to .40, *slight*; .41 to .60, *fair*; .61 to .80, *moderate*; and .81 to 1.0, *substantial reliability*.

Statistical Remedies for Low Reliability

If an investigator discovers that a quantitative measure is not sufficiently reproducible, there are several remedies that have been mentioned briefly before. The measure itself can be changed, the training of those administering it can be improved, or perhaps some special instructions can be developed for the respondents that improve the purity of the measurement outcome. These are examples of procedural remedies that are often effective. There is also a statistical remedy: Obtain several independent replicate measurements and average their results. The idea is simple: Averages of replicate measures are by definition more systematic than the individual measures themselves, so the reliability of the sum or average of items or ratings will be consistently higher than that of the components. The degree to which reliability is expected to improve in the composites is described mathematically by Spearman (1910) and Brown (1910). Let the sum of k ratings or items $(X_1, X_2, X_3, \ldots, X_k)$ be called $W(k)$. Then the expected reliability of $W(k)$ can be written as a function of k and the reliability of the typical measurement, R_X, according to the Spearman-Brown formula,

$$R_{W(k)} = \frac{kR_X}{1+(k-1)R_X} \qquad (33.3)$$

Equation 33.3 is based on assumptions about the comparability of the measurements that are averaged or summed into $W(k)$, not on the form or distribution of the individual measurements. Because the result is not limited by the distribution of the X measures, the formula is even useful in calculating the expected reliability of a scale composed of k binary (0,1) items, as well as scales composed of quantitative ratings or items. Averaging measures is a remedy for low reliability only if there is some evidence of replicability. It is clear that R_W will be zero if R_X is zero, regardless of the magnitude of k.

The relationship described in the Spearman-Brown formula can be used in studies of rater reliability to determine how many independent ratings need to be averaged to obtain an ideal level of reliability, say C_R. If the obtained level of reliability for a single rater is R_X, then the number of raters that are needed to produce an averaged-rater reliability of C_R is

$$k = \frac{C_R(1-R_X)}{R_X(1-C_R)} \qquad (33.4)$$

For example, if each rater only has a reliability of $R_X = .40$ and one wants a reliability of $C_R = .75$, then Equation 33.4 gives $k = 4.5$. This means that averages of four raters would be expected to have less than .75 reliability, while averages of 5 raters would exceed the target reliability of .75.

SPECIAL CONSIDERATIONS FOR BINARY MEASURES

Reliability theory does not make strong assumptions about the kind of measurement embodied in X, and many of the results just described can be used when the measurement X is yes/no, such as choice of a negotiation strategy or selection of a candidate for a prize as in Table 33.1. Kraemer (1979) showed explicitly how the results work with binary judgments, such as $X = 1$ for selection and $X = 0$ for not selected. From her mathematical analysis of the problem, the systematic component of X that we have called $T = E(X)$, will end up as a proportion falling between the extremes of 0 and 1. If replicate measures are obtained from independent raters, T represents the expected proportion of raters who would give the award to the respondent being evaluated. If T is close to 1, then most raters would say that the respondent deserves the award, and if T is close to 0, then most would say that the respondent does not deserve the award. Although X itself is binary, T is quantitative in the range $(0,1)$.

Because averages are quantitative (at least as n gets large), the psychometric results from the Spearman-Brown formula are applicable only when the composite of interest is quantitative. If the outcome of a panel of raters is a single binary selection, however, then the Spearman-Brown result does not apply. The single binary rule might depend on a consensus rule (award if all raters vote to give the award), or some similar arbitrary cut point. If the consensus rule is required, the result might be *less reliable* than some of the individual raters (Fleiss & Shrout, 1989). The total consensus rule is as weak as the least reliable rater because each has veto power regarding whether the consensual diagnosis is made.

Another special feature of binary measures is that the expected mean is related to the expected variance of that variable. For variables that are normally distributed, the mean contains no information about the variance of the variable, but for variables that are binomial (a very common distribution for binary variables), the variance is necessarily small for variables with means near 0 or 1. This fact has implications in the interpretation of Equation 33.1, the definition of the reliability coefficient. If the rate of endorsement of an item is low in a population, then σ_T^2 will be small. If the level of error variance is held constant, but σ_T^2 is made smaller, then R_X will be smaller. This is particularly important in clinical psychology where certain disorders are very rare in the population. One implication is that the level of error must be reduced to study disorders that have smaller base rates in the population. Any randomly false-positive diagnosis makes the diagnostic system seem unreliable for rare disorders. The fact that reliability is empirically related to prevalence has caused some commentators to question the utility of reliability measures in binary variables (Grove et al., 1981; Guggenmoos-Holzmann, 1993; Spitznagel & Helzer, 1985). Others have argued that dropping the statistic because of the challenge of measuring rare disorders is misguided (Shrout, 1998; Shrout et al., 1987) because the reliability statistic is useful in describing the effects of measurement error on statistical analyses. Kraemer (1992) provided a clear description of the rationale of reliability studies and showed how the challenge of establishing reliability for categorical data is affected by various features of the measurement situation and the design of the reliability study.

ESTIMATING RELIABILITY IN PRACTICE

To estimate R_X we need to distinguish systematic individual differences from measurement noise associated with sources of variation such as sampling a specific rater, random misunderstandings, or clerical errors. In practice, this is done by obtaining replicate measures of the latent variable T in Figure 33.1. In these replications, T presumably stays the same, but different E values occur. Classical psychometric theory defines the replication hypothetically. Suppose that a subject is selected and is measured over and over to produce the scores $X_1, X_2, X_3, \ldots, X_k$. These measures are taken independently without affecting the subject, or involving recall of previous X_j values (where j indexes each replicate measure). If the measurement were height or weight, then it would be easy to take many repeated measurements of this sort, but for self-reported moods or attitudes or for taxing cognitive tasks, this ideal is difficult to achieve, as the measurement process often affects the mood or attitude of interest.

Test–Retest Reliability

There are a variety of measurement designs for obtaining replicate measures. The most common approach is the *test–retest* design, which calls for making the X measurement at two points in time. Variation in the X values across replications and across respondents can be used to estimate σ_E^2, σ_T^2, and σ_X^2, and, therefore, R_X. The simplest estimate from this design is based on the Pearson product-moment correlation of the two measures, and Fisher's transformation can be readily applied to provide a confidence interval (e.g., Cohen et al., 2003, pp. 45–46). This interval is correct when the ratings are approximately normal in distribution. Sometimes only a sample of persons is selected for the retest phase of the reliability study (e.g., Jannarone et al., 1987). If the probability of selection is based on the scores from the first administration, then adjustment for the sampling design should be made when calculating the Pearson correlation (e.g., Shrout & Napier, 2011).

Although it is intuitively appealing, the test–retest design falls short of the ideal replication in at least two ways. On one hand, the second measurement is often affected by systematic psychological, biological, and social changes in the respondent. Insofar as one is interested in the quantity T at a given point in time (e.g., mood, baseline attitude, or memory at that instance), then legitimate change needs to be distinguished from measurement error. However, most test–retest studies confound legitimate change with error. In this case the estimate of the error variance is too large and the estimate of the reliability of the first assessment is too small. On the other hand, if the respondents remember their original responses, and then try to be *good* by reporting the same thing, then the reliability estimate may be too large. Methodologists who address these opposing biases recommend that the second assessments be carried out after a long enough period to reduce memory artifacts but promptly enough to reduce the probability of systematic changes. Recommendations of how long the period should be are more products of opinion than science, but 2 weeks often seems to work well.

Interrater Reliability

When measurements are ratings, then *interrater reliability* designs can be used. For example, if raters are evaluating the records of nominees for an award, then replicate measures are easily obtained by asking more than one rater to evaluate the same set of nominees. In this case each rater has exactly the same information about the nominee, and the differences in the ratings reflect unreliability of the rating protocol. There are other instances when raters have different information. For example, employees who are asked to evaluate the management style of their supervisor possibly may have different experiences. One might feel supported and charmed by the supervisor, whereas another might feel criticized and challenged. Although the test–retest reliability of each employee might be high, the interrater reliability of a randomly chosen employee could be low (see Murphy & Cleveland, 1995).

If the measurement design specifies that one or more raters evaluate all of the targets of study (e.g., nominees, film clips, essays), and if the same set of raters is used for all summary ratings, then we say that the rater is a *fixed effect*. To estimate the reliability of fixed raters, the reliability design should specify that a sample of targets each be rated by the same set of judges. This is a crossed design with n targets crossed with k raters. A common example of a fixed-effect rater would be an investigator hiring one or two raters to do all the ratings in a given study. In this case one can estimate the reliability by having a subsample of targets rated by an additional set of fixed raters. Because the inclination of a rater to use higher or lower scores on the average is applied to all the targets, the reliability analysis focuses on the consistency of the ratings rather than absolute agreement.

If raters are randomly sampled and each target is evaluated by different raters, then we say raters are *random effects*. The reliability of raters as random effects can be estimated using either the same crossed design mentioned above or a nested design in which replicate ratings are provided by different raters for each target. Because the tendency of the rater to use higher or lower scores has important implications if different targets have different raters, the reliability analysis is influenced by the absolute agreement of ratings rather than simple consistency.

Shrout and Fleiss (1979) recommended that reliability estimates from interrater studies be calculated as *intraclass correlations* (ICCs), and they described six different ICC versions (see also McGraw & Wong, 1996). Which version is appropriate depends on whether raters are considered to be fixed or random, whether we are interested in the reliability of a single rater or the average of k raters, and whether the reliability study design is crossed or nested. Table 33.3 shows the six different ICC forms expressed as variance ratios. Shrout and Fleiss also showed how these six versions can be calculated using information from an analysis of variance (ANOVA) applied to the rating data. There are two alternate ANOVA designs, a one-way design in which ratings are nested within each of n targets and a two-way design in which k raters are crossed with targets

TABLE 33.3

Versions of Intraclass Correlation Statistics for Various Reliability Designs

Type of reliability study design	Raters fixed or random?	Version of intraclass correlation
Part A. Reliability of single rater		
Nested: n subjects rated by k different raters	Random	$\text{ICC}(1,1) = \dfrac{\hat{\sigma}_T^2}{\hat{\sigma}_T^2 + \hat{\sigma}_w^2}$
Subject by rater crossed design	Random	$\text{ICC}(2,1) = \dfrac{\hat{\sigma}_T^2}{\hat{\sigma}_T^2 + \hat{\sigma}_J^2 + \hat{\sigma}_e^2}$
Subject by rater crossed design	Fixed	$\text{ICC}(3,1) = \dfrac{\hat{\sigma}_T^2}{\hat{\sigma}_T^2 + \hat{\sigma}_e^2}$
Part B. Reliability of an average of k raters		
Nested: n subjects rated by k different raters	Random	$\text{ICC}(1,k) = \dfrac{\hat{\sigma}_T^2}{\hat{\sigma}_T^2 + \hat{\sigma}_w^2/k}$
Subject by rater crossed design	Random	$\text{ICC}(2,k) = \dfrac{\hat{\sigma}_T^2}{\hat{\sigma}_T^2 + (\hat{\sigma}_J^2 + \hat{\sigma}_e^2)/k}$
Subject by rater crossed design	Fixed	$\text{ICC}(3,k) = \dfrac{\hat{\sigma}_T^2}{\hat{\sigma}_T^2 + \hat{\sigma}_e^2/k}$

Note. ICC(1,1) and ICC(1,k) are appropriate for reliability designs in which n targets are rated by k different raters (raters nested within target). The statistical model for the jth rating of the ith target is $Y_{ij} = T_i + W_{ij}$, where W_{ij} represents the deviation of each rating from the true score of the target. ICC(2,1) and ICC(2,k) are appropriate for reliability designs in which n targets are rated by the same k raters (raters crossed with target) but where raters are considered to be random and exchangeable. The statistical model for the jth rating of the ith target is $Y_{ij} = T_i + J_j + e_{ij}$, where J_j represents the average level of rating for the jth rater and e_{ij} represents the deviation of each rating from the true score of the target and the average rating level of the rater. ICC(3,1) and ICC(3,k) are also appropriate for reliability designs in which n targets are rated by the same k raters (raters crossed target) but where raters are considered to be fixed. The statistical model for the jth rating of the ith target is $Y_{ij} = T_i + J_j + e_{ij}$, where J_j represents the average level of rating for the jth rater and e_{ij} represents the deviation of each rating from the true score of the target and the average rating level of the rater.

in an n by k design. The formulas presented by Shrout and Fleiss assume that each of the n targets is rated by the same number (k) of judges. The more general formulas in Table 33.3 can be applied to data where there is not perfect balancing of ratings to targets, as we illustrate here.

The ICC equations in Table 33.3 essentially describe how variance component estimates can be combined to form reliability coefficients of the form described in Equation 33.1. ICC(1,1) is based on estimating variance components from a reliability design in which each target has its own raters. It refers to the expected reliability of a single rater. When k ratings are averaged, the reliability of the combined score is estimated using ICC(1,k). An example of this design would be admissions to graduate school where each applicant submits three recommendations. The estimate of the between target variance, σ_T^2, is based on the differences in the mean ratings of targets, after adjusting for the within-target error variance σ_W^2. This latter estimate is affected by both rater variation and error variation. A comparison of the expressions for ICC(1,1) and ICC(1,k) shows that the latter is always equal to or larger than the former. This is because averaging the ratings reduces the size of the error term by a factor of $(1/k)$.

We illustrate the calculation of ICC(1,1) and ICC(1,k = 3) coefficients using the data shown in Table 33.1. We obtained the variance component estimates using standard statistical software (in this case, the VARCOMP procedure of SPSS; IBM Corp., 2019; the syntax is shown in Appendix 33.1). In the example there is considerable variation between targets. Nominee 1 has an average rating of 7.67, whereas nominee 6 has an average rating of 2.00. As we show in Table 33.4, the estimated variation in the nominee true scores, σ_T^2, is 3.19, and the variability of ratings within candidates is 2.90. If one hoped to use a measurement procedure that samples only one rater per target, one could only expect a reliability of ICC(1,1) = 0.52. When 3 ratings are averaged the reliability goes up to ICC(1,3) = 0.77.

Even if the raters are considered to be random, an investigator might ask a set of k raters to make judgments on each of n targets in a preliminary reliability study. If the subsequent study samples one rater for each target, then we would use ICC(2,1), and if the subsequent study samples k raters, then we would use ICC(2,k). ICC(2,1) differs from ICC(1,1) in two important ways. First, the estimates of σ_T^2 and σ_E^2 are obtained from the rater × target crossed design, and second, the denominator of the ICC explicitly takes into account the variation in judges, which we call σ_M^2 (variation of measures). The crossed design allows us to learn more about the raters than we could in the nested design. As noted previously, the ratings of Judge 1 are systematically higher than the ratings of Judge 3, and Judge 2 appears to be midway between the other two. This new information allows us to decompose the sources of error into rater variation and residual error variation. Table 33.4 shows how the estimates of the variance components (see SPSS syntax in Appendix 33.1) can be combined to estimate the reliability of a randomly selected rater (ICC(2,1) = 0.58)

TABLE 33.4

Variance Decompositions and Estimated Intraclass Correlations for the Table 33.1 Example Data

Variance component	Nested Estimate	%	Crossed Estimate	%
σ_T^2	3.193	52.4	3.978	57.8
σ_W^2	2.900	47.6	—	—
σ_J^2	—	—	2.356	34.3
σ_E^2	—	—	0.544	7.9
Total	6.093	100	6.878	100
ICC(1,1)	0.52 (0.147, 0.831)		—	
ICC(1,3)	0.77 (0.341, 0.937)		—	
ICC(2,1)	—		0.58 (0.044, 0.877)	
ICC(2,3)	—		0.80 (0.121, 0.955)	
ICC(3,1)	—		0.88 (0.695, 0.965)	
ICC(3,3)	—		0.96 (0.873, 0.988)	

Note. Example has three judges evaluate 10 nominees on a 1-to-9 scale. The nested design treats each nominee as being rated by three unique judges. The crossed design treats nominees as being rated by the same three judges.

as well as the reliability of the average of three randomly selected raters (ICC(2,3) = 0.80).

The final ICC forms in Table 33.3 describe the reliability of ratings made by fixed raters. These forms use the same variance component estimates as ICC(2,1) and ICC(2,3), but they exclude the judge variance, σ_M^2, from the denominator of the reliability expression. Under this reliability model, any bias or tendency of a rater to be high or low applies equally to all the ratings and, therefore, does not affect the final ordering of the candidates. In this case ICC(3,1) is 0.88 and ICC(3,3) is 0.96. This indicates that after rater differences in scale usage are taken into account, the ratings in Table 33.1 are quite consistent. Therefore, a fixed rater might be reliable whereas a randomly selected rater might not.

In addition to the estimates of each ICC form, Table 33.4 shows 95% confidence intervals for the reliability results. These intervals are based on formulas reported in Shrout and Fleiss (1979), but they are easily obtained from standard software such as the RELIABILITY procedure of SPSS or the psych library of the R language (Revelle, 2020). In most cases we are not interested in whether the reliability is significantly different from 0—very low reliability that is estimated in a large sample might well be significant. Instead, we should be interested in how precise the reliability estimates are, and confidence intervals tell us what range of population values are consistent with the data at hand. The Shrout and Fleiss intervals are appropriate for ratings that are approximately normally distributed.

In addition to the ANOVA-based ICC measures of rater reliability, there is an extensive literature on measuring interrater agreement when the number of targets may be limited. For example, if ratings are being made of a few executives or leaders, applying the methods just reviewed might not be possible. LeBreton and Senter (2008) provided an overview of interrater agreement methods and how they relate to ICC reliability estimates.

Internal Consistency Estimates of Reliability

One of the most common ways that psychologists assess reliability is to use internal consistency estimates from measures that have multiple items. The best-known version of this approach is Cronbach's alpha (Cronbach, 1951), but the approach was developed by other measurement experts in the 1930s and 1940s (Guttman, 1945; Kuder & Richardson, 1937; see also Sijtsma, 2009, for more history). The approach essentially treats different items in a scale to be replicate measures of the same construct, and these items become the analogue to raters mentioned in the previous section. The justification for why different items should be considered replicate measures is part of the construct validity process (Chapter 35, this volume).

For many—if not most—self-report measurements in psychology, a scale is formed by summing or averaging a fixed set of items that are designed to relate to a single underlying psychological trait or symptom dimension. From the classical test theory perspective, the causal Model B, in Figure 33.1, is usually assumed. For example, if a latent variable is degree of anxiety, then the responses to items about nervousness, tenseness, sleep disturbance, and upset stomach are all caused by high or low levels of the trait. If a person were able to reduce their level of anxiety, then presumably all of the items in the scale would be endorsed with lower scores.

If it is reasonable to assume that all the items in a scale have the same degree of association with the latent variable, and if the overall measure is an average or sum of k items, then the intraclass form ICC(3,k), shown in Table 33.3, is appropriate. In fact, this is mathematically identical to Cronbach's alpha, even though the latter traditionally is computed using correlations among the k items. There are several advantages of carrying out the computations using the more general ICC approach. One is that confidence intervals can be computed in the same way as described. Another is that investigators can consider variations of standard reliability questions. Suppose that a measurement protocol is too long—is it possible to reduce the number of items from k to k' while still maintaining acceptable internal consistency? When the variance components for person, item (analogous to judge), and error have been estimated, it is simple to try different values of k in ICC(3,k).

We illustrate these calculations using the simulated data in Table 33.2. Using SPSS VARCOMP (see Appendix 33.1 at the end of the chapter for syntax), we estimated σ_T^2 to be .66, the variance of items σ_M^2 to be 2.15, and the residual variance σ_E^2 to be .53. Cronbach's alpha is computed by setting $k = 6$ for six fixed items in ICC(3,k) = .88. The 95% confidence interval is obtained by standard software as (.84, .92), indicating that the sample is consistent with a fairly narrow range of values of reliability (again, see Appendix 33.1 for syntax). If one wanted to shorten the measure to three items, how reliable would we expect the shortened scale to be? If we set $k = 3$, we obtain ICC(3,3) = [.659/(.659 + .525/3)] = 0.79. This is precisely the same result we would obtain by applying the Spearman Brown formula (Equation 33.3).

Although Cronbach's alpha is the most widely used measure of reliability in the substantive literature in psychology, it is often criticized by measurement experts (e.g., McNeish, 2018; Revelle & Condon, 2019; Revelle & Zinbarg, 2009; Sijtsma, 2009) as being overly simplistic and sometimes misleading. Authors, editors, and reviewers sometimes equate alpha with reliability itself, rather than as an estimate with documented shortcomings. Alpha is known to sometimes underestimate actual reliability (Cortina, 1993; Sijtsma, 2009), and other times to provide estimates that are too large (Raykov, 1997). Often the bias is relatively small, but sometimes it can be striking.

The conditions that allow alpha to be considered an unbiased estimate of reliability are quite restrictive: (a) Items must be replicate indicators of the same underlying latent trait; (b) responses to the items must be independent after adjusting for the level of the latent trait; and (c) the magnitude of error associated with each item must be the same. These conditions can be represented by a variation of the path in Model B in Figure 33.1, that explicitly states that the path from the latent variable (the circle) to each item (the box) has the same weight, and that the variance of each error term is identical across items. When these conditions hold, psychometricians say the items are *parallel* and acknowledge that, in this case, alpha is an excellent way to estimate reliability.

Alpha grossly underestimates reliability if it is applied to items for which the measurement Model B in Figure 33.1 does not hold. Bollen and Lennox (1991, p. 306) described Model B in Figure 33.1 as an *effects indicator model* because the item responses are effects of the latent variable, and they distinguished it from an alternate model in which the direction of the arrows between items and latent variable are reversed. They called the alternate model a *causal indicator model* (CIM). An example of a CIM is a life-stress inventory where some items are about stresses at home, others at work, and others in transition, such as transportation. Imagine a working mother who has a conflict with her adolescent daughter in the morning, then is delayed in arriving at work by a traffic jam caused by an accident, and finally arrives to her office to find that a deadline has been moved up by her boss. Responses to the life-stress measures of these events might be highly reliable, and the accumulation of these stressors into a single score might be valid, and yet alpha would not be high because the stressors are independent environmental events rather than something that is caused by a latent individual difference. When the CIM is appropriate, alpha should not be computed or reported. A test–retest design or alternate informant reliability design can be used to estimate reliability.

Alpha also underestimates reliability if the items vary in the strength of their association with the latent variable or if they are affected by more than one latent variable. For example, a scale of depression symptoms may contain some items on mood, others on psychophysiological complaints, and yet others on cognitive beliefs. Although these are all expected to be related to depression, they are not exact replications of each other. To the degree that the correlations among the items is due to the different item content rather than error, the overall reliability estimate will be smaller than it should be. Psychometricians have developed other estimators of reliability that overcome these limitations of alpha.

For example, *McDonald's omega* (McDonald, 1999) takes into account the possibility that items differ in their relation to a common latent variable, and Raykov and Shrout (2002) extended omega to take into account more than one latent variable. These alternate methods can be easily implemented in the context of structural equation models (Green & Yang, 2009) as well as in the psych or MBESS packages in the R language (Kelley, 2007; Revelle, 2020). Kelley and Pornprasertmanit (2016) provided comparisons among multiple reliability coefficients, with multiple corresponding confidence interval estimation methods, and make recommendations for their usage. Flora (2020) discussed the increasing attention to measurement, criticisms of coefficient alpha, and shift to more robust indices over the past decade, and he provides decision rules on which alternative to select.

For the gun data in Table 33.2, the analogous (unidimensional) omega reliability estimate, compared with the alpha estimate of .88, is .90, with a corresponding bias-corrected and accelerated bootstrap 95% confidence interval of (.86, .92) (Kelley, 2007; see Appendix 33.1 for syntax). In this case, alpha and omega estimates are quite similar. The omega point estimate is nominally larger, and its confidence interval is narrower. The qualitative conclusions of the two approaches are consequently similar, but that is because the assumptions of parallel items were minimally violated. At the very least, researchers should evaluate these assumptions before defaulting to the historical status quo of reporting alpha. Ideally, they would estimate and report both alpha and the appropriate omega, noting assumption violations and the context under which the measure is ultimately used (i.e., latent vs. observed scores; Thompson, 2003).

Reliability can also be overestimated by Cronbach's alpha if the whole item set is affected by irrelevant global response patterns, such as mood or response biases. For instance, some computer-administered questionnaires make it easy for a participant to endorse the same response alternative (e.g., "agree somewhat") repeatedly, regardless of item content. Unless steps are taken to counteract these response bias patterns, they will lead to correlated errors and inflated internal consistency reliability estimates. Response biases are often addressed by mixing the items across many conceptual domains, editing the items so that half are keyed as a symptom when the respondent says "no" and half are keyed the opposite way. Scales of yes-saying and need-for-approval are also sometimes constructed to identify those respondents who are susceptible to response biases. The validity of these scales, however, is a subject of discussion.

Proposed Standards of Evidence of Reliability

Given that coefficient alpha is susceptible to opposing biases, sometimes producing values that are too large and other times those that are too small, how can we evaluate this commonly reported estimate of reliability? If the results appear to indicate high reliability, look for response artifacts that might have inflated the estimate. If provisions have been taken to address response biases, then the high level of reliability might be real. If the results indicate that there is low reliability, then look to see if the items included within the internal consistency analysis are heterogeneous in content. It is possible that a set of items that are heterogeneous might have adequate test–retest reliability even though the internal consistency estimate is low.

Perhaps a more compelling piece of evidence is the track record of the measure being considered. If a measure has been widely used in various populations and investigators have reported high levels of test–retest and internal consistency reliability, then it might be adequate for a researcher to report an alpha coefficient or the results of a small reliability study, especially if the study design reduced the impact of response biases. Such evidence would satisfy our recommendation that reliability be studied in every new study population, and it would not impose a high burden on the investigator.

When a measure is being newly developed and proposed, the standards of evidence must be raised considerably. Suppose a measure is based on responses to k items, and the investigator hopes that an average response can be used as a scale score. In this case a simple report of coefficient alpha is inadequate. The effects indicator measurement Model B (Figure 33.1) should be justified, data collection should be structured to avoid response biases, and a factor analysis should be carried out. These analyses will indicate the number of latent variables needed to account for item correlations and the relation of each item to the loadings; and the structure should be evaluated from both reliability and validity perspectives, including their relative trade-offs (Clifton, 2020; see Chapter 36, this volume). If the item responses are binary, special nonlinear factor analysis called *item response theory* is needed (Embretson & Reise, 2000; Chapter 37, this volume). Unless the assumptions of coefficient alpha are met, the more flexible estimates of internal consistency reliability, such as McDonald's omega, should be used.

If the factor analysis step leads to selection of certain items and discarding of others, then a new sample should be drawn to get an unbiased estimate of internal consistency. Internal consistency measures, whether alpha or omega, are upwardly biased if based on the same sample that was used to select the items. If the measure development sample is large enough, it can be randomly split into an exploration sample and an estimation sample.

When developing new measures it is particularly useful to incorporate multiple designs into a reliability program. By systematically studying the kinds of replication, one can gain an insight into sources of measurement variation. This is what Cronbach et al. (1972) recommended in their comprehensive extension of classical test theory known as *generalizability theory* (GT). This theory encompasses both reliability and validity by asking about the extent to which a measurement procedure gives comparable results in different populations, at different times, and in different contexts (Chapter 34, this volume). When raters are involved, their level of training and their demographics are also considered. Insofar as a latent variable is considered theoretically to be a trait, the generalizability program expects test–retest to yield strong stability and reliability, whereas a latent variable that is a state might be internally consistent at several times but not highly correlated over retests. GT tends to blur the classic distinction of reliability and validity (see Brennan, 2001). How to interpret the blurred distinction has led to some controversy (Murphy & DeShon, 2000; Schmidt et al., 2000).

Reliability of Binary and Categorical Measures

When binary data such as the nominations for awards in Table 33.1 are collected, reliability can be estimated directly using a special reliability statistic called *Cohen's kappa* (Cohen, 1960). Fleiss and Cohen (1973) showed that kappa is conceptually equivalent to ICC(2,1) in Table 33.3. It can be calculated simply using the entries of a 2×2 table showing the diagnostic agreement. In general, this agreement table is laid out as shown in the top of Figure 33.2, where the four cells are designated, a through d. Cohen (1960) pointed out that while cells a and d represent agreement, it is not sufficient to evaluate reliability by reporting the overall proportion of agreement, $P_O = (a + d)/n$. This statistic may be large even if raters assigned diagnoses by flipping coins or rolling dice. His kappa statistic adjusts for simple chance mechanisms.

$$\text{kappa} = \frac{P_O - P_C}{1 - P_C} \quad (33.5)$$

where P_O is the observed agreement, $[(a + d)/n]$, and P_C is the expected agreement because of chance.

$$P_C = [(a+c)(a+b)+(b+d)(c+d)]/n^2 \quad (33.6)$$

When computing kappa by hand, it is sometimes more convenient to use the following equivalent expression:

$$\text{kappa} = \frac{ad - bc}{(ad - bc) + n(b + c)/2} \quad (33.7)$$

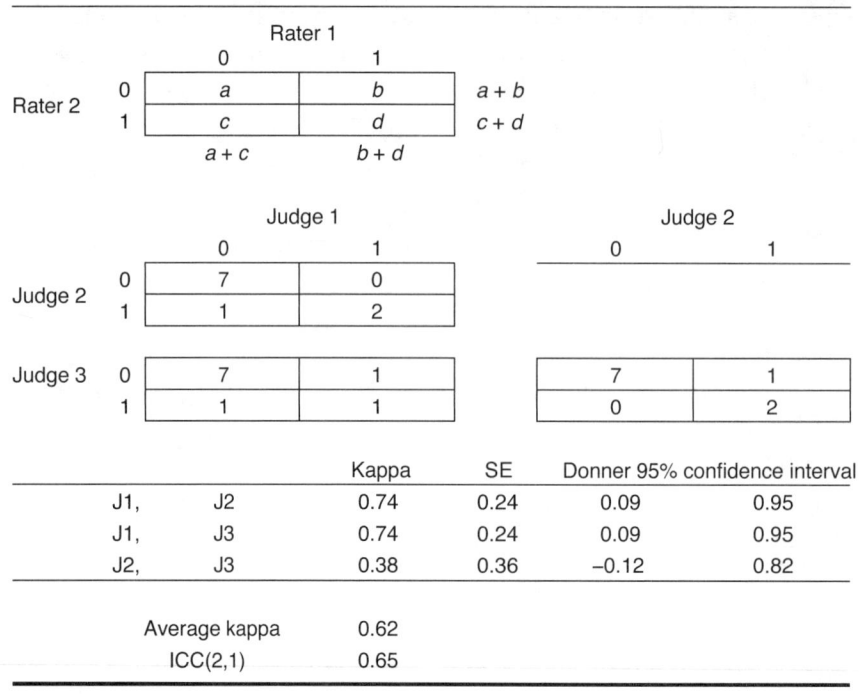

FIGURE 33.2. Illustration of prototype agreement table and numerical illustration based on binary outcomes in Table 33.1.

One advantage of calculating the reliability of binary judgments using kappa instead of intraclass correlation methods is that the expressions for kappa's standard error and confidence bounds are explicitly suited to binary data. Kappa can also be generalized to describe the overall reliability of classifications into multiple categories. Fleiss et al. (2003) provided an overview of many forms of kappa, and Donner and colleagues (Donner, 1998; Donner & Eliasziw, 1992, 1994, 1997; Donner et al., 1996, 2000) have done much to describe the sampling variation of kappa statistics.

The bottom section of Figure 33.2 illustrates the calculations with the binary ratings in the Table 33.1 example. Judges 1 and 3 each recommended that two persons be given an award, whereas Judge 2 recommended three persons. All three pairings of judges showed that they agreed that seven persons not be given the award, and overall agreement (calculated as $(a + d)/10$) was 90% for the pairing of Judge 1 with Judge 2 and with Judge 3 and 80% for the pairing of Judge 2 with Judge 3. Kappa, on the other hand took the value 0.74 for the first two pairings and 0.38 for the last. These represent estimates of how reliable a single randomly sampled rater would be in making judgments about the award. As shown in Figure 33.2, the 95% confidence bound computed using the method of Donner and Eliasziw (1992) was (0.09, 0.95) for the first two pairings and (–0.12, 0.82) for the last. The small sample does not give much closure about what the level of reliability is in this example. If a single summary measure of reliability were required, Fleiss et al. (2003) recommended averaging the three pairwise estimates or calculating the ICC(2,1) from Table 33.3. These approaches estimate the same quantity, although the unweighted average would be expected to be less efficient. The simple average in this case is 0.62, while the ICC(2,1) estimate is 0.65.

If an investigator asks participants to answer questions that have binary or ordinal responses, the appropriate class of psychometric analyses involve item response theory, and reliability estimates depend on individual response patterns. Average reliability indices are estimable, as are marginal reliabilities. See Chapter 37, this volume, for more information.

Extensions of Reliability Analysis

Although the estimation of reliability is an old topic in quantitative psychology, there continue to be new methodological developments in the psychometric and biostatistical literatures. One area of particular importance is the extension to longitudinal measures of change and development. For example, Laenen et al. (2007, 2009) introduced two reliability statistics that make use of longitudinal data when estimating the reliability of measures over time. One estimates the average reliability of a measure that is administered multiple times (R_T), and the other estimates the global reliability of a measure across all time points (R_Λ).

Other procedures have been developed to estimate the reliability of change in longitudinal measurements such as those collected in diary studies. Cranford and colleagues (2006) provided estimates of the reliability of change on the basis of a GT framework in which person-by-time variability is of particular interest. Wilhelm and Schoebi (2007) presented an alternate approach using multilevel modeling. These two approaches make strong assumptions about the equivalence of items in the diary scales, and so we (Lane & Shrout, 2010; Shrout & Lane, 2012) have suggested a less restrictive framework for estimating the reliability of change from a factor-analytic perspective. We have proposed longitudinal analogs of McDonald's (1999) omega to take into account possible heterogeneity of items both within and across individuals. Geldhof et al. (2014) subsequently proposed a similar multilevel factor-analytic approach that produces parallel versions of these omegas. More recently, Schuurman and Hamaker (2019) further developed between- and within-person reliability coefficients for intensive longitudinal data that account for stable autoregressive processes, which could otherwise bias estimates (e.g., violation of independent errors).

Other Ways to Quantify Precision and Measurement Error

As a summary of measurement quality, the reliability coefficient represented by Equation 33.1 has many positive features. It is easy to interpret, fairly easy to estimate, and is the relevant measure for understanding bias in statistical analysis caused by contamination with error. It has the disadvantage, however, of being a statistic that is relative to the population being studied. The amount of error in a measure is always considered in the context of the true score variation in the population. An alternate approach to studying precision and error is to focus on the relation of each item response pattern to the underlying dimension. When items are clearly phrased and related to the underlying (latent) dimension, the probability of endorsing an item category is systematically related to the latent dimension (e.g., see Embretson & Reise, 2000). Of special interest are the slope and location of each item, indicating the relevance and severity of each item with regard to the latent dimension. Item response theory (IRT) methods are especially useful for comparing the measurement equivalence of items across different groups (e.g., Gregorich, 2006; Chapter 37, this volume). These methods are related to factor analysis (McDonald, 1999; Raykov & Marcoulides, 2012), which also provides direct information about the quality of measures in relation to the latent variable of interest. Because the IRT models describe the probability of responding to an item conditional on (i.e., holding constant) the latent variable, the distribution of the latent variable in the population is considered to be less important. Some argue that IRT analyses should supplant traditional reliability analyses (e.g., Embretson & Reise, 2000).

CONCLUSION AND CLOSING COMMENTS

Inadequate reliability is a measurement problem that can often be rectified by improving interview procedures or by using statistical sums or averages of replicate measures. Determining the extent to which unreliability is a problem, however, can be challenging. There are various designs for estimating reliability, but virtually all have some biases and shortcomings. Studies of sampling variability of reliability statistics (Cantor, 1996; Donner, 1998; Dunn, 1989; Walter et al., 1998) suggest that sample sizes in pilot studies are often not adequate to give stable estimates about the reliability of key measurement procedures. Reliance on internal consistency measures of reliability, such as Cronbach's alpha, can give a false sense of security unless care is taken to evaluate sources of statistical bias.

When reliability is only modest, we know that validity studies and other empirical relationships will be biased. If properly specified, measurement models in structural equation methods can adjust for this bias, but often the adjustment comes at a price of less precise estimates of correlations and regression coefficients. Some researchers attempt to make ad hoc adjustments for unreliability by using Equation 33.2 to solve for the true correlation, corrected for attenuation. This can work if the reliability coefficient is known exactly, but in this chapter we have seen that estimates of reliability are often subject to bias or imprecision. If one uses conservative estimates of reliability with Equation 33.2, such as described in Revelle and Zinbarg (2009), one would make an anticonservative adjustment of the correlation. We recommend that corrections for attenuation be used with caution.

Far better than adjusting for unreliability is attention to the improvement of measures themselves. In this quest, one must evaluate critically reliability studies. Specifically, if the reliability of a measure appears to be very good, ask whether there are biases in the reliability design that might bias the results optimistically. Were the respondents sampled in the same way in the reliability study that they would be in the field study? Was the respondent given the chance to be inconsistent, or did the replication make use of archived information? If serious biases are not found, and the reliability study produced stable estimates, then one can put the issue of reliability behind them, at least for the population at hand.

If the reliability of a measure appears to be poor, one should also look for biases in the reliability design. How similar were the replications? Could the poor reliability results be an artifact of legitimate changes over time, heterogeneous items within a scale, or artificially different measurement conditions? Was the sample size large enough to be sure that reliability is in fact bad? Be especially suspicious if you have evidence of validity of a measure that is purported to be unreliable. Rather than dismissing a measure with apparently poor reliability, ask whether it can be improved to eliminate noise.

APPENDIX 33.1

SPSS syntax for Example 1 (Table 33.1)
```
*Importance ratings (continuous ratings).
*(SPSS comments start with asterisk and end in period).
*Data file should have targets in rows and raters or items in columns.
*First we estimate ICC(1,1) & ICC(1,k) and their confidence intervals.
RELIABILITY
/VARIABLES=Judge1 Judge2 Judge3
/ICC=MODEL(ONEWAY).
*Next we estimate ICC(2,1) & ICC(2,k) and their confidence intervals.
RELIABILITY
/VARIABLES=Judge1 Judge2 Judge3
/ICC=MODEL(MIXED) TYPE(ABSOLUTE).
*Finally, we estimate ICC(3,1) & ICC(3,k) and their confidence intervals.
RELIABILITY
/VARIABLES=Judge1 Judge2 Judge3
```

```
/ICC=MODEL(RANDOM) TYPE(CONSISTENCY).
*Next SPSS is asked to restructure the data file so that each rating is on a
separate line.
*An index for target and for rater identifies the rating that is named Score.
VARSTOCASES
/MAKE Score FROM Judge1 Judge2 Judge3
/INDEX=Judge(3)
/KEEP=Nominee
/NULL=KEEP.
*First we decompose the variance as a nested design (one-way ANOVA).
*This would be appropriate if each nominee has different raters.
VARCOMP Score BY Nominee
/RANDOM=Nominee
/DESIGN.
*Next we decompose the variance for a crossed design.
*This would be appropriate if the same raters judged all nominees.
VARCOMP Score BY Nominee Judge
/RANDOM=Nominee Judge
/DESIGN=Nominee Judge.
*Nominations (binary ratings).
*The next syntax assumes that Table 33.1 has been opened with each nominee
on a different line.
*Three binary rating variables are J1Nom, J2Nom, & J3Nom.
*Estimate kappa for each of the three combinations of judges.
CROSSTABS
/TABLES=J1Nom BY J2Nom
/STATISTICS=KAPPA .
CROSSTABS
/TABLES=J1Nom BY J3Nom
/STATISTICS=KAPPA .
CROSSTABS
/TABLES=J3Nom BY J2Nom
/STATISTICS=KAPPA .
*Estimate ICC(2,1) for agreement across all 3 judges.
RELIABILITY
/VARIABLES=J1Nom J2Nom J3Nom
/ICC=MODEL(MIXED) TYPE(ABSOLUTE).
*end of spss syntax example.
```

R syntax for Example 1 (Table 33.1)

```
## Importance ratings (continuous ratings)
# Comments in R follow a pound (cross hatch) symbol
# If not already loaded, get the psych package from
# https://cran.r-project.org/ and load the library before proceeding
install.packages("psych")
library("psych")
```

```r
# Construct data matrix of 3 judges' importance ratings of the 10 nominees
importance <- matrix(c(9, 9, 5,
8, 7, 6,
7, 5, 4,
5, 3, 2,
6, 5, 2,
4, 1, 1,
5, 4, 2,
4, 1, 1,
8, 8, 5,
6, 5, 3),
ncol=3, byrow = TRUE)
colnames(importance) <- paste0("J", 1:dim(importance)[2]) # column names = judges
rownames(importance) <- paste0("N", 1:dim(importance)[1]) # row names = nominees
print(importance) # print data to verify entered correctly
ICC(importance) # ICC function
#Nominations (binary ratings)
nominate <- matrix(c(1, 1, 0,
0, 1, 1,
0, 0, 0,
0, 0, 0,
0, 0, 0,
0, 0, 0,
0, 0, 0,
0, 0, 0,
1, 1, 1,
0, 0, 0),
ncol = 3, byrow = TRUE)
colnames(nominate) <- paste("J", 1:dim(importance)[2]) # column names = judges
rownames(nominate) <- paste("N", 1:dim(importance)[1]) # row names = nominees
print(nominate) # display nomination data
ICC(nominate)
```

R syntax for Example 2 (Table 33.2)
```r
## Gun ratings (continuous ratings)
# Packages for estimating omega
install.packages("GPArotation")
library(GPArotation) #required for psych package to estimate omega point estimate
install.packages("MBESS")
library(MBESS) #estimate multiple omegas and confidence interval types
#Load simulated data of 100 individuals' ratings on 6 gun items
setwd("C:/Data")
guns <- read.csv("Guns_Simulation.csv", header=TRUE, sep=",", dec=".")
#Subset data - remove ID
guns <- guns[c(2:7)]
omega(guns, nfactors=1) #psych package
ci.reliability(data=guns, type="omega", interval.type="bca", B=10000) #MBESS package
```

References

Baron, R. M., & Kenny, D. A. (1986). The moderator-mediator variable distinction in social psychological research: Conceptual, strategic, and statistical considerations. *Journal of Personality and Social Psychology, 51*(6), 1173–1182. https://doi.org/10.1037/0022-3514.51.6.1173

Bollen, K., & Lennox, R. (1991). Conventional wisdom on measurement: A structural equation perspective. *Psychological Bulletin, 110*(2), 305–314. https://doi.org/10.1037/0033-2909.110.2.305

Brennan, R. L. (2001). *Generalizability theory*. Springer. https://doi.org/10.1007/978-1-4757-3456-0

Brown, W. (1910). Some experimental results in the correlation of mental abilities. *British Journal of Psychology, 3*(3), 296–322. https://doi.org/10.1111/j.2044-8295.1910.tb00207.x

Cantor, A. B. (1996). Sample-size calculations for Cohen's kappa. *Psychological Methods, 1*(2), 150–153. https://doi.org/10.1037/1082-989X.1.2.150

Clifton, J. D. W. (2020). Managing validity versus reliability trade-offs in scale-building decisions. *Psychological Methods, 25*(3), 259–270. https://doi.org/10.1037/met0000236

Cochran, W. G. (1968). Errors in measurement in statistics. *Technometrics, 10*(4), 637–666. https://doi.org/10.2307/1267450

Cohen, J. (1960). A coefficient of agreement for nominal scales. *Educational and Psychological Measurement, 20*(1), 37–46. https://doi.org/10.1177/001316446002000104

Cohen, J. (1988). *Statistical power analysis for the behavioral sciences*. Erlbaum.

Cohen, J., Cohen, P., West, S., & Aiken, L. (2003). *Applied multiple regression/correlation analysis* (3rd ed.). Erlbaum.

Corp, I. B. M. (2019). *IBM SPSS statistics for Windows* (Version 26). IBM Corp.

Cortina, J. M. (1993). What is coefficient alpha? An examination of theory and applications. *Journal of Applied Psychology, 78*(1), 98–104. https://doi.org/10.1037/0021-9010.78.1.98

Cranford, J. A., Shrout, P. E., Iida, M., Rafaeli, E., Yip, T., & Bolger, N. (2006). A procedure for evaluating sensitivity to within-person change: Can mood measures in diary studies detect change reliably? *Personality and Social Psychology Bulletin, 32*(7), 917–929. https://doi.org/10.1177/0146167206287721

Crocker, L., & Algina, J. (1986). *Introduction to classical and modern test theory*. Wadsworth.

Cronbach, L. J. (1951). Coefficient alpha and the internal structure of tests. *Psychometrika, 16*(3), 297–334. https://doi.org/10.1007/BF02310555

Cronbach, L. J., Gleser, G. C., Nanda, H., & Rajaratnam, N. (1972). *The dependability of behavioral measurements: Theory of generalizability for scores and profiles*. Wiley.

Donner, A. (1998). Sample size requirements for the comparison of two or more coefficients of inter-observer agreement. *Statistics in Medicine, 17*(10), 1157–1168. https://doi.org/10.1002/(SICI)1097-0258(19980530)17:10<1157::AID-SIM792>3.0.CO;2-W

Donner, A., & Eliasziw, M. (1992). A goodness-of-fit approach to inference procedures for the kappa statistic: Confidence interval construction, significance-testing and sample size estimation. *Statistics in Medicine, 11*(11), 1511–1519. https://doi.org/10.1002/sim.4780111109

Donner, A., & Eliasziw, M. (1994). Statistical implications of the choice between a dichotomous or continuous trait in studies of interobserver agreement. *Biometrics, 50*(2), 550–555. https://doi.org/10.2307/2533400

Donner, A., & Eliasziw, M. (1997). A hierarchical approach to inferences concerning interobserver agreement for multinomial data. *Statistics in Medicine, 16*(10), 1097–1106. https://doi.org/10.1002/(SICI)1097-0258(19970530)16:10<1097::AID-SIM523>3.0.CO;2-8

Donner, A., Eliasziw, M., & Klar, N. (1996). Testing the homogeneity of kappa statistics. *Biometrics, 52*(1), 176–183. https://doi.org/10.2307/2533154

Donner, A., Shoukri, M. M., Klar, N., & Bartfay, E. (2000). Testing the equality of two dependent kappa statistics. *Statistics in Medicine, 19*(3), 373–387. https://doi.org/10.1002/(SICI)1097-0258(20000215)19:3<373::AID-SIM337>3.0.CO;2-Y

Dunn, G. (1989). *Design and analysis of reliability studies*. Oxford University Press.

Embretson, S. E., & Reise, S. P. (2000). *Item response theory for psychologists*. Erlbaum.

Fleiss, J. L., & Cohen, J. (1973). The equivalence of weighted kappa and the intra-class correlation coefficient as measures of reliability. *Educational and Psychological Measurement, 33*(3), 613–619. https://doi.org/10.1177/001316447303300309

Fleiss, J. L., Levin, B., & Paik, M. C. (2003). *Statistical methods for rates and proportions* (3rd ed.). Wiley. https://doi.org/10.1002/0471445428

Fleiss, J. L., & Shrout, P. E. (1989). Reliability considerations in planning diagnostic validity studies. In L. Robbins (Ed.), *The validity of psychiatric diagnoses* (pp. 279–291). Guilford Press.

Flora, D. B. (2020). Your coefficient alpha is probably wrong, but which coefficient omega is right? A tutorial on using R to obtain better reliability estimates. *Advances in Methods and Practices in Psychological Science*, *3*(4), 484–501. https://doi.org/10.1177/2515245920951747

Geldhof, G. J., Preacher, K. J., & Zyphur, M. J. (2014). Reliability estimation in a multilevel confirmatory factor analysis framework. *Psychological Methods*, *19*(1), 72–91. https://doi.org/10.1037/a0032138

Green, S. B., & Yang, Y. (2009). Reliability of summed item scores using structural equation modeling: An alternative to coefficient alpha. *Psychometrika*, *74*(1), 155–167. https://doi.org/10.1007/s11336-008-9099-3

Gregorich, S. E. (2006). Do self-report instruments allow meaningful comparisons across diverse population groups? Testing measurement invariance using the confirmatory factor analysis framework. *Medical Care*, *44*(11, Suppl 3), S78–S94. https://doi.org/10.1097/01.mlr.0000245454.12228.8f

Grove, W. M., Andreasen, N. C., McDonald-Scott, P., Keller, M. B., & Shapiro, R. W. (1981). Reliability studies of psychiatric diagnosis. Theory and practice. *Archives of General Psychiatry*, *38*(4), 408–413. https://doi.org/10.1001/archpsyc.1981.01780290042004

Guggenmoos-Holzmann, I. (1993). How reliable are chance-corrected measures of agreement? *Statistics in Medicine*, *12*(23), 2191–2205. https://doi.org/10.1002/sim.4780122305

Guttman, L. (1945). A basis for analyzing test-retest reliability. *Psychometrika*, *10*(4), 255–282. https://doi.org/10.1007/BF02288892

Hoyle, R. H., & Kenny, D. A. (1999). Sample size, reliability, and tests of statistical mediation. In R. H. Hoyle (Ed.), *Statistical strategies for small sample research* (pp. 195–222). SAGE.

Jannarone, R. J., Macera, C. A., & Garrison, C. Z. (1987). Evaluating interrater agreement through "case-control" sampling. *Biometrics*, *43*(2), 433–437. https://doi.org/10.2307/2531825

Kelley, K. (2007). Methods for the behavioral, educational, and social sciences: An R package. *Behavior Research Methods*, *39*(4), 979–984. https://doi.org/10.3758/BF03192993

Kelley, K., & Pornprasertmanit, S. (2016). Confidence intervals for population reliability coefficients: Evaluation of methods, recommendations, and software for composite measures. *Psychological Methods*, *21*(1), 69–92. https://doi.org/10.1037/a0040086

Kraemer, H. C. (1979). Ramifications of a population model for kappa as a coefficient of reliability. *Psychometrika*, *44*(4), 461–472. https://doi.org/10.1007/BF02296208

Kraemer, H. C. (1992). Measurement of reliability for categorical data in medical research. *Statistical Methods in Medical Research*, *1*(2), 183–199. https://doi.org/10.1177/096228029200100204

Kuder, G. F., & Richardson, M. W. (1937). The theory of estimation of test reliability. *Psychometrika*, *2*(3), 151–160. https://doi.org/10.1007/BF02288391

Laenen, A., Alonso, A., & Molenberghs, G. (2007). A measure for the reliability of a rating scale based on longitudinal clinical trial data. *Psychometrika*, *72*(3), 443–448. https://doi.org/10.1007/s11336-007-9002-7

Laenen, A., Alonso, A., Molenberghs, G., & Vangeneugden, T. (2009). Reliability of a longitudinal sequence of scale ratings. *Psychometrika*, *74*(1), 49–64. https://doi.org/10.1007/s11336-008-9079-7

Lane, S. P., & Shrout, P. E. (2010). Abstract: Assessing the reliability of within-person change over time: A dynamic factor analysis approach. *Multivariate Behavioral Research*, *45*(6), 1027. https://doi.org/10.1080/00273171.2010.534380

LeBreton, J. M., & Senter, J. L. (2008). Answers to 20 questions about interrater reliability and interrater agreement. *Organizational Research Methods*, *11*(4), 815–852. https://doi.org/10.1177/1094428106296642

Ledgerwood, A., & Shrout, P. E. (2011). The trade-off between accuracy and precision in latent variable models of mediation processes. *Journal of Personality and Social Psychology*, *101*(6), 1174–1188. https://doi.org/10.1037/a0024776

Lord, F. M., & Novick, M. R. (1968). *Statistical theories of mental test scores*. Addison-Wesley.

McDonald, R. P. (1999). *Test theory: A unified treatment*. Erlbaum.

McGraw, K. O., & Wong, S. P. (1996). Forming inferences about some intraclass correlation coefficients. *Psychological Methods*, *1*(1), 30–46. https://doi.org/10.1037/1082-989X.1.1.30

McNeish, D. (2018). Thanks coefficient alpha, we'll take it from here. *Psychological Methods*, *23*(3), 412–433. https://doi.org/10.1037/met0000144

Murphy, K. R., & Cleveland, J. N. (1995). *Understanding performance appraisal: Social, organizational, and goal-based perspectives*. SAGE.

Murphy, K. R., & De Shon, R. (2000). Progress in psychometrics: Can industrial and organizational psychology catch up. *Personnel Psychology*, *53*(4), 913–924.

Raykov, T. (1997). Scale reliability, Cronbach's coefficient alpha, and violations of essential tau-equivalence with fixed congeneric components. *Multivariate Behavioral Research, 32*(4), 329–353.

Raykov, T., & Marcoulides, G. A. (2012). *A first course in structural equation modeling*. Routledge.

Raykov, T., & Shrout, P. E. (2002). Reliability of scales with general structure: Point and interval estimation using a structural equation modeling approach. *Structural Equation Modeling, 9*(2), 195–212. https://doi.org/10.1207/S15328007SEM0902_3

Revelle, W. (2020). *psych: Procedures for psychological, psychometric, and personality research*. R package (Version 2.0.12) [Computer software]. https://CRAN.R-project.org/package=psych

Revelle, W., & Condon, D. M. (2019). Reliability from α to ω: A tutorial. *Psychological Assessment, 31*(12), 1395–1411. https://doi.org/10.1037/pas0000754

Revelle, W., & Zinbarg, R. E. (2009). Coefficients alpha, beta, omega, and the glb: Comments on Sijtsma. *Psychometrika, 74*(1), 145–154. https://doi.org/10.1007/s11336-008-9102-z

Schmidt, F. L., Viswesvaran, C., & Ones, D. S. (2000). Reliability is not validity and validity is not reliability. *Personnel Psychology, 53*(4), 901–912. https://doi.org/10.1111/j.1744-6570.2000.tb02422.x

Schuurman, N. K., & Hamaker, E. L. (2019). Measurement error and person-specific reliability in multilevel autoregressive modeling. *Psychological Methods, 24*(1), 70–91. https://doi.org/10.1037/met0000188

Shrout, P. E. (1998). Measurement reliability and agreement in psychiatry. *Statistical Methods in Medical Research, 7*(3), 301–317. https://doi.org/10.1177/096228029800700306

Shrout, P. E., & Fleiss, J. L. (1979). Intraclass correlations: Uses in assessing rater reliability. *Psychological Bulletin, 86*(2), 420–428. https://doi.org/10.1037/0033-2909.86.2.420

Shrout, P. E., & Lane, S. P. (2012). Psychometrics. In M. R. Mehl & T. S. Conner (Eds.), *Handbook of research methods for studying daily life* (pp. 302–320). Guilford Press.

Shrout, P. E., & Napier, J. L. (2011). Analyzing survey data with complex sampling designs. In K. H. Trzesniewski, M. B. Donnellan, & R, E. Lucas (Eds.), *Secondary data analysis: An introduction for psychologists*. American Psychological Association. https://doi.org/10.1037/12350-004

Shrout, P. E., Spitzer, R. L., & Fleiss, J. L. (1987). Quantification of agreement in psychiatric diagnosis revisited. *Archives of General Psychiatry, 44*(2), 172–177. https://doi.org/10.1001/archpsyc.1987.01800140084013

Sijtsma, K. (2009). On the use, the misuse, and the very limited usefulness of Cronbach's alpha. *Psychometrika, 74*(1), 107–120. https://doi.org/10.1007/s11336-008-9101-0

Spearman, C. (1910). Correlation calculated from faulty data. *British Journal of Psychology, 3*(3), 271–295. https://doi.org/10.1111/j.2044-8295.1910.tb00206.x

Spitznagel, E. L., & Helzer, J. E. (1985). A proposed solution to the base rate problem in the kappa statistic. *Archives of General Psychiatry, 42*(7), 725–728. https://doi.org/10.1001/archpsyc.1985.01790300093012

Thompson, B. (2003). *Score reliability: Contemporary thinking on reliability issues*. Sage. https://doi.org/10.4135/9781412985789

Walter, S. D., Eliasziw, M., & Donner, A. (1998). Sample size and optimal designs for reliability studies. *Statistics in Medicine, 17*(1), 101–110. https://doi.org/10.1002/(SICI)1097-0258(19980115)17:1<101::AID-SIM727>3.0.CO;2-E

Wilhelm, P., & Schoebi, D. (2007). Assessing mood in daily life: Structural validity, sensitivity to change, and reliability of a short-scale to measure three basic dimensions of mood. *European Journal of Psychological Assessment, 23*(4), 258–267. https://doi.org/10.1027/1015-5759.23.4.258

CHAPTER 34

GENERALIZABILITY THEORY

Xiaohong Gao and Deborah J. Harris

Generalizability (G) theory is a modern and powerful measurement theory. It is an extension of classical test theory (CTT) for evaluating the dependability of measurement procedures (Cronbach et al., 1972; see also Brennan, 2001a; Shavelson & Webb, 1991). G theory liberalizes CTT by providing a comprehensive conceptual framework and broad statistical procedures for addressing various measurement issues in behavioral, social, and health sciences. In particular, G theory broadens the conception and estimation of reliability in CTT. It enables people not only to identify and disentangle multiple sources of measurement error but also to understand the impact of measurement error on score interpretations. Furthermore, G theory, to some extent, presents a unified approach toward reliability and validity by both recommending careful construct explication and designing dependable measurement procedures.

The primary goals of this chapter are to enable readers (a) to understand the fundamental concepts in G theory and (b) to become familiar with basic models and designs under both univariate and multivariate G theory frameworks. In this chapter, we first present both single-facet and multifacet designs under univariate G theory and then briefly describe multivariate generalizability analysis. Both computational procedures and examples of generalizability analyses are presented. In addition, several computer programs and advanced issues are discussed to promote further exploration and applications of G theory.

CTT has been the dominant measurement theory in evaluating reliability of behavioral measurement (for more information about the treatment of CTT, see Chapter 33, this volume). The theory was developed in the early 20th century after scientists recognized error in scientific observations (Traub, 1997). The concept of *true score* is central in CTT, which is conceived as the average score that a person would get on an infinite number of independent and parallel measures (Feldt & Brennan, 1989; Haertel, 2006; Lord & Novick, 1968). A person's observed score (X), thus, consists of the person's true score (T) plus a random error (E), or $X = T + E$. Following from this equation, the total variance of observed scores is the sum of the true score variance and the error variance. In CTT, however, all error sources are indistinguishable. Reliability analyses are often conducted with a two-way table of data: persons (p) crossed by items (i) for internal consistency, raters (r) for interrater reliability,

---

The first author thanks both Richard J. Shavelson and Robert L. Brennan for leading her into the field of generalizability theory and for helping her gain an understanding of the richness and complexity it affords. The authors also acknowledge both Shavelson and Brennan for their insightful comments on an earlier version of this chapter.
https://doi.org/10.1037/0000318-034
APA Handbook of Research Methods in Psychology, Second Edition: Vol. 1. Foundations, Planning, Measures, and Psychometrics, H. Cooper (Editor-in-Chief)
Copyright © 2023 by the American Psychological Association. All rights reserved.

or occasions (o) for test–retest reliability. These indices of reliability are used to demonstrate consistency in differentiating or rank ordering individuals in behavioral measurement.

In the mid-1950s, Lord (1955) introduced the concept of randomly parallel tests. This led to the distinction between the reliability coefficient calculated from a single set of persons and items and the reliability estimate considered as the average over many random samples of items (Cronbach & Shavelson, 2004). Furthermore, the development of Fisher's analysis of variance (ANOVA) for experimental designs (Hoyt, 1941) and the need for handling more complex data structures than the two-way table motivated Cronbach and his colleagues to carry the approach in the direction of developing G theory (see Cronbach & Shavelson, 2004). Thus, G theory was born in the recognition of undifferentiable measurement error in CTT and the availability of ANOVA procedures to systematically estimate sources of error (for the history of G theory, see Brennan, 1997).

FUNDAMENTAL CONCEPTS IN GENERALIZABILITY THEORY

It has been almost a half century since the publication of the monograph *The Dependability of Behavioral Measurements: Theory of Generalizability for Scores and Profiles* (Cronbach et al., 1972). The conceptual complexity and terminologies in G theory may have impeded its quick adoption and widespread application to measurement issues in various disciplines. In this section, the basic but important concepts in G theory are introduced and illustrated using examples.

Generalizability Study

Generalizability analysis consists of two parts: *generalizability study* (G-study) and *decision study* (D-study). To appropriately apply G theory in research and practice, it is important to first understand the concepts and procedures associated with each of these components.

Random sampling is a fundamental assumption in interpreting behavioral measurement data and social science inquiries. It is also a central assumption in G theory. Under the G theory framework, any assessment outcome (e.g., a test score or behavioral rating) is a random sample from a *universe of admissible observations* (UAO). The universe consists of many measurement *facets* with various conditions analogous to factors and levels in ANOVA. In G theory, the facets are considered as potential sources of error from which the measurement samples are drawn. To evaluate the dependability or consistency of the behavioral measurement, a *generalizability study* (G-study) is designed to disentangle and to estimate as many facets of measurement error in the UAO as is reasonable and feasible. Although G theory uses experimental designs and applies ANOVA procedures, it focuses on the characterization and quantification of sources of variance associated with measurement facets rather than on traditional significance testing. Sampling variabilities or random effects associated with the *population* or *objects of measurement* and the measurement facets are estimated in the form of *variance components* in G-studies. These estimates are based on single observations (e.g., a single person on a single item scored by a single rater). They are building blocks in generalizability analysis and provide information about what sources contribute to measurement variance and the importance of the effects.

Consider a research study in which a psychologist is interested in self-regulation behavior in preschool children. The population can be defined as all preschool-age children (p). The psychologist may consider the UAO containing different observation conditions or measurement facets, such as a list of self-regulation behavior (items), measurement methods (e.g., direct observational checklists, indirect behavioral ratings), observers (e.g., caregivers, parents), session times (occasions), environmental settings (e.g., psychology laboratory, playground, home), and so forth. Thus, any measurement about a child's self-regulation behavior is only a sample from the universe of possible combinations of different items (i), measurement methods (m), raters (r), occasions (o), environmental settings (s), and so on. The measurement outcome can potentially be affected by all these sources because of random sampling.

In behavioral sciences, if a measurement model or a data collection design does not reflect or cannot capture the sources of variability that influence the observed responses, the resulting variance components will be incomplete and reliability estimates can be inappropriate. The goal of conducting a G-study, thus, is to anticipate the multiple uses of the measurement to provide as much information as possible about potentially important sources of variation. For example, behavioral ratings of self-regulation may be considered appropriate measures across different observers, occasions, and environmental settings. To investigate the magnitudes of the sampling variability and pinpoint major sources of error, a comprehensive G-study would include all the facets that potentially contribute to measurement error. Because of practical constraints in implementation such as time and cost, however, we cannot necessarily take account of all facets in a single G-study. The psychologist, in this case, may only be able to conduct a G-study with three random facets, treating other potential sources as hidden (see Cronbach et al., 1997). For example, a persons × items × raters × occasions G-study design may be considered where items, raters, and occasions are randomly sampled from all permissible items, raters, and occasions in the universe (× often stands for "crossed" in G theory notation). Alternatively, a persons × items × raters × settings G-study design can be used if the psychologist is more concerned about sampling error associated with different environmental settings than occasions. Moreover, the psychologist can conduct multiple G-studies to estimate *variance components* for the UAO and then decide where to focus future research efforts by dropping some less influential facets.

In the G-study analysis, the magnitudes of the variance components pinpoint the major sources of measurement error and identify how more reliable and efficient measurement procedures can be developed using these building blocks. For the psychologist, a persons × items × raters × occasions G-study would provide information about which of the three facets, item, rater, or occasion, contributes most to observation variability and, thus, can help them use this information to design accurate and efficient measurement procedures.

Decision Study

In the same way a G-study is associated with the UAO, a *decision study* (D-study) is related to the *universe of generalization* (UG), which is either similar to or smaller than the UAO. Under G theory, an investigator must define the UG to which they wish to generalize the measurement outcomes about the *objects of measurement* before addressing the issues of measurement error and reliability. G theory's D-study permits the investigator to have different UGs for different purposes. Thus, an individual may have different *universe scores* depending on how the investigator wants to interpret the measure within the UG. All measurement error and reliability estimates are also specific to and depend on the UG. There is no single number for the reliability applicable to all kinds of measurement procedures since a particular measurement procedure is a combination of specific facet conditions sampled from a UG. For the psychologist, the UG under a Persons × Items × Raters × Occasions design (with the uppercase letters representing D-study facets) is different from the UG for a Persons × Items × Raters × Settings design: generalizing the measurement over the items, raters, and occasions versus over the items, raters, and settings. Consequently, the reliability-like coefficients can be different under these two universes.

A D-study often deals with practical applications of measurement procedures, such as numbers of raters and occasions needed in behavioral observations, and it provides estimates of universe-score variance, error variances, and reliability-like coefficients associated with a specified UG and a particular measurement decision. True score in CTT is conceived as the average score that a person would get on an infinite number of parallel and independent measures. The concept of *universe score* in G theory is analogous to that of true score. It is defined as an expected value of the observed mean score over randomly parallel replications of the measurement procedure in the UG. For the psychologist, the universe score could be the expected value of the mean score over replications of the measurement procedure with 10 items, two raters, and three observation occasions randomly sampled from all admissible items, raters, and occasions. The variance of universe scores over all objects of measurement (e.g., persons in the population) is called *universe-score variance* and is analogous to true score variance in CTT.

G-Studies and D-Studies

In practice, the distinction between the G-study and D-study is often blurred. Usually, in a D-study, an investigator uses the estimates of variance components and information about their relative contributions to the total score variance obtained from a G-study to design a measurement procedure (D-study design and levels of conditions in the facets) that optimizes measurement precision for a particular purpose. Strictly speaking, we may call it a *D-study consideration* because no additional data are collected. In our example, a D-study or D-study consideration may contain some or all the facets (i.e., item, raters, occasions, and settings) and the same or different numbers of conditions within each facet as those in the G-study. Moreover, different D-study designs (e.g., nested) or models (e.g., mixed) can be considered to make the measurement more practical. For example, instead of a randomly crossed design, the psychologist may use a partially nested D-study design: Persons × Items × (Raters: Settings) where ":" usually stands for "nested within" in G theory notation. In other words, the children are observed by different raters (e.g., parents vs. day care staff) in different settings (home vs. day care center) using the same list of items. Alternatively, the psychologist may only be interested in generalizing the measurement outcomes to home, playground, and day care settings. In that case, the setting facet is considered as fixed. In generalizability analysis, fixing a facet often leads to decreased estimates of error variances due to a reduced UG.

Types of Measurement Error and Reliability Coefficients

When defining measurement precision, G theory also makes distinctions between two types of measurement decisions. The *relative decision*, as in CTT, concerns the differentiations or rank orders of the objects of measurement (e.g., norm-referenced interpretations of test scores for between-person comparisons). The *absolute decision* focuses on the interpretation of the response or performance levels, regardless of rank (e.g., within-person criterion-referenced or domain-referenced interpretations). The amount of measurement error and reliability depend not only on the UG but also on the type of measurement decision. Associated with these two types of decisions are two kinds of measurement error variances and reliability-like coefficients: *relative error variance* and *generalizability coefficient* for relative decisions and *absolute error variance* and *index of dependability* (or *dependability coefficient*) for absolute decisions, respectively. In our example, the psychologist may want to rank order a child's self-regulation behavior among other children (a relative decision) or decide whether the child's behavior is appropriate for his or her age (an absolute decision).

In CTT, each observation has a single true score belonging to one family of classical parallel observations (e.g., items, raters, occasions), which yields a single reliability coefficient. In G theory, however, the universe score is associated with a complex and multifaceted universe and reliability-like coefficients are associated with the UG. Furthermore, in CTT, a general equation for reliability is the ratio of true score variance to the observed score variance, which is the sum of true score variance and undifferentiated error variance. In G theory, the error variance is tied to the UG and decision type, and this variance is partitioned into different components associated with multiple sources of sampling error.

Estimates of the reliability-like coefficients are likely to fluctuate due to the universe-score variance especially when the study sample is relatively homogeneous and/or the sample size is small. Error variances or standard errors of measurement are more meaningful, stable, and easily interpretable indices of measurement precision (Brennan, 2021; Cronbach & Shavelson, 2004; Kane, 1996).

In summary, the development of G theory has extended CTT to assess multiple sources of measurement error so that a reliable and cost-efficient measurement can be built for appropriate interpretations and decisions. The following sections present some basic G theory models and designs as well as examples. After presenting the essentials, we briefly discuss some advanced issues in G theory and its applications.

UNIVARIATE GENERALIZABILITY ANALYSIS

The previous section presented the fundamental concepts in G theory. This next section shows how to conduct some univariate generalizability analyses.

Single-Facet Design and Analysis

Although the power of using G theory to evaluate measurement precision can be achieved best by using multifaceted data collection designs, a single-facet design connects G theory directly to CTT. In a single-facet generalizability analysis, the UAO consists of only one measurement facet such as items (i), raters (r), or occasions (o) instead of a combination of multiple facets. The objects of measurement are typically persons (p). Under CTT, a coefficient for internal consistency, interrater reliability, or test–retest reliability is estimated to differentiate or rank order the individuals. Within the G theory framework, we can estimate these reliability coefficients not only for rank ordering individuals (i.e., *generalizability coefficient for a relative decision*) but also for judging their response levels (i.e., *index of dependability for an absolute decision*) using a $p \times I$, $p \times R$, or $p \times O$ design. In addition, the investigator can conduct a D-study to examine the impact of using different levels of conditions such as the numbers of items or raters or employing a different design on measurement consistency.

Single-facet G-study. Consider a one-facet $p \times i$ design, or a two-way crossed design, in which each of n_p persons randomly sampled from the population responds to the same sample of n_i items in the UAO. Similarly, for a $p \times r$ design, n_p persons are scored by the same sample of n_r raters, or in a $p \times o$ design, n_p persons take a test or are observed on the same sample of n_o occasions. Because these are single-facet designs, only a single potential source of error is the focus of interest and other potential sources of error are unidentified in the universe. A linear model for decomposing the observed score X_{pi} for person p on item i can be represented as

$$X_{pi} = \mu \,(\text{grand mean})$$
$$+ \mu_p - \mu \,(\text{person effect})$$
$$+ \mu_i - \mu \,(\text{item effect})$$
$$+ X_{pi} - \mu_p - \mu_i + \mu \,(\text{residual effect}) \quad (34.1)$$

Under a single-facet design, all the effects above are considered random. In other words, it is conceptualized that persons are randomly sampled from the population, and items are randomly selected from the universe. Both the population and universe are often assumed to be essentially infinite.

Each score effect, except for the grand mean, is assumed to have a distribution with a mean of 0 and a variance of σ_p^2, σ_i^2, or σ_{pi}^2, respectively. More specifically,

$$\sigma_p^2 = E_p (\mu_p - \mu)^2 \quad (34.2)$$

$$\sigma_i^2 = E_i (\mu_i - \mu)^2 \quad (34.3)$$

$$\sigma_{pi}^2 = E_p E_i (X_{pi} - \mu_p - \mu_i + \mu)^2 \quad (34.4)$$

Under G theory, these variances are also assumed to be uncorrelated. Therefore, the total variance for the observed scores can be decomposed into the following *variance components*:

$$\sigma_{X_{pi}}^2 = \sigma_p^2 + \sigma_i^2 + \sigma_{pi}^2$$

These variance components are estimated using ANOVA procedures that involve setting the expected mean squares (MS) equal to the observed MSs to obtain the following estimated variance components:

$$\hat{\sigma}_p^2 = \frac{MS_p - MS_{pi}}{n_i}, \hat{\sigma}_i^2 = \frac{MS_i - MS_{pi}}{n_p}, \text{ and } \hat{\sigma}_{pi}^2 = MS_{pi}$$

Strictly speaking, the purpose of conducting a G-study is to estimate the variance components associated with the UAO and the population. After the variance components are estimated in the G-study, the investigator can identify the major source of the total variability by comparing the relative magnitudes of the variance components.

Single-facet D-study. After evaluating the G-study variance components, the investigator may ask what can be done to improve the measurement precision or to reduce the cost. Thus, the G-study variance components can be used further to design reliable and cost-effective measurement procedures. For example, short tests are becoming more popular in clinical and organizational psychology to reduce costs and increase administration flexibility. G theory can be used to examine the potential impact of reducing the test length on measurement precision. Similarly, the psychologist can predict the impact of increasing the numbers of observers or occasions on measurement error in the self-regulation study.

Because the variance components estimated in the G-study are based on a single observation (e.g., a single person on a single item), but measurement decisions are often based on the average or total scores over multiple observations (e.g., a set of items), G theory allows a decision maker to choose n items and to then estimate associated measurement error and reliability using the estimated G-study variance components. This is parallel with the Spearman–Brown formula and indicates that you can do what-if simulations varying the levels of one or more facets. Thus, the n_i' items used in the D-study are not required to be the same n_i in the G-study, and different numbers of n_i' can be tested to evaluate their impact on measurement precision. By convention, G theory uses mean scores in a D-study rather than total scores, as is common in CTT, although total scores can be used (see Brennan, 2001a). The mean score over a sample of n_i' items is denoted as X_{pI} in the $p \times I$ D-study for the single-facet design where the uppercase letter I designates a D-study design to distinguish it from a lower case i for the G-study design. Accordingly, the total variance for the $p \times I$ D-study design can be presented as $\sigma_{X_{pI}}^2 = \sigma_p^2 + \sigma_I^2 + \sigma_{pI}^2$, where $\sigma_I^2 = \sigma_i^2/n_i'$ and $\sigma_{pI}^2 = \sigma_{pi}^2/n_i'$, and the universe-score variance, σ_p^2, is unchanged. The variance component for persons (σ_p^2) indicates the variability of the expected person mean scores (i.e., universe scores) over different random samples of n_i' items. The variance component associated with items (σ_I^2) represents the variability among the means of randomly selected sets of n_i' items in the universe. The variance component σ_{pI}^2 shows the variability of rank ordering individuals based on their mean scores across the random samples of n_i' items as well as unmeasured random sources of variation. Because the D-study variance components are divided by n_i' based on the single-score G-study variance components, they are often smaller than the corresponding G-study variance components.

Depending on the UG and measurement decisions, the generalizability analysis provides different types of error variances (relative and absolute) and reliability-like coefficients (i.e., generalizability coefficient and index of dependability). If differentiating individuals is of concern (e.g., norm-referenced interpretations of test scores), then the relative error variance and generalizability coefficient can be used. If the focus is on the absolute level of individual performance (e.g., domain-referenced or criterion-referenced interpretations), then the absolute error variance and index of dependability should be computed.

Relative error variance is the expected variance of the discrepancies between observed deviation scores and universe deviation scores: $E E \delta_{pI}^2$ where $\delta_{pI} \equiv (X_{pI} - \mu_I) - (\mu_p - \mu)$ in a $p \times I$ D-study. Because the main effect of items affects all persons and does not change the relative standing of individuals, σ_I^2 is not a part of the relative error variance. For the D-study, relative error variance can be defined as $\sigma_\delta^2 = \sigma_{pI}^2 = \sigma_{pi}^2/n_i'$. *Absolute error variance*, on the other hand, is the expected variance of the discrepancies between observed scores and universe scores: $\underset{p}{E}\underset{I}{E}\Delta_{pI}^2$ where $\Delta_{pI} \equiv X_{pI} - \mu_p$. The sampling variability of items, σ_I^2, affects the level of performance; the absolute error variance for the $p \times I$ D-study is, thus, defined as $\sigma_\Delta^2 = \sigma_I^2 + \sigma_{pI}^2 = \sigma_i^2/n_i' + \sigma_{pi}^2/n_i'$. The square root of the error variance is the standard error of measurement (SEM) for a relative or absolute score interpretation, respectively.

The *generalizability coefficient* (G coefficient) for a relative decision is the ratio of universe-score variance (numerator) to the expected observed-score variance (denominator):

$$E\rho^2 = \frac{\sigma_p^2}{\sigma_p^2 + \sigma_\delta^2} \quad (34.5)$$

Similarly, the *index of dependability* (Φ) for an absolute decision is the ratio of the universe-score variance to the total variance:

$$\Phi = \frac{\sigma_p^2}{\sigma_p^2 + \sigma_\Delta^2} \quad (34.6)$$

Because σ_I^2 contributes to the absolute error variance, usually $\sigma_\delta^2 \leq \sigma_\Delta^2$ and $E\rho^2 \geq \Phi$.

In general, the estimates of error variances are more stable than the estimates of coefficients (see Gao & Brennan, 2001). Also, in test construction and use, the SEM has a clear meaning for score interpretation. Thus, an optimization procedure should also look at the impact of manipulating levels of a measurement facet on the SEM in addition to the coefficients.

Example. Consider an illustrative example of a generalizability analysis for a random-effects $p \times i$ design in which a 35-item mathematics test was administered to 100 examinees. Table 34.1 presents both the estimated G-study variance components $\hat{\sigma}^2(\alpha)$, where α denotes a G-study single score effect, and D-study variance components $\hat{\sigma}^2(\bar{\alpha})$, where $\bar{\alpha}$ represents the D-study average score effect. In the G-study, the variance component associated with items ($\hat{\sigma}_i^2$) is relatively small and accounts for about 6% of the total variance, indicating the mean of any one randomly selected mathematics item does not vary much from the mean of all items in the content domain. However, the variance component associated with the person-by-item interaction ($\hat{\sigma}_{pi}^2$) is large, suggesting that the relative ordering of persons differs by individual items. The results, therefore, suggest that a large number of items should be used in the assessment to reduce item sampling variability.

The D-study variance components are for average scores over replications of the measurement procedures in which samples of n_i' items

TABLE 34.1

Illustrative Example of Generalizability Analysis for a Random-Effects P × I Design

Effect (α)	MS	G-study $\hat{\sigma}^2(\alpha)$		D-study $n_i' = 20$		$n_i' = 35$	
P	1.13931	0.02688	(11.34%)	0.02688	(71.67%)	0.02688	(81.58%)
I	1.61114	0.01413	(5.90%)	0.00071	(1.88%)	0.00040	(1.22%)
pi	0.19836	0.19836	(82.87%)	0.00992	(26.44%)	0.00567	(17.20%)
$\hat{\sigma}_\delta^2$				0.00992		0.00567	
$\hat{\sigma}_\Delta^2$				0.01062		0.00607	
$E\hat{\rho}^2$				0.731		0.826	
Φ				0.717		0.816	

Note. Values in parentheses are the percentages of the total variance in the G-study and D-study. MS = mean square.

(e.g., 20 or 35) are randomly selected from the UG (e.g., content domain). The variance component associated with item samples ($\hat{\sigma}_I^2$) indicates the variability among the means of any random samples of n_i' items in the domain. The variance component, $\hat{\sigma}_{pI}^2$, estimates the variability of rank ordering of individuals based on their mean scores across the random samples. The percentages of the total variance in the D-study show the relative contribution of each mean score effect. For example, when a random sample of 35 items from the universe is used, the estimated universe-score variance contributes about 82% to the total variance and the error variances contribute less than 20% to the total variance. The D-study results, therefore, indicate that increasing the number of items can reduce measurement error and increase reliability. The use of the randomly sampled 35 items would result in a G coefficient greater than .80, which is considered sufficient in many practical situations (Crocker & Algina, 1986, p. 133; Researchgate, 2014).

Single-facet designs can take only one potential source of measurement error into account at a time. Here, only item sampling error is considered, but other error sources such as raters or occasions are not specified. Therefore, single-facet designs underestimate measurement error and overestimate reliability, if the true UG has more than one random facet.

Multifacet Designs and Analyses

Most behavioral assessments, such as the self-regulation example, contain multiple sources of error. G theory provides a powerful method for disentangling and quantifying measurement error and for developing appropriate measurement procedures under multifacet designs.

Multifacet G-study. Some researchers consider six types of error variance or facets as particularly applicable in behavioral measurement: item, dimension or category, rater, time, setting, and instrument or method (Bergeron et al., 2008). A UAO can consist of a combination of one or more of those measurement conditions (facets). For the self-regulation example, the behavior of a child (p) observed at one observation session, in one setting (e.g., playground), by one observer (e.g., caregiver), using one method (e.g., direct observation) would be considered only a sample of the child's self-regulation behavior from the multifaceted UAO. We can view the item (i) facet to be representative of the self-regulation behavioral category. The time or occasion (o) facet includes all possible occasions on which the psychologist would be equally willing to accept an observation result. We can consider the rater (r) facet as including all possible individuals (e.g., laboratory assistants, parents, caregivers) who could be trained to assign scores appropriately. The instrument or method (m) facet can include all possible ways of measuring the behavior, and the setting (s) facet includes all possible environmental contexts of collecting responses. Among these facets, some may be considered as random and infinite (e.g., items, raters, occasions) and others may be considered as fixed or finite (e.g., settings, methods). These facets can constitute various multifaceted universes of admissible observations with crossed ($\times$) or nested (:) designs, such as $i \times r \times o$, $i \times (r{:}s)$, or $i \times r \times (o{:}s)$. Thus, any measure should be viewed as a random sample of responses drawn from a complex universe.

After defining the universe of admissible observations, an investigator can design a G-study by considering resources and other constraints. For example, a $p \times i \times r \times o$ G-study can be conducted in which a random sample of individuals are administered a random sample of items on randomly selected occasions and the responses are scored by a random sample of raters defined in the UAO. The G-study can address such questions as what the major sources of measurement variability (items, rater, or occasion) are in assessing individual behavior. However, if administering the assessment across the three-facet $i \times r \times o$ is not feasible, a two-facet $p \times i \times r$, $p \times i \times o$, or $p \times r \times o$ G-study can be considered. In each of the two-facet G-studies, there can be a hidden facet: occasion facet in $p \times i \times r$, rater facet in $p \times i \times o$, or item facet in $p \times r \times o$.

To visually represent the relationship between objects of measurement and facets as well as the decomposed score effects (variance components), Venn diagrams can be used. Figure 34.1 represents a set of Venn diagrams for different two-facet designs in which p is normally not considered when describing the designs. Under the $p \times i \times r$ G-study design, p is designated as the population, which can be the object of measurement in a subsequent D-study, and i and r can be any two random facets. For example, a group of preschool children (p) are observed by two raters (r) on five different occasions (o) on their self-regulation behavior, or a group of raters (r) fills out observer ratings (i) for a sample of parent–child dyads (p) in terms of parent–child interaction. The observed scores X_{pir} have a variance of $\sigma^2_{X_{pir}}$, which can be partitioned into seven variance components under the $p \times i \times r$ G-study design as indicated in the Venn diagram in Figure 34.1A.

$$\sigma^2_{X_{pir}} = \sigma^2_p + \sigma^2_i + \sigma^2_r + \sigma^2_{pi} + \sigma^2_{pr} + \sigma^2_{ir} + \sigma^2_{pir} \quad (34.7)$$

These variance components can be estimated by setting the expected MS equal to the observed MS and solving the equations shown similar to those for the $p \times i$ design (for details, see Brennan, 2001a, Appendix B).

Multifacet D-study. Depending on the UG, the G-study variance components can be used to estimate universe-score variance and error variances of different measurement procedures and to examine the impact on generalizability of changing the number of levels in measurement facets. For the $p \times I \times R$ random-effects D-study design (e.g., a sample of individuals receive n'_i item scores or ratings from n'_r multiple raters), which is the same design as the $p \times i \times r$ G-study, error variance for relative decisions is

$$\sigma^2_\delta = \sigma^2_{pi}/n'_i + \sigma^2_{pr}/n'_r + \sigma^2_{pir}/n'_i n'_r \quad (34.8)$$

The number of levels (n') in the D-study can be any number that a decision maker considers appropriate or suitable for the UG. For absolute decisions, the error variance is

$$\sigma^2_\Delta = \sigma^2_i/n'_i + \sigma^2_r/n'_r + \sigma^2_{pi}/n'_i + \sigma^2_{pr}/n'_r$$
$$+ \sigma^2_{ir}/n'_i n'_r + \sigma^2_{pir}/n'_i n'_r \quad (34.9)$$

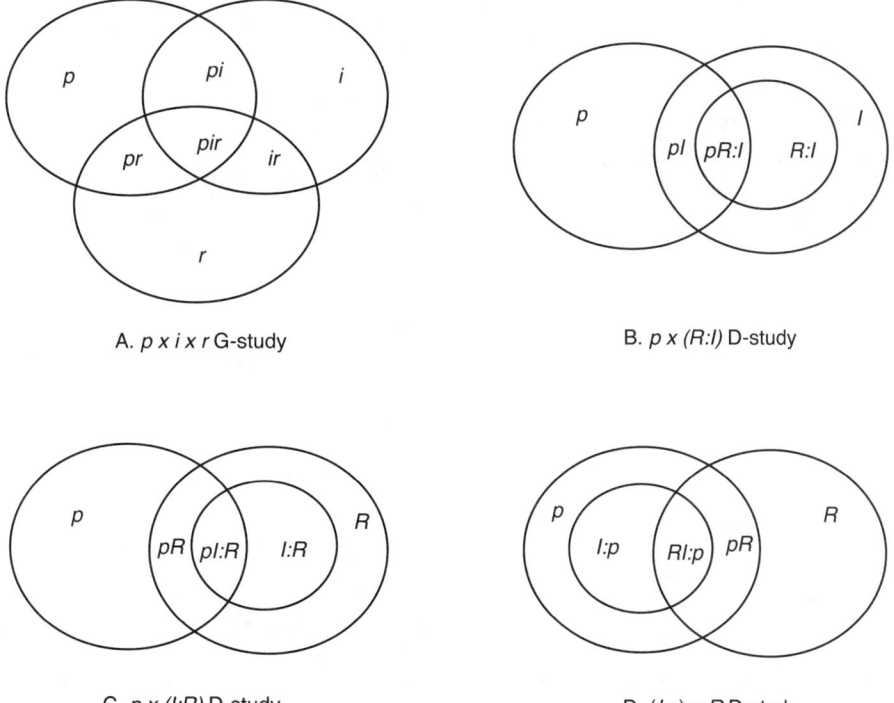

FIGURE 34.1. Venn diagrams for selected two-facet designs.

Equation 34.8 includes all variance components that are interactions with the objects of measurement (p), and that the denominator has one or more n' terms for the corresponding facets, while Equation 34.9 includes all variance components except the main effect of p (the objects of measurement) and includes in the denominator one or more n' terms for the corresponding facets.

The *main effects* of items (the difficulty of items) and raters (the strictness of raters) as well as the Rater × Item interaction do not contribute to the relative error variance for rank ordering individuals because any difference in item difficulty, rater strictness, or rank order of item difficulty by raters equally affects all individuals. However, these main effects and interactions do influence absolute performance levels and enter into the absolute error variance. The square roots of the error variances are measurement errors for relative and absolute decisions. Similarly, both the generalizability coefficient ($E\rho^2$) and index of dependability (Φ) can be computed using the general Equations 34.5 and 34.6.

One of the most important outcomes of a G-study is the quantification of the relative importance of sampling error in the UAO. Whenever possible, a crossed design should be used because both main effects and interaction effects can be fully examined (see Figure 34.1 for two-facet crossed and nested G-study and D-study designs). When interaction effects are small or negligible, in addition to changing the levels of a measurement facet (e.g., n'_i), we can also modify the D-study design by using a nested design for cost-efficiency considerations in future studies such as reducing the number of items scored by each rater. A crossed G-study can have both crossed and nested D-studies, but a nested G-study can only have limited nested D-studies if all facets in the G-study need to be considered (see Webb et al., 2006, for a list of possible two-facet designs). Similarly, a random-effects G-study can have either random- or mixed-effects D-studies, but a fixed facet in a G-study cannot become a random facet in D-studies. For example, the psychologist can evaluate children's self-regulation behavior under different settings by conducting a random-effects $p \times i \times r \times s$ G-study in which the universe for the setting facet may be conceptualized as various environmental conditions such as home, playground, classrooms, theme parks, movie theaters, and so forth. The psychologist can further modify the design to a mixed-effect $p \times I \times R \times S$ D-study with S fixed to estimate corresponding measurement precision. Under this measurement procedure, they do not have any intention of generalizing the observations to the contexts other than home and playground.

In understanding and interpreting estimated variance components and other associated statistics, investigators should keep in mind that these estimates may be unstable and subject to sampling variability, especially when the number of levels of each facet and the sample size from the population in the G-study are small and a design is complicated in which more MS terms are involved in computing variance components (Webb et al., 2006). Sampling variability of an estimated variance component can be estimated with different procedures, such as jackknife and bootstrap resampling procedures (see Brennan, 2001a, for details). For more information about resampling and Monte Carlo methods, see Chapter 23, this volume.

In addition, sometimes a negative variance component estimate can occur even though, by definition, variance components are positive. Negative estimates tend to arise when sample sizes are small, when the design involves a large number of facets, or when there is a very small score effect. Possible solutions for dealing with negative estimates may include (a) substituting 0 for the negative variance component estimate and carrying through the 0 in other expected mean square equations (Cronbach et al., 1972), or (b) setting all negative estimates of variance to 0 (Brennan, 2001a). From a practical perspective, however, choosing among these procedures is seldom a critical issue because the results are not very different.

Example. Although a UAO may contain many conditions, in behavioral measurement, often a two- or three-facet G-study design is used because of practical constraints. For illustration purposes, a *persons × items × raters* writing assessment example is presented. The discussion can be easily conveyed to other two-facet random effects designs.

In a study to evaluate measurement properties of a six-item (prompt) writing assessment, a sample ($n = 239$) of individuals (p) was administered the test and their short essays (i) were scored independently by two trained raters (r) on a 0 to 5 scale. A random-effects $p \times i \times r$ G-study was conducted to assess the multiple sources of variability. In that study, persons were considered randomly sampled from a target population and items and raters were assumed to be randomly selected from the UAO containing all admissible items and trained raters. The results are presented in Table 34.2.

The G-study results, $\hat{\sigma}^2(\alpha)$, indicate that variability among the test takers ($\hat{\sigma}^2_p$) contributes most to the performance differences. The person-by-item interaction ($\hat{\sigma}^2_{pi}$) is the second-largest variance component followed by $\hat{\sigma}^2_{pri}$ and $\hat{\sigma}^2_i$, and the variance components associated with the rater effects are relatively small. Thus, increasing the number of items (n'_i) in decision studies could greatly reduce measurement error and improve generalizability, whereas adding more raters (n'_r) may not show a large impact. Based on the $p \times I \times R$ D-study results, about six items would be needed to reach a coefficient of .80 with one rater. Nevertheless, decisions about how many raters and items are needed should be made based on both technical and practical considerations.

Furthermore, alternative D-study designs may be considered in addition to the $p \times I \times R$ D-study for various practical considerations, such as rater training and scoring. Table 34.3 presents the error variances and coefficients under the crossed and three nested designs (see Figure 34.1 for the Venn diagrams). The results show the impact of using different combinations of raters and items on measurement precision under these designs. More specifically, under the $p \times I \times R$ D-study design, each individual writes four or six short essays (n'_i), which are all scored by the same two raters (n'_r). Although only two raters were used in the study, it may not be feasible for the same raters to score all responses in a large-scale testing program. Under the $p \times (R:I)$ D-study design, each individual writes four or six short essays, but two different raters score each of the essays ($n'_{r:i}$). Thus, a total of eight or 12 raters (n'_{r+})

TABLE 34.2

Illustrative Example of Generalizability Analysis for a Random-Effects p × I × R Design

			D-study $\hat{\sigma}^2(\bar{\alpha})$			
		n'_r	1	1	2	2
G-study	$\hat{\sigma}^2(\alpha)$	n'_i	4	6	4	6
$\hat{\sigma}^2(p)$	0.31057	$\hat{\sigma}^2(p)$	0.31057	0.31057	0.31057	0.31057
$\hat{\sigma}^2(i)$	0.04913	$\hat{\sigma}^2(I)$	0.01228	0.00819	0.01228	0.00819
$\hat{\sigma}^2(r)$	0.00279	$\hat{\sigma}^2(R)$	0.00279	0.00279	0.00140	0.00140
$\hat{\sigma}^2(pi)$	0.27165	$\hat{\sigma}^2(pI)$	0.06791	0.04527	0.06791	0.04527
$\hat{\sigma}^2(pr)$	0.00167	$\hat{\sigma}^2(pR)$	0.00167	0.00167	0.00084	0.00084
$\hat{\sigma}^2(ri)$	0.00022	$\hat{\sigma}^2(RI)$	0.00006	0.00004	0.00003	0.00002
$\hat{\sigma}^2(pri)$	0.07655	$\hat{\sigma}^2(pRI)$	0.01914	0.01276	0.00957	0.00638
		$\hat{\sigma}^2(\delta)$	0.08872	0.05971	0.07832	0.05249
		$\hat{\sigma}^2(\Delta)$	0.10385	0.07072	0.09202	0.06209
		$E\hat{\rho}^2$	0.778	0.839	0.799	0.855
		$\hat{\Phi}$	0.749	0.815	0.771	0.833

TABLE 34.3

Alternative D-Studies Based on the p × i × r G-Study

Design	$p \times I \times R$		$p \times (R:I)$		$p \times (I:R)$		$(I:p) \times R$	
Total n'_r	2	2	8	12	2	2	2	2
Total n'_i	4	6	4	6	4	6	4p	6p
$\hat{\sigma}^2(\delta)$	0.07832	0.05249	0.07769	0.05179	0.08872	0.05971	0.09063	0.06070
$\hat{\sigma}^2(\Delta)$	0.09202	0.06209	0.09035	0.06023	0.10385	0.07072	0.09202	0.06209
$E\hat{\rho}^2$	0.799	0.855	0.800	0.857	0.778	0.839	0.774	0.837
$\hat{\Phi}$	0.771	0.833	0.775	0.838	0.749	0.815	0.771	0.833

Note. In the $p \times (R:I)$ design, $n'_{r:i} = 2$ for each item; in the $p \times (I:R)$ design, $n'_{i:r} = 2$ or 3 for each rater; and in the $(I:p) \times R$ design, $n'_{i:p} = 4$ or 6. 4p and 6p = four and six items per person, respectively.

need to be trained, but each one of them needs to score only one essay from each individual. This design requires training more raters but reduces individual rating time. Under the $p \times (I:R)$ D-study design, each individual still writes four or six short essays and half of the essays (two or three) are scored by the first rater, but the other half of the essays are scored by the second rater ($n'_{i:r}$). Thus, each of the two raters scores only two or three essays from each individual, but only a single rater scores each essay. Under the $(I:p) \times R$ D-study design, each individual chooses four or six different essay topics to write, and they are all scored by the same two raters. Under this design, however, many items (n'_{i+}) need to be developed and each rater would have to be trained to score all these different essays. Therefore, under these designs, even though the testing time and number of essays are the same for the individuals, the requirements for item writing, rater training, and scoring time are very different, which can have important practical implications.

When the objects of measurement (p) are nested within a measurement facet that contributes to measurement error, such as a $(p:R) \times I$ D-study where different samples of individuals are assigned to different raters, the variance component, $\hat{\sigma}^2_{p:R}$, would contain both $\hat{\sigma}^2_p$ (universe-score variance) and $\hat{\sigma}^2_{pR}$ (component of error variance). Consequently, both error variances and reliability-like coefficients cannot be appropriately estimated. However, persons can be nested within a group (e.g., class) where the objects of measurement are multilevel and nested ($p:c$). In that case, both $\hat{\sigma}^2_{p:c}$ and $\hat{\sigma}^2_c$ contribute to the universe-score variance (see Cardinet et al., 2010; Shavelson et al., 1996).

Mixed-Model G-Studies and D-Studies

G theory is perceived as essentially a random-effects theory in which objects of measurement are randomly sampled from an infinite population and measurement facets are randomly selected from an indefinitely large universe. In some practical situations, however, variations from both random and fixed sources are meaningful to measurement and can be incorporated in a generalizability analysis.

Generally speaking, in the following situations, a facet may be considered as fixed: (a) measurement levels are from a finite universe, such as content domains in a mathematics achievement test and categories or dimensions in a behavioral inventory, and all conditions in the universe are included in the measurement design; and (b) an investigator does not intend to, or it is not reasonable to, generalize the measurement outcome beyond the sampled conditions in the facet. When a study consists of at least one fixed facet in addition to at least one random facet, it has a mixed-effects model.

When a facet is fixed in a D-study, the universe score is based on an average score over the finite levels of the fixed facet. If persons are the objects of measurement, any person effects specific to the fixed facet, or the person-by-facet interaction, become part of the universe-score variance rather than the error variance. For example, in the self-regulation example, the psychologist could conduct a Persons × Items × Settings D-study with S fixed. If he or she is only interested in generalizing behavioral ratings to the specific settings such as playground and home in the S facet, the scores for that facet can be averaged over the two levels, and the Person × Setting interaction, or σ^2_{pS}, becomes part of the universe-score variance (σ^2_τ):

$$\sigma^2_\tau = \sigma^2_p + \sigma^2_{pS} = \sigma^2_p + \frac{\sigma^2_{pS}}{n'_s} \quad (34.10)$$

Note that σ^2_τ is the universe-score variance for a mixed-effects model when the same levels of the facet s are used in the G- and D-studies.

With the increase of the universe-score variance in the $p \times I \times S$ D-study when S is fixed, both relative and absolute error variances are decreased: $\sigma^2_\delta = \sigma^2_{pI} + \sigma^2_{pIS}$ and $\sigma^2_\Delta = \sigma^2_I + \sigma^2_{pI} + \sigma^2_{IS} + \sigma^2_{pIS}$. Consequently, the generalizability coefficient ($E\rho^2$) and index of dependability (Φ) are increased. Therefore, generalizations to narrow universes (or fixing a facet) reduce measurement error as compared with generalizations to broad universes (or random effects). Narrowing a universe, however, can restrict the extent to which inferences can be made about the measurement outcome. In other words, there can be trade-offs between reliability and validity. Ultimately, an investigator should define the extent to which observations can or should be generalized.

Fixed facets are often treated by averaging over their condition levels. When it does not make conceptual sense to average over the levels of a fixed facet, a separate G-study can be conducted for each condition (Shavelson & Webb, 1991) or a multivariate generalizability analysis may be considered.

Multivariate Generalizability Analysis

For behavioral measurement involving multiple scores on levels of a *fixed* facet, multivariate G theory (MGT) often provides a more powerful and flexible approach than the univariate G theory does. It can be more informative than univariate G theory by considering mutual dependence of the multiple scores and allowing for the evaluation of generalizability of composite and profile scores. Cronbach et al. (1972) and Brennan (2001a) provided an extensive treatment of MGT (also see Webb et al., 1983). Provided here is a brief introduction to some basic features. Notation is similar to that in Brennan (2001a).

The fundamental difference between MGT and univariate G theory is that MGT models two or more universe scores simultaneously. Under a multivariate generalizability model, each object of measurement has multiple universe scores, each of which is associated with one level of the fixed facet. For example, the psychologist may want to use two different instruments (or methods) such as a direct observational checklist and an indirect behavioral rating scale to obtain information regarding children's self-regulation behavior. The methods represent a fixed facet. Each child would have two observed scores, one from each measurement. Another common application of MGT is in the use of test batteries in which subscores are often derived (Raymond & Jiang, 2020). In addition to providing the univariate G-study and D-study statistics for each of the measurements, a multivariate generalizability analysis can (a) estimate correlations between the universe scores and possibly correlated errors on the distinct levels (e.g., two methods), (b) estimate measurement precision of composite or difference scores, and (c) estimate consistency between observed profile scores and universe profile scores (see Brennan et al., 1995; Clauser et al., 2006; Yin, 2005). In a multivariate G-study, both observed variances and covariances are decomposed into components for each score effect. An important feature in MGT is the distinction between *linked* and *unlinked* conditions, denoted as • and ∘, respectively. When the levels of conditions are linked or jointly sampled (e.g., the same behavior inventory is used across two observation settings), the expected values of covariance components are non-0.

However, when conditions for distinct levels are unlinked or selected independently (e.g., different items are used in the two instruments), the expected values of associated error covariance components are 0.

Many assessments are developed based on a table of specifications in which a different set of items is nested within each category of a fixed measurement facet, for example, a mathematics test with items nested within algebra and geometry, ratings of job analysis items in terms of frequency and importance, or behavioral ratings of multiple behavioral and emotional attributes. For these assessments, a $p \times i$ random-effects design is associated with each level of the fixed facet (Jarjoura & Brennan, 1983). If each person (p) responds to items (i) in n_v categories, but the items in these categories are different or sampled independently, the multivariate G-study design is designated as $p\bullet \times i^\circ$. However, in the study in which an investigator observes a sample of preschool children in different environmental settings using the same behavioral inventory, because the same items (i) were used, we can designate the G-study design as $p\bullet \times i\bullet$ to indicate the linked condition of the items.

The observed scores on two distinct levels (v and v') of the fixed facet can be modeled as $X_{piv} = \mu_v + \nu_p + \nu_i + \nu_{pi}$ and $X_{piv'} = \mu_{v'} + \xi_p + \xi_i + \xi_{pi}$, where ν and ξ are score effects for variables v and v'. The observed scores for the population and universe of admissible observations in the $p\bullet \times i\bullet$ G-study can be decomposed into three symmetric matrices:

$$\begin{bmatrix} \sigma_v^2(X_{pi}) & \sigma_{vv'}^2(X_{pi}) \\ \sigma_{vv'}^2(X_{pi}) & \sigma_{v'}^2(X_{pi}) \end{bmatrix}$$

$$= \begin{bmatrix} \sigma_v^2(p) & \sigma_{vv'}^2(p) \\ \sigma_{vv'}^2(p) & \sigma_{v'}^2(p) \end{bmatrix} \quad \text{(for person effect)}$$

$$+ \begin{bmatrix} \sigma_v^2(i) & \sigma_{vv'}^2(i) \\ \sigma_{vv'}^2(i) & \sigma_{v'}^2(i) \end{bmatrix} \quad \text{(for item effect)}$$

$$+ \begin{bmatrix} \sigma_v^2(pi) & \sigma_{vv'}^2(pi) \\ \sigma_{vv'}^2(pi) & \sigma_{v'}^2(pi) \end{bmatrix} \quad \text{(for residual effect)}$$

(34.11)

In this equation, the variance components are on the main diagonals and covariance components are off the diagonals: $\sigma_{vv'}(p)$ is the covariance between universe scores for v and v'. Dividing this covariance by the product of the square roots of the corresponding universe-score variances $\sigma_v^2(p)$ and $\sigma_{v'}^2(p)$ produces the disattenuated correlation between the two measures. The rest of the covariance terms are error covariance components. Similarly, correlated error can be estimated from the error variance and covariance components. In a $p\bullet \times i^\circ$ G-study design, the error covariance components for the item and residual effects are 0 because of the independent sampling of items.

After estimating the variance and covariance components in the G-study, the investigator can estimate variance–covariance matrices for a D-study. For any multivariate D-study, there are variance–covariance matrices for universe scores (Σ_τ), relative errors (Σ_δ), and absolute errors (Σ_Δ). The variance components in Σ_δ and Σ_Δ are the same as those in the univariate D-studies, and the covariance components are directly analogous to relative error and absolute error variance components, which are computed by dividing the G-study covariance components by the numbers of levels (n') in the D-studies.

In situations in which composite scores are of interest (e.g., an intelligence or achievement test with several subtests), a composite universe score can be defined as $\mu_{\tau C} = \Sigma_v w_v \mu_{\tau v}$, where the w_v are weights for the distinct levels (e.g., subtests) in the multivariate model and can be defined a priori by an investigator, usually such that $\Sigma_v w_v = 1$ and $w_v \geq 0$ for all v. In other cases, the weights are proportional to the number of items in each subtest. Sometimes the weights do not sum to 1; for example, $w_1 = 1$ and $w_2 = -1$ for difference scores. A composite universe-score variance is a weighted sum of the elements in the universe-score variance-covariance matrix Σ_τ.

$$\sigma_C^2(\tau) = \sum_v w_v^2 \sigma_v^2(\tau) + \sum_{v \neq v'}\sum w_v w_{v'} \sigma_{vv'}(\tau)$$

$$= \sum_v \sum_{v'} w_v w_{v'} \sigma_{vv'}(\tau), \quad (34.12)$$

where $\sigma_{vv'}(\tau) = \sigma_v^2(\tau)$ when $v = v'$. Similarly, the relative error variance for the composite is

$$\sigma_C^2(\delta) = \sum_v \sum_{v'} w_v w_{v'} \sigma_{vv'}(\delta) \quad (34.13)$$

and the absolute error variance for the composite is

$$\sigma_C^2(\Delta) = \sum_v \sum_{v'} w_v w_{v'} \sigma_{vv'}(\Delta) \quad (34.14)$$

The multivariate generalizability coefficient and index of dependability can be defined as the ratio of composite universe-score variance to itself plus composite relative error variance or composite absolute error variance, respectively.

$$E\rho^2 = \frac{\sigma_C^2(\tau)}{\sigma_C^2(\tau) + \sigma_C^2(\delta)} \quad (34.15)$$

and

$$\Phi = \frac{\sigma_C^2(\tau)}{\sigma_C^2(\tau) + \sigma_C^2(\Delta)} \quad (34.16)$$

Example. In a science achievement assessment, two different methods (hands-on experiment and computer simulation) with the same items were used (Gao et al., 1996). The investigators were interested in how exchangeable the different methods are.

Table 34.4 presents the variance–covariance matrices for this example from a $p\bullet \times i\bullet$ multivariate generalizability analysis with items linked across the assessment methods (v_1 and v_2). The estimated variance–covariance matrices for the person (p) effect, the item (i) effect, and the residual (pi) effect are denoted by $\hat{\Sigma}p$, $\hat{\Sigma}i$, and $\hat{\Sigma}pi$, respectively. Under the G-study results, the values on the diagonals of the matrices are variance component estimates, those below the diagonals are covariance component estimates, and those above the diagonals are correlation coefficients. The results show that the universe scores between the two measures are highly correlated (a .959 disattenuated or error-free correlation) and the errors associated with the

TABLE 34.4

Illustrative Example of Multivariate Generalizability Analysis for a p• × i• Design

Source	v	G-study		D-study ($n_i = 2$)		D-study ($n_i = 6$)	
		v_1	v_2	v_1	v_2	v_1	v_2
$\hat{\Sigma}p$	1	0.80526	0.95901	0.80526	0.95901	0.80526	0.95901
	2	0.68379	0.63134	0.68379	0.63134	0.68379	0.63134
$\hat{\Sigma}i$	1	1.82142	1.00503[a]	0.91071	1.00503[a]	0.30357	1.00503[a]
	2	1.15987	0.73122	0.57994	0.36561	0.19331	0.12187
$\hat{\Sigma}pi$	1	2.51712	0.34396	1.25856	0.34396	0.41952	0.34396
	2	0.67698	1.53902	0.33849	0.76951	0.11283	0.25650
Composite score weight (w_1, w_2)				(0.50, 0.50)	(0.25, 0.75)	(0.50, 0.50)	(0.25, 0.75)
$\hat{\sigma}_C^2(\tau)$				0.70105	0.66188	0.70105	0.66188
$\hat{\sigma}_C^2(\delta)$				0.67626	0.63844	0.22542	0.21281
$\hat{\sigma}_C^2(\Delta)$				1.28531	1.11849	0.42844	0.37283
$E\hat{\rho}^2$				0.509	0.509	0.757	0.757
$\hat{\Phi}$				0.353	0.372	0.621	0.640
Composite score weight (w_1, w_2)				(0.60, 0.40)	(0.40, 0.60)	(0.60, 0.40)	(0.40, 0.60)
$\hat{\sigma}_C^2(\tau)$				0.71913	0.68434	0.71913	0.68434
$\hat{\sigma}_C^2(\delta)$				0.73868	0.64087	0.24623	0.21362
$\hat{\sigma}_C^2(\Delta)$				1.40340	1.19657	0.46780	0.39886
$E\hat{\rho}^2$				0.493	0.516	0.745	0.762
$\hat{\Phi}$				0.339	0.364	0.606	0.632

[a] A correlation coefficient above 1.0 was set to the unity.

item variability are also highly correlated (e.g., the rank orders of item difficulty are similar across the two assessment methods). However, the rank orders of individuals on the items may vary between the two measures (a correlation of .344). These statistics indicate that the use of either method may not affect average performance but could impact individual performances. Table 34.4 also presents error variances and coefficients for composite scores across the two assessment methods when different numbers of items and weights are considered in the D-studies. The results demonstrate that different weights given to the different methods v_1 and v_2 could potentially change the reliability estimates. However, choice of measurement procedures including weights should be based on both theoretical and practical considerations instead of just maximizing generalizability coefficients.

COMPUTER PROGRAMS

Some general statistical packages, such as SAS or SPSS, provide G-study estimates of variance components. However, these programs have some limitations, such as (a) requiring specific data arrangements to fit the built-in routines, (b) missing D-study variance components and associated statistics, such as error variances and coefficients, and (c) having limited design options (see Mushquash & O'Connor, 2006). Some structural equation modeling programs such as Mplus and LISREL also can provide variance components and generalizability coefficients for certain designs (see Vispoel et al., 2019). Users should understand what estimation assumptions are made in these programs.

A few computer programs have been specifically developed and used for generalizability analyses (see Clauser, 2008; Vispoel et al., 2018, for a review). Two special programs are available for conducting univariate generalizability analysis under balanced designs with both random-effects and mixed-effects models: *GENOVA* (GENeralized analysis Of VAriance) originally developed by Crick and Brennan (1983) and *EDUG* designed by Jean Cardinet and associates (Cardinet et al., 2010). The functionality of these programs is similar in terms of providing both G-study and D-study variance components, error variances, and coefficients. *EDUG* has a simple user interface and directly implements the notions of symmetry (i.e., the same behavioral measurement may be used for different purposes with alternative roles of objects of measurement and facets) and nested objects of measurement (e.g., children are nested within schools) in the program (see Cardinet et al., 2010). *GENOVA* is combined with two other programs—*urGENOVA* (Brennan, 2001b) and *mGENOVA* (Brennan, 2001c)—into a *GENOVA* suite to conduct generalizability analysis under balanced and unbalanced designs on the basis of both univariate and MGT frameworks. In addition, GENOVA permits variance components as data input and calculates D-coefficients for cut scores. While GENOVA can estimate G-study variance components for group-level designs with multilevel objects of measurement (e.g., students nested within schools) and the D-study statistics when the groups are the objects of measurement, the program doesn't provide adequate D-study statistics when the objects of measurement are nested within another level (e.g., students nested within schools). Users would need to calculate these D-study statistics themselves.

For random-effects unbalanced designs mainly due to nesting, *urGENOVA* (Brennan, 2001b) provides univariate G-study variance components, but it has no D-study capabilities. A complementary program to *urGENOVA*, *G String V* (Bloch & Norman, 2018), can calculate generalizability coefficients based on variance component estimates from *urGENOVA*. Specifically, the menu-based *G String V* reads in tab-delimited or fixed format text files and executes *urGENOVA* to calculate the variance components. By varying levels of conditions in facets and types of facets, different D-study coefficients can be calculated. Like *ur*GENOVA, *G String V* doesn't allow missing data. It will replace, however, missing values by the grand mean which may not lead to adequate estimates of variance components and associated statistics. Moreover, *G String V* limits the sample size of objectives of measurement to 1,500. The software can be downloaded from the website G_String_V | MERIT (mcmaster.ca). But before downloading G_String_V.jar, the Java Runtime JRE 8 needs to be installed (see Teker, 2019).

Furthermore, *mGENOVA* (Brennan, 2001c), a program to conduct multivariate generalizability analyses, can be viewed as an extension of *GENOVA* for univariate balanced designs and an extension of *urGENOVA* for unbalanced designs. *mGENOVA* performs both multivariate G- and D-studies for a certain set of balanced or unbalanced designs. The programming command setups and input data conventions are similar across the three programs in the *GENOVA* suite.

All of the programs previously discussed can conduct various generalizability analyses. However, these specialized packages do not provide visualizations of the outcomes. The popular statistical software R (R Core Team, 2022) can be a useful tool in tabulating and visualizing results in addition to computing G theory statistics (Desjardins & Bulut, 2018). Huebner and Lucht (2019) provide a nice tutorial illustrating the applications of G theory in the R environment using the package *gtheory* (Moore, 2016). In the tutorial, they demonstrate how to use two R functions, *gstudy()* and *dstudy()* to conduct generalizability analyses under one- and two-facet random effect designs. They also illustrate how to format the data and visualize the analysis results. While R provides a rich environment for statistical modeling, analysis, visualization, and reporting, it does require a certain level of mastery of the software.

The availability of computer programs for conducting generalizability analyses can provide people easy access to the procedures and increase the applications of G theory in behavioral measurement. However, software cannot substitute for the conceptualization of measurement error, which is at the center of G theory.

SOME ADVANCED ISSUES

Since its introduction in Cronbach et al. (1972), G theory has emerged as one of the more frequently used modern test theories. Applications of G theory have extended into many scientific fields, including behavioral and social sciences (e.g., see Arterberry et al., 2014; Bergeron et al., 2008; Brennan & Liao, 2020; Briggs & Alzen, 2019; Christ et al., 2010; Clauser et al., 2020; Halvorsen et al., 2006; Lakes & Hoyt, 2009; Lee & Lewis, 2008; Lei et al., 2007; Shavelson et al., 1993; Vispoel et al., 2018; Wasserman et al., 2008). In addition, G theory has been linked to other techniques, such as structural equation modeling (see Ark, 2015, and Vispoel et al., 2018). In this chapter, however, we have only scratched the surface of the theory and provided a sampling of its uses. As challenges arise in behavioral measurement, some new concepts and procedures are being developed or explored. The following advanced topics deal with some important issues that have practical implications in using G theory.

Symmetry

G theory was developed from CTT, which focuses on differentiating individuals. Thus, its objects of measurement are often persons. In many practical situations, however, factors other than persons can be the focus of measurement (e.g., estimation of differences in performance tasks). In addition, there are not only nested facets of measurement (e.g., raters nested within occasions) but also nested objects of measurement (e.g., students nested within classes). During the 1970s and 1980s, Cardinet et al. (1976, 1981) introduced the concept of *symmetry,* which states that any factor in a measurement design can be selected as an object of measurement. This principle flexibly extends the practical applicability of G theory to a wide range of measurement contexts. They divided the factors in a generalizability analysis into two categories: *differentiation facet* (i.e., object of measurement) and *instrumentation facet* (i.e., error facets in the universe). Cardinet et al. (1976, 1981) recognized that the same behavioral measurement might be used for more than one purpose: A factor can be a differentiation facet under one measurement context but an instrumentation facet under another. For example, an achievement test can be used to evaluate individual student performance in which persons are the differentiation facet. The same observations, however, can also be used to evaluate generalizability of the variation in the item difficulty in which persons become an instrumentation facet and the variation among persons contributes to error. The intention behind developing the symmetry concept was to encourage the application of G theory to objects of study other than individuals (Cardinet et al., 2010).

The principle of symmetry has also led to the extensions of G theory in several directions by Cardinet et al. (2010), including analysis of multifaceted populations. In large-scale assessments and survey research as well as some behavioral measurement, individuals are often nested within group variables (e.g., classes, schools). For different uses of the measurement outcomes, different factors in the multifaceted objects of measurement can be of interest. The allocation of the variance components for the estimation of measurement error and reliability-like coefficients will be different. At the individual-level measurement, person variability is considered as true-score variance. At the group-level assessment, however, person variability introduces uncertainty about the group scores and contributes to the error variances (Cronbach et al., 1997). The 2014 Standards states,

> When average test scores for groups are the focus of the proposed interpretation of the test results, the groups tested should generally be regarded as a sample from a larger population, even if all examinees available at the time of measurement are tested. In such cases the standard error of the group mean should be reported, because it reflects variability due to sampling of examinees as well as variability due to individual measurement error. (American Educational Research Association et al., 2014, p. 46)

A generalizability analysis with stratified objects of measurement can provide appropriate estimates of measurement precision.

Reliability and Validity Coalesce

In behavioral sciences, assessments are designed for developing an understanding of what the observed responses mean and consequently deciding how the scores can or should be interpreted and used. As G theory liberalized CTT to broaden the conceptualization of reliability, certain aspects of validity have been mingled into the G theory framework. In other words, the theory of "reliability" and the theory of "validity" coalesce.

Although Cronbach et al. (1972) noted that G theory is part of validity, Kane (1982) highlighted the blurred distinction between reliability and validity from the perspective of two types of universes of generalization: (a) a restricted reliability-defining universe with standardized measurement procedures and (b) a broader validity-defining UG. According to Kane, standardization of measurement procedures can increase reliability but may lead to a decrease in some measures of validity (i.e., the reliability-validity paradox). Kane et al. (1999) extended the reliability–validity paradox notion in the context of performance assessments. Kreiter and Zaidi (2020) provided examples of applications of G theory in validity research of health science education.

Validity theory has evolved from separate models (i.e., criterion, content, and construct) to a unified model in which validation is viewed as a process of developing and evaluating evidence to support the proposed score interpretations and uses (Kane, 2006). Construct validation has become the basis for the unified model that includes various forms of validity evidence, such as content, criterion, generalizability, and theoretical argument (Messick, 1989).

G theory provides a broad conceptual framework and a useful tool for conceptualizing and estimating sources of measurement error and construct-irrelevant variance in supporting measurement validation. The 2014 Standards set by the American Educational Research Association et al. suggest that

> The test developer should set forth clearly how test scores are intended to

be interpreted and consequently used. The population(s) for which a test is intended should be delimited clearly, and the construct or constructs that the test is intended to assess should be described clearly. (p. 23)

Consistent with the 2014 Standards, G theory requires an investigator to specify the populations (objects of measurement), measurement conditions (facets) over which generalization will be made such as content domains, assessment and scoring methods, and other standardized contexts, as well as the types of decisions (uses) based on the measurement outcomes. All these specifications explicitly define the relevance of G theory in supporting score validation. The analysis of generalizability indicates how validly one can interpret a measure as representative of a certain set of possible measures (Cronbach et al., 1963). The use of *generalizability* and *dependability* instead of *reliability* in G theory reflects the interest in unifying reliability and validity. In fact, by acknowledging that the generalizability of the measurement depends on the universe about which the investigator intends to draw inferences or to make decisions, G theory, to a certain extent, overcomes the traditional distinction between reliability and validity. For example, the accuracy of domain specification and representativeness of the items (content validity) can affect sampling variability and consequently influence estimates of measurement errors and generalizability coefficients (Shavelson et al., 1996). Solano-Flores and Li (2009, 2013) found that the construct-irrelevant aspects of language such as *persons* × *item* × *language* interactions are very important sources of measurement error and can have an impact on measurement precision in the testing of English language learner populations. Their studies underscore the relevance of language and dialect variations in the design of assessments and developing testing policies that ensure valid interpretations of test scores for linguistic minorities. In addition, generalizability across different measures (e.g., assessment methods) refers to their exchangeability for measuring the same attribute and may be interpreted as an instance of convergent validity (Gao et al., 1996).

Moreover, almost all score interpretations involve generalization. Messick (1989) listed four types of generalizability of score interpretation as forms of validity evidence: *population, ecological, temporal,* and *task*. Kane et al. (1999) and Kane (2006) listed four components of interpretive argument for validity: *scoring* (from observed behavior to observed scores), *generalization* (from observed scores to universe scores), *extrapolation* (from universe scores to target scores or skill levels), and *implication* (from target scores to interpretations). Among these four inferences, G theory directly contributes to the generalization inference and facilitates the inferences for scoring and extrapolation (see Kreiter & Zaidi, 2020, for examples). G theory, especially MGT, provides a tool to quantify the uncertainty in the generalization and identify some sources of sampling variability and construct irrelevant variance in measured outcomes, such as variability associated with items, raters, occasions, as well as scoring rubrics, measurement methods, or observational settings. In other words, generalizability analyses give empirical checks on the degree of invariance from observations to expected performance in the universe of generalization, which is often a subset of the target domain for score validation. If sampling errors are substantial and the construct irrelevant variance is large, the inferences from the observed scores to the universe scores are uncertain and extrapolation may not be justified.

According to Kane et al. (1999), at least two issues in an assessment design can have a major impact on validity: standardization of the assessment and complexity and contextualization of the assessment. The former may increase generalization of observed scores to universe scores, whereas the latter could improve the extrapolation from universe scores to target scores. However, there is a clear trade-off between the two. For example, narrowing the domain or making the domain more homogeneous could increase measurement precision but may restrict the UG and, thus, limit the use of the measurement. Therefore, the goal is to strengthen generalization without weakening extrapolation. The more similar the UG is to the target domain, the better the inference would be in supporting validity of score uses and interpretations.

Generalizability Theory and Item Response Theory

G theory and item response theory (IRT) provide two powerful measurement frameworks for modeling measurement error and scaling latent traits. Fundamentally, G theory can be viewed as a macromeasurement model that focuses on test scores, and IRT can be considered principally as a scaling model that pays close attention to item scores (Brennan, 2001a). More specifically, G theory conceptualizes measurement precision on the basis of a sampling framework under the multifaceted universe. It assumes an additive linear model of independent score effects, and it focuses on disentangling and quantifying multiple sources of measurement error as well as designing optimized measurement procedures within a specified context (universe) of score inferences. IRT, on the other hand, emphasizes statistical properties of items and focuses on estimating a latent trait (e.g., a person's ability) under strong assumptions, such as unidimensionality and local independence. The test information function in IRT expresses the accuracy of the maximum likelihood estimate of the latent variable. Although the square root of the inverse of the test information function provides the standard error of the maximum likelihood estimate on the true value of the latent variable, IRT treats measurement error as undifferentiated and estimates both item and person parameters with other measurement conditions fixed. Consequently, standard errors of estimates in IRT are usually smaller than the SEM in G theory.

Because G theory and IRT view measurement from different perspectives, and have different assumptions in modeling responses, we should evaluate the merits and limits of each and consider using them jointly. Some efforts have been made to bring together the sampling model of G theory with the scaling model of IRT (see Bock et al., 2002; Briggs & Wilson, 2007; Choi, 2013; Kolen & Harris, 1987; Patz et al., 2002). Bock et al. (2002) acknowledged that the conditional standard error of estimates in IRT do not distinguish among multiple sources of error, and proposed an ad hoc solution to modify information functions on the basis of results from a generalizability analysis so that the standard error of estimates can be adjusted to consider both item and rater sampling errors. Li (2017) extended the Bock et al. (2002) methodology to obtain more accurate precision information for ability estimates in the context of testlets. Briggs and Wilson (2007) derived variance component estimates from estimates of item and person parameters obtained within the Rasch IRT framework, while Choi and Wilson (2018) used a generalized linear latent and mixed model approach. G theory and IRT have been used sequentially or simultaneously to exploit their relative strength in monitoring error variances and identifying specific incidences that contribute the most to the measurement variabilities to improve the quality of measurement (see Bachman et al., 1995; Iramaneerat et al., 2008; Jeon et al., 2009; Kim & Wilson, 2009; Li, 2017). Integrating IRT and G theory can be challenging and complex, but because both theories have their strengths, their combination can lead to a better understanding and interpretation of measurement outcomes, and efforts to utilize them both should be continued.

CONCLUDING REMARKS

When measuring a construct of interest (e.g., self-regulation), we typically can only obtain a sample of measurement data based on a specific measurement procedure. Our goal is to develop a measurement procedure that would allow us to obtain generalizable information from the sample to a larger universe of interest. G theory has introduced a change in the conceptualization of measurement error. It offers a powerful framework for understanding measurement error and the impact of measurement error on score interpretation in behavioral and social sciences as well as other fields in which measurements are not precise. Whether we are attempting to measure general ability or achievement, or to assess behavior or personality, our scores or observations are subject to measurement error. G theory provides a useful tool for quantifying multiple sources of error and offers building blocks to design reliable and efficient measurement procedures. Moreover, G theory not only regroups classical reliability indices within a unified conceptual framework and procedures but also helps us conceptualize our thinking about validity.

Born from CTT, G theory has several distinctive features from CTT. G theory (a) focuses on conceptualization of potential multiple sources of error (UAO), (b) provides detailed information about the relative importance of the different sources of measurement error by quantifying their variability (G-study and variance components), (c) casts measurement precision within a specific context (UG and relative vs. absolute decisions), (d) identifies how measurement procedures can be improved (D-study), (e) evaluates measurement precision beyond differentiations of individuals (symmetry), and (f) unifies some conceptualizations of traditional reliability and validity (reliability and validity coalescence).

While G theory has been perceived as an advanced approach towards reliability estimation, it can also be used as a general research paradigm for a broad range of measurement situations. In recent decades, the use of G theory has been extended to experimental and survey research, naturalistic studies, and instrument development in areas of education, psychology, social sciences, and medicine. Because of its diverse applications and its richness, G theory continues to play an important role in exploring and controlling sources of measurement error in behavioral and social sciences.

References

American Educational Research Association, American Psychological Association, & National Council on Measurement in Education. (2014). *Standards for educational and psychological testing*. https://www.testingstandards.net/open-access-files.html

Ark, T. K. (2015). *Ordinal generalizability theory using an underlying latent variable framework* [Unpublished doctoral dissertation]. The University of British Columbia.

Arterberry, B. J., Martens, M. P., Cadigan, J. M., & Rohrer, D. (2014). Application of generalizability theory to the big five inventory. *Personality and Individual Differences*, 69, 98–103. https://doi.org/10.1016/j.paid.2014.05.015

Bachman, L. F., Lynch, B. K., & Mason, M. (1995). Investigating variability in tasks and rater judgments in a performance test of foreign language speaking. *Language Testing*, 12(2), 238–257. https://doi.org/10.1177/026553229501200206

Bergeron, R., Floyd, R. G., McCormack, A. C., & Farmer, W. L. (2008). The generalizability of externalizing behavior composites and subscale scores across time, rater, and instrument. *School Psychology Review*, 37(1), 91–108. https://doi.org/10.1080/02796015.2008.12087911

Bloch, R., & Norman, G. (2018). *G String V user manual*. G_String_VI | MERIT (mcmaster.ca).

Bock, R. D., Brennan, R. L., & Muraki, E. (2002). The information in multiple ratings. *Applied Psychological Measurement*, 26(4), 364–375. https://doi.org/10.1177/014662102237794

Brennan, R. L. (1997). A perspective on the history of generalizability theory. *Educational Measurement: Issues and Practice*, 16(4), 14–20. https://doi.org/10.1111/j.1745-3992.1997.tb00604.x

Brennan, R. L. (2001a). *Generalizability theory*. Springer-Verlag. https://doi.org/10.1007/978-1-4757-3456-0

Brennan, R. L. (2001b). *Manual for mGENOVA*. Iowa Testing Programs, University of Iowa. (Available on https://education.uiowa.edu/centers/casma)

Brennan, R. L. (2001c). *Manual for urGENOVA*. Iowa Testing Programs, University of Iowa.

Brennan, R. L. (2021). Generalizability theory. In B. E. Clauser & M. B. Bunch (Eds.), *The history of educational measurement in the United States*. Routledge.

Brennan, R. L., Gao, X., & Colton, D. A. (1995). Generalizability analyses of Work Keys Listening and Writing tests. *Educational and Psychological Measurement*, 55(2), 157–176. https://doi.org/10.1177/0013164495055002001

Brennan, R. L., & Liao, J.-T. R. (February, 2020). *Generalizability theory references: The first sixty years* (CASMA Research Report No. 53). Center for Advanced Studies in Measurement and Assessment, The University of Iowa. (Available on https://education.uiowa.edu/centers/casma)

Briggs, D. C., & Alzen, J. L. (2019). Making inferences about teacher observation scores over time. *Educational and Psychological Measurement*, *79*(4), 636–664. https://doi.org/10.1177/0013164419826237

Briggs, D. C., & Wilson, M. (2007). Generalizability in item response modeling. *Journal of Educational Measurement*, *44*(2), 131–155. https://doi.org/10.1111/j.1745-3984.2007.00031.x

Cardinet, J., Johnson, S., & Pini, G. (2010). *Applying generalizability theory using EduG*. Routledge. https://www.routledge.com/Applying-Generalizability-Theory-using-EduG/Cardinet-Johnson-Pini/p/book/9781848728295

Cardinet, J., Tourneur, Y., & Allal, L. (1976). The symmetry of generalizability theory: Applications to educational measurement. *Journal of Educational Measurement*, *13*(2), 119–135. https://doi.org/10.1111/j.1745-3984.1976.tb00003.x

Cardinet, J., Tourneur, Y., & Allal, L. (1981). Extension of generalizability theory and its applications in educational measurement. *Journal of Educational Measurement*, *18*(4), 183–204. https://doi.org/10.1111/j.1745-3984.1981.tb00852.x

Choi, J. (2013). *Advances in combining generalizability theory and item response theory* [Unpublished doctoral dissertation]. University of California, Berkeley.

Choi, J., & Wilson, M. R. (2018). Modeling rater effects using a combination of generalizability theory and IRT. *Psychological Test and Assessment Modeling*, *60*, 53–80.

Christ, T. J., Riley-Tillman, T. C., Chafouleas, S. M., & Boice, C. H. (2010). Direct behavior ratings (DBR): Generalizability and dependability across raters and observations. *Educational and Psychological Measurement*, *70*(5), 825–843. https://doi.org/10.1177/0013164410366695

Clauser, B. E. (2008). A review of EDUG software for generalizability analysis. *International Journal of Testing*, *8*(3), 296–301. https://doi.org/10.1080/15305050802262357

Clauser, B. E., Harik, P., & Margolis, M. J. (2006). A multivariate generalizability analysis of data from a performance assessment of physicians' clinical skills. *Journal of Educational Measurement*, *43*(3), 173–191. https://doi.org/10.1111/j.1745-3984.2006.00012.x

Clauser, B. E., Kane, M. T., & Clauser, J. C. (2020). Examining the precision of cut scores within a generalizability theory framework: A closer look at the item effect. *Journal of Educational Measurement*, *57*(2), 216–229. https://doi.org/10.1111/jedm.12247

Crick, J. E., & Brennan, R. L. (1983). *Manual for GENOVA: A generalizability analysis of variance system* (American College Testing Technical Bulletin No. 43). ACT.

Crocker, L., & Algina, J. (1986). *Introduction to classical & modern test theory*. Holt, Rinchart, and Winston.

Cronbach, L. J., Gleser, G. C., Nanda, H., & Rajaratnam, N. (1972). *The dependability of behavioral measurements: Theory of generalizability for scores and profiles*. Wiley.

Cronbach, L. J., Linn, R. L., Brennan, R. L., & Haertel, E. H. (1997). Generalizability analysis for performance assessments of student achievement or school effectiveness. *Educational and Psychological Measurement*, *57*(3), 373–399. https://doi.org/10.1177/0013164497057003001

Cronbach, L. J., Rajaratnam, N., & Gleser, G. C. (1963). Theory of generalizability: A liberalization of reliability theory. *British Journal of Statistical Psychology*, *16*(2), 137–163. https://doi.org/10.1111/j.2044-8317.1963.tb00206.x

Cronbach, L. J., & Shavelson, R. J. (2004). My current thoughts on coefficient alpha and successor procedures. *Educational and Psychological Measurement*, *64*(3), 391–418. https://doi.org/10.1177/0013164404266386

Desjardins, C. D., & Bulut, O. (2018). *Handbook of educational measurement and psychometrics using R*. Taylor & Francis Group. https://doi.org/10.1201/b20498

Feldt, L. S., & Brennan, R. L. (1989). Reliability. In R. L. Linn (Ed.), *Educational measurement* (3rd ed., pp. 105–146). American Council on Education & Macmillan.

Gao, X., & Brennan, R. L. (2001). Variability of estimated variance components and related statistics in performance assessment. *Applied Measurement in Education*, *14*, 191–203. https://doi.org/10.1207/S15324818AME1402_5

Gao, X., Shavelson, R. J., Brennan, R. L., & Baxter, G. P. (1996, April). A multivariate generalizability theory approach to convergent validity of performance-based assessment. In G. Ensign (Chair), *Theory and practice in large-scale performance assessments* [Invited symposium]. Annual Meeting of the National Council on Measurement in Education, New York, NY, United States.

Haertel, E. H. (2006). Reliability. In R. L. Brennan (Ed.), *Educational measurement* (4th ed., pp. 65–110). American Council on Education/Praeger.

Halvorsen, M. S., Hagtvet, K. A., & Monsen, J. T. (2006). The reliability of self-image change scores in psychotherapy research: An application of generalizability theory. *Psychotherapy: Theory, Research, & Practice*, 43(3), 308–321. https://doi.org/10.1037/0033-3204.43.3.308

Hoyt, C. (1941). Test reliability estimated by analysis of variance. *Psychometrika*, 6(3), 153–160. https://doi.org/10.1007/BF02289270

Huebner, A., & Lucht, M. (2019). Generalizability theory in R. *Practical Assessment, Research & Evaluation*, 24, 1–12.

Iramaneerat, C., Yudkowsky, R., Myford, C. M., & Downing, S. M. (2008). Quality control of an OSCE using generalizability theory and many-faceted Rasch measurement. *Advances in Health Sciences Education: Theory and Practice*, 13(4), 479–493. https://doi.org/10.1007/s10459-007-9060-8

Jarjoura, D., & Brennan, R. L. (1983). Multivariate generalizability models for tests developed from tables of specifications. In L. J. Fyans, Jr. (Ed.), *Generalizability theory: Inferences and practical applications: New directions for testing and measurement* (pp. 83–101). Jossey-Bass.

Jeon, M., Lee, G., Hwang, J., & Kang, S. (2009). Estimating reliability of school-level scores using multilevel and generalizability theory models. *Asia Pacific Education Review*, 10(2), 149–158. https://doi.org/10.1007/s12564-009-9014-3

Kane, M. T. (1982). A sampling model for validity. *Applied Psychological Measurement*, 6(2), 125–160. https://doi.org/10.1177/014662168200600201

Kane, M. T. (1996). The precision of measurements. *Applied Measurement in Education*, 9(4), 335–379. https://doi.org/10.1207/s15324818ame0904_4

Kane, M. T. (2006). Validation. In R. L. Brennan (Ed.), *Educational measurement* (4th ed., pp. 65–110). American Council on Education/Praeger.

Kane, M. T., Crooks, T. J., & Cohen, A. (1999). Validating measures of performance. *Educational Measurement: Issues and Practice*, 18(2), 5–17. https://doi.org/10.1111/j.1745-3992.1999.tb00010.x

Kim, S. C., & Wilson, M. (2009). A comparative analysis of the ratings in performance assessment using generalizability theory and the many-facet Rasch model. *Journal of Applied Measurement*, 10(4), 408–423.

Kolen, M. J., & Harris, D. J. (1987). *A multivariate test theory model based on item response theory and generalizability theory*. Paper presented at the Annual Meeting of the American Educational Research Association, Washington, DC, United States.

Kreiter, C., & Zaidi, N. B. (2020). Generalizability theory's role in validity research: Innovative applications in health science education. *Health Profession Education*, 6(2), 282–290. https://doi.org/10.1016/j.hpe.2020.02.002

Lakes, K. D., & Hoyt, W. T. (2009). Applications of generalizability theory to clinical child and adolescent psychology research. *Journal of Clinical Child and Adolescent Psychology*, 38(1), 144–165. https://doi.org/10.1080/15374410802575461

Lee, G., & Lewis, D. M. (2008). A generalizability theory approach to standard error estimates for bookmark standard settings. *Educational and Psychological Measurement*, 68(4), 603–620. https://doi.org/10.1177/0013164407312603

Lei, P., Smith, M., & Suen, H. K. (2007). The use of generalizability theory to estimate data reliability in single-subject observational research. *Psychology in the Schools*, 44(5), 433–439. https://doi.org/10.1002/pits.20235

Li, F. (2017). *An information-correction method for testlet-based test analysis: From the perspectives of item response theory and generalizability theory* (Research Report No. RR-17-27). Educational Testing Service. https://doi.org/10.1002/ets2.12151

Lord, F. M. (1955). Estimating test reliability. *Educational and Psychological Measurement*, 15(4), 325–336. https://doi.org/10.1177/001316445501500401

Lord, F. M., & Novick, M. R. (1968). *Statistical theories of mental test scores*. Addison-Wesley.

Messick, S. (1989). Validity. In R. L. Linn (Ed.), *Educational measurement* (3rd ed., pp. 13–103). American Council on Education/Macmillan.

Moore, C. T. (2016). *gtheory: Apply generalizability theory with R*. R package version 0.1.2. https://CRAN.R-project.org/package=gtheory

Mushquash, C., & O'Connor, B. P. (2006). SPSS and SAS programs for generalizability theory analyses. *Behavior Research Methods*, 38(3), 542–547. https://doi.org/10.3758/BF03192810

Patz, R. J., Junker, B. W., Johnson, M. S., & Mariano, L. T. (2002). The hierarchical rater model for rated test items and its application to large-scale educational assessment data. *Journal of Educational and Behavioral Statistics*, 27(4), 341–384. https://doi.org/10.3102/10769986027004341

Raymond, M. R., & Jiang, Z. (2020). Indices of subscore utility for individuals and subgroups based on multivariate generalizability theory. *Educational and Psychological Measurement*, 80(1), 67–90. https://doi.org/10.1177/0013164419846936

R Core Team. (2022). *R: A language and environment for statistical computing*. R Foundation for Statistical Computing. https://www.r-project.org/

Researchgate. (2014). *What is the acceptable value for test retest reliability of a psychology test?* https://www.researchgate.net/post/What_is_the_acceptable_value_for_test_retest_reliability_of_a_psychological_test

Shavelson, R. J., Baxter, G. P., & Gao, X. (1993). Sampling variability of performance assessments. *Journal of Educational Measurement, 30*(3), 215–232. https://doi.org/10.1111/j.1745-3984.1993.tb00424.x

Shavelson, R. J., Gao, X., & Baxter, G. P. (1996). On the content validity of performance assessments: Centrality of domain specification. In M. Birenbaum & F. J. R. C. Dochy (Eds.), *Alternative in assessment of achievements, learning processes and prior knowledge* (pp. 131–141). Kluwer. https://doi.org/10.1007/978-94-011-0657-3_5

Shavelson, R. J., & Webb, N. M. (1991). *Generalizability theory: A primer*. Sage.

Solano-Flores, G., & Li, M. (2009). Language variation and score variation in the testing of English language learners, native Spanish speakers. *Educational Assessment, 14*(3-4), 180–194. https://doi.org/10.1080/10627190903422880

Solano-Flores, G., & Li, M. (2013). Generalizability theory and the fair and valid assessment of linguistic minorities. *Educational Research and Evaluation: An International Journal on Theory and Practice, 19*(2-3), 245–263.

Tasdelen Teker, G. (2019). Coping with unbalanced designs of generalizability theory: G String V. *International Journal of Assessment Tools in Education, 6*(5), 57–69. https://doi.org/10.21449/ijate.658747

Traub, R. E. (1997). Classical test theory in historical perspective. *Educational Measurement: Issues and Practice, 16*, 8–14. https://doi.org/10.1111/j.1745-3992.1997.tb00603.x

Vispoel, W. P., Morris, C. A., & Kilinc, M. (2018). Applications of generalizability theory and their relations to classical test theory and structural equation modeling. *Psychological Methods, 23*(1), 1–26. https://doi.org/10.1037/met0000107

Vispoel, W. P., Morris, C. A., & Kilinc, M. (2019). Using generalizability theory with continuous latent response variables. *Psychological Methods, 24*(2), 153–178. https://doi.org/10.1037/met0000177

Wasserman, R. H., Levy, K. N., & Loken, E. (2008). Generalizability theory in psychotherapy research: The impact of multiple sources of variance on the dependability of psychotherapy process ratings. *Psychotherapy Research, 19*(4-5), 397–408.

Webb, N. M., Shavelson, R. J., & Haertel, E. H. (2006). 4 Reliability coefficients and generalizability theory. *Handbook of Statistics, 26*, 81–124. https://doi.org/10.1016/S0169-7161(06)26004-8

Webb, N. M., Shavelson, R. J., & Maddahian, E. (1983). Multivariate generalizability theory. In L. J. Fyans (Ed.), *Generalizability theory: New directions for testing and measurement* (pp. 67–82). Jossey-Bass.

Yin, P. (2005). A multivariate generalizability analysis of the multistate bar examination. *Educational and Psychological Measurement, 65*(4), 668–686. https://doi.org/10.1177/0013164404273940

CHAPTER 35

CONSTRUCT VALIDITY

Kevin J. Grimm and Keith F. Widaman

In this chapter, we consider construct validity as an overarching idea with two broad aspects—internal validity and external validity—each of which has specific components. Various aspects of construct validation have been discussed in a number of key papers over the past half century (e.g., Borsboom et al., 2004; Cronbach, 1980; Cronbach & Meehl, 1955; McArdle & Prescott, 1992; Messick, 1989, 1995; Shepard, 1993), and we draw from this collection of work in framing the current chapter. *Construct validity*, or validity in general, has been regarded as the most fundamental and important aspect of psychometrics, the study of psychological measures and measurement encompassing direct assessments (e.g., fluid reasoning test and depression inventory), surveys of attitudes (e.g., political views), observations (e.g., classroom observations), among others (Angoff, 1988). However, despite its centrality to the scientific enterprise, few, if any, clear standards regarding construct validation have been proposed. This situation contrasts distinctly with procedures related to reliability (see Chapter 33, this volume), where several standard options for calculating reliability are routinely recommended, and reliabilities of .80 or higher are generally considered adequate to strong. One reason for the less structured approach to construct validity is because it is multifaceted; construct validity is often not considered to be a property of a test, but rather a property regarding the use of scores derived from a test or of inferences made from those test scores. Because researchers and practitioners can and do devise new ways to use test scores, construct validation is a lengthy process (Cronbach, 1989), one that is never finished (Cronbach, 1988).

A HISTORICAL SKETCH OF CONSTRUCT VALIDITY

To introduce the concept of construct validity, a brief sketch of the history of the notion is in order. Constructs and the validity of constructs were core aspects of psychological research for well over a half century before the term *construct validity* made its way into the scientific lexicon in Cronbach and Meehl (1955). In this brief introduction, we identify three phases in the history of construct validity, phases that we identify as the *preoperational*, *concrete operational*, and *formal operational*, with apologies to Piaget.

The preoperational phase of research related to construct validity encompasses the period from the emergence of psychology as a distinct discipline, during the 1870s, until the early 1920s. During the preoperational phase, researchers pursued wide-ranging studies of many different constructs but displayed little serious reflection on the tie between manifest measurements and the constructs that were assessed. For example, sensory thresholds and relations between sensation and perception were topics of great research interest, and many enduring methods of establishing thresholds (e.g., the method of constant stimuli) were developed during this phase. Little methodological criticism, however, was aimed at measurements, perhaps because the ties between manifest measures and the constructs they were to represent were very close in many domains of inquiry. This is not to say that research pursued during this period concerned only constructs subject to relatively direct measurement. Indeed, investigators were interested in initiating studies of rather nebulous concepts, such as the human soul and its relation to the mind–body problem. Still, arguments centered more on the experimental evidence produced for phenomena, rather than on qualities of the measurements themselves and their ties to the intended constructs.

The second phase, which we have termed the *concrete operational* phase, was occasioned by conflicting interpretations of results from the massive psychological testing enterprise undertaken by psychologists on behalf of the U.S. war effort during World War I (Yerkes, 1921). Early precursors of this phase can be seen in the behaviorist manifestos by Watson (e.g., 1913), which emphasized a hard-nosed approach to measuring behavior and dispensing with measures of unseen, latent, mentalistic constructs. But the concrete operational phase was forced onto the field of psychology by a nonpsychologist, Walter Lippmann, in the early 1920s. In a series of short articles in the *New Republic*, Lippmann (e.g., Lippmann, 1922) lambasted interpretations of results from the World War I testing enterprise. Based on their testing of recruits, psychologists had claimed that the mental age of the average Army recruit was 14 years, a value listed in the Yerkes (1921) volume. A later book by Brigham (1923) argued that Army recruits from Northern European countries were clearly above the mean in intelligence and that recruits from Southern European countries, on average, had mean intelligence levels that were on the borderline of intellectual disability. Lippmann argued that such conclusions could not be true; if they were true, the United States could not function as a modern society. If mean levels of performance by Army recruits were at the level of a 14-year-old, then perhaps intelligence was not what was being measured by the tests. Responses by psychologists were simple and direct, if less than stellar. Perhaps the most well-known came from Boring (1923), who stated that intelligence was what intelligence tests measure; if the tests indicate that the mean mental age of recruits was 14 years, then the emerging science of psychology would stand behind that claim.

This approach of emphasizing how a construct was operationalized—a given construct was what a measure of that construct measured—became central to the operational definition of constructs. This approach was propounded in notable contributions, such as Bridgman (1932), who wrote regarding operational definitions in physics. The operational definition of constructs was carried over directly into our field, providing an objective way of measuring constructs of importance to scientific psychology. Moreover, this operational approach was consistent with the emerging logical positivist movement associated with the Vienna Circle. A core tenet of the Vienna Circle was the verificationist theory of truth—the truth value of a statement was whether it was amenable to verification; statements that had no means of verification were not meaningful and, therefore, had no truth value. Translated into a scientific setting, the validity of a measurement was the way it was formulated or operationalized and the resulting experimental evidence associated with the resulting scores. Unfortunately, this emphasis on the operational definition of constructs led to a proliferation of constructs. Different ways of operationalizing a particular construct—whether it was rather abstract, like intelligence, or more concrete, such as hunger—resulted in different constructs, and different constructs might obey rather different psychological laws.

The third and most mature phase of work on construct validity—the *formal operational* phase—began officially with the publication of the seminal paper by Cronbach and Meehl (1955), which was an outgrowth of work by a committee of the American Psychological Association. Once again, however, this phase had a transition, with an earlier paper by MacCorquodale and Meehl (1948) on the distinction between hypothetical constructs and intervening variables being a clear precursor of the later, more celebrated, paper by Cronbach and Meehl (1955). MacCorquodale and Meehl argued for a distinction between two types of concepts. Intervening variables are simply shorthand verbal labels for objective phenomena or results, and the meaning of an intervening variable is shown by the empirical relations exhibited by the measurements and is limited by these relations. In contrast, hypothetical constructs imply certain forms of empirical relations, but they imply something beyond those empirical relations—some unseen processes that underlie the empirical relations. This idea about hypothetical constructs propounded by MacCorquodale and Meehl is quite consistent with the modern view of constructs and their validity.

One outcome of the continuing concerns about intervening variables and hypothetical constructs was the formation of a working group by the American Psychological Association headed by Cronbach and Meehl. The most well-known product of this working group was the statement by Cronbach and Meehl (1955) of the nature of construct validity, outlining the idea of construct validity and the various ways of investigating it. With this publication, the field entered the modern era, and the stage was set for future developments, such as validation using the multitrait–multimethod matrix (Campbell & Fiske, 1959) and reformulations of the nature of construct validity by Messick and others, described in the next section (see also American Educational Research Association et al., 2014).

Components of Construct Validity

Validity has been organized in several different ways, with *content validity*, *criterion-related validity*, and *construct validity* as the most prominent.

In 1995, Messick argued that all forms of validity fell under the umbrella of construct validity, and that construct validity had six facets: (a) content relevance and representation, (b) substantive theories underlying the sampling of domain tasks, (c) scoring models and their relation to domain structure, (d) generalizability and the boundaries of score meaning, (e) convergent and discriminant validity with external variables, and (f) consequences of validation evidence. The 2014 Standards for Educational and Psychological Testing organized validity evidence into five categories including evidence based on (a) test content, (b) response processes, (c) internal structure, (d) relations with other variables, and (e) consequences of testing.

In this chapter, we consider construct validity a multifaceted process revolving around two major axes. Following McArdle and Prescott (1992), the two major axes are *internal validity* and *external validity*. Similar to internal and external validity of a study, internal validity of a test is focused primarily on relationships internal to the test, whereas external validity is focused primarily on relationships external to the test. Specifically, the focus of internal validity is placed on relations among items constituting the test—how participants' responses to items function as a whole or in groups. The focus of external validity, on the other hand, is placed on relations of test scores with external criteria.

Internal validity can be part of determining whether test items measure the intended construct. However, common statistical approaches to examining internal validity (e.g., classical notions of reliability) focus narrowly on whether test items measure a hypothetical construct, although not necessarily the construct the test is intended to measure. To circumnavigate this issue, theoretical expectations regarding dimensionality, strength of factor loadings, discrimination, difficulty, etc., are important parts of internal validity in helping to determine whether items represent the intended construct.

External validity, on the other hand, revolves around a test score's association with additional variables, including measures of the same construct, measures of different constructs, and clinical diagnoses. The focus of external validity is placed on the extent to which the test measures the construct it is intended to measure. In this chapter, we consider external validity as having several components including criterion-related validity, composed of concurrent, predictive, and postdictive validity, as well as convergent and discriminant validity, change validity, score interpretation, and consequences.

Construct validity has also been organized around a set of goals or objectives, which is practical when taking on such an endeavor. The broad goal of construct validity is determining the extent to which the test measures the construct it is intended to measure (see Borsboom et al., 2004). However, recent treatments of validity (e.g., Messick, 1989) have focused on interpretations of test scores, and these can be considered two sides of construct validity. Examining internal and external validity is necessary for evaluating construct validity and both contribute, in different ways, to the broad goal of construct validity. Moreover, certain types of tests and test goals lend themselves to different evaluations of construct validity.

Internal validity is most applicable to the goal of determining the extent to which a test measures the construct it is intended to measure; however, external validity equally contributes to this endeavor. This objective can be seen as a more academic or research-oriented objective. A second objective is to determine the extent to which the interpretations and uses of test scores are appropriate. This objective relates more to the applied aspects of a test outside of a research setting and is closely aligned with evaluations of external validity. These objectives are strongly related to Embretson's (1983) construct representation and nomothetic span as well as Cronbach's (1971) two uses of tests: (a) making decisions about the person tested and (b) describing the person tested. These objectives are distinct, and evidence for one does not, in any way, provide evidence for the other. Both objectives are important to understanding construct validity of a test; however, one of the two objectives can take priority depending on the test purposes. For example, a primary use of the Scholastic Aptitude Test (SAT) is to predict freshman-year grade point average, so this objective should take priority over making sure the test measures writing, critical reading, and mathematics achievement.

INTERNAL VALIDITY

Internal validity of a test places the focus on the items that constitute the test and how they are theoretically derived, relate to each other, relate to the underlying construct(s), and whether they have the same meaning and difficulty for people with different background characteristics. These aspects of internal validity and methods for studying them are described next.

Content Validity

Content validity begins in the design phase of a psychological test. The creation of a psychological test or any test designed to generalize to a larger set of behaviors, occasions, situations, etc., should begin with precise definitions of the construct the test is intended to measure, the test's objectives, proposed uses of the test scores, as well as the range of abilities, attitudes, feelings, and attributes the test is supposed to cover and the population of individuals to whom the test is administered. Once these questions are answered, items are written to capture the underlying construct. In a sense, test makers attempt to build validity into the test (Anastasi, 1986).

Take, for example, the development of a child behavior scale. In this scale development project, we must first define the construct whether it be general behavior, behavior problems, and/or positive behaviors. Furthermore, we need to specify how finely or precisely we want to define our construct—is it behavior problems, distinct aspects of behavior problems such as externalizing and internalizing behavior problems, or even more specific aspects of externalizing and internalizing behaviors such as aggressive behaviors and withdrawal? Once the underlying construct is specified, we need to consider the objectives or goals for the test. Is it to distinguish between children who have clinical (exceptionally high) levels of behavior problems from children with normative levels of behavior problems; is it to measure accurately children along a continuum from little or no behavior problems up to high levels of behavior problems? These objectives may not be mutually exclusive; however, different objectives can change what items should be included in the scale. These objectives also lead to different uses of the scores obtained from the scale. Next, the population of children needs to be specified. The types of behavior problems that young children show differ markedly from the types of behavior problems that adolescents exhibit. If the scale is designed to be appropriate for young children and adolescents, then the scale needs to contain items appropriate for each age level, which may be weighted differentially based on age.

In the evaluation of content validity, no falsifiable statistical model is available, which has led some researchers to suggest content validity should not be used to defend a scale (Messick, 1975) because the evaluation is based on judgments, much like the scale development process (Shepard, 1993). A test developer must be able to defend whether the construct is appropriate, whether or not the items appropriately sample the construct, and whether the items are appropriate given the scale objectives and intended population. Usually, content validity is evaluated by a panel of "expert" judges. Expert is contained within quotes to indicate the term is sometimes used loosely, as expert judges may strongly disagree on certain aspects of scale.

Lawshe (1975) proposed a rater-agreement method to measure content validity in the job performance domain. In this method, each item was rated by a panel of expert judges on the degree to which the skill measured by the item was essential to job performance. Judges' ratings were made using a 3-point scale—(a) "essential," (b) "useful, but not essential," and (c) "not necessary." Lawshe suggested that if the majority of judges indicate the item is "essential," then the item has some degree of content validity and higher levels of content validity exist when a higher percentage of judges rate the item as "essential." Lawshe developed the *content validity ratio* (CVR) for each item, defined as

$$CVR = \frac{n_e - N/2}{N/2}, \qquad (35.1)$$

where n_e is the number of judges indicating the item is "essential" and N is the total number of judges. This formula yields values ranging from -1 to $+1$, where positive CVRs indicate at least half of the judges indicated the item is "essential." The mean CVR across items is a measure of the content validity of the scale. This method may be more difficult to implement with scales designed to measure psychological constructs because psychological constructs may not be as closely tied to observable behaviors such as those that occur in narrowly defined situations, such as job performance.

Another potential issue for this approach for psychological scales is that the construct the test measures may become too narrowly defined, which may make the test, in the end, less representative of the range of behaviors the construct defines and, thus, less valid. The issue of item selection is important, and there are several ways to approach this issue (e.g., Little et al., 1999).

Dimensionality

A first question once data are collected from a psychological test regards the dimensionality of the items. Often, the question is whether or not test items constitute a unidimensional scale. However, the main question is whether the theoretical dimensionality of the scale is supported. If so, a second step is checking whether items designed to measure each dimension do so in expected ways. If so, a third step is evaluating the degree of association between the various dimensions and whether the test dimensions relate in expected ways. If the theoretical dimensionality is not supported, the question turns to how many and what dimensions are assessed and how the items relate to each dimension. Once dimensionality is determined, additional aspects of internal validity can be studied, which include deeper assessments of item performance using item response methods (e.g., Embretson, 1983) to understand reliability, determinants of item performance, and item bias.

The study of dimensionality of a set of items is best studied with item factor analysis (see Chapter 36, this volume; Wirth & Edwards, 2007, for reviews). There are several types of item factor models, which are also referred to as (multidimensional) item response models (depending on the context of the model's derivation; see Chapter 37, this volume). The various types of models depend on the response type (e.g., ordered polytomous responses, dichotomous responses, or unordered polytomous responses), whether guessing is modeled, and desired model properties. All models, however, can be considered variants of the general item factor analytic framework (Thissen & Steinberg, 1986; Wirth & Edwards, 2007). Here, we describe two basic models often applied in psychological research. The first model is appropriate for dichotomous responses, such as cognitive items scored correct or incorrect, and the second is appropriate for ordered polytomous responses, such as rating scale items scored 0, 1, 2 for "never," "sometimes," and "often," respectively, and other scales that employ Likert-type response formats. Furthermore, these models are described in two frameworks—structural equation modeling (confirmatory factor model) and item response modeling; however, it is important to note that the two contexts can lead to functionally equivalent models.

Item Analysis Approaches

Item factor analysis models. In describing these models, we begin with dichotomous responses (e.g., incorrect/correct; disagree/agree) using the *probit* link specification, which is commonly employed in the structural modeling framework (Muthén, 1978). The factor analysis model for dichotomous responses can been viewed as having two parts. The first part relates the dichotomous response to a latent response distribution, an underlying continuous and normally distributed response propensity for each item, and the second part relates latent response distributions to the common factors. In the first part of the model, individual i's (dichotomous) response to item j, denoted x_{ij}, is considered a manifestation of individual i's latent continuous response for item j, denoted x_{ij}^*. At the sample level, the proportion of individuals who endorse each response category provide information about the latent response's threshold parameters, τ, which segment the latent response distribution for each response category. Mathematically, this is written as

$$x_{ij} = \begin{cases} 0 \text{ if } x_{ij}^* < \tau \\ 1 \text{ if } x_{ij}^* > \tau \end{cases}, \qquad (35.2)$$

such that the manifest response equals 0 or 1 depending on whether the individual's score on the latent response distribution is less than or greater than τ, respectively. Graphically, x_{ij}^* is considered to have a normal distribution and τ represents a location along this distribution. This relationship is depicted in Figure 35.1, where $\tau = .6$ suggesting that 27.4% of individuals endorsed the item (scored 1) and 72.6% did not endorse the item (scored 0). The threshold, therefore, provides information regarding how difficult the item was to endorse or answer correctly.

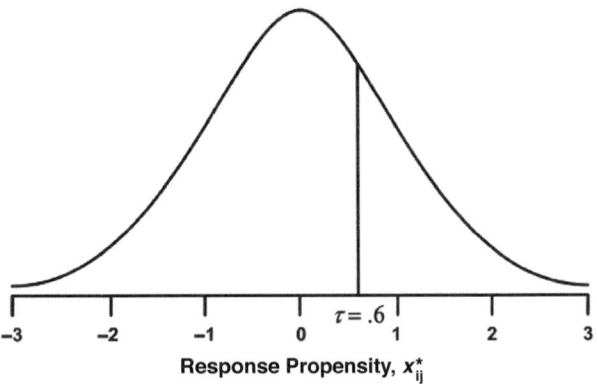

FIGURE 35.1. Representation of the relation between the latent response propensity and the observed response for a dichotomous item with a single threshold, τ.

The second part of the model relates latent response distributions to the common factors, such that

$$x_{ij}^* = \lambda_{j1}\eta_{1i} + \lambda_{j2}\eta_{2i} + \ldots + \lambda_{jk}\eta_{ki} + u_{ij}, \quad (35.3)$$

where λ_{jk} is the factor loading for the jth item on the kth factor, η_{ki} is the kth factor score for the ith individual, and u_{ij} is a residual for individual i's response to item j. The common factor model in Equation 35.3 can be written in matrix form as

$$\mathbf{x}_i^* = \mathbf{\Lambda}\boldsymbol{\eta}_i + \mathbf{u}_i, \quad (35.4)$$

where $\mathbf{x}_i^*$ is a $J \times 1$ vector of latent response propensities for individual i, $\mathbf{\Lambda}$ is a $J \times K$ matrix of factor loadings, $\boldsymbol{\eta}_i$ is $K \times 1$ vector of common factor scores for individual i, and $\mathbf{u}_i$ is a $J \times 1$ vector of residuals scores for individual i.

The population covariance matrix for the item factor analysis model is

$$\mathbf{\Sigma}_{xx}^* = \mathbf{\Lambda}\mathbf{\Phi}\mathbf{\Lambda}' + \mathbf{\Theta}, \quad (35.5)$$

where $\mathbf{\Sigma}_{xx}^*$ is a $J \times J$ matrix of population covariances between item response propensities (tetrachoric/polychoric correlations), $\mathbf{\Lambda}$ is a $J \times K$ matrix of factor loadings, $\mathbf{\Phi}$ is a $K \times K$ matrix of common factor covariances, and $\mathbf{\Theta}$ is a $J \times J$ matrix of unique factor variances and covariances, which is often specified to be an identity matrix. The $\mathbf{\Theta}$ matrix is often specified to be diagonal, which forces the item covariances to be accounted for by the common factor(s).

If the items are well represented by the common factor model, then the main questions addressed by the item factor analysis model are (a) the number of dimensions needed to adequately represent item correlations, (b) which items load onto which factor, (c) the strength of the associations between items and common factors (with standardized factor loadings of .4, .6, and .8 representing relatively low, medium, and high levels of communality, respectively), and (d) the magnitude and direction of associations among common factors. Often, a goal of test developers is to measure a single construct, and, therefore, they want to determine whether a single dimension underlies item responses. In certain situations, test developers may remove items that are more closely related to a secondary dimension, loosely related to the dominant factor, and/or multidimensional. However, this practice may limit the generalizability and validity of the measuring instrument by making the test's representation of the construct too narrowly defined. Little et al. (1999) discussed how some of these practices, while increasing estimates of reliability, decrease factor representation.

The item factor analysis model can be extended to model ordered polytomous responses (e.g., rating scales), often used in psychology, by means of invoking additional thresholds parameters that relate multiple categorical responses to the latent response propensity. For example, items with three response options (e.g., 0, 1, 2) have two thresholds (τ_1 and τ_2) to separate response categories. This relationship between the latent response distribution and a three-category item is depicted in Figure 35.2 and written as

$$x_{ij} = \begin{cases} 1 \text{ if } x_{ij}^* < \tau_1 \\ 2 \text{ if } \tau_1 < x_{ij}^* < \tau_2 \\ 3 \text{ if } x_{ij}^* > \tau_2 \end{cases}. \quad (35.6)$$

It is important to note that this relationship is considered a *cumulative response process* whereby

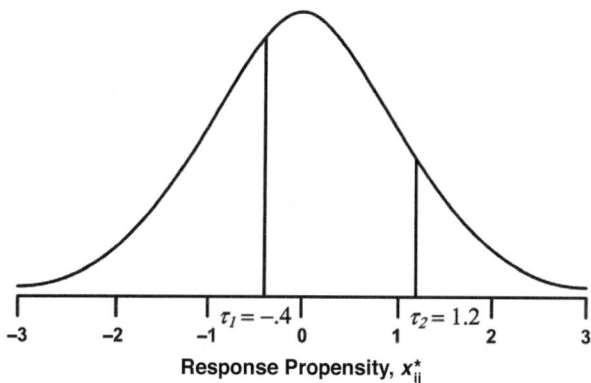

FIGURE 35.2. Representation of the relation between the latent response propensity and the observed response for a three-category item with two thresholds, τ_1 and τ_2.

each threshold distinguishes between responding at or below a given category versus above that category. This is opposed to an *adjacent response process* whereby the comparison is between two adjacent categories and conditioned on responding in one of those two response categories. In the cumulative model, all category responses aid in the estimation of the threshold parameters.

Item response models. The next series of models we describe were developed specifically to model item responses and come from the historical perspective of item response theory. More recently, these models have been shown to be quite similar to the models described earlier (Kamata & Bauer, 2008; Reise et al., 1993) with a constraint on the number of dimensions (e.g., one). However, models described here can and have been expanded to include multiple dimensions. Moreover, the item factor models described above can be specified using the logit link function as opposed to the probit link function and specified to be identical.

Again, we begin with a model appropriate for dichotomous item responses before presenting a model that can handle polytomous responses. The first item response model we describe is the two-parameter logistic model (2PLM), which models the probability of one of the two categories. Assuming a variable is coded 0/1, the two-parameter logistic model is written as

$$P(x_{ij}=1|\theta_i,\alpha_j,\beta_j)=\frac{\exp(\alpha_j(\theta_i-\beta_j))}{1+\exp(\alpha_j(\theta_i-\beta_j))}, \quad (35.7)$$

where $P(x_{ij}=1|\theta_i,\alpha_j,\beta_j)$ is the probability of individual i responding in category 1 (compared to 0) for item j conditional on item and person parameters. Item parameters include α_j, the *discrimination* parameter, and β_j, the *location* parameter. The only person parameter is θ_i, individual i's latent trait. The discrimination parameter indicates the strength of the association between the item and latent trait, and the location parameter is the point on the latent trait where there is a 50% chance of responding in category 1. Figure 35.3 is a plot of three-item characteristic curves that vary with respect to their discrimination

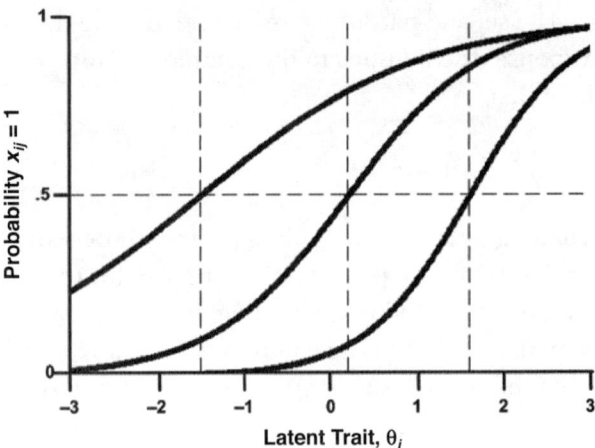

FIGURE 35.3. Item characteristic curve for a single item with $\alpha = 1$ and $\beta = 0$. Probability of endorsement is on the y-axis, and the latent trait is on the x-axis.

($\alpha_j = 0.8$, 1.3, and 1.7) and location ($\beta_j = -1.5$, 0.2, and 1.6) parameters. The midpoint of items with higher location parameters appears farther to the right, indicating a higher trait level is needed to have a 50% change of responding in the higher category. Items with stronger discrimination parameters show sharper differences in the likelihood of responding in the higher category (steeper slopes).

When an equality constraint is placed on the discrimination parameters, the model reduces to the one-parameter logistic model or Rasch model (Rasch, 1960). Item parameters from Equation 35.7 map onto the factor loading and threshold parameters from the item factor analysis model described earlier and can be derived from one another (see Kamata & Bauer, 2008). Moreover, Equation 35.7 is sometimes written with the constant 1.7 within the exponent terms (i.e., $\frac{\exp(1.7\cdot\alpha_j(\theta_i-\beta_j))}{1+\exp(1.7\cdot\alpha_j(\theta_i-\beta_j))}$), which makes the parameters of the two-parameter logistic model approximately equal to the parameters that would be obtained when using the probit link.

Several item response models are appropriate for polytomous response scales. Commonly specified polytomous item response models for ordered responses include the partial credit model (PCM; Masters, 1982), the generalized PCM (Muraki, 1992), and the graded response model (GRM; Samejima, 1969). These models differ in the number of item parameters, the number and type of constraints on parameters, and whether the response process is modeled as cumulative or adjacent. These differences cause the models to have different measurement properties, which can lead test developers to prefer one model over another. Here, we present the GRM as it is one of the most general models for polytomous responses and often used in psychological research. The graded response model is written as

$$P(x_{ij} \geq c | \theta_i, \alpha_j, \beta_{jc}) = \frac{\exp(\alpha_j(\theta_i - \beta_{jc}))}{1 + \exp(\alpha_j(\theta_i - \beta_{jc}))}, \quad (35.8)$$

where $P(x_{ij} \geq c | \theta_i, \alpha_j, \beta_{jc})$ is the probability of responding in or above category c conditional on person and item parameters. As with the 2PLM, item parameters include α_j, a discrimination parameter, and β_{jc}, the location parameter separating category $c - 1$ from c, and the person parameter is θ_i, the latent trait. The probability of responding in a given category can be calculating by subtracting the probability of responding in or above category $c + 1$ from the probability of responding in or above category c.

In addition to the use of these models in assessing dimensionality, researchers should pay close attention to the absolute and relative size of item parameters. For example, the Center for Epidemiologic Studies–Depression scale (CES-D) has an item that directly asks the respondent how depressed he or she has felt. In an item analysis of the CES-D, it is logical to expect this item to have a strong discrimination parameter and one that is greater than that for any other item. This would indicate the scale is appropriately centered on the construct. Furthermore, items such as "feeling blue" and "feeling sad" would be expected to also have strong discrimination parameters, but not as strong as the "feeling depressed" item. These items may represent a second tier in the magnitude of discrimination parameters because they are closely related to the construct. A collection of expectations regarding the size of discrimination and location parameters can be useful in establishing internal validity. Additionally, metrics,

such as those proposed by Westen and Rosenthal (2003), are discussed later in the chapter and can be used to quantify how an expected pattern of discrimination and location parameters matches the observed patterns.

Reliability and test information. Once the construct space is appropriately understood in terms of dimensionality, the next question is how reliably each dimension is measured. Often, researchers estimate coefficient α to assess reliability. However, this view of reliability only assesses internal consistency, and heavy reliance on coefficient α can lead to item homogeneity and a lack of construct representation. Item response theory offers another approach to reliability and recognizes that a test does not have a single reliability, but reliability is a function of (a) the strength of associations between items and construct (α_j, λ_j) and (b) the distance between item difficulty (location) and person's latent trait ($\theta_i - \beta_j$). If the test is not well targeted to the population, scores obtained from the test will not adequately represent the person's latent trait. In item response theory, item and test information are used to determine the standard error of measurement. For the 2PLM, item information is calculated as

$$I_j(\theta) = \alpha_j^2 P(\theta)(1 - P(\theta)), \quad (35.9)$$

where $I_j(\theta)$ is item information for item j at a trait level of θ, α_j is the item discrimination parameter, and $P(\theta)$ is the probability of endorsing (responding correctly, scoring 1 versus 0) the item at a trait level of θ. It's important to note that item information varies as a function of θ, which leads to reliability depending on θ. Test information is simply the sum of the item information curves (if local independence holds),

$$I(\theta) = \sum_{j=1}^{J} I_j(\theta). \quad (35.10)$$

Finally, the standard error is the square root of the reciprocal of test information at a specific trait level,

$$SE(\theta) = 1/\sqrt{I(\theta)}. \quad (35.11)$$

In terms of validity, it is important to know how reliability varies as a function of trait level—for a test to be valid, it should demonstrate adequate reliability for the range of trait levels assessed.

Measurement invariance and differential item functioning. Another important aspect of internal validity is whether items show any bias, whether it be related to gender, ethnicity, English language learner status, etc. The examination of item, and thus test, bias is a question of whether item parameters are invariant for people of different groups, controlling for trait level. In the structural modeling framework, this is referred to as a question of measurement or factorial invariance (Meredith, 1964, 1965, 1993; Meredith & Horn, 2001; Widaman & Reise, 1997) and in item response theory it is referred to as a question of differential item functioning (Thissen et al., 1986). Both the structural equation modeling and item response theory frameworks are appropriate for examining item and test bias. However, structural equation modeling and item response theory approaches to studying measurement invariance often proceed in different ways. In either framework, multiple analytic techniques for studying measurement invariance can be used (see Woods, 2009), and we briefly describe the multiple group method here because of its common usage and refer readers to Bauer (2017), Muthén (1985), Muthén and Lehman (1985), Woods (2009), Woods and Grimm (2011) for more in-depth discussions of alternative approaches.

A major analytic technique for studying measurement invariance is the multiple group approach where the data are separated in two (or more) nonoverlapping (mutually exclusive) groups and the item factor analysis model or item response model is fit to the data for each group. Researchers familiar with structural equation modeling often take an entire-test-based approach and begin with separately estimating all item parameters and identifying the model by fixing the mean and variance of the latent factor to 0 and 1, respectively. In the next model, factor loadings, Λ, are constrained to be equal over groups and the factor variance is estimated for all the groups except the first in the *weak* factorial invariance model. The fit of the *weak* (also known as the *metric*) invariance model is compared with the *baseline* (also known as the *configurally invariant*) model. If the fit of the weak invariance model does not fit significantly worse than the baseline model, then the process is continued. Next, item thresholds, τ, are constrained to be equal over groups and the factor mean is estimated for all the groups except the first in the *strong* (also known as the *scalar*) invariance model. The fit of the strong invariance model is compared to the fit of the weak invariance model. If the strong invariance model does not fit significantly worse than the weak invariance model, then the items do not show bias with respect to the grouping variable. If the comparisons of the weak and baseline or strong and weak invariance models lead to significant differences in model fit, then a more in-depth evaluation of the sources of noninvariance are studied and partial invariance models are considered. Occasionally, *strict* invariance, the invariance of residual variances, is examined at the item level; however, at the item level this investigation can lead to estimation issues and does not provide information regarding item or test bias. Strong invariance (invariance of loadings and thresholds) is needed to indicate that the item is not biased with respect to the grouping variable.

Researchers familiar with item response theory often take an item-by-item approach. The approach is initiated by fitting models for each group where discrimination and location parameters are constrained to be equal for all items and the mean and variance of θ_i are separately estimated for each group. This is considered the *invariance* model because all item parameters are equated across groups. Then, on an item-by-item basis, the discrimination and location parameters, referred to as the *target* item, are separately estimated for each group. The fit of this *alternative* model is compared with the fit of the invariance model. This process is repeated with each item serving as the *target* item. If the difference in model fit is significant, this is noted because the item *may* show bias. The goal of this procedure is to determine the *anchor items*—items whose parameters are invariant over groups. This process is iterative as all items are examined. If the fit of the alternative and invariance models is significant for multiple items, then the target item that led to the largest improvement in fit is set aside and the process is repeated until a set of anchor items is determined. Once the anchor items are determined, item parameters for all potentially biased items are reexamined for a lack of invariance with respect to the set of anchor items. If the alternative model fits significantly better than the invariance model, then the item parameters are examined separately to see if the discrimination and/or location parameter(s) are the source of the change in model fit. If the location parameter is the only source of the difference in model fit, then the item is said to show *uniform* differential item functioning. If the discrimination parameter is a source of the difference in model fit, then the item is said to show *nonuniform* differential item functioning.

Uniform differential item functioning indicates an item is universally easier (or harder depending on the direction of the group difference) to endorse (answer correctly) for one of the groups controlling for trait level. Figure 35.4A contains two-item characteristic curves from a reference and focal group for an item that shows uniform differential item functioning. As seen in this figure, a member of the focal group always needs a higher latent trait score (θ) to have the same probability of correctly responding (or agreeing) to the item as a member from the reference group. Nonuniform differential item functioning indicates that the item is easier at certain levels of θ and harder for others. Figure 35.4B contains two-item characteristic curves for an item that shows nonuniform differential item functioning. As seen in this figure, for lower values of θ, the reference group is more likely to correctly respond controlling for θ; however, for higher values of θ, the focal group is more likely to correctly respond controlling for θ. As with the factor analytic approach, the discrimination and location parameters need to be equal across groups to indicate that the item is not biased with respect to the grouping variable.

EXTERNAL VALIDITY

External validity of a test places the focus on a test score's association with additional variables including measures of the same construct, measures of different constructs, and clinical diagnoses. These associations provide information regarding whether the test measures the construct it is intended to measure and begins to examine the appropriateness of test score interpretations. Strong theoretical notions regarding expected associations are necessary for external validity to be demonstrated. We consider external validity as having several components including criterion-related validity, which is composed of concurrent, predictive, and postdictive validity, convergent and discriminant validity, change validity, as well as thorough examinations of the interpretations and consequences of test scores. We describe each of these components and how they can be studied.

Criterion-Related Validity

Criterion-related validity is the degree to which scores from the test under examination correlate in expected ways with a network of measures that have previously been validated. When examining criterion-related validity, it is important for criteria to have been previously validated and for researchers to know the degree of validity the criteria have demonstrated.

Criterion-related validity is composed of concurrent validity, predictive validity, and postdictive validity. Differences between them simply relate to when the criteria are taken. Correlations with criteria measured at the same time as the test under examination provide information regarding concurrent validity, correlations with criteria measured at some time in the future provide information regarding predictive validity, and correlations with criteria measured at some time in the past provide information regarding postdictive validity. When examining criterion-related validity, researchers often correlate the test under examination with a

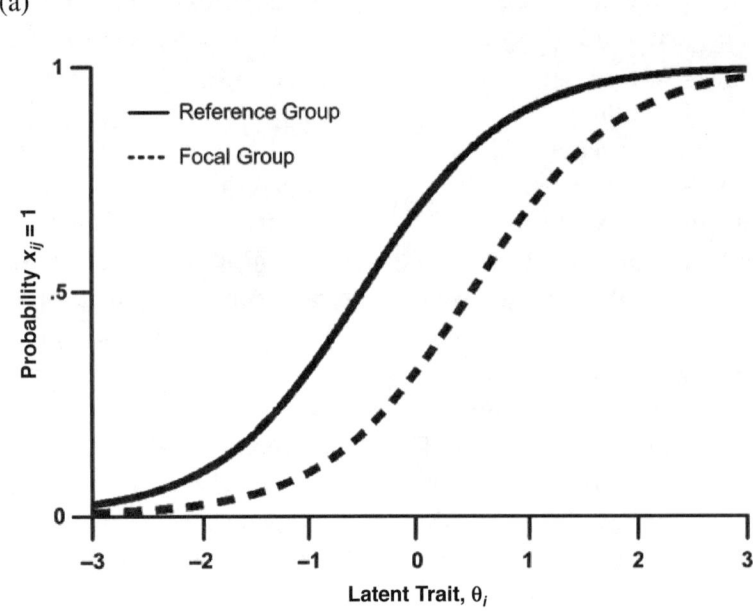

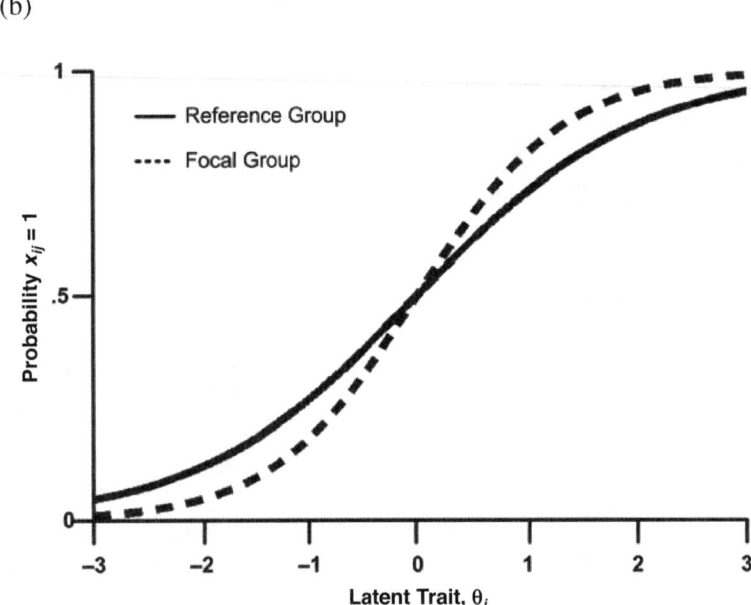

FIGURE 35.4. Item characteristic curves for an item with uniform differential item functioning (a) and nonuniform differential item functioning (b).

variety of measures that are expected to show a range of correlations—strong positive, weak positive, zero, weak negative, and strong negative. If the test correlates in expected ways with criteria then validity is demonstrated. However, it can be difficult to determine the degree of validity because test developers and researchers are often less-than-specific regarding the size of expected correlations. We propose some guidelines regarding the expected size of correlations and highlight Westen and Rosenthal's (2003) work on construct validity.

Theory often leads to expected correlations with criteria, and we agree that this should be the driving force. However, at the same time, it is important to have certain universal standards.

For example, in a given domain of research, investigators may argue that measures of the same construct should correlate at least .60 with one another; measures designed to measure different, but related, constructs should have correlations that range from .30 to .50. When testing whether the test correlates with additional variables in expected ways, it is important to specifically test whether the obtained correlation is significantly different from the expected correlation (as opposed to 0), and if so, by how much. In these cases, distance measures may be useful (see Westen & Rosenthal, 2003).

Westen and Rosenthal (2003) proposed two measures, based on the pattern of expected and obtained correlations, to quantify construct validity. The first measure, termed $r_{alerting\text{-}CV}$, is calculated as the correlation between expected and obtained correlations. Westen and Rosenthal noted that more accurate results can be obtained by first transforming expected and observed correlations into their *Fisher Z* equivalents. For example, if we are examining the external validity of a new measure of externalizing behavior, we might collect six additional measures for validation purposes. We expect the externalizing behavior measure to correlate with our criteria as follows (a) .60 with Child Behavior Checklist Externalizing, (b) .30 with Child Behavior Checklist Internalizing, (c) .10 with depression, (d) –.20 with nonverbal intelligence, (e) –.30 with teacher-rated academic skills, and (f) –.50 with Social Skills Rating System Cooperation. Data are then obtained and the following correlation pattern is found: (a) .40 with Child Behavior Checklist Externalizing, (b) .30 with Child Behavior Checklist Internalizing, (c) .30 with depression, (d) –.30 with nonverbal intelligence, (e) –.40 with teacher-rated academic skills, and (f) –.40 with Social Skills Rating System Cooperation. These correlations are then transformed into their Fisher Z equivalents and correlated. The resultant is the $r_{alerting\text{-}CV}$ and is .92. This value suggests that there is a good match between expected and obtained correlations. As more criterion variables are collected, $r_{alerting\text{-}CV}$ becomes more stable and, therefore, a more reliable index of criterion-related validity. One drawback of $r_{alerting\text{-}CV}$ is that the focus is on relative, not absolute, magnitudes of expected and observed correlations. For example, if the observed correlations in our example changed by –.20, then $r_{alerting\text{-}CV}$ would remain high even though the expected and observed correlations would be quite different. However, a distance measure would increase. This highlights why several measures should be used to assess validity.

The second index Westen and Rosenthal (2003) proposed is termed $r_{contrast\text{-}CV}$ and, like $r_{alerting\text{-}CV}$, is based on the match between the expected and observed correlations, but also includes information about the median intercorrelation among criteria and the absolute values of the correlations between the validating test and criterion measures. This measure is not described in detail here, and we refer readers to Rosenthal et al. (2000) and Westen and Rosenthal (2003) for details.

Convergent and Discriminant Validity

Convergent and discriminant validity are aspects of external validity and criterion-based validity whereby the test under examination is expected to correlate highly with measures of the same construct and not correlate highly with measures of different constructs. Campbell and Fiske (1959) presented a method for examining convergent and discriminant validity via the *multitrait-multimethod* (MTMM) *design*. An MTMM design is when multiple traits are assessed with multiple methods of data collection. This design can be very informative in psychology because many constructs can be assessed with a variety of assessment methods and the various methods of assessment may influence scores. For example, when attempting to measure externalizing behaviors, it is useful to observe the child at home and at school as well as ask their parents, teacher, friend's mother, and caregiver to complete questionnaires. These various methods of assessing the child's level of externalizing behavior are likely to show a degree of similarity because they are measures of externalizing behavior and show differences due to the method of assessment, the respondent making the ratings, and/or context of assessment. Differences due to the method and/or context of assessment can lead to biased correlations with additional variables depending on whether or not the additional variables share the method and/or context of assessment. When multiple traits are crossed with multiple methods of assessment, variability associated with the method and/or context can be accounted for and removed when examining relations among the traits.

Campbell and Fiske (1959) discussed how a systematic exploration of a correlation matrix derived from MTMM data can provide information regarding convergent and discriminant validity, and method effects. The correlation matrix from MTMM data can be decomposed into sections reflecting various combinations of traits and methods: monotrait-heteromethod, heterotrait-heteromethod, heterotrait-monomethod, and monotrait-monomethod. *Monotrait-heteromethod correlations* are obtained from measures of a given trait obtained from multiple methods; *heterotrait-heteromethod correlations* are obtained from different traits measured by different methods; *heterotrait-monomethod correlations* are obtained from different traits measured by a single method; and *monotrait-monomethod correlations* are reliability estimates. Comparisons between these configurations of correlations are used to examine convergent and discriminant validity, and evaluate method related variance in the observed scores. Specifically, convergent validity is shown by strong monotrait-heteromethod correlations; discriminant validity is shown by weak heterotrait-heteromethod correlations, and method effects are indicated by strong heterotrait-monomethod correlations.

Since Campbell and Fiske (1959) proposed the MTMM design, several statistical methods have been proposed to analyze MTMM data to supplement Campbell and Fiske's correlation comparison approach; include the analysis of variance, principal components analysis, and confirmatory factor models. Currently, confirmatory factor models are the most commonly utilized analytic technique and include various specifications including the correlated trait-correlated uniqueness (CT-CU) model (Marsh et al., 1992; Marsh & Grayson, 1995), correlated trait-correlated method (CT-CM) model (Kenny & Kashy; 1992; Marsh & Hocevar, 1983, Widaman, 1985), correlated trait-correlated method minus one (CT-C[M-1]) model (Eid, 2000), and direct product model (Browne, 1984; Cudeck, 1988; Wothke & Browne, 1990). Each of these models has benefits and drawbacks (Lance et al., 2002); however, we focus on the CT-CM model because of its common use, intuitive appeal, and because traits and methods are directly modeled with latent factors (Grimm, Pianta, & Konold, 2009).

The CT-CM model is a confirmatory factor model with trait, method, and unique factors. Trait factors are indicated by monotrait-heteromethod variables and method factors are indicated by heterotrait-monomethod variables. In a CT-CM model, trait factors covary with one another and method factors covary with one another, but trait factors are independent from method factors for identification purposes (Grayson & Marsh, 1994; Widaman, 1985). Unique factors account for variability that remains unexplained by trait and method factors. A CT-CM model with M methods and T traits can be written as

$$\mathbf{y}_i = \mathbf{\Lambda}_t \mathbf{\eta}_{ti} + \mathbf{\Lambda}_m \mathbf{\eta}_{mi} + \mathbf{u}_i, \qquad (35.12)$$

where $\mathbf{y}_i$ is an $MT \times 1$ vector of observed scores for individual i, $\mathbf{\Lambda}_t$ is an $MT \times T$ matrix of *trait* factor loadings, $\mathbf{\eta}_{ti}$ is a $T \times 1$ vector of latent *trait* factor scores for individual i, $\mathbf{\Lambda}_m$ is an $MT \times M$ matrix of *method* factor loadings, $\mathbf{\eta}_{mi}$ is an $M \times 1$ vector of latent *method* factor scores for individual i, and $\mathbf{u}_i$ is an $MT \times 1$ vector of residual scores for individual i.

The population covariance structure ($\mathbf{\Sigma}$) of the observed data is written as

$$\mathbf{\Sigma} = \mathbf{\Lambda}_t \mathbf{\Phi}_t \mathbf{\Lambda}_t' + \mathbf{\Lambda}_m \mathbf{\Phi}_m \mathbf{\Lambda}_m' + \mathbf{\Theta}, \qquad (35.13)$$

where $\mathbf{\Sigma}$ is an $MT \times MT$ population covariance matrix, $\mathbf{\Phi}_t$ is a $T \times T$ latent variable covariance matrix for the *trait* factors, $\mathbf{\Phi}_m$ is an $M \times M$ latent variable covariance matrix for the *method* factors, and $\mathbf{\Theta}$ is an $MT \times MT$ matrix of unique factor covariances. Figure 35.5 is a path diagram of the CT-CM model with three traits (internalizing, externalizing, and attention problems) and three methods or informants (self, mother, and father). In the CT-CM model, convergent validity is shown by strong trait factor loadings; discriminant validity is shown by weak trait factor correlations; and strong method factor loadings indicate that method effects are contaminating observed scores (Widaman, 1985).

CT-CM models have been fit to a variety of psychological measures, and many measures have shown considerable amounts of method variance, especially measures that rely on self- and other-reports (e.g., Grimm et al., 2009; Konold & Pianta, 2007). Indeed, measures occasionally show more method variance than trait variance. For example, in a longitudinal study of behavior changes during elementary school, Grimm et al. (2009) analyzed data from the National Institute of Child Health and Human Development's Study of Early Child Care and Youth Development. The institute's data included reports of child behavior by the child's mother, father, and teacher in first, third, fourth,

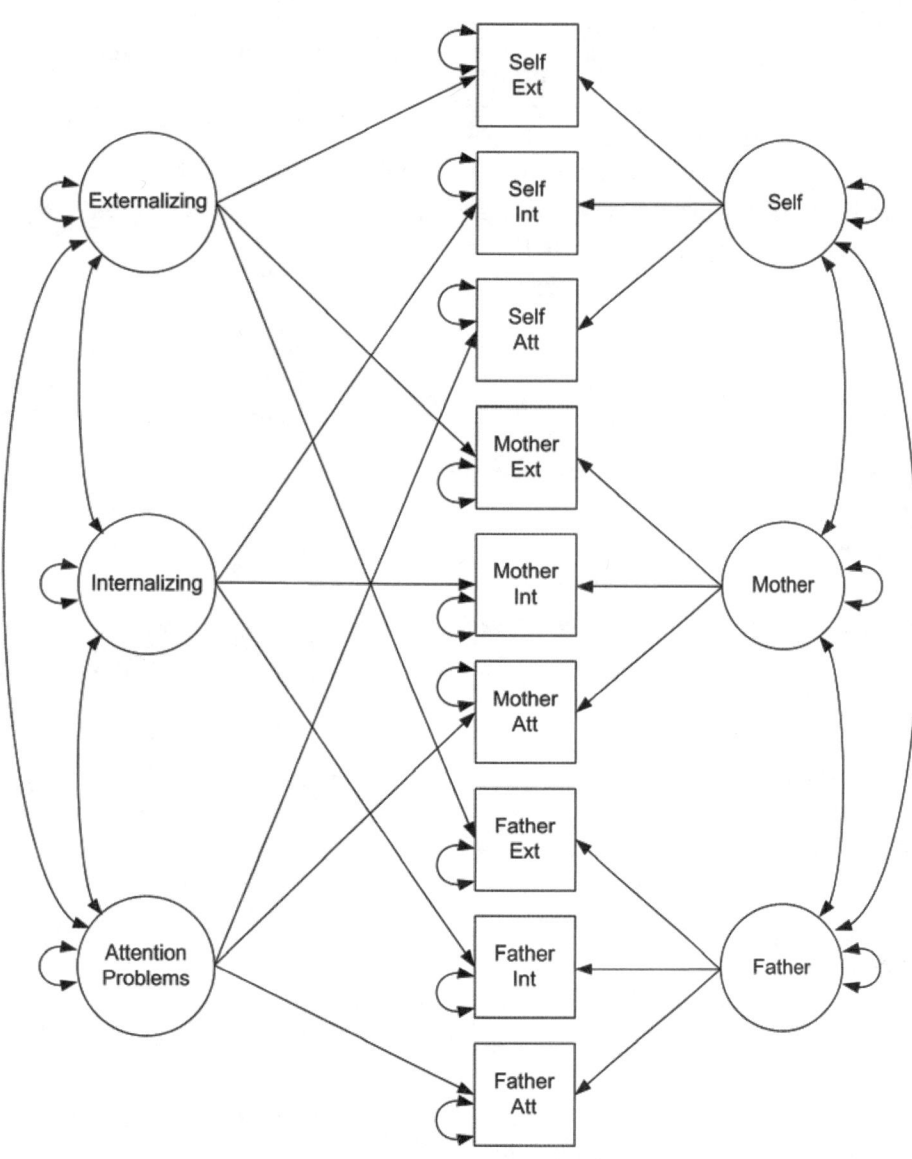

FIGURE 35.5. Path diagram of a correlated-trait correlated-method model with three traits and three methods or informants.

and fifth grades. Grimm et al. (2009) fit a longitudinal CT-CM model and found that 4% to 74% of the observed variance in child behavior ratings was related to the informant who completed the form, whereas 9% to 55% of the variance was associated with the trait being assessed.

The CT-CM factor model, along with other MTMM confirmatory factor models, can be embedded into analytic models to account for method variance and yield unbiased estimates of associations between traits and additional variables. For example, analyses conducted for Grimm et al. (2009), but not presented, included a series of child, mother, and father variables as predictors of the trait and method factors. Maternal depression, while predictive of children's behavior problems, also significantly predicted the mother method factor. Similarly, paternal depression was predictive of the father factor in addition to children's behavior problems. These results suggest that parental depression skewed their view of the child's level of behavior problems.

Change

Cronbach and Meehl (1955) discussed studying the change aspect of construct validity, but this has often been overlooked when examining construct validity. The way observed test scores change over time for the same individual should match theoretical notions regarding how the construct is expected to change (Grimm et al., 2011). Studying change requires theoretical notions regarding specific aspects of change, such as timing, tempo, acceleration, transitions, and asymptotes, as well as how these aspects are expected to vary over persons (Ram & Grimm, 2007). For example, many aspects of academic achievement follow elongated S-shaped developmental patterns that can be approximated by logistic, Gompertz, and Richards growth curves (Choi et al., 2009; Grimm & Ram, 2009). Measures of academic achievement that do not follow the predicted pattern of changes may lack construct validity related to change processes.

Change can be systematically examined using latent growth curves (McArdle & Epstein, 1987; Meredith & Tisak, 1990). Latent growth curves allow for modeling within-person change and between-person differences in change. Growth curves can be structured to take on many functional forms (e.g., linear and exponential), which describe specific patterns of change over time, and, as such, offer developmentalists a collection of models useful for testing specific hypotheses about change (Burchinal & Appelbaum, 1991). Growth curves can be fit in the structural modeling and multilevel modeling frameworks (Ferrer et al., 2004), each framework has its advantages and disadvantages (Ghisletta & Lindenberger, 2004), and mathematically identical models can be specified in each framework. As a structural model, the latent growth curve is specified as a restricted common factor model, which can be written as

$$\mathbf{y}_i = \mathbf{\Lambda}\mathbf{\eta}_i + \mathbf{u}_i, \quad (35.14)$$

where $\mathbf{y}_i$ is a $P \times 1$ vector of repeated measurements of variable y for individual i, $\mathbf{\Lambda}$ is a $P \times Q$ matrix of factor loadings, $\mathbf{\eta}_i$ is a $Q \times 1$ vector of latent factor scores, and $\mathbf{u}_i$ is a $P \times 1$ vector of unique variances. Latent factor scores are composed of sample-level means and individual deviations written as

$$\mathbf{\eta}_i = \mathbf{\alpha} + \mathbf{\zeta}_i, \quad (35.15)$$

where $\mathbf{\alpha}$ is a $Q \times 1$ vector of latent factor means and $\mathbf{\zeta}_i$ is a $Q \times 1$ vector of latent factor mean deviations. Specific hypotheses are tested by placing constraints on the $\mathbf{\Lambda}$ matrix, where the pattern of changes is structured. For example, a linear change model is specified by placing 1s in the first column of $\mathbf{\Lambda}$ to define the intercept and by placing linearly changing values in the second column to define the linear slope. Various constraints on the $\mathbf{\Lambda}$ matrix allow researchers to test specific expectations regarding how the change process unfolds, which can be used to evaluate change validity.

Interpretations and Implications of Test Scores

Much of the recent work on validity has focused on interpretations and implications of test scores.

It is often said that one does not validate a test, rather one validates the interpretations of test scores, which can have many implications. Test interpretations and the decisions based on those interpretations are the most far reaching aspect of validity because of their effect on people's lives. Important decisions are based on psychological and other types of tests. Examples include the use of intelligence tests to help determine whether a defendant is able to stand trial, the use of SAT scores to help determine college admissions, and a self-report depression measure to help determine whether a person should be referred for clinical help. We used the term *help determine* because most decisions are multifaceted; however, it is important to note that some important decisions are based almost entirely on a test score, such as state licensing exams.

In many cases, a criterion measure is categorical, such as a decision to be referred for additional services or a clinical diagnosis. Categorical criteria can be included to evaluate validity in the ways we previously discussed. Additional aspects of validity, however, should be examined when a test is used to make a yes-or-no decision (see Meehl & Rosen, 1955). For example, when validating a new measure of depression, it may be of interest to know what score best distinguishes between persons who are and are not diagnosed with depression.

Decision theory (Chernoff & Moses, 1959; Cronbach & Gleser, 1965; Meehl & Rosen, 1955) is a statistical framework for determining optimal cutoff scores that maximize prediction accuracy. To aid in this discussion, we provide simulated data partly based on empirical data on SAT scores and the likelihood of graduating from the University of California within 6 years. In the simulated data, we increased the strength of the association between SAT scores and the likelihood of graduation. This example is not ideal because admission decisions were partially based on the SAT, so we do not have a random sample of students who applied for admission and decided to attend the university, but a sample of students who had been accepted for admission and decided to attend.

Decision theory is largely based on logistic regression because the outcome is often dichotomous (e.g., graduation status or referral for special services). However, logistic regression alone does not provide information regarding an optimal cutoff score. When decisions are made regarding an unobservable dichotomy (e.g., gold standard) based on an observed test score, four outcomes are possible—two correct decisions and two incorrect decisions. The two correct decisions are true positive and true negatives. In our SAT example, a true positive is when we decide to accept the student based on their SAT score and the student graduates. A true negative is when we decide to reject the student based on their SAT score and, if accepted, the student would not graduate. The two incorrect decisions are false positives and false negatives. A false positive is when we decide to accept the student based on their SAT score, but the student does not graduate. A false negative is when we decide to reject the student based on their SAT score, but, if accepted, the student would graduate. These decisions highlight why a random sample collected before any decision criteria were imposed is necessary for conducting decision theory.

In practice, we often want to maximize the likelihood of true positives and true negatives and minimize the likelihood of false positives and false negatives. However, there are situations in which false positives and false negatives are not created equal as certain mistakes are seen as more detrimental than others (often in terms of cost or opportunity). For example, denying a student admission to the University of California who would have graduated (false negative) may be seen as a greater mistake than admitting a student who would not graduate (false positive). When conducting decision theory analyses, one must consider the relative weighting of false positive and false negatives because, as we will show, it can have a large impact on the cutoff score.

Going back to our example, we fit a logistic regression model predicting the likelihood of graduating from the students' high school SAT score. In these analyses, SAT scores were rescaled (divided by 100) to range from 4 to 16. Thus, a 1-point change in the rescaled variable represents a 100-point change in the SAT. High school SAT was a significant predictor of graduation ($\chi^2(1) = 3,063$) accounting for a maximum rescaled R^2 of .30. The odds ratio for high school SAT was 2.17 suggesting that students were 2.17 times more likely to graduate for every 100-point change in their observed SAT score. Figure 35.6 is a plot of the predicted relationship between the high school SAT score and the probability of graduating. As seen in this figure, there is a strong positive relationship between high school SAT scores and the probability of graduating; however, this plot does not provide any information regarding an appropriate location for a cutoff score.

A classification table was then constructed for various levels of the predicted probability of graduating, estimated from the relationship between graduation status and SAT scores. The columns in this table include the number of correct and incorrect events (graduates) and nonevents (nongraduates) as well as several percentages including (a) overall accuracy, (b) sensitivity, (c) specificity, (d) false positives, and (e) false negatives. These values vary as a function of the cutoff score, and researchers may pay closer attention to certain classification indices based on the specific goals for test. Overall accuracy is the percent of correctly predicted events and nonevents divided by the total number of events and nonevents. Put another way, it is the number of true positives and true negatives divided by the total number of decisions. Sensitivity is the ratio of true positives to the number of actual positive events (true positives and false negatives) and is a measure of whether the cutoff score correctly identifies the positive occurrences (graduation). For example, granting admission to everyone who applied to the University of California is 100% sensitive because everyone who would have graduated was admitted. Specificity, on the other hand, is the ratio of true negatives to the total number of actual negative events (true negatives and false positives) and is a measure of how well the cutoff score correctly identifies the negative outcomes (nongraduation).

The SAT is the only predictor variable in our logistic regression. Thus, we can calculate the SAT score that relates directly to the predicted probability. This classification table is presented in Table 35.1 for predicted probabilities between 0 and 1 in increments of .10. The table has four columns that contain information regarding correct and incorrect events (graduates) and nonevents (nongraduates). A *correct event* is an individual who was predicted to graduate, based on the SAT cutoff, and did graduate. A *correct nonevent* is an individual who was predicted not to graduate and did not graduate. An *incorrect event* is an individual who was predicted to graduate and did not graduate. An *incorrect nonevent* is an individual who was predicted not to graduate but did graduate. As seen from the classification table, the highest overall accuracy is obtained with a predicted probability of .50 or a cutoff score on the SAT of 909. If this cutoff score were implemented on these data, the overall accuracy would be 80.7% compared with 77.0%, the baseline accuracy representing the likelihood of graduating if everyone were admitted. A cutoff score of 909 yields a sensitivity of 95.0% and a specificity of 32.7%. Thus, the score is very sensitive—accepting students who will graduate. However, the score is not very specific—high

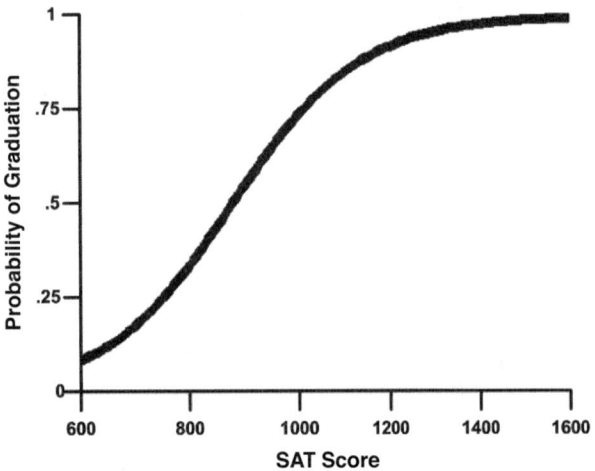

FIGURE 35.6. Predicted association between SAT score and probability of graduating within 5 years.

TABLE 35.1

Decision Information for Various Cutoff Scores Based on the Association Between SAT Score and Probability of Graduation

Predicted probability	SAT score	Correct		Incorrect		Percentages				
		Event	Nonevent	Event	Nonevent	Accuracy	Sensitivity	Specificity	False positives	False negatives
.00	—	15,075	0	4,493	0	77.0	100.0	0.0	23.0	—
.10	626	15,070	84	4,409	5	77.4	100.0	1.9	22.6	5.6
.20	730	15,022	307	4,186	53	78.3	99.4	9.6	21.3	18.3
.30	799	14,910	576	3,917	165	79.1	98.9	12.8	20.8	22.3
.40	857	14,690	1,005	3,488	385	80.2	97.4	22.4	19.2	27.7
.50	909	14,319	1,467	3,026	756	80.7	95.0	32.7	17.4	34.0
.60	961	13,524	2,078	2,415	1,551	79.7	89.7	46.2	15.2	42.7
.70	1,018	12,429	2,669	1,824	2,646	77.2	82.4	59.4	12.8	49.8
.80	1,087	10,336	3,396	1,097	4,739	70.2	68.6	75.6	9.6	58.3
.90	1,192	6,008	4,177	316	9,067	52.0	39.9	93.0	5.0	68.5
1.00	>1,600	0	4,493	0	15,075	23.0	0.0	100.0	—	77.0

likelihood of rejecting students who would have graduated.

The cutoff score of 909 is the optimal cutoff score if false positives and false negatives are considered to be equally poor outcomes. However, in applied work the different types of mistakes are not often considered equal. In our example, it is likely that denying a student admission who would graduate is considered a bigger mistake than granting admission to a student who would not graduate. The next question is "how much"? If the ratio is 2:1, with false negatives considered twice as bad of a mistake as false positives, then the cutoff score shifts to 830. At a 3:1 ratio, the cutoff score shifts to 750. If granting admission to a student who would not graduate is considered the bigger of the two mistakes and the ratio is 1:2, then the cutoff score shifts to 1010. A 1:3 ratio pushes the cutoff score higher to a value of 1040. The relative weights are often derived from the costs associated with mistakes; however, in certain applications costs are difficult to determine. This example is, of course, oversimplified as there are several criteria (e.g., high school grades, letters of recommendation) and constraints (e.g., class size, likelihood of attending if accepted) when making admissions decisions.

Consequences

A recent addition to discussions of construct validity is the idea of positive and negative consequences as well as intended and unintended consequences of assessment and score-based inferences at both the individual and societal levels (Messick, 1980, 1989; Shepard, 1993). For example, demographic (e.g., gender) differences in a score distribution may have unintended consequences if the test were used for selection. This is not to say there can never be any demographic-based differences in the score distributions; however, it is necessary to determine whether any differences are due to construct relevant or irrelevant test variance and/or criterion relevant or irrelevant test variance (Messick, 1989). A thorough examination of measurement invariance at the item and test level can help determine whether demographic-based differences are construct relevant or irrelevant. Additionally, a similarly thorough analysis of criterion-related validity can help determine whether demographic-based differences are criterion relevant or irrelevant.

Measurement, however, can bring about unintended consequences, which may be difficult or impossible to avoid. For example, through the No Child Left Behind Act, children in third through eighth grade are assessed annually in reading and mathematics achievement. School-level scores from these tests are made public, and important decisions are based on them. One possible unintended consequence of this measurement program is having class time set aside to review for these tests, possibly taking time away from topics such as science, art, physical education, and social studies. Another consequence is having teachers "teach to the test," which may artificially inflate scores making them less valid. In the grand scheme of measurement, all plausible foreseeable consequences need to be considered before implementation.

DISCUSSION

In this chapter, construct validity is conceived as having two broad areas—internal and external validity representing two axes of construct validity. This representation was chosen specifically to denote that the various components of construct validity do not always neatly fall in line with either one of these broad areas of construct validity. For example, item analyses, such as those described here, primarily examine internal validity; however, examining item and test bias can be seen as part of evaluating consequences of testing, which is primarily an aspect of external validity.

Properly validating psychological measurement is the most important aspect of academic and applied psychological research, because all inferences hinge on having scores with meaning that generalize to other situations and times. In this chapter, we highlighted several aspects of validity that should be considered when designing a new scale, creating a short-form, revising an existing scale, and/or considering using an existing test for new purposes. Validation, like reliability, falls on a continuum—a test score is neither fully valid nor invalid for a specific purpose. However, determining the degree of validity a test or scores from a test can be difficult. The most we can do is be explicit regarding how the validation process was conducted, including important study information, such as sample characteristics and test conditions. It is also important to be explicit regarding the outcomes of all validation studies including estimates of item parameters and the size of all associations along with their standard errors.

In this chapter, we focused on advanced quantitative methods that are useful for evaluating construct validity. These methods have long histories but have not always been specifically connected with studying construct validity. These advanced methods highlight aspects of construct validity or invalidity that simple correlation and regression analyses cannot. We hope that advanced quantitative methods will be more commonly utilized when investigating construct validity.

References

American Educational Research Association, American Psychological Association, & National Council on Measurement in Education. (2014). *Standards for educational and psychological testing*. https://www.testingstandards.net/open-access-files.html

Anastasi, A. (1986). Evolving concepts of test validation. *Annual Review of Psychology, 37*(1), 1–16. https://doi.org/10.1146/annurev.ps.37.020186.000245

Angoff, W. H. (1988). Validity: An evolving concept. In H. Wainer & H. I. Braum (Eds.), *Test validity* (pp. 19–32). Erlbaum.

Bauer, D. J. (2017). A more general model for testing measurement invariance and differential item functioning. *Psychological Methods, 22*(3), 507–526. https://doi.org/10.1037/met0000077

Boring, E. G. (1923). Intelligence as the tests test it. *New Republic, 35*, 35–37.

Borsboom, D., Mellenbergh, G. J., & van Heerden, J. (2004). The concept of validity. *Psychological Review, 111*(4), 1061–1071. https://doi.org/10.1037/0033-295X.111.4.1061

Bridgman, P. W. (1932). *The logic of modern physics*. Macmillan.

Brigham, C. C. (1923). *A study of American intelligence*. Princeton University Press.

Browne, M. W. (1984). The decomposition of multitrait-multimethod matrices. *British Journal of Mathematical & Statistical Psychology, 37*(Pt 1), 1–21. https://doi.org/10.1111/j.2044-8317.1984.tb00785.x

Burchinal, M., & Appelbaum, M. I. (1991). Estimating individual developmental functions: Methods and their assumptions. *Child Development, 62*(1), 23–43. https://doi.org/10.2307/1130702

Campbell, D. T., & Fiske, D. W. (1959). Convergent and discriminant validation by the multitrait-multimethod matrix. *Psychological Bulletin*, *56*(2), 81–105. https://doi.org/10.1037/h0046016

Chernoff, H., & Moses, L. E. (1959). *Elementary decision theory*. John Wiley.

Choi, J., Harring, J. R., & Hancock, G. R. (2009). Latent growth modeling for logistic response functions. *Multivariate Behavioral Research*, *44*(5), 620–645. https://doi.org/10.1080/00273170903187657

Cronbach, L. J. (1971). Test validation. In R. L. Thorndike (Ed.), *Educational measurement* (2nd ed., pp. 443–507). American Council on Education.

Cronbach, L. J. (1980). Validity on parole: How can we go straight? New directions for testing and measurement: Measurement achievement over a decade. *Proceedings of the 1979 ETS Invitational Conference* (pp. 99–108). Jossey-Bass.

Cronbach, L. J. (1988). Five perspectives on the validity argument. In H. Wainer & H. I. Braum (Eds.), *Test validity* (pp. 3–17). Erlbaum.

Cronbach, L. J. (1989). Construct validation after thirty years. In R. L. Linn (Ed.), *Intelligence: Measurement, theory, and public policy: Proceedings of a symposium in honor of Lloyd G. Humphreys* (pp. 147–171). University of Illinois Press.

Cronbach, L. J., & Gleser, G. C. (1965). *Psychological tests and personnel decisions*. University of Illinois Press.

Cronbach, L. J., & Meehl, P. E. (1955). Construct validity in psychological tests. *Psychological Bulletin*, *52*(4), 281–302. https://doi.org/10.1037/h0040957

Cudeck, R. (1988). Multiplicative models and MTMM matrices. *Journal of Educational Statistics*, *13*(2), 131–147.

Eid, M. (2000). A multitrait-multimethod model with minimal assumptions. *Psychometrika*, *65*(2), 241–261. https://doi.org/10.1007/BF02294377

Embretson, S. E. (Whitely). (1983). Construct validity: Construct representation versus nomothetic span. *Psychological Bulletin*, *93*(1), 179–197.

Ferrer, E., Hamagami, F., & McArdle, J. J. (2004). Modeling latent growth curves with incomplete data using different types of structural equation modeling and multilevel software. *Structural Equation Modeling*, *11*(3), 452–483. https://doi.org/10.1207/s15328007sem1103_8

Ghisletta, P., & Lindenberger, U. (2004). Static and dynamic longitudinal structural analyses of cognitive changes in old age. *Gerontology*, *50*(1), 12–16. https://doi.org/10.1159/000074383

Grayson, D. A., & Marsh, H. W. (1994). Identification with deficient rank loading matrices in confirmatory factor analysis: Multitrait-multimethod models. *Psychometrika*, *59*(1), 121–134. https://doi.org/10.1007/BF02294271

Grimm, K. J., Pianta, R. C., & Konold, T. (2009). Longitudinal multitrait-multimethod models for developmental research. *Multivariate Behavioral Research*, *44*(2), 233–258. https://doi.org/10.1080/00273170902794230

Grimm, K. J., & Ram, N. (2009). Nonlinear growth models in M*plus* and SAS. *Structural Equation Modeling*, *16*(4), 676–701. https://doi.org/10.1080/10705510903206055

Grimm, K. J., Ram, N., & Hamagami, F. (2011). Nonlinear growth curves in developmental research. *Child Development*, *82*(5), 1357–1371. https://doi.org/10.1111/j.1467-8624.2011.01630.x

Kamata, A., & Bauer, D. J. (2008). A note on the relation between factor analytic and item response theory models. *Structural Equation Modeling*, *15*(1), 136–153. https://doi.org/10.1080/10705510701758406

Kenny, D. A., & Kashy, D. A. (1992). Analysis of the multitrait-multimethod matrix by confirmatory factor analysis. *Psychological Bulletin*, *112*(1), 165–172. https://doi.org/10.1037/0033-2909.112.1.165

Konold, T. R., & Pianta, R. C. (2007). The influence of informants on ratings of children's behavioral functioning: A latent variable approach. *Journal of Psychoeducational Assessment*, *25*(3), 222–236. https://doi.org/10.1177/0734282906297784

Lance, C. E., Noble, C. L., & Scullen, S. E. (2002). A critique of the correlated trait-correlated method and correlated uniqueness models for multitrait-multimethod data. *Psychological Methods*, *7*(2), 228–244. https://doi.org/10.1037/1082-989X.7.2.228

Lawshe, C. H. (1975). A quantitative approach to content validity. *Personnel Psychology*, *28*(4), 563–575. https://doi.org/10.1111/j.1744-6570.1975.tb01393.x

Lippmann, W. (1922). The mental age of Americans. *New Republic*, *32*, 213–215.

Little, T. D., Lindenberger, U., & Nesselroade, J. R. (1999). On selecting indicators for multivariate measurement and modeling with latent variables: When "good" indicators are bad and "bad" indicators are good. *Psychological Methods*, *4*(2), 192–211. https://doi.org/10.1037/1082-989X.4.2.192

MacCorquodale, K., & Meehl, P. E. (1948). On a distinction between hypothetical constructs and intervening variables. *Psychological Review*, 55(2), 95–107. https://doi.org/10.1037/h0056029

Marsh, H. W., Byrne, B. M., & Craven, R. (1992). Overcoming problems in confirmatory factor analyses of MTMM data: The correlated uniqueness model and factorial invariance. *Multivariate Behavioral Research*, 27(4), 489–507. https://doi.org/10.1207/s15327906mbr2704_1

Marsh, H. W., & Grayson, D. (1995). Latent variable models of multitrait-multimethod data. In R. H. Hoyle (Ed.), *Structural equation modeling: Concepts, issues, and applications* (pp. 177–198). SAGE.

Marsh, H. W., & Hocevar, D. (1983). Confirmatory factor analysis of multitrait-multimethod matrices. *Journal of Educational Measurement*, 20(3), 231–248. https://doi.org/10.1111/j.1745-3984.1983.tb00202.x

Masters, G. N. (1982). A Rasch model for partial credit scoring. *Psychometrika*, 47(2), 149–174. https://doi.org/10.1007/BF02296272

McArdle, J. J., & Epstein, D. (1987). Latent growth curves within developmental structural equation models. *Child Development*, 58(1), 110–133. https://doi.org/10.2307/1130295

McArdle, J. J., & Prescott, C. A. (1992). Age-based construct validation using structural equation modeling. *Experimental Aging Research*, 18(3-4), 87–115. https://doi.org/10.1080/03610739208253915

Meehl, P. E., & Rosen, A. (1955). Antecedent probability and the efficiency of psychometric signs, patterns, or cutting scores. *Psychological Bulletin*, 52(3), 194–216. https://doi.org/10.1037/h0048070

Meredith, W. (1964). Notes on factorial invariance. *Psychometrika*, 29(2), 177–185. https://doi.org/10.1007/BF02289699

Meredith, W. (1965). A method for studying differences between groups. *Psychometrika*, 30(1), 15–29. https://doi.org/10.1007/BF02289744

Meredith, W. (1993). Measurement invariance, factor analysis and factorial invariance. *Psychometrika*, 58(4), 525–543. https://doi.org/10.1007/BF02294825

Meredith, W., & Horn, J. L. (2001). The role of factorial invariance in modeling growth and change. In L. M. Collins & A. Sayer (Eds.), *New methods for the analysis of change* (pp. 203–240). American Psychological Association. https://doi.org/10.1037/10409-007

Meredith, W., & Tisak, J. (1990). Latent curve analysis. *Psychometrika*, 55(1), 107–122. https://doi.org/10.1007/BF02294746

Messick, S. (1975). The standard problem: Meaning and values in measurement and evaluation. *American Psychologist*, 30(10), 955–966. https://doi.org/10.1037/0003-066X.30.10.955

Messick, S. (1980). Test validity and the ethics of assessment. *American Psychologist*, 35(11), 1012–1027. https://doi.org/10.1037/0003-066X.35.11.1012

Messick, S. (1989). Validity. In R. L. Linn (Ed.), *Educational measurement* (pp. 13–103). Macmillan Publishing Co.

Messick, S. (1995). Validity of psychological assessment: Validation of inferences form persons' responses and performances as scientific inquiry into score meaning. *American Psychologist*, 50(9), 741–749. https://doi.org/10.1037/0003-066X.50.9.741

Muraki, E. (1992). A generalized partial credit model: Application of an EM algorithm. *Applied Psychological Measurement*, 16(2), 159–176. https://doi.org/10.1177/014662169201600206

Muthén, B. (1978). Contributions to factor analysis of dichotomous variables. *Psychometrika*, 43(4), 551–560. https://doi.org/10.1007/BF02293813

Muthén, B. O. (1985). A method for studying the homogeneity of test items with respect to other relevant variables. *Journal of Educational Statistics*, 10(2), 121–132. https://doi.org/10.3102/10769986010002121

Muthén, B. O., & Lehman, J. (1985). Multiple-group IRT modeling: Applications to item bias analysis. *Journal of Educational Statistics*, 10(2), 133–142. https://doi.org/10.3102/10769986010002133

Pastore, N. (1978). The army intelligence tests and Walter Lippmann. *Journal of the History of the Behavioral Sciences*, 14(4), 316–327. https://doi.org/10.1002/1520-6696(197810)14:4<316::AID-JHBS2300140403>3.0.CO;2-N

Ram, N., & Grimm, K. J. (2007). Using simple and complex growth models to articulate developmental change: Matching method to theory. *International Journal of Behavioral Development*, 31(4), 303–316. https://doi.org/10.1177/0165025407077751

Rasch, G. (1960). *Probabilistic models for some intelligence and attainment tests*. Danish Institute for Educational Research.

Reise, S. P., Widaman, K. F., & Pugh, R. H. (1993). Confirmatory factor analysis and item response theory: Two approaches for exploring measurement invariance. *Psychological Bulletin*, 114(3), 552–566. https://doi.org/10.1037/0033-2909.114.3.552

Rosenthal, R., Rosnow, R. L., & Rubin, D. B. (2000). *Contrasts and effect sizes in behavioral research: A correlational approach*. Cambridge University Press.

Samejima, F. (1969). *Estimation of latent ability using a response pattern of graded scores*. Psychometric Society. https://doi.org/10.1007/BF03372160

Shepard, L. A. (1993). Evaluating test validity. *Review of Research in Education, 19*, 405–450.

Thissen, D., & Steinberg, L. (1986). A taxonomy of item response models. *Psychometrika, 51*(4), 567–577. https://doi.org/10.1007/BF02295596

Thissen, D., Steinberg, L., & Gerrard, M. (1986). Beyond group-mean differences: The concept of item bias. *Psychological Bulletin, 99*(1), 118–128. https://doi.org/10.1037/0033-2909.99.1.118

Watson, J. B. (1913). Psychology as the behaviorist views it. *Psychological Review, 20*(2), 158–177. https://doi.org/10.1037/h0074428

Westen, D., & Rosenthal, R. (2003). Quantifying construct validity: Two simple measures. *Journal of Personality and Social Psychology, 84*(3), 608–618. https://doi.org/10.1037/0022-3514.84.3.608

Whitely, S. E. (1983). Construct validity: Construct representation versus nomothetic span. *Psychological Bulletin, 93*(1), 179–197. https://doi.org/10.1037/0033-2909.93.1.179

Widaman, K. F. (1985). Hierarchically nested covariance structure models for multitrait-multimethod data. *Applied Psychological Measurement, 9*(1), 1–26. https://doi.org/10.1177/014662168500900101

Widaman, K. F., & Reise, S. P. (1997). Exploring the measurement invariance of psychological instruments: Applications in the substance use domain. In K. J. Bryant, M. Windle, & S. G. West (Eds.), *The science of prevention: Methodological advances from alcohol and substance abuse research* (pp. 281–324). American Psychological Association. https://doi.org/10.1037/10222-009

Wirth, R. J., & Edwards, M. C. (2007). Item factor analysis: Current approaches and future directions. *Psychological Methods, 12*(1), 58–79. https://doi.org/10.1037/1082-989X.12.1.58

Wothke, W., & Browne, M. W. (1990). The direct product model for the MTMM matrix parameterized as a second order factor analysis model. *Psychometrika, 55*(2), 255–262. https://doi.org/10.1007/BF02295286

Woods, C. M. (2009). Evaluation of MIMIC-Model methods for DIF testing with comparison to two-group analysis. *Multivariate Behavioral Research, 44*(1), 1–27. https://doi.org/10.1080/00273170802620121

Woods, C. M., & Grimm, K. J. (2011). Testing for nonuniform differential item functioning with multiple indicator multiple cause models. *Applied Psychological Measurement, 35*(5), 339–361. https://doi.org/10.1177/0146621611405984

Yerkes, R. M. (Ed.). (1921). Psychological examining in the United States Army. *Memoirs of the National Academy of Sciences, XV*, 1–890.

CHAPTER 36

ITEM-LEVEL FACTOR ANALYSIS

Nisha C. Gottfredson, Brian D. Stucky, and A. T. Panter

Fundamental research questions in psychology center on establishing the factor structure of new measures and understanding how unobserved constructs assessed by these measures relate to other constructs. The standard factor analytic model assumes that response data are based on continuously measured indicators of constructs, yet the individual items used in social science research rarely meet this assumption. Items appearing in surveys (such as in attitude or knowledge scales), obtained through observation codes or gathered in interview settings may be dichotomous, ordered categorical, censored counts, or zero-inflated counts. They may also have a variety of other distribution forms. This chapter addresses the historical traditions and current data analytic recommendations for conducting data analysis using latent variable models with item-level indicators.

The general topic of how to describe the factor structure and item-level characteristics of a collection of items emerged from two main theoretical routes (social sciences: item-level factor analysis [IFA]; education: item response theory [IRT]); the connection between these routes has been elucidated formally in the past few decades. In considering analytic options for modeling item-level data, we first discuss issues related to item measurement, response distributions, and estimation methods. We then address appropriate modeling conditions for focusing on individual items versus composites that are formed by the researcher from item subsets, such as item parcels or testlets, and we review methods for assessing measurement invariance across groups. Finally, specific recommendations are provided about appropriate research design conditions for modeling item-level data.

FACTOR ANALYSIS

The goal of factor analysis is to explain the relationships among the variables by a smaller set of underlying, or latent, variables; this is true for categorical and continuous variables. Traditionally, factor analysis emphasizes understanding the dimensionality of a set of variables (e.g., exploratory factor analysis [EFA] and confirmatory factor analysis [CFA]) and modeling the causal or correlational relationships among those dimensions (e.g., SEM). Although these analytic procedures are applicable for categorical response data, the key difference between the approaches lies in where the investigator places emphasis and the nature of the research questions. In the historical treatment of factor analysis

---

The authors thank members of the PROMIS pediatric network (funded by Grant 5U01AR052181) and Deb Irwin, Michelle Langer, David Thissen, Esi DeWitt, Jim Varni, Karin Yeatts, and Darren DeWalt for use of these data.

https://doi.org/10.1037/0000318-036
APA Handbook of Research Methods in Psychology, Second Edition: Vol. 1. Foundations, Planning, Measures, and Psychometrics, H. Cooper (Editor-in-Chief)
Copyright © 2023 by the American Psychological Association. All rights reserved.

for continuously measured items, idiosyncratic item-level characteristics were often seen as problematic (McDonald, 1967, 1999; McDonald & Ahlawat, 1974). For example, the very notion of item difficulty (the probability of endorsement) is conceptually challenging from a continuously distributed factor analytic perspective, and, hence, techniques such as data transformations and standardization are commonly used to mask item differences in response distributions and scales.

The IFA approach, on the other hand, appreciates item behavior and characteristics as intrinsically meaningful. Concepts such as *item discrimination* (the strength of the relationship between an item and its factor) and *item difficulty* are key tools that psychometricians use to analyze item response data. To further develop the importance of item characteristics, we provide some background on the traditional factor analysis model.

The common factor model (Jöreskog, 1969, 1970) is based on a set of assumptions that the observed variables $y = (y_1, \ldots, y_i)$ are continuous, normally distributed with mean μ and covariance Σ, and that the relationship between observed and latent variables $\xi = (\xi_1, \ldots, \xi_p)$ is best described by the linear model

$$y = \alpha + \Lambda\xi + \varepsilon, \; y = \alpha + \Lambda\xi + \varepsilon \quad (36.1)$$

where observed responses y are functions of factor loadings Λ, latent variables ξ, item means α, and uniquenesses (residuals; ε). Incorporating the covariance matrix of ξ, called Φ, and the covariance matrix of (typically uncorrelated) residuals, Ψ, the associations among y are represented by the covariance matrix Σ.

$$\Sigma = \Lambda\Phi\Lambda' + \Psi \quad (36.2)$$

Items appearing in research in psychology and the behavioral sciences typically have categorical response options that violate the assumption that residuals are normally distributed (Krosnick, 1999). In these situations, an appropriate alternative to the linear common factor model is IFA (Mislevy, 1986; Muthén, 1978; Wirth & Edwards, 2007).

Categorical confirmatory factor analysis (CCFA) assumes that a researcher is focused on the measurement features of responses to categorical items and that these items are "discrete representations of continuous latent responses" (Wirth & Edwards, 2007, p. 59). Items with these characteristics range from dichotomous responses common in education settings (e.g., correct or incorrect, true or false) to polytomous responses, or ordered categorical responses, now common in most psychological disciplines (i.e., Likert-type scales such as agreement, self-description).

Ignoring the categorical nature of items and apply the common factor model to such data is not statistically appropriate; attempting to do so can result in a variety of problems. Perhaps most central, categorical response variables are bounded by the minimum and maximum response options (e.g., 0 for an item that is not endorsed and 1 for an item that is endorsed), and only through nonlinear functions (such as the normal ogive and logistic cumulative distribution functions) is one able to place discrete item responses on the scale of the unobserved continuous latent variable (McDonald & Ahlawat, 1974). If ignored, the model is misspecified, and the linear approximation of the nonlinear relationship will be heavily influenced by the observed variable's mean (McDonald, 1999; Mislevy, 1986). Second, fitting a factor analysis linear model to categorical data often leads to biased parameter estimates (DiStefano, 2002). In addition, factor loadings may be attenuated in cases of sparse response coverage (such as skewness), which is typical of scale items with response options that measure only extreme trait locations. The accumulation of these problems results in untrustworthy model fit statistics.

In parallel with emergent developments for the factor analysis of dichotomous and ordered categorical data in the mid-1980s, important advances in the IRT tradition also allowed for analyses of these types of items (Mislevy, 1986). Examples from early adopters of these two traditions in psychology and related fields include assessment of depression (Childs et al., 1992; Schaeffer, 1988), need for cognition (Tanaka et al., 1988), self-monitoring (Panter & Tanaka, 1987), and psychopathology and personality (e.g., Reise & Waller, 1990) as well as several studies focusing on general issues in item order, scale design, and administration (Panter et al., 1992; Steinberg, 1994; Waller & Reise, 1989). Review articles and early conference presentations were specifically targeted at communicating these developments in the analysis item response data to psychological researchers (e.g., Panter et al., 1997; Reise et al., 1993; Steinberg & Thissen, 1995; Thissen, 1992).

Thissen and Steinberg (1986) described a taxonomy of models in the psychometric literature to analyze properly categorical response data in a confirmatory analytic setting allowing items to be linked to underlying latent variables. Many of these models originated in the IRT tradition, including one-, two-, and three-parameter logistic models for binary data, the graded-response model (GRM; Samejima, 1969), the generalized partial credit model (Muraki, 1992) for ordered categorical response items, models for nominal response data (Bock, 1972), and many others. For simplicity of discussion, however, we review the binary–dichotomous item response case (e.g., *agree* or *disagree*) as well as a generalization to model polytomous item responses (e.g., Likert-type items).

For dichotomous items, respondents' locations on the continuous underlying trait (ξ in factor analysis notation and θ in IRT notation) are expressed through their choice of response option. In other words, one's location on the latent variable, y_i^*, is modeled through the common factor and item-specific residual.

$$y_i^* = \lambda_i \xi + e_i \qquad (36.3)$$

where the continuous latent response y_i^* has a variance of 1.0. Assuming that higher scores reflect more of a given trait, the relationship between observed item responses y_i, location on the trait y_i^*, and the threshold parameters is

$$y_i = 1 \text{ if } y_i^* \geq \tau_i$$
$$0 \text{ if } y_i^* \geq \tau_i \qquad (36.4)$$

The answers that respondents provide to a given scale item can be arranged along the latent response distribution y_i^*, by thresholds, τ_i. Thus, a threshold represents the location on the latent continuum that separates discrete responses to a given item.

THE ITEM RESPONSE THEORY TRADITION

Chapter 37 of this volume reviews traditional IRT modeling and several new directions in the field. We discuss the more common set of IRT models, their assumptions, and their uses to motivate our discussion of the close relation between IFA and IRT. When binary data are modeled in an IRT context, one often uses logistic functions. While capitalizing on the mathematical convenience of the model (Birnbaum, 1968, p. 400), the logistic function closely follows the cumulative normal distribution. The two-parameter logistic (2PL) model may be written as

$$T\left(u_i = 1 | \theta = \frac{1}{(1 + \exp[-Da_i(\theta - b_i)])}\right) \qquad (36.5)$$

In keeping with Lazarsfeld's (1950) classic notation, T traces the probability of a correct response, $u = 1$, to item i conditional on ability θ, whereas an incorrect response has the probability $T(u = 0|\theta) = 1 - T(u = 1|\theta)$, or $T_0 = 1 - T_1(\theta)$ in more compact notation. The logistic function describes each response probability on the basis of the slope or discrimination parameter (a_i), which indicates the strength of association between the item response and latent dimension, and a difficulty or threshold parameter (b_i), which indicates the location on the ability continuum for which individuals' probability of correct response is 50%. The constant D (approximately 1.7) is commonly used to place the model on the same scale as the normal ogive, the precursor to the logistic representation (Lord, 1952).

For polytomous (ordered categorical) response data, a generalization of the 2PL, Samejima's (1969) GRM, is often used. The GRM describes the probability of a response in category k or higher, where $k = 0, 1, \ldots, m - 1$.

$$T*\left(y_i = k|\theta = \frac{1}{(1+\exp[-a_i(\theta - b_{ik})])}\right) \quad (36.6)$$

noting that $T^*(y = 0|\theta) = 1$ and $T^*(y = m|\theta) = 0$. Here the probability of responding in category k is the difference between the probabilities of responding in k or higher and the higher response.

$$T_i(k|\theta) = T_i^*(k|\theta) = T_i^*(k+1|\theta) \quad (36.7)$$

The model describes the response process by estimating one less threshold than the number of response alternatives. Each threshold or cutpoint marks the boundary between a response in category k from $k + 1$. Although such a model is useful for a variety of psychological scales with ordinal response category items, many other IRT models characterize item responses (for a review, see Embretson & Reise, 2000).

Relations Between the Two Traditions

The histories and notational differences between Jöreskog's (1969) common factor model and the IRT models popularized by Lord and Novick (1968) seem to indicate some inherent difference across the traditions. Actually, the relation between IRT and CCFA frameworks has been presented by Bartholomew (1983), Muthén (1983), and Muthén and Lehman (1985). Takane and de Leeuw (1987) provided the mathematical equivalence between the common models. Indeed, under certain conditions, IFA can be conducted entirely in an IRT framework. Given item parameters in either IRT or IFA, one may translate and back-translate between parameterizations. IRT-equivalent slopes and thresholds may be obtained easily from factor analysis notation.

$$a_i = \left(\frac{\lambda_i}{\sqrt{1+\lambda_i^2}}\right) D \text{ and } b_i = \frac{\tau_i}{\lambda_i} \quad (36.8)$$

where a and b are as previously defined, and τ_i represents the location on the latent variable scale that distinguishes between responses.

The square root of 1 minus the squared factor loading (λ_i) is the residual standard deviation of y_i^* (with y_i^* standardized to have a variance of 1.0, as is common in many IFA approaches). Additionally, if the IRT parameters are in the normal metric, the scaling factor D is not needed and drops out of the equation. With little algebra, one may translate the IRT parameters back into factor analysis notation loadings (Λ) and thresholds (τ).

$$\lambda_i = \left(\frac{a_i/D}{\sqrt{1+(a_i/D)^2}}\right) \text{ and } \tau_i = \left(\frac{(a_i/D)b_i}{\sqrt{1+(a_i/D)^2}}\right)$$
$$(36.9)$$

Many software programs estimate the model in a slope-intercept parameterization. This parameterization utilizes the logit, $Da_i(\theta - b_i)$, and after multiplying the slope through, provides the *intercept*, $-a_ib_i$, which, when $D = 1$, is the log odds of a correct response at $\theta = 0$. In typical IRT applications, however, intercepts are converted into the common slope-threshold parameterization by dividing the intercept by the negative slope.

As Wirth and Edwards (2007) made clear, there is some practical utility in these conversions. In many instances these translations help identify unreasonable parameter estimates. Item-level data are virtually never perfectly related to the latent trait. More often, items contain some degree of error variance, so when this error variance becomes suspiciously low, one can anticipate when item parameters are untrustworthy. Wirth and Edwards suggested cautiously interpreting factor loadings > .95 (and hence a parameters above about 3), and warned against trusting loadings > .97 (and a parameters above about 4). In both instances, such values would be considered near-Heywood (1931) cases.

Estimating Models Within the Two Traditions

If one considers IFA to be the intersection of traditional factor analysis and IRT, then it may be helpful to consider why these closely related techniques evolved from largely separate literatures. In part, the distinction has less to do with differences in the hypothesized models for item responses and more to do with differences in estimation employed within each tradition (Mislevy, 1986). Estimation methods for CCFA traditionally made use of the sample tetrachoric (for binary–dichotomous data) and polychoric (for polytomous–ordered categorical data) correlation matrix (Christofferson, 1975; Muthén, 1978, 1984) in addition to a weight matrix that grew substantially with the number of items. Mixtures of item types, which often occur in research settings in psychology, also could be handled as well as models with many factors (e.g., SEM). Two widely used least squares estimators that make use of the sample tetrachoric–polychoric correlation matrix are (a) diagonally weighted least squares (Jöreskog & Sörbom, 2001) as used in LISREL (Jöreskog & Sörbom, 2001), and (b) mean- and variance-adjusted weighted least squares (WLSMV; Muthén et al., 1997) as used in Mplus (Muthén & Muthén, 1998–2017). Both estimators use only the diagonal elements of a weight matrix (see Jöreskog, 1990; Muthén, 1984), thereby greatly reducing the burdensome operation of inverting a weight matrix for models with many items (for some other estimators see Christofferson, 1975; Jöreskog & Sörbom, 2001).

Only more recently have analysts in the factor analytic tradition begun to use an alternative to weighted least squares estimation: full-information maximum likelihood (FIML). Rather than employing a polychoric correlation matrix, FIML takes full advantage of the entire data matrix, not just covariance matrices. A benefit of this approach is that cases with missing data are not deleted listwise from analyses. With FIML, the underlying data structure is reproduced by way of the matrix of factor loadings (Λy), covariance matrixes of latent variables (Φ_ξ), and measurement errors (Θ_δ), and by factor means (α_ξ) and item intercepts (ν_y) or thresholds (t_{ky}). The FIML method produces unbiased standard errors for the model parameters (factor loadings, interrelations among latent variables, measurement errors) and model fit indexes, unlike adjusted weighted least squares approaches that require corrections for biased standard errors and fit indexes (see Satorra & Bentler, 1994). FIML introduces the problem of multiple dimensions, however. Specifically, integration—finding the area of a region defined by a function—must be approximated by a number of quadrature points (e.g., Gauss-Hermite) over the number of dimensions. So, for many reasonable-size models (and quadrature points), computing time is calculated in hours, a problem less often encountered when using least squares estimators.

Traditionally, IRT models have tended to focus on only one latent variable at a time. Estimation of IRT parameters has historically used maximum likelihood (Birnbaum, 1968; Bock & Lieberman, 1970; Rasch, 1960). Application of the expectation–maximization (EM) algorithm (Bock & Aitkin, 1981) alleviates much computational time for models with few factors and many items by iteratively estimating trial item parameters, then using these to find the expected number of responses and the proportions of individuals at given levels of the latent variable (E-step), and finally resubstituting these values back into the likelihood equation (M-step). The EM algorithm is used in widely available IRT software and is now widely used in SEM software with FIML estimation.

More recently, advances in parameter estimation have overcome the challenge of dimensionality posed by maximum likelihood and have made high-dimensional latent variable models more tractable (e.g., multidimensional IRT [MIRT]; Reckase, 2009). That is, when researchers measure categorical items, they can now model a larger number of underlying factors than was previously possible in traditional unidimensional IRT models. Here we briefly highlight three recent developments that, with time, may see more use from applied researchers in psychology and the behavioral sciences with high-dimensional data: (a) EM with adaptive quadrature (ADQ), (b) Markov chain Monte Carlo (MCMC), and (c) the Metropolis-Hastings Robbins-Monro (MH-RM) algorithm for maximum likelihood estimates (MLEs). For a moderate number of dimensions, ADQ is an attractive alternative to ML/EM. Instead of using fixed-point quadrature, ADQ adapts the number of points needed so that the estimation process becomes more efficient (Schilling & Bock, 2005). MH-RM (Cai, 2010a) used a Metropolis-Hastings (Hastings, 1970) Robbins-Monro algorithm (Robbins & Monro, 1951), which has enabled efficient estimation of high-dimensional models that had previously been intractable. Finally, MCMC algorithms allow for the inspection of the quality of maximum likelihood estimates by constructing a Markov chain with a stationary distribution as its target, at which point samples (i.e., random draws) taken from the chain serve as posterior estimates. Although MCMC is an attractive solution to dimensionality problems in FIML contexts, the efficiency of current MCMC techniques (i.e., the computational burden; Edwards, 2010) makes its use, from an applied researcher's perspective, somewhat limited. However, these newer estimation approaches and continued developments provide psychologists with the tools to test models whose complexity exceeded the boundaries of software in the past.

The preceding discussion highlights two analytic traditions that focus on understanding the underlying factor structure of item-level data with different measurement levels. The less than continuously measured items present more of an analytic challenge than do the continuously measured indicators. In the next section, we consider current research on a related approach that investigators have used to circumvent complexities associated with analyses conducted at the item level.

IF ITEMS ARE MORE COMPLICATED TO ANALYZE, WHY NOT PARCEL THEM?

Under certain circumstances, a researcher may decide to aggregate (i.e., create a sum score from) a collection of items to serve as factor indicators, rather than using individual items as indicators, before conducting their factor analysis. This practice is known as *parceling*.[1] Parceling involves splitting a relatively large number of items thought to represent a latent variable into a smaller set of sum scores. These sum scores are then used in place of the individual items to identify the latent variable.

Little, Cunningham, Shahar, and Widaman (2002) and Little, Lindenberger, and Nesselroade (1999) described a latent variable's domain as consisting of an infinite pool of potential items, each deviating to some degree from the centroid of the latent variable. Assuming that the expected value of these deviations is zero, and assuming that each item's error is uncorrelated with every other item's error, then a parcel that is constructed of a randomly selected sample of items should be, on average, a less biased and more reliable indicator of the latent construct. If, however, items are not conditionally independent from one another after accounting for the common factor (i.e., item responses are related for a reason other than the underlying dimension such as when two or three items share similar word stems or because they both cross-load on a different factor), then parcels of these correlated items are biased away from the latent variable's centroid.

If it makes sense to conceive of sampling from an infinite pool of *independently distributed* items in a single content domain, then using parcels represents the latent construct in a more stable, replicable way than if the same number of items were used to represent the same latent construct. Indeed, a frequently cited benefit of parceling is improved indicator reliability (Cattell & Burdsal, 1975). The Spearman–Brown prophecy formula reveals that if each item representing a latent construct consists partially of true score variability and partially of error variance, then the sum of several such items contain a higher proportion of true score variability than any individual item (Coffman & MacCallum, 2005).

Coffman and MacCallum (2005) advocated using parcels as latent variable indicators when

---

[1] In IRT, aggregated indicators of latent variables are called *testlets*. In this setting, testlets are formed to alleviate local dependence between correlated items that is irrelevant to the latent variable of interest, often resulting from related test sections or similar item stems (Wainer et al., 2007).

a large number of items are needed to achieve adequate representation of the latent variable domain and when it is implausible to use individual items as factor indicators. For example, if a researcher has a very large number of items to factor analyze, IFA estimation in both of the traditions (i.e., IRT and CFA) is more difficult. In such situations, when there are too many items to estimate a latent variable using individual items, researchers are forced to choose between (a) creating parcels so that model estimation is possible (because estimation with many discrete items is computationally intensive) or (b) aggregating the items into a single measured variable (e.g., by summing the items or outputting an estimated factor score). Coffman and MacCallum demonstrated that the parceling method is superior to alternative analysis options, such as path analysis, that do not allow the explicit modeling of unreliability of measurement.

Especially relevant to IFA, many researchers who use parcels do so to meet normality assumptions of their estimation method. When items are Poisson-distributed counts, dichotomous, or ordinal with only a few response categories (e.g., a 4-point Likert-type scale), then individual item distributions badly violates normality assumptions. If normality is assumed, parameters obtained by maximum likelihood (ML) or generalized least squares (GLS) estimation are downwardly biased. In other words, using this approach leads to serious consequences: standard errors for factor loadings are underestimated and chi-square tests of model fit are too high (West et al., 1995). West et al. (1995) suggested three potential solutions for handling nonnormal factor indicators. First, they suggested that researchers can use the Satorra–Bentler correction for nonnormal data in conjunction with the ML estimator for a better approximation of the model chi-square statistic, factor loadings, and associated standard errors (Satorra & Bentler, 1994). Second, it may be feasible to use an alternative estimator that does not require items to be normally distributed, such as WLSMV. Flora and Curran (2004) found that WLSMV works well even if the latent distribution underlying the discretely distributed observed variable is not normally distributed. Finally, West et al. (1995) suggested that a researcher may create parcels so that factor indicators more closely approximate a normal distribution to use with ML or GLS.

Hau and Marsh (2004) evaluated the use of parcels as a technique for handling nonnormally distributed items when the WLSMV assumption of continuous latent underlying variables is not plausible. They compared this method to the technique of using nonnormally distributed items as indicators with the Satorra–Bentler correction (Satorra & Bentler, 1994). The authors did not find support for the claim that factor loading estimates would be less biased when parcels are used, but they did find that estimates were less variable with this technique. The Satorra–Bentler correction resulted in less biased parameter estimates. Bandalos (2008) compared the parceling strategy to WLSMV estimation with nonnormal items and found that parameter estimates were biased when parcels were used, particularly when unidimensionality of parcels was violated. This result was obtained for both factor loadings and structural parameter estimates between latent factors. Furthermore, Bandalos showed that model fit was overestimated (i.e., thought to be better than it was) if parcels were used when unidimensionality was violated. In contrast, estimates obtained using WLSMV estimation without parcels were unbiased, particularly when sample size increased.

Several authors have shown that parceling leads to overly optimistic model fit indexes when multidimensionality is present (Bandalos, 2008; Little et al., 2002). When locally dependent items are combined into a parcel, the irrelevant item correlation is attributed to shared variance because of the common factor, thus masking multidimensionality and artificially inflating model fit. In addition to inflating model fit, the masking of a multidimensional factor structure leads to confounded and uninterpretable latent constructs (Hagtvet & Nasser, 2004). Given the potential pitfalls of parceling with locally dependent items, Coffman and MacCallum (2005) and Little et al. (2002) recommended testing the unidimensionality assumption and proceeding with parceling only if the assumption is reasonable.[2]

When the unidimensionality assumption is violated, the researcher should determine whether multidimensionality may be due to common method variance (e.g., the items start with the same stem). If so, these items should be included on separate parcels. Other times, multidimensionality is meaningful and should be modeled correctly using multiple latent variables.

When researchers decide whether they should factor analyze individual items that are not continuously measured, the current research suggests that parcels are more reliable than individual items and may allow researchers to represent more fully the domains of their latent constructs. Parcels seem to be the best option when too many items are present to estimate a full measurement model. On the other hand, if the relation between factors and individual items is substantively meaningful, parcels may mask true relations that exist within the data, such as local dependence or a complex factor structure (Little et al., 2002). Furthermore, alternative methods of estimation exist that negate the necessity of parceling in most circumstances, and these alternatives have been empirically demonstrated to produce less biased estimates than those obtained with parceling. Given these contrasting arguments, Little et al. (2002) suggested using parcels when unidimensionality is ensured, when constructs have been well established and defined, and when the measurement model is not of primary interest. That is, parceling may be a reasonable technique to use when the structural relations among latent variables are more interesting than the measurement model. Alternative methods, such as analyses from the factor analytic tradition, should be considered before proceeding with a parceling strategy.

MEASUREMENT INVARIANCE IN ITEM FACTOR ANALYSIS

Testing whether the factor structure of items is similar or invariant across independent groups is an important extension of the IFA problem.[3] Inferences about group differences are only accurate if the latent construct being measured is invariant across groups.

Types of Invariance

Configural invariance occurs when the same factor structure exists across groups (Thurstone, 1947). If factor loadings are equivalent across groups such that a one-unit increase in the latent variable mean is associated with an identical λ unit increase in the expected value for all items, regardless of group membership, then *weak factorial invariance* exists (Horn & McArdle, 1992; Millsap, 1997; Millsap & Kwok, 2004; Millsap & Meredith, 2007; Thurstone, 1947; Widaman & Reise, 1997). If weak factorial invariance is met and item intercepts and thresholds are constant across groups, then there is *strong factorial invariance* (Meredith, 1993; Millsap & Kwok, 2004; Millsap & Meredith, 2007; Steenkamp & Baumgartner, 1998). Strong factorial invariance is desirable because it means that no systematic differences are present in the measurement models across groups; thus, between-group comparisons of latent variable means are valid and measurement invariance is achieved.

---

[2] If violations of unidimensionality exist, the joint probability of item responses is no longer equal to the product of marginal probabilities, which leads to biased parameter estimates (Reckase, 1979) and overestimates of score precision (Thissen et al., 1989). Methods for detecting violations of unidimensionality may be broadly categorized as those stemming from unidimensional models that are diagnostic tests (e.g., Chen & Thissen, 1997; Yen, 1984), those that introduce additional model parameters and latent variables to account for local dependence (e.g., Bradlow et al., 1999; Hoskens & De Boeck, 1997), and those that test the assumption of conditional independence (e.g., Stout, 1987). Diagnostic methods are useful data analytic tools for researchers interested in identifying locally dependent pairs or subsets of items. Modeling the local dependence directly is useful in situations in which local dependence is expected and is a requirement of the test (e.g., the use of testlets in modeling passage-dependent items; Wainer & Kiely, 1987).

[3] The factor analytic idea of measurement invariance parallels the concept of *differential item functioning* within IRT. Differential item functioning exists when, controlling for individuals' true latent variable score, the conditional probability of answering an item correctly is not the same across groups of individuals (i.e., measurement noninvariance). This is a major concern for psychometricians who are responsible for creating bias-free standardized tests.

Partial invariance occurs when some, but not all, factor loadings, means, and thresholds are invariant (Millsap & Kwok, 2004). When strong invariance holds and unique factor variances are also equivalent across groups, then *strict factorial invariance* is present (Meredith, 1993; Millsap & Meredith, 2007). Strict factorial invariance implies that systematic group differences in item means and covariances are solely a function of group differences in factor means and covariances. According to McArdle (2007) and Meredith and Horn (2001), strong invariance should be expected to hold if two subgroups are equivalent with respect to the latent variable of interest; however, strict invariance is not necessarily expected to hold.

Partial Invariance

If strong measurement invariance is not met in studies involving predictive relations among latent variables, then regression parameter bias is present (Humphreys, 1986; Millsap, 1998). If item intercepts vary across groups, but the noninvariance is ignored such that the noninvariant measurement model is used to test structural hypotheses, then group differences in regression parameter estimates in the structural part of the model not only represents any true group differences in the relations between latent variables but also the structural parameter estimates are confounded with group differences in measurement. Thus, it is necessary to test for measurement invariance before proceeding to tests of predictive models and making inferences about true group differences. Millsap (1998) described a formal test of measurement invariance that is necessary to ensure that observed structural differences are due to differences in the population rather than to differences in measurement. Millsap and Tein (2004) extended this work to include simple factor models with ordered categorical or dichotomous response types.

If an analyst detects partial measurement invariance, there are three options. First, if there are enough items, and if removing the problematic item does not result in undercoverage of the domain of the latent variable, then the item(s) can be eliminated. Second, the analyst might find small noninvariance effects amongst several items, but the invariance might "cancel out" if there is no systematic direction of the invariance. For instance, if females are slightly more likely to endorse one item given their score on the latent factor and males are more likely to endorse a different item given their score on the latent factor, and, if these effects are of approximately the same magnitude, then the analyst may decide that it is reasonable to retain the full item set. Finally, the researcher may choose to retain the problematic item(s) but model the partial noninvariance. This option works best when there are fewer indicators for each factor, especially when noninvariance is scientifically meaningful. For instance, a researcher studying developmental trends in aggression across childhood may find that an item about biting peers is a fairly normative indicator of aggressive behavior in toddlers, but that its meaning is quite different for older children. Moderated nonlinear factor analysis (MNLFA) models extend traditional IFA models by allowing item parameters to be regressed on covariates (Bauer, 2017; Bauer & Hussong, 2009; Curran et al., 2016).

Before providing an IFA application, there are a variety of ways in which item factor analytic methods can be conducted depending on the analyst's goals. In situations in which researchers have little a priori knowledge of the factor structure of a set of items, the data analytic process might begin by fitting unrestricted EFA models where items have as many loadings as factors (see Jöreskog, 1990; Jöreskog & Moustaki, 2001; Muthén, 1984). It is more common in the IFA tradition to begin the data analysis process by fitting models that are restrictions on the general EFA framework (i.e., constraining some or many factor loadings to be 0 concurrent with the research hypothesis). Often these models are variations on hierarchical models, where all items receive a loading from a general factor that is assumed to underlie all the items, with subsets of the items receiving loadings that account for a shared association specific to the subset of items but that are above and beyond the relationship accounted for by the general factor.

As an alternative to bifactor or hierarchical models, and useful in situations in which multidimensionality may not be explicitly expected, there is often utility in beginning the data analytic process by fitting a single factor model and then considering local dependence (LD) statistics as evidence of nuisance or extra dimensionality. This approach may be preferred in situations in which the analyst does not begin with the expectation of multidimensionality. In less common situations, where the analyst has no prior beliefs about the structure of the items, EFA may still provide a satisfactory starting position. In the application that follows, we conduct EFA initially to show the strengths and weakness of such an approach and then move into more traditional IFA models.

AN APPLICATION OF IFA

In this final section, we provide a brief example of IFAs, involving less than continuously measured items, that merges the two IFA traditions that we have discussed. The data are from the Patient Reported Outcomes Measurement Information System, a multisite project that aims to develop self-reported item banks for clinical research. Although content domains in many areas of health are included as part of this project, for the purposes of our example, we focus on the emotional distress domain.

Anxiety and depressive symptoms items were split between two test administration forms. For brevity, we report only the results of Form 1, which had 759 children respond to 10 anxiety items and 10 depressive symptom items (Irwin et al., 2010). All items had the same 5-point response scale with the options *never* (0), *almost never* (1), *sometimes* (2), *often* (3), and *almost always* (4).

Our first step was to examine the factor structure of the individual items to determine whether there was a single dimension underlying them (a precondition for unidimensional IRT). Initial EFA models were fit to the Form 1 data (Table 36.1). The factor structure generally revealed depressive symptoms and anxiety factors but not simple structure. Simple structure occurs when items load strongly on only one dimension. A close inspection reveals many instances of items loading (in part) on the incorrect factor. Had commonly used techniques for deciding the number of factors been used (e.g., scree plot, fit indexes, magnitude of factor loadings, inspection of eigenvalues), two factors would have been extracted.

Taking an IFA approach to this problem would consider item-level characteristics (e.g., item content and the location of the item on the scale) to identify subsets of locally dependent items while resolving dimensionality concerns. In such instances, a bifactor model that estimates two loadings for all items, a nonzero general factor

TABLE 36.1

Exploratory Factor Loadings for 20 PROMIS Anxiety (A) and Depression (D) Items

	Factor	
Item	1	2
A1. I got scared really easy.	.88	−.12
A2. I felt afraid.	.89	−.10
A3. I worried about what could happen to me.	.65	.14
A4. It was hard for me to stop worrying.	.59	.24
A5. I woke up at night scared.	.55	.25
A6. I worried when I was away from home.	.42	.27
A7. I was afraid that I would make mistakes.	.34	.37
A8. I felt nervous.	.40	.27
A9. It was hard for me to relax.	.30	.42
A10. I felt afraid or scared.	.64	.23
D1. I wanted to be by myself.	−.08	.47
D2. I felt that no one loved me.	.04	.76
D3. I cried more than usual.	.39	.44
D4. I felt alone.	.06	.75
D5. I felt like I couldn't do anything right.	.08	.75
D6. I felt so bad that I didn't want to do anything.	.12	.64
D7. I felt everything in my life went wrong.	.06	.78
D8. Being sad made it hard for me to do things with my friends.	.28	.58
D9. It was hard to do school work because I felt sad.	.25	.59
D10. I felt like crying.	.42	.43

Note. Model fit using Crawford-Ferguson varimax rotation and mean- and variance-adjusted weighted least squares estimation. The correlation between factors is 0.55. $\chi^2(88) = 529$, comparative fit index = .91, Tucker-Lewis index = .97, and root-mean-square error of approximation = .08.

loading (here, emotional distress) and a group-specific loading (here, depressive symptoms and anxiety), serves as an excellent compromise between an EFA and traditional simple-structure CFA. In this case, a bifactor model is particularly relevant because the goal of the analysis is to determine whether depressive symptoms and anxiety are best treated as separate dimensions, and, hence scales, while also identifying sources of LD (i.e., violations of unidimensionality) that exist over and above the general and specific factors. Detecting LD in this manner allows the researcher to control the dimensionality of the scale. If LD is detected in either pairs or subsets of items, selecting one item from each grouping, and setting aside the LD-inducing items, should result in a unidimensional set of items, as the residuals of the offending items no longer covary with the selected item.

A modified bifactor model was then fit using M*plus* with WLSMV estimation. This model is considered a modified version of the traditional bifactor model because potential sources of LD identified in the expanded EFA were modeled as subfactors (i.e., three or more items receiving an additional factor loading) and correlated errors that represent correlations between the residuals after accounting for the covariance occurring for the general and domain-specific factor (Table 36.2).[4] Goodness-of-fit indexes suggested that the augmented bifactor model with three specific factors and four residual correlations fit the data well: $\chi^2(76, N = 621) = 247.83$, comparative fit index = .95, Tucker–Lewis index = .99, and root-mean-square error of approximation = .06.

Used in this fashion, the bifactor model provides information regarding the intended dimensionality and the presence of nuisance multidimensionality. The Patient Reported Outcomes Measurement Information System researchers were initially interested in determining whether these data provided evidence that emotional distress was a single dimension or whether distinguishable individual variation occurred between the anxiety items and then again between the depressive symptoms items. The fact that substantial loadings differed significantly from 0 on the group-specific factor for the depressive symptoms items in Table 36.2 indicated that the covariation among the item responses could not be adequately explained with the theory that a single emotional distress dimension of individual differences underlies responses to all of the items. It is a curiosity of the data that the general factor in Table 36.2 is an anxiety-dominated negative affect, leaving little unique variance for the anxiety group-specific factor. This fact is noted by comparing the ratio of the general factor to the domain-specific factors and demonstrated in the large number of nonsignificant loadings on the anxiety factor.

The analysis also highlights the precision with which IFA can detect nuisance dimensionality. Researchers who rely on EFA to determine the dimensionality of the items may have settled on the set of depressive symptoms and anxiety items originally hypothesized; however, a closer inspection reveals that the general and group-specific factors are not (all) conditionally independent. In Table 36.2, note that a cluster of items involves being "scared or afraid" with responses that are more correlated than expected given the general factor and the anxiety-specific factor, and four more pairs of items have significant residual correlations. Beginning at the top of Table 36.2, the pairs of items modeled with residual correlations are about "worrying," "feelings of loneliness," "sadness," and "crying." Items in these pairs or triplets are (in part) like asking the same question twice. In each instance, including a single item on the scale is sufficient and providing both (or all three in the case of the triplet) would violate assumptions of unidimensionality.

---

[4]If using FIML estimation, the Gibbons and Hedeker (1992) method would apply. In this context, integration would occur over eight orthogonal dimensions (1 general, 2 domain specific, 1 subfactor, and 4 error correlations), which with four quadrature points per dimension amounts to 65,536 points. Cai (2010b) considered a similar analytic problem, and using a prototype of IRTPRO with the MH-RM algorithm, reached model convergence in under 3 minutes compared with an ML/EM solution with adaptive quadrature, which took more than 4 hours.

TABLE 36.2

Factor Loadings and Residual Correlations for an Augmented Bifactor Model Fitted to the Items on Form 1

		Orthogonal group: specific factors			
Item stem	General factor	Anxiety	Depressive symptoms	Afraid/ scared	Doublet residual correlations
I felt afraid.	.68	*.11*		.67	
I got scared really easy.	.64	.30		.38	
I felt afraid or scared.	.76	.15		.20	
It was hard for me to stop worrying.	.73	*.11*			.32
I worried about what could happen to me.	.70	*.10*			
I woke up at night scared.	.72	.40			
I was afraid that I would make mistakes.	.70	−.39			
It was hard for me to relax.	.68	−.15			
I worried when I was away from home.	.64	*.10*			
I felt nervous.	.63	−.19			
I felt everything in my life went wrong.	.61		.56		
I felt like I couldn't do anything right.	.62		.55		
I felt so bad that I didn't want to do anything.	.57		.48		
I felt alone.	.59		.50		.27
I felt that no one loved me.	.60		.47		
Being sad made it hard for me to do things with my friends.	.72		.28		.26
It was hard to do school work because I felt sad.	.66		.31		
I felt like crying.	.66		.24		.49
I cried more than usual.	.64		.23		
I wanted to be by myself.	.27		.30		

Note. Italicized entries are less than 2 standard errors from 0. From "An Item Response Analysis of the Pediatric PROMIS Anxiety and Depressive Symptoms Scales," by D. E. Irwin, B. D. Stucky, M. M. Langer, D. Thissen, E. M. DeWitt, J. S. Lai, J. W. Varni, K. Yeatts, and D. A. DeWalt, 2010, *Quality of Life Research, 19*(4), p. 600. Copyright 2010 by Springer Science+Business Media. Reprinted with permission.

Conducting IFA in this careful manner is useful for identifying and eliminating violations of local independence. However, this modeling approach is not without its own complexities. In the present application, knowledge of the factor structure served as a foundation for later unidimensional IRT parameter calibration (i.e., after setting aside locally dependent items, the factors anxiety and depressive symptoms were separately fit with unidimensional IRT models). If the modified bifactor model is considered in a MIRT framework, however, many difficult interpretation and scoring issues remain. If IRT-based scores are desired, then, including residual correlations, there are eight dimensions of integration required. When IFA is conducted to explore or identify multidimensionality that often occurs in psychological data, it serves as a useful alternative to traditional EFA models. Had our previous analyses concluded after the EFA, we would have missed seeing that our item responses involved a great deal of LD. The situation shown in this data example is not rare. In well-constructed, expert-reviewed scales, LD is often missed, and it may be too minor to be identified via an EFA but large enough to affect item calibration. With recent advances in both efficient algorithms and computational speed, we expect IFA to continue to grow as more researchers become aware of the benefits of considering both scale dimensionality and item effects.

References

Bandalos, D. L. (2008). Is parceling really necessary? A comparison of results from item parceling and categorical variable methodology. *Structural Equation Modeling, 15*(2), 211–240. https://doi.org/10.1080/10705510801922340

Bartholomew, D. J. (1983). Latent variable models for ordered categorical data. *Journal of Econometrics, 22*(1–2), 229–243. https://doi.org/10.1016/0304-4076(83)90101-X

Bauer, D. J. (2017). A more general model for testing measurement invariance and differential item functioning. *Psychological Methods, 22*(3), 507–526. https://doi.org/10.1037/met0000077

Bauer, D. J., & Hussong, A. M. (2009). Psychometric approaches for developing commensurate measures across independent studies: Traditional and new models. *Psychological Methods, 14*(2), 101–125. https://doi.org/10.1037/a0015583

Birnbaum, A. (1968). Some latent trait models and their use in inferring an examinee's ability. In F. M. Lord & M. R. Novick (Eds.), *Statistical theories of mental test scores* (pp. 395–479). Addison-Wesley.

Bock, R. D. (1972). Estimating item parameters and latent ability when responses are scored in two or more nominal categories. *Psychometrika, 37*(1), 29–51. https://doi.org/10.1007/BF02291411

Bock, R. D., & Aitkin, M. (1981). Marginal maximum likelihood estimation of item parameters: An application of the EM algorithm. *Psychometrika, 46*(4), 443–459. https://doi.org/10.1007/BF02293801

Bock, R. D., & Lieberman, M. (1970). Fitting a response model for n dichotomously scored items. *Psychometrika, 35*(2), 179–197. https://doi.org/10.1007/BF02291262

Bradlow, E. T., Wainer, H., & Wang, X. (1999). A Bayesian random effects model for testlets. *Psychometrika, 64*(2), 153–168. https://doi.org/10.1007/BF02294533

Cai, L. (2010a). High-dimensional exploratory item factor analysis by a Metropolis-Hastings Robbins-Monro algorithm. *Psychometrika, 75*(1), 33–57. https://doi.org/10.1007/s11336-009-9136-x

Cai, L. (2010b). Metropolis-Hastings Robbins-Monro algorithm for confirmatory item factor analysis. *Journal of Educational and Behavioral Statistics, 35*(3), 307–335. https://doi.org/10.3102/1076998609353115

Cattell, R. B., & Burdsal, C. A., Jr. (1975). The radial parcel double factoring design: A solution to the item-vs.-parcel controversy. *Multivariate Behavioral Research, 10*(2), 165–179. https://doi.org/10.1207/s15327906mbr1002_3

Chen, W. H., & Thissen, D. (1997). Local dependence indices for item pairs using item response theory. *Journal of Educational and Behavioral Statistics, 22*(3), 265–289. https://doi.org/10.3102/10769986022003265

Childs, R. A., Dahlstrom, W. G., Kemp, S., & Panter, A. T. (1992). *Item response theory in personality assessment: The MMPI-2 Depression Scale* (Report 92-1). Thurstone Psychometric Laboratory, University of North Carolina at Chapel Hill.

Christofferson, A. (1975). Factor analysis of dichotomized variables. *Psychometrika, 40*(1), 5–32. https://doi.org/10.1007/BF02291477

Coffman, D. L., & MacCallum, R. C. (2005). Using parcels to convert path analysis models into latent variable models. *Multivariate Behavioral Research, 40*(2), 235–259. https://doi.org/10.1207/s15327906mbr4002_4

Curran, P. J., Cole, V., Bauer, D. J., Hussong, A. M., & Gottfredson, N. (2016). Improving factor score estimation through the use of observed background characteristics. *Structural Equation Modeling, 23*(6), 827–844. https://doi.org/10.1080/10705511.2016.1220839

DiStefano, C. (2002). The impact of categorization with confirmatory factor analysis. *Structural Equation Modeling, 9*(3), 327–346. https://doi.org/10.1207/S15328007SEM0903_2

Edwards, M. C. (2010). A Markov chain Monte Carlo approach to confirmatory item factor analysis. *Psychometrika, 75*(3), 474–497. https://doi.org/10.1007/s11336-010-9161-9

Embretson, S. E., & Reise, S. P. (2000). *Item response theory for psychologists*. Erlbaum.

Flora, D. B., & Curran, P. J. (2004). An empirical evaluation of alternative methods of estimation for confirmatory factor analysis with ordinal data. *Psychological Methods, 9*(4), 466–491. https://doi.org/10.1037/1082-989X.9.4.466

Gibbons, R. D., & Hedeker, D. R. (1992). Full-information item bi-factor analysis. *Psychometrika, 57*(3), 423–436. https://doi.org/10.1007/BF02295430

Hagtvet, K. A., & Nasser, F. M. (2004). How well do item parcels represent conceptually-defined latent constructs? A two-facet approach. *Structural Equation Modeling, 11*(2), 168–193. https://doi.org/10.1207/s15328007sem1102_2

Hastings, W. K. (1970). Monte Carlo simulation methods using Markov chains and their applications. *Biometrika, 57*(1), 97–109. https://doi.org/10.1093/biomet/57.1.97

Hau, K. T., & Marsh, H. W. (2004). The use of item parcels in structural equation modelling: Non-normal data and small sample sizes.

British Journal of Mathematical and Statistical Psychology, 57(Pt. 2), 327–351. https://doi.org/10.1111/j.2044-8317.2004.tb00142.x

Heywood, H. B. (1931). On finite sequences of real numbers. *Proceedings of the Royal Society of London: Series A. Mathematical and Physical Sciences, 134*(824), 486–501. https://doi.org/10.1098/rspa.1931.0209

Horn, J. L., & McArdle, J. J. (1992). A practical and theoretical guide to measurement invariance in aging research. *Experimental Aging Research, 18*(3), 117–144. https://doi.org/10.1080/03610739208253916

Hoskens, M., & De Boeck, P. (1997). A parametric model for local dependence among test items. *Psychological Methods, 2*(3), 261–277. https://doi.org/10.1037/1082-989X.2.3.261

Humphreys, L. G. (1986). An analysis and evaluation of test and item bias in the prediction context. *Journal of Applied Psychology, 71*(2), 327–333. https://doi.org/10.1037/0021-9010.71.2.327

Irwin, D. E., Stucky, B., Langer, M. M., Thissen, D., Dewitt, E. M., Lai, J. S., Varni, J. W., Yeatts, K., & DeWalt, D. A. (2010). An item response analysis of the pediatric PROMIS anxiety and depressive symptoms scales. *Quality of Life Research, 19*(4), 595–607. https://doi.org/10.1007/s11136-010-9619-3

Jöreskog, K. G. (1969). A general approach to confirmatory maximum likelihood factor analysis. *Psychometrika, 34*(2), 183–202. https://doi.org/10.1007/BF02289343

Jöreskog, K. G. (1970). A general method for analysis of covariance structures. *Biometrika, 57*(2), 239–251. https://doi.org/10.1093/biomet/57.2.239

Jöreskog, K. G. (1990). New developments in LISREL: Analysis of ordinal variables using polychoric correlations and weighted least squares. *Quality & Quantity: International Journal of Methodology, 24*(4), 387–404. https://doi.org/10.1007/BF00152012

Jöreskog, K. G., & Moustaki, I. (2001). Factor analysis of ordinal variables: A comparison of three approaches. *Multivariate Behavioral Research, 36*(3), 347–387. https://doi.org/10.1207/S15327906347-387

Jöreskog, K. G., & Sörbom, D. (2001). *LISREL user's guide*. Scientific Software International.

Krosnick, J. A. (1999). Survey research. *Annual Review of Psychology, 50*, 537–567. https://doi.org/10.1146/annurev.psych.50.1.537

Lazarsfeld, P. F. (1950). The logical and mathematical foundation of latent structure analysis. In S. A. Stouffer (Ed.), *Measurement and prediction*. Princeton University Press.

Little, T. D., Cunningham, W. A., Shahar, G., & Widaman, K. F. (2002). To parcel or not to parcel: Exploring the question, weighing the merits. *Structural Equation Modeling, 9*(2), 151–173. https://doi.org/10.1207/S15328007SEM0902_1

Little, T. D., Lindenberger, U., & Nesselroade, J. R. (1999). On selecting indicators for multivariate measurement and modeling with latent variables. *Psychological Methods, 4*(2), 192–211. https://doi.org/10.1037/1082-989X.4.2.192

Lord, F. M. (1952). *A theory of test scores*. Psychometric Society.

Lord, F. M., & Novick, M. R. (1968). *Statistical theories of mental test scores*. Addison-Wesley.

McArdle, J. J. (2007). Five steps in the structural factor analysis of longitudinal data. In R. Cudeck & R. C. MacCallum (Eds.), *Factor analysis at 100: Historical developments and future directions* (pp. 99–130). Erlbaum.

McDonald, R. P. (1967). Nonlinear factor analysis. *Psychometric Monograph, 15*.

McDonald, R. P. (1999). *Test theory: A unified treatment*. Erlbaum.

McDonald, R. P., & Ahlawat, K. S. (1974). Difficulty factors in binary data. *British Journal of Mathematical & Statistical Psychology, 27*(1), 82–99. https://doi.org/10.1111/j.2044-8317.1974.tb00530.x

Meredith, W. (1993). Measurement invariance, factor analysis and factorial invariance. *Psychometrika, 58*(4), 525–543. https://doi.org/10.1007/BF02294825

Meredith, W., & Horn, J. L. (2001). The role of factorial invariance in modeling growth and change. In A. G. Sayer & L. M. Collins (Eds.), *New methods for the analysis of change* (pp. 203–240). American Psychological Association. https://doi.org/10.1037/10409-007

Millsap, R. E. (1997). Invariance in measurement and prediction: Their relationship in the single-factor case. *Psychological Methods, 2*(3), 248–260. https://doi.org/10.1037/1082-989X.2.3.248

Millsap, R. E. (1998). Group differences in regression intercepts: Implications for factorial invariance. *Multivariate Behavioral Research, 33*(3), 403–424. https://doi.org/10.1207/s15327906mbr3303_5

Millsap, R. E., & Kwok, O. M. (2004). Evaluating the impact of partial factorial invariance on selection in two populations. *Psychological Methods, 9*(1), 93–115. https://doi.org/10.1037/1082-989X.9.1.93

Millsap, R. E., & Meredith, W. (2007). Factorial invariance: Historical perspectives and new problems. In R. Cudeck & R. C. MacCallum (Eds.), *Factor analysis at 100: Historical developments and future directions* (pp. 131–152). Erlbaum.

Millsap, R. E., & Tein, J. Y. (2004). Assessing factorial invariance in ordered-categorical measures. *Multivariate Behavioral Research*, *39*(3), 479–515. https://doi.org/10.1207/S15327906MBR3903_4

Mislevy, R. J. (1986). Recent developments in the factor analysis of categorical variables. *Journal of Educational Statistics*, *11*(1), 3–31. https://doi.org/10.3102/10769986011001003

Muraki, E. (1992). A generalized partial credit model: Application of an EM algorithm. *Applied Psychological Measurement*, *16*(2), 159–176. https://doi.org/10.1177/014662169201600206

Muthén, B. (1983). Latent variable structural equation modeling with categorical data. *Journal of Econometrics*, *22*(1–2), 43–65. https://doi.org/10.1016/0304-4076(83)90093-3

Muthén, B. O. (1978). Contributions to factor analysis of dichotomous variables. *Psychometrika*, *43*(4), 551–560. https://doi.org/10.1007/BF02293813

Muthén, B. O. (1984). A general structural equation model with dichotomous, ordered categorical, and continuous latent variable indicators. *Psychometrika*, *49*(1), 115–132. https://doi.org/10.1007/BF02294210

Muthén, B. O., du Toit, S. H. C., & Spisic, D. (1997). *Robust inference using weighted least squares and quadratic estimating equations in latent variable modeling with categorical and continuous outcomes* [Unpublished manuscript]. https://www.gseis.ucla.edu/faculty/muthen/psychometrics.htm

Muthén, B. O., & Lehman, J. (1985). Multiple group IRT modeling: Application to item bias analysis. *Journal of Educational Statistics*, *10*(2), 133–142. https://doi.org/10.3102/10769986010002133

Muthén, L. K., & Muthén, B. O. (1998–2017). *Mplus user's guide* (8th ed.). Muthén & Muthén.

Panter, A. T., Swygert, K., Dahlstrom, W. G., & Tanaka, J. S. (1997). Factor analytic approaches to item-level data. *Journal of Personality Assessment*, *68*(3), 561–589. https://doi.org/10.1207/s15327752jpa6803_6

Panter, A. T., & Tanaka, J. S. (1987, April). *Statistically appropriate methods for analyzing dichotomous data: Assessing self-monitoring*. Paper presented at the Eastern Psychological Association, Arlington, VA, United States.

Panter, A. T., Tanaka, J. S., & Wellens, T. R. (1992). The psychometrics of order effects. In S. Sudman & N. Schwarz (Eds.), *Context effects in social and psychological research* (pp. 249–264). Springer-Verlag. https://doi.org/10.1007/978-1-4612-2848-6_17

Rasch, G. (1960). *Probabilistic models for some intelligence and attainment tests*. University of Chicago Press.

Reckase, M. D. (1979). Unifactor latent trait models applied to multifactor tests: Results and implications. *Journal of Educational Statistics*, *4*(3), 207–230. https://doi.org/10.3102/10769986004003207

Reckase, M. D. (2009). *Multidimensional item response theory*. Springer. https://doi.org/10.1007/978-0-387-89976-3

Reise, S. P., & Waller, N. G. (1990). Fitting the two-parameter model to personality data. *Applied Psychological Measurement*, *14*(1), 45–58. https://doi.org/10.1177/014662169001400105

Reise, S. P., Widaman, K. F., & Pugh, R. H. (1993). Confirmatory factor analysis and item response theory: Two approaches for exploring measurement invariance. *Psychological Bulletin*, *114*(3), 552–566. https://doi.org/10.1037/0033-2909.114.3.552

Robbins, H., & Monro, S. (1951). A stochastic approximation method. *Annals of Mathematical Statistics*, *22*(3), 400–407. https://doi.org/10.1214/aoms/1177729586

Samejima, F. (1969). Estimation of latent ability using a response pattern of graded scores. *Psychometrika, Monograph No. 17*.

Satorra, A., & Bentler, P. M. (1994). Corrections to test statistic and standard errors in covariance structure analysis. In A. von Eye & C. C. Clogg (Eds.), *Analysis of latent variables in developmental research* (pp. 399–419). Sage.

Schaeffer, N. C. (1988). An application of the item response theory to the measurement of depression. In C. C. Clogg (Ed.), *Sociological methodology* (pp. 271–307). American Sociological Association. https://doi.org/10.2307/271051

Schilling, S., & Bock, R. D. (2005). High-dimensional maximum marginal likelihood item factor analysis by adaptive quadrature. *Psychometrika*, *70*(3), 533–555. https://doi.org/10.1007/s11336-003-1141-x

Steenkamp, J. E. M., & Baumgartner, H. (1998). Assessing measurement invariance in cross-national consumer research. *The Journal of Consumer Research*, *25*(1), 78–107. https://doi.org/10.1086/209528

Steinberg, L. (1994). Context and serial-order effects in personality measurement: Limits on the generality of measuring changes the measure. *Journal of Personality and Social Psychology*, *66*(2), 341–349. https://doi.org/10.1037/0022-3514.66.2.341

Steinberg, L., & Thissen, D. (1995). Item response theory in personality research. In P. E. Shrout &

S. Fiske (Eds.), *Personality research, methods, and theory: A Festschrift honoring Donald W. Fiske* (pp. 161–181). Erlbaum.

Stout, W. F. (1987). A nonparametric approach for assessing latent trait dimensionality. *Psychometrika, 52*(4), 589–617. https://doi.org/10.1007/BF02294821

Takane, Y., & de Leeuw, J. (1987). On the relationship between item response theory and factor analysis of discretized variables. *Psychometrika, 52*(3), 393–408. https://doi.org/10.1007/BF02294363

Tanaka, J. S., Panter, A. T., & Winborne, W. C. (1988). Dimensions of the need for cognition: Subscales and gender differences. *Multivariate Behavioral Research, 23*(1), 35–50. https://doi.org/10.1207/s15327906mbr2301_2

Thissen, D. (1992, August). *Item response theory in psychological research*. Invited address at the 100th Annual Convention of the American Psychological Association, Washington, DC, United States.

Thissen, D., & Steinberg, L. (1986). A taxonomy of item response models. *Psychometrika, 51*(4), 567–577. https://doi.org/10.1007/BF02295596

Thissen, D., Steinberg, L., & Mooney, J. (1989). Trace lines for testlets: A use of multiple-categorical response models. *Journal of Educational Measurement, 26*, 247–260. https://doi.org/10.1111/j.1745-3984.1989.tb00331.x

Thurstone, L. L. (1947). *Multiple factor analysis*. University of Chicago Press.

Wainer, H., Bradlow, E. T., & Wang, X. (2007). *Testlet response theory and its applications*. Cambridge University Press. https://doi.org/10.1017/CBO9780511618765

Wainer, H., & Kiely, G. L. (1987). Item clusters and computerized adaptive testing: A case for testlets. *Journal of Educational Measurement, 24*(3), 185–201. https://doi.org/10.1111/j.1745-3984.1987.tb00274.x

Waller, N. G., & Reise, S. P. (1989). Computerized adaptive personality assessment: An illustration with the Absorption scale. *Journal of Personality and Social Psychology, 57*(6), 1051–1058. https://doi.org/10.1037/0022-3514.57.6.1051

West, S. G., Finch, J. F., & Curran, P. J. (1995). Structural equation models with non-normal variables: Problems and remedies. In R. Hoyle (Ed.), *Structural equation modeling: Concepts, issues, and applications* (pp. 56–75). Sage.

Widaman, K. F., & Reise, S. P. (1997). Exploring the measurement invariance of psychological instruments: Applications in the substance use domain. In K. J. Bryant, M. Windle, & S. G. West (Eds.), *The science of prevention: Methodological advances from alcohol and substance abuse research* (pp. 281–324). American Psychological Association. https://doi.org/10.1037/10222-009

Wirth, R. J., & Edwards, M. C. (2007). Item factor analysis: Current approaches and future directions. *Psychological Methods, 12*(1), 58–79. https://doi.org/10.1037/1082-989X.12.1.58

Yen, W. M. (1984). Effects of local item dependence on the fit and equating performance of the three-parameter logistic model. *Applied Psychological Measurement, 8*, 125–145. https://doi.org/10.1177/014662168400800201

CHAPTER 37

ITEM RESPONSE THEORY

Steven P. Reise and Tyler M. Moore

Item response theory (IRT; Baker & Kim, 2017; Cai et al., 2016; Embretson & Reise, 2000; Van der Linden, 2018) refers to a class of mathematical models relating individual differences on one or more latent variables to the probability of responding to a scale item in a specific response category. A response of 3 on a 5-point personality item, a correct answer on a multiple-choice item, and a clinician's rating of an adolescent's anxiety are all item responses that can potentially be related (probabilistically) to a latent variable. IRT models, which focus on characterizing how individual differences on a latent variable interact with item properties to produce a response, contrast sharply with classical test theory (Lord & Novick, 1968) procedures, which focus on understanding the statistical properties of a composite scale score (e.g., estimating reliability of a test score).

The development of IRT models and associated methods (Birnbaum, 1968; Lord, 1952; Thurstone, 1925) was originally motivated by applied problems in large-scale, multiple-choice aptitude testing (e.g., how to efficiently administer different test items to individuals but still compare them on the same scale, how to link different sets of items measuring the same construct onto the same scale). However, applications of IRT models to personality, psychopathology, and patient reported outcomes (PRO) measurement have been increasing (see Cella et al., 2019; O'Hara et al., 2020; Segawa et al., 2020).

Regardless of context, researchers from a variety of fields have been keenly interested in the potential of IRT modeling as an alternative to traditional psychometric approaches to scale construction, item analysis, scale administration, and scoring individual differences. As reviewed in Foster et al. (2017), Reise et al. (2005), and Thomas (2019), IRT models potentially offer many attractive features. For example, through inspection of item and scale information statistics, a researcher can gain a better understanding of how well an item, or scale, functions (e.g., measurement precision) across different ranges of a latent variable. Moreover, because of the IRT item and person invariance properties, IRT models can be used to either place items from different instruments onto a common scale, or place individuals who responded to different items onto a common scale (Boulton et al., 2019; Lee et al., 2020; Schalet et al., 2020; Victorson et al., 2019). In turn, this facilitates the analysis of differential item functioning across demographic groups (i.e., exploring whether the items measure the same latent variable in the same way across different groups (Crins et al., 2019; Flens et al., 2021; Hays et al., 2018; Liegl et al., 2020; Taple et al., 2020)), as well as the creation of "item banks" that can be administered efficiently via computerized adaptive testing (Gibbons et al., 2020; Granziol et al., 2022; Moore et al., 2019; Thomas et al., 2020).

Nevertheless, this chapter does not focus on the strengths of IRT and its applications nor does it compare IRT with traditional psychometric procedures. Such articles are plentiful (e.g., Embretson, 1996; Reise & Henson, 2003). Rather, this chapter is divided into two sections. In the first, we describe commonly applied unidimensional IRT models appropriate for dichotomous or polytomous item response data; space considerations prevent us from extending these to the multidimensional or bifactor models (see Cai & Hansen, 2013; Reckase, 2009; Reise, 2012; Toland et al., 2017). Our primary goal in this section is to inform readers of the most popular unidimensional IRT models and the interpretation of their parameters. In the second section, we discuss some "lessons learned" thus far from the research literature on application of IRT. This second section is oriented toward both novice researchers who are considering applying IRT to their data and more experienced investigators who may not have considered some of the issues raised herein.

UNIDIMENSIONAL DICHOTOMOUS IRT MODELS

Item response theory modeling begins with a persons ($s = 1 \ldots S$) by items ($i = 1 \ldots I$) matrix of item responses (X_{si}). When items are dichotomously scored, such as correct versus incorrect or endorsed versus not endorsed, the item response matrix consists entirely of 0s and 1s. Given this matrix, the chief objective of IRT modeling is to fit a mathematical function that characterizes the relation between individual differences on an assumed latent variable (labeled θ) and the probability of endorsing an item. Herein, for dichotomous items, this function is termed an *item response curve* (IRC). The goal of fitting IRT models is to find a model such that the estimated IRC "best represents" or "fits" the observed item response data. In this section, we provide detailed descriptions of the most common unidimensional IRT models for dichotomous item response data.

As noted, the basic goal of IRT modeling is to find a function, that is, an IRC, that relates an individual's standing on a latent variable (θ) with the probability of endorsing an item. One such IRC must be found for each scale item. In considering an appropriate model, note that it has long been assumed, reasonably, that as individual trait levels increase, the probability of item endorsement should increase monotonically. Stated differently, groups of individuals who are higher on the latent variable measured by an item should have higher item endorsement rates relative to groups of individuals who are lower on the latent variable.

At first blush, the above observation may suggest that a straight line function could be used to describe the relation between the latent variable and item endorsement probability. However, a straight line function does not suffice because probabilities are bounded between 0 and 1, and any line eventually predicts values above 1 as the latent variable increases and predicts values below 0 as the latent variable decreases. Alternatively, a function that increases monotonically and is bounded between 0 and 1 is the two-parameter logistic model (2PLM).

$$P(x_{si}=1|\theta) = \frac{\exp(\alpha_i(\theta_s - \beta_i))}{1 + \exp(\alpha_i(\theta_s - \beta_i))} \quad (37.1)$$

Equation 37.1 states that the probability of endorsement ($x = 1$) conditional on a latent variable (θ), is a logistic regression with two parameters. The scale for the latent variable is arbitrary and must be identified by setting the mean and standard deviation. Values of 0 and 1 are typically chosen. The slope (*a*) parameter controls how rapidly the probability of endorsement increases as trait levels increase. Slope values typically range between 1.5 and 2.5 with higher values indicating a more discriminating item. Stated differently, the slope in the logistic model is interpreted as the slope of the line relating the latent variable to the log-odds of item endorsement, that is log(*P*/(*1-P*)). The location (β) parameter determines where along the trait scale the inflection point lies (i.e., where the probability of endorsement is .50). Location parameters typically range between –2 and 2 with positive values shifting the IRC to the right (reflecting a more "difficult" item—an item requiring higher values of θ) and negative values shifting the IRC to the left (reflecting an "easier" item—an item requiring lower values of θ).

Specifically, Equation 37.1 states that the probability of an endorsement changes as a function of the difference between a person's trait level and the item's location, weighted by the item slope. Different items are associated with different IRCs that reflects items that vary in discrimination and location. Modern statistical estimation software such as *mirt* (Chalmers, 2012) and *flexmirt* (Cai, 2017) include only logistic models. Equation 37.1 shows the 2PLM in the familiar slope and location form. By rearranging terms, however, the model can be written in the so-called slope-and-intercept form as shown in Equation 37.2.

$$P(x_{si} = 1|\theta) = \frac{\exp(\alpha_i \theta_s - \tau_i)}{1 + \exp(\alpha_i \theta_s - \tau_i)} \quad (37.2)$$

We can rewrite Equation 37.1 to be in slope-and-intercept form by defining an intercept as τ = –αβ; the intercept in the 2PLM is the predicted *log-odds* of the proportion endorsed for individuals at the mean on the latent variable (theta = 0). Equations 37.1 and 37.2 express exactly the same thing; both are two-parameter logistic models. Equation 37.1 is the parameterization most frequently reported and discussed, but Equation 37.2 is critically important to understand because (a) it is the model that is most easily transformed in a factor analytic model (i.e., slopes transformed into factor loadings and intercepts transformed into factor thresholds (Kamata & Bauer, 2008; McLeod et al., 2001, p. 199)), and, thus, (b) it is the model that generalizes most easily to multidimensional models (i.e., models with more than one latent variable, such as a bifactor model; Toland et al., 2017). Almost all major IRT software report parameter estimates in both slope-and-location and slope-and-intercept form.

To illustrate and better define the 2PLM, we report on item parameter estimates for 25 items taken[1] from the Taylor Manifest Anxiety Scale (TMAS; Taylor, 1953) based on 5,410 responses. Data were from the https://openpsychometrics.org/_rawdata/ website, and item content is shown in Table 37.1. Item parameters were estimated

TABLE 37.1

Item Content for 25 Items From the Taylor Manifest Anxiety Scale

Item #	Item content
1	I cannot keep my mind on one thing.
2	I worry quite a bit over possible misfortunes.
3	I have periods in which I have lost sleep over worry.
4	My sleep is fitful and disturbed.
5	I am easily embarrassed.
6	I am more sensitive than most other people.
7	I frequently find myself worrying about something.
8	I wish I could be as happy as others seem to be.
9	I am usually calm and not easily upset.
10	I feel anxiety about something or someone almost all the time.
11	I am happy most of the time.
12	It makes me nervous to have to wait.
13	I have sometimes felt that difficulties were piling up so high that I could not overcome them.
14	I must admit that I have at times been worried beyond reason over something that really did not matter.
15	I have very few fears compared to my friends.
16	I have been afraid of things or people that I know cannot hurt me.
17	I certainly feel useless at times.
18	I find it hard to keep my mind on a task or job.
19	I am inclined to take things hard.
20	Life is a trial for me much of the time.
21	At times I think I am no good at all.
22	I am certainly lacking in self confidence.
23	I sometimes feel that I am about to go to pieces.
24	I shrink from facing crisis of difficulty.
25	I am entirely self-confident.

Note. Item # is item order number.

---
[1]We selected 25 items based on psychometric criteria.

using marginal maximum likelihood as implemented using default specifications in the *mirt()* function in the *mirt* package (Chalmers, 2012) in R. The first two columns of Table 37.2 report the item-test correlations and the item means (proportions endorsed). Item-test correlations vary widely between 0.34 (Item 4, "My sleep is fitful and disturbed") and 0.58 (Item 23, "I sometimes feel that I am about to go to pieces"), and the proportions endorsed are all fairly low, from 15% for Item 25 ("I am entirely self confident") to a maximum of 38% for Item 16 ("I have been afraid of things and people that I know cannot hurt me"). The remaining columns of Table 37.2 show the IRT parameter estimates from the 2PLM for the TMAS. Consistent with the classical "proportion correct" parameters, the location (τ and β) estimates are almost all in the high end of the trait (theta) spectrum, reflecting the relatively low endorsement rates for the TMAS (i.e., the items are not popular and rarely endorsed). While not as obvious, the slope (α) estimates are also consistent with the classical item-test correlations.

Figure 37.1A contrasts two items that differ in both slope and location parameters: Item 4 My sleep is fitful and disturbed (slope = 0.46 location = 0.83), and Item 14 ("I must admit that I have at times been worried beyond reason over something that really did not matter") (slope = 1.60, location = 1.74). Clearly, not only is the IRC for Item 14 shifted far to the right—suggesting that only high trait individuals endorse this content, but relative to Item 4, the curve is much steeper suggesting that probabilities of endorsement change rapidly. These differences are of great consequence in terms of the items' relative contributions to measurement precision. In Figure 37.1B, we display the item information curves for these two items. These curves show the "discrimination power" (ability to lower the standard error) for these two items. Item 14 provides a lot of information in the high trait range, while Item 4 provides much less in the middle trait range. The concept of psychometric information is critically important in IRT modeling because test information is the sum of item information, and, in turn, the conditional standard error in IRT is related to one over the square root of the test information.

TABLE 37.2

Classical and 2PLM Parameter Estimates for the TMAS

| | Item-test | Proportion | 2PLM | | |
Item	r	endorsed	τ	β	α
1	0.38	0.22	−1.56	1.08	1.44
2	0.53	0.16	−2.65	2.03	1.31
3	0.38	0.22	−1.57	1.11	1.42
4	0.34	0.42	−0.38	0.83	0.46
5	0.42	0.34	−0.84	1.17	0.72
6	0.40	0.21	−1.70	1.21	1.41
7	0.56	0.10	−4.31	2.92	1.48
8	0.55	0.17	−2.62	2.16	1.21
9	0.46	0.36	−0.74	1.30	0.57
10	0.56	0.20	−2.27	2.11	1.08
11	0.48	0.35	−0.88	1.49	0.59
12	0.40	0.28	−1.16	1.12	1.03
13	0.53	0.17	−2.47	2.00	1.23
14	0.47	0.13	−2.78	1.74	1.60
15	0.42	0.21	−1.68	1.25	1.35
16	0.42	0.38	−0.63	1.15	0.55
17	0.54	0.22	−2.08	2.04	1.02
18	0.43	0.31	−1.00	1.20	0.83
19	0.46	0.21	−1.83	1.43	1.27
20	0.52	0.34	−1.01	1.69	0.60
21	0.58	0.29	−1.56	2.26	0.69
22	0.54	0.29	−1.38	1.87	0.74
23	0.58	0.25	−1.83	2.16	0.85
24	0.52	0.38	−0.75	1.68	0.45
25	0.44	0.15	−2.46	1.57	1.56

Note. α is the slope, β is the location, and τ is the intercept. 2PLM = two-parameter logistic model; TMAS = Taylor Manifest Anxiety Scale.

Reduced and Expanded Dichotomous Models

The 2PLM allows IRCs to vary in two ways: location and slope. Other IRT models for dichotomous responses can be viewed as either expansions of these models or as nested models derived by placing restrictions on the item slopes. For example, now we consider two types of restricted models. In the first, we constrain all slopes to be 1 and free up the variance for the latent factor (estimated to be 2.18 in this example). This is called a Rasch model (Bond & Fox, 2001; De Ayala, 2019; Rasch, 1960) and is shown in

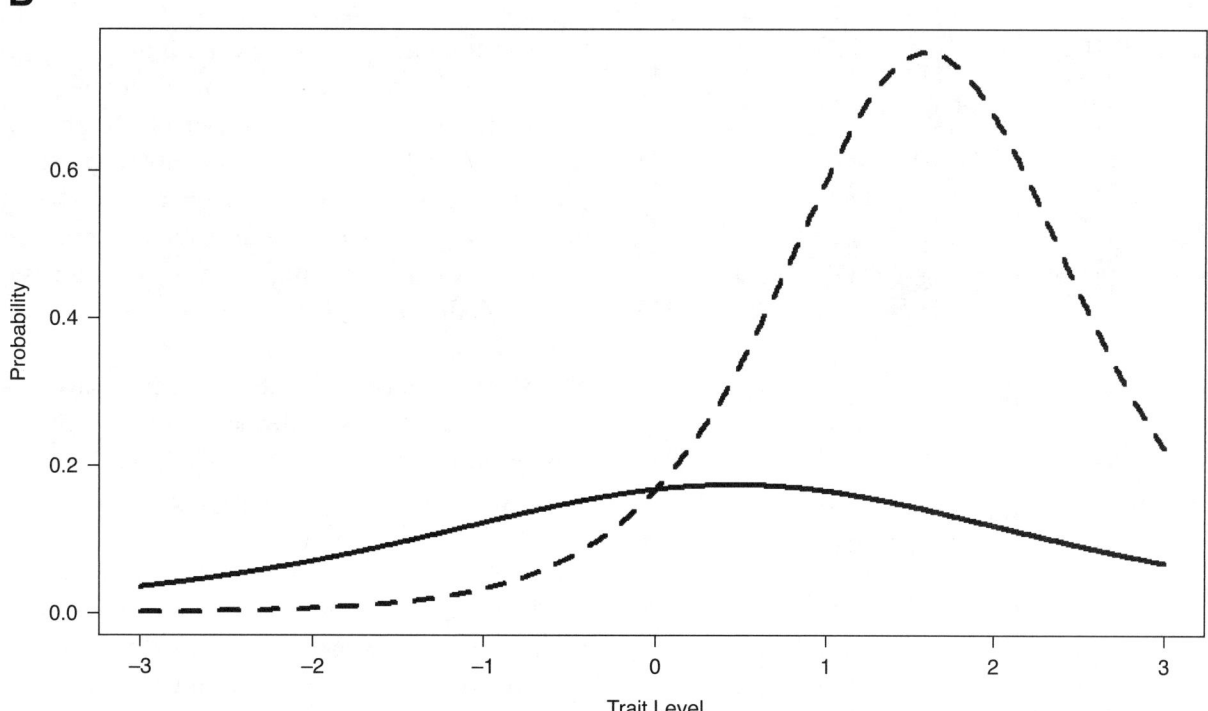

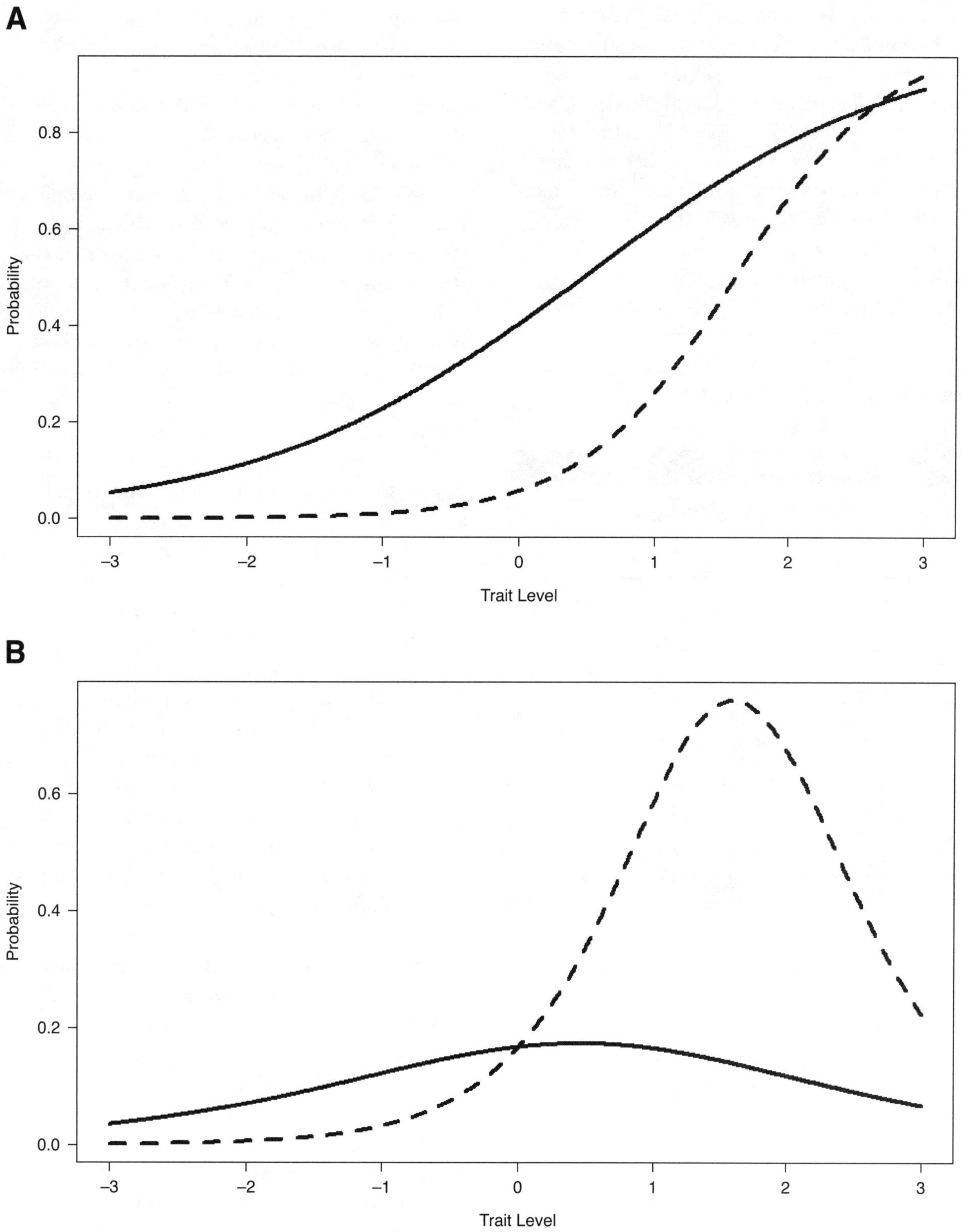

FIGURE 37.1. (A) Item response curves for Items 4 and 14. (B) Item information curves for Items 4 and 14.

the left of Table 37.3. In the second, we retain the identification constraint that the mean of the latent variable is 0 with standard deviation of 1 in the population, and impose the constraint that all the items have the same slope parameter. This is called the one-parameter logistic model (1PLM) and shown in the right of Table 37.3. In these models, the IRCs do not intersect because they are all constrained to have the same slope. Moreover, in the 1PLM and Rasch, the probability of endorsement is solely a function of the difference between an individual's trait standing and the item's location, weighted by a constant (the item slope, 1.47 or 1.00 in this example)

Over the last 40 years, there have been many researchers championing the potential virtues of Rasch models (e.g., sufficient statistics for estimating item parameters, nonintersecting IRCs, specific objectivity), and an equal number questioning their utility in real-world psychological data. Such debates are beyond the present treatment (for extended discussion, see Borsboom, 2005; Harvey, 2016; Petrillo et al., 2015), but two features of Rasch modeling are worth noting presently.

First, Rasch modeling, by its nature, emphasizes the meaningfulness and interpretability of the latent variable metric and items arrayed along that dimension. Second, as a general philosophy, following the factor analytic tradition, IRT modeling typically focuses on finding a model that "best fits" the data. On the other hand, a Rasch model is usually considered the only "correct" measurement model, and the goal of research is to find a set of items that provide responses fitting that model. In short, the philosophies underlying application of Rasch and non-Rasch models can be very different (Wilson, 2005).

Moving beyond restricted models, we now consider models that *add* parameters to the 2PL. Consider that on multiple-choice tests, it is arguable that the 2PLM is inadequate to describe the item response process because individuals may produce a correct response by chance, regardless of their levels on the latent variable. Notice that in a 2PLM, the IRC has a lower asymptote of zero (very low-scoring individuals have zero chance of answering the item correctly) and an upper asymptote of one (very high scoring individuals always get the item right). Thus, the model may be unrealistic in describing certain types of multiple-choice tests. Some personality researchers have argued that a 2PLM is inadequate because individuals at low levels of the latent variable may have a nonzero probability of endorsing the item (Reise & Waller, 2003; Waller & Faeuerstahler, 2017; Waller & Reise, 2010). To accommodate this fact in either cognitive or noncognitive measurement, the canonical 2PLM can be expanded to include a lower-asymptote parameter, as in Equation 37.3.

$$P(x_{si}=1|\theta) = \gamma_i + (1-\gamma_i)\frac{\exp(\alpha_i(\theta_s - \beta_i))}{1+\exp(\alpha_i(\theta_s - \beta_i))}$$

(37.3)

TABLE 37.3

Rasch and 1PLM Parameter Estimates of the TMAS

Item	Rasch			1PLM		
	τ	α	β	τ	α	β
1	−1.75	1	1.75	−1.75	1.48	1.19
2	−2.26	1	2.26	−2.26	1.48	1.53
3	−1.74	1	1.74	−1.75	1.48	1.18
4	−0.45	1	0.45	−0.45	1.48	0.31
5	−0.91	1	0.91	−0.92	1.48	0.62
6	−1.83	1	1.83	−1.84	1.48	1.24
7	−2.91	1	2.91	−2.92	1.48	1.97
8	−2.14	1	2.14	−2.15	1.48	1.45
9	−0.76	1	0.76	−0.77	1.48	0.52
10	−1.88	1	1.88	−1.88	1.48	1.27
11	−0.86	1	0.86	−0.86	1.48	0.58
12	−1.28	1	1.28	−1.28	1.48	0.87
13	−2.11	1	2.11	−2.11	1.48	1.43
14	−2.58	1	2.58	−2.58	1.48	1.75
15	−1.80	1	1.80	−1.8	1.48	1.22
16	−0.68	1	0.68	−0.68	1.48	0.46
17	−1.75	1	1.75	−1.76	1.48	1.19
18	−1.07	1	1.07	−1.08	1.48	0.73
19	−1.85	1	1.85	−1.85	1.48	1.25
20	−0.93	1	0.93	−0.93	1.48	0.63
21	−1.22	1	1.22	−1.22	1.48	0.82
22	−1.21	1	1.21	−1.22	1.48	0.82
23	−1.48	1	1.48	−1.48	1.48	1.00
24	−0.69	1	0.69	−0.69	1.48	0.47
25	−2.39	1	2.39	−2.39	1.48	1.62

Note. Variance of latent trait = 2.18 in the Rasch model. 1PLM = one-parameter logistic model; TMAS = Taylor Manifest Anxiety Scale.

In this three-parameter logistic model (3PLM), the lower asymptote parameter (γ) places a lower boundary on the IRC. For example, if γ is estimated to be .20, then regardless of how low an individual's standing is on the latent variable, the IRC goes no lower than .20. The location (β) in Equation 37.3 is no longer the point on the latent trait continuum at which the probability of endorsing is .50. Rather, the probability of endorsing at $\theta = \beta$ is $(1 + \gamma)/2$ (Hambleton & Swaminathan, 1985).

To illustrate, in the first set of columns in Table 37.4 are shown the 3PLM parameters estimated for the TMAS data. It is clear that for most items, there is no γ parameter indicating that as levels on the latent variable decrease, response probabilities go to 0. However, there are some items for which there is evidence for a γ parameter, especially Item 4 ("My sleep is fitful and disturbed") where the γ parameter estimates show that even examinees with very low theta level have a 13% chance of endorsing the item. Note that the 3PLM can also be parameterized such that the estimated asymptote parameter is at the high end rather than the lower end. That is, rather than estimating a lower asymptote > 0 to account for guessing, the 3PLMu ("u" for "upper") estimates an upper asymptote < 1.0 to account for "carelessness" or that the rate of the behavior never goes to 1.0 even for very high trait individuals. The right half of Table 37.4 shows the parameters estimates for this model using the TMAS data. Only four items have meaningful upper asymptotes of less than 1.0 with Item 25

TABLE 37.4

3PLM and 3PLMu Parameter Estimates of the TMAS

Item	3PLM				3PLMu (upper asymptote)			
	τ	α	β	γ	τ	α	β	δ
1	−1.63	1.13	1.44	0.01	−1.55	1.08	1.44	0.99
2	−2.96	2.29	1.29	0.01	−2.63	2.02	1.30	1.00
3	−1.63	1.15	1.42	0.01	−1.55	1.10	1.41	0.99
4	−0.90	1.12	0.81	0.13	−0.38	0.83	0.45	1.00
5	−0.96	1.26	0.77	0.02	−0.84	1.17	0.71	1.00
6	−1.71	1.23	1.40	0.00	−1.68	1.20	1.39	0.99
7	−4.40	3.01	1.46	0.00	−4.28	2.90	1.48	1.00
8	−2.65	2.20	1.21	0.00	−2.57	2.22	1.16	0.96
9	−0.96	1.46	0.65	0.04	−0.73	1.30	0.56	1.00
10	−2.37	2.21	1.07	0.00	−2.25	2.10	1.07	1.00
11	−0.91	1.51	0.60	0.00	−0.85	1.51	0.57	0.99
12	−1.18	1.14	1.03	0.00	−1.14	1.12	1.02	0.99
13	−2.49	2.03	1.23	0.00	−2.35	2.25	1.04	0.87
14	−2.93	1.86	1.57	0.00	−2.76	1.73	1.60	1.00
15	−2.12	1.56	1.36	0.04	−1.67	1.24	1.35	1.00
16	−0.77	1.25	0.62	0.03	−0.62	1.15	0.54	1.00
17	−2.10	2.06	1.02	0.00	−1.96	2.35	0.84	0.88
18	−1.01	1.21	0.83	0.00	−0.79	1.36	0.58	0.88
19	−1.98	1.56	1.27	0.01	−1.81	1.42	1.27	1.00
20	−1.03	1.71	0.60	0.00	−0.94	1.78	0.53	0.97
21	−1.58	2.28	0.69	0.00	−1.46	2.76	0.53	0.90
22	−1.40	1.89	0.74	0.00	−1.25	2.15	0.58	0.91
23	−1.86	2.2	0.85	0.00	−1.81	2.16	0.84	1.00
24	−0.77	1.70	0.45	0.00	−0.74	1.70	0.43	1.00
25	−2.47	1.59	1.55	0.00	−2.12	1.90	1.11	0.72

Note. α is item slope, β is item location, τ is item intercept, and γ and δ are lower and upper asymptotes, respectively. 3PLM = three-parameter logistic model; TMAS = Taylor Manifest Anxiety Scale.

("I am entirely self-confident"; reversed) having the lowest at .72. In Figure 37.2 we display the IRCs for Item 4 in the 3PL and Item 25 in the 3PLMu to illustrate the concepts of lower and upper asymptotes, respectively.

Moving beyond the 3PLM and 3PLMu, many researchers (Feuerstahler & Waller, 2014; Guo et al., 2020; Meng et al., 2020; Reise & Waller, 2003; Waller & Feuerstahler, 2017; Waller & Reise, 2010) have used a 4PLM that includes an upper asymptote parameter (δ) as well as a lower asymptote (γ) for psychopathology items.

$$P(x_{si} = 1|\theta) = \gamma_i + (\delta_i - \gamma_i) \frac{\exp(\alpha_i(\theta_s - \beta_i))}{1 + \exp(\alpha_i(\theta_s - \beta_i))} \quad (37.4)$$

This model was motivated by inspection of empirical IRCs and by theoretical considerations. For example, even in clinical populations (e.g., depressed populations), it would be unrealistic to expect that 100% of patients display any one symptom (e.g., suicide ideation, hopelessness). Hence, the upper asymptote for an item may not be 100%, as in the 2PLM or 3PLM but rather some smaller value, as in the 3PLMu. Relative to the 2PLM, the interpretation of the item parameters in this 4PLM model changes slightly. Specifically, the location (β) is now the point on the latent scale where the response proportion is ($\gamma + \delta$)/2. When the 4PLM was applied to the present data, no item was found to have both a nonzero lower asymptote and a non-one upper asymptote and, thus, to save space we do not display the results in a table.

At this point, an obvious question, then, is how to choose among the various IRT models available. One method is to compare the fit of the models, and Table 37.5 shows several common model fit indices available for this purpose (see Maydeu-Olivares et al., 2011, for description of structural modeling fit indices used in an IRT context); specifically, the M2 overall model-fit statistic (Maydeu-Olivares & Joe, 2006), root mean-square error of approximation (RMSEA), and comparative fit index (CFI). Based on

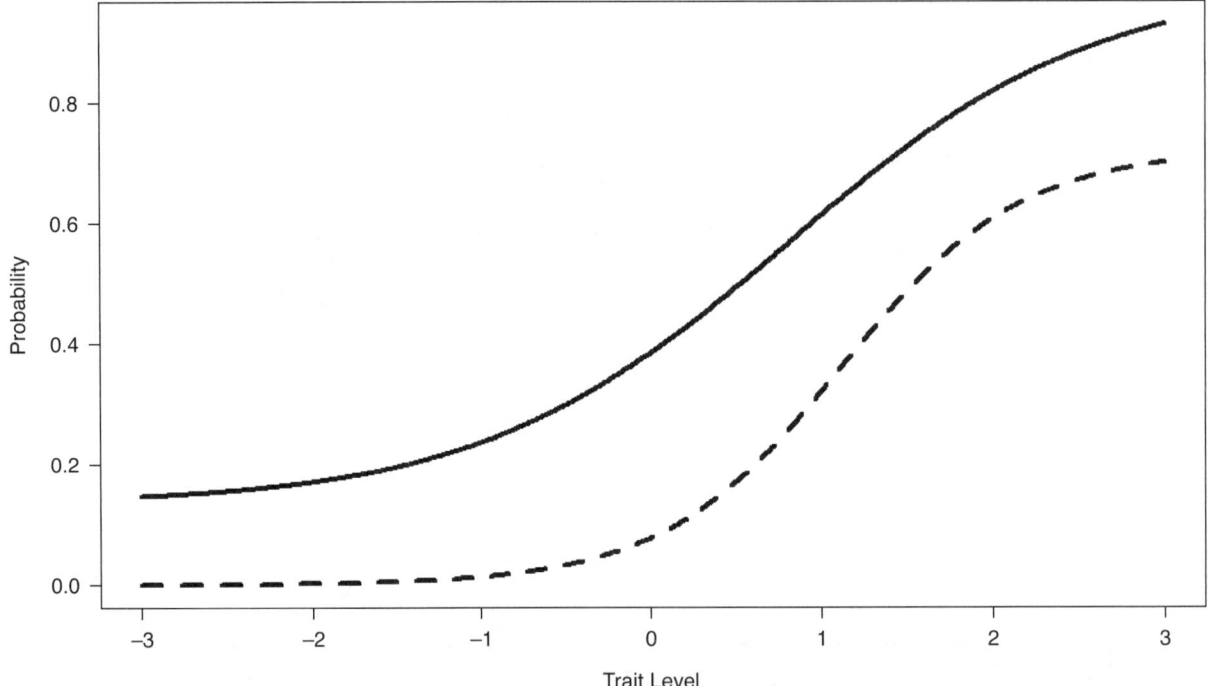

FIGURE 37.2. Item response curves for Items 4 and 25.

TABLE 37.5

Fit Indices and Information Criteria for Five Item Response Theory Models

Model	M2	df	p	RMSEA	CFI	AIC	BIC	PEst	Deviance (−2 LL)
1PLM	6811.26	299	~0	0.06	0.94	124292.5	124464.0	26	124240.5
2PLM	5325.73	275	~0	0.06	0.96	122924.1	123253.9	50	122824.0
3PLM	4449.77	250	~0	0.06	0.96	122948.7	123443.4	75	122798.7
3PLMu	3839.56	250	~0	0.05	0.97	122932.7	123427.4	75	122782.7
4PLM	3384.01	225	~0	0.05	0.97	122961.3	123620.9	100	122761.3

Note. PLM = parameter logistic model; PLMu = parameter logistic model upper; *RMSEA* = root mean square error of approximation, *CFI* = comparative fit index, *AIC* = Akaike's information criterion, *BIC* = Bayesian information criterion, *PEst* = the number of parameters estimated in the model, and *LL* = log likelihood.

commonly available "cutoff" values (Hu & Bentler, 1999; many other recommendations are available), the RMSEA and CFI suggest that all models fit about the same. M2 is highly significant in all models suggesting no model is adequate. Both Akaike's information criterion and the Bayesian information criterion suggest that the 2PLM is perhaps the best in terms of fit relative to parsimony, and statistical comparisons indicate that the 3PLM, 3PLMu, and 4PLM are not significant improvements in fit $p < .01$.

We would never suggest, however, that the choice of model rest on statistical tests alone. At the least, fit plots should be generated and inspected. In practice, however, the real test of the appropriateness of a model is whether it optimizes various forms of validity—for example, how well does the score predict important outcomes like suicide attempts or school grades? It is not uncommon to find that the various models presented here produce scores that are interchangeable—that is, they correlate extremely highly (in the present data trait level estimates from all models correlated > .99) and have nearly identical relationships with validity criteria. Even basic sum scores that do not take advantage of IRT methodology often perform comparably to IRT scores derived from highly complex models. It is, therefore, our recommendation that the appropriateness of an IRT model be judged based mostly on practical considerations such as improvements in validity and clinical decision making. Of course, this is not to downplay the many other practical advantages of IRT, such as test and score linking (Kolen & Brennan, 2004), computer adaptive testing (Weiss, 1982), and more efficient and flexible ways of investigating item bias (Thissen et al., 1993).

Unidimensional Polytomous Item Response Models

While dichotomously scored multiple-choice tests continue to dominate cognitive assessment, the fields of personality, psychopathology, and patient-reported outcomes assessment rely heavily on measures with ordered multicategory response options. The goals of this section are to introduce the logic of polytomous IRT models and to highlight important differences. There are many important polytomous models, but here we focus discussion on only a small subset. Readers interested in fuller treatment of the diverse family of polytomous IRT models should consult Ostini and Nering (2006), Nering and Ostini (2010), and Tutz (2020).

Just as the basic goal of IRT modeling for dichotomous items is to estimate an IRC that "best" represents the data, the chief objective of polytomous IRT models is to estimate a set of best fitting category response curves (CRCs). These CRCs model the relation between level on a latent variable and the probability of responding in a particular response category for an item. A central distinction between polytomous IRT models is the distinction between difference models and divide-by-total models (Thissen & Steinberg,

1986). Difference models require a two-stage computation procedure to derive CRCs, whereas divide-by-total models require only a single equation. Moreover, although there is only a single commonly used difference model, there is an entire class of nested divide-by-total models.

Graded response model. We begin by describing the graded response model (GRM; Samejima, 1969), which is the most frequently applied polytomous IRT model in the noncognitive assessment domain (Reise & Waller, 2009). One way to view the GRM is to think of it as an extension of the 2PL to the polytomous response case. Consider that, with a dichotomous item, there are only two response options, and, thus, there is only a single boundary or "threshold" between a response of 0 and 1. As a consequence, only a single IRC is needed to describe how increases on the latent variable increase the chances of an individual endorsing the item (i.e., responding 1 instead of 0).

```
0 . . . . . . . . . 1
Incorrect    Correct
0 . . . . . . 1 . . . . . . . . . . 2 . . . . . . . . 3
None     Somewhat    Mostly    Always
```

Now consider an item with four ordered response options (0, 1, 2, 3). This item can be thought of as containing three (number of categories minus one) dichotomies: 0 versus 1, 2, 3; 0, 1 versus 2, 3; and 0, 1, 2 versus 3. When represented in this way, it is easy to understand that the first step in estimating a GRM is to estimate the number of categories minus one threshold response curves (TRCs), one for each of the possible dichotomizations. These TRCs, shown in Equation 37.5, are simply 2PL model IRCs with equal slopes within an item (but not necessarily between items).

$$P^*(x_{si}|\theta) = \frac{\exp(\alpha_i(\theta_s - \beta_{ij}))}{1 + \exp(\alpha_i(\theta_s - \beta_{ij}))} \quad (37.5)$$

where $x = j = 1 \ldots$ number of response categories minus one.

Given that they are 2PLM functions, the TRCs indicate how the probability of responding in or above a given category changes as a function of the latent variable. In other words, for a four-category item, in the GRM model, each item is described by one item slope parameter (α) and the number of categories minus one location parameters (β_j) – 1 for each threshold between the response categories. The TRCs are important, but they do not directly yield the desired category response curves. Rather, once the parameters of the TRCs are estimated, computing the conditional category response probabilities for $x = 0 \ldots 3$ is done by subtraction as

$$P_x(\theta) = P^*_{(x)}(\theta) - P^*_{(x+1)}(\theta) \quad (37.6)$$

By definition, the probability of responding in or above the lowest response category is $P^*_{(x=0)}(\theta) = 1.0$, and the probability of responding above the highest response category is $P^*_{(x=3)}(\theta) = 0.0$. The curves derived from Equation 37.6 are CRCs, and they represent the probability of an individual responding in a particular category conditional on the latent variable. Again, the CRCs (Equation 37.6) are what we ultimately want, but we must first calculate the TRCs (Equation 37.5), which is why "difference" models like the GRM are sometimes called "indirect" models.

The item parameters in the GRM dictate the shape and location of the TRCs (and, thus, the CRCs). The higher the slope parameters (α), the steeper the TRCs and the narrower and peaked the CRCs, indicating that the response categories differentiate among individuals at different levels of the latent variable well. The location parameters (β_j) determine the location of the TRCs along the latent variable continuum and where each of the CRCs for the middle response options peak. Specifically, the CRCs peak in the middle of two adjacent location parameters.

To illustrate the model, we used 3,376 responses to the Sexual Compulsivity Scale (SCS; Kalichman & Rompa, 1995; https://openpsychometrics.org/_rawdata/) comprising items with four response options (0 = *Not at all like me*, 1 = *Slightly like me*, 2 = *Mainly like me*, 3 = *Very much like me*).

TABLE 37.6

Item Content of the Sexual Compulsivity Scale

Item	Item content
1	My sexual appetite has gotten in the way of my relationships.
2	My sexual thoughts and behaviors are causing problems in my life.
3	My desires to have sex have disrupted my daily life.
4	I sometimes fail to meet my commitments and responsibilities because of my sexual behaviors.
5	I sometimes get so horny I could lose control.
6	I find myself thinking about sex while at work.
7	I feel that sexual thoughts and feelings are stronger than I am.
8	I have to struggle to control my sexual thoughts and behavior.
9	I think about sex more than I would like.
10	It has been difficult for me to find sex partners who desire having sex as much as I do.

Table 37.6 displays the item content, and Table 37.7 displays the estimated item parameters for the GRM. Item 8 ("I have to struggle to control my sexual thoughts and behaviors") is most discriminating ($\alpha = 2.99$), and Item 10 ("It has been difficult for me to find sex partners who desire having sex as much as I want to") is the least discriminating ($\alpha = 1.15$). Item 6 ("I find myself thinking about sex while at work") is the easiest with thresholds shifted to the left, and Item 4 ("I sometimes fail to meet my commitments and responsibilities because of my sexual behaviors") is the hardest with thresholds shifted to the right.

In Figure 37.3 we display the category response curves for both Item 1 and Item 8 to illustrate the differences between a low discriminating item and a higher one. It is clear that the CRCs are much more peaked in the higher discriminating item indicating that position on the latent trait is much more prognostic of category response than in the low discriminating item. To make this more concrete, in Figure 37.4 we display the item information functions for these same items. Clearly, Item 8 is worth at least 3 times as much as Item 1 in terms of contribution to information and, thus, reducing error variance. It is also clear that, as typical of polytomous items, item information is more spread out across the trait continuum.

Nominal response model. We now turn our attention to a set of nested models that belong to a distinct class of "divide-by-total" or "direct" polytomous IRT models. We begin by introducing the most general direct model, namely, Bock's (1972) nominal response model (NRM). It is called a "nominal" response because the model does not assume that category responses are ordered within an item. Rather, the model treats

TABLE 37.7

Estimated Parameters in the Graded Response Model for the Sexual Compulsivity Scale

Item	r	mean	α	β_1	β_2	β_3	τ_1	τ_2	τ_3
1	0.62	1.31	1.72	−0.79	0.33	1.20	1.36	−0.57	−2.07
2	0.70	1.23	2.38	−0.59	0.38	1.17	1.40	−0.91	−2.79
3	0.74	1.23	2.68	−0.56	0.38	1.09	1.49	−1.02	−2.92
4	0.62	0.94	1.84	−0.19	0.81	1.60	0.36	−1.49	−2.95
5	0.66	1.24	1.98	−0.55	0.39	1.12	1.10	−0.78	−2.23
6	0.53	2.09	1.41	−2.31	−0.89	0.20	3.25	1.25	−0.29
7	0.71	1.20	2.56	−0.51	0.39	1.21	1.30	−0.99	−3.09
8	0.75	1.29	2.99	−0.59	0.26	1.02	1.76	−0.78	−3.05
9	0.57	1.46	1.56	−0.83	0.02	0.93	1.30	−0.04	−1.45
10	0.50	1.51	1.15	−1.00	−0.03	0.94	1.15	0.03	−1.09

Note. r is the item-test correlation, α is the item slope, $\beta_1 \ldots \beta_3$ are location parameters, and $\tau_1 \ldots \tau_3$ are the intercept parameters.

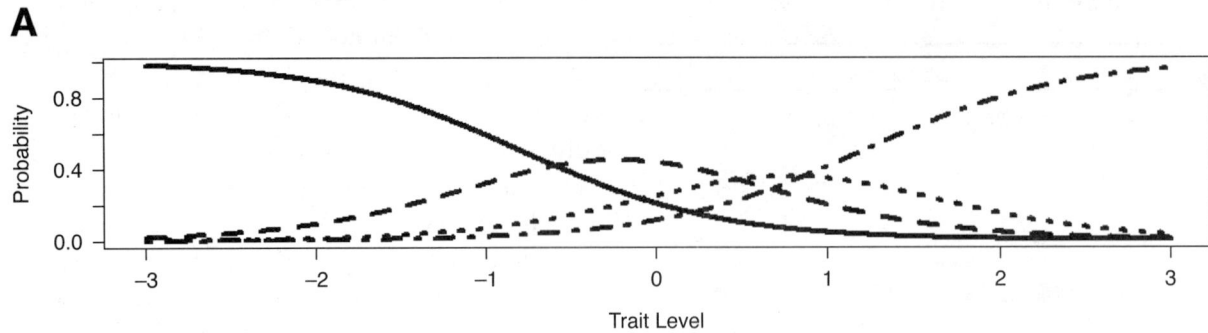

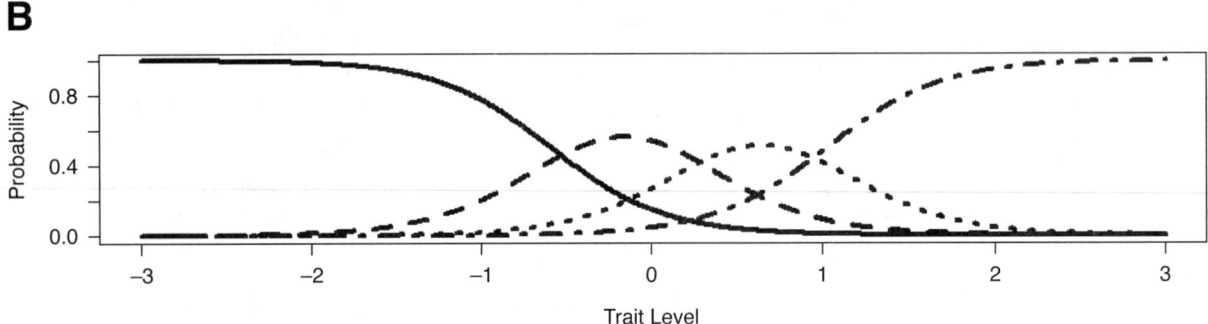

FIGURE 37.3. (A) Category response curve for Item 1. (B) Category response curve for Item 8.

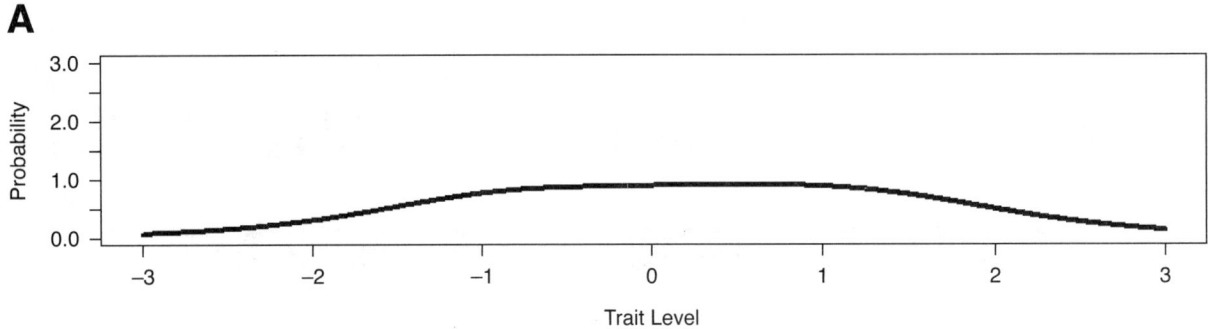

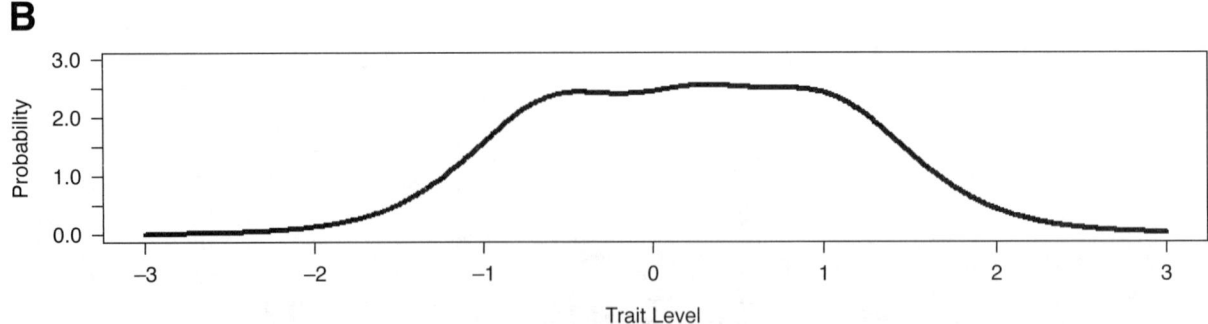

FIGURE 37.4. (A) Item information curve for Item 1. (B) Item information curve for Item 8.

category ordering, if any, as a property to be discovered, as we will see. In contrast, the GRM described above assumed that response categories are strictly ordered.

In the NRM the probability of an individual responding in category x ($x = 0 \ldots$ number of categories minus one) on an item, conditional on the latent variable (θ) is

$$P_x(\theta) = \frac{EXP(a_x\theta + c_x)}{\sum_{x=0}^{NCAT-1} EXP(a_x\theta + c_x)} \quad (37.7)$$

To identify the model, a constraint must be set: $\sum \alpha_x = \sum c_x = 0$. This constraint forces one response option (the one with the most positive a) to have a monotonically increasing CRC, and one response option (the one with the lowest a) to have a monotonically decreasing CRC. In Equation 37.7, c_x is an intercept parameter for category x, and the α_x is the slope of the linear regression of the latent variable on the log-odds of the probability of responding in a particular category. The c_x parameters reflect the "popularity" of a particular response category, where larger values reflect more popular options (Thissen et al., 1989).

The above description of the NRM does not readily reveal some of its most intriguing properties (see also Ju & Falk, 2019, and Falk & Ju, 2020). However, Thissen et al. (1989, 2010) showed how the NRM can be thought of in terms of the choice between two response categories. Specifically, if one thinks of an item response as a choice between two options x and $x - 1$ (3 vs. 2), then the NRM for this choice can be written in the form of the 2PLM model.

$$P_x|x = x \text{ or } x - 1 = \frac{1}{1 + \exp(-\alpha^*(\theta_s - c^*))} \quad (37.8)$$

where $a^* = a_x - a_{x-1}$ and $c^* = c_{x-1} - c_x/(a_x - a_{x-1})$. That is, the difference between the category slope parameters for two categories functions like a slope parameter in 2PLM, indicating how discriminating the choice between two categories is. Clearly, if a_x is larger than a_{x-1}, then a^* is positive, and the response categories are ordered along the latent variable; higher levels of the latent variable mean one is more likely to select x than $x - 1$.

Thus, inspection of the a^* parameters in the NRM allows an empirical test of the ordering of response categories (see also Murray et al., 2016). Preston and Reise (2015) called the a^* parameters category boundary discriminations (CBDs) and argued that inspection of these values is important not only to test for the ordering of categories but also to determine whether the item contains too many response categories (e.g., when an a^* is near zero; see Preston et al., 2011). It can also be used to evaluate whether the response categories are equally differentiating. For example, they cited examples of multipoint items where the CBD between the first and second category is very high, but the remaining CBDs are very low, suggesting that only the first response distinction is meaningful. Finally, they argued that a lack of consistency between the CBDs within an item may call into question the application of models that specify only a single item slope parameter (e.g., the generalized partial credit model to be described shortly, or the GRM discussed above).

The top panel of Table 37.8 displays the category slopes and category intercepts for the SCS. The more variable the slopes, the more discriminating the item. The distance between the slopes reflects how discriminating each transition between response categories is. This becomes clearer in the bottom panel that displays the three CBDs (a^*) for each item. Simply "eyeballing" the CBDs, it appears that there is little evidence of differential category discrimination and it appears that all categories (0 = *Not at all like me*, 1 = *Slightly like me*, 2 = *Mainly like me*, 3 = *Very much like me*) provide some useful "ordered" discrimination (Preston et al., 2011). There may be a slight tendency for the transition between 3 and 4 to be relatively more discriminating; more on this shortly.

Finally, it can be shown that the category intercepts in the NRM can be transformed into useful and interpretable information by taking $c^* = (c_{x-1} - c_x/a_j^*)$ to obtain category intersection parameters. These intersection parameters,

TABLE 37.8

Estimated Parameters in the NRM for the SCS

Item	α_1	α_2	α_3	α_4	c_1	c_2	c_3	c_4
1	−1.63	−0.53	0.53	1.63	0.04	0.62	0.07	−0.73
2	−2.52	−0.81	0.78	2.55	0.23	0.96	0.22	−1.42
3	−2.91	−1.07	0.86	3.12	0.34	1.14	0.24	−1.72
4	−1.86	−0.67	0.51	2.02	1.07	0.89	−0.17	−1.79
5	−1.92	−0.49	0.49	1.92	0.25	0.64	0.03	−0.93
6	−1.08	−0.56	0.31	1.33	−1.47	0.00	0.58	0.88
7	−2.8	−0.76	1.00	2.55	0.26	0.97	0.21	−1.43
8	−3.35	−0.97	1.10	3.22	−0.05	1.07	0.43	−1.45
9	−1.26	−0.41	0.27	1.41	−0.01	0.14	0.16	−0.29
10	−0.87	−0.3	0.25	0.92	0.03	−0.04	−0.03	0.04

Item	α_1^*	α_2^*	α_3^*	c_1^*	c_2^*	c_3^*
1	1.11	1.06	1.10	−0.52	0.51	0.74
2	1.71	1.60	1.77	−0.43	0.46	0.92
3	1.83	1.93	2.27	−0.44	0.46	0.87
4	1.19	1.17	1.51	0.15	0.90	1.07
5	1.43	0.99	1.43	−0.27	0.62	0.67
6	0.52	0.87	1.02	−2.83	−0.67	−0.29
7	2.04	1.76	1.55	−0.35	0.43	1.06
8	2.38	2.07	2.12	−0.47	0.31	0.89
9	0.85	0.68	1.14	−0.17	−0.03	0.39
10	0.57	0.56	0.67	0.14	−0.03	−0.10

Note. $\alpha_1 \ldots \alpha_4$ are category slopes, $c_1 \ldots c_4$ are category intercepts, $\alpha_1^* \ldots \alpha_3^*$ are category boundary discriminations, and $c_1^* \ldots c_3^*$ are category intersection. NRM = nominal response model; SCS = Sexual Compulsivity Scale.

of which there are the number of categories minus one, indicate the point on the latent variable scale where two CRCs intersect. Category intersections are important in all divide-by-total polytomous IRT models, including Rasch models. These parameters contrast sharply with the location parameters in the GRM. Specifically, locations in the GRM indicate where the probability of responding in and above a category is .50, while intersections indicate where the selection of one response category becomes more likely than the previous category. Moreover, category intersections are not necessarily ordered, but locations in the GRM must be. Yet, unordered category intersections do not indicate that the response options are unordered; recall that the ordering of response options is dictated solely by the a_j^* parameters.

More recently, Thissen et al. (2010) suggested a new and perhaps much more useful parameterization of the NRM in terms of (a) determining how influential each response is on the trait level estimate, and (b) studying category functioning. Specifically, define the logit z_k as

$$z_k = a_i^* a_k \theta + c_k \quad (37.9)$$

where a_i^* is the item slope reflecting the overall discrimination capacity of the item, a_k is the "scoring coefficient" (Muraki, 1992) for response category k, and c_k is the intercept parameter equal to the original parameterization. To identify the model for estimation, a_0 and c_0 are set to 0, and a_k for the highest category equals $K - 1$ where K is the number of categories.

In the top panel of Table 37.9 is shown this new parameterization of the NRM. The a_i^* values in the first column are "slope" and can be thought of as overall "impact" weights. Items 3 ("My desires

TABLE 37.9

Estimated Parameters in the NRM, GPCM, and PCM Under the New Parameterization

Item	α_i^*	α_{k0}	α_{k1}	α_{k2}	α_{k3}	c_1	c_2	c_3	c_4
1	1.09	0	1.02	1.99	3	0	0.58	0.03	−0.77
2	1.69	0	1.01	1.95	3	0	0.73	−0.01	−1.65
3	2.01	0	0.91	1.87	3	0	0.80	−0.1	−2.06
4	1.29	0	0.92	1.83	3	0	−0.18	−1.24	−2.86
5	1.28	0	1.12	1.89	3	0	0.39	−0.22	−1.18
6	0.80	0	0.65	1.73	3	0	1.47	2.05	2.35
7	1.78	0	1.14	2.13	3	0	0.71	−0.05	−1.69
8	2.19	0	1.09	2.03	3	0	1.12	0.48	−1.40
9	0.89	0	0.95	1.72	3	0	0.15	0.17	−0.28
10	0.60	0	0.95	1.88	3	0	−0.08	−0.06	0.00
1	1.08	0	1	2	3	0	0.57	0.02	−0.78
2	1.68	0	1	2	3	0	0.73	−0.04	−1.61
3	1.95	0	1	2	3	0	0.84	−0.09	−1.79
4	1.24	0	1	2	3	0	−0.17	−1.28	−2.65
5	1.27	0	1	2	3	0	0.35	−0.32	−1.20
6	0.87	0	1	2	3	0	1.82	2.36	2.68
7	1.83	0	1	2	3	0	0.63	−0.10	−1.99
8	2.22	0	1	2	3	0	1.06	0.39	−1.58
9	0.87	0	1	2	3	0	0.17	0.16	−0.17
10	0.59	0	1	2	3	0	−0.07	−0.06	0.03
1	1.21	0	1	2	3	0	0.64	0.08	−0.83
2	1.21	0	1	2	3	0	0.48	−0.13	−1.25
3	1.21	0	1	2	3	0	0.47	−0.22	−1.23
4	1.21	0	1	2	3	0	−0.17	−1.26	−2.61
5	1.21	0	1	2	3	0	0.33	−0.31	−1.14
6	1.21	0	1	2	3	0	2.28	2.99	3.20
7	1.21	0	1	2	3	0	0.34	−0.19	−1.47
8	1.21	0	1	2	3	0	0.49	0.08	−0.98
9	1.21	0	1	2	3	0	0.40	0.37	−0.21
10	1.21	0	1	2	3	0	0.35	0.35	0.03

Note. α_i^* is overall slope, $\alpha_{k0} \ldots \alpha_{k3}$ are scoring coefficients, and $c_1 \ldots c_4$ are category parameters. NRM = nominal response model; GPCM = generalization of the partial credit model; PCM = partial credit model.

to have sex have disrupted my daily life") and 8 ("I have to struggle to control my sexual thoughts and behavior") have the highest slopes. Items 10 ("It has been difficult for me to find sex partners who desire having sex as much as I want to") and 6 ("I find myself thinking about sex while at work") have the lowest.

The values for α_{k0}, α_{k1}, α_{k2}, and α_{k3} are "scoring coefficients." These are a little tricky to interpret, but basically, they are the "impact" of the response on the trait level estimate. Stated differently, they are the weights by which to multiply a category response (i.e., to score) to obtain an optimally weighted composite; optimally weighted means a weighted composite that has a nonlinear correlation of 1.0 with the trait level estimate (see Reise et al., 2023). As such, they can also be thought of as reflecting category discrimination. For example, for Item 6

Not at all like me = 0 weight = 0.80 × 0 = 0
Slightly like me = 1 weight = 0.80 × 0.65 = 0.52
Mainly like me = 2 weight = 0.80 × 1.73 = 1.38
Very much like me = 3 weight = 0.80 × 3 = 2.40

Now let's consider the more discriminating Item 8.

Not at all like me = 0 weight = 2.19 × 0 = 0
Slightly like me = 1 weight = 2.19 × 1.09 = 2.39
Mainly like me = 2 weight = 2.19 × 1.72 = 3.76
Very much like me = 3 weight = 2.19 × 3 = 6.57

So not only is Item 8 "worth more" than Item 6 in terms of categorical response increasing the "score" (trait level estimate or weighted composite), even within an item some categories are worth more than others. For example, in Item 8 going from a 0 to 1 response is worth 2.39 points, while going from 1 to 2 is worth 3.76 − 2.39 = 1.37 points. In Figure 37.5 are shown the CRCs for Items 6 and 8 under the NRM. These are contrasted to highlight the visual differences between a high and lower discriminating item, as well as to illustrate the meaning of category intersections. For example, for Item 8 the intersections are −0.47, 0.31, and 0.89. These are where the category response curves meet and the response in the higher category is equally likely as the one in the lower category. For Item 6 the intersections are −2.83, −0.67, and −0.29, and the same principles apply.

In sum, there are several ways to use the weights in Table 37.9. First, the weights should be increasing. When this occurs, the categories are ordered and higher responses correspond to higher trait levels. Second, the distance between the weights indicate the relative importance of increasing responses. Overall, examining the means shows that a 0, 1, 2, and 3 raw category score should translate roughly into 0, 1.36, 2.59, and 4.08 optimal score on average. This confirms our rough estimate earlier—going from a response of 2 to 3, is most discriminating or informative in terms of trait standing. Third, it is clear that more discriminating items, like 8, spread out scores (0 to 6.57; 2.19 × 3) considerably more than the less discriminating items, like 10, limit scores (0 to 1.80; 0.60 × 3).

Generalized Partial Credit Model

It may seem odd to describe Muraki's (1992) generalization of the partial credit model (GPCM) prior to describing the partial credit model

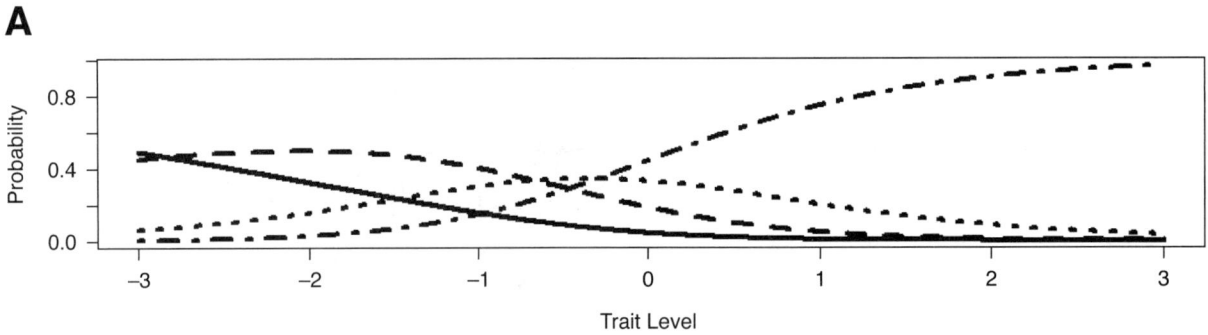

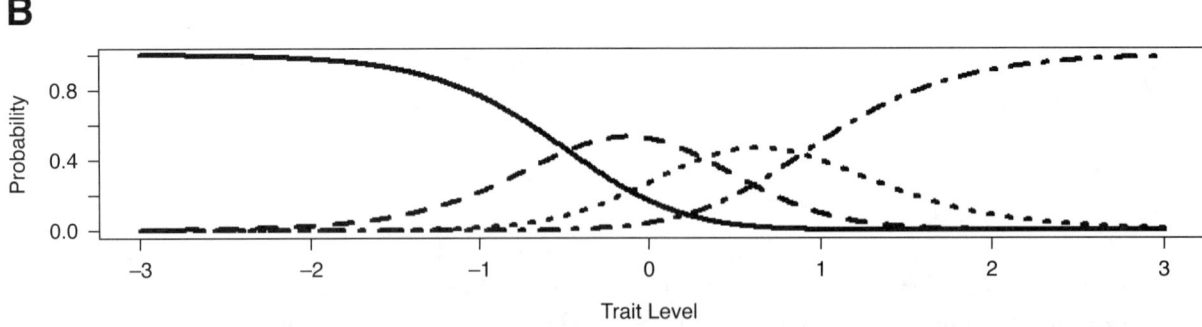

FIGURE 37.5. (A) Category response curve for Item 6. (B) Category response curve for Item 8.

(PCM; Masters, 1982). Our decision to include this model here, however, is based on the fact that the NRM highlighted in the previous section is the most general direct polytomous IRT model, and Muraki's model is a restricted version of the NRN, where CBD parameters are set equal within an item. Thus, while the NRM allows within item response category distinctions to vary in slope, the GPCM assumes CBDs are equally differentiating within an item, but items can vary in their overall discrimination. The GPCM can be written as

$$P_x(\theta) = \frac{EXP\sum_{j=0}^{x}\alpha(\theta-\delta_j)}{\sum_{x=0}^{NCAT-1}\left[EXP\sum_{j=0}^{x}\alpha(\theta-\delta_j)\right]} \quad (37.10)$$

where $\sum_{j=0}^{0}\alpha(\theta-\delta_j) \equiv 0$.

Equation 37.10 makes clear from where "divide-by-total" derives; the numerator is the probability of responding in a specific category and the denominator is a scaling factor that results in the conditional probability of each possible category response summing to one. For the GPCM, one unique slope parameter (α) and one minus the number of categories intersection parameters (δ) are estimated for each item. The category intersection parameters (δ) in this model are interpreted in the same way as the c^* parameters in the NRM—as the intersection point of two adjacent CRCs. They are the points on the latent variable scale where one category response becomes relatively more likely than the preceding response. No order is imposed on the intersection parameters. The slope (α) parameters have the usual interpretation as a kind of "discrimination" parameter, that is, they "indicate the degree to which categorical responses vary among items as θ level changes" (Muraki, 1992, p. 162).

Rather than show this traditional parameterization of the GPCM model with slopes and intersections, we display the new parameterization version (Equation 37.9). Specifically, in the middle panel of Table 37.9 are shown that the items still vary in their discrimination with Item 8 being high and Item 6 being low. However, the scoring coefficients are now simply integers. The major difference between the NRM and GPCM is that in the NRM category distinctions can vary in discrimination whereas in the GPCM, they do not. The "optimal weights" in the GPCM are simply the overall discriminations times the integer for the category. Finally, the NRM and GPCM are nested. In the present case, the chi-square test comparing the model is 65.73 on 20 df, which is significant, with $p = .01$.

In closing this section, we note that the GPCM and the GRM are very similar models but are derived from two different families. Models like the GPCM are built by considering the choice between two adjacent response categories x and $x - 1$—ignoring all other categories—and then deriving how the latent variable interacts with item slope and intersection parameters to determine the response choice. This is different than the GRM where all response options are considered in deriving each within-item TRC.

A Polytomous Rasch Model

The PCM (Masters, 1982) is the prototypical direct model suitable for analyzing ordered polytomous items. The PCM is an extension of the Rasch model for dichotomous items. Recall that the GRM discussed earlier is built around dichotomizing items at the boundaries between the response categories (e.g., 1, 2 vs. 3, 4), and then fitting 2PLM to each of the number of categories minus one boundaries between the categories. The PCM is also built around dichotomizing items at the boundaries between categories, but this process differs from the GRM in important ways. Specifically, the PCM is based on fitting 1PLM to the number of categories minus one ordered dichotomies, but considering only two response categories at a time. Specifically, with a four-category item, the PCM fits a Rasch model considering the dichotomies 0 versus 1, 1 versus 2, and 2 versus 3.

Interestingly, it is easy to show that the PCM is simply Equation 37.9 without the slope parameter. Thus, in the PCM the probability of response is determined solely by the difference between an individual's level on the latent variable and the category intersections. An interesting feature of the PCM is that the category intersections are not necessarily ordered. Recall that in the GRM, locations (β) must be ordered. When the intersection parameters are not ordered, this phenomenon is known as a *reversal* (Dodd & Koch, 1987). As a rule, if the intersection parameters are ordered within an item, then there is at least one location on the latent variable where every response option is most likely. If there is a reversal in intersection parameters, this guarantees that there will be at least one category that is never the most likely option conditional on the latent variable (Andrich, 1988).

As for the GPCM, we do not show the traditional parameterization of the PCM. Rather, in the bottom panel of Table 37.9 it is clear that in the PCM all items have equal discrimination (1.21) and scoring coefficients are simply category integers. Clearly, the raw score is a sufficient statistic in Rasch models. In the present data, the chi-square tests comparing GPCM with PCM was 1059 on 9 *df* ($p < .01$). In conclusion, the divide-by-total or direct polytomous IRT models are a nested family going from least restricted NRM, to allowing items to vary in slope (GPCM), to allowing items to vary only in category intersection parameters (PCM).

PRACTICAL APPLICATIONS AND CONSIDERATIONS

The first section of this chapter was dedicated to introducing important IRT models, their properties, and their interpretation. Understanding the mechanics of the above models is crucial because all applications of IRT (e.g., computerized adaptive testing, analysis of item and scale information functions, linking distinct measures onto a common scale, analysis of differential item functioning) rest squarely on the validity of the above representations. By *validity of the model*, we mean that term in the broadest sense to include the viability of IRT model assumptions, the accuracy of item parameter estimates, and the proper representation of the construct (i.e., is there really a latent variable that mediates the relations among the items?). With this in mind, the following section is geared toward applied research. Specifically, we consider (a) the applicability of unidimensional IRT models across various levels of the construct hierarchy, and (b) some "lessons learned" thus far from the research literature on application of IRT to noncognitive measures.

The Applicability of IRT Models

Researchers in both cognitive and noncognitive domains have long recognized the hierarchical nature of psychological constructs (Kotov et al., 2020). Accordingly, it has long been recognized that constructs and their associated measures vary in conceptual bandwidth ranging from narrow (physical attractiveness self-esteem, tooth brushing self-efficacy, math test anxiety) to broad (general self-esteem, negative affectivity). Commonly applied IRT models are unidimensional—they assume the existence of a single common variable affecting item responses. As pointed out by multiple authors over the years (see Humphreys, 1970; Gustafsson & Aberg-Bengtsson, 2010), attempting to create purely "unidimensional" scales can create quite a quandary and actually lead to poor measurement.

A way to achieve unidimensionality, and thus be consistent with IRT modeling, is to focus on a narrow construct and write items that are essentially replicates (this can increase coefficient alpha as well). Yet, it is questionable whether we really need the power of IRT to measure such conceptually narrow constructs where the correlations among the items can be explained merely by the semantic similarity of the items, rather than by the need to postulate an underlying psychological trait (Tellegen, 1991). On the other hand, the measurement of broadband constructs demands the inclusion of content-diverse indicators; indeed, if constructs are hierarchical, how would it even be possible to measure a broader band construct without multidimensionality caused by items tapping slightly different manifestations of the trait? In turn, this fact of multidimensionality almost guarantees violations of the IRT unidimensionality assumption (Anderson et al., 2017). Yet, it appears to us that for these types of substantively complex constructs, this is exactly where the power of IRT and other latent variable methods are most needed and interestingly applied. One possible solution to this "conundrum" of dimensionality is to recognize that even highly multidimensional measures can yield highly unidimensional scale scores or trait level estimates (Gustafsson & Aberg-Bengtsson, 2010).

A second approach to dealing with multidimensionality has been through the application of bifactor measurement models (Cai, 2011). For example, the bifactor model described by Gibbons and Hedeker (1992) has seen increased use of late as a tool for exploring the applicability of IRT models (Reise, 2012; see also Reise et al., 2007, 2010; Rodriguez et al., 2016a, 2016b). This model allows each item to reflect two things (hence, *bi*factor): (a) a single common latent variable causing all item responses, and (b) one additional latent variable causing only items that share item content. The latter, more specific latent variables in a bifactor model are sometimes referred to as content parcels. Thus, when a measure consists of multiple content parcels necessary to validly measure complex constructs, the bifactor model can easily accommodate such a structure. In other words, a bifactor framework affords the ability to use multidimensional item response data to achieve unidimensional measurement (see also Toland et al., 2017). Thus, we view the bifactor model as a tool not only for evaluating the distorting effects of forcing multidimensional data into a unidimensional model (Reise et al., 2007, 2011, 2015) but also as expanding the range of constructs that can be accommodated by IRT models.

LESSONS LEARNED FROM THE APPLICATION OF IRT TO NONCOGNITIVE MEASURES

Although impossible to document precisely because the literature is vast, we have observed that several interesting phenomena occur relatively frequently when polytomous IRT models are applied to personality, health outcomes, and psychopathology measures, namely, (a) high item slopes, (b) extreme item locations, (c) bunched item locations, and (d) a large range of item slopes. In this section, we discuss each of these phenomena in turn and propose reasons why they occur. For simplicity and continuity, we discuss these issues in the context of the slope and location parameters resulting from application of the GRM. These same issues arise in application of any model.

We begin with the phenomena of extremely high item slope parameters. To be conservative, we define high slopes as any value larger than 3 (logistic metric), but note that even a slope of 2 is relatively large compared to what is typically found in dichotomous IRT models. It is easy to demonstrate that as an item slope parameter moves beyond 3 the response categories are providing a high degree of discrimination among individuals; in other words, with a slope of 3 in the GRM, if a researcher knew an individual's trait level, they could predict in which category the individual is likely to respond with high accuracy. Another way of thinking about this issue is as follows: As item slopes increase beyond 3, the TRCs begin to look more like Guttman step functions than monotonically increasing ogives. Do such high slopes mean "good" measurement or is there something wrong here?

We argue that the answer to this question depends on understanding the causes of the high slope parameters. To begin, it is well known that one possible source of a high item slope is a problem known as *local dependency*. Local dependency means that two (or more) items share common variance above and beyond that due to the latent trait being measured. Local dependence can be caused by item content redundancy (i.e., asking essentially the same question twice) and results in inflated item slope parameters (Steinberg & Thissen, 1996). To the extent that slopes are inflated by local dependencies, the slope parameter estimates provide a misleading gauge of measurement precision. However, local dependence is not an explanation for high slopes when all or most of the items on a scale display exceptionally high slopes. In this situation we need to turn to other explanations.

A second possible explanation for high slopes is that the measured construct has a narrow conceptual bandwidth (e.g., knee joint pain). Sparing the reader the technical details, in IRT the magnitude of an item's average correlation with other items determines the item's slope (or factor loading in factor analysis). In measures of narrowband constructs, homogeneous item content is expected. In addition, due to a lack of diverse trait manifestations, in measures of narrowband constructs the conceptual distance between the item and the construct is often very small (e.g., "*I experience pain when bending my knee*" arguably suffices to cover the entire construct of knee joint pain). These factors result in narrow measures containing items with very high intercorrelations, which in turn, result in high IRT slope parameters. This is especially true if a 5-, 7-, or 9-point rating scale is used for each item because the more response options, the more room is left for individual differences in response style to operate, further inflating correlations.

When high item slopes are caused by the narrowband nature of the measured construct, their values are perfectly valid indicators of measurement precision. However, there is one big caveat—namely, that measurement precision should not be viewed as resulting from quality measurement but rather as resulting from the narrow construct that is being measured. It is unsurprising to observe high slopes on narrowband measures because individual differences are much easier to discriminate in that context. Consider this example: The items 3 + 4 = ?, 2 + 6 = ?, and 1 + 3 = ? would form a highly discriminating set of indicators of the construct of adding two single digits. In short, the fewer and more homogeneous the trait (or ability) manifestations, the easier it is to discriminate between those who are high or low on the trait with high precision, but the less meaningful those discriminations are.

A narrow construct and the resulting item content homogeneity can explain some cases of extremely high slopes, but it is irrelevant when high slopes are observed on measures of complex and multifaceted broadband constructs that contain diverse item content. In this situation, we propose an additional source as possible explanation, namely, a mixture of extreme groups (e.g., clinical and nonclinical) included in the calibration sample. In the measurement of psychopathology or health outcomes, psychometricians have long warned against the use of combined clinical and nonclinical samples in judging the psychometric properties of instruments. The obvious danger is that if a nonclinical group with a floor effect is combined with a clinical group with a ceiling effect, an instrument can look deceptively good in terms of item intercorrelations, item-test correlations, factor loadings, and coefficient alpha. In short, in mixed clinical and nonclinical samples strong psychometrics reflect merely the fact that the item differentiates between extreme groups (Waller, 2008). This is not the same thing as being a good measure of a dimensional construct across the entire range of the construct. Because IRT slope parameters are complex transformations of interitem correlations, a mixed clinical and nonclinical sample can easily result in very high slope parameter estimates. Because sampling has received almost no attention in the IRT literature, we cannot offer any guidance in this regard.

The next topic we consider is the issue of "bunched" item location parameters. By bunched item location parameters, we mean location parameters (e.g., in the GRM) that are clumped closely together along the latent variable (usually at the trait extremes) rather than spread out over the trait continuum. When location parameters are bunched together, this implies that the instrument affords measurement precision in only a narrow trait range. Note that this is an extremely odd occurrence given that the only real purpose of having a multipoint response format is to allow people to make discriminations across the continuum. If a researcher uses a multipoint response scale in a diverse sample, and location parameters still clump together, this is evidence that either there are too many response options, or more likely, what is being measured is a highly skewed or unipolar trait (Lucke, 2013, 2015).

It appears that many researchers are operating under the assumption that all constructs are fully continuous, defined at both ends of the construct, and that items can be found that measure (have location parameters) across an entire trait range. For example, Fraley et al. (2000), upon observing that in attachment measures item locations are highly bunched together on one end of the trait, suggested that new items be written to better spread the measurement precision out over the complete range of the latent variable. But what if such a search for new items or measures is fruitless? As discussed by Reise and Rodriguez (2016), if the trait has no meaning at one end of the spectrum, then there is no reason to expect any item to capture information about said meaningless range.

With a highly skewed construct or a unipolar trait, it may not be possible to find items with location parameters spread out across the range. Consider a research study by Gray-Little et al. (1997), who applied the GRM to a 5-point version of the Rosenberg self-esteem scale (Rosenberg, 1965). This study is fascinating because although the items contain five response options, the four location parameters per item are closely bunched at the low end of the latent trait (i.e., low self-esteem). For example, even the third location ($x = 1, 2, 3,$ vs. $4, 5$) was in the negative range for 8 out of the 10 items. To make this more concrete, the third location parameter for Item 1 (On the whole, I am satisfied with myself) was $\beta = -1.48$ implying that even individuals who are a standard deviation and a half below the mean on the trait are most likely to respond in the highest fourth or fifth category! In other words, even people far below the mean on self-esteem rate themselves highly self-satisfied. Although reasonable minds can disagree, one explanation for this effect is that it is not due to poor items or poor choice of response options. Rather, it is due to the nature of the self-esteem construct; items only differentiate people with low self-esteem because that is the only end of the construct that is meaningful. For instruction's sake, it might help to imagine two examples from cognitive testing: (a) It is impossible to know less than nothing about a topic, creating a natural floor effect for any knowledge test, and (b) there are some narrow constructs (e.g., two-digit addition) that require understanding of very few concepts to do well, resulting in a natural ceiling effect.

Related to the topic of bunched item location parameters is the topic of extreme item locations. By extreme we mean that the location parameters do not fall within a reasonable range of values, say −2 to 2 (assuming that the latent variable has a mean of 0 and standard deviation of 1). As mentioned previously, one reason why an extreme location may occur is if an item has a relatively low slope parameter (recall that the location is a function of the intercept divided by the slope). A second obvious reason is that either the lowest or highest response category is too extreme given the content of the item. A third, more interesting reason is that the latent variable is either highly skewed or a unipolar trait. We will again use the results of the Gray-Little et al. (1997) study to illustrate the phenomenon.

In their calibration of the Rosenberg Self-Esteem Scale, not only were the category locations bunched in the low end of the latent variable, they were also very extreme. For example, for all 10 items the first category location ($x = 1$ vs. $2, 3, 4, 5$) was a very low value. For example, for Item 1 (On the whole, I am satisfied with myself) the estimated location was $\beta = -3.45$, suggesting that even individuals who are nearly three and a half standard deviations below the mean are likely to respond in at least category 2. Moreover, for many items, even the fourth location ($x = 1, 2, 3, 4$ vs. 5) is barely above the trait mean. For example, for Item 3 (I feel that I have a number of good qualities) the fourth location is only $\beta = 0.22$. Thus, even people barely above the mean on self-esteem are most likely to respond in the highest category on this item. The only item that displayed a more reasonable fourth location was Item 9 (All in all I am inclined to feel that I am a failure—reversed) that had a fourth threshold of 2.13.

Our final issue is the observation that on some measures we noticed a very wide spread of item slopes. For example, van der Ark (2001) reported slopes of 0.8, 3.6, 0.4, 6.4, and 0.2 for a measure of coping strategy to industrial odor annoyance. We call this a *steep descent pattern* where one or two items have a relatively high slope, and then the value of the slope parameter decreases rapidly for the remainder of the items. Although it is reasonable that different trait indicators can be related to the latent trait to different degrees, a wide variance in slopes may also be a sign of problems. For example, in Hall et al. (2007), a 9-item "spiritual instability" measure had GRM slopes ranging from 2.63 ("When I sin, I am afraid of what God will do to me") to 0.74 ("When I sin, I tend to withdraw from God"). The remaining items had slopes (in decreasing order) of 1.9, 1.9, 1.5, 1.5, 1.4, 1.0, and 0.9.

Such a variable pattern of slopes is troubling in a number of respects. First, one could argue that the construct is so narrow, that one item essentially defines the latent variable, and the other items are only tangentially related. If that were true, one could argue that the remaining items are unnecessary or redundant. More technically, a second potential problem is that if IRT methods were used to estimate standing on the construct, in this example the best item has 3.7 times the influence compared with the worst item because the sufficient statistic for the latent trait estimate is the raw item response times the item slope. Moreover, because an item contributes to measurement precision by the square of the slope parameter, such results argue that the best item contributes 12.7 times more error reduction than the worst item; that is, it takes almost 13 items like the worst item to equal one item like the best.

This wide-ranging slope phenomenon is not unique to spirituality constructs and their associated measures. In fact, the phenomenon is rather easy to observe in the IRT literature and non-IRT literature (in the form of variable item-test correlations or factor loadings). Ignoring multidimensionality as a possible cause, we propose that this phenomenon is due to a combination of narrow-band constructs (where one or two good items essentially define the construct), combined with limited item pools. Many constructs in personality, health, and psychopathology have an extremely limited indicator pool (e.g., how many ways are there to react to industrial odor?). Even a relatively complex and multifaceted construct such as depression has a very finite set of indicators (e.g., sad moods, social isolation, suicide cognitions, feelings of hopelessness, somatic disturbances). Importantly, when only a few items have high slopes and the remainder have much lower slopes, a researcher must be very cautious in interpreting the latent variable. It could well be that the latent variable does not reflect variance on a common latent variable shared by all the items but rather merely reflects individual differences on the item with the highest slope.

In sum, our goal in this section was to draw attention to some interesting challenges that researchers may face in applying models to noncognitive constructs. Some of these challenges are due to working with constructs of varying conceptual breath, for which a set of very limited indicators exist, and for which the underlying distribution cannot possibly be normally distributed. To the degree that IRT applications in noncognitive settings raise issues that have not caught the attention of previous researchers or call into question the quality of legacy measures developed under traditional coefficient alpha–centric scale construction practices, this is a positive development for the field of psychometrics. Indeed, part of the excitement of current IRT research lies in identifying new problems and working toward their solutions.

References

Anderson, D., Kahn, J. D., & Tindal, G. (2017). Exploring the robustness of a unidimensional item response theory model with empirically multidimensional data. *Applied Measurement in Education, 30*(3), 163–177. https://doi.org/10.1080/08957347.2017.1316277

Andrich, D. (1988). A general form of Rasch's extended logistic model for partial credit scoring. *Applied Measurement in Education, 1*(4), 363–378. https://doi.org/10.1207/s15324818ame0104_7

Baker, F. B., & Kim, S.-H. (2017). *Item response theory: Parameter estimation techniques*. Marcel Dekker.

Birnbaum, A. (1968). Some latent trait models and their use in inferring a examinee's ability. In F. M. Lord & M. Novik (Eds.), *Statistical theories of mental test scores* (pp. 397–424). Addison-Wesley.

Bock, R. D. (1972). Estimating item parameters and latent ability when responses are scored in two or more latent categories. *Psychometrika, 37*(1), 29–51. https://doi.org/10.1007/BF02291411

Bond, T. G., & Fox, C. M. (2001). *Applying the Rasch model*. Erlbaum. https://doi.org/10.4324/9781410600127

Borsboom, D. (2005). *Measuring the mind: Conceptual issues in contemporary psychometrics*. Cambridge University Press. https://doi.org/10.1017/CBO9780511490026

Boulton, A. J., Tyner, C. E., Choi, S. W., Sander, A. M., Heinemann, A. W., Bushnik, T., Chiaravalloti, N., Sherer, M., Kisala, P. A., & Tulsky, D. S. (2019). Linking the GAD-7 and PHQ-9 to the TBI-QOL Anxiety and Depression Item Banks. *The Journal of Head Trauma Rehabilitation, 34*(5), 353–363. https://doi.org/10.1097/HTR.0000000000000529

Cai, L. (2017). *flexMIRT: Flexible multilevel multidimensional item analysis and test scoring* (Version 3.5) [Computer software]. Vector Psychometric Group.

Cai, L., Choi, K., Hansen, M., & Harrell, L. (2016). Item response theory. *Annual Review of Statistics and Its Application, 3*(1), 297–321. https://doi.org/10.1146/annurev-statistics-041715-033702

Cai, L., & Hansen, M. (2013). Limited-information goodness-of-fit testing of hierarchical item factor models. *British Journal of Mathematical and Statistical Psychology, 66*(2), 245–276. https://doi.org/10.1111/j.2044-8317.2012.02050.x

Cai, L., Yang, J. S., & Hansen, M. (2011). Generalized full-information item bifactor analysis. *Psychological Methods, 16*(3), 221–248. https://doi.org/10.1037/a0023350

Cella, D., Choi, S. W., Condon, D. M., Schalet, B., Hays, R. D., Rothrock, N. E., Yount, S., Cook, K. F., Gershon, R. C., Amtmann, D., DeWalt, D. A., Pilkonis, P. A., Stone, A. A., Weinfurt, K., & Reeve, B. B. (2019). PROMIS® adult health profiles: Efficient short-form measures of seven health domains. *Value in Health, 22*(5), 537–544. https://doi.org/10.1016/j.jval.2019.02.004

Chalmers, R. P. (2012). mirt: A Multidimensional Item Response Theory Package for the R Environment. *Journal of Statistical Software, 48*(6), 1–29. https://doi.org/10.18637/jss.v048.i06

Crins, M. H. P., Terwee, C. B., Ogreden, O., Schuller, W., Dekker, P., Flens, G., Rohrich, D. C., & Roorda, L. D. (2019). Differential item functioning of the PROMIS physical function, pain interference, and pain behavior item banks across patients with different musculoskeletal disorders and persons from the general population. *Quality of Life Research, 28*(5), 1231–1243. https://doi.org/10.1007/s11136-018-2087-x

De Ayala, R. J. (2019). Item response theory and Rasch modeling. In G. R. Hancock, L. M. Stapleton, & R. O. Mueller (Eds.), *The reviewer's guide to quantitative methods in the social sciences* (2nd ed., pp. 145–163). Routledge.

Dodd, B. G., & Koch, W. R. (1987). Effects of variations in item step values on item and test information in the partial credit model. *Applied Psychological Measurement, 11*(4), 371–384. https://doi.org/10.1177/014662168701100403

Embretson, S. E. (1996). The new rules of measurement. *Psychological Assessment, 8*(4), 341–349. https://doi.org/10.1037/1040-3590.8.4.341

Embretson, S. E., & Reise, S. P. (2000). *Item response theory for psychologists*. Erlbaum.

Falk, C. F., & Ju, U. (2020). Estimation of response styles using the multidimensional nominal response model: A tutorial and comparison with sum scores. *Frontiers in Psychology, 11*, 72. https://doi.org/10.3389/fpsyg.2020.00072

Feuerstahler, L. M., & Waller, N. G. (2014). Estimation of the 4-parameter model with marginal maximum likelihood. *Multivariate Behavioral Research, 49*(3), 285. https://doi.org/10.1080/00273171.2014.912889

Flens, G., Smits, N., Terwee, C. B., Pijck, L., Spinhoven, P., & de Beurs, E. (2021). Practical significance of longitudinal measurement invariance violations in the Dutch-Flemish PROMIS item banks for depression and anxiety: An illustration with ordered-categorical data. *Assessment, 28*(1), 277–294. https://doi.org/10.1177/1073191119880967

Foster, G. C., Min, H., & Zickar, M. J. (2017). Review of item response theory practices in organizational research: Lessons learned and paths forward. *Organizational Research Methods, 20*(3), 465–486. https://doi.org/10.1177/1094428116689708

Fraley, R. C., Waller, N. G., & Brennan, K. A. (2000). An item response theory analysis of self-report measures of adult attachment. *Journal of Personality and Social Psychology, 78*(2), 350–365. https://doi.org/10.1037/0022-3514.78.2.350

Gibbons, R. D., & Hedeker, D. (1992). Full-information item bi-factor analysis. *Psychometrika, 57*(3), 423–436. https://doi.org/10.1007/BF02295430

Gibbons, R. D., Kupfer, D. J., Frank, E., Lahey, B. B., George-Milford, B. A., Biernesser, C. L., Porta, G., Moore, T. L., Kim, J. B., & Brent, D. A. (2020). Computerized adaptive tests for rapid and accurate assessment of psychopathology dimensions in youth. *Journal of the American Academy of Child & Adolescent Psychiatry, 59*(11), 1264–1273. https://doi.org/10.1016/j.jaac.2019.08.009

Granziol, U., Brancaccio, A., Pizziconi, G., Spangaro, M., Gentili, F., Bosia, M., Gregori, E., Luperini, C., Pavan, C., Santarelli, V., Cavallaro, R., Cremonese, C., Favaro, A., Rossi, A., Vidotto, G., & Spoto, A. (2022). On the implementation of computerized adaptive observations for psychological assessment. *Assessment, 29*(2), 225–241. https://doi.org/10.1177/1073191120960215

Gray-Little, B., Williams, V. S. L., & Hancock, T. D. (1997). An item response theory analysis of the Rosenberg self-esteem scale. *Personality and Social Psychology Bulletin, 23*(5), 443–451. https://doi.org/10.1177/0146167297235001

Guinart, D., de Filippis, R., Rosson, S., Patil, B., Prizgint, L., Talasazan, N., Meltzer, H., Kane, J. M., & Gibbons, R. D. (2021). Development and validation of a computerized adaptive assessment tool for discrimination and measurement of psychotic symptoms. *Schizophrenia Bulletin, 47*(3), 644–652. https://doi.org/10.1093/schbul/sbaa168

Guo, S., Zheng, C., & Kern, J. L. (2020). IRTBEMM: An R package for estimating IRT models with guessing or slipping parameters. *Applied Psychological Measurement, 44*(7–8), 566–567. https://doi.org/10.1177/0146621620932654

Gustafsson, J. E., & Aberg-Bengtsson, L. (2010). Unidimensionality and the interpretability of psychological instruments. In S. E. Embretson (Ed.), *Measuring psychological constructs* (pp. 97–121). American Psychological Association. https://doi.org/10.1037/12074-005

Hall, T. W., Reise, S. P., & Haviland, M. G. (2007). An item response theory analysis of the spirituality assessment inventory. *The International Journal for the Psychology of Religion, 17*(2), 157–178. https://doi.org/10.1080/10508610701244197

Hambleton, R. K., & Swaminathan, H. (1985). *Item response theory*. Kluwer-Nijhoff. https://doi.org/10.1007/978-94-017-1988-9

Harvey, R. J. (2016). Improving measurement via item response theory: Great idea, but hold the Rasch. *The Counseling Psychologist, 44*(2), 195–204. https://doi.org/10.1177/0011000015615427

Hays, R. D., Calderón, J. L., Spritzer, K. L., Reise, S. P., & Paz, S. H. (2018). Differential item functioning by language on the PROMIS® physical functioning items for children and adolescents. *Quality of Life Research, 27*(1), 235–247. https://doi.org/10.1007/s11136-017-1691-5

Hu, L. T., & Bentler, P. M. (1999). Cutoff criteria for fit indexes in covariance structure analysis: Conventional criteria versus new alternatives. *Structural Equation Modeling, 6*(1), 1–55. https://doi.org/10.1080/10705519909540118

Humphreys, L. G. (1970). A skeptical look at the factor pure test. In C. E. Lunneborg (Ed.), *Current problems and techniques in multivariate psychology: Proceedings of a conference honoring Professor Paul Horst* (pp. 23–32). University of Washington.

Ju, U., & Falk, C. F. (2019). Modeling response styles in cross-country self-reports: An application of a multilevel multidimensional Nominal Response Model. *Journal of Educational Measurement, 56*(1), 169–191. https://doi.org/10.1111/jedm.12205

Kalichman, S. C., & Rompa, D. (1995). Sexual sensation seeking and Sexual Compulsivity Scales: Reliability, validity, and predicting HIV risk behavior. *Journal of Personality Assessment, 65*(3), 586–601. https://doi.org/10.1207/s15327752jpa6503_16

Kamata, A., & Bauer, D. J. (2008). A note on the relation between factor analytic and item response theory models. *Structural Equation Modeling, 15*(1), 136–153. https://doi.org/10.1080/10705510701758406

Kolen, M. J., & Brennan, R. L. (2004). *Test equating, scaling, and linking: Methods and practices* (3rd ed.). Springer. https://doi.org/10.1007/978-1-4757-4310-4

Kotov, R., Jonas, K. G., Carpenter, W. T., Dretsch, M. N., Eaton, N. R., Forbes, M. K., Forbush, K. T., Hobbs, K., Reininghaus, U., Slade, T., South, S. C., Sunderland, M., Waszczuk, M. A., Widiger, T. A., Wright, A. G. C., Zald, D. H., Krueger, R. F., Watson, D., & the HiTOP Utility Workgroup. (2020). Validity and utility of Hierarchical Taxonomy of Psychopathology (HiTOP): I. Psychosis superspectrum. *World Psychiatry, 19*(2), 151–172. https://doi.org/10.1002/wps.20730

Lee, M. K., Schalet, B. D., Cella, D., Yost, K. J., Dueck, A. C., Novotny, P. J., & Sloan, J. A. (2020). Establishing a common metric for patient-reported outcomes in cancer patients: Linking patient reported outcomes measurement information system (PROMIS), numerical rating scale, and patient-reported outcomes version of the common terminology criteria for adverse events (PRO-CTCAE). *Journal of Patient-Reported Outcomes, 4*(1), 106. https://doi.org/10.1186/s41687-020-00271-0

Liegl, G., Rose, M., Knebel, F., Stengel, A., Buttgereit, F., Obbarius, A., Fischer, H. F., & Nolte, S. (2020). Using subdomain-specific item sets affected PROMIS physical function scores differently in cardiology and rheumatology patients. *Journal of Clinical Epidemiology, 127,* 151–160. https://doi.org/10.1016/j.jclinepi.2020.08.003

Lord, F. (1952). *A theory of test scores* (Psychometric Monograph No. 7). Psychometric Corporation. https://www.psychometricsociety.org/sites/main/files/file-attachments/mn07.pdf?1576607452

Lord, F. M., & Novick, M. R. (1968). *Statistical theories of mental test scores*. Addison-Wesley.

Lucke, J. F. (2013). Positive trait item response models. In R. E. Milsap, L. A. Ark, D. M. Bolt, & C. M. Woods (Eds.), *New developments in quantitative psychology* (pp. 199–213). Springer. https://doi.org/10.1007/978-1-4614-9348-8_13

Lucke, J. F. (2015). Unipolar item response models. In S. P. Reise & D. A. Revicki (Eds.), *Handbook of item response theory modeling: Applications to typical performance assessment* (pp. 272–284). Routledge/Taylor & Francis Group.

Masters, G. N. (1982). A Rasch model for partial credit scoring. *Psychometrika, 47*(2), 149–174. https://doi.org/10.1007/BF02296272

Maydeu-Olivares, A., Cai, L., & Hernández, A. (2011). Comparing the fit of item response theory and factor analysis models. *Structural Equation Modeling, 18*(3), 333–356. https://doi.org/10.1080/10705511.2011.581993

Maydeu-Olivares, A., & Joe, H. (2006). Limited information goodness-of-fit testing in multidimensional contingency tables. *Psychometrika, 71*(4), 713–732. https://doi.org/10.1007/s11336-005-1295-9

McLeod, L. D., Swygert, K. A., & Thissen, D. (2001). Factor analysis for items scored in two categories. In D. Thissen & H. Wainer (Eds.), *Test scoring* (pp. 189–216). Erlbaum.

Meng, X., Xu, G., Zhang, J., & Tao, J. (2020). Marginalized maximum a posteriori estimation for the four-parameter logistic model under a mixture modelling framework. *British Journal of Mathematical and Statistical Psychology, 73*(S1, Suppl. 1), 51–82. https://doi.org/10.1111/bmsp.12185

Moore, T. M., Calkins, M. E., Satterthwaite, T. D., Roalf, D. R., Rosen, A. F. G., Gur, R. C., & Gur, R. E. (2019). Development of a computerized adaptive screening tool for overall psychopathology ("p"). *Journal of Psychiatric Research, 116*, 26–33. https://doi.org/10.1016/j.jpsychires.2019.05.028

Muraki, E. (1992). A generalized partial credit model: Application of an EM algorithm. *Applied Psychological Measurement, 16*(2), 159–176. https://doi.org/10.1177/014662169201600206

Murray, A. L., Booth, T., & Molenaar, D. (2016). When middle really means "top" or "bottom": An analysis of the 16PF5 using Bock's nominal response model. *Journal of Personality Assessment, 98*(3), 319–331. https://doi.org/10.1080/00223891.2015.1095197

Nering, M. L., & Ostini, R. (Eds.). (2010). *Handbook of polytomous item response theory models*. Taylor & Francis.

O'Hara, N. N., Richards, J. T., Overmann, A., Slobogean, G. P., & Klazinga, N. S. (2020). Is PROMIS the new standard for patient-reported outcomes measures in orthopaedic trauma research? *Injury, 51*(Suppl. 2), S43–S50. https://doi.org/10.1016/j.injury.2019.10.076

Ostini, R., & Nering, M. L. (2006). *Polytomous item response theory models*. Sage. https://doi.org/10.4135/9781412985413

Oude Voshaar, M. A. H., Vonkeman, H. E., Courvoisier, D., Finckh, A., Gossec, L., Leung, Y. Y., Michaud, K., Pinheiro, G., Soriano, E., Wulfraat, N., Zink, A., & van de Laar, M. A. F. J. (2019). Towards standardized patient reported physical function outcome reporting: Linking ten commonly used questionnaires to a common metric. *Quality of Life Research, 28*(1), 187–197. https://doi.org/10.1007/s11136-018-2007-0

Petrillo, J., Cano, S. J., McLeod, L. D., & Coon, C. D. (2015). Using classical test theory, item response theory, and Rasch measurement theory to evaluate patient-reported outcome measures: A comparison of worked examples. *Value in Health, 18*(1), 25–34. https://doi.org/10.1016/j.jval.2014.10.005

Preston, K., Reise, S., Cai, L., & Hays, R. D. (2011). Using the nominal response model to evaluate response category discrimination in the PROMIS emotional distress item pools. *Educational and Psychological Measurement, 71*(3), 523–550. https://doi.org/10.1177/0013164410382250

Preston, K. S., & Reise, S. P. (2015). Detecting Faulty Within-Item Category Functioning with the Nominal Response Model. In S. P. Reise & D. A. Revicki (Eds.), *Handbook of item response theory modeling: Applications to typical performance assessment* (pp. 272–284). Routledge/Taylor & Francis Group.

Rasch, G. (1960). *Probabilistic models for some intelligence and attainment tests*. Danmarks Paedagogiske Institut.

Reckase, M. D. (2009). *Multidimensional item response theory*. Springer. https://doi.org/10.1007/978-0-387-89976-3

Reise, S., Moore, T., & Maydeu-Olivares, A. (2011). Target rotations and assessing the impact of model violations on the parameters of unidimensional item response theory models. *Educational and Psychological Measurement, 71*(4), 684–711. https://doi.org/10.1177/0013164410378690

Reise, S. P. (2012). The rediscovery of bifactor measurement models. *Multivariate Behavioral Research, 47*(5), 667–696. https://doi.org/10.1080/00273171.2012.715555

Reise, S. P., Ainsworth, A. T., & Haviland, M. G. (2005). Item response theory: Fundamentals, applications, and promise in psychological research. *Current Directions in Psychological Science, 14*(2), 95–101. https://doi.org/10.1111/j.0963-7214.2005.00342.x

Reise, S. P., Cook, K. F., & Moore, T. M. (2014). Evaluating the impact of multidimensionality on unidimensional item response theory model parameters. In S. Reise & D. Revicki (Eds.), *Handbook of item response theory modeling* (pp. 131–158). Routledge.

Reise, S. P., Du, H., Wong, E. F., Hubbard, A. S., & Haviland, M. G. (2021). Matching IRT models to patient-reported outcomes constructs: The graded response and log-logistic models for scaling depression. *Psychometrika, 86*(3), 800–824. https://doi.org/10.1007/s11336-021-09802-0

Reise, S. P., & Henson, J. M. (2003). A discussion of modern versus traditional psychometrics as applied to personality assessment scales. *Journal of Personality Assessment, 81*(2), 93–103. https://doi.org/10.1207/S15327752JPA8102_01

Reise, S. P., Hubbard, A. S., Wong, E. F., Schalet, B. D., Haviland, M. G., & Kimerling, R. (2021). Response category functioning on the Healthcare Engagement Measure using the nominal response model. *Assessment*, 1–15. https://doi.org/10.1177/10731911211052682

Reise, S. P., Hubbard, A. S., Wong, E. F., Schalet, B. D., Haviland, M. G., & Kimerling, R. (2023). Response category functioning on the Healthcare Engagement Measure using the nominal response model. *Assessment, 30*(2), 375–389. https://doi.org/10.1177/10731911211052682

Reise, S. P., Moore, T. M., & Haviland, M. G. (2010). Bifactor models and rotations: Exploring the extent to which multidimensional data yield univocal scale scores. *Journal of Personality Assessment, 92*(6), 544–559. https://doi.org/10.1080/00223891.2010.496477

Reise, S. P., Morizot, J., & Hays, R. D. (2007). The role of the bifactor model in resolving dimensionality issues in health outcomes measures. *Quality of Life Research, 16*(Suppl. 1), 19–31. https://doi.org/10.1007/s11136-007-9183-7

Reise, S. P., & Rodriguez, A. (2016). Item response theory and the measurement of psychiatric constructs: Some empirical and conceptual issues and challenges. *Psychological Medicine, 46*(10), 2025–2039. https://doi.org/10.1017/S0033291716000520

Reise, S. P., & Waller, N. G. (2003). How many IRT parameters does it take to model psychopathology items? *Psychological Methods, 8*(2), 164–184. https://doi.org/10.1037/1082-989X.8.2.164

Reise, S. P., & Waller, N. G. (2009). Item response theory and clinical measurement. *Annual Review of Clinical Psychology, 5*(1), 27–48. https://doi.org/10.1146/annurev.clinpsy.032408.153553

Rodriguez, A., Reise, S. P., & Haviland, M. G. (2016a). Applying bifactor statistical indices in the evaluation of psychological measures. *Journal of Personality Assessment, 98*(3), 223–237. https://doi.org/10.1080/00223891.2015.1089249

Rodriguez, A., Reise, S. P., & Haviland, M. G. (2016b). Evaluating bifactor models: Calculating and interpreting statistical indices. *Psychological Methods, 21*(2), 137–150. https://doi.org/10.1037/met0000045

Rosenberg, M. (1965). *Society and the adolescent self-image*. Princeton University Press. https://doi.org/10.1515/9781400876136

Samejima, F. (1969). Estimation of latent ability using a response pattern of graded scores. *Psychometrika, Monograph Supplement 17*.

Schalet, B. D., Janulis, P., Kipke, M. D., Mustanski, B., Shoptaw, S., Moore, R., Baum, M., Kim, S., Siminski, S., Ragsdale, A., & Gorbach, P. M. (2020). Psychometric data linking across HIV and substance use cohorts. *AIDS and Behavior, 24*(11), 3215–3224. https://doi.org/10.1007/s10461-020-02883-5

Segawa, E., Schalet, B., & Cella, D. (2020). A comparison of computer adaptive tests (CATs) and short forms in terms of accuracy and number of items administrated using PROMIS profile. *Quality of Life Research, 29*(1), 213–221. https://doi.org/10.1007/s11136-019-02312-8

Steinberg, L., & Thissen, D. (1996). Uses of item response theory and the testlet concept in the measurement of psychopathology. *Psychological Methods, 1*(1), 81–97. https://doi.org/10.1037/1082-989X.1.1.81

Taple, B. J., Chapman, R., Schalet, B. D., Brower, R., & Griffith, J. W. (2020). The impact of education on depression assessment: Differential item functioning analysis. *Assessment, 29*(2), 272–284. https://doi.org/10.1177/1073191120971357

Taylor, J. A. (1953). A personality scale of manifest anxiety. *Journal of Abnormal and Social Psychology, 48*(2), 285–290. https://doi.org/10.1037/h0056264

Tellegen, A. (1991). Personality traits: Issues of definition, evidence, and assessment. In D. Cichetti & W. Grove (Eds.), *Thinking clearly about psychology: Essays in honor of Paul Everett Meehl* (pp. 10–35). University of Minnesota Press.

Thissen, D., Cai, L., & Bock, R. D. (2010). The nominal categories item response model. In M. Nering & R. Ostini (Eds.), *Handbook of item response theory models* (pp. 43–75). Taylor & Francis.

Thissen, D., & Steinberg, L. (1986). A taxonomy of item response models. *Psychometrika, 51*(4), 567–577. https://doi.org/10.1007/BF02295596

Thissen, D., Steinberg, L., & Fitzpatrick, A. R. (1989). Multiple-choice models: The distractors are also part of the item. *Journal of Educational Measurement, 26*(2), 161–176. https://doi.org/10.1111/j.1745-3984.1989.tb00326.x

Thissen, D., Steinberg, L., & Wainer, H. (1993). Detection of differential item functioning using the parameters of item response models. In P. W. Holland & H. Wainer (Eds.), *Differential item functioning* (pp. 67–113). Erlbaum.

Thomas, M. L. (2019). Advances in applications of item response theory to clinical assessment. *Psychological Assessment, 31*(12), 1442–1455. https://doi.org/10.1037/pas0000597

Thomas, M. L., Brown, G. G., Patt, V. M., & Duffy, J. R. (2020). Latent variable modeling and adaptive testing for experimental cognitive psychopathology research. *Educational and Psychological Measurement, 81*(1), 155–181. https://doi.org/10.1177/0013164420919898

Thurstone, L. L. (1925). A method of scaling psychological and educational tests. *Journal of Educational Psychology, 16*(7), 433–451. https://doi.org/10.1037/h0073357

Toland, M. D., Sulis, I., Giambona, F., Porcu, M., & Campbell, J. M. (2017). Introduction to bifactor polytomous item response theory analysis. *Journal of School Psychology, 60*, 41–63. https://doi.org/10.1016/j.jsp.2016.11.001

Tutz, G. (2020). A taxonomy of polytomous item response models. *arXiv preprint* arXiv:2010.01382.

van der Ark, L. A. (2001). Relationships and properties of polytomous item response theory models. *Applied Psychological Measurement, 25*(3), 273–282. https://doi.org/10.1177/01466210122032073

van der Linden, W. J. (Ed.). (2018). *Handbook of item response theory, three volume set*. CRC Press. https://doi.org/10.1201/9781315119144

Victorson, D., Schalet, B. D., Kundu, S., Helfand, B. T., Novakovic, K., Penedo, F., & Cella, D. (2019). Establishing a common metric for self-reported anxiety in patients with prostate cancer: Linking the Memorial Anxiety Scale for Prostate Cancer with PROMIS Anxiety. *Cancer, 125*(18), 3249–3258. https://doi.org/10.1002/cncr.32189

Waller, N. G. (2008). Commingled samples: A neglected source of bias in reliability analysis. *Applied Psychological Measurement, 32*(3), 211–223. https://doi.org/10.1177/0146621607300860

Waller, N. G., & Feuerstahler, L. (2017). Bayesian modal estimation of the four-parameter item response model in real, realistic, and idealized data sets. *Multivariate Behavioral Research, 52*(3), 350–370. https://doi.org/10.1080/00273171.2017.1292893

Waller, N. G., & Reise, S. P. (2010). Measuring psychopathology with non-standard item response theory models: Fitting the four parameter model to the MMPI. In S. Embretson (Ed.), *New directions in psychological measurement with model-based approaches* (pp. 147–174). American Psychological Association.

Weiss, D. J. (1982). Improving measurement quality and efficiency with adaptive testing. *Applied Psychological Measurement, 6*(4), 473–492. https://doi.org/10.1177/014662168200600408

Wilson, M. (2005). *Constructing measures: An item response modeling approach*. Erlbaum.

CHAPTER 38

MEASURING TEST PERFORMANCE WITH SIGNAL DETECTION THEORY TECHNIQUES

Teresa A. Treat and Richard J. Viken

The development and evaluation of assessment and prediction strategies designed to distinguish two mutually exclusive states are central enterprises in psychological science. For example, we might want to assess diagnostic status (present or absent) or child maltreatment (present or absent). Alternatively, we might be interested in predicting whether violence is likely or whether treatment relapse will occur. Once classic psychometric methods have been used to develop one or more assessment devices, the predictive or criterion validity of the measurement strategies must be evaluated (see Clark & Watson, 2019). Widely used indexes of test performance include *sensitivity* (the proportion of positive cases correctly classified as positive), *specificity* (the proportion of negative cases correctly classified as negative), *positive predictive power* (the proportion of cases classified as positive that actually are positive), and *negative predictive power* (the proportion of cases classified as negative that actually are negative). These indexes vary widely, however, as a function of cutoff scores, the base rates of the phenomenon of interest, and the costs and benefits associated with a particular assessment or prediction context, as we will see.

As a result, researchers increasingly are relying on the methods of signal detection theory, particularly receiver operating characteristic (ROC) analysis and utility-based decision theory approaches. ROC methods can be used to quantify and compare the discriminative power of measurement devices independently of cutoff scores, base rates (BRs), and costs and benefits. Decision theory methods then can be used to determine optimal cutoff scores for particular contexts, given specification of the BRs and the values placed on different kinds of correct and incorrect decisions.

After presenting background on the role of BRs in assessment and prediction as well as traditional accuracy indexes, we provide an overview of the use of ROC and decision-theory approaches for examination and enhancement of decision making in psychology. We close with recommendations regarding the reporting of the development of new measures, especially with regard to optimal cutoff values for a range of BRs and several common decision goals.

TRADITIONAL INDEXES OF TEST PERFORMANCE

In this chapter, we illustrate issues in evaluating test performance with a data set from the National Comorbidity Survey Replication (NCS-R; Kessler & Merikangas, 2004; Kessler et al., 2004). The NCS-R is a nationally representative survey

https://doi.org/10.1037/0000318-038
APA Handbook of Research Methods in Psychology, Second Edition: Vol. 1. Foundations, Planning, Measures, and Psychometrics, H. Cooper (Editor-in-Chief)
Copyright © 2023 by the American Psychological Association. All rights reserved.

of English-speaking adults in the United States that was conducted from 2001 to 2003. *Diagnostic and Statistical Manual of Mental Disorders*, 4th edition (*DSM–IV*; American Psychiatric Association, 1994) diagnoses were determined for 9,282 respondents. The K6 is a six-item screening scale that was completed by 6,656 of the participants in the data set, which we use as our predictive test. The K6 contains questions about the frequency with which various aspects of psychological distress were experienced during the respondent's worst month emotionally in the past year (Kessler et al., 2002, 2003). Respondents indicated how often they felt worthless, depressed, restless, hopeless, nervous, and that everything was an effort. Responses were made on a 5-point scale ranging from 1 = *all the time* to 5 = *none of the time*. Responses were summed to obtain a total score on both scales, with lower scores indicating greater psychological distress. The large size and the high quality of the NCS-R sample make it an excellent database to provide examples for the methods described in this chapter. The K6 data in the sample are not missing at random with respect to the full sample, so the results of the analyses in this paper should be considered illustrative only.

Evaluating the performance of the K6 screening scale requires selection of a gold standard of psychological distress. The gold standards used in test evaluation typically are higher quality or more expensive indicators of the phenomenon of interest, although they still may contain error (Swets et al., 2000). In the current analyses, we used the presence or absence of the 12-month *DSM–IV* anxiety and mood disorders that were assessed for all respondents and included in the current public release of the NCS-R data set: agoraphobia with or without panic disorder, generalized anxiety disorder, panic disorder, specific phobia, social phobia, major depression, dysthymia, and bipolar I and II disorders. We considered participants to be positive for a disorder if they met criteria for at least one of these disorders. This chapter examines the extent to which the K6 scale provides far lower cost and less time-intensive assessments of psychological distress than the gold standard.

Figure 38.1 provides an initial look at the association between the interview-based diagnostic outcomes and the K6 screen. The two interview-based outcomes (disorder present or absent) are depicted in the rows of the figure. The two K6-based predictions (disorder present or absent) are depicted in the columns of the figure. Of the 6,656 subjects with data on both the screen and the interview, 1,899 (28.5%) met criteria for at least one of the disorders. The percentage (or proportion) of the sample meeting criteria for a disorder according to the gold standard interview is referred to as the *base rate* (BR) or, in conventional clinical terms, the *prevalence of the disorder*. This BR is reflected in the BR entry to the far right in the disorder present row of the figure. With 28.5% of the sample meeting criteria for a disorder, this means that 71.5% (100 − BR) did not. All technical terms used in the chapter are listed chronologically with a brief definition in Exhibit 38.1.

The columns of Figure 38.1 depict the predictions made on the basis of the K6. In this example, we used a cutoff value on the K6 of 22: Anyone with a score of 22 or lower (recall that lower K6 scores indicate more distress) is predicted to have a disorder. This value was selected for illustrative purposes because it optimizes the percentage of correct classifications in the current sample. The last entry in the first column shows that 1,420 (21.3%) of K6 respondents were predicted to have a disorder. The percentage (or proportion) of a sample predicted to have the characteristic of interest is often called the *selection ratio* because in many practical applications of test prediction this group is being selected for further action. In the current context, for example, respondents scoring at or below 22 might receive further evaluation or referrals for treatment. The remaining 78.7% of the sample (100 − selection ratio) is predicted not to have a disorder.

The shaded cells of Figure 38.1 provide the core information about test performance. In this sample, 911 (13.7%) persons were predicted to have a disorder on the basis of the K6 and were found to have a disorder on the basis of

		K6-based classification		
		Disorder present (K6 < 22)	Disorder absent (K6 > 22)	
Interview-based classification ("Truth")	Disorder present	Valid positives (Hits) Frequency = 911 Percentage = 13.7%	False negatives (Misses) Frequency = 988 Percentage = 14.8%	Base rate Frequency = 1,899 Percentage = 28.5%
	Disorder absent	False positives (False alarms) Frequency = 509 Percentage = 7.7%	Valid negatives (Correct rejections) Frequency = 4,248 Percentage = 63.8%	100 − Base rate Frequency = 4,757 Percentage = 71.5%
		Selection ratio Frequency = 1,420 Percentage = 21.3%	100 − Selection ratio Frequency = 5,236 Percentage = 78.7%	Frequency = 6,656 Percentage = 100%

FIGURE 38.1. Matrix of interview-based classifications by K6-based classifications for National Comorbidity Survey Replication data set. The percentages in the figure do not sum perfectly because of rounding issues.

EXHIBIT 38.1

Glossary of Technical Terminology

Base rate (or prevalence): Percentage (or proportion) of cases identified by the gold standard as positive.
Cutoff (or threshold): Value of assessment or prediction measure that distinguishes cases classified as positive and negative.
Selection ratio: Percentage (or proportion) of cases classified as positive.
Valid positives (or hits): Cases identified by the gold standard as positive who are classified as positive.
Valid negatives (or correct rejections): Cases identified by the gold standard as negative who are classified as negative.
False negatives (or misses): Cases identified by the gold standard as positive who are classified as negative.
False positives (or false alarms): Cases identified by the gold standard as negative who are classified as positive.
Percent correct: Percentage of correctly classified cases.
Percent correct by chance: Percentage of cases that can be classified correctly by chance.
Predicting from the base rate: Predicting the more frequently occurring outcome for all cases.
Sensitivity: Proportion (or percentage) of positive cases correctly classified as positive.
Specificity: Proportion (or percentage) of negative cases correctly classified as negative.
Positive predictive power: Proportion of cases classified as positive who actually are positive.
Negative predictive power: Proportion of cases classified as negative who actually are negative.
Hit rate (or valid positive rate): Probability of correctly classifying a positive case as positive.
False alarm rate (or false positive rate): Probability of correctly classifying a negative case as positive.
Area under the curve: The probability that a randomly selected pair of positive and negative cases is ranked correctly by the assessment method.
Utility: Value placed on a specific decision-making outcome (i.e., user-perceived benefit or cost).
Overall utility: A utilities-weighted sum of the probabilities of the four decision-making outcomes.
Utility ratio: User-perceived relative importance of decisions about negative versus positive cases.
Information gain: The reduction of uncertainty about the true classification of a case that results from administering an assessment or prediction measure.

the interview-based "truth." In clinical prediction contexts, such persons would be referred to as the *valid positive*, or *true positive*, cases, and in the signal detection theory context, they would be referred to as *hits*. The remaining 509 respondents who were predicted to have a disorder on the basis of the K6 did not, in truth, have a disorder. In clinical prediction contexts, these respondents would be referred to as the *false positive* cases, and in signal detection theory contexts, they are referred to as *false alarms*. Among those predicted to have no disorder on the basis of the K6, 988 (14.8%) were found actually to have a disorder present on the basis of the interview. In clinical prediction contexts, such persons are referred to as *false negatives*, whereas in signal detection theory, they would be referred to as *misses*. The 4,248 remaining people who were predicted to have no disorder on the basis of the K6 (63.8%) were indeed found to have no disorder as judged by the interview. These respondents are referred to as *valid negative* or *true negative* cases in clinical prediction, and as correct rejections in signal detection theory.

One of the first things to evaluate in a table like this (see Figure 38.1) is the percentage of cases for which the K6-predicted classification was correct. There are two ways to be correct: (a) valid positive and (b) valid negative classifications. We can add the percentage of respondents in these two cells (13.7 and 63.8) to find that the K6-based prediction was correct 77.5% of the time. Although 77.5% accuracy sounds pretty good, one must compare percentage correct when using the K6 predictor to the percentage correct expected by chance. Conceptually, percentage correct by chance would be equivalent to making our predictions on the basis of a random process like a set of coin tosses rather than on the basis of the predictor. How often would we be correct if we randomly assigned 21.3% (the same percentage reflected in the selection ratio used for the K6) of participants to a prediction of disorder present? We can compute this expected percentage correct by considering the marginal percentages associated with each of the two ways of being correct. The percentage of valid positives expected by chance will be the product of the BR and selection ratio (i.e., 28.5% × 21.3% = 6.1%) because the BR and selection ratio are the marginal percentages associated with the valid positive cell in Figure 38.1. The percentage of valid negative cases expected by chance is the product of (100 − BR) and (100 − selection ratio; i.e., 71.5% × 78.7% = 56.2%). Summing these two ways of being correct (6.1 + 56.2) gives us an expected percent correct by chance of 62.3%. Thus, in our example, it does appear that the K6 is modestly more accurate than expected by chance (77.5% vs. 62.3%). As first discussed by Meehl and Rosen (1955), as BRs decrease, making predictions that are better than chance becomes more difficult. For instance, if the actual BR or prevalence of disorder in the current example were 5% rather than 28.5%, then the expected percent correct by chance would be 75.9% [i.e., (5% × 21.3%) + (95% × 78.7%)]. Expected percent correct by chance is an important baseline against which to judge test performance.

There is another way to consider the effects of BR on our success in making accurate predictions on the basis of tests (Meehl & Rosen, 1955). As the BR of an outcome decreases, it becomes easier to obtain a high degree of accuracy just by predicting that no one will be in the affected group. In our current example, we would be accurate 71.5% of the time just by predicting that the disorder will never be present (in essence, setting the selection ratio to 0). We will always be wrong for respondents who do develop a disorder (the percentage of valid positive cases will be 0, because no positive cases are predicted to develop a disorder), but we will always be right for the far more numerous respondents who do not have a disorder (the percentage of valid negative cases will be 71.5, because all negative cases are predicted not to develop a disorder). This strategy is sometimes called *predicting from the base rate*. If the BR of the disorder were 5%, then we could achieve 95% accuracy just by predicting that no one will develop the disorder. Finding a real predictor that can match the 95% accuracy obtained by predicting from the BR will be difficult to. This BR problem is a particular challenge in psychology, where many of the phenomena of interest have low BRs, frequently prompting researchers to conduct studies with high-risk populations for which the BRs are higher.

The problem with measures of overall percentage correct (whether observed or expected by chance) is that they treat different kinds of correct predictions and different kinds of errors as though they are equal in importance. This assumption of equal importance is rarely true. For instance, in a clinical prediction setting, because successfully recognizing a disorder can lead to appropriate treatment, we might place high value on maximizing the percentage of valid positive cases and minimizing the percentage of false negative cases. At the same time, we may view the cost of false positives to be relatively low, consisting primarily of the time and expense it takes to follow up with our gold standard assessment. Once we begin placing different values on the four cells in the prediction × outcome matrix, overall percentage correct is no longer a good index of our success. In the example in Figure 38.1, 13.7% of the sample are valid positive cases, more than twice the 6.1% that would be expected by chance and much more than the 0% we would identify by assuming that no one will have a disorder (i.e., setting the selection ratio to 0). If maximizing valid positives is important to us, then the test will do much better than the other strategies, because a far greater percentage of valid positive cases will be identified. Thus, even when low BRs make it difficult to achieve better than chance accuracy, or better accuracy than predicting from the BR, a test can still be useful if it can help us to exchange certain types of errors for others. In most assessment and prediction settings, it is the *profile* of correct predictions and errors that matters most, not overall percentage correct.

There are several indexes of test performance that recognize our interest in particular types of correct predictions and particular types of errors. *Sensitivity* (expressed as either a proportion or a percentage) is an index that focuses attention on our accuracy in correctly predicting disorder among those who have a disorder. It is based on the disorder present row of the matrix for the interview-based classification, and it is computed as the valid positive percent/BR percent. In the current example, sensitivity is relatively low: Less than half (48.1%) of the individuals who had a disorder according to the interview were predicted to have a disorder on the basis of a K6 score of 22 or below. *Specificity* (expressed as either a proportion or a percentage) is an index that focuses attention on our ability to avoid mistaken predictions of disorders among individuals in whom disorders are absent. Specificity is based on the disorder absent row of the matrix and is computed as valid negative percent/(100 − BR percent). With a cutoff of 22 or lower on the K6, specificity in this example is very high at .892.

Although sensitivity and specificity reflect, in part, the accuracy of a predictive instrument, they are also strongly influenced by the cutoff or threshold at which we predict that a disorder will be present. If we were to increase the cutoff score in our example from a K6 score of 22 or less to a score of 26 or less (thereby including individuals with less severe K6 scores among those predicted to have a disorder), our sensitivity will increase, and our specificity will decrease. To see why this is so, consider Figure 38.2, which shows frequency distributions of K6 scores for the sample described in Figure 38.1, split into people with no diagnosis (white bars) and people with at least one mood or anxiety disorder (black bars). Consider the cutoff of 22 or lower, which is the basis of Figure 38.1. Clearly, most individuals without a diagnosis have scores higher than 22, which is reflected in the high specificity of the K6 using this cutoff. Although individuals with diagnoses predominate in the part of the distribution at or below 22, it is obvious that about half of diagnosed individuals actually have K6 scores higher than 22. This is reflected in the relatively low sensitivity of the K6 at this cutoff level. If we were to raise our cutoff to 26 (moving to the right on the x-axis and including individuals who show less extreme responses to the K6), we would increase sensitivity from .481 to .758. The reason is obvious in Figure 38.2. By moving our cutoff to the right, we include all of the additional diagnosed individuals with scores between 22 and 26 on the K6. These individuals, who previously were false

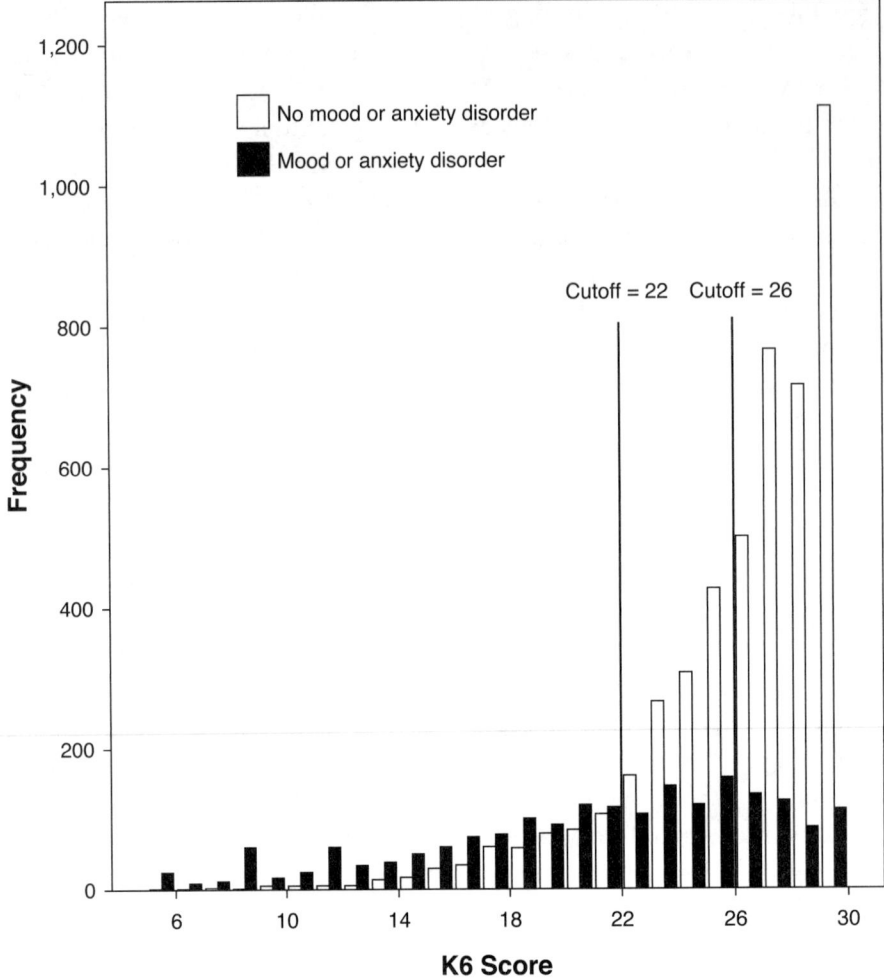

FIGURE 38.2. Histograms of K6 scores for respondents who did and did not receive a mood or anxiety disorder diagnosis. Lower scores indicate greater psychological distress.

negatives, now are converted to valid positives. But this increase in true positives comes at a cost, because setting the cutoff K6 score to 26 means that we are also including many individuals who do not have diagnoses. Indeed, most of the people added by moving our cutoff from 22 to 26 are not diagnosed. Those individuals were previously valid negatives and are converted to false positives. Accordingly, specificity drops from .892 to .649. In general, as we make our threshold for predicting diagnosis more liberal (i.e., as we increase the selection ratio), sensitivity increases, and specificity decreases. Figure 38.3 shows this inverse relationship across a wide range of cutoff values. If we set a conservative threshold that demands strong evidence of problems (in the case of the K6, this means a low score) before predicting disorder, then specificity is high and sensitivity is low. As we make our threshold more liberal, requiring less evidence of problems before we predict disorder, specificity decreases and sensitivity increases. It should be clear that general statements like "the sensitivity of this scale when predicting depression is .8" are not very informative, given that sensitivity depends on the cutoff that we choose.

Sensitivity and specificity are conditional on outcomes (the interview-based classifications of present and absent expressed as the rows in Figure 38.1). Two additional indexes of test performance are conditional on our predictions (the columns of Figure 38.1). Positive predictive

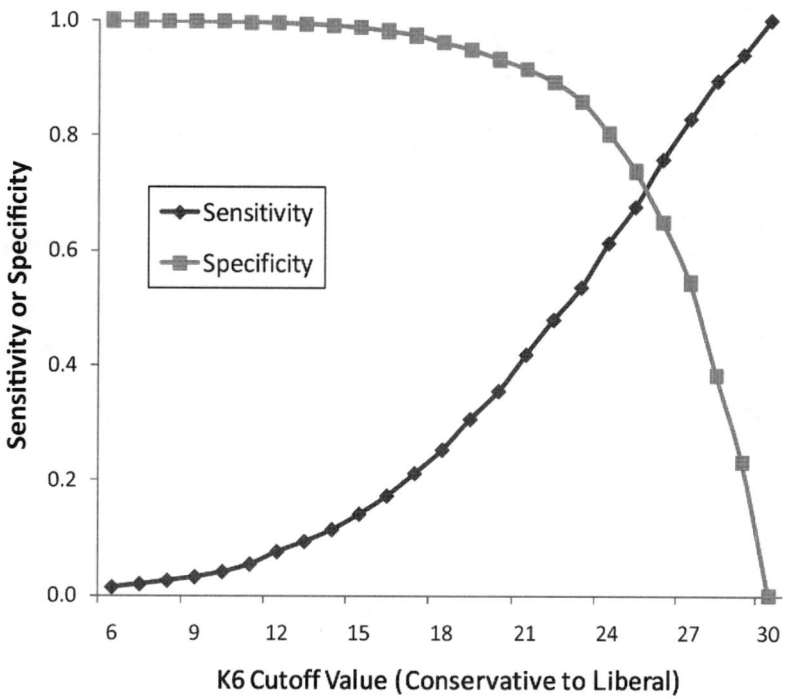

FIGURE 38.3. Sensitivity and specificity as a function of K6 cutoff values.

power is the probability that someone we predict to have a disorder actually has a disorder. It is computed as valid positive percent/selection ratio, which in the current example equals .643. Negative predictive power is the probability that someone we predict not to have a disorder in fact does not have a disorder. It is computed as valid negative percent/(100 − selection ratio), which in the current example equals .811. Like sensitivity and specificity, predictive power is influenced by our cutoff for predicting disorder. Making a cutoff more liberal usually decreases positive predictive power because as we move toward the not-disordered side of the distribution (the right side of Figure 38.2), we usually pick up more not-disordered individuals relative to those with disorders. This increases the percentage of false positives more than the percentage of valid positives. The same change to a more liberal threshold usually results in an increase in negative predictive power because as we move toward the not-disordered end of the distribution, we lose a higher percentage of false negative individuals than valid negative individuals. Figure 38.4 shows the empirical relationship between the selected cutoff and both positive and negative predictive power for the current sample.

Positive and negative predictive power are also strongly influenced by the BR or prevalence of a phenomenon. At a given threshold, increasing prevalence implies relatively more valid positive than false positive cases, and relatively fewer valid negative than false positive cases. Thus, as prevalence increases, positive predictive power increases and negative predictive power decreases. Figure 38.5 shows the expected change in positive and negative predictive power with increasing prevalence in the current sample. The discussion thus far shows why sensitivity, specificity, positive predictive power, and negative predictive power provide better information about test performance than an overall measure of percent correct. They focus our attention on specific goals (e.g., finding people who need help vs. not squandering resources on people who do not need help) rather than on a general goal of overall accuracy. But because these indexes refer to test performance at only one of many possible criteria or thresholds, and because they refer to test performance at only one observed BR, their

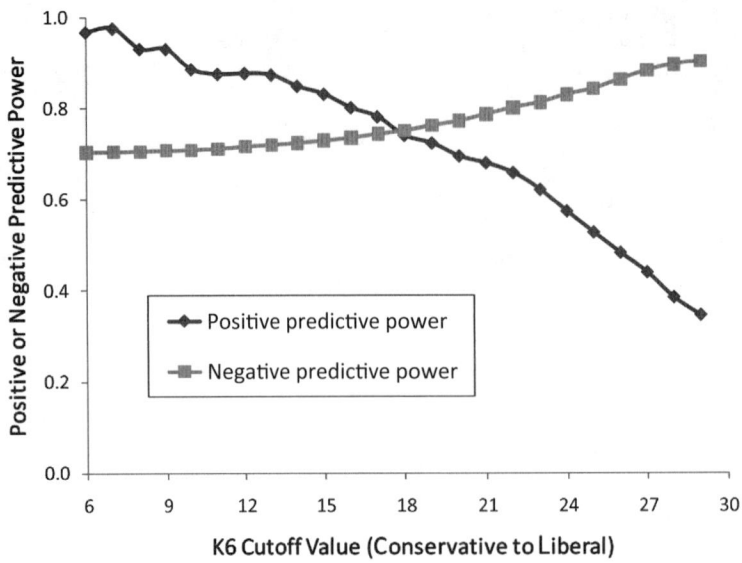

FIGURE 38.4. Positive and negative predictive power as a function of K6 cutoff values.

generalizability to new samples and applications is questionable. If the relative importance of avoiding false negative versus false positive mistakes differs in a new setting, thereby implying a different cutoff score, or if the prevalence differs in the new setting, then it will be difficult to predict how a scale will function in the new setting on the basis of reports of sensitivity, specificity, positive predictive power, and negative predictive power in previous studies. It would be far more useful to have a measure of test performance that better generalizes across samples and thresholds. Next, we provide an overview of just such an index, the area under the ROC curve. Subsequently, we describe how decision-theory methods can be used to select a threshold or cutoff value that optimizes practical utility in a context characterized by a particular BR and set of values.

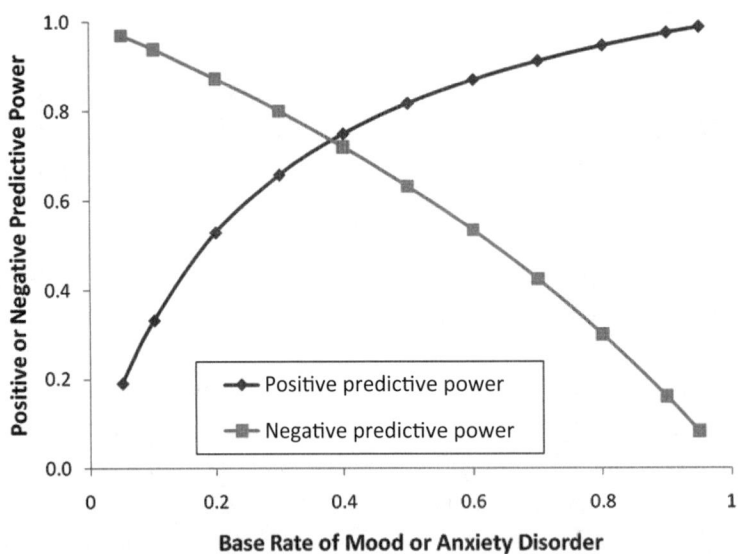

FIGURE 38.5. Positive and negative predictive power as a function of the base rate (or prevalence) of a mood or anxiety disorder, assuming a cutoff of 22 on the K6.

QUANTIFYING DISCRIMINATORY POWER: APPLICATION OF ROC ANALYSIS

ROC analysis, an analytic approach based on signal detection theory, yields a quantitative index of how well an assessment strategy detects or predicts a signal of interest or discriminates two signals of interest (e.g., the presence of a disorder, the occurrence of violence, response to treatment, recidivism). Originally, engineers developed ROC analysis to quantify how well a human receiver detected electronic signals in the presence of noise, and ROC analysis acquired its name from its application to radar-detection problems during World War II. Unlike the indexes of test performance reviewed thus far, the ROC-based index is independent of the BRs or prevalence of a phenomenon, the selected cutoff score, and the values or utilities placed on the four potential decision-making outcomes. Subsequent decision-theory approaches then can be used to optimize cutoff selection for the assessment strategy with maximal discriminatory power in a particular context, which necessarily is influenced by phenomenon BRs and user-specified values. The sequential employment of ROC analysis and decision-theory approaches provides psychologists with a powerful pair of tools for the selection and application of valid and practically useful assessment and prediction methods (e.g., Swets, 1996; Swets et al., 2000).

We illustrate the use of ROC methods by continuing our analysis of the K6 screen for psychological distress and illness. We now use the language of signal detection theory to refer to the four cells in Figure 38.1 (e.g., hits, misses, false alarms, and correct rejections rather than valid positives, false negatives, false positives, and valid negatives). Figure 38.6 presents the ROC curve for the K6 scale as a predictor of the interview-based diagnostic outcome discussed thus far. The axes of the ROC plot are the hit and false alarm rates (i.e., the proportions of valid positives and false positives, respectively), and

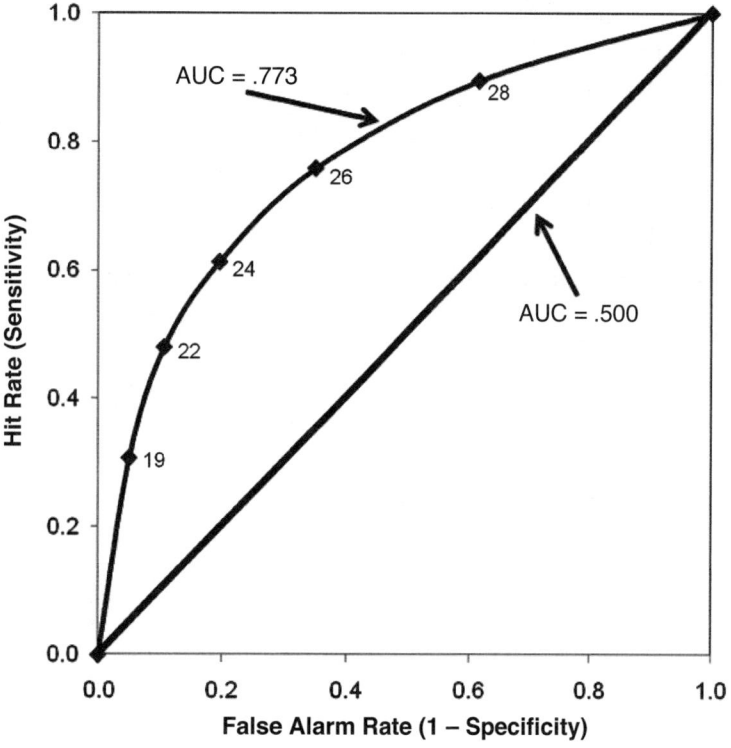

FIGURE 38.6. Receiver operating characteristic curve for K6 scale, with five labeled cutoff values ranging from conservative (19) to liberal (28). AUC = area under the curve.

each point on the ROC curve corresponds to a pair of hit and false alarm rates that results from the use of a specific cutoff value. The hit rate can be computed as hits/(hits + misses), and the false alarm rate corresponds to false alarms/(false alarms + correct rejections). In more traditional language, the ROC curve is a plot of sensitivity against 1 − specificity at all possible cutoff values. A few pairs of false alarm and hit rates are indicated by their associated K6 cutoff values. For example, counting K6 scores less than or equal to 22 as positive cases (because lower scores indicate more distress on the K6) produces a false alarm rate of .107 and a hit rate of .480, and a cutoff score of 28 produces false alarm and hit rates of .616 and .895, respectively. The cutoff value of 28 corresponds here to a liberal criterion or cutoff, which results in a substantial hit rate but also a high false alarm rate. In contrast, the markedly conservative cutoff value of 19 results in a very low false alarm rate (.050) but also an unimpressive hit rate (.307). Thus, the cutoff changes from maximally conservative to maximally liberal as one moves along an ROC curve from the lower left corner (where false alarm and hit rates both are 0.0) to the upper right corner (where false alarm and hit rates both are 1.0). Because lower K6 scores indicate greater pathology, lower scores index more conservative cutoffs. On other measures in which higher scores indicate greater pathology, however, higher scores correspond to more conservative cutoffs because fewer positive cases are identified by high cutoff scores.

The area under the ROC curve (AUC) quantifies the discriminative power of an assessment or prediction method independently of the cutoff value, unlike traditional accuracy indexes. The values for AUC can range from 0.0 (when the ROC curve passes from the lower left corner through the lower right corner to the upper right corner) to 1.0 (when the ROC curve passes from the lower left corner through the upper left corner to the upper right corner). An ROC curve that lies on the main diagonal (see Figure 38.6) indicates that the diagnostic system is operating at the level of chance because the hit and false alarm rates are equal across the range of possible cutoff values. Chance performance corresponds to an AUC of 0.5. As the performance of the diagnostic system increases, the distance of the observed ROC curve from the chance line increases.

The AUC for the K6 as a predictor of mood or anxiety disorder diagnoses in the current illustrative data set is .773, with a standard error of .007 and a 95% confidence interval estimate ranging from .763 to .783. The AUC value has a readily interpretable probabilistic meaning: It corresponds to the probability that a randomly selected pair of observations drawn from the two underlying distributions will be ranked correctly by the assessment method. In the current context, this value indicates that the K6 score will be lower 77.3% of the time for a randomly selected individual with a mood or anxiety disorder than for a randomly selected individual without a mood or anxiety disorder. A z test demonstrates that the observed AUC value is significantly greater than the chance value of .500 ($z = 41.949$, $p < .0001$), indicating that K6 scores are a significant signal of the presence of a mood or anxiety disorder.

It is important to note that AUC is a measure of discrimination, or accuracy, in assessing relative risk. It indexes our ability to distinguish people who have a condition from those who do not have the condition. If, instead, the goal of prediction is to assign absolute levels of risk, for example to assign a prognosis of 30% risk of an outcome for an individual patient, then we would need to use a different type of model that assesses the calibration between predicted and actual probabilities of the outcomes (see e.g., Alba et al., 2017; Cook, 2007).

Figure 38.7 juxtaposes the ROC curve for the K6 with that for the K10, a 10-item screen that includes four additional items (Kessler et al., 2002, 2003). The AUC value for the K10 is .782 ($SE = .006$, 95% confidence interval [CI] = .772–.792), and it is significantly greater than the chance value of .50, $z = 44.373$, $p < .0001$. The difference between the AUC values for the K10 and K6 is .008 ($SE = .002$, 95% CI = .005–.012) and is significantly greater than 0, $z = 5.004$,

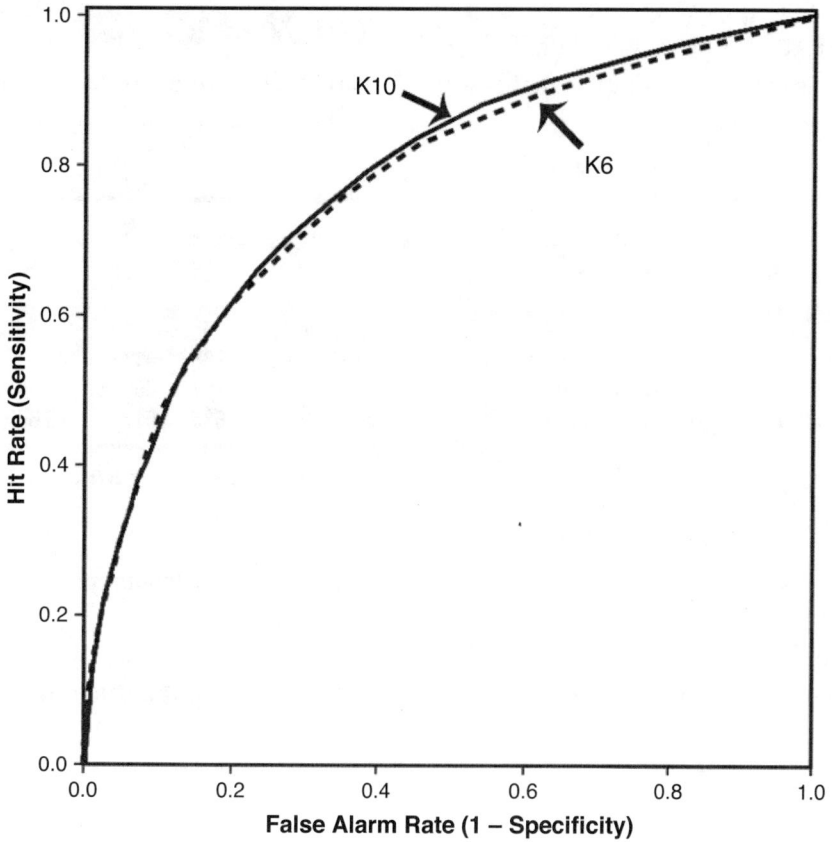

FIGURE 38.7. Receiver operating characteristic curves for K6 and K10 scales.

$p < .001$. This set of results indicates that the K10 shows a statistically but not practically significant advantage over the K6 for detection of the presence of a mood or anxiety disorder. Inspection of Figure 38.7 suggests that the K10 may have a small advantage over the K6 when more liberal cutoff values are employed (e.g., 24 and greater). Thus, when the practical goal in a particular context is to use a screening device to distinguish those with very few symptoms from those with more than very few symptoms, the K10 may be slightly preferable to the K6, in spite of the inclusion of four addition items. When the goal instead is to distinguish those reporting significant symptoms from the remainder of respondents, the K6 and K10 perform very similarly. Formal methods are available to compare two ROC curves according to several criteria, including (a) at a single hit or false alarm rate point on the curve or (b) across a range of user-specified false alarm rate values. For example, we could use these methods to evaluate whether the sensitivity of the K10 is significantly greater than the sensitivity of the K6 at a false alarm rate of .500. Or, we could evaluate whether the discriminatory power of the K10 is significantly greater than that of the K6 for false alarm rate values ranging from .500 to .800. In their initial report on the psychometric properties of the K6 and K10, Kessler et al. (2002) reported AUC values of .876 and .879, respectively. The notably higher values presumably reflect in part their use of a broader gold standard index: the 12-month diagnosis of any anxiety disorder, any mood disorder, or any nonaffective psychosis as well as a global assessment of functioning score between 0 and 70. Similar to the present findings, however, administration of the K10 did not enhance substantially the information acquired from administering the K6. Given the negligible increase in discriminatory power associated with use of the longer K10 in both Kessler et al.'s initial report and the current illustrative analyses, we hereafter use the K6 in all analyses.

Of course, the AUC value for a scale will depend on the outcome that it is predicting. For illustrative purposes, Figure 38.8 presents K6 ROC curves for four of the six anxiety disorder diagnoses that currently are available in the NCS-R: generalized anxiety disorder, panic disorder, specific phobia, and social phobia. Table 38.1 lists the AUC values, standard errors, 95% CIs, and z statistics and evaluates whether discriminatory power is significant for each diagnosis. The discriminatory power of the K6 is significantly greater than chance for all four diagnoses. Not surprisingly, the performance of this six-item screening measure varies across diagnoses; it is significantly worse for detection of specific phobia than for the other three diagnoses, all $p < .001$, and it is significantly better for detection of generalized anxiety disorder than for panic disorder, social phobia, and specific phobia, all $p < .05$.

ROC methods initially were parametric and assumed to be appropriate only when the underlying distributions were normal and showed homogeneous variances. Fortunately, parametric

TABLE 38.1

Receiver Operating Characteristic Analysis Results for K6 Screening of Four Anxiety Disorders

Disorder	AUC	SE	z	P	95% CI
Generalized anxiety disorder	.825	.0102	31.899	.0001	815–.834
Panic disorder	.788	.0141	20.430	.0001	778–.797
Social phobia	.751	.00985	25.454	.0001	740–.761
Specific phobia	.686	.0100	18.608	.0001	675–.698

Note. AUC = area under the curve; CI = confidence interval.

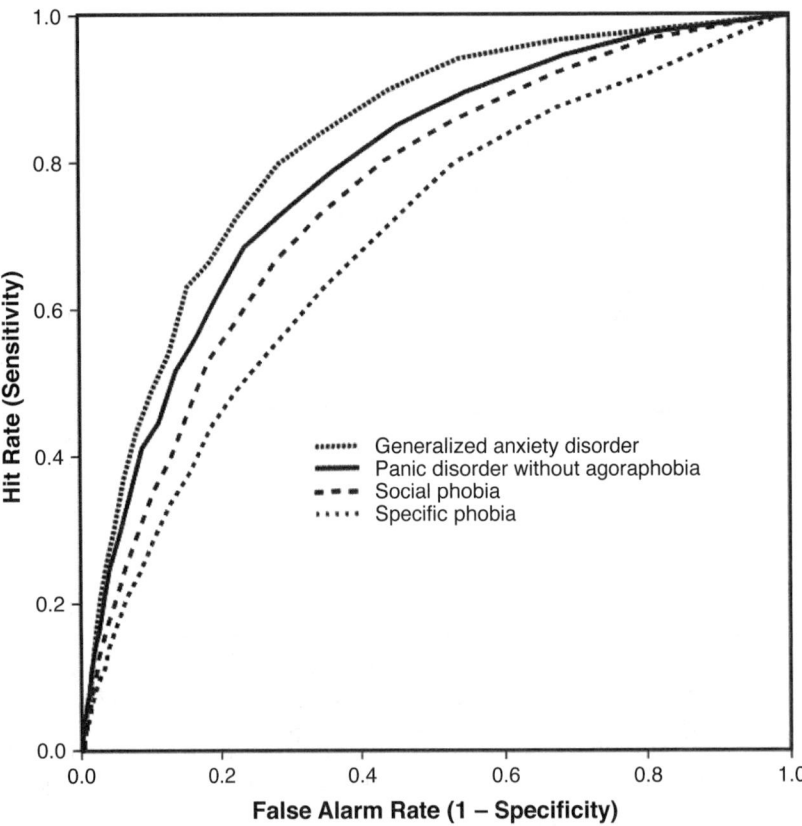

FIGURE 38.8. Receiver operating characteristic curves for K6-based detection of four anxiety disorders.

estimation appears to be robust to violations of these assumptions, and nonparametric estimation methods also are available when either or both of these assumptions are violated. Both parametric and nonparametric methods allow the user to compare AUC values with chance performance values, to compare two independent or dependent AUC values, and to evaluate whether the AUC for a new measure is not inferior to the AUC for an established measure (see Obuchowski & Bullen, 2018; Zhou et al., 2011).

ROC curves can be generated in a variety of ways. First, multiple pairs of hit and false alarm rates can be calculated from a single data set by varying the cutoff. Second, the assessment method may be used repeatedly with different decision criteria employed on each occasion (i.e., from conservative to liberal). Each occasion provides a unique set of hit and false alarm rates. Third, a rating scale method may be used, in which raters not only classify the person (or other stimulus) into one of two categories but also indicate their confidence level for the accuracy of their classification, typically on a 5- or 7-point scale. In this case, multiple pairs of hit and false alarm rates can be obtained by treating each confidence level as a separate cutoff value (see Macmillan & Creelman, 1991). When ROC analysis is used to quantify the performance of assessment and prediction strategies, the first strategy most commonly is employed.

A variety of software programs are available for ROC analysis. Commercially available programs with extensive options include SAS, Stata, and MedCalc, whereas ROC-related features within SPSS are less well-developed. All analyses for this chapter were conducted using MedCalc version 11.2.1.0. Robin et al. (2011) introduced a widely used open-source R package, pROC, which allows the user to plot and smooth ROC curves, to compute and compare paired and unpaired AUC and partial-AUC values (both parametrically and nonparametrically), and to compute confidence interval estimates for a variety of statistics (e.g., the ROC curve, the AUC, sensitivity at a particular specificity, specificity at a particular sensitivity, thresholds). More recently,

Goksuluk et al. (2016) introduced easyROC, a free web-based tool that provides a user-friendly graphical interface (rather than the R command-based interface) to access pROC and several other related R programs. EasyROC also incorporates OptimalCutpoints (López-Ratón et al., 2014), an R package that estimates optimal cutoffs on the basis of a wealth of potential criteria, including the overall utility function discussed in the latter half of this chapter (labeled CB for cost–benefit analysis within OptimalCutpoints). Finally, easyROC implements sample size determination procedures when evaluating a single test, when comparing two tests, and when determining whether a new test is not inferior to an established test (see Zhou et al., 2011, for more information on power analyses for ROC studies).

In recent decades, ROC methods have been generalized to address a wide variety of more complex circumstances of interest to psychological scientists: (a) analysis of assessment and prediction tasks including two or more response options; (b) analysis of assessment and prediction tasks including continuous, rather than discrete, response options; (c) meta-analysis of test performance across multiple samples; (d) treatment of clustered data (e.g., multiple tests within a sampling unit or multiple judges of a sampling unit); and (e) ROC-based regression methods, which incorporate potential predictors of test performance and facilitate development of prediction equations. Zhou et al. (2011) and Obuchowski and Burren (2018) provided comprehensive coverage of these issues and pointers to relevant literature for interested readers.

SELECTING A CUTOFF: APPLICATION OF DECISION AND INFORMATION THEORY

Although ROC analysis provides an index of discriminatory power that is independent of cutoff values, BRs, and the values or utilities placed on the four decision-making outcomes, it does not provide the optimal cutoff value or illustrate how the ideal cutoff value varies as a function of the hit and false alarm rates, BRs, and values (Hsiao et al., 1989; Mossman &

Somoza, 1989; Murphy et al., 1987; Somoza et al., 1994; Swets et al., 2000). Having first used ROC methods to identify the assessment or prediction strategy with the greatest discriminatory power, users next must select an optimal cutoff value, which necessarily involves specification of a function to be maximized. Thus, there is no true and unique optimal cutoff value, and the usefulness of a diagnostic test can vary widely across the contexts in which it is employed as a function of cutoff selection. In the next section, we provide an overview of two common approaches to selecting optimal cutoff values that incorporate hit and false alarm rates, BRs, and utilities in their criterion function.

Decision Theory Approach to Cutoff Specification

Meehl and Rosen (1955) and Somoza and Mossman (1991), among others, have advocated the use of an approach that combines a signal detection theory (SDT) analysis with utility-based decision theory (see also Metz, 1978; Swets, 1992). This approach allows the user to place a differential value on (i.e., to specify the differential utility of) hits (H), false alarms (FA), correct rejections (CR), and misses (M). Frequently, the user does not value these four possible outcomes equally because of their differential implications (i.e., variation in the perceived benefits and costs associated with the four outcomes). As summarized in the following equation, the overall utility of a specific cutoff value is a function of the hit rates and false alarm rates (HR and FAR) that result from a given cutoff value, a BR estimate (expressed as a proportion), and the values or utilities placed on each of the four decision-making outcomes (UH = utility for hits, UM = utility for misses, UFA = utility for false alarms, and UCR = utility for correct rejections):

$$U_{overall} = (BR)(HR)(UH) + (BR)(1-HR)(UM)$$
$$+ (1-BR)(FAR)(UFA)$$
$$+ (1-BR)(1-FAR)(UCR). \quad (38.1)$$

Each term in $U_{overall}$ is the product of the probability of a particular outcome (e.g., the probability of a Hit is BR * HR) and the utility of that outcome (e.g., UH). Thus, $U_{overall}$ is a utilities-weighted sum of the probabilities of the four decision-making outcomes. Utilities typically range between 0 and 1, where a value of 0 represents the least desired outcome and a value of 1 indicates the most desired outcome. Typically, therefore, hits and correct rejections are assigned utilities ≥ .5, whereas misses and false alarms are assigned utilities ≤ .5. Suppose, for example, that we wanted to instantiate the common decision goal of maximizing percent correct in the previous example. We would assign the maximal value of 1 to correct detection of individuals with an anxiety or mood disorder (i.e., UH = 1) and to correct rejection of individuals without an anxiety or mood disorder (i.e., UCR = 1). The minimal value of 0 would be assigned to failure to detect individuals with an anxiety or mood disorder (i.e., UM = 0) and to failure to reject individuals without an anxiety or mood disorder (i.e., UFA = 0). We then would compute $U_{overall}$ for all possible cutoff values (e.g., the 25 potential K6 cutoff scores) and a range of prevalence rates. These steps readily can be instantiated in Excel.

Figure 38.9 depicts how the overall utility of various K6 cutoff values changes as a function of phenomenon BRs in a specific decision context, assuming that the decision goal is to maximize percent correct. As the BR of either a mood or anxiety disorder increases from .100 to .900, the optimal cutoff value increases markedly from 13 to 30. More generally, whenever the decision goal is to maximize percent correct, the ideal cutoff value necessarily becomes more conservative and results in fewer positive classifications as the BR of a phenomenon decreases, so that false alarms do not become too frequent.

The potentially marked influence of changes in BRs on the utility of cut scores commonly is ignored in both research and applied contexts. Cutoff scores determined to be optimal during scale development may be reified and used without modification across contexts in which BRs vary widely. For example, an optimal cut score might be determined in an initial study in which the BRs for the phenomenon of interest are higher

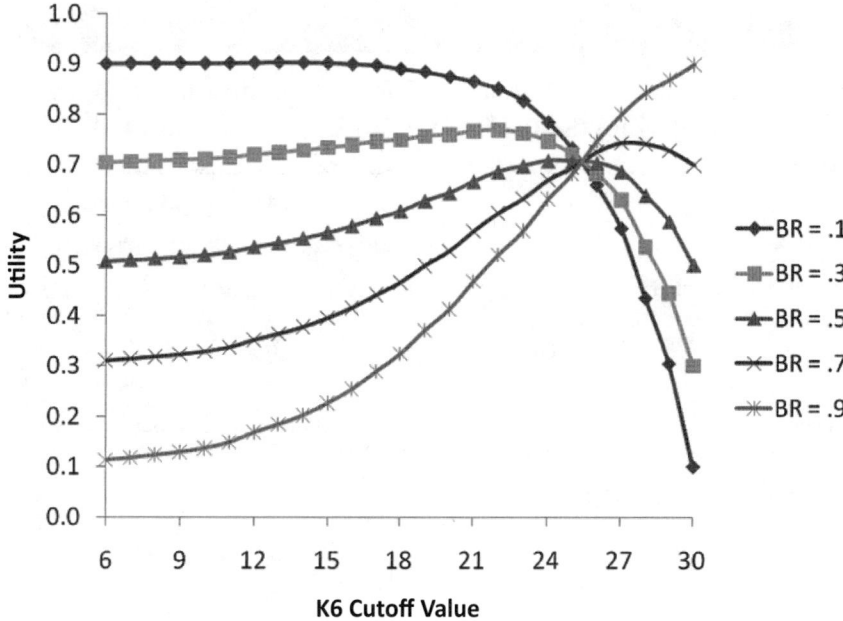

FIGURE 38.9. Utility of K6 cutoff values as a function of the base rate (BR) of mood or anxiety disorders while maximizing percent correct.

(perhaps because of oversampling persons with disorders) than in the context in which the resulting measure and cut score commonly are applied. As a result, the cut score that was optimal in the higher BR context is too liberal in the lower BR context, resulting in a notable increase in the relative frequency of false alarms. Alternatively, the ideal cutoff score for a measure that emerges from work with a large community sample might be unacceptably conservative when applied within a clinical context.

Exhibit 38.2 illustrates the potential impact of ignoring the influence of disorder prevalence on the practical utility of the K6. Exhibit 38.2A presents the classification results for the 6,656 individuals in the current sample, given two assumptions. First, the BR of a mood or anxiety disorder is assumed to be .285, the observed value for the current sample. Second, the cutoff score is 22, the optimal value assuming that the proportion correct is being maximized for the given prevalence. This cutoff is associated with a hit rate of .480 and a false alarm rate of .107. Overall proportion correct is .775 (i.e., [911 + 4248]/6656). Exhibit 38.2B then presents the results if the same cutoff value of 22 is employed in a context in which the BR of mood or anxiety disorders is .500, rather than .285. This might occur in a clinical context, for example. Overall proportion correct drops to .686. Finally, Exhibit 38.2C presents the results if the ideal cutoff value is used for a context in which the BR of mood or anxiety disorders is .500. This cutoff value is higher (24), as would be expected when the proportion of positive cases increases, and it is associated with a hit rate of .613 and a false alarm rate of .197. Notably, overall proportion correct now increases to .708, and a significantly greater proportion of positive cases is detected. Thus, it is critical for researchers both to provide and to make use of BR-specific guidance on the cutoff values that optimally balance correct and incorrect decisions.

A decision goal of maximizing percent or proportion correct frequently is selected to sidestep the need to specify values or utilities for each of the four decision-making outcomes. This default approach makes equally strong implicit assumptions, however. In the present context, choosing to maximize percent correct is predicated on the assumption that correctly identifying those without mood or anxiety disorders

EXHIBIT 38.2

Influence of Base Rates on Proportion Correct Classification of Mood or Anxiety Disorders on the Basis of K6 Scores, Using a Cutoff of 22

		K6-based classification		
		Disorder present	Disorder absent	Total
A: Base rate = .285, cutoff = 22 (HR = .480, FAR = .107), proportion correct = .775				
Interview-based classification ("truth")	Disorder present	911	988	1,899
	Disorder absent	509	4,248	4,757
	Total	1,420	5,236	6,656
B: Base rate = .500, cutoff = 22 (HR = .480, FAR = .107), proportion correct = .686				
Interview-based classification ("truth")	Disorder present	1,597	1,731	3,328
	Disorder absent	356	2,972	3,328
	Total	1,953	4,703	6,656
C: Base rate = .500, cutoff = 24 (HR = .613, FAR = .197), proportion correct = .708				
Interview-based classification ("truth")	Disorder present	2,040	1,288	3,328
	Disorder absent	654	2,674	3,328
	Total	2,694	3,962	6,656

Note. HR = hit rate; FAR = false alarm rate.

is just as important as correctly identifying those with mood or anxiety disorders, although some might argue the latter is more valuable.

Analogously, this approach stipulates that erroneously classifying a person as having a mood or anxiety disorder is just as problematic as failing to identify a person with a mood or anxiety disorder, although some might perceive the latter to be more serious. Consideration of plausible value specifications is facilitated by inspection of the following utility ratio (Somoza & Mossman, 1991):

$$\text{utility ratio} = (UCR - UFA)/(UH - UM). \quad (38.2)$$

Maximizing percent correct essentially specifies a utility ratio of 1.0, whereby the difference between the values placed on correct versus incorrect decisions about negative cases in the numerator is the same as the difference between the values placed on correct versus incorrect decisions about positive cases in the denominator. Alternative value specifications could capture the greater perceived importance of decisions about positive cases than negative cases, however. For example, we might stipulate that $UH = 1$, $UCR = .75$, $UM = 0$, and $UFA = .25$, resulting in a utility ratio of .5 (i.e., we care twice as much about decisions regarding positive cases than negative cases). Alternatively, pronounced concerns about the negative consequences or side effects of case identification or treatment might lead one to place greater value on decisions about negative cases ($UH = .75$, $UM = .25$, $UCR = 1$, $UFA = 0$), thereby specifying a utility ratio of 2.0 (i.e., we care twice as much about decisions regarding negative than positive cases). Thus, value configurations that weight decisions about positive and negative cases equally correspond to a utility ratio of 1.0, configurations that weight decisions about positive cases far more than negative cases produce utility ratios less than 1.0, and configurations that weight decisions about negative cases far more than positive cases produce utility ratios greater than 1.0. Figure 38.10 illustrates how the overall utility of various K6 cutoff values changes as a function of the utility ratio, or the relative value placed on decisions about positive versus negative cases. The BR is held fixed at .285 for all computations, as this is the probability of a mood or anxiety disorder in the current data set. As greater importance is placed on decisions about

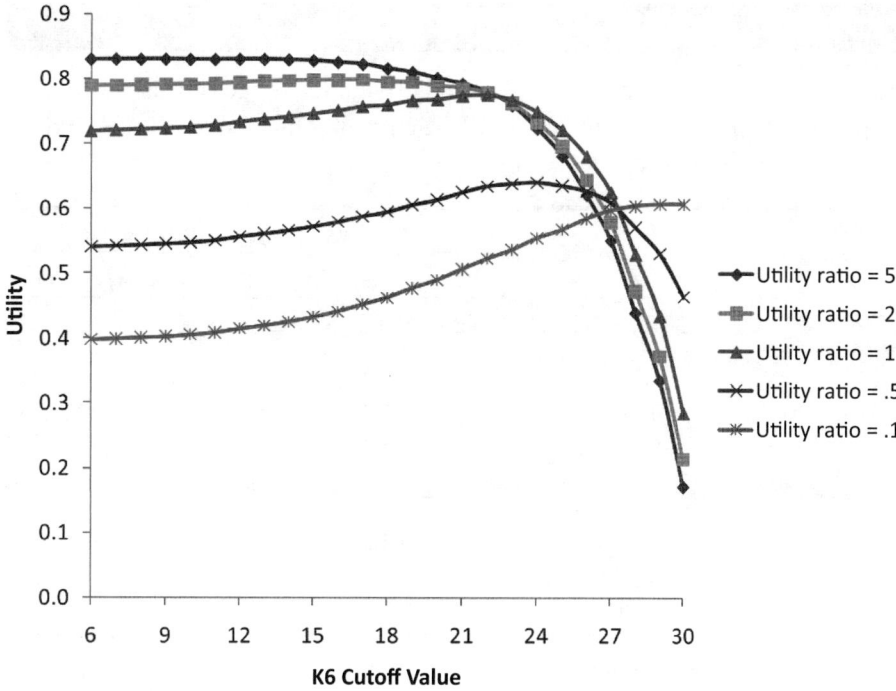

FIGURE 38.10. Utility of K6 cutoff values as a function of the relative value placed on positive versus negative cases, assuming the base rate of mood or anxiety disorders is .285. See text for more information.

positive cases (i.e., as the utility ratio decreases), the most useful threshold increases in value from 13 for a utility ratio of 5.0 (decisions about negative cases more important) to 30 for a utility ratio of 0.1 (decisions about positive cases more important). When decisions about positive and negative cases are valued equally (i.e., the utility ratio = 1.0), the optimal cutoff value is 22. Not surprisingly, as the value placed on positive cases increases, the cutoff becomes more liberal.

Exhibit 38.3 illustrates how ignoring implicit assumptions about the equal importance placed on decisions about positive and negative cases when maximizing proportion correct may result in the selection of unnecessarily conservative cutoff scores. Exhibit 38.3A presents the classification results for the 6,656 individuals in the current sample, given two assumptions. First, the prevalence of a mood or anxiety disorder is assumed to be .285, the observed value for the current sample. Second, the cutoff score is 22, which is the optimal value assuming that proportion correct is being maximized for the given prevalence rate (i.e., UH = 1, UCR = 1, UM = 0, and UFA = 0; the utility ratio = 1.0). Using a cutoff of 22 produces a hit rate of .480 and a false alarm rate of .107. Under these conditions, the proportion correct for positive cases (sensitivity) is .480, and the proportion correct for negative cases (specificity) is .893. Exhibit 38.3B then presents the results if the cutoff score is 24, which is ideal in a context in which accurate decisions about those with a mood or anxiety disorder are construed as twice as important as accurate decisions about those without a mood or anxiety disorder (i.e., UH = 1, UCR = .75, UM = 0, and UFA = .25; the utility ratio = .5). The cutoff score of 24 is associated with a hit rate of .613 and a false alarm rate of .197. Under these conditions, the proportion correct for positive cases increases to .613 (an increase of 13 percentage points), whereas the proportion correct for negative cases declines to .803 (a decrease of 9 percentage points). This example highlights how implicitly placing equal importance on decisions about positive and negative cases when one in actuality places far greater importance on positive than negative decisions may result in the use of unnecessarily

EXHIBIT 38.3

Influence of Relative Value Placed on Positive and Negative Cases on Proportion Correct Classification of Presence or Absence of Mood/Anxiety Disorders on the Basis of K6 Scores

		K6-based classification		
		Disorder present	Disorder absent	Total
A: Cutoff = 22 (HR = .480, FAR = .107), proportion correct (positive case) = .480, proportion correct (negative case) = .893				
Interview-based classification ("truth")	Disorder present	911	988	1,899
	Disorder absent	509	4,248	4,757
	Total	1,420	5,236	6,656
B: Cutoff = 24 (HR = .613, FAR = .197), proportion correct (positive case) = .613, proportion correct (negative case) = .803				
Interview-based classification ("truth")	Disorder present	1,164	735	1,899
	Disorder absent	935	3,822	4,757
	Total	2,099	4,557	6,656

Note. HR = hit rate; FAR = false alarm rate.

conservative cutoff scores, resulting in decreased accuracy for positive cases.

More generally, the practical utility of assessment and prediction devices could be enhanced greatly if researchers routinely provided optimal cutoff scores for a range of BRs and utility ratios during measure development. Although the utility approach has been criticized because it requires the user to quantify both BRs and utility ratios,[1] it is important to recognize that proceeding instead by ignoring BR effects and maximizing percent correct also makes stringent assumptions that can exert marked influences on overall accuracy. In other words, no absolute optimal cutoff value exists in the absence of prevalence information and assumptions about the meaning of optimal.

INFORMATION THEORY APPROACH TO CUTOFF SPECIFICATION

To finesse the use of subjective utilities, Metz et al. (1973) proposed that an information theory (Shannon & Weaver, 1949) analysis of the ROC curve provides a natural optimization function (information gain, or I_{gain}) for the selection of an optimal threshold (see also Mossman & Somoza, 1989; Somoza et al., 1994)

$$I_{gain} = (BR)(HR)(\log 2(HR/G))$$
$$+ (BR)(1-HR)(\log 2[(1-HR)/(1-G)])$$
$$+ (1-BR)(FAR)(\log 2(FAR/G))$$
$$+ (1-BR)(1-FAR)(\log 2[(1-FAR)/(1-G)]), \qquad (38.3)$$

where G = selection ratio (expressed as a proportion).

According to Metz et al.'s (1973) approach, information gain refers to the reduction of uncertainty about the true classification of a person that results from administering the diagnostic measure. For our example, information gain refers to the difference between the uncertainties about the mood or anxiety disorder status of an individual before and after knowing the individual's K6 score.

---

[1] In some settings, there may be data available on the relative cost (time, expense, productivity) of false positives and false negatives that can be used to facilitate utility specification. When such data are not available, expert ratings may provide subjective utilities that are useful as a starting point.

Inspection of the criterion functions specified by decision theorists ($U_{overall}$) and information theorists (I_{gain}) reveals that both incorporate the false alarm rate, the hit rate, and the BR (expressed as a proportion). I_{gain} maximizes information gain, however, whereas $U_{overall}$ maximizes utility. Interestingly, $U_{overall}$ is a general case of I_{gain}, because I_{gain} provides an alternative specification of the utilities of the four outcomes (Metz et al., 1973; Somoza & Mossman, 1992a, 1992b). Thus, Metz et al.'s (1973) approach to criterion selection sidesteps the necessity of explicitly specifying the outcome utilities. Variability in prevalence continues to exert an influence on cutoff selection in the information theory approach, however.

Figure 38.11 depicts the influence of BRs on information gain for K6 cutoff values. Two effects are visible in the figure. First, information gain from administering the K6 is maximal for a BR of .5 and declines markedly when BRs are extremely low or high. This reflects the far greater a priori uncertainty about a case in which both positive and negative outcomes are equally likely. In contrast, markedly unequal BRs for positive and negative outcomes provide extensive a priori information about the most likely outcome (i.e., one could simply predict the more prevalent category for each case and be correct the overwhelming majority of the time). Second, the optimal cutoff becomes more liberal as BRs increase. For the K6, ideal cutoffs range from 22, when the prevalence of a mood or anxiety disorder is 5%, to 26, when the prevalence is 95%. Ignoring the influence of BRs on information gain has similarly deleterious effects to those illustrated in Exhibit 38.2 for overall utility.

Another approach that focuses on the information value of the predictor at different thresholds involves computing diagnostic likelihood ratios (in the typical case, sensitivity/[1 −specificity]), which reflect the degree to which exceeding a certain threshold or range of thresholds is associated with the probability of having the condition of interest relative to the probability of not having the condition (Youngstrom, 2014). In combination with information about BR, diagnostic likelihood ratios provide another way of choosing thresholds for particular goals when specific information on the relative utility of different outcomes is not available.

Comparison of Two Approaches and Recommendations

Table 38.2 contrasts the optimal K6 cutoff scores for varying BRs for four optimization functions: I_{gain}, $U_{overall}$ assuming decisions about positive cases

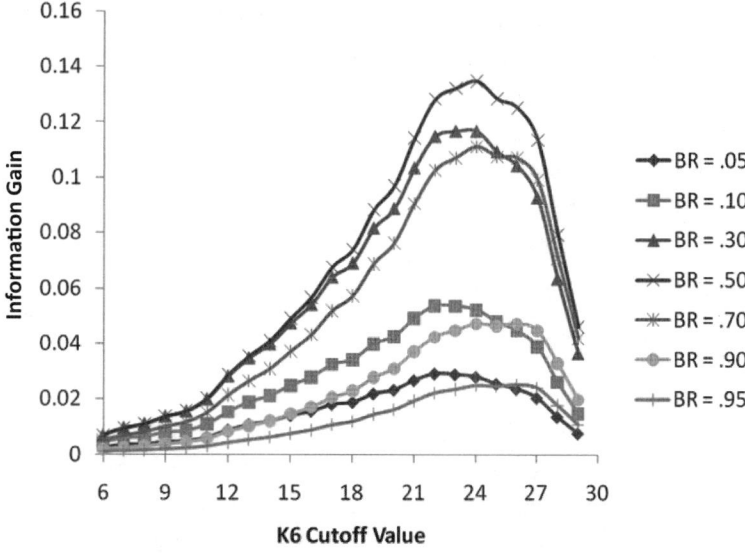

FIGURE 38.11. Information gain associated with K6 cutoff values as a function of the base rate (BR) of a mood or anxiety disorder.

TABLE 38.2
Optimal K6 Cutoff Values as a Function of Base Rates and Optimization Function

Optimization function	Base rate						
	.05	.10	.30	.50	.70	.90	.95
Maximizing I_{gain}	22	22	23	24	24	26	26
Maximizing $U_{overall}$: Decisions about positive cases twice as important as decisions about negative cases	13	17	24	27	30	30	30
Maximizing $U_{overall}$: Decisions about positive and negative cases equal in importance	7	13	22	24	27	30	30
Maximizing $U_{overall}$: Decisions about negative cases twice as important as decisions about positive cases	7	9	17	22	26	30	30

Note. I_{gain} = information gain; $U_{overall}$ = overall utility.

are twice as important as decisions about negative cases, $U_{overall}$ assuming decisions about positive and negative cases are equivalent in value, and $U_{overall}$ assuming decisions about negative cases are twice as important as decisions about positive cases. These values range from 7 to 30, making it evident that both users and developers of assessment and prediction devices benefit from attending to three factors when selecting a cutoff score that maximizes practical utility: (a) the BRs of the phenomenon in the context in which the device is employed, (b) whether maximizing utility or information is preferred, and (c) the relative importance of decisions about positive versus negative cases of the phenomenon if maximizing utility is preferred. It is not critical to the profitable use of this information that either exact BRs be known or utility ratios be specified precisely. If the user is wholly unable to specify even an approximate utility ratio, then the cutoff value that maximizes information for the approximate prevalence rate should be selected. We suspect that most users are in a position to articulate a clear preference between the three options provided in the table, however. In this case, cutoffs predicated on utility maximization are recommended. More generally, we urge those developing assessment and prediction devices to provide a similar table of ideal cutoff values rather than a single cutoff value that may not be robust to variations in BRs and utility ratios.

CONCLUSION

Contemporary evaluation of the performance of assessment and prediction strategies in psychological science entails the completion of a two-step strategy that distinguishes the discriminative and decisional aspects of psychological measurement. First, ROC methods can be used to quantify the power of our measures to discriminate between two mutually exclusive states of interest. Indexes drawn from signal detection theory, such as AUC, assess performance independently of the selected cutoff value, the BRs of the phenomenon of interest, and the values placed on the four decision-making outcomes, unlike traditional indexes such as sensitivity, specificity, positive predictive power, and negative predictive power. Second, decision-theory methods can be employed to select a cutoff value that maximizes either the practical utility of or the information gained by test administration in a particular decision-making context, as defined by both BRs and the relative values or utilities placed on the different outcomes. This approach highlights the context specificity of optimal cutoffs or thresholds, prompting a recommendation that researchers who develop new measurement strategies routinely report optimal cutoff values for a range of potential BRs and four potential decision-making goals. Notably, precise specification of local BRs or utilities is not critical to the profitable use of this information, which will obviate the need to make stringent assumptions about the generalizability of BRs and utilities across decision-making contexts and will enhance the practical applicability of our measurement strategies.

References

Alba, A. C., Agoritsas, T., Walsh, M., Hanna, S., Iorio, A., Devereaux, P. J., McGinn, T., & Guyatt, G. (2017). Discrimination and calibration of clinical prediction models: Users' guides to the medical literature. *Journal of the American Medical Association, 318*(14), 1377–1384. https://doi.org/10.1001/jama.2017.12126

American Psychiatric Association. (1994). *Diagnostic and statistical manual of mental disorders* (4th ed.).

Clark, L. A., & Watson, D. (2019). Constructing validity: New developments in creating objective measuring instruments. *Psychological Assessment, 31*, 1412–1427. https://doi.org/10.1037/pas0000626

Cook, N. R. (2007). Use and misuse of the receiver operating characteristic curve in risk prediction. *Circulation, 115*(7), 928–935. https://doi.org/10.1161/CIRCULATIONAHA.106.672402

Goksuluk, D., Korkmaz, S., Zararsiz, G., & Karaagaoglu, A. E. (2016). easyROC: An interactive web-tool for ROC curve analysis using R language environment. *The R Journal, 8*(2), 213–230. https://doi.org/10.32614/RJ-2016-042

Hsiao, J. K., Bartko, J. J., & Potter, W. Z. (1989). Diagnosing diagnoses. Receiver operating characteristic methods and psychiatry. *Archives of General Psychiatry, 46*(7), 664–667. https://doi.org/10.1001/archpsyc.1989.01810070090014

Kessler, R. C., Andrews, G., Colpe, L. J., Hiripi, E., Mroczek, D. K., Normand, S.-L. T., Walters, E. E., & Zaslavsky, A. M. (2002). Short screening scales to monitor population prevalences and trends in non-specific psychological distress. *Psychological Medicine, 32*(6), 959–976. https://doi.org/10.1017/S0033291702006074

Kessler, R. C., Barker, P. R., Colpe, L. J., Epstein, J. F., Gfroerer, J. C., Hiripi, E., Howes, M. J., Normand, S. L., Manderscheid, R. W., Walters, E. E., & Zaslavsky, A. M. (2003). Screening for serious mental illness in the general population. *Archives of General Psychiatry, 60*(2), 184–189. https://doi.org/10.1001/archpsyc.60.2.184

Kessler, R. C., Berglund, P., Chiu, W.-T., Demler, O., Heeringa, S., Hiripi, E., Jin, R., Pennell, B. E., Walters, E. E., Zaslavsky, A., & Zheng, H. (2004). The US National Comorbidity Survey Replication (NCS-R): Design and field procedures. *International Journal of Methods in Psychiatric Research, 13*(2), 69–92. https://doi.org/10.1002/mpr.167

Kessler, R. C., & Merikangas, K. R. (2004). The National Comorbidity Survey Replication (NCS-R): Background and aims. *International Journal of Methods in Psychiatric Research, 13*(2), 60–68. https://doi.org/10.1002/mpr.166

López-Ratón, M., Rodríguez-Álvarez, M. X., Cadarso-Suárez, C., & Gude-Sampedro, F. (2014). OptimalCutpoints: An R package for selecting optimal cutpoints in diagnostic tests. *Journal of Statistical Software, 61*(8), 1–36. https://doi.org/10.18637/jss.v061.i08

Macmillan, N. A., & Creelman, C. D. (1991). *Detection theory: A user's guide*. Cambridge University Press.

Meehl, P. E., & Rosen, A. (1955). Antecedent probability and the efficiency of psychometric signs, patterns, or cutting scores. *Psychological Bulletin, 52*(3), 194–216. https://doi.org/10.1037/h0048070

Metz, C. E. (1978). Basic principles of ROC analysis. *Seminars in Nuclear Medicine, 8*(4), 283–298. https://doi.org/10.1016/S0001-2998(78)80014-2

Metz, C. E., Goodenough, D. J., & Rossmann, K. (1973). Evaluation of receiver operating characteristic curve data in terms of information theory, with applications in radiography. *Radiology, 109*(2), 297–303. https://doi.org/10.1148/109.2.297

Mossman, D., & Somoza, E. (1989). Maximizing diagnostic information from the dexamethasone suppression test. An approach to criterion selection using receiver operating characteristic analysis. *Archives of General Psychiatry, 46*(7), 653–660. https://doi.org/10.1001/archpsyc.1989.01810070079013

Murphy, J. M., Berwick, D. M., Weinstein, M. C., Borus, J. F., Budman, S. H., & Klerman, G. L. (1987). Performance of screening and diagnostic tests. Application of receiver operating characteristic analysis. *Archives of General Psychiatry, 44*(6), 550–555. https://doi.org/10.1001/archpsyc.1987.01800180068011

Obuchowski, N. A., & Bullen, J. A. (2018). Receiver operating characteristic (ROC) curves: Review of methods with applications in diagnostic medicine. *Physics in Medicine and Biology, 63*(7), 07TR01. https://doi.org/10.1088/1361-6560/aab4b1

Robin, X., Turck, N., Hainard, A., Tiberti, N., Lisacek, F., Sanchez, J.-C., & Müller, M. (2011). pROC: An open-source package for R and S+ to analyze and compare ROC curves. *BMC Bioinformatics, 12*(1), 77. https://doi.org/10.1186/1471-2105-12-77

Shannon, C. E., & Weaver, W. (1949). *The mathematical theory of communication*. University of Illinois Press.

Somoza, E., & Mossman, D. (1991). "Biological markers" and psychiatric diagnosis: Risk-benefit balancing using ROC analysis. *Biological Psychiatry, 29*(8), 811–826. https://doi.org/10.1016/0006-3223(91)90200-6

Somoza, E., & Mossman, D. (1992a). Comparing and optimizing diagnostic tests: An information-theoretical approach. *Medical Decision Making, 12*(3), 179–188. https://doi.org/10.1177/0272989X9201200303

Somoza, E., & Mossman, D. (1992b). Comparing diagnostic tests using information theory: The INFO-ROC technique. *The Journal of Neuropsychiatry and Clinical Neurosciences, 4*(2), 214–219. https://doi.org/10.1176/jnp.4.2.214

Somoza, E., Steer, R. A., Beck, A. T., & Clark, D. A. (1994). Differentiating major depression and panic disorders by self-report and clinical rating scales: ROC analysis and information theory. *Behaviour Research and Therapy, 32*(7), 771–782. https://doi.org/10.1016/0005-7967(94)90035-3

Swets, J. A. (1992). The science of choosing the right decision threshold in high-stakes diagnostics. *American Psychologist, 47*(4), 522–532. https://doi.org/10.1037/0003-066X.47.4.522

Swets, J. A. (1996). *Signal detection theory and ROC analysis in psychological diagnostics: Collected papers*. Erlbaum.

Swets, J. A., Dawes, R. M., & Monahan, J. (2000). Psychological science can improve diagnostic decisions. *Psychological Science in the Public Interest, 1*(1), 1–26. https://doi.org/10.1111/1529-1006.001

Youngstrom, E. A. (2014). A primer on receiver operating characteristic analysis and diagnostic efficiency statistics for pediatric psychology: We are ready to ROC. *Journal of Pediatric Psychology, 39*(2), 204–221. https://doi.org/10.1093/jpepsy/jst062

Zhou, X. H., Obuchowski, N. A., & McClish, D. K. (2011). *Statistical methods in diagnostic medicine*. John Wiley & Sons. https://doi.org/10.1002/9780470906514

Index

AAALAC, International, 90
ABCD Study. *See* Adolescent Brain Cognitive Development Study
Abducting eye movements, 470
Abelson, R. P., 199
ABI/INFORM, 159
Ability, on Rasch model, 181
Ability tests, 383–384, 418
Abortion studies, question order effects in, 279–280, 288, 291, 292
ABRs (auditory brainstem responses), 609
Absolute decision, 748, 749
Absolute errors, variance–covariance matrix for, 758
Absolute error variance, 748, 751, 753, 759
Absolute risk, 846
Absolute threshold, 517
Academic achievement, norm-referenced, 409–410
Academic community, 138, 228
Academic Search Ultimate, 160
Acceptable responses to projective tests, 434
Accessible language, for findings, 6
Accountability testing, 428
Accuracy
 and base rate, 840–841
 classification, 427, 461
 decoding, 615
 defined, 196–197
 of fast guesses, 498
 of hormone assays, 567
 and observer agreement, 262
 overall, in decision theory, 786
 and response times, 494
 and sensitivity/specificity, 841

Accuracy in parameter estimation (AIPE) approach, 195–197
 for omnibus effect, 204–205
 organizational behavior example, 204–205
 parameter specification for, 200
 research goals appropriate for, 190, 193
 for targeted effect, 204
ACE (average causal effect), 28–30, 45
Acetylcholine, 547
Acquiescence, 394
Acquisition orientation, fMRI, 632–633
Action potentials, 581, 616
Action research, 9–10
Activational hormone effects, 566
Active electrode systems, 583, 621
Active listening, 305
Activity dimension, for emotion words, 369
Adams, R. B., Jr., 551
Adaptation
 dark, 518–519
 data analysis related to, 522–523
 defined, 517
 in psychophysical experiments, 513, 517–520
Adaptive ICA, 701
Adaptive optics, 524
Adaptive quadrature (ADQ), 797–798
Adaptive staircase method, 521–522
Additivity of stimulus-centered measurements, 177
Adducting eye movements, 470
Adjacency matrix, 706
Adjacent response processes, 776
Adjusted residual, 269
Adjusting, on causal graph, 34

Adjustment, method of, 521–523
Adjustment criterion, for structural causal models, 37–38
Administration bias, 100
Adolescent Brain Cognitive Development (ABCD) Study, 227, 642, 649
Adolescents, privacy and consent for, 61, 71
ADQ (adaptive quadrature), 797–798
Advice for a Young Investigator (Cajal), 147
AERA. *See* American Educational Research Association
AES (automated essay scoring), 363
AFC task. *See* Alternative forced choice task
Affect, facial expression and, 550
Affect and blood glucose levels in diabetic patients study, 339, 350–352
Affective disorders, ERP studies of, 614
Affective-valence model, 592–595, 661
Affirmative action studies, 291
AFNI toolbox. *See* Analyses of Functional Neuroimages toolbox
African Americans, 110, 237
Age and aging, 288, 614
Age-equivalent scores, 418–419
Agency for Healthcare Research and Quality (AHRQ), 155, 229
Aggression
 and asymmetric alpha power, 594–595
 conceptual and operational definition of, xxxviii–xxxix
 multiple operational definitions of, xxxix–xl
 TMS studies of, 660

Index

Aggression Questionnaire, 593
Agreement, with interviewer, 300, 308, 310
Agreement matrix, 262
AIPE approach. *See* Accuracy in parameter estimation approach
Akaike's information criterion, 817
Aliasing, 585
Alignment kappa, 263
Aliquoting saliva samples, 573
Allen, J. J. B., 593
Allen, K. M., 541
Allen, L. K., 367
Almeida, D. M., 337
Alpha
    coefficient/Cronbach's. *See* Coefficient alpha
    Krippendorff's, 266
Alphabetic writing systems, reading, 471, 473, 475
Alpha frequency band, 591–595
α-amylase, 567, 568, 572–574
Alternative distribution for statistical power, 194, 195
Alternative forced choice (AFC) task, 517, 519–520, 522
Alternative IRT model, 778–779
Altman, D. G., 205
ALT models, 353
Alvesson, M., 138
Ambient noise, in physiological measures, 533–534
Ambiguous stimuli, 464–436
Ambiguous temporal precedence, threat of, 26
Ambivalence, 290–291
American and Communist reporter question studies, 280–281, 287–289, 292
American Educational Research Association (AERA), 384–385, 762–763, 771
American Psychiatric Association, 386, 454, 838
American Psychological Association (APA)
    Committee on Animal Research and Ethics, 91
    construct validity research by, 771
    databases created by, 157, 158, 161, 164
    Dissertation Research Awards, 239
    Early Graduate Student Researcher Award, 239

    "Ethical Principles of Psychologists and Code of Conduct," 59, 60, 63–77
    Journal Article Reporting Standards, 196
    Publication Manual, xliii, 195
    Standards for Educational and Psychological Testing, 384–385, 771
    Task Force on External Funding, 75
    Task Force on Statistical Inference, xlii, 574
    training grants from, 239
American Psychological Foundation, 239
Amodio, D. M, 596
Amplification and amplifiers, 621, 688
Amplitude
    of EMG signal, 549
    of skin conductance responses, 545
Amygdala, 536
α-Amylase, 567, 568, 572–574
Analgesics, withholding of, 89
Analyses of Functional Neuroimages (AFNI) toolbox, 635, 700, 710
Analysis of covariance (ANCOVA), 574
Analysis of variance (ANOVA)
    directionality information from, 192
    in generalizability theory, 746
    intraclass correlation statistics from, 730–731
    in latent trait analysis, 184, 185
    omnibus vs. targeted effect sizes for, 191
    one-way, 191, 192, 730
    and outliers in RT distributions, 499–500
    in single-facet generalizability analysis, 750
    stimulus-centered focus of scaling and, 174
    two-way, 730–731
Analytic units, xxxvii–xxxix, 251, 252
Anastasi, A., 143–144, 410–411, 419
Anatomical regions of interest, 638
"Ancestors," causal graph, 32, 33
Ancestry search, 165
Anchor item, 779
ANCOVA (analysis of covariance), 574
Anderson, S. F., 202
Andy's Brain Book (Jahn), 700, 709
Anesthetics, withholding of, 89
Anger, 551, 593, 594
Angoff, W. H., 416–418

Angoff method, 428
Animal and Plant Health Inspection Service (APHIS), 87, 89, 90
Animal rights, 85
Animal studies. *See* Nonhuman animals, research with
Animal welfare, 85–87, 89–90. *See also* Laboratory animal welfare
Animal Welfare Information Center, 91
Annual protocol reviews, for animal studies, 89–90
Annual Report of Animal Usage 2018 (APHIS), 89
Anonymization, of interviewees, 319
ANOVA. *See* Analysis of variance
Anterior N2 ERP component, 612
Antibodies, 568
Anticipatory anxiety, 658
Anticipatory processes, ERP studies of, 607
Anticonvulsive agents, evaluating effects of, 685
Antigens, 568
Antipathy, 288
Anxiety, anticipatory, 658
Anxiety disorders, nonhuman animal studies of, 83
Anxious–joy scale example, 395–396
APA. *See* American Psychological Association
a^* parameters, nominal response model, 821
Apartheid, 110
APF/COGDOP Graduate Research Scholarships, 239
APHIS. *See* Animal and Plant Health Inspection Service
Apocrine sweat glands, 543
Appelbaum, M., 196
Appelbaum, P. S., 70
Appetitive stimuli, 595
Approach criteria, for grants, 239, 242
A priori method of knowing, xxv
AR1 (first-order autoregressive residual) structure, 348
Arabic language, 473
Archimedes, 139
Architect role, of researcher, 13
Arc-shaped arrays, visual search in, 481
Area under the curve (AUC), 839, 846–848
Aristotle, 546
Arousal, pupil dilation and, 483–484
Arterial system, 536

Artifacts
    ballistocardiac, 680
    from combination of NIBS and EEG, 687–688
    in EEG/MEG signals, 586–588
    in ERP studies, 622, 626–627
    eye blink, 622, 688
    eye movement, 586–588, 622
    in physiological measures, 534, 539, 541
    principal component analysis for removal of, 702
    scanner, 680
Artificial neural networks, 525
Asmundson, G. J. G., 391
Assay, defined, 568
Assignment mechanism, PO framework, 29–30
Assignment probability, 29
Assimilation effect, 281–283, 292
Association
    between-person, 328, 329, 351–352
    causal, xxxii, 34, 709
    collider, 34, 35
    confounding, 34
    and dimensionality of test items, 773
    mutual, 343
    noncausal, 34
    of projective tests and performance-based measures, 445
    within-person, 328, 329, 348–349, 351
Associational question order effects, 227, 292–293
Assurance parameter, 205
Asymmetrical data analysis, EEG–fMRI studies, 680
Atlas-based approaches to functional connectivity, 643
Atlas-based nodes, 706
Atlas-based regions of interest, 638
Attention, 471, 538
Attention-deficit/hyperactivity disorder, 595, 658
Attenuation effect of unreliability, 726
Attenuation paradox, 384, 393–394
Attitude crystallization, 290–291
Attitude statements, stimulus-centered measurements of, 176
Attrition, threat of, 26
AUC (area under the curve), 839, 846–848
Audio recordings, interview, 321
Auditory brainstem responses (ABRs), 609

Auditory stimulus
    calibration for psychophysical experiments with, 516
    ERP components evoked by, 609, 610
    mismatch negativity with, 612
Augmented reality, 524
Auscultatory method of measuring blood pressure, 540
Auspurg, K., 286
Authentic assessment, 423
Authorities, knowing through, xxv
Authors, contacting, 165
Authorship, 107
Autism, 606–607
Automated essay scoring (AES), 363
Automated facial recognition systems, 551–552
Automated language analysis, 361–375
    challenges with writing evaluation via, 366
    of essay responses, 363–366
    future of, 375
    for intelligent tutoring systems, 370–375
    in research on psychological attributes and processes, 367–370
    response scoring with NLP, 362–367
    of short natural language response, 362–363
Automated writing evaluation (AWE) systems, 365–366, 374–375
Automaticity, of face processing, 606
Autonomy, 37, 74
Autoregressive effect, 346
AutoTutor, 369–373
Average causal effect (ACE), 28–30, 45
Averaged ears, 589
Averaged ERPs, 622–625, 627
Average experiences, investigating, 328–329, 341–346
Average fixation duration, 472
Average quantiles, 503
Average reference, EEG, 588, 589
Average reliability indices, 736
Average reliability measures, 737
Averaging
    in ERP research, 607–608
    of measures with low reliability, 727
    of quantiles over subjects, 503–505
Awards
    career development, 233, 236–237
    fellowship, 229, 234–236, 239
    multiproject, 241–242

AWE (automated writing evaluation) systems, 365–366, 374–375
Axes of inequality, 115, 116
Ayidiya, S. A., 294

Backdoor criterion, 37
Back-translation approach, 122–124
Backwards search, 165
Bae, G. Y., 615
Bakeman, R., 252–253, 255, 263–265
Baker, E. L., 424
Ballistocardiac artifacts, 680
Bandalos, D. L., 799
Bandpass filtering, 584–585
Bandura, A., 147
Barba, L. A., 212
Barclay, A., 285
Bareinboim, E., 46
Bare remote repository, 218
Baron, R. M., 726
Baroreceptors, 537
Barrett, L. F., 337
Bartholow, B. D., 596
BAS dysregulation theory, 595
Baseline, physiological, 533
Baseline model, 778
Base rate (BR; prevalence)
    and accuracy of prediction, 840–841
    in cutoff value specification, 855
    defined, 838
    and information gain, 855
    and overall utility of cutoff values, 850–852
    and positive/negative predictive power, 843–844
    predicting from, 839–841
    on Taylor–Russell tables, 420
BAS (Behavioral Activation System) scales, 593
Batchelder, W. H., 411–412
Bateson, P., 253
Bayesian information criterion, 817
Beauchamp, T. L., 84
Beck Depression Inventory, 25
Beckmann, C. F., 701
Behavioral Activation System (BAS) scales, 593
Behavioral-assessment approaches, short forms and, 458
Behavioral Inhibition System (BIS) scales, 593
Behavioral observation, 251–272
    code-unit grid for representing, 260–261
    coding schemes for, 253–256

Behavioral observation (continued)
    contingency indexes for analyzing, 268–271
    as measurement, 251
    observer agreement for, 262–266
    reasons for using, 252–253
    recording coded data on, 256–260
    sessions as analytic units, 252
    statistical analysis of, 266–268
Behavioral science databases, 158–159
Behavior counts, scaling, 173
Belmont Report, 60, 84
Bender Visual Motor Gestalt Test, 433
Beneficence and Nonmaleficence (Principle A), 63
Benign behavioral interventions, Common Rule on, 62
Bennett, A. J., 84
Bennett, J., 426
Benning, S. D., 551
Bereitschaftspotential, 614
Berger, Hans, 581
Berk, R. A., 426, 427
Berntson, G. G., 537
BERT (Bidirectional Encoder Representations from Transformers), 365
Beta frequency band, 591
    oscillatory behavior in, 686–687
    theta–beta ratio, 595–596
Beta values, 637, 698
Between-person associations, 328, 329, 351–352
Between-person reliability, 340, 737
Between-persons model (Level 2 model)
    for investigating average experiences, 341–342, 345–346
    for investigating change across time, 346–348
    moderation effects in, 349–350
    for statistical stimulation study, 353
Between-person variation, 341
Between-subject research factors, 251, 252
Beuckelaer, A., 102
Bevans, G. E., 327
Bias(es), 97–100. See also specific types
    and AIPE approach, 197
    defined, 98
    and internal validity, 778
    in parameter values, 198
    a posteriori procedures to deal with, 106
    a priori procedures to reduce, 103–106

publication, 156
    in reliability design, 738
    in research with marginalized groups, 116
    response scales to study, 105–106
Bias uncertainty corrected sample size (BUCSS) approach, 199–200, 202–204
Bidirectional Encoder Representations from Transformers (BERT), 365
BIDS (Brain Imaging Data Structure) format, 649
Bifactor models, 802–804, 827
Big data, 142, 361
Bilingual translators, 122–123
Binary adjacency matrix, 706
Binary measures, 256, 727, 728, 735–736
Binet, A., 408
Binet-Simon scale, short form of, 458
Bing, 157
Binocular coordination, of eye movements, 470–471
Binomial distribution, 728
Biobehavioral research, on hormones, 565–567
Biofeedback therapies, 83
Biographical interviews, 298
Biomarkers, ERPs as, 614
Biophysical balloon model, 699
Biosketches, 233
Biphasic pulse circuit, 655, 656
BIPOC (Black, Indigenous, people of color) participants, 333
Bipolar alignment for electromyography, 548
Bipolar disorder, 70, 76, 593
Biserial correlation coefficient, 413
Bishop, G., 279–280, 287
BIS (Behavioral Inhibition System) scales, 593
Black, Indigenous, people of color (BIPOC) participants, 333. See also African Americans
Black Lives Matter movement, 136, 420
Blalock, H. M., 42
Block design tasks, 639
Blocked path, on causal graph, 33
Blocking, 34, 35
Blood glucose levels, study of affect and, 339, 350–352
Blood oxygenation, fNIRS and changes in, 646

Blood oxygen level-dependent (BOLD) signals, 631, 675
    electrical neural activity and, 678
    in epilepsy, 680
    ERPs vs., 616
    modeling, 699
    in real-time fMRI, 645
    in task-based fMRI, 639–640
Blood pressure, 537, 540–541
Blood volume, 541
Blurring, in visual search, 481
Bock, R. D., 176, 764, 819
Body language and postures, 306–307, 594, 598
Boehnke, K., 105
Boker, S. M., 329, 352
BOLD signals. See Blood oxygen level-dependent signals
Bolger, N., 329, 352
Bollen, K., 353, 733
Bond, L., 421
Bond, M. H., 103, 105
Bonett, D. G., 195
Bonferroni correction, 646, 698, 699
Bookmark technique, 428
Boolean operators, 162
Borderline approach, 428
Boring, E. G., 770
Bornstein, R. F., 438
Bottom-up processes, 6, 105
Boundaries, target construct, 385
Boundary technique, 473–474, 481
Bowling, A., 284
Box, Joan Fisher, 42
Box-and-whisker plot, 269
BR. See Base rate
Bradburn, N. M., 281
Brain activity
    and electrodermal activity, 544
    functional neuroimaging to investigate, 631
    and intensity of sensation, 531
    multivariate pattern analysis of, 614–616
    and psychogenic sweating, 543–544
    and psycho-physiological measures, 553
    reverse inference from, 648
Brain Connectivity Toolbox, 710
BrainIAK, 710
Brain Imaging Analysis Kit, 703
Brain Imaging Data Structure (BIDS) format, 649
Brain Innovation B. V., 700
Brain Modulyzer, 710

Brain stimulation. *See* Noninvasive brain stimulation (NBS)
Brainstorming, 136
BrainVoyager, 635, 700, 702, 710
Branching, functions for, 220
Brannigan, G. B., 144, 147–148
Brennan, R. L., 757, 760
Bridging, in iSTART, 372
Bridgman, P. W., 770
Brief instruments, 451–464. *See also* Short forms
    creating, 455–456
    defining, 451
    and item response theory, 462–463
    limitations on use of, 456–457
    and Spearman-Brown prophecy formula, 452, 453
    validity of, 452–455
Brief telephone interviews, 336–338
Briggs, D. C., 764
Brigham, C. C., 770
British Education Index, 158
Brito, C., 39
Broadband implicit techniques, 436
Broad consent, 63
Broad tests, 384
Broderick, J. E., 333
Brown, W., 727
Browsing literature, 165
Bryk, A. S., 345, 353
Buckheit, J. B., 212
BUCSS (bias uncertainty corrected sample size) approach, 199–200, 202–204
Buffer questions, 292
Bullen, J. A., 849
Bunched item location parameters, 828–829
Burch, R. L., 88
Burden, participant, 332, 333, 336
Burisch, M., 453, 454
Burns, R. C., 443
Burstein, J., 365
Business Source Complete, 159
Business technology grants, 241
Buss, A. H., 593
Buxton, R. B., 699

C1 wave, in oddball paradigm, 610
Caching results, 217
Cacioppo, J. T., 147, 212, 283, 532, 533
Calculated results, in text, 215–216
Calibration, of stimulus, 516, 518
California Achievement Tests, 419

California Health Interview Survey (CHIS), 285
Camerer, C. F., 212–213
Campbell, C. G. G., 84n2
Campbell, D. T., 23, 25, 26, 40, 46, 398–400, 781, 782
Campbell Collaboration, 156, 163, 165
"Can you tell me" format, questions with, 300–301
"Can you tell me more about" format, follow-ups with, 305–306
Captioning, for online interviews, 322
Cardiac cycle, 535–537
Cardiac output, measuring, 542
Cardinet, J., 760–762
Cardioacceleratory center, 536
Cardioinhibitory center, 536
Cardiovascular system
    anatomy and physiology of, 535–536
    measuring activity of, 537–542
    neural control of, 536–537
    physiological measures of activity, 535–542
Career development awards (K awards), 233, 236–237
Carroll, E. J., 436
Carrot2 search engine, 163
Carryover effects, 350, 533
Cartwright, N., 24
Carver, R. P., 484
Cases, defined, 251
Castelloe, J., 198–199
Castillo, L. G., 127
Casual assumptions, 24
Categorical confirmatory factor analysis (CCFA), 794, 796, 797
Categorical data, xli
    coders of, 256
    construct validity of, 785
    factor analysis for, 794–795
    in intensive longitudinal studies, 352
    reliability of, 728, 736
Categorical judgment, law of, 176, 182
Category boundary discriminations (CBDs), 821, 825
Category intersection parameters, 821–822, 826
Category ordering, in nominal response model, 821
Category response curves (CRCs), 817–820, 824
Category scaling, 517, 520, 523
Cattell, J. McK., 408, 409
Cattell, R. B., 398
Causadias, J. M., 115

Causal association, xxxii, 34, 709
Causal assumptions, 44–45
causaleffect package, 37, 48
Causal effects, 44–45
Causal explanatory research, xxxi–xxxiv
Causal generalization, 45–46
Causal graphs
    defined, 23, 34
    and definition of causal effects, 44
    and joint use of frameworks, 50
    origins of, 31–32
    for treatment selection, 38–39
Causal identification, 44–45
Causal indicator model (CIM), 392, 733
Causal inference
    from intensive longitudinal studies, 334, 350–351
    and internal validity, 25
    in psychological theory, 23
Causal inference frameworks, 23–50
    causal generalization and replication for, 45–46
    causal identification in, 44–45
    definition of causal effects in, 44
    estimation of causal effects and statistical inference in, 45
    integration and formalization of subject matter theory in, 46–48
    joint use of, 50
    key components of, 24–25
    philosophies of causation in, 40–43
    potential outcomes, 28–31
    research designs associated with, 48–49
    structural causal models, 31–40
    theory of cause for, 43–44
    validity typology/threats, 25–28
Causal mediation analysis, 39
Causal modeling, xxxiii, xxxvii
Causal path, 33–35
Causal replication, 27, 46
Causal search, 39
Cause
    in experimental designs, xxxiv
    INUS condition for, 40, 41, 43
    philosophies of causation, 40–43
    theory of, 25, 43–44
CBDs (category boundary discriminations), 821, 825
CBPR (community-based participatory research), 119
CCFA. *See* Categorical confirmatory factor analysis
Ceiling effect, 828

Index

Center Core Grants (P30), 241
Center for Brains, Minds, and Machines, 703, 709
Center for Epidemiologic Studies–Depression scale (CES-D), 777
Center for Scientific Review (CSR), 242
Center grants, 241–242
Centers of Excellence Environmental Health Disparities research (P50), 241
Centrifugation, of saliva samples, 573
Cerebellum, rTMS of, 664
Cerebral cortex
    connectivity between hemispheres of, 658
    excitability of, 664–665
    flexibility of, 540
    noninvasive stimulation of. *See* Noninvasive brain stimulation (NBS)
    pyramidal cells of, 616
    tDCS and excitability of, 664–665
Certificates of Confidentiality, 74–75, 118–119
CES-D (Center for Epidemiologic Studies–Depression scale), 777
CFI (comparative fit index), 816, 817
CFR (*Code of Federal Regulations*), 60–61, 65–66
Chain, causal graph, 33
Chain searching, 165
Challenging interviewees, 311–313
Chance
    percent correct by, 839, 840
    in research, 147
    ROC curve for operation at, 846
Chang, A. C., 212
Change aspect of construct validity, 784
Change prediction, 350–352
Change processes, 329, 350–352
Changes across time, 346–350
Charities, public, 229–230, 232
Checksums, 220
Chemoreceptors, 537
Chen, B., 39
Chewing gum, for saliva collection, 572
Child Development & Adolescent Studies database, 158
Childers, R., 507
Children
    debriefing with, 73
    HIPAA rules for, 61
    rational informed consent from, 71
"Children," causal graph, 32, 33
Children's Appercetion Test, 441

Chinese language, 472–474
Chinese reading model (CRM), 477
CHIS (California Health Interview Survey), 285
Chronic pain, animal studies of treatment for, 83
Chronometric measures
    eye movements, 469–486
    response times, 493–508
Chunks of statistical commands, 214–215
CI. *See* Confidence interval
CIM (causal indicator model), 392, 733
CINAHL (Cumulative Index to Nursing and Allied Health Literature), 160
Circadian patterns of hormone secretion, 566
Citation management tools, 154
Citation mining, 165
Citric acid, 572
Claerbout, J. F., 212
Clarification, in interviews, 300–301, 308–309
Clark, L. A., 386, 389, 390, 400
Clark, Rudy, 227
Classical paradigm of measurement, 186
Classical reliability theory, 391, 394, 395
Classical test theory (CTT)
    generalizability theory and, 745, 748–749, 761, 762, 765
    on internal consistency, 732
    item selection based on, 388–389
    norm-referenced measures in, 410
    reliability in, 391, 723–727, 732, 745–746
    short forms and, 458
    stimulus-centered scaling and, 174–175, 186
    true score in, 747–748
Classification accuracy, 427, 461
Classroom discussions, research ideas from, 140
Cleaning data sets, 215
Client/Patient, Student, and Subordinate Research Participants (Standard 8.04b), 69
Cliff, N., 461
Clinical significance, xlii
Clinical Trial Planning Grant Program (R34), 239–241
Clinical trials, 62, 240
ClinicalTrials.gov, 164

Closed-loop procedures, 533
Closed path, causal graph, 33
Closed questions, 301–302
Cloud storage, 218
Clustering coefficient, 707
Cluster samples, 416
Cluster-threshold correction, 646
Coaching, to improve test performance, 421
Cocchi, L., 708
Cochrane Collaboration, 156, 163–165
Cochrane Library, 160
Cocktail party effect, 597, 700–701
Coconstruction of interview data, 323
Code of Federal Regulations (CFR), 60–61, 65–66
Coders, 254, 256, 257
Code-unit grid, 260–261, 264
Coding
    for behavioral observation, 253–256
    multidimensional, 258–259
    for muscle activity studies, 551
    post hoc, 259
    for Rorschach inkblot responses, 437–438
    and statistical workflow, 220–224
Coding manual, 255
Coefficient alpha (Cronbach's alpha), 340
    attenuation paradox and, 394
    defined, 413
    for heterogeneous items, 396
    homogeneity of scale and, 392–393
    impact of additional items on, 454
    for new measures, 732–735
    for norm-referenced measures, 413–414
    for objective tests, 394–397
Coefficient of reproducibility, 180
Coefficient of variation (CV), 568
Coefficient omega. *See* McDonald's omega
Coffman, D. L., 798–800
Cognition
    combined neuroimaging studies of, 673, 678
    electric current stimulation to study emotion and, 668
    in schizophrenia, 618–619
Cognitive ability, 384, 411
Cognitive accessibility, 282
Cognitive involvement, elaboration-likelihood model and, 284
Cognitive load, 484, 485
Cognitive neuroscience, 685–686

864

Cognitive processing
  eye movements and, 469
  and fixation time, 476
  and question order effects, 278
  for scene perception, 478
  of skipped words during reading, 476
Cognitive sophistication, question order effects and, 288–290
Cognitive state, MVPA sensitivity to, 703
Cognitive strategies for research question development, 136
Cohen, D., 581
Cohen, J., xlii, 196, 461, 726, 735
Cohen, P., 461
Cohen's kappa, 262–264, 735–736
Coherence analysis, 596–597
Cole, D. A., 334
Colearning approach, 76
Collaboration, 136, 205–206, 227
Collectivism, 118
College admission tests, 420
College student samples, scale development with, 391
Collider association, 34, 35
Collider path, 33–35
Collider variables, 33
Collins, L. M., 331
Colzato, L. S., 540
Combined neuroimaging methods, 673–690
  EEG and MEG uses and limitations, 674–675
  EEG/MEG–fMRI, 678–681
  fMRI uses and limitations, 675–676
  NIBS–EEG, 686–689
  NIBS–fMRI, 681–686
  NIBS uses and limitations, 676–677
Comfort, during fMRI, 634
Comments, in code, 215
Commercial hormone assay services, 573
Commercially published tests, 146–147
Common causes, on causal graphs, 32, 33
Common drive process, 547
Common factor model, 775, 784, 794, 796, 798
Common Rule. *See* Federal Policy for the Protection of Human Subjects
Communication, with participants, 534–535, 634
Communication and Mass Media Complete database, 159

Communication Source, 159
Communist and American reporter question studies, 280–281, 287–289, 292
Community, impact of research on, 110–111
Community Advisory Boards, 120
Community-based participatory research (CBPR), 119
Community consultation, 76
Community detection, 707
Comparative decision making tests, 419–420
Comparative fit index (CFI), 816, 817
Comparative judgment, law of, 176, 182
Compensation, for participants, 67–69, 228
Complex factor structure, parceling and, 800
Complexity, question order effects and, 286
Complex pattern-matching research designs, 27
Compliance tracking, 335–338
Component-independent experimental designs, 614–616
Composite universe scores, 758
Composite variables, xli
Comprehension, 372, 477
Comprehensive item pools, 386
Comprehensive searches, 152
Comprehensive System (CS), 437–439
Computer-adaptive tests, 390
Computer monitors, 513, 516, 524
Computer programs. *See* Software
Concealed information test, 538
Concept inequivalence, 101
Concept maps, 136
Conceptual definitions, xxxviii–xxxix
Conceptual equivalence, 121–122
Concomitant measures, 532
Concrete codes, 255–256
Concrete operational phase of construct validity research, 770
Concurrent combination
  of EEG and fMRI, 679–681
  of NIBS and EEG, 688–689
  of NIBS and fMRI, 683–686
Concurrent editing, version control for, 218
Concurrent validity, 385, 400, 779
Conditional probability, 268
Conditional question order effects, 227, 292–293
Conditioning, 34, 37

Conference papers, 163, 164
Conferences, research ideas generated by, 136
Confidence interval (CI)
  AIPE approach to obtain narrow, 196, 197
  and effect size, 190
  for effect size, 195–196
  for magnitude estimates, 192–193
  for reliability estimates, 732
  width of, 192–193, 196, 197, 204
Confidence level, 197, 849
Confidentiality
  APA Ethics Code standards on, 74–75
  and brief telephone interviews, 337
  in cross-cultural research, 108
  informed consent and, 66–67
  interviews with limits on, 319
Configural invariance, 126, 778, 800
Confirmation, degree of, 26
Confirmatory factor analysis (CFA), xli, 793
  categorical, 794, 796, 797
  convergent and discriminant validity determinations with, 782–784
  multigroup, 126
  refining scales with, 389
  single-factor model fit testing with, 393
Conflicts of interest, 75
Confounding association, 34
Confounding path, 33–35
Confounding variables
  on causal graphs, 33
  in fMRI studies, 635–636
  in hormone assays, 574
  in intensive longitudinal studies, 351
Confusion matrix, 262
Conjoint measurement, theory of, 181
Connectivity analysis, 596–597, 643, 708–709
Connectome workbench, 710
Conner, T. S., 352
CONN toolbox, 700, 702, 709, 710
Conscientiousness scale, 383–384
Consensus accounts, 310–311
Consensus rule, 728
Consent capacity, 70, 71, 75–76
Consent rate, for linkage questions, 289
Consequences of measurement programs, 787–788
Consistency
  in classical reliability theory, 391
  in statistical workflow, 211–212

Index

Consistency assumption, 37, 43
Consistency effect, 281, 287, 290
Consolidated Standard of Reporting Trials (CONSORT), 196
Constant stimuli, method of, 520–521
Constrained PCA, 703
Construct affective models, 369
Construct bias, 98–100
Constructed responses, 362–363, 367–368
Construct homogeneity
　for brief instruments, 454–455
　defined, 392
　for objective test items, 388, 392–393
　in short forms, 458
Construct inequivalence, 100–101
Constructs
　conceptualization of, 386
　defining, 453, 770, 772
　hypothetical, 771
　representation of, 454, 458
Construct validity, 769–788
　attenuation paradox for, 394
　for causal inference findings, 46
　centrality of, in psychometrics, 769
　change aspect of, 784
　components of, 771–772
　and consequences of measurement programs, 787–788
　content validity, 772–773
　convergent and discriminant validity, 781–784
　criterion-related validity, 779–781
　dimensionality, 773–774
　of EEG reference, 589
　external, 779–788
　facets of, 771
　historical perspective on, 385, 769–771
　internal, 772–779
　and interpretations of test scores, 784–787
　item analysis approaches to, 774–779
　and measurement equivalence, 125
　reliability analysis to establish, 391–398
　for short forms, 459–461
　standards for, 769
　in validity typology/threats framework, 25, 43–44
Construct validity invariance, 125, 126
Consulting librarians, 154–155, 166
Contaminants, in response time distributions, 493

Content
　homogeneity, 828
　reliability evidence related to, 425
　validity evidence related to, 419
Content browsing, 165
Content category, in LIWC, 368
Content domain coverage, by short forms, 459–460
Content parcels, 827
Content-standard test scores, 423. See also Criterion-referenced testing
Content validity, 772–773
　of brief instruments, 453
　in history of psychometrics, 385
　of norm-referenced tests, 419
　and substantive phase of scale development, 385
Content validity ratio (CVR), 773
Context
　in happiness studies, 282–283
　in hypothesis-testing studies, 102
　in qualitative research, 6–7
　in research question formulation, 143
　and validity of assessment, 763–764
Context-aware experience sampling, 332, 338–339
Context-dependent validity typology/threats framework, 42–43
Context effects, 277, 289–292. See also Question order effects
Contextual constraint, skipping effects and, 476
Contextual constructionist research, 19
Contingency, questions of, 253
Contingency indexes, 268–271
Contingency statistics, 266
Contingency tables, 268–271
Contingent valuation studies, 285
Continuous performance task, 610
Continuous recording, 257–261
Continuous scale, 256
Continuous timed event recording, 259–261
Continuous untimed event recording, 258–261
Contralateral delay activity, 612
Contrasted Group approach, 428
Contrast effect, 279, 281–283, 292, 517
Control
　over cardiovascular activity, 536–537
　over eye movements, 475–477, 480, 482–483
　over muscular activity, 547–548

　over stimulus, in psychophysics, 511–512, 514, 516, 523–524
　over sudomotor activity, 543–544
Controlled random-walk with inhibition for saccade planning (CRISP) model, 486
Convenience samples, 227–228
Conventions, research ideas generated by, 136
Convergent correlation, 399–400
Convergent validity, 763
　context and acceptable level of, 401
　in CT-CM model, 783
　MTMM designs to examine, 781–784
　for objective tests, 398–399
Conversational context, in happiness studies, 282–283
Conversations, interviews vs., 297, 306
Co-occurrence, 254, 269
Cook, T. D., 40, 46
Coombs, C. H., 178, 180
Cooper, H., xliii, 115
Coping potential, skin conductance and, 545–546
Coping strategies, 328. See also Stress and coping during preparation for professional licensing exam survey
Copying data, for statistical analysis, 221–222
Coregistration process, 636
Core self-evaluations, job performance and, 201–206
Cornell, F. G., 416
Correct events, 786
Correction(s)
　of baseline physiological data, 533
　Bonferroni, 646, 698, 699
　cluster-threshold, 646
　for ERP artifacts, 622
　false discovery rate method, 646, 698–699
　for fMRI data, 635, 636
　Greenhouse-Geisser epsilon, 626
　for point-biserial correlation coefficients, 413
　Satorra–Bentler, 799
Correct nonevents, 786
Correct rejections. See Valid negatives
Correlated error, 758
Correlated trait–correlated method minus one (CT-C[M-1]) model, 782
Correlated trait–correlated method (CT-CM) model, 782–784

Correlated trait–correlated uniqueness (CT-CU) model, 782
Correlational data
　from behavioral observation, 251
　in brain and behavior studies, 676
　in intensive longitudinal studies, 334
Correlational question order effects, 227, 292–293
Correlation coefficient, 420
Correlations, criterion-related validity and, 780–781
Cortical excitability, 664–665
Cortical flexibility, 540
Cortical silent period (CSP), 657–658
Cortical stellate cells, 598
Cortina, J. M., 393
Cortisol, 566, 568, 570, 572–574
CosMoMVPA toolbox, 705, 710
Cost(s)
　of hormone assays, 571
　for research participants, 67
Costa, P. T., Jr., 146
Council review, 243–244
Count data, scaling, 184
Counterfactual analysis, 39
Counterfactual outcomes, 28, 42
Counting tasks, pupillometric response in, 484
Couples, interviews with, 314
Coursera, 700, 703
Covariance
　analysis of covariance, 574
　in fMRI studies, 637
　in multivariate generalizability analysis, 758
　of short form and original measure scores, 461
Covariance matrix, for common factor model, 794
COVID-19 pandemic
　remote interviewing in, 316
　research animal care in, 90
　research questions generated by, 136
　selection test administration during, 420
　venture investors during, 228
Cox, D. R., 256, 257
C-PAC software, 710
cPPI package, 709
Cramér's V, effect size for, 191n4
Cranford, J. A., 340, 344, 737
CRCs (category response curves), 817–820, 824
C-reactive protein, 568
Credible inference, 47

Crick, J. E., 760
CRISP (controlled random-walk with inhibition for saccade planning) model, 486
Critchley, H. D., 543–544
Criterion (portfolio system), 364, 365
Criterion, in signal detection theory, 517
Criterion keying, 388
Criterion-referenced testing, 422–429
　history of, 422–423, 429
　with norm-referenced tests, 425
　norm-referenced vs., 407, 423, 427
　psychometric issues in, 425–429
　switching to, 426
　uses of, 423–425
Criterion validity, 385, 400–401, 779–781
Critical realist approaches, 14
Critical thinking, xxviii
CRM (Chinese reading model), 477
Cronbach, L. J., 385, 735, 746, 757, 761, 762, 769, 771, 772, 784
Cronbach's alpha. See Coefficient alpha
Cross-cultural comparative research, 97–111
　and bias, 97–100
　ethical issues in, 106–110
　impact of, on community, 110–111
　and inequivalence, 100–102
　interpreting data in, 109–110
　methodological issues with, 97–102
　a posteriori procedures to deal with bias in, 106
　a priori procedures to reduce bias/ inequivalence in, 103–106
　sensitive topics in, 108–109
　taxonomy of, 102–103
Cross-cultural effects, in scene perception, 480
Cross-cultural psychology, 97
Crossed generalizability studies, 754
Crossed reliability studies, 730–731
Crossed time-based designs, 331
Cross-level interaction model, 349–350
Cross-linguistic studies, 285
Cross-reactivity, in hormone assays, 567, 568
Crowdsourced research funding, 228–229
Crystallized attitude, 290, 291
CS (Comprehensive System), 437–439
CSD (current-source density), 589
Csikszentmihalyi, M., 327

CSP (cortical silent period), 657–658
CSR (Center for Scientific Review), 242
CT-CM (correlated trait–correlated method) model, 782–784
CT-C(M-1) model, 782
CT-CU (correlated trait–correlated uniqueness) model, 782
Cultural and societal issues
　cross-cultural research methods, 97–111
　research with individuals from marginalized groups, 115–127
Cultural attribution fallacy, 105
Cultural biases, 109–110
Cultural competence, 118
Cultural informants, 107
Cultural-level studies, 103
Culturally informed theory, 125–126
Cultural psychology, 97
Culture
　and group interviews, 314
　psychological constructs specific to, 101
　and question order effects, 285
　research on, 97
Cumulative density function, 495–497
Cumulative Index to Nursing and Allied Health Literature (CINAHL), 160
Cumulative response processes, 775–776
Cunningham, S., 39
Cunningham, W. A., 798
Curran, P. J., 353, 799
Current-source density (CSD), 589
Curricular alignment, with test, 425
Curricular validity, 425
Cutoff scores
　for criterion-referenced testing, 428, 429
　decision theory to determine, 785–787
　defined, 839
　impact of utility ratio on, 852–854
　overall utility vs. information gain-based, 855–856
　and positive/negative predictive power, 843, 844
　ROC curve and, 846
　and sensitivity/specificity, 841–842
　specifying, for test performance, 849–856
Cutter, M. G., 475
CVR (content validity ratio), 773
Czopp, S. T., 439

Daft, R. L., 135, 138
DAG (directed acyclic graph), 32
dagitty package, 36, 48
Dao, T. K., 439
DAP:SPED (Draw-A-Person: Screening Procedure for Emotional Disturbance), 443
DAP (Draw-A-Person) test, 443
Dark adaptation, 518–519
Darker, C. D., 285
DARPA (U.S. Defense Advanced Research Projects Agency), 229
Darwin, Charles, 546
Data
    critique of interviews as, 322–323
    realist vs. relativist position on, 9
Data analysis
    for adaptive methods, 522–523
    for fMRI, 636–639, 644–645, 710. *See also* Neuroimaging analysis methods
    for intensive longitudinal methods, 339–341
    observer agreement during, 265–266
    for salivary hormone assays, 574
Databases, 151
    bibliographic, 159
    developing search for most relevant, 161–162
    health sciences and medicine, 160
    multidisciplinary, 159–160
    for non-English citations, 160
    selecting, for literature search, 157–160
    social and behavioral sciences, 158–159
    translating search to other, 162, 163
Data collection
    observer agreement during, 265–266
    for resting-state fMRI, 642–643
Data-driven approach, 648, 706
Data entry, for longitudinal studies, 336
Data extraction tools, 155
Data integrity, 220
Data interpretation, in cross-cultural research, 109–110
Data preparation, in statistical workflow, 213
Data quality, response time, 494
Data security, 66–67, 74
Data set cleaning, 215
Data smoothing, 549, 636, 700, 703
Data smuggling, 108
Davidson, R. J., 593
Davison, M. L., 184

Davison, W. P., 290
Day-to-day variability, investigating, 329, 341–346
Debra P. case, 424–425
Debriefing, 73–74, 321
Debriefing (Standard 8.08), 73
Decentering, 123
Deception research, 72–73, 109
Decision making
    comparative tests of, 419–420
    ethical, 59
    interpretations of test scores in, 785
    pupil dilation during, 553
    relative vs. absolute, 748
    value-based, 687
Decision region of perceptual span, 481
Decision study (D-study), 746–748
    generalizability study vs., 748
    mixed-model, 756–757
    multi-facet, 753–756
    multivariate, 758–759
    partially nested, 748
    single-facet, 750–752
Decision theory, 785
    in evaluation of test performance, 837, 850–856
    with ROC analysis, 845
Declaration of Helsinki, 60
Decoding accuracy, 615
Decoding analyses, 614–616, 704–705
Decoding Toolbox, 710
Deductive model for qualitative research, 8
Deep brain regions, TMS and, 663
Defense Mechanism Manual (DMM), 441, 442
Definitive studies, reliability values for, 727
DeGrazia, D., 84
Degree distribution, 707
Degree of correlation, 412
Degree of node, 707
Dehoaxing, 73
Dehydroepiandrosterone (DHEA), 568
De Incessu Animalium (Aristotle), 546
Delaney, H. D., 184
Delays to discourage fast guessing, 498
Delgado, M. Y., 123–124
Delta frequency band, 591
Democracy, science and, xxviii
Demographic-based differences, in scores, 787
De Motu Animalium (Aristotle), 546
Denial scale, of Defense Mechanism Manual, 441

Density function. *See* Probability density function
Denver, J. W., 539
Department of Defense (DoD), 229
Department of Veterans Affairs, 229
Dependability, 398, 763. *See also* Index of dependability
The Dependability of Behavioral Measurements (Cronbach), 746
Dependence
    local, 800, 802–804, 827
    in multi-informant diaries, 353
Dependent variables
    hormone levels as, 570
    in response time distributions, 506–508
Depression, 83, 593
Dermis, 543
"Descendants," causal graph, 32, 33
Description, in qualitative approaches, 8
Descriptive phenomenology, 8, 12, 15
Descriptive research designs, xxxi, xxxvii
Design replication studies, 27. *See also* Within-study comparisons (WSCs)
Dess, N. K., 84
Detection thresholds, 514
Deterministic models of scaling, 178–180
Deviant case analysis, 19
Device-contingent designs, 330, 332, 338
DHEA (dehydroepiandrosterone), 568
DHHS (U.S. Department of Health and Human Services), 60–61, 74–75
Diabetic patients, study of, 339, 350–352
Diagnostic and Statistical Manual of Mental Disorders, 4th edition (DSM-IV), 838
Diagnostic and Statistical Manual of Mental Disorders, 5th edition (DSM-5), 386, 454, 457
Diagnostic likelihood ratios, 855
Diao, H., 428
Diary format, 327, 334–339
Diary studies, 737
Diastolic blood pressure (DP), 540, 541
Dichotomous IRT models, 810–817
Dichotomous research questions, 189–190
Dichotomous responses
    factor analysis for, 794, 795
    item factor analysis models for, 774–776
    testing ordinal-level assumption for, 179
Diener, E., 334

DIF. *See* Differential item functioning
Difference because of memory (*Dm*), 613
Difference models, polytomous IRT, 817–818
Difference scaling task, 517, 520, 523
Difference waves, 618–619
Differential item functioning (DIF)
 and internal validity, 779, 780
 as item bias, 99, 100
 item response theory to assess, 391
Differential psychology, 146, 410–411
Differentiation facet, 761–762
Difficult moments, member checking after, 318
Diffusion decision models, 506–507
Diffusion tensor imaging (DTI), 683
Digital audio recorders, 321
Digital files, for continuous timed-event recording, 259–260
Dignity. *See* Respect for People's Rights and Dignity (Principle E)
Dimensionality
 and internal validity, 773–774
 and item-level factor analysis, 797–798, 803
Dipole-fit model, 679
Direct cause, on causal graphs, 33
Direct costs of research, 230–231
Directed acyclic graph (DAG), 32
Directed edges, causal graph, 32
Directed matrix, 707
Direct endocrine assessment, 565–566
Direction of effect
 null hypothesis significance testing for, 191–192
 sample size for determining, 189, 193–195
Directories, 220–221
Direct physical measurement, observation vs., 252, 253
Direct product model, 782
Direct realist approaches, 14, 19
Disabilities, students with, 420
Disagreements
 with interviewees, 311–313
 between observers of untimed events, 263
Discomfort, in physiological experiments, 534–535
Discourse analysis, 13, 477
Discovery orientation, 11–12, 144
Discredited participants, 320–321
Discriminal differences, in stimulus-centered measurements, 176–177

Discriminant validity
 for brief instruments, 453
 in CT-CM model, 783
 MTMM design to examine, 781–784
 for objective tests, 399–400
Discrimination, individuals targeted by, 119
Discrimination parameter, item response model, 776, 777, 825
Discrimination thresholds, 514, 517
Discriminatory power, 812, 845–849
Discussing the Limits of Confidentiality (Standard 4.02), 66
Disenfranchised communities, consultation with, 76
Dispensing With Informed Consent for Research (Standard 8.05), 71, 72
Dissertation project, funding for, 234–235
Dissertations, literature searches for, 164
Distance of interval scales, 172
Distracting information, in interviews, 303
Distress, of nonhuman animals, 88, 89
Distributional assumption, xl, 39
Distribution shape, 505–506
Diversity Research Grant for Predoctoral Candidates, 239
Divide-by-total models, 817–825
Dixon, D., 453
DLPFC (dorsolateral prefrontal cortex), 682, 685
Dm (difference because of memory), 613
D'Mello, S. K., 369
DMM (Defense Mechanism Manual), 441, 442
Documentation
 of data set cleaning, 215
 of literature search, 165–166
 and replicability, 213
 and reproducibility, 212
 of software version, 221
 of statistical workflow, 211, 213–217
DoD (Department of Defense), 229
Doll, E. A., 458
Domain-referenced testing. *See* Criterion-referenced testing
Dominance relation, 171, 182
Dong, Y., 391
Donnelly, C. A., 256, 257
Donner, A., 736
Donoho, D. L., 212

Do(.) operator, 31, 34, 36–37, 41, 44
Dopamine level, blink rate and, 552
Doppelt, J. E., 462
Dorans, N. J., 428
Dorsal medial prefrontal cortex, 683
Dorsolateral prefrontal cortex (DLPFC), 682, 685
Dotsch, R., 545
Double-coded observational data, 265
Double-dipping, with fMRI data, 646
Double interview method, 317
Double translation approach, 122
Douglass, William, 251
DP (diastolic blood pressure), 540, 541
d' (sensitivity index), 514–517
Draw-A-Person: Screening Procedure for Emotional Disturbance (DAP:SPED), 443
Draw-A-Person (DAP) test, 443
Drift, during fixations, 470
Drisko, J. W., 7
Dry electrode systems, EEG, 583
d-separation, on causal graph, 34–36
DSM-IV (*Diagnostic and Statistical Manual of Mental Disorders,* 4th edition), 838
DSM-5. *See* Diagnostic and Statistical Manual of Mental Disorders, 5th edition
D-study consideration, 748. *See also* Decision study (D-study)
dstudy() function, 761
DTI (diffusion tensor imaging), 683
Duality, 192n7
Dual roles, for interviewers, 320
Dual-site tDCS, 667
Duara, R., 317
DuBois, P. H., 407, 408
Duchenne de Boulogne, Guillaume, 546
Dumas, D., 391
Dupré, D., 551
Duration of observational data, 267
Duty, 201–202
Duty-to-warn requirements, 67, 74, 75
Dyadic Adjustment Scale, 328, 341
Dyads, longitudinal methods with, 353
Dynamic causal modeling, 709
Dynamic intersubject correlation (ISC), 644
Dynamic programming, 263
Dynamic scene perception, 479
Dynamic structural equation modeling, 205, 329
Dynamic systems, 352

Early-career researchers, NIH awards for, 236–237
Early Child Care and Youth Development Study, 783–784
Early posterior negativity, 613
Eastern cultures, scene perception in, 480
easyROC, 849
Eating expectancy inventory, 454
EBSCO, 157–160
Eccentric vision, 471
Eccrine sweat glands, 543
ECG (electrocardiogram), 535, 537–540
Echo planar image (EPI), 633
Echo time (TE), 633
Eckman, S., 289
Ecological fallacy, 103
Ecological-level studies, 103
Ecological momentary assessment (EMA) studies, 327, 330, 331
Ecological validity, 328
EDA (electrodermal activity), 544–545
Editing stage of response, 278
Education, question order effects and, 288–290
Educational Administration Abstracts database, 158, 164
Educational grants, 232
Educational Measurement series, 418–419
Educational testing, 407
Educational Testing Service (ETS), 363, 365
Education policy, 164
Education Resources Information Center (ERIC), 157, 158, 161
Education Source, 158
EDUG program, 760
Edumetric testing. *See* Criterion-referenced testing
Edwards, M. C., 796
EEG. *See* Electroencephalography
EEG/MEG signals
 coherence and connectivity analyses of, 596–597
 defined, 581
 frequency bands of interest, 591–592
 method of recording, 582–585
 obtaining frequency of, 590–591
 reducing artifact effects for, 586–588
 sequential combination of fMRI, 678–679
EFA. *See* Exploratory factor analysis
Effect, in experimental designs, xxxiv
Effective connectivity analysis, 709
Effects indicator model, 733

Effect size (relation strength)
 in cross-cultural research, 106
 defined, 190
 in fixed-interval studies, 330
 interpretation of, xli–xlii
 and interpretation of results, 191–193
 literature review approach to specifying, 199–200
 for magnitude estimation, 192–193
 MIES approach to specifying, 198–199
 omnibus, 191, 203–205
 quantifying, 191
 reporting confidence intervals for, 195–196
 role of, in research, 190–193
 for sample-size planning, 197–200
 and statistical power, 193, 194
 targeted, 191, 202–204
Efficiency, of short forms, 457, 459–462
Egalitarian social agenda, 9–10
EIAs (enzymatic immunoassays), 569, 572
Eigenvalues, 702
Einthoven, Willem, 535
EIS (Ethnic Identity Scale), 127
Either–or questions, 299
Ekman, Paul, 255
Elaboration, in iSTART, 372
Elaboration-likelihood model, 283
Elapsed time, 351
Electrical conductivity of skin, 542. *See also* Sudomotor activity
Electrical neural activity, 678
Electrical potential, recording, 619
Electrocardiogram (ECG), 535, 537–540
Electrochemical toxins, 666
Electrodermal activity (EDA), 544–545
Electrodes
 number of, for ERP studies, 621
 for recording EEG, 583–585
 sites of, in ERP studies, 626, 627
Electroencephalographic (EEG) signals. *See also* EEG/MEG signals
 about, 581–582
 event-related desynchronization effects for, 596
 extracting averaged ERPs from, 622–625
 psychological studies using, 592–595
 recording, 583–585, 619–622
 referencing, 588–589
 relations among frequency bands of, 595–596

 time–frequency analysis of, 591
 transcranial magnetic stimulation with, 663
Electroencephalography (EEG), 581–598
 defined, 581
 EEG/MEG–fMRI, 678–681
 extraction of ERPs from, 607–608
 magnetoencephalography vs., 674
 NIBS–EEG, 686–689
 other neuroimaging methods vs., 597–598
 preparing participants for, 585–586
 simultaneous fMRI and, 634
 uses and limitations of, 674–675
Electromagnetic induction, 655–656
Electromyography (EMG), 546–552
 EEG/MEG artifacts and, 586–587
 facial, 550–552, 587
 history of, 546
 integrated, 549–550
 muscle action potential and, 547
 in reflex probe, 550–551
 sensors, 548
 signal conditioning, 548–549
 signal representation, 549
 video-based alternatives to, 551–552
Electronic response formats, for longitudinal studies, 337–339
Electronic response skin conductance responses (ER-SCR), 545
Electrooculography (EOG), 552, 583–584, 587
Electrophysiological markers of value-based decision making, 687
Elementary and Secondary Education Act (ESEA), 415, 426
Elemente der Psychophysik (Fechner), 531
Eliasziw, M., 736
Eligibility criteria, literature search, 156–157
ELISAs (enzyme-linked immunosorbent assays), 569, 572
Elizabeth Munsterberg Koppitz Child Psychology Graduate Student Fellowship, 239
ELSA (English Longitudinal Study of Ageing), 284
Elwert, F., 39
EM (expectation–maximization) algorithm, 797–798
EMA (ecological momentary assessment) studies, 330, 331
Embase, 160
Embretson, S. E., 185, 772

Emerald Insight, 158
EMG. *See* Electromyography
Emic approach, xxxi
Emotion
  alpha frequency band and processing of, 592
  combined neuroimaging methods to study, 673
  electric current stimulation to study, 668
  ERP components related to, 613–614
  heart rate/interbeat interval and, 538
  muscle artifacts and evocation of, 587
  and muscular activity, 546
  rTMS studies of, 661
  single-pulse TMS studies of, 657–659
Emotional difficulties, figure drawing by individuals with, 443–444
Emotional part of scene, eye movements to, 479
Emotional state
  and asymmetric alpha power, 504
  and cardiac reactivity, 535
  and startle eyeblink reflex, 550–551
Emotion regulation, heart rate variability in, 539–540
Empirical data, fitting response-time models to, 500–501
Empirical documentation of cultural influences, 104
Empirically based concept inequivalence, 101
Empirical research on ethics, 75–76
Empowerment agenda, 9
Empty room recordings, 588
Encoding-related ERPs, 613
Endocardium, 535
Endogenous ERP components, 608, 611–612
English language, 160, 474. *See also* Alphabetic writing systems
English Longitudinal Study of Ageing (ELSA), 284
Entwisle, D. R., 442
Environment criteria for grants, 242
Enzymatic immunoassays (EIAs), 569, 572
Enzyme-linked immunosorbent assays (ELISAs), 569, 572
EOG. *See* Electrooculography
EPI (echo planar image), 633
Epidermis, 542–543
Epilepsy, EEG–fMRI studies of, 680

Epistemological assumptions, 10–11, 17–18
Epistemological bases for qualitative research, 5–21
  definition of qualitative research, 5–7
  differences among approaches, 7–10
  in evaluation of research quality/value, 18–20
  phenomenological knowledge, 12, 14–16
  realist knowledge, 11–14
  social constructionist knowledge, 12–13, 16–18
  varieties of knowledge related to, 13–18
Epoch measure, 539, 590–591
Equal importance, assumption of, 841, 852–854
Equal-variance assumption, 515, 517
Equipment, as direct research cost, 231
Equivalence. *See also* Inequivalence
  conceptual, 121–122
  defined, 98
  full score, 102
  functional, 101, 551
  item response theory models for studying, 737
  measurement, 124–127
  metric/measurement unit, 101–102, 126
  scalar, 102
  semantic, 121, 122
  structural, 101, 106
  of translated materials, 121, 124
Equivalency rule, 171
Equivalent-current dipole, 617
e-rater, 363–365
ERD (event-related desynchronization), 596
ERFs. *See* Event-related fields
Ergonomics, 513
ERIC. *See* Education Resources Information Center
Eriksen flanker task, 612
ERN (error-related negativity), 609, 612
ERP components
  defined, 608
  described, 605
  emotion-related, 613–614
  exogenous sensory, 609–611
  as focus of research, 608
  language-related, 613
  memory-related components, 613
  N2 family of, 612

  N170 component and face processing, 605–608
  overlapping, 625, 627
  P3 family of, 611–612
  polarity of, 616
  quantifying magnitude and timing of, 625
  response-related, 614
ERPs. *See* Event-related potentials
ERP waveforms, plotting, 606
Error-related negativity (ERN), 609, 612
Errors
  assumption of equal importance for, 841
  in classical test theory, 725, 726
  with functional neuroimaging, 648
  with repeated calculations, 221–223
  in statistical analysis, 211–212
  version control and correcting, 217
Error terms
  in probabilistic models, 178, 180–181
  in stimulus-centered models, 177
Error variance
  absolute, 748, 751, 753, 759
  in classical test theory, 726
  in common factor model and IRT, 796
  model, 193
  relative, 748, 750–751, 753, 759
  in single-facet generalizability analysis, 750–751
  and test–retest reliability, 729
Error variation, in classical test theory, 725, 726
ER-SCR (electronic response skin conductance responses), 545
ESEA (Elementary and Secondary Education Act), 415, 426
ESP (Experience Sampling Program), 337
Essay responses, automated analyses of, 363–366
Estimation
  in item-level factor analysis vs. item response theory, 796–798
  of magnitude of effect, 189, 195–197
  of reliability, 728–737
Estimation algorithms, for ICA, 701
Estradiol, 568
Ethical considerations
  in nonhuman animal research, 83–91
  research guidelines and regulations, 59–77

Ethical decision making, 59
Ethical dilemmas, 110
Ethical issues
    with conducting interviews, 318–321
    in cross-cultural research, 106–110
    in interviews, 312
"Ethical Principles of Psychologists and Code of Conduct" (APA Ethics Code), 59, 63–77
    and Belmont Report, 60
    Beneficence and Nonmaleficence principle, 63
    on confidentiality, 74–75
    on conflicts of interest, 75
    for cross-cultural research, 98
    on deception research, 72–73
    and evidence-based/participant-informed research, 75–77
    Fidelity and Responsibility principle, 63–64
    on informed consent, 64–72
    Integrity principle, 64
    Justice principle, 64
    on research debriefing, 73–74
    Respect for People's Rights and Dignity principle, 64
Ethical research guidelines and regulations, 59–77
    in APA Ethics Code, 59, 60, 63–77
    federal regulations, 60–61
    and institutional oversight, 61–63
Ethics cascade, 84
Ethnic identity, longitudinal studies of, 329
Ethnic Identity Scale (EIS), 127
Ethnographic interviews, 298
Ethnography, 10, 12
Etic approach, xxxi, xxxvii
ETS (Educational Testing Service), 363, 365
European Society of Cardiology, 539
Evaluation dimension, for emotion words, 369
Evaluative threat, 541
Even-handedness, norm of. See Reciprocity, norm of
Event-based designs (event-contingent designs), 330–332
Event-based kappa, 264
Event codes, for ERP studies, 622
Event-recorded data
    Cohen's kappa and, 262–263
    continuous timed, 259–260
    continuous untimed, 258–259

Event-related desynchronization (ERD), 596
Event-related fields (ERFs), 582, 674
Event-related potential (ERPs)
    evaluating studies of, 626–627
Event-related potentials (ERPs), 605–627, 674. See also ERP components
    cognition in schizophrenia experiment, 618–619
    concurrent TMS-EEG studies of, 688–689
    defined, 605
    in EEG, 582
    EEG–fMRI investigations of variability in, 681
    EEG/MEG and fMRI to model, 678, 679
    emotion-related components, 613–614
    and event-related fields, 582
    exogenous sensory components, 609–611
    generation of, 616–617
    language-related components, 613
    localization of, 617–618
    memory-related components, 613
    multivariate pattern analysis with, 614–616
    N2 family of components, 612
    N170 component and face processing experiment, 605–608
    naming conventions for, 608–609
    neural origins of, 616–618
    P3 family of components, 611–612
    recording and analysis of, 619–626
    response-related components, 614
    in special populations, 614
Events
    defining, 332
    as recording units, 257–260
Event sequential data, 261
Evidence-based research, 75–77
Evidence maps, 153
Excitotoxicity, 666
ExGaussian response time distributions, 496–498, 507–508
Existence of effect
    null hypothesis significance testing for, 191–192
    sample size for determining, 189, 193–195
Exner, J. E., Jr., 437, 442

Exogenous sensory ERP components, 608–611
Expectancy effects, 350
Expectation–maximization (EM) algorithm, 797–798
Expectations, in AutoTutor, 371
Expected correlations, 780–781
Expected frequency, 268–269
Expected mean, 728
Expected percentage correct, 840
Experienced observers, 519
Experiences, grounding interview responses in, 303–304
Experience sampling methods. See Ecological momentary assessment (EMA) studies
Experience Sampling Program (ESP), 337
Experimental control
    causal inference frameworks favoring, 48, 49
    removing, for cost reduction, 228
Experimental designs, xxxiii–xxxiv, xxxvii, 640–641
Experimental psychology, 146
Experimental studies, behavioral observation in, 251
Experimenter, in psychophysical experiments, 518
Expert, role of, 10, 773
Expertise, 321, 606
Explanation, seeking, during interviews, 308–309
Explanatory research, causal, xxxi–xxxiv
Explicit distribution functions, 507–508
Exploratory/Development Research Grant Program (R21), 239, 240
Exploratory factor analysis (EFA), xli, 793
    dimensionality detection with, 803
    for item selection, 389, 390
    in PROMIS example, 802
    starting model fitting with, 801–802
Exploratory searches, 152, 166
Exploratory studies, cross-cultural comparisons in, 102
Extension strategy for research question formulation, 144–145
External funding sources, 228–230, 232–233
External validity, 779–788
    change aspect of, 784
    components and focus of, 771–772, 779

and consequences of measurement programs, 787–788
convergent and discriminant validity, 781–784
criterion-related validity, 779–781
and interpretations of test scores, 784–787
of new objective tests, 398–401
of phenomenological knowledge, 12
in validity typology/threats framework, 25
Extrafoveal masks, 478
Extrapolation, generalization and, 763–764
Extratest behavior, 435–436
Extreme groups, samples with, 828
Extreme location parameters, 829
Eye blinks
    artifacts due to, 622, 688
    EEG signals and, 587
    measuring, 552
Eye movements, 469–486
    artifacts due to, 586–588, 622
    and attention, 471
    binocular coordination of, 470–471
    control of, 475–477
    fixational, 470
    measuring, 471
    physiological measurement of, 552
    and pupillometry, 483–486
    in reading, 471–477
    saccades, 469–470
    during scene perception, 477–480
    and visual acuity, 471
    and visual cognition, 483
    and visual search, 480–483
Eyes-closed rest, 642
Eyes-open rest, 642
Eye-trackers, fMRI with, 634, 642
E-Z Reader model, 477

F31 fellowship (Individual Predoctoral Fellowship to Promote Diversity), 238
F31 NRSA training award, 234–235
F32 NRSA training award, 235
Face processing, 605–608
Face-to-face contact, with members of marginalized populations, 118
Facets
    content validity analyses for, 460
    of decision studies, 748
    differentiation, 761–762
    of generalizability studies, 746–748
    of homogeneous traits, 455
    instrumentation, 761–762
    multifacet generalizability analysis, 752–756
    single-facet generalizability analysis, 749–752
Facial Action Coding System (FACS), 550
Facial electromyography, 550–552, 587
Facial expression, 550, 594
Facial mimicry, 552
Facilities and administrative (F&A) costs, 231–232
F&A (facilities and administrative) costs, 231–232
FACS (Facial Action Coding System), 550
Factor analysis. See also Item-level factor analysis (IFA)
    confirmatory. See Confirmatory factor analysis (CFA)
    exploratory. See Exploratory factor analysis (EFA)
    item-level vs. other types of, 793–795
    for item selection, 389
    moderated nonlinear, 801
    principal, 389
    quantifying precision/measurement error with, 737
    reliability determination with, 735, 737
    slope-intercept parameterization for, 811
    standard model for, 793
    testing unidimensionality with, 456
Factorial invariance, 125, 126, 778
Factor structure of short form, 460
Fairness behavior, 665
Faithfulness assumption, 37
False alarm rate (false positive rate), 839. See also False positives
    in cutoff value specification methods, 855
    in ROC analysis, 845–846
    and sensitivity index/response bias, 515
    in signal detection theory, 517
False discovery rate (FDR) correction method, 646, 698–699
False negatives (misses)
    cutoff score and weighing of, 785
    in decision theory, 785
    defined, 839, 840
    utility assigned to, 850
    value of valid positives vs., 841
False positives (false alarms). See also False alarm rate
    cutoff score and weighing of, 787
    in decision theory, 785
    defined, 839, 840
    in fMRI data, 646
    and multiple comparison issue, 698
    utility assigned to, 850
Families
    group interviews with, 314
    intensive longitudinal methods with, 353
Family-wise error rate (FWE), 698
Faraday, Michael, 655
Fast-event related paradigm, 699
Fast Fourier transform (FFT), 591
Fast-frequency rTMS, 660, 661
Fast guesses, on response time distributions, 498
FATCAT toolbox, 709
Fatigue, pupillometric response and, 485
F Awards, 234–235
FDA (U.S. Food and Drug Administration), 164, 663–664
Feasibility issues with intensive longitudinal methods, 333
FEAT software tool, 700
Feature selection, decoding analysis, 704
Fechner, G. T., 175, 511, 531
Fechner's law, 516
Federal ethics regulations, 60–61
Federal funding, 229, 232–233
Federal Policy for the Protection of Human Subjects (Common Rule)
    2017 revision of, 62–63, 65
    on confidentiality, 74
    history of, 61
Feedback
    from intelligent tutoring systems, 373, 374
    in real-time fMRI, 645
Feldman-Barrett, D. J., 337
Fellowship awards, 229, 239
    grant review for, 242
    from NIH, 234–236
Feminist analysis, 8, 9
Féré, Charles, 542
Feredoes, E., 685
Ferris, Timothy, xxviii
Ferromagnetic metals, in fMRI scanner, 634
FFT (fast Fourier transform), 591
Fibrils, 547

Index

Fidelity and Responsibility (Principle B), 63–64
Fields, database, 158
Figure drawings, 442–444
Filenames, relative, 221
Filial piety, 100
Filters
    database, 162
    for ERP data, 621, 626
FIML (full-information maximum likelihood) method, 797
Findlay, J. M., 482
Finger-clip photoplethysmograph, 541
Finlay, L., 19
First-level GLM analysis, 637
First-order autoregressive residual (AR1) structure, 348
Fisher, C. B., 72
Fisher, D. F., 476
Fisher's analysis of variance (ANOVA), 746
Fisher Z equivalents, for correlations, 781
Fiske, D. W., 398–400, 781, 782
FIT (Fusion ICA), 702, 710
Fixational eye movements (fixations), 469–472
Fixation duration
    measures of, 472–473
    for reading, 476–477
    for scene perception, 479–480
    for visual search, 480–482
Fixed effect, in Level 2 model, 345, 347, 348
Fixed-effects analysis, with GLM, 637
Fixed facets
    in decision studies, 756–757
    in generalizability studies, 754, 757
    in mixed-model analysis, 756–757
    in multivariate generalizability analysis, 757–760
Fixed-interval schedules, 330–331
Fixed-n approach to sample-size planning, 189, 193
Fixed raters, 729, 730, 732
Fixed schedule electronic response formats, 337–338
Fleiss, J. L., 730–732, 735
flexmirt software, 811
Flip angle, fMRI, 633
Floor effect, 828
Flora, D. B., 734, 799
Florida, graduation test in, 424–425
F-measures, for AESs, 365

fMRI. *See* Functional magnetic resonance imaging (fMRI)
fMRIprep tool, 635
fNIRS (functional near-infrared spectroscopy), 632, 646–647
FOAs (funding opportunity announcements), 232–233
Focality, of TMS vs. tES, 677
Focus groups, 313–314
Follow-up interviews, 317–318
Follow-up questions, 305–306
Foltin, R. W., 84
Food and Agricultural Organization of the United States, 86
Food cravings, tDCS studies of, 665–666
Forgetfulness, diary completion and, 335, 336
Fork, causal graph, 33
Formal operational phase of construct validity research, 770–771
Formation stage of response, 278
Formative feedback, 374
Formative indicators, 392
Formulations, within interviews, 309–310
Fornito, A., 706–708
Forward search, 165
Forward translation, 122
Foundations, 229–230, 232, 239
Fourier transform, 590
Four-parameter logistic model (4PLM), 816, 817
Fovea, 471
Fowler, J. C., 436
Fraley, R. C., 829
Frame switching, 123
Framing effect, 290–292
France, S. L., 411–412
Frank, L. K., 434, 436
Franklin, M. S., 484
Free-association narrative interviews, 298
FreeSurfer, 635, 710
Freezing, of saliva samples, 573
Fregni, F., 665–666
Frequency
    of EEG/MEG signals, 590–591
    expected, 268–269
    of nonspecific skin conductance responses, 545
    of observational data, 266, 268
    observed joint, 268
Frequency bands of interest, 591–592, 595–596
Frequency distribution, norm-referenced measure, 409–411

Frequency domain measures, heart rate variability, 539
Frequency polygon of response times, 502
Frequentist framework for sample-size planning, 189
Freud, S., 434–435
Fringe benefits, 231
Friston, K. J., 699
Frontal areas, TMS targeting, 677
Frontal lateralization theories of motivation, 657, 661, 665
Front-end editor, 214, 216, 218, 219
Frozen statements, 373
FSFAST version 6.0 toolbox, 709
FSL toolbox, 635, 700, 710
F tests, 698
Fuente Academica, 160
Fuligni, A. J., 329
Full-information maximum likelihood (FIML) method, 797
Full score equivalence, 102
Fully unconditional model, 345
Fulmer, G. W., 425
Functional connectivity analysis, 643, 708–709
Functional equivalence, 101, 551
Functional localizer, 382
Functional magnetic resonance imaging (fMRI), 25, 631–646
    correlations of EEG/MEG measures with, 597–598
    EEG/MEG–fMRI, 678–681
    EEG/MEG vs., 597, 598
    ERPs vs. signals in, 616
    experimental design for, 640–641
    fNIRS vs., 647
    history of, 697
    multivariate pattern analysis in, 614–615
    naturalistic task, 643–645
    NIBS–fMRI, 681–686
    participant safety and comfort during, 634
    real-time, 645
    resting-state, 641–643
    scan parameters for, 632–634
    task-based, 639–641
    uses and limitations, 675–676
Functional magnetic resonance imaging (fMRI) data
    analyzing, 636–639, 644–645, 710. *See also* Neuroimaging analysis methods

challenges with analyzing, 645–646
preprocessing, 635–636
Functional near-infrared spectroscopy (fNIRS), 632, 646–647
Functional networks, PCA to extract, 702
Functional neuroimaging methods, 631–649
  common errors with, 648
  functional magnetic resonance imaging, 631–646
  functional near-infrared spectroscopy, 646–647
  positron emission tomography, 647–648
  robust and reproducible results from, 648–649
Functional PCA, nonlinear, 702
Functional regions of interest, 639
Functions, coding with, 223–224
Function words, in LIWC, 368
Fundamental problem of causal inference, 28
Funding, 227–245
  business technology and innovation, 241
  center grants and multiproject awards, 241–242
  conflicts of interest related to, 75
  external sources of, 228–230, 232–233
  and grant review process, 242–244
  for investigators from traditionally underrepresented backgrounds, 237–239
  and IRB approval, 62
  NIH fellowship and training grants, 234–239
  non-NIH training grants, 239
  project-focused grants, 239–241
  and research cost categories, 230–232
  selecting the right grant program/mechanism for, 232–233
  for training, career development, and workforce diversity efforts, 233
Funding opportunity announcements (FOAs), 232–233
Fusion ICA (FIT), 702, 710
FWE (family-wise error rate), 698

GABA-mediated processes, TMS studies of, 659–660
Gable, P., 595

Gable, S. L., 335
Galton, F., 143, 185, 408, 411
Gamma frequency band, 591, 596
Gamma probability density functions, 699
Gandrud, C., 214
Garbarski, D., 284–285
Gardner, M. J., 205
Gardner, W., 264–265
Gaskell, G. D., 290
Gates, Bill, 139
Gaussian noise term, in ICA, 701
Gaussian random field theory (GRFT), 698
Gauss-Markov theorem, 697
gee package, 352
Geldhof, G. J., 737
Gender differences, in control of cardiovascular activity, 536
Gender-specific norms, 415–416
Generality, defined, 532
Generalizability, 25. See also External validity
  of causal inference findings, 45–46
  of qualitative research, 6
  of research with marginalized populations, 127
Generalizability analysis
  computer programs for conducting, 760–761
  decision study in, 747–748
  generalizability study in, 746–748
  for mixed-model studies, 756–757
  for multifacet designs, 752–756
  multivariate, 757–760
  for single-facet designs, 749–752
  univariate, 749–757
Generalizability coefficient
  for absolute decision, 749
  multivariate, 759
  for relative decision, 748, 749, 751, 754
Generalizability study (G-study), 746–748
  decision study vs., 748
  goal of, 746–747
  mixed-model, 756–757
  multi-facet, 752–753, 755
  multivariate, 757–758
  single-facet, 749–751
Generalizability theory (GT), 174, 745–765
  and classical test theory, 748–749
  fundamental concepts of, 746–749
  and item response theory, 764

and reliability, 344–345, 735, 737, 762–764
  symmetry as issue in, 761–762
  types of measurement error and reliability coefficients in, 748–749
  and validity, 462, 762–764
Generalization
  causal, 45–46
  of Comprehensive System, 437
  and extrapolation, 763–764
  of ROC methods, 849
Generalized partial credit model (GPCM), 776–777, 824–825
Generalized Sequential Querier (GSEQ), 261, 264
General linear model (GLM), 697–700
  fMRI analysis with, 636–638
  modeling hemodynamic response with, 699
  multiple comparison issue with, 698–699
  MVPA vs., 703
  software tools for implementing, 700
  statistical inferences based on, 698
  temporal autocorrelation in, 699–700
General (whole) question
  on abortion, 279–280
  avoiding question order effects with, 292
  on happiness, 281–282
General Social Survey (GSS), 279, 281–282
Generative games, in intelligent tutoring systems, 372, 374
GENOVA (GENeralized analysis Of VAriance) program, 760, 761
German language, 474
Gescheider, G. A., 512
ggplot2 package, 216–217, 339
Gianotti, L. R., 661–662
Gibbons, R. D., 827
GIFT extension, 702, 710
Gill, A., 369
Ginther, D. K., 237
Girvan, M., 707
git, version control with, 218–220
GKT (guilty knowledge test), 538, 544
Gladwell, Malcolm, 139
Glaser, B., 7
Glaser, R., 423, 425
Gleason, M. E. J., 329, 353
Gleser, G. C., 735
GLM. See General linear model

Global efficiency, in network analysis, 708
Global reliability measure, 737
Global response patterns, 734
Global signal regression (GSR), 643
Glutamate-mediated processes, TMS studies of, 659
GMAT (Graduate Management Admission Test), 364, 421
Goals of research. *See also* Objectives of research
    and interpretation of study results, 191–193
    parameter specification method and, 198
    sample size and, 189–190
Goksuluk, D., 849
Gold, R. S., 285
Goldfried, M. R., 433
Gomez, R., 100
Goodness-of-fit approach to informed consent, 76
Goodness-of-fit measures, outliers and, 507
Google, 163
Google Scholar, 151, 157–158, 163, 165
Go-past time, 473
Gordon Commission, 423
Gottman, J. M., 253, 255, 263, 264, 352
Gough, B., 19
Government agencies, funding from, 229, 230
GPCM (generalized partial credit model), 776–777, 824–825
gPPI package, 709
Graded response model (GRM)
    for noncognitive measures, 827–830
    for polytomous responses, 777, 795–796
    threshold response curves in, 818–819
Grade-equivalent scores, 418, 419
Graduate Management Admission Test (GMAT), 364, 421
Graduate Record Examination (GRE), 421
Graduate Research Fellowship Program (GRFP), 239
Graduate school admission tests, 421
Graduate school research, funding for, 239
Grammatical category, in LIWC, 368
Grand average waveforms, 619

Granger causality, 709
Grant, A. M., 201–206
Grant, D., 285
Grants
    application review process, 242–244
    business technology, 241
    center, 241–242
    from foundations/charities vs. government agencies, 230
    innovation, 241
    project-focused, 239–241
    selecting the right program, 232–233
    training, 233, 236–239
Granularity, of codes, 255
Graphical identification analysis, 45
Graphical rules, for structural causal model, 31
Graphical user interface (GUI), 213
Graph metrics, network analysis, 707
Graphs, programming to create, 216–217
Graph theory, 706
Graph Theory GLM Toolbox, 710
GraphVar, 710
Gratitude, 201–202
Gray literature resources, 162–164
Gray-Little, B., 829
GRE (Graduate Record Examination), 421
Green, D. M., 512
Greenhouse-Geisser epsilon correction, 626
Green science, 642
GRFP (Graduate Research Fellowship Program), 239
GRFT (Gaussian random field theory), 698
Grimes, D. A., 199
Grimm, K. J., 783–784
Grisso, T., 70
GRM. *See* Graded response model
Groat, M., 436
Grønnerød, C., 438
Grounded theory methodology, 8, 12, 319
Grounding, of interviewee responses, 303–305
Grounding, to reduce EEG artifacts, 588
Ground truth value of stimulus, 514
Group-difference research, xxxiv–xxxvi
Group interviews, 313–314
Group-level generalizability analysis, 762

Groups
    behavioral observation in, 252
    intensive longitudinal methods with, 353
    norm, 414–417, 439
GSEQ (Generalized Sequential Querier), 261, 264
GSR (global signal regression), 643
GSS (General Social Survey), 279, 281–282
G String V program, 760–761
G-study. *See* Generalizability study
gstudy() function, 761
GT. *See* Generalizability theory
gtheory software package, 761
Guesses, on response time distributions, 498
Guessing parameter, 422
GUI (graphical user interface), 213
Guide for the Care and Use of Laboratory Animals (National Research Council), 87, 90
Guidelines for Ethical Conduct in the Care and Use of Animals (APA), 91
Guilt, 594
Guilty knowledge test (GKT), 538, 544
Gun Attitude Scale, 177
Guttman scale model, 178–180

Haas, G.-C., 289
Habituation, 252–253, 334, 545
Haddock, C., 270
Hagemann, D., 589
Hajcak, G., 658
Hales, S., 539
Half recovery time, 545
Hall, T. W., 830
Hallgren, K. A., 265
Hamaker, E. L., 329, 737
Hambleton, R. K., 105
Hamming window, 591
Handbook of Research Methods in Psychology (Cooper), 115
Handsearching, 165
Hanslmayr, S., 681, 686–687
Happiness, 281–283, 551
Harlow, H. F., 139
Harmon-Jones, E., 593–595
Harris, C. W., 425, 426
Harvard-Oxford anatomical atlas, 643
Harvey, William, 535
Hau, K. T., 799
Haynes, S. N., 453
Hayward, Clare, 314
Hazard rate function, 495–497

H-coil (Hesed coil), 664
Headcases, neuroimaging, 589, 636
Head coils, fMRI, 633
Head Start program, 415
Health and safety studies, question order effects in, 283–286
Health disparities, reducing, 241–242
Health Information Technology for Economic and Clinical Health Act, 61
Health Insurance Portability and Accountability Act (HIPAA), 61
Health sciences databases, 160
Hearing protection, 634
Heart, anatomy and physiology, 535–536
Heart period, 537
Heart rate (HR), 532, 537
Heart rate variability (HRV), 538–540
Hebrew language, 473, 474
Hedeker, D., 827
Heinze, H. J., 678
Helmreich, R., 252–253
Hemodynamic response
  GLM for modeling, 699
  in rapid event-related tasks, 639–640
Hemodynamic response function (HRF), 637, 699
Henderson, J. M., 479–480
Hendrickson, A. T., 494–495
Hepburn, A., 323
Hermans, F., 212
Hermeneutics of meaning recollection, 8
Hermeneutics of suspicion, 8
Hermiller, M. S., 686
Hernández, M. G., 118
Herndon, T. C., 212
Hesed coil (H-coil), 664
Hess, U., 551
Heterogeneity
  in classical reliability theory, 395–396
  in covariance, for ERP data, 626
Heterotrait-heteromethod correlations, 782
Heterotrait-monomethod correlations, 782
Hibbard, S., 441, 442
HICs (homogeneous item composites), 387
Hierarchical constructs, applying IRT models to, 826–827
Hierarchical factor analytic models, 801–802

High slope parameters, for noncognitive measures, 827–828
Hill, C. A., 287, 683
Hill, N. J., 512
Hillegas, M. R., 409
HIPAA (Health Insurance Portability and Accountability Act), 61
Hippler, H.-J., 287
Hippocampus, theta burst stimulation and, 686
Hiskey-Nebraska Test of Learning Aptitude, 415
History, threat of, 26
Hit rate (valid positive rate), 839
  in cutoff value specification methods, 855
  in ROC analysis, 845–846
  and sensitivity index/response bias, 515
  in signal detection theory, 517
Hits. See Valid positives
HLM program, 339, 346n6
Ho, A. D., 425
Ho, D. Y. E., 100
Hodos, W., 84n2
Hofstede, G. H., 103
Holland, P. W., 23, 28, 45
Hollway, W., 10
Holtzman Inkblot Technique, 436
Homogeneity
  construct. See Construct homogeneity
  content, 828
Homogeneous item composites (HICs), 387
Horizontal eye movements, 587
Hormonal contraceptives, 570
Hormone assay methods, 568–569
Hormones
  bidirectional relationship of behavior and, 566
  in biobehavioral research, 565–567
  function of, 565
  sources of, 565
Horn, J. L., 801
House-Tree-Person (H-T-P) technique, 443
How Working Men Spend Their Time (Bevans), 327
Hox, J. J., 352
Hoyle, R. H., 726
HR (heart rate), 532, 537
HRV (heart rate variability), 538–540
H-T-P (House-Tree-Person) technique, 443
Hu, J., 682

Huebner, A., 760
Huff, A. S., 138
Hugh-Jones, Siobhan, 323
Hulin, C. L., 410
Human Animal Use Categories, 89
Human-centric design, 513
Human Connectome Project, 642, 649
Human participants, 336
  burden for, 332, 333
  communication with, 534–535, 634
  compensation for, 67–69, 228
  discredited, 320–321
  ethical issues related to use of, 107–108
  ethical research with, 59–60
  physiological measures from, 534–535
  preparing, for EEG/MEG, 585–586
  research ethics with nonhuman animals vs., 83–84
  safety and comfort of, during fMRI, 634
  screening, for salivary hormone assays, 569–571
  training for, in intensive longitudinal studies, 332
Human Resources Abstracts database, 159
Human rights, 109
Hume, David, xxxii–xxxiii
Hunter, J. E., 139, 141
Husek, T. R., 414, 426, 427
huxtable package, 216
Hybrid intensive longitudinal designs, 332
Hyman, H. H., 281
Hyperscanning, 596–597
Hypomania, 595
Hypothalamus, cardiovascular activity and, 536
Hypotheses
  plausible rival, 26
  prerequisites to creating, 141–142
Hypothesis testing, xxvii–xxviii, xli–xlii
  cross-cultural comparisons in, 102
  data-driven research vs., 648
  measurement process for, 169
Hypothetical constructs, 771
Hypothetico-deductive research, 7

IACUC (Institutional Animal Care and Use Committee), 87–90
IAPS (International Affective Picture System), 658
IBI (interbeat interval), 537, 538

Index

ICC. *See* Intraclass correlation coefficient; Item characteristic curve
ICC Calculator, 265
ICE (individual causal effect), 28
ICF (intracortical facilitation), 659
IC (Individualism versus Collectivism) framework, 104–105
ICI (intracortical inhibition), 659
IDAS (Inventory of Depression and Anxiety Symptoms), 387
IDE (integrated development environment), 214
Identification games, in intelligent tutoring systems, 372, 374
Identified causal effect, 37
Idiosyncratic responses, 434, 443
IFA. *See* Item-level factor analysis
IFG (inferior prefrontal cortex), 681, 686–687
Iida, M., 334
ILAR (Institute for Laboratory Animal Research), 90–91
Ilmoniemi, R. J., 663
Image-computable models, 525
Image-led interviews, 317
Imbens, G., 24, 28
Immigrants, recruitment of, 117–118
Immunoassays, 568–569
Impedance cardiography, 542
Impedance reduction, for EEG, 585
Implications, in quantitative descriptive research, xxxiii
Implicit Association Test, 436
Implicit attitude task, 550
Implicit contrast, 280
Important research questions, 137–143
    and concern about practical problems/implications of basic research, 139
    and knowledge of research/theoretical literature, 139
    new methods of inquiry and, 142
    sources of ideas for formulating, 139–141
    as worthwhile, 137–138
Impulsivity, facets of, 455
Inattentional blindness, 485
Incentives, for research participation, 118
Inclusion of others in the self (IOS) scale, 349–350
Incomplete sentences blank, 434
Inconsistency, in classical reliability theory, 391, 395–396
Incorrect events, 786

Incorrect nonevents, 786
Independence, local, 177, 180
Independence relations, on causal graphs, 32
Independent component analyses, 700–702
    artifact removal via, 688
    correcting for eye blink artifacts with, 587, 588
    probabilistic, 701–702
    with resting-state fMRI data, 643
    standard, 700–701
Independent investigators, grants for, 237, 239–240
Independently distributed items, parceling, 798
Independent Scientist Award (K02), 237
Independent variables, in GLM, 636–637
Indexes of test performance, 837–844
Index of dependability (dependability coefficient), 748, 751, 754, 759
Indirect cause, on causal graphs, 33
Indirect costs of research, 230–232
Individual causal effect (ICE), 28
Individual differences
    in change processes, 329
    cross-cultural comparisons in studies of, 103
    in function word use, 368
    question order effects due to, 288–291, 293
    research on group differences vs., xxxiv–xxxvi
    in response to state manipulations, 595
Individual growth models, 347
Individualism versus Collectivism (IC) framework, 104–105
Individualistic assignment mechanism, 30
Individual Predoctoral Fellowship to Promote Diversity (F31), 238
Inducements, for participants, 68–69
Inductive model, 7–8
Industrial psychology, 421
Industry-funded research, 228
Inequality, axes of, 115, 116
Inequivalence
    a priori procedures to reduce, 103–106
    in translations, 105
    types of, 100–101
Infants
    asymmetric alpha power for, 504
    ERP studies with, 614

    fNIRS studies with, 647
    mismatch negativity studies with, 612
Inferences, from physiological measures, 532–533
Inferior prefrontal cortex (IFG), 681, 686–687
Inflammation markers, 567
Informal interviews, 310
Information gain, 839, 854–856
Information theory, 854–856
Informative parts of scene, eye movements to, 479
Informed consent
    APA Ethics Code standards on, 64–72
    and confidentiality, 74
    for cross-cultural research, 107–108
    and deception research, 72
    empirical research on, 75–76
    in interviews, 319
    IRB approval of forms for, 62
    language/format for obtaining, 65
Informed Consent (Standard 3.10b), 71
Informed Consent to Research (Standard 8.02b), 67
"Informed" requirement, for consent, 65–67
Infrared corneal reflections, 471
Infrared Purkinje image tracking, 471
Inion, 585–586
Initial elevation bias, 334
Initial item pool, 385–388
Inline results, programming for, 215–216
Innovation grants, 239, 241, 242
Innovative research questions, 138
Input-computable models of psychophysics, 525
Inquiry methods, 142
Inscapes (film), 644
Insider knowledge, 15
In situ data collection, 7
Institute for Laboratory Animal Research (ILAR), 90–91
Institute of Education Sciences, 158
Institutional Animal Care and Use Committee (IACUC), 87–90
Institutional Approval (Standard 8.01), 62
Institutional oversight, 61–63
Institutional review board (IRB)
    and cross-cultural research, 107
    on deception research, 109
    determinations by, 62–63

oversight by, 61–63
  protocol submission to, 62
  Revised Common Rule and, 63
  waiver of informed consent from, 72
Instructional validity, 425
Instrumental variable estimators, 48–49
Instrumentation, threat of, 26
Instrumentation facet, 752, 761–762
Instrument bias, 100
Instruments, gray literature on, 164
Integer scale, 256
Integrated development environment (IDE), 214
Integrated electromyography, 549–550
Integration, of EMG signal, 549
Integrity (Principle C), 64
Intellectual disabilities, individuals with, 70, 76
Intelligence, as construct, 770
Intelligence tests, 383, 408–409, 415, 443
Intelligent Essay Assessor, 363–365
Intelligent tutoring systems (ITSs), 370–375
  automated analysis of constructed responses for, 362–363
  AutoTutor, 370–372
  iSTART, 372–374
  Writing Pal, 374–375
IntelliMetric, 363, 364
Intensity, for tDCS, 666–667
Intensive longitudinal methods, 327–355
  with categorical variables, 352
  data analysis issues with, 339–341
  described, 327
  in device-contingent designs, 332
  diary format for, 334–339
  disadvantages with, 332–334
  with dyads, families, and groups, 353
  and dynamic systems models, 352
  in event-based designs, 331–332
  examining changes across time with, 346–350
  examples of, 341–352
  history of, 327–328
  investigating average experiences with, 341–346
  and multivariate multilevel analysis, 353
  predicting change/investigating change process with, 350–352
  research questions answered by, 328–329
  simulation with, 353–354
  in time-based designs, 330–331

Interactive Strategy Trainer for Automated Reading and Thinking (iSTART), 372–374
Interactive voice response (IVR), 336–338
Inter-assay coefficient of variation, 568
Interbeat interval (IBI), 537, 538
Intercept-only model, 345
Intercepts, invariance in, 126
Intercultural Adjustment Potential Scale, 109
Interitem correlation, 389, 393–394, 460
Interleukins, 568
Intermittent theta burst (iTBS), 663–664
Internal coherence, of radical constructionist research, 19
Internal consistency
  and construct homogeneity, 456
  and content validity, 453
  for criterion-referenced testing, 427
  of intensive longitudinal data, 340
  of new measure, 735
  of new objective tests, 388–389
  in norm-referenced testing, 413–414
  of objective tests, 392–393
  and reliability, 732–734, 738
  of short forms, 460
Internal noise, 515, 522
Internal reliability
  of Rorschach inkblots, 438
  of Thematic Apperception Test, 441–442, 444–445
Internal validity, 772–779
  content validity, 772–773
  dimensionality, 773–774
  and interpretations of test scores, 772
  item analysis approaches to, 774–779
  and measurement equivalence, 124
  of research with marginalized populations, 120
  statistical approaches to examining, 771
  threats to, 26
  in validity typology/threats framework, 25
International Affective Picture System (IAPS), 658
International Clinical Trials Registry Platform, 164
International Federation of Clinical Neurophysiology, 662

International Personality Item Pool, 146
Interpretation
  in critical realist approach, 14
  in qualitative approaches, 8
  question order effects and, 289
Interpretation stage of response, 278
Interpretive phenomenology, 8, 12, 15–16, 19
Interpretive research, xxx–xxxi
Interrater agreement, 732
Interrater reliability, 437–438, 441, 729–732
Interrupted interval recording, 258
Interrupting interviewees, 307–308
Intersectional identities, individuals with, 115, 116, 124–125
Interstimulus intervals, ERP study, 626
Intersubject correlation (ISC) analyses, 644
Intersubject functional correlation, 644–645
Intersubject representational similarity analysis, 645
Intertrial intervals, pupillometric research, 485
Intertrial phase-locking value analysis, 596
Interval data, summary statistics for, 268
Interval judgments, 517, 520
Interval length, in fixed time-based designs, 330–331
Interval recorded data
  basic statistics for, 266, 267
  Cohen's kappa for, 262–263
  representing, 261
Interval recording, 257–258, 260
Interval scale, 171, 184, 256
  described, 172
  and Rasch model, 181
  statistical analysis for data in, 183, 186
  for stimulus-centered measurements, 176
Interval sequential data, 261
Intervening variables, 771
Intervention, in structural causal model, 31, 34, 36
Intervention distribution, 36
Interventionist account of causation, 41
Interview-based diagnostic tests, 838–839
Interviewees
  disagreeing with/challenging, 311–313
  discredited participants as, 320–321

Interviewees (continued)
  interrupting, 307–308
  number and characteristics of, 313–314
  seeking explanation from, 308–309
Interviewer-administered surveys, 286–288
Interviewer–interviewee consensus accounts, 310–311
Interviewers
  dual roles for, 320
  expertise and reaction of, 321
  with "not-knowing" stance, 308–309
  number and characteristics of, 314–315
  responses completed by, 308
  self-disclosure by, 310–311
  technique improvements for, 323
Interviews, 297–323
  critique of interviews as data, 322–323
  defined, 297
  and design of interview studies, 313–318
  disagreeing with/challenging interviewee in, 311–313
  ethical issues with conducting, 318–321
  formulations within, 309–310
  grounding responses in examples in, 303–305
  nonleading questions in, 299–300
  not-knowing stance of interviewer in, 308–309
  open and closed questions in, 300–302
  prompts and follow-up questions in, 305–306
  recording and transcribing, 321–322
  schedules for, 298–299
  self-disclosure by interviewer in, 310–311
  semistructured, 7, 298–313
  short question technique in, 302–303
  silence as tool in, 306–308
  study design including, 313–318
  types of, 297–298
Interview schedules, 298–299
Intille, S. S., 332
Intra-assay coefficient of variation, 568
Intraclass correlation coefficient (ICC)
  Cohen's kappa and, 735–736
  internal consistency estimates of reliability vs., 732
  for observational data, 265

  for reliability estimates, 730–731
  for R-PAS variables, 438
Intracortical facilitation (ICF), 659
Intracortical inhibition (ICI), 659
Intraindividual change, intensive longitudinal studies of, 329
Intrasubject correlation analyses, 645
Intrinsically photosensitive retinal ganglion cells (ipRGCs), 524
INUS condition for cause, 40, 41, 43
Invariance
  configural, 126, 778, 800
  construct validity, 125, 126
  factorial, 125, 126, 778, 800
  measurement, 778–779, 800–802
  partial, 126, 801–802
  strict, 126, 778, 801
  strong, 126, 778, 800
  types of, 800–801
  weak factorial, 800
Invariance assumption, 37
Invariance model, in IRT, 778–779
Invariant measures, defined, 532
Invariant research procedures, 116
Inventory of Depression and Anxiety Symptoms (IDAS), 387
Inverse Gaussian response time distributions, 496–498
Inverse problem, with EEG/MEG, 675
Investigator criteria for grants, 242
IOS (inclusion of others in the self) scale, 349–350
Iowa Tests of Basic Skills, 419
ipRGCs (intrinsically photosensitive retinal ganglion cells), 524
Ipsilateral silent period (iSP), 658
IRB. See Institutional review board
IRC. See Item response curve
Iris dilator muscle, 552
Iris sphincter muscle, 552
Irregular assignment mechanism, 30–31, 45, 48–49
ISC (intersubject correlation), 644
ISETBio model framework, 525
iSP (ipsilateral silent period), 658
iSTART (Interactive Strategy Trainer for Automated Reading and Thinking), 372–374
"Is there anything you'd like to add?" interview question, 302
iTBS (intermittent theta burst), 663–664
Item analysis approaches to internal validity, 774–779
Item banks, 810

Item bias, 99, 100
Item characteristic curve (ICC), 178–181
  item selection based on, 390
  for performance assessment items, 422
  tailored testing approach based on, 462–463
Item correlation, homogeneity of scale and, 393
Item difficulty (item location)
  in criterion-referenced testing, 425–426
  in factor analysis, 794
  in item-level factor analysis, 794
  in item response theory approaches, 421
  for norm-referenced measures, 411–412
  on Rasch model, 181
  in two-parameter IRT model, 390
Item discrimination
  for criterion-referenced testing, 426–427
  in item-level factor analysis, 794
  in item response theory approaches, 422
  in two-parameter IRT model, 390
Item discrimination indices, 412
Item easiness, 411
Item facet, in generalizability analysis, 752
Item information curves, 812, 813
Item-level factor analysis (IFA), 773–776, 793–804
  and item response theory, 793, 795–798
  measurement invariance in, 800–802
  other types of factor analysis vs., 793–795
  parceling items for, 798–800
  PROMIS study example of, 802–804
Item location. See Item difficulty
Item-objective congruence, 426
Item pool size, 830
Item recognition task, 494–495
Item response curve (IRC), 810, 812, 813, 816
Item response matrix, 810
Item response theory (IRT)
  and brief instruments/short forms, 462–463
  defined, 809
  differential item functioning in, 778
  and generalizability theory, 764
  item difficulty in, 412

and item-level factor analysis, 793, 795–798
item selection based on, 389–391
and norm-referenced testing, 421–422
reliability in, 777
Item response theory (IRT) models, 186, 809–830
applicability of, 826–827
comparing measurement equivalence with, 737
development of, 809–810
features of, 809–810
generalized partial credit model, 824–825
of internal validity, 776–777
for noncognitive measures, 827–830
polytomous Rasch model, 825–826
reduced and expanded dichotomous, 812–817
for reliability determination, 735
and response-centered measurement, 180–182
statistical inference for latent traits with, 185
unidimensional dichotomous, 810–812
unidimensional polytomous, 817–824
Item revision, for criterion-referenced test, 427
Item selection, for criterion-referenced test, 426–427
Item-standard congruence, 426
Item statistics, for criterion-referenced test, 426
Iterative proportional fitting (IPF) algorithm, 263
ITSPOKE, 370
ITSs. *See* Intelligent tutoring systems
IVR (interactive voice response), 336–338

Jäckle, A., 286
Jacobson, Edmund, 546
Jahn, Andrew, 700, 709
James, William, 531, 546
Japan, question order effects in, 280
Japanese language, 473
JARS (Journal Article Reporting Standards), 196
Jefferson, T., 10
Jiroutek, M. R., 190
JNDs. *See* Just noticeable differences

Joanna Briggs Institute, 153
Job performance, core self-evaluations and, 201–206
John, L. K., 213
Johnson, T., 105–106
Johnston, M., 453
Jones, L. V., 176
Jonker, Z. D., 665
Jöreskog, K. G., 142, 796
Journal Article Reporting Standards (JARS), 196
Journal Storage (JSTOR), 158
JSTOR (Journal Storage), 158
Judgmental dependency, 292–293
Jung, Carl, 542
Justice (Principle D), 64
Just noticeable differences (JNDs), 175, 514, 517

K01 award, 236
K02 award, 237
K6 screening scale, 838–839
K08 award, 236–237
K10 screening scale, 846–847
K23 award, 236–237
K99/R00 award (NIH Pathway to Independence Award), 237
Kahneman, D., 195
Kane, M. T., 762, 763
Kang, S.-M., 185
Kappa
acceptable values for, 264–265
alignment, 263
Cohen's, 262–264, 735–736
event-based, 264
with rating scales, 265
for R-PAS, 438
time-unit, 264
Kappa agreement scores, 365
KappAcc program, 265
Kappenman, E. S., 608
Karrenbach, M., 212
Kartman, B., 285
Kastendieck, T., 552
Kaufman, S. H., 443
K awards (career development awards), 233, 236–237
Kelley, K., 190, 195, 200, 202, 734
Kenny, D. A., 726
Kent, R. N., 433
Kernal PCA, 702
Kessler, R. C., 847–848
KFD (Kinetic Family Drawing) test, 443
Kinetic Family Drawing (KFD) test, 443
Kingdom, F. A. A., 512, 513, 522

Kirschstein-Institutional National Research Service Award (T32 grant), 235–236
Kirschstein-NRSA Individual Fellowships, 234–235
Kivisalu, T. M., 438
$K \times K$ table, 262
Kleck, R. E., 551
Klein, R. A., 281
Kliegl, R., 469
Knauper, B., 288
knit function, 216
knitr package, 213, 214, 217
Knoblauch, K., 522
Knoch, D., 661–662, 665
Knowing, methods of, xxv–xxvi
Known assignment mechanism, 29–30
Knuth, D. E., 213
Kolaczyk, E., 707
Kolen, M. J., 416, 419
Konner, Mel, 258
Koppitz scores, 443
Korean language, 473, 474
Kotov, R., 384
K–R 20 index, 392
Kraemer, H. C., 728
Krantz, D. H., 192
Kreiter, C., 762
Kriegeskorte, N., 705
Krippendorff's alpha, 266
Krosnick, J. A., 289, 291
Kuchinke, L., 484
Kulesz, D., 212
Kurtz, J. E., 383

Laboratory analysis, for hormone assay, 575
Laboratory animal welfare, 85–87, 89–90
Laboratory Animal Welfare Act (AWA), 87
Laenen, A., 737
Lag sequential analysis, 271
LAN (left anterior negativity), 613
Landing position effects, 475–476
Lane, P. E., 333, 340
Lane, S. P., 737
Lange, Carl, 531
Language
NLP analysis of style of, 368
Language(s)
comprehension of, 613
construct validity and use of, 25
in cross-cultural research, 105

Language(s) *(continued)*
   ERP components related to, 613
   recruiting marginalized populations of other, 117–118
   social constructionist studies of, 13
   target population's ability with, 124
Language network, MEG research on, 596
Larkin, M., 15
Larson, R., 327
Latency, of skin conductance responses, 545
Latency–probability plots, 506
Latency variability, in ERP trials, 623–625
Latent growth curves, 784
Latent method factor scores, in CT-CM model, 782
Latent scores, observed and, 184–185
Latent semantic analysis (LSA), 364–365, 369, 372–373
Latent traits
   complexity of measuring, 170
   factor scores in CT-CM model for, 782
   in item response theory, 764
   response-centered scaling for, 174
   statistical inferences about, 184–186
   stimulus-centered measurement of, 173–175
   and subject-centered scaling, 175
Latent trait theory, 180, 186
Latent variables
   data analysis to uncover, xli
   defined, 725
   in factor analysis, 793
   fit of measurement to, xxxviii
   IRT on individual responses and, 809
   parceling for, 798–799
   reliability estimation and association with, 733
   scale levels for, 171
   scaling psychological data related to, 173
Late positive potential, 613–614
Lateralized readiness potential (LRP), 614, 618–619
Latin American & Caribbean Health Sciences Literature (LILACS), 160
Latinx individuals, 118, 237–238
Laurenceau, J.-P., 329, 352
Law of categorical judgment, 176, 182
Law of comparative judgment, 176, 182
Law of small numbers, 195
Law School Admission Test (LSAT), 421

Lawshe, C. H., 773
Lazarsfeld, P. F., 795
LC (liquid chromatography), 569
LC-MS systems, 569
LD. *See* Local dependence
LDA (linear discriminant analysis), 704
Leading questions, 299–300
LeBreton, J. M., 732
Ledgerwood, A., 727
Lee, D. S., 29–30
Lee, S., 285
Left anterior negativity (LAN), 613
Leish, F., 213
Lemieux, T., 29–30
Lennox, R., 733
Leong, F. T. L., 135–137
Lesion approach to studying the brain, 677
Letter spaces, 471n3
Level 1 model. *See* Within-persons model
Level 2 model. *See* Between-persons model
Level of analysis, in cross-cultural studies, 104
Level-oriented studies, 103, 106
Levinson, A. J., 659
Levy, P., 462
Lexical chaining, 259
Lexical databases, 369
Lexical decision task, 494–495
Lexical variables, fixation duration and, 476–477
LGBTQ issues, research on, 108–109
Li, F., 764
Li, M., 763
Li, P., 212
Li, X., 682
Librarians, 154–155, 166
Library(-ies), 221, 222
Lie detection, 544
Light, R. J., 27
Likelihood, defined, 500
Likert scales, 172, 176, 460
LILACS (Latin American & Caribbean Health Sciences Literature), 160
Limits
   database, 162
   method of, 521
Lindenberger, U., 798
Linear coregistration, 636
Linear discriminant analysis (LDA), 704
Linearity assumption, 39
Linear model of trajectory, 329

Linear model with second-order nonlinear Volterra series, 699
Linear relationships, for observed and latent scores, 184
Linear support vector machine (SVM), 704
Linear trajectory, 347–348
Linear transformations, of data, 172, 175, 417–418
Line numbers, database, 162
Linguistic features of words, 368
Linguistic inquiry word count (LIWC) tool, 368
Linguistics and Language Behavior Abstracts (LLBA), 159
Linkage questions, 289
Linked conditions, 757
Linked earlobes reference, EEG, 588–589
Linn, R. L., 423–425
Lippmann, Walter, 770
Liquid chromatography (LC), 569
LISREL, 760
Literate programming, 213–217
Literature
   contribution of research to, 136
   knowledge of, 139
Literature reviews
   for initial item pool development, 385–386
   for parameter specification, 198, 199, 202–203
   research questions and, 136–138
Literature search process, 151–166
   completing, documenting, and reporting search, 165–166
   consulting librarian and selecting software tools, 154–155
   determining search parameters, 156–157
   determining type and purpose of search, 152–153
   developing search for most relevant database, 161–162
   searching for related reviews, 160
   selecting databases, 157–160
   selecting gray literature resources, 162–164
   translating search to other databases, 162, 163
   using other search techniques, 164–165
Litt, M. D., 334
Little, T. D., 775, 798–800
Live observation, 256–257

LIWC (linguistic inquiry word count) tool, 368
LLBA (Linguistics and Language Behavior Abstracts), 159
LLRs (long-latency responses), 609
Loading, on unrotated factor, 393
Loan repayment programs, 237
Loan Repayment Programs (LRPs), 237
Local customs, research violating, 111
Local dependence (LD)
    considering in factor analysis, 802–804
    and high slope parameters, 827
    parceling and, 800
Local independence, 177, 180
Localization
    of ERPs, 617–618
    in NBS experiments, 663
    in tDCS experiments, 666–667
Localizer scans, fMRI, 639
Local regulations, on animal research, 88
Local repositories, 218
Location, interview, 315–316
Locational cues, 475, 479, 482
Location parameters
    bunched, 828–829
    extreme, 829
    in item response model, 776, 777, 811, 816, 822
    for noncognitive measures, 828–829
Locus coeruleus, 484
Locus of Control Scale, 101
Loevinger, J., 383, 385, 386, 401
Logical deduction, xxv–xxvi
Logical positivism, 770
Logistic regression, 785–786
Logistic relationships, for observed and latent scores, 184
Logit link function, 776
Log odds, 270, 271
Lohman, D. F., 407
Long, J. S., 220
Longitudinal data, 737. *See also* Intensive longitudinal methods
Long-latency responses (LLRs), 609
Long outliers, 493, 498–500
Long-separation channels, 647
Long-term memory, 613, 686–687
Lookup searches, 152
Lord, F. M., 182, 746, 796
LORETA (low-resolution brain electromagnetic tomography), 25
Lower asymptote parameter, 815, 816
Lower limit of detection, 567
Low-income individuals, recruiting, 117

Low-resolution brain electromagnetic tomography (LORETA), 25
LRP (lateralized readiness potential), 614, 618–619
LRPs (Loan Repayment Programs), 237
LSA. *See* Latent semantic analysis
LSAT (Law School Admission Test), 421
Luce, R. D., 181
Lucht, M., 760
Luck, S. J., 608
Ludwig, C., 539
Ludwig, J., 288–289
Luminance, of stimuli, 485, 553
Lun, V. M.-C., 103
Lundberg, C. C., 141–142
Lykken, D. T., 538, 544

MacCallum, R. C., 798–800
MacCorquodale, K., 771
Mackenzie, D., 24, 40, 42
Mackie, J. L., 40, 43
Madill, A., 19, 20, 318
Magliano, J. P., 363, 367
Magnetic field strength, 633, 656–657
Magnetic resonance imaging (MRI). *See also* Functional magnetic resonance imaging (fMRI)
    fNIRS and PET vs., 632
    history of, 697
    sequential combination of NIBS with, 683
    structural vs. functional, 631
    in transcranial magnetic stimulation experiments, 664
Magnetoencephalography (MEG), 581–598
    defined, 581
    EEG/MEG–fMRI, 678–681
    electroencephalography vs., 674
    ERPs from, 617
    online combinations of fMRI and, 679
    other neuroimaging methods vs., 597–598
    preparing participants for, 585–588
    preventing electrode position shifts in, 589
    use of EEG vs., 581
    uses and limitations of, 674–675
Magnetoencephalography (MEG) signals. *See also* EEG/MEG signals
    about, 581–582
    method of recording, 582–583

Magnitude, of ERP component, 625
Magnitude estimation, 517
    interpreting study results for, 192–193
    psychophysical experiments for, 520, 523
    sample size for, 189, 195–197
    sample-size planning for, 190
Magnusson, D., 410, 418
Mail surveys, 286–288
Main effects, 754
Maisel, N. C., 335
Major depressive disorder, TMS studies of, 659–660
Maloney, L. T., 522
Manipulability of cause, 41, 43
Manual versions of files, controlling, 218
Many Labs, 206
mapca software, 710
Mapping reviews, 153
Mapping the Language of Racism (Wetherell and Potter), 313
MAPs (muscle action potentials), 547
Marginalized individuals and communities, 115–127
    future topics for effective research with, 127
    improving representativeness of samples involving, 117–121
    measurement equivalence for, 124–127
    naïve realist approaches with, 14
    translation of measures for, 121–124
Marianismo Beliefs Scale, 127
markdoc package, 214
Markers, defined, 532
Markers of inflammation, in saliva, 567
Markov assumption, 37
Markov chain Monte Carlo (MCMC) algorithms, 798
markstat package, 214
Markup language, writing text in, 214
Marsh, H. W., 799
"Martian perspective" strategy, 136
Martin, P., 253
Marxist analysis, 8
Masling, J. M., 438
Mass spectrometry (MS), 569
Mass univariate model. *See* General linear model (GLM)
Master file, in working directory, 221
Mastery testing. *See* Criterion-referenced testing

Mastoid process, 621
The Mathematics of Marriage (Gottman), 352
Matsumoto, D., 106
Matteucci, Carlo, 546
Maturation, threat of, 26
Matzke, D., 507
Maximum likelihood conjoint measurement (MLCM), 517, 523
Maximum likelihood difference scaling (MLDS), 517, 523
Maximum likelihood estimates (MLEs), 500, 797–798
Maxwell, S. E., 184, 202, 334
Maxwellian viewing conditions, 516
Mayer, R. E., 147
MBESS package, 203–205
McArdle, J. J., 771, 801
MCAT (Medical College Admission Test), 329, 421
McClendon, M. J., 282, 287
McCrae, R. R., 146
McDonald's omega, 414, 734, 735, 737
McGill, W. J., 507
McGrath, R. E., 436, 454
MCMC (Markov chain Monte Carlo) algorithms, 798
McNamara, D. S., 373
McNeish, D., 329
Mean
  of binary measures, 728
  of exGaussian distribution, 497
  regression to, 26
Mean amplitude, ERP, 625
Mean- and variance-adjusted weighted least squares (WLSMV) estimation, 799
Mean arterial blood pressure, 541
Mean bout duration, 267
Mean difference, 197, 200
Meaning, in qualitative research, 6–7
Meaning recollection, 8
Mean response times, 493–494
Mean scores, decision study, 750
Measurement
  behavioral observation as, 251
  defined, 251
  gray literature on, 164
  for hypothesis testing, 169
  in psychophysical experiments, 513–514, 517
  relationship of theory and, 169
Measurement bias, 98
Measurement equivalence, 124–127

Measurement error
  in classical test theory, 391
  with fixed-facet design, 757
  and generalizability theory, 745, 748–749, 764–765
  in G-studies, 747
  quantifying, 723, 737. *See also* Reliability
  in single-facet design, 749, 752
  and universe of generalizability, 747
Measurement invariance, 778–779, 800–802
Measurement methods, xxxvii–xl
Measurement paradigms, 183–184
Measurement quality, 737
Measurement reactivity, 333–334
Measurement scales, 169–186
  levels of, 170–173
  and measurement paradigms, 183–184
  permissible statistics based on, 182–183
  for psychological data, 173
  response-centered focus of, 174, 177–183
  and statistical inferences for latent traits, 184–185
  stimulus-centered focus of, 173–177
  subject-centered focus of, 173–175
  taxonomies of, 170
Measurement unit (metric) equivalence, 101–102, 126
Measurement windows, in ERP studies, 626, 627
Measuring instruments, described, 253
MedCalc, 849
Medial brain regions, NIBS for studying, 677
Media messages, 290
Medians, 499
Mediating mechanisms, xl, 140–141, 145
Mediation analysis, 726–727
Medical College Admission Test (MCAT), 329, 421
Medical gray literature, 164
Medical Subject Headings (MeSH) thesaurus, 160
Medicine databases, 160
MedicLatina, 160
Medline, 160
Medulla, cardiovascular activity and, 536
ME&E (mutually exclusive and exhaustive) codes, 254–255, 262

Meehl, P. E., 385, 769, 771, 784, 840, 850
MEG. *See* Magnetoencephalography
Mehl, M. R., 352
Mehta, P. H., 574
Melmoth, D., 512
MELODIC module, 702–703
Member check interviews, 318
Memory. *See also* Working memory
  ERP components related to, 613
  long-term, 613, 686–687
  theta burst stimulation in studies of, 686
Memory hypothesis of question order effects, 288
Memory work, 13
Menstrual cycle, hormone levels over, 570
Mental activity, monitoring, 607
Mental disorders, ERP studies of, 614
Mental effort, pupil dilation and, 553
Mental extensity, 408
Mental Health Research Dissertation Grant to Enhance Workforce Diversity (R36), 238
Mental load, pupil dilation and, 483–484
Mental maps, 136
Mental Measurements Yearbook, 164
Mental retardation, measures of, 408
Mentored Clinical Scientist Research Career Development Award (K08), 236–237
Mentored Patient-Oriented Research Career Development Award (K23), 236–237
Mentored Research Scientist Development Award (K01), 236
MEP. *See* Motor-evoked potential
Meredith, W., 801
Merge conflicts, git, 219–220
mergetools, git, 220
Merrens, M. R., 144, 147–148
MeSH (Medical Subject Headings) thesaurus, 160
Messick, S., 385, 763, 771
Meta-analysis, xli, xliii
Method, in psychophysical experiments, 517, 520–522
Method bias, 99, 100
Method facet. *See* Instrumentation facet
Method factor loadings, CT-CM model, 782
Method of adjustment, 521–523
Method of constant stimuli, 520–521

Method of limits, 521
Method of tenacity, xxv
Methodology, effect size and, xlii
Method variance, of measures, 783
Metric (measurement unit) equivalence, 101–102, 126
Metric invariance model, 778
Metropolis-Hastings Robbins-Monro (MH-RM) algorithm, 798
Metropolitan Achievement Tests, 419
Metz, C. E., 854
Meyer, G. J., 383, 438
Meyer, S. S., 589
mGENOVA program, 760, 761
MGT (multivariate generalizability theory), 757–758
MH-RM (Metropolis-Hastings Robbins-Monro) algorithm, 798
Michell, J., 185
Microsaccades, 470
Microsoft Stream transcript VTT file cleaner, 322
Mid-latency responses (MLRs), 609
MIES (minimally important effect size) approach, 198–200, 203
Mihura, J. L., 438–439
Mill, John Stuart, 40
Miller, D. T., 199
Millionshort, 163
Millman, J., 423
Millsap, R. E., 801
Mind wandering, 469
Minerva Research Initiative, 229
Minimally important effect size (MIES) approach, 198–200, 203
Minimal risk classification, 63
Minnesota Multiphasic Personality Inventory (MMPI), 438, 439
Minnesota Multiphasic Personality Inventory, 3rd edition (MMPI-3), 415
Minors, HIPAA rules for, 61
mirt software, 811
Mischel, W., 433
Mismatch negativity (MMN), 612
Misses. *See* False negatives
Mistakes, in longitudinal study diaries, 336
Mitchell, J., 169
Mitra, A., 680
Mixed-effects decision studies, 754
Mixed-methods approach, research questions for, 144
Mixed-model studies, generalizability analysis for, 756–757

Mixed-mode surveys, 293
MIXED procedure, 345–346
Mixed processes, response time for, 496
MLCM (maximum likelihood conjoint measurement), 517, 523
MLDS (maximum likelihood difference scaling), 517, 523
MLEs (maximum likelihood estimates), 500, 797–798
MLRs (mid-latency responses), 609
MMN (mismatch negativity), 612
MMPI (Minnesota Multiphasic Personality Inventory), 438, 439
MMPI-3 (Minnesota Multiphasic Personality Inventory, 3rd edition), 415
MNI (Montreal Neurological Institute) atlas, 636
MNLFA (moderated nonlinear factor analysis) models, 801
Mobile web surveys, 287–288
Model building, 144
Model-dependence of inference frameworks, 42–44
Model development, in workflow, 213
Model error variance, 193
Model fitting, 500–501
Moderated nonlinear factor analysis (MNLFA) models, 801
Moderated regression analysis, 185
Moderate relationships, odds ratios for, 270
Moderate social constructionism, 16, 17
Moderation effects, 349–350
Moderation strategy, for research questions formulation, 145
Modularity, of network, 707–708
Modularity index (Q), 707–708
Module, of nodes, 707
Module detection, 707
Momentary codes, 259
Momentary sampling, 257
Monotonic relationships, 184, 200, 810
Monotonic transformation, 172
Monotrait-heteromethod correlations, 782
Monotrait-monomethod correlations, 782
Monte Carlo simulations, 501
Montreal Neurological Institute (MNI) atlas, 636
Mood biases, 734
Morgan, M. J., 512
Morgan, S. L., 39
Morlet wavelet, 591

Mossman, D., 850
Mosteller, F., 505
Motion correction, fMRI, 636
Motivation
  affective-valence model of, 592–595, 661
  frontal lateralization theories of, 657, 661, 665
  heart rate/interbeat interval and, 538
  in intensive longitudinal studies, 332–333
  rTMS studies of emotion and, 661
  single-pulse TMS studies of emotion and, 657–659
Motivational direction model of frontal asymmetry, 593–595
Motor cortex, TMS/tES and fMRI studies of, 683
Motor ERP components, 608, 614
Motor-evoked potential (MEP), 657, 658, 660, 663, 664, 682
Motor theories of thinking, 546
Motor unit of muscle, 547
Movement, neuroimaging artifacts due to, 534, 587, 636
Moving-mask technique, 473, 478, 481
Moving-window technique, 473, 478, 481
Mplus, 339, 353, 760
MRI. *See* Magnetic resonance imaging
MS (mass spectrometry), 569
MTMM (multitrait–multimethod) design, 399–400, 781–784
Muccio, D. J., 135–137
Müller, Johannes, 546
Müller-Frommeyer, L. C., 368
Multiband fMRI, 634
Multidimensional coding, 258–259
Multidimensionality
  IRT models for constructs with, 826–827
  item-level factor analysis to explore, 804
  length of measure and, 457
  parceling with, 799–800
  and stimulus-centered approach, 175
Multidimensional language analysis, 375
Multidimensional measures, short forms for, 460
Multidisciplinary databases, 159–160
Multiecho fMRI, 634
Multievent data, 261, 266–268
Multifaceted populations, 762

Multifacet generalizability analysis, 752–756
   decision study, 753–756
   generalizability study, 752–753
   random-effects $p \times i \times r$ example, 754–756
Multigroup confirmatory factor analysis, 126
Multi-informant diaries, 353
Multilevel analysis, 345–346
Multilevel modeling, 106, 341, 737
Multilevel studies, 103, 106
Multimodal automated language analysis, 375
Multimodal imaging, 663, 673–674. *See also* Combined neuroimaging methods
Multiple comparison issue, 626, 698–699
Multiple-document comprehension, 367–368
Multiple group approach to measurement invariance, 778–779
Multiple interviewers, projects with, 314–315
Multiple operationism, xxxix–xl
Multiple regression
   in analysis of latent traits, 184
   for fMRI data, 636–637
   omnibus vs. targeted effect sizes for, 191
   sample-size planning for, 201–206
Multiproject awards, 241–242
Multi-pulse protocols, 684
Multisite studies, 206, 227
Multitasking, ERP studies of, 607
Multitrait–multimethod (MTMM) design, 399–400, 781–784
Multivariate analysis
   brief instruments for, 452
   independent component analysis, 700–702
   multilevel, 353
   multivoxel pattern analysis, 703–706
   of neuroimaging data, 700–706
   principal component analysis, 702–703
   unreliable measurement in, 726
Multivariate generalizability analysis, 757–760
   computer programs for, 761
   decision study, 758–759
   generalizability study, 757–758
   $p^\bullet \times i^\bullet$ example, 759–760

Multivariate generalizability theory (MGT), 757–758
Multivariate pattern analysis, 614–616
Multivoxel pattern analysis, 703–706
Munafò, M. R., 213
Muraki, E., 824
Murdock, B. B., Jr., 501
Murphy-Hill, E., 212
Murray, H. A., 434, 435, 439, 441, 442
Muscle action potentials (MAPs), 547
Muscle artifacts, 586–587
Muscular activity
   anatomy and physiology related to, 547
   measurement of, 548–553
   neural control over, 547–548
   physiologic measures of, 546–553
Music, synchronization of neural oscillations to, 597
Muthén, B., 205
Mutual associations, 343
Mutually exclusive and exhaustive (ME&E) codes, 254–255, 262
Mutually exclusive states, distinguishing, 837
MY Access, 364

N1 wave, in oddball paradigm, 611
N2a ERP component, 612
N2c ERP component, 612
N2pc ERP component, 612
N170 ERP component, 605–608
N400 ERP component, 613
Naber, M., 485
Naglieri, J. A., 443
Naison, 585–586
Naïve observers, 519
Naïve realist approaches, 13–14
Nakayama, K., 485
Naming conventions
   EEG electrode, 583, 584
   ERP, 608–609
   and projective tests, 434–437
Nanda, H., 735
Narayan, S., 289
Narrative analysis, 13
Narrative interviews, 298
Narrative reviews, 152–153
Narrow conceptual bandwidth, 828, 830
Narrow tests, 384
Nasal application of oxytocin, 566

National Academies of Science, Engineering, and Medicine, 90
National Center for Posttraumatic Stress Disorder, 158
National Center for Veterans Affairs, 158
National Commission for the Protection of Human Subjects of Biomedical and Behavioral Research (Belmont Report), 60
National Comorbidity Survey Replication (NCS-R), 837–838
National Council on Measurement in Education (NCME), 385, 771
National Defense Science and Engineering Graduate (NDSEG) Fellowship Program, 229
National Institute of Child Health and Human Development, 783–784
National Institute of Mental Health (NIMH), 229
National Institute on Minority Health and Health Disparities (NIMHD), 241
National Institutes of Health (NIH), 74–75, 87
   business technology and innovation grants from, 241
   fellowship and training grants from, 234–239
   funding opportunity announcements, 232
   grant review process of, 242–244
   grants for investigators from underrepresented backgrounds from, 237–238
   multiproject and center funding from, 241–242
   project-focused grants from, 241
   research funding by, 229
Nationalism, 289
National Library of Medicine, 160
National Opinion Research Center (NORC), 279
National Preparedness System, 90
National Research Act (1974), 60, 62
National Research Council, 87, 90
National Science Foundation (NSF), 229, 239, 337
National Television System Committee (NTSC) standard, 259, 261
Natural behavior, 252–253
Naturalistic task fMRI, 643–645

Natural language processing (NLP)
  for emotional state prediction, 368–369
  of essay responses with, 363–366
  in intelligent tutoring systems, 370–375
  modeling psychological processes with, 369–370
  overview of assessment with, 366–367
  in research on psychological attributes and processes, 367–370
  response scoring with, 362–367
  of short responses, 362–363
Nazi war crimes, 59, 60
NBS. *See* Noninvasive brain stimulation (NIBS)
NCLB. *See* No Child Left Behind Act
NCME (National Council on Measurement in Education), 385, 771
NCS-R (National Comorbidity Survey Replication), 837–838
NDSEG (National Defense Science and Engineering Graduate) Fellowship Program, 229
Necessary connection, in causal relationship, xxxii
Need for Cognition, 147
Needleman–Wunsch algorithm, 263
Needs, TAT as indicator of, 442
Negative predictive power, 837, 839, 843–844
Negative variance components, 754
Neighborhood safety studies, 284
Neocortex, EEG sensitivity to, 674
NEO Personality Inventory Revised, 146
NEO Personality Inventory Revised (NEO PI-R), 457
Nerve tissue, in tDCS, 664, 666
Nervous system, origin of ERPs in, 616–618
Nesselroade, J. R., 798
Nested analytic units, 251
Nested studies
  decision, 754, 756
  generalizability, 754
  reliability, 730
  with time-based designs, 331
Network analyses, xli, 706–709
  basics of, 706
  of functional and effective connectivity, 708–709
  metrics for, 706–708
  software packages for, 709
Network metrics, 706–708
Neural activity, BOLD signals and, 675–676
Neural control
  over cardiovascular activity, 536–537
  over muscular activity, 547–548
  over sudomotor activity, 543–544
Neural decoding, 704
Neural networks, for decoding analysis, 704–705
Neural oscillations model, 597
Neurohackademy lecture series, 706
Neuroimaging analysis methods, 697–710
  general linear model, 697–700
  independent component analysis, 700–702
  multivariate models, 700–706
  multivoxel pattern analysis, 703–706
  network analyses, 706–709
  principal component analysis, 702–703
  software for fMRI analysis, 710
Neuroimaging studies
  with combined methods. *See* Combined neuroimaging methods
  data analysis in. *See* Neuroimaging analysis methods
  functional. *See* Functional neuroimaging
Neurons, EEG/MEG activity and, 582
Neurophysiology, 513, 685
Neuropredict package, 705, 710
Neuroscientific measures
  from combined neuroimaging methods, 673–690
  from electro- and magneto-encephalography, 581–598
  event-related potentials, 605–627
  from functional neuroimaging, 631–649
  and neuroimaging analysis methods, 697–710
  noninvasive brain stimulation for, 655–668
NeuroSynth, 638
Neurovisceral integration model, 540
New areas of interest, F32 award for research in, 235
Newman, M. E. J., 707
New research skills and expertise, F33 award for, 235
New settings, F32 NRSA award for research in, 235
Newtonian viewing conditions, 516
Neyman, J., 28
Neyman-Rubin model. *See* Potential outcomes (PO) framework
NHST (null hypothesis significance testing), 191–192
NIBS. *See* noninvasive brain stimulation (NBS)
NIH. *See* National Institutes of Health
NIH Pathway to Independence Award (K99/R00), 237
NIH Research Supplements to Promote Diversity, 238
Nilearn package, 705
NIMH (National Institute of Mental Health), 229
NIMHD (National Institute on Minority Health and Health Disparities), 241
Nipype tool, 635, 700, 710
Nix, B., 574
nlme package, 352, 700
NLP. *See* Natural language processing
No Child Left Behind Act (NCLB), 415, 426, 787–788
Nock, M. K., 332
No hidden variation of treatments assumption, 29
No interference assumption, 29
Noise
  and ERP data, 619, 621, 623
  explicit modeling of fMRI, 699–700
  fixational eye movements as, 470
  Gaussian term for, 701
  internal, 515, 522
  in physiological measures, 533–534
  signal-plus-noise distribution, 515
  signal-to-noise ratio, 633, 647
Nominal response model (NRM), 819–825
Nominal scale, 256
  described, 170–171
  statistical analysis for data in, 183, 186
  statistical inference with, 173
Nomological networks, 101
Nonability tests, 383–384
Nonadaptive methods, 520
Nonbiological artifacts, 588
Noncausal association, 34
Noncausal path, 33–35
Noncentrality parameter, 193–195
Noncognitive measures, IRT model for, 827–830

Nonexperiments (observational studies), 30, 47, 251
Nonhuman animals, research with, 83–91
  alternatives to, 85–86
  and animal rights vs. animal welfare, 85
  annual reviews and reporting concerns related to, 89–90
  concern for laboratory animal welfare, 85–87
  IACUC approval for, 88–89
  pain and distress classifications for, 89
  researchers' responsibilities related to, 91
  and research ethics vs. regulations, 83–85
  U.S. oversight of, 87–88
  voluntary accreditations for programs, 90–91
Nonindependence, in multi-informant diaries, 353
Noninvasive brain stimulation (NBS; NIBS), 655–668
  developments in field of, 663–664
  limitations of, 668
  limitations with, 676–677
  NIBS–EEG, 686–689
  NIBS–fMRI, 681–686
  spatial resolution and localization in experiments with, 663
  transcranial direct-current stimulation, 664–668
  transcranial magnetic stimulation, 655–664
  uses of, 655, 668, 676–677
Nonleading questions, 299–300
Nonlinear coregistration, 636
Nonlinear functional PCA, 702
Nonlinear ICA, 702
Nonlinear relationships, for observed and latent scores, 184, 185
Nonlinear SVM, 704–705
Nonmaleficence. See Beneficence and Nonmaleficence (Principle A)
Nonnormal distributions, parceling in, 799
Nonparametric statistics, 183, 186, 849
Nonparametric structural model, 31
Nonpolarizable electrodes, EEG, 583
Nonprototypic content, short forms omitting, 458–459
Nonreductionism, 41
Nonspecific skin conductance responses (NS-SCRs), 545

Nonuniform differential item functioning, 779, 780
Nonverbal organisms, studies with, 252
NORC (National Opinion Research Center), 279
Normal curve, 410–411
Normality assumptions, 799
Normalization transformation, 418
Norm groups, 414–417, 439
Norm of reciprocity (even-handedness), 281, 283, 286, 289, 292
Norm-referenced testing, 174, 407–422
  criterion-referenced vs., 407, 423, 427
  in early modern psychological testing, 408–410
  history of, 429
  internal consistency reliability in, 413–414
  item response theory approaches to, 421–422
  norms and norm groups in, 414–417
  score distributions for, 417–419
  switching from, 426
  test item as unit of assessment in, 411–413
  uses of, 419–421
Norms, 414–417
North American Society of Pacing and Electrophysiology, 539
North Korea, 281
Notes, of interviews, 321
"Not-knowing" stance, of interviewers, 308–309
Novelty P3 component, 612
Novelty Seeking scale, Temperament and Character Inventory, 453
Novice investigators, research ideas for, 139–141
Novick, M. R., 796
NRM (nominal response model), 819–825
NSF. See National Science Foundation
NS-SCRs (nonspecific skin conductance responses), 545
NTSC (National Television System Committee) standard, 259, 261
Nucleus tractus solitarius, 537
Nuijten, M. B., 211–212
Null distribution, for statistical power, 194
Null hypothesis, xli–xlii
Null hypothesis significance testing (NHST), 191–192
Null networks, generating, 708

Numerosity tasks, 494–495
Nuremberg Code, 60
Nyquist theorem, 585

OB1-reader model, 477
Objectives-based testing. See Criterion-referenced testing
Objectives of research, xxv–xliv. See also Goals of research
  causal explanatory research, xxxi–xxxiv
  on construct validity, 772
  and democracy/science, xxviii
  finding methods that fit, xxix–xxx
  on individual change vs. group difference, xxxiv–xxxvi
  and interpreting effect size/relation strength, xli–xlii
  interpretive research, xxx–xxxi
  and methods of knowing, xxv–xxvi
  and multiple operationism, xxxix–xl
  and nature of scientific investigation, xxvii–xxviii
  quantitative data analysis, xl–xliv
  relationship between research design and question, xxxvi–xxxvii
  and transparency, xliii–xliv
Objectives of test, content validity and, 773
Objective tests, 383–401
  classifications of, 383–384
  external validation of, 398–401
  in history of psychometrics, 384–385
  projective vs., 383, 434
  structural validation of, 388–398
  substantive validation of, 385–388
Objectivity, 19, 182
Objects of measurement
  in G-studies, 746–747
  in principle of symmetry, 761
  in universe of generalization, 747
O'Brien, D. J., 282
O'Brien, R. G., 198–199
Observation
  behavioral. See Behavioral observation
  knowing through, xxv
Observational sessions, as analytic units, 252
Observational studies (nonexperiments), 30, 47, 251
Observed joint frequency, 268
Observed scores, relationship of latent and, 184–185

Observers
    agreement between, 262–266
    defined, 256
    in psychophysical experiments, 517–519
Obuchowski, N. A., 849
Occasion facet, in generalizability analysis, 752
Oddball paradigm and stimulus, 610
Odds ratio, 269–271
Offering Inducements for Research Participation (Standard 8.06), 69
Office of Human Research Protections, 61
Office of Laboratory Animal Welfare (OLAW), 87, 88, 91
Offline combination. *See also* Sequential combination
    of EEG/MEG and fMRI, 678–679
    of TMS and tES, 677, 687
Offline reference, for EEG, 589
Offset time, 258–260
O'Key, Victoria, 314, 315
OLAW. *See* Office of Laboratory Animal Welfare
Older participants, study diaries for, 337
OLS (ordinary least squares) method, 697
Omega, McDonald's, 414, 734, 735, 737
Omission, to eliminate question order effects, 292
Omnibus effect size, 191, 203–205
One-parameter logistic model (1PLM), 421, 814, 817
One-shot approach to community research, 110–111
One-way analysis of variance (ANOVA)
    directionality information from, 192
    intraclass correlation statistics from, 730
    omnibus vs. targeted effect sizes for, 191
Online assessment, with variable-interval designs, 331
Online combinations. *See also* Simultaneous combinations
    of EEG and fMRI methods, 679–680
    of NIBS and EEG methods, 689
Online interviews, 316–317, 322
Online psychophysical experiments, 516, 519
Onset time, 258–260
Open fields, 582
Open-minded skepticism, xxviii
OpenNeuro, 649

Open path, causal graph, 33, 35
Open questions, 300–302
Open science, xliii, xliv, 525
Open Science Framework, 212, 649
Operational definitions, xxxix–xl
Operational paradigm of measurement, 186
Opinion extraction, 369
Optical illusions, xxvi–xxviii
OptimalCutpoints package, 849
Optimal global alignment algorithm, 263
Optimizing behavior, question order effects and, 289
Optodes, 646
Optseq, 639
Oral hormone administration, 566
Order effects, 350
Ordinal scale, 256
    described, 171–172
    for Guttman scale model, 179
    judgments on, 517, 520
    kappa with, 265
    perceptual, 520
    raters using, 256
    reliability estimates for responses on, 736
    statistical analysis for data in, 183, 186
    statistical inference with, 173
Ordinary least squares (OLS) method, 697
Organizational behavior example of sample-size planning, 201–206
    AIPE approach, 204–205
    power analytic approach, 202–203
Organizational hormone effects, 565–566
Organization for Human Brain Mapping, 709
Origin, for ratio scale, 172
Orthogonal rotations, for item selection, 389
Oscillations
    EEG/MEG studies of, 674
    ERP studies with, 623–625, 627
    NIBS–EEG studies of, 689
Oscillometric method of measuring blood pressure, 540
Outcomes, defined, 532
Outcome variable, effect size and value of, xlii
Outlier response times, 498–500
    and goodness-of-fit measures, 507
    long, 493, 498–499
    power of ANOVA and, 499–500

and shape of hazard function, 496
    short, 498, 501
    and skewness of distribution, 506
Outliers (Gladwell), 139
Outside events, in causal systems, xxxii
Overall accuracy, 786
Overall utility
    base rate and, 850–852
    cutoff scores based on, 850, 855–856
    defined, 839
    information gain vs., 855
    and utility ratio, 852–854
Overgeneralization, of cross-cultural findings, 110
Overinclusiveness, 386, 388
Overlapping ERP components, 625, 627
Oversight
    by institution, 61–63
    of nonhuman animal studies, 84, 87–88
Overt behavior, measures of, xxxviii
Oxytocin, 566, 568
Ozdemir, R. A., 689

P01 grant (Research Program Project Grant), 241
P1 wave, in oddball paradigm, 610–611
P3a ERP component, 612
P3b ERP component, 611–612, 614
P3 ERP component, 609, 611–612
    averaging trials in studies of, 623
    difference wave for, 618, 619
P30 grants (Center Core Grants), 241
P50 grant (Specialized Center Grant), 241
P50 research (Centers of Excellence Environmental Health Disparities research), 241
P300 ERP component, 609, 611
Pain, in research with nonhuman animals, 88, 89
Paired-pulse TMS, 659–660, 663
Pairwise comparison tasks, 517, 520
PAL (Phase Alternating Line) standard, 259
PANAS-X. *See* Positive and Negative Affect Schedule
Panicker, S., 84
Paper-and-pencil recording
    of behavioral observations, 260
    in longitudinal study diaries, 335–336
PAR (postauricular reflex), 551
Parafilm®, 572
Parafovea, 471, 474

Parafoveal-on-foveal effects, 474–475
Parallel ICA, 702
Parallel items, reliability for, 733
Parallel processing, saccades in, 482
Parameters
  estimating, for ex- and inverse Gaussian distributions, 497–498
  for literature search, 156–157
  specification of, 197–201
Parametric statistics, scales permitting use of, 183, 186
Parametrization of stimuli, 514
Paraphrasing, in iSTART, 372
Parceling items, 798–800
Parent announcements, 233
Parents, consent from, 71
"Parents," causal graph, 32, 33
Parietal cortex, rTMS of, 664
Partial construct validity invariance, 125–126
Partial correlation, for network analysis, 709
Partial credit model (PCM), 776–777, 824–826
Partial-interval sampling, 257, 258
Partial invariance, 126, 801–802
Partially nested decision studies, 748
Participant burden, 332, 333, 336
Participant considerations
  with fMRI, 634
  with physiological measures, 534–535
Participant information sheet, 319
Participant-informed research, 75–77
Participant screening, for hormone assays, 569–571
Participant training, for intensive longitudinal studies, 332
Participant validation, 318
Part-part effect, 281, 292
Part (specific) question, 279–282
Part-whole effect, 280, 292
Pascual-Leone, A., 662
Passband, EMG, 549
Passive consent, 71
Passive drooling, 572
Passive electrode systems, EEG, 583
Path analysis, 799
Path length, in network analysis, 708
Paths, causal graph, 33, 34
Patient-Centered Outcomes Research Institute (PCORI), 232
Patient Reported Outcomes Measurement Information System (PROMIS) study, 802–804

Pattern Recognition for Neuroimaging Toolbox (PRoNTo), 705, 710
Pavlovia (platform), 519
P awards (Program Project/Center Grants), 241
Payment in-kind, 69
PCA. See Principal components analysis
PCORI (Patient-Centered Outcomes Research Institute), 232
Peabody Picture Vocabulary Test, 415
Peak amplitude, ERP, 625, 627
Peak latency, ERP, 625
Peaks, ERP, 605
Pearl, J., 23, 24, 39, 40, 42, 46
Pearl growing, 165
Pearson Assessments, 409
Pearson correlation, 340, 397, 709
Pearson Knowledge Technologies, 363
Pearson's second skewness measure, 506
Pearson's skewness measure, 497
Pecchinenda, A., 545–546
Peer effects, 29
Peer Review of Electronic Search Strategy (PRESS) checklist, 161
Peer writing evaluations, 366
Peirce, Charles, xxv–xxvii
Pember-Reeves, M., 327
Pennebaker, J. W., 368
Peptide hormones, 567
Perceived control, 535
Percent correct
  by chance, 839, 840
  cutoff values to maximize, 850–852
  defined, 839, 840
Percentile rank, 417
Perception, 511
  psychophysics to predict mechanisms of, 513
  psychophysics to quantify, 512–513
  signal detection theory and, 515
  stimulus-centered approach to studying, 175
Perceptual contour integration, 682
Perceptual span, 473, 478, 481
Performance-based measures, 408, 444, 445
Perimetric physiological measures, 531–553
  ambient noise and, 533–534
  artifacts in, 534
  baselines for, 533
  of cardiovascular activity, 535–542
  inferential challenges with, 532–533

  of muscular activity, 546–553
  participant considerations when using, 534–535
  of sudomotor activity, 542–546
Peripheral nerve stimulation, artifacts due to, 688
Peripheral vision, 471
Perry, M., 593
Personal experience, questions based on, 135–136
Personality traits
  brief instruments for, 457
  performance-based measures of, 444
  temporal instability in, 397–398
Personal Problem-Solving System–Revised, 442
Personal representatives for minors, 61
Person-centered counselor role, 12
Personnel selection, norm-referenced testing for, 421
PET. See Positron emission tomography
Peterson, N. S., 419
Pet Protection Act, 87
Petty, R. E., 137, 138, 144–147, 283
Peytchev, A., 287
PFA (principal factor analysis), 389
Pfabigan, D. M., 679
PFC (prefrontal cortex), 661, 665
Phase Alternating Line (PAL) standard, 259, 261
Phase locking, 667–668, 689
Phase variability, in ERP trials, 623–625
Phenomenological knowledge, 11, 12, 14–16
PHI (protected health information), 61
Phi coefficient, 270
Philosophical issues
  causal inference frameworks, 23–50
  epistemological bases for qualitative research, 5–21
Phosphenes, 682
Photo-elicitation methods, 317
Photorealistic rendering, 524
Photovoice methods, 317
PHS (U.S. Public Health Service), 87, 89
Physically based codes, 255
Picture Frustration Study, 433
Pierce, G. L., 479–480
Pilot studies
  coding scheme in, 253–254
  of diary format, 339
  in initial item pool development, 387
  publication bias for, 199–200
  reliability estimates in, 738
  of translated materials, 124

$p \times i \times r$ study design, 754–756
$p^\bullet \times i^\bullet$ study design, 758–760
$p^\bullet \times i^\circ$ study design, 758
$p \times i$ study design, 751–752
Piswanger, K., 100
Plant-based research, 86
Plausible rival hypotheses, 26
Plesser, H. E., 212
Plethysmography, 541
Pluralistic qualitative research designs, 20–21
PO framework. See Potential outcomes framework
Point-biserial correlation coefficient, 412–413
Point estimates, effect size, 195
Point of subjective equality (PSE), 514, 517
Poisson model, 699
Polanía, R., 687
Polarity, ERP component, 616
Polarizable electrodes, EEG, 583
Polarization, of nerve tissue, 664
Poldrack, R. A., 633
Politics
  qualitative research involving, 9–10
  question order effects in, 278–283, 290
Polychoric correlation matrix, 797
Polyester rolls, for saliva collection, 572, 573
Polytomous IRT models
  Rasch model, 825–826
  unidimensional, 817–824
Polytomous responses
  factor analysis for, 794–796
  item response theory models for, 776–777
Polyvagal theory, 538–539
Ponterotto, J. G., 17
Popham, W. J., 414, 424, 426, 427
Popularity of response category, 821
Population, defining, 416
Population-based surveys, 278
Population covariance structure, CT-CM model, 782
Population effect size, 204
Porcerelli, J. H., 442
Porges, S. W., 538
Pornprasertmanit, S., 734
Porter, G., 484
Positive affect, alpha power and, 595
Positive and Negative Affect Schedule (PANAS-X), 389, 393, 397

Positive predictive power, 837, 839, 842–844
Positivist approach, 18
Positivity assumption, 29
Positron emission tomography (PET), 647–648
  correlations between EEG/MEG measures and, 597–598
  MRI and fNIRS vs., 632
  sequential combination of EEG/MEG and, 678
  transcranial magnetic stimulation with, 663
Postauricular reflex (PAR), 551
Postdictive validity, 779
Postdoctoral trainees, 235, 237
Post hoc coding, 259
Postpositivist approach, 18
Postqualitative research, 18
Postsynaptic potentials (PSPs), 581–582, 616
Posttraumatic stress disorder (PTSD), 454, 455, 457
Potency dimension, for emotion words, 369
Potential outcomes, defined, 28, 41–42
Potential outcomes (PO) framework, 23
  causal generalization and replication in, 46
  causal identification in, 45
  definition of causal effects, 44
  described, 28–31
  estimation of causal effects/statistical inference in, 45
  joint use of, 50
  philosophy of causation for, 41–43
  research designs for causal interference in, 48–49
  subject matter theory in, 46, 47
  theory of cause for, 43–44
  VT and SCM vs., 48–50
Potter, J., 313, 323
Powell, S. G., 212
Power
  alpha, 595
  of ANOVA, 499–500
  discriminatory, 812, 845–849
  and interview location, 315, 316
  in interviews, 309, 319–320
  predictive, 837, 839, 842–844
  statistical, 88, 193–195, 198, 641
Power analytic approach to sample-size planning, 193–195
  organizational behavior example, 202–203

  parameter specification for, 198–200
  research goals appropriate for, 190, 193
  statistical power for omnibus effect, 203
  statistical power for targeted effect, 202–203
Power-law distribution, 707
Power spectra, converting EEG signals to, 590
Practical significance, xlii, 139
Pratt, H., 611
Preacher, K. J., 190
Precision. See also Reliability
  of code-unit grid, 260
  of estimates from intensive longitudinal studies, 333
  in generalizability theory, 764
  of hormone assays, 568
  of interval data, 257
  and narrowband constructs, 828
  quantifying, 737
Prediction
  from base rate, 839–841
  change, 350–352
  in iSTART, 372
  validity and, 420
Predictive power
  negative, 837, 839, 843–844
  positive, 837, 839, 842–844
Predictive validity, 385, 400, 779
Predictors. See Independent variables
Predoctoral students, 234–235, 239
Preferred Reporting Items for Systematic Reviews and Meta-Analyses (PRISMA), 153, 166
Preferred viewing location, 475
Prefrontal cortex (PFC), 661, 665
Prejudice, 545, 550
Preliminary studies, reliability values for, 727
Prentice, D. A., 199
Preoperational phase of construct validity research, 769–770
Preprocessing, of fMRI data, 635–636, 643, 645
Prescott, C. A., 771
Prescott, S., 327
PRESS (Peer Review of Electronic Search Strategy) checklist, 161
Presser, S., 277–282, 288–291
Prestimulus baseline period, 619–620, 623, 626
Preston, K. S., 821
Prevalence. See Base rate

891

Preview benefit
  in reading, 473–474
  in scene perception, 478–479
  for visual search, 481–482
Preview region, of perceptual span, 481
Prewhitening method, 700
Primary motor cortex, 663, 682
Priming, 285, 474
PRIM&R (Public Responsibility in Medicine and Research), 91
Princeton MVPA Toolbox, 705, 710
Principal components analysis (PCA), 389, 700, 702–703
Principal factor analysis (PFA), 389
Prins, N., 512, 513, 522
Priori, A., 664
PRISMA (Preferred Reporting Items for Systematic Reviews and Meta-Analyses), 153, 166
Privacy, confidentiality and, 74
Privilege, 115–117
Probabilistic assignment mechanism, 29, 30
Probabilistic independent component analyses, 701–702
Probabilistic maps, regions of interest defined by, 638–639
Probabilistic models of scaling, 180–182
Probability, for observational data, 267, 268
Probability density function, 495, 497, 505
Probit link function, 774–776
Procedural remedies for low reliability, 727
Professional services, 68, 69
Progesterone, 568, 570
Program Project/Center Grants (P awards), 241
Progressive enhancement, 689
Project-focused grants (R awards), 239–241
Projective hypotheses, 434, 436
Projective tests, 433–445
  alternatives to name for, 436–437
  association of performance-based measures with, 445
  features of, 434
  figure drawings in, 442–444
  objective vs., 383, 434
  optimal, 444
  problems with name of, 434–436
  Rorschach inkblots in, 437–440
  Thematic Apperception Test, 439, 441–442

Project MUSE, 158
Prolific (platform), 519
PROMIS (Patient Reported Outcomes Measurement Information System) study, 802–804
Prompts, interview, 305
PRoNTo (Pattern Recognition for Neuroimaging Toolbox), 705, 710
Propensity scores, 30, 31
Proportional thresholding, 707
Proprioceptors, 537
ProQuest, 157–159
Protected health information (PHI), 61
Protocol scoring, for Rorschach inkblots, 437
Protocol submission to IRB, 62
Provisional causality, 42
Proximity operators, 162
PSE (point of subjective equality), 514, 517
PSPs (postsynaptic potentials), 581–582, 616
PsycArticles, 158
PsycBooks, 158
Psychiatric conditions, informed consent from individuals with, 70, 75–76
Psychoanalytic theory, 8, 12, 14
Psychogenic sweating, 543–544
Psychological Bulletin, 137, 140
Psychological category, in LIWC, 368
Psychological Review, 137
Psychological Science Accelerator, 206
Psychological tests. *See also* Test performance
  brief instruments and short-form, 451–464
  norm- and criterion-referenced testing, 407–429
  objective, 383–401
  projective, 433–445
  research question and selection of, 146
Psychology (field)
  causal inference in, 23
  measurements from outside discipline of, xxxviii
  objective tests in other areas vs., 401
  opportunities for research in, 227
Psychology and Behavioral Sciences Collection, 158
Psychometric analysis, xxxvii–xl
  of intensive longitudinal data, 340–341

issues with criterion-referenced testing, 425–429
  objective tests in history of, 384–385
  with projective tests, 433–434
Psychometric function, 515, 517, 522
Psychometricians' fallacy, 185
Psychopathology
  hierarchical models of, 384
  resting frontal asymmetry and, 593
Psychophysical experiments, 513–523
  analysis in, 522–523
  measure in, 513–514
  method in, 520–522
  observer in, 518–519
  stimulus in, 514, 516, 518
  task in, 519–520
  terminology for, 517–518
Psychophysical measures, 511–525
  defined, 511–512
  experiments with, 513–523
  future research directions for, 523–525
  selecting, 513–514
  terminology related to, 517–518
  uses of, 512–513
Psychophysics (field), 512, 516, 525
Psychophysics Toolbox, 525
Psychophysiological measures, xxxviii
  perimetric measures, 531–553
  salivary hormone assays, 565–575
PsychoPy, 525
PsycInfo database, 157, 158, 161, 164
PsycNet, 157
PTSD. *See* Posttraumatic stress disorder
PTSDpubs, 158
Publication bias, 156, 199
Publication Manual of the American Psychological Association (APA), xliii, 195
Public charities, 229–230, 232
Public opinion studies, 277–283
Public Responsibility in Medicine and Research (PRIM&R), 91
Public trust, 60, 64, 75
PubMed, 157, 160, 163
Pulmonary circuit of cardiac cycle, 535, 536
Pulse rate, 535
Pulse sequence, fMRI, 633
Pulse volume, 541
Pupillometry, 483–486, 552–553
Pupil reactivity, 483
p values, 174, 191, 411, 698
PyMVPA package, 705, 710
Pyramidal cells, of cerebral cortex, 616

Q (modularity index), 707–708
Q-Q plots, 505
Quadratic trajectory, 348–349
Qualitative feedback, iSTART, 373
Qualitative research, xxxvi, xxxvii
  definition of, 5–7
  differences among approaches to, 7–10
  in emic approach, xxxi
  epistemological bases for, 5–21
  forms of, 5
  quality and value of, 18–20
  quantitative vs., 18
Qualitative variables, 171
Quality criteria, for hormone assays, 567–568
Quality of speech, 436
Quality of thought, 436
Quantile-probability plots, 502–503
Quantile response times
  averaging, over subjects, 503–505
  fitting RT distributions with, 500–501
  Q-Q plots, 505
  representing shape of RT distributions with, 501–505
  skewness of, 506
Quantitative research
  data analysis, xl–xliv
  descriptive, xxxiii, xxxvii
  estimating reliability for, 728
  qualitative vs., 18
Quasi-experimental designs, xxxiv, 46–49, 105
Quera, V., 253
Question design, cross-cultural, 105–106
Questionnaire design, 291–293
Question order effects, 277–293
  conditional, 227, 292–293
  defined, 277
  in health and safety studies, 283–286
  individual differences in participants and, 288–291
  and questionnaire design, 291–293
  for social and political topics, 278–283
  survey modes and, 286–288
  in vignette research, 286
Questions
  follow-up, 305–306
  leading, 299–300
  nonleading, 299–300
  open and closed, 300–302
Quetelet, Adolph, 410–411
Quota samples, 416

R (language)
  intensive longitudinal data in, 339, 352
  literate programming in, 213–214
  resources for coding in, 220
  switching compiler to interpret commands in, 214
  syntax for reliability examples, 739–740
  visualizing generalizability analysis outcomes with, 761
R01 grant (Research Project Grant), 239–240
R03 program (Small Grant Program), 239, 240
R21 grant program (Exploratory/Developmental Research Grant Program), 239, 240
R34 grant program (Clinical Trial Planning Grant Program), 239–241
R36 grant (Mental Health Research Dissertation Grant to Enhance Workforce Diversity), 238
R41 and R42 grants (Small Business Technology Transfer [STTR] Grants), 241
R43 and R44 grants (Small Business Innovation Research [SBIR] Grants), 241
Radical social constructionism, 16–17, 19
Radioactive isotopes, 647, 648
Radioimmunoassays (RIAs), 568–569, 572, 573
Rafaeli, S., 335
Rajaratnam, N., 735
$r_{alerting-CV}$ measure, 781
Ramon y Cajal, Santiago, 147, 148
Random assignment, 29
Random effects, in Level 2 model, 345, 347–348
Random-effects analysis, with GLM, 637–638
Random-effects decision studies, 754
Random-effects generalizability studies, 751–752, 754–756
Randomized block design, 26
Randomized controlled trials (RCTs), 48–49
Randomized group assignment, 67
Randomized matched pairs design, 26
Randomized question order, 292
Random jitter, in fMRI studies, 641
Randomly arranged arrays, visual search in, 481

Randomly parallel tests, 746
Randomly-selected raters, 730–732
Random number generator, setting seed for, 220
Random sampling, 416, 746
Rank order, 184, 517, 520
Rapid event-related task, fMRI during, 639–641
Rapport building
  for intensive longitudinal studies, 333
  in interviews, 309, 310, 312, 313
  in physiological experiments, 534–535
Rasch IRT model
  category intersection parameters in, 822
  described, 181–182, 186
  estimating latent scores with, 185
  PCM and, 825–826
  as reduced dichotomous model, 812, 814
  2PLM models with equality constraints and, 776
Rasinski, K. A., 285
Ratcliff, R., 493–495, 499–502, 506, 507
Rate of observational data, 266, 267
Rater-agreement method of measuring content validity, 773
Rater facet, 752
Raters, defined, 256
Rating scales, kappa with, 265
Rational analysis, xxvii
Rational informed consent, 65, 69–72
Rationalization, questions that elicit, 304–305
Ratio scales, 171–173, 183, 184, 186, 256
Rausch, J. R., 200
Raudenbush, S. W., 345, 353
R awards (project-focused grants), 239–241
Raw data, reading, 215
Raw residuals, 269
Raw scores, psychometric value of, 417
Raykov, T., 734
Rayner, K., 469, 480, 482
R_{Change} measure, 344–345
RCMI (Research Centers in Minority Institutions; U54 award), 241–242
$r_{contrast-CV}$ measure, 781
RCTs (randomized controlled trials), 48–49
RDM (representational dissimilarity matrix), 705

Reactance, 334
Reaction time analysis, 523
Read, J. C., 512
Reader evaluation, 19
Readiness potential, 614
Reading, eye movements in, 471–477
    control of eye movements, 475–477
    fixational, 471–472
    and fixation time, 476–477
    parafoveal-on-foveal effects, 474–475
    and perceptual span, 473
    and preview benefit, 473–474
    and pupillometric responses, 484
    saccades, 471–472
Reading skill, 472, 473
Reading Strategy Assessment Tool (RSAT), 363, 367
Real, K., 283–284
Realism, in qualitative approaches, 8–9
Realist knowledge, 11–14, 19
Real-time fMRI, 645
Real-world reflection, questions based on, 136, 139
Real-world studies, in qualitative research, 7
Reardon, S. F., 425
Recall scores, 365
Recall stage of response, 278
Receiver operating characteristic (ROC) analysis, 515. *See also* ROC curves
    and cutoff selection, 849–850
    development of, 845
    of discriminatory power, 845–849
    functions of, 837
    parametric limitations of, 848–849
Reciprocal fairness, 662
Reciprocity, norm of, 281, 283, 286, 289, 292
Recording
    of behavioral observations, 256–260
    of EEG/MEG signals, 582–585
    of EMG signals, 548
    of ERPs, 605, 619–626
    of interviews, 321–322
    of sudomotor activity, 544–546
Recovery coefficients, 567
Recruitment, 107, 117–121, 333
Reduced interference distributions (RIDs), 591
Reduction, in three Rs for animal research, 88
Reductionism, 40–41
Redundant content, removing, 459

Reference effects, with tDCS, 667
Reference electrode, EEG, 621
Reference searching, 165
Reference site, in ERP studies, 621–622, 626
Referencing EEG signals, 588–589
Refinement, in three Rs for animal research, 88
Refixation, 472
Reflexivity, of qualitative research, 19–20
Reflex probe, 550–551
Region-of-interest (ROI) analyses, 638–639, 698, 706
Regression analysis, xli, 569, 587–588, 849
Regression discontinuity design, 27, 48, 49
Regressions, in reading, 471–472
Regression to the mean, 26
Regressors. *See* Independent variables
Regularity account of causation, 40
Reichardt, C. S., 27
Reicher, S., 19
Reinhart, C. M., 212
Reise, S. P., 821, 829
Rejection, of ERP trials with artifacts, 622, 626–627
Relation strength. *See* Effect size
Relative decision, 748, 749, 751
Relative duration, of observational data, 267
Relative error variance, 748, 750–751, 753, 759
Relative error variance–covariance matrix, 758
Relative filenames, 221
Relative frequency, of observational data, 266–267
Relative risk, 846
Relativism, 8–9, 16
Relevance, initial item pool, 387
Reliability, 723–740. *See also specific types*
    and attenuation paradox, 393–394
    of bar exam data set, 344–345
    of behavioral observation, 252
    of binary measures, 728, 735–736
    of brief vs. longer measures, 451
    of categorical measures, 736
    classical test theory and, 745–746
    classical test theory view of, 723–727, 745
    coefficient alpha as index of, 394–397
    in criterion-referenced testing, 427

    defined, 384, 413, 723
    estimating, 728–737
    extensions of, 737
    general equation for, in CTT, 748
    and generalizability theory, 745, 762–764
    in history of psychometrics, 384
    of hormone assays, 568
    of intensive longitudinal data, 340
    internal consistency, 392–393, 732–734
    and internal validity, 777–778
    in norm-referenced testing, 413–414
    of objective tests, 391–398
    proposed standards of evidence of, 734–735
    of realist research, 19
    of Rorschach inkblots, 437–438
    R syntax for examples, 739–740
    of short forms, 459
    Spearman–Brown prophecy formula on, 452
    SPSS syntax for example, 738–739
    statistical remedies for low, 727
    of Thematic Apperception Test, 441–442
    trait level and, 778
    and universe of generalizability, 747
Reliability coefficients
    ad hoc adjustments to, 738
    between- and within-person, 737
    in classical test theory, 726
    disadvantages of using, 737
    and generalizability theory, 748–749
    for intensive longitudinal data, 340
    and measurement quality, 737
    for new objective measures, 734–735
    and origins of generalizability theory, 745–746
    in single-facet generalizability analysis, 749–751
    variance component estimates for, 731
RELIABILITY procedure, SPSS, 732
Reliability–validity paradox, 762
Remote areas, impact of NIBS on, 686, 689
Remote interviews, 316–317
Remote repositories, 218, 219
Repetition, in code, 221–223
Repetition time, fMRI, 633
Repetitive transcranial magnetic stimulation (rTMS), 660–662, 664, 683

Replacement, in three Rs for animal research, 88
Replicability, xliv, 212–213
Replications, reliability and, 727–729
Replication studies, 137, 142, 144
Reporting
  of animal welfare concerns, 89–90
  on literature search, 155, 165–166
  of observer agreement, 266
  on salivary hormone assays, 574–575
  standards for, xliii
Reporting biases, 334
Reporting stage of response, 278
Reports, literature searches for, 164
Repositories, fMRI data, 649
Representational dissimilarity matrix (RDM), 705
Representational similarity analysis (RSA), 705
Representation paradigm of measurement, 186
Representativeness, 25, 117–121, 387, 391. See also External validity
Reproducibility
  coefficient of, 180
  of functional neuroimaging results, 648–649
  of hormone research, 574
  and statistical workflow, 212
Reproductive status, of hormone assay participants, 570
Requests for applications (RFAs), 233
Requests for proposals (RFPs), 233
Research, defined, 59
Research Centers in Minority Institutions (RCMI; U54 award), 241–242
Research costs
  categories of, 230–232
  reducing, 227–228
Research design(s)
  analytic units and research factors in, 251
  for causal inference, 26, 48–49
  for cross-cultural studies, 104–107
  ethical issues related to, 106–107
  for interview studies, 313–318
  research question and, xxxvi–xxxvii
  with salivary hormone assays, 569–571
Research discussions, 140
Researchers
  ethical responsibilities of, 59, 91
  mindset of, 585
  reflexivity of, 7, 16
Research ethics, 83–85

Research factors, 251, 252
Research groups, contacting, 165
Research ideas
  examples of, in psychology, 141–142
  and knowledge of research/theoretical literature, 139
  new methods of inquiry and, 142
  and practical problems/implications of basic research, 139
  sources of, for novice investigators, 139–141
Research method(s). See also specific types
  matching research question to, xxix–xxx
  objectives of research and, xxv–xliv
  transparency in, xliii–xliv
Research participants. See Human participants
Research planning, xxx
Research priorities, of external funding sources, 232
Research Program Project Grant (P01), 241
Research Project Grant (R01), 239–240
Research question(s), 135–148
  for cross-cultural research, 104
  developing, 135–138
  for ERP studies, 607–608
  finding a method that fits, xxix–xxx
  important, 137–143
  for intensive longitudinal studies, 328–329
  for members of marginalized populations, 119–120
  new methods of inquiry and, 142
  for qualitative research, 5–6
  research design and, xxxvi–xxxvii
  and research ideas, 141–142
  for resting-state fMRI studies, 641–642
  sample-size planning based on, 189–190
  search concepts resulting from, 156
  sources of ideas for formulating, 139–141
  statistical workflow and, 211
  in studies with hormone assays, 570
  testable, 143–147
  worthwhile, 137–138
Research regulations, 83–87
Research strategy, 233
RESEL unit, 698
Residual error, 348
Residuals, 269

Residual variance–covariance matrix, 348
Resolution. See Spatial resolution; Temporal resolution
Respect for People's Rights and Dignity (Principle E), 64
Respiratory sinus arrhythmia (RSA), 539
Respondent behavior, during projective tests, 435–436
Response biases
  in brief telephone interviews, 337
  and Cronbach's alpha, 394, 734
  defined, 517
  signal detection theory on, 515
  with yes–no tasks, 519, 522
Response-centered focus of scaling, 170, 174, 177–183
Response method, in fMRI studies, 641
Response-related ERP components, 614
Response scales, for cross-cultural research, 105–106
Response scoring, with NLP, 362–367
Response selection process, 618
Response time distributions
  cumulative density function for, 495–496
  exGaussian and inverse Gaussian, 496–498
  explicit functions for, 507–508
  fitting models of, to empirical data, 500–501
  hazard rate function for, 495, 496
  insights from, 508
  and mean response times, 494
  measures of shape for, 505–506
  probability density function for, 495
  quantiles to represent shapes of, 501–505
  relationships among dependent variables in, 506–508
Response times (RTs), 493–508
  and cognition in schizophrenia, 618–619
  defined, 493
  ERP studies of multitasking and, 607
  mean, 494
  outlier, 498–500
  P3b latency and, 611–612
  stability across session of, 494–495
Responsibility. See Fidelity and Responsibility (Principle B)
Resting EEG asymmetry, 592
Resting eye blink rate, 552

895

Index

Resting-state fMRI, 641–643
Resting state networks (RSNs), 680
REST software, 710
Resubmission, grant, 244
Retinotopic localizer scans, 639
Retinotopic visual cortex, 682
Retrospection bias, 328
Return sweeps, 472
Revelle, W., 738
Reversal, in partial credit model, 826
Reverse inference, 648
Reviews, types of, 152–153
Review software, 155
Review team, translation, 123
Reward processing, 665–666, 679
Reymond, Du-Bois, 546
RFAs (requests for applications), 233
RFPs (requests for proposals), 233
RIAs. *See* Radioimmunoassays
RIASEC measure, 146
RIDs (reduced interference distributions), 591
Rights, respect for. *See* Respect for People's Rights and Dignity (Principle E)
Right temporal parietal junction (rTPJ), 683
Rimal, R. N., 283–284
RIR (Rochester interaction record), 332
Rise time, skin conductance response, 545
Risk–benefit analysis, for informed consent, 65–66
Risk difference, 270–271
Risk judgments, question order effects for, 285
Risk-taking behaviors, rTMS studies of, 661–662
R_{KF} measure, 344, 345
R markdown, 214
RMSE. *See* Root of mean square error
R-noweb, 214
Robinson, W. S., 103
Robustness, 220–221, 648–649
ROC analysis. *See* Receiver operating characteristic analysis
ROC curves
 area under, 846–848
 defined, 517
 generating, 849
 information theory analysis of, 854–855
 in terms of specificity and sensitivity, 846

Rochester interaction record (RIR), 332
Rodgers, J. L., xxxiii
Rodriguez, A., 829
Rogoff, K. S., 212
Rohrer, J. M., 40
Rondoni, J., 332
Roosa, M. W., 120–121
Root of mean square error (RMSE), 196–197, 816, 817
R-Optimized instructions, for R-PAS, 437, 438
Rorschach inkblots, 433, 437–440
 ambiguity of, 436
 features of, 434
 reliability of, 437–438
 scoring system for figure drawing vs., 444
 validity of, 438–439
Rorschach Performance Assessment System (R-PAS), 434, 437–440, 445
Rosen, A., 840, 850
Rosenbaum, P. R., 27
Rosenberg Self-Esteem scale, 829
Rosenthal, R., 199, 777, 780, 781
Rosenzweig Picture Frustration Study, 433
Ross, B. H., 503, 505
Rossini, A., 214
Round About Pound a Week (Pember-Reeves), 327
R-PAS. *See* Rorschach Performance Assessment System
RSA (representational similarity analysis), 705
RSA (respiratory sinus arrhythmia), 539
RSAT (Reading Strategy Assessment Tool), 363, 367
RSA toolbox, 710
RSNs (resting state networks), 680
RStudio, 214, 216, 218
rTMS. *See* Repetitive transcranial magnetic stimulation
rTPJ (right temporal parietal junction), 683
RTs. *See* Response times
Rubin, D. B., 23, 28
Rubin causal model. *See* Potential outcomes (PO) framework
Rubinov, M., 707
Ruiz-Padial, E., 539–540
Runs, fMRI, 634
Russell, W. M. S., 88

Russia. *See* Communist and American reporter question studies
Ruth L. Kirschstein National Research Service Awards Individual Fellowships (F Awards), 234–235

S_A (sinoatrial node), 536, 537
sAA. *See* Salivary α-amylase
Sabourin, G., 551
Saccades, 469–470
 and attention, 471
 defined, 469
 integration of visual information across, 483
 latency for, 470
 memory across, 478–479
 and parafoveal-on-foveal effect, 475
 in parallel processing, 482
 and pupillary dimensions, 485–486
 in reading, 471–472
Saccadic suppression, 470
Safari approach to community research, 110–111
Safety, 316, 634, 662, 666
SAGE Online, 158
Saklofske, D., 443
Salaries, as research costs, 230–231
Saliency map model of eye-movement control, 480
Saliva collection methods, 571–573, 575
Salivary α-amylase (sAA), 567, 568, 572–574
Salivary hormone assays, 565–575
 data analysis and report writing involving, 574–575
 and hormones in biobehavioral research, 565–567
 methods of assaying hormones, 568–569
 quality criteria for, 567–568
 sample collection and processing for, 571–574
 screening questionnaire for, 571
 study design and participant screening for, 569–571
Salivettes, 572
Samejima, F., 795
Sample bias, 100
Sample processing, salivary hormone assay, 573–575
Sample size, 189, 193, 354
Sample-size planning, 189–206
 AIPE approach to, 195–197, 204–205
 for determining existence/direction of effect, 193–195

for estimating magnitude of effect, 195–197
for multiple regression, 201–206
parameter specification and, 197–201
power analytic approach to, 193–195, 202–203
role of effect sizes in research, 190–193
Sample storage, 575
Sampling errors, 416–417, 754
Sampling rate, EEG/MEG, 585
Sampling units, defined, 251
Sampling variability, 754
Sanctions for animal mistreatment, 90
Sandberg, J., 138
Santos, H. C., 103
SAS (language), 214
analyzing intensive longitudinal data in, 339
generalizability analysis with, 760
intensive longitudinal categorical data in, 352
ROC analysis with, 849
statistical simulation studies in, 353
syntax for intensive longitudinal data analysis in, 354–355
SASweave tool, 214
SAT (Scholastic Aptitude Test), 772
Satisfaction With Life Scale, 127
Satisficing behavior, 289–290
Satorra–Bentler correction, 799
Satterthwaite estimates, 349
SBIR (Small Business Innovation Research) Grants (R43/R44), 241
SBPF. *See* Spearman–Brown prophecy formula
Scalar equivalence, 102
Scalar invariance model, 778
Scale development and validation process, 385–401
external phase in, 398–401
structural phase in, 388–398
substantive phase in, 385–388
Scaling, defined, 518
Scaling function, 518, 523
Scalogram, 179
Scanner artifacts, 680
Scanner drift, 635
Scan parameters, fMRI, 632–634
Scan path, scene perception, 478
SCAW (Scientific Center for Animal Welfare), 91
Scene perception, 477–480, 482, 485
Schedules, interview, 298–299

Schizophrenia
cognition in, 618–619
consent capacity of individuals with, 75
ERP studies of, 614
face processing by individuals with, 607
Schmidt, F. L., 139, 141
Schmitt, N., 393
Schneider, A. M. de A., 438
Schneider, B., 523
Schoebi, D., 737
Scholastic Aptitude Test (SAT), 772
Schools
informed consent to research in, 71
norm-referenced tests in, 416, 419
Schultheiss, O., 442, 565, 574
Schultz, K. F., 199
Schultzberg, M., 205
Schuman, H., 277–282, 288–292
Schuurman, N. K., 737
Schwarz, N., 282–283, 286, 287
ScienceDirect, 158
Scientific Center for Animal Welfare (SCAW), 91
Scientific method, xxvi–xxviii
Scientific Review Group (SRG), 242–244
SCL (skin conductance level), 545
SCM framework. *See* Structural causal models framework
Scoping reviews, 153, 165
Scopus, 157, 160, 165
Score distributions, norm-referenced testing, 414, 417–419
Score variation, in classical test theory, 726
Scoring
in AutoTutor, 371–372
of figure drawings, 443–444
of grant proposals, 242–243
for norm-referenced measures, 411–412
of responses. *See* Response scoring
of Rorschach inkblots, 437
Scoring coefficients, nominal response model, 822–823
SCORS-G (Social Cognition and Object Relations Scale-Global Rating Method), 441, 442
SCR (skin conductance response), 545
Screening questionnaires, 571
SCS (Sexual Compulsivity Scale), 818–819, 821
SDIS (Sequential Data Interchange Standard) format, 261

SDT. *See* Signal detection theory
Search array, 481
Search coils, 471
Search concepts, literature review, 156–157
Search engines, 157, 163–164
Searchlight fMRI analyses, 638
Search platforms, databases vs., 157, 158
Search techniques, 164–165
sEBR (spontaneous eye blink rate), 552
Secondary data analysis, xli
Secondary sources, 137
Second-level GLM analysis, 637
Second-order isomorphism, 705
Second-order linear oscillator modeling, 352
Seed-based functional connectivity, 643
SEI (severe exposures index), 392
Seizure induction, with rTMS, 662
Selection, threat of, 26
Selection ratio, 420, 838, 839
Selective attention, 596
Selective searches, 152
Self-administered surveys, 286
Self-consciousness, 586
Self-criticism, xxvii–xxviii
Self-deprecating interview strategies, 309
Self-Directed Search assessment, 146
Self-disclosure, in interviews, 310–311
Self-explanation(s)
inferring psychological processes from, 369–370
iSTART assessments of, 372–373
natural language processing of, 366–367, 369–370
Self-interested behavior, 682
Self-reflective processes, 334
Self-reported health (SRH) questions, 284–286
Self-report measures
automated language analysis of, 361–375
in intensive longitudinal methods, 327–355
interviews as, 297–323
question order effects with, 277–293
SEM. *See* Structural equation modeling
SEM (standard error of measurement), 751, 764
Semantic analysis, 369
Semantic equivalence, 121, 122
Semantic incongruity, 613
Semantic violations, detecting, 479
Semi-blind ICA, 702

Semistructured interviews
  defined, 297–298
  disagreeing with/challenging interviewee in, 311–313
  formulations within, 309–310
  grounding responses in examples in, 303–305
  nonleading questions in, 299–300
  not-knowing stance of interviewer in, 308–309
  open and closed questions in, 300–302
  prompts and follow-up questions in, 305–306
  for qualitative research, 7
  schedule for, 298–299
  self-disclosure by interviewer in, 310–311
  short question technique in, 302–303
  silence in, 306–308
  techniques for conducting, 298–313
Senior fellows, F32 NRSA award for, 235
Senn, S. J., 198
Sensation
  defined, 511
  intensity of, 531
  predicting mechanisms of, 513
  quantifying, 512–513
Sense making, 15–16
Sensitive topics
  in cross-cultural research, 108–109
  interviewer self-disclosure on, 311
  and interview schedule, 299
  research with marginalized populations on, 119
  vulnerability of interviewee related to, 320
Sensitivity
  and cutoff score, 841–842
  in decision theory, 786
  defined, 837, 839, 841
  of hormone assays, 567
  in psychophysics, 518
  ROC curve in terms of, 846
Sensitivity index (d'), 514–517
Sensors
  electrocardiogram, 537–538
  electromyogram, 546, 548
  for measuring electrodermal activity, 544–545
Sensory scale, suprathreshold measures on, 514
Sentence processing studies, 477

Senter, J. L., 732
Sentiment analysis, 369
Sequential combination
  of EEG/MEG and fMRI, 678–679
  of NIBS and EEG, 686–687
  of NIBS and fMRI, 682–683
  simultaneous combinations vs., 690
Sequential Data Interchange Standard (SDIS) format, 261
Sequential estimation method of sample-size planning, 189, 193
SES (socioeconomic status), of translators, 124
Setting facet, 752
Severe exposures index (SEI), 392
Sexual Compulsivity Scale (SCS), 818–819, 821
Sexuality, cross-cultural research on, 108–109
Shadish, W. R., 18, 23, 24, 46
Shahar, G., 798
Sham stimulation condition, 662, 666
Shape of response time distribution
  diffusion decision models accounting for, 506–507
  explicit functions for modeling, 507–508
  impact of mean response time on, 494
  measures of, 505–506
  RT quantiles to represent, 501–505
  skewness, 505–506
Share, D. L., 484
Sharma, A. R., 184
Sheatsley, P. B., 281
Shebilske, W. L., 476
Shechter, A., 484
Shermis, M. D., 363, 364
Sherwood, A., 542
Shortage areas, T32-funded programs in, 236
Shortest path length for network, 707
Short forms, 457–464
  as brief instruments, 451
  and item response theory, 462–463
  removal of valid content in, 459–462
  and Spearman-Brown prophecy formula, 452, 453
  validity of, 458–459
Short outlier response times, 498, 501
Short question technique, 302–303
Short responses, automated language analyses of, 362–363
Short-separation channels, 647
Short-time Fourier transform (STFT), 591

Shrout, P. E., 333, 334, 340, 727, 730–732, 734, 737
Sieber, J. E., 73
Sigelman, J., 594
Sigelman, L., 289
Signal conditioning, EMG, 548–549
Signal detection theory (SDT), 837. *See also* Test performance
  for cutoff specification, 850
  defined, 518
  and psychophysics, 515
  terminology in, 839, 840
Signaling devices, in variable-interval designs, 331
Signal-plus-noise distribution, 515
Signal representation, EMG, 549
Signal-to-noise ratio (SNR), 633, 647
Sign approach to figure drawings, 443
Significance criteria, for grants, 239, 242
Silberzahn, R., 211
Silence, as interview tool, 306–308
Similarity assessment, iSTART, 372
Simmons, J. P., 211
Simms, L. J., 392
Simon, T., 408
Simple event data, 258, 267–268, 271
Simple feelings, 531
Simulation, 353–354
Simultaneous combinations of neuroimaging techniques, 687–690
Singelis, T., 105
Singer, J. D., 348
Single binary rule, 728
Single-facet generalizability analysis, 749–752
Single-gender groups, interviews with, 314
Single-pulse TMS, 656–659, 663
Single-subject behavioral observations, 252
Singular value decomposition (SVD), 365, 702
Sinoatrial node (SA), 536, 537
Sireci, S. G., 428
Skaff, M. M., 339, 350–352
Skepticism, xxviii
Skewness, 505–506, 829
Skin, electrical conductivity of, 542. *See also* Sudomotor activity
Skin cancer studies, 283–284
Skin conductance level (SCL), 545
Skin conductance response (SCR), 545
Skipped words, in reading, 472
Skipping effects, 476
Sleeping, during fMRI scans, 642

Sleep studies, EEG–fMRI, 680
Slice order of acquisition, fMRI, 633
Slice prescription, fMRI, 632
Slice-timing correction, 635
Slope
    of category boundary discriminations, 821
    invariance in, 126
    in IRT, for noncognitive measures, 827–828
    location parameters and, 829
    spread of, 829–830
    of two-parameter logistic model, 810–811
Slope-intercept parameterization, 796, 811
Slow event-related task, fMRI during, 639
Slow-frequency rTMS, 660, 661
Small Business Innovation Research (SBIR) Grants (R43/R44), 241
Small Business Technology Transfer (STTR) Grant (R41/R42), 241
Small Grant Program (R03), 239, 240
Small numbers, law of, 195
Smart vagus, 539
Smith, C. A., 545–546
Smith, G. T., 453–455, 459, 461, 462
Smith, S. M., 701
Smith, T., 281–282
Smith, T. W., 279, 292
Smith v. Regents of the University of California, 420
Smoothing, data, 549, 636, 700, 703
Snapshots, for version control, 218
Snowballing, 165
SNR (signal-to-noise ratio), 633, 647
SNS (sympathetic nervous system), 567, 570
Social behavior, resting EEG asymmetry and, 592
Social Cognition and Object Relations Scale-Global Rating Method (SCORS-G), 441, 442
Social constructionist knowledge, 11–13, 16–19
Social desirability, 394
Social identity, 119, 123–125
Socially based codes, 255
Social processes, realist studies of, 11
Social science databases, 158–159
Social support, intensive longitudinal studies of, 329
Social topics, question order effects for, 278–283

Society for Psychophysiological Research, 544
Society for the Advancement of Psychotherapy, 239
SocINDEX, 158
Socioeconomic status (SES), of translators, 124
Sociological Abstracts database, 158
Sociology Source Ultimate, 158, 159
Software. *See also specific languages and programs*
    for analyzing intensive longitudinal data, 339
    for coding, 256
    and continuous timed-event recording, 259–260
    documenting version of, 221
    for generalizability analysis, 760–761
    for implementing GLM, 700
    for literature search, 154–155
    for multivoxel pattern analysis, 705–706
    for natural language processing, 361
    for network analyses, 709
    for neuroimaging analysis, 700, 703, 705–706, 709, 710
    for ROC analysis, 849
Solano-Flores, G., 763
Solomon, J. A., 512
Somoza, E., 850
Song, F., 156
Sound, artifacts due to, 688
South Africa, 110
SP (systolic blood pressure), 540, 541
Spangler, W., 442
Sparsity feature, ICA with, 701
Spatial attention, 612
Spatial extent of preview benefit, 474
Spatial ICA, 701
Spatial intersubject correlation (ISC), 644
Spatial resolution
    of ERP data, 607, 615
    in fMRI studies, 632, 638, 675
    in NBS experiments, 663
    in tDCS experiments, 666–667
    with TMS, 656
Spatial smoothing, 636, 703
Spearman, C., 391, 726, 727
Spearman–Brown prophecy formula (SBPF)
    assumptions underlying, 463
    and binary measures, 728
    and brief instruments/short forms, 452, 453, 460

    and D-study for single-facet analysis, 750
    and internal consistency, 733
    and parceling, 798
    and remedies for low reliability, 727
Spearman correlation distance, 705
Specialized Center Grant (P50), 241
Specialized Centers of Excellence on Minority Health and Heath Disparities (U54), 241
Special populations, 415, 614
Specific aims document, 233
Specificity
    and cutoff score, 841–842
    in decision theory, 786–787
    defined, 532, 837, 839, 841
    of hormone assays, 567–568
    ROC curve in terms of, 846
Specific objectivity, 182
Specific (part) question, 279–282
Speculation, questions requiring, 304
Speech, 436, 597
Sperry, Roger W., 532
Spill-over effects, 29
Spiraling test forms, 416
Split-ballot experiments, 279–280, 282
SPM toolbox, 635, 700, 710
Spoken conversational computer, 370
Spontaneous eye blink rate (sEBR), 552
Sporns, O., 707
SportDiscus, 160
Spread of intercepts, 346
Spreadsheet errors, 212
Sprites, P., 23
SPSS
    analyzing intensive longitudinal data in, 339
    generalizability analysis with, 760
    intensive longitudinal categorical data in, 352
    ROC analysis with, 849
    syntax for reliability example, 738–739
Squared errors, in criterion-referenced testing, 427
Squires, D., 425
SRC (Survey Research Center), 279, 291
SRG (Scientific Review Group), 242–244
SRH (self-reported health) questions, 284–286
ss.aipe.R2() function, 205
ss.aipe.src() function, 204
ss.power.reg1() function, 203
ss.power.R2() function, 203

Stability
- dependability of test vs., 398
- of response times across sessions, 494–495

Stable-unit-treatment-value assumption (SUTVA), 28–29, 41, 43

Staircase method, 521–522

Standard deviation, 499, 501

Standard error
- and adjusted residual, 269
- of estimate, 764
- and internal validity, 777

Standard error of measurement (SEM), 751, 764

Standard independent component analyses, 700–701

Standardization
- of effect size, 191
- of electrodermal measurement, 544
- of projective test administration, 444–445
- and validity of assessment, 763–764

Standardized mean difference, 197, 200

Standardized regression model, 201

Standards
- for criterion-referenced testing, 428, 429
- of evidence of reliability, 734–735
- for short forms, 458

Standards-based assessments. *See* Criterion-referenced testing

Standards for Educational and Psychological Testing (AERA, APA, and NCME), 384–385, 771

Standard stimulus, oddball paradigm, 610

Stanford Achievement Tests, 409, 419

Stanford Revision of the Binet-Simon Scale (Stanford-Binet test), 408–409

Stanley, J. C., 26

Stanton, S. J., 574

Stark, K., 443, 444

Stark, T. H., 280

Startle eyeblink reflex, 550–551

Stata, 214, 220, 849

Statements, questions delivered as, 299–300

State research funding, 229

State sequential data, 261

Static functional connectivity, 643

Stationary attractor points, 352

Statistical analysis
- of behavioral observation, 266–268
- description of, for hormone assay, 575
- in ERP studies, 625–626
- from intensive longitudinal studies, 333
- scale level of data and, 170, 182–183, 186
- tasks in, 213
- workflow of. *See* Statistical workflow

Statistical conclusion validity, 25

Statistical inference
- β as basis for, 698
- with causal inference frameworks, 45
- for latent traits, 184–185
- and scale level, 173, 182–183
- and statistical conclusion validity, 25

Statistical power, 88
- defined, 193, 194
- of fMRI experiments, 641
- and MIES approach to parameter specification, 198
- in null hypothesis significance testing, 195
- for omnibus effect, 203
- for targeted effect, 202–203

Statistical significance, in cross-cultural research, 106

Statistical workflow, 211–224
- coding issues that impact, 220–224
- consistency in, 211–212
- documenting, 211, 213–217
- and replicability, 212–213
- and reproducibility, 212
- subjective view of improving, 213
- and version control, 217–220

Statistics, coding to combine text and, 214–215

Stedman, J. M., 436–437

Steegen, S., 211

Steep descent pattern, 830

Steinberg, L., 795

Steiner, P. M., 28, 46

Stellate cells, 598

Stem cell research, 84

Stereotypes, 106–107, 110

Steroid hormones, 566

Stevens, S. S., 170, 182, 256, 257

Stevens' power law, 514, 516

STFT (short-time Fourier transform), 591

Stimulation intensity, rTMS, 661

Stimulus, in psychophysical experiments
- calibration of, 516, 518
- control over, 511–512, 514, 516, 523–524
- defined, 514, 518
- realistic, naturalistic, and immersive, 524

Stimulus-attribution tests, 436

Stimulus-centered focus of scaling, 169–170, 173–177, 179, 182

Stimulus magnitude, 518

Stimulus reduction, 514, 518

Stochastic theory of causal effects, 31

Stodden, V., 212

Storytelling, turn conversation units in, 306

Strack, F., 282

Strasburger, H., 512

Strategic social behavior, 683

Stratified random sampling, 416

Stratum corneum, 542–543

Stratum germinature, 543

Strauss, M. E., 455

Stress and coping during preparation for professional licensing exam survey, 339
- average experience and day-to-day variability for, 342–346
- GT approach to reliability analysis with, 344–345
- linear trajectory for, 347–348
- moderation effects with, 349–350
- multilevel analyses of, 345–346
- preliminary steps in data analysis, 342–344
- quadratic trajectory for, 348–349
- trajectories for, 346–350

Striated muscle tissue, 547

Strict invariance, 126, 778, 801

Stroke volume, 542

Strong ignorability assumption, 30

Strong Interest Inventory, 146

Strong invariance, 126, 778, 800

Strong relationships, odds ratios for, 270

Stroop task, 612

Structural assignments, 36

Structural causal models (SCM) framework, 23
- causal generalization and replication in, 46
- causal identification in, 45
- definition of causal effects, 44
- described, 31–40
- joint use of, with other frameworks, 50
- philosophy of causation for, 41–43
- research designs for causal interference in, 49
- subject matter theory in, 46, 48
- theory of cause for, 43–44
- VT and PO vs., 48–50

Structural equation modeling (SEM), xxxiii, 709
  adjusting unreliable measurement with, 727
  generalizability theory and, 761
  with intensive longitudinal data, 353
  McDonald's omega for, 734
  omnibus vs. targeted effect sizes for, 191
  reliability coefficients from, 396–397
  research question development for, 142
Structural equivalence, 101, 106
Structural fidelity, 388
Structural magnetic resonance imaging, 631
Structural modeling fit indices, 816
Structural modeling framework
  for defining causal effects, 44
  generalizability analysis with, 760
  measurement/factorial invariance in, 778
Structural validation
  and classical test theory, 388–389
  and item response theory, 389–391
  of objective tests, 388–398
  reliability, 391–398
  and sampling for item selection, 391
  structural fidelity, 388
  test–retest reliability, 397–398
Structured interviews, 298
Structured reviews, 153
Structure-oriented studies
  bias in, 106
  cross-cultural comparisons in, 103
STTR (Small Business Technology Transfer) Grant (R41/R42), 241
Studies in Word Association (Jung), 542
Study selection software, 154–155
Subcortical brain regions, NIBS studies of, 677
Subject-centered scaling, 169, 173–175
Subject databases, 157
Subjective experience, phenomenological studies of, 12
Subjectivity analysis, 369
Subject-level summaries, 343
Subject matter theory, 30, 31, 46–50
Subjects, defined, 251. *See also* Human participants
Subsequent memory effect, 613
Substance use disorder, 76
Substantive validation, 385–388
Subtraction order hypothesis, 279–281, 283, 292

Sudman, S., 281
Sudomotor activity
  anatomy and physiology related to, 542–543
  measurement of, 544
  neural control over, 543–544
  physiological measures of, 542–546
  recording, 544–546
"Sufficiently large" convergent correlations, 398
"Sufficiently narrow" confidence interval, 196, 197
Sullivan, P., 318
Sultan, S., 438
Summarization, learning, 372
Summary scores, observational data, 266
Summary Sheet system, 365
Summary statement, grant review, 243
Summary statistics, 258, 265, 267–268
Supplementary information, for council review, 243–244
Support vector machine (SVM), 704
Suprathreshold metrics, 514, 518, 520, 523
Surface electrodes, measuring eye movements with, 471
Survey modes, 286–288, 293
Survey Research Center (SRC), 279, 291
Surveys
  behavioral observation vs., 252, 253
  diary entries vs., 335
  mechanism underlying response to, 278
  question order effects and knowledge about topic of, 290
Suspicion, hermeneutics of, 8
Sutton, S. K., 593
SUTVA. *See* Stable-unit-treatment-value assumption
SVD (singular value decomposition), 365, 702
SVM (support vector machine), 704
Sweat glands, 543
Sweave package, 213, 217
Swensen, C. H., 443
Swets, J. A., 512
SWIFT model, 477
Switching replications, 27
Symmetrical data analysis, EEG–fMRI studies, 680
Symmetry, generalizability theory and, 761–762
Symons, F., 253
Sympathetic nervous system (SNS), 567, 570

Syntactic positive shift, 609, 613
Syntactic violations, detecting, 479
Syntax, for search, 162
Systematic biases, 416
Systematic change, 329, 729
Systematic errors, 394, 461
Systematic research methods, 116, 165
Systematic Review Data Repository, 155
Systematic reviews, 153–154, 160
Systematic Review Toolbox, 154
Systemic circuit of cardiac cycle, 536
Systolic blood pressure (SP), 540, 541
Szondi Test, 433

$T1$-weighted images, 633
$T2^*$-weighted images, 633
T32 grant (Kirschstein-Institutional National Research Service Award), 235–236
Tables, programming to generate, 216
Taboo subjects, cross-cultural research on, 108–109
tACS. *See* Transcranial alternating current stimulation
Tactical language and culture training system, 370
Tactile scalp sensation, artifacts due to, 688
Taijin kyofusho, 101
Tailored testing approach to brief assessment, 462–463
Talairach atlas, 636
Tang, A., 622
Tangling process, 213
Tarchanoff, Ivan Romanovish, 542
Target acquisition model, 482–483
Targeted effect size, 191, 202–204
Target items, for assessing invariance, 778–779
Target population, 119–120, 122
Task, psychophysical experiment, 518–520
Task-based fMRI, 639–643
Task-defined probability, sensitivity of P3b to, 611–612
Task engagement, 545–546, 634
Task Force of the European Society of Cardiology and the North American Society of Pacing and Electrophysiology, 539
Tassinary, L. G., 532, 533
TAT. *See* Thematic Apperception Test
Taylor, D. W., 142
Taylor Manifest Anxiety Scale, 811–812, 815–816

Taylor–Russell tables, 420
TBS (theta burst stimulation), 663, 686
TCI (transcallosal inhibition), 658–660
TCUs (turn construction units), 306–307
tDCS. See Transcranial direct-current stimulation
t distribution, 698
TE (echo time), 633
Technology
  for intensive longitudinal studies, 336
  research ideas driven by, 142
  for stimulus control, 511–512
Tein, J. Y., 801
Telephone interviews, 336–337
Telephone surveys, 286, 287
Temperament and Character Inventory, 453
Temple Lang, D., 213
Temporal autocorrelation, 646, 699–700
Temporal correlation, 643
Temporal ICA, 701
Temporal intersubject correlation (ISC), 644
Temporal resolution
  in fMRI study, 632, 633, 675
  with PET scans, 648
  in tES studies, 677
  in TMS studies, 677
Temporal stability, measures of, 397–398
Tenacity, method of, xxv
Tennen, H., 328
Tenure-track faculty, K99/R000 award for, 237
Teresi, J. A., 391
Terman, L. M., 408, 409
tES. See Transcranial electric stimulation
Testable research questions, 143–147
Test batteries, generalizability analysis for, 757
Test design, content validity in, 772–773
Testing, threat of, 26
Testing set, for AES model, 363
Test item(s)
  dimensionality of, 773–774
  as unit of assessment, 411–413
Testosterone, 566, 568, 570
Test performance, 837–857
  cutoff value specification, 849–856
  decision theory in evaluation of, 850–856
  information theory in evaluation of, 854–856

ROC analysis of discriminatory power, 845–849
  traditional indexes of, 837–844
Test–retest reliability, 729
  of criterion-referenced test, 414
  of intensive longitudinal data, 340
  for objective tests, 397–398
  of Rorschach inkblots, 438
Tests, uses of, 772
Test scores, interpreting, 772, 784–787
Test statistic, null hypothesis testing, 193
Test validity, 420, 453
Tetrachoric correlation matrix, 797
Text, programming to combine statistics and, 214–215
Text difficulty, 472, 473
Tharinger, D. J., 443, 444
Thematic Apperception Test (TAT), 433, 439
  Card 16 and ambiguity in, 436
  reliability of, 441–442
  standardization in administration of, 444–445
  validity of, 442
Thematic material, in projective test responses, 435
Theme of figure drawing, 443
Theoretical literature, 138, 139
Theoretical models, in cross-cultural studies, 104–105
Theory
  coding scheme as reflection of, 253
  relationship of measurement and, 169
Theory-driven research, xxxvii, 7–8
Theory of cause, 23, 43–44
Theory of conjoint measurement, 181
Therapeutic drugs, nonhuman animal studies of, 83
Therapeutic misestimation, 66
Thermoregulatory sweating, 543
Thesaurus terms, 157, 161
Theses, literature searches for, 164
Theta-band oscillatory synchronization, 685
Theta–beta ratio, 595–596
Theta burst stimulation (TBS), 663, 686
Theta frequency band, 591, 595–596
Thibodeau, M. A., 391
Third person effect, 290
Thissen, D., 795, 821, 822
Thoemmes, F., 24
Thomas, D. L., 334
Thomas, E. A. C., 503, 505
Thomas, L., 138
Thorndike, E. L., 409

Thorndike, R. M., 407
Thought, quality of, 436
Threats
  and action readiness, 658
  evaluative, 541
  to validity, 25–27. See also Validity typology/threats (VT) framework
Three-parameter logistic model (3PLM), 182, 814–817
Three Rs for animal research, 88
Thresholding, for network analysis, 707
Threshold response curves (TRCs), 818
Thresholds. See also Cutoff scores
  absolute, 517
  analysis for, 522
  defined, 839
  methods associated with, 521
  observers in experiments related to, 519
  in psychophysics, 512–513
  suprathreshold metrics vs. measures of, 514
  tasks associated with, 520
Thurstone, R. R., 175–176, 182, 523
Thut, G., 689
Tibetan language, readers of, 473
Time-based intensive longitudinal designs, 330–331
Timed-event data
  aligning, 264
  basic statistics for, 266, 267
  recording, 259–261
  representing, 261
  sequential, 261
  summary statistics for, 267
  time-unit and event-based kappas for, 264
  time-window sequential analysis for, 271
Time domain measures, of HRV, 539
Time facet, in generalizability analysis, 752
Time–frequency analysis, 591, 625
Time-locking, 608, 623
Time-sampling. See Interval recording
Time-unit kappa, 264
Time-validity tradeoff, with short forms, 462
Time-window sequential analysis, 271
Timing
  of ERP component, 607, 625
  of rest-state fMRI data collection, 642–643
Tissue culture, 86

TMS. *See* Transcranial magnetic stimulation
TMS-evoked potentials, 689
Tonic heart rate, 538
Top-down cultural influence, 104–105
Torgerson, W. S., 176–177
Total variance, 750
Tourangeau, R., 278, 283
Trace line, 178
Tracers, 568–569
Training, participant, 332
Training awards, 234–235, 242
Training grants, 232, 233, 236–239
Training set, 363, 704
Trait factor loadings, in CT-CM model, 782
Trait variance, 783
Trajectory of experiences, investigating, 329, 346–350
Transcallosal inhibition (TCI), 658–660
Transcranial alternating current stimulation (tACS), 667–668
   combination of EEG and, 687, 688
   concurrent use of fMRI and, 685
   uses of, 676
Transcranial direct-current stimulation (tDCS), 664–668
   developments in field of, 667–668
   safety risks with, 666
   sham stimulation condition for experiments using, 666
   spatial resolution and localization in experiments with, 666–667
   uses of, 676
Transcranial electric stimulation (tES). *See also* transcranial alternating current stimulation (tACS); transcranial direct-current stimulation (tDCS)
   combination of EEG and, 688
   combination of fMRI and, 634, 682
   uses and limitations of, 676–677
Transcranial magnetic stimulation (TMS), 655–664
   combination of EEG and, 687–689
   combination of fMRI and, 682–686
   and electromagnetic induction, 655–656
   paired-pulse, 659–660
   repetitive, 660–662
   safety risks with, 662
   sham stimulation condition for experiments using, 662
   single-pulse, 656–659
   uses and limitations of, 676–677

Transcription, interview, 322
Transdisciplinary Collaborative Centers for Health Disparities Research (U54), 242
Transformation of data
   linear, 172, 175, 417–418
   for long outlier response times, 499
   monotonic, 172
   normalization, 418
Transient error, 394–395
Translation
   approaches to, 121–123
   in cross-cultural research, 105
   for members of marginalized communities, 121–124
   of search, to other databases, 162, 163
Translators, selecting, 123–124
Transparency
   of code for statistical analysis, 221–224
   in hormone assay analysis, 574
   in research methods, xliii–xliv
Transparent Reporting of Evaluations with Nonrandomized Designs (TREND), 196
Transportability, 39, 46
Transsaccadic memory, 478
Travel costs, 231
TRCs (threshold response curves), 818
Tremor, eye, 470
Trenado, R. M., 263
TREND (Transparent Reporting of Evaluations with Nonrandomized Designs), 196
Treutwein, B., 512
Trial registries, 164
Trial set, 704
Trial-to-trial variability, ERP, 681
Tricco, Andrea, 154
Trimming long outliers, 498–500
True negatives. *See* Valid negatives
True positives. *See* Valid positives
True score, 391, 458, 745, 747–748
Truth, verificationist theory of, 770
Tuerlinckx, F., 493, 501, 507
Tukey, J. W., 181, 505
Turn construction units (TCUs), 306–307
Tuskegee syphilis study, 59, 64
Tversky, A., 195
21st Century Cures Act, 74
Twitch, muscle, 547
2 × 2 tables contingency tables, 269–271
Two-alternative forced-choice tasks (2AFC), 520

Two-choice tasks, RT distribution for, 506–507
Two-parameter (2PL) logistic models, 182, 776, 777, 795
   fit of other IRT models vs., 817
   graded response model as extension of, 818
   item discrimination in, 422
   nominal response model and, 821
   for unidimensional dichotomous responses, 810–812
Two-way analysis of variance (ANOVA), 730–731
Type I error rate, 191–193, 195, 626
Type II error, 194, 195
Typographical variables, eye movements and, 472

U54 awards, 241–242
UAO. *See* Universe of admissible observations
UG (universe of generalization), 747
UK Biobank, 642
Ulrich, R., 453, 454
Umaña-Taylor, A. J., 115
Uncertainty, 196, 199, 591
Unconditional question order effects, 227, 291–292
Unconfounded assignment mechanism, 30
Unconfoundedness assumption, 47
The Undaunted Psychologist (Brannigan & Merrens), 144, 147–148
Underrepresented backgrounds, investigators from
   center-based awards for, 241–242
   research funding for, 233, 234, 237–239
Understanding checking, in interviews, 309–310
Undirected matrix, 706–707
Undocumented immigrants, recruiting, 118–119
Unfolding model, 178, 180
Unidimensional IRT models
   dichotomous, 810–812
   polytomous, 817–824
Unidimensionality
   content validity and, 456
   internal consistency and, 392–393
Unidimensionality assumption, 800
Uniform differential item functioning, 779, 780
Unintended consequences, 787–788
Unipolar depression, 70

Unipolar traits, location parameters for, 829
United States. *See also* Communist and American reporter question studies
  ethical issues regarding research participation in, 107–108
  government spending on research in, 229
  oversight of nonhuman animal studies in, 87–88
  sensitive topics in other countries vs., 107–108
United States Department of Agriculture (USDA), 87, 89, 91
United States House Appropriations Committee, 229
Units of analysis, xxxvii–xxxix, 251, 252
Univariate generalizability analysis, 749–757
  computer programs for, 760–761
  for mixed-model studies, 756–757
  for multifacet designs, 752–756
  for single-facet designs, 749–752
Universe of admissible observations (UAO), 746
  G-studies to estimate variance components in, 747
  for multifacet generalizability analysis, 752
  for single-facet generalizability analysis, 749
  universe of generalization and, 747
Universe of generalization (UG), 747
Universe score(s)
  composite, 758
  with fixed facets, 756–757
  in generalizability theory, 748
  in multivariate generalizability analysis, 757
  and reliability coefficients, 748–749
  variance–covariance matrix for, 758
Universe-score variance, 748, 753, 757
University-based research, participation in, 69
University of California system, 420
Unlinked conditions, generalizability theory for, 758
Unmixing matrix, 701
Unpackaging variables, 105
Unreliability, attenuation effect of, 726
Unstandardized effect size, 191
Unstandardized mean difference, 197, 200

Unstandardized regression coefficient, 204n16
Unstructured interviews, 298
Untimed-event data, 258–261, 263
Unusual parts of scene, eye movement to, 479
Unwarping fMRI data, 635
Upper asymptote parameter, 815–816
Urbina, S., 419
Urdu language, 473
urGENOVA program, 760, 761
U.S. Army Research Institute for Behavioral and Social Sciences, 229
U.S. Defense Advanced Research Projects Agency (DARPA), 229
U.S. Department of Education, 158
U.S. Department of Health and Human Services (DHHS), 60–61, 74–75
U.S. Food and Drug Administration (FDA), 164, 663–664
U.S. Public Health Service (PHS), 87, 89
USDA. *See* United States Department of Agriculture
Utility, 839, 856
Utility-based decision theory, 850
Utility ratio, 839, 852–854

Valid content
  removal of, from short forms, 459–462
Validity. *See also specific types*
  of behavioral observation, 252
  of brief instruments, 451, 452–455
  of criterion-referenced testing, 428–429
  defined, 385, 723
  and generalizability theory, 745, 762–764
  in history of psychometrics, 384–385
  of hormone assays, 567
  of intensive longitudinal data, 340–341
  of IRT models, 826
  and reliability, 723, 738
  of research with marginalized populations, 127
  of Rorschach inkblots, 438–439
  of short forms, 457–459
  Spearman–Brown prophecy formula on, 452
  of Thematic Apperception Test, 442
Validity generalization research question, 141–142
Validity theory, 762

Validity–time tradeoff, short form, 462
Validity typology/threats (VT) framework, 23
  causal generalization and replication, 45–46
  causal identification in, 44–45
  definition of causal effects, 44
  described, 25–28
  joint use of, with other frameworks, 50
  philosophy of causation, 40–43
  PO and SCM vs., 48–50
  research designs for causal interference in, 48
  subject matter theory in, 46–47
  theory of cause for, 43–44
Valid negatives (correct rejections; true negatives), 785, 839, 840, 850
Valid positive rate. *See* Hit rate
Valid positives (hits; true positives), 839–841, 850
Value-based decision making, 687
Van den Berg, H., 313
Van der Ark, L. A., 829–830
Van de Vijver, F. J. R., 101, 105
Van Haaften, E. H., 101
Vanman, E. J., 551
Vantage Learning, 363
VARCOMP procedure, 344, 731, 733
Variability
  day-to-day, 329, 341–346
  in group-level generalizability analysis, 762
  heart rate, 538–540
  latency, 623–625
  phase, 623–625
  sampling, 754
  trial-to-trial, 681
Variable ambulatory electronic response formats, 338
Variable-interval schedules, 330, 331
Variables, causal graph, 32. *See also specific types*
Variance, 517. *See also* Analysis of variance (ANOVA); Error variance; Invariance
  in classical test theory, 725–726
  in criterion-referenced testing, 426
  equal-variance assumption, 515, 517
  and expected mean, of binary measures, 728
  method, 783
  negative components, 754
  of norm-referenced test items, 412

relative error, 748
in resting EEG, 593
total, 750
trait, 783
universe-score, 748, 753, 757
Variance components
G-study, 746–747
in multifaceted populations, 762
in multivariate generalizability analysis, 758
negative, 754
in single-facet generalizability analysis, 749–750
in universe of admissible observations, 747
Variance–covariance matrices, 348, 758
Variation
between-person, 341
in classical test theory, 726
coefficient of, 568
within-person, 341
Veldkamp, C. L. S., 211
Velocity of saccades, 470
Venables, P. H., 544
Venn diagrams, generalizability analysis, 753
Venous system, 536
Ventro-medial prefrontal cortex, 683
Venture investors, research funding by, 228
Verbal accounts, in qualitative research, 6
Verificationist theory of truth, 770
Verschuere, B., 538
Version control, 217–220
Vertical eye movements, 587
Video-based pupil monitoring, 471, 553
Video recording
of interviews, 321
of muscle activity, 551–552
during physiological experiments, 534, 535
Viewing conditions, for psychophysical experiments, 514, 516
Vigilance state studies, 681
Vignette research, 286
Vigoroux, Romain, 542
Vincent averaging, 503–504
Vincentiles, 503
Vindication of stereotypes, 106–107
Violante, I. R., 685
Virtual reality, 524
Visual acuity, 471
Visual cognition, eye movements and, 483

Visual psychophysics, 516, 523–525
Visual search, 174, 480–485
Visual stimulus, ERP evoked by, 609–611
Visual working memory, 478, 685
Vocational Preference Inventory, 146
Voltage, EEG as measure of, 621
Voluntary accreditations, for animal research programs, 90–91
Voluntary control of pupil, 485
Voluntary informed consent, 65, 67–69
Voxel-based nodes, 706
Voxels, 631
VT framework. *See* Validity typology/threats framework
Vulnerability, in interviews, 319–320
Vulnerable populations
participant-informed approach to research with, 76–77
rational informed consent for, 69, 70
voluntary informed consent from, 68

Wagenmakers, E.-J., 507
Wagner, S., 212
Waiver of informed consent, 72
Wald z-test, 348
Walker, R., 482
Waller, N. G., 185
Wang, D., 127
Watson, D., 386, 389, 390, 393, 399–400
Watson, J. B., 770
Wavelet transform, 591
Waves, ERP, 605
Weak factorial invariance, 800
Weak invariance model, 778
Weak relationships, odds ratios for, 270
Wearable monitoring systems, 532, 541
Weaving process, 213
Webb, E. J., xxxix
Weber, E. H., 175
Weber–Fechner law, 516
Weber's law, 516
Web of Science, 157, 160, 165
Web surveys, 287, 288, 292
Wechsler, D., 458
Wechsler Adult Intelligence Scale, 4th Edition, 457
Wechsler Individual Achievement Test, 366
Wechsler Intelligence Scale for Children, 5th edition (WISC-V), 415
Weighted adjacency matrix, 706
Weighted response, in nominal response model, 823–824

Weiner, I. B., 436
Well-being of research animals, 86–87
West, S. G., 24, 799
Westen, D., 777, 780, 781
Western cultures, scene perception in, 480
Wet electrode systems, EEG, 583
Wetherell, M., 313
"What you *see* is what you get" editing software, 214
Wheeler, L., 332
White grant applicants, 237–238
White matter tracts, EEG coherence and, 596
White, R. M. B., 127
Whole-brain fMRI analysis, 638, 698
Whole-brain functional connectivity, 643
Whole-interval sampling, 257–258
Whole question. *See* General question
Why-Atlas, 370
"Why" questions, in interviews, 304–305
Wicherts, J. M., 212
Wichmann, F. A., 512
Wickens, T. D., 271
Wicker, A. W., 140–141, 143–145, 147
Widaman, K. F., 798
Width of confidence intervals, 192–193, 196, 197, 204
Wigboldus, D. H. R., 545
Wild, D., 574
Wiley Online Library, 158
Wilhelm, P., 737
Willig, C., 19
Willowbrook hepatitis study, 59, 64
Wilson, D. C., 291
Wilson, M., 764
Windowing, in EEG research, 591
Window of opportunity, 271
Windsor, J., 284
Windsor Deception Checklist, 72
Windsorized data, 499
Winship, C., 39
Wirth, R. J., 796
WISC-V (Wechsler Intelligence Scale for Children, 5th edition), 415
Within-group diversity, for marginalized groups, 116
Within-person associations
in intensive longitudinal research, 328, 329, 351
quadratic trajectory for, 348–349
Within-person reliability coefficients, 737

Within-persons model (Level 1 model)
  for investigating average experiences, 341, 343, 345
  for investigating change across time, 347
  moderation effects in, 349
  for statistical stimulation study, 353
Within-study comparisons (WSCs), 27–28, 46
Within-subject research factors, 251, 252
WLSMV (mean- and variance-adjusted weighted least squares) estimation, 799
Wong, V. C., 28, 46
Woodcock-Johnson test, 366
Word2Vec, 365
WordCat, 163
Word length, 472, 475–476
WordNet-Affect, 369
Workforce diversity, 233, 237–239, 241–242
Working directories, 221
Working memory, 596, 613
  PET studies of, 648
  and question order effects, 288
  theta-band oscillatory synchronization and, 685
  visual, 478, 685
World Health Organization, 164
World Medical Association, 60
World War I, 419–420, 770
World War II, 60, 419–420, 845
Worsley, K. J., 698, 699
Wrap-up effects, 477
Wright, S., 23
Wright, T. J., 485
Wrightson, L., 443
Write.csv command, 220
Writing evaluation, automated, 366
Writing Pal, 374–375
Wrzesniewski, A., 201–206
WSCs (within-study comparisons), 27–28, 46
Wundt, W., 408, 531

Xie, Y., 213, 214

Yale Law School Roundtable on Data and Code Sharing, 212
Yeo functional atlas, 643
Yerkes, R. M., 139
Yes–no task, 518, 519, 522
Yeung, N., 612
Yip, T., 329
Yoder, P. J., 253
Young children, ERP studies with, 614
Young Faculty Award Program, DARPA, 229
Yule's Q, 270, 271

Zaidi, N. B., 762
Zalesky, A., 708
Zeligman, R., 439
Zelinsky, G. J., 482–483
Zenisky, A. L., 105
Zero-one sampling, 257, 258
Zeros, in contingency tables, 271
Zhou, X. H., 849
Zimbardo, P. G., 139
Zinbarg, R. E., 738
z_k parameterization, of nominal response model, 822–823
Z-lines (Z-bands), of muscle, 547
z-scores, 177